Practical Oracle E-Business Suite

An Implementation and Management Guide

Syed Zaheer and Erman Arslan

Apress®

Practical Oracle E-Business Suite: An Implementation and Management Guide

Syed Zaheer
Bahadurpura, Hyderabad
India

Erman Arslan
Tesvikiye, Istanbul
Turkey

ISBN-13 (pbk): 978-1-4842-1423-7
DOI 10.1007/978-1-4842-1422-0

ISBN-13 (electronic): 978-1-4842-1422-0

Library of Congress Control Number: 2016952811

Managing Director: Welmoed Spahr
Acquisitions Editor: Susan McDermott
Developmental Editor: Laura Berendson, Douglas Pundick
Technical Reviewer: Maris Elsins
Editorial Board: Steve Anglin, Pramila Balen, Laura Berendson, Aaron Black, Louise Corrigan, Jonathan Gennick, Robert Hutchinson, Celestin Suresh John, Nikhil Karkal, James Markham, Susan McDermott, Matthew Moodie, Natalie Pao, Gwenan Spearing
Coordinating Editor: Rita Fernando
Copy Editor: Kim Wimpsett
Compositor: SPi Global
Indexer: SPi Global
Cover image selected by Freepik.com.

Distributed to the book trade worldwide by Springer Science+Business Media New York, 233 Spring Street, 6th Floor, New York, NY 10013. Phone 1-800-SPRINGER, fax (201) 348-4505, e-mail orders-ny@springer-sbm.com, or visit www.springer.com. Apress Media, LLC is a California LLC and the sole member (owner) is Springer Science + Business Media Finance Inc (SSBM Finance Inc). SSBM Finance Inc is a Delaware corporation.

For information on translations, please e-mail rights@apress.com, or visit www.apress.com.

Apress and friends of ED books may be purchased in bulk for academic, corporate, or promotional use. eBook versions and licenses are also available for most titles. For more information, reference our Special Bulk Sales–eBook Licensing web page at www.apress.com/bulk-sales.

Any source code or other supplementary materials referenced by the author in this text is available to readers at www.apress.com. For detailed information about how to locate your book's source code, go to www.apress.com/source-code/.

Printed on acid-free paper

This book is dedicated to my mother, Asuman Arslan,
and to my father, Osman Ertuğrul Arslan.
—Erman Arslan

This book is dedicated to my parents.
—Syed Zaheer

Contents at a Glance

About the Authors..xxi

About the Technical Reviewer xxiii

Acknowledgments..xxv

Introduction xxvii

■Chapter 1: Architecture 1

■Chapter 2: Installation and Configuration 35

■Chapter 3: Oracle E-Business Suite Upgrades.. 103

■Chapter 4: Oracle E-Business Suite 12.2 File System 155

■Chapter 5: Patching Concepts 199

■Chapter 6: Working with the Applications DBA Online Patching Tool (adop) 245

■Chapter 7: Managing FMW/WebLogic.. 351

■Chapter 8: AutoConfig to Manage EBS System Configuration Changes............. 441

■Chapter 9: SYSADMIN Fundamentals.. 483

■Chapter 10: Oracle EBS Concurrent Managers 531

■Chapter 11: Cloning Oracle EBS Systems 579

■Chapter 12: An Introduction to Oracle EBS Security 641

■Chapter 13: Oracle E-Business Suite 12.2 Performance Recommendations..... 675

■Chapter 14: Oracle E-Business Suite 12.2 on Engineered Systems................... 735

Index... 765

Contents

About the Authors...xxi

About the Technical Reviewer xxiii

Acknowledgments..xxv

Introduction...xxvii

■Chapter 1: Architecture 1

Introduction to Oracle E-Business Suite.. 1

CRM Applications Family... 2

Service Management Family.. 2

Financial Management Family 3

Human Capital Management Family 4

Project Portfolio Management Family 5

Advanced Procurement Family 5

Supply Chain Management Family... 6

Understanding the Oracle E-Business Suite's Three-Tier Architecture Model 7

Concurrent Processing 11

Database Tier and EBS Data Model 11

Understanding the EBS 12.2 Technology Stack Components....................................... 15

Oracle EBS 12.2 File System Structure 19

Application Tier File System 23

Technology Stack Changes in EBS 11i/12.1/12.2.. 32

Summary.. 34

■Chapter 2: Installation and Configuration 35

New Features in Release 12.2's Rapidwiz Install Wizard 35

Preparing for Installation 37

Hardware Prerequisites 37

Computing Requirements 38

Space Requirements 38

Software Requirements 39

Software Tools Requirements 39

Kernel Version 39

Operating System Packages 40

Configuring the yum Repository for EBS 12 Package Installation 42

Get the Repository File with Wget 42

Oracle EBS 12.2 Stage Directory Structure 49

Build Stage Menu Options 51

Copy Patches to Existing Stage Area 53

List Files in the TechPatches Directory 53

Copy Patches to Existing Stage Area 54

Single-Node Installation 54

Before Running Rapidwiz 54

Multinode Installation 73

Key Points Related to Multinode Installation 74

Rapidwiz Install: RAC Database Option 74

Shared APPL_TOP in Oracle EBS 12.2 75

Post-installation Steps 76

Post-installation Steps for the Application 76

Client PC Requirements 79

Post-installation Steps for the Database 80

How to Deal with Failed Installations 81

Rapidwiz Installation Process 81

How to Deal with Corrupted/Lost Technology Stack Components 83

Replacing the Oracle EBS Database Technology Stack (RDBMS Oracle Home).......................... 83

Replacing the Oracle EBS 10g AS (10.1.2: Tools) Technology Stack 92

Replacing the Oracle Fusion Middleware Technology Stack 102

Summary 102

■Chapter 3: Oracle E-Business Suite Upgrades 103

Introduction to the Oracle E-Business Suite Upgrade Process 103

Road Map to 12.2 Upgrade 103

Preparation of an Oracle EBS 12.2 Upgrade 105

Operating System and Server Upgrade 105

Virtualization Considerations 105

Space and Computing Capacity Considerations 106

Upgrade the Database 106

Purge/Archive Data 107

Upgrade Dependent EBS Integrated Applications 107

Upgrading Oracle E-Business Suite: 12.2.0 to 12.2.5 108

Patching Utilities Used for Different Tech Stack Components 110

Upgrade Demonstration 110

Execution of checkMTpatch.sh 110

Execution of checkDBpatch.sh 113

Installation of the RDBMS Patches 115

Applying Latest AD and TKX Patches 120

Apply WebLogic Patches 121

Installation of 12.2.5 Upgrade Patch 121

Post-upgrade Tasks 124

Upgrading from 12.1.3 to 12.2.0 126

Phase 1 126

Phase 2 126

Phase 3 126

Phase 4 126

Upgrade Environment Details 127

    Oracle EBS Database Upgrade 128

    Oracle Application Upgrade 129

    Install 12.2.0 Tech Stack Components 129

    Prepare for 12.2.0 Upgrade Patch 142

    Apply Main Upgrade Patch 143

    Configure the EBS Upgrade Using Rapidwiz 144

    Finishing the Upgrade 150

    Enable Online Patching 151

    Post-upgrade Steps 153

    EBS Upgrade Timing Summary 153

Summary 154

■Chapter 4: Oracle E-Business Suite 12.2 File System 155

Oracle E-Business Suite File System Architecture Overview 155

Understanding the Application Dual and Noneditioned File Systems 157

Oracle EBS 12.2 Environment Variables 166

Working with Environment Variables on the Application Tier and Navigating the
Application File System 177

    Scenario 1: Starting the Application Services 177

    Scenario 2: You Want to Check the SMTP Server Settings in CONTEXT_FILE 180

    Scenario 3: You Want to Connect to the EBS Database Remotely from the EBS
    Application Tier Node 181

Working with Environment Variables on the Database Tier and Navigating the Database
File System 183

    Scenario 1: Restarting the EBS Database and the Database Listener 185

    Scenario 2: Modifying the Database Configuration Using AutoConfig 187

EBS 12.2 Applications Log Files 189

EBS 12.2 Database Log Files 191

Summary 198

■Chapter 5: Patching Concepts 199

Introduction to Oracle Patching in EBS 12.2 199

Types of the Patches and Deciding the Patching Order 201

The Manual Method...203

The Patch Application Assistant Method 210

Different Patching Utilities Under Oracle EBS 12.2 220

Patching WebLogic with BSU (BEA Smart Update)................................. 221

Patching the Application Tier Oracle Homes and the Database with Opatch 223

Applying the Applications Patches with the ADOP Utility 225

Introduction to Online Patching Utility (adop)....................................... 226

Technological Changes for Supporting Online Patching.....................................227

Understanding Edition-Based Redefinition Usage in Online Patching.................229

Phases of Online Patching...234

Backup Best Practices for EBS 12.2 Patching....................................... 237

Summary.. 244

■Chapter 6: Working with the Applications DBA Online Patching Tool (adop) 245

Overview of adop 245

Working with the adop Utility 247

adop Command-Line Parameters and Options.. 252

Executing the Patching Cycle 262

Prepare Phase 263

List of Restricted Functionalities in the Online Patching Cycle 266

Apply Phase...267

Finalize Phase...269

Cutover 270

Cleanup...272

Abort Phase 273

Hotpatch Mode 275

Downtime Mode 279

Merging Oracle Application Patches 282

Applying Patches in a Multinode Environment... 289

Adding a New Language, Patching for NLS and HRMS 298

Localization Patches 316

Patch Reporting Utilities... 324

Summary.. 350

■Chapter 7: Managing FMW/WebLogic.. 351

Introduction to Fusion Middleware in EBS 12.2 351

Architecture and Components.. 352

Advantages of FMW.. 359

FMW Directory Structure in EBS 12.2 360

Controlling Admin Server, Node Manager, and
Managed Servers 364

Using the FMW Control and the WebLogic Console.. 371

WLST and Its Typical Usages in EBS 12.2.. 397

Best Practices for Tuning Fusion Middleware in EBS 12.2.............................. 401

Best Practices for FMW Performance and Managing the Configuration
of WebLogic Server in EBS 12.2 403

Managing the Configuration of Oracle HTTP Server....................................... 417

EBS 12.2 FMW Diagnostics 421

Summary.. 440

■Chapter 8: AutoConfig to Manage EBS System Configuration Changes............ 441

Introduction to the AutoConfig Utility 441

Understanding Configuration Management Tools and Utilities.......................... 442

AutoConfig Scripts... 442

Context File.. 443

Template Files 444

Driver Files 444

Working with AutoConfig 445

Working with the Context File... 447

Running AutoConfig in Preview Mode 450

File System 453

Database 453

Running AutoConfig for Configuration Changes 458

Executing AutoConfig on the Database Tier 463

Rolling Back AutoConfig Configuration Changes 464

Using AutoConfig for Managing Customizations 465

Customizing Existing AutoConfig Template 466

Advanced AutoConfig Features and Utilities 468

AutoConfig Command-Line Options 469

Using Profiling with AutoConfig 469

Running AutoConfig in Parallel Mode in Multinode Environment 472

adconfig Execution on dbTier with parallel Option 472

adconfig Execution on appsTier with parallel Option 473

AutoConfig and Fusion Middleware Home 474

The Feedback Loop 475

Adding Custom Top to EBS 12.2 480

Summary 481

■Chapter 9: SYSADMIN Fundamentals 483

Introduction to Application Technology Layer 483

Using AD Utilities 484

Using the adadmin Utility 487

Generate Applications Files Menu 491

Maintain Applications Files Menu 491

Compile/Reload Applications Database Entities Menu 492

Maintain Applications Database Entities Menu 492

Important DB Objects 493

Using Application DBA Reporting Utilities 493

    adutconf.sql: Utility for Displaying Application Configuration 493

    adident: File Version Identification Utility 494

    adchkdig.. 494

Oracle Application Diagnostic.. 495

    Application Diagnostic Responsibility.. 498

Working with the SYSADMIN Responsibility.. 502

Alert Manager Responsibility 504

    Clicking Action Details... 507

Workflow Admin Responsibility.. 508

    Status Monitor 508

    Administration 509

    Vacation Rule... 510

    Notification Search 511

Working with Oracle Applications Manager 512

    Administration 516

    How to License a Product... 517

    Reports 518

    Workflow Mailer Configuration 519

    Monitoring 521

User, Role, and Responsibility Management... 523

Managing Profiles and Profile Levels 525

Using Printers in EBS 526

    Printer Types.. 528

Summary.. 530

■Chapter 10: Oracle EBS Concurrent Managers 531

Introduction to Oracle Concurrent Processing 531

Understanding Terms Concurrent Requests, Program, and Processes 531

Service Management Architecture 532

How the Service Manager Works 532

Different Types of Concurrent Managers 535

Internal Concurrent Managers 535

Standard Manager 535

Conflict Resolution Manager 535

Transaction Manager 535

Understanding Concurrent Request Phases 537

Parent Request and Child Request 537

Working with Concurrent Requests (Standard Requests, Custom Requests,
and Request Arguments) 539

Submitting a Standard Concurrent Request 539

Request Arguments 545

Upon Completion 550

Working with Concurrent Request Sets 551

Managing Concurrent Manager Incompatibilities 559

Creation of Custom Concurrent Manager 562

Working with the Specialization Rule and Work Shifts 566

Understanding Parallel Concurrent Processing (PCP) 569

Role of ICM in Parallel Concurrent Processing 570

Role of Service Manager (FNDSM) in PCP 571

Role of Internal Monitor Process (FNDIMON) in PCP 571

Using the CLI for Submitting Concurrent Requests 571

Troubleshooting Concurrent Manager Issues 572

From the Back End 574

Concurrent Manager Process log File 574

Internal Manager Log File 575

Using Concurrent Manager Recover Wizard 575

Problems with Printing Reports 576

Proactive Maintenance 576

Important Concurrent Manager Tables 577

Summary 577

■Chapter 11: Cloning Oracle EBS Systems 579

Introduction to OracleApplication Cloning and Its Purpose 579

Using Rapid Clone and Its Options 579

High-Level Clone Process with AD and TKX Delta6 580

High-Level Clone Process with AD and TKX Delta7 580

adpreclone.pl Operations 580

adcfgclone.pl Operations 581

adpreclone.pl and adcfgclone.pl Options 581

Prerequisites for a New Clone Environment 582

Prepare the Clone Systems 582

Verify Disk Space 582

OS Prerequisites 582

Apply Required Patches 582

Oracle EBS Inventory Requirements 583

Validate AutoConfig on the Source System 583

Execute and Maintain Snapshot Information from adadmin 583

Cloning from a Single Node to a Single Node 584

Steps of Rapid Clone EBS 12.2 on the Source and Target Systems 584

Environment Details 585

Prepare the Clone on the Source System 586

Execute the Clone Preparation Script on the Database Tier (dbTier) 586

Execute the Clone Preparation Script on the Application Tier (appsTier) 587

Configure the Clone on the Target System 589

Create a Group and Users on the Target System 591

Change Ownership of the Target System Directories 592

Execute the Clone Configuration Script on the Database Tier on the Target System 592

Execute the Clone Configuration Script on the Application Tier on the Target System...................... 594

Cloning from a Single Node to a Multinode 600

Execute the Clone Preparation Script on the Source System 601

Execute the Clone Configuration Scripts on the Database and Application Tiers 601

Cloning from a Multinode to a Single-Node Clone Using Online Backup 608

Prepare the Clone on the Source System 610

Execute the adpreclone.pl Script on dbTier 610

Perform a Full Database rman Backup... 611

Execute a Full Database Backup rman Script 612

Execute the adpreclone.pl Script on appsTier (Run Edition).. 614

Configure the Target System 615

Execute the adcfgclone.pl Script with the dbTechStack Option 616

Execute rman duplicate.. 618

Configure the Target System Application Tier 622

Cloning in RAC-Enabled Systems 624

Prepare the Clone 626

Execute the adclone.pl Script for Staging 626

Configure the Clone on the Target System 628

Execute adclone.pl on the Target System.. 631

Adding Nodes and Configuring Shared APPL_TOP 632

Points to Be Considered for Shared APPL_TOP Deployment 632

Post-cloning Steps 637

Change Passwords for All Superusers... 637

Configure the Workflow Mailer 637

Size the Target System 637

Change System Profiles... 637

Update Printer Settings 638

Cancel Scheduled Concurrent Requests 638

Troubleshooting Cloning Issues 638

    Log Files on the Source System 638

    Log Files on the Target System 638

Summary 639

■Chapter 12: An Introduction to Oracle EBS Security 641

Configuring SSL/TSL with Oracle EBS 12.2 642

    Creation of a Wallet 642

    Configuration of the Web Tier (FMW) 648

    Conclusion 649

Using a DMZ and Reverse Proxy with Oracle EBS 12.2 649

    DMZ Configuration with External and Internal Application Tiers (Option 1) 650

    DMZ Configuration with Reverse Proxy and External Application Tier (Option 2) 651

    DMZ Configuration with Multiple Internal/External Application Tiers Within the Intranet and DMZ (Option 3 and Option 4) 652

Using TDE with Oracle EBS 12.2 Database 660

    Key Points for Transparent Data Encryption 661

    Transparent Data Encryption Column Level (CE) 661

    Configuration of TDE Wallet 662

Users and Password Management in Oracle EBS 12.2 665

    Use the FNDCPASS Utility for Changing Passwords 666

    Use AFPASSWD for Changing the APPS Password 666

Securing the Database and Application Files 670

    Securing Oracle Database 671

    Oracle EBS Security Profile Options 671

Oracle EBS Proxy Users 672

Summary 674

■Chapter 13: Oracle E-Business Suite 12.2 Performance Recommendations..... 675

Introduction to Oracle EBS Performance Tuning 675

EBS 12.2 Client-Side Performance Tuning 676

EBS 12.2 Middle Tier Performance Tuning 679

EBS 12.2 Database Structure and Performance 688

Initialization Parameters 690

Tablespaces, Data Files, and Redolog Files... 698

EBS 12.2 SQL Access Paths 713

EBS 12.2 Network Performance Tuning 720

EBS 12.2 Tuning the Concurrent Processing 721

Performance Recommendations for Reporting, Workflow, and Application
Debug Profiles 731

Summary... 734

■Chapter 14: Oracle E-Business Suite 12.2 on Engineered Systems................... 735

Introduction to Oracle Engineered Systems 735

Exadata Fresh Installation 738

Exadata Migration 741

Configuring and Managing EBS 12.2 on Exadata 747

Benefits of Running EBS on Exadata Systems 752

Oracle Database Appliance Implementations... 754

    Installing EBS 12.2 on ODA Bare Metal 755

    Installing EBS 12.2 on Virtualized ODA 758

Exalogic Implementations 761

Summary... 763

Index.. 765

About the Authors

Syed Zaheer is an engineering graduate in computer science and information technology with a decade of experience in the implementation and management of Oracle databases since Version 8i till 12c, Oracle E-Business Suite, Oracle HA Stack, and Oracle Fusion Middleware. He has domain knowledge in diversified business streams including financials, FMCG, manufacturing, and consulting. He is currently working as a senior Oracle apps DBA in the largest stock exchange in the Middle East and Africa. He also has excellent skills in managing the Oracle Enterprise Linux and Oracle Solaris operating environments. He has been part of 15+ successful implementations of Oracle E-Business Suite from version 11i until R12.2.5. He has 14 Oracle certifications covering operating systems, databases, engineered systems, applications, and Fusion Middleware. He is an active contributor on OTN Forums with a status of GURU. He is a speaker at public conferences like MEOUG, TROUG, OUGF and he writes articles related to Oracle technologies on his blog (http://appsdbaworkshop.com) and the Toadworld community.

Erman Arslan is currently working as "Applications and Database Operations Manager" and "Leading Oracle Consultant" for one of the biggest Oracle Partner Company in Turkey. He is a "Principle Apps Dba", "Oracle-certified Linux" and Certified Exadata Admin" with lots of field experience in several Oracle projects implemented in several sectors as banking, healthcare, insurance, manufacturing, retail, telecommunications, transportation, oil and gas, TV, and more.

He studied Computer Engineering and received an MBA in istanbul Turkey. He is a blogger who has written about Oracle Technologies ("Erman Arslan' Oracle Blog - www.ermanarslan.blogspot.com") since 2013. Arslan also answers the questions of his readers and provides support for their problems in his Oracle forum. ("Erman Arslan's Oracle Forum http://ermanarslan.blogspot.com.tr/p/forum.html")

In addition to the administration and implementation works, Arslan has developed applications for helping the Oracle Dbas in routine administration works such as backup and recovery, deployments and performance.

As part of the consultancy work, Arslan has done several Oracle environment healthchecks and general recoverability assessments in critical customer environments.

Arslan has completed several EBS migrations, Core Database migrations and replatforming projects. He also played part as the Apps DBA Lead in 5 EBS 12.2 projects, which have gone live in 2015 and in 2016.

As part of the Apps Dba, Core Dba and Engineered Systems support responsibilities, he has managed more than 15 Critical Customer Production Environments (mostly EBS, but also including Exadata, Oracle Database Appliance, SSO, OID, and Weblogic Application Servers as well). Arslan also has worked as DB SME in very critical assesment and migration projects which are done by EMC in Banking Sector.

About the Technical Reviewer

Maris Elsins is an experienced Oracle applications DBA currently working as the lead database consultant at The Pythian Group. His other responsibilities include supervising the technical solutions provided by one of Pythian's apps DBAs teams to the clients. Maris' main areas of expertise are maintenance, troubleshooting, and performance tuning of Oracle Database and E-Business Suite systems. He is a blogger and a frequent speaker at Oracle-related conferences such as UKOUG, Collaborate, HotSos, Oracle OpenWorld, and others. Maris is an Oracle ACE and Oracle Certified Master. He's a coauthor of *Practical Oracle Database Appliance* (Apress, 2014) and also a member of the board at the Latvian Oracle User Group (LVOUG).

Acknowledgments

Writing this book in parallel to my job has required lots of efforts. I have spent lots of time not only on writing it but also on reviewing the content and making corrections.

It was a long run, and by considering these circumstances, this book would not have been written without superior motivation.

So, first, many thanks to my mother, Asuman Arslan, and my father, Osman Ertuğrul Arslan, for their continuous support, for providing me with a suitable and peaceful home office environment, and for their understanding. Many thanks to them for believing in me and giving me the motivation that I needed every time I felt the weight of writing this book on my shoulders.

I would also like to thank the Apress editors, especially Susan McDermott and Rita Fernando, for believing in us and supporting this project, making us gain the advanced knowledge for writing and reviewing a book, and also keeping up with us from the beginning to the end.

Our technical reviewer, Maris Elsins, helped us to remove several obscure and misleading statements. So, I would like to thank him for reading our book carefully and making his valuable comments when necessary.

I want to thank to Alp Çakar, who was my first supervisor and has believed in and supported me since the first day I started working as an Oracle DBA.

I would like to thank to my bosses, especially Savaş Yeleser, for creating the environment that I need for improving my skills, and Ferhan Ezer, for his understanding about my book work.

I want to send my greetings to my friend and colleague Barış Saltık, who has influenced me by his personality and his true engineering approaches. Barış helped me gain a different kind of engineering perspective by giving his valuable support and by making his comments about things every time I needed.

I want to thank to my teammates Ali, Cihan, Hülya, and Eren for trying to work as efficiently as possible and decreasing the additional pressure on my shoulders caused by being the manager of the team.

Thanks to Nişantaşı Starbucks, as I have written a significant number of pages there.

Lastly, many thanks to all the people who directly or indirectly, consciously or unconsciously, have helped me to arrive today.

—Erman Arslan

Becoming an author was my dream, and this is my first book written with my friend Erman Arslan. First I would like to thank Jonathan and Susan for providing this wonderful opportunity to be a part of Apress and making this dream a reality.

I would like to thank my wife and sweet daughters, Ameema and Amina, for their perpetual and prolonged patience and support while I was writing this book.

I would like to thank the Apress editorial team, especially Rita, Douglas, and SPi Global for their tremendous support in editing our chapters and guiding us all the way.

I would also like to thank Maris Elsin for reading and reviewing our work patiently, correcting our work as necessary, and providing feedback for delivering better content.

I would also like to thank Nassyam Basha who supported and encouraged me in all aspects throughout my Oracle career. I cannot forget Venkat venu with whom my journey in Oracle Application products has been started. I would like to thanks Tauseef Ali, Syed Mahmood, Khaja majid and Ameen Ali who supported and guided me whenever its required.

At last I am thankful to all the individuals who supported our work directly or indirectly in completing this book.

—Syed Zaheer

Introduction

Years have passed dealing with Oracle products. The first days were database days for us, as in those days Oracle was mostly a database company, or maybe it is better to say, Oracle applications were not so widely used in our environment. But, later a new era came to our DBA world, as Oracle increased the importance of the application stack massively and developed and purchased business applications to deliver best-in-class business solutions, which covered almost every aspect of technology from application to disk.

In the initial stages, people who managed and maintained databases were called DBAs, and the job role of DBA became a globally recognized role in the IT industry. Database administrators have always played a critical role in organizations.

Although some might consider the database to be a component in the application layer, we have always considered Oracle Database as a system—a relational database management system that is tightly integrated with the application tier above it and the operating system beneath it. While Oracle is tightly integrated with the application and operating system technologies, this tight integration has turned Oracle Database into sophisticated software that needs additional skills at the operating system and application layers for proper administration. So, it was expected that expert DBAs know the operating system and the application technology as well.

Once Oracle started growing and moving toward the development of business applications, new roles in the IT industry started to emerge. That is, we started learning how to manage, maintain, and administer these applications.

We actually started working with Oracle E-Business Suite 11i and continued with R12 and the administration of these application suites with the job title of Oracle Apps DBA.

At that time (and maybe still), it was clear that Oracle EBS was a complex and a tightly coupled application with its technology stack components and database, and it required significant experience in implementation and management, in addition to the knowledge required for being an expert on it.

So, over the years we installed, administered, maintained, and supported EBS systems. The Apps DBA role (and the complexity of EBS itself) has dragged us into the Oracle EBS technology stack components, the database model, and all the relationships in between technology and business.

EBS 11i was the first release we worked on. EBS 12.0 (R12) and 12.1 (R12) were the subsequent releases on which we learned EBS truly. We have installed, upgraded, and supported these EBS releases several times and continued to work on them until EBS 12.2 was released. When we had the opportunity for the first look at EBS 12.2, we saw the changes in it. At that time, we understood that there is no finish line. We had to continue to keep ourselves up-to-date, we had to continue learning, and we had to continue being release-independent Apps DBAs.

Although it sounds like that it was a requirement, the things like the desire to work with Oracle, the interest to analyze the new features and the great wish to become an expert on Oracle products were always coming from inside of us. Again, we were very excited for our first contact with the new release, EBS 12.2, as it brought lots of new features and almost a completely new application tier technology stack. We were excited to administer the new FMW components of EBS 12.2 and especially wondering about the new online patching concept.

Although we were experts on EBS 11i and R12, EBS 12.2 brought us lots of challenges with the new technological enhancements in its software and database stack.

The changes in administration methods also increased the level of these challenges and thus motivated us to deal with something new, something that could be considered an innovation in EBS world.

While we were dealing with the new EBS 12.2, EBS has continued to evolve. During these evolutions we have seen that the first bugs have been fixed and administration has become more stabilized.

When agreeing to write this book, EBS 12.2 was already started to be used in new ERP projects, and EBS 12.2 upgrades were being planned for existing/former EBS environments.

Moreover, Oracle engineered systems have been utilized with EBS 12.2 systems, and even the Oracle VM templates were made available for deploying EBS 12.2 to Oracle virtualized environments.

So, today, when you are an Apps DBA, you are always connected to all the layers, from hardware to software. When you are on your EBS stack, you know that you are using the Oracle technologies by pushing their limits.

That's why, after all the database administration, OS administration, storage administration, and sometimes even the software development, we have decided to stick with the Apps DBA role and that was our most significant motivation for writing this book.

Writing this book was harder than we thought, but we think we have produced something useful, something that can be used for learning EBS administration and more importantly, something that will shed a light on the new EBS 12.2 releases and their administration activities.

We hope you enjoy reading this book; get to know EBS 12.2 by the explanations, examples, and recommendations we provide; and enhance your apps DBA skills eventually.

CHAPTER 1

Architecture

In this chapter, we will introduce Oracle E-Business Suite (EBS). We will first cover the history and evolution of EBS. We will then cover the EBS applications and the technical architecture of EBS by exploring the architectural model, EBS file system, database tier, and application tier, including the technological components and technological stack changes from the earlier releases to the latest release, EBS 12.2. For such a complex product as EBS, we believe this foundation is necessary in order to administer and troubleshoot it properly.

Introduction to Oracle E-Business Suite

Oracle E-Business Suite, also known as Oracle Applications or Oracle EBS, is sophisticated software that works like a software system, which as a whole supplies the enterprise resource planning (ERP), customer relationship management (CRM), and supply chain planning application families. It is a software system that consists of global business applications with built-in integrity.

E-Business Suite is a product of Oracle Corporation and was created in late 1980s. The first name of the product was Oracle Financials. After Oracle Financials, the product name changed to Oracle Applications; the next release was called Oracle Application Release 1, introduced in August 1987. Following Oracle Application Release 1, Oracle released its first ERP application called Accounting System in 1988; this application was considered Release 2. After that, the release numbers increased linearly. Oracle continued to enhance the product over the years, and at the time of writing this book, the latest release version is 12.2.5.

Recent Oracle EBS software versions consist of three or four digits. Versions such as 11.5.10.2, 12.1.3, 12.2.3, 12.2.4, and 12.2.5 are all examples of the EBS software versions used by organizations today. The first digit is the release number, so versions starting with 11 imply Release 11, which is called 11i. Likewise, versions starting with 12 imply Release 12.

Although release numbers describe the general capabilities of the application, there are some exceptions. For example, version 11.5.10.2 is the latest version for the former release EBS 11i (referred to as Release 11), but it is much more enhanced than other 11i releases. The situation is the same for EBS 12.2. EBS 12.2 actually has a different technology and architectural design compared to earlier releases. It is really different, and in our perspective, this enhanced new-generation EBS 12.2 is not Release 12 anymore. The enhancements, changes in the technology components, new administration methods, utilities, and innovations in EBS 12.2 are so exciting that they're the reason we're writing this book.

There are several applications in E-Business Suite's application families. We will introduce these applications in the forthcoming sections.

Electronic supplementary material The online version of this chapter (doi:10.1007/978-1-4842-1422-0_1) contains supplementary material, which is available to authorized users.

S. Zaheer and E. Arslan, *Practical Oracle E-Business Suite*, DOI 10.1007/978-1-4842-1422-0_1

EBS can be called a *software system* because it is software as a whole and includes its own database, application server, and software running on top of this stack. By using the cross-industry capabilities of EBS, organizations can make decisions in a better, faster, reliable, and more cost-efficient way. Some of the business applications are already in EBS, and some of the applications are separate but tightly integrated with it. We describe the applications in EBS in the following sections.

■ **Note**   Some of the EBS applications in the application families covered next are actually solutions, so they have no short product codes. They are considered as extensions to the other applications and are created by using the capabilities of other EBS applications. These *solutions*, as we call them, may contain more than one product across different EBS modules. They can be enabled by performing some of the setup with the dependent Oracle E-Business applications and some of the setup within the solutions themselves.

CRM Applications Family

The applications and solutions delivered within the CRM applications family provide strong customer relationship management features inside EBS.

- *Oracle Channel Revenue Management*: This supplies consistent, accurate information and advanced tools for managing revenues of both direct and in-direct channels. Oracle Channel Revenue Management contains the Accounts Receivable Deductions Settlement, Channel Rebates and Point-of-Sale Management, Partner Management, Price Protection, and Supplier Ship and Debit products.

- *Oracle Marketing*: This supplies a robust environment for managing marketing information and processes.

- *Oracle Order Management*: This supplies a platform for driving the order fulfillment process of any business.

- *Oracle Service*: This supplies customer service based on true information.

Service Management Family

The applications and solutions delivered within the service management family provide information-driven customer service features inside EBS.

- *Advanced Inbound Telephony*: This enables telephony integration to all major telephone systems. It is part of the product family named Oracle Interaction Center, which consists of the Advanced Inbound Telephony, Advanced Outbound Telephony, Email Center, and Scripting applications.

- *Advanced Outbound Telephony*: This supplies tools such as list management and predictive dialing for executing outbound calling campaigns.

- *Advanced Scheduler*: This supplies productive and cost-effective scheduling for field service reps.

- *Depot Repair*: This supplies the ability for automating the in-house repair processes.

- *Email Center*: This is an e-mail response management system for managing the high volume of incoming messages.

- *Field Service*: This supplies the ability for automating the dispatching processes in field services, which is required for servicing the service calls in remote locations.

- *Interaction Center*: This provides an interaction center for integrating the customer interaction channels.

- *iSupport*: This provides a secure, self-service web portal for enabling the self-service functionality to both customer and employees.

- *Mobile Field Service*: This makes the information accessible to the agents via both handheld and laptop devices. This application is part of the Oracle Service application.

- *Scripting*: This provides scripting and survey capabilities.

- *Service Contracts*: This provides contract management and a centralized repository for entitlement information.

- *Spares Management*: This provides logistics and planning for selecting and delivering the spare parts to field locations.

- *Tele Service*: This supplies the ability for automating the resolutions by using the integrated CRM applications. This application is part of the Oracle Service application.

Financial Management Family

The applications and solutions delivered within the financial management family are the financial applications for increasing the efficiency and reducing the costs of all the financial processes.

- *Cash and Treasury Management*: This provides management for treasury operations. This application includes the Cash Management (CE) and Treasury (XTR) applications.

- *Asset Lifecycle Management*: This provides an effective environment for managing the assets of the organization. This solution consists of Enterprise Asset Management, Self-Service Work Requests, Asset Tracking, and Property Manager.

- *Credit-To-Cash*: This provides customer data management, credit decision making, standard invoicing/billing and electronic bill presentment, revenue recognition, cash receipt, cash application, collections, audit and financials compliance, and reporting. Credit-To-Cash is a solution for managing credit, collections, and receivables for the Advanced Collections, Oracle Financial Analytics, iReceivables, Loans (LNS), Credit Management, Financials Centralized Solution Set, Payments (IBY), Receivables (AR), and Accounts Receivables Deductions Settlement applications.

- *Financial Control and Reporting*: This provides financial control for creating and managing the transactions and provides the ability for reporting the results. This solution works with the Oracle Financial Analytics, Oracle Hyperion Financial Management, Financials Accounting Hub, Governance, Risk and Compliance Management, and Oracle Financials (General Ledger and Financials Centralized Solution Set) applications.

- *Financial Analytics*: This provides business intelligence in the financial area. This application is an Oracle Business Intelligence (OBIEE) application that gets its data from EBS. So, it is used with EBS financial applications to bring the business intelligence into the EBS environments.

- *Governance, Risk, and Compliance*: This provides enterprise risk management, compliance, and controls enforcement. Governance, Risk, and Compliance (GRC) includes applications such as Advanced Controls for E-Business Suite, Application Access Controls Governor, Application Access Controls for E-Business Suite, Configuration Controls Governor, Configuration Controls for E-Business Suite, Transaction Controls Governor, and Preventive Controls Governor.

- *Lease and Finance Management*: This supplies the ability for automating lease and load portfolio.

- *Procure-To-Pay*: This supplies integration between purchasing and payables. This solution can be implemented with the following applications: Oracle Financial Analytics, Internet Expenses, iProcurement, iSupplier Portal, Landed Cost Management, Oracle Financials, Payables, Payments, Procurement Contracts, Projects, Purchasing, Services Procurement, Sourcing, and Supplier Network.

- *Travel and Expense Management*: This provides an automated and simplified travel and expense management solution. This solution can be implemented using the included applications: Oracle Financial Analytics, Internet Expenses, Oracle Financials, Payables, and Payments.

Human Capital Management Family

The human capital management family delivers business applications and solutions for constructing a global and sophisticated human resource environment to increase productivity, manage labor, increase the motivation of employees, analyze the workforce efficiency, and reduce the costs of service delivery. The processes of these applications also comply with local laws and regulations. The main application in this family is called Human Resources.

- *Global Core Human Capital Management*: This solution delivers a complete, worldwide HR management system, which includes these applications: Human Resources, Self-Service Human Resources, Advanced Benefits, Compensation Workbench, iRecruitment, Payroll, Performance Management, Time and Labor, and Succession Planning.

- *Workforce Management*: This provides a detailed workforce management solution that addresses such needs as labor forecasting, schedule management, capturing the labor data, tracking the workforce, and adhering to labor laws and pay rules. It is a solution for managing the workforce using the HRMS applications and other EBS solutions such as Time and Labor, Advanced Scheduler, Project Resource Management, and Mobile Field Service.

- *Talent Management*: This is a talent management solution that provides talent management requirements such as planning, recruiting, performance, learning, career development, succession planning, compensation, talent reviews, and measuring and reporting. It is a solution for delivering talent management using the HRMS applications.

- *HR Analytics*: This provides business intelligence for analyzing workforce staffing and productivity. This application is an OBIEE application that gets its data from EBS. So, it is used with EBS HR applications to bring the business intelligence into the EBS environments.

Project Portfolio Management Family

The applications and solutions in the project portfolio management family provide project and portfolio management features including forecasting, budgeting for the profitability, resource assignments, and so on. The main application in this family is called Projects.

- *Project Analytics*: This provides business intelligence for analyzing important project data such as forecasts, budgets, cost, revenue, billing, and profitability. This application is an OBIEE application that gets its data from EBS. So, it is used with EBS to bring business intelligence into the EBS environments.

- *Project Billing*: This provides the ability to measure the profitability of contract projects, as well as simplified client invoicing and improved cash flow. It is an option to be implemented under the Project Costing solution of the Projects application.

- *Project Contracts*: This provides the ability to deliver complex, project-driven commercial and government contracts.

- *Project Collaboration*: This provides a platform for project members to collaborate and communicate. It is a solution to be implemented within the Projects application.

- *Project Costing*: This provides an integrated cost management solution for all projects and activities. It is a solution to be implemented within the Projects application.

- *Project Management*: This is a consolidated project management solution for planning the work, assigning the resources, forecasting the competition, and communicating with stakeholders.

- *Project Resource Management*: This fulfils a management need for the capacity and deployment of people and assets for project work. It is a solution to be implemented within the Projects application.

- *Project Portfolio Analysis*: This supplies the ability to analyze, prioritize, and choose the right set of projects.

Advanced Procurement Family

The applications and solutions in the advanced procurement management family are there to support the whole process for procurements.

- *iSupplier Portal*: This is an Internet-based portal that provides all the supplier communication. It is an option to be implemented within the Purchasing application.

- *iProcurement*: This is a self-service solution for controlling employee spending.

- *Oracle Procurement and Spend Analytics*: This offers business intelligence for procurement. This application is an OBIEE application that gets its data from EBS and is used with EBS to bring business intelligence into the EBS environments.

- *Oracle Spend Classification*: This supplies accurate categorization of past spending data. It is a component of Oracle iProcurement.

- *Oracle Supplier Network*: This is a secure online service that provides automated electronic document exchange with suppliers.

- *Oracle Supplier Hub*: This provides critical supplier information for quickly onboarding, evaluating, and managing suppliers.

- *Landed Cost Management*: This enables the financial visibility into the extended supply chain costs.

- *Procurement Contracts*: This is a solution that is part of the advanced procurement family and provides the ability to create and enforce better purchasing contracts.

- *Purchasing*: This delivers a modern purchase order processing for professional buyers. Purchasing includes optional solutions to be implemented with it, such as Sourcing, Sourcing Optimization, iSupplier Portal, Procurement Contracts, Services Procurement, and Advanced Pricing.

- *Services Procurement*: This is an EBS solution that provides control for the services spending.

- *Supplier Lifecycle Management*: This is an EBS solution that supplies the ability to streamline registration, review the potential suppliers, evaluate the cross-functional performance, assure effective governance, and mitigate risk.

- *Oracle Contract Lifecycle Management for Public Sector*: This is a solution that provides a procure-to-pay system with automated and auditable processes.

Supply Chain Management Family

The applications and solutions in the supply chain management family provide integrated supply chain processes for delivering complete and information-driven value chains.

- *Advanced Procurement*: This provides supply management applications and solutions for managing goods and services and procure-to-pay processes spending.

- *Value Chain Execution*: This is a solution for logistics needs. Value Chain Execution includes Transportation Management, Landed Cost Management, Warehouse Management, Global Trade Management, Mobile Supply Chain, and Inventory Management. The products for the value chain execution family are also considered EBS products, even though there are value chain execution applications such as Oracle Transportation Management, which is integrated with the EBS products but resides outside of the EBS environment.

- *Order Orchestration and Fulfillment*: This provides support for planning, configuration, pricing, and orchestration and fulfillment processes.

- *Asset Lifecycle Management*: This provides effective asset management. This solution consists of Enterprise Asset Management, Self-Service Work Requests, Asset Tracking, and Property Manager.

- *Manufacturing*: This provides a complete manufacturing solution with capabilities such as configure-to-order, project manufacturing, outsourcing, and quality management capabilities.

- *Product Value Chain Management*: This provides the ability to innovate, develop, and commercialize compliant products.

- *Value Chain Planning*: This provides demand-driven planning. It includes applications such as Advanced Planning Command Center, Advanced Supply Chain Planning, Collaborative Planning, Demand Management, Demand Signal Repository, Global Order Promising, Inventory Optimization, and more.

- *Business Intelligence and Analytics: Business Intelligence for Oracle Supply Chain and Order Management*: This application is an OBIEE application that gets its data from EBS.

As you can see, within Oracle EBS there are many application families and quite a few applications to support today's business needs. This big and integrated application environment is modular in deployment, so it saves time and increases the efficiency for organizations.

Because the modules and supplementary system are tightly integrated, the solutions provided seem to be served from a single source. This of course is accomplished by the ultimate application design, high-level software engineering, and power within the Oracle technologies.

Exposing such an application ecosystem is a big job, but the duties of deploying, managing, troubleshooting, tuning, supporting, and maintenance are also important responsibilities. As you may imagine, all of these duties fall on the shoulders of the applications DBA; that's why the job requires a high-level understanding of EBS-specific features as well as the underlying technologies.

The technology stack starts from the features in EBS and includes the Oracle data model stored in Oracle Database as a built-in data store for EBS. The separation of duties means applications DBAs can be focused on the EBS-specific technologies and leave the database administration to the core database administration. Still, we believe applications DBAs should know the core DDA activities and have the experience in those activities as well.

Understanding the architectural model of Oracle E-Business Suite is as important as knowing commands and which actions to take for administrating an Oracle E-Business Suite environment properly. Thus, it is better to start with understanding the Oracle E-Business Suite architectural model before going into further detail about the E-Business Suite components.

Understanding the Oracle E-Business Suite's Three-Tier Architecture Model

The Oracle EBS architecture is based on multitier computing and consists of three tiers.

- In the *desktop tier*, you have PCs or any supported desktop clients that are able to run a browser, which provides the HMTL or HTML-based applications as well as a Java applet for opening Oracle Forms–based applications.

- The *application tier* consists of Fusion Middleware (FMW), web services, forms services, Java application services, and the concurrent processing server. This tier sits between the desktop and database tiers and drives the business logic. It is also referred to as the *middle tier* because it supplies the communication between the desktop and database tiers.

- The *database tier* sits in the back end; it consists of Oracle Database and its services for storing and managing all the data maintained by Oracle EBS.

Figure 1-1 shows the tree-tier model; it illustrates the technologies and tools that provide the related application services in each tier. You can see that the client interface is provided by the web browser and the Sun Java plug-in, the application services are provided by FMW and the concurrent processing server, and lastly the database tier is actually Oracle Database 11g R2 or 12c.

Web Browser
with Oracle/Sun
Java Plug-In

Fusion
MiddleWare (FMW)
-Web Services
-Forms Services
-Java Application Services

Concurrent
Processing
Server

Oracle Database
11g R2 or 12c

Figure 1-1. *Tree-tier model presenting the EBS tree-tier architecture*

So you have a better understanding of the three-tier architecture, we will go into the details of the each tier and explain the components specific to each tier. Let's start with the desktop tier.

The desktop tier is about the browser, but we can't say it is all about the browser because running the Forms Java applet is also an important role of desktop clients. When using EBS HTML pages, all of the processing is done by the web server of EBS, but when it comes to the forms pages/screens, the desktop client plays the big role. The forms screen works in the client by transferring the related JAR files from the network on the fly. So, whenever a client wants to open an EBS forms-based application, the relevant JAR files are transferred automatically from the server to the client machine and the client's JVM, which can be considered to be a Java plug-in integrated into the browser; it executes the code inside these JAR files and displays the forms screen through an applet running on the client machine.

Forms are widely used within the applications of EBS, but there are some applications (such as self-service applications) that are processed through HTML-based pages and don't require clients to open any forms screens.

Figure 1-2 shows a closer look at the process needed to establish a client's form session and shows what is happening between the client tier and the application tier when a form session is created.

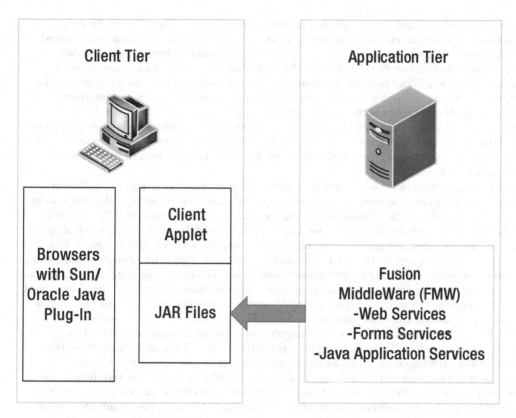

Figure 1-2. *JAR fies supplied to clients*

As shown in Figure 1-2, JAR files are supplied to the clients by the Fusion Middleware server. During the form execution, JAR files are obtained and executed by the client's Sun J2SE plug-in enabled browser through a Java applet.

The purpose of the application tier is to serve HTTP, Java, forms, and concurrent processing services. The application tier can consist of multiple servers, which can be configured to run in a load balancing and failover manner. A load balancing and failover configuration can be used for web, forms, and concurrent processing services.

The application tier consists of Oracle HTTP Server, Oracle Application Server 10.1.2, Oracle Fusion Middleware, and concurrent processing services. Although all major services are started from the Fusion Middleware, using two application servers is a design choice. These four main technologies work together for supplying EBS services.

When serving HTML-based applications, Oracle HTTP Server provides the web listener for accepting the client requests and directs them to the WebLogic Server present in Fusion Middleware if needed. Oracle WebLogic Server supplies the Oracle Applications Framework and creates the database interaction through a servlet engine. That is, WebLogic validates the user access, obtains the metadata UI definition and relevant data for the page, creates the HTML, and sends the page to the browser.

When serving forms-based applications, EBS uses a forms listener servlet or traditionally a forms server in socket mode. Using servlet or socket mode is a matter of preference and also a requirement for using some features that are not available in socket mode, such as SSL. However, the form servlet is the latest technology in this area. It is more convenient for Internet connections because it offers more robustness and security and because it has the ability to reestablish dropped network connections and requires fewer ports. Oracle EBS 12.2 uses forms servlet by default, but configuring forms socket mode is also possible.

In forms servlet mode, the web listener triggers the forms listener servlet, which creates the forms runtime processes for each client and manages the communication between the client and its associated forms runtime process. The forms listener servlet also communicates with the Oracle database server using Oracle Net, but actual database work is done by the forms runtime process. So, you can consider the forms listener servlet as a bridge between the client, the forms runtime process, and the database. The communication from the client appears to be based on the HTTP responses through the web services. Besides, the forms servlet architecture is compatible with the application industry standards.

In forms socket mode, the client action data such as a clicking a button is passed to the associated form server, in which the UI interface logic runs. This communication is made using the TCP/IP network protocol, so desktop clients access the forms server directly. On the back end, the Oracle Forms runtime process makes the database interaction.

Apart from the applications based on the user interaction, which employs Oracle Fusion Middleware components and the Oracle Forms services, there are long-running batches and reporting and data updating programs inside an EBS environment. These programs may be run as scheduled or triggered from the web interfaces such as forms or HTML-based applications, but they run in the background and are handled by the concurrent processing server. The *concurrent processing* term is specific to Oracle EBS. The processing done here is actually the management of the back-end program executions. That is, the concurrent processing consists of program managers called *concurrent managers*, which run on their own operating system processes. These concurrent managers are programs for managing other programs called *concurrent requests*. Any type of program that is instructed to be executed by the concurrent manager is accepted to be a concurrent program, and its start, finish, termination, and scheduling are managed by its associated concurrent manager.

By default, there are a number of concurrent managers, that come pre-configured with the EBS installation. Of course, these default concurrent managers can be configured and tuned according to the workload. Also, custom concurrent managers for executing some custom programs can be created.

The first concurrent manager started is the Internal Concurrent Manager (ICM), as it controls all the other concurrent managers. Conflict Resolution Manager (CRM) is also an important one because it deals with the conflicts among the runnable concurrent programs. Standard Manager is the default concurrent manager for all the concurrent programs. If a concurrent program is not configured to be executed by a specific concurrent manager, Standard Manager runs it.

As mentioned earlier, there are a number of concurrent managers, and we will go into the details of them in Chapter 10.

The database tier in EBS actually means Oracle Database. It has the technology of Oracle Database, where the EBS data model and EBS-specific database objects such as indexes and tables are stored. There are special database schemas for the use of apps DBAs, the EBS tech stack, and the application modules inside of EBS database.

There is no direct communication between the clients and the database. The services, or servers run in the application tier, communicate with the database for storing, updating, deleting, structuring, and querying the data. We will give the details about the data model later in this chapter.

So, basically, the HTML services, Java-based services, forms services, concurrent processing services, and Oracle Database are components used in EBS. The HTML, Java-based, and forms services are almost transparent; there are almost no details for you to analyze, the configuration of these services is straightforward, and the actions for managing them are more like starting, stopping, and troubleshooting.

By contrast, this is not the case for concurrent programs. To manage the concurrent tier, you need to know more details.

Concurrent Processing

Concurrent processing in EBS implies the completion of tasks in the background, while maintaining work done by the clients using the EBS web and forms interfaces. Besides, the works in background are done concurrently in concurrent processing, which makes *concurrent processing* an optimal term for describing this technology. In Chapter 10, we will go into the details of concurrent managers, but it is important to know the general information now.

Concurrent processing is supplied by the concurrent managers, as they are the parent programs that are responsible for managing the program executions. Programs defined to be run by the concurrent managers are called the *concurrent programs*. The term used for describing the request for running a concurrent program is *concurrent request*. When a program is requested to run or is scheduled to run, a concurrent request for that program is created and placed in its associated concurrent manager's queue. The concurrent manager by design checks its queue and meets the concurrent request waiting in its queue. To meet the request, a concurrent manager actually runs the associated concurrent program with its supplied arguments by interpreting the associated concurrent request, as concurrent requests carry this information. There is also a mechanism for controlling the concurrency between these concurrent requests; a separate concurrent manager is dedicated to this work. Any requests that must not be run while another concurrent request is running are placed in this concurrent manager's queue and wait there until the incompatible concurrent request finishes running. This mechanism is supplied and configured with the rules that are used to define the incompatibility settings.

We'll now identify the concurrent managers so you have a clearer picture about concurrent processing. The main concurrent managers come predefined in EBS. The most important of these managers are Internal Manager, Standard Manager, Conflict Resolution Manager, and Transaction Managers.

Internal Manager is the main concurrent manager that is programmed to do the internal work. Internal Manager is started by the concurrent manager start script, and it is responsible for starting up, verifying, resetting, and shutting down all other concurrent managers.

Standard Manager is the default concurrent manager of all requests. It accepts and runs all the concurrent requests if they are not configured to run by another manager and excluded explicitly from Standard Manager.

Conflict Resolution Manager is responsible for managing the conflicts between the concurrent requests. Any request breaking the compatibility rules is placed in its queue and waits there until the environment become appropriate for it to run.

Transaction Managers are predefined managers. They support synchronous processing, and they are dedicated to the concurrent request triggered by the client applications. That is, a form interface may have the option to run a concurrent program to do a transaction, and if that is the situation, this concurrent program may be configured to run by the associated Transaction Manager.

In addition, custom concurrent managers can be created and configured to run the custom concurrent programs. Custom managers are often preferred for separating the queues of the standard and custom concurrent programs. This type of configuration guarantees the standard programs to be run without any unpredictable delays that may be caused by the high number of ready-to-run custom concurrent programs filling Standard Manager's queue.

Database Tier and EBS Data Model

The database tier and the EBS data model make up one of the important layers of EBS. All the application tier components and processes work by considering the EBS data model, and they do all their database activities by connecting to Oracle Database, which comes packaged with EBS.

EBS uses the world's leading relational database management system (RDBMS), Oracle Database. The database version included with the installation depends on the EBS release. For example, in EBS 12.1, the default database that comes with the installation is 11.1.0.7; in EBS 12.2, Oracle Database 11.2.0.3, 11.2.0.4, or 12.1.0.2 (with the latest installation package) comes as the default database.

Needless to say, the database in EBS can be upgraded to the higher releases, even to 12c, which is supported by all major releases such as EBS 11.5.10.2, 12.1, and 12.2.

EBS's Oracle Database is managed just like a standard Oracle Database, but there are some extras for DBA's management activities. This includes a role named Apps DBA.

To manage Oracle Database, DBAs (namely, apps DBAs in EBS environments) need to know the standard core DBA activities. In addition, apps DBAs should know the EBS data model, which is stored inside the database and how to use tools such as Autoconfig and Rapid Clone to manage the apps-specific configuration and apps schema structure. There are important differences even in managing database accounts such as managing database schema passwords. That is, apps DBAs should use a tool for changing a user's password; they can't just execute an alter user command from SQL*Plus to accomplish that.

We will go into detail about these tools and management activities later in this book, but here we'll introduce the EBS data model.

The EBS data model consists of base product schemas. These base product schemas are the database representation of EBS applications. For storing the General Ledger, there are schemas like GL, the INV schema is used for Inventory, AP is used for Account Payables, PO for Purchase and Orders, and so on. The base product schemas continue in this way, and they store data objects such as tables, sequences, indexes, constraints, and queues of their associated product.

So, the base product schemas store the data, and the schema called APPS stores the product code objects. The APPS schema is the most important schema for apps DBAs because it is used in almost every applications DBA operation. The APPS schema is also important for EBS because it is the schema that drives the application. The APPS schema has the grants and synonyms for accessing the entire Oracle E-Business Suite data model, which consists of all the objects of the base product schemas. This makes the APPS schema special and also is used by the EBS system internally.

After the login, the EBS system uses the APPS schema to connect to the database and do the database-related operations using this schema. No matter what application is used, EBS uses the APPS schema internally to get through the related data model.

There are also other EBS schemas that provide the integrity and make it work. The APPLSYS schema is an example of these kinds of schemas. APPLSYS stores the objects of the applications technology layer products such as Foundation (FND) and Applications DBA (AD).

The GUEST and APPLSYSPUB accounts are important accounts too. GUEST is an EBS account and is used internally by EBS to access and display EBS web pages like the login page when there is no application authentication present.

APPLSYSPUB is a public database account, and it is used for EBS authentication. The supplied application's usernames and passwords are authenticated inside the database, and this database connection is made using the APPLSYSPUB schema.

The APPLSYSPUB and GUEST schemas are transparent to the APPS DBAs. They have default passwords, do not require any administration operations, and work internally. The base product schemas are managed by EBS actually, but it is important to know the structures of them and their relation with APPS in order to have the full control over an EBS database.

APPLSYS is the application system schema. As mentioned earlier, it stores the APPS systems objects, but it is not involved intensely in administration operations.

Of course, there are also schemas such as SYS and SYSTEM inside the database because they are the system schemas for the Oracle Database itself. In addition, there are schemas to support optional database features such as MDSYS, ORDSYS, OLAPSYS, and CTXSYS. Even the famous sample schema named SCOTT comes with the installation.

Also, custom database schemas can be created for storing the objects related to customizations and the data produced by customized code, but care must be taken here as the custom schema should be added appropriately. We will cover this topic in Chapter 8.

The main focus of an apps DBA is the APPS schema because it means the same thing as the SYSTEM schema for Oracle Database. It has the access rights for reaching the other schemas, it used internally by the EBS system, and it is used in almost every kind of administration operation.

Figure 1-3 is a good representation for describing the relationship between APPS, APPLSYS, and base product schemas.

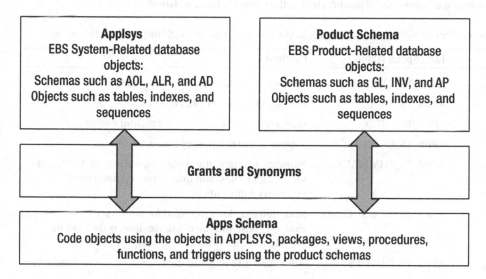

Figure 1-3. Relationship between APPS, APPSYS, and PRODUCT schemas in EBS 12.2 SCHEMA

As shown in Figure 1-3, the APPS schema accesses both the base product and APPLSYS schemas to make the EBS system run properly. EBS application tier components use the APPS schema to access all the base product schemas and APPLSYS through grants and synonyms.

There are some situations that require you to re-create these grants and synonyms. Fortunately, an administration tool called Adadmin can be used for accomplishing this task. We will explain this kind of operation in detail in Chapter 9.

Because the data store of EBS is an Oracle database, it is needless to say that the EBS data model stands on the tablespaces. The block size used for the tablespace, actually for the whole EBS database, is 8KB. EBS releases 12.1 and 12.2 both require tablespaces with 8KB in size. This is because having the EBS database with 8KB block sizes makes the whole system perform well, and Oracle E-Business Suite indexes accommodate 8k block size.

In an EBS database, the standard tablespaces such as System, Undo, and Temporary are normally present. The Undo tablespace and the System tablespace are used instance wide.

The Temporary tablespace in an EBS database can be more than one. That is, dedicated Temporary tablespaces can be created to separate the temp usages of each EBS product.

However, creating dedicated temporary tablespace is not an effective method. Since EBS uses the APPS schema to connect to the database, the Temporary tablespace of the APPS schema becomes the default Temporary tablespace for all the EBS products.

EBS 12.2 uses 12 tablespaces including Temporary, System, and Undo. So, there are nine EBS-specific tablespaces present in EBS 12.2.

These tablespaces are locally managed, and they are delivered to have 128Kb uniform extent sizes by default. Alternatively, you can auto-allocate extent management, which is a simpler and more efficient method and can be used for managing the extent sizes of EBS tablespaces. If auto-allocate extent management is your choice, you can accomplish it by re-creating the tablespaces with the auto-allocate extent management option and re-migrating the objects to these tablespaces. This is required because the Oracle RDBMS server does not support changing the extent management of a locally managed tablespace.

In EBS 12.2, the object-tablespace classifications are based on the Oracle Applications Tablespace Model (OATM).

Table 1-1 summarizes the tablespace types, tablespace names, and related contents. The database objects in EBS 12.2 are categorized based on their contents and stored in the relevant tablespaces, which have the desired tablespace type whose definition meets the content characteristics.

Table 1-1. *EBS Tablespaces Providing the Tablespace and Content Types for the Standard EBS Tablespaces*

Tablespace Type	Tablespace Name	Content
Transaction tables	APPS_TS_TX_DATA	Tables that contain transactional data
Transaction indexes	APPS_TS_TX_IDX	Indexes on transactional tables
Reference	APPS_TS_SEED	Reference and setup-based data and indexes
Interface	APPS_TS_INTERFACE	Interface and temporary data and indexes
Summary	APPS_TS_SUMMARY	Summary management objects, such as materialized views, fact tables, and other objects that record summary information
No logging	APPS_TS_NOLOGGING	Materialized views not used for summary management and the database objects that can be rebuilt, in other words, do not require recovery
Advanced queuing	APPS_TS_QUEUES	Advanced queuing and dependent tables and indexes
Media	APPS_TS_MEDIA	Multimedia objects
Archive	APPS_TS_ARCHIVE	Tables that contain archived and purged data
Undo	APPS_UNDOTS1	Undo tablespace with automatic undo management
Temporary	TEMP tablespace group with tablespaces TEMP1 and TEMP2	Temporary tablespace for global temporary tables, sorts, and hash joins
System	SYSTEM	Standard System tablespace of Oracle Database

As shown in Table 1-1, the objects are grouped into tablespaces. OATM makes this classification based on rules called Explicit and Implicit Classification rules. In Implicit Classification rules, OATM classifies the objects based on their object types. That is, while it stores the AQ tables (Queue tables used by Oracle Advanced Queuing) in APPS_TS_QUEUE, which is a dedicated tablespace for advanced queuing objects, it stores the transaction table indexes in APPS_TS_TX_IDX, which is a dedicated tablespace for indexes on transactional tables.

Table 1-2 shows the implicit rules and the distribution of the objects to the tablespaces.

Table 1-2. *Object Types and Tablespace Type Associations*

Object Type	Tablespace Type
AQ tables	AQ
IOTS	Transaction tables
Materialized views	Summary
Materialized view logs	Summary
All other indexes	Same tablespace type as the table
Domain indexes	Transaction indexes
Indexes on transactional tables	Transaction indexes

Explicit rules take this distribution into a higher level because these rules are based on the I/O characteristics of an object. These classifications are seeded by Oracle.

In addition to the information provided earlier, the objects that are not mentioned in the implicit rules are stored in the default tablespace of their owner schemas. It is also important to know that the default tablespace for all the EBS schemas are set to APPS_TS_TX_DATA.

So, you have seen the database tier by going through the database schemas and tablespace model. At this point, you have detailed information about what an EBS database looks like.

Let's continue with the technology stack components and take a detailed look at them now.

Understanding the EBS 12.2 Technology Stack Components

E-Business Suite's technology stack consists of application tier technology components and database tier technology components. These components come installed and configured when the installation is complete.

As for technology stack components, there are various technologies to support the diversity of the services that EBS offers to the clients.

The technology stack components in version EBS 12.2 (the latest release 12.2.5) can be categorized as Oracle technologies, Java technologies, technologies delivered in applications (APPL_TOP technologies), and external technologies.

Table 1-3 summarizes these groups of technologies with the versions delivered with the latest EBS 12.2.5 installation.

Table 1-3. *Oracle Technologies and Their Component Versions in EBS 12.2.5, Deployed with the Latest Installation Package (startCD–startCD 51)*

Oracle Technology	Version
Oracle Database	12.1.2.0
JDK on concurrent processing node	1.7.0_85
JDK version used by AD utilities	1.7.0_85
Sun JDK client version	1.6.0_27
JDK version on HTTP server node	1.7.0_85
JDK version on HTTP server node	1.7.0_85
OA Framework version	12.2.5
Oracle Application Server	10.1.2.3
Database client library version in Oracle Application Server	10.1.0.5.0
Oracle Application Server/Oracle Fusion Middleware	11.1.1.9
Oracle WebLogic Server	Oracle WebLogic Server 10.3.6
XDK for the database tier	11.1.1.9
Oracle HTTP Server	11.1.1.9

■ **Note**   EBS 12.2 is installed as the base release 12.2.0, which is not supported and required to be immediately upgraded to a supported patchset (currently 12.2.2 and upward). At the time of writing this book, the latest patchset level of EBS 12.2 was 12.2.5, so although EBS 12.2.5 is not directly installable because it is provided with an upgrade patch, the following version information provided is based on this patchset level, 12.2.5, because it is currently the most stable and latest patchset among all the supported patchsets of EBS 12.2.

The database tier technology component in EBS 12.2 basically implies Oracle Database.

As for the latest EBS 12.2 release installed with the latest startCD (currently startCD 51), EBS's database tier is Oracle Database 12.1.0.2, which is a stable release of Oracle Database. As for the EBS 12.2 environments, which are deployed using earlier startCD versions, the database tier can be deployed as Oracle Database 11.2.0.3 or 11.2.0.4 according to the version of the startCD that is used for the installation. On the other hand, as using Oracle Database 12c is supported with EBS 12.2, the database tier can be upgraded to 12c for these environments, as well.

The XML Development Kit (XDK) for Java is a database feature that contains a set of components, tools, and utilities for building, deploying, and supporting XML-enabled applications. These components can be for various XML processing operations such as parsing XML, validating XML, transforming XML documents into another format, and generating Java and C++ classes from input XML schemas.

So, EBS uses the XDK through Oracle XML Gateway in certain transactions such as inbound transactions; it is used to get the XML files/messages and parse and import the data into the application tables for further processing.

Oracle Application Server 10.1.2.3, also called as Developer Home in EBS 12.2, is used for providing forms and reports services. Forms services are provided by cooperating with FMW. It is in the form of an Oracle Home, which has several binaries, libraries, and configuration files to provide its services.

You can take a deeper look at this process by referring to Figure 1-4, where the cooperation between the FMW components and Oracle 10.1.2 Home (needed for providing the form services) is described.

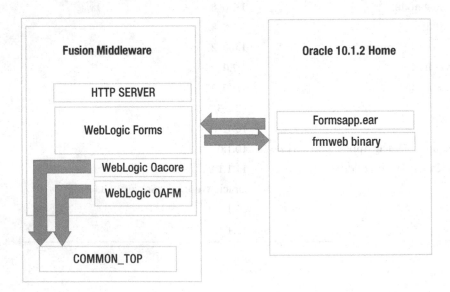

Figure 1-4. *The relationship between 10.1.2 Oracle Home and WebLogic forms services*

As shown in Figure 1-4, there is a relationship between 10.1.2 Oracle Home and the WebLogic form services. Figure 1-4 also shows the WebLogic Oacore and OAFM services reaching the Java classes, HTML pages, and other files and directories stored in the COMMON_TOP directory. (We will explain COMMON_TOP later in this chapter.)

The EBS modules (formsapp.ear) and the actual forms executable (frmweb) runs on this 10.1.2 application tier Home, but all the major services for frmweb are served by the Oracle Fusion Middleware. So, when an Oracle report program is executed or a client request is made for opening an Oracle form-based EBS screen, the binaries in this Oracle Home are triggered.

Oracle Fusion Middleware (FMW) 11.1.1.9.0 is the application server for applications that provide the core functionalities in EBS Java code. Using the WebLogic Server that resides in it, FMW hosts the Oacore server to provide the pages developed with Oracle Application Framework (OAF), which is a framework supplied by Oracle to be used for development within the Oracle E-Business Suite OAFM to provide such as web services and a secure enterprise search agent. In addition, it hosts the forms server for services, all the forms functionality, and forms-c4ws to expose forms-based functionalities as web services.

A JSP compiler and JSP engine are also included in FMW.

The WebLogic JSP compiler, weblogic appc, is used for the precompilation of JSP pages in EBS. The SP engine is used for processing the JSP pages and converting them to the servlets.

FMW also includes control mechanisms/utilities for its core WebLogic services, as well as all the JRF files needed by EBS and Oracle HTTP Server to be used as a web entry point for EBS.

So, Oracle HTTP Server, WebLogic Server, 10.1.2 Home services, and the binaries stored in application directories such as COMMON_TOP and APPL_TOP are used together for the application tier processing. Figure 1-5 shows the FMW components such as Oracle HTTP Server and WebLogic Server, as well as the other technologies such as 10.1.2 Oracle Home and three important top-level EBS directories such as APPL_TOP, COMMON_TOP, and INST_TOP working together.

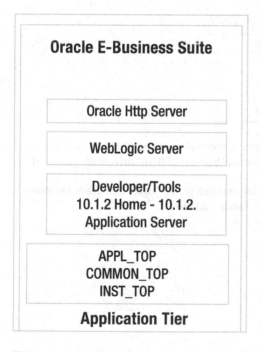

Figure 1-5. *Oracle E-Business Suite application and database tier components*

The XDK is also present in the application tier. The XDK in the application tier is used mostly in the application reports such as the Account Analysis report. Data gathering activities of these kinds of applications are based on XML publisher technology that relies on XDK in the back end.

Oracle FMW comes with Oracle HTTP Server 11.1.1.9.0 for accepting HTTP requests and passing them to the related WebLogic services if needed.

Oracle HTTP Server can provide responses for basic requests, without passing them to the WebLogic servers.

Table 1-4 summarizes the Java technologies that come with the latest version, EBS 12.2 (12.2.5).

Table 1-4. *Java Technologies and the Versions Used in EBS 12.2.5*

Java Technology	Version
Java SE development kit	7
Native Java plug-in	6

There are two JAVA SE developments kits (JDKs) present in EBS 12.2. One of them is used for the programs related to concurrent processing, which are not provided by WebLogic Server. The second JDK is used for Oracle application tier Java code and the application framework.

There is also a native Java plug-in stored in the EBS application tier. This plug-in is used for client-side forms interfaces. That is, if a client requests opening a form-based interface, then this plug-in is transferred to the client on the fly, and by using this plug-in, the client browser can open the forms through the Java applet.

Also, there are technologies deployed in the Oracle applications APPL_TOP directory. Table 1-5 summarizes technology components delivered within the Oracle applications directory, APPL_TOP.

Table 1-5. *Technology Components in APPL_TOP Directory [CAPTION]*

Technology Delivered in APPL_TOP	Version
Oracle JDeveloper runtime libraries	10.1.3
Oracle BI beans	3.1.1.14
Oracle thin JDBC drivers	11.2.0.3

In the APPL_TOP directory of EBS12.2, standard JDeveloper runtime libraries and BI beans are delivered to support applications leveraged from them. In addition, Oracle thin JDBC drivers are provided for use in the database connections.

In addition to the technologies delivered with EBS, there are external technologies that are considered to be part of an EBS environment but are not deployed with an EBS installation.

Table 1-6 lists these technologies and their supported versions.

Table 1-6. *External Technologies and Their Latest Versions Certified with EBS 12.2.5*

Externally Installed Oracle Technology	Versions Certified with EBS 12.2.5 as of April 2016
Oracle Internet Directory	11g Release 1 (11.1.1.9.0)
Oracle Access Manager	11.1.2.3
Oracle Business Intelligence Enterprise Edition	12.2.1.1
Oracle Discoverer	11.1.1.7
Oracle WebCenter Portal	11.1.1.9
Oracle Portal	11.1.1.7
Oracle BPEL Process Manager	11.1.1.9
Oracle Enterprise Manager for EBS	12.1.0.4

Oracle Internet Directory when used with Oracle Access Manager supplies the single sign-on for EBS. Oracle Business Intelligence is a separate program for delivering the business intelligence but can also be integrated into EBS.

Oracle Discoverer brings a reporting solution into an EBS environment. Discoverer is a powerful reporting tool that supplies a reporting platform for creating reports with almost any details and advanced reporting capabilities.

Oracle WebCenter Portal is used to create websites and portals, and the integration of EBS applications to a WebCenter Portal application is certified with EBS. Oracle Portal is a Fusion Middleware component used for creating enterprise portals, and these portals too can be in conjunction with EBS.

With the Release 12.2, Oracle BPEL Process Manager 11.1.1.9 can be used for the integration. Systems like Oracle Transportation Manager can be integrated to EBS using this method.

Oracle Enterprise Manager 12c provides an Oracle EBS plug-in for managing the EBS system using Oracle Enterprise Manager. Enterprise Manager 12c has EBS-specific capabilities such as performance monitoring and cloning support.

We've now introduced the technology components, so let's proceed with the EBS 12.2 file system structure; looking the components explained earlier from the file system may provide a better understanding of them.

Oracle EBS 12.2 File System Structure

The EBS 12.2 file system structure can be classified in two groups: the database tier file system and the application tier file system.

Database Tier File System

The database tier file system consists of a directory structure called Oracle Home, similar to a directory structure that comes after a standard database installation.

The EBS database tier file system structure is similar to a standard database file system structure, but they are not the same. The database tier in EBS has some additions on top of the standard database Home file system structure to support EBS-specific configurations.

The EBS database, when installed using the latest startCD, is delivered as an Enterprise Edition 12.1.0.2 64-bit Oracle Database patched with a list of the latest technology bug fixes required for Oracle E-Business Suite Release 12.2, as well as a set of recommended patches. Oracle Home contains the Oracle Database 12c products (12.1.0.2) delivered with the 12c examples CD, as well. Using a Real Application Cluster (RAC) for the database tier is also an option; it brings a multinode configuration ability to the database tier. Rapidwiz, which is the installation tool of EBS, has an optional Oracle RAC installation, too.

The big difference in an EBS Oracle Home is the existence of an appsutil directory. The appsutil directory inside an Oracle EBS Oracle RDBMS Home contains Perl scripts, bash scripts, SQL scripts, a Java runtime environment, JAR files, a clone directory, and a log directory for the use of application-specific database activities, such as database tier cloning and AutoConfig, as well as pure database-oriented activities such as starting/stopping database and the listener.

The appsutil directory comes with the installation, but it can be rebuilt if needed.

Rebuilding it is easy. To do that, you create an appsutil zip file in the application tier using application utilities designed for this purpose and then copy this zip file to the Oracle Home of the database with the proper file permissions, which lets the Oracle Database software owner use the scripts and all the other files contained in it.

Once the copying is done, you just unzip to extract the content of it. The content is actually the appsutil directory.

So, you have an appsutil directory in the database tier for supporting the EBS-specific database operations. We have mentioned the types of file stored in the appsutil directory. We'll now cover them in detail.

The appsutil directory consists of several subdirectories and a context file, as listed next.

■ **Note** There may be some new terms in the following list that will be explained in the coming chapters. We are just walking through the directories and files for now.

Sql: Stores SQL scripts that can be used in apps DBA activities (such as adgrants. sql, which is used for granting necessary privileges on a selected SYS object to the APPS user).

Java: Stores JAR files (xmlparserv2.jar) and classes (AutoConfigProcess.class, AutoConfigSynchronizer.class, and so on) for use by EBS-specific database utilities such as AutoConfig.

Media: Contains four standard GIF files for use by Oracle applications, such as the Oracle log. This directory is not relevant to the database tier, but it is there for use by applications, just in case.

Perl: Contains Perl modules such as AutoConfig.pm for use by TXK utilities such as TXKScript.pl, as well as modules such as Sysutil.pm for use by AD utilities such as adgentns.pl.

Html: Contains XML and XSL files for use by AutoConfig-related Java classes such as AppltopDrivers.class.

jre: Provides Java runtime environments for use by Java classes inside the appsutil directory.

temp: Is a temporary folder for use by application utilities present inside the appsutil directory. This folder acts as temporary file storage. The utilities inside the appsutil directory are designed for placing their temp files within directories related to their core.

■ **Note** txkEBSWrapper.pl sets its temp directory destination to $ORACLE_HOME/appsutil/temp/TXK.

Clone: Stores the file adcrdb.zip, which contains the scripts adcrdb.sh and adcrdbclone.sql to re-create the control file and start up the database. These script files are used by rapid clone Java classes such as ApplyRmanDatabase.class while creating a clone database. Also, its subdirectory bin (clone/bin) is created by the preclone and stores the post clone-related Perl scripts. Cloning and all these scripts will be explained in detail in Chapter 11.

Bin: Provides the bash and Perl scripts for application-specific database activities such as AutoConfig. These scripts are normally run by following the directions in the Oracle Support documents, and some of them are used internally, but it is still worth knowing what they're for. The scripts and their definitions are as follows:

- adbldxml.pl: This is an AutoConfig tool to generate the context file for the database's Oracle Home.

- adchkcfg.sh/adchkcfg.cmd (for Windows): This runs the AutoConfig tool to test reconfiguration on the apps tier and the database tier.

- adchkutl.sh: The checks the system for ld, ar, cc, and make.

- adclonectx.pl: This is a Perl script that clones the context file.

- adclone.pl: This runs the AutoConfig tool to clone applications.

- adclone.sh: This is an obsoleted script for the same purpose as adclone.pl. It runs the AutoConfig tool to clone applications.

- adconfig.pl: This runs the AutoConfig tool to reconfigure the APPL_TOP directory and the database Oracle Home.

- adconfig.sh: This runs the AutoConfig tool to reconfigure APPL_TOP.

- adcustomizer.sh/adcustomizer.cmd (for Windows): This is an obsolete script that performs the task of migrating the customizations done by users to AutoConfig-generated files to the custom template. This script has been obsoleted in 12.2 because beginning-to-end customizations are not supported in Release 12.2.

- adcvm.sh/adcvm.cmd (for Windows): This manages changes in values of the context file because of changes in the template.

- addlnctl.pl: This enables/disables password protection for the RDBMS password and changes the password of the already password-protected listener.

- adgendisks.pl: This creates a database staging area for Rapidwiz, which is the installation tool of EBS.

- adgentns.pl: This script is used to generate the tnsnames.ora with all the necessary tns entries, dynamically.

- adtmplreport.sh/adtmplreport.cmd (for Windows): This is a wrapper script for running ATTemplateReport.java, which is a utility to list the template names and their target file names and locations.

- adxerr.pl: This displays the cause and action sections of ADX error messages. It uses $AD_TOP/html/adxmsg.xml or <RDBMS_ORACLE_HOME>/appsutil/html/adxmsg.xml as an ADX message repository.

- txkDBSecUserAuditActionBanner.pl: This script is used to generate the banner file txkDBSecUserAuditActionBanner.txt in the appsutil/template during an AutoConfig run in the database tier.

- txkGenCtxInfRep.pl: This script is used to search for a keyword in all product top templates and generate a detailed report (text/HTML).

- txkHealthCheckReport.pl: This generates a health check report that contains current versions of the technologies installed, the latest version of the technologies installed, and recommendations, if necessary.

- txkInventory.pl: This generates a report containing versions of various technology components in the Oracle applications tech stack.

- txkrun.pl: This is a simple wrapper script to create a TXK::Script object and run the supplied script.

- TXKScript.pl: This is a simple wrapper script to create a TXK::Script object and run the supplied script. This script is similar to txkrun.pl, but it takes different arguments like a full path of the script to be executed and the logfile path. This script is generally used within txkInventory.pl for giving an output file to txkInventory.pl to write its report output.

Admin: Stores some scripts that are transferred from the application tier. Certain patches provide action plans such as "copy the adgrants.sql from Application Server to Database Server and place it inside the $ORACLE_HOME/appsutil/admin directory and run it from there."

Out: Stores the output files. This is used for apps utilities in operations such as database cloning. Certain intermediate scripts and their logs that are generated during the cloning operations are placed here (such as restore-single2.rman and run_utlrp.sql).

log: Stores log files generated during the executions of utilities. An example is the adconfig.log file, which provides the logs generated during an AutoConfig run.

Template: Stores AutoConfig template files, which are the sources for creating site-specific configuration files. AutoConfig reads the context file and creates the final configuration files by filling these template files with the values it gets from the context file.

Scripts: Contains scripts for executing AutoConfig, executing preclone, and stopping and starting the database and the listener.

- adautocfg.sh: This is a script for executing an AutoConfig. It is a wrapper for executing adconfig.sh stored in $ORACLE_HOME/appsutil/bin directory. adconfig.sh in turn calls the adconfig.pl Perl script, which does the actual job.

- adchknls.pl: This checks for the existence of the RDBMS $ORACLE_HOME/nls/data/9idata directory and the cr9idata.pl file in that directory.

- addbctl.sh: This is a script for starting and stopping the database.

- addlnctl.sh: This is a script for starting and stopping the database listener.

- adexecsql.pl: This executes all SQL scripts that update the profiles in an AutoConfig run.

- adlsnodes.sh: This is a wrapper on lsnodes to check whether the cluster manager is available in a RAC environment.

- adpreclone.pl: This is a Perl script that runs the source system cloning preparation.

- adstopdb.sql: This is used by addbctl.sh to stop the database.

- adstrtdb.sql: This is used by addbctl.sh to start the database.

Outbound: Stores file created from inside the database. It is pointed at by the database directory named APPS_DATA_FILE_DIR. It is used as a directory for storing the files created by extracting the data from the database.

Install: Stores various scripts for EBS-specific database activities such as cleaning the concurrent manager's queues, creating database directories, and setting some database-related EBS profile options.

In addition to the appsutil directory, there are two special files in the database tier: the context file and the environment file.

Context file: The context file is an XML file that stores the inputs mostly used while configuring the EBS system using the autoconfig tool. Its name is in the form of <s_systemname>_<s_hostname>.xml. The context file is used by AutoConfig to make the necessary system-wide configurations for the tier where it is executed. So, it can be considered an input file for the AutoConfig utility. Like the application tier, the context file is also used in the database tier. The context file in the database tier includes configurations for the EBS database. As, various configurations such as the listener port, the domain name can be done using AutoConfig, there are XML tags associated with the configuration of them in the context file. We will explain the context file with all its details in Chapter 8.

Environment file: The environment file is stored in the $ORACLE_HOME directory and used for setting the environment variables for managing EBS's Oracle database tier from the operating system. Once this file is sourced, you can do the database activities using the environment variables such as ORACLE_HOME, TNS_ADMIN, and so on. Its name is in the form of <s_systemname>_<s_hostname>.env.

So, as shown, the database tier of EBS consists of a standard Oracle RDBMS Home that has some EBS-related additions/utilities on it. EBS-specific utilities bring a need for competence in managing the EBS database stack, as these utilities are used for critical operations. A problem or a misconfiguration in this layer can break down the application tier connections as they rely on apps-specific configurations inside the database. In addition, this adds a new level on top of standard database administration and makes things a little hard. On the other hand, the good news is that once you know what to do and understand the logic, these apps-specific additions (explained earlier) inside the database home make it almost automatic to manage the EBS database.

Well, then, we have explained the database tier file system structure and given the necessary details where needed. Let's continue with the application file system structure.

Application Tier File System

The root directory of the EBS 12.2 application tier file system is called the *base directory*. The directory structure branches out from the base directory. The base directory is specified during the installation, and the branches are derived from the base directory.

Just under the base directory, there are three directories named fs1, fs2, and fs_ne and one file called EBSapps.env.

EBSapps.env is the environment file for EBS 12.2. It is EBS 12.2 file system aware and is used by apps DBAs to set the environment for EBS 12.2. EBSapps.env knows the dual file system architecture used in EBS 12.2 and sets the appropriate environment accordingly. That is, when it is executed with the "run" argument,

23

it sets the run time (active file system) environment, and when it is executed with the "patch" argument, it sets the patch environment with all the environment variables pointing to the patch file system directories and files. We will explain the run and patch file system later in this book, but let's take a quick look now.

The fs acronym is used for referring to the file system, and the numbers denote file system 1, file system 2, and a noneditioned file system. This fs-based file system architecture was introduced in EBS 12.2, and these file system directories, together called a *dual file system*, are the result of implementing an online patching mechanism. In the online patching mechanism, which is a new feature of EBS 12.2, these file system directories are used to store both the active and patched files in a different directory structure. That is, the fs1 and fs2 directories are used for storing the active (run) file system and patch file system in their subfolders. Thus, they are enabling an environment that can be switched from active to patch and from patch to active. Besides, these directories are switching their roles.

For example, suppose fs1 is the active, and suppose fs2 is the patch file system at time t0; then suppose the apps DBA applies a patch at time t1 and as a result of this patch initiates a cutover operation, which switches the file system from active to patch and from patch to active. So, at time t2, fs2 becomes the active (run), and fs1 becomes the patch file system.

In addition to these active and patch file systems, there is an fs_ne directory just under the base directory.

The directory fs_ne is a noneditioned file system for storing the noneditioned file system objects. Noneditioned here means the fixed files such as concurrent processing log files, adop log files, patch files, and adop wrapper script, which are not changed by any patching operations.

Figure 1-6 shows the run edition, patch edition, and noneditioned filesystems by providing the top-level directories named fs1, fs2, and fs_ne with their main subdirectories, which store the files that EBS application tier services rely on.

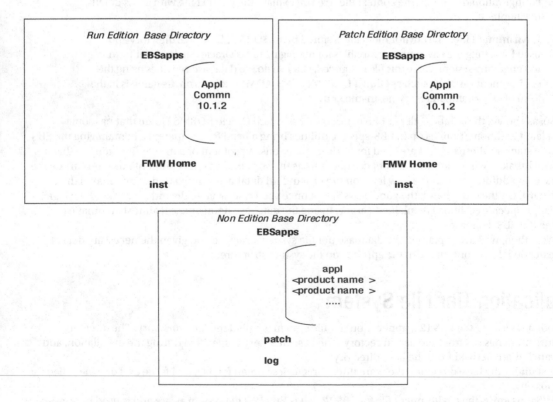

Figure 1-6. *EBS 12.2 dual filesystem and noneditioned filesystem directories: fs1, fs2, and fs_ne*

The following environment variables can be used to retrive to full directory paths of fs1, fs2, and fs_ne directories;

- NE_BASE is the environment variable which is set to the full path of the non-editioned file system (fs_ne).

- PATCH_BASE is the environment variable which is set to the full path of the current patch file system (fs1 or fs2, whichever is the patch file system at that time).

- RUN_BASE is the environment variable which is set to the full path of the current run file system (fs1 or fs2, whichever is the run file system at that time).

■ **Note**   We will explain the details of online patching and the structure that supports it in Chapter 5.

Under the fs1 and fs2 directories, there are three important top-level directories in an EBS 12.2 application file system structure.

These directories are inst (instance home), EBSapps, and the Fusion Middleware Home (FMW_Home).

The inst directory, also called *instance home* and pointed at by the $INST_TOP environment variable, contains most of the configuration files created by AutoConfig, configuration files for Oracle Application Server 10.1.3 (which is used by form and reports), and the other files such as forms log files (in the subdirectory pointed by $LOG_HOME), application services start/stop script logs (pointed at by ADMIN_SCRIPTS_HOME environment variable), 10.1.2 make logs, application listener log file, reports cache files, oam diagnostic files, and the context file for the use of AutoConfig.

Figure 1-7 shows the directory structure of the inst directory and its subdirectories.

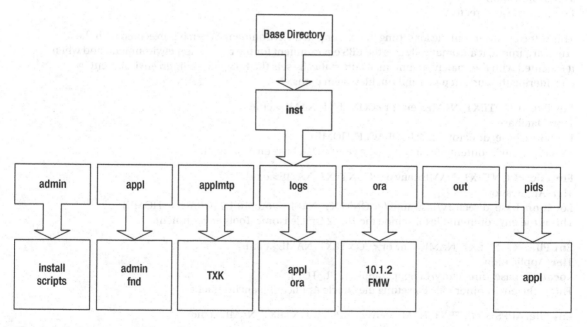

Figure 1-7. *Structure of the inst directory ($INST_TOP)*

The EBSapps directory is one of the directories in the base directory and at the same level with the instance home directory.

EBSapps consists of three subdirectories. These directories are the appl directory, which is pointed at by the $APPL_TOP environment variable; the common directory, which is pointed at by the $COMMON_TOP environment variable; and the 10.1.2 directory, which is pointed at by the $ORACLE_HOME environment variable.

The appl directory, also known as applications top (APPL_TOP), stores core technology directories, all the product directories, the main EBS environment file (which is in the form of <s_systemname>_<s_hostname>.env and <s_systemname>_<s_hostname>.cmd for Windows), and the consolidated env file in the form of APPS<s_systemname>_<s_hostname>.env and APPS<s_systemname>_hostname.cmd for Windows.

Environment files are for setting the APPS-related environment variables for the executing shells. The APPS<s_systemname>_<s_hostname>.env file is used for setting both the Oracle E-Business Suite and Oracle technology stack environments, whereas the <s_systemname>_<s_hostname>.env file sets the environment for applications only.

That is, the environment file named in the form of <s_systemname>_<s_hostname>.env does not set the environment variable for 10.1.2 Oracle Home that is used by forms and reports.

There are four different environment files for setting the shell environments in EBS 12.2, and each environment file is used for setting a different environment for administrating a different set of Oracle technology products.

Table 1-7 lists the environment files present in EBS 12.2 and gives information about what they are used for.

Table 1-7. *EBS 12.2 Environment Files*

Env File: EBSapps.env
Tier: Application
Location: base_directory

This is the environment file for setting the run or patch environment. When it is executed with the "run" argument, it automatically sets the EBS environment for the run edition environment, and when it executed with the "patch" argument, it automatically sets the EBS patch edition environment by considering the current patch and run filesystem paths.

Env File:<CONTEXT_NAME>.env or <CONTEXT_NAME>.cmd
Tier: Database
Location: base_directory/11.2.0 (ORACLE_HOME)
This is the environment file for setting the Oracle Database environment.

Env File: <CONTEXT_NAME>.env or <CONTEXT_NAME>.cmd
Tier: Application
Location: base_directory/inst/apps/<CONTEXT_NAME>/ora/10.1.2 (ORACLE_HOME)
This is the environment file for setting the 10.1.2 Oracle Home-Tools environment.

Env File: <CONTEXT_NAME>.env or <CONTEXT_NAME>.cmd
Tier: Application
Location: base_direectory/EBSapps/appl (APPL_TOP)
This is the environment file for setting the Oracle Application environment.

Env File: APPS<CONTEXT_NAME>.env or APPS<CONTEXT_NAME>.cmd
Tier : Application
Location: base_directory/EBSapps/appl (APPL_TOP)
This is the consolidated environment file used for setting the Oracle applications and tech stack environments.

As mentioned earlier, the appl directory consists of several subdirectories, such as the admin directory that stores the adovars.env file to set the location of various files such as Java files, HTML files, and JRE files. The admin directory under the appl directory contains upgrade-related files for all products.

Besides, the appl directory stores several subdirectories for storing the product files.

For every product, there is a subdirectory named with the associated product's short name. These product directories are used for storing product-specific files and pointed at by the environment variables named with the form <PROD>_Top. <PROD>_Top points to the 12.0.0 directory, which is stored in the product directory. In every product directory, there is a subdirectory named with the release number, which is defined as 12.0.0 for EBS 12.2.

To understand it better, let's take a look at an example. For example, for General Ledger product files, the gl directory inside the appl directory is used. Thus, the environment variable GL_TOP points to the gl/12.0.0 directory, which resides in the appl directory.

This makes GL_TOP to be $APPL_TOP/gl/12.0.0, and all the GL files are stored there.

Thus, <PROD_TOP> becomes $APPL_TOP/<Product_shortname>/12.0.0.

Figure 1-8 shows the directory structure of the appl directory, which is pointed at by the APPL_TOP environment variable in a general manner.

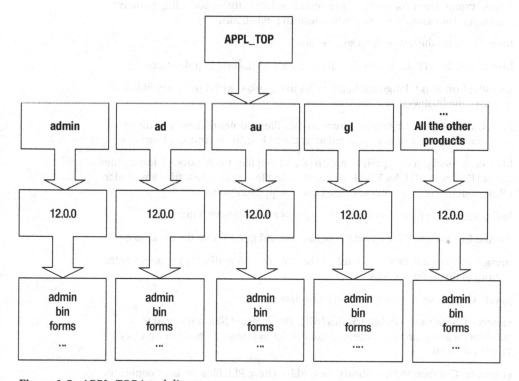

Figure 1-8. *APPL_TOP/appl directory structure*

As shown in Figure 1-8, all the product directories contain subdirectories.

In most of the product directories, there are directories named admin, bin, forms, help, html, java, lib, log, mds, media, mesg, out, patch, reports, and sql.

The following list summarizes these subdirectories with the type of files stored in them.

admin: Contains product-specific files used to upgrade the associated product. This is in distinction to the following.

driver: Contains driver files (.drv files) to be used in an upgrade.

import: Contains DataMerge files to be used in seed data upgrades.

odf: Contains object description files (.odf files) used to create database objects.

sql: Contains SQL scripts for upgrading and concurrent processing, as well as PLSQL scripts for creating PLsql objects/PL/SQL stored procedures.

bin: Contains concurrent programs, C programs, and shell scripts.

forms: Contains Oracle Forms runtime (.fmx) files to be executed by the forms engine. These forms files are stored in subdirectories according to their languages, for example, US to store American English forms.

help: Contains the online help source files.

html: Contains HTML, JavaScript, and JSP for HTML-based applications.

include: Contains C language header files to be linked with the library files stored in the lib directory.

java: Contains JAR files and Java dependency files. Copies of these JAR files are also located in the directory pointed at by the $AF_JLIB environment variable.

lib: Contains object files (.o files for UNIX and .obj files for Windows), library files (.a for UNIX and .DLL for Windows), and make files (.mk). These files are used to relink concurrent programs with the Oracle-supplied libraries.

log: Contains log files for concurrent requests and concurrent managers.

media: Contains GIF files used to display text and graphics on the desktop tier.

mesg: Contains message files (msb) to be used by EBS to display messages at the bottom of the forms screens.

patch: Contains patch files to the data or data model.

reports: Contains report binary files (rdf). These report files are stored in subdirectories according to their languages, for example, US to store American English Reports.

resource: Contains PLSQL library files (PLL). These PLL files are later copied to.

Before continuing with the common directory, we want to include some specific information about three subdirectories of the appl directory. That is, there are three important subdirectories inside the appl directory: the ad, au, and fnd directories.

The ad directory is the directory for the AD (Applications DBA product), and it stores the ad utilities such as adadmin and AutoConfig. The au directory is pointed at by AU_TOP, and its name comes from the application utilities.

AU_TOP contains important files such as PL/SQL libraries used by Oracle Forms, forms source files, a copy of all Java files used when regenerating the desktop client JAR, and certain reports needed by products such as Discoverer.

FND is short for Foundation, and the fnd directory pointed by FND_TOP contains important files for building data dictionaries, forms, and C object libraries.

The common directory is also known as COMMON TOP and pointed at by the COMMON_TOP environment variable; it stores files that can be used by several EBS products and even third-party tools. It is called common because it stores the common files such as Java classes, HTML pages, and other files and directories used by multiple products.

Figure 1-9 represents the COMMON TOP directory structure with all the main subdirectories of it.

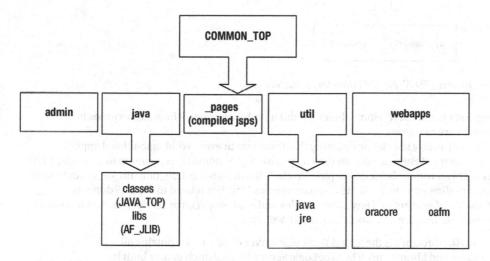

Figure 1-9. *Structure of COMMON_TOP/comn directory*

The last subdirectory in the EBSapps directory is 10.1.2, and it is pointed at by the $ORACLE_HOME environment variable. As you can probably guess because of its associated environment variable's name, it is a 10.1.2 Oracle Home, which provides an environment for the server-side 10g forms and report binaries to run properly.

Executables such frmweb, which is the server-side forms process, and rwrun (reports binary) are started from this directory. The application listener, which is used for the FNDFS and FNDSM connections, is also started from this directory.

The Fusion Middleware Home (FMW_Home) directory consists of the Fusion Middleware components and is pointed at by the $FMW_HOME environment variable. The most important component in this Oracle Home is WebLogic Server, which is the main application server used by the core application services.

There are subdirectories in FMW_Home such as user_projects, wls_10.3, utils, oracle_common, webtier, modules, and Oracle_EBS-appl, as shown in Figure 1-10.

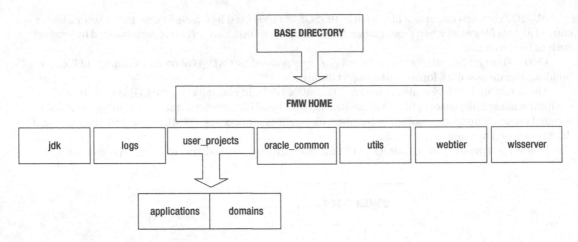

Figure 1-10. *FMW_Home($FMW_HOME) directory structure*

Figure 1-10 represents the FMW_Home directory and its subdirectories. The subdirectories in the FMW_HOME directory are as follows.

The user_projects directory is a classic directory that is present in every WebLogic-related application environment. It contains the WebLogic domain directory named EBS_domain_<s_systemname> used by EBS application services. This directory is used to deploy Oracle E-Business Suite. EBS_domain_<s_systemname> inside the user_projects directory stores all the configuration and log files related to the EBS domain.

Moreover, all the WebLogic-related environment files and start/stop/control scripts such as setDomain. env and startWebLogic.sh are normally stored in the FMW directory.

The Wls_10.3 directory is the actual WebLogic server directory. It contains all the binaries and libraries used by WebLogic Server 10.3.6, which comes built in to EBS 12.2.

The Utils directory contains FMW utilities, such as bsu (Smart Update), which is the patching tool for WebLogic Server.

The Oracle_common directory contains the JRF files used by Oracle EBS. A JDK comes deployed under this directory, as well.

The Webtier directory contains all the configuration and log files used by Oracle HTTP Server. Oracle HTTP Server started from this directory, namely, from the ohs subdirectory (webtier/ohs/bin/). In addition, opmn (Oracle Process Manager) for managing the OHS server is stored in here. In addition, this directory has its own JDK stored in its subdirectory named jdk.

The modules directory contains WebLogic modules, which are presented as JAR files. It also contains applications such as Apache ant, which supplies operations such as compiling, assembling, testing, and running Java applications.

The last Fusion Middleware directory in the list is the Oracle_EBS-appl directory, which contains the Oracle EBS WebLogic components and the core technology components, which are forms, forms-c4ws, oacore, and oafm. So, they are deployed into this directory. Thus, WebLogic Server inside EBS runs them as applications from this directory. Normally, there is a JDK stored in this Oracle Home. In addition, all the configuration files of these EBS WebLogic components/applications are stored in the Oracle_EBS-appl directory.

You have now seen the main directories in the EBS file system structure. We have gone through the main directories and described their contents. You have seen the important EBS directories, and we have listed their contents with the names and content types of their important subdirectories. Although EBS's directory structure is a complex one, you have seen the environment variables to reach the desired locations in the directory structure easily.

Important environment variables in this context are listed here:

IAS_ORACLE_HOME: FMW web tier home directory.

ORACLE_HOME: 10.1.2 Oracle Home used for forms and reports.

CONTEXT_FILE: The context file used by the AutoConfig utility. AutoConfig uses it as an input for configuring the EBS system.

EBS_DOMAIN_HOME: WebLogic domain in where EBS WebLogic deployments are stored.

ADMIN_SCRIPTS_HOME: Shell scripts for starting/stopping/controlling EBS services.

EBS_ORACLE_HOME: EBS WebLogic components/applications are stored in this Oracle_EBS-appl directory.

RW: Oracle Reports directory.

APPS_VERSION: Returns the EBS version.

NE_BASE: Nonedition file system base directory.

APPL_TOP_NE: The appl directory in the nonedition file system.

RUN_BASE: The run file system directory.

PATCH_BASE: The patch file system directory.

APPL_TOP: The appl directory stores core technology directories, all the product directories, and the main EBS environment file.

COMMON_TOP: The common directory stores files that may be used by several EBS products and even third-party tools.

In addition, you have learned about the EBSapps.env script for setting these environment variables automatically.

When sourced, EBSapps.env sets more than 300 environment variables and thus eases the apps DBA's work. After connecting to the system using the application owner operating system user and executing EBSapp.env, you can start using these environment variables immediately.

As EBS 12.2 has a dual file system architecture, EBSapps.env is executed by an argument specifying the edition type. When executed with the "run" argument, EBSapps.env sets the environment variable according to the run edition file system. As you may imagine, when executed with the "patch" argument, EBSapps.env sets the environment variable according to the patch edition file system.

```
Following is an example for setting the run edition environment.
. EBSapps.env run
  E-Business Suite Environment Information
  -----------------------------------------
  RUN File System : /u01/install/APPS/fs2/EBSapps/appl
  PATCH File System : /u01/install/APPS/fs1/EBSapps/appl
  Non-Edition File System: /u01/install/APPS/fs_ne

  DB Host: ermanhost.ermandomain.com Service/SID: ORATEST

Sourcing the RUN File System
. EBSapps.env patch
  E-Business Suite Environment Information
  -----------------------------------------
  RUN File System          : /u01/install/APPS/fs2/EBSapps/appl
  PATCH File System        : /u01/install/APPS/fs1/EBSapps/appl
  Non-Editioned File System: /u01/install/APPS/fs_ne

  DB Host: ermanhost.ermandomain.com Service/SID: ORATEST

Sourcing the PATCH File System
```

Having a general knowledge about the directory structure is important, but memorizing all the directories inside this huge directory structure is unnecessary because the environment variables do this job.

Later in this book, we will expand on all the information provided in this chapter by providing practical examples such as installation, upgrade, patching, and so on. Lastly in this chapter, we will look at the technological differences between the major EBS releases.

Technology Stack Changes in EBS 11i/12.1/12.2

Since the first release of EBS, while the product capabilities have improved, so have the technologies used in EBS. In this section, we will explain the technology stack changes in the major EBS releases.

We will cover the technological architectures of EBS 11i (11.5.10.2), EBS 12 (12.1.3), and EBS 12.2(12.2.4/12.2.5) and explain the differences between them. Although mostly the same Oracle technologies are used in almost all of these releases, the versions of the technological components differ according to EBS release, as shown in Figure 1-11.

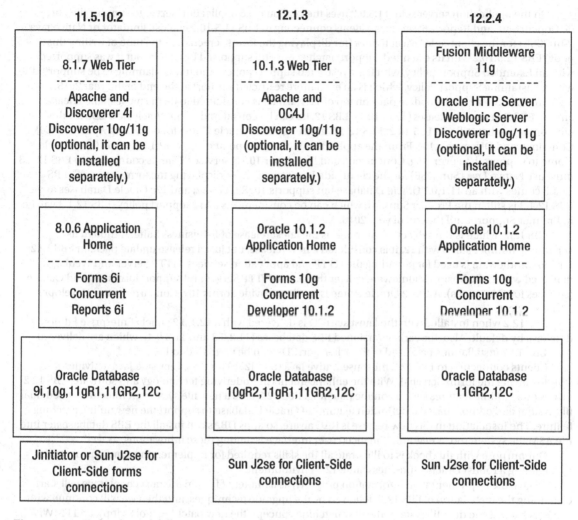

11.5.10.2

8.1.7 Web Tier

Apache and
Discoverer 4i
Discoverer 10g/11g
(optional, it can be
installed
separately.)

8.0.6 Application
Home

Forms 6i
Concurrent
Reports 6i

Oracle Database
9i,10g,11gR1,11GR2,12C

Jinitiator or Sun J2se for
Client-Side forms
connections

12.1.3

10.1.3 Web Tier

Apache and
OC4J
Discoverer 10g/11g
(optional, it can be
installed
separately.)

Oracle 10.1.2
Application Home

Forms 10g
Concurrent
Developer 10.1.2

Oracle Database
10gR2,11gR1,11GR2,12C

Sun J2se for Client-Side
connections

12.2.4

Fusion Middleware
11g

Oracle HTTP Server
Weblogic Server
Discoverer 10g/11g
(optional, it can be
installed
separately.)

Oracle 10.1.2
Application Home

Forms 10g
Concurrent
Developer 10.1.2

Oracle Database
11GR2,12C

Sun J2se for Client-Side
connections

Figure 1-11. Technological differences between the major EBS releases

The database versions displayed in Figure 1-11 are the supported/certified database versions classified according to the EBS releases. In this manner, while EBS 11.5.10.2 is certified with 9i and 10g databases, EBS 12.1.3 is not. However, Figure 1-11 does not give any information regarding to the certifications for the exact four-digit database versions like 9.2.0.8 or 10.2.0.5. That is, EBS 12.1.3 is certified with 10g R2, but it is certified only with the specific 10g R2 releases such as 10.2.0.4 and 10.2.0.5. Also, EBS 12.1.3 and 12.2 are up-to-date EBS releases, so these certifications may be updated soon. That's why we don't give details about certified database versions here; we recommend you check the Oracle Support Certifications tab for the exact supported database versions for your EBS instances.

EBS 11.5.10.2 is one of the major releases that is still in use in production environments. EBS 11.5.10.2 is a maintenance pack sits on top of 11.5.10, and it is the latest version of EBS 11i. EBS 11.5.10.2 supports 11g R2 and 12c Oracle Database for the database tier. It utilizes 8.1.7 Web HTTP, which contains the Apache and Discoverer 4i products.

On the application server side, 11.5.0.2 uses the version 8.0.6 application server to support the Forms 6i, Concurrent, and Reports 6i services. Clients connecting to EBS 11.5.10.2 can use Jinitiator or Native Java (Sun J2SE) for the client-side Java activities (for displaying the forms screens). At the time of writing this book, EBS 11.5.10.2 with its extended support patches was still supported by Oracle, but it was supported with an Extended Support policy, which is a restricted support policy, and it was planning to be supported with a Sustaining Support Policy, which is an even more restricted support at the end of the year 2015.

EBS 12.1.3 is a release update pack on top of 12.1, which is considered to be the most stable release among EBS Release 12 releases (12.0, 12.1). EBS 12.1.3 can be considered a completely new EBS for the environments that still use 11.5.10.2. EBS 12.1.3 utilizes a 10.1.3 Oracle Home for delivering Apache, OC4J Container, and Discoverer 10g. From the application technology point of view, 12.1.3 uses a 10.1.2 Oracle Home to support the Forms 10g, Concurrent, and Developer 10.1.2 services. Clients connecting to EBS 12.1.3 must use Native Java (Sun J2SE) for the client-side Java activities (for displaying the forms screens). EBS 12.1.3 comes with an 11.1.0.7 Oracle Database but supports 10gR2, 11GR2, and 12c Oracle Databases as well. EBS 12.1.3 is still in the Premier Support, which can be considered as a full support policy. EBS 12.1.3 will be in Premier Support until the end of year 2016.

EBS 12.2, which is the subject of this book, is the latest release of E-Business Suite. Although its versioning number starts with 12, it is considered a new release, not just a release update pack. In EBS 12.2 Fusion Middleware is used for providing the HTTP and application services. HTTP Server and WebLogic delivered within the Fusion Middleware deliver the Oracle HTTP Server and support forms 10g and Oacore (services for OAF pages). A 10.1.2 Oracle Home is used to provide Forms 10g, Concurrent, and Developer 10.1.2 services.

EBS 12.2 when installed with the latest startCD is delivered with a 12.1.0.2 Oracle Enterprise Edition database by default. Also, the earlier versioned EBS databases (11.2.0.3 and 11.2.0.4), which are delivered with EBS 12.2 installations packaged with earlier startCDs, can be upgraded to 12C.

Clients connecting to EBS 12.2 must use Native Java (Sun J2SE) for the client-side Java activities (for displaying the forms screens). With the enhancements in underlying technology and software, EBS 12.2 brings outstanding features such as online patching. EBS 12.2 uses a new file system architecture called dual file system and edition-based redefinition features of Oracle Database to support the new online patching feature. The installation in this new release is RAC aware, so apps DBAs can install the EBS database tier into the ASM file system too. A new and enhanced user interface is among these innovations, as well.

Our purpose with this book is to illustrate all the skills required for implementing, configuring, and maintaining a robust Oracle E-Business Suite 12.2 environment.

To give the implementation information properly, as a matter of fact, in the next chapter we will start explaining the installation of EBS 12.2, followed by the upgrade techniques, and then we will continue with subjects such as the dual filesystem, the new patching concept, the new patching tool (adop), and FMW, which are introduced in EBS 12.2 and can considered as enhancements. Subsequently, we will explain the general EBS subjects such as Sysadmin fundamentals, AutoConfig, and performance tuning by focusing on these subjects in the context of EBS 12.2. Lastly, we will take a look at the implementation processes for implementing EBS 12.2 on Oracle-engineered systems because utilizing engineered systems such as the EBS platforms is the new trend.

Summary

In this first chapter, we introduced to you Oracle EBS by taking a look at the brief history of EBS and listing the EBS 12.2 applications and their product families.

We also explained EBS's three-tier architectural model, the client-server communication model used in EBS 12.2, and the application and database tier components. We shed a light on the EBS 12.2 file system structure and gave you the technology stack changes from EBS 11i to the latest release EBS 12.2.

With the information we gave you in this chapter, you now have a general idea about an EBS 12.2 environment, so we think that it is time to proceed with more technical subjects.

CHAPTER 2

Installation and Configuration

In the previous chapter, we discussed in detail Oracle E-Business Suite and its underlying architecture. In this chapter, we will talk about the Oracle E-Business Suite installation process. Planning for the installation and preparing the system are the key factors for a successful installation and for successful project rollouts. Inappropriate system design and incorrect configuration will lead to many problems during implementation and the go-live phase.

Oracle E-Business Suite (EBS) is a highly scalable environment, and it can have multiple database and application nodes. The system topology is based on the number of users, the utilization, and the business requirements. Oracle EBS can be installed on a stand-alone single server, and it can be deployed on multiple nodes to maximize its availability and performance.

This chapter will provide insight into the different supported installation options available with Oracle E-Business Suite 12.2 and how you can deploy these options on a production system.

New Features in Release 12.2's Rapidwiz Install Wizard

The Rapidwiz Install Wizard is the only utility that supports the installation of Oracle E-Business Suite 12.2. It will install and configure the database, application, and Fusion Middleware and lay out all the application/configuration files. Rapidwiz is located on the "StartHere" CD. Starting with EBS 12.2, there are significant changes in Rapidwiz. The following are the new features of Rapidwiz and their benefits.

- *New version of Oracle Database 12.1.0.2*: The earlier version 12.1 shipped with the 11.1.0.7 database; the current version of Rapidwiz ships with the 12.1.0.2 database.

- *RAC and ASM support*: Oracle Real Application Cluster (RAC)/Automatic Storage Management deployment is supported from the Rapidwiz Install Wizard. In earlier releases, this process was tedious and time-consuming because you needed to first install and create the database on a standard supported file system and then migrate it to RAC/ASM using supported tools.

■ **Note** Rapidwiz will not install and configure any Grid Infrastructure components. To use the RAC/ASM option provided by Rapidwiz, you need to configure all the Grid Infrastructure services with the required ASM disk space and get all the services up and running first.

© Syed Zaheer and Erman Arslan 2016

S. Zaheer and E. Arslan, *Practical Oracle E-Business Suite*, DOI 10.1007/978-1-4842-1422-0_2

- *Dual file system*: As discussed in the previous chapter, a dual file system is required for online patching, and this will be laid out by the Rapidwiz Install Wizard. The dual file system, consisting of fs1 and fs2, will be configured on two different ports.

- *WebLogic Server*: In EBS 12.2 Rapidwiz will install and configure the Oracle Fusion Middleware 11g WebLogic Server, whereas in 12.1, Rapidwiz installed Oracle 10g Application Server 10.1.3. Rapidwiz 12.2 will also configure the EBS domain, admin, and managed servers.

- *Password enhancement*: Rapidwiz will allow you to configure and set up passwords for all critical application and database user accounts during the installation phase, whereas in prior releases the application was installed with default passwords and they had to be changed as a post-install step.

■ **Note**   It's been noticed with too many customers uses the default passwords for EBS installations. This is a high risk to the system. It's highly recommended to utilize this option of Rapidwiz and configure the new passwords during the install phase.

The Rapidwiz Install Wizard will lay out the complete file system and configure the database and technology stack components. It will allow you to enable licenses for the products that an organization is entitled to use. Country-specific functionalities and localization settings can also be configured using Rapidwiz during the initial install.

Specifically, Rapidwiz will install and configure the following components:

- It will install the 12.1.0.2 RDBMS Oracle software.

- It will create a 12.1.0.2 database (Fresh or Vision based on your selection).

- It will install and lay out the dual application file system consisting of fs1 and fs2 for online patching and the fs_ne file system.

- It will install and configure the WebLogic admin and managed server.

Figure 2-1 explains how the Rapidwiz Install Wizard will lay out the database and application file system at the OS level.

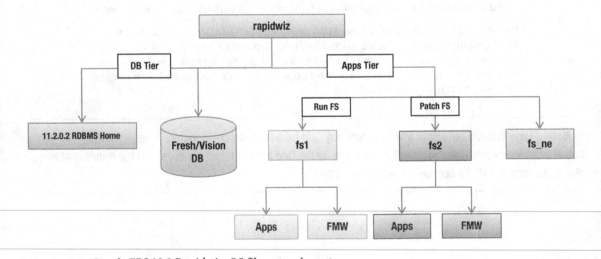

Figure 2-1. *Oracle EBS 12.2 Rapidwiz: OS file system layout*

Before we begin showing how to install Oracle E-Business Suite, we'll define the terms *single node* and *multinode*. In the previous chapter, we discussed the three-tier architecture (the database tier, the application tier, and the client tier). It's a general perception that these tiers will be three different physical entities. However, this is not true; the architecture is all about the distribution of services. All three tiers can be deployed on a single server, or they can be deployed on multiple servers.

- *Single-node installation*: All E-Business Suite components will be deployed on one physical server that includes database services, application services, and concurrent processing services. Such a type of installation is usually deployed in a small-scale organization and in test/dev/user acceptance test (UAT) environments.

- *Multinode installation*: Oracle E-Business Suite components will be distributed across multiple servers. These installations can have multiple database nodes, multiple applications, and middle tier nodes. Such a type of installation typically will be deployed in medium-scale and large-scale organizations. But the number of nodes in the deployment topology varies, and it will be defined based on the number of users, transaction load, and application availability. But multinode installation is supported only for the database tier (RAC). Starting with startCD 49, multimode installation for the application tier is no longer supported.

■ **Note**   No older versions of startCDs are supported, and they're not available for download from MOS. That includes startCD 46, 47, 48, 49, and 50. The only supported version is startCD 51 at the time of writing this book.

Preparing for Installation

All software products are developed with some specific installation requirements, and to install any software, you need to make sure that all installation prerequisites are in place for a successful installation. An installation of the Oracle E-Business Suite should be planned appropriately to avoid any issues during the install phase. Incorrect configuration will lead to a failed installation and will cost time and resources. You will see now what prerequisites are required for installing Oracle EBS 12.2. The prerequisites are usually classified in two major categories: hardware prerequisites and software prerequisites. Both of the prerequisites should be configured appropriately for a hassle-free installation.

Hardware Prerequisites

Hardware prerequisites include the processor architecture, minimum required memory, and storage capacity required for hosting the EBS installation files. Different installation options are available with the Oracle EBS 12.2 Rapidwiz Install Wizard, and space should be planned according to the type of installation you want.

Table 2-1 lists the certified operating systems and the version required for installing EBS 12.2. You should plan in advance to meet these operating system requirements. (This information may change, so it's always recommended that you check the Certification tab on your My Oracle Support portal.)

Table 2-1. *Oracle EBS 12.2 Software Certification on Different OS/Platform Versions*

Operating System	Certified Version
HP-UX Itanium	1 version: 11.3
IBM AIX - Power (64-Bit)	2 versions: 7.1, 6.1
Linux X86-64	8 versions: SLES 11 and 10, RHEL 7, 6 and 5, OEL 7, 6, and 5
Oracle Solaris on SPARC (64-bit)	2 versions: 11, 10
Microsoft Windows x64	2 versions: 2012 R2, 2008 R2

Computing Requirements

No specific benchmark is available for deployment. This is because of multiple products, mixed workload, number of customizations, and so on. The best strategy for designing a system is to create an identical testing environment for production and conduct load testing to create a benchmark. This will be helpful in designing a production environment appropriately. You should have a clear road map for the next five years for the configuration changes, the increase in the number of users, and the increase in workload/ transactions based on data growth. This five-year road map will help in designing the system with the correct computing requirements.

Table 2-2 lists the general guidelines for sizing the computing requirements for Oracle E-Business Suite 12.2.

Table 2-2. *Oracle EBS 12.2 Hardware Sizing (CPU and Memory)*

Number of Users	Database Node		Application Node	
	CPU Cores	System Memory	CPU Cores	System Memory
0 to 100	2	4	2	12GB
100 to 200	2	8	2	24GB
200 to 400	4	12	4	40GB
400 to 800	8	20	8	72GB

■ **Note** These are just the generic guidelines for sizing. You can determine the correct sizing by running realistic test cases for a single-node/multinode deployment.

Space Requirements

Oracle E-Business Suite is complex software and consists of many technology and application components; thus, it requires considerable disk capacity for installation. As we've discussed, Oracle EBS supports different installation options (Fresh/Vision), and each option has its own respective space requirements.

Table 2-3 explains the disk space requirements for different installation options.

- For online patching, an additional 25GB of space is required for the System tablespace.

- The upgrade space requirements will be discussed in Chapter 3.

Table 2-3. *Rapidwiz EBS 12.2 Installation Disk Space Requirements*

Installation Type	Application Node Disk Space	Database Node Disk Space	Stage and Patching
Fresh	64GB for dual file system	90GB: 11.2.0.3 Home + database	55GB + 50GB (recommended)
Vision	64GB for dual file system	200GB: 11.2.0.3 Home + database	55GB + 50GB (recommended)

Software Requirements

Oracle E-Business Suite 12.2 has specific software prerequisites for database nodes and application nodes. These prerequisites should be configured on the respective nodes based on the target deployment topology. Each operating system has its own software prerequisites, and they should be configured as mentioned for a successful installation. In this chapter, we will discuss the high-level operating system software requirements that should be configured before beginning the installation. The installation is demonstrated on an Oracle Enterprise Linux 6 64-bit server.

The following are the prerequisites before installation:

- Configure software tools requirements

- Configure the kernel version

- Configure the operating system packages

- Configure the kernel parameters

- Configure the operating system files

- Create group and users

- Create directories

- Prepare the 12.2 software stage

Now you will see each of these configurations in detail. This prerequisites checklist applies to other operating systems as well. The differences are in the settings and packages.

Software Tools Requirements

These tools should be installed on all servers that will be part of the deployment topology. These software locations should be in the PATH variable of the shell and user account from which EBS 12.2 will be installed.

Linux x86-64 -ar, gcc, g++, ld, ksh, make, X Display Server

These software tools will be installed by default with installation, and if they don't exist on the system, then you should install them.

Kernel Version

Table 2-4 lists the supported kernel version with the respective Linux operating system. As mentioned, in this book, Oracle Enterprise Linux 6 64-bit is used for installing Oracle EBS 12.2.Table 2-4 lists the minimum versions that are supported for installation, and if the version of the kernel is higher than the default, then it's supported by Oracle.

Table 2-4. *Supported Linux Kernel Versions for EBS 12.2*

Operating System	Kernel
Oracle Linux 5	2.6.18-194.0.0.0.3.EL5
Oracle Linux 6	2.6.32-131.0.15.el6, 2.6.32-100.34.1.el6uek
Oracle Linux 7	3.10.0-123.el7, 3.8.13-35.3.1.el7uek
Red Hat Enterprise Linux AS/ES 5	2.6.18-194.0.0.0.3.EL5
Red Hat Enterprise Linux 6	2.6.32-131.0.15.el6, 2.6.32-100.34.1.el6uek
Red Hat Enterprise Linux 7	3.10.0-123.el7, 3.8.13-35.3.1.el7uek
SUSE Linux Enterprise Server 10	2.6.16.60-0.21
SUSE Linux Enterprise Server 11	3.0.13-0.27-de

Operating System Packages

Installing prerequisite operating system packages is a tedious job for a system admin/DBA. If the installation of the operating system is performed with the minimum package selection, then installing the Oracle EBS 12.2 prerequisite packages will check for many dependencies. The best way to configure the operating system packages is to use the yum repository. Oracle provides the oracle-ebs-server-R12-pre-install package. It is recommended you install this package on an operating system with the minimum package selection. This will install only the packages that are required for running Oracle E-Business Suite.

This pre-install RPM package is available only for Oracle Enterprise Linux 5 and Oracle Enterprise Linux 6. If using other distributions, it is recommended that you use a vendor-specific yum repository to install all the OS prerequisite packages. Individual RPM packages can also be installed, but that requires some extra time and effort.

Table 2-5 lists the prerequisite RPMs on OEL5/OEL6/OEL7.

Table 2-5. *Release 12.2 OS Package Requirements for OEL and RHEL*

Operating System	Required Packages (Minimum Versions)
Oracle Linux 6* Red Hat Enterprise Linux 6*	• openmotif21-2.1.30-11.EL6.i686 (32-bit) • xorg-x11-libs-compat-6.8.2-1.EL.33.0.1.i386 (32-bit) • libXrender-0.9.5-1.el6.i686 • binutils-2.20.51.0.2-5.20.el6.x86_64 • compat-libstdc++-296-2.96-144.el6.i686 • compat-libstdc++-33-3.2.3-69.el6.i686 • gcc-4.4.5-6.el6.x86_64 • gcc-c++-4.4.5-6.el6.x86_64 • glibc-2.12-1.7.el6.i686 (32-bit) • glibc-2.12-1.7.el6.x86_64 • glibc-common-2.12-1.7.el6.x86_64 • glibc-devel-2.12-1.7.el6.i686 (32-bit)

(continued)

Table 2-5. (*continued*)

Operating System	Required Packages (Minimum Versions)
	• glibc-devel-2.12-1.7.el6.x86_64
	• libgcc-4.4.4-13.el6.i686
	• libgcc-4.4.4-13.el6.x86_64
	• libstdc++-devel-4.4.4-13.el6.i686
	• libstdc++-devel-4.4.4-13.el6.x86_64
	• libstdc++-4.4.4-13.el6.i686
	• libstdc++-4.4.4-13.el6.x86_64
	• libXi-1.3-3.el6.i686
	• libXp-1.0.0-15.1.el6.i686
	• libXp-1.0.0-15.1.el6.x86_64
	• libaio-0.3.107-10.el6.i686
	• libaio-0.3.107-10.el6.x86_64
	• llbgomp-4.4.4-13.el6.x86_64
	• make-3.81-19.el6.x86_64
	• gdbm-1.8.0-36.el6.i686
	• gdbm-1.8.0-36.el6.x86_64
	• redhat-lsb-4.0-3.0.1.el6.x86_64
	• sysstat-9.0.4-11.el6.x86_64
	• util-linux-ng-2.17.2-6.el6.x86_64
	Oracle RDBMS RPMs
	• compat-libcap1-1.10-1.x86_64
	• compat-libstdc++-33-3.2.3-69.el6.x86_64
	• elfutils-libelf-devel-0.148.1-el6.x86_64
	• libaio-devel-0.3.107-10.el6.i686
	• libaio-devel-0.3.107-10.el6.x86_64
	• unixODBC-2.2.14-11.el6.i686
	• unixODBC-devel-2.2.14-11.el6.i686
	• xorg-x11-utils-7.4-8.el6.x86_64

■ **Note** In this chapter, only Oracle Enterprise Linux 6 prerequisites are discussed. For other vendor operating systems, please refer to the MOS tech note "Oracle E-Business Suite Installation and Upgrade Notes Release 12 (12.2) for Linux x86-64" (Doc ID 1330701.1).

Configuring the yum Repository for EBS 12 Package Installation

The pre-install package for EBS will install and configure most of the required prerequisites. The following actions will be performed by the pre-install package:

- Download and install all OS package dependencies that are required for the Oracle EBS 12.2 installation

- Configure kernel parameters in the /etc/sysctl.conf file

- Configure hard and soft shell resource limits

- Create the users named oracle and applmgr with the respective groups dba and oinstall

- Configure /etc/resolv.conf with the required settings

- Set numa=off in the kernel command line

- Disable the Transparent Huge Pages option if it's enabled (Linux 6 only)

Get the Repository File with Wget

The Wget utility is responsible for downloading the repository file. To download this file, the server should be connected to the Internet.

```
[root@erpnode1 ~]# cd /etc/yum.repos.d
[root@erpnode1 yum.repos.d]# wget http://public-yum.oracle.com/public-yum-ol6.repo
--2015-07-04 14:38:05--  http://public-yum.oracle.com/public-yum-ol6.repo
Resolving public-yum.oracle.com... 79.140.95.219, 79.140.95.217
Connecting to public-yum.oracle.com|79.140.95.219|:80... connected.
HTTP request sent, awaiting response... 200 OK
Length: 5046 (4.9K) [text/plain]
Saving to: "public-yum-ol6.repo.1"

100%[=============================================>] 5,046        --.-K/s   in 0

2015-07-04 14:38:06 (170 MB/s) - "public-yum-ol6.repo.1" saved [5046/5046]

[root@erpnode1 yum.repos.d]#
```

Once the file is downloaded, modify the file settings with the parameters enabled=0 to enabled=1. The parameter enabled=0 will not allow system to use that repository.

Repository File Before Update

Once the file has downloaded, you should edit the file for the repositories that you want to use for installing the RPM packages. You have to update the value for the parameter enabled=0 to enabled=1.

```
enabled=0 (Disables the repository)
enabled-1 (Enabled the repository)
[root@erpnode1 yum.repos.d]# cat public-yum-ol6.repo
```

```
[public_ol6_latest]
name=Oracle Linux $releasever Latest ($basearch)
baseurl=http://public-yum.oracle.com/repo/OracleLinux/OL6/latest/$basearch/
gpgkey=file:///etc/pki/rpm-gpg/RPM-GPG-KEY-oracle
gpgcheck=1
enabled=0
```

Repository File After Update

After modifying the repository file, verify the settings are saved, as shown here:

```
[root@erpnode1 yum.repos.d]# cat public-yum-ol6.repo
[public_ol6_latest]
name=Oracle Linux $releasever Latest ($basearch)
baseurl=http://public-yum.oracle.com/repo/OracleLinux/OL6/latest/$basearch/
gpgkey=file:///etc/pki/rpm-gpg/RPM-GPG-KEY-oracle
gpgcheck=1
enabled=1
```

Check the Available yum Repository

The yumrepolist command can be used to check the available yum repositories. To install the package, you should use yum install <pkg-name>. This will install the required RPM packages, and it will also resolve all dependencies required for installing the main package.

```
Installing  the package using repository:
[root@erpnode1 yum.repos.d]# yum install oracle-ebs-server-R12-pre-install
---
---
---
  openmotif21.i686 0:2.1.30-11.EL6                          readline.i686 0:6.0-4.el6
  unixODBC.i686 0:2.2.14-14.el6                             unixODBC-devel.i686
0:2.2.14-14.el6
  xorg-x11-libs-compat.i386 0:6.8.2-1.EL.33.0.1.0.2

Dependency Updated:
  glibc.i686 0:2.12-1.149.el6_6.9          glibc.x86_64 0:2.12-1.149.el6_6.9
glibc-common.x86_64 0:2.12-1.149.el6_6.9
  glibc-devel.x86_64 0:2.12-1.149.el6_6.9 glibc-headers.x86_64 0:2.12-1.149.el6_6.9

Complete!
[root@erpnode1 yum.repos.d]#

[root@erpnode1 yum.repos.d]#yum install oracle-rdbms-server-12cR1-pre-install
```

The RPM package oracle-rdbms-server-12cR1-pre-install can be used for Oracle Database 12c prerequisites. startCD 51 will install Oracle Database 12c, and all the prerequisites should be in place for the database as well.

Check the Swap Space of the Server

Swap space should be configured with a minimum of 16GB, but it is recommended you use the same value as the system memory. For example, if the server RAM size is 64GB, then the recommended value of the swap space is 128GB; however, you should configure at least the same as the system memory, as in 64GB.

To check the existing swap space on a Linux system, you can use the following command:

```
[root@erpnode1 rapidwiz]# grep SwapTotal /proc/meminfo
SwapTotal:      17407996 kB
[root@erpnode1 rapidwiz]#
```

Verify Kernel Parameters Configured by the Pre-install Package

Check for the entries in the /etc/sysctl.conf file that are added by the pre-install package and related to oracle-ebs-server-R12-pre-install.

```
# oracle-ebs-server-R12-pre-install setting for fs.file-max is 6815744
fs.file-max = 6815744

# oracle-ebs-server-R12-pre-install setting for kernel.sem is '256 32000 100 142'
kernel.sem = 256 32000 100 142

# oracle-ebs-server-R12-pre-install setting for kernel.shmmni is 4096
kernel.shmmni = 4096

# oracle-ebs-server-R12-pre-install setting for kernel.shmall is 1073741824 on x86_64
# oracle-ebs-server-R12-pre-install setting for kernel.shmall is 2097152 on i386

# oracle-ebs-server-R12-pre-install setting for kernel.shmmax is 4398046511104 on x86_64
# oracle-ebs-server-R12-pre-install setting for kernel.shmmax is 4294967295 on i386
kernel.shmmax = 4398046511104

# oracle-ebs-server-R12-pre-install setting for kernel.msgmni is 2878
kernel.msgmni = 2878

# oracle-ebs-server-R12-pre-install setting for net.core.rmem_default is 262144
net.core.rmem_default = 262144

# oracle-ebs-server-R12-pre-install setting for net.core.rmem_max is 4194304
net.core.rmem_max = 4194304

# oracle-ebs-server-R12-pre-install setting for net.core.wmem_default is 262144
net.core.wmem_default = 262144

# oracle-ebs-server-R12-pre-install setting for net.core.wmem_max is 1048576
net.core.wmem_max = 1048576

# oracle-ebs-server-R12-pre-install setting for fs.aio-max-nr is 1048576
fs.aio-max-nr = 1048576
```

```
# oracle-ebs-server-R12-pre-install setting for net.ipv4.ip_local_port_range is 9000 65500
net.ipv4.ip_local_port_range = 9000 65500

[root@erpnode1 rapidwiz]#
```

Verify the Soft and Hard Shell Limits

The pre-install package will configure these settings in the file /etc/security/limits.d/oracle-ebs-server-R12-pre-install.conf for Linux 6 and in the file /etc/security/limits.conf for Linux 5.

```
[root@erpnode1 ~]# cat /etc/security/limits.d/oracle-ebs-server-R12-pre-install.conf

# oracle-ebs-server-R12-pre-install setting for nofile soft limit is 4096
oracle    soft    nofile    4096
applmgr   soft    nofile    4096

# oracle-ebs-server-R12-pre-install setting for nofile hard limit is 65536
oracle    hard    nofile    65536
applmgr   hard    nofile    65536

# oracle-ebs-server-R12-pre-install setting for nproc soft limit is 16384
# refer orabug15971421 for more info.
oracle    soft    nproc     16384
applmgr   soft    nproc     16384

# oracle-ebs-server-R12-pre-install setting for nproc hard limit is 16384
oracle    hard    nproc     16384
applmgr   hard    nproc     16384

# oracle-ebs-server-R12-pre-install setting for stack soft limit is 10240KB
oracle    soft    stack     10240
applmgr   soft    stack     10240

# oracle-ebs-server-R12-pre-install setting for stack hard limit is 32768KB
oracle    hard    stack     32768
applmgr   hard    stack     32768
[root@erpnode1 ~]#
```

Verify DNS Resolver Parameters

You have to make sure that the options attempts and options timeouts parameters are configured as shown here. These parameters are added by the pre-install package.

```
[root@erpnode1 rapidwiz]# vi /etc/resolv.conf
[root@erpnode1 rapidwiz]# cat /etc/resolv.conf
# Generated by NetworkManager
search oralabs.com
nameserver 192.168.2.80
options attempts:5
options timeout:15
[root@erpnode1 rapidwiz]#
```

45

Verify System Configuration Files

The /etc/hosts file should be configured as listed with a loopback address and fully qualified domain name, and you should verify that the hostname and IP address is pinging.

```
[root@erpnode1 ~]# cat /etc/hosts
127.0.0.1 localhost localhost.localdomain
192.168.2.81 erpnode1.oralabs.com erpnode1 localhost
[root@erpnode1 ~]#
```

The /etc/sysconfig/network file should contain the fully qualified hostname.

```
[root@erpnode1 ~]# cat /etc/sysconfig/network
NETWORKING=yes
HOSTNAME=erpnode1.oralabs.com
GATEWAY=192.168.2.80
[root@erpnode1 ~]#
```

The /etc/sysconfig/networking/profiles/default/network file should not exist on the system. If it exists, then you should remove it.

```
[root@erpnode1 ~]# ls -l /etc/sysconfig/networking/profiles/default/network
ls: cannot access /etc/sysconfig/networking/profiles/default/network: No such file or directory
[root@erpnode1 ~]#
```

Unlink and Relink Library

This is a prerequisite step that is required for successful configuration of middleware components. So, to avoid this issue, you must unlink and create a new link, as shown here:

```
[root@erpnode1 ~]# ls -l /usr/lib/libXtst.so.6
lrwxrwxrwx. 1 root root 16 Jul  4 15:07 /usr/lib/libXtst.so.6 -> libXtst.so.6.1.0
[root@erpnode1 ~]# unlink /usr/lib/libXtst.so.6
[root@erpnode1 ~]# ln -s /usr/X11R6/lib/libXtst.so.6.1 /usr/lib/libXtst.so.6
[root@erpnode1 ~]# ls -l /usr/lib/libXtst.so.6
lrwxrwxrwx. 1 root root 29 Jul  4 16:29 /usr/lib/libXtst.so.6 -> /usr/X11R6/lib/libXtst.so.6.1
[root@erpnode1 ~]#
```

All prerequisites steps are completed at this stage, and it is recommended that you reboot the server once, but it is not mandatory.

■ **Note**   These prerequisite steps should be performed on all nodes in a multinode installation.

Create Directories and Change Permissions and Ownership

As mentioned, the database and application file system will be installed on two different directories, and you must create these directories and then change the ownership/permissions for these respective directories. In this example for database and application users, different operating system groups are used for segregating the file system group ownership.

```
[root@erpnode1 ~]# mkdir -p /u01/ora_prod
[root@erpnode1 ~]# mkdir -p /u01/appl_prod
[root@erpnode1 ~]# chmod -R 775 /u01/ora_prod/
[root@erpnode1 ~]# chmod -R 775 /u01/appl_prod/
[root@erpnode1 ~]# chown -R oracle:dba /u01/ora_prod/
[root@erpnode1 ~]# chown -R applmgr:oinstall /u01/appl_prod/
```

Verify the Inventory File Has Been Created

Rapidwiz requires an empty oraInventory directory to be in place, and the inventory location is stored in the /ect/oraInst.loc file.

```
[root@erpnode2 ~]# cat /etc/oraInst.loc
inventory_loc-/u01/ora_prod/oraInventory/
inst_group=dba
[root@erpnode2 ~]# mkdir -p /u01/ora_prod/oraInventory/
[root@erpnode2 ~]#chown -R oracle:dba /u01/ora_prod/oraInventory/
[root@erpnode2 ~]#chmod -R 777 /u01/ora_prod/oraInventory/
```

Keep full permissions on the oraInventory directory until the installation is complete; you can change this after the successful installation.

Failing to provide inst_group will fail the pre-installation validation checks. This issue is discussed in much more detail here: https://www.toadworld.com/platforms/oracle/b/weblog/archive/2016/03/04/oracle-e-business-suite-r12-2-installation-issues-with-start-cd-51.

Preparing the Stage Area

The stage area is where all software installation binaries will be placed. Usually the stage area will be a single directory location where all the software installation files are located. In earlier releases, installing directly from media (CD/DVD) was supported, but with the current releases, performing installation using CD/DVD media is not supported. The size of the software is big: almost 55GB. Installing such large software using a CD/DVD will cause many problems for reading, mounting, and unmounting the media.

The software is available for download from the Oracle Software Delivery Cloud (http://edelivery.oracle.com) under the E-Business Suite section. You need to select the appropriate platform applicable as per your environment and download the media. Usually you will download the software on the local PC that is connected to Internet and then upload it to the server. If the server is connected to Internet, then you can download the software directly onto the server.

To download the media, log in to https://edelivery.oracle.com with valid credentials.

Figure 2-2 displays the main login page from the Oracle Software Delivery Cloud from which you can download the Oracle E-Business Suite 12.2 files.

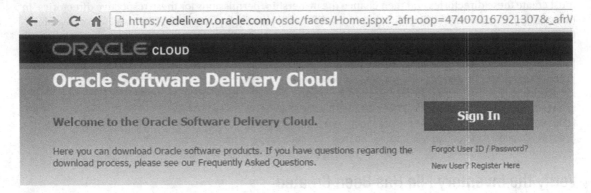

Figure 2-2. *Oracle Software Delivery Cloud login page*

Search for *Product E-Business suite* and select the appropriate platform.

Figure 2-3 shows the media pack search screen, which provides a drop-down list for all available the products and platforms. You can type any of the Oracle EBS product names, for example, *order management* or any other product name.

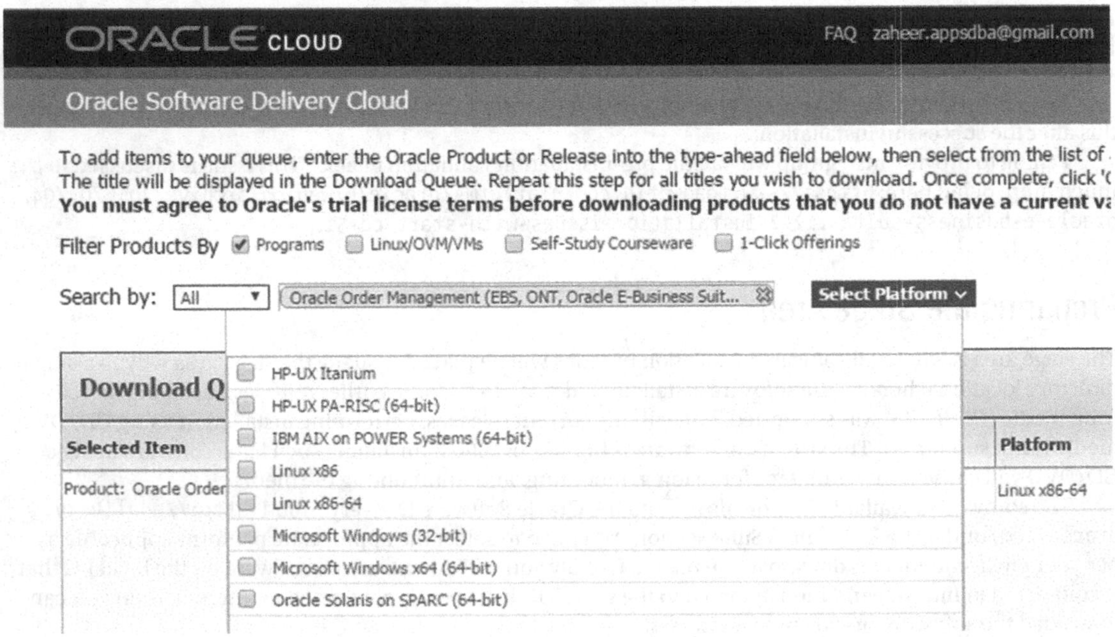

Figure 2-3. *Oracle Software Delivery Cloud media pack search screen*

Figure 2-4 lists the available versions and software with respect to E-Business Suite. You should select Oracle E-Business Suite (12.2.5), Linux X86-64. Don't think that the following stage for 12.2.5 will install EBS 12.2.5 by default. This media pack only includes patch software for 12.2.5. It will only install the 12.2.0 base release, and later you can use the downloaded media pack to upgrade it to 12.2.5.

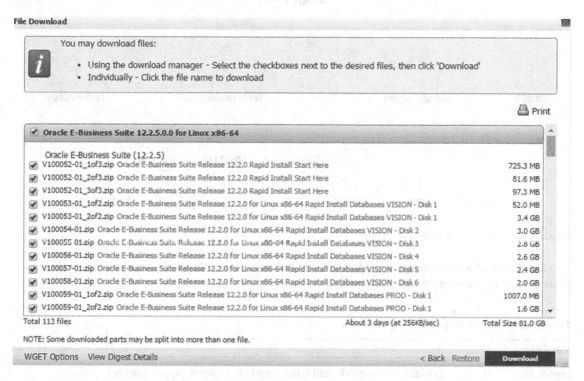

Figure 2-4. *Oracle EBS 12.2.5 media pack download page*

Oracle EBS 12.2 Stage Directory Structure

You should download all the required files including the NLS files based on the additional language requirements, and all these zip files should be copied to a single directory.

Certain files are not required to be downloaded at the initial install, but they may be needed based on the business requirements. For example, if you are performing a Fresh installation, then you don't need files related to the Vision database. Similarly, if you are performing a Vision install, then files for the production database are not required.

Oracle E-Business Suite 12.2 stage software will be distributed across different directories. Figure 2-5 depicts the directory structure for different components created by the 12.2 staging script.

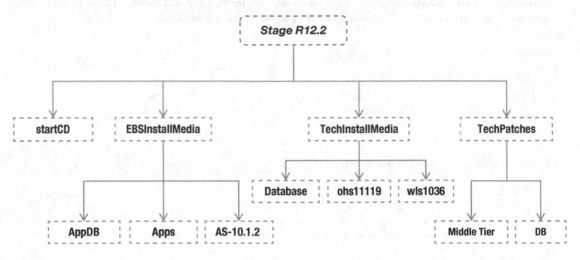

Figure 2-5. *Stage 12.2 directory structure*

The Oracle EBS 12.2 staging area contains the multiple underlying directories required for installation. Table 2-6 lists the directory structure that will be created by the Rapidwiz staging script.

Table 2-6. *EBS 12.2 Stage Directory Contents*

startCD	
rapidwiz	Contains the Rapid Install Wizard and all required supporting files
EBSInstallMedia	
AppDB	Oracle E-Business Suite 12.2 database
Apps	Oracle E-Business Suite application products
AS10.1.2	Oracle Application Server 10.1.2
TechInstallMedia	
database	Oracle RDBMS 12.1.0.2 ORACLE_HOME
Ohs11119	Oracle HTTP Server
wls1036_generic	Oracle WebLogic Server (Oracle Fusion Middleware)
TechPatches	
Middle Tier	Application tier patches
DB	Database tier patches

Build Stage Menu Options

The buildstage.sh script should be used for creating the EBS 12.2 staging area, and this script provides multiple options related to the creation and management of the staging area. Table 2-7 lists the options available with the 12.2 buildstage.sh script.

Table 2-7. *EBS 12.2 buildstage.sh Script Menu Options*

S. No.	Menu Option	Description
1.	Create new stage area	This option is used for creating a new software stage area.
2.	Copy patches to existing area	If a stage area is created, then additional patches can be copied using this option.
3.	List files in TechPatches directory	This will provide a list of patches in the TechPatches directory.
4.	Exit	This will exit from the build stage menu.

Figure 2-6 describes how to execute and use the buildstage.sh script. This script will be located in the startCD /rapidwiz/bin directory.

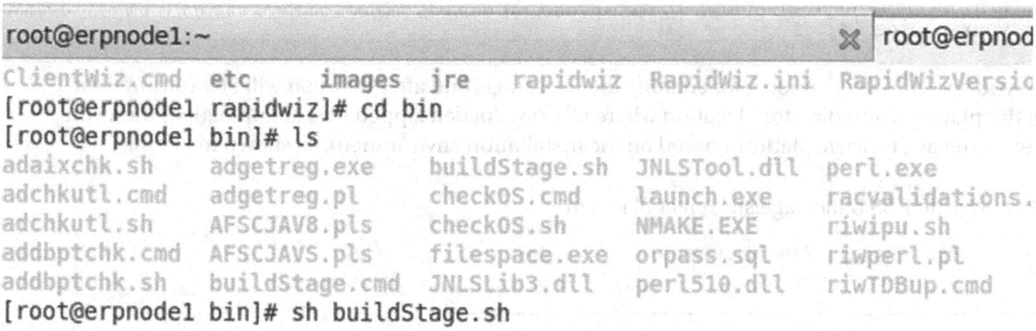

```
root@erpnode1:~                                          ✕  root@erpnod

ClientWiz.cmd   etc      images   jre    rapidwiz  RapidWiz.ini  RapidWizVersio
[root@erpnode1 rapidwiz]# cd bin
[root@erpnode1 bin]# ls
adaixchk.sh     adgetreg.exe    buildStage.sh   JNLSTool.dll   perl.exe
adchkutl.cmd    adgetreg.pl     checkOS.cmd     launch.exe     racvalidations.
adchkutl.sh     AFSCJAV8.pls    checkOS.sh      NMAKE.EXE      riwipu.sh
addbptchk.cmd   AFSCJAVS.pls    filespace.exe   orpass.sql     riwperl.pl
addbptchk.sh    buildStage.cmd  JNLSLib3.dll    perl510.dll    riwTDBup.cmd
[root@erpnode1 bin]# sh buildStage.sh
```

Figure 2-6. *Rapidwiz build stage main menu, "Create new stage area" menu*

Starting with EBS 12.2, the "StartHere" CD provides a utility called buildstage.sh for preparing the EBS 12.2 stage. This utility has its own menu and multiple functions available from the menu options. The major task for preparing the stage is to create directories and subdirectories and unzip the files in the relevant stage directories. Listing 2-1 illustrates the main menu option of the buildstage.sh script.

```
buildstage.sh script will be located under  "<R122_Stage>/"
```

Listing 2-1. EBS 12.2 buildstage.sh Main Menu Option

```
[root@erpnode1 bin]# pwd
/u01/stage/stage_R1225/startCD/Disk1/rapidwiz/bin
[root@erpnode1 bin]# ls -l buildStage.sh
-rwxr-xr-x 1 root root 17325 Jun 15 10:16 buildStage.sh
[root@erpnode1 bin]# sh buildStage.sh
```

```
                    Copyright (c) 2002, 2013 Oracle Corporation
                         Redwood Shores, California, USA

                      Oracle E-Business Suite Rapid Install

                                Version 12.2.0

Press Enter to continue...

                         Build Stage Menu

    -------------------------------------------------------

    1.      Create new stage area

    2.      Copy patches to existing stage area

    3.      List files in TechPatches directory

    4.      Exit menu

Enter your choice [4]: 1
```

Here you should select option 1 for creating the new stage, and after this, you will be prompted for selecting the platform and directory location where all downloaded zipped files are uploaded; then you should select the appropriate platform based on the installation environment, as shown in Listing 2-2.

Listing 2-2. Oracle EBS buildstage.sh: Select Platform

```
           Rapid Install Platform Menu

    -------------------------------------------------------

    1.     Oracle Solaris SPARC (64-bit)

    2.     Linux x86 (64-bit)

    3.     IBM AIX on Power Systems (64-bit)

    4.     HP-UX Itanium

    5.     Exit Menu

Enter your choice [5]: 2

Specify the directory containing the zipped installation media:/u01/1225_Stage
```

Copy Patches to Existing Stage Area

Oracle will release newer versions of the startCD, and each new version of the startCD will include multiple bug fixes and enhancements. To copy these patches into the existing stage area, you have to use the option "Copy patches to existing stage area." If you're using the latest version of the startCD, you have to remove the existing startCD directory from the existing stage area.

At the time of writing this book, the latest available startCD version is 51, so this option cannot be tested at this stage, but when startCD 52 is available, then you can use this option.

■ **Note** After the release of startCD 51, Oracle decommissioned all previous versions of startCD patches, so they are not available to be downloaded from the MOS website. The first startCD introduced was 46, and then there were consecutive releases 47, 48, 49, 50, and 51. But currently the only supported version of the startCD is 51.

List Files in the TechPatches Directory

Listing 2-3 shows the last option of the buildstage.sh script; this option will list the patches for the database and the middle tier that exist in the stage directory.

Listing 2-3. Oracle EBS: Listing Database and Middle Tier Patches from the Stage Area

```
                    Build Stage Menu


    -------------------------------------------------------

    1.      Create new stage area
    2.      Copy patches to existing stage area
    3.      List files in TechPatches directory
    4.      Exit menu

    Enter your choice [4]: 3


Directory /u01/stage/stage_R122_51/startCD/Disk1/rapidwiz/bin/../../../../TechPatches

|--DB
|    |--17257305
|    |    |--p17257305_R12_LINUX.zip
|    |--18485835
|    |    |--p18485835_121020_Linux-x86-64.zip
....
....
|--MiddleTier
|    |--10152652
|    |    |--p10152652_10123_LINUX.zip
|    |--11669923
|    |    |--p11669923_10123_GENERIC.zip
|    |--11781879
|    |    |--p11781879_103607_Generic.zip
```

Copy Patches to Existing Stage Area

Oracle will release newer versions of the startCD, and each new version of the startCD will include multiple bug fixes and enhancements. To copy these patches into the existing stage area, you have to use the option "Copy patches to existing stage area." If you're using the latest version of the startCD, you have to remove the existing startCD directory from the existing stage area.

At the time of writing this book, the latest available startCD version is 51, so this option cannot be tested at this stage, but when the startCD 52 is available, then you can use this option.

■ **Note**   After the release of startCD 51, Oracle decommissioned all previous versions of startCD patches, and they are not available to be downloaded from the MOS website. The first startCD introduced was 46, and then there were consecutive releases 47, 48, 49, 50, and 51. But currently the only supported version of the startCD is 51.

Single-Node Installation

As discussed earlier, in single-node installation, all services will be configured on a single server. Before actually beginning with the installation, you should verify all prerequisites are in place. Missing prerequisites or incorrect configuration of any of these prerequisites may make the installation fail. If there is a plan to use the single-node installation in production, then you have to size the system appropriately for database and application users based on the earlier guidelines in the section "Computing Requirements."

Before Running Rapidwiz

The Oracle E-Business Suite installation will be performed using the root user, so you need to have access to that user account.

- There should be an X Display shell working to support the GUI installation.

- Verify that sufficient space is available in the /usr/tmp or /tmp directory.

- Execute Rapidwiz.

Figure 2-7 displays the execution of the Rapidwiz script, which will be used for the Oracle E-Business Suite installation.

```
[root@erpnode1 rapidwiz]# ./rapidwiz


Rapid Install Wizard is validating your file system......
CMDDIR=/u01/R1224_Stage/startCD/Disk1/rapidwiz
Rapid Install Wizard will now launch the Java Interface.....

[root@erpnode1 rapidwiz]# ▯
```

| 🖳 root@erpnode1:/u01/... | ⚙ Install Oracle E-Busine... |

Figure 2-7. EBS 12.2: execution of Rapidwiz

Figure 2-8 shows the first and main installation screen that will list the tech stack components that will install Oracle EBS.

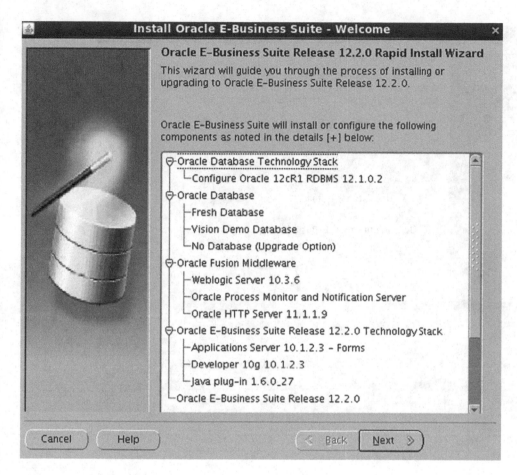

Figure 2-8. Rapidwiz: first installation screen

Two options are available (see Figure 2-9): Install and Upgrade. You are performing a Fresh installation here, so you should choose the Install option. You will see how the Upgrade option works later.

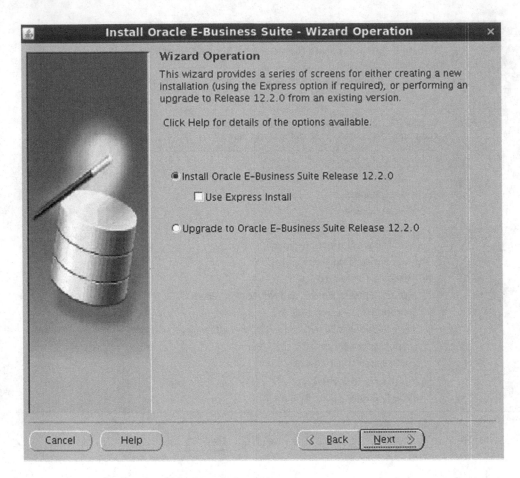

Figure 2-9. *Rapidwiz: Install and Upgrade options*

Figure 2-10 shows the Rapidwiz screen for configuring the Oracle Support credentials, which are required for Oracle Configuration Manager. If you have valid credentials and the server is connected to the Internet, then you should provide these details. Otherwise, you can skip this option and configure them after installation.

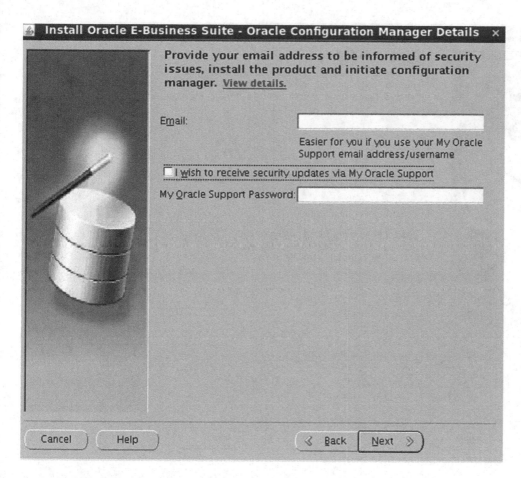

Figure 2-10. *Rapidwiz: Oracle Configuration Manager credentials*

The Rapidwiz Install Wizard will use the default values for almost all parameters, but this option is not recommended for production installation. Using the Rapidwiz Install Wizard, you can perform a Fresh or Vision EBS installation.

Figure 2-11 provides a configuration screen with two options: "Create a new configuration" and "Load the following saved configuration." If you are performing a Fresh install, then you should select the first option for creating a new configuration. "Load the following saved configuration" is required for multinode installations.

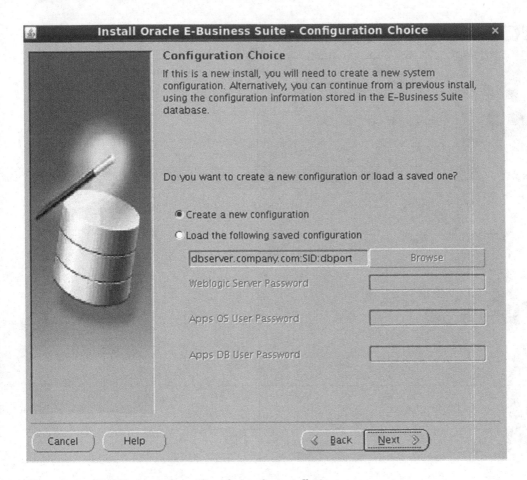

Figure 2-11. *Rapidwiz: configuration choices for installation*

"Create a new configuration" will store all the provided configuration settings in a text file, and later it will save this information into a database during the database tier configuration phase.

Figure 2-12 allows you to choose the database type (Fresh or Vision) based on selecting "Vision demo database/Fresh database will be installed." The Vision database option will install sample business data that can used for evaluating the product and performing Proof of concept (POC). The Fresh database option will not install any business data, and this is the only option that will used for a production implementation.

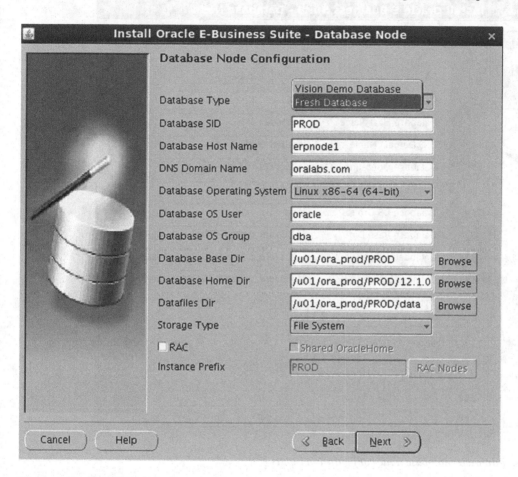

Figure 2-12. *Installation choices: Fresh Database and Vision Demo Database*

The Database Node Configuration screen shown in Figure 2-13 requires inputs for configuring the database, and it displays the provided input parameter used in the current installation.

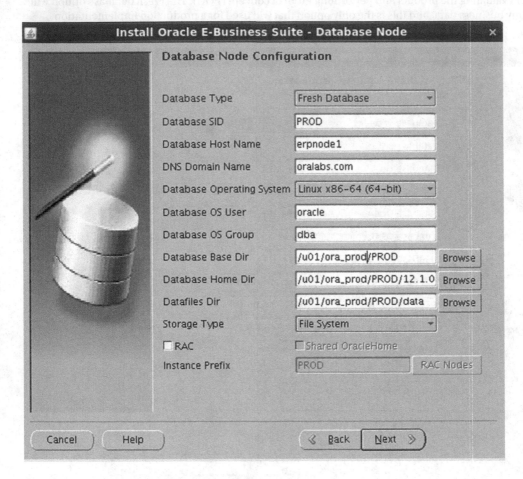

Figure 2-13. *Rapidwiz: database node configuration inputs*

It also requires inputs for the operating system database username, group, and location for installing Oracle RDBMS (12.1.0.2) Home and the database.

You can choose to store files on the file system or ASM based on your requirements. When using the ASM option for Storage Type, you should configure the ASM instance and ASM disk groups with the required capacity in advance, and the database OS user should have access to write to the ASM disk group.

The "Configuration of RAC database" option is also available on the Database Node configuration screen, but we will explain this option in Chapter X.

Figure 2-14 provides two options: Suite Licensing and Component Licensing. You have to choose an option based on your company's license agreement. If your organization is entitled to use suite licensing, then by default Rapidwiz will register all products included in the application price bundle.

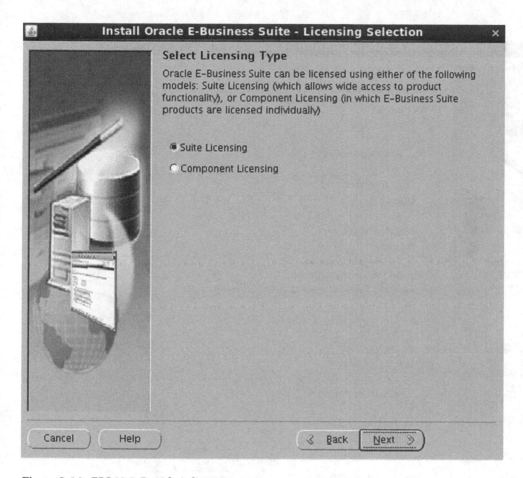

Figure 2-14. *EBS 12.2: Rapidwiz licensing options*

The Component Licensing option will allow you to choose individual components to license, and you have to select components based on your organization's license agreement.

Figure 2-15 displays a list of licensed products; the products that are checked and grayed out are licensed as part of suite licensing. On this screen you can license additional products, but these additional products will not be part of the suite licensing bundle. You need to have a separate license for any additional products.

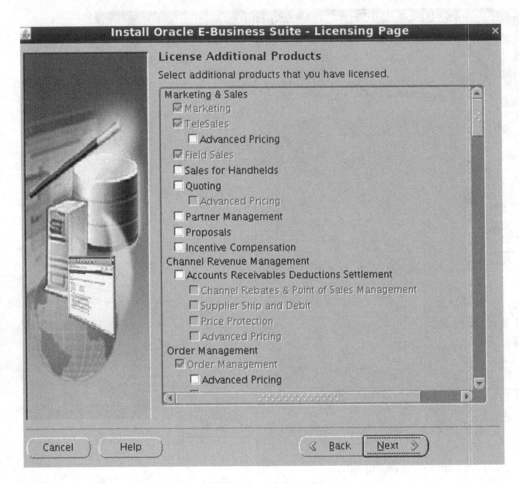

Figure 2-15. *Rapidwiz : licensing additional products*

The screen shown in Figure 2-16 provides a list of all the available country-specific functionalities, and it will allow you to choose a country specific to your localization. Consider that a company is running in the United States, Australia, and Brazil. The localization rules and labor laws will be different across these countries, so this option will allow the application to accommodate other country-specific functionalities in Oracle E-Business Suite.

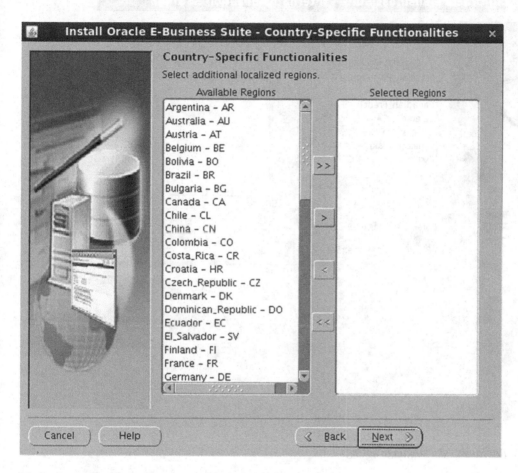

Figure 2-16. Rapidwiz: country-specific functionalities options

All supported country-specific functionalities are listed within the installation screen, and this will allow to add/remove any additional functionalities.

The Internationalization Settings screen in Figure 2-17 allows you to add any additional language to your Oracle E-Business Suite installation. Based on other languages, you should choose the character set for the database and applications.

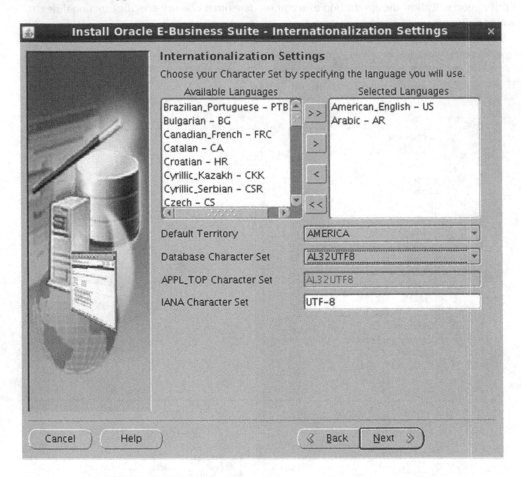

Figure 2-17. *Rapidwiz: NLS language settings*

Rapidwiz enables you to add any additional languages based on the country-specific language requirements. In Figure 2-16, by default U.S. English is selected, and Arabic is selected as an additional language. You should select the supported character set with respect to additional selected languages.

You should select the character set type carefully. It is difficult to change the character set after installation, and there are many restriction for character set conversion. For example, you can convert the character set from USASCII7 to AL32UTF8, but you cannot convert the character set from AL32UTF8 to USASCII7. AL32UTF8 supports almost all languages, so it's recommended that you use AL32UTF8 if there is a chance of using more than two different languages.

NLS stands for National Language Settings, and additional languages should be enabled based on the country-specific language settings.

At this stage, you can provide the information about the primary application tier node. It can be different server, but there should be network communication between the primary application server and the database tier nodes. All OS prerequisites should be performed on the primary application server. But in this demonstration we have used a single server for both the database and primary application tiers.

The Primary Applications Node configuration screen shown in Figure 2-18 allows you to provide inputs for OS user, group, and directory locations for installation. It requires locations for Apps Base Dir and Apps Instance Dir. Rapidwiz will not allow you to select two different locations for the RUN and PATCH file systems.

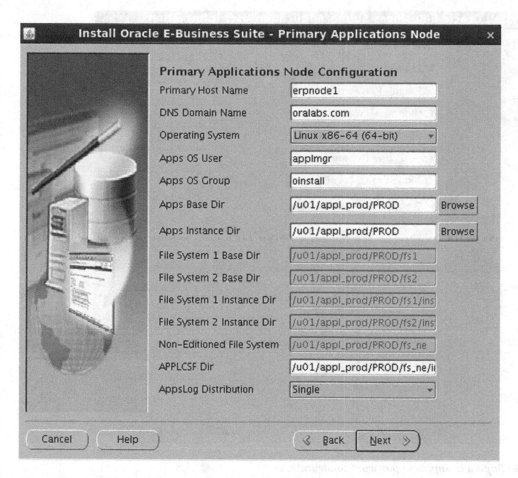

Figure 2-18. *Rapidwiz: primary application node configuration*

As we are performing a single-node installation here, the hostname for the database node and application node is the same. By default all application services will be enabled on the primary application tier node.

The Application User Information screen shown in Figure 2-19 allows you to configure all application superuser passwords. In earlier releases, the superuser password was configured by default, and you had to change these passwords as a post-install step.

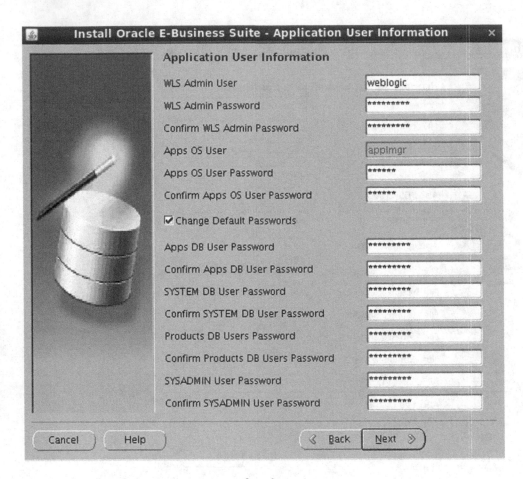

Figure 2-19. *Rapidwiz: superuser password configuration*

The Node Information screen shown in Figure 2-20 summarizes the nodes that are used in the EBS installation topology.

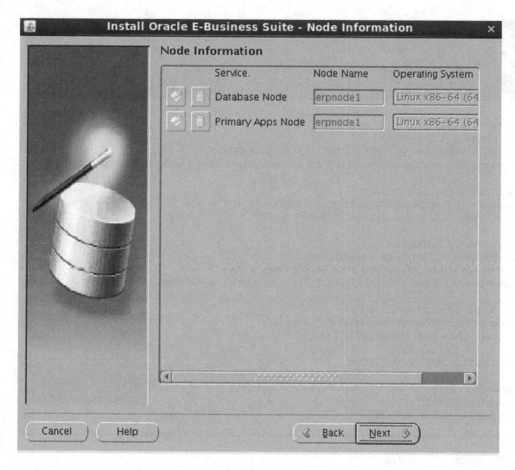

Figure 2-20. *Rapidwiz: node information summary*

Rapidwiz will perform the full pre-install checks that are required to be in place to avoid issues during the installation process. Figure 2-21 illustrates the Rapidwiz pre-install checks.

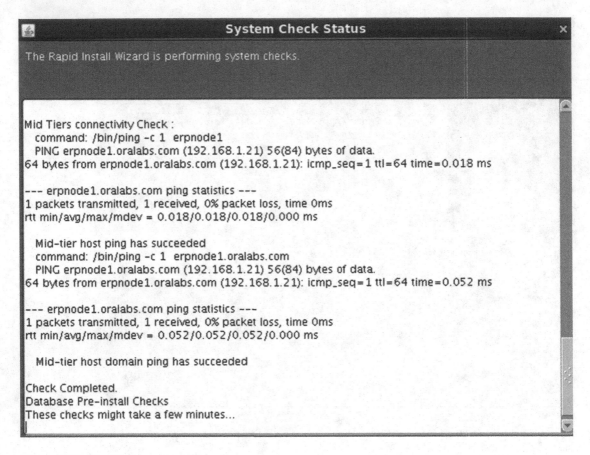

Figure 2-21. *Rapidwiz: pre-install checks*

The Validate System Configuration screen shown in Figure 2-22 will perform the prerequisites checks for all the previously listed settings, and all these items should have green check mark to proceed with the installation. If there are any errors or warnings for any of this configuration, then you should fix them before proceeding with the installation.

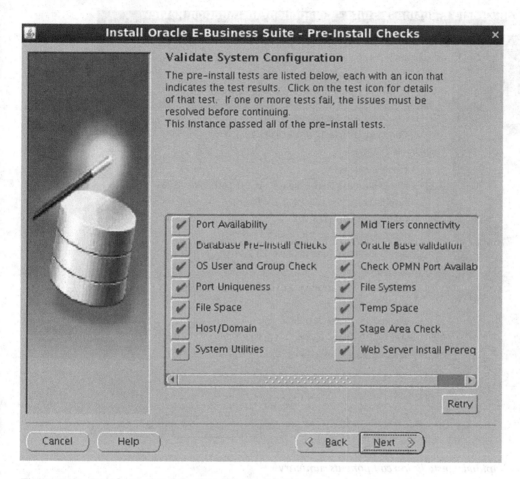

Figure 2-22. Rapidwiz: system configuration validations

As discussed earlier in this chapter, Rapidwiz is responsible for installing the multiple technology stack components and application products. Figure 2-23 provides the list of technology stack components that Rapidwiz will install and the configuration of the language setting that Rapidwiz will perform.

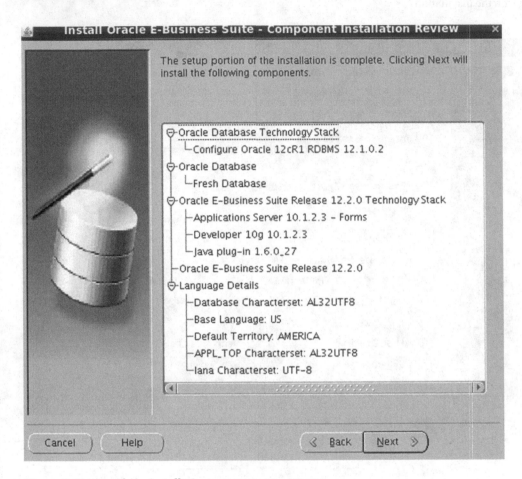

Figure 2-23. *Rapidwiz: installation components summary*

Rapidwiz will install different technology stack components in different stages. There are a total of eight steps for installation, and for a successful installation, all these steps should complete successfully. Figure 2-24 shows the installation progress.

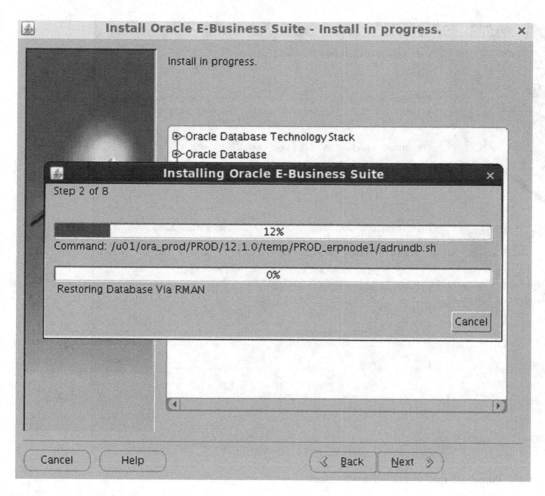

Figure 2-24. *Rapidwiz: installation progress summary*

After all the installation steps are performed, Rapidwiz will perform the post-installation checks to validate the system configuration and services. Figure 2-25 displays the components that Rapidwiz will check during the system validation process.

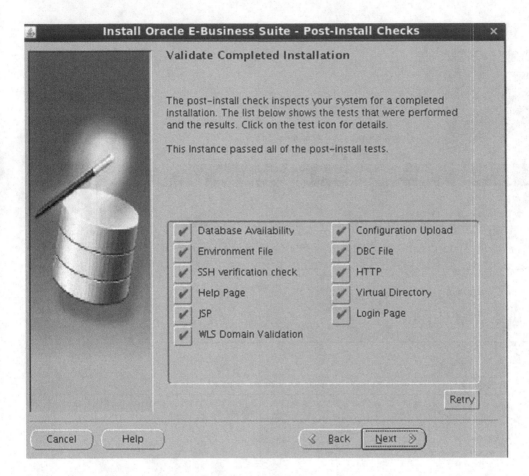

Figure 2-25. *Rapidwiz: post-install validation check*

▓ **Note**   Our installation completed in five hours with 24GB RAM and four vCPUs, but your installation time may vary based on different computing resources.

With this, you are done with the single-node installation process, but you should perform the post-installation steps once the installation is completed. Figure 2-26 shows the main installation completion screen; note the radio button Connect to Oracle E-Business Suite 12.2. Clicking it will open a browser and connect to the application URL.

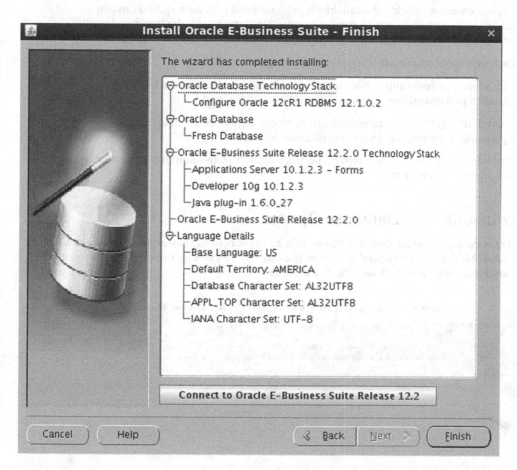

Figure 2-26. Rapidwiz: installation completion summary

Multinode Installation

The term *multinode* is self-explanatory. In such installations the database and application services are distributed across multiple database and application nodes. The full multinode installation was supported until startCD 48, where you can have multiple database nodes (RAC) and application nodes. However, the latest version of the startCD doesn't support the multiple application node installation.

Starting with startCD 49, the Rapidwiz Install Wizard cannot configure the multiple application tier nodes. The database services can be installed on a single node or multiple nodes (using RAC), and application services can be on separate nodes. But at the time of writing this book, startCD 51 is available only for download from MOS.

Key Points Related to Multinode Installation

Remember the following key points:

- Multiple database nodes are supported by the Rapidwiz install process provided that the same version of Grid Infrastructure is preconfigured with the required capacity on ASM disk groups on all EBS database nodes. Until startCD 50, the Rapidwiz install process delivered database version 11.2.0.3; since startCD 51, it delivers 12.1.0.2.

- Only one application node is supported, starting with startCD 49.

- Any additional application node should be added after upgrading the freshly installed EBS system from version 12.2.0 to 12.2.3/12.2.4/12.2.5.

- Shared APPL_TOP and parallel concurrent processing can be configured after upgrading to the target supported application release.

- The Add Server install option is available until startCD 48; this option is not available starting from startCD 49.

Rapidwiz Install: RAC Database Option

Figure 2-27 shows the participating cluster nodes for EBS database deployment. ebsnode1 is the local cluster node, and ebsnode2 is the secondary database node. You can choose a storage option of ASM or other supported shared storage options such as NFS, OCFS2, or ZFS.

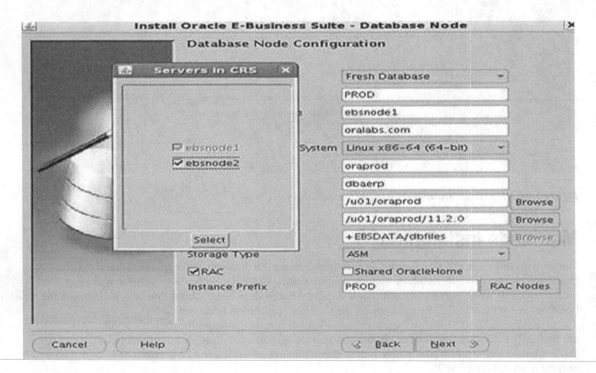

Figure 2-27. *Rapid install: RAC database option*

In Oracle 12c, Grid Infrastructure Flex Cluster and Flex ASM were introduced, so you can configure EBS database nodes to use the Flex Cluster option. In a traditional cluster environment, there will be an ASM instance running on each cluster node, but in Flex Cluster ASM instances are not required to run on each cluster node. ASM instances will be running on hub nodes, and leaf nodes will share the ASM instance running on the hub node.

Shared APPL_TOP in Oracle EBS 12.2

The Oracle EBS system supports shared APPL_TOP terminology starting from application version 11i, and it's supported until 12.2. Generally, the shared APPL_TOP concept is simple, and it's helpful in large deployments. It will simplify the management of the application tier nodes and reduce the patching efforts and downtime.

In a shared application tier configuration, the node on which the application tier is configured initially will be considered as the *primary* application tier node, and the nodes that are configured later are called the *secondary* application tier nodes. In Figure 2-28, you can see EBSApps (appl, comn, 10.1.2), FMW_Home (webtier, wls), and INST_TOP are shared across application nodes.

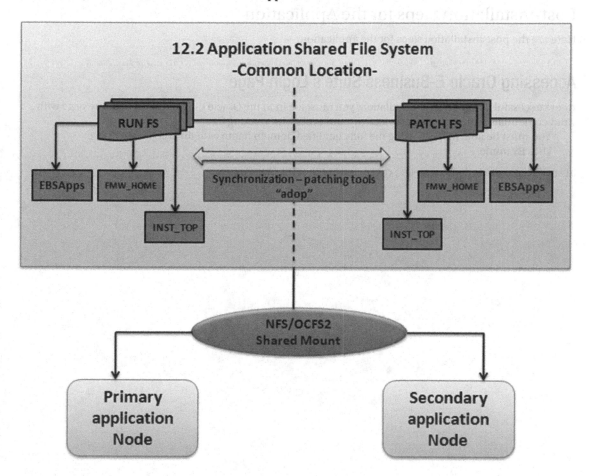

Figure 2-28. *Rapidwiz install: shared application tier*

The Rapidwiz Install Wizard starting with startCD 49 doesn't support shared APPL_TOP configuration; it can be configured after upgrading it to the supported target releases of 12.2.3/12.2.4/12.2.5. But you can configure the shared location on all application nodes from the Rapidwiz Install Wizard itself, and later this shared location can be configured on other participating application tier nodes. This will help in configuring the shared location of the application tier on the primary node. Currently NFS and OCFS2 are the only certified shared file system options with the 12.2 application tier.

In Chapter 11, you will see in detail how you can configure the shared APPL_TOP for the secondary application tier.

Post-installation Steps

These are the series of steps that must be executed after a successful installation of Oracle E-Business Suite. Some of these steps are mandatory, and some are optional based on the business requirements and implementation plan.

Post-installation Steps for the Application

Here are the post-installation steps for the application.

Accessing Oracle E-Business Suite's Login Page

After successful completion of installation, you must log in to the Oracle E-Business Suite home page with valid credentials and verify that connectivity and access are working fine.

You must be able to log in using the fully qualified domain name with the web listener port.

URL Example

```
http://<hostname.domian-name>:<http port>/OA_HTML/AppsLogin
```

URL Specific to Installation Shown in Figure 2-29

```
http://erpnode1.oralabs.com:8000/OA_HTML/AppsLogin
```

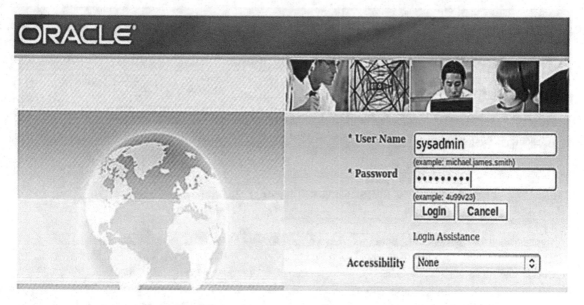

Figure 2-29. *EBS 12.2: main login page*

The Oracle Application Manager's Applications Dashboard displays the host and services status. Figure 2-30 shows the Applications Dashboard for the single-node installation performed earlier in this chapter.

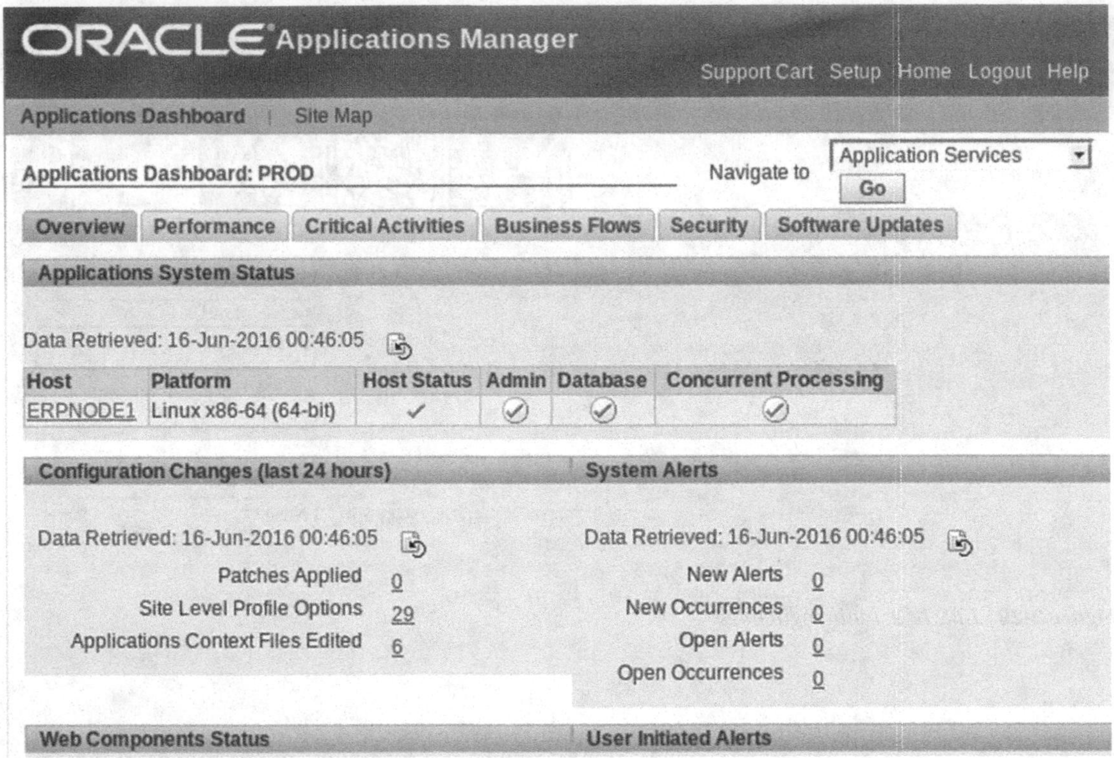

Figure 2-30. EBS 12.2: Application Dashboard

You should verify the installed version and list of products using OAM Dashboard | Site Map configuration overview, as shown in Figure 2-31.

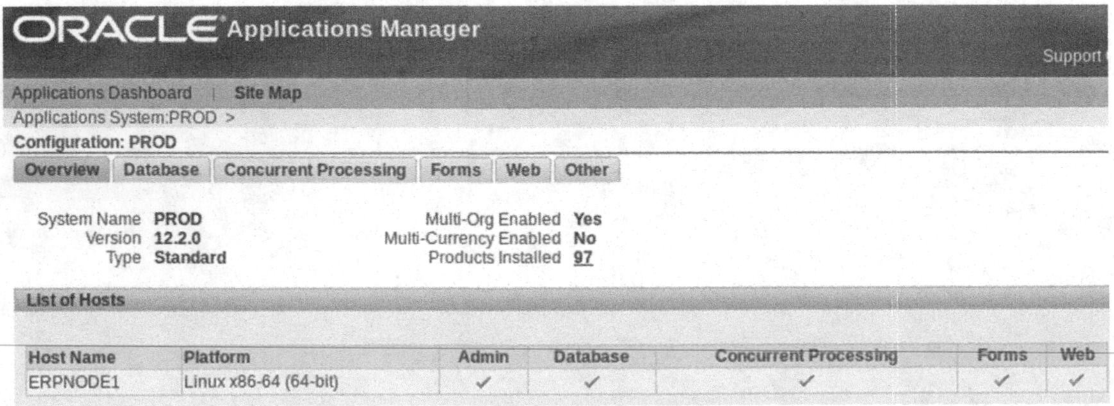

Figure 2-31. EBS 12.2: application version and installed products

Change Default Passwords

As discussed earlier, all super-privileged account passwords can be configured using the Rapidwiz Install Wizard. If these passwords are not set up using the Rapidwiz Install Wizard, you must change them manually. The following are the list of users for which passwords must be changed:

```
Database - sys, system, apps
Application - sysadmin, weblogic (WLS admin user)
```

The sys and system account passwords can be changed using the alter user command, but for other users, there is a specific procedure for changing the passwords. You will see this procedure in Chapter 12.

Implement Product and Country-Specific Functionalities

Based on the selected products and country-specific functionalities you are planning to use within the installation, you may need to perform additional steps or may need to apply additional patches. You will see how to implement these options later in this book.

Implement Additional NLS Language

As discussed earlier, the Rapidwiz Install Wizard will not configure the NLS language in EBS 12.2. By default the base installation base language will be American English. If you select any additional language during the installation phase, then the Rapidwiz Install Wizard will configure the required site-level profiles for the additional selected language and territory.

Set Up Printers

Oracle E-Business Suite provides reporting capabilities, and reports can be printed based on the business's user requirements. Oracle E-Business Suite supports printing directly from applications. To use this feature, you have to configure the printers within Oracle E-Business Suite, and if using additional NLS languages, then you may need to perform some additional configuration steps to print reports in languages other than U.S. English. You will see the detailed configuration and setup of printers within Oracle E-Business Suite in Chapter 9.

Oracle Workflow Mailer Configuration

Oracle E-Business Suite can send e-mail notifications and Oracle e-mail alerts for business events and configured alerts, respectively. To utilize this functionality workflow, the mailer should be configured with the required SMTP and IMAP (for inbound e-mail processing) accounts. Later in this book you will see the detailed configuration of the Workflow mailer.

Client PC Requirements

Here are the requirements for the client PC.

JRE Client

You need to make sure that clients are running the certified version of the JRE client software on a certified browser. This Java applet is required for launching the form-based applications. Oracle continues to release new versions of the JRE that include enhancements, bug fixes, and security vulnerabilities. But you cannot use the latest available version of the JRE on client machines until it's been certified by Oracle against the respective release of Oracle E-Business Suite.

You should always refer to MOS tech note "Deploying JRE (Native Plug-in) for Windows Clients in Oracle E-Business Suite Release 12" (Doc ID 393931.1) for deploying the correct version of the JRE on client machines.

■ **Tip**   In certain organizations there may be other applications that need a Java client to run, so you should always choose the appropriate certified version that can be compatible with the other Java-enabled application.

Ports Access

You need to ensure that all required ports are open, from the client PC to application servers. If there is a requirement for developers/technical consultants to establish a direct database connection, then you also need to ensure that the database listener port is open from the required PC.

Post-installation Steps for the Database

Here are the post-installation steps for the database.

Oracle Database Initialization Parameters

Oracle Database initialization parameters are configured by the default installation, which uses the init<SID>.ora initialization parameter file. All required and relevant database initialization parameters are listed in MOS tech note "396009.1 - Database Initialization Parameters for Oracle Applications Release 12." After setting up the required parameters, you must create the server parameter file spfile, which you must use for all future changes.

You must also refer to MOS tech note "bde_chk_cbo.sql - EBS initialization parameters - Healthcheck (Doc ID 174605.1)" before configuring the new parameters related to the database.

Update PL/SQL Log and Out Directory

By default the /usr/tmp directory is used on the database server for log and output files from pl/sql concurrent programs, and this directory may contain sensitive data. You need to make sure that proper privileges exist on this directory for other operating system users.

This value is specified in the database initialization parameter as utl_file_dir=/usr/tmp, and the same value will be assigned to the APPLTMP environment variable. It is recommended that you use some other directory of your choice because there are limitations for using /usr/tmp location. For example, there may be a problem for access rights, or you may face space pressure during heavy transactions, and during reboots the content will be lost from the /usr/tmp directory.

You can configure the directory of your choice using the following steps:

1.   Configure the database initialization parameter utl_file_dir=<target directory.

2.   Update the APPLTMP variable to the same directory value configured for utl_file_dir.

3.   Run AutoConfig and verify the changes.

Resize the Database

Database tablespaces will be configured with the default sizes. Based on the selected products, data growth considerations, and business requirements, you need to resize the database accordingly.

Back Up the Database and Application

After all post-installation steps are completed, then it is highly recommended to perform a cold backup for the application and database. Once you have a full backup of the system, it is recommended that you plan and design the backup policy for the database and application that meets your company's service level agreement or operational level agreement.

Upgrade EBS to 12.2.4 or 12.2.5

The installation will deliver the base release 12.2.0, which is not supported at the moment, so one of the major post-installation steps is to upgrade the current release from 12.2.0 to 12.2.4/12.2.5. At the time of writing this book, 12.2.5 is the latest maintenance pack available. The upgrade steps from 12.2.0 to 12.2.5 are discussed in detail in Chapter 3.

How to Deal with Failed Installations

Oracle E-Business Suite failed installations are often reported on community forums and many other places including in the creation of service requests on My Oracle Support. At the beginning of the chapter, we discussed the conditions for a successful installation. The key for a successful installation is to perform all the prerequisites successfully before beginning the installation. However, there may be certain situations where installation fails because of some other reasons such as hardware failure, power failure, media corruption, and so on. In such situations, the actions you perform as a DBA are extremely important.

As you know, Oracle E-Business Suite installations are time-consuming, and if the installation fails in the middle or at the last stage, then it will cost you a lot of time. First you have to find the problem, and then you have to fix the problem before resuming the installation.

Starting with Oracle E-Business Suite 12.2, Rapidwiz does not support the restart option like previous releases (rapidwiz -restart). If there is a failure during the installation or in the post-install check, then you must identify the problem that caused error, clean the system with the installed database and application files, fix the problem, and start the installation again from the beginning. This information is clearly published in MOS tech note "R12.2: How to Create Stage In Preparation for installation" (Doc ID 1596433.1).

Rapidwiz will install and configure the database and technology stack components in different phases. Each phase of installation will have its own log file. In the case of a failure during the Rapidwiz install, you have to analyze the respective log files to identify the problem. The stage area is one of the crucial parts of installations. Corrupted or missing files in the stage area will create errors during installation, and installation will be halted. Starting from EBS 12.2, the stage area will be verified by the buildstage.sh script. If there is still a problem and installation is producing errors, then you should run a checksum against your staging area. To run a checksum for the 12.2 stage, you can use MOS tech note "MD5 Checksums for R12.2 Rapid Install Media" (Doc ID 1505510.1).

Rapidwiz Installation Process

Here is the Rapidwiz installation process.

Database Tier

Here are the steps for the database tier:

1. Rapidwiz collects information required for configuring the database tech stack and database.

2. Rapidwiz performs a prerequisite check required for database configuration.

3. Files from the 12.2 stage area are extracted onto the file system.

4. dbTeckStack will be installed using scripts called by Oracle Universal Installer (OUI).

5. The control file will be restored from the 12.2 stage area backup.

6. Data files will be restored and renamed using RMAN using the 12.2 stage area backup.

7. Start the listener and database.

8. Execute AutoConfig for any further configuration.

Application Tier

Here are the steps for the application tier:

1. Install WebLogic Server from shiphome using scripts that invoke the native installer.

2. Install web tier utilities (OHS) and patches using native the installer from shiphome.

3. Configure Tools Oracle Home (Forms).

4. The APPL_TOP file system is extracted from the 12.2 stage zip files.

5. Reconfigure the application tier using cloning and AutoConfig.

6. Create WebLogic domain and assign managed server to newly created domain.

7. Create and configure WebLogic Server properties.

8. Services are started on the RUN file system.

■ **Note** Rapidwiz will Install and configure both file systems (RUN and PATCH), named fs1 and fs2. fs2 will be configured first, and then fs1 will be configured. Services will be started from the RUN file system; by default it will be fs1.

■ **Tip** If the application node restarted/failed for any reason, then it is not required to delete the database. Rapidwiz will load the configuration from the database and start the installation on that specific node. This option is possible only once the database node installation has completed successfully.

■ **Note** The best note for understanding and troubleshooting the Rapidwiz install process is "Troubleshooting Rapid Install for E-Business suite Release R12.2" (Doc ID 1378579.1). This tech note provides a detailed description of each phase of installation and its relevant log files for troubleshooting in the of a failure during installation.

How to Deal with Corrupted/Lost Technology Stack Components

Oracle E-Business Suite consists of technology stack components that were discussed in detail in Chapter 1. There may be a situation where these technology stack components get corrupted or lost. In such a situation, there is a new feature in Rapidwiz 12.2 to replace the existing technology stack components in an existing instance. This option can be used to replace the technology stack executables belonging to Oracle EBS RDBMS Home, Oracle FMW WebLogic Server, and Oracle Application Server 10.1.2.

This option is helpful only after a Fresh installation of the system. After installation, if you applied patches on technology stack components, then Rapidwiz cannot restore the newly applied patches. For example, if you applied patches on the existing 12.1.0.2, then Rapidwiz cannot restore all the patches applied on 12.1.0.2 RDBMS Oracle Home.

The following section covers how you can replace the different technology stack components.

Replacing the Oracle EBS Database Technology Stack (RDBMS Oracle Home)

These are the steps:

1. Remove the Rapidwiz install stage area from the RDBMS $ORACLE_HOME/temp/* directory.

   ```
   [oracle@erpnode1 ~]$ echo $ORACLE_HOME
   /u01/ora_prod/PROD/12.1.0
   [oracle@erpnode1 ~]$ cd /u01/ora_prod/PROD/11.2.0/temp/
   [oracle@erpnode1 temp]$ pwd
   /u01/ora_prod/PROD/12.1.0/temp
   [oracle@erpnode1 temp]$ rm -rf *
   [oracle@erpnode1 temp]$ ls
   [oracle@erpnode1 temp]$
   ```

2. Source the environment file and detach the RDBMS Oracle Home from the inventory.

   ```
   [oracle@erpnode1 temp]$ $ORACLE_HOME/oui/bin/detachHome.sh
   Starting Oracle Universal Installer...

   Checking swap space: must be greater than 500 MB. Actual 16979 MB    Passed
   The inventory pointer is located at /etc/oraInst.loc
   The inventory is located at /u01/ora_prod/oraInventory/
   'DetachHome' was successful.
   ```

3. Remove the existing RDBMS Oracle Home.

   ```
   [oracle@erpnode1 ~]$ echo $ORACLE_HOME
   /u01/ora_prod/PROD/12.1.0
   [oracle@erpnode1 ~]$ rm -rf $ORACLE_HOME
   [oracle@erpnode1 ~]$ cd $ORACLE_HOME
   -bash: cd: /u01/ora_prod/PROD/12.1.0: No such file or directory
   [oracle@erpnode1 ~]$
   ```

83

4. Execute Rapidwiz with the -techstack option from a database-owned OS user.

```
[oracle@erpnode1 rapidwiz]$ ./rapidwiz -techstack

Rapid Install Wizard is validating your file system......
CMDDIR=/u01/R1225_Stage/startCD/Disk1/rapidwiz
Rapid Install Wizard will now launch the Java Interface.....

[oracle@erpnode1 rapidwiz]$
```

Using Rapidwiz, you can replace the technology stack components if they are lost or corrupted. Figure 2-32 displays the option for replacing the RDBMS technology stack.

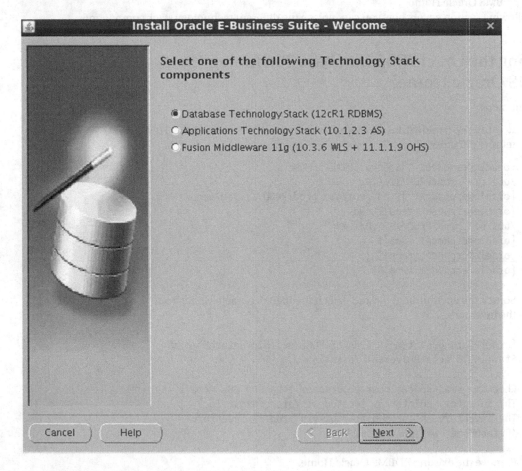

Figure 2-32. *Rapidwiz: replacing RDBMS technology stack*

In Figure 2-33, you provide all the inputs the same as they were configured before. For replacing the RDBMS tech stack in this demonstration, we have used the single-node installation performed earlier in this chapter.

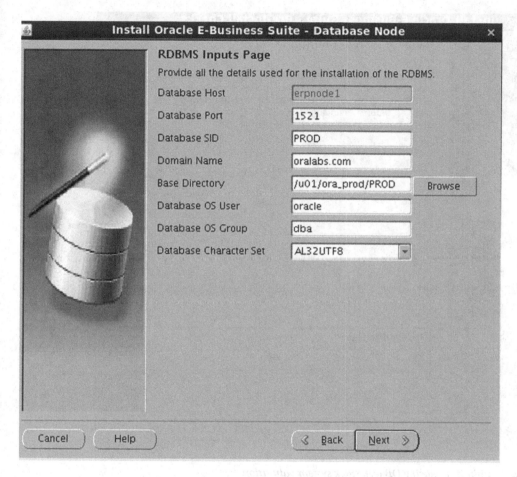

Figure 2-33. *Rapidwiz: replacing database tech stack inputs*

As per the process, Rapidwiz will perform the system validation checks before performing the install actions. In Figure 2-34, Rapidwiz is checking the availability of the provided port number.

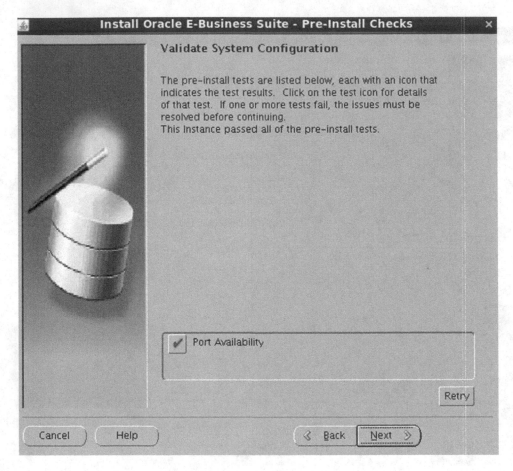

Figure 2-34. *Rapidwiz: replacing DB tech stack system validation*

Oracle 12c R1 (12.1.0.2) will be installed by default using this option, as shown in Figure 2-35.

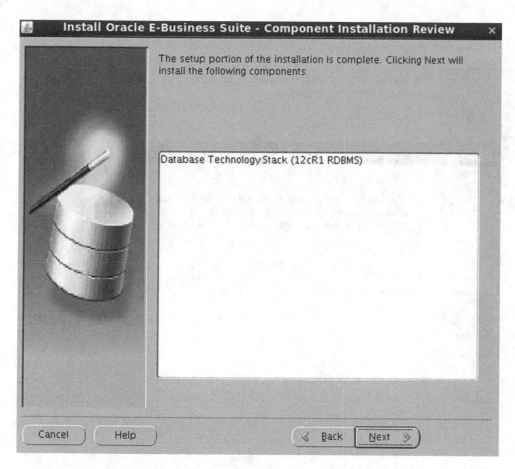

Figure 2-35. *Rapidwiz: replacing DB tech stack installation*

Rapidwiz will confirm before proceeding with the installation of the selected products, as shown in Figure 2-36.

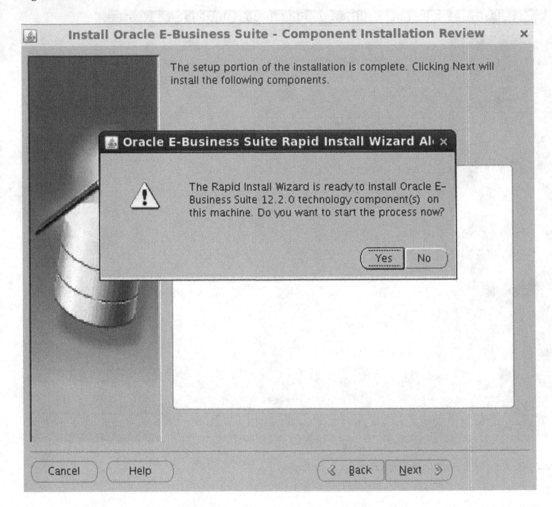

Figure 2-36. *Rapidwiz: replacing the database tech stack installation confirmation*

You are replacing only RDBMS Home; hence, only one step is listed in Figure 2-37, which is showing the installation progress.

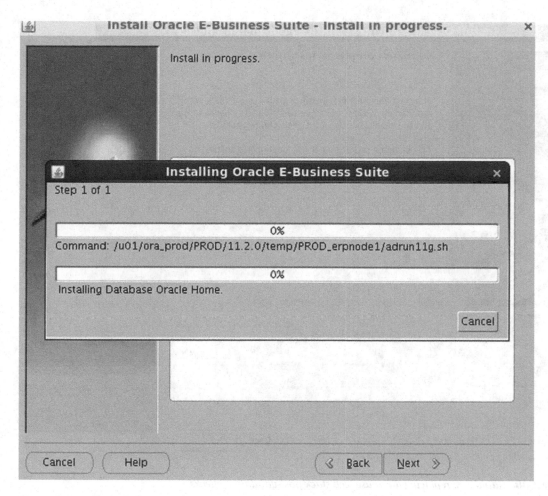

Figure 2-37. *Rapidwiz: replacing database tech stack installation progress*

After installation is complete, Rapidwiz will perform the post-validation checks and list the installed components, as shown in Figures 2-38 and 2-39.

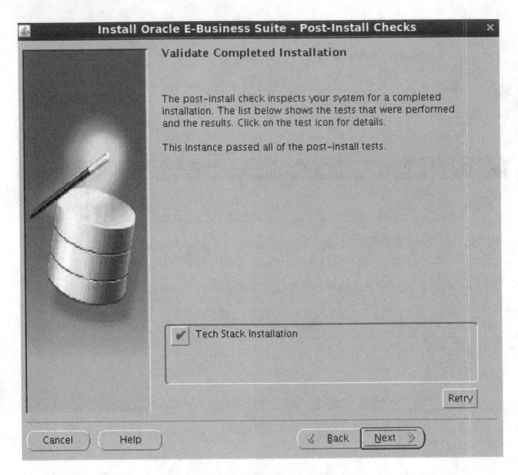

Figure 2-38. *Rapidwiz: replacing database tech stack post-validation checks*

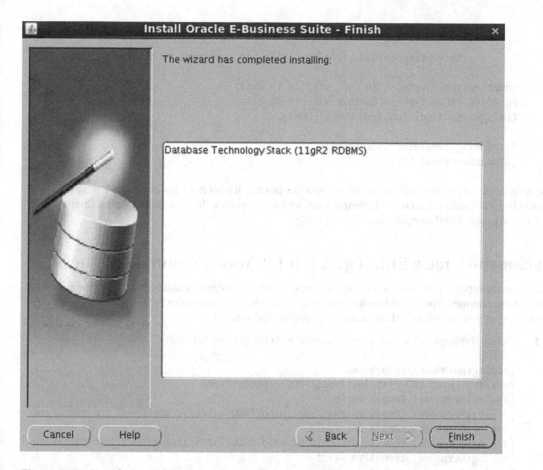

Figure 2-39. Rapidwiz : replacing database tech stack installation completion

Installation of RDBMS techstack component completed successfully using Rapidwiz.

5.   Execute AutoConfig (adconfig.sh).

```
[oracle@erpnode1 bin]$ adconfig.sh
Enter the full path to the Context file: /u01/ora_prod/PROD/12.1.0/appsutil/
PROD_erpnode1.xml
Enter the APPS user password:
The log file for this session is located at: /u01/ora_prod/PROD/12.1.0/appsutil/
log/PROD_erpnode1/06160222/adconfig.log

AutoConfig is configuring the Database environment...

AutoConfig will consider the custom templates if present.
        Using ORACLE_HOME location : /u01/ora_prod/PROD/12.1.0
        ....
 /u01/ora_prod/PROD/12.1.0/appsutil/PROD_erpnode1.xml

Context Value Management will now update the Context file
```

```
        Updating Context file...COMPLETED

        Attempting upload of Context file and templates to database...COMPLETED

    Updating rdbms version in Context file to db121
    Updating rdbms type in Context file to 64 bits
    Configuring templates from ORACLE_HOME ...

    AutoConfig completed successfully.
    [oracle@erpnode1 bin]$
```

The tech stack installation will create the context file, but it will not create the environment files. To validate the installation of the tech stack components, you must execute the AutoConfig script. Chapter 8 will explain the process and components of AutoConfig.

Replacing the Oracle EBS 10g AS (10.1.2: Tools) Technology Stack

The procedure for replacing/restoring the 10g AS Oracle Home is similar to replacing the database tech stack with some small changes. The procedure for detaching 10.1.2 Oracle Home from the inventory should be run twice because you have the dual application file systems fs1 and fs2.

1. Delete the Rapidwiz install stage area from both file systems fs1 and fs2.

```
[applmgr@erpnode1 temp]$ pwd
/u01/appl_prod/PROD/fs1/inst/apps/PROD_erpnode1/temp
[applmgr@erpnode1 temp]$ rm -rf *
[applmgr@erpnode1 temp]$ cd /u01/appl_prod/PROD/fs1/inst/apps/PROD_erpnode1/temp
[applmgr@erpnode1 temp]$ ls
[applmgr@erpnode1 temp]$ cd /u01/appl_prod/PROD/fs2/inst/apps/PROD_erpnode1/temp
[applmgr@erpnode1 temp]$ rm -rf *
[applmgr@erpnode1 temp]$
```

2. Detach 10.1.2 Oracle Home from oraInventory from both file systems.

To remove Oracle Homes from oraInventory, you need to identify the names of the Oracle Homes first. You can use following command to find out the configured Oracle Homes for both file systems:

```
[root@erpnode1 ContentsXML]# grep PROD_TOOLS__u01_appl_prod_PROD_* inventory.xml
<HOME NAME="PROD_TOOLS__u01_appl_prod_PROD_fs2_EBSapps_10_1_2" LOC="/u01/appl_prod/PROD/fs2/
EBSapps/10.1.2" TYPE="O" IDX="5"/>
<HOME NAME="PROD_TOOLS__u01_appl_prod_PROD_fs1_EBSapps_10_1_2" LOC="/u01/appl_prod/PROD/fs1/
EBSapps/10.1.2" TYPE="O" IDX="9"/>
[root@erpnode1 ContentsXML]#

[applmgr@erpnode1 bin]$ runInstaller -removeHome ORACLE_HOME=$ORACLE_HOME ORACLE_HOME_
NAME=PROD_TOOLS__u01_appl_prod_PROD_fs1_EBSapps_10_1_2
Starting Oracle Universal Installer...
No pre-requisite checks found in oraparam.ini, no system pre-requisite checks will be executed.
[applmgr@erpnode1 bin]$
```

runInstaller will be located under the 10.1.2/oui/bin directory, and you should execute this command from their respective file systems.

```
[root@erpnode1 ContentsXML]# grep PROD_TOOLS__u01_appl_prod_PROD_* inventory.xml
<HOME NAME="PROD_TOOLS__u01_appl_prod_PROD_fs2_EBSapps_10_1_2" LOC="/u01/appl_prod/PROD/fs2/
EBSapps/10.1.2" TYPE="O" IDX="5"/>
<HOME NAME="PROD_TOOLS__u01_appl_prod_PROD_fs1_EBSapps_10_1_2" LOC="/u01/appl_prod/PROD/fs1/
EBSapps/10.1.2" TYPE="O" IDX="9" REMOVED="T"/>
[root@erpnode1 ContentsXML]#
```

After detaching a Home, it will add the entry REMOVED for the Oracle Home Name value in the inventory file. Perform the same procedure for detaching the Oracle Home from the other file system.

3.   Delete the 10.1.2 Oracle AS Home from both file systems (fs1 and fs2).

```
[applmgr@erpnode1 EBSapps]$ pwd
/u01/appl_prod/PROD/fs1/EBSapps
[applmgr@erpnode1 EBSapps]$ ls
10.1.2  appl  comn
[applmgr@erpnode1 EBSapps]$ mv 10.1.2 10.1.2.orig
[applmgr@erpnode1 EBSapps]$ cd /u01/appl_prod/PROD/fs2/EBSapps
[applmgr@erpnode1 EBSapps]$ mv 10.1.2 10.1.2.orig
[applmgr@erpnode1 EBSapps]$ ls
10.1.2.orig  appl  comn
[applmgr@erpnode1 EBSapps]$
```

4.   Execute Rapidwiz with the tech stack option for installing 10.1.2 Home on both file systems.

```
[applmgr@erpnode1 rapidwiz]$ ./rapidwiz -techstack

Rapid Install Wizard is validating your file system......
CMDDIR=/u01/R1224_Stage/startCD/Disk1/rapidwiz
Rapid Install Wizard will now launch the Java Interface.....

[applmgr@erpnode1 rapidwiz]$
```

In Figure 2-40 we have selected the tools (10.1.2) Home for replacement.

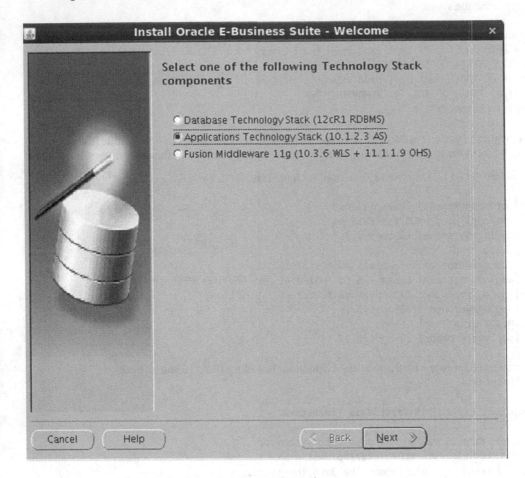

Figure 2-40. *Rapidwiz: replacing tools tech stack (10.1.2)*

You have to provide the location of the context file for both file systems, as shown in Figure 2-41.

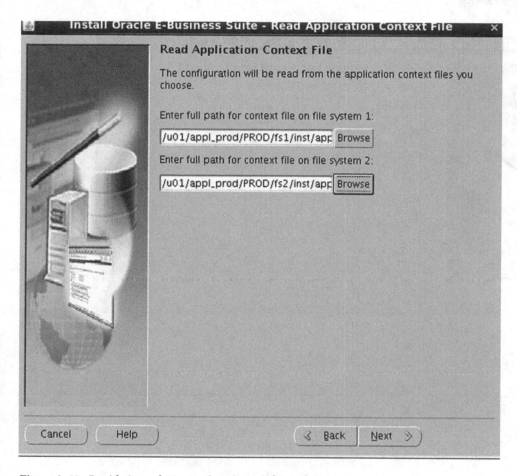

Figure 2-41. *Rapidwiz: replacing tools tech stack (10.1.2) file system*

After reading the context file, it will take the locations of the 10.1.2 Home by default for installation, as shown in Figure 2-42.

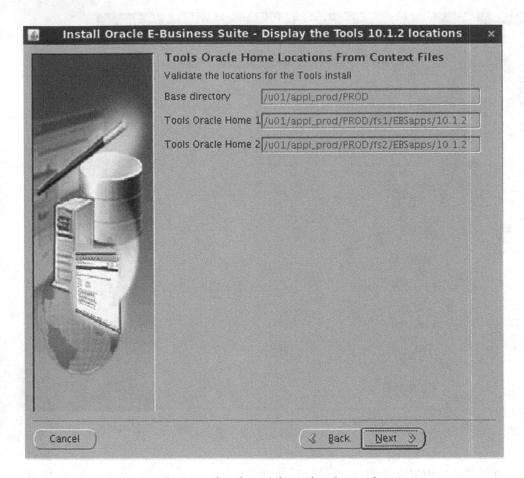

Figure 2-42. *Rapidwiz: replacing tools tech stack (10.1.2) tool Home locations*

Once Rapidwiz identifies both tools Oracle Home locations, it will proceed with the installation of the 10.1.2 tech stack components with a series of steps, as shown in Figures 2-43 to 2-47.

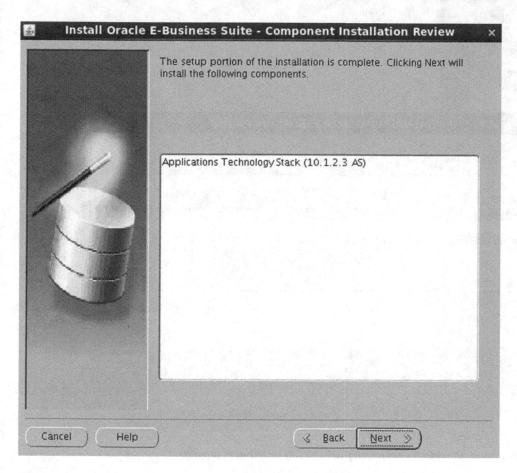

Figure 2-43. *Rapidwiz: replacing tools tech stack (10.1.2) component list*

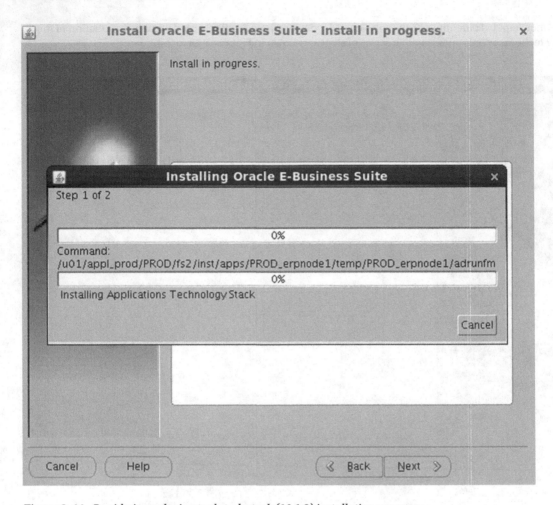

Figure 2-44. Rapidwiz: replacing tools tech stack (10.1.2) installation progress

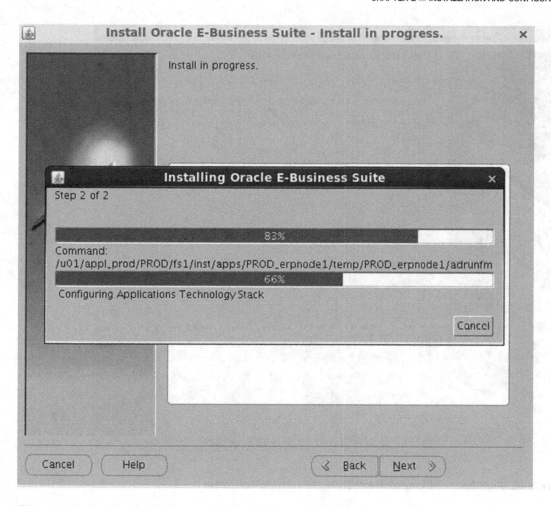

Figure 2-45. *Rapidwiz: replacing tools tech stack (10.1.2) installation progress step 2*

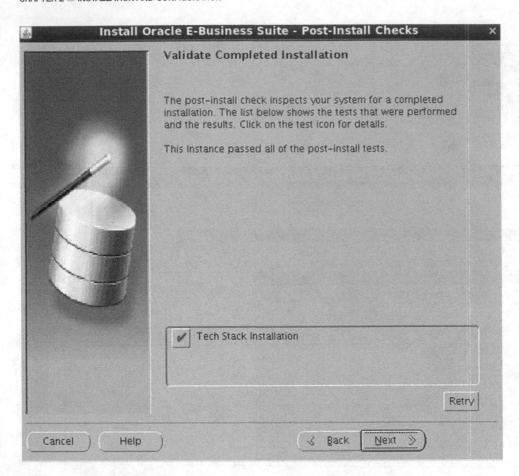

Figure 2-46. *Rapidwiz: replacing tools tech stack (10.1.2) post-validation*

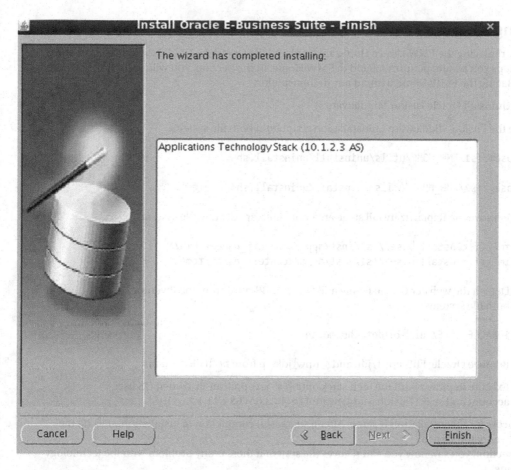

Figure 2-47. *Rapidwiz: replacing tools tech stack (10.1.2) installation completion*

The installation of the 10.1.2 Home on both file systems completed successfully. After installation, you should start application services and verify the system.

```
[root@erpnode1 PROD]# ls
fs1 fs2 fs_ne
[root@erpnode1 PROD]# cd fs1
[root@erpnode1 fs1]# ls
EBSapps  FMW_Home  inst
[root@erpnode1 fs1]# cd EBSapps/
[root@erpnode1 EBSapps]# ls
10.1.2  10.1.2.orig  appl  comn
[root@erpnode1 EBSapps]# pwd
/u01/appl_prod/PROD/fs1/EBSapps
[root@erpnode1 EBSapps]# cd /u01/appl_prod/PROD/fs2/EBSapps
[root@erpnode1 EBSapps]# ls
10.1.2  10.1.2.orig  appl  comn
[root@erpnode1 EBSapps]# pwd
/u01/appl_prod/PROD/fs2/EBSapps
[root@erpnode1 EBSapps]#
```

Replacing the Oracle Fusion Middleware Technology Stack

The steps for replacing the FMW Oracle Home are similar to the Oracle AS 10.1.2 Home. There are some additional steps you should perform related to FMW Home. In this section, you will see only the required steps for replacing the FMW Home without any demonstration.

1. Uninstall Oracle Fusion Middleware.

Execute the Fusion Middleware uninstallation script from both file systems.

```
<Install_Base>/fs1/FMW_HOME/utils/uninstall/uninstall.sh
```

```
<Install_Base>/fs2/FMW_HOME/utils/uninstall/uninstall.sh
```

2. Remove the Rapidwiz install stage area from both application file systems.

    ```
    rm -rf <Install_base>/fs1/inst/apps/<context_name>/temp/*
    rm -rf <Install_base>/fs1/inst/apps/<context_name>/temp/*
    ```

3. Detach the web tier Oracle Home and Oracle_EBS-app1 from the inventory for both file systems.

    ```
    $ORACLE_HOME/oui/bin/detachHome.sh
    ```

4. Remove Oracle_EBS-app1/jdk and s_fmw_jdktop from both file systems.

5. Execute Rapidwiz with the tech stack option as an application-owned OS user account and select Fusion Middleware 11g (10.3.6 WLS + 11.1.1.6 OHS).

The process for the installation is same. After a successful completion of installation, start up the services and verify the system.

In this section, you saw how you can recover the system if there is any problem with the technology stack component.

Summary

The installation of Oracle E-Business Suite is a long and time-consuming process. If there are failures during installation, then you may need additional time for finding the problem, fixing it, and restarting the installation. Hence, to avoid any issues during installation, it is highly recommended that you perform and configure all prerequisites successfully. In this chapter, you walked through an installation on Oracle Enterprise Linux only, but the installation process will be similar on other operating system platforms. The only difference is that you have to verify the OS prerequisites.

In this chapter, you learned about the new features introduced in Rapidwiz in 12.2, such as the preparation of the system before installation, single-node installation, post-installation steps, and the replacement of the technology stack components in the case of loss or corruption in existing tech stack components.

CHAPTER 3

■■■

Oracle E-Business Suite Upgrades

If you're an experienced Apps DBA and aware of Oracle EBS patching utilities in versions 12.1 and 12.2, including FMW patching, then you should proceed with this chapter. If you're not aware of patching utilities in Oracle EBS 12.1 or 12.2, then we recommend you skip this chapter and return to it after reading Chapters 5 and 6.

There is ongoing development in software industry, and software development companies define certain lifetimes for specific releases of software. Their customers are advised to be on the supported version for better utilization of the software capabilities. As you know, every new release of the software contains a good number of bug fixes for problems, and at the same time, it will deliver new features to cope with the business expectations and requirements. To be on a supported version of the software and use the new features delivered by a specific release of software, you always have to keep upgrading your software. In this chapter, you will see how the upgrade process works for Oracle E-Business Suite applications and what the key areas are that you should focus on to simplify the overall upgrade process.

This chapter is not a detailed step-by-step guide for upgrading your Oracle EBS systems, but it will navigate you through the general process of upgrading Oracle EBS systems.

Introduction to the Oracle E-Business Suite Upgrade Process

An Oracle E-Business Suite upgrade is a complex process, and for success there should be a lot of planning before you start. Oracle E-Business Suite upgrades will upgrade the technology stack components and introduce new functionality, and they may change how the existing functionality works with a different methodology. The biggest challenge in all upgrade projects is managing the customizations during and after the upgrade. If a customization is not deployed as per the Oracle standards, then it will cost your organization.

The Oracle E-Business Suite upgrade process needs excellent teamwork for a successful rollout of the project. The team members will be from different areas and have different job roles; they include the Oracle Apps DBA, the Oracle technical consultant, the Oracle functional consultant, the core business users, the project manager, and the end users.

The upgrade procedure should go through at least two to three iterations, and you should note the exact duration of each activity; this will be helpful in estimating the required downtime/upgrade time for the whole activity.

Road Map to 12.2 Upgrade

We discussed in earlier chapters the different releases of Oracle E-business Suite. First you need to identify the current version of the database, applications, technology stack components, and other integrated applications. There are different paths available for a 12.2 upgrade, but choosing the correct upgrade path will minimize your effort and time.

© Syed Zaheer and Erman Arslan 2016
S. Zaheer and E. Arslan, *Practical Oracle E-Business Suite*, DOI 10.1007/978-1-4842-1422-0_3

There is always a generic question that arises: "Our current EBS release is stable and running without any issues. Why should we upgrade to a newer release?" Software development is a continuous process, and you need to align with current and future information technology trends. You need to ensure you are moving forward and ready to accept these changes. Moreover, Oracle stopped development on the release 12.1.3, and all future enhancements are focused on the 12.2 release.

Figure 3-1 shows the different upgrade paths supported for different Oracle application releases to reach 12.2. Oracle has its own policy for supporting the specific release of software for specific timelines. There are three different types of support policies provided for all Oracle software releases.

- *Premier support*: For this policy, there will be default fees for respective products; usually they are 20 percent of the product license fees.

- *Extended support*: You need to add an extra 20 percent to the existing support fees to use this option.

- *Sustaining support*: You have to contact your Oracle account manager to use the sustaining support.

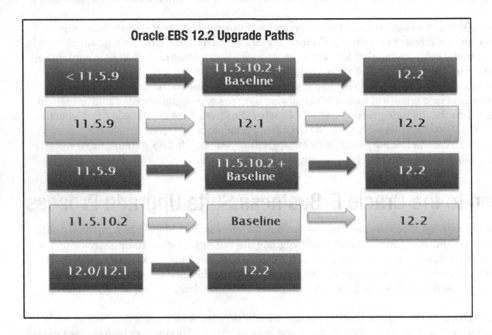

Figure 3-1. Oracle EBS upgrade paths

The same support policies apply to different Oracle E-Business Suite releases. Table 3-1 shows the support timeline for respective versions.

Table 3-1. *Oracle EBS Support Timeline*

Release	Version Release Date	Premier Support Ends	Extended Support Ends	Sustaining Support Ends
11.5.10	November 2004	November 2010	December 2014	Indefinite
12.0	January 2007	January 2012	January 2015	Indefinite
12.1	May 2009	December 2016	December 2019	Indefinite
12.2	September 2013	September 2018	September 2021	Indefinite

In this chapter, we will discuss two different upgrade scenarios. First you will see an upgrade from 12.2.0 to 12.2.5, and later you will see the upgrade procedure from 12.1.3 to 12.2.0. Before we jump to the upgrade process, we'll cover the steps you should consider in preparation for a 12.2 upgrade.

Preparation of an Oracle EBS 12.2 Upgrade

As discussed earlier, proper planning is the key to a successful upgrade. There are certain technology areas that should be considered on existing systems for an easier upgrade transition.

Operating System and Server Upgrade

Oracle E-Business Suite 12.2 is certified on specific releases of different operating systems, as discussed in detail in Chapter 2. You need to evaluate the current operating system type, version, and resource sizing in advance. If the current operating system type, version, and sizing are not meeting the Oracle EBS 12.2 requirements, then you have to plan to upgrade/migrate respective areas in advance. This will help you in minimizing the overall upgrade downtime.

For example, Oracle 11i/R12 is certified on Linux 32-bit, but Oracle EBS 12.2 is not certified on the 32-bit version of Linux. Therefore, you have to migrate the existing application to 64-bit hardware and the operating system to the EBS 12.2 supported version.

■ **Tip**   Oracle will not certify products against specific hardware. All certification will be announced for the operating system level. You need to cross-check the OS certification with the target hardware.

Virtualization Considerations

Currently, virtualization is one of the major components of data centers. If you have any plan to deploy/enable virtualization for an existing EBS system, then you must ensure that it's certified with the OS and virtualization technology. As of today, Oracle supports only Oracle virtualization technology (this means Oracle VM for X86 and SPARC architectures). There are many customers who are running EBS environments on VMware, Azure, and other virtualization platforms; for other platforms, the support for the VM technology will be limited.

The following are key points with respect to virtualization:

- The Oracle virtualization platform is supported.

- Microsoft Hyper-V Server 2012 R1 is supported.

- Check the certification for virtualization and upgrade the VM ahead of time.

- The minimum Oracle VM for X86 is 3.2.3.0.0.

- The minimum Oracle VM for SPARC is 1.3.

Space and Computing Capacity Considerations

There will be additional space required on the server while performing an upgrade, so you must ensure that appropriate space is allocated to the server in advance.

The following are the key considerations for space requirements:

- You'll need additional space for the dual file system.

- You'll need additional space for the new RDBMS Home and database.

- You'll need additional space for the 12.2 software stage (50GB).

Upgrade the Database

Oracle EBS 11i ships with version 9i, Oracle EBS 12.0 ships with 10g, and Oracle EBS 12.1 ships with 11.1. We have seen many customers running the same version of databases in production as shipped with the base release of an application. Database upgrades are always a time-consuming activity; you can save a significant amount of downtime if you plan ahead and upgrade the database before upgrading EBS.

Oracle EBS 12.2 is supported on version 11.2.0.4 as a minimum, but it's highly recommended that you upgrade it to 12.1.0.2. This is the latest certified version that can be used with EBS 12.2 at the time of writing this book; it may change at a later stage.

The upgrade paths may vary based on the current release of the database, and there are different upgrade methods available for upgrading the database. Table 3-2 shows the different upgrade paths that must be followed for performing an upgrade.

Table 3-2. *Oracle Database Upgrade Paths*

Source Database	Upgrade Path	Target Database
9.2.0.7 (or lower)	10.2.0.5	12.1.0.x
10.2.0.4 (or lower)	10.2.0.5	12.1.0.x
11.1.0.6		12.1.0.x
11.2.0.1		12.1.0.x

So, based on the current database release, you can decide on your upgrade path; this will also help you to calculate how much time is required for upgrading the current release of the database.

Purge/Archive Data

Data is the most important piece of all systems across the enterprise. This is the right time to identify and purge any unwanted data from the system before performing an EBS upgrade. You can use all seeded purge concurrent programs to purge the unwanted data from the system. If there is a plan to purge/archive business transactional data, then you must ensure that a robust testing methodology is implemented before purging the transactional data.

MOS tech note "Purging Strategy for E-Business Suite" (Doc ID 732713.1) is helpful for purging EBS data using seeded concurrent programs.

To purge/archive EBS transaction data, refer to MOS tech note "Reducing Your Oracle E-Business Suite Data Footprint using Archiving, Purging, and Information Lifecycle Management" (Doc ID 752322.1).

Upgrade Dependent EBS Integrated Applications

The current release of an EBS system may be integrated with other Oracle application software or other third-party application. You should ensure all existing third-party applications are certified with EBS 12.2, and if they are not certified, then you must plan the upgrade for the integrated applications.

The upgrade of these integrated applications should be decided purely based on the software releases and certification. Consider you are currently using 10g AS/SSO on EBS 11i and Linux 4, but the latest version of Oracle Access Manager may not be supported with 11i and Linux 4. In such situations, you have to do the SSO migration after the successful completion of the EBS 12.2 upgrade. Figure 3-2 displays the list of integrated applications that should be migrated before a 12.2 upgrade.

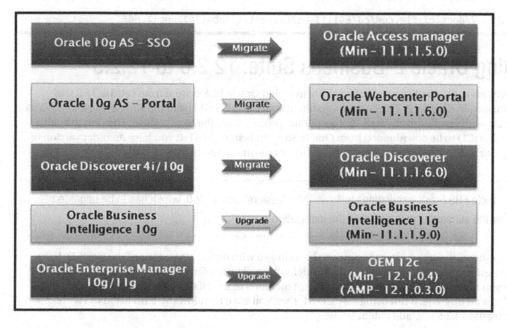

Figure 3-2. *Oracle EBS integrated applications*

This section discussed some of the key factors you must consider during the planning/preparation phase of an Oracle E-Business Suite upgrade; you should perform all necessary actions on the existing release. For any reason if you are not able to perform any of the actions, then you must plan for doing so in the upgrade or post-upgrade phase.

```
┌─────────────────────────────────────────────────────────────────┐
│              MOS TECH NOTES FOR AN EBS UPGRADE                    │
└─────────────────────────────────────────────────────────────────┘
```

- "Oracle Applications Release 12 Upgrade Sizing and Best Practices" (Doc ID 399362.1)

- "Database Initialization Parameters for Oracle E-Business Suite Release 12" (Doc ID 396009.1)

- "Oracle E-Business Suite Release 12.2: Consolidated List of Patches and Technology Bug Fixes" (Doc ID 1594274.1)

- "Oracle E-Business Suite Release 12.2: Suite-Wide Rollup and AD/TXK Delta Information" (Doc ID 1583092.1)

- "Applying the Latest AD and TXK Release Update Packs to Oracle E-Business Suite Release 12.2" (Doc ID 1617461.1)

- "Oracle E-Business Suite Release 12.2: Upgrade Sizing and Best Practices" (Doc ID 1597531.1)

- "R12.1 and 12.2 Oracle E-Business Suite Preinstall Patches Report [Video]" (Doc ID 1448102.2)

- "Oracle E-Business Suite Release 12.2: Technical Planning, Getting Started, and Go-Live Checklist" (Doc ID 1585857.1)

- `http://docs.oracle.com/cd/E51111_01/current/acrobat/122upg12.pdf`

Upgrading Oracle E-Business Suite: 12.2.0 to 12.2.5

This section covers the upgrade process of a freshly installed Oracle EBS system from release 12.2.0 to 12.2.5, as discussed in Chapter 2. The current version of startCD (51) will install the 12c database with FMW 11.1.1.9, and this will simplify the overall 12.2.5 upgrade process from the base release. The only available version of the startCD to be downloaded from Oracle Support is startCD 51. If you have an older version of the startCD, prior to 51, that you have downloaded, its not recommeded to use.

■ **Note** All Oracle EBS Fresh installations will configure base release 12.2.0, which has to be upgraded separately after the successful completion of the installation.

Figure 3-3 shows the 12.2.5 upgrade paths to be followed with different versions of the startCD. If the installation is performed using startCD 51, then by default it will install Oracle Database 12.1.0.2 and FMW 11.1.1.9.0, so you have to apply all patches that are not included in any of the startCDs, and then you are ready to perform an upgrade. If not using startCD 51, then you have to follow the path listed in Figure 3-3 before applying the 12.2.5 upgrade patch.

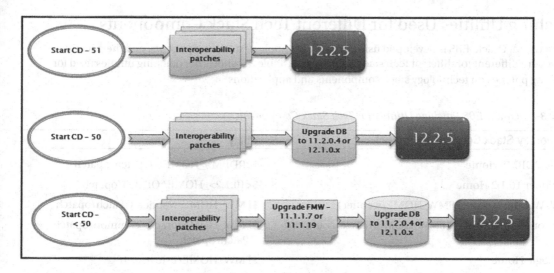

Figure 3-3. *Upgrade path using different versions of the startCD*

In this chapter, the Oracle EBS 12.2.5 upgrade is performed on a Fresh installation using startCD 51. The database version should be 11.2.0.4 or 12.1.0.*x*, and the FMW version should be 11.1.1.7 or 11.1.1.9 in order to upgrade to the 12.2.5 release. So, the major prerequisites will be available if the installation is performed using startCD 51, and you have to install all patches that are not included in any of the startCDs, as listed in MOS note "Oracle E-Business Suite Release 12.2: Consolidated List of Patches and Technology Bug Fixes" (Doc ID 1594274.1). You should also install all database and FMW technology stack patches listed in the ETCC output file.

Basically, you have to install patches on the following tech stack components:

- Oracle RDBMS Home

- Developer 10.1.2 Home

- FMW: Webtier Home ($FMW_HOME/webtier)

- FMW: oracle_common ($FMW_HOME/oracle_common)

- WebLogic Home

■ **Note** You should ensure that every step is performed carefully to avoid issues during the major patch installation.

Now you will see the upgrade steps from EBS 12.2.0 to 12.2.5. The number of patches listed and installed in this demonstration may change in the future, so it's always recommended that you read all the listed MOS tech notes before performing an upgrade.

In this chapter, we are not going to discuss patching utilities, as there are specific chapters in this book that cover the patching tools in great detail.

Patching Utilities Used for Different Tech Stack Components

As discussed, Oracle EBS is developed using different technology stack components, and the patching utilities are different for different tech stack components. Table 3-3 shows the patching utilities used for installing patches on technology stack components and applications.

Table 3-3. *Oracle EBS Patching Utilities for Tech Stack Components*

Technology Stack Component/Product	Utility
Oracle RDBMS Home	$<RDBMS_HOME>/OPatch/opatch
Developer 10.1.2 Home	$<10.1.2>_HOME/ OPatch/opatch
FMW: Webtier Home ($FMW_HOME/webtier)	$FMW_HOME/webtier/OPatch/opatch
FMW: oracle_common ($FMW_HOME/oracle_common)	$FMW_HOME/oracle_common/opatch OPatch/opatch
WebLogic Home	$FMW_HOME/bsu/bsu.sh
Application products and dependent components	$AD_TOP/bin/adop

Upgrade Demonstration

As the first step, you should install patch 17537119, which will provide output of all the latest available patches that are missing on the current instance. You should ensure that you have downloaded the latest version of this patch from Oracle Support.

The EBS Technology Code Checker (ETCC) patch will provide two scripts, one for the database tier (checkDBpatch.sh) and another for the application tier (checkMTpatch.sh), that will check the patches on the tech stack components. These scripts are provided with patch 17537119. Listings 3-1 and 3-2 show the execution of the ETCC scripts.

Execution of checkMTpatch.sh

The script in Listing 3-1 will check all middle tier components and generate a summary with the list of patches that need to be installed.

Listing 3-1. EBS Upgrade: EBS Technology Code Checker: Middle Tier

```
[applR12@erpnode2 ETCC]$ sh checkMTpatch.sh


+=================================================================+
|      Copyright (c) 2005, 2016 Oracle and/or its affiliates.     |
|                   All rights reserved.                          |
|            Oracle E-Business Suite Release 12.2                  |
|          Middle Tier Technology Codelevel Checker               |
+=================================================================+

Using context file from currently set applications environment:
/d01/appl_prod/PROD/fs1/inst/apps/PROD_erpnode2/appl/admin/PROD_erpnode2.xml
```

```
Starting Middle Tier Technology Codelevel Checker, Version: 120.0.12020000.27.
Mon Mar 14 17:19:55 AST 2016
Log file for this session: /d01/appl_prod/PROD/fs_ne/EBSapps/patch/ETCC/checkMTpatch_3929.log

Bugfix XML file version: 120.0.12020000.22
This file will be used for identifying missing bugfixes.

Mapping XML file version: 120.0.12020000.3
This file will be used for mapping bugfixes to patches.

Checking for prerequisite bugfixes in File Edition: run

Enter the password for the APPS user:
Connecting to database.
Database connection successful.
The installed AD.C codelevel does not support storing the results in the database.

================================================================================
Oracle Forms and Reports
================================================================================
Now examining product Oracle Forms and Reports.

Oracle Home = /d01/appl_prod/PROD/fs1/EBSapps/10.1.2.
Product version = 10.1.2.3.0.
Checking required bugfixes for Oracle Forms and Reports 10.1.2.3.0.
  Missing Bugfix: 17353142  ->  Patch 21539521
  Missing Bugfix: 20643256  ->  Patch 21539521
  Missing Bugfix: 16041055  ->  Patch 21539521
  Missing Bugfix: 16910762  ->  Patch 21539521
  Missing Bugfix: 20270659  ->  Patch 21539521
  Missing Bugfix: 17372642  ->  Patch 21539521
  Missing Bugfix: 17566694  ->  Patch 21539521
  Missing Bugfix: 20240480  ->  Patch 21539521
  Missing Bugfix: 19304738  ->  Patch 21539521
  Missing Bugfix: 20391574  ->  Patch 21539521
The above list shows missing bugfixes for Oracle Forms and Reports.

Checking required bugfixes for RSF within Forms 10.1.0.5.0.
All required bugfixes are present for RSF within Forms.

================================================================================
Oracle Fusion Middleware (FMW) - Web Tier
================================================================================
Now examining product Oracle Fusion Middleware (FMW) - Web Tier.

Oracle Home = /d01/appl_prod/PROD/fs1/FMW_Home/webtier.
Product Version = 11.1.1.9.0
Checking required bugfixes for FMW - Web Tier 11.1.1.9.0.
  Missing Bugfix: 21300463  ->  Patch 22107540
The above list shows missing bugfixes for FMW - Web Tier.
```

Checking required bugfixes for RSF within FMW Web tier 11.1.0.7.0.
All required bugfixes are present for RSF within FMW Web tier.

```
================================================================================
```
Oracle Fusion Middleware (FMW) - oracle_common
```
================================================================================
```
Now examining product Oracle Fusion Middleware (FMW) - oracle_common.

Oracle Home = /d01/appl_prod/PROD/fs1/FMW_Home/oracle_common.
Product Version = 11.1.1.9.0
Checking required bugfixes for FMW - oracle common 11.1.1.9.0.
  Missing Bugfix: 21366277 -> Patch 21366277
  Missing Bugfix: 21628307 -> Patch 21628307
The above list shows missing bugfixes for FMW - oracle common.

```
================================================================================
```
Oracle WebLogic Server (WLS)
```
================================================================================
```
Now examining product Oracle WebLogic Server (WLS).

Oracle Home = /d01/appl_prod/PROD/fs1/FMW_Home/wlserver_10.3.
Product Version = 10.3.6.0.7

Note that for Oracle WebLogic Server, patches rather than bugfixes are verified.

Checking required patches for Oracle WebLogic Server (WLS) 10.3.6.0.7.
  Missing Patch ID: 20780171
The above list shows missing patches for Oracle WebLogic Server.
If you have applied other Oracle WebLogic Server patches, they may have included the
bugfixes needed.
Contact Oracle Support if you require assistance in determining whether this is the case.

```
================================================================================
```
Generating Patch Recommendation Summary.
```
================================================================================
```
PATCH RECOMMENDATION SUMMARY
```
================================================================================
```
One or more products have bugfixes missing.
The default patch recommendations to install these missing bugfixes are:

```
--------------------------------------------------------------------------------
```
Oracle Forms and Reports 10.1.2.3.0
```
--------------------------------------------------------------------------------
```
  Patch 21539521
    - Filename: p21539521_101232_LINUX.zip

```
--------------------------------------------------------------------------------
```
Oracle Fusion Middleware (FMW) - Web Tier 11.1.1.9.0
```
--------------------------------------------------------------------------------
```
  Patch 22107540
    - Filename: p22107540_111190_Generic.zip

```
-----------------------------------------------------------------------------
Oracle Fusion Middleware (FMW) - oracle_common 11.1.1.9.0
-----------------------------------------------------------------------------

  Patch 21366277
    - Filename: p21366277_111190_Generic.zip

  Patch 21628307
    - Filename: p21628307_111190_Generic.zip


-----------------------------------------------------------------------------
Oracle WebLogic Server (WLS) 10.3.6.0.7
-----------------------------------------------------------------------------

  Patch 20780171 [SU Patch [EJUW]: WLS PSU 10.3.6.0.12]
    - Filename: p20780171_1036_Generic.zip

Apply the required patches and rerun this script.


+---------------------------------------------------------------------------+
[WARNING]  Patch 20780171 [SU Patch [EJUW]: WLS PSU 10.3.6.0.12] is missing.
This is the recommended minimum WLS patch set.
You should install it now, and then rerun this script to check for any
further fixes available.
+---------------------------------------------------------------------------+

See Doc ID 1594274.1 for any special instructions regarding these patches.
Footnotes in Doc ID 1594274.1 also apply to corresponding overlay patches.

Finished checking prerequisite patches for File Edition: run.
Mon Mar 14 17:20:20 AST 2016

Log file for this session: /d01/appl_prod/PROD/fs_ne/EBSapps/patch/ETCC/checkMTpatch_3929.log

================================================================================
[applR12@erpnode2 ETCC]$
```

Execution of checkDBpatch.sh

The script in Listing 3-2 will check all the latest available RDBMS patches and generate a summary with the list of patches that should be installed on the RDBMS Home.

Listing 3-2. EBS Upgrade: ETCC: Database Tier

```
[oraR12@erpnode2 ETCC]$ checkDBpatch.sh


+===================================================================+
|      Copyright (c) 2005, 2016 Oracle and/or its affiliates.        |
|                     All rights reserved.                          |
|              Oracle E-Business Suite Release 12.2                  |
|            Database EBS Technology Codelevel Checker               |
+===================================================================+
```

```
Using context file from currently set database environment:
/d01/ora_prod/PROD/12.1.0/appsutil/PROD_erpnode2.xml

Starting Database EBS Technology Codelevel Checker, Version 120.32
Mon Mar 14 17:22:14 AST 2016
Log file for this session : ./checkDBpatch_5582.log

Bugfix XML file version: 120.0.12020000.29
This file will be used for identifying missing bugfixes.

Mapping XML file version: 120.0.12020000.2
This file will be used for mapping bugfixes to patches.

Identifying database release.
Database release set to 12.1.0.2.

Connecting to database.
Database connection successful.

Checking for DB-ETCC results table.
Creating DB-ETCC results table.
Created the table to store DB-ETCC results.

Checking if InMemory option is enabled.
InMemory option is not enabled in the Database.

Obtained list of bugfixes to be applied and the list to be rolled back.
Now checking Database ORACLE_HOME.

The opatch utility is at the required version.

Found patch records in the inventory.

  Missing Bugfix: 21028698  ->  Patch 22098146
  Missing Bugfix: 21286665  ->  Patch 21286665
  Missing Bugfix: 21614112  ->  Patch 21841318

Generating Patch Recommendation Summary.

================================================================================
PATCH RECOMMENDATION SUMMARY
================================================================================
The default patch recommendations to install these missing bugfixes are:
--------------------------------------------------------------------------------
Oracle Database Release 12.1.0.2  (No PSU applied)
--------------------------------------------------------------------------------
  Patch 22098146
     - Filename: p22098146_121020_Linux-x86-64.zip
```

```
Patch 21286665
  - Filename: p21286665_121020_Linux-x86-64.zip

Patch 21841318
  - Filename: p21841318_121020_Linux-x86-64.zip

Apply the required patches and rerun this script.

See Doc ID 1594274.1 for any special instructions for these patches.
Note: Footnotes in Doc ID 1594274.1 also apply to corresponding overlay patches.

Stored Technology Codelevel Checker results in the database successfully.

Finished prerequisite patch testing : Mon Mar 14 17:22:23 AST 2016

Log file for this session: ./checkDBpatch_5582.log

================================================================================
[oraR12@erpnode2 ETCC]$
```

There is no interdependency for installing these patches. You can install the patches in the database Home or any of the middle tier Homes. But in this demonstration, the database Home is patched first followed by middle tier Home patching and finally the WebLogic Home patching.

Installation of the RDBMS Patches

The patches listed in the ETCC output and the patches listed in the tech note with Doc ID 1594274.1 need to be installed. Follow these steps:

1. Perform an RDBMS Home and inventory backup.

2. Shut down the database and listener.

3. Install all the required RDBMS patches.

4. Perform any patch post-installation steps.

5. Start the database and listener.

Table 3-4 lists the patches that should be installed on the existing RDBMS Home, and Listing 3-3 shows the installation of the patches that were not included in any of the startCD and ETCC summaries.

Table 3-4. *ETCC Summary RDBMS Patches*

	Linux x86-64
Not included in any startCD or ETCC summary output	21841318
	22098146
	21286665

Listing 3-3. EBS: Installation of Missing Database Patches

```
[oraR12@erpnode2 21286665]$ opatch apply
Oracle Interim Patch Installer version 12.1.0.1.10
Copyright (c) 2016, Oracle Corporation.  All rights reserved.

Oracle Home        : /d01/ora_prod/PROD/12.1.0
Central Inventory : /d01/ora_prod/oraInventory/
   from            : /d01/ora_prod/PROD/12.1.0/oraInst.loc
OPatch version    : 12.1.0.1.10
OUI version       : 12.1.0.2.0
Log file location : /d01/ora_prod/PROD/12.1.0/cfgtoollogs/opatch/21286665_
Mar_14_2016_18_05_03/apply2016-03-14_18-05-03PM_1.log

Verifying environment and performing prerequisite checks...
OPatch continues with these patches:   21286665

Do you want to proceed? [y|n]y

You have not provided an email address for notification of security issues.
Do you wish to remain uninformed of security issues ([Y]es, [N]o) [N]:   Y

Please shutdown Oracle instances running out of this ORACLE_HOME on the local system.
(Oracle Home = '/d01/ora_prod/PROD/12.1.0')

Is the local system ready for patching? [y|n]y
User Responded with: Y
Backing up files...
Applying interim patch '21286665' to OH '/d01/ora_prod/PROD/12.1.0'
Patching component oracle.rdbms, 12.1.0.2.0...
Patch 21286665 successfully applied.
Log file location: /d01/ora_prod/PROD/12.1.0/cfgtoollogs/opatch/21286665_
Mar_14_2016_18_05_03/apply2016-03-14_18-05-03PM_1.log
OPatch succeeded.
[oraR12@erpnode2 21286665]$
```

Sometimes you may see patch conflicts with critical patch updates (CPUs)/patchset upates (PSUs) installed; in that case, you may need to roll back certain patches and install certain patches with patch conflict resolution. The detailed process for managing patch conflicts is discussed in MOS tech note "Database Patch Conflict Resolution" (Doc ID 1321267.1).

ETCC output for database listed above contains more patches, here we demonstrated installation of only one patch on RDBMS home. We should follow the same process for Installing other RDBMS patches.

After installing the patches, copy the adgrants.sql script from $APPL_TOP/admin/ to the database tier and execute the script from the database tier. Listing 3-4 shows the execution of the adgrants.sql script.

Listing 3-4. EBS Upgrade: Execution of adgrants.sql

```
SQL> @adgrants.sql APPS
Connected.
----------------------------------------------------
--- adgrants.sql started at 2016-03-14 18:07:34 ---

Creating PL/SQL profiler objects
----------------------------------------------------
--- profload.sql started at 2016-03-14 18:07:34 ---

Session altered.
Package created.
```

After execution of adgrants.sql, execute the $ORACLE_HOME/rdbms/admin/utlrp.sql script for compiling invalid objects in the database.

You should ensure that there are no invalid objects after the execution of utlrp.sql.

Installation of Middle Tier Patches

The patches listed in the ETCC output summary should be installed on the respective middle tier Homes.

Install Oracle 10g Developer Home Patch (10.1.2.3.0)

The patch will be applied using the opatch utility from 10.1.2 Home. This patch will be available only on 32-bit platforms. So, 64-bit platform servers should also download the 32-bit patch only. Table 3-5 lists the patch that should be installed on the developer Home.

Table 3-5. *ETCC Summary 10g Developer Home*

	Linux x86-64
Not included in any startCD or ETCC summary	21539521

$ORACLE_HOME for 10.1.2 will be set by default after sourcing the consolidated application environment file. Still, you should ensure that the correct ORACLE_HOME and opatch utility are set up before installing the patch. Listing 3-5 illustrates the installation of 10g Developer Home patches.

Listing 3-5. EBS Upgrade: Installation of 10g DEV Home Patch

```
[applR12@erpnode2 FMW_patches]$ which opatch
/d01/appl_prod/PROD/fs1/EBSapps/10.1.2/OPatch/opatch
[applR12@erpnode2 FMW_patches]$ cd 21539521/
[applR12@erpnode2 21539521]$ opatch apply
```

```
Oracle Interim Patch Installer version 1.0.0.0.64
Copyright (c) 2011 Oracle Corporation. All Rights Reserved..

Oracle Home            : /d01/appl_prod/PROD/fs1/EBSapps/10.1.2
Oracle Home Inventory  : /d01/appl_prod/PROD/fs1/EBSapps/10.1.2/inventory
Central Inventory      : /d01/ora_prod/oraInventory/
   from                : /etc/oraInst.loc
OUI location           : /d01/appl_prod/PROD/fs1/EBSapps/10.1.2/oui
OUI shared library     : /d01/appl_prod/PROD/fs1/EBSapps/10.1.2/oui/lib/linux/
liboraInstaller.so
Java location          : /d01/appl_prod/PROD/fs1/EBSapps/10.1.2/jdk/jre/bin/java
Log file location      : /d01/appl_prod/PROD/fs1/EBSapps/10.1.2/.patch_storage/<patch ID>/*.log

Creating log file "/d01/appl_prod/PROD/fs1/EBSapps/10.1.2/.patch_storage/21539521/
Apply_21539521_03-14-2016_19-10-15.log"
Invoking fuser to check for active processes.
..........
..........
Applying patch 21539521...

Patching archive files...
Patching copy files...
Running make for target install.
Inventory is good and does not have any dangling patches.
Updating inventory...
Verifying patch...
Backing up comps.xml ...
OPatch succeeded.
[applR12@erpnode2 21539521]$
```

Install Fusion Middleware (FMW): Webtier (11.1.1.9) Patches

To install these patches, you need to set the ORACLE_HOME web tier directory, and the version of the
Opatch utility should be 11.1.0.9.0 or higher. Table 3-6 shows the patch that is not included in any of the
startCDs and needs to be installed.

Table 3-6. *ETCC Summary FMW_HOME: webtier*

	Linux x86-64
Not included in any startCD	22107540

Listing 3-6 shows the installation of FMW Home (web tier) patches.

Listing 3-6. EBS Upgrade: Installation of FMW (Web Tier) Patches

```
[applR12@erpnode2 FMW_Home]$ export ORACLE_HOME=/d01/appl_prod/PROD/fs1/FMW_Home/webtier
[applR12@erpnode2 FMW_Home]$ export PATH=$ORACLE_HOME/OPatch:$PATH
[applR12@erpnode2 FMW_Home]$ which opatch
/d01/appl_prod/PROD/fs1/FMW_Home/webtier/OPatch/opatch
[applR12@erpnode2 FMW_Home]$
```

```
[applR12@erpnode2 FMW_patches]$ cd 22107540
[applR12@erpnode2 22107540]$ opatch apply
Oracle Interim Patch Installer version 11.1.0.12.9
Copyright (c) 2016, Oracle Corporation.  All rights reserved.

Oracle Home        : /d01/appl_prod/PROD/fs1/FMW_Home/webtier
Central Inventory : /d01/ora_prod/oraInventory/
   from             : /d01/appl_prod/PROD/fs1/FMW_Home/webtier/oraInst.loc
OPatch version     : 11.1.0.12.9
OUI version        : 11.1.0.11.0
Log file location : /d01/appl_prod/PROD/fs1/FMW_Home/webtier/cfgtoollogs/opatch/22107540_
Mar_14_2016_19_18_53/apply2016-03-14_19-18-53PM_1.log

OPatch detects the Middleware Home as "/d01/appl_prod/PROD/fs1/FMW_Home"
Applying interim patch '22107540' to OH '/d01/appl_prod/PROD/fs1/FMW_Home/webtier'
Verifying environment and performing prerequisite checks...

Conflicts/Supersets for each patch are:

Patch : 22107540

........
.......
Patching component oracle.as.clone.ohs, 11.1.1.9.0...

Verifying the update...
Patch 22107540 successfully applied
OPatch succeeded.
[applR12@erpnode2 22107540]$
```

Install Fusion Middleware (FMW): Oracle_common (11.1.1.9) Patches

To install these patches, you need to set ORACLE_HOME to the oracle_common directory, and the version of the OPatch utility should be 11.1.0.9.0 or higher. Table 3-7 displays the list of patches not included in the startCD or ETCC summary. Listing 3-7 shows the installation of patches on the FMW Home (oracle_common).

Table 3-7. *ETCC Summary FMW_HOME: oracle_common*

Not included in any startCD or ETCC summary	Linux x86-64
	21366277
	21628307

Listing 3-7. EBS Upgrade: Installation of FMW Home (oracle_common) Patches

```
[applR12@erpnode2 FMW_Home]$ export ORACLE_HOME=/d01/appl_prod/PROD/fs1/FMW_Home/oracle_common
[applR12@erpnode2 FMW_Home]$ export PATH=$ORACLE_HOME/OPatch:$PATH
[applR12@erpnode2 FMW_Home]$ which opatch
/d01/appl_prod/PROD/fs1/FMW_Home/oracle_common/OPatch/opatch
[applR12@erpnode2 FMW_Home]$
```

```
[applR12@erpnode2 21366277]$ opatch apply
Oracle Interim Patch Installer version 11.1.0.12.9
Copyright (c) 2016, Oracle Corporation.  All rights reserved.
Oracle Home        : /d01/appl_prod/PROD/fs1/FMW_Home/oracle_common
Central Inventory : /d01/ora_prod/oraInventory/
   from            : /d01/appl_prod/PROD/fs1/FMW_Home/oracle_common/oraInst.loc
OPatch version     : 11.1.0.12.9
OUI version        : 11.1.0.11.0
Log file location : OPatch detects the Middleware Home as "/d01/appl_prod/PROD/fs1/FMW_Home"

Applying interim patch '21366277' to OH '/d01/appl_prod/PROD/fs1/FMW_Home/oracle_common'
Verifying environment and performing prerequisite checks...
All checks passed.
You have not provided an email address for notification of security issues.
Do you wish to remain uninformed of security issues ([Y]es, [N]o) [N]:  Y
Backing up files...
Patching component oracle.as.common.clone, 11.1.1.9.0...
Verifying the update...
Patch 21366277 successfully applied
OPatch succeeded.
```

You have to apply the latest AD and TKX patches before installing the WebLogic patches.

Applying Latest AD and TKX Patches

The patch sequence, patch numbers, and options may change, so it's recommended that you refer to MOS tech note "Applying the Latest AD and TXK Release Update Packs to Oracle E-Business Suite Release 12" (Doc ID 1617461.1) before applying these patches. The patching sequence and options provided should be used as mentioned or the patching cycle may encounter issues.

The following are the patches that should be installed:

- Patch 20745242 (R12.AD.C.Delta.7)

- Patch 22123818:R12.AD.C

- Patch 20784380 (R12.TXK.C.Delta.7)

- Patch 22363475:R12.TXK.C

- Patch 22495069:R12.TXK.C

All these patches should be copied to the $PATCH_TOP -<BASE>/fs_ne/EBSapps/patch directory, or if you're using nondefault location, then you can provide the patch TOP location. Follow these steps:

1. Ensure a system backup is performed before applying these patches.

2. Start the WebLogic admin server from the RUN file system.

3. Run adgrants.sql from the respective patch directories before applying the patch.

The patch 20745242 (R12.AD.C.Delta.7) contains a newer version of the adgrants.sql script, so it's mandatory to execute this script from the database tier as mentioned earlier in this chapter. After completion of this script, you should install the patch.

4. Set the following: adop phase=apply patches=20745242 hotpatch=yes.

Similarly, the patch 22123818:R12.AD.C also contains the adgrants.sql script. Execute the script before applying this patch.

5. Set the following: adop phase=apply patches=22123818 hotpatch=yes.

After installing these patches, you can merge patches 20784380, 22363475, and 22495069 and install it.

6. Set the following: adop phase=apply patches=20784380,22363475,22495069 hotpatch=yes merge=yes.

7. Execute AutoConfig on the database tier.

8. Migrate the latest code on the database tier using $AD_TOP/bin /admkappsutil.pl.

9. Restart the database and application tiers.

Apply WebLogic Patches

The following list of patches must be installed on WebLogic Server before proceeding with the upgrade. These patches may conflict with other existing patches, so you must remove all conflicts and apply these patches using the bsu.sh utility. Table 3-8 lists the patches that should be installed on WebLogic Home. The Installation of weblogic patches is demonstrated in chpater 7.

- Ensure the WebLogic admin and managed servers are working without issue.

- After successful installation of the listed patches, execute the ETCC script on the database and middle tiers to ensure that all patches are in place.

Table 3-8. *ETCC Summary WebLogic*

	19687084	8FBW
Not included in any startCD or ETCC summary	13964737	YVDZ
	20780171	EJUW
	13729611	L34G
	17319481	N5FK
	22128205	GK5N

Installation of 12.2.5 Upgrade Patch

The preparation of the EBS 12.2.5 patch upgrade is complete. Now the system is almost ready for installing an upgrade patch. Follow these steps:

■ **Note** Make sure there is enough space available in all data mount points and file systems.

1. Set optimizer_adaptive_features to FALSE.

   It's recommended that you set this to FALSE because of performance issues during upgrade; this is listed in MOS tech notes Doc ID 1349240.1 and Doc ID 1983050.1.

2. Source the RUN file system.

3. Stop all application services.

4. Ensure there is no active patching cycle.

5. Install 12.2.

6. Upgrade patch 19676458 in downtime mode. Listing 3-8 shows the installation of the 12.2.5 patch in downtime mode.

Listing 3-8. EBS Upgrade: Installation of 12.2.5 Patch

```
[applR12@erpnode2 PROD]$adop phase=apply apply_mode=downtime patches=19676458

Enter the APPS password:
Enter the SYSTEM password:
Enter the WLSADMIN password:
Validating credentials.
Initializing.
    Run Edition context  : /d01/appl_prod/PROD/fs1/inst/apps/PROD_erpnode2/appl/admin/PROD_
erpnode2.xml
    Patch edition context: /d01/appl_prod/PROD/fs2/inst/apps/PROD_erpnode2/appl/admin/PROD_
erpnode2.xml
Reading driver file (up to 50000000 bytes).
    Patch file system free space: 35.29 GB

Checking for existing adop sessions.
    Application tier services are down.
    Continuing with the existing session [Session ID: 2].


===========================================================================
ADOP (C.Delta.7)
Session ID: 2
Node: erpnode2
Phase: apply
Log: /d01/appl_prod/PROD/fs_ne/EBSapps/log/adop/2/adop_20160325_012312.log
===========================================================================

Applying patch 19676458.
    Log: /d01/appl_prod/PROD/fs_ne/EBSapps/log/adop/2/apply_20160325_012312/PROD_
erpnode2/19676458/log/u19676458.log
Running finalize actions for the patches being applied.
    Log: @ADZDSHOWLOG.sql "2016/03/25 05:13:26"
Running cutover actions for the patches being applied.
    Creating additional workers to process cutover DDL in parallel
    Log: /d01/appl_prod/PROD/fs_ne/EBSapps/log/adop/2/apply_20160325_012312/PROD_erpnode2/
log/cutover.log
```

```
      Performing database cutover in Quick mode
Generating post apply reports.
Generating log report.
      Output: /d01/appl_prod/PROD/fs_ne/EBSapps/log/adop/2/apply_20160325_012312/PROD_
erpnode2/adzdshowlog.out
The apply phase completed successfully.
adop exiting with status = 0 (Success)
[applR12@erpnode2 PROD]$
```

7. Verify the patch log files for any warnings and errors.

8. Execute the cleanup phase. Listing 3-9 shows the cleanup phase after the 12.2.5 patch installation.

Listing 3-9. EBS Upgrade: adop Cleanup Phase

```
[applR12@erpnode2 scripts]$ adop phase=cleanup
Enter the APPS password:
Enter the SYSTEM password:
Enter the WLSADMIN password:
Validating credentials.
Initializing.
      Run Edition context  : /d01/appl_prod/PROD/fs1/inst/apps/PROD_erpnode2/appl/admin/PROD_
erpnode2.xml
      Patch edition context: /d01/appl_prod/PROD/fs2/inst/apps/PROD_erpnode2/appl/admin/PROD_
erpnode2.xml
      Patch file system free space: 23.60 GB
Checking for existing adop sessions.
=====================================================================
ADOP (C.Delta.7)
Session ID: 2
Node: erpnode2
Phase: cleanup
Log: /d01/appl_prod/PROD/fs_ne/EBSapps/log/adop/2/adop_20160325_103220.log
=====================================================================
Processing cleanup actions in parallel.
      Log: /d01/appl_prod/PROD/fs_ne/EBSapps/log/adop/2/cleanup_20160325_103220/PROD_erpnode2/
log/cleanup.log

Generating report of queued DDL actions.
      Output: /d01/appl_prod/PROD/fs_ne/EBSapps/log/adop/2/cleanup_20160325_103220/PROD_
erpnode2/adzdallddls.out
Running cleanup in STANDARD mode.
      Log: @ADZDSHOWLOG.sql "2016/03/25 10:33:26"
Generating log report.
      Output: /d01/appl_prod/PROD/fs_ne/EBSapps/log/adop/2/cleanup_20160325_103220/PROD_
erpnode2/adzdshowlog.out
The cleanup phase completed successfully.
adop exiting with status = 0 (Success)
```

9. Execute the fs_clone phase. Listing 3-10 shows the execution of the fs_clone phase after patch installation.

Listing 3-10. EBS Upgrade: Execution of fs_clone

```
[applR12@erpnode2 scripts]$ adop phase=fs_clone

Enter the APPS password:
Enter the SYSTEM password:
Enter the WLSADMIN password:

Validating credentials.

Initializing.
    Run Edition context  : /d01/appl_prod/PROD/fs1/inst/apps/PROD_erpnode2/appl/admin/PROD_
erpnode2.xml
.................
.................
.................

Generating log report.
    Output: /d01/appl_prod/PROD/fs_ne/EBSapps/log/adop/3/fs_clone_20160325_103853/PROD_
erpnode2/adzdshowlog.out

The fs_clone phase completed successfully.

adop exiting with status = 0 (Success)
[applR12@erpnode2 scripts]$
```

10. Set backoptimizer_adaptive_features to TRUE.

The upgrade of Oracle EBS 12.2.0 to 12.2.5 has completed successfully.

Post-upgrade Tasks

Post-upgrade tasks include the following:

- Ensure all admin and managed servers are working properly.

- Ensure the login page and system access are working properly.

- Ensure the concurrent managers are working properly.

- Apply the 12.2.5 online help patch 19676460 in hotpatch mode.

Figures 3-4 and 3-5 display the new interface login interface of EBS 12.2.5 and the OAM dashboard displaying the installed version of EBS.

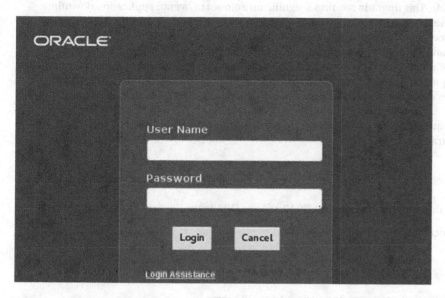

Figure 3-4. *EBS 12.2.5 login screen*

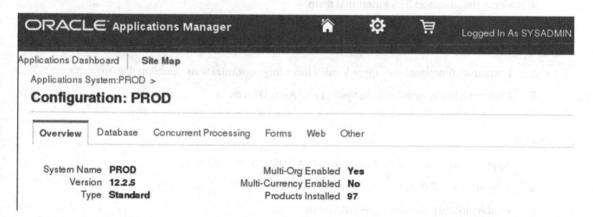

Figure 3-5. *OAM Dashboard: EBS installed version*

The upgrade of Oracle EBS 12.2.0 to 12.2.5 is complete. The process of upgrading is simple provided that you have read all the referenced Oracle documents carefully and installed all the prerequisite steps as mentioned.

Now you will see how you can perform an upgrade from release 12.1 to 12.2.

Upgrading from 12.1.3 to 12.2.0

This one is a major upgrade. This upgrade requires a significant amount of overall application downtime. The number and list of patches may differ from environment to environment, So I would highly recommend to follow oracle support tech notes for applying patches on your systems. This section of this chapter will give you a better understanding of the upgrade process to help you upgrade your Oracle EBS environment.

Oracle EBS is a major upgrade, and the Apps DBA is not the only person who will complete the upgrade process. The upgrade requires teamwork from Oracle EBS technical, functional, and core application business users. The duties should be segregated between different teams, which will help in creating a successful rollout.

The segregation of duties listed next was followed in a real customer environment and helped the whole team create a successful transition.

Phase 1

1. Upgrade the database on the existing EBS 12.1: Apps DBA team

2. Execute a functional test: EBS functional team

Phase 2

3. Install all application pre-upgrade patches: Apps DBA team

4. Verify the instance: EBS functional team

Phase 3

5. Execute all functional pre-upgrade tasks including customizations: functional team

6. Perform a full system backup: System and Apps DBA team

Phase 4

7. Apply localization and 12.2 pre-upgrade patches: Apps DBA team

8. Upgrade to 12.2.0: Apps DBA team

9. Enable online patching: Apps DBA team

10. Apply tech stack patches: Apps DBA team

11. Upgrade to 12.2.4/12.2.5: Apps DBA team

12. Perform all post-upgrade tasks: Apps DBA and functional teams

13. Application function test cases: core business users

Figure 3-6 shows the high-level steps that should be followed for upgrading pre-12.2 Oracle EBS environments.

Figure 3-6. EBS 12.2 upgrade process

■ **Note** A direct upgrade to 12.2.4/12.2.5 is not possible. You have to first upgrade to 12.2.0 and then upgrade to any later version.

Before we begin with the upgrade demonstration, here are the key points to help in minimizing the overall upgrade downtime:

- Disable archive log mode.
- Appropriately size the redo log files.
- Disable TDE, Database Vault, and auditing.
- Enable degree of parallelism (DOP).
- Tune database initialization parameters appropriately.
- Purge irrelevant data before the upgrade.
- Disable the RAC database during the application upgrade.
- Use a higher value for the batch size.
- Merge patches wherever it's possible.
- Record issues and their solutions for future quick reference.

Upgrade Environment Details

Table 3-9 displays the current and target releases of the database and applications.

Table 3-9. EBS Upgrade Environment Details

	Current Release	Target Release
Operating system	OEL 6.6: 64-bit	OEL 6.6: 64-bit
Database	11.2.0.3	12.1.0.2
Applications	12.1.3	12.2.0
Database size	1.2 TB	1.28 TB
NLS language	English	English

Oracle EBS Database Upgrade

An Oracle EBS database upgrade is a separate activity that can be performed ahead of the application upgrade. This will reduce the downtime during the application upgrade. In this section, you will see the high-level steps for upgrading an Oracle database in Oracle EBS environments.

1. Perform OS prerequisites for Oracle Database 12c installation.

2. Install the Oracle 12.1.0.2 database software.

3. Install the Oracle 12.1.0.2 examples CD on the newly installed 12.1.0.2 RDBMS Home.

4. Install any additional Oracle application patches (adpatch).

5. Install the 12.1.0.2 database patches (opatch) on the newly installed Oracle Home.

6. Run the pre-upgrade tool from the 12c Database Home.

7. Perform all changes recommended by the upgrade tool.

8. Configure the Oracle networking files in the 12c Database Home.

9. Back up the database and application.

10. Use DBUA/manual upgrade tools for upgrading the database.

11. Compile all invalid objects.

12. Build a database context file in the Database 12c Oracle Home.

13. Enable AutoConfig in the Oracle Database 12c Home.

14. Execute AutoConfig in the application nodes.

15. Start up application services and verify the upgrade.

THE DETAILED STEPS FOR THE DATABASE UPGRADE ARE LISTED IN THESE MOS TECH NOTES:

- "Interoperability Notes EBS 12.0 or 12.1 with RDBMS 12cR1" (Doc ID 1524398.1)

- "Interoperability Notes EBS 11i with RDBMS 12cR1" (Doc ID 1524399.1)

- "Interoperability Notes Oracle EBS 11i with Oracle Database 11gR2" (11.2.0) (Doc ID 881505.1)

- "Interoperability Notes Oracle EBS 12.2 with Oracle Database 12c Release 1" (Doc ID 1926201.1)

There certain steps that should be considered while performing a database upgrade.

1. If you're using the DBUA utility for performing an upgrade, then ensure the oratab file contains a valid entry of SID, which will be upgraded to 12c.

2. DBUA will lock and expire all users except sys and system, so you may need to reset the password manually.

3. Start the listener from 12c Home before running DBUA. The recompilation of network-dependent objects will face performance issues if the listener is not started from the 12c Home.

Oracle Application Upgrade

Now we will proceed with the application upgrade demonstration. This demonstration will give you an overall look at performing an EBS upgrade. This not a step-by-step, detailed demonstration. In this demo, a number of application patches are installed that cannot be considered as reference for other upgrade environments. The patch number will be updated in respective MOS upgrade notes, and those notes should be the reference for applying these patches.

There are certain situations during an upgrade project where the upgrade patches will be different in different iterations.

The following is the list of high-level steps that must be performed for an EBS upgrade from version 12.0.x/12.1.x to 12.2.0:

1. Install the 12.2.0 tech stack components.

2. Prepare for the 12.2.0 upgrade patch.

3. Apply the main application upgrade patch.

4. Configure an EBS upgrade using Rapidwiz.

5. Finish the upgrade.

6. Enable online patching.

7. Perform the post-upgrade steps.

Install 12.2.0 Tech Stack Components

For laying out the application file system, the stage area should be prepared, and all the operating system prerequisites should be performed in preparation of the 12.2 installation. Before installing the new file system, back up the existing global inventory files. At the time of writing this book, startCD 51 is the latest version available.

Execute Rapidwiz as Root User

Figure 3-7 will list the components that going to be installed by Rapidwiz.

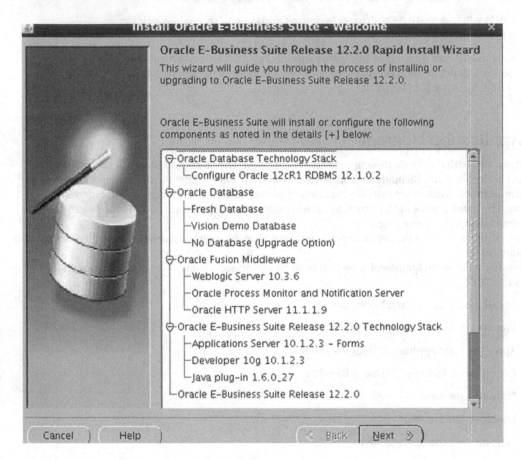

Figure 3-7. Rapidwiz install upgrade file system

Figure 3-8 displays the Rapidwiz choices, and you must choose the Upgrade option for installing the file system.

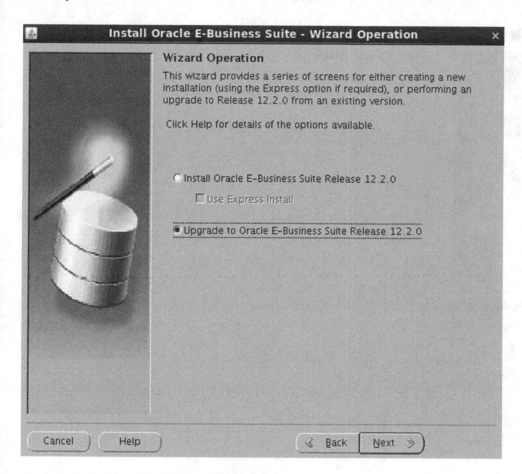

Figure 3-8. *Rapidwiz: Install/Upgrade choice*

Figure 3-9 shows that Rapidwiz provides two options for upgrade. The first one will create the upgraded file system, and the second option will configure the upgraded 12.2.0 file system.

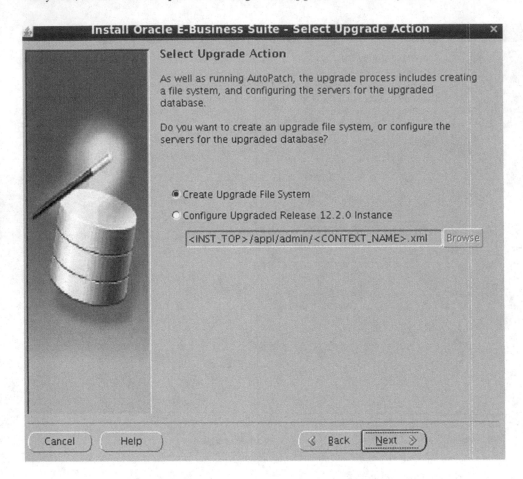

Figure 3-9. *Rapidwiz upgrade actions*

The screen shown in Figure 3-10 will allow you to configure the ports for a 12.2 file system. If using the same ports as 12.1 in that target file system, then services running on the source system (12.1) must be stopped or installation of the upgraded file system will fail because of a port conflict.

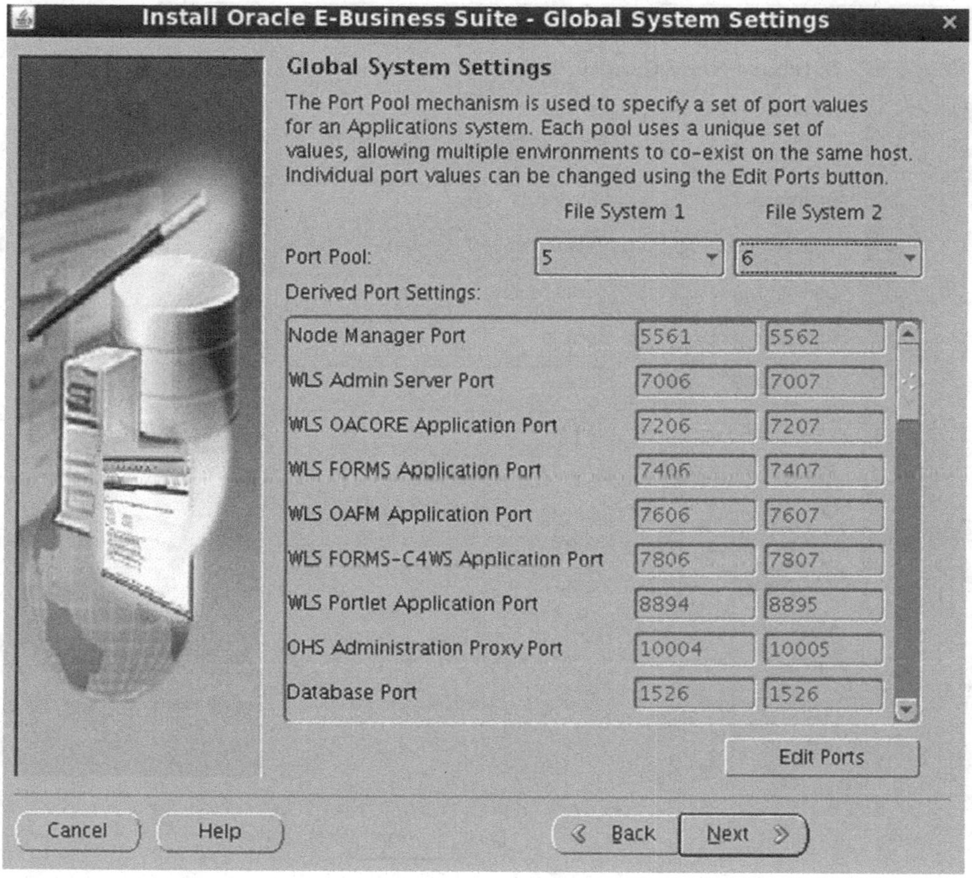

Figure 3-10. Rapidwiz ports configuration

■ **Note** Ensure the database port is configured correctly.

Figure 3-11 shows the screen that needs information for the database node. There is an option to install a new Oracle_Home, or you can choose an existing Home. In this case, the database is already upgraded to 12.1.0.2, so you can select Use Existing Oracle Home and it will not install the new Home.

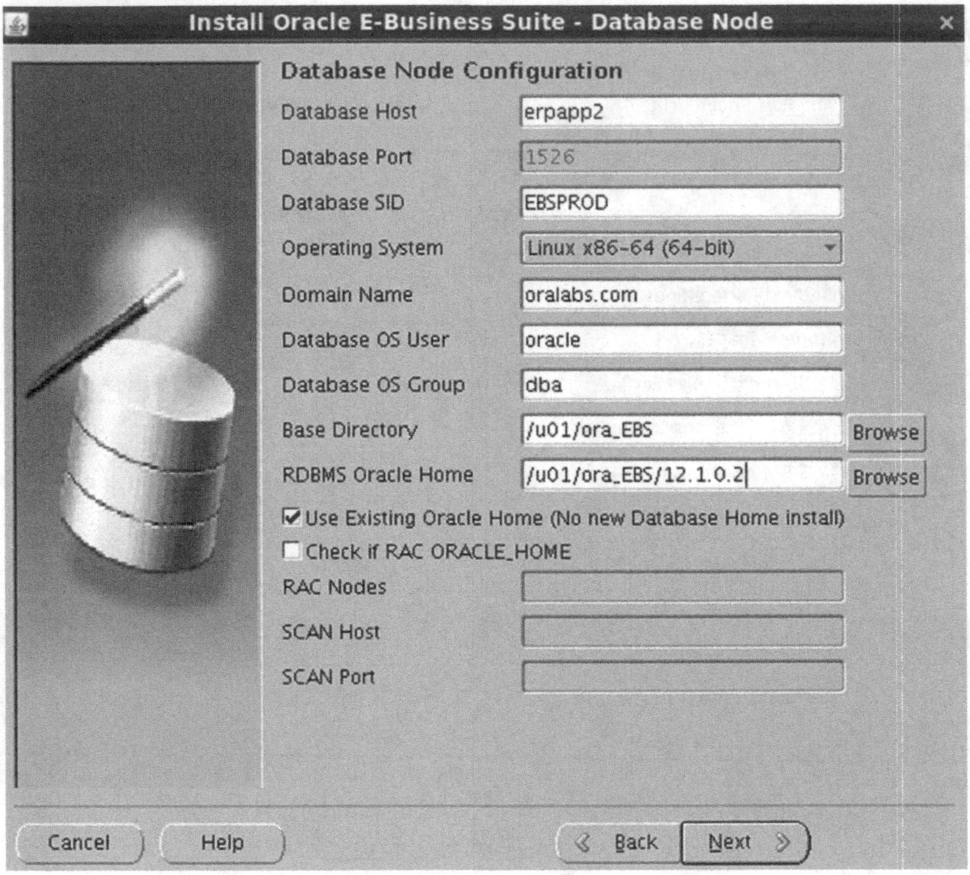

Figure 3-11. *Rapidwiz database node configuration*

Rapidwiz will configure WebLogic Server as part of installing the upgrade file system. So, a WebLogic admin password must be provided, as shown in Figure 3-12.

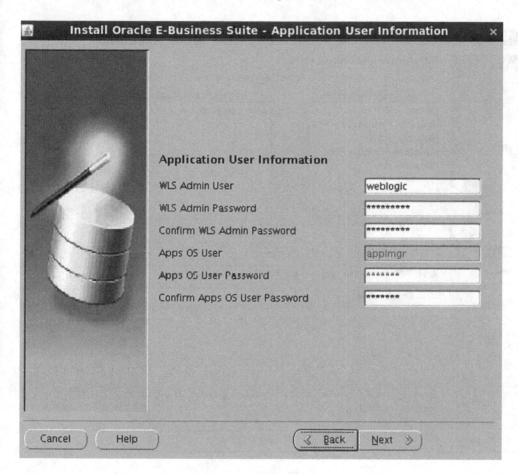

Figure 3-12. Rapidwiz WebLogic password configuration

The upgrade file system must be installed using the same character set as the source system (12.1) for the application and database (Figure 3-13).

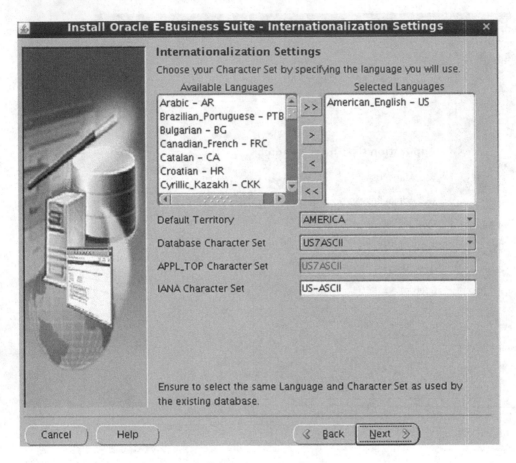

Figure 3-13. *Rapidwiz language and character set configuration*

Rapidwiz will configure the dual file system for the application tier, as shown in Figure 3-14.

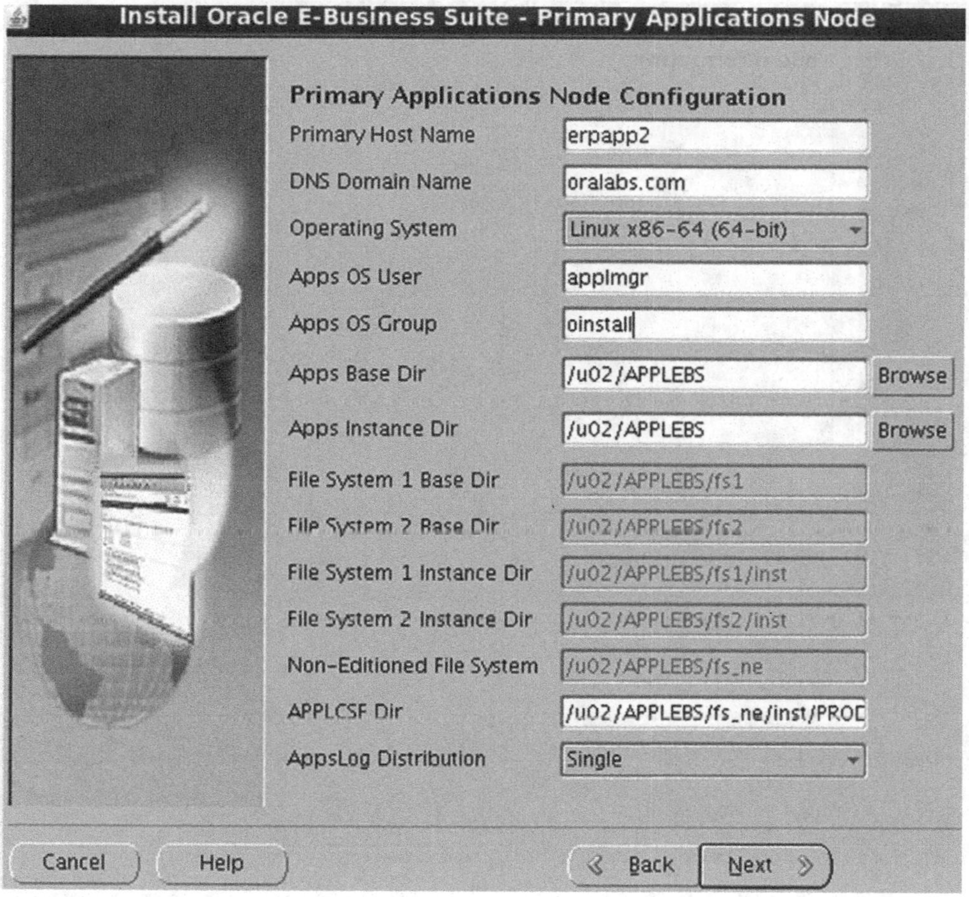

Figure 3-14. *Rapidwiz application node configuration*

The node summary will be listed after providing all the required inputs, as shown in Figure 3-15.

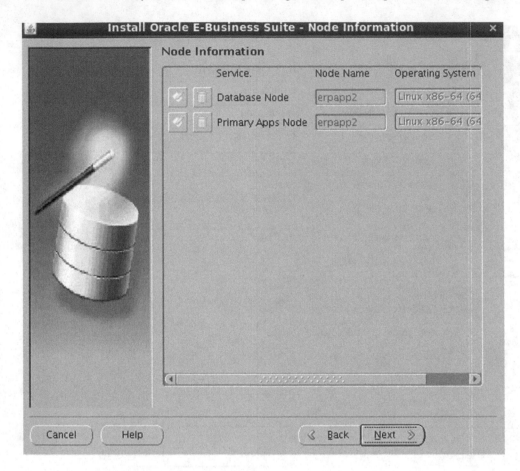

Figure 3-15. *Rapidwiz node information summary*

Rapidwiz will check the prerequisites before laying down the upgraded file system, as shown in Figure 3-16.

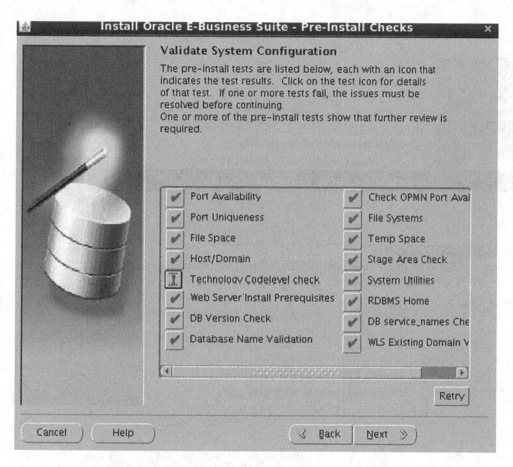

Figure 3-16. *Rapidwiz prerequisite check summary*

Figure 3-17 shows the installation progress of the upgraded file system.

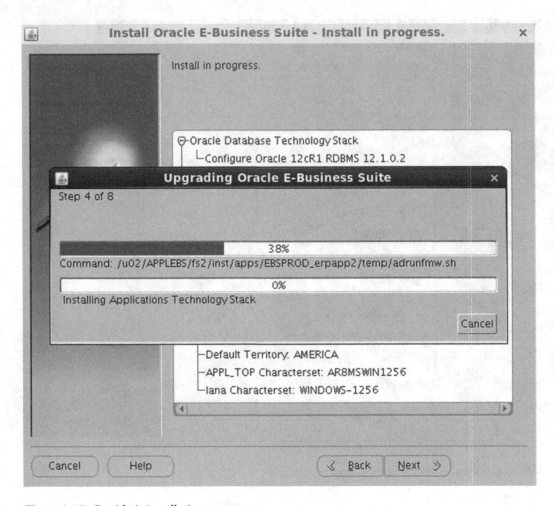

Figure 3-17. Rapidwiz installation progress

After installation completes, Rapidwiz will validate the upgraded file system, as shown in Figure 3-18.

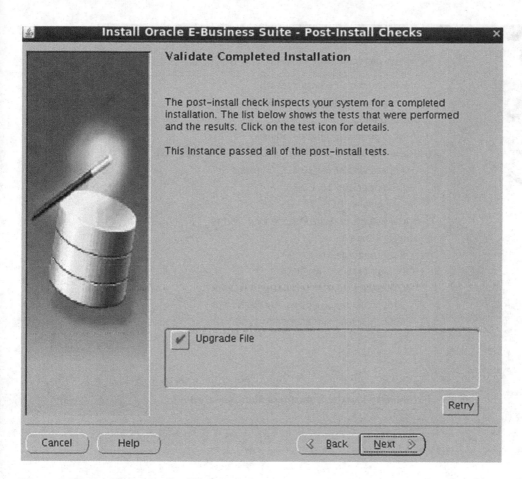

Figure 3-18. *Rapidwiz install validation*

Figure 3-19 lists the technology stack components installed by Rapidwiz.

Figure 3-19. *Rapidwiz installation summary*

Prepare for 12.2.0 Upgrade Patch

Before starting the layout of the file system, you must perform a set of actions on the database in preparation of an EBS upgrade.

The MOS tech note "Database Preparation Guidelines for an E-Business Suite Release 12.2 Upgrade" (Doc ID 1349240.1) covers the detailed steps that should be performed on the current database, which will prepare the database to be ready for an application upgrade.

You should disable the AOL audit trial as suggested in Chapter 3 of the Oracle EBS upgrade guide.

The next step is to download the pre-install patch report from MOS tech note "R12.1 and 12.2 Oracle E-Business Suite Preinstall Patches Report [Video]" (Doc ID 1448102.2). This document consists of three tabs, so you should use the 12.2 tab from this document. You should also ensure that you are downloading the latest pre-install patch report from the MOS as this report is updated every month until all patches that are going to be installed are finalized. All applicable patches from this report should be installed.

The latest CUPS patch 10117518 is also included in MOS tech note 1448102.2. You should ensure that the latest version of the patch is being downloaded until all patches are frozen. Oracle continuously updates this patch.

To identify the prerequisite application patches, refer to section 3 of MOS tech note "Oracle E-Business Suite Release Notes, Release 12.2" (Doc ID 1320300.1). It provides instructions for installing CUPS and the newly merged application driver patches. Listing 3-10 shows the merging of patches.

Apply Main Upgrade Patch

Follow these steps:

1. Apply the AD upgrade patch with other required patches as the merged patch.

2. Apply CUPS and all other patches identified in note 1448102.2. These patches should be installed in pre-install mode. Listing 3-11 shows the AD and 12.2 upgrade merging of patches.

Listing 3-11. EBS Upgrade: Merge AD and 122 Upgrade Patches

```
AD CUP5 patch (patch#18040523:R12.AD.C) superseded by 19796564:R12.AD.C
patch#19477748:R12.AD.C
patch#20937084:R12.AD.C.
R12.AD.C 20029957:R12.AD.C
p21670164_R12.AD.C_R12_GENERIC
Source patch directory ==> /d01/appl_EBS/ebs_patches/AD_Source
Target patch directory ==> /u02/APPLEBS/122_upgrade_patches

[applmgr@erpapp2 ~]$ admrgpch -s /d01/appl_EBS/ebs_patches/AD_Source -d /u02/APPLEBS/122_
upgrade_patches/10117518_CUP6  -merge_name 10117518_cup6 -admode

Executing the merge of the patch drivers
 -- Processing patch: /d01/appl_EBS/ebs_patches/AD_Source/21670164
 -- Processing file: /d01/appl_EBS/ebs_patches/AD_Source/21670164/u21670164.drv
 -- Done processing file: /d01/appl_EBS/ebs_patches/AD_Source/21670164/u21670164.drv
 -- Done processing patch: /d01/appl_EBS/ebs_patches/AD_Source/21670164

95% complete. Copied 886 files of 932...
100% complete. Copied 932 files of 932...

Character-set converting files...
  6 unified drivers merged.
Patch merge completed successfully
Please check the log file at ./admrgpch.log.
[applmgr@erpapp2 ~]$
```

Merge the Pre-install Patches with the Main Upgrade Driver

Do the following:

```
$admrgpch -d . -preinstall -master u10124646.drv
```

At this point, ensure all prerequisite steps are performed and the system is ready for upgrade. It's always a best practice to keep the check list for the prerequisite steps. We also recommend that you perform a full system backup, which will be helpful in case of patch failures.

Installation of Main Upgrade Driver

The main upgrade driver should be installed with the nocopyportion and nogenerate portion options. The following command can be used for applying the main driver patch:

```
$adpatch options=nocopyportion,nogenerateportion
```

■ **Note**   The main patch installation and other pre-patches, including fixes, took us about nine hours.

Configure the EBS Upgrade Using Rapidwiz

You can use the Rapidwiz Install Wizard to configure the upgraded file system. This option will configure the WebLogic domain, configure the RUN and PATH file systems, and verify the configuration of the tech stack components. Execute Rapidwiz from the same stage area, as shown in Figure 3-20.

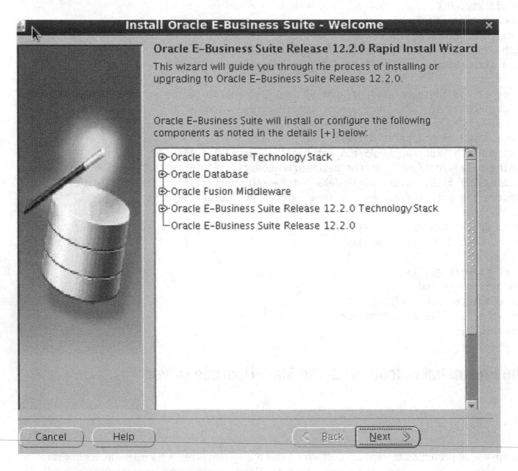

Figure 3-20. Rapidwiz upgrade configuration

Choose to upgrade to Oracle EBS 12.2.0, as shown in Figure 3-21.

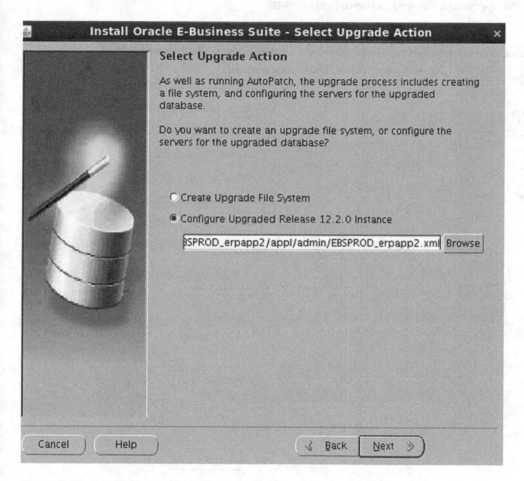

Figure 3-21. Rapidwiz upgrade configuration option

Rapidwiz will request for the APPS and WebLogic admin passwords for review, which are required for configuring the upgraded file system, as shown in Figure 3-22.

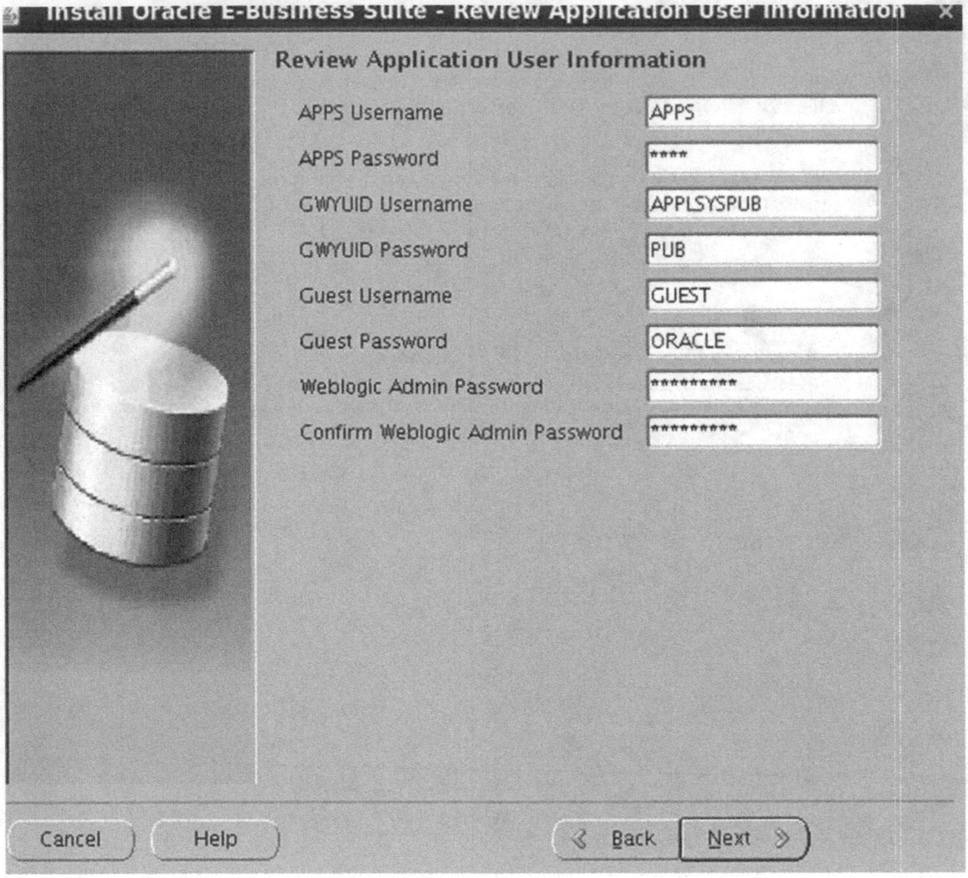

Figure 3-22. Rapidwiz upgrade configuration: application user review

After the configuration completes, it will perform the pre-install check that is required for the upgraded configuration, as shown in Figure 3-23.

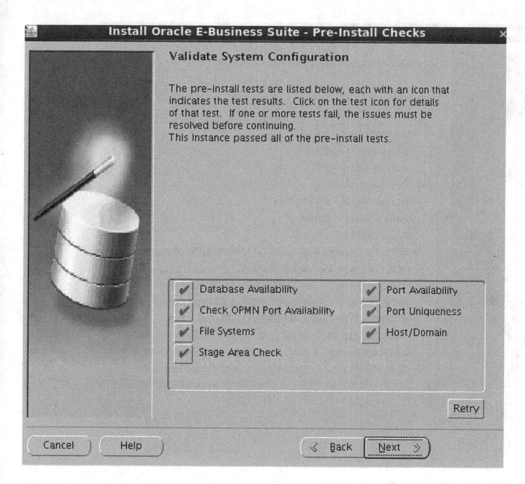

Figure 3-23. Rapidwiz upgrade configuration validation

Rapidwiz will list the components it's going to configure. Figure 3-24 shows the configuration items that will be configured as part of the upgraded configuration.

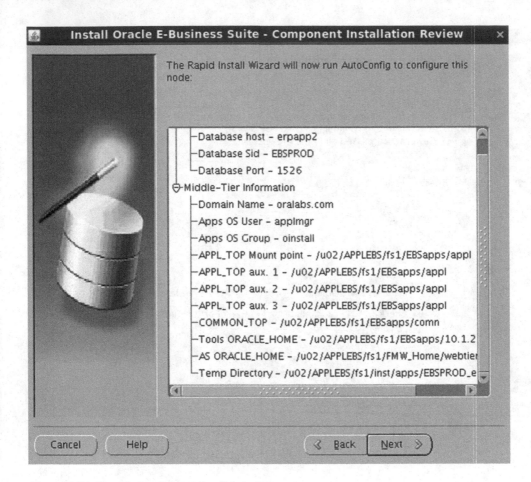

Figure 3-24. *Rapidwiz configuration list summary*

Rapidwiz will perform the post-install check for the tech stack components, as shown in Figure 3-25. Figure 3-26 shows the Rapidwiz upgrade configuration summary.

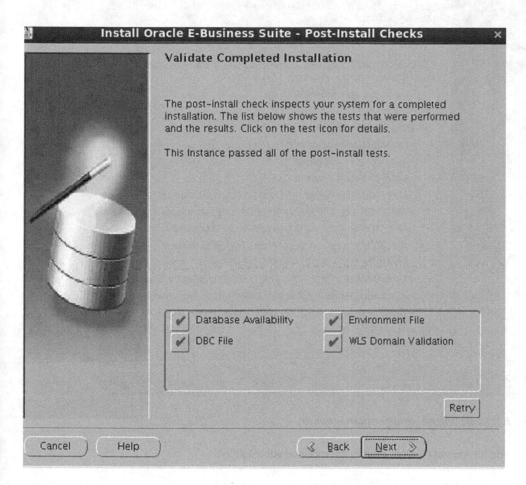

Figure 3-25. Rapidwiz upgrade configuration post-install validations

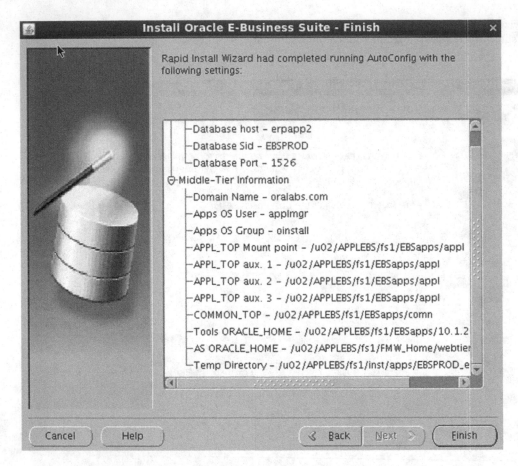

Figure 3-26. *Rapidwiz upgrade configuration summary*

The upgrade file system configuration has completed successfully.

Finishing the Upgrade

Follow these steps:

1. After the completion of the patch installation, disable maintenance mode because maintenance mode is not available in EBS 12.2.

2. Enable AutoConfig on the database tier.

3. Generate a new context file using adbldxml.pl.

4. Execute AutoConfig.

5. You should now configure/add the custom database objects (optional).

6. Reenable custom triggers, constraint, and indexes (optional).

Enable Online Patching

Online patching is one of the major changes introduced in Oracle EBS 12.2. This is not an optional step; online patching must be enabled at this stage. There are several steps and scripts that need to be executed for enabling online patching. In this section, we will cover the high-level process that will give you an idea of how you can enable online patching.

After successful enablement of online patching, the applications DBA can apply patches online when the application is up and running. Chapter 6 of this book gives detailed information about online patching.

Let's see the steps required for enabling online patching.

Verify the database version minimum; it can be 11.2.0.3, but 12.1.0.2 is recommended. All recommended patches are applied from the note.

Execute Online Patching Enablement/Readiness Report

The main reference document for enabling online patching is "Online Patching Readiness Report in Oracle E-Business Suite Release 12.2" (Doc ID 1531121.1).

- The report will list violations of objects that don't comply with the EBR rule about noneditioned objects and referencing editioned objects.

- ADZDPSUM.sql provides the summary of objects that depend on EBS code and are recommended to be editioned.

- ADZDPMAN.sql provides a list of objects with different categories of violations to EBR rules that must be fixed prior to running the enablement process.

- ADZDPAUT.sql lists objects with violations to EBR that will be fixed automatically from the enablement process.

Fix Violations

Fix all violations those are incompatible with online patching. These violations will be listed in the online patching readiness report that require manual intervention.

1. Review the sections listed in ADZDPSUM.sql.

2. Many violations will be fixed automatically by registering CUSTOM schemas with (SYS, SYSTEM, and CTXSYS schemas should not be registered).

3. Perform the fix recommended by Oracle by customizing $AD_TOP/sql/ADZDPCUST.sql.

4. Execute the online patching enablement report until all violations are fixed.

Verify the Free Space in Tablespaces

Follow these steps:

1. The edition-based redefinition feature of Oracle Database 11gR2 requires additional space for the dictionary tables that are used to manage editioned objects.

2. Run the following report to retrieve the current tablespace free space:

```
perl $AD_TOP/bin/adzdreport.pl apps
```

3. Select option 3, Other Generic Reports.

4. Select the next option, Free Space in Important Tablespaces.

   • Ensure there is enough space available in the database to accommodate the following sizing:

      a. SYSTEM: 25GB of free space

      b. APPS_TS_SEED: 5GB of free space

   • Add space to the tablespace to meet the minimum requirement.

Execute Online Patching Enablement Report

Follow these steps:

1. Capture the list of invalid objects and ensure there were no invalids with AD_ZD names.

2. Execute sqlplus <apps username> @$AD_TOP/sql/ADZDEXRPT.sql.

   a. Shut down all application services.

   b. Install the online patching enablement patch.

      • Apply 13543062.12.AD.C using adpatch.

   While applying the Online Enablement patch, you may receive the following error: "Attention: Adpatch should no longer be used to apply patches. Please use ADOP tool for applying patches." If you receive this error, then you must use adop in hotpatch mode to apply the enablement patch.

      • Monitor the Online Patching enablement patch application.

The enablement patch application may take several hours to finish. You can monitor its progress at any time by running the DDL Status Report (ADZDSHOWDDLS.sql) as follows:

```
sqlplus <apps Username> @$AD_TOP/sql/ADZDSHOWDDLS.sql
```

   a. Compile invalid objects.

   b. Execute the online patching enablement status report (ADZDEXRPT.sql) after completing the patch installation.

   c. Execute the online patching enablement readiness report called ADZDPSUM.sql after completing the patch installation.

   d. Execute online patching database compliance checker report called ADZDDBCC.sql to check the coding standard violations.

   e. Add the initialization parameter ebs_patch to support online patching.

Post-upgrade Steps

The upgrade guide contains a specific section for post-upgrade activities. There are certain activities from the list that are mandatory; others are optional. The post-upgrade steps that are categorized as conditional may vary in different environments; for example, there are certain organizations using only supply chain, and for such organizations applying HR legislative data may not be applicable.

For detailed post-upgrade tasks, refer to https://docs.oracle.com/cd/E26401_01/doc.122/e48839/T579510T579526.htm.

The following are the additional post-upgrade steps that should be considered:

1. Enable the database and application backup.

2. Integrate all third-party applications.

3. If the disaster recover site was in place, then reconfigure it.

4. Execute an empty patching cycle to ensure that it's working successfully.

5. Gather statistics for all schemas.

6. Verify all log files including for the database, middleware, and operating systems.

7. Configure/verify the Workflow mailer.

8. Clients using Windows XP are no longer supported, so you must upgrade to the supported client operating system.

9. Ensure all critical concurrent requests such as create accounting, payroll run, and so on, are working without issues.

10. Verify all connected printers are printing from concurrent requests.

11. Verify reports in other NLS languages are working properly.

After every upgrade generally you may need to apply many other patches to fix any issues or to avoid issues in the future. But the process of bugs and fixes is a never-ending process, and it's not possible to list all the patches that are required to be installed after an upgrade; moreover, data/functionalities varies from each other environment. However, we have added the list of patches applied after an upgrade for a real customer running Oracle EBS as one of their core business applications. You can download the list of patches from the Source Code tab at www.apress.com/978-1-4842-1423-7.

EBS Upgrade Timing Summary

The upgrade has been performed on a system with 12 core processors and 48GB RAM.

Here are the hardware details:

- *Processors*: INTEL XEON E5 (2.6GHz) processors

- *Disks*: EMC Storage FC SAS disks (15K) with 8GB connectivity

Table 3-10 shows the duration summary for the upgrade activities.

Table 3-10. *EBS Upgrade Activities: Duration Summary*

Serial Number	Upgrade Activity	Duration (in Hours)
1	Database upgrade from 11.2.0.3 to 12.1.0.2	6
2	Laying out the 12.2 file system	3.5
3	Installation of pre and main 12.2 upgrade driver	7
4	Configuration of upgraded file system	1
5	Compilation of invalid objects	1.5
6	Enablement of online patching	5
7	Installation of 12.2.5 pre and main patches	6

Summary

In this chapter, you learned how you can upgrade from Oracle EBS 12.1.*x* and 12.2.0 to 12.2.5. The upgrade process for 12.2 is identical, but the prerequisite patch numbers may vary for different releases. The customization should be handled carefully during the upgrade process. As discussed in the beginning of this chapter, prepare the system ahead for the activities that can be performed on the existing system before the 12.2 upgrade.

■ ■ ■

## CHAPTER 4

Oracle E-Business Suite 12.2 File System

The file system in EBS 12.2 is a crucial topic, so it is impossible not to mention it in this book. In earlier chapters, we introduced the file system structure of EBS 12.2, as well as the EBS environment variables, which are tightly related with the file system directories used in EBS 12.2. This chapter is dedicated to the file system; having a deeper understanding of the file system will give you a better understanding of all the technology components of EBS 12.2.

Specifically, we will explain the application file system, including the Fusion Middleware directory structure (in addition, we will be focusing on FMW in EBS 12.2 in Chapter 7). We will also cover the environment variables used in EBS 12.2 and give you the directory navigations and log file locations.

We'll start by defining the important environment variables used in EBS 12.2 so you know which directory to use for specific file system operations.

Oracle E-Business Suite File System Architecture Overview

The EBS file system architecture4 is based on an application file system and a database file system, as mentioned in Chapter 1. The database file system is delivered as a standard Oracle Home, with a directory named appsutil residing it. The data files, control files, redo log files, and the parameter file that contributes Oracle Database can be placed anywhere in the database file system as well as in the ASM file system.

In the RAC installations, there is also a Grid Home in the database tier that gets delivered with the EBS installation. The Grid Home can be considered part of the database file system, as it supplies the clustering and it hosts other critical utilities such as listeners and ASM. So, EBS's database file system is a typical Oracle Database file system that any core DBA can understand and manage (with the exception of the application-related database management activities such as using AD utilities in the database tier).

The EBS application file system architecture, on the other hand, has become a bit more complex with the 12.2 release. A dual file system and the noneditioned file system were introduced with this release, and there are also new technologies such as Fusion Middleware delivered with the standard installation.

Moreover, online patching was introduced in this release, and also some of the application tier technologies such as 10.1.3 Oracle Home have been retired.

As a result of these changes, EBS 12.2 has become more powerful than its ancestors, but its file system architecture, especially for the application tier, has become complex.

With Release 12.2, there are two file systems, named fs1 and fs2, representing the dual file system architecture. The dual file system is used for supporting online patching, as only one of these file systems can be active (run) at a certain time. The patching activities are done in the inactive file system, which can also be called the patch file system because it provides the ability to patch the EBS system online without disturbing the applications in use.

For supporting online patching properly, EBS houses two identical file systems, synchronized using the new online patching tools in its application tier. These file systems host most of the EBS files including the directories. These directories include the directory hosting Fusion Middleware, APPL_TOP, COMMON_TOP, and INST_TOP.

That means there are two application file systems, two sets of binaries, and two editions (the run and patch) but one EBS database. So, the binaries that reside on these two application file systems connect to the same EBS database but see the database objects differently according to their roles at a certain time.

That is, there is an isolation mechanism in the EBS database that makes binaries that reside in the active (run) file system use the runtime database objects and makes the binaries that reside in the patch file system use the copies of the runtime database object without interrupting the database work that active applications do. This database-level isolation mechanism is the edition-based redefinition (EBR) feature that comes with the Oracle Database 11g R2 and 12c. EBR is in the EBS database, so it is not part of the database file system, but it is tightly integrated with the application tier, so we will explain it while we are explaining the file system architecture in EBS 12.2.

There is also a non-edition file system called fs_ne to store the non-editioned objects such as the concurrent request log and out files as well as the adop log files, which are not changed according to the active (run) file system being fs1 or fs2.

Figure 4-1 represents the synchronized file system architecture that is used in the EBS application tier, as well as the usage of EBR for database-level isolation for supporting the online patching in the database tier.

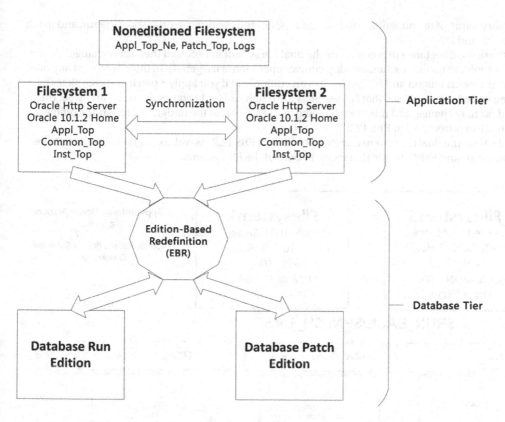

Figure 4-1. *EBS file system architecture*

Understanding the Application Dual and Noneditioned File Systems

The file system architecture in the EBS application tier is based on the dual and nonedition file systems. It is a completely new file system architecture compared to EBS 12.1, 12.0, and 11i, and it is also a unique file system architecture design compared to the file system design of any other Oracle product.

While the concepts of the dual file system and nonedition file system are new, calling the file systems that constitute the dual file system architecture the *run* and *patch* file systems according to their roles at a certain time is exciting. Also, the noneditioned file system, which gets its name from not being required to be synchronized, is also part of the file system design.

■ **Note**   The run file system is used by the Oracle applications in runtime. The patch file system is a copy of the run file system and is there to support online patching. The noneditioned file system is a file system that stores the files needed by both the run and patch file systems but is not patched during the online patching cycles; thus, it does not need to be synchronized.

The directory name of the nonedition file system is fs_ne, and the directory names of the run and patch file systems are fs1 and fs2.

fs1 and fs2 are the directories that constitute the dual file system in EBS, and their roles change when a patch cycle is completed (actually when an adop cutover operation is triggered). In other words, at any one time fs1 can be the patch edition and fs2 can be the run edition, but if you apply a patch and complete the online patching cycle for it, you'll see that fs2 becomes the patch and fs1 becomes the run edition. So, the roles of fs1 and fs2 may change, and this interchanging of roles is part of the design to support the online patching mechanism introduced in EBS 12.2.

Figure 4-2 shows the dual file system architecture used in EBS 12.2, as well as the main top directories named EBSapps, inst, and FMW_Home that reside in both of the file systems.

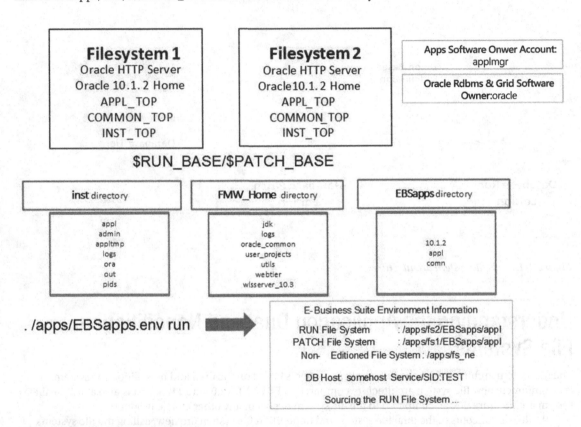

Figure 4-2. *EBS dual file system architecture*

So, all the application files and directories that constitute the application file system architecture of EBS 12.2 are located in the subdirectories of these three directories (run file system, patch file system, and noneditioned file system), as shown in Figure 4-2.

These three top-level directories, however, are also located in a directory called the base directory, which you define by specifying the application base directory (the Apps Base Dir box) during the installation or cloning of EBS 12.2.

Figure 4-2 also shows the usage and output of the EBSapps.env script used to set the runtime environment. From the output of the EBSapps.env script provided in the bottom-right corner of Figure 4-2, you can see the current run, patch, and the noneditioned file system directories as well as the database SID of the environment.

So, as shown with the example tree command output in Listing 4-1, the base directory /u01/install/APPS consists of three directories: fs1, fs2, and fs_ne. It also consists of an environment file named EBSapps. env, which can be used to source the run or patch environment files easily. As we explained earlier, fs1 and fs2 may change roles, and that's why there cannot be a fixed environment file to source the run and patch environments.

However, EBSapps.env is intelligent; thus, you can set your environment using it. You can use EBSapps. env to set your environment to the run edition for administrating the running EBS services; likewise, you can set your environment to be the patch environment for doing some patching activities.

Listing 4-1 shows a tree command and its output that lists the base directory and its main subdirectories.

■ **Note**   tree is a tool for Linux OS that lists the contents of directories in a tree-like structure. It is widely used in this chapter to display the directory structures in a simple tree format.

Listing 4-1. tree Command Output Representing the base directory

```
tree /u01/install/APPS  -L 1    --charset=ANSII -l

APPS
|-- EBSapps.env
|-- fs1
|-- fs2
|-- fs_ne
```

Inside the fs1 and fs2 folders, you see the same directory structures because they are copies of each other. There are three top-level directories in fs1 and fs2.

EBSapps is the key directory for Oracle EBS applications, and it stores three main directories: appl, 10.1.2, and comn. The famous $APPL_TOP environment variable points to the directory named appl in EBSapps, as this directory stores the EBS product files in its subdirectories named with the product short names. The files that belong to the custom applications that are defined for enabling the customizations inside EBS are also stored in the subdirectories located in the directory named appl. There are also environment variables for defining for these custom directories; it is a rule of thumb to name these environment variables and directories with XX (for stating that it is a custom directory) followed by the EBS style of three-letter short names for the companies. For a company named EXAMPLE, the names for the environment variable and the corresponding custom directory would be XXEXP_TOP and xxexp.

■ **Note**   Adding custom applications will be explained in Chapter 8.

The comn directory pointed at by the $COMMON_TOP environment variable stores the files used by several different Oracle E-Business Suite products and third-party products. The 10.1.2 directory also known as Oracle Application Server 10.1.2 Oracle Home is pointed at by the $ORACLE_HOME environment variable, and as the name implies, it stores the Oracle Home files that are there for executing processes such as frmweb, which plays a part in enabling forms services for the clients.

FMW_Home is the base directory for Fusion Middleware that is present in EBS 12.2. It stores the files that constitute the WebLogic domain, WebLogic Server, and Oracle HTTP Server used in EBS 12.2.

The inst directory pointed at by the $INST_TOP environment variable is called Instance Home. Oracle Application Server 10.1.2 ORACLE_HOME configuration files, the application's context file pointed at by the $CONTEXT_FILE, application control script pointed at by $ADMIN_SCRIPTS_HOME, and log files such as AutoConfig log files are stored in this directory.

Listing 4-2 shows an example tree command and its output displaying the directory structures of fs1 and fs2. Notice that fs1 and fs2 have the same subdirectory structures because they are copies of each other.

Listing 4-2. tree Command Output Representing the Contents of fs1 and fs2 Directories

```
tree fs1/ fs2/ -d -L 1    --charset=ANSII

fs1/
|-- EBSapps
|   |-- 10.1.2
|   |-- appl
|   |-- comn
|-- FMW_Home
|   |-- logs
|   |-- modules
|   |-- oracle_common
|   |-- Oracle_EBS-app1
|   |-- patch_wls1036
|   |-- user_projects
|   |-- utils
|   |-- webtier
|   |-- wlserver_10.3
|-- inst
    |-- apps
fs2/
|-- EBSapps
|   |-- 10.1.2
|   |-- appl
|   |-- comn
|-- FMW_Home
|   |-- logs
|   |-- modules
|   |-- oracle_common
|   |-- Oracle_EBS-app1
|   |-- patch_wls1036
|   |-- user_projects
|   |-- utils
|   |-- webtier
|   |-- wlserver_10.3
|-- inst
    |-- apps
```

Of course, the fs_ne directory pointed at by the $NE_BASE environment variable has a different set of subdirectories than fs1 and fs2, as the fs_ne is the noneditioned file system. There are two main directories under the fs_ne directory: EBSapps and inst. In the EBSapps directory, there are three subdirectories named appl, log, and patch.

In the appl directory, there are two important wrapper scripts named adop and adopreports for executing the adop utility (the patching tool) and the adop reports (the AD reporting tool). adop_sync.drv, the custom synchronization driver that is called during the prepare phase of adop is also located here. This driver file is used by adop for syncing the custom apps objects across the editioned file systems (fs1 and fs2).

■ **Note**   We will explain the usage of adop_sync.drv in detail while we are explaining the customizations in Chapter 9.

Some code signing/JAR signing–related files such as adkeystore.dat and appltop.cer are also located in this directory.

The log directory stores the log and output files used by the patch-related AD utilities. This includes the log files produced by the adop utility, the log and output files of the adadmin utility, and the log files of AD workers (which are used by adop while patching). In addition, the status outputs of adop status commands are stored in this directory.

The directory named patch stores the zip files and the unzipped states of these files, as this directory can be reached by the cd $APPL_TOP_NE/../patch command; it is the default directory where you as an apps DBA uploads and unzips patches to be applied and also where adop, when executed, looks for the patches to be applied. The inst directory is the location where concurrent request logs and output files are stored. The log files of concurrent managers and the workflow notification mailer's log, both inbound and inbound threads, are also stored in this directory.

If you need a little more detail, the log files are stored in inst/<SID>_<hostname>/logs/appl/conc/log, and the outputs are located in the inst/<SID>_<hostname>/logs/appl/conc/out directory.

Listing 4-3 shows the fs_ne directory and its contents.

Listing 4-3.   tree Command Output Representing the Contents of fs_ne

```
fs_ne/
|-- EBSapps
|   |-- appl
|   |-- log
|   |-- patch
|-- inst
    |-- EBSDB_apps
    |-- TEST_somehost
```

We already explained these directories and the type of files stored in them, as well as the purposes of these directories. Now we will give you some details about them. In this context, the 10.1.2 directory in the EBSapps directory is the 10.1.2 Oracle Home, and the subdirectories of this directories are the same as you can find almost in any 10.1.2 Oracle Home.

The appl and comn subdirectories of the EBSapps directory are EBS-specific directories, as mentioned earlier, and by just looking at the subdirectories residing in them, you can probably understand their purposes. As shown in the tree command output, in the appl directory you have all the EBS product directories, and in the comn directory you have directories such as utils and shared_libs that are there to be used by the application stack.

The FMW_Home directory delivers the Fusion Middleware technology, with its subdirectories that contain the EBS domain, web tier, and WebLogic-related utilities. So, FMW_Home delivers the Fusion Middleware that comes bundled with EBS 12.2 and has the classic FMW directory structure inside of it.

Lastly, the inst directory is another EBS-specific directory, which was introduced with EBS R12. The inst directory, as explained earlier, stores some of the configuration files, the context file, and application service control scripts.

When you take a deeper look at one of the dual file system directories with the tree command, which produces more detailed output (as shown in Listing 4-4), you see that there are also several directories under the main subdirectories; they are named EBSapps, appl, comn, FMW_Home, and inst.

Listing 4-4 shows the output of a tree command that is used for listing the subdirectories of the fs1 file system; this is what the directory structure of the EBS dual file system looks like.

Listing 4-4. Directory Structure for Representing the Subdirectories of fs1

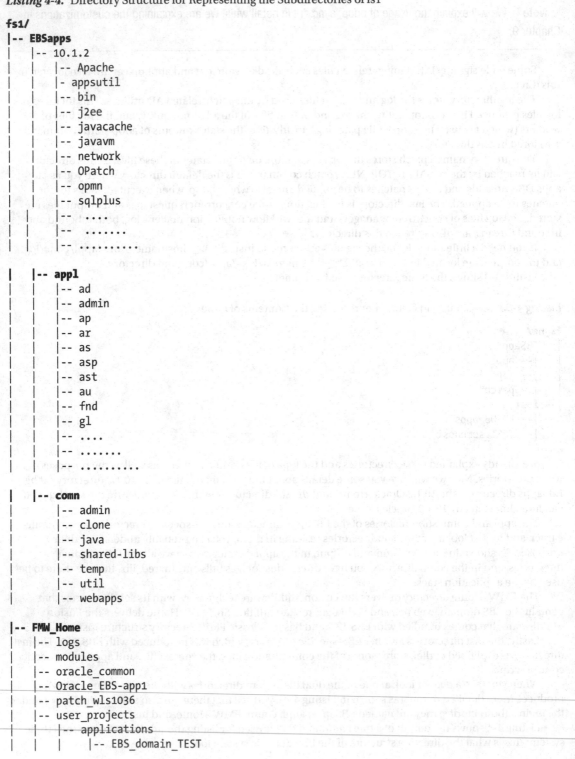

```
fs1/
|-- EBSapps
|   |-- 10.1.2
|   |   |-- Apache
|   |   |- appsutil
|   |   |-- bin
|   |   |-- j2ee
|   |   |-- javacache
|   |   |-- javavm
|   |   |-- network
|   |   |-- OPatch
|   |   |-- opmn
|   |   |-- sqlplus
|   |   |-- ....
|   |   |-- .......
|   |   |-- .........
|
|   |-- appl
|   |   |-- ad
|   |   |-- admin
|   |   |-- ap
|   |   |-- ar
|   |   |-- as
|   |   |-- asp
|   |   |-- ast
|   |   |-- au
|   |   |-- fnd
|   |   |-- gl
|   |   |-- ....
|   |   |-- .......
|   |   |-- .........
|
|   |-- comn
|       |-- admin
|       |-- clone
|       |-- java
|       |-- shared-libs
|       |-- temp
|       |-- util
|       |-- webapps
|
|-- FMW_Home
|   |-- logs
|   |-- modules
|   |-- oracle_common
|   |-- Oracle_EBS-app1
|   |-- patch_wls1036
|   |-- user_projects
|   |   |-- applications
|   |   |   |-- EBS_domain_TEST
```

```
|   |   |   |     |-- ebs-3rdparty
|   |   |   |     |-- ebs-forms
|   |   |   |     |-- ebs-product
|   |   |   |     |-- servers
|   |   |-- domains
|   |   |   |-- EBS_domain_TEST
|   |   |   |     |-- autodeploy
|   |   |   |     |-- bin
|   |   |   |     |-- config
|   |   |   |     |-- console-ext
|   |   |   |     |-- init-info
|   |   |   |     |-- lib
|   |   |   |     |-- opmn
|   |   |   |     |-- pending
|   |   |   |     |-- security
|   |   |   |     |-- servers
|   |   |   |     |-- sysman
|   |   |   |     |-- tmp
|   |-- utils
|   |   |-- bsu
|   |-- webtier
|   | -- wlserver_10.3
|-- inst
    |-- apps
```

As shown in the tree command output, many directories are present in the EBS 12.2 application file system architecture. In fact, there are more directories than displayed in the previous tree command output, as the tree command output used for producing the previous output shows the directory level with only a depth of 3.

Nevertheless, you don't need to memorize all these directories, their full paths, and their usages. You don't even need to cd to most of these directories during your daily administration work. The only thing you need to know is the environment variables that are set when the EBS environment file (in other words, EBSapps.env) is sourced.

The database tier has a simpler file system architecture that core DBAs are already familiar with, as shown in Listing 4-5.

In Listing 4-5, you see a tree command and its output, which displays the database tier base directory with all of its main subdirectories. The output in Listing 4-5 is a bit consolidated, and some of the directories that reside in Oracle Home have been extracted, as these directories are not special for EBS 12.2 and can be found in any Oracle Database installation. Also in Listing 4-5, we focus on EBS-specific database directories and describe critical directories near their directory names.

Listing 4-5. tree Command Output Representing the Contents of Database File System

```
[oracle@somehost /u01]$ cd install
[oracle@somehost install]$ tree -A -L 4 oraInventory PROD

PROD
|-- 11.2.0                  : ORACLE_HOME directory
|   |-- admin
|   |--apex
```

```
|   |-- appsutil              : appsutil directory that accommodate the application utilities
|   |   |-- admin
|   |   |-- bin
|   |   |-- clone
|   |   |   |--bin             : directory that stores the cloning scripts such as adcfgclone.
|   |   |                        pl (The cloning scripts and the cloning process itself will be
|   |   |                        explained with all of their details in Chapter 11.)
|   |   |   |--context
|   |   |   |--data
|   |   |   |--dbts
|   |   |   |--html
|   |   |   |--jlib
|   |   |   |--jre
|   |   |   |--oui
|   |   |-- driver
|   |   |-- html
|   |   |-- install
|   |   |-- java
|   |   |-- jre
|   |   |-- log
|   |   |-- media
|   |   |-- <sid>_<hostname>.xml     : CONTEXT_FILE for the database
|   |   |-- out
|   |   |-- outbound
|   |   |-- perl
|   |   |-- scripts            : Directory containing the scripts that can
|   |   |                        be used for EBS related database management
|   |   |                        activities.
|   |   |   |--<sid>_<hostname>
|   |   |   |   |-- adautocfg.sh      : Autoconfig script
|   |   |   |   |-- adchknls.pl       : script for checking existence of ORACLE_HOME/nls/
|   |   |   |                           data/9idata and cr9idata.pl in that directory.
|   |   |   |   |-- addbctl.sh        : Wrapper script for stopping and starting the
|   |   |   |                           database
|   |   |   |   |-- addlnctl.sh       : Script for starting and stopping the database
|   |   |   |                           listener
|   |   |   |   |-- adexecsql.pl      : Script that executes all sql scripts that
|   |   |   |                           update the profiles in an AutoConfig run
|   |   |   |   |-- adlsnodes.sh      : Wrapper script to check if the cluster manager
|   |   |   |                           is available in a RAC environment
|   |   |   |   |-- adpreclone.pl     : Script for taking a preclone
|   |   |   |   |-- adstopdb.sql      : Actual script that is used by addbctl.sh for
|   |   |   |                           stopping the database
|   |   |   |   |-- adstrtdb.sql      : Actual script that is used by addbctl.sh for
|   |   |   |                           starting the database
|   |   |   |--sql
|   |   |-- bin
|   |   |-- css
|   |   |-- ctx
|   |   |-- dbs
|   |   |-- inventory
```

```
|   |-- j2ee
|   |-- javavm
|   |-- jdbc
|   |-- jdev
|   |-- jdk
|   |-- jlib
|   |-- lib
|   |-- log
|   |-- network                              : directory that accommodates the network
|                                              configuration file of EBS database tier.
|   |   |-- admin
|   |   |   |-- <sid>_<hostname>
|   |   |   |   |-- listener.ora             : configuration file for the database listener.
|   |   |   |   |-- listener_ifile.ora       : additional configuration file for the
|   |   |   |   |                               database listener
|   |   |   |   |-- sqlnet_ifile.ora         : sqlnet additional configuration file
|   |   |   |   |-- sqlnet.log               : sqlnet log file
|   |   |   |   |-- sqlnet.ora               : sqlnet configuration file
|   |   |   |   |-- tnsnames.ora             : TNS configuration file
|   |-- install
|   |-- jlib
|   |-- lib
|   |-- log
|   |-- mesg
|   |-- tools
|   |-- trace
|   |-- Opatch                               : Directory where opatch tool, that is used for
|                                              patching EBS database tier resides.
|   |-- opmn
|   |-- <SID>_<hostname>.env                 : environment file that can be source for setting
|                                              Oracle Home environment.
|   |-- oraInst.loc                          : file that points to the oraInventory location of EBS
|                                              database tier. (
|   |-- owm
|   |-- perl
|   |-- rdbms
|   |-- root.sh
|   |-- sqlplus
|   |-- xdk
|-- data                                     : directory that contains the database files
|   |-- a_archive01.dbf
|   |-- a_int01.dbf
|   |-- a_int02.dbf
|   |-- a_media01.dbf
|   |-- a_media
...
....
....... - - list continues.
```

165

As shown in the directory tree represented in Listing 4-5, there are two main directories named oraInventory and PROD that reside in the main installation directory (in this example /u01/install) in the database tier.

If you take a look at the directory structure represented in Listing 4-5 more specifically, you see that the database tier consists of an Oracle Home (PROD/11.2.0) directory for supplying the Oracle RDBMS software, an inventory (oraInventory) directory for storing the inventory information of the EBS database, and database files (PROD/data) that contribute Oracle Database.

Inside these directories, you have lots of subdirectories such as TNS configuration files, control scripts, and database files, which will be known, used, and managed by you.

It is important to know that the paths for the main directories can be specified during the installation of EBS 12.2, so the directory names may differ according to the installation. Also, if you use ASM to store your database files, then naturally the database files are placed in the ASM disk groups rather than traditional operating system directories. So, if ASM is used for storing the database files, you can't see the database file on your traditional file systems. And if that's the case, then you can only see the database files by using the asmcmd command or by querying the respective v$ views, which can be used to get information from the ASM file system.

Lastly, it is important to mention that most of the EBS configuration files such as TNS files or environment file can be re-created using the AutoConfig utility, which is explained in Chapter 8.

The appsutil directory can also be re-created in the application tier using the admkappsutil.pl script and then can be transferred to the database tier, as explained in Chapter 3.

As explained earlier, EBS has a complex directory structure consisting of several subdirectories. It is complex because it has several subdirectories, and you use the files and scripts stored in these subdirectories in your daily administration works. It is hard to memorize these directory paths, and it is also not necessary to memorize them, as they may change according to the EBS installations. Thanks to Oracle, you have environment variables that point to the relevant directories and that save you from memorizing the whole directory structure of EBS 12.2 with all the subdirectories.

That is, using EBS environment variables, it is much easier to navigate to both the application and database file systems, as you can directly cd to the directories using the environment files or open a file such as the context file using the environment variable called $CONTEXT_FILE, rather than dealing with long directory paths and trying to find where the directory or file that you need to work with is located.

Let's now take a look at these environment variables, see how to set them, and get to know the most important environment variables that you will use in your daily administration work.

Oracle EBS 12.2 Environment Variables

As mentioned while explaining the directory structures previously in this chapter, there are environment variables both in the application tier and in the database tier, and they are defined to make your job easier while dealing with the file system directories and files.

These environment variables are set by apps DBAs using the relevant scripts that come with the EBS installations. You usually execute or source these environment scripts just after logging in to the environment with the relevant application or database OS user. Alternatively, you sometimes add these scripts to the bash files that are sourced automatically by the operating system during every login operation. The advantage of using these bash files for automatic execution or sourcing these scripts and files is that it also automates the settings needed for the environment variables; thus, you can log in to the operating system and start using an environment variable without a need to source or execute any environment scripts or files. Using such an automated environment setting method eases your job as an apps DBA because it saves you from executing a script to set the relevant environment in every login.

So, let's start with the application tier by getting the know the script that sets the environment variables, the descriptions of most important environment variables themselves, and the automated method for setting these environment variables in every login.

In the application tier, the environment variables are set using the EBSapps.env file, which resides in the base directory at the same directory level as fs1, fs2, and fs_ne, as shown in Listing 4-6.

Listing 4-6. tree Command Output Displaying the EBSapps.env Script, Which Is Located Under the base directory

```
|-/u01/install/APPS/   (The base directory)
|------ EBSapps.env    (Script that is used for setting application Tier environment variables)
|------ fs1
|------ fs2
|------ fs_ne
```

We already explained the EBSapps.env file in previous chapters, but we will give an example of its usage because it is the main file that sets the application environment in EBS 12.2.

To set all the application tier environment variables at once, the EBSapps.env file can be executed, and it must be executed with an argument. The argument can be patch or run. That is, if you source the environment file with the command . EBSapps.env run, it sets the run environment. Alternatively, if you execute it with the command . EBSapps.env patch, it sets the patch environment.

The patch environment should be set in cases when you as the apps DBA wants to operate on the patch file system. In other words, when the patch environment is set, the environment variables are defined to point to the directories or files that reside in the patch file system. So, if you use the APPL_TOP environment variable to cd to the directory that stores the EBS product files, then you will find yourself in the EBSapps/appl directory that resides in the patch file system environment. Similarly, if you use the CONTEXT_FILE environment variable to reach the context file of the environment, you will reach the context file that resides in the patch file system. Moreover, if you use sqlplus command to connect to the database, you will find yourself in the patch edition of the EBS database.

Listing 4-7 shows the values of the APPL_TOP, CONTEXT_FILE, and TWO_TASK environment variables as well as the TNS entry that is defined for the patch edition after setting the patch environment using the EBSapps.env script.

Also in Listing 4-7, you can see that if you use sqlplus, it directly tries to connect to the patch edition in the EBS database; however, it can't connect to the database because there is no patch edition because the system in Listing 4-7 is not in a patching cycle (adop patching cycle).

The way to make sqlplus connect to the patch edition is using the TWO_TASK environment variable, which is the default environment variable used by the sqlplus utility to retrieve the database connection information. When TWO_TASK is set to the TNS alias that points to the patch edition service name defined in tnsnames.ora, sqlplus will try to connect to the patch edition of the EBS database.

That is, as the patch environment sets TWO_TASK to be the TNS alias defined for the patch edition of the database, sqlplus tries to connect to the database patch edition if it is invoked without specifying a connect identifier. This behavior of sqlplus should not be your focus, but it clearly shows the effect of setting the patch environment, as shown in Listing 4-7.

Listing 4-7. The environment Variables, the TNS Entry for the Patch Edition and the behavior of sqlplus when the patch environment is set

```
[applmgr@somehost ~]$ . /u01/install/APPS/EBSapps.env patch

E-Business Suite Environment Information
----------------------------------------
RUN File System           : /u01/install/APPS/fs1/EBSapps/appl
PATCH File System         : /u01/install/APPS/fs2/EBSapps/appl
Non-Editioned File System : /u01/install/APPS/fs_ne

DB Host: somehost.somedomain  Service/SID: TEST
```

Sourcing the **PATCH** File System ..

[applmgr@somehost ~]$ echo $APPL_TOP
/u01/install/APPS/**fs2**/EBSapps/appl

[applmgr@somehost ~]$ echo $CONTEXT_FILE
/u01/install/APPS/**fs2**/inst/apps/TEST_somehost/appl/admin/TEST_somehost.xml

[applmgr@somehost ~]$ echo $TWO_TASK
TEST_patch

Contents of tnnames.ora stating the TEST_patch(TWO_TASK) TNS entry:

```
TEST_patch=
        (DESCRIPTION=
                (ADDRESS=(PROTOCOL=tcp)(HOST=somehost.somedomain.)(PORT=1521))
            (CONNECT_DATA=
                (SERVICE_NAME=ebs_patch)
                (INSTANCE_NAME=TEST)
            )
        )
```

[applmgr@somehost ~]$ sqlplus apps/apps

sqlplus: Release 10.1.0.5.0 - Production on Sat Aug 22 16:15:05 2015

Copyright (c) 1982, 2005, Oracle. All rights reserved.

ERROR:
ORA-00604: error occurred at recursive SQL level 1
ORA-20099: E-Business Suite Patch Edition does not exist.
ORA-06512: at line 29

Setting the patch environment is needed only in rare cases. Investigating a patch failure or implementing a DMZ configuration are some examples where you would set the patch environment, but normally you won't use the patch environment often.

So, you normally do your administration work using the run environment, which can be set by sourcing EBSapps.env with the run argument, as mentioned earlier.

Listing 4-8 shows how to set the run file system using EBSapps.env, as well as the values of the environment variables and behavior of sqlplus after setting the run environment.

Listing 4-8. The environment Variables, the TNS Entry for the Run Edition and the behavior of sqlplus when the run environment is set

```
[applmgr@somehost APPS]$ . EBSapps.env run

  E-Business Suite Environment Information
  --------------------------------------
  RUN File System          : /u01/install/APPS/fs1/EBSapps/appl
  PATCH File System        : /u01/install/APPS/fs2/EBSapps/appl
  Non-Editioned File System : /u01/install/APPS/fs_ne

  DB Host: somehost.somedomain  Service/SID: TEST
```

Sourcing the RUN File System ...

```
[applmgr@somehost APPS]$ echo $APPL_TOP
/u01/install/APPS/fs1/EBSapps/appl
[applmgr@somehost APPS]$ echo $CONTEXT_FILE
/u01/install/APPS/fs1/inst/apps/TEST_somehost/appl/admin/TEST_somehost.xml
[applmgr@somehost APPS]$ echo $TWO_TASK
TEST
```

Contents of tnsnames.ora stating the TEST(TWO_TASK) TNS entry:

```
TEST=
        (DESCRIPTION=
                (ADDRESS=(PROTOCOL=tcp)(HOST=somehost.somedomain(PORT=1521))
            (CONNECT_DATA=
                (SERVICE_NAME=TEST)
                (INSTANCE_NAME=TEST)
            )
        )
 [applmgr@somehost APPS]$ sqlplus apps/apps
SQL>
```

As shown, the directory and file paths for the environment variables shown in Listing 4-2 and Listing 4-1 differ from each other. That is, as the patch edition is in fs2 and the run edition is in fs1, you see the directory pointed at by APPL_TOP and the file pointed at by the CONTEXT_FILE environment variables are different from each other. Also, you see a similar difference in TWO_TASK that points to the default TNS entry used by sqlplus to get the connection information for the EBS database.

Moreover, you see a failure in the sqlplus output as shown in Listing 4-7, as it tries to connect to the patch edition that does not even exist, and you see a successful sqlplus connection in Listing 4-8, as TWO_TASK is set to the service that is defined for connecting to the current/run edition of the database.

So, we have explained how to set the environment variables in the EBS 12.2 application tier, and we have shown the difference between the run and patch edition environments by providing you with the values of some of the environment variables and by showing the situation in sqlplus connections after setting each of these environments.

Let's now take a closer look at the environment variables used in the EBS 12.2 application tier and get to know their values and descriptions. As every standard product has its own directory named with its short name and pointed at by an environment variable in the form of SHORTNAME_TOP and also as there are several technologies and tools used in EBS 12.2, there are several environment variables used in EBS application tier.

Fortunately, it is not required that you know every single environment variable and the cases where they may be needed; usually apps DBAs do not need to use most of them.

But know that you can use the env command at any time to the display the environment variables that are set by executing the EBSapps.env file, just to satisfy your curiosity. Listing 4-9 shows a truncated env command output that shows a bunch of environment variables set by the EBSapps.env script.

Listing 4-9. env Command Output That Shows Application Tier Environment Variables

```
[applmgr@somehost APPSDEVEL]$ env|more
PRP_TOP=/u01/install/APPSDEVEL/fs2/EBSapps/appl/prp/12.0.0
OA_DOC=/u01/install/APPSDEVEL/fs2/EBSapps/comn/doc
PJI_TOP=/u01/install/APPSDEVEL/fs2/EBSapps/appl/pji/12.0.0
IGC_TOP=/u01/install/APPSDEVEL/fs2/EBSapps/appl/igc/12.0.0
```

```
FPA_TOP=/u01/install/APPSDEVEL/fs2/EBSapps/appl/fpa/12.0.0
EGO_TOP=/u01/install/APPSDEVEL/fs2/EBSapps/appl/ego/12.0.0
ASG_TOP=/u01/install/APPSDEVEL/fs2/EBSapps/appl/asg/12.0.0
APPL_TOP=/u01/install/APPSDEVEL/fs2/EBSapps/appl
AFJSMARG=-server -Xmx384m -Doracle.apps.fnd.common.Pool.leak.mode=stderr:off -verbose:gc
APPLLIB=lib
IRC_TOP=/u01/install/APPSDEVEL/fs2/EBSapps/appl/irc/12.0.0
ANT_CONTRIB=/u01/install/APPSDEVEL/fs2/FMW_Home/modules/net.sf.antcontrib_1.1.0.0_1-0b2
APPLSQL=sql
INV_TOP=/u01/install/APPSDEVEL/fs2/EBSapps/appl/inv/12.0.0
IEC_TOP=/u01/install/APPSDEVEL/fs2/EBSapps/appl/iec/12.0.0
....
.......
......... list continues...
```

Although we already mentioned that apps DBAs should not memorize every single environment variable in EBS 12.2 as most of the environment variables are not used during the administration work, this does not mean that most of the environment variables in EBS 12.2 are not critical.

In fact, most of these environment variables are used internally by EBS applications for actions such as setting their class paths or realizing the places where their binaries reside. That's why if an application or technology component cannot use an environment variable that it needs to use, then it may not behave well and will probably crash.

In addition, there are some environment variables that every apps DBA should know by heart. You can cd to the directories they point at and use the files residing in the directories they point at when needed during your daily administration work. Some of these environment variables, such as the CONTEXT_FILE environment file, point directly to the files rather than that directories, and also some of them such as FILE_EDITION can be used only for getting information about the environment.

Also, it is important to remind you that these environment variables are set automatically when you execute the EBSapps.env script. So, the directories or files that are pointed at by the environment variables can differ according to the environment being patched or run. That is, if the EBSapps.env script is executed with the run argument, it sets the run edition, and if the EBSapps.env script is executed with the patch argument, it sets the patch edition. So, naturally the environment variables are set accordingly.

The most important environment variables that an apps DBA will use during daily administration work are listed in Table 4-1. Table 4-1 summarizes the environment variables for both the run edition and the patch edition, provides the associated directories, and describes the environment variables. Note that the term <base> in Table 4-1 is used for describing the base directory that is specified by installing EBS 12.2 using the Rapidwiz Install Wizard. So, it is the root directory for EBS, where all the other directories reside.

Table 4-1. *Environment Variables, Directories, and Descriptions*

Environment Variable	Directory/File/Value	Description
RUN_BASE	<base>/fs1 or <base>/fs2 (it can point to fs1 or fs2, according to the fact that it points to the current run file system)	Base directory of the run edition file system.
PATCH_BASE	<base>/fs1 or <base>/fs2 (it can point to fs1 or fs2, according to the fact that it points to the current patch file system)	Base directory of the patch edition file system.
CONTEXT_NAME	Example: TEST_somehost	Context name of the environment in the form of <SID>_<hostname>.
NE_BASE	<base>/fs_ne	Base directory of the noneditioned file system (fs_ne).
APPL_TOP	Run edition: $RUN_BASE/EBSapps/appl Patch edition: $PATCH_BASE/EBSapps/appl	Directory that stores the EBS product files. Product directories pointed at by the PRODUCT_TOP environment variables are also located in this directory.
APPL_TOP_NE	$NE_BASE/EBSapps/appl	Noneditioned APPL_TOP directory.
COMMON_TOP	Run edition: $RUN_BASE/EBSapps/comn Patch edition: $PATCH_BASE/EBSapps/comn	Directory that stores their common libraries.
INST_TOP	Run edition: $RUN_BASE/ inst/apps/$CONTEXT_NAME Patch edition: $PATCH_BASE/inst/apps/$CONTEXT_NAME	Directory that stores the configuration files and also files like application service control scripts.
ORACLE_HOME	Run edition: $RUN_BASE/EBSapps/10.1.2 Patch edition: $PATCH_BASE/EBSapps/10.1.2	10.1.2 Oracle Home directory.
FMW_HOME	Run edition: $RUN_BASE/EBSapps/FMW_Home Patch edition: $PATCH_BASE/EBSapps/FMW_Home	Fusion Middleware Home directory.
JAVA_TOP	$COMMON_TOP/java/classes	Resides in the directory pointed at by COMMON_TOP and stores the Java classes used by the applications.
EBS_DOMAIN_HOME	$FMW_HOME/ FMW_Home/user_projects/domains/EBS_domain_<SID>	Directory that stores the EBS WebLogic domain.
ADMIN_SCRIPTS_HOME	$INST_TOP/apps/$CONTEXT_NAME/admin/scripts	Directory that stores the application service control scripts.
FND_TOP	$APPL_TOP/fnd/12.0.0	Foundation top directory.
AD_TOP	$APPL_TOP/ad/12.0.0	Applications DBA directory.

(continued)

Table 4-1. (*continued*)

Environment Variable	Directory/File/Value	Description
CUSTOM_TOPS Ex: XXABC_TOP	$APPL_TOP/<custom_module_short_name>12.0.0	Custom products directories.
CONTEXT_FILE	$INST_TOP/ apps/$CONTEXT_NAME/appl/admin/$CONTEXT_NAME.xml	Application context file.
PRODUCT_TOPS Ex: PO_TOP	$APPL_TOP/<standard_module_short_name/12.0.0 Example: $APPL_TOP/po/12.0.0	Standard EBS product directories.
LOG_HOME	$INST_TOP/apps/$CONTEXT_NAME/logs	Directory that stores application service control script log files, as well as 10.1.2 Oracle Home–related forms log files.
ADOP_LOG_HOME	$NE_BASE/EBSapps/log/adop	Directory that stores the log file of the adop utility.
IAS_ORACLE_HOME	$FMW_HOME/webtier	FMW web tier Home directory.
FORMS_TRACE_DIR	$INST_TOP/ apps/$CONTEXT_NAME/logs/ora/10.1.2/forms	Directory that stores the forms traces produced when forms runtime diagnostics is enabled.
APPLCSF/$APPLLOG	$NE_BASE/inst/$CONTEXT_NAME/logs/appl/conc	Directory that stores the concurrent request and manager log files.
FILE_EDITION	Returns "run" or "patch" according to the environment that is set	Shows current file system in use (patch or run).

As shown in Table 4-1, even if you consolidated the list of environment variables and make it include only the environment variables that you use often, there are actually more than 300 application tier environment variables that are set by sourcing the environment file (EBSApps.env) in the EBS 12.2 application tier.

One thing that may attract your attention is that the files or directories the environment variables point at when the environment is set to the patch edition. As shown in Table 4-1, it is not hard to guess the corresponding patch edition value of an environment variable, because for most of the environment variables that point to an application directory, the only difference between the patch and run edition values of them is the root directory in the path being fs1 or fs2, in other words, the run base or patch base. That is, if the run file system is fs2 and if a run edition environment variable is defined to point to a directory /u01/fs2/directory_name, then its corresponding patch edition version should be pointing to /u01/fs1/directory_name.

In the next sections, you will see how to use these environment variables and strengthen your knowledge about them, but before going there, let's take a look at the database tier and explain how to set the environment variables for working in the database node. We will also describe the database environment variables. The database tier relies on a simpler file system architecture, as mentioned earlier. It is simpler because it is based on the classic Oracle RDBMS file system that every Oracle core DBA and even Oracle database operators are familiar with.

So, just like a stand-alone Oracle database node, the EBS database node is based on an Oracle Home, an Oracle inventory (oraInventory), and a file system that stores the database files. The database files in EBS 12.2 may be put on a cooked file system that is supported by the underlying operating system (for example, ext3, ext4 for Linux, or NTFS for Windows).

The database files may also be placed on ASM, which is based on the Grid Infrastructure; in other words, it comes with the Grid Installation, which is available in the EBS 12.2 Rapidwiz Install Wizard.

Using ASM is a requirement for multinode database installations, in other words, for EBS Real Application Clusters (RAC) installations. Using ASM to store the database files is preferred for single-node installations too.

In this manner, if you use ASM to store your database files, you definitely need to add the Grid Home to the directories that contribute the EBS database file system.

So if you use ASM to store your database files, then you can say that the database file system in EBS 12.2 is based on an Oracle Home, a Grid Home (optional), an Oracle inventory (oraInventory), and a file system(a cooked file system or ASM) that stores the database files.

As mentioned, there are three or four main directories in the EBS 12.2 database file system, which looks like a classic Oracle RDBMS Home. There are also some additional directories in the EBS database file system not found in standard Oracle Home installations.

The appsutil directory and the directory pointed at by the TNS_ADMIN environment variable are the additional directories. These EBS database-related directories reside in the Oracle Home directory, which is the main directory that constitutes the biggest part of the EBS 12.2 database file system architecture.

Let's take a look at the environment variables in the EBS 12.2 database tier, learn how to set them, see their values, and understand what they are used for. The database tier environment variables are set using the env script named <SID>_<hostname>.env (for example, TEST_somehost.env) that resides in the Oracle Home.

The environment script is created by AutoConfig and can be sourced after logging in to the database node operating system with the Oracle Database owner OS user account (for example, oracle), as shown in Listing 4-10. Note that, in this example, the Oracle Home directory is /u01/install/TEST/11.2.0.

Listing 4-10. Setting the Database Environment

```
[oracle@somehost ~]$ . /u01/install/TEST/11.2.0/TEST_somehost.env
```

After sourcing the environment file that resides in the ORACLE_HOME, if you use the env command to display the environment variables defined for your operating system terminal session, you will see the environment variables shown Listing 4-11.

Note that the env command output in Listing 4-11 is truncated to discard the unnecessary environment variables such as the environment variables named term or SHELL that are by default set by the operating system because they are not your focus since they are not related to EBS 12.2.

Listing 4-11. env Output Showing the Database Environment Variable Set After Sourcing the EBS Database Environment File

```
[oracle@somehost ~]$env | sort
ADJREOPTS=-Xms128M -Xmx512M
ADJVAPRG=/u01/install/TEST/11.2.0/appsutil/jre/bin/java
ADPERLPRG=/u01/install/TEST/11.2.0/perl/bin/perl
CONTEXT_FILE=/u01/install/TEST/11.2.0/appsutil/TEST_somehost.xml
CONTEXT_NAME=TEST_somehost
LANG=en_US.UTF-8
LD_LIBRARY_PATH=/u01/install/TEST/11.2.0/lib:/usr/X11R6/lib:/usr/openwin/lib:/u01
/install/TEST/11.2.0/lib:/usr/dt/lib:/u01/install/TEST/11.2.0/ctx/lib
LIBPATH=/u01/install/TEST/11.2.0/lib:/usr/X11R6/lib:/usr/openwin/lib:/u01
/install/TEST/11.2.0/lib:/usr/dt/lib:/u01/install/TEST/11.2.0/ctx/lib
NLS_DATE_FORMAT=DD-MON-RR
NLS_LANG=American_America.US7ASCII
NLS_NUMERIC_CHARACTERS=.,
```

```
NLS_SORT=binary
ORA_NLS10=/u01/install/TEST/11.2.0/nls/data/9idata
ORACLE_HOME=/u01/install/TEST/11.2.0
ORACLE_SID=TEST
PATH=/u01/install/TEST/11.2.0/perl/bin:/u01/install/TEST/11.2.0/bin:/usr/bin:/usr/sbin:/u01
/install/TEST/11.2.0/appsutil/jre/bin:/bin:/usr/bin/X11:/usr/local/bin:/u01/install/
TEST/11.2.0/perl/bin:/u01
/install/TEST/11.2.0/bin:/usr/bin:/usr/sbin:/u01/install/TEST/11.2.0/appsutil/jre/bin:/bin:/
usr/bin/X11:/usr
/local/bin:/usr/lib64/qt-3.3/bin:/usr/local/bin:/bin:/usr/bin:/usr/local/sbin:/usr/sbin:/
sbin:/home/oracle/bin:.:.
PERL5LIB=/u01/install/TEST/11.2.0/perl/lib/5.10.0:/u01/install/TEST/11.2.0/perl/lib/site_
perl/5.10.0:/u01
/install/TEST/11.2.0/appsutil/perl
SHLIB_PATH=/u01/install/TEST/11.2.0/lib:/usr/lib:/u01/install/TEST/11.2.0/ctx/lib
TNS_ADMIN=/u01/install/TEST/11.2.0/network/admin/TEST_somehost
```

The environment variables that are highlighted with bold in Table 4-2 are the environment variables you use during your daily administration work, and the remaining list of environment variables such as ADPERLPRG, LANG, and PERL5LIB, are the environment variables that are transparent but still needed in order to administer the database tier components properly.

Table 4-2 explains these environment variables, Table 4-2 explains these environment variables, with corresponding example values and descriptions.

Table 4-2. *Environment Variables, the Example Environment Variable Values, and Descriptions*

Environment Variable	Example Directory/File/Value	Description
NLS_SORT	Binary	Environment variable to specify the sort mechanism for enabling the linguistic sorting of results. It can be used by any operating system tool and also by some scripts residing in appsutil to set their environments and produce their outputs accordingly.
ADJREOPTS	-Xms128M -Xmx512M	This is used for specifying Java command-line options. Scripts like adconfig.pl use this environment variable for executing their Java commands with the desired options.
NLS_LANG	American_America.US7ASCII	Oracle's standard environment variable in the form of language_territory.character set. It is used for specifying the locale for Oracle tools running on the database node. It is used by most of the Oracle binaries, libraries, and scripts that reside in Oracle Home. For example, sqlplus produces its output in the language specified by NLS_LANG.
PERL5LIB	/u01/install/TEST/11.2.0/ perl/lib/5.10.0:/u01/install/ TEST/11.2.0/perl/lib/ site_perl/5.10.0:/u01/install/ TEST/11.2.0/appsutil/perl	Environment variable that specifies the list of directories that store Perl library files. Since Perl is used often in Oracle products, the PERL5LIB environment variable is required for the Perl scripts residing in Oracle Home to run properly.

(continued)

Table 4-2. (*continued*)

Environment Variable	Example Directory/File/Value	Description
LD_LIBRARY_PATH	/u01/install/TEST/11.2.0/lib:/usr/X11R6/lib:/usr/openwin/lib:/u01/install/TEST/11.2.0/lib:/usr/dt/lib:/u01/install/TEST/11.2.0/ctx/lib	The LD_LIBRARY_PATH environment variable is used for specifying the linker in Linux OS to search for libraries. It is used by OS, and it is set to include the directories in Oracle Home that store the Oracle libraries. It is used by the OS linker to find the needed shared libraries, as these shared libraries are used widely in the Oracle RDBMS.
ORA_NLS10	/u01/install/TEST/11.2.0/nls/data/9idata	ORA_NLSXX environment variables are used to indicate where the Oracle RDBMS/client software can locate the definitions of character sets stored in .nlb files in ORA_NLS** directories.
		EBS has a requirement for ORA_NLS10 to set the directory where the needed nlb files are located, as well as the $ORACLE_HOME/nls/data/9idatis that directory used in all of the EBS 12.2 installations.
ORACLE_SID	TEST	Database SID of the EBS database that is used by command-line tools like sqlplus when executed in your terminal sessions.
LIBPATH	/u01/install/TEST/11.2.0/lib:/usr/X11R6/lib:/usr/openwin/lib:/u01/install/TEST/11.2.0/lib:/usr/dt/lib:/u01/install/TEST/11.2.0/ctx/lib	LIBPATH is used in AIX and is the equivalent of the LD_LIBRARY_PATH environment variable in Linux. Although you are focused on Linux OS in this book and although it is unnecessary, you can see that the environment script sets the LIBPATH for Linux too.
TNS_ADMIN	/u01/install/TEST/11.2.0/network/admin/TEST_somehost	This environment variable points to the directory where the sqlnet configuration file for the EBS database is stored. Tools like sqlplus or the listener use this environment variable to get the network configuration information for use in their operations.
PATH	/u01/install/TEST/11.2.0/perl/bin: /u01/install/TEST/11.2.0/bin: /u01/install/TEST/11.2.0/appsutil/jre/bin :/bin: /usr/local/bin . . .	Standard Linux PATH environment variable that is used by the shell (for example, bash) to determine the directories to search for executable files. It is appended to include the binary directories in Oracle Home.
ADJVAPRG	/u01/install/TEST/11.2.0/appsutil/jre /bin/java	Environment variable set to Java in the appsutil directory. It is used by AD scripts located in appsutil to run Java commands with the appropriate Java version that comes bundled with appsutil.

(*continued*)

Table 4-2. (*continued*)

Environment Variable	Example Directory/File/Value	Description
CONTEXT_NAME	TEST_somehost	The context name that is used for naming the subdirectories of some main directories residing in Oracle Home. It is in the form of <SID>_<db_hostname>. The directory pointed at by TNS_ADMIN is an example of its usage. In a standard installation, the sqlnet configuration files are placed in the $ORACLE_HOME/network/admin directory. On the other hand, in an EBS database node, the sqlnet configuration files are put in to the $ORACLE_HOME/network/admin/$CONTEXT_NAME directory.
CONTEXT_FILE	/u01/install/TEST/11.2.0/appsutil/TEST_somehost.xml	The environment variable that points to the database context file that is used by AutoConfig.
ADPERLPRG	/u01/install/TEST/11.2.0/perl/bin/perl	The environment variable that points to the Perl executable, which should be used for executing the Perl scripts that reside in Oracle Home.
NLS_NUMERIC_CHARACTERS	.,	Environment variable that specifies the characters to use as the group separator and decimal character. It is used commonly by the tools in Oracle Home.
ORACLE_HOME	/u01/install/TEST/11.2.0	Environment variable that points to the directory where the Oracle software is installed.
NLS_DATE_FORMAT	DD-MON-RR	Environment variable that specifies the default date format to use with the TO_CHAR and TO_DATE database functions. It is used commonly by the tools and binaries in Oracle Home to set the date format used in database sessions.

Although the environment variable list given in Table 4-2 seems a little long, there are actually a few environment variables that are used in your daily administration work in the database tier. That is, apps DBAs mostly use the ORACLE_HOME, ORACLE_SID, and TNS_ADMIN environment variables to connect and administer the database tier components. The work done varies according to the situation, but mostly the database tier work is based on standard maintenance operations such as patching the database tier and stopping or starting the database and listeners.

At this point, we have explained the EBS file systems by giving an overview of both the application and database file system architectures, including the file system concepts such as dual and nonedition file systems in the application tier. We also introduced the important environment variables and gave general information about the environment variables used in EBS 12.2. Now that you have gotten to know the file system architecture and the environment variables used in both the EBS application and the database tiers, let's continue with some examples so you can learn how to navigate the application and database tiers and accomplish certain administration tasks.

Working with Environment Variables on the Application Tier and Navigating the Application File System

As mentioned earlier, you just need to use the environment variables to accomplish your admin tasks in EBS 12.2. Using environment variables rather than memorizing and navigating the directories and files is a more efficient way to perform administration work. When you need to use the OS terminal to do some maintenance work such as stopping/starting the EBS services, running AutoConfig, executing cloning scripts, and so on, environment variables ease your job, because they save you from dealing with several important factors such as complex directory names, paths, and file names.

In addition to environment variables' general handiness, dealing with the directory names or file names may be a headache in multitier EBS 12.2 environments, which consists of multiple applications and/ or multiple database nodes. Also, if there are multiple EBS environments for you to administer such as the DEV, TEST, and PROD environments, actions such as navigating in the varying directory paths will be troublesome. That is, although the directory skin that comes with the standard installation may seem similar, it actually differs because most of the directory paths in EBS 12.2 contain the context name that is derived by the application server's hostname and the database SID of the EBS environments.

In this manner, the directory names, important file names (for example, context file), and paths in a TEST EBS instance may not be the same as the directories names, important file names, and paths in a PROD EBS instance. So, you are probably responsible for administrating all the EBS instances in your corporate networks, and using the environment variables is a more logical way for you to deal with these varying directory and file names.

In EBS 12.2 almost all the technology components and scripts use these environment files; it is impossible to administer these components or run these scripts without an environment (like a shell or terminal) where the EBS environment variables are set. So, as using the environment variables are crucial for administrating EBS 12.2, we'll give you a better understanding of their usages and see how they ease your jobs in the OS terminal by walking through the following scenarios.

Scenario 1, Scenario 2, and Scenario 3 in the following sections show how to use the environment variables in the EBS 12.2 application tier for accomplishing certain administration tasks.

Scenario 1: Starting the Application Services

Log in as the applmgr user, set your runtime environment using the EBSapps.env script, and then change your current working directory to the administration scripts.

Set your runtime environment using EBSapps.env, which is located in the base directory as follows. Suppose the base directory is /u01/install.

```
[applmgr@somehost ~]$cd /u01/install

[applmgr@somehost ~]$. EBSapps.env run

  E-Business Suite Environment Information
  ----------------------------------------
  RUN File System          : /u01/install/TEST/fs2/EBSapps/appl
  PATCH File System        : /u01/install/TEST/fs1/EBSapps/appl
  Non-Editioned File System : /u01/install/TEST/fs_ne

  DB Host: somehost.somedomain  Service/SID: TEST

  Sourcing the RUN File System ...
```

At this point, your runtime environment is set, and you can start using EBS-specific environment variables. For this example, you need to change your working directory where the administration script is located. So, you use the $ADMIN_SCRIPTS_HOME environment variable with the cd command.

```
[applmgr@somehost ~]$ cd $ADMIN_SCRIPTS_HOME
[applmgr@somehost scripts]$
```

Your current working directory is set to the directory where the administration scripts are located. As shown by the following pwd command, you can use the ADMIN_SCRIPTS_HOME environment variable to set the actual directory without knowing the full path of it.

```
[applmgr@somehost scripts]$
pwd
/u01/install/TEST/fs2/inst/apps/TEST_somehost/admin/scripts
```

As mentioned earlier, the administration scripts are located in the directory pointed at by ADMIN_SCRIPTS_HOME, and the following ls command output lists these scripts as a confirmation. Note that the following ls output is truncated to exclude some unnecessary files.

```
[applmgr@somehost scripts]$ ls
adadminsrvctl.sh  adapcctl.sh   adcmctl.sh    adformsrvctl.sh    adnodemgrctl.sh
adpreclone.pl     adstrtal.sh   jtffmctl.sh   mwactl.sh
adalnctl.sh       adautocfg.sh  adexecsql.pl  admanagedsrvctl.sh  adopmnctl.sh     adstpall.sh
gsmstart.sh       java.sh       mwactlwrpr.sh
```

Before going forward and using some of these scripts in the remaining part of this example, it is worthwhile to take a look at these administration scripts by going through their definitions and usages, as shown in Table 4-3.

Table 4-3. application Tier Administration Scripts Located in the $ORACLE_HOME/appsutil/scripts/$CONTEXT_NAME Directory

Script	Definition	Usage
adadminsrvctl.sh	Script for controlling WebLogic admin server.	sh adadminsrvctl.sh {start|stop|status} [forcepatchfs] [-nopromptmsg] [-silent]
adalnctl.sh	Script for controlling applications RPC listener.	sh adalnctl.sh {start|stop|status}
adapcctl.sh	Script for controlling Oracle HTTP Server.	sh adapcctl.sh {start|stop|status}
adautocfg.sh	Applications AutoConfig script.	sh adautocfg.sh
adcmctl.sh	Script for controlling concurrent managers.	sh adcmctl.sh {start|stop|abort|status} <apps_username>/<apps_password> or <Applications username/Applications password> There are additional parameters normally not used but may also be required in some fine-grained configurations: [sleep=<seconds>] [restart=<N|minutes>] [pmon=<iterations>] [quesiz=<pmon_iterations>] [diag=Y|N] [wait=Y|N]

(*continued*)

Table 4-3. (*continued*)

Script	Definition	Usage
adformsrvctl.sh	Script for controlling forms server in socket mode.	sh adformsrvctl.sh {start|stop|status}
admanagedsrvctl.sh	Script for controlling WebLogic managed servers.	sh admanagedsrvctl.sh {start|adminmode|resume|suspend|force_ suspend|stop|abort|status} <managed_server_ name> [-nopromptmsg] Or for starting all the managed servers that are parts of a service type at once: sh admanagedsrvctl.sh {startall|stopall} <servicetype> [-nopromptmsg]
adnodemgrctl.sh	Script for controlling the Node Manager.	sh adnodemgrctl.sh {start|status|stop} [-nopromptmsg]
adopmnctl.sh	Script for controlling opmn.	sh adopmnctl.sh {start|stop|status}
adstpall.sh	Script for stopping all the application services at once.	sh adstpall.sh <apps_username>/<apps_ password>
adstrtal.sh	Script for starting all the application services at once.	sh adstrtal.sh <apps_username>/<apps_ password>
gsmstart.sh	Script for starting FNDSM.	This must not be run from the command line. This script is referenced in the application tier's listener configuration file ($TNS_ ADMIN/listener.ora).
java.sh	Java script used by opmn and Java concurrent programs. It is used like a wrapper for calling Java with additional arguments.	This is used by opmn and Java concurrent programs, so is not used by apps DBAs.
jtffmctl.sh	Script for controlling the fulfillment server.	sh jtffmctl.sh {start|stop}
mwactl.sh	Script for starting and stopping the Telnet server used in EBS mobile applications.	sh mwactl.sh start/stop <PORT> There are additional parameters normally not used but may also be required in some fine-grained configurations: [-java_config "VM Settings"] [-mwatop MWA_ TOP] [-login username/password]
adpreclone.pl	Script for executing the preclone, which is a critical prerequisite operation for cloning EBS environments.	perl adpreclone.pl { appsTier	atTechStack	dev10gHome	fmwHome	wlsConfig	ohsConfig	appltop }
adexecsql.pl	Script used by AutoConfig for executing the SQL scripts that update the application profiles.	We as apps DBAs don't use this, but nevertheless the usage is as follows: perl adexecsql.pl sqlfile=<file> <apps_user> <apps_password>

So, once you reach the appsutil directory, where all the application control scripts listed in Table 4-3 reside, you use the relevant administration script to accomplish the required administration task.

As shown in Table 4-3, while you can stop, start, and check the statuses of all the application services using the application administration scripts, you can also take some critical action such as taking a preclone or executing an AutoConfig using the relevant application administration scripts.

In this example scenario, you use adstrtal.sh script for starting all the application services, as follows:

```
[applmgr@somehost scripts]$ sh adstrtal.sh apps/apps_password
```

Note that, as the security best practice, you can just execute the sh adstrtal.sh command without providing the apps/apps_password value.

The adstrtal.sh script will request the password for the apps user when it starts its execution, as shown next. This way, you can prevent the apps password from being saved in the Linux command history from which the password could be retrieved later.

```
[applmgr@somehost scripts]$ sh adstrtal.sh
You are running adstrtal.sh version 120.24.12020000.10
Enter the APPS username: apps
Enter the APPS password:
Enter the WebLogic Server password:
```

Scenario 2: You Want to Check the SMTP Server Settings in CONTEXT_FILE

Again, you log in as the applmgr user, set your runtime environment using the EBSapps.env script, and then change your current working directory to the directory that stores the administration scripts. You then just use the $CONTEXT_FILE environment variable to open the context file whose name may differ according to the environment and that is located in the $INST_TOP/ apps/$CONTEXT_NAME/appl/admin/ directory.

So, you use your favorite editor (vi for us) to open the context file and view its contents accordingly. In Figure 4-3, we see the part of the context file, which is related to the workflow mailer's smtp server(outbound) configuration.

```
[applmgr@somehost ~]$ vi $CONTEXT_FILE
```

```
</oa_cp_server>
<!-- Workflow -->
<oa_workflow_server>
   <hostname oa_var="s_javamailer_imaphost">someimapserver</hostname>
   <domain oa_var="s_javamailer_imapdomainname">somedomain</domain>
   <username oa_var="s_wf_admin_role">SYSADMIN</username>
   <username oa_var="s_javamailer_reply_to" customized="yes">oracle@someappsserver.com.tr</username>
   <username oa_var="s_javamailer_imap_user">oracle@somedomain.com.tr</username>
   <username oa_var="s_javamailer_outbound_user" customized="yes">oracle@someappsserver.com.tr</username>
</oa_workflow_server>
<oa_smtp_server>
   <hostname oa_var="s_smtphost" customized="yes">somesmtpserver</hostname>
   <domain oa_var="s_smtpdomainname" customized="yes">somedomain</domain>
```

Figure 4-3. *Applications context file*

Scenario 3: You Want to Connect to the EBS Database Remotely from the EBS Application Tier Node

Let's first try to connect to the database without setting the environment.

```
[applmgr@somehost ~]$ sqlplus apps/apps
-bash: sqlplus: command not found
```

As shown, the shell can't find the sqlplus executable without the environment settings.

Let's set the ORACLE_HOME variable and then set the PATH environment variable to include the $ORACLE_HOME/bin directory where sqlplus resides and try connecting to the database.

```
[applmgr@somehost bin]$ export ORACLE_HOME=/u01/install/APPS/fs1/EBSapps/10.1.2
[applmgr@somehost bin]$ export PATH=$PATH:$ORACLE_HOME/bin
```

```
[applmgr@somehost bin]$ sqlplus apps/apps
sqlplus: Release 10.1.0.5.0 - Production on Tue Aug 25 11:23:27 2015
Copyright (c) 1982, 2005, Oracle.  All rights reserved.
ERROR:
ORA-12162: TNS:net service name is incorrectly specified
Enter user-name:
```

Now, the problem is the TNS names, as you did not pass the TNS entry or any connection string to sqlplus, so it could not find the service name and thus could not connect to the database.

You know that the TNS entry of the EBS database is defined in the tnsnames.ora file located in the $INST_TOP/ora/10.1.2/network/admin directory, which is pointed at by the TNS_ADMIN environment variable, but you don't have the TNS_ADMIN or INST_TOP environment variable set for your shell environments.

Pretend you somehow navigate to the directory where the tnsnames.ora file resides manually without using environment variables, open tnsnames.ora, and get the EBS database connection information presented to you like in the example tnsnames.ora file shown in Figure 4-4.

```
 [applmgr@somehost ~] cd /u01/install/APPS/fs1/inst/apps/TEST_somehost/ora/10.1.2/network/admin
[applmgr@somehost admin]$ vi tnsnames.ora
```

```
###############################################################
#
# Do not edit settings in this file manually. They are managed
# automatically and will be overwritten when AutoConfig runs.
# For more information about AutoConfig, refer to the Oracle
# E-Business Suite Setup Guide.
#
#$Header: NetServiceHandler.java 120.28.12020000.6 2014/05/14 07:55:23 mmanku ship $
#
###############################################################

ORATEST=
        (DESCRIPTION=
                (ADDRESS= (PROTOCOL=tcp) (HOST=somehost) (PORT=1521))
            (CONNECT_DATA=
                (SERVICE_NAME=TEST)
                (INSTANCE_NAME=TEST)
            )
        )
```

Figure 4-4. A part of the tnsnames.ora file located in the application tier, showing the EBS database connection information

After getting the database connection information, let's retry executing sqlplus by supplying the connection string to it.

```
[applmgr@somehost admin]$ sqlplus apps/oracleR12@somehost:1521/TEST

sqlplus: Release 10.1.0.5.0 - Production on Tue Aug 25 11:39:18 2015

Copyright (c) 1982, 2005, Oracle.  All rights reserved.
SQL>
```

At last, you reached your goal and connected to the database. But you have taken a lot of actions to accomplish such an easy task like connecting to the database from the application tier. This is not acceptable and fortunately not the case in an apps DBA's life, as you use the environment variables and set them all at once using the EBSapps.env script.

Let's do the same database connection with sourcing the environment file and see how easy it actually is.

```
[applmgr@somehost ~]$ . /u01/install/APPS/EBSapps.env run
 E-Business Suite Environment Information
 ----------------------------------------
  RUN File System          : /u01/install/APPS/fs1/EBSapps/appl
  PATCH File System        : /u01/install/APPS/fs2/EBSapps/appl
  Non-Editioned File System : /u01/install/APPS/fs_ne
  DB Host: somehost.somedomain  Service/SID: TEST
  Sourcing the RUN File System ...

[applmgr@somehost ~]$ sqlplus apps/apps

SQL>
```

As shown in the previous code, after sourcing EBSapps.env to set the EBS-related environment variables in the application tier, there is no need to set PATH manually, no need to check the tnsnames.ora file for getting the database connection information, and no need to specify the connection string while executing sqlplus for connecting to the EBS database. Actually, the environment variables PATH, ORACLE_HOME, TNS_ADMIN, TWO_TASK, and several more are set by the EBSapp.env script, and they are used when you execute sqlplus to connect to the database from your application tier terminal connection.

So, as shown in the previous scenarios, you just use the environment variables to navigate the application file system. Using the environment variables, you don't even need to know things like the directory that stores the application tier administration scripts or the full path of the context file in which you make some modifications for AutoConfig. Moreover, you don't even know the database SID of the EBS database to establish a sqlplus connection to it.

As the bottom line, as explained earlier, in addition to the example scenarios, almost any administration task that needs some navigation in the application tier can be done using the environment variables. You have seen how the environment variables eases your job while working in applications' OS terminals. In addition, you have seen that there are some tasks that can be done only when the environment is set properly.

Let's continue with the database tier and see how the environment variables used in the database tier nodes accomplish administration tasks.

Working with Environment Variables on the Database Tier and Navigating the Database File System

Like in the application tier, environment variables are widely used for doing the administration work in the database tier. Although there are a few environment variables present in the database tier, they are crucial for administrating the most important technology, Oracle Database, which resides in the database tier of EBS 12.2 environments.

As mentioned earlier, the biggest part of an EBS 12.2 database tier is Oracle Database. Looking from the OS side, excluding the EBS database model, which resides in EBS database, you can say that EBS 12.2 delivers a standard Oracle Database Enterprise Edition hosted by a database file system that includes a standard Oracle Home, with the exception of some additional tools and some additional directories.

So, the EBS database consists of an Oracle Home that all the Oracle core DBAs and most of the Oracle database operators are familiar with. As core DBAs or Oracle database operators already know, to administer an Oracle database, there should be at least tree environment variables defined properly in your shells or terminals where you execute the administration commands. That is, the environment variables named ORACLE_HOME, ORACLE_SID, and PATH constitute the minimum set of environment variables that should be set to the proper values for being able to administer Oracle Database through OS terminals.

However, when we talk about an EBS database, we actually need to talk about more than these three environment variables, as the EBS database is an AutoConfig-enabled environment in which all the management for its configurations is done using the AutoConfig tool. From init.ora parameters such as sga_target to listener port numbers and from the listener name to the values to be set for environment variables, almost all the configuration is done using AutoConfig in the EBS 12.2 database tier.

For example, the sqlnet configuration files such as sqlnet.ora, tnsnames.ora, and listener.ora are created by AutoConfig, and these sqlnet files are placed in the relevant subdirectories named in the form of <sid>_<hostname> located in the default directories where they normally reside in standard Oracle Homes.

That is, while the sqlnet files are located in the $ORACLE_HOME/network/admin directory in standard Oracle Database environments, they are located in the $ORACLE_HOME/network/admin/<sid>_<hostname> directory in EBS database environments.

Because EBS database environments utilize this kind of nondefault directory, you need to have additional environment variables such as TNS_ADMIN to point to the locations they are located. Without TNS aliases, for instance, you can only connect to the EBS database using EZ-connect (sqlplus apps/pwd@<db_host>:<listener_port</<SERVICE_NAME>), which is not a preferred method because it requires you to supply the database hostname, the listener port, and the service name of the database each time you want to connect to the database remotely. So, without setting the TNS_ADMIN environment variable properly, you can't use sqlplus without supplying a connection string to connect to your database through the database listener in EBS 12.2. Also, you can't even administer the listener in the EBS database tier without the TNS_ADMIN environment variable set properly.

Database- and listener-related log and trace files are also placed in the relevant subdirectories named in the form of <sid>_<hostname> located inside the default directories where they normally reside in standard Oracle Homes, and that's why it is better to use the environment variable CONTEXT_NAME, which is actually set to <sid>_<hostname> while navigating the database tier.

Also, as AutoConfig is based on a context file, there is a context file stored in EBS Oracle Home, and it is pointed at by an additional environment variable named CONTEXT_FILE. Thus, you use this CONTEXT_FILE variable to open the context file for your EBS database whenever you want to check the value of the context variables it.

Moreover, as EBS databases are cloned using a tool called Rapid Clone, the Oracle Home used in EBS 12.2 also includes the Rapid Clone scripts that are not present in standard database Oracle Homes. As these kinds of scripts are located in the directory named appsutil, which is an additional directory deployed as part of the Oracle Home of the EBS database tier, you need to navigate to this directory from time to time.

■ **Note** The script for executing the autoconfig and administration scripts for controlling the database tier are also located in the appsutil directory.

Before giving some examples about using the environment variables and navigating in the database tier file system for accomplishing some admin tasks, we'll introduce the administration scripts delivered in the $ORACLE_HOME/appsutil/scripts/$CONTEXT_NAME directory, as you will see some of them in action while you are going through the scenarios that will be described in the next paragraphs.

Table 4-4 describes these administration scripts and gives usages.

Table 4-4. *Database Tier Administration Scripts Located in the $ORACLE_HOME/appsutil/ scripts/$CONTEXT_NAME Directory*

Script	Description	Usage
adautocfg.sh	AutoConfig script	sh adautocfg.sh
adchknls.pl	Script to check the existence of $ORACLE_HOME/nls/data/9idata and cr9idata.pl in that directory	perl adchknls.pl
addbctl.sh	Database stop/start script	To stop: sh addbctl.sh stop <shutdown mode> (normal|immediate|abort) To start: sh addbctl.sh start
addlnctl.sh	Listener stop/start script	To stop: sh addlnctl stop <listener_name> To start: sh addlnctl start <listener_name>
adexecsql.pl	Script to execute all SQL scripts that update the profiles in an AutoConfig run	Normally gets executed by AutoConfig, not by apps DBAs Nevertheless, the usage is as follows: perl adexecsql.pl sqlfile=<file> <apps_user> <apps_password>
adlsnodes.sh	Wrapper script to check whether the cluster manager is available in a RAC environment	sh adlsnodes.sh
adpreclone.pl	Script for executing the preclone, which is a critical prerequisite operation for cloning EBS environments	perl adpreclone.pl (dbTier | database | dbTechStack)
adstopdb.sql	Script for stopping the database used by the addbctl.sh script internally	Used by addbctl.sh; nevertheless, here is an example usage: sqlplus /nolog @adstopdb.sql "sys as sysdba" immediate
adstrtdb.sql	Script for starting the database used by the addbctl.sh script internally	Used by addbctl.sh; nevertheless, here is an example usage: sqlplus /nolog @adstrtdb.sql "sys as sysdba"

So, as the environment variables must be used in the database tier for administrating the EBS 12.2 databases and as the context file and scripts for enabling the EBS-specific database tools such as AutoConfig and Rapid Clone are located in the appsutil directory located in the database Oracle Home directory, we'll give you a better understanding about both the environment variables and the use of the scripts in the appsutil directory by walking through some scenarios. The following scenarios show different use cases for the environment variables through the administration scripts addlnctl.sh and addbctl.sh located in the appsutil directory in the EBS 12.2 database tier for accomplishing the related administration tasks required to be done in certain scenarios.

Scenario 1: Restarting the EBS Database and the Database Listener

You log in as the RDBMS owner OS user (for example, oracle), set your runtime environment using the environment script (named in the form of <sid>_<hostname>.env) located in Oracle Home directory, and then change your current working directory to the administration scripts. Also, as you have the opportunity to administer the database and listener using the sqlplus and lsnrctl executables, you will also see the method for starting the database and listener using sqlplus and lsnrctl in this example scenario.

In this scenario, the Oracle Home is the /u01/install/TEST/11.2.0 directory.

■ **Note** Although it is not crucial and the approaches in the database tier won't differ according to the database release, we still feel the need to give you the following information at this point.

The directory name used in this example is 11.2.0 because the EBS environment used in this example has an 11g R2 database.

You first source the <sid>_<hostname> environment file that is stored in the directory pointed at by the $ORACLE_HOME environment variable and set the proper environment consisting of the environment variables such as ORACLE_HOME, ORACLE_SID,TNS_ADMIN, PATH, LD_LIBRARY_PATH, CONTEXT_FILE,CONTEXT_NAME, and NLS_SORT, as follows:

```
[oracle@somehost ~]$ . /u01/install/TEST/11.2.0/TEST_somehost.env
```

After setting the proper environment, you follow this action plan to restart the listener and EBS database:

1. Stop the listener.
2. Stop the database.
3. Start the listener.
4. Start the database.

To stop the listener, you use the addlnctl.sh script, which can be used to stop and start the database.

You first navigate to the $ORACLE_HOME/appsutil/scripts/$CONTEXT_NAME directory where all the database administration scripts are located and then run the addlnctl.sh script by supplying it with the string stop and the name of the EBS listener that you want to stop as arguments.

```
[oracle@somehost ~]$  cd $ORACLE_HOME/appsutil/scripts/$CONTEXT_NAME
[oracle@somehost TEST_somehost]$ sh addlnctl.sh stop TEST
```

Note that the listener name provided in this scenario is TEST. However, the value of the listener can be derived by the context variable named s_db_listener, defined in the database tier context file. Note that as for the RAC instances, we recommend using srvctl for stopping the database listener, but still, the names of the RAC listener can be derived by the database tier context file.

In this context, the local listener of a RAC node is written in the context variable named s_instLocalListener, and the remote listener, also known as the scan listener of a RAC node, is written in the context variable named s_instRemoteListener.

After stopping the listener, you use the addbctl.sh script to shut down the EBS database. addbctl.sh uses adstopdb.sql located in the same directory ($ORACLE_HOME/appsutil/scripts/$CONTEXT_NAME) in conjunction with sqlplus to shut down the EBS database.

So, you run addbctl.sh with "stop" and the shutdown mode (in this example, you use "immediate") arguments to shut down an EBS database, described as follows:

```
[oracle@somehost TEST_somehost]$ sh addbctl.sh stop immediate
```

As you may realize by looking the previous addbctl.sh command that although the default shutdown mode used in the addbctl.sh script is normal mode, you have initiated an immediate shutdown by supplying the argument immediate to the addbctl.sh script. This is because usually you stop the application tier services and wait for all the application processes to be cleared before stopping an EBS database. Moreover, you take your downtime and are usually sure that no one does anything critical in the EBS environment while you are stopping it.

So, as all the services are stopped and there is no need to wait for uncommitted transactions to commit or open sessions to quit, you just initiate an immediate mode shutdown rather than initiating a normal one to shut down the EBS databases.

As for the RAC instances, we recommend using srvctl for stopping the database. The database name can be derived by the context variable named s_dbGlnam defined in the database tier context file.

After stopping the database, you use the addlnctl.sh script again to start the listener, but this time you run the addlnctl.sh script with the argument "start" rather than "stop" because your goal is to start the listener TEST that you just stopped.

```
[oracle@somehost TEST_somehost]$ sh addlnctl.sh start TEST
```

For the RAC instances, we recommend using srvctl for starting the database listener, but still, the names of the RAC listener can be derived by the database tier context file. In this context, the local listener of a RAC node is written in the context variable named s_instLocalListener, and the remote listener, also known as the scan listener of a RAC node, is written in the context variable named s_instRemoteListener.

After starting the listener, you use the addbctl.sh script once again. But this time, you use it to start the EBS database. For the start operation, addbctl.sh uses adstrtdb.sql located in the same directory with it. The addbctl.sh script uses adstrtdb.sql in conjunction with sqlplus to start the EBS database.

This time, you run addbctl.sh with the "start" argument to start the EBS database, as follows:

```
[oracle@somehost TEST_somehost]$ sh addbctl.sh start
```

At this point, your listener and database start servicing again, and you have reached your goal: completing the restart operation of the listener and the EBS database.

As for the RAC instances, we recommend using srvctl for starting the EBS database. The database name can be derived by the context variable named s_dbGlnam defined in the database tier context file.

Now, let's take a look at the alternative manual method for accomplishing such a restart operation. In the manual method, you just execute the lsnrctl command for controlling the listener and execute the sqlplus command to control the EBS database.

To stop the listener, you use the lsnrctl command directly by supplying the operation (stop) and the listener name (the listener name is TEST in this example) arguments, as shown here:

```
[oracle@somehost TEST_somehost]$ lsnrctl stop TEST
```

After stopping the listener with lsnrctl, you initiate an "sqlplus as sysdba" connection to the database and issue a "shutdown immediate" command to shut down the EBS database with the immediate option.

```
[oracle@somehost TEST_somehost]$ sqlplus "/as sysdba"

SQL> shutdown immediate;
Database closed.
Database dismounted.
ORACLE instance shut down.
```

After stopping the database, as your goal is to restart the listener and the database, you just start the listener using lsnrctl and then start the database again by using the sqlplus, as follows.

■ **Note**   To start the listener, you run the lsnrctl command by supplying it with the type of operation you want to do (start) and the listener name you want to administer (TEST).

```
[oracle@somehost TEST_somehost]$ lsnrctl start TEST
```

To start the EBS database, you first execute the sqlplus "/as sysdba" command and get your SQL prompt. Then, you execute the startup command in the SQL prompt to start the EBS database, as follows:

```
[oracle@somehost TEST_somehost]$ sqlplus "/as sysdba"
SQL> startup
ORACLE instance started.
Total System Global Area 5.0241E+10 bytes
Fixed Size                   2240016 bytes
Variable Size             1879048688 bytes
Database Buffers          4.8318E+10 bytes
Redo Buffers                40890368 bytes
Database mounted.
Database opened.
```

Scenario 2: Modifying the Database Configuration Using AutoConfig

You log in as the RDBMS owner OS user (for example ,oracle) and set your shell environment using the environment script (<sid>_<hostname>.env) located in the Oracle Home directory. Next, you open the database context file by using the CONTEXT_FILE environment variable and your favorite text editor (for example, vi in Linux) and then make the modification in that file, as shown in Figure 4-5. Lastly, you run the autoconfig to propagate the change you have made in the context file.

Let's take a look at the commands and environment variables you use to change the listener name of the EBS 12.2 database, by changing the value associated with it in the context file and running AutoConfig afterward.

First, you source the environment file as follows:

```
[oracle@somehost ~]$ . /u01/install/TEST/11.2.0/TEST_somehost.env
```

Next, you open the database context file pointed at by the $CONTEXT_FILE environment variable using the vi editor and update the relevant context variable stored in the context file, as shown here:

```
[oracle@somehost ~]$ vi $CONTEXT_FILE
```

Figure 4-5 shows part of the database context file, where you update the s_db_listener context variable to the new listener name. (In this example, you change the listener name from TEST to TESTNEW.)

```
<db_logfiles oa_var="s_dbhome2">/u01/install/TEST/data</db_logfiles>
<db_datfiles oa_var="s_dbhome3">/u01/install/TEST/data</db_datfiles>
<db_ndxfiles oa_var="s_dbhome4">/u01/install/TEST/data</db_ndxfiles>
</oa_environment>
<oa_env_file type="db_home" oa_var="s_db_home_file" osd="unix">/u01/install/TEST/11.2.0/TEST_somehost.env</oa_env_file>
<oa_env_file type="custom" oa_var="s_custom_file" osd="unix">/u01/install/TEST/11.2.0/customTEST_somehost.env</oa_env_file>
<oa_environment type="db_home">
<ORACLE_HOME oa_var="s_db_oh">/u01/install/TEST/11.2.0</ORACLE_HOME>
<PATH oa_var="s_db_path" osd="LINUX_X86-64">/u01/install/TEST/11.2.0/bin:/usr/bin:/usr/sbin:/u01/install/TEST/11.2.0/appsutil/jre
<JAVA_HOME oa_var="s_db_java">/u01/install/TEST/11.2.0/appsutil/jre</JAVA_HOME>
<LD_LIBRARY_PATH oa_var="s_db_ldlib" osd="LINUX_X86-64">/u01/install/TEST/11.2.0/lib:/usr/X11R6/lib:/usr/openwin/lib:/u01/install
/ctx/lib</LD_LIBRARY_PATH>
<SHLIB_PATH oa_var="s_db_shlib" osd="LINUX_X86-64">/u01/install/TEST/11.2.0/lib:/usr/lib:/u01/install/TEST/11.2.0/ctx/lib</SHLIB_
<LIBPATH oa_var="s_db_libpath" osd="LINUX_X86-64">/u01/install/TEST/11.2.0/lib:/usr/X11R6/lib:/usr/openwin/lib:/u01/install/TEST/
ib</LIBPATH>
<LINK_CNTRL oa_var="s_db_linkctrl"/>
<ORA_NLS oa_var="s_db_oranls" osd="unix">/u01/install/TEST/11.2.0/nls/data/9idata</ORA_NLS>
<TNS_ADMIN oa_var="s_db_tnsadmin">/u01/install/TEST/11.2.0/network/admin/TEST_somehost</TNS_ADMIN>
<TWO_TASK oa_var="s_db_twotask">TEST</TWO_TASK>
<DB_LISTENER oa_var="s_db_listener">TESTNEW</DB_LISTENER>
<ALTERNATE_SERVICE_INSTANCES oa_var="s_alt_service_instances"/>
<IFILE oa_var="s_ifile">/u01/install/TEST/11.2.0/network/admin/TEST_somehost/TEST_somehost_ifile.ora</IFILE>
<INIT_IFILE oa_var="s_init_ifile">/u01/install/TEST/11.2.0/dbs/TEST_somehost_ifile.ora</INIT_IFILE>
<LSNR_IFILE oa_var="s_lsnr_ifile">/u01/install/TEST/11.2.0/network/admin/TEST_somehost/listener_ifile.ora</LSNR_IFILE>
<SQLNET_IFILE oa_var="s_sqlnet_ifile">/u01/install/TEST/11.2.0/network/admin/TEST_somehost/sqlnet_ifile.ora</SQLNET_IFILE>
<SQLNET_EXPIRE_TIME oa_var="s_sqlnet_expire_time">10</SQLNET_EXPIRE_TIME>
```

Figure 4-5. *A part of the database context file pointed at by the $CONTEXT_FILE environment variable in the database tier, showing the change made in the database listener name*

Lastly, after modifying and saving the database context file, you navigate to the $ORACLE_HOME/appsutil/scripts/$CONTEXT_NAME directory and run the AutoConfig script by supplying the appspass argument to it.

Note that the appspass argument is not mandatory, as the AutoConfig script asks for the apps password anyway. However, we have used it in the following example command because we wanted to give a one-line command for the AutoConfig execution:

```
[oracle@somehost ~]$ cd $ORACLE_HOME/appsutil/scripts/$CONTEXT_NAME
[oracle@somehost TEST_somehost]$ sh adautocfg.sh appspass=apps
```

So, AutoConfig re-creates the sqlnet configuration files, and as a result, the listener name specified in the listener configuration file (listener.ora) gets changed.

At this moment, you have reached your goal, and you may now stop the already running listener, which can be considered as the old listener, and then start the new listener using addlnctl.sh as follows:

```
[oracle@somehost TEST_somehost]$ sh addlnctl.sh stop TEST
Logfile: /u01/install/PROD/11.2.0/appsutil/log/TEST_somehost/addlnctl.txt

[oracle@somehost TEST_somehost]$ sh addlnctl.sh start TESTNEW
Logfile: /u01/install/PROD/11.2.0/appsutil/log/TEST_somehost/addlnctl.txt
```

```
You are running addlnctl.sh version 120.4
Starting listener process TESTNEW ...
...
.....
.......

addlnctl.sh: exiting with status 0
```

So far, you have seen the file system architecture delivered in EBS 12.2 and also seen the environment variables. You understand their usages because you have navigated both the application tier and the database tier using them as well as accomplished the tasks explained in the examples. Before going to the next chapter, let's take a look at the log files in EBS 12.2 and complete this chapter by having a complete awareness of the entities on the EBS 12.2 file system.

EBS 12.2 Applications Log Files

Because EBS environments are generally based on two tiers, named the application tier and the database tier, and because different kinds of technology components and applications run on each of these tiers, the log files in EBS 12.2 are placed in the directories according to the components they are produced for. In other words, the log files related to application tier components are placed in the application tier file system, and the log files related to the database components are placed in the database tier file system.

Application log files in EBS 12.2 are produced for FMW components, the concurrent processing server, patching tools, and administration utilities such as logs for ad utilities, application service control scripts, and AutoConfig scripts.

Let's start with the directory pointed at by the environment variable named LOG_HOME. $LOG_HOME is an important environment variable, and it points to the log directory located in the instance top directory ($INST_TOP).

$LOG_HOME stores different types of log files, and these log files are categorized by the directories they reside in, as follows:

- *$LOG_HOME/appl/admin/log*: Stores administration scripts' log files such as the log files produced for starting and stopping the managed servers as well as the AutoConfig log file and the log files for adstrtal.sh, adstpall.sh, and adnodemgrctl.sh scripts.

- *$LOG_HOME/appl/rgf*: Stores the log files produced while registering WLS listeners and also stores the TXK configuration log files such as log files for the txkSetAppsConf.pl script.

- *$LOG_HOME/ora/10.1.2/forms*: Stores forms rti files, which contain metric data about the forms' runtime processes.

- *$LOG_HOME/ora/10.1.2/install*: Stores the make/compilation logs of the binaries in 10.1.2 Oracle Home.

- *$LOG_HOME/ora/10.1.2/network*: Stores the application rpc listener's log files.

- *$LOG_HOME/ora/10.1.2/reports/cache*: Stores Oracle Reports server's cache files. That is, when concurrent requests that run Oracle Reports are submitted, temporary files are created under this directory.

So, the log file for the administration scripts, AutoConfig, TXK configurations, WLS listener registrations, forms runtime metrics, 10.1.2 Oracle Home compilations, RPC listener, and the reports cache are placed in the $LOG_HOME directory.

The log files for FMW components such as Oracle Process Manager (opmn), Oracle HTTP Server (OHS), and the WebLogic server logs are stored in the subdirectories of the directory pointed at by the FMW_HOME environment variable.

The following is a list describing the important Fusion Middleware log directories and the type of the logs files stored in them:

- *$IAS_ORACLE_HOME/instances/EBS_web_<SID>_OHS<INSTANCE_NUMBER> / diagnostics/logs*: Stores Oracle HTTP Server and OPMN logs.

- *$FMW_HOME/wlserver_10.3/ common/nodemanager/nodemanager.log*: Stores Node Manager log files.

- *$EBS_DOMAIN_HOME/<server_name>/logs*: Stores the HTTP transaction logs, as well as diagnostic, log, and output files for WebLogic admin and managed servers. Actually, the directory $EBS_DOMAIN_HOME/AdminServer stores much more than that; $EBS_DOMAIN_HOME/AdminServer/log/ stores the WebLogic domain log (DomainName.log), which contains forwarded information from the defined servers within the EBS WebLogic domain. Oracle WebServices Manager (owsm) logs are also stored in the $EBS_DOMAIN_HOME/AdminServer/log/owsm/msglogging directory.

- *$EBS_DOMAIN_HOME/AdminServer/data*: Stores the Embedded Ldap server and Ldap access logs.

- *$EBS_DOMAIN_HOME/servers/server_name/adr/diag/ofm/EBS_ domain_<sid>/<server_name>/incident*: Stores the incident files created by the Diagnostic Framework, which is explained in Chapter 7 of this book.

In addition to IAS_ORACLE_HOME, LOG_HOME, and FMW_HOME, there are log files stored in other application directories such as directories pointed at by the ADOP_LOG_HOME and APPLCSF environment variables.

The directory pointed at by ADOP_LOG_HOME is stored in noneditioned file system (fs_ne), and the EBS 12.2 application patching tool's log files are stored here.

The directory skin of the adop log files is as follows:

```
$ADOP_LOG_HOME/<adop_session_id>/<phase_timestamp>/<context_name>
```

The directory pointed at by the APPLCSF environment variable is also stored in the noneditioned file system (fs_ne), and the concurrent processing log and output files are stored in this directory. The log and output files stored in this directory are actually separated into two subdirectories as follows:

```
Concurrent manager and concurrent program/request log files: $APPLCSF/$APPLLOG, typically
$APPLCSF/log
Concurrent program/request output files: $APPLCSF/$APPLOUT, typically $APPLCSF/outt
```

Lastly, the logs generated by the adadmin utility, which can be used to do several administration tasks such as compiling forms and compiling apps schema, are also stored in the noneditioned file system (fs_ne), in the directory pointed at by $APPL_TOP_NE/../log/adadmin.

So, you have seen the important log directories and what kind of log files are stored in them. By knowing this log file and log directory mapping, an apps DBA can easily navigate to the right directory and start analyzing the related log files, without navigating the complex application file system directory structure and trying to find the related log file by listing the contents of all the log directories one by one. That is, by knowing the directories and the type of the log files stored in them, the apps DBA can directly navigate to the directory that contains the related log file, list the log files by timestamp, open the related log file using their favorite text editor, and start analyzing it.

So far, you have gained the knowledge to investigate the problems that may arise in the application tier components by going through the application tier log directories and the type of log files stored in them.

Let's continue with the database tier and gain knowledge about the log files that can be used to investigate database tier problems.

EBS 12.2 Database Log Files

The Oracle database delivered within EBS 12.2 is not so different from any standard Oracle Database.

The EBS database has almost the same file system architecture as the file system that is deployed when you use runInstaller to install a stand-alone Oracle Database. So, it is just an Enterprise Edition Oracle Database 11GR2 (or 12c, if the installation is done with the latest startCD) that has almost the same logging mechanisms, log files, and directories that can be found in any Oracle Database environment.

As we have explained, the database file system architecture used in EBS 12.2 is almost the same but not exactly the same as the standard Oracle database file systems. The reason is that there are some application-aware AD utilities and scripts that are stored in the appsutil directory in the Oracle Home of the EBS database, and these utilities and scripts are normally not delivered in a standard Oracle Database file system architecture. Moreover, these scripts and utilities produce log files that also can't be found in standard Oracle Database log file directories.

So, although it seems like a standard Oracle Database file system, and even if the log mechanism used in the EBS database is the same as the mechanism used in all the Oracle databases, we will explain the EBS log files in this chapter.

By considering some exceptional log directories, which can't be found in non-EBS databases, you will take a look at the log files produced in the database tier, and we will explain where to look in the EBS database file system to find the related log files while diagnosing a database tier problem.

As for the database tier logging, EBS 12.2 uses the standard Oracle Database logging mechanism that core DBAs are already familiar with.

The EBS 12.2 database uses a diagnostic destination specified by the database parameter diagnostic_dest, which introduced with the release of Oracle Database 11g, to store all of its log files. While the diagnostic_dest parameter can be changed to point to any directory that the Oracle database OS user has necessary privileges for, the EBS installer named Rapidwiz by default sets the diagnostic_dest parameter to the directory named /<sid>_hostname>, stored in $ORACLE_HOME/admin ($ORACLE_HOME/admin/<sid>_hostname>).

The current value of the diagnostic_dest parameter can be checked at any time to display the diagnostic directory used in an EBS 12.2 database. The value of the diagnostic_dest parameter can be displayed using a sqlplus connection and the show parameter command, as shown in Listing 4-12.

■ **Note** As we have already explained the environment variables and environment setting earlier, we won't show how to set the database environment before using the sqlplus command or any other command displayed in the upcoming examples.

Listing 4-12. The Output of show parameter diagnostic_dest Used with sqlplus to Display the Value of the diagnostic_dest Database Initialization Parameter

```
[oracle@somehost ~]$ sqlplus "/as sysdba"

SQL> show parameter diagnostic_dest

NAME                             TYPE        VALUE
-------------------------------- ----------- -------------------------------
diagnostic_dest                  string      /u01/install/PROD/11.2.0/admin /TEST_somehost
```

So, the EBS Oracle database uses the directory pointed at by the diagnostic_dest parameter to store Oracle Database log files, and it has the subdirectories as shown in the ls output provided in Listing 4-13. Note that in Listing 4-13 we are using the same EBS database that we used to show the diagnostic_dest value in Listing 4-12.

Listing 4-13. ls command Output Showing the Subdirectories of the diagnostic dest Directory

```
[oracle@somehost ~]cd /u01/install/PROD/11.2.0/admin//TEST_somehost
[oracle@somehost TEST_somehost]$ ls
bdump  cdump  diag  oradiag_applmgr  oradiag_oracle  udump
```

Although there are six subdirectories named bdump, cdump, diag, oradiag_applmgr, oradiag_oracle, and udump inside the diagnostic dest directory as listed in Listing 4-13, only three of them are in use. That is, the bdump, cdump, and udump directories that come with the installation are just there to support the old-style Oracle database logging, and they are not used by the EBS Oracle database to store its log files. The diag, oradiag_applmgr (in the form of oradiag_ApplicationOSUser), and oradiag_oracle (in the form of oradiag_databaseOSUser) directories are the actual directories where the database tier log files are created.

Let's start with the diag directory stored in the directory pointed at by the diagnostic_dest parameter ($ORACLE_HOME/admin/<sid>_<hostname>). The diag directory is the main and actual directory where the EBS database log files are stored. To analyze a database problem, you usually check the log files stored in the diag directory, as the diag directory contains the logs created for user sessions, background processes and database alerts, and the listener. To store several type of log file in a meaningful manner, the log files stored in the diag directory are categorized and stored in the subdirectories according to their types and the database tier components they are created for.

The tree command output shown in Listing 4-14 shows the important subdirectories that reside in the diag directory. Also, the information displaying the type of log files that are stored in these subdirectories, can be found on the right side of each directory listed in the tree command output shown in Listing 4-14.

■ **Note**   There are Automatic Diagnostic Repository (ADR)–related directories in the output provided by the tree command used in Listing 4-14. You should stick to them for now, as we will explain ADR just after Listing 4-14.

Listing 4-14. tree Command Output Showing the Subdirectories of the Diag Directory by Giving the Information About the Types of Log Files Stored in Them

```
tree $ORACLE_HOME/admin/TEST_somehost/diag/ -L 4 -A

diag/
|-- rdbms                            : root directory that stores rdbms log and trace files
|-- |-- TEST                         : directory named with the Database name in order
                                       to separate the log files according to the
                                       Oracle Database SIDs in case where there are
                                       multiple databases uses the same diagnostic
                                       destination directory.
|-- |-- |-- TEST                     : directory named with the Database sid in order
                                       to separate the log files according to the
                                       Oracle Database SID in case where there are
                                       multiple RAC instances uses the same diagnostic
                                       destination directory.
```

`|-- |-- |-- |-- alert`	:	directory where xml formatted database alert log files reside (log.xml ,log1.xml and so on).
`|-- |-- |-- |-- cdump`	:	directory that stores the core dumps.
`|-- |-- |-- |-- incident`	:	directory that stores the ADR incident files created when an important database error is encountered such as ORA-00600, ORA-01578, ORA-07445 and consist of error stacks, call stacks, block dumps etc..
`|-- |-- |-- |-- incpkg`	:	directory that stores the ADR packages created by packaging incidents into bundles.
`|-- |-- |-- |-- trace`	:	directory that stores user and background traces (aa replacement for the old udump and bdump directories). The text based database alert log file named with the format alert_<SID>.log, is also stored in trace directory.
`|-- tnslsnr`	:	root directory that stores listener log and trace files
`|-- |-- somehost`	:	directory named with the hostname (database server's hostname) that listener is working on.
`|-- |-- TEST`	:	The service name that the listener listens for.
`|-- |-- |-- alert`	:	directory where xml formatted listener log files resides (log.xml, log1.xml and so on).
`|-- |-- |-- cdump`	:	directory that stores the core dumps.
`|-- |-- |-- incident`	:	directory that stores the ADR incident files created when an important listener error is encountered.
`|-- |-- |-- incpkg`	:	directory that stores the ADR packages created by packaging incidents into bundles.
`|-- |-- |-- lck`		
`|-- |-- |-- trace`	:	Listener trace files and the text based listener log file named with the format <listener_name>.log are stored in this directory

As shown in Listing 4-14, you have two main subdirectories named tnslsnr and rdbms in the diag directory. The database-related diagnostic files (logs, trace, core dumps, and so on) are placed in the related subdirectories of the rdbms directory, and the listener-related diagnostic files are placed in the related subdirectories of the tnslsnr directory.

As it is important to know the directory structure where the EBS database log files are stored, it is also crucial to know how to analyze the log files created in these log directories.

As apps DBAs, you can always use your favorite text editors to analyze these log files, as shown in Figures 4-6 and 4-7.

```
Wed Jun 25 04:42:28 2014
Starting ORACLE instance (normal)
****************** Large Pages Information *****************

Total Shared Global Region in Large Pages = 0 KB (0%)

Large Pages used by this instance: 0 (0 KB)
Large Pages unused system wide = 0 (0 KB) (alloc incr 16 MB)
Large Pages configured system wide = 0 (0 KB)
Large Page size = 2048 KB

RECOMMENDATION:
  Total Shared Global Region size is 2050 MB. For optimal performance,
  prior to the next instance restart increase the number
  of unused Large Pages by atleast 1025 2048 KB Large Pages (2050 MB)
  system wide to get 100% of the Shared
  Global Region allocated with Large pages
*************************************************************
LICENSE_MAX_SESSION = 0
LICENSE_SESSIONS_WARNING = 0
Shared memory segment for instance monitoring created
Picked latch-free SCN scheme 3
Autotune of undo retention is turned on.
IMODE=BR
ILAT =44
LICENSE_MAX_USERS = 0
SYS auditing is enabled
Starting up:
Oracle Database 11g Enterprise Edition Release 11.2.0.3.0 - 64bit Production
With the Partitioning, OLAP, Data Mining and Real Application Testing options.
ORACLE_HOME = /u01/install/TEST/11.2.0
/ORA-
```

Figure 4-6. Using the vi editor to search for database errors in alert_<sid>.log file, using "ORA-" as the search item

```
ORA-16014: log 7 sequence# 2411 not archived, no available destinations
ORA-00312: online log 7 thread 1
Mon Aug 31 10:19:14 2015
ARC0: Closing local archive destination LOG_ARCHIVE_DEST_1
Mon Aug 31 10:19:29 2015
ARCH: Archival stopped, error occurred. Will continue retrying
ORACLE Instance    TEST - Archival Error
ORA-16038: log 7 sequence# 2411 cannot be archived
ORA-19502: write error on file "",
ORA-00312: online log 7 thread 1:
Mon Aug 31 10:19:29 2015
Archiver process freed from errors. No longer stopped
ARCH: Archival stopped, error occurred. Will continue retrying
ORACLE Instance    TEST - Archival Error
ORA-16014: log 7 sequence# 2411 not archived, no available destinations
ORA-00312: online log 7 thread 1
Archiver process freed from errors. No longer stopped
Mon Aug 31 10:21:27 2015
Incremental checkpoint up to RBA [0x96f.795cc.0], current log tail at RBA [0x96f.797de.0]
Mon Aug 31 10:25:10 2015
Archived Log entry 412 added for thread 1 sequence 2411 ID 0xc9da88c7 dest 1:
krse_arc_driver_core: Successful archiving of previously failed ORL
Mon Aug 31 10:26:09 2015
Archived Log entry 413 added for thread 1 sequence 2414 ID 0xc9da88c7 dest 1:
Mon Aug 31 10:27:12 2015
Archived Log entry 414 added for thread 1 sequence 2412 ID 0xc9da88c7 dest 1:
Mon Aug 31 10:27:41 2015
Archived Log entry 415 added for thread 1 sequence 2413 ID 0xc9da88c7 dest 1:
Mon Aug 31 10:42:54 2015
Incremental checkpoint up to RBA [0x96f.79fae.0], current log tail at RBA [0x96f.7a170.0]
Mon Aug 31 11:03:11 2015
```

Figure 4-7. vi editor placing the cursor in the first database error returned from the search shown in Figure 4-6

As depicted in Figure 4-6, you use the vi editor to check the text-based database alert log (alert_<sid>.log) to see whether any errors are reported by the database by making a search using the string "ORA-," as you know that the database error messages start with "ORA-" (for example, ORA-600, ORA-07445, and so on).

By using such a search method, you can directly jump to the log lines created when the database errors are encountered, as shown in Figure 4-7.

So, using text editors and their capabilities can be an efficient way to analyze the log files and find the causes of the database problems. Sometimes you need to check the database's alert log to see what's wrong in the database, like the archival problem shown in Figure 4-7, and sometimes you need to check several trace files to gather a bunch of diagnostic information and state the problem accordingly.

In addition to a text editor, the Oracle database used in EBS 12.2 offers a tool called Automatic Diagnostic Repository for analyzing the logs and finding problems. Using ADR to diagnose problems is much easier than navigating in the directory structure and dealing with the huge number of files using text editors.

Even though ADR is beyond the scope of this chapter, let's take a look at its usage, as shown in Listing 4-15.

■ **Note**   In Chapter 7, which is focused on FMW, we will explain ADR in more detail. Although Chapter 7 is not related to Oracle Database, the logic behind ADR and its usage is similar to the database tier.

In Listing 4-15, we use ADR to view the contents of the database alert log file, without navigating the diagnostic directories and dealing with a text editor.

First, you execute the adrci command to open the Automatic Diagnostic Repository Command Interpreter (adrci) utility, which is the utility for executing ADR commands.

```
[oracle@somehost ~]$ adrci
adrci>
```

After opening the adrci utility, you use the show alert command to display the alert log of the database, as follows:

```
adrci>show alert
```

The adrci utility lists the available diagnostic homes present in the diagnostic repository and waits for you to choose the diagnostic home, which is your focus right now.

Choose the alert log from the following homes to view:

     1: diag/rdbms/test/TEST

     Q: to quit

Please select option: 1
You choose the diagnostic home, and the alert log is displayed, as shown in Listing 4-15.

Listing 4-15. Using ADRCI to Display the Contents of the Database Alert Log File (alert_<sid>.log File)

```
Output the results to file: /tmp/alert_8084_14034_TEST_1.ado
2014-06-25 04:42:28.610000 -04:00
Starting ORACLE instance (normal)
LICENSE_MAX_SESSION = 0
LICENSE_SESSIONS_WARNING = 0
Shared memory segment for instance monitoring created
Picked latch-free SCN scheme 3
Autotune of undo retention is turned on.
IMODE=BR
ILAT =44
LICENSE_MAX_USERS = 0
SYS auditing is enabled
Starting up:
Oracle Database 11g Enterprise Edition Release 11.2.0.3.0 - 64bit Production
With the Partitioning, OLAP, Data Mining and Real Application Testing options.
ORACLE_HOME = /u01/install/TEST/11.2.0
...
.....
........
```

■ **Note**   The adrci utility internally uses the vi editor to display the alert log contents.

The adrci utility can do much more than displaying alert log contents. Listing 4-16 shows an example output produced by adrci when you execute the show incident command.

Listing 4-16. An Example adrci Output Showing the Incidents

```
adrci> show incident

ADR Home = /u01/install/TEST/11.2.0/admin/TEST_somehost/diag/rdbms/test/TEST:
*************************************************************************
INCIDENT_ID           PROBLEM_KEY                                        CREATE_TIME
------------------    --------------------------------------------    -----------
26457                 ORA 7445 [__intel_new_memcpy()+2960]               2014-09-11
    13:49:55.196000 -04:00
26465                 ORA 7445 [__intel_new_memcpy()+2960]               2014-09-11
13:51:15.144000 -04:00
26489                 ORA 7445 [__intel_new_memcpy()+2960]               2014-09-11
13:52:18.166000 -04:00
26409                 ORA 7445 [__intel_new_memcpy()+2960]               2014-09-11
13:53:24.305000 -04:00
26425                 ORA 7445 [__intel_new_memcpy()+2960]               2014-09-11
11:21:28.188000 +03:00
161116                ORA 600 [kktget2: no updCol]
2015-04-08 15:20:29.230000 +03:00
```

As shown in Listing 4-16, adrci can list all the incidents encountered in the database with their timestamp and problem key information. There are many more things that can be done using adrci such as going into the details of these incidents, creating packages from them, and so on, but the bottom line is that it brings you efficiency and it definitely should be used in diagnosing database problems because it saves you time in navigating the database directories and checking the trace files one by one manually in the OS terminals using a text editor.

So, you have seen the database tier log files and the diagnostic directories, log files, and methods for analyzing these log files used in an EBS 12.2 database environment. Now let's take a look at the database tier log files produced for applications DBA utilities and scripts.

The applications DBA utilities and scripts are the scripts and utilities delivered with the appsutil directory, which resides in the database tier Oracle Home. There are database stop/start scripts, listener stop/start scripts, AutoConfig scripts, cloning scripts, and several others. Most of these scripts and utilities create log files, and unlike Oracle Database itself, which has a diagnostic repository consisting of several directories, the log files created by application DBA scripts and utilities are placed in a single directory called log that resides in the appsutil directory.

Although most of the application scripts write the information for their log file paths to the terminal from where they are executed, Listing 4-17 shows a tree command output that lists the log directory located in the $ORACLE_HOME/appsutil directory.

Listing 4-17. tree Command Output Showing the Log Directories and Files Located in the $ORACLE_ HOME/appsutil/log Directory

```
tree -A $ORACLE_HOME/appsutil/log

log
|-- CloneContext_0115002604.log
|-- CloneContext_0115012653.log
|-- TEST_somehost/
|-- |-- 08261526
|-- |-- |-- adconfig.log
|-- |-- |-- adcvmlog.xml.08260827
|-- |-- |-- NetServiceHandler.log
|-- |--   adcrdb_TEST.txt
```

```
|-- |--  adcrobj.txt
|-- |--  adcvmlog.xml
|-- |--   addbprf.txt
|-- |--  addbupdgsm.txt
|-- |--  addlnctl_tmp.txt
|-- |--  addlnctl.txt
|-- |--  adupdlib.txt
|-- |--  afdbprf.txt
|-- |--  ApplyDBTier_06250438.log
|-- |--  make_06250440.log
|-- |--  NetServiceHandler.log
|-- |--  ohclone.log
|-- |--  StageDBTier_08311120.log
```

As shown in the output displayed in Listing 4-17, the log files are named with the name of the scripts and the name of the utilities that they are produced for. In this manner, it is easy to understand that addlnctl.txt is the log file for the addlnctl.sh script used for controlling the database listener. There are also some directories named with the format <sid>_<hostname> and located in the $ORACLE_HOME/appsutil/log directory. These directories are for storing log files such as adconfig.log, which is the log file produced by the AutoConfig script.

The other log files located in $ORACLE_HOME/appsutil/log are named with the scripts and utilities they are produced for. The log file named make_06250440.log shown in Listing 4-17, for example, is the log file for produced for a Linux make command that is executed probably by a script located in appsutil.

So, most of the time navigating the $ORACLE_HOME/appsutil/log directory is enough for locating the log files of application DBA scripts and tools, as the log files are mostly named according to the script and tool names. However, there are also some log files in the appsutil/log directory named with some strings that don't give you any clues about the tool or script they are produced for. StageDBTier_08311120.log, shown in Listing 4-17, is one of them, and it is produced for a preclone activity, but by looking its name, you can't predict that.

So, whether the log file name gives you a clue or not, it is not so important to memorize which file in the appsutil/log directory to look for when an error is encountered in an applications DBA script or utility. That's because, as already mentioned, most of the applications DBA scripts and utilities report their log file location when they are executed.

Listing 4-18 shows an example AutoConfig run. By looking at the output of AutoConfig script, you can see that the AutoConfig script reports its log file location just after it starts its execution.

Listing 4-18. AutoConfig Script Reporting Its Log File

```
[oracle@somehost TEST_somehost]$ sh adautocfg.sh
Enter the APPS user password:
The log file for this session is located at: /u01/install/TEST/11.2.0/appsutil/log/TEST_
somehost/08311817/adconfig.log
```

Summary

In this chapter, you learned about the file system architecture of EBS 12.2, as well as the environment variables used to describe the directories and used to get the EBS-specific values while working in the OS terminals. We explained how to work with the environment variables by giving specific examples, and we explained the log files by going into the details and giving some examples . You looked at the EBS file system and related topics such as environment variables and log files, from both the application and the database perspectives.

In the next chapter, you will continue with Oracle E-Business Suite patching concepts, which are almost completely changed in EBS 12.2.

CHAPTER 5

■ ■ ■

Patching Concepts

In this chapter, we will explain patching concepts in EBS 12.2. We will provide the information about the components and utilities used in patching and shed light on the logic behind the patching methods. In addition, we will cover the usages and roles of the dual file system and edition-based redefinition in EBS 12.2 patching. Further, we will introduce the new patching cycle concept in EBS 12.2 as well as the patch phases used in the online patching concept and explain best practices for EBS 12.2 patching. Both application tier and database tier patching will be covered in this chapter.

Introduction to Oracle Patching in EBS 12.2

Patching in Oracle E-Business Suite is an inescapable activity because bug fixes and enhancements are published by Oracle every day. Patching is required in critical projects such as an EBS release or Family Pack upgrades. Patches can be related to any component present in an E-Business Suite system, and as a matter of fact, the tools and the methods used for patching differ according to the type of patches.

Although you have different kind of patches in an EBS patching context such as applications patches, database tier patches, WebLogic patches, and application tier Oracle Home patches, the most common patching work is done for the applications patches. In other words, except the big upgrades, the things that usually need patching are the applications.

For example, a form failing to deliver expected contents or an OAF page working slow will require patching most of the time. It is less necessary to apply patches in the application technology stack and database tier once EBS is deployed with its latest Family Packs. This is a result of EBS being a packaged application. So, as EBS 12.2 uses stable versions of the technology stack components, most of the patching activity is done for the EBS code changes.

Before EBS version 12.2, the approaches used in patching were similar. Versions 11i and 12 (12.0 and 12.1) were similar in their patching concepts. In these releases, when a patch needed to be applied to the application tier, you stopped the application services, enabled the maintenance mode, and applied the required patch with the relevant tool. If the patch could be applied while the application services were running, you applied it as a hotpatch without needing to stop any services, but this was not a scenario that was encountered much.

The method for applying database tier and application tier Oracle Home patches was also similar and straightforward. For database and application tier Oracle Home patches, you used the opatch utility. Actually, this has not changed with EBS 12.2.

However, patching in the application tier has changed with the release of EBS 12.2. As you may imagine, this was expected. Because EBS 12.2 has introduced almost a complete new technology stack in the application tier, the tools for patching and the methods had to be changed.

But this was not the big change in the subject of patching EBS 12.2. The most important change in EBS 12.2 is the new online patching concept.

© Syed Zaheer and Erman Arslan 2016
S. Zaheer and E. Arslan, *Practical Oracle E-Business Suite*, DOI 10.1007/978-1-4842-1422-0_5

In 12.1, there was an option named Staged APPL TOP to make the system be available while patching. But even with Staged APPL TOP, if a patch required changes in the database objects, the system had to be taken offline.

As the name itself implies, the online patching concept introduced in EBS 12.2 allows the applications patches, as well as the application tier technology stack patches (WebLogic and application tier Oracle Home–based components), to be applied online with a near-zero downtime. This online patching feature applies even for the patches that require some database object changes.

There is still a minimal downtime, but it is only required for restarting application services. There is also a downtime option, which was first introduced with EBS 12.2.4 (or AD-TXK Delta 5) for applying patches with downtime. However, to apply a patch with this option, the patch must be compatible with it. In other words, it should be explicitly documented in the patch readme file or in the relevant Oracle Support documents. That is, unless the Oracle Support documents or the readme of the patch declare something like "This patch can be applied using apply_mode=downtime," you must use online patching.

Patching with downtime should be preferred only where the downtime is not an issue and there is a need to increase the patching speed. Patching with downtime is used in operations such as Fresh installations, upgrades, and some specific product upgrades at the moment. It is not something that should be used frequently, and this makes online patching the main way to apply patches in EBS 12.2.

To able to create an EBS environment with the online patching feature, Oracle has used its own technologies. EBS 12.2 employs edition-based redefinition (EBR), a feature of Oracle Database 11g R2 and 12c (12c R1) in the database tier, and a dual file system in the application tier to support online patching.

In addition to these new technologies, the patching utility and the patching concepts have also been changed according to the online patching methodology. EBS 12.2 brings a new patching utility for applying the application tier patches called *adop* (which stands for "applications DBA online patching"), which replaces the adpatch utility used in EBS 12.1 and 11i. Although adop seems like a wrapper for executing adpatch in the back end, it is far more than that.

It is the tool that drives the online patching cycle and affects both the database tier EBR and the dual file system because it makes them become involved in the patching process. In addition to the adop utility, the new patch cycle concept is at the top of this online patching stack. Every time a patch needs to be applied, a patch cycle is created. Patching cycles in EBS 12.2 consist of five main phases: prepare, apply, finalize, cutover, and cleanup.

So, adop, the dual file system, EBR, and the patching cycle and phases together supply the online patching used in applying EBS 12.2 application patches. We will explain these terms and the adop utility itself in detail in the coming sections. Also, we will walk you through the online patching process in conjunction with the dual file system explained in Chapter 4.

The method used in patching the database tier is the same as the old releases. As you may imagine, the opatch utility is used for database tier patching in EBS 12.2. The tool opatch is also used in the application tier Oracle Home patches in EBS 12.2.

Using opatch is a familiar approach for core DBAs and former apps DBAs. However, there are also new utilities like BSU for patching the new EBS application tier components such as WebLogic. These utilities will be covered later in this chapter, while we explain the different patching utilities.

So, although patching seems to consist of downloading the required patches from Oracle Support, uploading them to the server, and using the utilities to apply them, the technology and the infrastructure behind them are highly complex. In addition to the complex patching infrastructure consisting of utilities and a bunch of technologies supporting them introduced in the previous paragraphs, patching EBS is not a straightforward operation every time.

Downloading the patches from Oracle Support is certainly the first and easiest step in a patching operation. The only point to be considered while downloading a patch is that you must download the patches according to the platform and release level of the corresponding environment. Choosing the correct patch that will fix the related problem is also important here.

After choosing and downloading the patches, the second step is placing the patches in the corresponding directory and configuring their ownerships. This is also easy.

However, the action begins after this point. Once the patches are in place, you need to choose the correct patching order and proceed with applying them. You can apply patches one by one or merge them into a single patch and apply all the patches in one go. Even if the order and action plan are correct, there may be other issues while patching, so you need to know the whole patching process, the architecture behind it, and the tools used in patching.

Let's start by identifying how and why these patches in EBS are created by Oracle and how to decide on the patching order in general.

Types of the Patches and Deciding the Patching Order

Patches for EBS are created by Oracle as bug fixes or as enhancements. A patch may address a single issue or multiple issues and enhancements.

The story behind the patch creation is based on Oracle Support service requests. A customer or an Oracle Support analyst opens a service request to report his or her findings. If there are no patches available or if the reported problem is not an expected behavior, the problem is logged as a bug and transferred to the development team at Oracle. The development team makes its research and creates a new patch for the reported bug. Afterward, the patch becomes available for all the required Oracle applications, platforms, and all the required languages, and the patch become ready to be released for the customer use.

There are six main patch types present for EBS products: one-off patches, Recommended Patch Collection (RPC) patches, Mini Packs, Family Packs, Release Update Packs, and Maintenance Packs. One-off patches are usually the smallest patches, and they are created to fix specific issues. Recommend Patch Collection patches are used for applying multiple recommended one-off patches in one go. RPC patches combine the latest recommended patches with all their prerequisite patches for the EBS products.

Mini Packs are created by assembling multiple one-off patches and can be considered cumulative bug fixes and enhancements related to a specific EBS product. Family Packs are collections of Mini Packs to provide cumulative bug fixes and enhancements for a group of EBS products. The grouping of products is based on the product family. For example, a Family Pack for financials has fixes and enhancements for the products such as AR, AP, GL, and FA, as these products constitute the financials family. Release Update Packs are a collection of Family Packs that are created for a given codeline after the initial EBS release. For example, upgrading from 12.1.1 to 12.1.2 is done by applying 12.1.2 Release Update Pack.

Maintenance Packs are the collection of Family Packs to be used for the release upgrades. For example, a release upgrade from 12.0 to 12.1.1 is done by applying the 12.1.1 Maintenance Pack.

In addition to the EBS product patches, there are patches for the technology components that come bundled with EBS. The application tier technology components such as WebLogic, FMW, and Oracle 10.1.2.3 Home and Oracle Database are the components in this category, and they have their own patching needs, terminology, and methods. For these components, the nomenclature is as follows:

- *Interim patch*: This is the same as the one-off patch explained earlier. These patches contain one or more fixes.

- *Diagnostic patch*: This is an interim patch that does not fix any problems but is used to diagnose a specific problem.

- *Bundle patch*: This is a cumulative patch for the corresponding product. These patches include fixes and sometimes some minor enhancements.

- *Patchset update (PSU)*: This is a quarterly patch that contains the most critical fixes.

- *Security patch update (SPU)*: This is a cumulative patch that contains the security fixes for the corresponding product.

As explained in Chapter 2, EBS 12.2.0, which is installed as the base release, is not supported by Oracle. So, EBS 12.2.0 must be upgraded to the latest release immediately after the installation, as we covered in Chapter 2. Thus, within the installation (actually just before the upgrade), the technological components become stable as there are many prerequisite patches for these components to be applied in order to upgrade EBS to the latest release, which is 12.2.5 currently.

However, patching these components is still required. Sometimes because of a bug, sometimes because of security vulnerability, and sometimes just because of the need to adapt the support policies, these components require patching.

As long as there is time to wait until the next patchset to get a fix, applying PSU and SPU patches is enough for the technological components in EBS. As we have mentioned about the adop utility for applying application product patches, technology components have their own tools to be used in patching.

To apply a patch to Oracle Database, Oracle 10.1.2.3 Home, the FMW web tier, or oracle_common, you use the tool opatch. This is a well-known utility in the Oracle world, and core DBAs are quite familiar with it. However, to be able to apply a patch the WebLogic Server environment, you must use the BSU utility.

Although there is a detailed information regarding the installation instructions present in the readme files residing in the patches, we will explain these utilities in detail in the next section, "Different Patching Utilities Under Oracle EBS 12.2."

Deciding on the patching order is as important as applying the patches. The key to deciding the order of patches is identifying whether any prerequisite patches are required to be applied before the patch that you want applied. If there are prerequisite patches for the desired patch, another check should be done to identify whether those prerequisite patches require other prerequisite patches to be applied before applying them. This process of identifying goes on until all the prerequisites are identified. It seems tough, but normally it does not take so much time. There are some scenarios such as upgrading ATG family products that require a lot of prerequisite patches to be applied, but these kinds of operations are rare. So, most of the time, one patch requires one or two prerequisites and that's it. In addition, if the required prerequisite patch is already applied to your system, normally there is no need to apply it again.

However, there are situations where a single patch requires several prerequisite patches. These situations are most likely caused by not keeping the EBS system up-to-date with patching. That is, if the system is not patched often, then the most of the recent bug fixes will be missing, and when a problem that requires a patch to be applied as a fix arises, the prerequisites of that patch will most likely be required to be applied. Moreover, if there are several prerequisites for that patch, this will increase the patching time and also increase the testing effort because there will be more things to test after applying several patches. In this context, we recommend you keep the EBS system up-to-date by applying the latest Mini Packs and recommended patch collections, as long as the business has the ability to give you the required approval for these maintenance operations and the resources for testing them.

There are two methods that can be used to check the prerequisites and decide the patching order. The first one is the manual method, which is the preferred method of the two. It is preferred because of old habits. That is, apps DBAs have administrated the EBS environment since version 11i, and they are accustomed to these methods. The second method is using the Patch Application Assistant (admsi. pl), which is a tool/Perl script for generating the customized installation instructions according to the environment. With Release 12.2, using admsi.pl for determining patching actions has started to become widespread. As a result, even the readme files of the latest patches in EBS 12.2 redirect to admsi.pl for determining the prerequisite actions and patches. In the readme files of these patches, the redirection is made by the statement "run the Patch Application Assistant by entering admsi.pl."

Almost every application patch in 12.2 uses admsi.pl, but for some patches like patches technology stack components, there is still a requirement to read and follow the readme files for the prerequisite actions and installation instructions.

In addition, unfortunately there are some EBS 12.1 patches that can be applied on EBS 12.2 systems. To apply these kinds of patches or determine whether they can be applied to EBS 12.2, you need to follow their readme files carefully. These patches may contain a statement like "For 12.2.X patches (using adop), you can perform the tasks in this section without shutting down the Application tier services," which proves that they can be applied to EBS 12.2 systems.

Therefore, because of these important causes, it is good to know both of these methods and read the readme files carefully even if the patch in question is admsi.pl-compatible.

Let's start with the manual method.

The Manual Method

In the manual method, you connect to Oracle Support and check the readme file of the patch you want to apply. In the readme file, there is a section named "Prerequisites" that lists the prerequisite actions and the prerequisites patches, if there any.

To give you an example of this method, let's walk through the Fusion Middleware patch 17555224: OHSTLS 1.2 WITH CLIENT CERTIFICATE AUTHENTICATION, which is an example for a patch that requires the readme file to be followed.

As shown in Figure 5-1, you connect to My Oracle Support using the URL https://support.oracle.com.

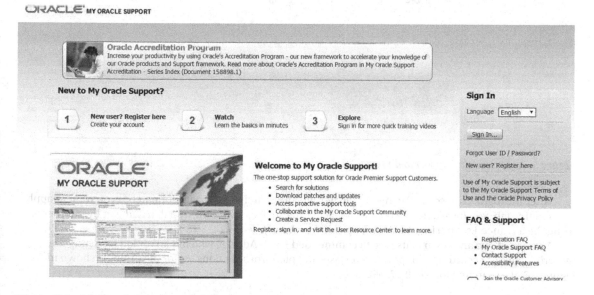

Figure 5-1. *My Oracle Support web page*

Click the Sign In button and supply your credentials on the login page shown in Figure 5-2. The account name you are using to log in to My Oracle Support needs to have at least one valid customer support identification (CSI) associated with it. (The CSI is provided by Oracle when purchasing license and support services.)

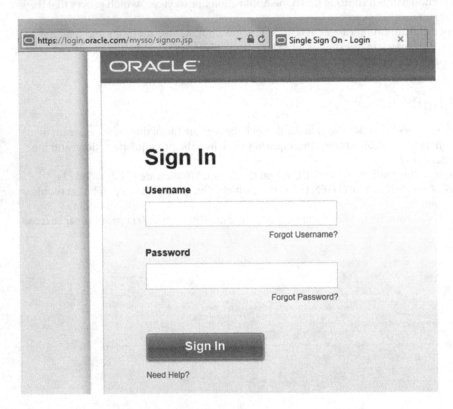

Figure 5-2. *My Oracle Support login page*

After the login, choose the Patches & Updates tab and search for the patch or patches you want to apply.

On this tab, you have different options for searching such as searching by patch name or by number or using the advanced search for searching by product or family.

You even have an option to use the Recommended Patch Advisor, which is an option for listing the required patches according your product, release, and platform selections. As for the example shown in Figure 5-3, we searched for patch 17555224.

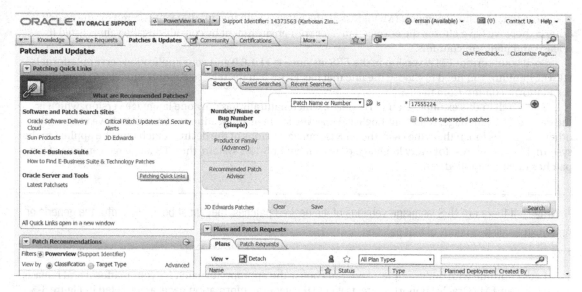

Figure 5-3. *My Oracle Patches & Updates tab*

When the search finishes, you will the list of patches with this number, as depicted in Figure 5-4.

Description	Patch Name	Release	Platform (Language)	Classification	Product
OHSTLS 1.2 WITH CLIENT CERTIFICATE AUTHENTICATION (Patch)	17555224	11.1.1.7.0	Linux x86-64 (American English)	General	Oracle Securit Service
OHSTLS 1.2 WITH CLIENT CERTIFICATE AUTHENTICATION (Patch)	17555224	11.1.1.7.0	HP-UX Itanium (American English)	General	Oracle Securit Service
OHSTLS 1.2 WITH CLIENT CERTIFICATE AUTHENTICATION (Patch)	17555224	11.1.1.7.0	Oracle Solaris on SPARC (64-bit) (American English)	General	Oracle Securit Service
OHSTLS 1.2 WITH CLIENT CERTIFICATE AUTHENTICATION (Patch)	17555224	11.1.1.6.0	HP-UX Itanium (American English)	General	Oracle Securit Service
OHSTLS 1.2 WITH CLIENT CERTIFICATE AUTHENTICATION (Patch)	17555224	11.1.1.6.0	Microsoft Windows x64 (64-bit) (American English)	General	Oracle Securit Service
OHSTLS 1.2 WITH CLIENT CERTIFICATE AUTHENTICATION (Patch)	17555224	11.1.1.6.0	IBM AIX on POWER Systems (64-bit) (American English)	General	Oracle Securit Service
OHSTLS 1.2 WITH CLIENT CERTIFICATE AUTHENTICATION (Patch)	17555224	11.1.1.7.0	IBM AIX on POWER Systems (64-bit) (American English)	General	Oracle Securit Service
OHSTLS 1.2 WITH CLIENT CERTIFICATE AUTHENTICATION (Patch)	17555224	11.1.1.6.0	Oracle Solaris on SPARC (64-bit) (American English)	General	Oracle Securit Service
OHSTLS 1.2 WITH CLIENT CERTIFICATE AUTHENTICATION (Patch)	17555224	11.1.1.7.0	Microsoft Windows x64 (64-bit) (American English)	General	Oracle Securit Service
OHSTLS 1.2 WITH CLIENT CERTIFICATE AUTHENTICATION (Patch)	17555224	11.1.1.6.0	Linux x86-64 (American English)	General	Oracle Securit Service

Figure 5-4. *My Oracle Support patch search page*

Note that My Oracle Support (MOS) lists all the patches with the number you entered for the search criteria; here we have chosen the correct patch for your environment by considering the values listed in release and platform columns.

So, if your current FMW version in the EBS instance is 11.1.6.0 and your application server platform is HP-UX Itanium, you need to choose the line that has 11.1.6.0 in the release column and HP-UX Itanium in the Platform column from the list.

The patch in this example is an FMW patch, which naturally has only one language version, which is the default EBS language, American English. However, some of applications patches may have versions for other languages too. If that's the case, the NLS language versions of the desired patch must be applied to the system. In other words, for every language present in an EBS 12.2 system, the NLS language versions of the patches must be applied, too.

■ **Note** If there are NLS language versions of the desired patches, they must be applied after the generic or American English versions of that patches.

Let's continue with our example. Once you choose the appropriate patch for your platform and release, you click it and My Oracle Support redirects you to the general information page, as depicted in Figure 5-5, where you can see options such as downloading the patch itself, see the bugs resolved by that patch, and see the readme file of it.

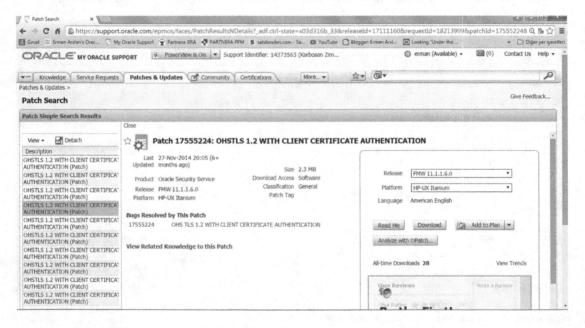

Figure 5-5. *My Oracle Support patch information page*

Click the Read Me button, and My Oracle Support opens the readme file of that patch in a new browser tab, as shown in Figure 5-6.

```
===============================
Interim Patch for Bug: 17555224
===============================

Date: Oct 30, 2014
---------------------------------
Platform Patch for   : HP-UX Itanium
Product Patched      : Oracle Security Service
Product Version      : 11.1.1.6.0
Auto Enabled         : No

This document describes how to install the interim patch for
bug # 17555224. It includes the following sections:

        Section 1, "Prerequisites"

        Section 2, "Pre-Installation Instructions"

        Section 3, "Installation Instructions"

        Section 4, "Post-Installation Instructions"

        Section 5, "Deinstallation Instructions"

        Section 6, "Post Deinstallation Instructions"

        Section 7, "Bugs Fixed by This Patch"

1 Prerequisites
----------------

Ensure that you meet the following requirements before you install or
deinstall the patch:

1. Before applying the non-mandatory patches, ensure that you have the
   exact symptoms described in the bug.

2. Review and download the latest version of OPatch 11.1.x via Bug 6880880.
   (OPatch version 11.1.0.8.3 or higher)
   a. Oracle recommends that all customers be on the latest version of OPatch.
      Review the My Oracle Support note 224346.1, and follow the instructions
      to update to the latest version if needed. Click the following link to
```

Figure 5-6. *My Oracle Support patch readme file*

As you can see, you have several sections in a patch readme. The section names and counts change according to the type, platform, effect, and importance of the patches. But generally, the format in the readme file is like the format displayed in Figure 5-6.

Once the readme file is opened, check the prerequisites first. You take the actions specified in the "Prerequisites" section and continue with the pre-installation, installation, and post-installation instructions. Note that there are de-installation instructions for some of the patches, as well. These instructions may be followed if a patch must be uninstalled because of errors while applying it or because some side effects were discovered after applying it.

So, the previous example shows determining the prerequisites and patching order of a single patch, which is dependent on some prerequisite patches. Naturally the patch order for this patch is to apply prerequisite patches and then to apply the actual patch.

But there can be some cases, especially in applying Oracle applications patches, where you have to apply several prerequisite patches that have several prerequisites as well. If that is the case, you should make a list, and by performing a cross-patch analysis, you must apply the prerequisite patches first. You can merge and apply several prerequisite patches in one go; this approach, which will be explained in Chapter 6, makes the patching easier and faster.

One more thing that makes your job easy is that, nowadays, Oracle Support supplies documents for big patches. Patches like latest AD and TXK Release Updates are documented through their separate Oracle Support documents, which list the prerequisites for them and even the post actions related to them. So, for these kinds of big and important patches, Oracle does these analyses for you and releases them in Oracle Support documents, which makes your lives easier.

Figure 5-7 shows an example of this kind of documentation from Oracle. It is used for upgrading the AD and TXK product releases to their latest versions. It is detailed, and the patching order is present in it.

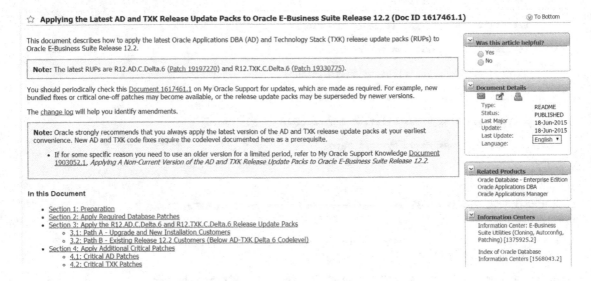

Figure 5-7. *Documentation applying the latest AD and TXT release update packs*

Actually, the update packs AD and TXK Delta 7 were just released, so the latest release for these update packs can be considered as Delta 7. However, the versions of these update packs do not change the approach. Also, the document to be followed (1617461.1) does not change either, because the document 1617461.1 is updated frequently so that it always points to the AD and TXK update pack patches for the latest release.

We mentioned the patches that redirect you to admsi.pl for determining the prerequisite and installation instructions; AD.C.Delta.6 is one of those patches, as shown in the example screen in Figure 5-8.

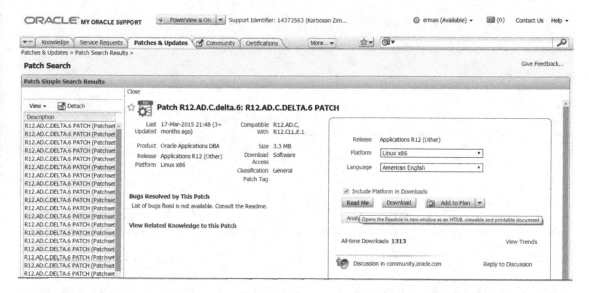

Figure 5-8. *My Oracle Support patch general information page for the AD.C.Delta.6 patch*

When you open the readme file of these kinds of patches, you see instructions that say the following:

1. Source the Applications environment file.

2. Run the Patch Application Assistant by entering "admsi.pl"

The example readme file shown in Figure 5-9 is for patch 19197270, and as shown, the instructions for applying the patch and preparation tasks are clearly specified.

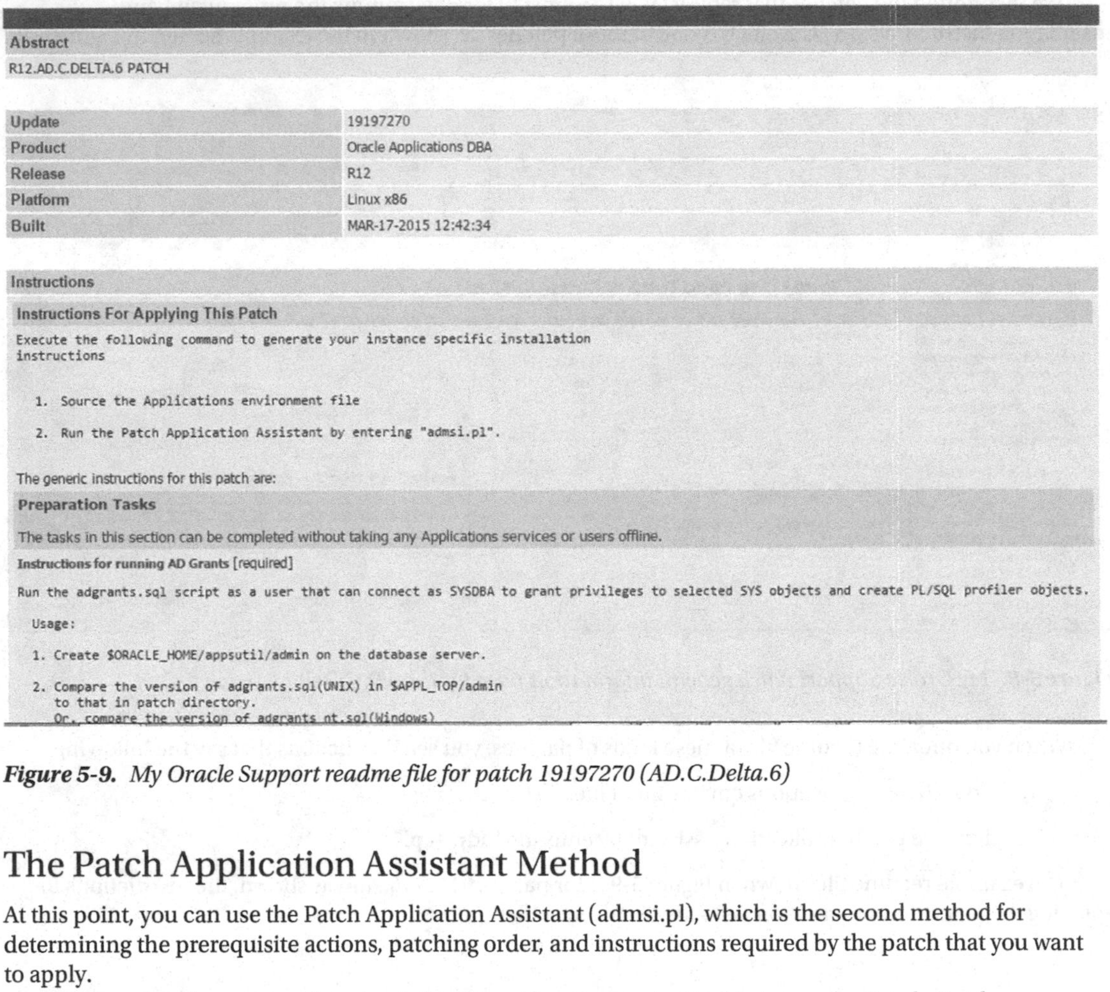

Abstract	
R12.AD.C.DELTA.6 PATCH	

Update	19197270
Product	Oracle Applications DBA
Release	R12
Platform	Linux x86
Built	MAR-17-2015 12:42:34

Instructions

Instructions For Applying This Patch

Execute the following command to generate your instance specific installation instructions

1. Source the Applications environment file

2. Run the Patch Application Assistant by entering "admsi.pl".

The generic instructions for this patch are:

Preparation Tasks

The tasks in this section can be completed without taking any Applications services or users offline.

Instructions for running AD Grants [required]

Run the adgrants.sql script as a user that can connect as SYSDBA to grant privileges to selected SYS objects and create PL/SQL profiler objects.

Usage:

1. Create $ORACLE_HOME/appsutil/admin on the database server.

2. Compare the version of adgrants.sql(UNIX) in $APPL_TOP/admin to that in patch directory.
   Or, compare the version of adgrants_nt.sql(Windows)

Figure 5-9. My Oracle Support readme file for patch 19197270 (AD.C.Delta.6)

The Patch Application Assistant Method

At this point, you can use the Patch Application Assistant (admsi.pl), which is the second method for determining the prerequisite actions, patching order, and instructions required by the patch that you want to apply.

We'll explain how to use the admsi.pl utility with an example. To able to use the Oracle Patch Application Assistant, an X Desktop Viewer such as Vncserver must be used, and the desired patches must be placed in the application file system. So, after downloading the patch zip files, you need to be transferred to a location in the application server with the file ownerships set to application OS user.

In this example, create a folder named ADCDELTA6 in the home directory of the application OS user and unzip the patch there.

```
[applmgr@somenode ~]$ pwd
[applmgr@somenode ~]$ /home/applmgr
[applmgr@somenode ~]$ mkdir ADCDELTA6
--we transfer the patch zip file in to the newly created folder, ADCDELTA6 using our
favorite file transfer utility such as Winscp.
[applmgr@somenode ~]$ cd ADCDELTA6
[applmgr@somenode ADCDELTA6]$
[applmgr@somenode ADCDELTA6]$ ls
p19197270_R12.AD.C_R12_LINUX.zip
--once we upload the patch zip file, we use unzip utility for extracting the patch contents.
```

```
[applmgr@somenode ADCDELTA6]$ unzip p19197270_R12.AD.C_R12_LINUX.zip
[applmgr@somenode ADCDELTA6]$ls
19197270 p19197270_R12.AD.C_R12_LINUX.zip
```

By the way, not all the patches contain the same directories and files, but an application patch typically contains the following files:

README.txt and README.html files: These include the instructions and prerequisite actions required by the corresponding patch. README.txt is in text format, and README.html is in HTML format.

Unified driver file: This is a driver file named with the <patch_name>.drv format, which is used by the patching utility to perform actions such as copying, generating the application objects, and taking database-related actions.

Patch metadata files: These are ldt files in b.<patch-number>.ldt and f.<patch-number>.ldt naming formats. These files are used by the patching utilities for determining prerequisite patches, analyzing the impact of the patch, and comparing the file versions of patch with the file versions present in the system.

The replacement files: These files are usually in the folders named with the related product names such as ad, ar, ap, and so on, and these are the actual files used by the patching utility through the unified driver to replace the files the objects such as SQL, forms, reports, and HTML files with their patched versions.

patch_metadata.xml file: This contains the metadata information about the patch to be applied. admsi.pl reads this file and populates its screens accordingly.

Java files: These are the Java files delivered by the patch. These files are in zip format with names like j<patch_number>_<related_product_short_name>.zip, and they contain Java files such as Java classes.

marker1.txt: This contains the name of the patch zip file.

JRIMETA.dat: This file is an encrypted binary file located in the META-INF directory. The patching utility reads this file to compare the version of the Java class present in the system with the Java class file delivered with the patch to determine whether the update of the relevant Java class is required.

You've now seen the contents of an application patch, so let's continue with the example. When you unzip the patch zip file, the unzip utility will create a folder named with the patch number and extract the content of the zip files into it.

Just after unzipping the downloaded patch file and sourcing the EBS environment file, you run Oracle Patch Application Assistant by executing admsi.pl using the applications operating system user (usually applmgr).

```
[applmgr@daroratestappsrv1 ~]$ . /u01/install/APPS/EBSapps.env run
[applmgr@daroratestappsrv1 ~]$ admsi.pl
```

Once the Oracle Patch Application Assistant is executed, it opens an initial screen with two options (viewing instance-specific or generic instructions for a new patch) and lists the incomplete tasks remaining from the previous patches, as shown in Figure 5-10.

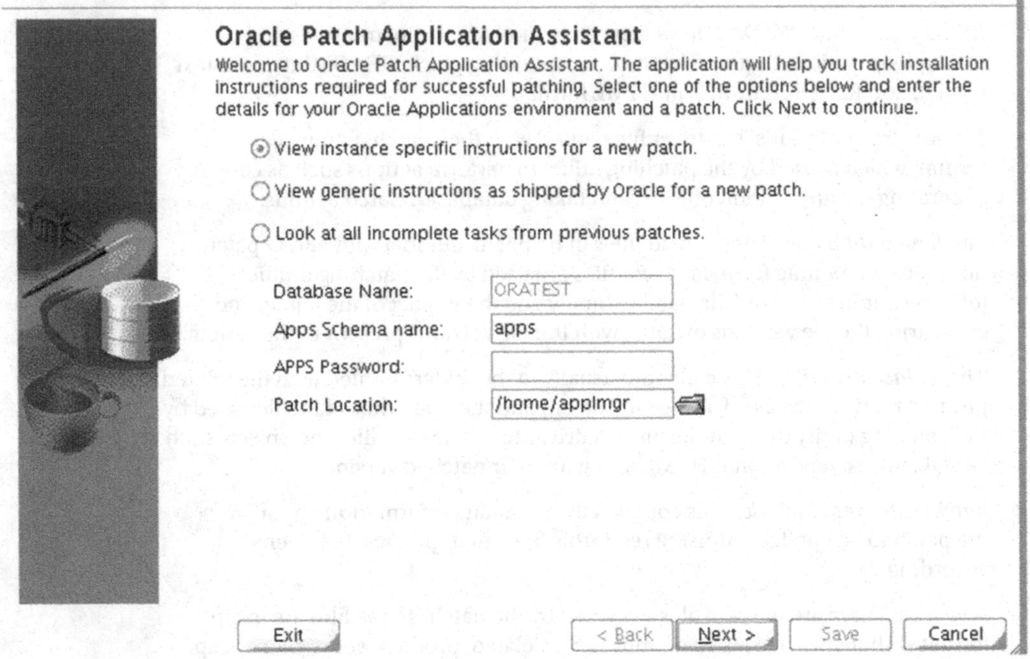

Oracle Patch Application Assistant

Welcome to Oracle Patch Application Assistant. The application will help you track installation instructions required for successful patching. Select one of the options below and enter the details for your Oracle Applications environment and a patch. Click Next to continue.

- ⦿ View instance specific instructions for a new patch.
- ◯ View generic instructions as shipped by Oracle for a new patch.
- ◯ Look at all incomplete tasks from previous patches.

Database Name:	ORATEST
Apps Schema name:	apps
APPS Password:	
Patch Location:	/home/applmgr

Exit   < Back   Next >   Save   Cancel

Figure 5-10. Oracle Patch Application Assistant initial screen

At this point, you choose "View instance specific instructions for a new patch" and specify the apps password and the location of the patch that you unzipped earlier, as shown in Figure 5-11.

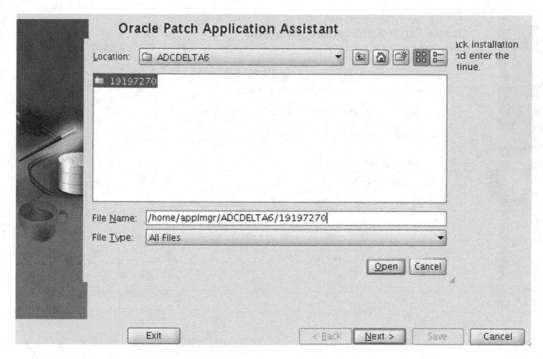

Figure 5-11. *Oracle Patch Application Assistant: viewing instance-specific instructions for a patch and specifying the patch location*

After filling in the APPS Password text box and choosing the location of the patch, click Next, as depicted in Figure 5-12.

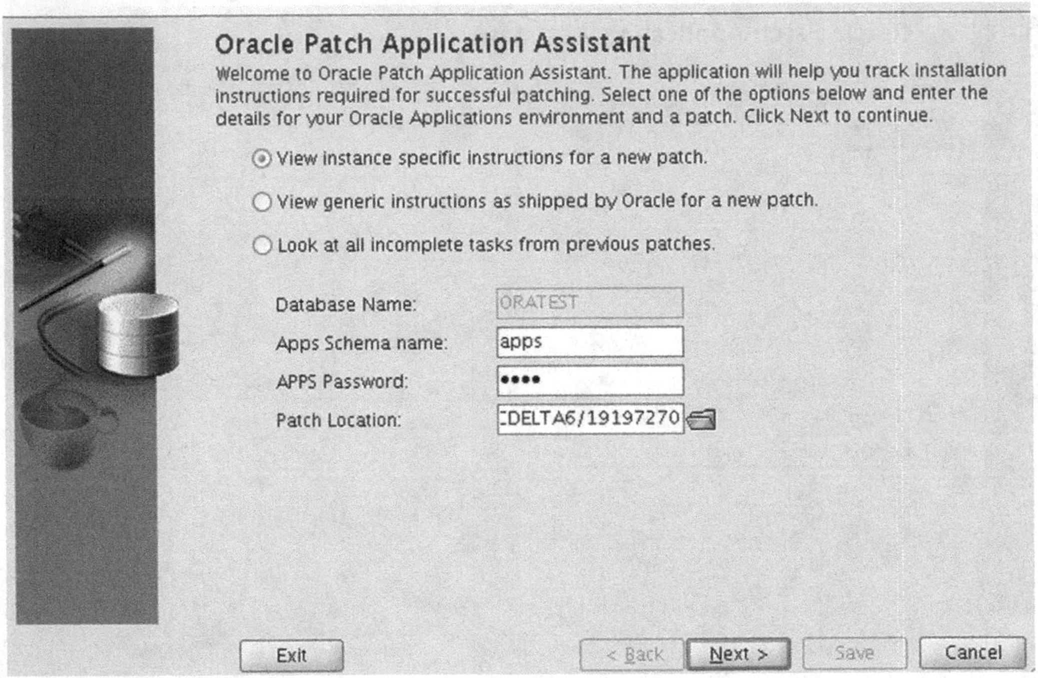

Figure 5-12. *Oracle Patch Application Assistant, viewing instance-specific instructions for patch 19197270 and specifying the apps schema name, password, and patch location*

On the next screen (see Figure 5-13), the Oracle Applications Patch Assistant lists the prerequisite actions and installation instructions with the subtitles Preparation Tasks and Apply the Patch.

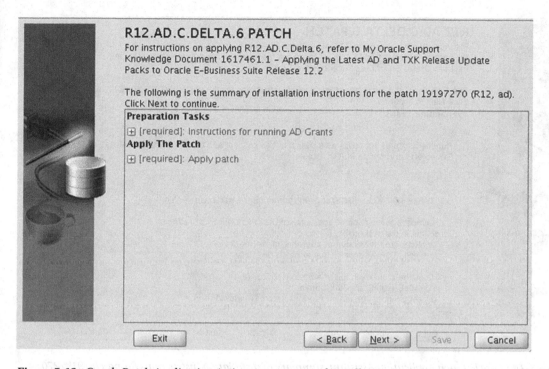

Figure 5-13. *Oracle Patch Application Assistant, summary of installation instructions for patch 19197270*

When a subtitle is expanded, the instructions specific to the environment can be displayed, as shown in Figure 5-14 and Figure 5-15.

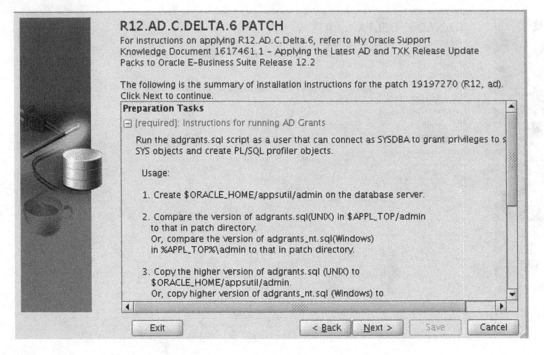

Figure 5-14. Oracle Patch Application Assistant, summary of installation instructions for patch 19197270, continued

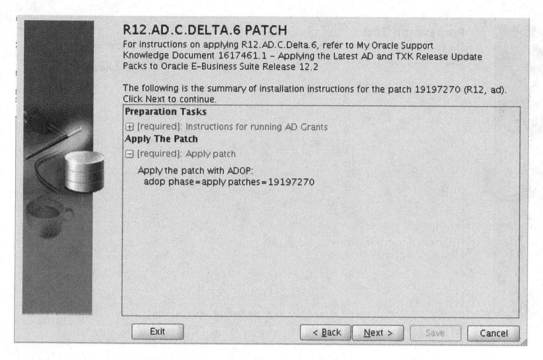

Figure 5-15. *Oracle Patch Application Assistant, summary of installation instructions for patch 19197270, continued*

So, the instructions displayed on this screen are the main function of the Oracle Patch Application Assistant. With this view, the Oracle Patch Application Assistant generates a detailed and clearly explained instruction list, which contains the manual steps for applying a patch in an EBS 12.2 environment. Additional steps may also be detailed depending on the patch, the state of the system, and the products installed.

When you click Next, the instructions come one by one. Once you complete an instruction, you have the opportunity to click the Completed check box and save your work, as shown in Figure 5-16.

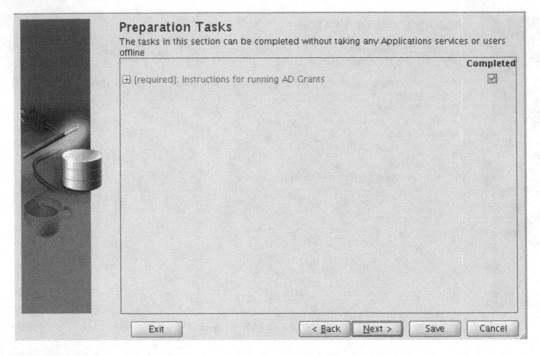

Figure 5-16. *Oracle Patch Application Assistant, completing the preparation tasks*

In addition, the Oracle Patch Application Assistant provides a summary screen, as shown in Figure 5-17, to display the actions that have been done so far or that remain for a patch to become properly applied to the system.

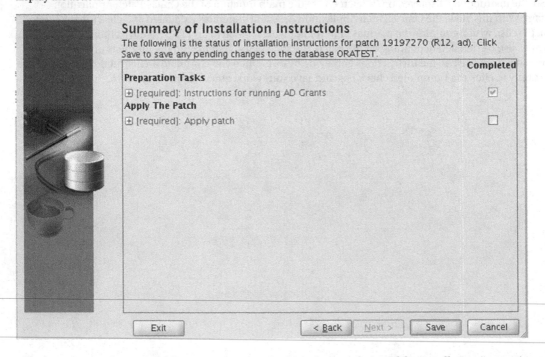

Figure 5-17. *Oracle Patch Application Assistant, checking the completion of the installation instructions*

The Summary of the Installation Instructions screen is the last screen of the Oracle Patch Application Assistant, where you can save the work for a patch in the database and later continue following the patching instructions for that patch from where the assistant left off.

Figure 5-18 shows the summary screen for patch 19197270 where the preparation task of the patch is finished and the current state of the work for this patch is saved.

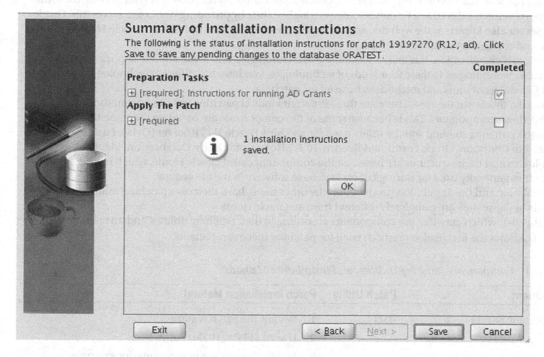

Figure 5-18. *Oracle Patch Application Assistant, saving the work*

As shown in Figure 5-18, the Oracle Patch Application Assistant is really like an assistant who helps both identify the custom actions required by patches and track the work done during the patch applications. So, we and Oracle strongly suggest using this utility for EBS 12.2 patching activities, as recommended in the readme files of EBS 12.2 patches.

Even so, the best approach for determining the instructions needed for patching and deciding on the patching order is using the Oracle Patch Application Assistant in conjunction with reading the readme files of the patches. This is because there are some patches that aren't compatible with the Oracle Patch Application Assistant or using it is not explicitly defined in their readme files. In addition, there may be some important instructions in the readme files of those patches.

The bottom line is that it is important to deal with patching as a whole as it takes more than only using the relevant patching utility to apply an EBS patch properly. Things like determining the required patch, the correct patching order of the actions, and the instructions are the most important parts of the patching activities in EBS 12.2. In other words, these duties constitute 50 percent of the actual patching work, but still there is other important work for applying a patch properly to an EBS 12.2 system. This remaining 50 percent is applying patches using related utilities.

There are different kinds of utilities for different kinds of patches in EBS 12.2. Let's continue with the next section and start getting to know them.

Different Patching Utilities Under Oracle EBS 12.2

As EBS 12.2 is comprised by a bunch of different technological components, patching methods, and utilities for patching, the method of patching differs from one component to other.

These are the components in the technology stack of an EBS 12.2 instance: EBS 12.2 employs Oracle Database (Oracle RDMBS) as the database tier, Oracle Application Server (Oracle AS) for serving the forms and reports services, the Oracle Fusion Middleware architecture by providing WebLogic Server and Oracle HTTP Server also known as the web tier, and an Oracle Common Home (which is an Oracle Home for storing and serving the common modules).

With this classification, this makes four different technologies, and if you add the applications/EBS products as technologies to these four kinds of technologies, you have five different technologies and may expect five different tools and methods to be used for patching.

Luckily, this is not the case. There are three different kinds of patching utilities and methods for patching these components. This is because some of the components are based on the same technologies. That is, the patching method and the utility used for patching Oracle HTTP Server (OHS), Fusion Middleware Common, Oracle Forms and Reports 10.1.2 Home, and Oracle Database are identical, as these technologies and their structures are based on the component called Oracle Home, which is a file system architecture generally used for storing Oracle Database software in the file system.

WebLogic and the application products, on the other hand, have their own patching utilities and methods because they are completely different from an Oracle Home.

Table 5-1, which classifies the components according to their patching utilities and installation methods, shows the installation methods used for patching these components.

Table 5-1. *Components, Patching Utilities, and Installation Methods*

Component	Patch Utility	Patch Installation Method
• WebLogic Server	BSU	1. Review the patch readme.
		2. Use cd $FMW_HOME/utils/bsu.
		3. Follow the readme instructions, for example, by running the command $ bsu.sh.
• OHS (web tier)	opatch	1. Review the patch readme.
• Oracle Common		2. Set ORACLE_HOME.
• Oracle Forms and Reports 10.1.2 Home		3. Include $ORACLE_HOME/OPatch in the PATH.
		4. Change the directory to the patch directory.
• Database (Oracle RDBMS)		5. Follow the readme instructions.
• Oracle applications/product patches	adop	1. Review the patch readme.
		2. Source the application environment file (run edition env).
		3. Prepare the system for patching (adop phase=prepare); this must be done before applying a patch if a patching cycle is not present.
		4. Apply the patch (adop phase=apply).
		5. Complete the patching cycle (adop phase=finalize, adop phase=cutover and adop phase=cleanup).
		6. Synchronize the file systems (adop phase=fs_clone), which is optional.

As shown in the previous table, the components can be categorized into three categories according to the patching utilities and the patching methods.

Patching WebLogic with BSU (BEA Smart Update)

WebLogic patches are applied online by following the online patching process of EBS 12.2, which we will explain in detail in the next section. To apply a patch to WebLogic Server inside an EBS 12.2 system, you basically create an online patching cycle, source the patch edition, and use BSU utility, which is also known as Smart Update. Actually, we prefer to call this utility BEA Smart Update, because the letter *B* in BSU stands for the company BEA, which Oracle acquired in 2008. BEA was the owner of WebLogic Server, before it was acquired by Oracle.

To patch the WebLogic instance, you normally start by downloading the required patches from Oracle Support and placing them in the application server or servers where your WebLogic instance resides. Once the patches are downloaded and unzipped in the $FMW_HOME/utils/bsu/cache/dir location in the patch file system, BSU can be run from the $FMW_HOME/utils/bsu directory as follows:

1. With the application OS user (for example, applmgr), open a VNC server connection.

2. Create an online patching cycle and set the patch edition environment using the EBSapps.env script using the command . EBSapps.env patch. Alternatively, the utility can be run from the run edition environment, if the purpose of running it is just to control the WebLogic patching information (for example, checking the applied patches).

   - cd /u01/install/APPS

   - . EBSapps.env run

   - adop phase=prepare

   - . EBSapps.env patch

3. Change the directory where the bsu.sh resides using a command like cd $FMW_HOME/utils/bsu.

4. Execute the bsu script using the command . /bsu.sh.

Once the BSU utility starts, it will list the patches present in the cache directory where you have unzipped them. BSU makes patching easier because it provides you with the opportunity to apply the desired patch or patches by just clicking a button. Figure 5-19 shows an example of the BSU initial screen.

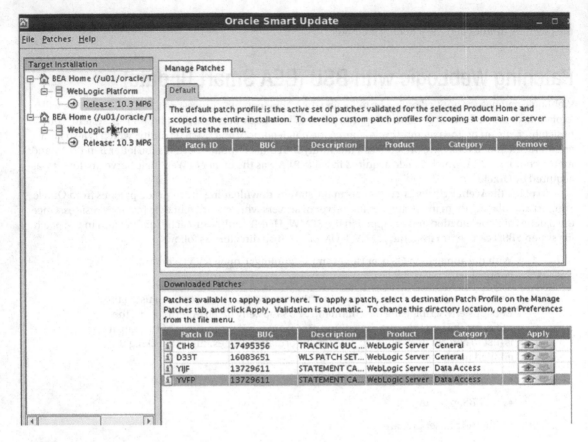

Figure 5-19. BSU utility

As an alternative for the interactive BSU screen, you can apply the WebLogic patches using terminal screens in noninteractive mode using the following command format:

```
bsu.sh \
-prod_dir=<path>/FMW_Home/wlserver_10.3 \
-patchlist=<patchID>
-verbose -install
```

After installing the WebLogic patches, you proceed with the adop finalize, cutover, and cleanup phases to complete the online patching cycle as follows:

- adop phase=finalize

- adop phase=cutover

- adop phase=cleanup

So, the approach for patching WebLogic in EBS 12.2 is pretty straightforward because it is based on the standard WebLogic patching tool BSU, which can be executed easily from the command line and which also has a user-friendly graphical user interface.

Patching the Application Tier Oracle Homes and the Database with Opatch

The required actions for patching the technology stack components such as Oracle Forms and Reports Home, Oracle HTTP Server (web tier), and Oracle Common are pretty straightforward, too. These components can be classified as application tier Oracle Home–based components, and the utility used for patching them is opatch, which is an Oracle-supplied tool well-known by core database administrators. Like with WebLogic inside EBS 12.2, these components are patched online.

The required patching actions for the Oracle Database component is similar to the technology stack components. The only difference is you create any online patching cycle before patching the database, as the database patches are not handled with the online patching feature of EBS 12.2.

To patch a technology stack component with opatch, you need to create an online patching cycle, set the patch edition environment, set the Oracle Home to the Base directory (ORACLE_HOME directory) of the component, set the PATH for its terminal session to include the Opatch directory present in the corresponding ORACLE_HOME directory, change the current working directory to the directory where the patch is unzipped, and issue an opatch apply command from there. Lastly, once the patch application is finished, you need to complete the patching cycle to complete the patching process.

In this context, follow these steps:

1. To patch OHS (web tier), Forms and Reports Home, and Oracle Common Home, follow these steps:

   - Connect to the application server using the application OS user, create an online patching cycle, set the patch environment using the EBSapps.env script located in the Base EBS apps tier directory, set the ORACLE_HOME and PATH environment variables accordingly, and execute the opatch apply command.

   Here's an example:

   ```
   cd /u01/install/APPS
   . EBSapps.env run
   adop phase=prepare
   . EBSapps.env patch
   ```

2. For patching the web tier, the required environment settings are as follows:

   ```
   export ORACLE_HOME= $FMW_HOME/webtier/
   export PATH=$ORACLE_HOME/OPatch: $PATH
   ```

3. For patching Oracle Common, the required environment settings are as follows:

   ```
   export ORACLE_HOME=$FMW_HOME/oracle_common/
   export PATH=$ORACLE_HOME/OPatch:$PATH
   ```

4. For patching Forms and Reports 10.1.2 Oracle Home, the required environment settings are as follows:

   ```
   export PATH=$ORACLE_HOME/OPatch: $PATH
   ```

Note that you don't need to set ORACLE_HOME for 10.1.2 Home patches, as it is the default Oracle Home sourced by the EBSapps.env environment file.

After setting the environment, you change your directory to the directory where you unzipped the patch and execute opatch for applying the patch or patches to the patch edition from there.

- cd /patch_dir

- opatch apply

After applying the patch or patches using the opatch apply command, you proceed with the adop finalize, cutover, and cleanup phases to complete the patching cycle.

- adop phase=finalize

- adop phase=cutover

- adop phase=cleanup

Note that we have given opatch apply as the command that should be used to apply Oracle Home patches using the opatch utility. However, there may be some exceptional situations where you may need to execute opatch using arguments such as napply or auto. The requirements for using these kinds of arguments are explicitly stated in the patch readme files or Oracle Support documents, which direct you to apply the patches.

As mentioned earlier, you don't create an online patching cycle or set the patch environment before applying EBS 12.2 database patches (there is no patch environment in the database tier anyway). What you do for patching the EBS 12.2 database is not different from any other Oracle database. You just source the database environment and execute Opatch. Following the readme files of the patches is also important, as most of the database patches require the database to be shut down, and some of the database patches require manual actions as well.

To patch Oracle Database (RDBMS), follow these steps:

- Connect to the database server using the database OS user, also known as the Oracle software owner, and set the runtime environment, present in the Oracle Home of the database. Once the general environment is set, set the PATH environment variable properly to include the Opatch directory and lastly execute the opatch apply command.

For patching Oracle Database Home, the required environment settings are as follows:

```
cd <ORACLE_HOME directory> (For example: /u01/install/PROD/11.2.0)
Source the database environment : . <s_systemname>_<s_hostname>.env
export PATH=$ORACLE_HOME/OPatch: $PATH
```

- cd /patch_dir

- opatch apply

Just like the application tier component patches, there may be some exceptional situations in the database tier. That is, for some patches, you may need to execute opatch using arguments like napply or auto; the requirements for using these kinds of arguments are explicitly stated in the patch readme files or Oracle Support documents that direct you to apply the patches.

opatch is an easy-to-use utility despite its wide range of capabilities. The utility is based on an inventory mechanism and may list the patches and bug fixes currently present in the system using the inventory it maintains. Like BSU, opatch provides an ability to roll back/remove the patches applied without depending on the time the patches in question are applied. But in contrast with BSU, opatch does not require a vncserver connection. So, it is a tool that works in the text terminal.

You can use the opatch -help command to display the usage for different options present in opatch.

```
opatch -help
Oracle Interim Patch Installer version 11.2.0.3.0
Copyright (c) 2012, Oracle Corporation.  All rights reserved.
 Usage: opatch [ -help] [ -report ] [ command ]


          command := apply
                     lsinventory
                     lspatches
                     napply
                     nrollback
                     rollback
                     query
                     version
                     prereq
                     util
...
```

It is important to know that the patches may have pre-installation and post-installation instructions, too. As explained in the introduction of this chapter, patching is not all about executing the appropriate tool for the component to be patched.

An example of this is a database patch, which may require a SQL script to be executed with a database user who has SYSDBA privileges, as instructed in the readme file. In these cases, you need to apply the desired patch using the opatch utility and execute the SQL pointed at by the readme file of that patch. This kind of situations applies to the Forms and Reports, Oracle Common, and OHS patches, too. That's why we remind you of the importance of reading the readme files, once again.

Applying the Applications Patches with the ADOP Utility

After explaining the opatch and BSU utilities, we'll continue with the adop utility, which is the tool for applying the application product patches.

adop is an acronym for "applications DBA online patching" and was introduced in EBS 12.2. Although adop internally uses the adpatch utility, which is used for patching in earlier releases, it replaces adpatch in general.

As mentioned earlier, patches for the database and other technological components patches are applied to the EBS 12.2 systems rarely. That is, once the installation and upgrade to the latest available release of a new EBS 12.2 are complete, you'll rarely need to apply technology component and database patches.

But this is not the case for application product patches, as EBS 12.2 is a huge system consisting of several products, and product codes are at the top level of its technology stack. As a result, application product patches are the most frequently applied patches in an EBS 12.2 environment during and after the initial deployment. As stated earlier, these patches are applied using the adop utility.

In EBS 12.2, the application patches are applied online, and as the name of the utility implies, the adop utility is used for online patching in EBS 12.2.

The instructions for applying a patch with adop are as follows:

1. Log in to the application server using the application OS user (for example, applmgr).

2. Set the environment <EBS_ROOT>/EBSapps.env run.

3. Unzip the patch to the $APPL_TOP_NE/../patch directory pointed at by the $PATCH_TOP environment variable.

4. Run the Oracle Patch Application Assistant (admsi.pl) and follow the instructions.

5. Run the adop utility.

- adop phase=prepare

- adop phase=apply patches=123456

- adop phase=finalize

- adop phase=cutover

- . <EBS_ROOT>/EBSapps.env run

- adop phase=cleanup

Note that you set the environment again just before the cleanup phase. This is because during the cutover phase, the current run edition becomes the patch edition, and vice versa. The details of this operation will be given later in this chapter.

So far, you have seen the different patching utilities used in EBS 12.2. As you can see, the adop utility is based on a more complex structure than others. It governs the phases, and it is based on the dual file system and edition-based redefinition feature in the back end.

As mentioned, the application product patches are mostly applied patches in an EBS 12.2 environment, which makes the adop utility important. To understand this complexity, you have to take a closer look at the utility, understand the technologies supporting it, and understand its own logic and terms, especially the phases.

Introduction to Online Patching Utility (adop)

Online patching in EBS 12.2 is a big advancement, and it brings some changes to support this completely new patching architecture and method for apps DBAs. Using the adop utility is one of the major changes in EBS 12.2, and it actually drives the online patching architecture supplied by EBS 12.2.

The online patching architecture is provided by Oracle, and it is provided by having a dual file system consisting of two apps tier file systems named fs1 and fs2 in the application tier and using the edition-based redefinition feature of RDBMS 11g R2 and 12C in the database tier. Moreover, the new patching methodology in EBS 12.2 brings five phases: prepare, apply, finalize, cutover, and cleanup. The term *patching cycle* is used to describe the new patching process consisting of these five phases. adop is the tool that creates this patching cycle, advances the phases, and applies the patch files to the system.

We will use all these terms while discussing online patching in EBS 12.2 later in this chapter, and Chapter 6 is devoted to adop. Right now we'll introduce the adop utility and explain the method used for applying application patches in EBS 12.2.

Just like the other patches, to apply an application patch using the adop utility, the patch must be downloaded from Oracle Support and placed in an appropriate location in the application file system. Unlike the case with the opatch, there is no need to execute the adop command from the directory where the patch file resides. You can run adop from any directory as long as the environment is set properly.

Patches can be placed into the $APPL_TOP_NE/../patch directory, which is the default location where adop looks for patches when invoked, or the patches can be placed in any directory where the application OS user has the appropriate file permissions.

Note that if the patches are located in a nondefault directory, that directory should be given as an input to adop. This is accomplished using the patchtop argument, which you will see in Chapter 6.

So, the environment must be set before applying the patches. Setting the environment for adop is only about setting the application environment. Before trying to apply a patch with adop, you set the environment with the script EBSapps.env by supplying "Run" as an argument to it. Here's an example:

```
EBSapps.env Run
```

Once your patch is in place (unzipped and the ownerships configured) and the prerequisites mentioned in the readme file of the patch are met, you start by executing adop phases in the following sequence:

1. adop phase=prepare

2. adop phase=apply

■ **Note** In addition to the application patches applied using adop, you can apply WebLogic and other application technology stack component patches at this point before going any further in the patching cycle.

---

3. adop phase=finalize

4. adop phase=cutover

5. adop phase=cleanup

We will cover the phases in detail in the next section, but here we'll give you some introductory information about them. The first phase, which is the prepare phase of adop, is used for preparing the system for online patching, and it starts a new patch cycle. Continuing with the apply phase, you actually apply the patch in question. With the finalize phase, you finalize things with actions such as compilations.

Until the time you execute the cutover phase, all the things done by adop can be rolled back, but once the cutover phase is finished, there is no option for rolling back anymore. At this point, you execute adop phase=cutover, and the patched files are actually activated. By design, a near-zero downtime occurs. This downtime is caused by the need to restart application services for making them use the patched files.

In the last phase, which is the cleanup phase, the objects created for the use of online patching are cleaned up. After the cutover phase is completed, the patch becomes applied, and the patched files and database objects can be used by the applications.

Besides the phases, adop have several capabilities. It can abort a patching activity/patching cycle, and it can initiate a file system clone operation, all of which will be covered in Chapter 6.

As the bottom line, the logic used in online patching in EBS 12.2 is to patch the nonactive files and nonactive database objects without touching any of the active ones and doing a file system and database edition switch-over, once the patching work finishes. The separation of these activities is done by using the phases and is driven by the adop utility.

The logic is clear; however, the structure that makes the online patching available is a complex one. Let's take a look at the structure by explaining the technologies behind online patching.

Technological Changes for Supporting Online Patching

To provide online patching, EBS 12.2 uses two major technologies. There are two technologies because there are two major tiers in an EBS environment: the application tier and the database tier. EBS 12.2 uses an additional file system as a copy/patch file system to build a file system structure for supplying the online patching requirements in the application tier. As for the database tier, EBS 12.2 uses the edition-based redefinition feature of Oracle Database to provide the online patching requirements of the database objects.

These two major technologies introduced in EBS 12.2 are tightly integrated, and they are orchestrated by the new patching utility, adop, as mentioned in the previous section. Using these two technologies, EBS 12.2 applies the patches into the copy of the production system, does not interfere the production environment, and thus provides the business continuity even while a patching is being applied. In other words, patching any module does not cause the entire system to be down.

The phrase "copy of production system" is used for describing a patch file system in the application tier and a patch edition in the database tier. So, when an application tier code change is required by the patch, this change is made in the patch file system, and when a database object needs to be changed, the action is done in the patch edition of the EBS database.

The editioned objects and file system structures are created by the copies of the production objects, and during an online patching operation, only the objects to be changed by the patches are copied; in other words, application data is not copied during an EBS 12.2 online patching operation. As mentioned earlier, the idea behind online patching in EBS 12.2 is to apply the patch to the copy and then to switch the copy to be the real one, and vice versa.

Switching the copy to be the real one with near-zero downtime requires restarting the application services, which is automatically done by the adop utility and which creates a downtime measured in minutes. Although there is downtime in switching the file system and editions, the control of the downtime is in your hands. That is, you as the apps DBA may complete the online patching operations during office hours and then execute the cutover phase, which makes the switch, during night time when downtime is acceptable. Of course, following such a method like applying a patch and waiting for the switch for a long time has some side effects to the application; we will explain these effects in Chapter 6.

So, let's explore the dual file system structure in EBS 12.2 so you have a better understanding of online patching. In EBS 12.2, in addition to the application file system, a secondary file system is used. This secondary file system, called the patch file system, is a copy of the application's currently active file system called the run file system, and it is kept synchronized by the patching tools.

Although the name dual file system implies two file systems, there is another file system, called the noneditioned file system, present in the EBS 12.2 application tier to support online patching architecture. Therefore, you actually have three file systems in EBS 12.2: fs1, fs2, and fs_ne (noneditioned). fs1 and fs2 can switch roles by design. The switching of file systems, which is done by adop in the cutover phase, makes this happen. That is, in the cutover phase of adop, the run file system becomes the new patch file system, and the patch file system becomes the new run file system. So, at any one time, fs1 or fs2 can be the run file system or the patch file system.

Nevertheless, the EBSapps.env script mentioned earlier in this chapter eases your work to determine and operate on these file systems. If it is executed with the run argument, the EBSapps.env script sets your environment to point at the run file system, and if it is executed with the patch argument, the EBSapps.env script sets your environment to point at the patch file system.

The third file system is fs_ne, the noneditioned file system. It contains the types of files that are not changed during the application patches, such as log files, report outputs, and data import/export files. As the files in fs_ne are not changed by the patches, they are not synchronized during patching activities.

Figure 5-20 represents the dual file system and the fs_ne file system (noneditioned file system).

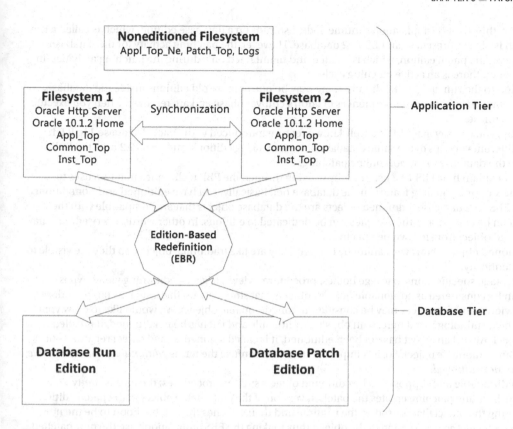

Figure 5-20. *Dual file system and noneditioned file system*

As shown in Figure 5-20, you have three file systems but one database. The run and patch file systems are shown as Filesystem 1 and Filesystem 2. They connect to the same database although their roles are different from each other, and that's why you see the edition-based redefinition feature in the figure; the editions created using the edition-based redefinition feature make multiple database editions available for multiple application tier file systems. Thus, EBR lets EBS have a patch file system that connects to the patch edition and a run file system that connects to the run edition.

In other words, like adop makes its patching activities on the copies of the application objects, the work needed for patching the database objects is done on the copies of the corresponding database objects.

Understanding Edition-Based Redefinition Usage in Online Patching

EBR is an isolation mechanism that supplies the online patching of database objects. The editions created in the EBS database define what you view. That is, EBR allows applications such as EBS 12.2 to use the application definitions and the changes in different editions inside the Oracle Database.

Thus, there may be two copies of the same database object in a single database, and the patching utility adop may use the patch editions to make the database changes required by the patches on copies of the database objects. This brings with it an opportunity to upgrade or patch the database objects online without interrupting the end users.

To support this, the EBS application runtime code also runs on a database edition, which is called a run edition, which is always present in an EBS 12.2 database. However, the patching activity for the database objects is done in the patch edition, which is created and maintained only during the patching activities, in other words, when there is an active patching cycle.

In addition to the run and patch editions, there may be one or more old editions inside the database. These old editions arise from the consequences of adop's cutover phase and are removed when you execute adop's cleanup phase.

To sum up, you can say that EBR is a well-known feature introduced with Oracle Database 11g R2. It isolates the different versions of the same database objects by using editions, and EBS 12.2 uses the EBR feature inside the database to support online patching.

We'll now explain how EBS 12.2 uses EBR by walking through the EBR techniques that EBS uses to support the new online patching feature in the database tier. Basically, you have editioned and noneditioned objects in an EBS 12.2 database. Editioned objects are the database objects that are compatible with the EBR, so they can be copied, and these copies can be dedicated to editions. In other words, every edition may see an editioned object from its own perspective.

Noneditioned objects, however, cannot be copied. They are like traditional objects, so they are visible to all editions identically.

While package specifications, package bodies, procedures, views, triggers, editioning views, types, and synonyms can be considered as editionable objects, objects that store data on them such as tables, indexes, materialized views, and sequences may be considered noneditionable objects. We would like to draw your attention to the terminology used here. If an object is editonable and if it has been editioned, it is called an editioned object. Also, if an object has not been editioned, it is called a noneditioned object regardless of whether it is an editionable object. So, it is important to not to confuse the terms *editionable*, *noneditionable*, *editioned*, and *noneditioned*.

For the editionable and supposed to be editioned objects such as procedures, the idea is pretty straightforward. Online patching creates the patched version of the editionable object in the patch edition without touching the object that is used by the runtime and then switches the patch edition to be the new run edition to activate the new version of the object, thus making the EBS applications use the new patched version instantaneously.

As you may have noticed, EBS 12.2 supplies the online patching feature even though there are noneditioned objects inside an EBS database. EBS handles these noneditionable objects by using advanced features of EBR such as editioning views, cross-edition triggers, and editioned data storage in the back end.

In the case of the patching table structure, rather than copying the tables and using the copies for patching, EBS uses different ways to alter the tables without breaking the online patching methodology. By using editioning views, the tables in an EBS 12.2 database can be seen in different forms according to the editions. So, these editioning views are the keys for the structure to support online patching, and that's why by design all the code in EBS 12.2 uses these editioning views to access the database tables. Even the custom codes and third-party product codes must not access EBS 12.2 tables directly; rather, the EBS tables must be accessed via synonyms defined in the APPS schema.

Any third-party schema, either from third-party products or custom code, must access Oracle E-Business Suite tables via the synonyms in the APPS schema. Direct access to Oracle E-Business Suite tables may produce incorrect results.

In this context, when a patch needs to alter a column of a database table, it is actually a new column with the desired attributes into that database table. As a result, changing a column does not affect the application because the application continues to see the table the way it was before the new column was added. This is accomplished by using the editioning views.

■ **Note**   EBS 12.2 can use the old format without any admin intervention, as EBS uses editioning views to reach the tables.

To support online patching, the application tables in EBS have editioning views in front of them. These editioning views are named almost identically with their corresponding tables. The only difference in naming is that editioning views have # characters added as suffixes on their names. For example, the EBS 12.2 database uses an editioned view named FND_NODES # for reaching the FND_NODES table in an editioned manner.

The FND_NODES table belongs to the APPLSYS schema, and it stores the node information in an EBS 12.2 environment. When EBS needs to use the FND_NODES table, it uses the APPS schema, and since the APPS schema has synonyms defined for the application tables and because these synonyms are defined with the same names as their corresponding tables, FND_NODES is accessed through the synonym.

The important thing here is that the synonyms are not created to directly point to the tables they are created for. These synonyms in the EBS 12.2 environment actually point to the editioning views, which are created to reach the underlying table according to the editions. So, in the case of FND_NODES, the synonym in the APPS schema named FND_NODES points to the editioning view, which is named FND_NODES#. The FND_NODES# editioning view reaches the FND_NODES table according to the editions.

As the editioning views are used to reach the tables, the session (or let's say the applications operating on the tables) sees the tables in the format according to their editions.

To have a better understanding about this, suppose a column is altered during a patch application. Suppose that the patch changes the column type from number(10) to number(15). In EBS 12.2, to make this operation, the online patching mechanism does not change the actual column. Rather than doing that, the mechanism adds a new column with a type of number(15) to the underlying table.

By doing so, the patching tools or patch edition may work on the table while the application or run edition actually uses it. The patching tools see the table with its new structure, and the application continues to see the tables like it has never changed. This happens without any invalidations or code breaks.

Figure 5-21 represents this scenario, where the patch edition view sees the table with a newly added column named ID2, while the run edition view continues to see the table as unchanged, with its run edition columns.

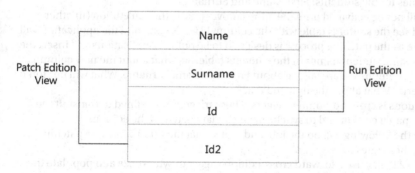

Figure 5-21. Patch edition view vs. run edition view of application tables

As shown, the patch edition and run edition view the same table at the same time, but they see different columns, so this makes sure patching and the running applications do not conflict with each other. This makes the system remain stable, and patching can continue while the applications are running.

In addition to the editioning views, using the cross-editioning trigger feature of EBR is crucial for building an online patching environment in modern systems like EBS 12.2. Cross-editioning triggers are triggers that are triggered when the data in the actual edition changes and populates the tables in other editions with these new data changes to make them be synchronous with the base table. Figure 5-22 depicts the scenario where a cross-edition trigger is triggered to propagate the changes done in the original column named ID to the new version of it named ID2, which is added by a patch.

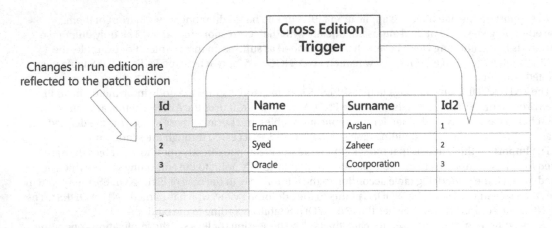

Figure 5-22. Cross-edition triggers populating newly added column

These triggers are used in EBS 12.2 to propagate the changes to a table during a patch application. As explained earlier, in such a patching scenario like changing the definition of a column to a table, this change will first be added in the patch edition. While the new table structure remains in the patch edition, the run edition (in other words, the applications) won't see this column with its new description. Consider a scenario that changing the column description actually affects the data. That is, consider that a patch is used for changing the way the full name of the students in the student table is stored. That is, consider that there was only one column named FULL NAME to store the full names of the students before the patch.

Now consider that with the new structure that comes with the patch, the student table will have two columns for storing the full names for the students: First Name and Surname.

So, as the new structure will not be activated until the adop cutover phase, the run edition (in other words, the application) will still see the students table with the column FULL NAME, and the application will continue to operate on this table as the patching process is designed to be online. Applications will insert the new student name or update existing student names in the students table. So, what about the new columns defined by the patch in the patch edition? We are talking about First Name and Surname. What will be stored there? What about the new inserts? What about the updated data?

The answer for these questions is cross-editioning triggers. These triggers are defined to transmit the data from the run edition to the patch edition and to synchronize the data between the editions.

A cross-edition trigger like the following will do the job, and that's what the EBS 12.2 online patching mechanism uses for answering these questions.

In a scenario like this, EBS 12.2 may use a forward cross-edition trigger to syncronize and populate the new column.

```
CREATE OR REPLACE STUDENTS_FTRG
BEFORE INSERT OR UPDATE
ON FULL_NAME
FOR EACH ROW
FORWARD CROSSEDITION
DISABLE
BEGIN
:NEW.FIRSTNAME := TRIM(SUBSTR(:NEW.FULLNAME, 1, INSTR(:NEW.FULLNAME, ' ', -1)));
:NEW.SURNAME := TRIM(SUBSTR(:NEW.FULLNAME, INSTR(:NEW.FULLNAME, ' ', -1)));
END STUDENTS_ FTRG;
/
```

The previous trigger can be used in making newly inserted or updated values in the old edition be synchronized with the new edition.

So, as you may have noticed, there is a forward cross-edition statement in the previous code, which defines the trigger STUDENTS_FTRG as a forward cross-edition trigger.

It is important to mention that forward cross-edition triggers are not the only type of cross-edition triggers used in EBS 12.2.

That is, although the general logic of online patching in EBS 12.2 is having only one way to synchronize, which is from the new edition to the old edition, there are some exceptional cases where you also see reverse cross-edition triggers come into play. This is rare, but there are cases where online patching needs synchronizing with the old edition from the data stored in the new edition. In such cases like "updating a column in a seed table, that has a not null constraint, with no default value" or "updating a column which is part of an unique index," you can see reverse cross-edition triggers for synchronizing the updated data from the patch edition to the run edition.

■ **Note**   You may see the reverse cross-edition triggers in some exceptional cases, but you see the forward cross-edition triggers almost in every case where a table structure is changed via online patching.

During online patching, forward cross-edition triggers are created in the patch edition, and they are triggered when the changes are made in the old (run) edition. Oracle has chosen to use cross-edition triggers for these type of operations as they can be reexecuted automatically for all the rows that are inserted or changed by the running application. As for the patches that change the structure of application tables, forward cross-edition triggers are used for synchronizing the old rows as well. In this context, a simple update like update example_table set dummy=dummy will trigger the forward cross-edition trigger that is defined on top of the table named example_table, and as a result, all the current rows of example_table are synchronized.

In the case of the tables that store the seed data, the method is different. The table data is actually copied during a patch application, and EBS uses the virtual private database (VPD) feature to create views of data according to the edition that queries the data. The copying of data is done in the table. That is, seed tables have an additional column named ZD_EDITION_NAME to store the edition type of a row. So, the seed data (the rows residing on the seed table, which is in the target of the patch) is copied into the same table, and the values of the ZD_EDITION_NAME columns for these copied rows are set to the patch edition's name. Thus, with the VPD based on the ZD_EDITION_NAME column, the online patching mechanism makes the patch edition see and operate on the copy of the data without touching any of the actual data that is used by the running EBS applications.

There must be sufficient space in the EBS 12.2 database to hold the duplicate copy of the seed data. This is also required for the patches that are changing the columns of the application tables. In this manner, the System tablespace should have at least 25GB of free space available, and the APPS_TS_SEED tablespace should have a minimum of 5GB of free space available before starting an online patching cycle. We also recommend you have at least 10 percent free space available in all other standard EBS tablespaces.

Later, within the cutover phase, the modified data becomes the actual data, and the former actual data becomes the old data, which is removed in the cleanup phase. Oracle calls this method *editioned data storage*, which allows an online patch to modify the seed data online.

Using this approach, what happens basically is that the data in seed data tables is replicated into the same tables where it resides, and the patch operates on the private copy of the data. Thus, any change in the seed data won't affect the running application.

Oracle must have chosen this approach for the seed data, because the seed data is the data used by the code itself, and unlike the application data stored in the application tables, the seed data is created and patched by Oracle.

That is, the patches written for the seed data probably change the data. As you may recall, the patches for the application tables, as explained earlier, usually change the table structures of the related tables, and this is where seed data patches differs. As the patches for seed data usually operate on the data, the online patching mechanism does not follow a method based on the editioning views for supplying the online patching; the purpose of the editioning views is not preventing the data from being accessed concurrently. So, with this design, Oracle does not want to have two database editions to operate on the same data concurrently; a VPD-based operation called *editioned data storage* is used for applying the patches that have seed tables on their targets.

Figure 5-23 represents how the run and patch editions see the data in a single seed table differently.

Seed Table

	Column1	Column2	Column3	Zd_Edition_Name
Run Edition				Run Edition Name
				Run Edition Name
				Run Edition Name
				Run Edition Name
Patch Edition				Patch Edition Name
				Patch Edition Name
				Patch Edition Name
				Patch Edition Name

Figure 5-23. Run edition vs. patch edition view of seed data stored in seed tables

Lastly, the forward cross-edition triggers are used to synchronize the copy of the data that is used by the patch edition and the data used by the run edition, as there may be updates to the actual seed data during a patching cycle, exactly between the apply and cutover phases.

■ **Note** The reverse cross-edition triggers could also be used in such scenarios. In a scenario like seed data loading, reverse cross-edition triggers may be used for ensuring the old NOT NULL or UNIQUE constraints on the old run edition columns are satisfied while the rows are being loaded in the patch edition. However, as no changes in the patch edition are propagated to the run edition, reverse cross-edition triggers are not your concern.

If you pay attention, you'll see we are talking about phases all the time. We explained the phases in general in the introduction of this chapter, but you need to have detailed knowledge about them, as they as a whole may be considered one of the most important systems that the online patching architecture is based on.

So, let's take a closer look at the phases of online patching, also known as the adop phases.

Phases of Online Patching

Unlike earlier releases, EBS 12.2 uses a patching cycle for applying the patches. The patching cycle consists of five major phases, which the online patching mechanism follows for applying any of the application product patches. There is another mechanism, which is the downtime option, that we have already explained in general but you will learn more about in Chapter 6.

So, all the patches except the patches applied with the downtime option can be considered as online patches in EBS 12.2. The patching activities required for these online patches are maintained by the online patching phases also known as adop phases.

To apply a patch online, a patching cycle must be created, which is created by putting the system into the first phase of online patching. The first phase is the prepare phase. To put the system into this prepare phase, as it is applicable for putting the EBS system into any other phases, is done by executing the adop phase=prepare command.

Once adop puts the system into the prepare phase, the patching cycle begins. After the prepare patch, any patches can be applied using adop phase=apply in the patch edition of the EBS system online without touching the runtime codes and objects. Once the application of the patches finish, in other words, once the apply phase is completed, you can proceed with the finalize and cutover phases to activate those changes brought by the patches. What is actually done by proceeding with the finalize and cutover phases is making the EBS 12.2 application start using the newly deployed versions of both the code objects and data structures.

Lastly, in the cleanup phase, all the objects and data created for patching the EBS 12.2 online are cleared from the system, and the patching cycle completes.

■ **Note**   Any time before the cutover, you can abort the patching cycle by using the adop phase=abort command. However, a patching cycle cannot be aborted once the cutover phase is completed.

Figure 5-24 depicts what the phases and methodology followed by online patching looks like.

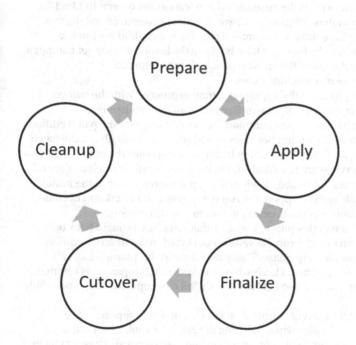

Figure 5-24. *Phases of online patching*

Let's get into the phases in more depth. Starting with the prepare phase (adop phase=prepare), the file system gets synchronized. It is an incremental synchronization, so only the required file system objects are copied from run to patch. The required files for the synchronization are files changed after the last patch is applied to the system. Moreover, a new patch edition is created during the prepare phase. The new database edition is created by making copies of the editioned objects in the database, and the copies don't consume space, as they are like pointers to the runtime objects. In other words, these copies are only the virtual representations of the corresponding runtime objects and actualized only when they are patched. Although the editioned objects do not consume space until they get actualized, this is not true for the patches designed to change the seed data or application table definitions.

The seed data is also copied in this phase, and this copy of rows consumes space inside the database. Thus, it is better to say that, except the seed data and the application table definitions, objects that are supposed to be patched get actualized and start using space in the database patch edition only after they are actually patched/changed.

Continuing with the apply phase, the patches are applied. The adop phase=apply command starts the application of one more patches. While the patching actions required for changing a file system object are done in the patch file system of the application tier, database actions taken by the patch are done in the patch edition for the database tier. So, the apply phase is where the patches are actually applied online to an EBS 12.2 system. However, the patches are applied to the patch edition and patch file system, so they are not activated yet.

Even custom patches that are created by developers to deploy customized objects are applied in this phase. Custom patches are prepared by developers, as well as using Application Management Pack (AMP), which extends the capabilities of Oracle Enterprise Manager 12c Cloud Control to manage an Oracle E-Business Suite 12.2 system more effectively. Note that you can refer to "Developing and Deploying Customizations in Oracle E-Business Suite Release 12.2" (Doc ID 1577661.1) for details about developing and deploying customized database objects, as well as the customized application tier objects in EBS 12.2.

Before activating the patched files and database objects, you have one more phase to complete; this phase is called the finalize phase. The adop phase=finalize command puts the system into the finalize phase, which can be considered a staging point. The finalize phase is where the invalid objects get compiled, derived objects are generated, and DDLs for the use of the cutover phase are precomputed.

The finalize phase is also a terminal phase in a patching cycle.

You can wait as long as you want in this phase for the appropriate time to proceed with the cutover phase, where the application services gets restarted, in other words, where downtime is needed.

Cutover, which is executed by the adop phase=cutover command, is the phase where the patch edition becomes the new run edition and the previous run edition becomes an old edition. In this phase, the patch file system becomes the new run file system, and the patch edition in database becomes the new run edition.

As a result of the cutover, application services are restarted, and that's why downtime is felt by the end users of the EBS applications. That is, end users are logged off when the application services in the middle tier are stopped. When the application middle tier is stopped, the run file system and run edition become old, and the patch file system and patch edition become the run file system and run edition.

Also, some final maintenance is performed in this phase, and after that, users are brought back online when the application services are restarted on the new run file system connected to the new run edition.

The last phase of the patching cycle is the cleanup phase. The action done in this phase is basically cleaning up the environment after applying the patches. This is where the System tablespace gets cleaned, unnecessary objects are deleted, and even the old edition gets deleted if a full cleanup (cleanup_mode=full) is performed.

So far, we have explained the online patching architecture, dual file system, EBR supporting the architecture, and the phases that you need to consider while patching the EBS 12.2 application online. Before continuing with Chapter 6, we will show these concepts in action and discuss backup best practices for EBS 12.2 patching.

Backup Best Practices for EBS 12.2 Patching

You have learned the methodology behind the patching activities in EBS 12.2. You have seen the different methods, different tools, and different patching components along the way. You have seen the opatch and BSU utilities for patching the technological components in EBS 12.2, and you have learned the new online patching mechanism used in EBS product patches and the architecture supporting this mechanism in the previous chapters. So, here we will explain the best practices for backup.

Backing up the system before applying patches to the technology components such as WebLogic and Oracle Home such as 10.1.2 Home and RDBMS is not so crucial, as the utilities used in patching them have the ability to roll back the action they made while patching.

BSU can remove a patch, which has been already applied to WebLogic, and opatch can roll back a patch, which has been applied into an Oracle Home. These are pretty straightforward operations, and removal or de-installation instructions for them can be found in the patch readme files.

Nevertheless, it's worth mentioning the patch de-installation steps for patches that are applied using BSU and opatch. To de-install a WebLogic patch that was applied using BSU utility, you basically execute the BSU with a special argument called remove.

Here is an example of its usage:

```
./bsu.sh3 -remove -patchlist=<patchID1> \ prod_dir=<path>/FMW_Home/wlserver_10.3 -verbose
```

The command to be used removing a WebLogic patch is generally in this format, but there may be some special instructions for the patches. That's why we always recommend reading the readme files, even though the actions needed for installation or de-installation can be memorized.

The following is a snippet from the readme of a WebLogic patch, which is actually a PSU. As you can see, it says to stop the WebLogic server, navigate to MW_HOME/utils/bsu, and execute the command bsu. sh -remove.

```
Uninstalling Oracle WebLogic Server Patch Set Update 10.3.6.0.7
----------------------------------------------------------------

- Stop all WebLogic Servers
- Navigate to the {MW_HOME}/utils/bsu directory.
- Execute bsu.sh -remove -patchlist={PATCH_ID} -prod_dir={MW_HOME}/{WL_HOME}
```

Alternatively, the remove operation can be done using the BSU utility interactively. As you see in Figure 5-25, there is a Remove button for every patch listed in the BSU inventory. So, these Remove buttons can also be used to remove a WebLogic patch from the WebLogic instance of an EBS 12.2 system.

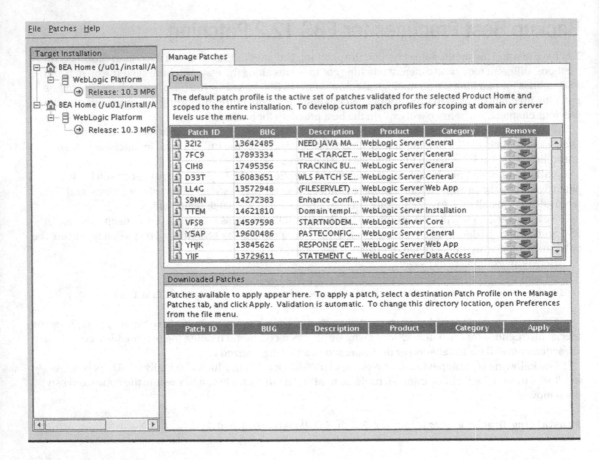

Figure 5-25. BSU Remove buttons

To de-install an Oracle Home patch that was applied using the opatch utility, you basically execute the opatch with the special argument called rollback. Here's an example:

opatch rollback -id <patch number>

Reading the readme file applies for these patches too.

The following is the de-installation part of a patch readme file that belongs to a database patch. As you can see, it requires a SQL script to be executed for the patch to be installed.

```
To deinstall
    Connect to the database using sqlplus / as sysdba
    sqlplus> @catnomgdidcode   (NOTE: file is located in $OH/md/admin)
```

Again, it is straightforward. The principle is just "Read the readme file and execute commands." However, the situation is a little different or a little complicated when it comes to online patching.

That is why we will focus on the backup best practices of online patching in this section.

The online patching mechanism introduced by the new release has an option to roll back the patches up to the cutover phase. The adop utility, when run with the abort option, results in the special phase called the abort phase to be executed for the active patching cycle. Thus, all the changes that occurred by doing the patching activities up to the cutover phase can be rolled back.

The benefits of the online patching mechanism emerge again, but this time in the form of supporting the ability to roll back the changes created by the results of the patching activities.

"Ability to roll back the changes created by patching" means the ability to roll back the patches actually. So, the patches in EBS 12.2 can be rolled back, but the ability to roll back is available up to the cutover phase. Once the cutover is executed, the changes made in the apply phase become committed, and they cannot be rolled back. In other words, a patch or bunch of patches applied as one in one go can be rolled back even after applying them with the opatch phase=apply command.

By knowing this, you could say that if the online patching cycle consisted of only the prepare and apply phases, the EBS 12.2 online patches could be rolled back. However, in reality, there is a phase called cutover in online patching, and the changes cannot be rolled back once they are committed in the cutover phase.

This constraint brings a requirement to take a backup before patching. A cold backup could work, but there is a big downtime for taking a cold backup. An online backup could also work, but it is a time-consuming process and will increase the backup maintenance cost in the environment, so taking an online backup for every patch is not so rational.

The problem here is not actually the method of the backup. It is the backup operation itself that creates the cost. In other words, taking a backup before applying every online patch in EBS 12.2 is not so applicable, as it costs so much that it complicates the patching operation and it increases the backup maintenance operations; therefore, it even reduces the benefits of using online patching.

Therefore, you can use a different method for taking backups and for guaranteeing the ability to roll back the EBS system to a state before the patching activities. The method you should follow to accomplish this involves using the Flashback Database feature of Oracle Database in the database tier and restarting the application services from the relevant file system edition depending on whether the decision to roll back the system is done before the file systems were switched.

To explain this approach properly, let's walk through on a scenario in which you actually need to roll back the system after the cutover phase has been run. Suppose you want to apply a patch to your EBS 12.2 instance and started the patching cycle using the adop phase=prepare command. After the prepare phase, you continue with the adop phase=apply command and apply the patch to the database patch edition and application patch file system. Then you use the adop phase=finalize command to finalize the things before running the adop's cutover phase.

After the finalize phase suppose you execute adop phase=cutover, but cutover fails. Also suppose you try to fix the problem, causing cutover to fail (Oracle suggests so) but could not fix it. Thus, as a last resort, you decide to go back to a state before you ran the cutover phase.

To able to go back to that state, you have to roll back the changes done in the database and application tiers.

In such a scenario, you need to start by rolling back the database to a state before you ran the cutover phase, and to able to do so, you need to have a backup that can restored and used for recovering the database just before running the cutover phase.

If the point-in-time recovery is not preferred, you can also take a full online backup before running the cutover phase. However, taking an online backup in the cutover phase extends the time needed for patching, and therefore it is not applicable for every patch. Suppose you need to apply a patch 10KB in size, but to guarantee the ability to roll back in case of a failure that may be encountered during the cutover phase, you need to take a backup of your EBS environment, which is 500GB in size.

So, backing up the environment would increase the duration of the patch application, and it could take hours to apply a small patch to this system. Without even mentioning the side effects like heavy I/O that backup jobs create, you can understand that taking a full backup before applying a small patch is not a great idea. Similarly, restoring a full backup taken just before the cutover or restoring a full backup that has been taken earlier and doing a point-in-time recovery will be a long process, and it is not applicable to be used in the case of a patching failure.

Let's go back where you started and illustrate this scenario again, but this time you'll use the flashback option and a couple of application tier operations to restore your EBS 12.2 system to the state it was in before the online patching cutover phase was run.

Enable flashback and configure it with four settings accordingly, before starting the patching cycle, as follows:

```
sqlplus "/as sysdba"
```

```
SQL>alter system set db_recovery_file_dest = '/some_path/some_directory' scope=BOTH SID='*';
```
db_recovery_file_dest is set to a directory where the flashback logs are placed. It can set to an ASM disk group, as well.

```
SQL> alter system set db_recovery_file_dest_size = 100G scope=BOTH SID='*';
```

db_recover_file_dest_size is where flashback is placed; the size of the db_recovery_file_dest should be set according to our needs. It actually depends on how long we want to store the flashback logs. Also in addition to the flashback logs if we place our rman backups and online redologs in the database recovery file destination, then we also need to consider them for setting the db_recovery_file_dest_size.

```
SQL> alter system set db_flashback_retention_target=120;
```
db_flashback_retention_target is set to a value which actually represents the upper limit in minutes on how far back in time the database may be flashed back.

```
SQL> alter database flashback on;
```
By executing "alter database flashback on", flashback in the Database gets activated.

At this point, you can say that configuring and enabling flashback in the EBS 12.2 database is completed. The next thing to do is to create a flashback restore point, which is a point in time where you want to restore your database using the flashback techniques. In such EBS 12.2 online patching scenarios, this restore point may be created just before starting the patching cycle or preferably just before the cutover phase.

Before continuing with the creation of the restore point, let's take a look at the recommendations for this phase.

It is better to put the scheduled concurrent requests on hold before creating the request point and do a log switch before and after creating the restore point.

Also, it is recommended you shut down the web services before creating the restore point to ensure that there is no loss of data. So, by shutting down the web services and putting the critical concurrent requests on hold, you can ensure that you won't lose any important transactional data. Also, if there are any other database applications that reach the EBS database via database links or any other non-EBS products using the EBS database (actually there should not be), then they should be stopped or their EBS-related activities should prevented by their application owners.

Another thing to consider is that rather than creating a normal restore point, a guaranteed restore point should be created, as a guaranteed restore point assures that the database will maintain enough flashback logs to flash back the database to the restore point. To accomplish this, you should use the guarantee flashback database statement to create the restore point.

Lastly, it is important to ensure that no third-party application changes the data during the cutover phase, so these kinds of third-party applications should be stopped before creating the restore point.

So, to summarize the requirements mentioned in the previous paragraphs, you have the following action plan:

1. Stop the web services.

2. Stop the concurrent managers or put the schedule concurrent requests on hold.

3. Stop database-bound third-party applications or cut off their database connections.

4. Force a log switch.

5. Create a guaranteed restore point.

6. Force another log switch.

Although you have the ability to choose when to create the restore point, it is advisable to create the restore point just before the cutover phase, because as you can see in the previous action plan, there are some requirements to stop the application services, which will increase the downtime for the patching operation. So, it is better to create the restore point as late as possible.

After reviewing and ensuring the recommendations are in place, you continue with creating the patching cycle and completing phases one by one until you reach the cutover phase and creating the restore point as follows.

To start patching, you create the patching cycle using the adop phase=prepare command and complete the phases one by one as shown here, until the cutover phase:

```
adop phase=prepare
adop phase=apply
adop phase=finalize
```

Just before the cutover phase, you create the restore point as follows:

```
SQL>alter system switch logfile;
System altered.
SQL>create restore point BEFORE_PATCH guarantee flashback database;
Restore point created.
SQL>alter system switch logfile;
System altered.
```

Once the restore point is created, you have a database backup that was taken exactly at the time you wanted and can be restored if needed.

At this point, you have a backup; thus, you can continue with the critical cutover phase.

```
adop phase=cutover
```

Now suppose you face an unsolvable error during the cutover phase and decide to roll your EBS 12.2 environment back to the state before the patching cycle was started. This time, rather than a costly standard database and application file system restore, you can use flashback to restore the database to the restore point named BEFORE_PATCH, which was created just before the cutover phase.

To accomplish this, you follow this action plan:

1. Shut down the database.

   • SQL>shutdown immediate

2. Start the database in mount mode.

   • SQL>startup mount

3. Restore the database to the restore point BEFORE_PATCH using the flashback feature.

   • SQL>flashback database to restore point BEFORE_CUTOVER;

4. Start the database in read-only mode.

- SQL>alter database open read only

5. Check the database with simple queries and ensure that there are no abnormalities.

6. Shut down the database and open it using the resetlogs option.

   - SQL>shutdown immediate

   - SQL>startup mount

   - SQL>alter database open resetlogs;

By doing the previous actions, you roll back your database to a state before the cutover phase.

After rolling back your database using flashback, you should disable the flashback in the database and leave it to be disabled until the next patching operation. By doing so, you eliminate the risk of running out of space in FRA, which may be caused by retaining the flashback logs. Note that running out of space will cause the EBS database to hang.

The following action plan can be used to accomplish that:

1. Disable flashback.

   - SQL>alter database flashback off;

2. Drop the restore point.

   - SQL>drop restore point BEFORE_CUTOVER;

3. Set recovery file destination.

   - SQL>alter system set db_recovery_file_dest='';

So far, so good. We have explained how to roll back an EBS 12.2 database using the flashback option in case of a failure that may be encountered during the cutover phase. But what about the application tier file systems? To fully roll back an EBS 12.2 system in the case of a cutover failure, you need to roll back the file systems of the application nodes, too.

As patching activities change the database objects in the database, they change the file objects in the application file system. Until the cutover phase, all the file objet changes are done in the patch file system; likewise, all the database objects changes are done in the patch edition. So, any time before the cutover phase, you can use adop phase=abort and roll back those changes. However, once you start the cutover phase, abort will no longer work, and that's why you need to do some special actions to roll back the changes done in the cutover phase.

For the database tier, it is a little complicated. An operation like rolling back the changes that occurred before the cutover employs using the flashback option, restore points, and so on. However, it is pretty simple for the application tier.

Suppose you execute the cutover phase during a patching activity and encounter some errors. So, you decide to roll back your EBS system to a state before the cutover phase. To roll back the changes for the database tier, suppose you use the flashback restore point that you created earlier.

Just after the database is restored, you continue with rolling back the application tier. To do that, you need to know whether the cutover failed before the file systems were switched. You can identify this using the cutover logs stored in the adop cutover log file ($NE_BASE/EBSapps/log/adop/<current_session_id>/cutover_<timestamp>/ for your session ID).

If the cutover failed before the file systems were switched, then you are lucky, as you just need to shut down all the application services and then start all the application services using the run edition environment like in your standard startup procedure.

If the log file indicates that cutover failed after the file systems were switched, then you have to follow a different action plan. That is, if the file systems were switched, then you need to switch back the file systems in order to roll back your application tier to its state before the cutover phase.

What you need to do is as follows:

1. Source the environment on the current run file system.

2. Shut down all the application services using the standard procedure (adstpall.sh).

3. Switch back the file system using txkADOPCutOverPhaseCtrlScript.pl.

   ```
   Usage :
   perl $AD_TOP/patch/115/bin/txkADOPCutOverPhaseCtrlScript.pl \
   -action=ctxupdate \
   -contextfile=<full path to new run context file> \
   -patchcontextfile=<full path to new patch file system context file> \
   -outdir=<full path to out directory>
   ```

4. Start up all services from the new run file system using the standard procedure. (Source run edition environment and use the adstrtal.sh script to start all the application services.)

Figure 5-26 represents the approach we have explained so far for rolling back a patch after executing the adop's cutover phase in EBS 12.2.

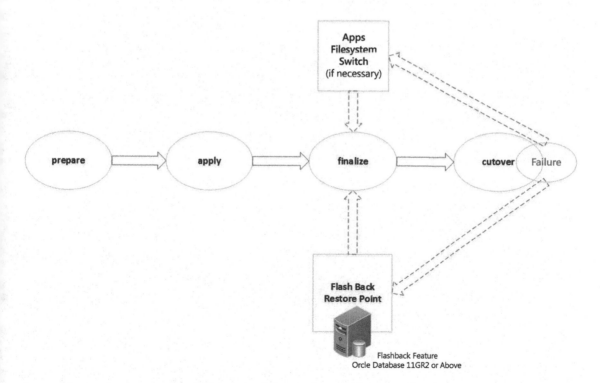

Figure 5-26. *Using the Oracle Database flashback feature to roll back an EBS 12.2 system in case of patch failure*

Once you flash back the database and restart the application services from the file system that was your run file system before the last cutover phase, your EBS 12.2 system is rolled back to the state before the cutover phase. At this point, you can decide whether to continue or abort the patching cycle.

If you fix the issues causing cutover to fail, you may decide to continue the patching. In that case, you can just execute the adop phase=cutover command. However, if you decide not to continue, you can use adop phase=abort and abort the patching cycle.

Summary

In this chapter, you were introduced to the online patching concept used in EBS 12.2. You saw how to decide the patching order in cases where you need to apply multiple patches in one go. Also, you learned about merging patches and the different patching utilities available in EBS 12.2.

You took a deep dive into online patching and saw the phases that you go through while applying applications patches online.

Lastly, you saw a recommended approach to be used in special recovery scenarios, where the database work that is done in online patching is already committed.

Our goal in this chapter was to make you familiar with the Oracle E-Business Suite patching concepts by concentrating on the newly introduced online patching concept. It is important to understand the patching concepts of EBS 12.2 before going forward with Chapter 6, in which we will give you more specifics on applying applications patches in EBS 12.2.

CHAPTER 6

■ ■ ■

Working with the Applications DBA Online Patching Tool (adop)

In the previous chapter, you learned about the patching utilities used for applying different kind of patches in EBS 12.2, the new online patching concept, and the patching tools and technology improvements delivered in this new release of EBS to support the new patching concepts. In that chapter you also focused on online patching because it is a new concept delivered with EBS 12.2 and it is the most common patching activity that you will use in terms of EBS 12.2 patching.

We also introduced the new online patching tool, adop. In this chapter, you will focus on the adop utility and learn more about its usage. We will also explain the details of online patching activities in EBS 12.2. In this context, we will be showing you common usages of the adop tool that you may face in your daily work.

Specifically, we will cover the following topics: adop's command-line parameters and options, how to create patching cycles, adop's remote invocation, hotpatch mode, downtime mode, how to merge the patches, how to create patch reports, and diagnostics and troubleshooting.

Overview of adop

adop stands for "applications DBA online patching," and it is the new patching utility in EBS 12.2. adop takes the place of its ancestor, the adpatch utility, which was used for applications patching in earlier releases. This does not mean adpatch has been retired. adop uses the adpatch utility in the back end transparently to do some of its work. But adop is much more than a wrapper. The biggest difference of adop is that it uses a new patching capability to support the online patching concept introduced in EBS 12.2.

adop is executed using the adop wrapper script named adop located in $APPL_TOP_NE/ad/bin. You don't need to remember this path, as the directory $APPL_TOP_NE/ad/bin comes included in your $PATH environment variable when you source the applications environment using the EBSapps.env script.

So, wherever you're in the file system and execute the adop command, the adop wrapper script $APPL_TOP_NE/ad/bin/adop is executed by your shell, and this wrapper script executes the Perl script named adzdoptl.pl located in the $AD_TOP/bin directory, which does the real work. The adzoptl.pl script is a Perl script and uses several Perl libraries located in $AU_TOP/perl/ADOP, which, as you may guess, comes in your $PERL5LIB environment variable when you source the applications environment. So, by using the Perl libraries in the $AU_TOP/perl directories, adzoptl.pl drives the patching cycles, does the patching work, and even executes some Java commands when necessary.

Topics such as the internals of adop, how it does the processing, the Perl scripting language behind it, the wrappers, the actual scripts, and the environment variables are good to know and will bring you the perspective on what you are dealing with; however, these things are mostly transparent to you.

© Syed Zaheer and Erman Arslan 2016
S. Zaheer and E. Arslan, *Practical Oracle E-Business Suite*, DOI 10.1007/978-1-4842-1422-0_6

The important things to know for your administration work are what you can do with adop, how you drive the patching cycle using it, how to use the adop utility consciously, what kinds of options are in this utility, and how to diagnose the patching problems that may be encountered while using it.

Patching in EBS is done both on the application tier and on the database tier. That is, patches are prepared by Oracle to change, modify, or create objects located both in the application tier and in the database tier. Some patches may modify a forms objects or a report object located in the application tier file system, and others may modify a PL/SQL package inside the database. Some of the application patches are for adding a new language to the EBS system, and some of them are for adding the localizations for the EBS products.

So, no matter the types of application patches and no matter their size or how big their effects are, the patching is done by following some standards and a patching mechanism. These standards and the patching mechanism are called *online patching* and come built-in with EBS so that the adop utility drives this patching mechanism and applies the application patches in respect to the standards in EBS 12.2.

The patching standards and the mechanism used in EBS application patching are quite sophisticated. The sequences of events that are performed during the EBS application patching are as follows. First, EBS application patches are applied by analyzing the patch metadata to determine the dependencies and requirements. After analyzing the patch metadata, the patch driver files are read to determine the patching actions, and the product objects are compared with their correlates that come with the patch that is about to be applied.

Next, the object definitions that will be changed by the patch are backed up, and actions are specified in the patch driver file such as the following: copying files, compiling JSPs and invalid objects in the database, relinking application tier executables, and generating forms, reports, messages, and JAR files. Also, the database objects are updated if necessary, and lastly an AutoConfig is triggered to update the configuration files if the patch delivers a new template or any existing template files are updated. As the patching session finishes, the patch information is saved to the database to be queried for the next time.

So, all of these standards that are based on the patching mechanism in EBS 12.2 are followed by the adop utility. In other words, adop in conjunction with the patch files, the patch metadata repository, and the version information all work in respect to this mechanism to apply the application patches to the EBS 12.2 system in a supported way. adop does the heavy work, and you as the apps DBA just execute it and try to fix any problems encountered in the adop executions. adop is an application-aware online patching utility that can also sets its environment automatically and has capabilities such as recovering a failed patching session, logging all of its activities, reporting its status, and doing other things such as validating the connection to EBS schemas and making its operations in parallel.

The adop tool has additional modes such as preinstall mode, which is generally used in special situations when instructed, such as when a patch needs to upgrade an AD utility. There is also a test mode of adop, which can be used when you want to see the effects of a patch before applying it.

The adop tool can run interactively or noninteractively except for prompting for a password. Prompting for a password can also be disabled during execution by passing passwords as inputs to adop using the capabilities of the underlying shell. (For example, you can use Linux pipes to supply the passwords to adop while executing it.)

In addition, the adop utility in EBS 12.2.5 (or in earlier 12.2 releases, which are at AD-TXK Delta 5 patch levels) has the ability to apply patches offline using the downtime option.

To summarize, adop is a sophisticated tool that drives the complex patching process used in EBS 12.2. It is also important to mention that, in addition to the adop's capabilities, there are supporting AD tools such as admerge for merging several patches to a single one and adctrl for controlling the adop workers that are often used while working with adop. Thus, they will also be explained in this chapter.

Working with the adop Utility

As the adop tool utility is used for applying application patches to an EBS 12.2 system, the utility is located in the application tier and run from the application tier's run edition file system.

To run the adop utility and apply patches, you just log in to the application node or nodes using the application owner OS user (for example, applmgr), set the run edition environment, and execute the adop command. Listing 6-1 describes sourcing the runtime environment using the famous EBSapps.env script and running the adop utility.

Listing 6-1. Setting the Runtime Environment and Running adop

```
[applmgr@somehost ~]$ . /u01/install/TEST/EBSapps.env run

    E-Business Suite Environment Information
    ----------------------------------------
    RUN File System          : /u01/install/TEST/fs1/EBSapps/appl
    PATCH File System        : /u01/install/TEST/fs2/EBSapps/appl
    Non-Editioned File System : /u01/install/TEST/fs_ne
    DB Host: somehost.somedomain.com  Service/SID: TEST
    Sourcing the RUN File System ...

[applmgr@somehost ~]$ adop
Enter phase:
```

As shown in Listing 6-1, when executed without any command-line parameters, adop requests to enter the phase. This means adop can't be executed without specifying the phase; this is a logical requirement because the patching in EBS 12.2 is based on a new concept, the patching cycle.

The patching cycle and the phases of it were explained in Chapter 5, but it is worth reviewing them before you start working with adop in this chapter.

The patches can be applied online by following the phases in the patching cycle. The patching cycle consists of five phases named prepare, apply, finalize, cutover, and cleanup. The phase abort is also a main phase in this patching cycle concept, but it is used for quitting an ongoing patching activity by aborting the patching cycle. In addition, there are two more phases named fs_clone and actualize_all, which can be used in special situations and will be explained when we talk about the adop command-line parameters and options.

So, to start online patching an EBS 12.2 system with adop, you first need to execute the adop prepare phase. The adop tool prepare phase creates a patching cycle, which can then be used for patching the EBS system by following the remaining adop phases in sequence. In other words, to apply a patch, you start a patching cycle using adop phase=prepare, and after that you continue with the phase=apply, phase=finalize, phase=cutover, and phase=cleanup commands.

Listing 6-2 shows how to set the runtime environment and execute the adop phases one by one in sequence to apply a patch online to an EBS 12.2 system.

The outputs of the adop commands provide lots of the details about their executions and display the log file paths of the ongoing adop operations and scripts executed along the way, but we won't list the logs here, as they are beyond the scope of this section. Rather than concentrating on the outputs and logs at this point, you will see them later this chapter while we explain diagnostics and troubleshooting in online patching.

Another thing that may catch your attention is that, as shown in Listing 6-2, adop requests you to enter the APPS schema, SYSTEM schema, and WLSADMIN passwords before it starts executing the phases.

Listing 6-2. Executing adop with Phases

```
[applmgr@somehost ~]$ . /u01/install/APPS/EBSapps.env run
[applmgr@somehost ~]$ adop phase=prepare

Enter the APPS password:
Enter the SYSTEM password:
Enter the WLSADMIN password:

[applmgr@somehost ~]$ adop phase=apply
Enter the APPS password:
Enter the SYSTEM password:
Enter the WLSADMIN password:

[applmgr@somehost ~]$ adop phase=finalize
Enter the APPS password:
Enter the SYSTEM password:
Enter the WLSADMIN password:

[applmgr@somehost ~]$ adop phase=cutover
Enter the APPS password:
Enter the SYSTEM password:
Enter the WLSADMIN password:

[applmgr@somehost ~]$ adop phase=cleanup
Enter the APPS password:
Enter the SYSTEM password:
Enter the WLSADMIN password:
```

So, each time an adop phase completes, it gives you the OS terminal prompt back so you can continue with the next phase by running adop again by supplying the desired phase as an argument. That is, when adop phase=prepare completes, you execute the adop phase=apply command, and after the apply phase is complete, you continue by executing the adop phase=finalize command, and so on.

Actually, you can execute the adop phases one by one in sequence like a script without waiting in the OS terminal for each phase to complete.

Listing 6-3 shows an adop command that instructs adop to execute the five main adop phases one after another.

Listing 6-3. Executing All the adop Phases in One Go

```
[applmgr@somehost ~]$ adop phase=prepare,apply,finalize,cutover,cleanup
Enter the APPS password:
Enter the SYSTEM password:
Enter the WLSADMIN password:
```

As you may see in the Listings 6-2 and 6-3, adop wants you to provide the APPS schema, SYSTEM schema, and WebLogic admin passwords every time it runs. You can use the shell trick in Listing 6-4 to automate specifying these passwords. Note that this method brings an opportunity to execute adop with less effort from the shell scripts or any other code that has the ability to connect to the operating system.

Listing 6-4. Executing adop by Supplying the APPS Schema, SYSTEM Schema, and WebLogic Passwords in the Command Line

```
[applmgr@somehost ~]$ { echo appspassword; echo systempassword; echo adminpassword; } | adop
phase=prepare,apply,finalize,cutover,cleanup
```

You can even go further and create an input file for adop to specify things such as the parallel worker counts, the number of the patch to be applied, and the directory that the patch to be applied is located, as shown in Listing 6-5. In Listing 6-5, we are using an input file in conjunction with an automated password specification method to apply patch 20863040 by only pressing the Enter button. To do this, you create an input file named test_input and add the lines shown in the listing in it.

Listing 6-5. Executing adop phases as a one liner by piping the passwords and giving an input file as a command line argument

```
workers=12
patches=20863040
phase=prepare,apply,finalize,cutover,cleanup
patchtop=/home/applmgr
[applmgr@somehost ~]$ { echo appspassword; echo systempassword; echo adminpassword; } | adop
input_file=/home/applmgr/input_test
```

Note that the patch used in Listing 6-5 is located in the /home/applmgr directory and is unzipped.

As described in Listing 6-5, after creating the input file, you supply it to adop using the command-line argument named input_file.

So, as shown in Listing 6-5, there are different forms of executions for adop, and even though we have not explained them yet, there are several command-line arguments that can be supplied for it.

Another important thing is that we did not specify any patch numbers or point adop to look for a patch in a specific directory while we were showing the adop phases in Listing 6-2. However, in Listing 6-5, we supplied the patch location and the number of the patch to be applied using an input file. So, you may ask, "How does adop know which patch to apply without specifying the patch directory and patch number as showing Listing 6-2?"

The answer is simple. adop looks to a default directory pointed at by $APPL_TOP_NE/../patch to determine the patch or patches to be applied.

As long as there are no command-line arguments or any input files that specify the patch directory or the number of the desired patch, adop checks the $APPL_TOP_NE/../patch directory and applies the patches located as unzipped in that directory.

Knowing this, you can just download the desired patch from Oracle Support and unzip it into the $APPL_TOP_NE/../patch directory and then execute adop without specifying any arguments for patch locations and patch numbers. That's why you may see a sentence like the following in most of the Oracle Support documents that are written for big upgrade patches: "Download and unzip all the patches to the default Patch Top location for R12.2 ($APPL_TOP_NE/../patch)."

Listing 6-6 shows unzipping patch 21140485, which was downloaded to a directory named /downloads, to the default patch directory for adop and executing the adop apply phase afterward (we have already completed the adop=prepare phase).

Listing 6-6. Unzipping an Application Patch into the Default Patch Top Location for adop ($APPL_TOP_NE/../patch) and Executing the adop apply Phase

```
[applmgr@somehost ~]$ cd /downloads
[applmgr@somehost ~]$ ls
p21140485_R12.CLE.C_R12_GENERIC.zip
[applmgr@somehost ~]$ unzip  p21140485_R12.CLE.C_R12_GENERIC.zip -d $APPL_TOP_NE/../patch
[applmgr@somehost ~]$ adop phase=apply
```

As shown in Listing 6-6, for your convenience you can unzip the patch or patches to be applied to the default patch directory and thus execute adop without specifying any patch-related arguments. Also, as in Listing 6-5, you can always apply a patch located in a nondefault directory by specifying that directory using the patchtop and patches arguments. That is, if you unzip a patch with the number 123456 to a directory named /home/applmgr, you should supply patchtop as /home/applmgr and the patches argument as patch number to adop, as shown in Listing 6-7.

In Listing 6-7, you unzip patch 21140485 to a nondefault patch directory named /home/patches and then execute adop by specifying that directory using the patchtop argument. (We have already completed the adop=prepare phase.)

Listing 6-7. Unzipping an Application Patch into a Nondefault Patch Location (/home/applmgr/patches) and Executing adop Apply Phase with the patchtop Argument

```
[applmgr@somehost ~]$adop=prepare phase
[applmgr@somehost ~]$cd /downloads
[applmgr@somehost ~]$ls
p21140485_R12.CLE.C_R12_GENERIC.zip
[applmgr@somehost ~]$ unzip  p21140485_R12.CLE.C_R12_GENERIC.zip -d /home/applmgr/patches
[applmgr@somehost ~]$ adop phase=apply patchtop=/home/applmgr/patches
```

■ **Note**   Whether using the default patch top, the patches that are unzipped and applied in an online patching cycle must not be deleted and must be located in the same location where they are unzipped and applied from. These patches will be used in the next prepare phase, in other words, in the next patching cycle for synchronizing the patch file system. So, the patches that are applied in an online patching cycle should not be deleted from the patch top directory (default or nondefault) until the next prepare phase is complete.

As there are different phases to be executed for applying a patch online with the adop utility and as there is no need to execute the phases of adop immediately one after another, there is a status option for adop that gives the current statuses of adop patching cycles.

In this context, the adop –status command can be used anytime there is a need for checking the current status of the patching cycle to understand which phases are executed, which are pending, and so on. The adop tool –status command requests you to supply only the APPS password when it gets executed.

Listing 6-8 shows the adop –status command and its output for a patching cycle where all the phases are completed and patch 20863040 is applied.

■ **Note**   The output of the adop –status command has been trimmed here in order to display the statuses in a better format.

Listing 6-8. adop -status Command and Its Output Displaying That Patch 20863040 Has Been Applied

```
[applmgr@somehost ~]$adop -status
Enter the APPS password:

Node Name  Node Type  Phase     Status     Started            Finished           Elapsed
---------  ---------  --------  ---------  -----------------  -----------------  -------
somehost              PREPARE   COMPLETED  14-APR-15 04:11:19  14-APR-15 05:32:38  1:21:19
master                                     +03:00              +03:00
v1
                      APPLY     COMPLETED  14-APR-15 05:33:03  14-APR-15 05:35:32  0:02:29
                                           +03:00              +03:00
                      FINALIZE  COMPLETED  14-APR-15 05:35:42  14-APR-15 05:36:07  0:00:25
                                           +03:00              +03:00
                      CUTOVER   COMPLETED  14-APR-15 05:36:17  14-APR-15 05:50:51  0:14:34
                                           +03:00              +03:00
                      CLEANUP   COMPLETED  14-APR-15 05:50:53  14-APR-15 05:51:34  0:00:41
                                           +03:00              +03:00
================================================================================
            Patches Applied in the Current Patching Cycle
================================================================================
Node Name  Node Type  Status   Run ID File System  File System Applied  Session Type
           Patch               Patch Base          Base Adpatch Parameters
---------  ---------  -------  -----------------  -------------------------  ------------
somehost   20863040   Y        78344                /u01/install/APPS/fs1    ONLINE
master
```

So, you have seen how to execute adop from the OS terminal as well as how to unzip patches and supply the needed information such as patch directories and patches to be applied for adop to operate. Remember, execute the adop phases one by one and execute all the phases by running only one adop command.

Also, you have seen some advanced topics such as piping the passwords to adop using the command line, using an input file in conjunction with the command-line password piping method, and specifying all the phases in a comma-separated list in adop's phase argument to execute the whole patching cycle process using only a one-liner. You have also seen how to report the status of the adop phases executed in patching cycles by seeing an example of the adop –status command.

So far, you should realize that it is easy to execute adop, but there are different forms for its executions. That is, by seeing the previous examples, you may already start feeling that there are several command-line options for adop and several use cases that may be required according to the different patching scenarios. Even though the adop tool is easy to use, there are lots of things it can do.

Although adop can be executed using only a simple command like adop phase=desired_phase, there are several command-line options for adop that change the behavior of this patching tool.

Well, we have started fast and you already seen some of the command-line options for adop while seeing how you work with adop in this section. Until now, you have seen a couple of these command-line parameters, and you used them to make your job easier. In the examples provided earlier, it was optional to use the command-line options such as input file, patchtop, and patches. However, there are some command-line parameters that are required in some special cases.

So, there are several command-line parameters for the adop utility, and it is crucial to know them all. We will explain the command-line parameters and options in the next section.

adop Command-Line Parameters and Options

adop command-line arguments can be classified into two categories: command-line parameters and command-line options.

The main difference between command-line parameters and command-line options is that command-line options can be used to change the way adop operates. That is, you can supply options to adop and change its default behavior when applying application patches such as skipping compiling invalid database objects after taking the necessary patching actions in the database or reapplying a patch even if it is already applied. Normally adop detects the patches if they are already applied and gives the type of warnings shown in Listing 6-9.

Listing 6-9. adop Warnings for Already Applied Patches

```
[WARNING]   Skipping the application of patch 18060329 since it has been already applied
[WARNING]   Hint: Patches can be applied again by specifying options=forceapply when
invoking adop
```

Command-line parameters, however, can be used to make adop use the provided values in its executions. That is, you can tell adop to execute only the prepare phase in a patching cycle, or you can increase the log level of adop by supplying it with the necessary command-line parameters. To summarize, the command-line options can be used to change the standard behavior of adop, and the command-line parameters can be used to specify the standards to be applied by adop.

In addition to this main difference, there are some more differences in using the command-line parameters and options. That is, while all the command-line options are optional, there are some command-line parameters such as phase that are required to be supplied to adop in order to apply a patch.

The ways of using these options and parameters at the command line also differ from each other. That is, options are supplied using the options argument (for example, adop options=nocopyportion, nogenerateportion).

However, the parameters are supplied directly (for example, adop phase=apply or adop phase=apply loglevel=STATEMENT). Nevertheless, there is still a big similarity between them, as options are specified as using the command-line parameter named options, so this makes the command-line options can be considered command-line parameters in a way.

After this quick introduction, let's examine the adop command-line parameters and options in detail so you can see what options you have and what you can do using the parameters. Table 6-1 describes the available command-line parameters for adop and provides examples of how to use them in command line. The adop tool command-line options are also declared and explained in Table 6-1, as the command-line options are specified using the command-line parameter named options.

■ **Note** The usages of these parameters can also be viewed by using the adop –help command. In addition, using the adop –examples command, you can view the example usages of these parameters.

Table 6-1. *The adop Tool Command-Line Parameters and Options with Their Descriptions, Possible Values, and Usage Examples*

Parameter	Possible Values	Description	Example of Usage
phase	• prepare • apply • finalize • cutover • cleanup • fs_clone • abort • actualize_all	Used for specifying the phase to be executed by adop. Except abort and fs_clone, other phases can be specified together like a comma-separated list.	adop phase=prepare adop phase=prepare,apply adop phase=abort adop phase=fs_clone adop phase=prepare,apply, finalize,cutover,cleanup
loglevel	• statement • procedure • event (default) • warning • error • unexpected	Used to adjust the log level for adop. statement is the highest level, where adop logs almost everything, and unexpected is the lowest level, where adop logs only the unexpected situations.	adop phase=prepare log_level=warning adop log_level=statement
apply_mode	• online (default) • downtime • hotpatch • bootstrap	Used to specify how the patch is applied. This parameter can be used only for the apply phase. The default value of online is for specifying the online patching, the value of downtime is for applying a patch while the application services are down, and the value of hotpatch is for applying the patch directly to the run edition while the application services are running. Bootstrap mode is an undocumented mode, but it applies the patches in hotpatch mode and, when used, adop makes you deal with the adpatch dialogs just like in earlier releases. So, it is just a way to use adpatch through adop. Bootstrap mode must not be used unless instructed by Oracle.	adop phase=apply apply_mode=downtime

(continued)

Table 6-1. (*continued*)

Parameter	Possible Values	Description	Example of Usage
cleanup_mode	• quick • full • standard (default)	Used in the cleanup or prepare phase, where the cleanup action takes place. Used to tell adop how much to clean up. Quick cleanup mode has the shortest execution time by removing the cross-edition triggers and obsolete data and skipping some other essential cleaning actions such as dropping old editions and obsolete columns. Standard cleanup mode has the second shortest execution time. The difference between quick and standard cleanup modes is, in standard mode, obsolete; editioned code objects are also removed. Full cleanup mode is the slowest cleanup mode. In a full cleanup, in addition to all the cleanup work that is done in standard cleanup mode, the old editions and obsolete columns are also removed.	adop phase=prepare cleanup_mode=full adop phase=cleanup cleanup_mode=quick
finalize_mode	1. full 2. quick (default)	This parameter can be used both in the finalize and cutover phases. (There is a finalize operation in cutover phase too.) Quick finalize mode has the shortest execution time. The difference between full and quickest finalize modes is that quick finalize mode skips some essential finalizing actions such as gathering statistics. In full finalize mode, the finalize phase may take a long time (like an hour) according to the performance of the database system, as statistics are gathered in full finalize mode to improve performance.	adop phase=finalize finalize_mode=full adop phase=cutover finalize_mode=full

input_file	User-specified file with full path	An input file prepared by users (apps dbas) for adop. Using input files, apps DBAs can specify several parameters in a file called the input file and use the input file command-line parameter to make adop interpret that file and get its parameters.	Input file name: /tmp/test.in Input file contents: workers=12 patches=20863040 phase=prepare,apply,finalize,cutover,cleanup patchtop=/home/applmgr Specifying the input file: adop input_file=/tmp/test.in
maxworkers	User-specified value for telling adop the maximum parallel worker count that it can use in its patching activities	This parameter can be used in the apply phase. Normally, maxworkers are automatically calculated by adop according to the CPU core counts, but by using the maxworkers parameter, apps DBAs can overwrite it. Note that to overwrite the automatically calculated workers value, the value of the maxworkers parameter should be used in conjunction with workers parameters, and it must be set greater than the automatically calculated and desired worker value. Otherwise, adop will use the automatically calculated one.	adop phase=cleanup workers=8 maxworkers=12 adop phase=prepare workers=40 maxworkers=50 adop phase=prepare,apply,finalize,cutover,cleanup workers=20 maxworkers=30
patches	Patch number or comma-separated list of patch numbers, used to tell adop the patches to be applied	This parameter is required in the apply phase. Using the patches parameter, apps DBAs can tell adop which patch or patches to apply in an apply phase.	Adop phase=apply patches=123456 Adop phase=apply patches=123456,112233,445566 In case of translation patches, the patch number is specified with the short name of the language and the driver file of the patch. The following example shows specifying the patch 111111 and Turkish version of patch 123456: adop phase= apply patches=111111, 123456_TR:123456.drv

(continued)

Table 6-1. (*continued*)

Parameter	Possible Values	Description	Example of Usage
hotpatch	yes no (default)	If stated in their readme files, the patches can be applied in hotpatch mode. In hotpatch mode, apps DBAs directly execute the apply phase without starting a patching cycle using the prepare phase. In hotpatch mode, the patch application takes place directly in the run edition rather than the patch edition. The hotpatch parameter is used to specify whether to apply the patch in hotpatch mode.	adop phase=apply patches=123456 hotpatch=yes
flags	hidepw (default) nohidepw trace notrace (default) logging nologging (default) autoskip noautoskip (default)	Flags to specify a comma-separated list of options. hidepw can be used to tell adop to hide the passwords in the log files. trace can be used to log all the database operations to a trace file. logging can be used to create indexes in logging mode. nologging can be used to create indexes in nologging. autoskip can be used to make adop continue even in the case of a failure in patch driver actions. Note that the flags prefixed with "no" can be thought of as direct opposites of the flags that are not prefixed with "no." For example, logging can be used to create indexes in logging mode, and nologging can be used to create indexes in nologging mode. (nologging is the direct opposite of logging in this case.) Similarly, autoskip can be used to make adop continue even in the case of a failure, but noautoskip makes adop not continue in the case of a failure.	adop phase=prepare flags=nohidepw adop phase=apply patches=111111 flags=hidepw,logging adop phase=apply patches=111111 flags=autoskip
prompt	yes (default) no	Used to specify whether adop should continue without taking the user's confirmation in case of a warning situation. The default behavior (prompt=yes) is to take the user's confirmation on warnings.	adop phase=prepare prompt=no adop phase=apply patches=1111 prompt=no

options		
	adop options that can be specified in a comma-separated list.	adop phase=apply patches=11111 options=nocompiledb
	Although these options can be specified in any phases, the options are relevant to the apply phase. The options parameter is used to specify the command-line options for adop, and the definition of these options are as follows:	adop phase=apply patches=123456 options=nodatabaseportion, nogenerateportion
checkfile(default) nocheckfile	checkfile: Skip running exec, SQL, and exec:er in case they are detected as already run.	
compiledb(default) nocompiledb	compiledb: Compile invalid objects after completing the actions in the patch's database driver.	
compilejsp(default) nocompilejsp	compilejsp: Compile outdated JSP files, if the patch has actions related to JSP files.	
copyportion(default) nocopyportion	copyportion: Run commands residing in the copy portion of the unified driver.	
databaseportion(default) nodatabaseportion	databaseportion: Run commands residing in the database portion of the unified driver.	
generateportion(default) nogenerateportion	generateportion. Run commands found in the generate portion of the unified driver	
integrity nointegrity(default)	integrity: Perform patch integrity checking.	
autoconfig(default) noautoconfig	autoconfig: Run AutoConfig.	
actiondetails(default) noactiondetails	actiondetails: Display patch action details.	
parallel(default) noparallel	parallel: Do database updates and patch actions that generate files in parallel.	
prereq(default) nopreprereq	prereq: Perform prerequisite checking before running the patch drivers.	
validate novalidate(default)	validate: Connect to the database using EBS-registered schemas to make a kind of a validation before applying the patches.	
phtofile nophtofile(default)	phtofile: Save patch history to a file	
forceapply noforceapply(default)	forceapply: Reapply a patch even if it is already applied.	
	Note that these options can be prefixed with 'no" in order to make adop behave in the opposite way.	

(continued)

Table 6-1. (*continued*)

Parameter	Possible Values	Description	Example of Usage
cm_wait	User-specified value representing the minutes	Sets how much time in minutes to wait for the running concurrent requests to finish before shutting down the internal concurrent manager as part of the application shutdown operation that adop initiates during the cutover phase. If not specified, adop waits indefinitely.	adop phase=cutover cm_wait=10
workers	User-specified value for specifying the number of parallel workers	This option can be used in all phases. It is used for specifying the number of parallel workers to execute patching tasks. workers and maxworkers should be used and specified in conjunction for overriding the automatically calculated worker count. That is, for example, when workers=12 and maxworkers=16, adop will use 12 workers. If not specified, adop calculates the number of workers automatically according to the CPU core count.	adop phase=prepare workers=8 maxworkers=12 adop phase=apply patches=11111 workers=12 maxworkers=16
defaultsfile	The file name representing the user prepared defaultsfile In case of an application of a hotpatch, defaultsfile must be located in the run edition's $APPL_TOP/admin/$TWO_TASK directory In case of an online patch application, defaultsfile must be located in patch edition's $APPL_TOP/admin/$TWO_TASK directory	A parameter for specifying the patchtop parameter by using a file (rather than using it as a command-line argument). Actually it is not a preferred parameter as only one parameter (patchtop) can be specified by using it. It is more preferable to use an input file if it is needed to specify the command-line parameters through a file. Note that the parameters supplied directly by the command line overwrite the parameter specified using an input file, and the parameters specified using an input file overwrite the parameters supplied using defaultsfile. So, defaultsfile has the lowest level of precedence.	Defaultsfile name: $APPL_TOP/admin/$TWO_TASK/test.df Specifying defaultsfile: adop phase=apply patches=11111 defaultsfile =$APPL_TOP/admin/$TWO_TASK/test.df (the patch edition's APPL_TOP and TWO_TASK values) adop phase=apply hotpatch=yes patches=11111 defaultsfile =$APPL_TOP/admin/$TWO_TASK/test.df (the run edition's APPL_TOP and TWO_TASK values)

Parameter	Values	Description	Example
patchtop	User-specified directory path where patch directories reside; in other words, the directory where the patches to be applied are unzipped $APPL_TOP_NE/../patch (default)	The directory where you unzip the patches, in other words, where the patch directories reside. Used in the apply phase, and if not specified, the default $APPL_TOP_NE/../patch directory is searched by adop to find the patches to be applied. Actually using this default directory to unload the patches is recommended by Oracle.	adop phase=apply patchtop=/home/applmgr/ad_patches patches=11111
merge	yes / no (default)	Used to tell adop to merge patches rather than apply the patch drivers sequentially. By default this parameter is set to "no." In earlier EBS releases, using the tool called Ad merge patch was the only way for merging the application patches. In 12.2, the patching tool adop includes this merging capability.	adop phase=apply patches=11111,22222 merge=yes
abandon	yes / no (default)	Used to tell adop whether to abandon a previously failed patching attempt. This parameter can be set to "yes" in cases where the previous patching attempt was stopped with errors, which you can't correct and want adop to abandon your previous adop session. Note that this parameter can't be specified with the restart parameter.	adop phase=apply patches=11111 abandon=yes
restart	yes / no (default)	This parameter works like the opposite of the abandon parameter. If it is set to yes, adop restarts the previous failed attempt, when it is executed again. If it is set to "no," adop continues the patch application from the point where it encountered errors previously. Note that this parameter can't be specified with the abandon parameter.	adop phase=apply patches=111111 restart=yes

(continued)

Table 6-1. (*continued*)

Parameter	Possible Values	Description	Example of Usage
skipsyncerror	yes no (default)	This parameter can be used for specifying whether to expect any synchronization errors in the prepare phase to be fixed automatically in the next patching activities. Synchronization errors may appear after a patching activity in which you continued and completed the patching cycle although there were errors in the apply phase. Note that this parameter should be used after analyzing the log files and concluding that the errors will be fixed later by the synchronization actions which will be taken by adop while applying the subsequent patches. If this can't be concluded, the patching cycle should be aborted (adop phase=abort), and then the application file systems should be synchronized using the fs_clone phase.	adop phase=prepare skipsyncerror=yes
mtrestart	yes (default) no	The parameter name comes from the middle tier restart. It is used in the cutover phase to tell adop to restart the application services after the cutover phase. The default behavior of adop is to restart the application services after the cutover phase. Normally this parameter should not be changed and left as default, but if you want to do some manual actions after completing the cutover phase, then you can set this parameter to "no" and restart the application services using the adstrtall.sh script manually after taking or manual actions.	adop phase=cutover mtrestart=no
allowcoredump	yes no (default)	This parameter can be used in any adop phase, but it should be left as default unless there is a need to debug adop code itself.	adop phase=cutover allowcoredump=yes
analytics	yes no (default)	Enables generation of reports that are not needed normally but can be used for debugging purposes. This parameter can be specified in the apply, finalize, cutover, and cleanup phases.	adop phase=apply patches=11111 analytics=yes adop phase=finalize analytics=yes

Parameter	Values	Description	Example
allnodes	yes (default) No	This parameter can be used in multimode environments to tell adop to take some specific actions on specific nodes. For example, you can use allnodes=no with phase=prepare to make adop take specific actions on the current node only. Using allnodes=yes makes adop take actions on all the nodes in a multinode environment, and it can be specified only when running adop on the admin node.	adop phase=prepare allnodes=no
action	db (default) nodb	This parameter can be used in multimode environments to tell adop whether to take database actions. actions=db can be specified only while running adop in the admin node.	adop phase=prepare action=nodb This makes adop take only the file system actions on the current node. In other words, using action=nodb makes adop not take any database-related actions while running in the current node.
wait_on_failed_job	Yes No (default)	This parameter can be used to tell adop whether to exit when all the patch workers have failed in noninteractive mode. By default, this parameter is set to no, so adop exists when all the adpatch workers have failed.	Adop phase=apply patches=1111 wait_on_failed_job=yes

As shown in Table 6-1, there are lots of parameters and options that can be specified while running adop. Although the parameter list is a long one, only some of these parameters are actually used often. That is, while mandatory parameters such as phase, patches, and patchtop are used in applying almost every patch, some of the parameters such as cleanup_mode, analytics, abandon, and restart are used only in rare cases.

Nevertheless, it is good to know all of these parameters and keep in mind that they may be needed one day.

So, after having this information, let's take a look at the patching cycle and see how to use adop commands and parameters by going through the adop commands used in EBS patching. In the next section, you will take a look at the creation of a patching cycle and learning what you can do after creating the patching cycle by seeing the adop options you have and the adop parameters you can use while proceeding with the phases in the patching cycle.

You will be focusing on the online patching, as it is the default patching method/mode in EBS 12.2, but you will also see more about the patching methods/modes named hotpatch and downtime, which can be specified using the apply_mode parameter. Hotpatch and downtime mode will be explained in the next sections.

Executing the Patching Cycle

In Chapter 5 we explained the patching cycle and the five main phases of the patching cycle: prepare, apply, finalize, cutover, and cleanup. In this chapter, we will go through the adop commands by giving their usages along with quick reviews of the adop phases and explain subjects such as creating the patching cycle, commands that can be used in different phases of the patching cycle, and the available adop command-line options/parameters that can be used according to the conditions.

As explained in Chapter 5, the online patching introduced in EBS 12.2 is based on a patching cycle concept. Patches are applied online by creating the patching cycles and executing the phases in the patch cycles. The five phases must be executed sequentially in order to apply an application patch online in EBS 12.2. Executing each phase puts the patching activity into the relevant state in the patching cycle. That is, when you execute the prepare phase, your system becomes prepared so you are in the prepare state in the patching cycle and later continue with the apply state, which comes after the prepare state according to the order of the patching cycle.

The term *patching cycle* is used to describe this flow because it is a cycle that starts from a certain point each time it is created and has to go through all steps for applying a patch online.

Figure 6-1 shows all the adop phases in an online patching cycle and the connections between these phases, which will be explained later in this chapter.

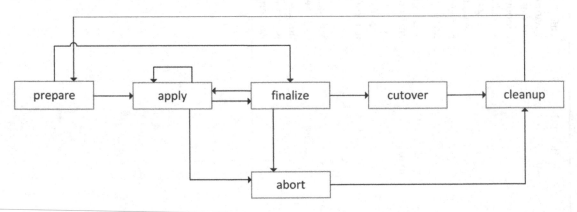

Figure 6-1. *Online patching cycle and adop phases*

Note that multiple patches can be applied in a single online patching cycle. This patching cycle concept is used only for applying the patches online.

Prepare Phase

The patching cycle is created and started by the prepare phase. After sourcing the runtime environment, a simple adop phase=prepare command must be executed to create the patching cycle, and once it is completed, the system becomes prepared for online patching.

During the execution of the adop phase=prepare command, adop does the following. adop first checks to see whether any cleanup is needed as there may be some unnecessary objects in the system that can be left out in case you forget to run the cleanup phase at the end of the previous patching cycle.

After checking and executing the cleanup phase if necessary, adop validates the system and makes necessary checks in the database and in the application tier in order to be sure that the environment is ready for online patching. The adop tool also ensures that the Online Patching In Progress (short name: ADZDPATCH) concurrent program exists, as this program is used to prevent some certain concurrent programs from running during an online patching operation. The adop tool starts this concurrent program even if a small number of concurrent managers are running in the system during the patching cycle.

Then, adop synchronizes the applied patches in the patch edition APPL_TOP using the repository information for patches that have been applied to the run edition APPL_TOP.

Lastly, adop creates a patch edition if it does not exist and confirms that the database connection to the patch edition can be established without any problems.

To run the prepare phase without any problems, there should be at least 25GB free space in SYSTEM and at least a 5GB free space in APPS_TS_SEED, as per the requirements in the maintenance guide "Oracle E Business Suite Maintenance Guide Release 12.2 Part Number E22954-20."

$AD_TOP/sql/ADZDSHOWTS.sql, shown in Listing 6-10, is an easy way to check these tablespace requirements.

■ **Note**   ADZDSHOWTS.sql shows the tablespace utilization for APPS_TS_TX_IDX and APPS_TS_TX_DATA as well, because as you may recall Chapter 1, these tablespaces are where the objects that are directly related to the transactional data are. In addition, ADZDSHOWTS is not only designed to be used in patching. This script can be used in any time for controlling purposes, because it shows the tablespace utilization for these two important tablespaces and because a lack of free space in them could create a system-wide hang situation.

Listing 6-10. Running ADZDSHOWTS.sql and Checking the Free Space in Important Tablespaces

```
[applmgr@somehost ~]$ sqlplus apps/apps @$AD_TOP/sql/ADZDSHOWTS.sql
SQL*Plus: Release 10.1.0.5.0 - Production on Mon Sep 14 11:20:18 2015
Copyright (c) 1982, 2005, Oracle.  All rights reserved.

=======================
    Important Tablespace Status
=======================
```

TABLESPACE_NAME	TOTAL_SPACE	(GB) USED_SPACE (GB)	FREE_SPACE (GB)	PCT_USED
APPS_TS_SEED	8.96	7.07	1.90	78.85
APPS_TS_TX_DATA	29.19	27.31	1.87	93.58
APPS_TS_TX_IDX	10.07	8.24	1.83	81.78
SYSTEM	38.60	32.00	6.60	82.89

■ **Note**   ADZDSHOWTS.sql is not autoextend-aware, so if you have autoextend-enabled data files, then it is better to check the free space in these important tablespaces by considering the auto extendable/allocatable space using a query like described in Listing 6-11.

Listing 6-11. Custom Tablespace Check Query and Its Output

```
select "TBS_NAME","TOTAL GB" as "TOTAL GB(autoextend included)" ,"TOTAL GB"-"USED GB" as
"ALLOCATABLE/FREE SPACE" from
(
select tablespace_name as "TBS_NAME",
round(sum(decode(autoextensible,'NO',bytes,'YES',maxbytes))/1024/1024/1024,0) as "TOTAL GB"
,(select round(sum(bytes)/1024/1024/1024,0)
from dba_segments where tablespace_name=d.tablespace_name) as "USED GB"   from dba_data_
files d
where tablespace_name in('SYSTEM','APPS_TS_SEED','APPS_TS_TX_DATA','APPS_TS_TX_IDX') group
by tablespace_name
);
```

TBS_NAME	TOTAL GB(autoextend included)	ALLOCATABLE/FREE SPACE
APPS_TS_TX_IDX	9	3
APPS_TS_SEED	9	2
SYSTEM	69	39
APPS_TS_TX_DATA	41	31

Also, it is important to know that, in addition to the free space requirements of the tablespaces, EBS 12.2 requires the patch file system to have at least 25GB of free disk space for executing adop operations.

So, adop phase=prepare is the starting point for an online patching operation. Normally, you execute it without any parameters, but there are some optional parameters that you can supply to adop while running the prepare phase. The optional parameters that can be used in the prepare phase are workers, input_file, loglevel, defaultsfile, allowcoredump, analytics, cleanup_mode, and skipsyncerror. Although you don't usually use these parameters often, there are some conditions when you might need them.

The parameter skipsyncerror is a good example of these conditions you may face. The parameter skipsyncerror can be used to prevent adop from failing against some synchronization errors that are expected as a result of a previously failed patching attempt.

```
These types of synchronization errors can be seen while adop was running the /
txkADOPPreparePhaseSynchronize.pl script to synchronize the filesystems and following
command can be executed as a workaround. adop phase=prepare skipsyncerror=yes
```

■ **Note**   If the skipsyncerror parameter is used, it is the apps DBA's responsibility to make sure the file systems are correctly in sync after the patching is done.

An alternative and safer method that can be used in case of an error in the synchronization that is done in the prepare phase can be aborting the patching cycle using the adop abort phase, cloning the file system using the adop fs_clone clone phase, and then reexecuting the prepare phase in the exact sequence as follows:

```
adop phase=abort
adop phase=fs_clone
adop phase=prepare
```

When executed with phase=abort, adop aborts the patching cycle by dropping the patch edition, canceling the ADZDPATCH concurrent program, and deleting the rows representing the existence of the ongoing patching cycle in the ad_adop_sessions and ad_adop_session_patches tables. When executed with phase=fs_clone, adop re-creates the patch edition file system by copying the active/run file system.

To summarize, adop's prepare phase can be executed with the parameters named workers, input_file, loglevel, defaultsfile, allowcoredump, analytics, cleanup_mode, and skipsyncerror.

■ **Note**   These parameters, their descriptions, and their usage examples were already documented in Table 6-1.

In addition, the patching cycle that is created using adop's prepare phase can be aborted by the adop phase=abort command, and the synchronization error that may be encountered in the adop prepare phase can be fixed using adop's file system cloning ability (adop phase=fs_clone). Once the prepare phase is completed, you can proceed with the next phase, called apply.

Figure 6-2 shows the prepare phase, which can be used with other adop parameters to start a new patching cycle and its relationship between the fs_clone, prepare, and apply phases as well as the finalize and abort phases, which can be used to abort the patching cycle.

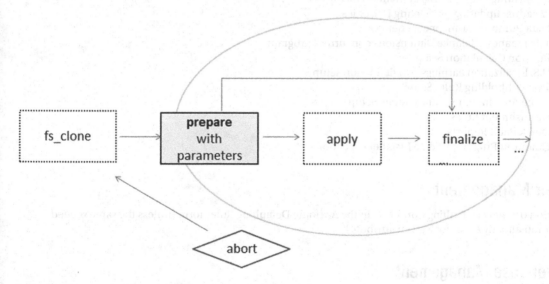

Figure 6-2. *Online patching cycle: prepare phase and its relation with other phases*

■ **Note** Normally you continue executing the patching operations with the apply phase after completing the prepare phase successfully.

In the case of manual patching operations such as deploying new custom packages and procedures, you may continue with the finalize phase without running the apply phase, as represented with the arrows that connect the prepare and finalize phases in both Figure 6-1 and Figure 6-2.

One more thing about the prepare phase is that it is possible to execute an adop phase and leave the system prepared for upcoming patching activities. The system can be left in the prepare state for days or weeks in order to gain time in case you need to apply a patch. However, as being in the prepare state means being in an online patching cycle, it is not so reasonable to do that. Product functionalities will be restricted during an online patching cycle, and there will be an error reported to users if they try to use these functionalities.

List of Restricted Functionalities in the Online Patching Cycle

When a new patching cycle is created with the adop phase=prepare command (in other words, when a patching cycle is active in EBS), some of the EBS application functionalities are affected and cannot be performed properly. The following is a list of these restricted functionalities categorized according to the products they belong.

Payroll

Defining Fast Formulas or using the Fast Formula Assistant.

    Performing dynamic trigger maintenance
    Creating, updating, or deleting U.S. cities
    Data Pump meta-mapper generator
    The Japanese Balance Dimensions concurrent program
    Pension Calculation Setup
    U.S. localization earnings and deduction setup
    Tax Withholding Rules Setup
    Wage Attachment Earnings Rules Setup
    Garnishment Rules Setup
    Quick Paint Reports
    Quantum Program Update Installer execution

Order Management

Creation of a new Defaulting Condition in the Attribute Defaulting Rules form (unless the same seeded condition already exists for a given attribute)

Warehouse Management

WMS Rule creation

Inventory

Concurrent program Generate Stock Locator Flexfield Definition for Mobile Transactions

Public Sector Financials International

Concurrent program named Subledger Security: Apply Security

Concurrent program named Subledger Security: Import/Export Data Fix

Subledger Accounting

Validating the Application Accounting definitions

Accounts Receivable

Creating new Transaction Sources

Incentive Compensation

Transaction collection process for new mappings

Synchronize Classification Rulesets program
Formula Generation feature
Specifying new formulas or changes to compensation rules

Oracle Demand Planning

Demand plans

Apply Phase

Continuing with the apply phase in the online patching cycle, you can make adop apply the patches by taking patching actions in the patch file system and patch edition in the database. File system objects such as forms, reports, and PLLs are placed in the patch edition, and database objects such as tables and packages are created or altered in the patch edition of the EBS database, which is created in the prepare phase.

In the apply phase, you usually execute the adop phase=apply command with just a few parameters such as the patches parameter to specify the patch number to be applied and the patchtop parameter in cases where you unload the patches into some other directory rather than the default one.

You sometimes use an input file to make adop read its parameters from a file that contains these parameter and their values, as demonstrated in Listing 6-5.

Also, in big patching activities, you use adop's merge parameter to merge some of the patches that are suitable for merging with each other into a single patch, which eases your work by letting you deal with only one patch rather than a list of patches. In addition, you have a downtime option that can be specified in the apply phase using an additional parameter called apply_mode. That is, when you use the adop phase=apply apply_mode=downtime patches=11111 command, adop applies patch 11111 in downtime mode, which is faster than online patching and requires fewer system resources. However, with downtime mode, you will have more system downtime.

■ **Note**　These two capabilities of adop will be explained later in this chapter.

To summarize, adop's apply phase is the phase where adop applies patches to the patch edition file system and patch edition of the database tier.

In an apply phase, in addition to applying a single patch, you have the ability to apply multiple patches or a merged patch that contains several patches.

The next phase that comes after the apply phase is the finalize phase. Of course, you have the ability to abort patching in the case of an error in the apply phase or in case you just decide to do so.

The apply phase can be executed with the following parameters: workers, loglevel, defaultsfile, allowcoredump, analytics, prompt, patchtop, apply_mode, maxworkers, merge, abandon, restart, options (checkfile, compiledb, compilejsp, copyportion, databaseportion, generateportion, integrity, autoconfig, actiondetails, parallel, prepreq, validate, phtofile, forceapply), and flags (preinstall, wait_on_failed_job, printdebug, uploadph).

■ **Note** These parameters, their descriptions, and their usage examples were already documented in Table 6-1.

Figure 6-3 shows the apply phase, which can be used to apply patches in an online patching cycle. The figure also shows the relationship of the prepare and finalize phases as well as the abort phase, which can be used to abort the patching cycle, as already mentioned.

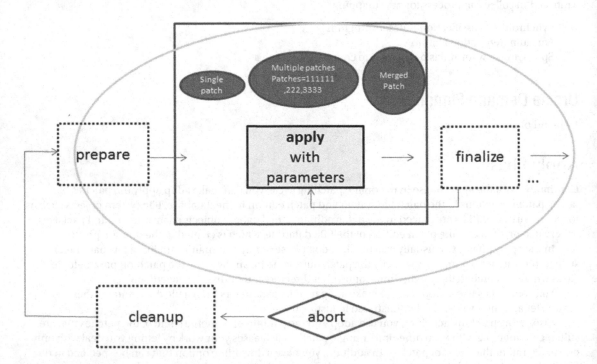

Figure 6-3. *Online patching cycle: apply phase and its relation with other phases*

■ **Note** It is recommended that you run the prepare phase after the abort phase, so if there is a need to abort the patching cycle, it is advisable to use the adop phase=abort,cleanup cleanup_mode=full command to abort the patching cycle and do a full cleanup afterward.

Finalize Phase

Continuing with the finalize phase, you make adop prepare the system for the next phase, the cutover phase. In the finalize phase, adop triggers the work that needs to be done for compiling the invalid objects and preparing the DDL statements to be used in the cutover phase.

Also, before the completion of this phase, some validations/checks are done for making sure that the system is ready for the cutover. Lastly, if this phase is executed with the additional parameter finalize_mode set to full, the statistics for the important data dictionary tables are also gathered.

The finalize phase can be executed with the parameters named workers, loglevel, defaultsfile, allowcoredump, analytics, prompt, finalize_mode, mtrestart, and cm_wait.

Figure 6-4 shows the finalize phase and its relationship with the prepare, apply, and cutover phases as well as the abort phase, which can be used to abort the patching cycle. As shown with the arrow that directly connects the prepare and finalize phases in Figure 6-4, and as mentioned earlier in this chapter, you can execute the finalize phase just after the prepare phase in the case of a manual patching operation such deploying new custom packages and procedures.

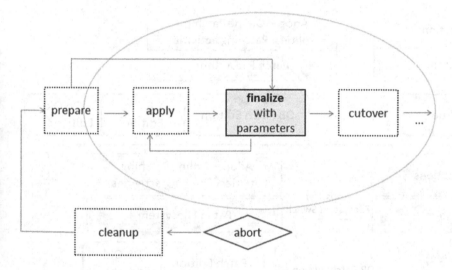

Figure 6-4. *Online patching cycle: finalize phase and its relation with other phases*

Also note that as shown with the arrow that directly connects the finalize phase back to the apply phase, you can execute the apply phase even after completing the finalize phase. That is, you can go back from the finalize phase to the apply phase in the standard sequence of the patching cycle if you decide to apply another patch just after the finalize phase is completed.

■ **Note** In the case of aborting the patching cycle during the finalize phase, it is recommended that you run the prepare phase after the abort phase, so if there is a need to abort the patching cycle, it is advisable that you use the adop phase=abort,cleanup cleanup_mode=full command to abort the patching cycle and do a full cleanup afterward.

Cutover

Continuing with cutover phase, you in general tell adop to make the patch file system, which was patched and prepared for the cutover in the previous adop phases, to be the new run file system and the patch edition in the database to be the new run edition. Also, as a result of running cutover, the current run file system becomes the new patch file system.

It sounds simple, but adop does several things by invoking the txkADOPCutOverPhaseCtrlScript.pl script to complete this cutover operation. First, adop shuts down the concurrent managers and all the other application services. Then, using the AD script named adzdpmgr.pl script located in the $AD_TOP/bin directory, adop makes the patch edition the new run edition in the database. After switching the database editions, adop also makes the patch file system to be the new run file system, and vice versa, by configuring the environment variable accordingly by using the AutoConfig utility.

Lastly, adop terminates all the database sessions that work on the old run edition and starts the application services.

Figure 6-5 shows the processing that is done in the cutover phase.

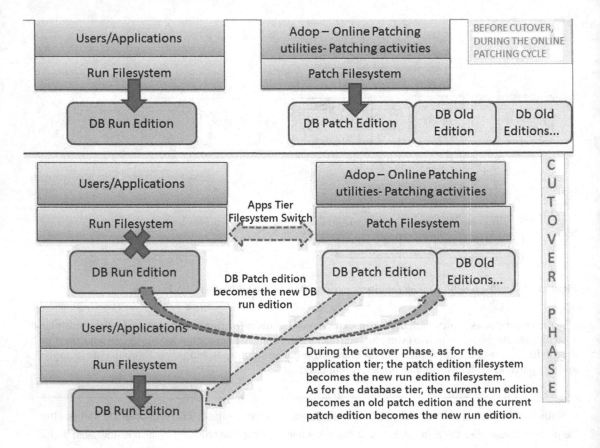

Figure 6-5. *Online patching cycle: cutover*

As you may already notice by the blue *X* located on the connection between users, applications, and the run edition in Figure 6-5, there is downtime caused by running the cutover phase. The downtime equals the time needed to stop the application services, make the database patch edition the new database run edition (the current database run edition becomes an old database edition), make the patch file system the new run file system, kill the old database sessions, and start the application services.

The cutover phase can be executed with the parameters named workers, loglevel, defaultsfile, allowcoredump, analytics, prompt, and finalize_mode.

Cutover is the most critical phase, as once it is executed, it is not possible to roll back unless using the flashback database method explained in Chapter 5.

After completing the cutover phase, the patching is finished as the patched application and database objects are activated and the application user can start using them. However, to complete the patching cycle, the last phase of it named cleanup should be executed too.

Figure 6-6 shows the cutover phase, which can be used to activate the patched file system and database edition in an online patching cycle. Figure 6-6 also displays the relationship between the cutover and other online patching cycle phases.

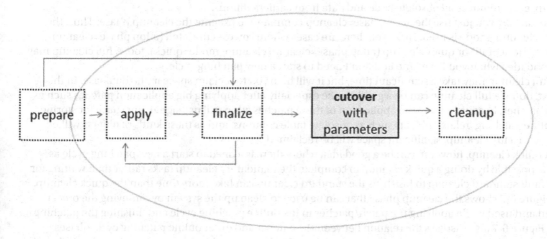

Figure 6-6. *Online patching cycle: cutover phase and its relation with other phases*

Note that in Figure 6-6 you don't see the abort phase. This is because Figure 6-6 is focused on the cutover phase, and once the cutover phase is run, the patching cycle can't be aborted.

Also, it is important to mention that as you can't execute the abort phase once you enter the cutover phase, you have to solve any problems encountered in this phase to complete the online patching cycle properly.

Cleanup

Continuing with the cleanup phase by executing the command adop phase=cleanup, you tell adop to clean the objects created and used for online patching.

The cleanup phase can be executed with the parameters named workers, loglevel, defaultsfile, allowcoredump, analytics, prompt, and cleanup_mode.

The most used one of these parameters is the cleanup mode.

Various database objects such as cross-edition triggers, editioned code objects, indexes, columns, editions, and obsolete seed data are dropped in this phase. The list of dropped objects actually changes according to the cleanup_mode parameter.

Normally, when you execute the adop phase=cleanup command, the default value of cleanup_mode, standard, is taken into account, and a standard cleanup, including removal of obsolete cross-edition triggers, obsolete editioned code objects, and seed data, is done on the database side.

In addition, when you set cleanup_mode to quick (adop phase=cleanup cleanup_mode=quick) to make adop do a quick cleanup, adop leaves the obsolete editioned code objects in the database.

Lastly, when you set the value of the cleanup_mode parameter to full, adop does a full cleanup. In a full cleanup, adop removes all obsolete code and data from earlier editions.

So, usually you just use the adop phase=cleanup command to execute the cleanup phase. Thus, the default cleanup_mode is used. However, there are cases where you execute a full (adop phase=cleanup cleanup_mode=full) or quick cleanup (adop phase=cleanup cleanup_mode=quick), too. A full cleanup may be a good idea when you have time and don't need to start a new patching cycle.

Full cleanup may take a significant time, but it will help you to reclaim space in the database. In this context, doing a full cleanup can be a good choice especially after applying big application patches such as rollup patches, because during the application of these patches adop will use significant space for storing the online patching–related objects such as obsolete table columns, and as these kinds of objects will be dropped in a full cleanup, significant space will be reclaimed.

A quick cleanup, however, can be a good idea where there is a need to start a new patching cycle as soon as possible by doing a quick cleanup to complete the mandatory cleanup tasks rather than waiting for the default standard cleanup to finish, as the standard cleanup can take more time than the quick cleanup.

Figure 6-7 shows the cleanup phase that can be used to clean up the system by removing the object created and used while applying the patch/patches in the online patching cycle and finishing the patching cycle. Figure 6-7 also displays the relation between the cutover and other online patching cycle phases.

Note that in Figure 6-7 you see two cleanup boxes, for describing the cleanup operations that is done in a online patching cycle.

You see the cleanup phase depicted in the most right box, for giving you the place of the cleanup phase in an online patching cycle. Also, you see a dotted cleanup box drawn just between the prepare and apply phases. So this dotted cleanup box actually represents another cleanup (a cleanup operation in prepare phase) operation that can be kicked in in cases where, adop phase=cleanup command which should have been executed in a previous patch cycle, was not executed or failed with an error. So, in those cases, a standard mode cleanup will be executed as part of the prepare phase that will be used to start the next patching cycle, as depicted in Figure 6-7.

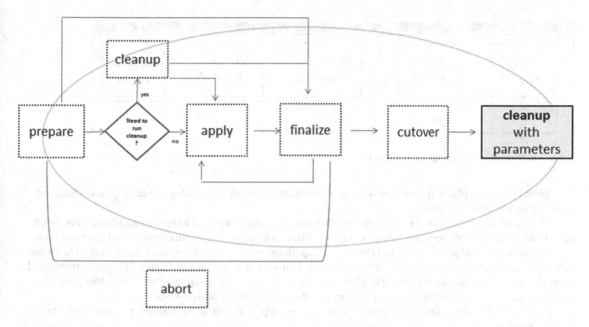

Figure 6-7. *Online patching cycle: cleanup phase and its relation with other phases, as well as the phases in which the online patching cycle can be aborted*

Well, you have now seen all the phases that contribute to the online patching cycle. We have explained how to apply a patch online by executing the online patching cycle through the phases named prepare, apply, finalize, cutover, and cleanup.

We also explained the things happening in the back end while you are executing the phases and the connections between these phases by giving you detailed diagrams for each of these phases. We also explained the fs_clone phase, which can be used in certain scenarios. We explained the abort phase too, but it was just a brief introduction, so we will explain the abort phase in more detail in the following section.

Abort Phase

When you execute the adop phase=abort command to terminate a patching cycle as mentioned earlier, adop checks to see whether an online patching cycle is active and whether any online patching is in-progress, and adop checks the patch edition in the database and removes it if it is exists. adop also cancels the ADZDPATCH concurrent program and deletes the rows in the ad_adop_sessions and ad_adop_session_patches tables.

The abort phase can be executed after the prepare, apply, and finalize phases; in other words, it can be executed until you run the cutover phase.

Figure 6-8 shows the abort phase and represents that it can be executed until you run the cutover phase.

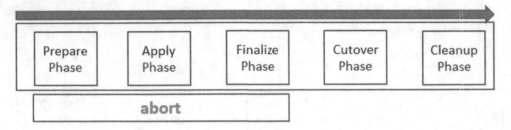

Figure 6-8. *Online patching cycle: abort*

When the adop phase is executed, you need to execute a full cleanup using the adop phase=cleanup cleanup_mode=full command.

Also, if abort is called after executing the adop phase=apply command to apply patches into the patch edition and patch file system, then there is a need to run an fs_clone too. In this case, the adop phase=abort command should be followed by a full cleanup (adop phase=cleanup cleanup_mode=full) and an fs_clone (adop phase=fs_clone) to make the database be in a clear state and to make the patch file system re-created from the run/active file system. Using fs_clone, the patch file system is re-created to be in a clear state (without patches applied) and also in a synchronized state with the run file system.

Here's a summary of the things you do while you are applying a patch or multiple patches in an online patching cycle:

1. You start by executing the prepare phase (adop phase=prepare with or without additional parameters).

■ **Note**   In the prepare phase, you have the ability to abort the patching. So if you choose to abort the patching cycle because of a failure or because you change your mind and decide not to apply any patches, you execute the abort phase (adop phase=abort), do a full cleanup (adop phase=cleanup cleanup_mode=full), and then leave the system in a clean state ready for a new patching cycle.

---

2. You continue with the apply phase (adop phase=apply patches=<patch_number> or adop phase=apply patches=<patch_number>,<patch_number>... with or without additional parameters).

■ **Note**   In the apply phase, you have the ability to abort the patching. So, if you choose to abort the patching cycle because of a failure or because you change your mind and decide not to apply any patches, you execute the abort phase (adop phase=abort), do a full cleanup (adop phase=cleanup cleanup_mode=full), and lastly do fs_clone (adop phase=fs_clone) to leave the system in a clean state ready for a new patching cycle.

---

    3.   Then you finalize (adop phase=finalize with or without additional parameters).

■ **Note**   Until this point, you have the ability to abort the patching. So, if you choose to abort the patching cycle because of a failure or because you change your mind and decide not to apply any patches, you execute the abort phase (adop phase=abort) and then do a full cleanup (adop phase=cleanup cleanup_mode=full) to leave the system in a clean state ready for a new patching cycle.

You can wait as long as you want in the finalize phase. That is, you can postpone the execution of the cutover phase until you have the needed downtime for it.

---

    4.   After the finalize phase, you continue with the cutover phase (adop phase=cutover with or without additional parameters).

■ **Note**   You have no ability to abort the patching if you start executing this phase.

---

    5.   Lastly, you execute the cleanup phase and complete the patching cycle (adop phase=cleanup -- with or without additional parameters).

Hotpatch Mode

adop's hotpatch mode gives you an opportunity to apply the.patches online to the run edition directly rather than following the steps in an online patching cycle to apply the patches to the patch edition and then cut over to make the patched file system and database edition the run edition.

Hotpatch mode is activated through the adop parameter hotpatch and supplying the value yes for it (hotpatch=yes). This parameter can be specified only while running the apply phase. In other words, hotpatch mode is valid for the apply phase only, and it should be used only when directed by the patch readme or by Oracle Support.

Not that if it is not directed by Oracle to apply a patch with the hotpatch option, then applying that patch with the hotpatch option can be considered an unsafe operation.

This means it has not been tested by Oracle or the patch is not suitable for applying with the hotpatch option. So, if you apply a patch that is unsafe with the hotpatch option, you'll need to take the risk yourself and be ready for the consequences such as invalid objects, missing code dependencies, mismatches between the code level of the file system and database, missing column data, other data integrity problems, out-of-date indexes and materialized view definitions, and invalid data in runtime caches.

After applying a safe patch (documented in Oracle Support docs or the readme of the patch, suitable for hotpatch mode) with the hotpatch option, the files in the run file system will be directly patched. These patched files in the run file system get synchronized with the patch file system in the next online patching cycle, when the prepare phase is executed. As part of the prepare phase, adop syncs the patch file system using the findings of the adop config change detector, which will detect the newly applied patches to the run file system.

Of course, if you want to synchronize the file system immediately after applying a patch in hotpatch mode, without waiting for the next prepare phase to be executed, you can execute a file system clone operation using the adop phase=fs_clone command.

There is no need to synchronize the patched database objects with the patch edition, and that's why there is no option available for that.

Also, to apply a patch in hotpatch mode, you must not have any patching cycle active; otherwise, you end up with the following error:

```
[UNEXPECTED]Cannot apply hotpatch as another online patching cycle is going on.
```

To apply a patch in hotpatch mode, you just set your runtime environment and use the hotpatch_mode=yes parameter in conjunction with parameters phase=apply, patches, and patchtop if the patch is not located in the default patch top directory.

Like the patches that are applied online following the phases in online patching cycle, whether using the default patch top, the patches that are unzipped and applied in hotpatch mode must not be deleted and must be located in the same location where they are unzipped and applied from. These patches will be used in the next prepare phase, in other words, in the next patching cycle for synchronizing the patch file system. So, the patches that are applied in hotpatch should not be deleted from the patch top directory (default or nondefault) until the next online patching cycle's prepare phase is completed.

■ **Note** If the patches that are applied in hotpatch mode are deleted from the PATCH_TOP before the next prepare phase, adop will report an error and complain about the missing patch directories, as the prepare phase will try to sync the patch file system from the run file system, and it will not be successful on this. So in this case, you can always restore the deleted patches by downloading them from Oracle Support and retrying the prepare phase.

Although restoring the patches is the recommend approach, there is an alternative for this problem. That is, in the case of a synchronization problem encountered in an adop prepare phase that is caused by the missing patch folders in PATCH_TOP, you can also abort the patching cycle and run an fs_clone. After the fs_clone is completed, you can run the prepare phase again. The fs_clone will build the patch file system from the run file system.

Also, if any other parameters are specified in the readme file or in the related Oracle Support documents, then those parameters should be supplied to adop.

■ **Note** Before going any further, it is important to mention that although the EBS 12.2.5 was recently released and it is the latest release of EBS 12.2, you may find EBS 12.2.4–related patches in the examples given in this chapter. You may also find EBS 12.2.4–related reference documents for patching-related activities, which are the main focus of this chapter. What we would like to stress is that the methods and statements referenced from all the MOS documents in this chapter are correct for EBS 12.2.5 as well. Only the patch numbers may differ.

In Listing 6-12, you see the hotpatch mode in action for patch 5584908.

As documented in the Oracle document 2036816.1 ("HOW TO RUN SLA HOT PATCH IN EBS R12.2.4 USING ADOP?"), which is applicable for EBS 12.2.5, too, you see the additional options (patchtop and option=nocopyportion) and a different kind of usage for the patches parameter with the hotpatch parameter.

Listing 6-12. Using Hotpatch Mode for Applying the SLA Patch (5584908)

```
adop phase=apply options=nocopyportion patchtop=$XLA_TOP/patch/115
patches=driver:xla5584908.drv hotpatch=yes
```

In Listing 6-12, nocopyportion is used as the patch files are already located in APPL_TOP (XLA_TOP/patch/115), and patchtop is used in order to specify the location of the patch files. The driver is used to specify the patch driver for adop, as when the adop is executed with hotpatch=yes, adop runs the adpatch with a command such as adpatch workers=16 options=hotpatch, and adpatch asks its classic questions such as the name of the patch driver.

In Listing 6-13, you see hotpatch mode in use for another patch, the consolidated seed table upgrade patch 17204589 as documented in the Oracle E-Business Suite Release Notes, Release 12.2 (Doc ID 1320300.1) readme file.

This time you see a plain adop command specifying only the patches and hotpatch parameters, supposing the patch was unloaded to the default patch top directory and it is a classical patch for which you don't need to specify any options like nocopyportion, and so on.

Listing 6-13. Using Hotpatch Mode for Applying Consolidated Seed Table Upgrade (17204589)

```
adop phase=apply patches=17204589 hotpatch=yes
```

Listing 6-14 shows a different example in which the hotpatch_mode parameter is used in conjunction with the merge parameter in order to merge multiple patches and apply them into the run file system and run edition of the EBS database in a single run.

In Listing 6-14, the 12.2.4 online help patch and an online help–related grants patch are merged and applied in hotpatch mode, as documented in MOS document "Oracle E-Business Suite Release 12.2.4 Readme" (Doc ID 1617458.1).

■ **Note** Applying an online help patch using the hotpatch option is also recommended for EBS 12.2.5, as per the MOS documentation "Oracle E-Business Suite Release 12.2.5 Readme" (Doc ID 1983050.1).

Listing 6-14. Using Hotpatch and Merge Parameter

```
adop phase=apply patches=17919162,19290141 hotpatch=yes merge=yes
```

■ **Note** We will explain adop's merge parameter in detail in the section "Merging Oracle Application Patches." For now, you may recall the definition of it given in Table 6-1: "merge: Used tell adop to merge patches rather than apply the patch drivers sequentially."

In general, online help patches consolidate update patches, and as stated in MOS document "Oracle E-Business Suite NLS Release Notes, Release 12.2" (Doc ID 1314621.1), the NLS patches can be applied using hotpatch mode. It is also possible to merge the NLS patches while applying them in hotpatch mode.

Listing 6-15 shows an example adop command for applying the Russian translation that can be considered as a base NLS patch.

Listing 6-15. Using Hotpatch Parameter for Applying the Russian Translation Patch (10124646)

```
adop phase=apply patches=10124646_RU:u10124646.drv hotpatch=yes
```

■ **Note** In Listing 6-15 you use the patches parameter to supply the directory name of the patch, which is unloaded into the default patch top directory, and the driver file for the patch to adop, as adop uses adpatch in hotpatch mode, which will ask for the driver file anyway. So, rather than giving the driver name when it is asked for by adop, you can choose to supply the driver file while running the adop command in this example.

It is also important to mention that if there is a requirement to apply an online patch after applying a patch in hotpatch mode, then it is required to execute the prepare phase. This is because if you apply a patch in hotpatch mode, adop marks the apply phase as active, but it also marks the cutover phase not applicable, as shown in the adop –status command output provided in Figure 6-9.

```
Node Name    Node   Type     Phase     Status           Started           Finished
-----------  ----   ------   -------   --------------   ------------      -----------------------
somehost            master   PREPARE   NOT APPLICABLE
                                       APPLY            ACTIVE            20-DEC-14 09:18:18 -04:00
                                                                         20-DEC-14 09:30:18

                                       FINALIZE         NOT STARTED
                                       CUTOVER          NOT APPLICABLE
                                       CLEANUP          NOT STARTED
```

Figure 6-9. *A snippet from the output of the adop –status command showing the apply phase is in active status*

This active apply phase shown in Figure 6-9 is not like the one used in an online patching cycle. It is there for hotpatches, as no online patching cycle is created or started in hotpatch mode.

In this manner, you can continue by applying patches in hotpatch mode, as this apply phase is active for applying hot patches. However, if you try to apply a patch using the online patching cycle, you need to execute the prepare phase to create an online patching cycle. Likewise, you can't execute the finalize, cutover, or cleanup phase once you apply a patch using hotpatch mode.

Lastly, if you apply a patch using hotpatch mode and if there are manual post-patch instructions for the patch that you are applying or in the Oracle Support note that you are following, then those post-patch installation actions should be taken just after the hotpatch apply operation. In addition, the scripts or commands represented as the post-patch instruction should be executed from the run edition environment.

Before continuing with the next section, we want to clarify one more thing. As you may have realized, we did not mention using the options=hotpatch and apply_mode=hotpatch parameters in this section, but if you recall the parameters and their definitions given in Table 6-1, these two parameters are also for enabling hotpatch mode. So, does something seem wrong? Well, it is not actually. We mentioned the hotpatch=yes parameter when we were explaining the hotpatch mode in this section because options=hotpatch is actually an adpatch parameter, which was the patching tool used in releases before 12.2. Although it can be used for enabling hotpatch mode in EBS 12.2, it is not recommended by any Oracle Support document.

apply_mode=yes is an adop parameter that Oracle introduced with R12.AD.C.delta.4 as a replacement for hotpatch=yes, but it is very new and not used in Oracle documents.

So, using hotpatch=yes is the best method for enabling hotpatch mode at this time; because it is the adop parameter introduced in the initial days of adop implementation, it is a way for achieving backward compatibility (for AD.C levels lower than AD.C.Delta.4), and it is the parameter used in Oracle Support documents that specify patches to be applied in hotpatch mode (at the time of writing this book).

Downtime Mode

Downtime mode gives you the ability to apply an application patch using adop offline.

Oracle must have been thinking that with online patching, there will no need for any downtime when EBS 12.2 was first released, but then when Oracle saw that using online patching and executing the patching cycle made the customers lose time in applying big patches in the release upgrades, it provided an downtime option to adop with the AD-TXK Delta 5 level.

■ **Note** When we started writing this book, the latest EBS release was 12.2.4, and the latest AD-TXK Delta 5 level was Delta 5.

At that time, being on AD-TXK Delta 5 level was a must for EBS 12.2.4 environments, since EBS 12.2.4 could be installed only by upgrading from an earlier release (for example, upgrading from 12.2.0, 12.2.3, or so on), and the latest AD and TXK levels have always been a prerequisite for these EBS 12.2 upgrades.

However, at the time of bringing this book to print, the latest EBS release is now 12.2.5, and the latest AD-TXK Delta level has become Delta 7. So, at this time, being on AD-TXK-Delta 7 level is the prerequisite for installing the latest EBS release (EBS 12.2.5).

So, what the downtime option does is to tell adop to apply patches without executing the patching cycle. As the name implies, in downtime mode, the application patches are applied when application services are down. Like in the hotpatch mode, adop applies the patches directly to the run file system and run edition of the EBS database.

The benefit of the downtime option is its speed, but the disadvantage of it is the downtime. Downtime mode can be specified only with the apply_mode parameter.

Listing 6-16 shows how to make adop apply a patch using the downtime option.

Listing 6-16. Applying Patch 123456 with the downtime Option

```
adop phase=apply patches=123456 apply_mode=downtime
```

Like the hotpatch mode, downtime mode can be used only with the apply phase, and it should be used only when directed by the patch readme or by the Oracle Support documents.

Actually, all the patches can be applied using the downtime mode, but unless it is documented in Oracle Support with a statement like "This patch can be applied using apply_mode=downtime," you may need to solve problems during the adop downtime patching. This is because of the fact that most of the Release 12.2 patches are not normally tested by Oracle in downtime mode; thus, unless it is documented, patches must not be applied in downtime mode. So, in case of a problem when using downtime mode in an application of a patch, which is not suitable/tested for downtime mode, you may even need to restore to a backup.

In general, downtime mode has been created by Oracle to speed up the EBS 12.2.4 and EBS 12.2.5 upgrades that are performed as part of the EBS 12.2 installations to be on the latest supported EBS release levels.

Downtime mode is considered faster, even faster than the hotpatch mode, because during a downtime mode patch, the system resources are not used by EBS users and application services.

As already mentioned in Chapter 2, upgrading EBS is a mandatory task immediately after installing it. So, using downtime is an option that can increase the speed of the EBS 12.2.4 or 12.2.5 upgrades that are done just after installing the EBS 12.2.0 base release.

In this manner, if EBS is installed as the base release, which is EBS 12.2.0, and if it is about to be upgraded to a higher release such as 12.2.4 or 12.2.5 without opening the services to the users (in other words, before you put data into it), then the downtime option can be used for the patches that are applied for upgrading to EBS 12.2.4 or 12.2.5. Downtime mode can also be used for all the post-12.2.4 and 12.2.5 upgrade patches as long as the application tier processes have not been started after the EBS 12.2.4 or 12.2.5 upgrades.

However, if the system is used after the installation, then all the subsequent patches must be applied online using the standard online patching cycle unless there is a possibility of using the downtime option for those patches as stated in Oracle Support documents.

Using the downtime option also has some restrictions. That is, a failed patch cannot be aborted, and it is not supported to apply patches with downtime mode in multinode application tier environments.

Listing 6-17 shows the EBS 12.2.4 upgrade applied with the downtime option as documented by Oracle Support note "Oracle E-Business Suite Release 12.2.4 Readme" (Doc ID 1617458.1).

Listing 6-17. Applying EBS 12.2.4 Upgrade Patch Using the downtime Option

1. You first source the run edition.

    ```
    $ . /u01/install/TEST/EBSapps.env run
    ```

2. Stop the application services.

    ```
    cd $ADMINS_SCRIPTS_HOME
    sh adstpall.sh apps/apps
    ```

3. Apply the upgrade patch in downtime mode.

    ```
    adop phase=apply apply_mode=downtime patches=17919161
    ```

4. Start the application services.

    ```
    cd $ADMINS_SCRIPTS_HOME
    sh adstrtal.sh apps/apps
    ```

5. Execute a cleanup operation.

    ```
    adop phase=cleanup
    ```

6. Lastly, execute an fs_clone operation.

    ```
    adop phase=fs_clone
    ```

Listing 6-17 clearly shows the process of applying a patch with the downtime option. As shown in Listing 6-17, you first stop the application tier service if it is running because the downtime option requires the application services to be down. This is where the downtime for the patch application begins.

Then you apply the upgrade patch using the adop downtime option with the command adop phase=apply apply_mode=downtime patches=17919161 (the patchtop parameter is not used, supposing the upgrade patch is placed in the default patch top $APPL_TOP_NE/../patch as recommended by Oracle).

After the patch application, you start all the application services so the users can log in and start using the applications. This is where the downtime ends.

After starting the services, you execute the cleanup phase (adop phase=cleanup) to remove the database-side objects used for applying the upgrade patch. You execute cleanup just after you apply the upgrade patch, as the upgrade patch is a very big one, so you want to clear the objects and gain free space as well as being ready for the prepare phase, which will be executed in the next patching cycle.

Lastly, you execute an fs_clone operation, as it is essential for big patches applied to the run edition using the hotpatch or downtime option. This is again done for being ready for the prepare phase, which will be executed in the next patching cycle.

■ **Note** In the prepare phase, these kinds of synchronizations are already done, but it can take a long time and extend the time for creating the next patching cycle. Because of these reasons, Oracle Support note "Oracle E-Business Suite Release 12.2.4 Readme" (Doc ID 1617458.1) instructs you to execute this fs_clone phase.

Also, there are some patches that can be applied in downtime even if the EBS users have already started using EBS applications and have put some data into the EBS database through the applications they use.

Listing 6-18 shows the application of R12.HR_PF.C.Delta.6 (19193000) and two other patches, 21055497 and 21055497, in downtime mode sequentially, as documented in Oracle document "Steps to Apply R12. HR_PF.C.Delta.6(19193000) in Downtime Mode" (Doc ID 2041006.1).

■ **Note** This document was written for both upgrading to Oracle E-Business Suite Release 12.2 from Release 11i, 12.0, or 12.1 and installing a new Oracle E-Business Suite system, which means this patch can be applied in downtime mode even when the EBS system to be patched has already been used by users.

Listing 6-18. Applying Multiple Downtime Patches in downtime Mode

1. You first source the run edition.

   ```
   $ . /u01/install/TEST/EBSapps.env run
   ```

2. Stop the application services.

   ```
   cd $ADMINS_SCRIPTS_HOME
   sh adstpall.sh apps/apps
   ```

3. Apply the patches in downtime mode.

   ```
   adop phase=apply apply_mode=downtime patches=19193000
   adop phase=apply apply_mode=downtime patches=21055497
   adop phase=apply apply_mode=downtime patches=21055497
   ```

4. Start the application services.

   ```
   cd $ADMINS_SCRIPTS_HOME
   sh adstrtal.sh apps/apps
   ```

5. Execute a cleanup operation.

   ```
   adop phase=cleanup
   ```

6. Lastly, execute an fs_clone operation

   ```
   adop phase=fs_clone
   ```

So, downtime mode is something to use when documented by Oracle. Unless documented, it should not be used, as Oracle knows in which cases it may be needed and tests those cases, stating that the downtime option can be used for them.

Using the downtime option is similar to using the hotpatch option. They both should be used if documented by Oracle, they both apply the patches to the run edition file system and the run edition of the EBS database, they can both be used only in adop's apply phase, and there is no need to create a patching cycle in order to use them.

The only difference between them is hotpatch mode is used when the application services are online, but the downtime option is used when the application services are offline.

Merging Oracle Application Patches

Merging Oracle application patches is an option for applying EBS application patches. It has always been an option for minimizing the patching downtime and is considered one of the best practices for EBS patching in older releases such as EBS 11i and 12 (12.0, 12.1). It was a tradition for apps DBAs, who were managing the EBS 11i and 12 environments. Whenever possible, multiple patches were merged into a single one and applied as a single patch, especially in big upgrades where there were a lot patches to be applied in a sequence.

Well, this tradition is still around in EBS 12.2, because merging is also considered as one of the most important patching best practices, and it is even documented in release upgrade Oracle Support documents to merge patches when appropriate.

One of the benefits of merging the patches is that as there is a single merged patch rather than several patches to be applied to EBS system, there is only a single use of the patching tool. Thus, activities such as answering the questions asked by the patching tool and executing the patching tool itself through the command line is only done for once, even if you apply ten patches as a single merged patch. This saves time for apps DBAs.

However, the biggest benefit of merging the application patches is that it saves time as some patching actions such as compiling database objects and relinking executables are done only for the merged patches. That is, once you merge several patches into a single one and apply that single merged patch into your EBS system, these kinds of actions are executed only once as adop treats this merged patch as a single patch, even if that merged patch consists of several patches.

However, without merging, you need to execute those compiling and relinking activities for every patch over and over again.

Also, there are some patches that need to be merged and applied as a single patch in order to be applied properly, fix the things they were created for, or bring the enhancements that need to brought.

The situations where you can merge the application patches vary. The patches should be merged for sure when stated by the Oracle documents, but also sometimes you can just decide to merge a patch with another patch or patches.

In general, the patches that are part of the same product can be merged. Except the AD product, which should be merged with AD patches only, almost all the patches in EBS can be merged. That means you can have cross-product patches in a merged patch, as well. For example, multiple NLS patches can be merged, or a big patch can be merged with a small-size patch, which may be a post-requisite of that big patch.

Also, you need to execute the prerequisite of every patch that is merged into a single merged patch before you start adop's apply phase. Likewise, you should do the actions specified as the post-installation tasks stated in the readme files of each patch or, if it is available, stated in the related Oracle Support document for each patch, after completing the adop's apply phase.

■ **Note** You should not do the same actions repeatedly. For example, if you merge two patches and both of them require the same script to be run as their post-installation or pre-installation task, then you should run that script once only.

Like in EBS 11i and 12, the tool AD Merge Patch (admrgpch) can be used in EBS 12.2 to merge application patches. Additionally, adop has the ability to merge patches. So, now you have two options to merge application patches in EBS 12.2. That is, if you are an old-style apps DBA, you can just use the admrgpch tool to merge the patches and give the generated merged patch to adop and make it apply the merged patch in a single run, or you can use the optional adop parameter (merge) to offload this merging activity to adop and make adop merge the patches and apply them as a single patch in EBS 12.2.

Let's take a look of these two methods by starting with the AD Merge Patch utility as it is the traditional merging utility used in EBS 11i and 12, as well as the latest release. AD Merge Patch is invoked using the admrgpch command, and it is used for merging several patches into a single one. It takes two mandatory parameters: the source directory, which is where the patches to be merged reside, and the destination directory, where the merged patch will be located.

Listing 6-19 shows the general usage of the admrgpch utility, as it has several additional parameters, which are not used mostly.

Listing 6-19. Applying Multiple Downtime Patches in downtime Mode

```
admrgpch  -s <source_directory -d <destination_directory>
```

Note that the optional parameters of the admrgpch utility can be displayed with their definitions using the admrgpch –help command. Table 6-2 defines the optional parameters that can be used as parameters for admrgpch.

Table 6-2. *admrgpch Parameters and Descriptions*

Parameter Name	Description
-verbose	This parameter can be used for increasing or decreasing the verbosity level of the admrgpch tool. This parameter can be set to the value 0, 1, 2, or 3. 3 is for specifying the highest verbosity level. 0: Silent. 1: Quiet (default). 2: Verbose. 3: Loud.
-merge_name	This parameter can be used to name the merged patch name. (The default name for a merged patch is merged.) This affects the name of the merged patch driver. By default the name of the patch driver is u_merged.drv. We strongly recommend using this parameter for naming the merged patches, as when you name the merged patches, it is easier to identify the merged patches by checking the ad_ tables with their names when there is need to check the applied patches later.
-s	This is a mandatory parameter that should be used for specifying the source directory where the patches that are wanted to be merged reside.
-d	This is a mandatory parameter that should be used for specifying the destination directory where the emergent merged patch will reside.

(*continued*)

Table 6-2. (*continued*)

Parameter Name	Description
-preinstall	This parameter is used for merging the preinstall patches. It is used with the master parameter to merge the preinstall patch drivers with the master driver.
	Note: When you use the preinstall parameter, you don't specify the –s parameter to specify the source directory as your source automatically becomes as follows:
	$APPL_TOP/admin/$TWO_TASK>/preinstall
	For example, the following command merges the preinstall patches with the driver of patch 6678700:
	admrgpch -d /u01/install/patches_dir/dest -preinstall -master u6678700.drv
-driveronly	This parameter can be used for merging the patch drivers only. When used, admrgpch only merges the patch drivers but does not copy the patch files to the destination directory. This parameter must be used only when directed by Oracle (via Oracle Support documents, patch readme files, or Oracle service requests).
	A possible use of this parameter can be in such a scenario where you want to execute the scripts and commands delivered with the patch driver but do not want the patch files to copied to the application file system.
-master	This parameter is used for merging the preinstall patches. It is used with the preinstall or driveronly parameters to merge the preinstall patch drivers with the master driver.
	When you use the preinstall parameter, you don't need to specify the –s parameter to specify the source directory as your source automatically becomes as follows:
	$APPL_TOP/admin/$TWO_TASK>/preinstall
	For example, the following command merges the preinstall patches with the driver of patch 6678700:
	admrgpch -d /u01/install/patches_dir/dest -preinstall -master u6678700.drv
	Note that using this parameter is required in cases like 12.2.0 upgrades, where there is a need to merge the preinstall patches with the consolidated upgrade patch to apply all of them in a single run. So, this parameter is used when you want to merge preinstall patches with a normal patch.
-admode	This parameter must be used when you want to merge the AD patches.
	For example:
	admrgpch -s /u01/install/patches_dir/source/ -d /u01/install/patches_dir/dest/ -admode
	For instance, if you want to merge the AD patch (9179588:R12.AD.B) with other AD patches such as 9477107:R12.AD.B and R12.AD.B.1 (patch 7461070), you should use the –admode parameter.

Table 6-2. (*continued*)

Parameter Name	Description
-manifest	This parameter can be used when you don't want to or are not able to (consider 100 patches to be unzipped and suppose there is no disk available for that) unzip the patches and put them to the source directory for merging. Using the manifest parameter, you tell admrgpch to unzip the patches on the fly and merge them.
	To use the –manifest parameter properly, you download the patch zip files into a directory and use the –manifest parameter to specify the full paths of the downloaded patches that you want to merge.
	Here's an example:
	Contents of /u01/patchlist.txt:
	/u1/install/patches_dir/downloads/p19290141_R12_GENERIC.zip
	/u1/install/patches_dir/downloads/p17919162_R12_GENERIC.zip
	Merge command:
	admrgpch -s /u01/install/patches_dir/source manifest /u01/patchlist.txt
	-d /u01/install/patches_dir/dest
-logfile	This parameter can be used to specify the log file. By default admrgpch creates its log file named admrgpch.log in the current directory where it was executed.

So, as shown in Table 6-2, there are various parameters that can be used with the admrgpch tool. Knowing their descriptions and their usages is good. However, to be honest, you just use the -s and –d parameters to merge the patches most of the time.

As shown in Listing 6-19, you need to supply the source directory and destination directory paths for executing admrgpch successfully.

When you execute the admrgpch command, admgrpch looks to the source directory, finds the patch directories residing in it, merges them by merging the patch files and merging the patch drives files, and creates a single merged patch in the destination directory.

■ **Note**   If the same files are delivered by multiple patches, then only the file with the highest version is packaged into the merged patch.

So, as admrgpch uses the source directory for locating the patches to be merged, all the patches that you want to be merged should be located in the source directory supplied to the admrgpch utility using the –s parameter. That's why you need to unzip the patches you want to merge into the source directory before executing the admrgch command.

In addition, another important requirement of using the admrgch utility is that the destination directory and the source directory must be on the same directory level. That is, if the source is /u01/PATCHES/source, then the destination directory must be located in the /u01/PATCHES directory too. (For this example, the destination directory may be /u01/patches/dest.)

Listing 6-20 shows an example of real-life usage for the admrgpch utility to merge the 12.2.4 online help patch (17919162) and the help patch of Oracle grants (19290141).

Listing 6-20 also shows the application of the merged patch using adop as follows:

1.   You first create your source and destination directories in the same top-level directory (/u01/patches_dir).

```
[applmgr@somehost /]$ mkdir -p /u01/patches_dir/source
[applmgr@homehost /]$ mkdir -p /u01/patches_dir/dest
```

2.   Next, you cd into the directory where you downloaded the patches to be merged and unzip them into your source directory.

```
[applmgr@somehost/]$ cd /downloads

[applmgr@somehost downloads]$ ls
p17919162_R12_GENERIC.zip  p19290141_R12_GENERIC.zip

[applmgr@somehost downloads]$ unzip p17919162_R12_GENERIC.zip -d /u01/ /patches_
dir/source/
[applmgr@somehost downloads]$ unzip  p19290141_R12_GENERIC.zip  -d /u01/ /patches_
dir/source/
```

3.   Once you unzip the patch zip files into your source directory, the subdirectories for the patch files are created as shown in the ls command output.

```
[applmgr@somehost downloads]$cd /u01/ /patches_dir/source/
 [applmgr@somehost source]$ ls
17919162   19290141
```

4.   Next, you execute the admrgpch utility by supplying the source and destination directories to it.

5.   Note that the output of the following admrgpch is truncated to fit on the page.

```
[applmgr@somehost source]$ admrgpch -s /u01 /patches_dir/source/ -d /u01/patches_
dir/dest/

Executing the merge of the patch drivers
  -- Processing patch: /u01/patches_dir/source/17919162
  -- Processing file: /u01/patches_dir/source/17919162/u17919162.drv
  -- Done processing file: /u01/patches_dir/source/17919162/u17919162.drv
  -- Done processing patch: /u01/patches_dir/source/17919162

  -- Processing patch: /u01/patches_dir/source/19290141
  -- Processing file: /u01/patches_dir/source/19290141/u19290141.drv
  -- Done processing file: /u01/patches_dir/source/19290141/u19290141.drv
  -- Done processing patch: /u01/patches_dir/source/19290141

Copying files...

5% complete. Copied 26 files of 519...
10% complete. Copied 52 files of 519...
  ...
```

```
Character-set converting files...
2 unified drivers merged.
Patch merge completed successfully
Please check the log file at ./admrgpch.log.
```

6. Once admrgpch executes successfully, it gives you a message saying "Patch merge completed successfully," and it displays a message saying where the log file for this merging session is located: "Please check the log file at ./admrgpch.log."

7. So, before going further and applying the merged patch, you check admrgpch.log to see if there are any error reported in it. (just in case)

```
[applmgr@somehost source]$ tail -f ./admrgpch.log
Please check the adncnv logfile at admrgpch.log.
STOP_TASK: [Character-set converting files] [Mon Sep 21 2015 15:45:01]
2 unified drivers merged.
Patch merge completed successfully
Please check the log file at ./admrgpch.log.
```

8. Then, you cd to the destination directory and check the files and subdirectories located in it to see that the merged patch files are placed properly.

```
[applmgr@somehost source]$ cd /u01/patches_dir/dest

[applmgr@somehost dest]$ ls
17919162_README.html  ad    ap    az              bom  cs   csi  edr             fa   frm
gmd  gmp  iby  imc  je   lns           okc  ont  per  po   qot             wip  xtr
17919162_README.txt   ahl  ar   b17919162.ldt  cct  csd  csp  ego             flm  fv
gme  gms  icx  inl  jl   metadata_files  oke  ota  pji  pon  qp              wms  zx
19290141_README.html  ak   asn  b19290141.ldt  ce   cse  csr  f17919162.ldt  fnd
ghg  gmf  hxt  ieu  inv  jmf  msc           okl  ozf  pjm  pos  rrs             wsh
19290141_README.txt   ame  ast  bne            cmi  csf  eam  f19290141.ldt  fpa  gl
gmo  ibu  iex  ja   jtf  mth           oks  pa   pn   qa   u_merged.drv  xnp
```

9. While you are in the destination directory, you execute adop phase=apply and apply the merged patch.

```
applmgr@somehost dest]$ adop phase=apply
```

adop executes adpatch, and adpatch detects the patch directory. You just press Enter and accept the default, as adpatch considers your current working directory as the default patch directory.

The default directory is [/u01/patches_dir/dest].

- adpatch requests you give the name of the patch driver file; in this case, you enter the merged patch driver file, u_merged.drv, and continue.

```
Please enter the name of your AutoPatch driver file : u_merged.drv
```

- adop (the adpatch in the background actually) starts applying the merged patch.

Once the patch is applied, it is required that you copy the source patch directories to the destination merged patch directory, as adop will look for these patches in the destination merged patch directory in the next prepare phase to use for synchronizing the patch file system.

Listing 6-20. Merging Patches with admrgpch and Applying the Merged Patch with adop

```
Following move commands can be used for accomplish this.
[applmgr@somehost dest]$ cd /u01/patches_dir/source/
[applmgr@somehost source]$  mv 17919162/ ../dest/
[applmgr@somehost source]$ mv 19290141/ ../dest/
```

As well as using admrgpch as an option for merging the patches, the new patching tool adop can be used for merging patches and applying them at the same time. Actually, using adop to merge patches is the default merging method in EBS 12.2, and a similar command such as adop phase=apply merge=yes patches=1111,2222 can be found in any Oracle Support document (especially in release upgrade documents) where there are some instructions for some patches to be merged.

adop is a sophisticated patching tool, as it can apply patches when application services are down or while applications are running. The adop tool can apply patches online without affecting the actively running applications, as explained in detail in this chapter and also in Chapter 5.

adop calls the admrgpch internally using $AD_TOP/bin/admerge.pl to accomplish the merging. That's why adop uses the same merging principles, even the same merging tool, for the merging the patches.

Using adop for merging patches in straightforward. Besides, when using adop for merging the patches, you can apply the merged patch at the same time.

To merge patches with adop, you use the merge option and set its value to yes, as explained in Table 6-1.

Listing 6-21 shows an example of merging with adop, as it is used in the EBS 12.2.4 upgrade and documented in Oracle Support document "Oracle E-Business Suite Release 12.2.4 Readme" (Doc ID 1617458.1).

To apply patches 17919162 and 19290141, you first download these patches from Oracle Support, and then you unzip them into the $APPL_TOP_NE/../patches folder. Then execute the adop command.

Listing 6-21. Merging the Patches and Applying Them Using adop

```
adop phase=apply patches=17919162,19290141 hotpatch=yes merge=yes
```

■ **Note**   In this example, you have used hotpatch mode by specifying hotpatch=yes while running adop. Any parameter that can be used with the apply phase can be used in conjunction with the merge parameter.

For instance, you could apply these patches using adop's merge by unzipping them to another directory and specifying that directory using patchtop as well.

Listing 6-22. Merging and Applying Patches Located in a Nondefault Directory Using adop

```
adop phase=apply patchtop=/u01/patches_dir patches=17919162,19290141 hotpatch=yes merge=yes
```

So, the standard EBS 12.2 patching principle applies for merged patched too. If you apply some patches with the merge=yes option, you need to follow the procedure for the patching method that you prefer. That is, if you need to apply some patches in the online patching cycle, you need to create a patching cycle and follow the online patching cycle phases exactly like when you follow it for applying a single patch or multiple patches sequentially. The only difference while applying a patch with merging is that in the apply phase you use the merge=yes option with adop, as shown in Listings 6-21 and 6-22. Likewise, when you apply multiple patches with merging while using the downtime option or the hotpatch option at the same time, you only specify the merge=yes parameter in your adop command to tell adop that patches specified with the patches parameter should be merged and then applied.

In short, the only difference in the process of applying a patch with the adop merge option is to specify the parameter merge=yes in the adop phase=apply command.

Applying Patches in a Multinode Environment

Multinode EBS 12.2 environments consist of at least two application nodes. Also, there may be multiple database nodes in the database tier in EBS 12.2, as it is supported to use Oracle Real Application Clusters (RAC) in the database tier of EBS, but it is not related to application patches. So, what we mean by *multinode* is an EBS 12.2 environment that consists of at least two application nodes.

The application nodes in a multinode configuration may have all the services running on each of them to provide load balancing and failover configuration, or one of the application nodes may have a list of services running, and the other nodes may have a list of other services running. Also, the application nodes may share the same application file system (shared application tier file system), or they may have their own dedicated application file systems (nonshared APPL_TOP). So, it depends on the configuration and your choice, but for patching it is not so important. The most important thing for patching multinode configurations is that adop should be executed from the admin node, which is the first application node that is created during the installation.

■ **Note** Multinode installation is not supported for EBS 12.2. To have multinode environments, you need to install a single-node EBS and then clone its application tier to the other nodes, as described in Chapter 2. Terms such as nonshared APPL_TOP and shared APPL_TOP were also introduced in Chapter 2 while explaining the multinode environments.

So, after that review of what a multinode configuration is, let's focus on the next topic.

Applying patches into multiple node environments is not so hard, as adop handles the multinode environments very well.

Applying a patch in an EBS 12.2 environment, which consists of several application tier nodes, is almost the same as applying patches into a single-node system, as you just execute the adop commands from only one node (from the admin node of the configuration) and adop deals with the patching actions required in the other application nodes. So, it is transparent, and the process of patching a multinode system is not different from what we have explained so far.

Of course, there are some special requirements when we talk about multinode patching. Let's take a look at the procedure that needs to be followed for applying patches in a multinode environment.

We have mentioned that you just execute the command from the admin node of the application tier and adop deals with the other nodes and takes patching actions in those other nodes transparently to you. To do that, there should be password-less SSH configured between the admin node and the other application nodes. Setting up password-less SSH to provide a password-less SSH connection from the admin node to all the secondary nodes is a requirement for multinode patching in EBS 12.2, as adop runs in admin node, uses remote APIs, and needs SSH connections to execute the patching actions in the remote/other application nodes.

So, to use SSH, adop requires the SSH equivalency from the admin node to all the application nodes in a multinode environment setup, because adop is not designed to supply a password while connecting the application nodes using SSH.

To set up the SSH equivalency (in other words, to configure the application OS user of the admin node to be able to connect all the other application nodes without needing to supply a password), you can use the ssh-keygen utility to create private and public key pairs. You place the private key pairs into the admin node and the public key pairs into all the application nodes in the configuration, thus letting the admin node connect all the application nodes using SSH without a password.

Setting up the password-less SSH connection is an easy operation, as shown in Listing 6-23.

■ **Note**   In Listing 6-23, we are setting up a password-less SSH from node1 to node2.

Listing 6-23. Setting Up Password-less ssh from node1 to node2 in a Two-Node Application Tier Configuration

If .ssh directories are not present in the nodes, create them as follows:

```
[applmgr@node1 ~]$mkdir ~/.ssh
[applmgr@node1 ~]$chmod 755 ~/.ssh
[applmgr@node2 ~]$mkdir ~/.ssh
[applmgr@node2 ~]$chmod 755 ~/.ssh
```

Create the RSA key pair and copy it from node1 to node1.

```
[applmgr@node1 ~]$ ssh-keygen -t rsa
Generating public/private rsa key pair.
Enter file in which to save the key (/home/applmgr/.ssh/id_rsa):
Enter passphrase (empty for no passphrase):
Enter same passphrase again:
Your identification has been saved in /home/applmgr/.ssh/id_rsa.
Your public key has been saved in /home/applmgr/.ssh/id_rsa.pub.
The key fingerprint is:
aa:73:97:2b:a0:c9:ce:6e:db:8d:2f:18:ba:11:00:c2
applmgr@node1
The key's randomart image is:
+--[ RSA 2048]----+
|+                |
|oE               |
|.                |
|.                |
|.        S       |
| ...  .          |
|.o = ..  .       |
|.o*.o+o o        |
|.==.+=oo..       |
+-----------------+
```

```
[applmgr@node1 ~]$ scp -pr  /home/applmgr/.ssh/id_rsa.pub node2:/home/applmgr/.ssh/authorized_keys
applmgr@node2 password:
id_rsa.pub
100%   420       0.4KB/s   00:00
```

Test the password-less connection from the applmgr user in node1 to the applmgr user in node2.

```
[applmgr@node1 ~]$ ssh node2
Last login: Tue Sep 15 15:56:13 2015 from 10.10.10.111
```

The method described in Listing 6-23 overwrites the authorized keys file, but you have an alternative method if you don't want to overwrite it. This may be necessary for the environments that have other keys present in their authorized_keys file.

Listing 6-24 shows how to build a password-less configuration from node1 to node2 in a two-node system, without overwriting the content of the authorized_keys file.

Listing 6-24. Setting Up Password-less SSH from node1 to node2 in a Two-Node Application Tier, Without Overwriting the authorized_keys Files in node2

If the .ssh directory is not present in node1, create is as follows;

```
[applmgr@node1 ~]$mkdir ~/.ssh
[applmgr@node1 ~]$chmod 755 ~/.ssh
```

Create the rsa key pair in node 1 and append the contents of authorized_keys file in node2;

```
[applmgr@node1 ~]$ /usr/bin/ssh-keygen -t rsa
[applmgr@node1 ~]$ cat ~/.ssh/id_rsa.pub >> ~/.ssh/authorized_keys
[applmgr@node1 ~]$ ssh applmgr@node2  cat ~/.ssh/id_rsa.pub >> ~/.ssh/authorized_keys
```

■ **Note**   In Listings 6-23 and 6-24, we have set up this password-less configuration (only from node1, the admin node, to node2) in a two-node system, but even for the EBS environments that consist of several nodes, the procedure is the same. That is, you just create the private and public pairs in the admin node and copy the public pairs created in the admin node to all the other nodes.

Once you configure the password-less SSH, there is actually nothing special when applying application patches in multinode.

The same principles and procedures that we have explained in this chapter while explaining the online patching and hotpatch modes still apply. That is, adop can apply patches online or in hotpatch mode regardless of the environment being a single-node environment or a multinode environment.

Using the downtime option, however, is not tested or supported by Oracle. So, unless it is documented or explicitly stated in readme of a patch, adop's downtime option is not applicable for multinode environments.

The adop commands and the methodology of patching are also similar in multinode configurations. Application patches are applied in the same way they are applied in a single-mode configuration. The only difference is that this time the application patches are applied to all the application nodes rather than a single one.

In addition, there is no need to specify an extra parameter for adop to tell that environment is a multinode environment, as adop detects the topology and uses SSH to connect to the other environment and takes the patch actions in all the application nodes.

Of course, there are some multinode-specific adop parameters that can be used in a few scenarios. The parameters named actions and allnodes are the multinode-specific adop parameters, as documented in Table 6-1, and you may need to use them in some situations that will be explained in the next paragraphs.

There is also a requirement for using adop in a multinode environment. That is, if the application nodes are not sharing the APPL_TOP, (in other words, if the multinode configuration is based on the nonshared APPL_TOPs), then you need to place the patches in the same directory that you have specified with the patchtop parameter while executing adop from the admin node. In other words, you need to copy the patches to be applied to all the nodes and place them in the same directory paths so that the patch files are available in the same directory paths on all the nodes.

■ **Note** The difference between nonshared APPL_TOP and shared APPL_TOP configurations was explained in Chapter 2, we explained the Shared appl_top and in Chapter 11 you will see how to configure shared appl_top.

So, as mentioned, the adop commands that are used for applying patches in multinode configurations are the same in single-node configurations, as adop deals with them transparently. However, the question is what happens if adop fails while applying a patch in a multinode configuration? Scenarios may vary, as adop may fail on one node but may complete successfully on other nodes, or adop may patch a node successfully but may fail in all the other nodes.

This kind of situation is where the difference between multinode and single-node configurations appears and where the term *abandoned nodes* comes into play.

When a patch cannot be applied in an application node due to a failure in the prepare, finalize, apply, or cutover phases, you have an opportunity to stop at that point and restart the patching after correcting the failure in the related application nodes.

For example, if there is a failure encountered in a nonadmin application node while executing adop phase=prepare in a multinode environment, adop will report the following warning and request that you to give an instruction for it:

```
Prepare phase failed on node secondarynode.If you choose to proceed with cutover, node will
be marked as abandoned.
Do you want adop to continue with other completed nodes [y/n]?
```

If you say "n" to this warning, then adop will exit with error, and you can restart the same phase after correcting the problem in the relevant application node (in this case it is secondarynode).

Once you correct the problem, you can execute the prepare phase again, but this time you need to supply the allnodes parameters as follows:

```
adop phase=prepare allnodes=yes.
```

■ **Note** The allnodes parameter, as explained in Table 6-1, tells adop to take the patching actions for all the nodes in a multinode environment.

The situation is the same for the apply phase. That is, if there is a failure encountered in a nonadmin application node while executing adop phase=apply in a multinode environment, adop will display the following question in a warning and request you give an instruction for it: "Do you want adop to continue with other completed nodes [y/n]?" If you say "no" to this question, adop will exit with an error, and you can restart the same phase using the following command after correcting the problem in the relevant application node:

```
adop phase=apply allnodes=yes.
```

For the cutover phase, the situation is a little different. If there is a failure encountered in a nonadmin application node while executing adop phase=cutover in a multinode environment, adop will just continue by skipping that problematic node and report that problematic node in the subsequent prepare, apply, or fs_clone phase.

You also have an opportunity to ignore these kinds of failures encountered in a nonadmin application node while executing adop's prepare and apply phases. Any errors in the nonadmin application nodes can be ignored as long as the services that are configured in the application node don't break the availability of EBS applications.

For example, if a failure node is the only node that has the concurrent processing tier, then you can't ignore a patching failure in that node and continue patching, because this will reduce the capabilities of EBS applications. So, if all the essential services are available on other nodes and if the available nodes have the capacity to handle the workload until the failed node is added to the configuration, then the failed node can be ignored at this time.

You can always execute the failed adop phase or adop command in the same patching cycle for the failed node to synchronize it with the other nodes where the relevant phase was successful.

Consider the following scenario. The prepare phase was successful on node1 but failed on node2, and you skipped the failure, completed the prepare phase, and continued with the apply phase. If that's the case, the apply phase will be executed only for node1, as node2 was skipped due to the failure in the prepare phase.

After completing the apply phase (before running cutover), you decide to correct the failure in node2, which caused the previous prepare phase to fail for it. After correcting the problem on node2, you run the prepare and apply phases only for node2 by executing the adop command from node2 and using the allnodes=no parameter to synchronize it with node1 before you execute the cutover phase.

However, if you ignore and continue patching without correcting the problem on that failed node and make it sync with the other nodes, once you execute the cutover phase, the application node that was skipped will be marked as abandoned after the execution of the cutover phase.

■ **Note** If the patch or patches cannot be applied because of a failure in the cutover phase, the application node that has failures is marked as abandoned just after restarting the application services, which is an operation that is done in the cutover phase. However, the admin node can't be marked as abandoned, so if it is the admin node in which adop is failing while applying the patches, the problem that causes the failure should be corrected and that patching operation should be retried.

Also, by design, the admin node should not have an abandoned status at any time, so if you see this, you need to contact Oracle Support by raising a service request.

In these kinds of scenarios, the abandoned nodes must be removed from the system, or they should be re-created using by cloning techniques.

After the patching session is completed, the abandoned nodes can be identified by checking the log file $ADOP_LOG_HOME/<latest_session_id>/adop_latest_timestamp.log located in the admin node.

The log file will report the phase and the status of that phase for all the nodes with a format like the following:

```
Node <Node name> : <COMPLETED or ABANDONED>
<Phase_name1> status = <COMPLETED or FAILED or RUNNING>
<Phase_name2> status = <COMPLETED or FAILED or RUNNING>
```

To clean the abandoned nodes, they should be removed from the EBS configuration and added back using Rapid Clone.

We will explain the cloning process in EBS 12.2 in Chapter 11, but here we will give the instructions for deleting and re-creating an application node using Rapid Clone in this chapter.

After completing the patching (in the case of online patching after completing the online patching cycle), you log in to the node that needs to be deleted, source the run edition environment, and execute the following command:

```
. /u01/install/EBSapps.env run (sourcing the run edition env, EBSapps.env script path may
differ according to your installation)

perl $AD_TOP/patch/115/bin/adProvisionEBS.pl ebs-delete-node \

-contextfile=<CONTEXT_FILE> -logfile=<LOG_FILE>
```

Next, if the environment is based on a nonshared application file system architecture, you delete the $FMW_HOME/webtier, $FMW_HOME/oracle_common, and $FMW_HOME/Oracle_EBS-app1 directories.

If the environment is based on a shared application file system, you remove the Fusion Middleware Home and 10.1.2 Oracle Home entries from oraInventory by changing your directory to $FMW_HOME/oracle_common/oui/bin and running runInstaller as follows:

```
cd $FMW_HOME/oracle_common/oui/bin
$ ./runInstaller -detachhome ORACLE_HOME=$FMW_HOME/oracle_common –silent
$ ./runInstaller -detachhome ORACLE_HOME=$FMW_HOME/webtier-silent
$ ./runInstaller -detachhome ORACLE_HOME=$FMW_HOME/Oracle_EBS-app1
$./runInstaller -removeHome ORACLE_HOME=$ORACLE_HOME –silent
```

After removing the inventory entries, if the TXK level of the environment is on R12.TXK.C.Delta.4 or lower, you source the patch edition environment and execute the adProvisionEBS.pl script to delete the managed WebLogic servers, OHS instance, and Node Manager from the WebLogic domain in the patch file system, as follows:

```
. /u01/install/EBSapps.env patch (sourcing the patch edition env, EBSapps.env script path
may differ according to your installation)

perl $AD_TOP/patch/115/bin/adProvisionEBS.pl ebs-delete-node \
-contextfile=$CONTEXT_FILE -logfile=<LOG_FILE>
```

Lastly, if the node configuration is based on nonshared application file systems, remove the inventory entries for $FMW_HOME/webtier, $FMW_HOME/oracle_common, $FMW_HOME/Oracle_EBS-app1, and $ORACLE_HOME (10.1.2 Home) from the patch environment, as follows:

```
cd $FMW_HOME/oracle_common/oui/bin
$ ./runInstaller -detachhome ORACLE_HOME=$FMW_HOME/oracle_common –silent
$ ./runInstaller -detachhome ORACLE_HOME=$FMW_HOME/webtier-silent
$ ./runInstaller -detachhome ORACLE_HOME=$FMW_HOME/Oracle_EBS-app1
$./runInstaller -removeHome ORACLE_HOME=$ORACLE_HOME –silent
```

The abandoned node is now deleted from the configuration.

The next thing you should do is clone an application node to this cleaned node; thus, it will be added back to the configuration.

Before starting the cloning operation, you run adop phase=fs_clone to synchronize the patch file system with the run file system by using an exact copy of the run file system.

After cloning the file system, you start your application cloning operation by taking a preclone both in the run and patch editions of the admin node as follows:

```
. /u01/install/EBSapps.env run
cd $ADMIN_SCRIPTS_HOME
perl adpreclone.pl appsTier

. /u01/install/EBSapps.env patch
cd $ADMIN_SCRIPTS_HOME
sh adadminsrvctl.sh start forcepatchfs
perl adpreclone.pl appsTier
```

■ **Note**   You supply the appsTier argument to tell the adpreclone.pl script that you want to take the preclone of the application tier as a whole.

After taking a preclone using the adpreclone.pl script in the admin node, you just copy $APPL_TOP, $COMMON_TOP, and ORACLE_HOME (10.1.2 Oracle Home) from the admin node to the cleaned/new second node.

The following is a demonstration of this copying process.

You log in to the second node using the application owner (for example, applmgr), create the necessary root directory (/u01/install/APPS/fs2/EBSapps) if it is not already created, and then copy the necessary directories from both the patch edition and the run edition of the admin node using the scp tool as follows:

```
secondnode>mkdir -p /u01/install/APPS/fs2/EBSapps
secondode>cd /u01/install/APPS/fs2/EBSapps
secondnode>scp -r  applmgr@adminnode1: /u01/install/APPS/fs2/EBSapps/appl   .
secondnode>scp -r  applmgr@adminnode1: /u01/install/APPS/fs2/EBSapps/comn  .
secondnode>scp -r  applmgr@adminnode1: /u01/install/APPS/fs2/EBSapps/10.1.2 .
secondnode>mkdir -p /u01/install/APPS/fs1/EBSapps
secondode>cd /u01/install/APPS/fs1/EBSapps
secondnode>scp -r  applmgr@adminnode1: /u01/install/APPS/fs1/EBSapps/appl   .
secondnode>scp -r  applmgr@adminnode1: /u01/install/APPS/fs1/EBSapps/comn  .
secondnode>scp -r  applmgr@adminnode1: /u01/install/APPS/fs1/EBSapps/10.1.2 .
```

■ **Note**   You make the directory paths in the secondary node the same as the admin node, as this is required in EBS 12.2. Also, you configure the run edition and patch edition file systems of the secondary to be the same as the admin node.

Also note that you don't copy any FMW directories, as they will be created by the post-clone, which is done by running adcfgclone.pl, as explained in the next paragraphs.

So, after copying the necessary directories from the admin node to the secondary node, you run the adcfgclone.pl script in the secondary node from both the run edition and patch edition environments, as demonstrated next.

■ **Note** You supply the appsTier argument to tell the adcfgclone.pl script that you want to clone the application tier as a whole. The adcfgclone.pl script is executed in this phase to configure the newly added node (secondary node) using the copied directories and create the necessary FMW directories on this secondary node.

You first set the run environment and execute the adcfgclone script.

```
. /u01/install/EBSapps.env run
cd <COMMON_TOP>/clone/bin
$ perl adcfgclone.pl appsTier
```

■ **Note** The answers for the questions that will be asked by adcfgclone.pl when executed from the run edition are as follows:

Target System File Edition type: run

Do you want to add a node: yes

Do you want to startup the Application Services ...: y

After running adcfgclone in the run environment, you set the patch environment and execute the adcfgclone script once again, but this time for the patch environment.

```
. /u01/install/EBSapps.env patch
cd <COMMON_TOP>/clone/bin
$ perl adcfgclone.pl appsTier
```

■ **Note** The answers for the questions that will be asked by adcfgclone.pl when executed from the patch edition follow:

Target System File Edition type: patch

Do you want to add a node: yes

Next, you make the WebLogic managed servers–related configurations in the newly cloned secondary node by using the txkSetAppsConf.pl script located in $FND_TOP/bin.

The following is the manual version of txkSetAppsConf.pl, which can be used to add or remove managed servers in this phase:

```
perl <FND_TOP>/patch/115/bin/txkSetAppsConf.pl \
  -contextfile=<CONTEXT_FILE> \
  -configoption=addMS \
  -oacore=<host>.<domain>:<port> \
  -oafm=<host>.<domain>:<port> \
  -forms=<host>.<domain>:<port> \
  -formsc4ws=<host>.<domain>:<port>
```

For example, if you want this newly configured secondary node to provide oacore and oafm services from ports 7206 and 7606, you just set the run edition in the secondary node and execute txkSetAppsConf.pl as follows:

```
perl $FND_TOP/patch/115/bin/txkSetAppsConf.pl -contextfile=$CONTEXT_FILE \
-configoption=addMS -oacore=secondarynode.somedomain.com:7206 -oafm= secondarynode.
somedomain.com:7606
```

Also, you may need to delete some managed server information from the secondary in case the secondary node is supposed to provide the Oracle HTTP Server services. If that's case, the old references (managed server information) that will be present in the secondary node as a result of the cloning activity should be deleted.

As mentioned, the txkSetAppsConf.pl script can be used for removing the managed servers, as well. For example, if you want delete the reference for the oacore and oafm managed servers that are actually running from ports 7202 and 7602 in the admin node, you just set the run edition in the secondary node and execute txkSetAppsConf.pl as follows:

```
perl $FND_TOP/patch/115/bin/txkSetAppsConf.pl -contextfile=$CONTEXT_FILE \
-configoption=removeMS -oacore=adminserver.somedomain.com:7202 -forms= adminserver.
somedomain.com:7602
```

The next thing you should do is to register the newly added secondary node to admin servers and its own application tier listener. To do that, you connect to both nodes (adminnode and secondarynode) and execute AutoConfig after sourcing the run edition env, as demonstrated here:

```
. /u01/install/EBSapps.env run
cd $ADMIN_SCRIPTS_HOME
sh adautocfg.sh
```

After running AutoConfig on each node, you reload the application listeners on each node and make them aware of the newly added host by executing the following command with the application owner OS user (for example, applmgr):

```
lsnrctl reload APPS_<TWO_TASK> (TWO equals the SID of the environment. For example : TEST)
```

Next, you stop the Node Manager if it is running on the patch edition of the secondary node.

```
./u01/install/APPS/EBSapps.env patch
sh <ADMIN_SCRIPTS_HOME>/adnodemgrctl.sh stop
```

Also, you stop the WebLogic administration server and the Node Manager that is running on the patch edition of the admin node. Remember, you started them in the pre-clone phase earlier.

```
./u01/install/APPS/EBSapps.env patch
sh $ADMIN_SCRIPTS_HOME/adadminsrvctl.sh stop
sh $ADMIN_SCRIPTS_HOME /adnodemgrctl.sh stop
```

Lastly, you run AutoConfig on the database node (in other words, in all the database nodes of the EBS environment, considering the EBS database may be a RAC database) and reload the database listener/listeners running in all the database nodes, as demonstrated next.

You connect to the database node using Oracle RDBMS owner OS user (for example, oracle). Source the database env using the environment script located in the $ORACLE_HOME.

```
. /u01/install/TEST/11.2.0/TEST_somehost.env
sh $ORACLE_HOME/appsutil/scripts/$CONTEXT_NAME/adautocfg.sh
lsnrctl reload <listener_name> (listener name may be $ORACLE_SID by default, but may change
according to our environment, as it may be changed.)
```

At this point, you have deleted the abandoned node and added it back to the system in a clean state. We explained how to deal with abandoned nodes in EBS 12.2 by showing how to delete and add back the abandoned one to make it clean again.

Of course, there are other steps according to the complexity of the EBS configuration such as configuring the load balancer to direct the connection to the newly added/secondary node too (if the newly added/secondary node has the Oracle HTTP Server service). Please see Section 5.4 of Oracle Support document "Cloning Oracle E-Business Suite Release 12.2 with Rapid Clone" (Doc ID 1383621.1) to see the action plans that can be used for deleting and application node in different cases, and please see Section 5.3 of the same document for detailed action plans and references that can be used for adding an application node in different cases.

Our focus in this section was on dealing with the abandoned nodes in a nonshared application file system EBS 12.2 environment, but if you are interested in knowing how to deal with the abandoned nodes in a shared file system EBS 12.2 environment, the same logic applies, as you still need to delete the node and add it back to the configuration. However, the method and commands you use in shared application file system configuration are different from the nonshared application file system configuration, so if you are interested, please see Section 4 in Oracle Support document "Sharing The application tier File System in Oracle E-Business Suite Release 12.2" (Doc ID 1375769.1).

Adding a New Language, Patching for NLS and HRMS

In this section, we will explain three topics. First, we will explain the action plan to follow for adding a new language to EBS 12.2. Then we will explain NLS patching in EBS 12.2. While explaining NLS patching, rather than applying the NLS versions of every patch that you apply in an EBS system to keep the NLS part of the system synchronized with the generic part (the objects and data in default language), we will give an alternative approach. Lastly, we will explain the action plan to follow for installing the HRMS legislations to your EBS 12.2, as installation HRMS legislations are done in almost every EBS project done in multinational customer environments.

We will explain these topics by giving examples that fully describe the required steps and by showing screenshots to provide a clear picture of the enablement processes.

Adding Human Resources Management System (HRMS) legislations for enabling country-specific legislations and adding National Language Support (NLS) for enabling additional languages are crucial tasks in EBS 12.2 projects, as most EBS customers are multinational companies that run their business processes according to their own legislations and their employees prefer to use their own languages while doing their work using Oracle applications.

Enabling HRMS legislations and adding an NLS language to an EBS 12.2 environment are based on patching. That is, you use adop to patch the EBS system for adding a new language; likewise, you use adop to patch the EBS system with the related legislative patch for enabling the HRMS legislations. Patches for HRMS legislations and NLS bring new data and application tier objects such as forms and reports to the EBS 12.2 system. Thus, the application screens get translated, new business rules are defined, and objects like new reports get deployed. Basically, these are standard patches that load data into the EBS database and create new objects such as the NLS version of the standard forms in the application tier.

The reason why we have reserved this section for these two crucial activities (considering that NLS patching and adding a language are almost the same) is that although HRMS legislations and a new language are deployed to EBS 12.2 system by applying the relevant patches with adop, there are some additional things that need to be done before applying those patches for their enablement.

Let's start by explaining how you install an additional language to your EBS 12.2 system. The method for adding an additional language is done in six phases.

1. License the additional language.

2. Maintain the multilingual tables.

3. Update the snapshot information for the complete APPL_TOP.

4. Create a translation patch synchronization request.

5. Apply the translation synchronization patch.

6. Generate message files.

Let's take a look at the steps given in this list.

First, you license the language that you want to add as an additional language using Oracle Applications Manager (OAM). Then, you use adadmin tool to maintain multilingual tables.

Next, you update the snapshot information to generate a manifest file, which includes the up-to-date file versions, and request a translation synchronization patch from Oracle Support using this manifest file.

Lastly, you apply the translation synchronization patch that is prepared by Oracle Support in response of your request to your EBS 12.2 system using adop and generate message files using the adadmin tool.

We'll give an example of adding a new language to an EBS 12.2 system by going through the required steps called licensing, running adadmin, requesting a translation synchronization patch, and applying the translation synchronization patch.

As mentioned, licensing a new language is done using OAM in EBS 12.2.

You log in with the SYSADMIN user and choose the License Manager, which resides in the System Administrator responsibility. The full navigation for the License Manager is System Administrator ➤ Oracle Applications Manager ➤ License Manager.

To license a language, you first click the License Manager link using the System Administrator ➤ Oracle Applications Manager ➤ License Manager, as shown in Figure 6-10.

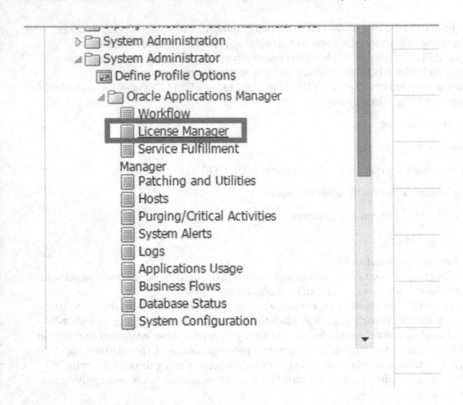

Figure 6-10. *Opening the license manager using the EBS screen navigation*

In the License Manager OAF page, you click the Languages link, as shown in Figure 6-11.

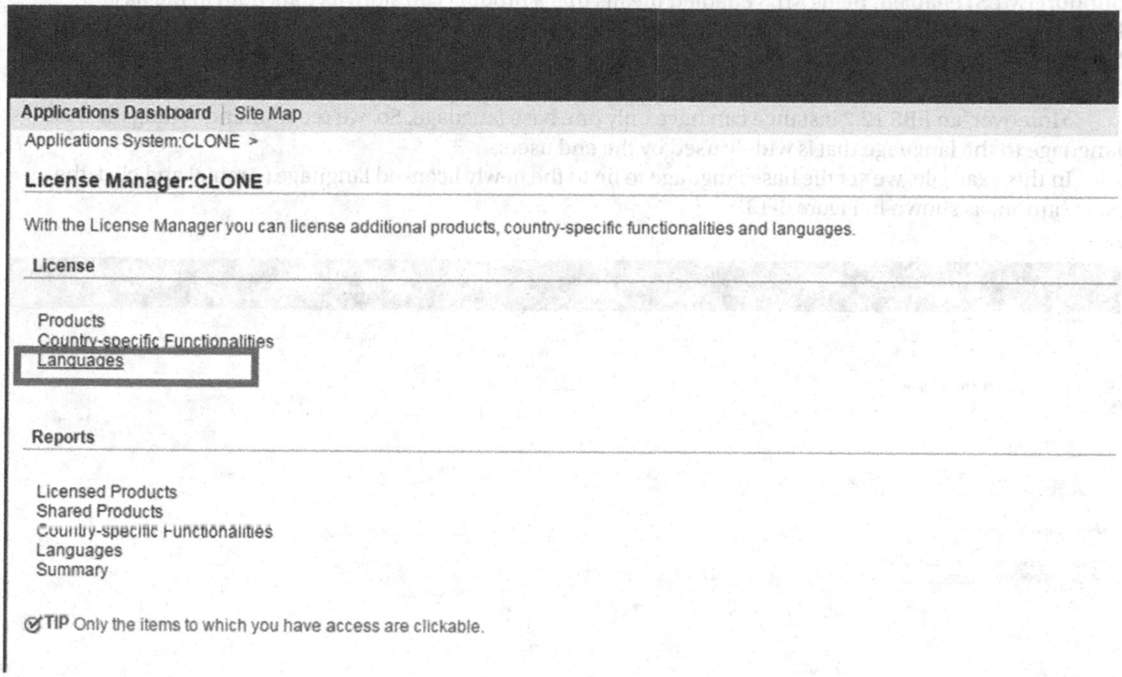

Applications Dashboard | Site Map

Applications System:CLONE >

License Manager:CLONE

With the License Manager you can license additional products, country-specific functionalities and languages.

License

Products
Country-specific Functionalities
Languages

Reports

Licensed Products
Shared Products
Country-specific Functionalities
Languages
Summary

✓TIP Only the items to which you have access are clickable.

Figure 6-11. *Clicking the Languages link on the License Manager page*

After clicking the Languages link, an OAF page showing the available languages is displayed. On this page you can choose which additional languages to add to your EBS 12.2 environment.

We chose Arabic for this example, as shown in Figure 6-12; then click the Next button on the top right of the page.

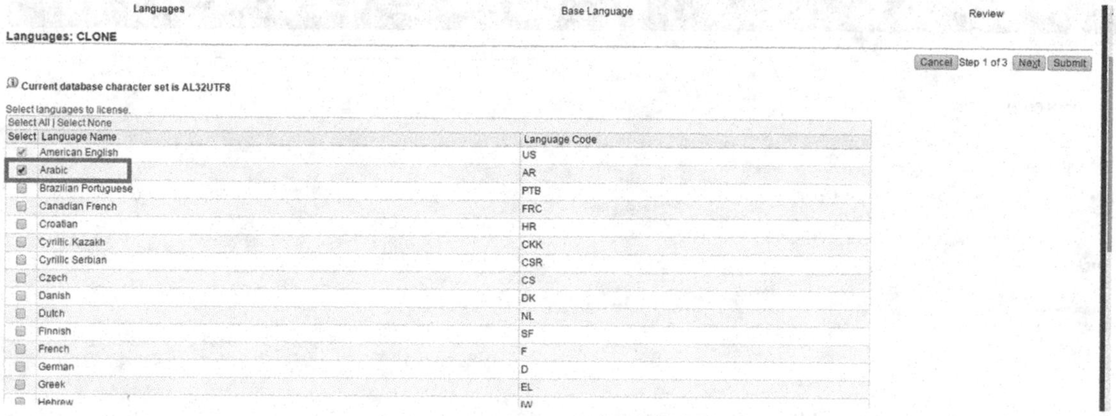

| Languages | Base Language | Review |

Languages: CLONE

Cancel Step 1 of 3 Next Submit

ⓘ Current database character set is AL32UTF8

Select languages to license.
Select All | Select None

Select	Language Name	Language Code
✔	American English	US
✔	Arabic	AR
☐	Brazilian Portuguese	PTB
☐	Canadian French	FRC
☐	Croatian	HR
☐	Cyrillic Kazakh	CKK
☐	Cyrillic Serbian	CSR
☐	Czech	CS
☐	Danish	DK
☐	Dutch	NL
☐	Finnish	SF
☐	French	F
☐	German	D
☐	Greek	EL
☐	Hebrew	IW

Figure 6-12. *Licensing an additional language, page 1 of 3*

301

On the next screen, OAM wants you to choose the base language. Selecting the base language as the default language or as the additional language matters only for the products that are not Multi Language Support (MLS) enabled. Being MLS enabled means that a product can store its data both in the base language and in additional languages. That is, if a product is not MLS enabled, then it stores all its data in the base language. The MLS-enabled products, however, store their data both in the base language and in any installed languages, so it does not matter for MLS-enabled products what value the base language is set to.

Moreover, an EBS 12.2 instance can have only one base language. So, we recommend setting the base language to the language that is widely used by the end users.

In this example, we set the base language to be to the newly licensed language (Arabic) and click the Next button, as shown in Figure 6-13.

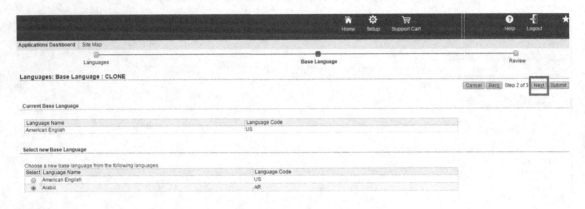

Figure 6-13. Licensing an additional language, page 2 of 3

After clicking the Next button, an OAF page will appear, where you can review your licensing task, submit that task, and finish the licensing work.

As shown in Figure 6-14, the OAF page shows that Arabic will be licensed, and the base language will also be set to Arabic.

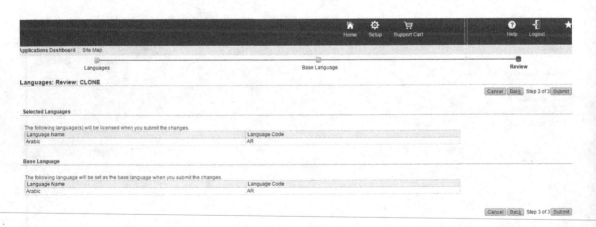

Figure 6-14. Licensing an additional language, page 3 of 3

So, after you submit your licensing request, the language you want to add becomes licensed and your work with OAM is finished.

After the licensing, you continue with the next step by executing the admin to maintain the multilingual tables. So, you use the AD utility named adadmin, which will be explained in detail when we explain the AD utilities in Chapter 9. For now, we will give the information needed for running adadmin and cover the choices you need to make for updating the current view snapshot for APPL_TOP using adadmin.

To run adadmin, you source the run edition environment and then execute the adadmin command, as shown in Listing 6-25.

Listing 6-25. Sourcing the run Edition Environment and Running the adadmin Tool

```
[applmgr@somehost ~]$ . /u01/install/APPS/EBSapps.env run
[applmgr@somehost ~]$ adadmin
```

Once adadmin is executed, it asks some questions such as "What is the system schema password?" and "What is the apps schema password?" and "Is this the correct APPL_TOP?" and so on. Supposing the environment is correct, you should only enter the APPS and SYSTEM schema passwords for your environment. That is, you can accept the default answers for all the other questions by using the Enter key.

Once these questions are answered, you reach the AD Administration main menu, where you can choose the general actions that you want to take and reach other submenus.

To maintain the multilingual tables, your choices must be in the order of 4 and 3, as shown next.

■ **Note** You can accept the default for the worker count, or you can increase or decrease the worker count according to the load of your environment.

Listing 6-26 shows the choices that need to be made to make adadmin maintain the multilingual tables.

Listing 6-26. adadmin for Maintaining Multilingual Tables

```
            AD Administration Main Menu
    -------------------------------------------------

    1.    Generate Applications Files menu
    2.    Maintain Applications Files menu
    3.    Compile/Reload Applications Database Entities menu
    4.    Maintain Applications Database Entities menu
    5.    Exit AD Administration

Enter your choice [5] : 4

            Maintain Applications Database Entities
    -------------------------------------------------

    1.    Validate APPS schema
    2.    Re-create grants and synonyms for APPS schema
    3.    Maintain multi-lingual tables
    4.    Check DUAL table
    5.    Return to Main Menu

Enter your choice [5] : 3
```

```
AD utilities can support a maximum of 999 workers. Your
current database configuration supports a maximum of 531 workers.
Oracle recommends that you use between 8 and 32 workers.

Enter the number of workers [8] : 8
```

At this point, adadmin starts working and makes the multilingual tables prepared for the NLS patch, which will be executed to load the NLS data into the EBS 12.2 database in the next steps.

After finishing the operation for maintaining the multilingual tables, you exit from adadmin and continue with creating the translation patch synchronization request.

Translation patches are the patches that can be applied for adding a new language in an EBS 12.2 environment. To gather a translation patch for your EBS 12.2 environment, you first request a translation patch from Oracle Support and then apply the translation synchronization patch when Oracle Support completes preparing it.

In other words, translation synchronization patches include translations for the current situation of your EBS environment, and they are delivered by Oracle Support. To receive them, you first need to send the current file versions of your EBS environment to Oracle Support. In this manner, the current file version of your EBS environment is written in a file called the *manifest file*. In reply to the manifest file that you send within your translation patch request, Oracle Support sends you the translation synchronization patch that is suitable for your environments.

As mentioned, the versions of the files such as form files, report files, and ldt files are recorded in a file called manifest, and this manifest file can be created using the manifest generation tool, which is a Perl script named adgennls.pl.

```
adgennls.pl perl script is located in $AD_TOP/bin directory.
```

The full process for requesting the translation patch is documented in Oracle Support document "R11i / R12 : Requesting Translation Synchronization Patches" (Doc ID 252422.1), but what you will find here will be based on a practical example.

Before starting with the generation of the manifest file, it is required that you check the prerequisite section of Oracle Support document 252422.1, as that document may be updated from time to time. However, currently the only thing that you find advisable in the prerequisite section of document 252422.1 is to update the snapshot information for the complete APPL_TOP.

An APPL_TOP snapshot lists and records the patches and versions of files located in the $APPL_TOP directory, so updating it and making it reflect the current view is useful for adgennls.pl. The script as adgennls.pl uses this snapshot information to generate the manifest file.

To update the current view snapshot, you use the adadmin utility, which will be explained in detail in Chapter 9, as mentioned earlier.

To execute adadmin, you source the run edition environment and run adadmin using the adadmin command, as depicted in Listing 6-26 earlier. Again, once adadmin is executed, it asks some questions such as "What is the system schema password?" and "What is the apps schema password?" and "Is this the correct APPL_TOP?" and so on. Supposing the environment is correct, you should only enter the APPS and SYSTEM schema passwords for your environment, as you have done while maintaining the multilingual tables using adadmin earlier. That is, you can accept the default answers for all the other questions by using the Enter key.

Once these questions are answered, you reach the AD Administration main menu, where you can choose the general actions that you want to take and reach other submenus.

To update the current view snapshot for the complete APPL_TOP, your choices must be in the order of 2, 4, 2, and 1, as shown in Listing 6-27.

Listing 6-27. adadmin for Updating the Current View Snapshot for Complete APPL_TOP

```
            AD Administration Main Menu
   ----------------------------------------------------
   1.     Generate Applications Files menu
   2.     Maintain Applications Files menu
   3.     Compile/Reload Applications Database Entities menu
   4.     Maintain Applications Database Entities menu
   5.     Exit AD Administration
Enter your choice [5] : 2

            Maintain Applications Files
   -----------------------------------------
   1.     Relink Applications programs
   2.     Copy files to destinations
   3.     Convert character set
   4.     Maintain snapshot information
   5.     Check for missing files
   6.     Return to Main Menu
Enter your choice [7] : 4

            Maintain Snapshot Information
   --------------------------------------------
   1.     List snapshots
   2.     Update current view snapshot
   3.     Create named snapshot
   4.     Export snapshot to file
   5.     Import snapshot from file
   6.     Delete named snapshot(s)
   7.     Return to Maintain Applications Files menu

Enter your choice [7] : 2

            Maintain Current View Snapshot Information
   --------------------------------------------
   1.     Update Complete APPL_TOP
   2.     Update JAVA_TOP only
   3.     Update a PRODUCT_TOP
   4.     Return to previous Menu

Enter your choice [4] : 1
```

So, after updating the current view snapshot for the complete APPL_TOP, you continue with executing adgennls.pl, as shown in Listing 6-28.

You should run adgennls.pl from the run edition environment, so you first source the run edition environment.

```
[applmgr@somehost ~]$ . /u01/install/APPS/EBSapps.env run
```

Then, you execute adgennls.pl to create your manifest file. Note that adgennls.pls requests you to supply the APPS user and password.

Listing 6-28. Generating the Manifest File for Requesting NLS Synchronization Patch

```
[applmgr@somehost ~]$ perl $AD_TOP/bin/adgennls.pl
Please enter the APPS User [APPS]:
Please enter the APPS password: Manifest file generation is in progress...

Manifest generated in: /u01/install/APPS/fs1/EBSapps/appl/admin/ORATEST/out/adgennls.txt
```

Once the execution of adgennls.pl script is finished, adgennls.pl reports the full path of the generated manifest file. In this example it is located the full path of the file manifest file is "/u01/install/APPS/fs1/EBSapps/appl/admin/ORATEST/out/adgennls.txt".

In Figure 6-15, you can see a snippet from a manifest file generated by adgennls.pl.

```
# Release: R12
# Active languages: TR, US
# TWO_TASK: ORATEST
# Manifest generated by adgennls.pl 120.9 on Fri Oct  2 11:53:04 2015

ad patch/115/import/US addiag.ldt 120.1 TR:120.1:-99999
ad patch/115/import/US addrimt2.ldt 120.2 TR:120.2:-99999
ad patch/115/import/US addrpimt.ldt 120.6 TR:120.6:-99999
ad patch/115/import/US addrpobs.ldt 120.1 TR:120.1:-99999
ad patch/115/import/US admenutemp.ldt 120.3 TR:120.3:-99999
ad patch/115/import/US adpacp.ldt 120.0.12020000.3 TR:120.0.12020000.4:-99999
ad patch/115/import/US adpacp_fnd.ldt 120.2.12020000.2 TR:120.2.12020000.2:-99999
ad patch/115/import/US adpacpdp.ldt 120.0 TR:120.0:-99999
ad patch/115/import/US adpadvsrreg.ldt 120.0.12020000.2 TR:120.0.12020000.3:-99999
ad patch/115/import/US adparepa.ldt 120.1 TR:120.1:-99999
ad patch/115/import/US adparg.ldt 120.0 TR:120.0:-99999
ad patch/115/import/US adparg_fnd.ldt 120.2 TR:120.2:-99999
ad patch/115/import/US adpars.ldt 120.3 TR:120.3:-99999
ad patch/115/import/US adzdpatch.ldt 120.2.12020000.2 TR:120.2.12020000.5:-99999
ad patch/115/import/US sequence_ad_R12.ldt 120.0 TR:120.0:-99999
ad patch/115/import/US table_ad_building_block_R12.ldt 120.0 TR:120.0:-99999
ad patch/115/import/US table_ad_code_levels_R12.ldt 120.0 TR:120.0:-99999
ad patch/115/import/US table_ad_compile_R12.ldt 120.0 TR:120.0:-99999
ad patch/115/import/US table_ad_concurrent_sessions_R12.ldt 120.0 TR:120.0:-99999
ad patch/115/import/US table_ad_event_registry_R12.ldt 120.0 TR:120.0:-99999
ad patch/115/import/US table_ad_merge_parameters_R12.ldt 120.0 TR:120.0:-99999
ad patch/115/import/US table_ad_merged_tables_R12.ldt 120.0 TR:120.0:-99999
ad patch/115/import/US table_ad_padvsr_R12.ldt 120.0 TR:120.0:-99999
ad patch/115/import/US table_ad_patch_history_R12.ldt 120.0 TR:120.0:-99999
```

Figure 6-15. *Licensing an additional language, page 3 of 3*

As shown in the figure, the manifest file reports the active languages (Turkish and American English in this example) that are present in the EBS system as well as the files and their versions.

To receive the NLS translation synchronization patch, you send the manifest file to Oracle Support, as shown by the following example.

To send the manifest to Oracle Support, you use your browser to go to the following URL:

```
https://updates.oracle.com/TransSync
```

In addition to the Request a New Patch button, the first web page that is reached by the URL https://updates.oracle.com/TransSync displays the translation synchronization patches that have been sent for your previous translation synchronization patch requests. So, you can also download and use them again if you need.

To request a new translation synchronization patch using your newly created manifest file, you click the Request a New Patch button, as shown in Figure 6-16.

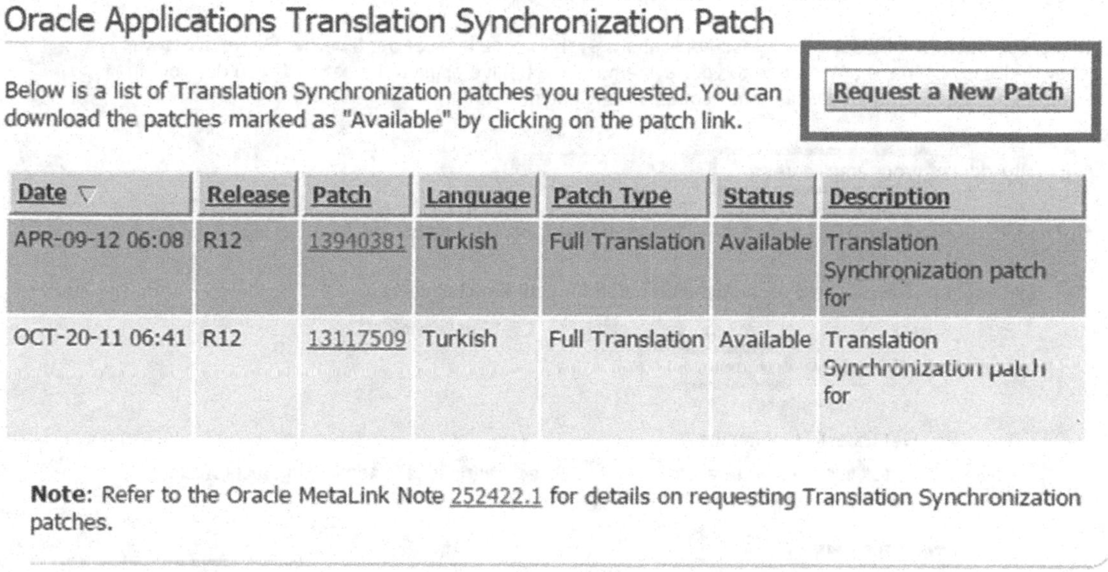

Oracle Applications Translation Synchronization Patch

Below is a list of Translation Synchronization patches you requested. You can download the patches marked as "Available" by clicking on the patch link.

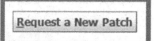

Request a New Patch

Date ▽	Release	Patch	Language	Patch Type	Status	Description
APR-09-12 06:08	R12	13940381	Turkish	Full Translation	Available	Translation Synchronization patch for
OCT-20-11 06:41	R12	13117509	Turkish	Full Translation	Available	Translation Synchronization patch for

Note: Refer to the Oracle MetaLink Note 252422.1 for details on requesting Translation Synchronization patches.

Figure 6-16. Requesting translation synchronization patches, the first web page

After clicking the Request a New Patch button, a new page where you can submit your newly generated manifest file to Oracle Support appears.

As shown in Figure 6-17, you enter your e-mail address and description in the relevant text boxes and choose your manifest file, which you have transferred from the EBS application server to your desktop client; then click the Submit button.

Oracle Applications Translation Synchronization Patch

The Translation Synchronization Patch Utility generates a patch for each of your active languages with the exact version of the files present in your environment. The resulting patches allow you to synchronize the language file versions with the American English file versions. In order to request your Translation Synchronization patches, you must provide the file manifest of your environment. See Oracle MetaLink Note 252422.1 for information about generating the file manifest.

Note: The patch will be specific to your Applications system code level at the time the file manifest was generated. Do not make any change to your system until you have applied the patch. If you do, you should generate the manifest again and request a new patch.

Email Address your email adress

A confirmation email will be sent to this email address. If the email address populated by default is not correct, provide a valid email address, and update your user profile in Oracle MetaLink.

Description Translation Synchronization patch for your email address

(ex. Translation Synchronization patch for 11.5.10 environment)

File Manifest Dosya Seç adgennls.txt

(ex. c:\adgennls.txt)

☑ Get Latest Translations

Check this box if you want to receive the latest translations in addition to synchronizing your active languages with your American English file versions.

Submit   Clear   Cancel

Figure 6-17. *Requesting translation synchronization patches, submitting the translation patch request*

Once you enter your e-mail address, choose your manifest file, and click the Submit button, a web page is displayed. This web page confirms that your request is in progress and a translation synchronization patch will be prepared by Oracle. This web page also gives you the patch number to be used for the upcoming translation synchronization patch and informs you about the e-mail you'll receive when your patch will be ready, as shown in Figure 6-18.

Oracle Applications Translation Synchronization Patch

Confirmation

Translation Synchronization patches will be generated for the active languages that require synchronization, using patch 21935187. When a patch is available, an email will be sent to you with the password and instructions on how to download that patch.

View your Translation Synchronization patches Close

Figure 6-18. *Requesting translation synchronization patches, confirmation page*

At this point, you need to wait for approximately 30 minutes to get the notification e-mail from Oracle Support, stating the link for downloading the translation synchronization patch that is created for your environment and the password that is required for downloading it. Figure 6-19 shows an example for these kinds of e-mails.

Translation Synchronization Patch 21935187 for Turkish is now available

Translation Synchronization Notification <isd_do_not_reply@oracle.com>

Dear Customer,
Your R12 Translation Synchronization patch 21935187 for Turkish is available at:
https://updates.oracle.com/ARULink/SimpleSearch/process_form?
search_type=patch&patch_number=21935187&plat_lang=116L

If you have enabled this language in Lightweight mode, do not apply the Translation Synchronization patch. The current authorization password is "XXXXXXXX". It is valid for 7 days from the date of this email. You may access all your Translation Synchronization patches at any time, with up-to-date passwords, at the following URL:

https://updates.oracle.com/TransSync

Contact Oracle Support if you have any issue or concern with this patch.

Figure 6-19. *Requesting translation synchronization patches, translation synchronization notification e-mail*

After downloading the translation synchronization patch using the download link and password delivered by the translation synchronization notification email, you apply the patch by following the instructions in the readme file delivered with the patch. If there are no specific actions stated in the readme file, then you create an online patching cycle and apply the translation synchronization patch following the standard procedure for applying patches online in EBS 12.2, as explained earlier in this chapter.

After applying the translation synchronization patch, it is advised by Oracle to run adadmin and generate the message files by selecting Generate Applications Files Menu (option 1 in the main menu) followed by selecting the Generate Message Files menu option (option 1 in the Generate Applications Files menu). So, once you complete generating the message files, you have completed adding a new language to your EBS 12.2 environment.

Translation patches can be used as alternatives for situations where you need apply several NLS patches. The NLS patches are applied the same way as the normal patches. Almost all the EBS 12.2 patches created for fixing some problems or bringing some new functionality to the EBS products have their translated versions called NLS patches. Technology patches are an exception for this as they do not need to have NLS translated versions, because they are mostly written for making some code or configuration changes in EBS technological products or internal codes of EBS so that there is nothing to translate after applying them.

The need for applying NLS patches comes from having additional languages in an EBS 12.2 system. In this manner, after applying EBS product patches, the NLS-translated version of those patches must be applied as well. For example, suppose you use Arabic and Russian in addition to American English (the default language that comes with the installation) in your EBS 12.2 environment and suppose you want to apply patch 11111, which has a translated version. Then you need to apply the Russian and Arabic versions of patch 11111 after applying patch 11111. If you don't, then the user who logs in using Arabic or Russian languages will not see the benefit of the changes that are supposed to be brought by the applied patch.

Figure 6-20 shows the patch search in Oracle Support for displaying the NLS patches and the base patch for patch 19677379.

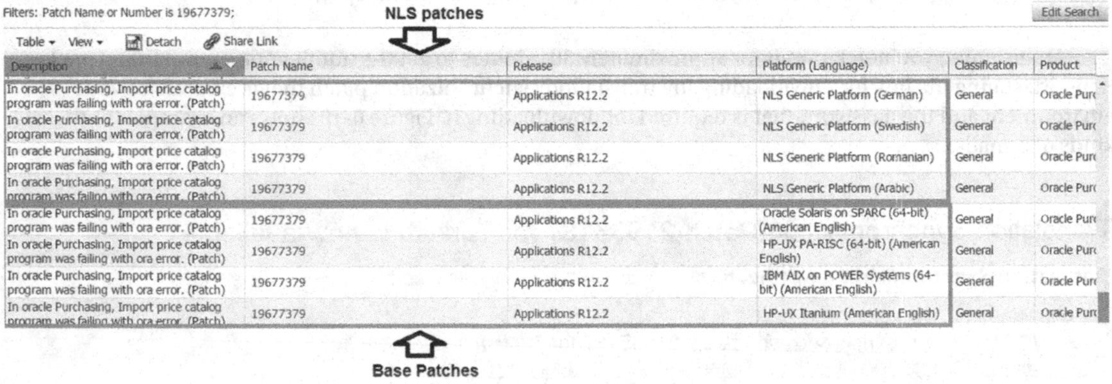

Figure 6-20. *Oracle Patch Search displaying the NLS and Base versions of patch 19677379*

So, as shown in Figure 6-20, you need to download and apply a base patch suitable for your application server's operating system from Oracle Support using the patch search, and if you have additional languages, then you need to download and apply the NLS version of that patch for your additional language/languages too.

The need for applying an NLS translated version of an EBS patch is so clear, but it may become a problem in some cases.

Consider a scenario where you want to apply 20 EBS product patches and all these patches have their translated versions, as well. Also suppose you have three additional languages, in total four languages (including the default one, American English) in your EBS system, which makes 80 patches to apply. Applying 80 patches may be a time-consuming process, unless they are merged. In fact, although merging is an option for this, merging in such a scenario can be considered as a complex process, which includes downloading of several patches.

Another example scenario is the installation process of EBS 12.2. As mentioned earlier, EBS 12.2 is installed as EBS 12.2.0, and it is mandatory to upgrade it to at least a stable EBS 12.2 release such as 12.2.3. In this context, there are patches that need to be applied, and if you have licensed and added additional languages in your newly installed EBS 12.2.0 system, then there are several NLS translation patches that you need to apply for these upgrade patches too.

In other words, for every patch that needs to be applied during the upgrade and that has an NLS translation patch available, an NLS translation patch (if it is available) should be applied, as well.

This is also a heavy process, as you need to apply several patches during the upgrade, and having the requirement for applying the NLS translation version of them just extends the time needed for the upgrade. Even if you can merge these patches and decrease the patch count, it still requires lots of preparation steps as it involves downloading and merging dozens of NLS patches, as explained earlier.

Fortunately, you have another way, which is applying the translation synchronization patch by following almost the same steps as for adding a language.

There is no licensing needed in this situation, and you apply the NLS patches for the additional languages that you already have in your EBS 12.2.

So, the steps for applying a translation synchronization patch rather than applying several NLS patches to synchronize the NLS files of the EBS applications with the default files are as follows:

1. Use adadmin to update the current view snapshot for the complete APPL_TOP.

2. Use adgennls.pl to generate a manifest file.

3. Upload the generated NLS file to Oracle Support by creating a translation synchronization request.

4. Download and apply the translation synchronization patch when it is ready.

So, we have explained how to add a new language to EBS 12.2 using the translation synchronization patch for synchronizing the NLS files of the EBS 12.2, both for cases where you need to add a new language to your EBS system and where you need an alternative for applying several NLS patches.

Translation synchronization patches can also be considered a maintenance operation in some environments where the environment is managed by many apps DBAs and where the history of patch applications and the patching procedures is not reliable. In these kinds of environments, the translation synchronization patch may save the environment from being incomplete in terms of translations, as some of the translation patches can be forgotten in one of the previous patching operations.

Let's continue with enabling the HRMS legislations by taking a look at the things you need to do for enabling the country-specific HRMS legislations.

As mentioned earlier in this section, HRMS legislations are installed for enabling country-specific legislations for multinational companies that run their business processes according to their own HR legislations. This definition is sufficient, as you are the apps DBA responsible for the technical stuff.

To install the HRMS legislations to an EBS 12.2 system, you first create an online patching cycle using the adop phase=prepare command; then you use the DataInstall utility to choose the country you want to install the legislations for, and lastly you use the driver hrglobal.drv to install the HRMS legislations data that by default comes with the data files that are present in the application file system of EBS 12.2 instances. hrglobal.drv is a patch driver that loads only the legislation-specific data into the database, and this data is present in the data files located in the application file system.

So, you don't need to download a patch for enabling HRMS legislations, as the data files for enabling the legislations are already present in the application tier, and hrglobal.drv knows what to do with them.

If you look at this process a little more closer, you can see that after creating the online patching cycle with the adop phase=prepare command, you invoke the DataInstall utility and choose the country that you want to install the legislations for. Then you save your choice and use adop to apply the hrglobal.drv by executing the apply phase. Once the apply phase is completed, you continue with the finalize, cutover, and cleanup phases for completing the online patching cycle and finish.

The DataInstall utility should be invoked from the patch environment.

Also, hrglobal.drv should be applied in an online patching cycle unless you are upgrading to EBS 12.2 from an earlier release (11i, 12.0, or 12.1).

■ **Note** If you are upgrading to EBS 12.2 from earlier releases, you can apply hrglobal.drv in downtime mode after applying R12.HR_PF.C.Delta.5 or above.

In Listing 6-29, we are demonstrating how to install HRMS legislations for Saudi Arabia.

You first set your run environment using the EBSApps.env script and create the online patching cycle as follows;

Listing 6-29. Installing HRMS Legislations Using DataInstall and hrglobal.drv

```
[applmgr@somehost ~]$ . /u01/install/APPS/EBSapps.env run
[applmgr@somehost ~]$ adop phase=prepare
Then, we  set our patch environment using EBSApps.env script again. This time we supply
"patch" as an argument to the environment script.
[applmgr@somehost ~]$ . /u01/install/APPS/EBSapps.env patch

Next, we invoke the DataInstall utility as follows;
Note that: The format for executing the DataInstall utility is as follows;
 java oracle.apps.per.DataInstall appsuser appspassword thin <database_server_
hostname>:<database_listener_port>:<database_sid>

[applmgr@somehost ~]$ java oracle.apps.per.DataInstall apps oracleR12 thin
daroratestdbsrv1:1521:ORATEST

When executed, DataInstall welcome us with a Main Menu as follows;
DataInstall for hrglobal
+----------------------------------------------------+
|                 DataInstall Main Menu              |
+----------------------------------------------------+
1.    Select legislative data to install/upgrade
2.    Select college data to install/upgrade
3.    Select JIT to install/upgrade
4.    Exit to confirmation menu

Enter your choice :
Enter your choice (for example 2I) : 1

We choose option 1 to choose the country that we want to install the legislations for.
When we write 1 as our choice and press enter, a list of available legislations appears, as
shown below.
Note that: Global localization comes installed by default.  So, if the country that you want
to install the legislations for is not in this list and if you still need to run hrglobal
driver as a post requisite action after a patch application, then you should choose the
Global and install the Global once again, even if it is already installed.

 # Localisation          Product(s)               Leg. Data? Action
 -- ------------------    ------------------------ ---------- -------------
 1 Global                Human Resources          Installed
 2 Australia             Human Resources
 3 Belgium               Human Resources
 4 Canada                Human Resources
 5 China                 Human Resources
 6 Denmark               Human Resources
 7 Finland               Human Resources
 8 France                Human Resources
 9 Germany               Human Resources
10 Hong Kong             Human Resources
```

```
11 Hungary                Human Resources
12 India                  Human Resources
13 Ireland                Human Resources
14 Italy                  Human Resources
15 Japan                  Human Resources
16 Korea, Republic of     Human Resources
17 Kuwait                 Human Resources
18 Mexico                 Human Resources
19 Netherlands            Human Resources
20 New Zealand            Human Resources
21 Norway                 Human Resources
22 Poland                 Human Resources
23 Romania                Human Resources
24 Russian Federation     Human Resources
25 Saudi Arabia           Human Resources
26 Singapore              Human Resources
27 South Africa           Human Resources
28 Spain                  Human Resources
29 Sweden                 Human Resources
30 United Arab Emirates Human Resources
31 United Kingdom         Human Resources
32 United States          Human Resources
33 United States          US Federal Human Resources

<Product #><Action> - Change Action
where <Action> is [I : Install, C : Clear]

[Return]      - To return to main menu.
```

Enter your choice (for example 2I) :

We check the list and check the number residing on the name of the country that we want to install legislations for, and use that number with the "I" letter to make the DataInstall marks it as a legislation to be installed.

In this example, we make our choice as "25I" to install the legislations for Saudi Arabia and when we write 25I as our choice and press enter, DataInstall display a list showing the legislations for Saudi Arabia is marked for install as shown below;

Note that: we can always use the letter "C" to clear a marked legislation. (for example: using "25C" , we can clear the previous choice that we made for installing legislations for Saudi Arabia, and then using 30I, we can mark legislations for United Arab Emirates for the installation.)

```
Enter your choice (for example 2I) :25I
# Localisation            Product(s)                  Leg. Data? Action
-- --------------------   ------------------------ ---------- -------------
 1 Global                 Human Resources             Installed
 2 Australia              Human Resources
 3 Belgium                Human Resources
 4 Canada                 Human Resources
 5 China                  Human Resources
 6 Denmark                Human Resources
 7 Finland                Human Resources
 8 France                 Human Resources
```

```
 9 Germany               Human Resources
10 Hong Kong             Human Resources
11 Hungary               Human Resources
12 India                 Human Resources
13 Ireland               Human Resources
14 Italy                 Human Resources
15 Japan                 Human Resources
16 Korea, Republic of    Human Resources
17 Kuwait                Human Resources
18 Mexico                Human Resources
19 Netherlands           Human Resources
20 New Zealand           Human Resources
21 Norway                Human Resources
22 Poland                Human Resources
23 Romania               Human Resources
24 Russian Federation    Human Resources
25 Saudi Arabia          Human Resources                     Install
26 Singapore             Human Resources
27 South Africa          Human Resources
28 Spain                 Human Resources
29 Sweden                Human Resources
30 United Arab Emirates  Human Resources
31 United Kingdom        Human Resources
32 United States         Human Resources
33 United States         US Federal Human Resources

<Product #><Action> - Change Action
where <Action> is [I : Install, C : Clear]

[Return]      - To return to main menu.
```

At this point, we see that the word "Install" appears in the line representing the
legislations for Saudi Arabia and we can consider our work is done in DataInstall.
So, we press "enter/return" to go back in the DataInstall Main Menu where we exit to the
confirmation menu using option 4 .

```
Enter your choice (for example 2I) :
+---------------------------------------------------+
|              DataInstall Main Menu                |
+---------------------------------------------------+
1.    Select legislative data to install/upgrade
2.    Select college data to install/upgrade
3.    Select JIT to install/upgrade
4.    Exit to confirmation menu

Enter your choice : 4
```

When we exit to the confirmation menu, DataInstall displays a confirmation dialog where we
can write the letter "Y" and press the enter button to confirm and save the changes we have
done, as shown below.

```
          DataInstall - Actions confirmation
Do you really wish to exit and save your changes?
```

```
[Y]       - Yes, save then exit
[N]       - No, don't save but exit
[Return] - To return to the DataInstall Main Menu

Enter your choice (for example Y) : Y
```

After confirming the choice for the legislations installation that we have just done, DataInstall displays a summary for the actions that will be performed and exits.

```
 DataInstall - Actions summary
 -----------------------------
The following actions will be performed:
Localisation         Product(s)                    Leg. Data? Action
------------------   ------------------------   ----------   -------------

Saudi Arabia         Human Resources                           Install

Localisation    College Data? Action
--------------  ------------- -------------
United Kingdom
United States

Option                                 Data?          Action
------------------------------------   -------------  -------------
JIT/Geocode
```

After performing these actions, you tell the EBS environment that you will install the legislations for Saudi Arabia. In other words, your EBS environment becomes ready for the legislations-related data that will be installed by patching with the hrglobal driver, which is actually your next step for legislations-related data installation.

Next, you execute adop by supplying hrglobal.drv, located in the $PER_TOP/patch/115 directory, as the patch driver.

■ **Note**   We refer to the patch edition's $PER_TOP environment variable used as the patchtop in the adop command.

```
adop phase=apply patchtop=$PER_TOP/patch/115 patches=driver:hrglobal.drv options=nocopyporti
on,nogenerateportion,forceapply
```

You execute the adop command from the patch environment (considering adop will set the necessary environment variables by itself) and start the apply phase in the online patching cycle that you have created by the adop phase=prepare command in the beginning of this example.

Note that you use the nocopyportion, nogenerateportion, and forceapply options in the adop command, as it is unnecessary to copy or generate anything after a data installation.

After completing the apply phase, you execute the online patching cycle phases (finalize, cutover, and cleanup) one by one, as shown here in sequence, and complete the patching cycle.

```
adop phase=finalize
adop phase=cutover
adop phase=cleanup
```

After completing the online patching cycle, your work is done because the legislations that you want to install are installed into your EBS 12.2 system. However, there is still one optional point that you may need to consider if there is a need to install the translation patch for the legislations that you have just installed. That is, the NLS-translated version of hrglobal should be applied at this point if you have additional languages installed with the NLS translation patches in your EBS system.

For example, if you have an Arabic translation in your EBS system, then you need to install the Arabic translation version of hrglobal.drv after completing the HR legislations installation.

The translated version of hrglobal is available via patch 21055497, and it is applied using a simple adop command adop phase=apply patches=21055497 in a newly created online patching cycle, just like any standard EBS application patch.

Listing 6-29 explains the complete process for installing HRMS legislations in EBS 12.2. So after applying hrglobal and its NLS version (if it is available for the country in question), your work for installing HRMS legislations is done.

Let's continue with the next section, in which you will see how to apply localization patches and see the additional actions that need to be done before applying them.

Localization Patches

The localization patches are created by Oracle to provide country-specific code and applications objects that allow multinational countries to do their country-specific work using Oracle applications. As Oracle is an American company, by default the business rules and the interfaces such as forms, batch jobs, and reports that are delivered within EBS 12.2 are targeted to the United States.

If you are in a different country than the United States, you will not have application functionality such as country-specific reports and batch processes in a newly installed EBS 12.2 system. As you may guess, these kinds of functionalities that enable localization of the EBS products are delivered using localization, which are available on Oracle Support (http://support.oracle.com).

The localization patches are standard patches that are downloaded from Oracle Support and applied using the standard patching tool, adop.

Localizations are installed in two phases in EBS 12.2. First you need to apply the prerequisite patches, and then you apply the actual localization patches.

However, the prerequisite patches that you are dealing with in the case of localizations are a little special. The document to follow for prerequisite actions is "Creating CLE Product & Applying Mandatory Patches for R12.2 EMEA Add-on Localizations" (Doc ID 1628719.1). There is a mandatory action for creating the CLE product, which is the EBS product that is used for the localization. As the localization-related database tier objects are created in the CLE schema and application tier localization objects are created in $CLE_TOP, you need to create the CLE product before applying the localization patches.

Knowing that, the action plan for applying the localization patches is to install or create the CLE product, apply the prerequisite patch, and then apply the localization patches.

To create the CLE product, you first need to connect to the EBS database using a sqlplus as sysdba connection initiated from the database server, create the CLE schema, and then grant the necessary privileges to it, as shown in Listing 6-30.

Listing 6-30. Creating the CLE Schema

```
[oracle@somedbhost ~]$ sqlplus "/as sysdba"
SQL> create user CLE identified by CLE default tablespace APPS_TS_TX_DATA;
User created.
SQL> grant connect , resource to CLE;
Grant succeeded.
```

After creating the CLE schema, you download patch 13725897 (CLE: Adsplice Patch for R12.2) to your application server. Patch 13725897 is required for installing the CLE (localizations) product, as it installs the CLE product using the adsplice tool, which will be explained in detail in Chapter 9. For now, it is enough to know that the adsplice utility reads an information file for a product that you want to splice into your EBS environment, and according to that information file, adsplicer adds that product into the EBS database. So, as you want to enable the localization and as the localization must be stored in the CLE product, which is not installed by the EBS installer (Rapidwiz), you need to use adsplice to add the CLE product to your EBS 12.2 system.

The information file that adsplicer will read when adding the CLE product in EBS 12.2 is gathered from patch 13725897, as this patch contains the information file specific to the CLE product.

So, using this information file gathered from patch 13725897, you make the adsplice utility splice the CLE product into your EBS 12.2 system.

To add CLE using the adsplice utility, you first unzip patch 13725897 and copy the .txt files from the patch directory (13725897\cle\admin to the $APPL_TOP/admin directory), as shown in Listing 6-31.

You first log into the application server using the application owner OS user (for example, applmgr) and set your run environment.

Listing 6-31. Unzipping Patch 13725897 and Copying the newprods.txt, cleprod.txt, and cleterr.txt Files to the $APPL_TOP/admin Directory

```
[applmgr@somehost ~]$ . /u01/install/APPS/EBSapps.env run
```

Then you change your directory to where you downloaded patch p13725897 (the patch zip file is p13725897_R12_GENERIC.zip) and unzip the patch as follows:

```
[applmgr@somehost ~]$ unzip p13725897_R12_GENERIC.zip Archive:  p13725897_R12_GENERIC.zip
```

Then you change your directory to 13725897/cle/admin/ and copy the text files located in that directory to the $APPL_TOP/admin directory.

```
[applmgr@somehost ~]$ cd 13725897/cle/admin/
[applmgr@somehost admin]$ ls
cleprod.txt  cleterr.txt  newprods.txt
[applmgr@somehost admin]$ cp * $APPL_TOP/admin/
```

After copying the patch .txt files, you open the newprods.txt file and modify it as necessary. Listing 6-31 shows an example of unzipping patch 13725897 and copying the text files delivered with the patch files to the $APPL_TOP/admin directory. The default newprods.txt file and the modified newsprods.txt, which can be used for adding the CLE product into an EBS 12.2 system, are also shown in Listing 6-32.

You can open newsprod.txt using a text editor (for example, vi editor) to modify it for use by adsplicer.

Listing 6-32. The default contents of a newprods.txt file

```
[applmgr@somehost admin]$ vi newsprod.txt
# Add Product,EMEA Add-On Localizations
product=cle
base_product_top=*APPL_TOP*
oracle_schema=cle
sizing_factor=100
# Table spaces may need to be editted to fit database setup
main_tspace=CLED
index_tspace=CLEX
temp_tspace=TEMP
default_tspace=CLED
```

By default, you see the CLED and CLEX tablespaces in newsprods.txt. In other words, the default version of newsprods.txt is prepared by Oracle to instruct adsplice to create CLE tables in the tablespace named CLED and to create CLE indexes in the tablespace named CLEX.

So, as you don't have these tablespaces and as it is instructed by Oracle Support ("Creating CLE Product & Applying Mandatory Patches for R12.2 EMEA Add-on Localizations" [Doc ID 1628719.1]), you modify the lines starting with main_tspace and index_tspace according to your environment. main_tspace is used for specifying the tablespace where CLE tables will reside, and index_tspace is used for specifying the tables where CLE indexes will reside. You also set default_tspace to be APPS_TS_TX_DATA in order to make the adsplice scripts that have no tablespace definitions in them create the objects in the APPS_TS_TX_DATA tablespace.

So after the modification, newsprod.txt looks like Listing 6-33.

Listing 6-33. A modified newprods.txt file

```
product=cle
base_product_top= *APPL_TOP*
oracle_schema=cle
sizing_factor=100
main_tspace= APPS_TS_TX_DATA
index_tspace=APPS_TS_TX_IDX
temp_tspace=TEMP
default_tspace= APPS_TS_TX_DATA
```

Once you finish modifying newsprod.txt, you continue by running the adsplice command from the $APPL_TOP/admin directory, as shown in Listing 6-34.

Listing 6-34. Running adsplicer to Add the CLE Product to the EBS 12.2 System

```
[applmgr@somehost admin]$. /u01/install/APPS/EBSapps.env run
[applmgr@somehost admin]$ cd $APPL_TOP/admin
[applmgr@somehost admin]$ adsplice
```

Note adsplice normally asks the following questions. The questions are self-explanatory, and you can accept the defaults for most of them.

- *Is this the correct APPL_TOP [Yes]?*: Accept the default by pressing Enter.

- *Filename [adsplice.log]*: Accept the default by pressing Enter. (By default, the log file for the adsplice session is created in the $APPL_TOP/admin/<SID>/log directory, with the name adsplice.log.)

- *Is this the correct database [Yes]?*: Accept the default by pressing Enter.

- *Enter the password for your 'SYSTEM' ORACLE schema*: Supply the password of the SYSTEM schema.

- *Enter the ORACLE password of Application Object Library [APPS]*: Supply the password of the APPS schema.

- *The default directory is [/u01/install/APPS/fs1/EBSapps/appl/admin]*: Accept the default by pressing Enter.

- *Please enter the name of your AD Splicer control file [newprods.txt]*: Accept the default by pressing Enter.

- *Do you wish to regenerate your environment file [Yes]?*: Accept the default by pressing Enter.

After you answer these questions, adsplice runs and splices the CLE product into your EBS 12.2 environment.

■ **Note** You don't apply 13725897 patch using adop. That's because you only need to use the .txt files delivered with this patch for the adsplice operations.

The CLE schema password that you specified while you were creating the CLE schema can be changed using the FNDCPASS utility, if desired.

At this point, you log in again to the application server using the application owner account and check whether adsplicer has created the CLE product successfully. Listing 6-35 shows the SQL queries and OS commands to check whether the CLE product has been added to the EBS 12.2 system properly.

Connect to the database using sqlplus apps/<apps_password> and query for the following SQL statements:

```
SQL> select application_id, product_code from  fnd_application where application_short_name = 'CLE';

APPLICATION_ID PRODUCT_CODE
-------------- --------------------------------------------------------
         13014 CLE

SQL> select application_id, patch_level from  fnd_product_installations where APPLICATION_ID = 13014;

APPLICATION_ID PATCH_LEVEL
-------------- ------------------------------
         13014 R12.CLE.C

SQL> select username,account_status from dba_users where username='CLE';

USERNAME                             ACCOUNT_STATUS
------------------------------------ ------------------------------
CLE                                  OPEN
```

All of these SQL statements should return one row. If each of them returns one row, then proceed with the following check.

With the application OS user (for example, applmgr), check the value of CLE_TOP and change the directory to $CLE_TOP to check whether it has the admin, forms, log, mds, mesg, out, patch, and sql subdirectories.

Listing 6-35. Checking CLE After Splicing It with adsplice

```
[applmgr@somehost ~]$ echo $CLE_TOP
/u01/install/APPS/fs1/EBSapps/appl/cle/12.0.0
[applmgr@somehost ~]$ cd $CLE_TOP
[applmgr@somehost 12.0.0]$ ls
admin  forms  log  mds  mesg  out  patch  sql
```

The next thing to do is to run the adop phase=fs_clone command to propagate the changes done by adsplicer and you are done.

After you finish splicing the CLE product into the EBS 12.2 system and execute an fs_clone operation, you proceed by applying the prerequisite patches that need to be applied before starting the application of the localization patches. Specifically, after splicing the CLE product, you need to apply patch 13768679 (R12. CLE.C) and the latest CLE seed patch.

Apply patch 21279652 (R12.2 - CLE: SEED patch for Localization DFF/GDFF, Forms Personalization), as instructed in Oracle Support document "Creating CLE Product & Applying Mandatory Patches for 12.2 EMEA Add-on Localizations" (Doc ID 1628719.1).

■ **Note** There is only a generic version of patch 13768679 available in Oracle Support. However, there are translated versions of patch 21279652 available in Oracle Support. So, if the environment that you are patching has multiple languages, then you need to apply the NLS versions of patch 21279652, too.

To apply these patches, you follow the standard online patching cycle method. You execute adop phase=prepare and then unzip the patches to the $APPL_TOP_NE/../patch directory. After unzipping the patches, you use the adop phase=apply patches=13768679 and adop phase=apply patches=21279652 commands and apply these patches your EBS 12.2 environment.

After the apply phase, you continue by performing the adop phase =finalize, adop phase=cutover, and adop phase=cleanup commands to complete your patching activities and the online patching cycle. After you finish applying the prerequisite patches, you can continue with applying the localization patches.

To decide on the localization patches that need to be applied to your EBS 12.2 system, you first check the Oracle Support document "Introduction to Add-On Localizations for R12" (Doc ID 429042.1), as this document is the root document for localizations and it provides the links for the country-specific localization documents that state the number of localization patches that need to be applied for different kinds of product localizations.

In Oracle Support document 429042.1, there is a table that provides links both to the documents for reaching the country-specific installation documents that state the required patches for enabling the country-specific localizations and to the documents that state the country-specific data sheets for reviewing the changes that come with the enablement of the localization.

Figure 6-21 shows the table used in Oracle Support document 429042.1, which provides the links for country-specific localization documents.

Europe, Middle East & Africa	(Links to Countries Notes)		
Austria	Belgium	Bulgaria	Commonwealth of Independent States
Croatia	Czech Republic	Finland	Germany
Greece	Hungary	Israel	Italy
Netherlands	Norway	Poland	Portugal
Romania	Serbia	Slovakia	Slovenia
Spain	Sweden	Switzerland	Turkey
Europe, Middle East & Africa	(Links to Datasheets)		
Austria	Belgium	Bulgaria	Croatia
Czech Republic	Finland	Germany	Greece
Hungary	Israel	Italy	Kazakhstan
Netherlands	Norway	Poland	Portugal
Romania	Russia	Serbia	Slovakia
Slovenia	Spain	Sweden	Switzerland
Turkey	Ukraine		

Figure 6-21. *Table providing the links for country-specific localization documents*

As you can see in Figure 6-21, the table that provides the links for country-specific localization documents consists of two parts. The links in the first part, which are gathered under "Links to Countries Notes," let you reach the documents that state the country-specific localization patches. The links in the second part, which are gathered under "Links to Countries DataSheets," let you reach the documents that state the country-specific localization data sheets.

As the datasheets give the function information about the changes and abilities that EBS 12.2 achieves by installing the localizations for EBS 12, you can focus on the country notes, which give the patch numbers for enabling the localizations for EBS 12.2 products.

The following is an example of the Turkey localization document, which can be reached by clicking the Turkey link in the first part of the table (under "Links to Countries") used in Oracle Support document 429042.1.

The Oracle Support document that you reach using the Turkey link is "R12 EMEA Add-on Localizations - Turkey" (Doc ID 472686.1).

■ **Note** The process and the documentation logic are the same for all the other countries. For example, when you click the Bulgaria link, you reach the document "R12 EMEA Add-on Localizations - Bulgaria" (Doc ID 473626.1).

In "R12 EMEA Add-on Localizations – Turkey," you see the links for the patches labeled Latest Patch, and once you click the Latest Patch link associated with your EBS version, you find yourself in the Oracle Support page that gives you the ability to download the relevant localization patch.

Note that these localization patches have no generic versions, as they are available only for the additional languages. For instance, if you apply a Complete Set localization patch for Turkey, then you need to choose Turkish as the language for the patch that you want to download and apply that patch once it is downloaded.

Complete Set is the patch that delivers most of the localizations; you can think of it as the base. That is, if you want to enable localizations, you apply the Complete Set patch and then apply the localizations for the specific products if those localizations are not included in the Complete Set patch.

The same applies for the localization of all the countries.

Figure 6-22 shows a snippet from the document "R12 EMEA Add-on Localizations - Turkey" (Doc ID 472686.1), where you can see the links for reaching the Complete Set patch of all the EBS 12 versions. In Figure 6-22, you also see that links to the technical reference manuals, user guides, and installation instructions are provided in "R12 EMEA Add-on Localizations - Turkey" (Doc ID 472686.1).

Turkey Add-on Localizations - Complete Set

Use these links to download the complete set of Add-on Localizations for Turkey.

Installation and Documentation list	R12.0	R12.1	R12.2
Patch Set	Latest Patch	Latest Patch	Latest Patch
User Guide-PDF	User Guide	User Guide	User Guide
Technical Reference Manual	Technical Reference Manual	Technical Reference Manual	Technical Reference Manual
Installation Instructions	Forms Personalizations-Part1 Forms Personalizations-Part2	Included in User Guide	Included in User Guide

Figure 6-22. *A snippet from the Oracle Support document 472686.1 showing the links for reaching the Complete Set patch*

Figure 6-23 shows the download page that you reach when you click the Latest Patch link for the Complete Set patch in the Oracle Support document 472686.1.

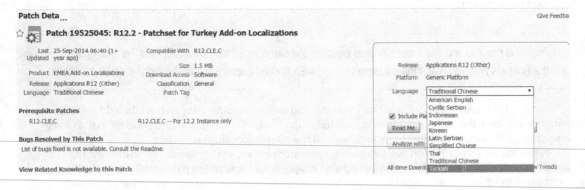

Figure 6-23. *Download page for the Complete Set patch*

As mentioned earlier, there are some localization patches for some of the application functions, such as the Supplier Credit Memo Report, which are delivered in the Complete Set patch. For these, you see the statement "Included In Patchset" in the table that provides the links for the localization patches of that application functionality, as shown in Figure 6-24.

Supplier Credit Memo Report

Supplier Credit Memo printing report will print all the credit memos entered for a Supplier, Accounting Period and Invoice Number. User can reprint already printed Credit Memos also.

R12.0	R12.1	R12.2
Included in Patchset	Included in Patchset	Included in Patchset

The "User Guide", "Technical Reference Manual" & "Installation Instructions" are common to all Turkey Add-on Localizations.

back to list of countries   back to list of Turkey features

Figure 6-24. The localization patch for Supplier Credit Memo Report is already included in the Complete Set patch

Here, you don't need to apply any additional patches; applying the Complete Set patch will install the localization for these kinds of application functionalities.

Of course, there are some localization patches for some of the application functionalities that are not included in the Complete Set patch. In these kinds of situations, in addition to the Complete Set patch, you need to apply the specific localization patches for that product.

The localization patch for "Periodic Prepaid Expenses Distribution" is an example for that kind of localization patch, as shown in Figure 6-25.

Periodic Prepaid Expenses Distribution

This feature allows allocation and accounting of a prepaid expense in periods. It calculates periodic amount and creates a journal for the period by debiting the actual expenses account and crediting the current year prepaid expense account.

For the first period, the system will calculate next year amount of the prepaid expense and create a journal. The accounts of this journal are next year prepaid expense account debit, current year prepaid expense account credit. A reverse of this journal will be created at the first period of next year.

Inflation adjustment can be applied to the journals created, so inflation adjustment index will be applied if given. User can also change the distribution periods to be distributed at any point of time; distribution amounts recalculated and appropriate adjustment accounting entries are created in the current period by the system.

R12.0	R12.1	R12.2
Latest Patch	Latest Patch	Latest Patch

The "User Guide", "Technical Reference Manual" & "Installation Instructions" are common to all Turkey Add-on Localizations.

Figure 6-25. The localization patch for "Periodic Prepaid Expenses Distribution"

So, you can apply the Complete Set patch and all the localization patches, but applying all the localization patches can be an unnecessary action, as the application functions for which you apply the localization patches may not be used in your EBS 12.2 environment. Moreover, the application itself may not be licensed in your EBS 12.2 environment.

Therefore, it is better to leave the decision to the functional administrators. That is, you should provide the information about the available localizations stated in the localization document and let the functional administrators choose the needed localization areas. Then, you can apply the needed patches using the adop online method for the chosen localizations.

■ **Note**   The instructions for applying the localization patches are in the patch readme files. However, the localization patches are mostly applied online using adop. That is, you create an online patching cycle using the adop phase=prepare command and then apply the localization patch or patches in question using adop phase=apply patches=<patch_number>.

You can apply multiple localization patches in one patching cycle.

Once you apply the localization patch or patches, you continue with the remaining adop online patching cycle phases and finish the work needed for enabling the localizations.

Before we continue with the next section, we want to share our experience from a real-life example. We have encountered a problem while applying the Complete Set patch for enabling the Turkish localization. The problem was a form that could not be compiled. To correct this problem, we opened a service request to Oracle Support for this patch, and Oracle Support sent us a patch, which was created on the fly especially for our problem. But even after applying the patch, the form could not be compiled. At the end of the day, we had to compile a flex field that was deployed by the localization patch (Complete Set) using EBS screens.

So, the localization patches in EBS 12.2 may be a little problematic sometimes, and you may need to open Oracle Support service requests and also deal with the problems in parallel with Oracle Support SRs to get the fix needed. In addition, the localization documents that we have mentioned in this section are updated daily. Remember to check these documents before applying the localization patches.

Patch Reporting Utilities

So far, we have given all the details about the patching process in EBS 12.2. Both in Chapter 5 and in this chapter, we have explained the patching process used in EBS 12.2 by giving you the basics, use case examples, and details about patching activities that you will do while administrating the EBS 12.2 environments.

Although we have given the core information about patching and covered several different kinds of patching methodologies, tools, and action plans used both in preparing the environment for patching and in applying the EBS 12.2 patches according to different scenarios and needs, we haven't introduced or explained the built-in patch reporting utilities that are delivered by default with the EBS 12.2 installations.

Analyzing the log files by navigating the EBS 12.2 application file system and gathering the necessary diagnostic information for solving the problems can be done manually by using the operating system tools and commands. However, using the EBS 12.2 patch reporting tools saves you from spending time and effort when reviewing the patch log files by navigating the numerous log directories in the complex directory structure of EBS 12.2.

In addition, using such sophisticated patch reporting tools gives you other benefits such as the ability to check the exceptions that are encountered while applying patches and patch-related timing information.

Unfortunately, there are still some log files such as the log files produced while executing the adop phases that can analyzed only from the application node where the application patches are applied. So, all the patch-related logs can be checked, and all the patch-related analysis can be done using the EBS patch reporting tools, but the log files of adop itself can be checked only by logging into the application node with the relevant OS user account.

We will explain the analysis that can be done from the application node later; first we will explain the EBS patch reporting tools. Reporting and analyzing are two different things, so we will explain the tools that can be used for reporting and analyzing as well. In this manner, we will explain the OAM pages that can be considered as the tools for viewing the log files and analyzing the patching actions, timings, and exceptions.

The tool that is used for patch reporting purposes in EBS 12.2 is called the Applied Patches Reporting tool. Using this, you can gather all the necessary information about the patching activities in the EBS 12.2 system, including patch numbers, driver names, EBS platform (OS and CPU architecture), APPL_TOP, contents and language of the patch, files changed with the patches, files copied with the patches, bug fixes delivered with the patches, timing information about the patches, and the status of the patching activities (success or fail). The Applied Patches Reporting tool is reached using OAM. The tool is simply available as an OAM web page, and it gives the information about patching activities using the patch-related information that the adop tool stores in the EBS database.

Normally, all the adop actions are stored in the EBS 12.2 database, as long as you don't use the preinstall=y and apply=no arguments with adop. (You can check Table 6-1 for the descriptions of these arguments.)

To use the Applied Patches Reporting tool, you log in to EBS and use the Patching and Utilities link defined in the System Administrator responsibility under Oracle Applications Manager, as shown in Figure 6-26.

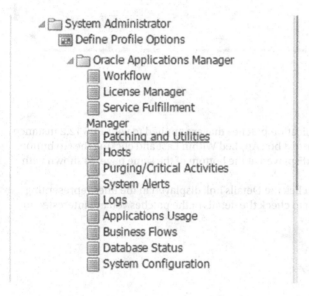

Figure 6-26. *Navigation for patching and utilities (Applied Patches Reporting tool)*

Once you reach this and click the Patches and Utilities link defined in the System Administrator responsibility, the Applied Patches page appears.

As shown in Figure 6-27, the Applied Patches page provides a search form where you can do a simple search or advanced search where you can provide the patch number and/or time range and/or a specific language as the search criteria, based on your needs.

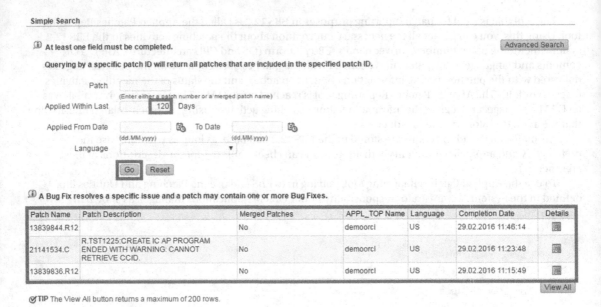

Figure 6-27. *Patch search*

In this search form, you can search all the application patches that are applied to your EBS 12.2 instance within last 120 days by entering the value 120 in the text box Applied Within Last and clicking the Go button. After clicking the Go button, the search results are displayed at the bottom of the same page, as shown with the big red rectangle.

After the search results are displayed, you can click the Details link displayed in the lines representing the patches that are returned from the patch search to check the details of the patches you are interested in, as shown in Figure 6-28.

Simple Search

ⓘ At least one field must be completed.

Advanced Search

Querying by a specific patch ID will return all patches that are included in the specified patch ID.

Patch [   ]
(Enter either a patch number or a merged patch name)

Applied Within Last [120] Days

Applied From Date [   ] 📇 To Date [   ] 📇
(dd.MM.yyyy)   (dd.MM.yyyy)

Language [▼]

Go   Reset

ⓘ A Bug Fix resolves a specific issue and a patch may contain one or more Bug Fixes.

Patch Name	Patch Description	Merged Patches	APPL_TOP Name	Language	Completion Date	Details
13839844.R12		No	demoorcl	US	29.02.2016 11:46:14	🔳
21141534.C	R.TST1225:CREATE IC AP PROGRAM ENDED WITH WARNING: CANNOT RETRIEVE CCID.	No	demoorcl	US	29.02.2016 11:23:48	🔳
13839836.R12		No	demoorcl	US	29.02.2016 11:15:49	🔳

View All

✅TIP The View All button returns a maximum of 200 rows.

Figure 6-28. *Search results and Details links*

When you click the Details link for a patch (in this example, we are clicking the Details link of patch 21141534.C), the details page is displayed.

In the details page, there are five tabs displaying details about the patch you are interested in. The first tab, which is the default tab, is like a summary of the details, showing the patch driver files, the adop options that were used while applying the patch, the platform of the environment, the directory where the patch files reside, and the start date and the end date of the patch application.

Figure 6-29 shows what the details page looks like.

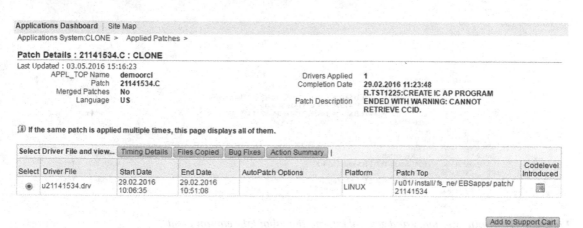

Applications Dashboard | Site Map

Applications System:CLONE > Applied Patches >

Patch Details : 21141534.C : CLONE
Last Updated : 03.05.2016 15:16:23

APPL_TOP Name	demoorcl	Drivers Applied	1
Patch	21141534.C	Completion Date	29.02.2016 11:23:48
Merged Patches	No		R.TST1225:CREATE IC AP PROGRAM
Language	US	Patch Description	ENDED WITH WARNING: CANNOT RETRIEVE CCID.

ⓘ If the same patch is applied multiple times, this page displays all of them.

Select Driver File and view... Timing Details Files Copied Bug Fixes Action Summary |

Select	Driver File	Start Date	End Date	AutoPatch Options	Platform	Patch Top	Codelevel Introduced
◉	u21141534.drv	29.02.2016 10:06:35	29.02.2016 10:51:08		LINUX	/u01/ install/ fs_ne/ EBSapps/ patch/ 21141534	🔳

Add to Support Cart

Figure 6-29. *Details page*

The second tab in the details page is the Timing Details tab, where you can see all the timing details for the patch you are interested in.

As shown in Figure 6-30, you can see all the timing details for all the specific patching actions that were taken while applying patch 21141534.

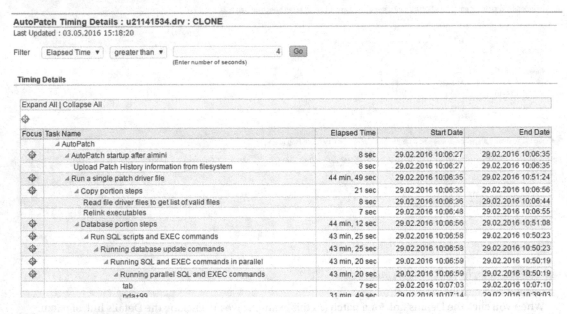

Figure 6-30. Timing Details tab

While you are in the Timing Details tab, you can also see general information about the environment that the patch was applied for, at the bottom of the page. You can also see a patch timing summary at the bottom of the page, as shown in Figure 6-31.

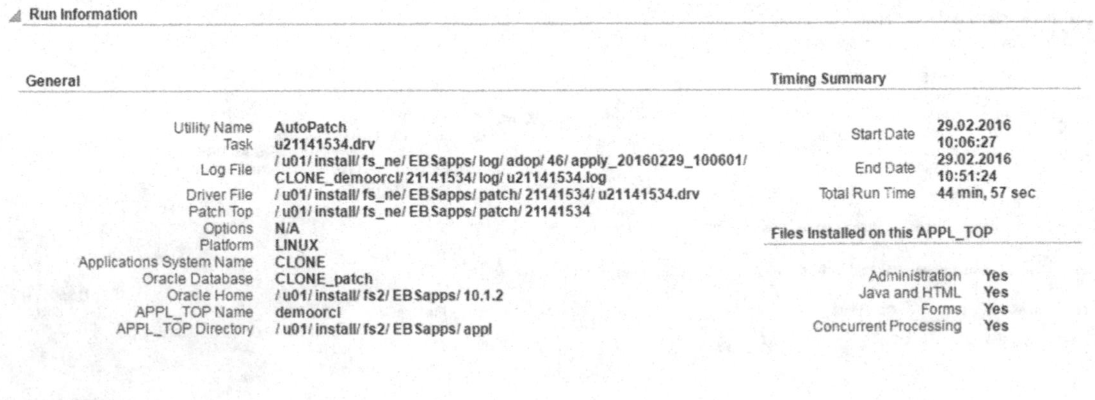

Figure 6-31. Timing summary and general information about the environment

Moreover, you can click some of these task names and open a job timing report, which displays the timing information for every single operation done.

To understand which of the tasks names are clickable and which aren't, just move your mouse on them. If the tasks have job timing reports available, the shape of your mouse pointer indicates that there is a link to click and EBS directs you to the job timing report page for that task.

Figure 6-32 shows a job timing report.

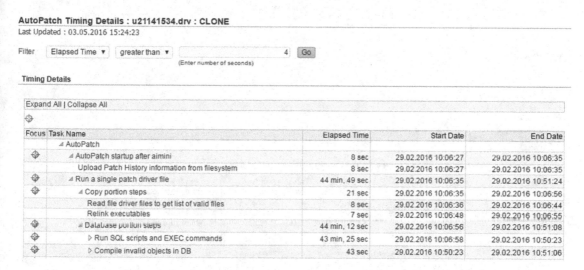

AutoPatch Timing Details : u21141534.drv : CLONE
Last Updated : 03.05.2016 15:24:23

Filter   Elapsed Time ▾   greater than ▾   [4] [Go]
                                             (Enter number of seconds)

Timing Details

Expand All | Collapse All

Focus	Task Name	Elapsed Time	Start Date	End Date
	◢ AutoPatch			
⊕	◢ AutoPatch startup after aimini	8 sec	29.02.2016 10:06:27	29.02.2016 10:06:35
	Upload Patch History information from filesystem	8 sec	29.02.2016 10:06:27	29.02.2016 10:06:35
⊕	◢ Run a single patch driver file	44 min, 49 sec	29.02.2016 10:06:35	29.02.2016 10:51:24
⊕	◢ Copy portion steps	21 sec	29.02.2016 10:06:35	29.02.2016 10:06:56
	Read file driver files to get list of valid files	8 sec	29.02.2016 10:06:36	29.02.2016 10:06:44
	Relink executables	7 sec	29.02.2016 10:06:48	29.02.2016 10:06:55
⊕	◢ Database portion steps	44 min, 12 sec	29.02.2016 10:06:56	29.02.2016 10:51:08
⊕	▷ Run SQL scripts and EXEC commands	43 min, 25 sec	29.02.2016 10:06:58	29.02.2016 10:50:23
⊕	▷ Compile invalid objects in DB	43 sec	29.02.2016 10:50:23	29.02.2016 10:51:06

Figure 6-32. Opening the job timing report of a task

The job timing report is a detailed report that gives information such as the products that the patching action affect, the files that the patching actions are related to, the start and end times of the patching actions, and the elapsed time of each patching action that are done within the scope of the subtask for which you want to get detailed information.

Figure 6-33 shows the job timing report for the subtask named "Running parallel SQL and EXEC commands," which was executed in the scope of applying patch 21141534 by the patch driver named u21141534.drv.

329

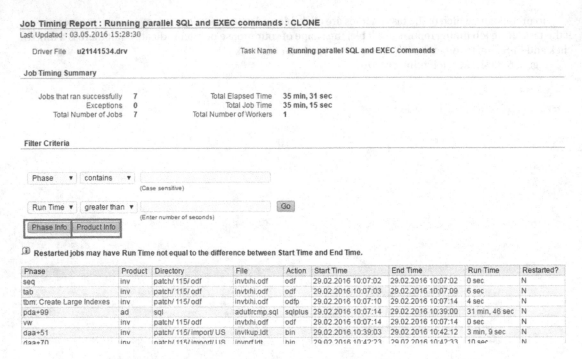

Job Timing Report : Running parallel SQL and EXEC commands : CLONE
Last Updated : 03.05.2016 15:28:30

| Driver File | u21141534.drv | | Task Name | Running parallel SQL and EXEC commands |

Job Timing Summary

Jobs that ran successfully	7	Total Elapsed Time	35 min, 31 sec
Exceptions	0	Total Job Time	35 min, 15 sec
Total Number of Jobs	7	Total Number of Workers	1

Filter Criteria

Phase ▼ contains ▼ [   ]
(Case sensitive)

Run Time ▼ greater than ▼ [   ] Go
(Enter number of seconds)

[Phase Info | Product Info]

ⓘ Restarted jobs may have Run Time not equal to the difference between Start Time and End Time.

Phase	Product	Directory	File	Action	Start Time	End Time	Run Time	Restarted?
seq	inv	patch/ 115/ odf	invtxhi.odf	odf	29.02.2016 10:07:02	29.02.2016 10:07:02	0 sec	N
tab	inv	patch/ 115/ odf	invtxhi.odf	odf	29.02.2016 10:07:03	29.02.2016 10:07:09	6 sec	N
tbm: Create Large Indexes	inv	patch/ 115/ odf	invtxhi.odf	odfp	29.02.2016 10:07:10	29.02.2016 10:07:14	4 sec	N
pda+99	ad	sql	adutlrcmp.sql	sqlplus	29.02.2016 10:07:14	29.02.2016 10:39:00	31 min, 46 sec	N
vw	inv	patch/ 115/ odf	invtxhi.odf	odf	29.02.2016 10:07:14	29.02.2016 10:07:14	0 sec	N
daa+51	inv	patch/ 115/ import/ US	invlkup.ldt	bin	29.02.2016 10:39:03	29.02.2016 10:42:12	3 min, 9 sec	N
daa+70	inv	patch/ 115/ import/ US	invprf.ldt	bin	29.02.2016 10:42:23	29.02.2016 10:42:33	10 sec	N

Figure 6-33. Job timing report for the action "Running parallel SQL and EXEC commands"

The Job Timing Report page gives you filters to narrow the actions that are displayed in this page. In addition, the information about the phase in which the actions are done, as well as the information about the products that the patched files belong, can be gathered using the Phase Info and Product Info buttons just above the action list, as marked with the red rectangles in Figure 6-33.

The Phase button, when clicked, opens the Phase Information page, which presents the general information about the patch that the actions belong to. Information such as the time required to complete the phase, the database processing phase name, the name of the patch driver, the task name, and the number of jobs in the phase are displayed on the Phase Information page.

Figure 6-34 shows an example Phase Information page, which presents the general phase information about the "Running parallel SQL and EXEC commands" patching action.

| Applications Dashboard | Site Map |

Applications System:CLONE > Applied Patches > Patch Details > AutoPatch Timing Details > Job Timing Report >

Phase Information : Running parallel SQL and EXEC commands : CLONE
Last Updated : 03.05.2016 15:32:18
Driver File   u21141534.drv   Task Name   Running parallel SQL and EXEC commands

Phase	Start Time	Elapsed Time	Jobs	Total Job Time	Restarted?	Skipped
seq	29.02.2016 10:07:02	0 sec	1	0 sec	N	0
tab	29.02.2016 10:07:03	6 sec	1	6 sec	N	0
tbm: Create Large Indexes	29.02.2016 10:07:10	4 sec	1	4 sec	N	0
vw	29.02.2016 10:07:14	0 sec	1	0 sec	N	0
pda+99	29.02.2016 10:07:14	31 min, 46 sec	1	31 min, 46 sec	N	0
daa+51	29.02.2016 10:39:03	3 min, 9 sec	1	3 min, 9 sec	N	0
daa+70	29.02.2016 10:42:23	10 sec	1	10 sec	N	0

Figure 6-34. Phase Information page for "Running parallel SQL and EXEC commands"

The Product Info button basically presents the information about the short names of the EBS 12.2 products that are affected by the patch action you are analyzing.

Figure 6-35 shows an example product info page that presents the short name of the products that are affected by the "Running parallel SQL and EXEC commands" patching action.

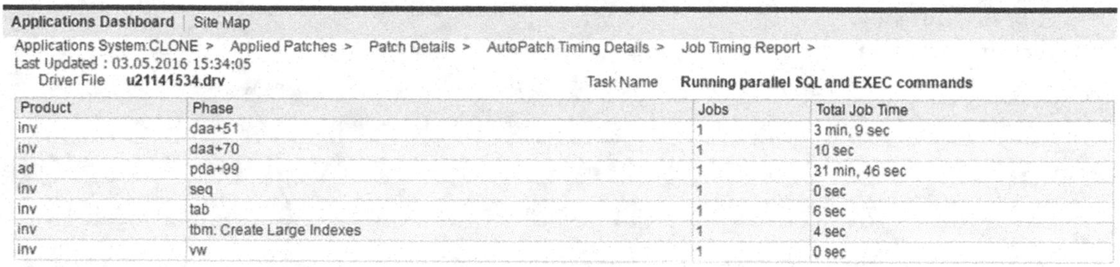

Applications Dashboard	Site Map			

Applications System:CLONE > Applied Patches > Patch Details > AutoPatch Timing Details > Job Timing Report >
Last Updated : 03.05.2016 15:34:05
Driver File **u21141534.drv**   Task Name   **Running parallel SQL and EXEC commands**

Product	Phase	Jobs	Total Job Time
inv	daa+51	1	3 min, 9 sec
inv	daa+70	1	10 sec
ad	pda+99	1	31 min, 46 sec
inv	seq	1	0 sec
inv	tab	1	6 sec
inv	tbm: Create Large Indexes	1	4 sec
inv	vw	1	0 sec

Figure 6-35. *Product information page for "Running parallel SQL and EXEC commands"*

As shown in Figure 6-35, only the products with the short names AD (Applications DBA) and INV (Inventory) are affected by the "Running parallel SQL and EXEC commands" action in this example.

The Files Copied tab, as shown in Figure 6-36, gives you the information about the files copied to your application file system as a result of the patch application.

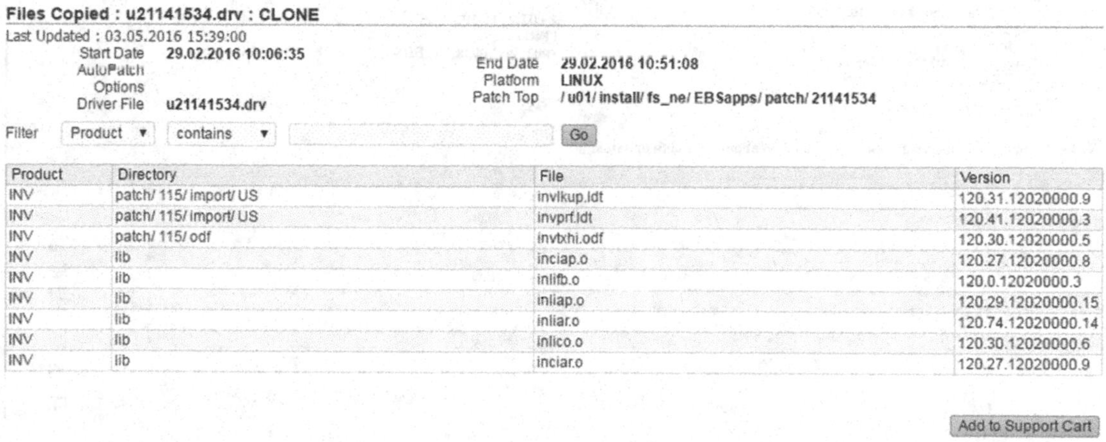

Files Copied : u21141534.drv : CLONE
Last Updated : 03.05.2016 15:39:00
Start Date **29.02.2016 10:06:35**   End Date   **29.02.2016 10:51:08**
AutoPatch   Platform   **LINUX**
Options   Patch Top **/ u01/ install/ fs_ne/ EB Sapps/ patch/ 21141534**
Driver File **u21141534.drv**

Filter | Product ▼ | contains ▼ | | Go |

Product	Directory	File	Version
INV	patch/ 115/ import/ US	invlkup.ldt	120.31.12020000.9
INV	patch/ 115/ import/ US	invprf.ldt	120.41.12020000.3
INV	patch/ 115/ odf	invtxhi.odf	120.30.12020000.5
INV	lib	inciap.o	120.27.12020000.8
INV	lib	inlifb.o	120.0.12020000.3
INV	lib	inliap.o	120.29.12020000.15
INV	lib	inliar.o	120.74.12020000.14
INV	lib	inlico.o	120.30.12020000.6
INV	lib	inciar.o	120.27.12020000.9

Add to Support Cart

Figure 6-36. *Files Copied tab*

The file list provided on the Files Copied tab gives you information about the products that the copied files are used by and the versions of the copied files, as well.

The Bug Fixes tab lists the bugs fixed by the patch you are interested in. Remember, one patch can fix several bugs.

Figure 6-37 shows the Bug Fixes tab displaying the bugs that were fixed by applying patch 21141534.

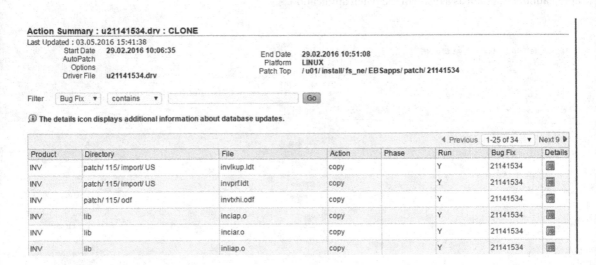

Bug Fixes : u21141534.drv : CLONE

Last Updated : 03.05.2016 15:40:32

Start Date	29.02.2016 10:06:35	End Date	29.02.2016 10:51:08
AutoPatch		Platform	LINUX
Options		Patch Top	/ u01/ install/ fs_ne/ EBSapps/ patch/ 21141534
Driver File	u21141534.drv		

Filter [Bug Fix ▼] [contains ▼] [   ] [Go]

Bug Fix	Product	Applied	Remarks
21141534	inv	Y	
9015477	ad	Y	
17857332	inv	Y	
17910010	bom	Y	
20920029	inv	Y	
9015477	inv	Y	

Figure 6-37. *Bug Fixes tab*

The last tab, Action Summary, displays the files delivered by the patch you are interested in, the directories where the patch files are deployed, the relationship with the files, and the bug fixes and the actions taken by the patch (for example, copy) for deploying the patch files. Figure 6-38 shows the Action Summary tab populated for patch 21141534.

Action Summary : u21141534.drv : CLONE

Last Updated : 03.05.2016 15:41:38

Start Date	29.02.2016 10:06:35	End Date	29.02.2016 10:51:08
AutoPatch		Platform	LINUX
Options		Patch Top	/ u01/ install/ fs_ne/ EBSapps/ patch/ 21141534
Driver File	u21141534.drv		

Filter [Bug Fix ▼] [contains ▼] [   ] [Go]

ⓘ The details icon displays additional information about database updates.

◀ Previous [1-25 of 34 ▼] Next 9 ▶

Product	Directory	File	Action	Phase	Run	Bug Fix	Details
INV	patch/ 115/ import/ US	invlkup.ldt	copy		Y	21141534	🖼
INV	patch/ 115/ import/ US	invprf.ldt	copy		Y	21141534	🖼
INV	patch/ 115/ odf	invtxhi.odf	copy		Y	21141534	🖼
INV	lib	inciap.o	copy		Y	21141534	🖼
INV	lib	inciar.o	copy		Y	21141534	🖼
INV	lib	inliap.o	copy		Y	21141534	🖼

Figure 6-38. *Action Summary tab*

You also have an advanced search option in the top-right corner of the Applied Patches page, as shown in Figure 6-39.

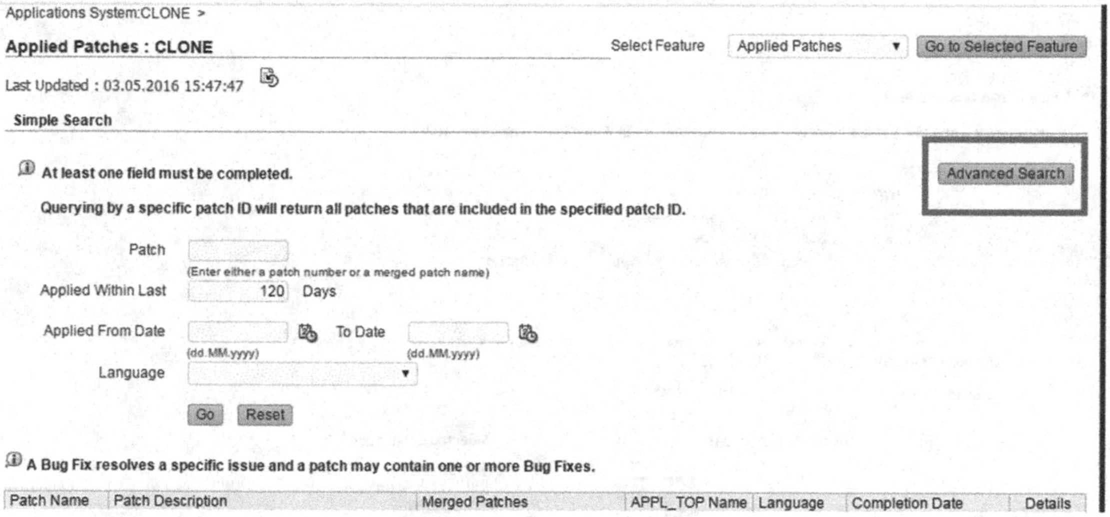

Applications System:CLONE >

Applied Patches : CLONE   Select Feature   Applied Patches   ▼   Go to Selected Feature

Last Updated : 03.05.2016 15:47:47

Simple Search

ⓘ At least one field must be completed.   Advanced Search

   Querying by a specific patch ID will return all patches that are included in the specified patch ID.

         Patch   [   ]
                  (Enter either a patch number or a merged patch name)
Applied Within Last   [120] Days

Applied From Date [   ] 📷   To Date   [   ] 📷
                   (dd.MM.yyyy)   (dd.MM.yyyy)
       Language   [▼]

                  Go   Reset

ⓘ A Bug Fix resolves a specific issue and a patch may contain one or more Bug Fixes.

Patch Name	Patch Description	Merged Patches	APPL_TOP Name	Language	Completion Date	Details

Figure 6-39. *Advanced Search button*

If you click the Advanced Search button, you reach the Advanced Search page, where you can make searches based on different filters, such as the patch languages, applied times, and products, as shown in Figure 6-40.

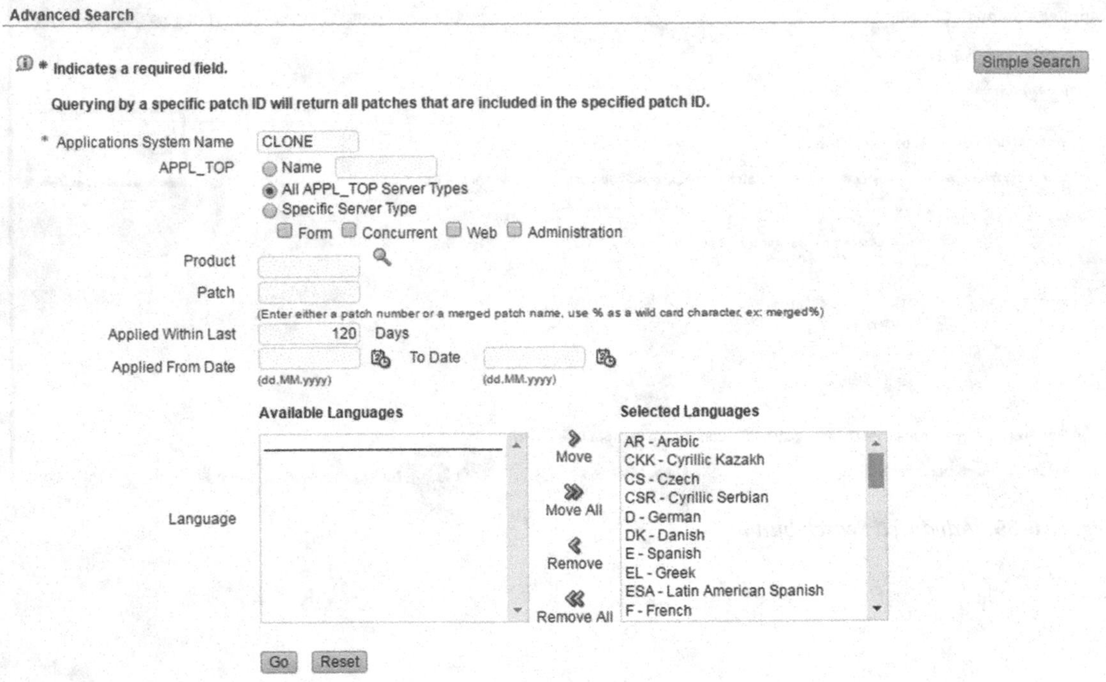

Figure 6-40. *Advanced Search page*

After choosing the necessary filters and clicking the Go button on the Advanced Search page to search for the patches, you can see the output of this search displayed at the bottom of the same page and the Details link displayed in the lines representing the patches that are returned from the patch search.

Figure 6-41 shows an example for the advanced search for patches that affect the "ad" product.

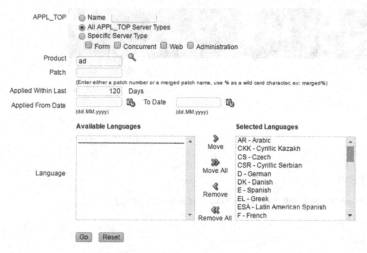

APPL_TOP	○ Name
	● All APPL_TOP Server Types
	○ Specific Server Type
	□ Form □ Concurrent □ Web □ Administration
Product	ad
Patch	
	(Enter either a patch number or a merged patch name, use % as a wild card character, ex: merged%)
Applied Within Last	120 Days
Applied From Date	To Date
	(dd.MM.yyyy) (dd.MM.yyyy)

Available Languages   **Selected Languages**

Move
Move All
Language   Remove
Remove All

AR - Arabic
CKK - Cyrillic Kazakh
CS - Czech
CSR - Cyrillic Serbian
D - German
DK - Danish
E - Spanish
EL - Greek
ESA - Latin American Spanish
F - French

Go   Reset

ⓘ A Bug Fix resolves a specific issue and a patch may contain one or more Bug Fixes.

Patch Name	Patch Description	Merged Patches	APPL_TOP Name	Language	Completion Date	Details
13839844.R12		No	demoorcl	US	29.02.2016 11:46:14	
21141534.C	R.TST1225:CREATE IC AP PROGRAM ENDED WITH WARNING: CANNOT RETRIEVE CCID.	No	demoorcl	US	29.02.2016 11:23:48	
13839836.R12		No	demoorcl	US	29.02.2016 11:15:49	

Figure 6-41. *Advanced search for "ad" patches*

So, the Applied Patches tool is a sophisticated patch reporting utility, as you have seen so far, but it is mostly used in reporting purposes, and it is not the only utility that can be used for analyzing the application of the patches.

The Timing Report is another utility that comes with OAM. Using the Timing Report utility, you can take a detailed look at the job timings to analyze the patching process as a whole, and you also can view the log files produced for the patching work and review all their details using a web interface without logging into the application server.

To reach the Timing Report tool, click the Site Map link located in the top-left corner of the Applied Patches web page.

Figure 6-42 shows the Site Map link in the Applied Patches web page.

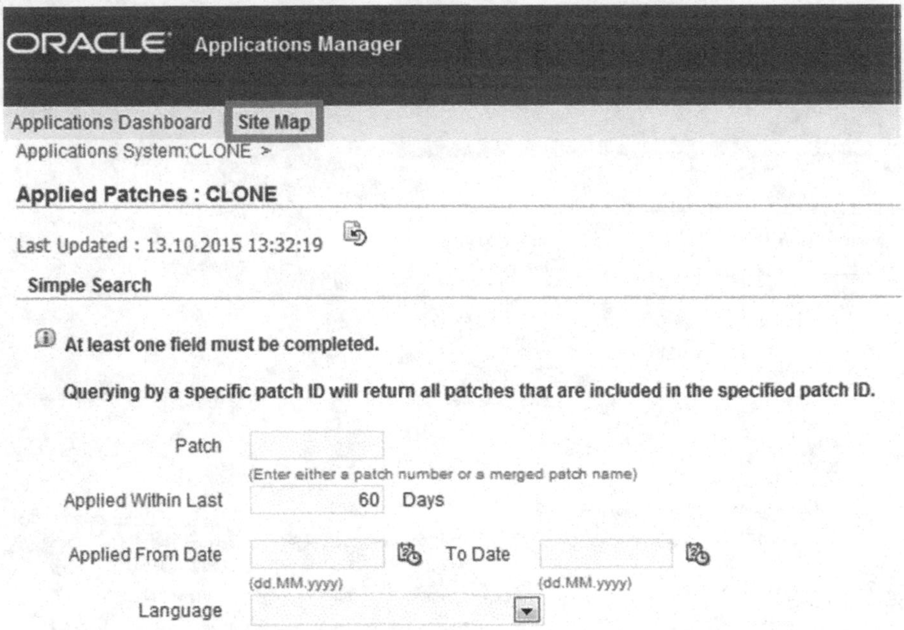

ORACLE Applications Manager

Applications Dashboard | Site Map |
Applications System:CLONE >

Applied Patches : CLONE

Last Updated : 13.10.2015 13:32:19

Simple Search

At least one field must be completed.

Querying by a specific patch ID will return all patches that are included in the specified patch ID.

Patch	
	(Enter either a patch number or a merged patch name)
Applied Within Last	60 Days
Applied From Date	To Date
	(dd.MM.yyyy) (dd.MM.yyyy)
Language	

Figure 6-42. Opening the Timing Report tool

When you reach the Site Map page, you click the Timing Report link located on the Maintenance tab, as shown in Figure 6-43.

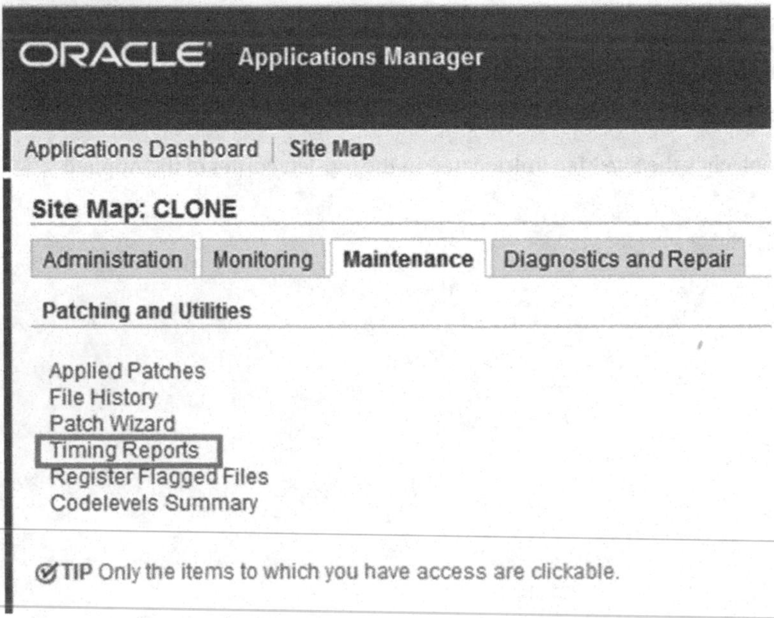

ORACLE Applications Manager

Applications Dashboard | Site Map

Site Map: CLONE

| Administration | Monitoring | **Maintenance** | Diagnostics and Repair |

Patching and Utilities

Applied Patches
File History
Patch Wizard
| Timing Reports |
Register Flagged Files
Codelevels Summary

☑ TIP Only the items to which you have access are clickable.

Figure 6-43. Timing Reports link in the Maintenance tab of the Site Map page

Once you click the Timing Reports link, you reach the Timing Reports page, where you can see the list showing the patching actions that were done in your EBS 12.2 environment. The list is ordered by the start dates of the patching actions, and it also displays the statuses of each action as well as the runtime information and the time for the last update of the information that is displayed. This list in Timing Reports page also gives you an opportunity to check the details as well as check the log files of each operation.

Figure 6-44 shows an example Timing Reports page displaying the patching actions and status of these actions. You can see there are some operations that completed with errors.

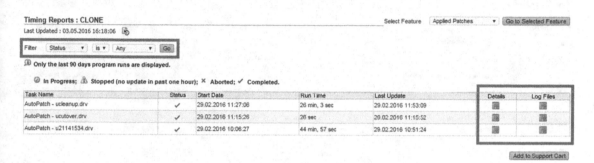

Figure 6-44. Timing Reports page

In Figure 6-44, the status of these problematic operations have an *X*, and the status of the operations that encountered some warnings have a warning sign. The successful operations have a check mark symbol.

So, the contents of the Timing Reports page are pretty self-explanatory, like the contents of almost all the EBS 12.2 web interfaces.

■ **Note** You can use the filters provided on the Timing Reports page to filter the patch tasks that are shown in the list. You can use a filter such as the status filter to list only the completed tasks or to list only the aborted tasks or even to list the tasks in progress.

As indicated with the red rectangle in Figure 6-44, the Timing Reports page gives you the opportunity to check the details and log files of the patching operations.

The links in the red rectangle in Figure 6-44 can be used in this manner.

Figure 6-45 shows the details page that is opened when you click the Details link of a patching operation. As shown in Figure 6-45, the detail page of an operation shows all the necessary information for the patch. It is a detailed overview displaying the elapsed times for the operations as well as the specifics such as the log file path and the driver name.

Timing Details

Expand All | Collapse All

Focus	Task Name	Elapsed Time	Start Date	End Date
	◢ AutoPatch			
	◢ AutoPatch startup after aimini	8 sec	29.02.2016 10:06:27	29.02.2016 10:06:35
	Upload Patch History information from filesystem	8 sec	29.02.2016 10:06:27	29.02.2016 10:06:35
	◢ Run a single patch driver file	44 min, 49 sec	29.02.2016 10:06:35	29.02.2016 10:51:24
	◢ Copy portion steps	21 sec	29.02.2016 10:06:35	29.02.2016 10:06:56
	Read file driver files to get list of valid files	8 sec	29.02.2016 10:06:36	29.02.2016 10:06:44
	Relink executables	7 sec	29.02.2016 10:06:48	29.02.2016 10:06:55
	▷ Database portion steps	44 min, 12 sec	29.02.2016 10:06:56	29.02.2016 10:51:08
	▷ Steps after generate portion	16 sec	29.02.2016 10:51:08	29.02.2016 10:51:24

◢ **Run Information**

General

Utility Name	AutoPatch
Task	u21141534.drv
Log File	/ u01/ install/ fs_ne/ EBSapps/ log/ adop/ 46/ apply_20160229_100601/ CLONE_demoorcl/ 21141534/ log/ u21141534.log
Driver File	/ u01/ install/ fs_ne/ EBSapps/ patch/ 21141534/ u21141534.drv
Patch Top	/ u01/ install/ fs_ne/ EBSapps/ patch/ 21141534
Options	N/A
Platform	LINUX
Applications System Name	CLONE
Oracle Database	CLONE_patch
Oracle Home	/ u01/ install/ fs2/ EBSapps/ 10.1.2
APPL_TOP Name	demoorcl
APPL_TOP Directory	/ u01/ install/ fs2/ EBSapps/ appl

Timing Summary

Start Date	29.02.2016 10:06:27
End Date	29.02.2016 10:51:24
Total Run Time	44 min, 57 sec

Files Installed on this APPL_TOP

Administration	Yes
Java and HTML	Yes
Forms	Yes
Concurrent Processing	Yes

Figure 6-45. *Details page*

■ **Note** These patch screens in EBS 12.2 are much more useful than they were in earlier releases. This is because in EBS 12.2 the patches are mostly applied online, and thus these screens, providing easy access to the patching details and logs, are accessible all the time.

Figure 6-46 shows the View Log Files page that is opened when you click the Log File icon for the patch task that you want to analyze.

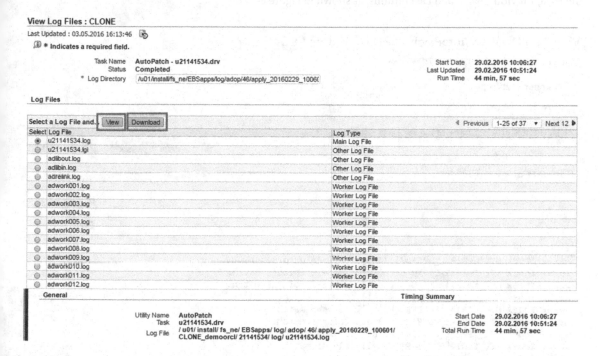

Figure 6-46. *View Log Files page*

The View Log Files page lists all the log files produced for all the subtasks of the patching tasks and gives you an opportunity to view these log files in your browser and to download these log files to your client machine. Viewing and downloading these log files can be done using the View and Download buttons, as marked with the rectangles in Figure 6-46.

When you select a log file and click the View button, the log file that you have selected is displayed in your browser. EBS calls this kind of page a View Log Details page, where it divides the log file into pages and displays the log files page by page.

You can configure the number of lines per pages using the text box "Number of lines per page," jump to a specific page using the text box "View specific page number," and navigate in the pages of the log file using the First, Previous, Next, and Last buttons, as shown in Figure 6-47.

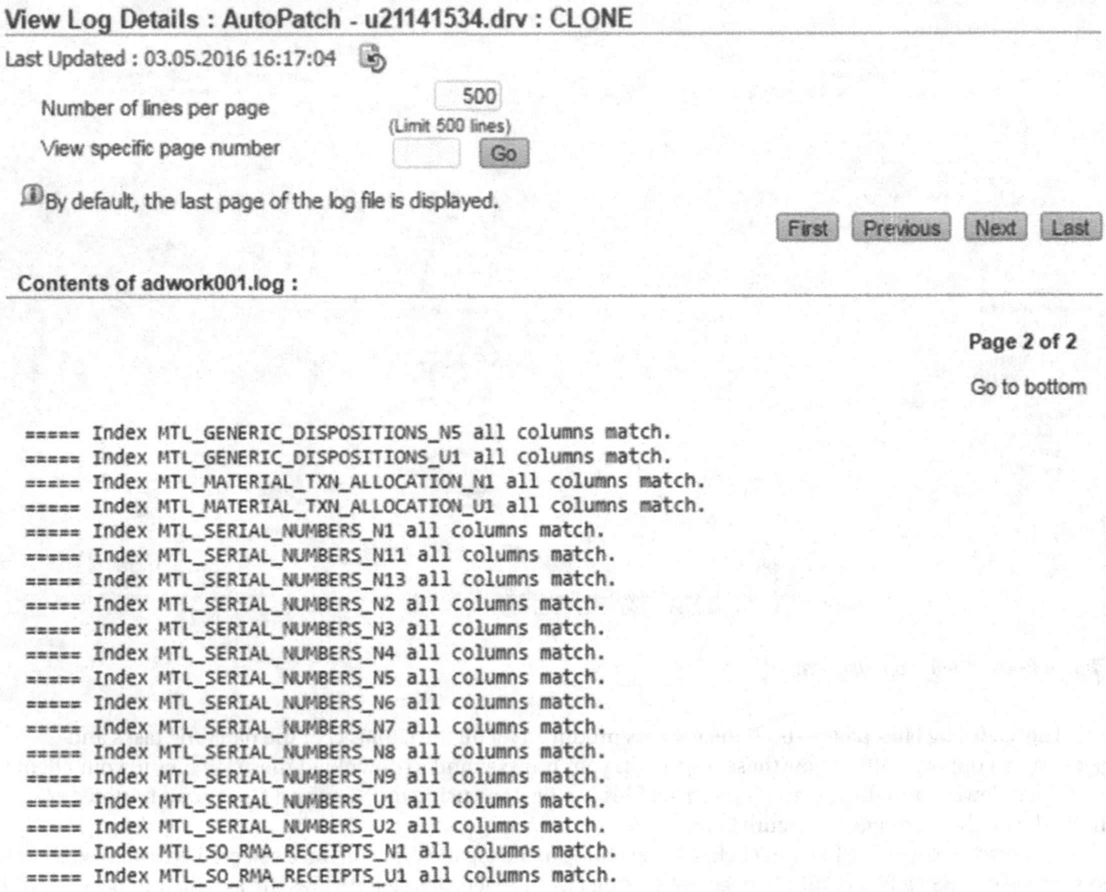

View Log Details : AutoPatch - u21141534.drv : CLONE

Last Updated : 03.05.2016 16:17:04

Number of lines per page   500
                          (Limit 500 lines)
View specific page number   [   ] Go

By default, the last page of the log file is displayed.

[First] [Previous] [Next] [Last]

Contents of adwork001.log :

Page 2 of 2

Go to bottom

```
===== Index MTL_GENERIC_DISPOSITIONS_N5 all columns match.
===== Index MTL_GENERIC_DISPOSITIONS_U1 all columns match.
===== Index MTL_MATERIAL_TXN_ALLOCATION_N1 all columns match.
===== Index MTL_MATERIAL_TXN_ALLOCATION_U1 all columns match.
===== Index MTL_SERIAL_NUMBERS_N1 all columns match.
===== Index MTL_SERIAL_NUMBERS_N11 all columns match.
===== Index MTL_SERIAL_NUMBERS_N13 all columns match.
===== Index MTL_SERIAL_NUMBERS_N2 all columns match.
===== Index MTL_SERIAL_NUMBERS_N3 all columns match.
===== Index MTL_SERIAL_NUMBERS_N4 all columns match.
===== Index MTL_SERIAL_NUMBERS_N5 all columns match.
===== Index MTL_SERIAL_NUMBERS_N6 all columns match.
===== Index MTL_SERIAL_NUMBERS_N7 all columns match.
===== Index MTL_SERIAL_NUMBERS_N8 all columns match.
===== Index MTL_SERIAL_NUMBERS_N9 all columns match.
===== Index MTL_SERIAL_NUMBERS_U1 all columns match.
===== Index MTL_SERIAL_NUMBERS_U2 all columns match.
===== Index MTL_SO_RMA_RECEIPTS_N1 all columns match.
===== Index MTL_SO_RMA_RECEIPTS_U1 all columns match.
```

Figure 6-47. *Viewing the log files in a browser*

Figure 6-47 shows the View Log Details page where you can view the log file of a patch subtask in your browser.

Alternatively, rather than viewing these log files in your browser, you can download them onto your client machines and analyze them using your favorite text editor.

Figure 6-48 shows how to use the Download button to download the log file of a patch task.

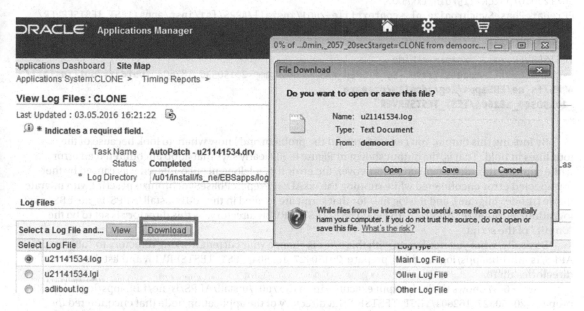

Figure 6-48. *Downloading the log files*

Well, you have seen the abilities you have when you use the patch reporting tools to analyze the patches that are applied or that are being applied to your EBS 12.2 system. So far, we gave a general overview about some patch reporting utilities and showed you all the practical OAM pages that can be used for patch reporting purposes. Using this information, you can get started with patch reporting and discover the details yourself. Any time you need extra information that you can't find here, you can consult the "EBS 12.2 Maintenance Guide" available at http://docs.oracle.com.

Continuing with the adop-related logs, the logs of the scripts that are executed by adop, and an analysis of these logs, the adop tool reports the place where you need to look in order to analyze a problem.

To explain how the analysis for adop errors should be done in EBS 12.2, we will present a real-life scenario. In this manner, starting from Listing 6-36 to 6-44, you will see a real adop problem, take a look at the analysis and diagnostics that can be done for that problem, and see the solution that we applied for that problem.

Listing 6-36 represents an example of the output that is produced by adop after stopping because of an error it encountered while executing the prepare phase (adop phase=prepare).

Listing 6-36. adop Command Output, Showing the Error and the Log File Directory

```
--------------------
Lines #(419-421):
TIME    : Mon May 30 16:38:12 2015
FUNCTION: main::migrateCloneComponentApply [ Level 1 ]
ERRORMSG: /u01/install/APPS/fs1/EBSapps/comn/adopclone_TESTSERVER/bin/adclone.pl did not go
through successfully.
-------------------------------------
```

In the adop log it first had its unexpected error while running
txkADOPPreparePhaseSynchronize.pl:
```
----------------
```

```
   [UNEXPECTED]Error occurred while executing "perl /u01/install/APPS/fs1/EBSapps/appl/
ad/12.0.0/patch/115/bin/txkADO
PPreparePhaseSynchronize.pl -contextfile=/u01/install/APPS/fs1/inst/apps/TEST_TESTSERVER/
appl/admin/IKYSDEV_T1VSTEBSAPP01.
xml -patchcontextfile=/u01/install/APPS/fs2/inst/apps/TEST_TESTSERVER/appl/admin/TEST_
TESTSERVER.xml -promptmsg=hide
 -console=off -mode=migrate -sessionid-=39 -timestamp=20150530_182604 -outdir=/u01/install/
APPS/fs_ne/EBSapps/log/adop/39/prepare
_20150540_182604/TEST_TESTSERVER"
-------------------------
```

By looking this output, you can understand the problem and know where to look because of the four lines in bold. That is, the output shown in Figure 6-33 clearly says that adop encountered an error while running the adclone.pl script. Moreover, the error that adclone.pl encountered was caused by the unexpected error encountered while running the txkADOPPreparePhaseSynchronize.pl script with migrate mode (mode=migrate), and the log files for that script are located in the /u01/install/APPS/fs_ne/EBSapps/log/adop/39/prepare_20150427_162604/TEST_TESTSERVER directory, as this directory is set to be the "outdir" of the script.

Basically, what you need to do with this error is change your current working directory to /u01/install/APPS/fs_ne/EBSapps/log/adop/39/prepare_20150427_162604/TEST_TESTSERVER and list the files and directories there.

Listing 6-37 shows the ls –l output executed from the /u01/install/APPS/fs_ne/EBSapps/log/adop/39/prepare_20150427_162604/TEST_TESTSERVER directory of the application node that encountered the problem described in Listing 6-36.

Listing 6-37. ls –l Command Output for Listing the Contents of the Output Directory Pointed at by adop

```
-rw-r--r--. 1 applmgr dba 1204 May 30 2015 adConfigChanges.log
-rw-r--r--. 1 applmgr dba 305145 May 30 2015 adconfig.log
-rw-r--r--. 1 applmgr dba 11444 May 30 2015 adzdshowlog_cleanup.out
-rw-r--r--. 1 applmgr dba 23852 May 30 2015 adzdshowlog.out
-rw-r--r--. 1 applmgr dba 1407 May 30 2015 adzdshowts.out
..
...
..
drwxr-xr-x. 7 applmgr dba 4096 May 30 2015 TXK_SYNC_migrate_Sat_May_30_16_35_11_2015
drwxr-xr-x. 2 applmgr dba 4096 May 30 2015 TXK_SYNC_update_Sat_May_30_16_35_11_2015
```

As stated, the txkADOPPreparePhaseSynchronize.pl script was executed by adop in migrate mode (mode=migrate), so you change your directory to TXK_SYNC_migrate_Sat_May_30_16_35_11_2015, which is shown in bold in Listing 6-37.

Listing 6-38 shows the ls –l output executed from the TXK_SYNC_migrate_Sat_May_30_16_35_11_2015 directory.

Listing 6-38. - ls –l Command Output for Listing the Contents of the Directory TXK_SYNC_migrate_Sat_May_30_16_35_11_2015

```
-rw-r--r--. 1 applmgr dba 175 May 30 2015 txkADOPCustomSyncUp.log
-rw-r--r--. 1 applmgr dba 1654 May 30 2015
txkADOPPreparePhaseSynchronize_Sat_May_30_16_35_11_2015.log
drwxr-xr-x. 3 applmgr dba 4096 May 30 2015 wlsConfig_apply
drwxr-xr-x. 3 applmgr dba 4096 May 30 2015 wlsConfig_stage
```

As you can see in Listing 6-36, the failed script was txkADOPPreparePhaseSynchronize.pl, so the log file that you need to analyze in this case is txkADOPPreparePhaseSynchronize_Sat_May_30_16_35_11_2015.log, as its name starts exactly with the same string as the failed script name (txkADOPPreparePhaseSynchronize).

After analyzing the txkADOPPreparePhaseSynchronize_Sat_May_30_16_35_11_2015.log, you can see that the next thing to look at is a log file located in the /u01/install/APPS/fs_ne/EBSapps/log/adop/39/prepare_20150530_163504/TEST_TESTSERVER/TXK_SYNC_migrate_Sat_May_30_16_35_11_2015/ohsConfig_apply directory.

Listing 6-39 shows the error lines in txkADOPPreparePhaseSynchronize_Sat_May_30_16_35_11_2015.log. The lines in bold say the log files for the failing commands are located in the /u01/install/APPS/fs_ne/EBSapps/log/adop/39/prepare_20150530_163504/TEST_TESTSERVER/TXK_SYNC_migrate_Sat_May_30_16_35_11_2015/ohsConfig_apply directory and the problem was encountered while running adclone.pl.

Listing 6-39. The Errors in TXK_SYNC_migrate_Sat_May_30_16_35_11_2015

```
/u01/install/APPS/fs1/EBSapps/comn/adopclone_TESTSERVER/bin/adclone.pl did not go through
successfully.
LOG DIRECTORY: /u01/install/APPS/fs_ne/EBSapps/log/adop/39/prepare_20150530_163511/TEST_
TESTSERVER/TXK_SYNC_migrate_Sat_May_30_16_35_11_2015/ohsConfig_apply
*******FATAL ERROR*******
PROGRAM : (/u01/install/APPS/fs1/EBSapps/appl/ad/12.0.0/patch/115/bin/
txkADOPPreparePhaseSynchronize.pl)
FUNCTION: main::migrateCloneComponentApply [ Level 1 ]
ERRORMSG: /u01/install/APPS/fs1/EBSapps/comn/adopclone_TESTSERVER/bin/adclone.pl did not go
through successfully.
```

After analyzing the txkADOPPreparePhaseSynchronize_Sat_May_30_16_35_11_2015.log file, you change your current working directory to /u01/install/APPS/fs_ne/EBSapps/log/adop/39/prepare_20150530_163511/TEST_TESTSERVER/TXK_SYNC_migrate_Sat_May_30_16_35_11_2015/ohsConfig_apply and use an ls command to list the files there.

Listing 6-40 show the ls –l command executed from the ohsConfig_apply directory.

Listing 6-40. – ls –l Command Output Showing the File in ohsConfig_apply for the Failed adop prepare Command

```
-rw-r--r--. 1 applmgr dba 2842 May 30 2015 FSCloneApplyAppsTier_07081115.log
drwxr-xr-x. 3 applmgr dba 4096 May 30  2015 ohsT2Papply
```

At this point, you open FSCloneApplyAppsTier_07081115.log as it is the first log file that you see in the ohsConfig_apply directory (considering ohsT2PApply is a directory).

In FSCloneApplyAppsTier_07081115.log, you see that the errors were encountered when running adadminsrvctl.sh to start the WebLogic admin server from the patch file system.

Listing 6-41 shows the important part of FSCloneApplyAppsTier_07081115.log that gives you the information about the failing script and the log file path for that script.

Listing 6-41. A Snippet of FSCloneApplyAppsTier_07081115.log Showing Which File to Analyze Next

```
Obfuscated Password log written to /u01/install/APPS/fs1/EBSapps/comn/adopclone_TESTSERVER/
FMW/obfuscatedPassword_05301637.log
START: Checking if AdminServer is Up and Running
AdminServer is currently not running.
AdminServer is not UP. Starting UP AdminServer...
Running...../u01/install/APPS/fs2/inst/apps/TEST_TESTSERVER/admin/scripts/adadminsrvctl.sh
start -nopromptmsg forcepatchfs
```

```
You are running adadminsrvctl.sh version 120.10.12020000.9
Starting WLS Admin Server...
Refer /u01/install/APPS/fs2/inst/apps/TEST_TESTSERVER/logs/appl/admin/log/adadminsrvctl.txt
for details
```
adadminsrvctl.sh: exiting with status 1
adadminsrvctl.sh: check the logfile /u01/install/APPS/fs2/inst/apps/TEST_TESTSERVER/logs/
appl/admin/log/adadminsrvctl.txt for more information ...

So, the problem is in adadminsrvctl.sh, and the log file /u01/install/APPS/fs2/inst/apps/TEST_TESTSERVER/logs/appl/admin/log/adadminsrvctl.txt should be analyzed to see the cause of the error.

The log file adadminsrvctl.txt is your last resort for your diagnostic work, as it is the script that actually fails in the back end and causes the adop prepare phase to complete with errors.

Listing 6-42 shows a snippet from adadminsrvctl.txt that clearly shows the actual error, in other words, the low level that caused the adop prepare phase to fail.

Listing 6-42. A Snippet from the adadminsrvctl.txt File Showing Which File the Has Low Level Errors

```
Validated the passed arguments for the option ebs-nmstart-adminsrv
Checking if the Admin Server is already up.
The Admin Server is not already up.
Checking if the Node Manager is already up..
Traceback (innermost last):
  File "<string>", line 1, in ?
  File "<iostream>", line 123, in nmConnect
  File "<iostream>", line 653, in raiseWLSTException
WLSTException: Error occured while performing nmConnect : Cannot connect to Node Manager. :
Unexpected end of stream
Use dumpStack() to view the full stacktrace

Connecting to Node Manager ...

ERROR: Cannot connect to Node Manager. Check if port 5557 is correct
ERROR: Unable to connect to the Node Manager. The Admin Server cannot be started up.
Successfully disconnected from Node Manager.
```

At this point, your diagnostic work is finished, as you have gathered the information representing the low level error that caused the adop prepare phase to complete with errors.

At this point, you can connect to Oracle Support and search for error strings such as "File <iostream>, line 123, in nmConnect" and "File <iostream>, line 653, in raiseWLSTException." Then check the related documents and take the appropriate actions.

If these errors are documented in Oracle Support, then your job is easy. You just find the related document by making an Oracle Support search for the error messages and apply the instructions documented by Oracle Support to fix the issue.

However, if the error is not a documented one, then you have two options. The first option is to make an analysis yourself, and the second option is to open an Oracle Support service request for the issue and wait for an action plan from the Oracle Support engineers.

For the error shown in the example, we analyzed the code of the adadminsrvctl.sh script and found the script was executed with the nopromptmsg argument, so the admin password should be supplied to it.

Listing 6-43 shows the if statement used in adadminsrvctl.sh to read the WebLogic admin password when executed with the nopromptmsg argument.

Listing 6-43. Portion of adadminsrvctl.sh Code That Reads the WebLogic Password if nopromptmsg Argument Is Used

```
if [ "$promptmsg" = "-nopromptmsg" ]; then
    read wlspass
    read appspass
```

So, as adop runs the command /u01/install/APPS/fs2/inst/apps/TEST _TESTSERVER/admin/scripts/adadminsrvctl.sh start -nopromptmsg forcepatchfs, it should supply the Weblogic Server admin password. At this point, we thought that the problem might be related to the password that is supplied to adadminsrvctl.sh by adop.

Moreover, as we could not see the password in the logs, we thought that the password that adop supplied to the adadminsrvctl.s might be wrong.

In addition, the following line

```
Obfuscated Password log written to /u01/install/APPS/fs1/EBSapps/comn/adopclone_TESTSERVER/
FMW/obfuscatedPassword_05301637.log
```

was drawing our attention.

So, the cause is probably a password corruption problem.

However, obfuscatedPassword_0501637.log did not give us any clues, as there was only a single line in it. That is, only the string "Object persisted successfully" was written in the obfuscatedPassword log file.

At this point, we decided to run the failing adadminsrvctl.sh manually to see whether it could start the admin server and Node Manager without any problems.

We ran the command ./u01/install/APPS/fs2/inst/apps/TEST_TESTSERVER/admin/scripts/adadminsrvctl.sh start -nopromptmsg forcepatchfs and supplied the password when asked by adadminsrvctl.sh. The result was success. adadminsrvctl.sh could start the admin server and Node Manager when invoked manually and when supplied with passwords manually.

At this point, we were pretty sure that the problem was password corruption, so we updated the password that was supplied to adadminsrvctl.sh using the standard password change method described next and tried the adop phase=prepare command again. This time, the command completed successfully, and the issue got resolved.

Listing 6-44 gives the necessary instructions for changing the Node Manager credentials (username and password) using the Weblogic Console.

Listing 6-44. Changing Node Manager credentials

1. Log in to the WebLogic console.

2. Click the domain name in the domain tree.

3. Choose the Security tab.

4. Click Lock & Edit.

5. Change the Node Manager credentials located under Advanced to match the WebLogic admin user and password that are used while logging in to the WebLogic console.

6. Activate the changes.

The analysis and the diagnostics are done using the log files that adop commands report. Sometimes the log files point to other log files, and sometimes there should be some insight to sense the problem while analyzing logs written in these log files. Curiosity is needed to solve the problem yourself, but it is good to know that Oracle Support is there to support you.

To summarize, you read the lines in the adop outputs and logs, read script logs if stated in the adop log files, run the scripts by taking the risk to see the error or to diagnose the script causing the error more closely, and apply the fix if you can find it using this analysis. The fix may be in Oracle Support documents, or it may be in your mind, but even if the fix is not anywhere, you can always create Oracle Support service request to get help from a support engineer.

So, you have seen a real-life problem and analysis to deal with that problem. Honestly, the way to deal the adop problems is not so different than we explained in the example scenario. It is manual.

However, there are still some adop tools that can be useful while dealing the adop problems. For example, the adop –status command can be used to get the adop phase information of the EBS 12.2 environment. In addition, when it is executed with the –detail argument, it gives you a detailed view of the adop phase information.

Listing 6-45 shows the execution and output of the adop –status –detail command in an EBS 12.2 environment where the online patching cycle was aborted after the apply phase.

Listing 6-45. adop –status –detail and Its Output

```
[applmgr@somehost]$ ./u01/install/APPS/EBSapps run
[applmgr@somehost ~]$ adop -status -detail
Enter the APPS password:

Current Patching Session ID: 36
Node Name        Node
Type        Phase              Status          Started                    Finished
                 Elapsed
--------------- --------------- --------------- --------------- ----------------------------
-- ----------------------------- ------------
somehost         master          PREPARE         SESSION ABORTED            18-SEP-15 15:42:51
+03:00      21-SEP-15 16:19:07 +03:00                            72:36:16
                                 APPLY           SESSION ABORTED            21-SEP-15 16:21:50
+03:00      22-SEP-15 13:11:52 +03:00                            20:50:02
                                 FINALIZE        SESSION ABORTED
                                 CUTOVER         SESSION ABORTED
                                 CLEANUP         NOT STARTED
File System Synchronization Used in this Patching Cycle: Light
INFORMATION: Patching cycle aborted, so fs_clone will run automatically on somehost node in
prepare phase of next patching cycle.
Generating full ADOP Status Report at location: /u01/install/fs_ne/EBSapps/log/status_
20151015_163502/adzdshowstatus.out
Please wait...
Done...!
```

Moreover, the adoreports utility can be used to complete actions related to EBS 12.2 patching. The adoreports utility is based on patching, but you can even check the table details or the index details in an EBS 12.2 environment using this tool. The adoreports utility generates several reports that can be used for diagnosing adop issues or simply gaining knowledge about the status of your EBS 12.2 systems.

Listing 6-46 shows an example usage of adoreports, where you check the indexes on the FND_NODES table.

Listing 6-46. adopreports Example

```
Listing 6-[applmgr@somehost]$ ./u01/install/APPS/EBSapps run
[applmgr@somehost]$ adopreports
Enter the APPS username: apps
Enter the APPS Password:

    Online Patching Diagnostic Reports Main Menu
    --------------------------------------------
    1.  Run edition reports
    2.  Patch edition reports
    3.  Other generic reports
    4.  Exit
    Enter your choice [4]: 3

    Other Generic Reports Sub Menu
    ------------------------------

    1.  Editions summary
    2.  Editioned objects summary
    3.  Free space in important tablespaces
    4.  Status of critical AD_ZD objects
    5.  Actual objects in current edition
    6.  Objects dependencies
    7.  Objects dependency tree
    8.  Editioning views column mappings
    9.  Index details for a table
    10. Inherited objects in the current edition
    11. All log messages
    12. Materialized view details
    13. Database sessions by edition
    14. Table details (Synonyms, EV, etc.)
    15. Count and status of DDL execution by phase
    16. Back to main menu

    Enter your choice [16]: 9
    Enter the object name : FND_NODES


================================================================================
================================================================================
=  Indexes for FND_NODES
================================================================================

OWNER           INDEX_NAME                   COL# COLUMN_NAME                    COLUMN_EXPRESSION
--------------- ---------------------------- ---- ------------------------------ ---------
--------------------------------------------------
APPLSYS         FND_NODES_N1                    1 NODE_ID
APPLSYS         FND_NODES_U1                    1 NODE_NAME
Above report is captured in file : /u01/install/APPSDEVEL/fs2/EBSapps/appl/admin/TEST/out/
adzdshowindex.out
```

The last utility that we want to explain is the adop Log File Scanner utility (adopscanlog). adopscanlog can be used to scan the adop log files and save you from checking all the log files to catch the error and warnings in case of a patch error.

adopscanlog is invoked by executing the adopscanlog command after setting the run edition environment. When executed without any parameters, adscanlog scans all the directories of the latest adop session and displays the errors if it can find any in the related log files.

When executed with the latest parameters (adopscanlog –latest=yes), adopscanlog scans the directories related to the latest run of adop in the latest session. When executed with the –latest and –phases parameters (adopscanlog -latest=yes -phase=apply), the adopscanlog utility scans all the log files located in the latest run of the phase specified with the –phases argument, and the parameter –session_id can be used to tell adopscanlog to scan all the log directories for a given session (session_id). adopscanlog –help can be used to display the help output, which can be thought as a manual for the supported adopscanlog parameters.

Figure 6-49 shows the output of adopscanlog. As you can see, adopscanlog is a sophisticated utility with many parameters that affect the output it generates.

```
[applmgr@ somehost ~]$ adopscanlog -help

ADOP Log File Scanner
---------------------
Usage:
  adopscanlog [<option_1> <option_2> ... <option_N>]
Examples:
  adopscanlog
  adopscanlog [session_id=<session_id>] [phase=<phase>] [loglevel=<loglevel>] [context=<# lines>]
Options:
  session_id - scans logs pertaining to a particular session ID, [default: latest]
               Note: Supplying session_id=0, results in scanning all the adop log files
                     under base log directory ($NE_BASE/EBSapps/log/adop)
  phase      - scans logs pertaining to a particular phase, [default: all]
  loglevel   - minimum log level to search (statement|procedure|event|warning|error|unexpected|generic), [default: error]
  latest     - scans logs of latest ADOP run only, [default: no]
  scan_dir   - specifies directory to scan
  rules      - specifies XML rules file including path
  context    - number of lines of output context for each match, [default: 4]
  help       - displays this help screen
```

Figure 6-49. *adopscanlog help*

In addition to reporting the errors and warnings, adopscanlog also displays diagnostic messages that help you identify the underlying problems easily.

Listing 6-47 shows an adopscanlog execution for diagnosing a failed apply phase.

Listing 6-47. Output of adopscanlog Produced for a Failed Apply Phase

```
/u01/install/APPS/EBSapps.env run
adopscanlog -latest=yes -phase=apply

Scanning /u01/install/APPS/fs_ne/EBSapps/log/adop/15/ directory ...
/u01/install/APPS/fs_ne/EBSapps/log/adop/15/apply_20140713_040605/ORATEST_somehost/18733711/log/adwork003.log:
------------------------------------------------------------------------------------------
----------------------------
Lines #(1100-1104):
Updating task with status 1
AD Worker error:
The utility FndXdfCmp returned error for the above task.
Lines #(1103-1107):
The utility FndXdfCmp returned error for the above task.
```

```
AD Worker error:
The above program failed.  See the error messages listed
above, if any, or see the log and output files for the program.
/u01/install/APPS/fs_ne/EBSapps/log/adop/15/apply_20140713_040605/ORATEST_somehost/18733711/
log/u18733711.log:
--------------------------------------------------------------------------------
---------------------------
Lines #(5056-5060):
   8 running, 65 ready to run and 304 waiting.
   FAILED: file cle_f220_ext_flex_edition_gt.xdf on worker  3 for product cle username APPS.
Time is: Sun Jul 13 2014 04:10:16
```

As shown in Listing 6-47, adopscanlog displays the names of the log files it has analyzed, the lines in which the errors are seen, the failed patching work, and even the adpatch work number that has failed. By just executing the adopscanlog after a failed session, you can see all the necessary information, and if this information is enough for finding the solution, you don't even need to check any log file or script code manually.

In Listing 6-47, you see that adpatch worker 3 failed while propagating object definitions residing in the cle_f220_ext_flex_edition_gt.xdf file.

As the name of the file starts with CLE, you know it is a localization-related file. At this point, you can make an Oracle Support search for the file name cle_f220_ext_flex_edition_gt.xdf to see whether that error is documented. If you can't find anything in the Oracle Support search, you can check the log file for adpatch worker number 3 and see why it failed in processing cle_f220_ext_flex_edition_gt.xdf.

The log file of adpatch worker number 3 is also displayed in the adopscanlog output given in Listing 6-48 (/u01/install/APPS/fs_ne/EBSapps/log/adop/15/apply_20140713_040605/ORATEST_somehost/18733711/log/adwork003.log).

Listing 6-48 shows the error lines in the adpatch worker's log file. As shown in Listing 6-48, an ORA-955 error was encountered while creating the sequence named CLE_F220_EXT_FLEX_EDITION_GT_S.

Listing 6-48. The Errors in adworker's Log

```
Applying XDF file : /u01/install/APPS/fs2/EBSapps/appl/cle/12.0.0/patch/115/xdf/cle_f220_
ext_flex_edition_gt.xdf
================================================================================

Creating the Sequence in schema CLE.
CREATE SEQUENCE  "CLE"."CLE_F220_EXT_FLEX_EDITION_GT_S"  MINVALUE 1 MAXVALUE
9999999999999999999999999999 INCREMENT BY 1 START WITH 2313 CACHE 20 NOORDER  NOCYCLE
Start time for statement above is Sun Jul 13 04:10:16 EDT 2014
Error Message is ORA-00955: name is already used by an existing object

Unable to create sequence CLE_F220_EXT_FLEX_EDITION_GT_S due to the error ORA-955
```

The corrective action is to connect to the EBS 12.2 database and find the description of the sequence named CLE_F220_EXT_FLEX_EDITION_GT_S. If the definition of this sequence is the same as the definition in adpatch worker 3's log, then you can safely drop this sequence and restart patching.

■ **Note**   These types of problems are normally not seen in EBS application patches, but unfortunately when it comes to the localization patches, sometimes these types of obvious problems may be encountered.

Summary

So, you have reached the end of this long chapter! In it, we explained all the EBS 12.2 patching-related topics that you will need.

In this chapter, you started by making a deep dive into EBS 12.2 patching. We went beyond the things explained in Chapter 5 while explaining the adop utility, and we explained the execution of the patching cycle deeply by taking a closer look. Also, we explained topics such as different patching modes supported in EBS 12.2, merging the applications patches, and applying patches in multinode environments. In addition, we covered topics like applying localization patches and adding additional languages in this chapter. Before finishing the chapter, we also explained reporting and diagnosing the patching process in EBS 12.2. These are all the topics needed by apps DBAs to manage the process in EBS 12.2.

CHAPTER 7

■ ■ ■

Managing FMW/WebLogic

In this chapter, we will introduce Oracle Fusion Middleware (FMW). We will explain the components and services provided by FMW and explain how to use the FMW components used in EBS 12.2. Furthermore, we will cover the advantages of using FMW in EBS 12.2 and go into the details of managing, tuning, diagnosing, and patching the FMW environment in EBS 12.2.

Introduction to Fusion Middleware in EBS 12.2

Oracle Fusion Middleware is a wide collection of software providing a range of services, such as Java EE, developer tools, integration, identity management, business intelligence (BI), and collaboration. In addition to these services, FMW supplies core services for the software stack placed on it, such as concurrency, transactions, threading, messaging, and the SCA framework. FMW also supplies scaling and has clustering options that applications like EBS 12.2 can benefit from.

With this software infrastructure and technology, FMW can be considered an application server, a BI platform, a content management repository, an SOA, a service bus called Integration and Business Process Management (BPM), a security and identity management platform, and a web portal. In addition, FMW offers a sophisticated management platform for managing the components provided with it.

While these components and solutions offered by FMW can be used together to provide an enterprise application and services environment, only some of them can be used to provide the services and applications needed by clients. That is, an FMW component can be placed in a client environment to provide a specific solution. As an example, a single FMW component such as FMW Application Server can be placed in an environment where a Java EE application server is needed, or BI alone can be implemented in an environment where only a BI solution is required.

That's actually what you see in EBS 12.2, too. EBS 12.2 uses the web server and application server components of FMW. The rest of the services EBS provides rely on other technologies such as Oracle Forms, Oracle Reports, and EBS product-specific software codes.

FMW components, Oracle HTTP Server, and WebLogic Server are standard FMW components in EBS 12.2. They are not specialized or customized for use with EBS. The only difference between the FMW components used in EBS 12.2 and the stand-alone FMW components is that EBS 12.2 has AutoConfig on top of these FMW components.

With Release 12.2, Oracle has replaced the 10.1.3 Oracle Home that was used by EBS 12.1 with Oracle HTTP Server (OHS) and WebLogic Server (WLS), which are parts of Fusion Middleware 11g.

© Syed Zaheer and Erman Arslan 2016
S. Zaheer and E. Arslan, *Practical Oracle E-Business Suite*, DOI 10.1007/978-1-4842-1422-0_7

Figure 7-1 shows the general EBS architecture, with attention on the Fusion Middleware 11g components.

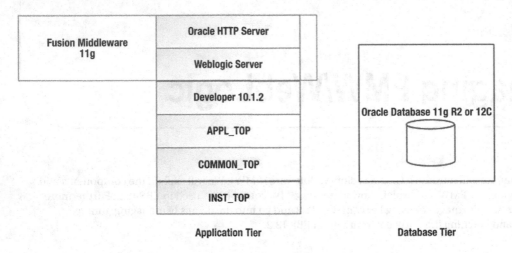

Figure 7-1. EBS 12.2 Fusion Middleware and general architecture

By using WLS in Fusion Middleware 11g, EBS gained a lot of new functionalities, as WLS has a lot of benefits when compared with the former application server, Oracle Application Server 10g. These benefits will be covered later in this chapter; let's now take a closer look at the FMW architecture and components in EBS 12.2.

Architecture and Components

In EBS 12.2, the FMW components of WebLogic Server and Oracle HTTP Server are used in the web tier, which can be called the *middle tier*, considering the three-tier architecture of EBS 12.2. Usually, these FMW components reside on the same server where the concurrent managing processes are running.

As the application server processing is done by Oracle HTTP Server and WebLogic Server in the middle tier, these two FMW components have a big role in the client-server communication in EBS 12.2. They act like middlemen between the client tier and the database tier.

In addition to WebLogic Server, FMW technologies like UIX 11g and JSP are used in EBS 12.2 to provide the web interfaces (in other words, the web pages) to EBS users.

Oracle HTTP Server stands at the forefront of the architecture and works like a web listener; it meets the URL requests sent by EBS users using their browsers. Once HTTP Server gets an HTTP request, it calls the Java Server Pages (JSP) through the use of WebLogic Server, which can be considered a servlet. JSP on WebLogic generates the web pages to be returned to the clients by obtaining the relevant contents of the tables and using the metadata information. Finally, the generated web pages are returned to the clients by HTTP Server.

Most of this work is done when the JSP generates the web pages to be returned to the clients by obtaining the relevant contents of the tables and by using the metadata information. If you take a closer look at this process, you can better understand the mechanism and FMW subcomponents used for constructing a web page.

Figure 7-2 depicts the subcomponents and technologies used, with JSP constructing the web page by using the contents from the EBS database.

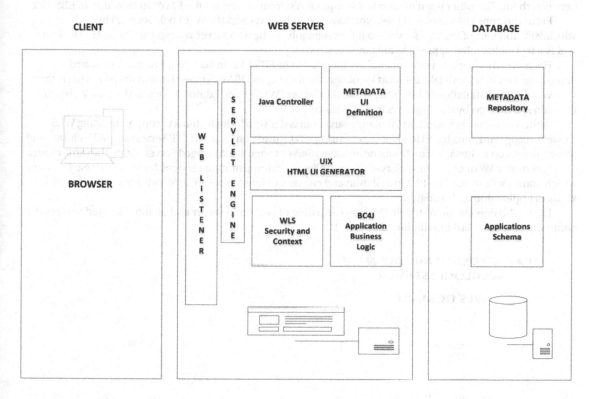

Figure 7-2. *EBS 12.2 Fusion Middleware subcomponents and technologies*

As shown in Figure 7-2, the web listener meets the user's HTTP request and passes it to the servlet engine, which validates the user and decides whether the user has rights to access the page. After the validation, the metadata UI definition is retrieved from the metadata repository that resides on the database tier, and the Business Components for Java (BC4J) objects, which are used for transparently storing and retrieving data, are initialized.

The Java controller acts as the controller in the Model-View-Controller architecture and modifies the page definitions according to the dynamic UI rules. Lastly, HTML UI Generator (UIX) reads the final page definition and creates the web page accordingly.

So, the FMW architecture supplied by WebLogic and Oracle HTTP Server in EBS 12.2 internally works more or less in this manner. Oracle HTTP Server passes the work to WebLogic Server, and WebLogic Server, by cooperating with the various FMW components such as UIX and JSP, retrieves the data, constructs the HTML, and passes the resultant web page back to the client via Oracle HTTP Server.

If you take a look at this mechanism from a higher level, you see the web listener called Oracle HTTP Server that is powered by Apache and a Java servlet engine called Oracle WebLogic Server (WLS).

Oracle WebLogic Server used in EBS 12.2 is a WebLogic Server Basic Edition, which includes usage rights for several WebLogic features such as Core WebLogic Application Server, Java EE/EJB, WebLogic Server Management tools, WebLogic JDBC Drivers, WebLogic Server Client, WebLogic and Apache Web Server plug-in, basic JMS messaging, deployment, high availability functionality, and streamlined storing of important objects to data stores.

There are actually two points of views for the architecture and the components. One of them is the general technical view, which describes the general architecture, the technologies used, and the relationship between them. The other point of view is the apps DBA's point of view for the FMW architecture in EBS 12.2.

From the apps DBA's point of view, you have the web server and the WebLogic server. The administration part of the web server is a lightweight job, as the web server is a typical Oracle HTTP Server and is a technology that apps DBAs are familiar with.

However, WebLogic is a new technology introduced in EBS 12.2. In addition, EBS has a standard deployment on it. So, let's take a look at WebLogic from the apps DBA's perspective and find out what is there.

Within the installation of EBS 12.2, WebLogic Server (WLS) Basic Edition is installed, and a Weblogic Domain is delivered by the Rapidwiz Install Wizard.

WebLogic Server is a standard WebLogic server but is delivered with features to support building WLS clusters, using hardware-based load balancers, using a WLS proxy on Oracle HTTP Servers in a WLS cluster, and using the session re-instantiation from one Managed Server to another Managed Server within the same cluster.

You have a WebLogic Admin Server that supplies the administration services for the Weblogic Domain, which comes within the EBS 12.2 installation and consists of four Managed Servers for servicing different kinds of application technologies.

Figure 7-3 depicts the Weblogic Domain consisting of an Admin server and all the Managed Servers that come with the standard installation of EBS 12.2.

**ORACLE FUSION MIDDLEWARE
WEBLOGIC SERVER**

WLS DOMAIN

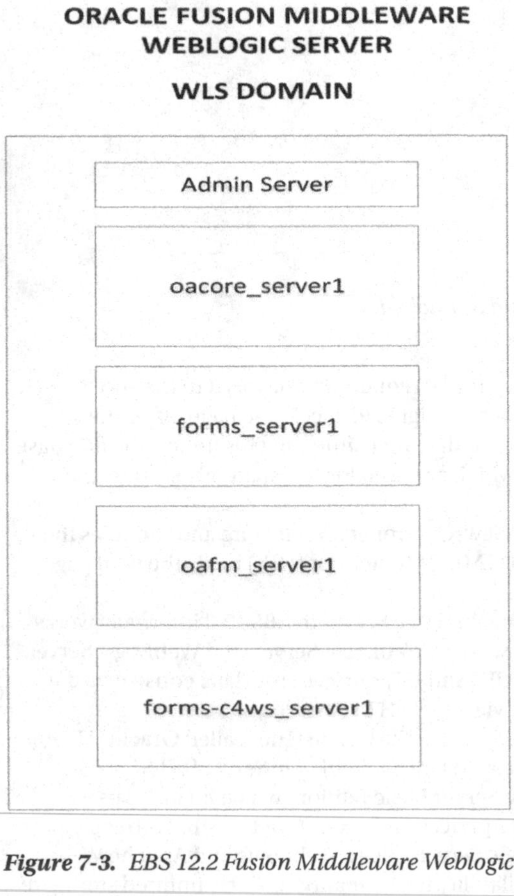

Figure 7-3. EBS 12.2 Fusion Middleware Weblogic Domain

Normally, the Managed Servers are named according to their services and with number suffixes representing application nodes they belong to, considering the multinode configurations. Most of the time, by looking at a name such as oacore_server1, you can understand that it is the Managed Server that supplies the OAF functionality and it is running on the first application node.

However, a Managed Server named oacore_server2 can be running on the first application node, too. Therefore, it is important to know that there may be more than one Managed Server for a single-node application tier.

So, when you look the Weblogic Domain that comes with a standard EBS 12.2 installation, you see a Weblogic Domain with one administration server, a Node Manager, four Weblogic Server Clusters, and four Managed Servers deployed by EBS 12.2. At this point, if you look at the WebLogic terminology, you have three standard components in a WebLogic environment. One of them is the domain that is a logically related group of WebLogic Server resources. The second component is an administration server that is used to configure all server instances and resources in the domain. Finally, there is a Node Manager, which is used to perform operation tasks for a Managed Server.

If you leave the standard things such as the domain, administration server, and Node Manager aside, EBS 12.2 employs four Managed Servers to meet the demands of different EBS application types. These four Managed Servers within the EBS WebLogic instance are oacore, oafm, forms, and forms-c4ws. Managed Servers in a WebLogic environment are the servers that supply the components and associated resources that constitute the applications. Roughly speaking, the applications run on these Managed Servers.

In this context, oacore_server (Oracle Applications Core) is used for servicing the requests coming from application tier Java code objects such as Java code for OAF pages, in other words, for the OAF functionality.

oafm_server (Oracle Applications Fusion Middleware) is the Managed Server that is used by the web services, secure enterprise search, Oracle transport agent, and other components such as map viewer.

forms_server is the Managed Server for managing the creation of forms runtime processes, which actually execute the code of the forms applications. The forms server also manages the network communication between clients and the associated forms runtime processes. forms-c4ws_server provides the business logic contained within Oracle Forms to be exposed as web services. In addition to these four Managed Servers, there is a Managed Server named oaea, which can be provisioned if the relevant applications are installed. The server oaea is the Managed Server for serving additional applications such as E-Business Suite Access Gate, eKanban, and Spatial.

As EBS 12.2 builds Weblogic Server Clusters with the default installation, it is important to mention that these WebLogic Managed Servers provisioned by EBS 12.2 are grouped into Weblogic Server Clusters. Although such a cluster configuration is most effective in a multinode configuration, Weblogics clusters are in use even in the single-node EBS configurations. In this context, one cluster is created for each Managed Server in the EBS Weblogic Domain.

oacore_cluster1 is the cluster for oacore Managed Servers. For a multimode configuration, this cluster has members for each node in the cluster such as oacore_server1 for Node1, oacore_server2 for Node 2, and so on.

Similarly, oafm_cluster1 is the cluster for oafm Managed Servers, forms_cluster1 is there for forms Managed Servers, forms-c4ws_cluster1 is the cluster for forms-c4ws Managed Servers, and oaea_cluster1 is the cluster for grouping the oaea Managed Servers.

So, EBS 12.2 uses Weblogic Server Clusters to increase both the scalability and the reliability in the middle tier, as the Weblogic Server Clusters consist of multiple WebLogic Managed Servers running simultaneously. Moreover, the members of a cluster can be in different application nodes. As shown in Figure 7-4, there are two Managed Servers for servicing every single application type, and these Managed Servers are distributed into two different nodes, supplying both the load balancing and the high availability.

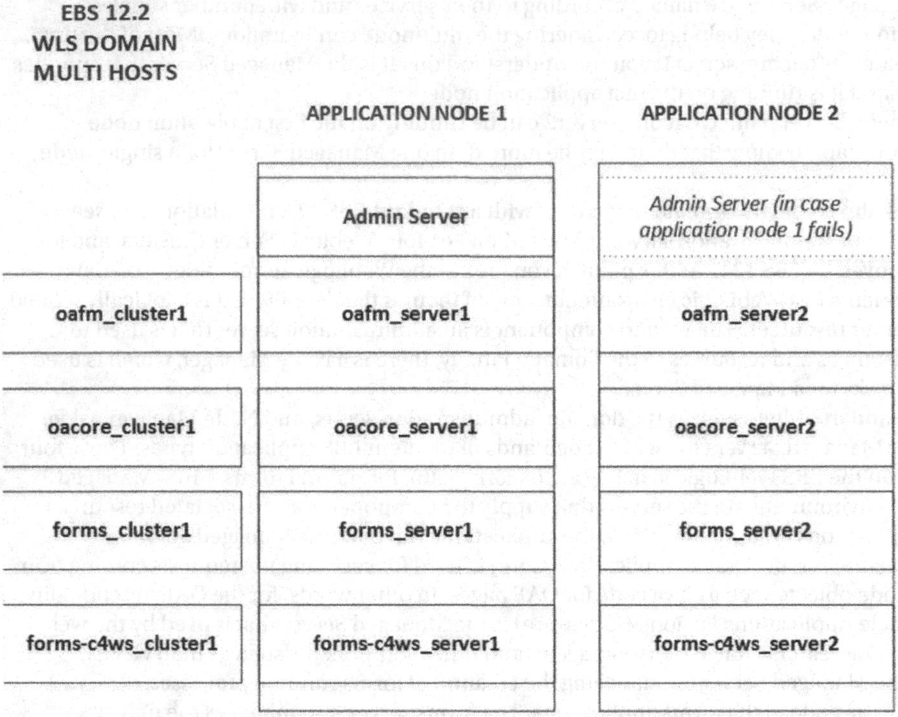

EBS 12.2
WLS DOMAIN
MULTI HOSTS

	APPLICATION NODE 1	APPLICATION NODE 2
	Admin Server	Admin Server (in case application node 1 fails)
oafm_cluster1	oafm_server1	oafm_server2
oacore_cluster1	oacore_server1	oacore_server2
forms_cluster1	forms_server1	forms_server2
forms-c4ws_cluster1	forms-c4ws_server1	forms-c4ws_server2

Figure 7-4. *EBS 12.2 Fusion Middleware Weblogic Domain consisting of multiple hosts*

The Admin Server, as shown in Figure 7-4, can run on a single server even though WebLogic is implemented as a multinode cluster. In this manner, the Admin Server's high availability can be considered as active-passive high availability, as it cannot run simultaneously on multiple nodes but can be started on one of the available nodes in the case of a node failure.

In general, to supply the continuity of the services and application processing, you need high availability setups, and if you want your processing power to be increased by horizontally scaling up the processing , you need load balancing. You can think of load balancing as a way to provide the continuity and to increase the fault tolerance. When we talk about load balancing in WebLogic, we actually need to talk about the load balancing of its components one by one. As we have different major software components like servlets, JSPs, JDBC data stores, JMS, EJB, and RMI objects in WebLogic, there are some differences in their load balancing architecture.

Before explaining the load balancing in WebLogic by going through its software components, let's introduce you these components a little bit. Servlets are classes that can be invoked and executed on the server most likely on behalf of a client. The servlets you see mostly are the HTTP servlets, which are classes for handling the HTTP request and delivering an HTTP response.

Java Servlet Pages combine Java and HTML to provide dynamic content for web pages.

JDBC data sources provide access to the database and manage the database connections. Each data source maintains a connection pool and supplies the database connections to the applications using the connection pool.

Java Messaging Service (JMS) is an enterprise messaging system that supplies a message-based communication platform for the applications. By using JMS, applications can communicate with each other by exchanging messages.

Enterprise Java Beans (EJB) is a Java technology that enables rapid and simplified development of distributed, transactional, secure, and portable applications based on Java technology. EJBs are like APIs and EJB objects. EJB objects contain the business methods inside them.

Remote Method Invocation (RMI) allows an object running in one Java virtual machine to invoke methods on an object running in another Java virtual machine. In a way, it provides a distributed object-oriented programming. RMI objects, whose methods can be invoked remotely, are the products of this mechanism.

These different software technologies in a WebLogic environment have different load-balancing techniques.

Load balancing for servlets and JSPs can be accomplished using the WebLogic Proxy plug-in within Oracle HTTP Server or using an external load balancer. While the WebLogic Proxy plug-in is designed to load balance the traffic between Oracle HTTP Server and the EBS 12.2 WebLogic Managed Servers, a load balancer enables all the traffic between the client and Oracle HTTP Server to be load balanced, thus making EBS 12.2 load balanced on multiple application nodes.

In the WebLogic Proxy plug-in method, the WebLogic proxy plug-in attached to the Apache server maintains a list of available Managed Servers for the incoming HTTP requests and forwards the HTTP requests to these available Managed Servers in a round-robin fashion. So, using the WebLogic Proxy plug-in, you can load balance the traffic between Oracle HTTP Server and WebLogic Managed Servers.

In the external load balancer method, the requests first arrive to the load balancer, and the load balancer forwards them to the Oracle HTTP Servers, which in turn forward the HTTP requests to the available Managed Servers according to the configuration. The load-balancing algorithm used in the external load balancer method can be any method that the load balancer supports. So, using the load balancer, you actually get EBS 12.2 load balanced on multiple application nodes by load balancing the traffic between clients and Oracle HTTP Servers running on multiple EBS 12.2 application nodes.

As for the JMS, EJBs, and RMI objects, the load balancing comes built in, as it is configured from administration console, which you will see in the next sections. So, the load balancing for EJB and RMI is controlled inside WebLogic. The default load-balancing algorithm for these objects in the Weblogic Server Clusters in an EBS 12.2 is round robin. In round robin, requests are balanced across a list of available servers by selecting from the list sequentially.

Note that there is also a random style and a weighted-style load balancing for JMS, EJB, and RMI objects. The random algorithm balances the requests by selecting random servers. The weighted-style load balancing, on the other hand, can balance the requests with the percentages according to the predefined weights of the Managed Servers.

Lastly, normally in generic WebLogic instances, load balancing of JDBC connections is done using multiple data sources. The approach used in here is called *clustered JDBCs*, and these clustered JDBCs can be configured when configuring multiple data sources. However, for EBS 12.2, the load balancing of JDBC connections is done by the scan listeners of the EBS 12.2 database. (Note that scan listeners were introduced with Oracle Database Release 11g R2). They distribute the connections to the available database nodes transparently to the applications.

If the scan listeners are not used in the EBS 12.2 database site (which is not recommended for Oracle EBS 12.2 RAC databases), you can use multiple data sources in this manner, but you should ask Oracle Support whether this will be a supported move or not.

So, the load-balancing capabilities of Managed Servers supply the ability to distribute the application work to all of the available application servers. It can be considered like parallelization, and it also increases the scalability of the EBS environments.

These capabilities also provide high availability, in other words, business continuity.

If there are multiple application nodes and if these nodes are configured to host Managed Servers within clusters, a node failure won't affect the business continuity. However, as you can see in Figure 7-4, there is only one Administration Server in a Weblogic Domain. This is actually a rule in WebLogic, but it does not affect the high availability of the WebLogic resources. That is, the failure of the Administration Server for a domain does not affect the Managed Servers in that domain, as long as the Managed Servers are up and running. In such a scenario, the applications running on WebLogic will continue to run, and all the failover and load balancing capabilities will still be available for them.

Figure 7-5 represents a standard configuration for supporting the load-balancing and failover capabilities of the EBS 12.2 environment. Considering all the things we have mentioned about load balancing and high availability, the configuration provided by Figure 7-5 fulfills the requirements of the high availability and load balancing of WebLogic Managed Servers.

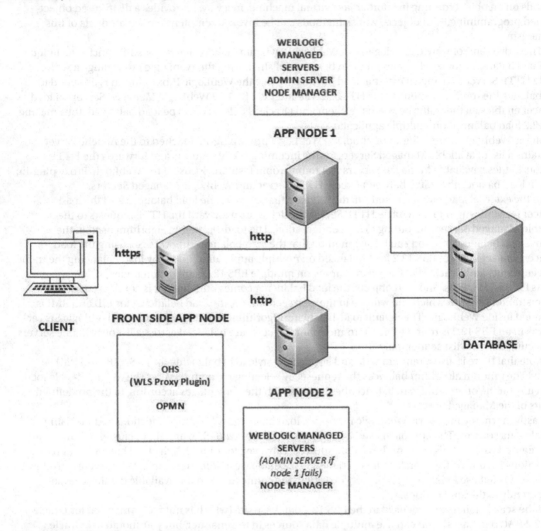

Figure 7-5. EBS 12.2 configuration for supporting load balancing and failover

In Figure 7-5 you can see one application node on the front side, and it balances the requests to the application nodes that run WebLogic Managed Servers in a clustered configuration. You can see two oacore, two forms, two oafm, and two forms-c4ws Managed Servers, and they are pairs of their associated Weblogic Server Clusters.

Also note that you can see one Node Manager located in each application node for managing these Managed Servers.

This configuration supplies a single web entry by the application node on the front side. This application node in the front runs OPMN and OHS with a WebLogic Proxy plug-in. The WebLogic proxy plug-in routes the requests to the relevant available Managed Servers in a round-robin fashion, thus providing load balancing and high availability at the same time.

So, you have seen the Fusion Middleware architecture so far. We have gone into some details about WebLogic, as it can be considered the key component of Fusion Middleware inside EBS 12.2. We explained the load balancing of the Managed Servers in WebLogic, and we actually will explain more about FMW and WebLogic later in this chapter, when we explain the directory structure and activities such as management and tuning.

Let's take a look at the advantages of FMW inside EBS 12.2.

Advantages of FMW

As EBS 12.2, Oracle's new-generation ERP system, uses FMW for its middleware technology stack, there should be some advantages of it, right? The advantages of using Oracle FMW for EBS 12.2 can be seen by analyzing its technological components one by one and then analyzing it as a whole.

Let's start with WebLogic 11. WebLogic Application Server 11g delivers high performance in the middleware technology stack, as it can benefit from the latest hardware architectures, including 64-bit addressable memory, multicore computing systems, and high-speed networks. Furthermore, WebLogic uses Oracle's Jrockit, which is one of the highest-performing JVMs in the industry.

In addition to performance, WebLogic provides scalability, reliability, and enterprise-level security. It is also an easy-to-use application server equipped with powerful administration facilities that provide easy application deployment routines and the monitoring and management of the WebLogic resources.

FMW also provides a powerful diagnostic framework called Fusion Middleware Diagnostic Framework (DFW) for detecting, diagnosing, and resolving problems. In this context, to recognize, analyze, and resolve critical errors, DFW can be configured to create incidents consisting of all the related diagnostic data automatically, thus easing the administrator's job.

Another advantage of FMW is its ability for real-time monitoring of the applications. The source of the mentoring in FMW is the WebLogic Diagnostic Framework. A dashboard called the Monitoring Dashboard, provided by the WebLogic Administration Console, uses charts and graphs to give administrators the ability to monitor the internal WebLogic resource, as well as the application resources such as JVM heaps, JDBC data sources, and the general metrics like HTTP request counts.

In addition, the tightly integrated administration tools, such as the Fusion Middleware console, WebLogic Administration Console, and WLST, that come within FMW enable consolidated administration of the server resource, as well as applications from deployment to configuration.

As mentioned, FMW supplies high availability, scalability, and failover by design. Within the Fusion middleware technology stack and software technologies used by FMW applications, Fusion Middleware provides a favorable environment for building highly available applications with scale-out and failover capabilities.

FMW also appears as an integration platform for other Fusion applications such as SOA, SSHR Organization Chart, and Oracle Business Intelligence. Today, it is possible to integrate these applications into EBS 12.2. So, it is one of the important advantages of FMW because these kinds of technology applications, when configured work together, can provide an important business value for the enterprise.

Lastly, the applications are designed and built using a single integrated and modular design tool in FMW. The design tool includes Oracle JDeveloper, Toplink, Oracle Application Development Framework, and Oracle Eclipse. In FMW, all the software design (including user interfaces, business logic, service composition, business processes, workflow, business rules, and business intelligence) is done using this design tool. This single design environment improves the productivity and makes designing and debugging easier.

Let's now dive into FMW on EBS 12.2 by reviewing the FMW directory structure in EBS 12.2.

FMW Directory Structure in EBS 12.2

FMW has a great place in the EBS 12.2 directory structure. Almost one-third of the application file system structures in EBS 12.2 consist of FMW directories and files. The root of the FMW directories is FMW_Home. FMW_Home resides just below the installation base directory, so it resides at the same directory level as the EBS-specific root directories named EBSapps and inst (which are not in the scope of this chapter). In addition, if you recall the dual filesystem that we talked about in previous chapters, FMW_Home resides in the patch and run filesystems.

We explained the FMW_Home directory in Chapter 4, so rather than giving the same explanations twice, we will explain some important FMW directories and configuration files in this section. Gaining such information specific to EBS 12.2 will increase your understanding of the FMW components residing in EBS 12.2.

As a reminder, the FMW_Home directory has the following subdirectories:

- *user_projects*: This directory contains the Weblogic Domain used by EBS.

- *wlserver_10.3*: This directory contains all the binaries and libraries for WebLogic Server that is part of the FMW. This directory contains WebLogic Server itself.

- *oracle_common*: This directory contains all the Java Required Files (JRFs) used by EBS and the binaries and libraries for the Oracle Enterprise Manager Fusion Middleware Control.

- *webtier*: This directory contains the Oracle HTTP Server component of FMW used by EBS.

- *Oracle_EBS-app1*: This directory is an Oracle Home that EBS deploys into. All the configuration files for the EBS FMW applications such as oacore, forms, oafm, and form-c4ws reside in this directory.

Even though there are several directories in the FMW directory structure of EBS 12.2, the previous directories are the main directories in the file system architecture. As an apps DBA, you won't often work on files in these directories, and you don't even need to know the internals of them. The EBS_Domain directory and the web tier are still our focus now, as they host the main configuration files, log files, and control programs.

Figure 7-6 shows the directory structure and related components. As you can see, there are five important directories: webtier, wlsserver_10.3, Oracle_EBS-app1, oracle_common, and EBS_Domain.

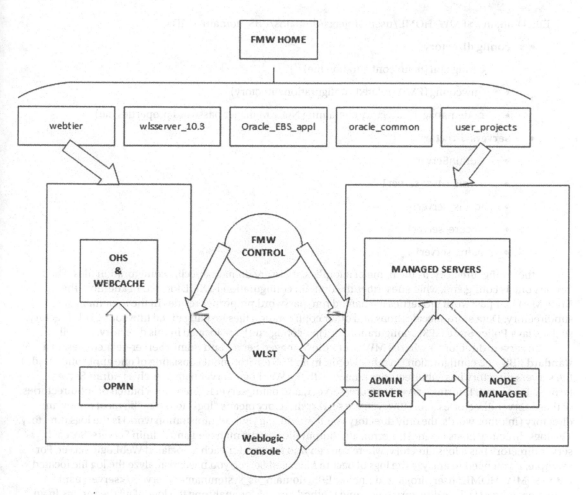

Figure 7-6. *EBS 12.2 Fusion Middleware directories, system components, and their relations with management utilities*

Among these five directories, there are two critical directories, which you may actually visit during your administration. One of them is webtier, which hosts opmn and controls the HTTP Server and web cache using it. The other one is the EBS_Domain directory where the Weblogic Domain of EBS resides. Managed Servers, the Node Manager, and the administration server are located in this directory.

At the bottom, in the middle of these system components, you can see the administration utilities, such as the FMW Control, WLST, and the WLS console for managing these components.

We will take a look at the administration utilities in this section and in "Using the WebLogic Console." Let's continue with the details of the important directories.

- The EBS WebLogic_Domain directory resides in the user_projects directory, located in $FMW_HOME/user_projects/domains/EBS_domain_<SID>.

In the EBS domain directory, there are two important directories; one of them is the config directory, and the other is the servers directory. These directories and their main contents are as follows;

EBS Domain / $FMW_HOME/user_projects/domains/EBS_domain_<SID>

- **config directory**
    - config.xml (main configuration file)
    - fmwconfig (FMW-related configuration directory)
    - nodemanager (directory containing Node Manager password properties file)
- **servers directory**
    - AdminServer
    - forms-c4ws_server1
    - forms_server1
    - oacore_server1
    - oafm_server1

In the config directory, as the name of it implies, there are domain-specific configuration files. The famous one is config.xml, which describes the domain configuration in XML format. In addition, the Node Manager password properties file named nm_password.properties resides in the nodemanager subdirectory. Data store specifications and other configuration files residing in the fmwconfig subdirectory, such as Java Policy Store (JPS) configuration file (jps-config.xml), are located in this directory, as well.

The servers directory is where FMW stores the Managed Server and Admin Server–related files. In a standard EBS 12.2 configuration (in other words, in an EBS environment consisting of one application node), the servers directory has subdirectories named with the WebLogic server names such as AdminServer, forms-c4ws_server1, forms_server1, oacore_server1, and oafm_server1. There are a bunch of subdirectories of these server directories, too. However, the servers directory means "logs" for you. The most important directory (in other words, the only directory you'll use during your administration work) is the logs directory. The logs directory hosts diagnostic, error, and output files for the managed and Admin Servers. So, each server directory has a logs directory, where you can find the logs for each associated WebLogic server. For example, if you need to analyze the logs of oacore Managed Server, you need to analyze the log file located in the $FMW_HOME/ user_projects/domains/EBS_domain_<s_systemname>/servers/<server_name> (i.e oacore_server1)/logs directory. The same method applies for analyzing the logs of all the servers in an EBS domain.

- EBS Oracle Home (in other words, Oracle_EBS-app1) is pointed at by the EBS_ORACLE_HOME environment variable, and it has three important subdirectories. The first is the applications folder, pointed by the $EBS_APPS_DEPLOYMENT_DIR environment variable, and it is the directory that EBS deploys into and where EAR/WAR deployments are located.

The $OAH_TOP environment variable points to the oacore subdirectory of Oracle_EBS-app1, and it is the top directory where HTML-based applications' HTML files are copied. Also, the environment variable defined for specifying the location of an Oracle application, named $OA_HTML, points to the applications/oacore/html subdirectory of Oracle_EBS-app1. HTML-based files are located in the applications/oacore/html directory.

Deployment descriptor files such as application.xml and weblogic-application.xml are also located in Oracle_EBS_app1.

The deployment-plans folder is another important subdirectory of Oracle_EBS-app1, as it hosts the default deployment plans. For each Managed Server in an EBS domain such as oacore and forms, a plan.xml file, which is an XML document used to define an application's deployment configuration for a specific WebLogic Server environment, can be found in the deployment-plan directory for each of the EBS applications.

The shared_libs directory is the third important subdirectory, in which the FMW shared libraries are pointed. The manifest files located in the shared_libs directory points to the JAR files located in the relevant FMW_HOME directories such as $FMW_Home/oracle_common and $FMW_HOME/modules.

- Oracle_EBS-app1
  - applications EAR/WAR deployments
  - deployment_plans Default deployment plans
  - shared_libs FMW Shared libraries

The last important thing residing in FMW_HOME is the web tier's instance home, in other words, the webtier directory. webtier is the directory where Oracle HTTP Server files reside.

Webtier

- instances
  - EBS_web_<context> EBS OHS Home
  - bin opmnctl
  - config
    - OHS
      - EBS_web_component Apache conf files
    - OPMN
  - opmn opmn.xml
    - diagnostics
      - logs
        - OHS
          - EBS_web_component Apache and OHS log files
        - OPMN
          - opmn OPMN logs

webtier may seem like a standard Oracle Home at first sight, but it has a different directory structure. It contains classic Oracle Home components such as sqlplus and opatch. However, the instances directory residing in it makes it special, as all the EBS FMW HTTP Server and OPMN files are located there. Although you use EBS admin scripts to manage all the services including Oracle HTTP Server, the opmn, which actually controls Oracle HTTP Server, resides in this directory. The Apache configuration files, such as the httpd.conf file, for instance, reside in this directory, too. All the log files for OHS and Apache are stored in the diagnostics subdirectory of webtier/instances/EBS_web_<context>.

In the case of an HTTP Server failure or a requirement for analyzing the HTTP requests or an opmn problem, you can analyze the logs and diagnostics files located in this directory. As you see, the directory is not so complicated, but it is important to know why the files are there and the tools that are using them. So, let's continue with understanding of management activities for WebLogic components, as you may need to perform them every day.

Controlling Admin Server, Node Manager, and Managed Servers

Controlling FMW system components in EBS 12.2 is done by using applications DBA (AD) scripts installed in the application nodes, in the directory pointed at by the $ADMIN_SCRIPTS_HOME environment variable. Actually, controlling all the EBS system components is done using these AD scripts.

When you change the current working directory to the directory pointed at by $ADMIN_SCRIPTS_HOME and list the files located in it, you see almost 16 shell scripts, as follows. Note that the AD scripts in bold in the following list, are actually the scripts for administrating the FMW system components.

- **adadminsrvctl.sh**: This script is used to start and stop the Admin Server.

- adalnctl.sh: This script is used to start and stop the applications RPC listener process.

- adapcctl.sh: This script is used to start, stop, and check the status of Oracle HTTP Server.

- adautocfg.sh: This script is used for executing AutoConfig.

- adcmctl.sh: This script is used to start, stop, and check the status of the concurrent managers.

- adformsrvctl.sh: This script is used to start, stop, and check the status of the forms server in socket mode.

- **admanagedsrvctl.sh**: This script is used to start and stop the Managed Servers.

- **adnodemgrctl.sh:** This script is used to start the Node Manager.

- **adopmnctl.sh:** This script is used to start, stop, and check the status of OPMN.

- adstpall.sh: This script is used to stop all the Oracle E-Business Suite services.

- adstrtal.sh: This script is used to start all the Oracle E-Business Suite services.

- gsmstart.sh: This script is used to source the APPSORA environment file and start the FNDSM process.

- java.sh: This script is used by opmn and Java concurrent programs to call the Java executable with additional arguments.

- jtffmctl.sh: This script is used to start and stop the fulfillment server process.

- mwactl.sh: This script is used to start and stop the Telnet server/MWA server.

- mwactlwrpr.sh: Wrapper script to start and stop the Telnet server/MWA server through AutoConfig.

While scripts like adstpall.sh and adstrtal.sh enable all the services to be stopped or started in one go, the individual service scripts can be used to start or stop service components individually. There are several service component control scripts in EBS 12.2, as you see in the previous list. However, only four of them (the ones in bold) are used for administering the FMW system components.

Note that we'll focus on the FMW-related administration scripts in this chapter but will explain all of these scripts with their usages in the following chapters.

Before giving the information about the scripts and their usages, we'll explain what needs to be administrated in the case of FMW in EBS 12.2. There are four different kinds of FMW system components that need to be controlled and administered by the apps DBAs.

- Oracle HTTP Server, as it is the web entry point for EBS 12.2 and is part of FMW.

- The WebLogic administration server, as it is the central configuration/monitoring controller for the Weblogic Domain and the application named Administration Console runs on this server. (The next section explains the Administration Console .)

- The Managed Servers, as the EBS applications such as oacore and oafm are deployed onto these separate server instances.

- The Node Manager, as it is Java utility that is used for operations such as starting, shutting down, and restarting the administration server and Managed Server instances.

To make your EBS applications accessible, you need to have only the Oracle HTTP Server and Managed Servers running. However, the Node Manager and administration server must also be running, as they enable the administration activities for the Managed Servers, which host the EBS applications.

While a failure in HTTP Server or the Managed Servers can impact the end users directly, a failure in a Node Manager or in the administration server may create a negative impact on your daily administration work. Because these four system components must be up and running all the time, they need to be monitored and under control.

As shown in Figure 7-7, there are utilities like the administration control, FMW control, and WLST for managing the FMW system components. To manage the applications running on the Managed Servers, these utilities all use the Node Manager in the back end, so they are operating by communicating with the Node Manager, as this is the method for managing the Managed Servers in WebLogic.

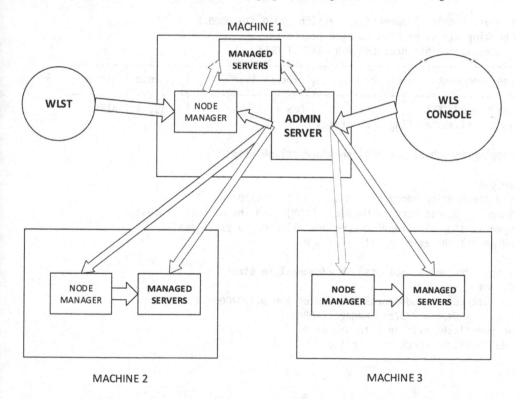

Figure 7-7. *EBS 12.2 Fusion Middleware management utilities and WebLogic servers*

These administration utilities are in the base and specific to WebLogic; however, you are on EBS (in other words, on top of the stack) and have the ability to use some EBS utilities to do this WebLogic administration.

Here, the applications DBA scripts comes into play, as one of the control mechanisms used for these FMW components is based on the applications DBA scripts, as mentioned earlier. These scripts enable apps DBAs to manage the FMW components without knowing the details of WebLogic administration.

That is, the apps DBAs should know how to use the related application's DBA administration script in case it is required to deal with an FMW component.

As mentioned earlier, the scripts for managing the FMW components are located together with the other administration scripts in the directory pointed at by $ADMIN_SCRIPTS_HOME, which is the usual administration scripts directory for apps DBAs since EBS release 12.1.

The scripts and usage examples are listed here:

- **adopmnctl.sh {start|stop|status}**: Used to start, stop, and check the status of the opmn process and processes managed by opmn; in EBS 12.2 this managed process is Oracle HTTP Server.

Here are some example usages:

```
[applmgr@somehost ~]$ cd $ADMIN_SCRIPTS_HOME
[applmgr@somehost scripts] sh adopmnctl.sh status
```

Here is the output:

```
You are running adopmnctl.sh version 120.0.12020000.2
Checking status of OPMN managed processes...
Processes in Instance: EBS_web_ORATEST_OHS1
---------------------------------+--------------------+---------+---------
ias-component                    | process-type       |     pid | status
---------------------------------+--------------------+---------+---------
EBS_web_ORATEST                  | OHS                |   19054 | Alive
adopmnctl.sh: exiting with status 0

[applmgr@somehost scripts] sh adopmnctl.sh stop

Output:
You are running adopmnctl.sh version 120.0.12020000.2
Stopping Oracle Process Manager (OPMN)  and the managed processes ...
opmnctl stopall: stopping opmn and all managed processes...
adopmnctl.sh: exiting with status 0

[applmgr@somehost scripts] sh adopmnctl.sh start
Output:
You are running adopmnctl.sh version 120.0.12020000.2
Starting Oracle Process Manager (OPMN)
adopmnctl.sh: exiting with status 0
adopmnctl.sh: check the logfile
```

- **adnodemgrctl.sh {start|status|stop} [-nopromptmsg]:** Used to start, stop, and check the status of the Node Manager process. It requires the WebLogic admin password supplied as input.

  Here are some example usages:

  ```
  [applmgr@somehost scripts]$ sh adnodemgrctl.sh status
  Output:
  You are running adnodemgrctl.sh version 120.11.12020000.11
  Enter the WebLogic Admin password:
  The Node Manager is running
  adnodemgrctl.sh: exiting with status 0

  [applmgr@somehost scripts]$ sh adnodemgrctl.sh stop
  Output:
  You are running adnodemgrctl.sh version 120.11.12020000.11
  Enter the WebLogic Admin password:
  adnodemgrctl.sh: exiting with status 0

  [applmgr@somehost scripts]$ sh adnodemgrctl.sh start
  Output:
  You are running adnodemgrctl.sh version 120.11.12020000.11
  Enter the WebLogic Admin password:
  Starting the Node Manager...
  adnodemgrctl.sh: exiting with status 0
  ```

- **adadminsrvctl.sh {start|stop|status} [forcepatchfs] [-nopromptmsg] [-silent]:** Used to stop, start, and check the WebLogic Admin Server. It requires the WebLogic admin password and the APPS schema password as inputs. The nopromptmsg parameter can be used while automating the script execution, as the adminsrvctl.sh script does not prompt for messages while the nopromptmsg argument is specified. The forcepatchfs argument lets the WebLogic Admin Server start on the patch filesystem, which may be required in procedures for certain operations such as adding an application node to the application tier.

  Here are some example usages:

  ```
  [applmgr@somehost scripts]$ sh adadminsrvctl.sh status
  Output:
  You are running adadminsrvctl.sh version 120.10.12020000.9
  Enter the WebLogic Admin password:
  Enter the APPS Schema password:
  The AdminServer is running
  adadminsrvctl.sh: exiting with status 0

  [applmgr@somehost scripts]$ sh adadminsrvctl.sh stop
  Output:
  You are running adadminsrvctl.sh version 120.10.12020000.9
  Enter the WebLogic Admin password:
  Enter the APPS Schema password:
  Stopping WLS Admin Server...
  adadminsrvctl.sh: exiting with status 0
  ```

```
[applmgr@somehost scripts]$ sh adadminsrvctl.sh start
Output:
You are running adadminsrvctl.sh version 120.10.12020000.9

Enter the WebLogic Admin password:
Enter the APPS Schema password:
Starting WLS Admin Server...
adadminsrvctl.sh: exiting with status 0
admanagedsrvctl.sh
```

- **admanagedsrvctl.sh{start|adminmode|resume|suspend|force_
  suspend|stop|abort|status} <managed_server_name> [-nopromptmsg]** : Used to
  stop, start, and check WebLogic Managed Servers in the EBS domain. In a standard
  installation consisting of one application tier, these servers are oacore_server1,
  oafm_server1, forms_server1, and forms-c4ws_server1. Additional arguments, which
  are not often used by apps DBAs, are available, too. You can use an argument such
  as suspend to suspend a Managed Server and can use resume to make it continue its
  work and change its state from suspend to running.

As you might have recognized, admanagedsrvctl.sh requires the Managed
Server's name for operating, and this makes it a utility that is operated server by
server. However, it has an alternative usage, as shown here:

admanagedsrvctl.sh {startall|stopall} <servicetype> [-nopromptmsg]

So, by using the startall and stopall arguments, server groups in crowded
EBS environments can be controlled. Using stopall and startall is handy in
environments where a bunch of Managed Servers are running for the same
service types.

By using the startall argument with a service type argument such as oacore,
all the oacore Managed Servers such as oacore_server1, oacore_server2, and
oacore_server3 can be started in one go. As you may guess, by using stopall with
a service type argument, all the Managed Servers for that service type can be
stopped, too.

Here are some example usages:

```
[applmgr@somehost scripts]$ sh admanagedsrvctl.sh status oacore_server1
Output:
You are running admanagedsrvctl.sh version 120.14.12020000.9
Enter the WebLogic Admin password:
oacore_server1 is running.
admanagedsrvctl.sh: exiting with status 0

[applmgr@somehost scripts]$ sh admanagedsrvctl.sh stop oacore_server1
Output:
You are running admanagedsrvctl.sh version 120.14.12020000.9
Enter the WebLogic Admin password:
Stopping oacore_server1...
admanagedsrvctl.sh: exiting with status 0
```

```
[applmgr@somehost scripts]$ sh admanagedsrvctl.sh start oacore_server1
You are running admanagedsrvctl.sh version 120.14.12020000.9
Output:
Enter the WebLogic Admin password:
Calling txkChkEBSDependecies.pl to perform dependency checks for oacore_server1
Perl script txkChkEBSDependecies.pl got executed successfully
Starting oacore_server1...
admanagedsrvctl.sh: exiting with status 0

[applmgr@somehost scripts]$ sh admanagedsrvctl.sh stopall oacore
Output:
You are running admanagedsrvctl.sh version 120.14.12020000.9
Enter the WebLogic Admin password:
Stopping all oacore Managed Servers...
admanagedsrvctl.sh: exiting with status 0

[applmgr@somehost scripts]$ sh admanagedsrvctl.sh startall oacore
Output:
You are running admanagedsrvctl.sh version 120.14.12020000.9
Enter the WebLogic Admin password:
Calling txkChkEBSDependecies.pl to perform dependency checks for       SERVER_NAME
Perl script txkChkEBSDependecies.pl got executed successfully
Starting all oacore Managed Servers...
admanagedsrvctl.sh: exiting with status 0
```

As you can see in the script execution example, there are some logs stating the operation in progress, such as "Stopping all oacore Managed Servers." Also, after every successful script execution, there is a log for stating the exit status of the executed script such as "admanagedsrvctl.sh: exiting with status 0."

Note that we did not include the outputs of these scripts fully, as the output in the example would not look nice and it would be hard to understand because the high number of log lines.

However, it is important to mention that, normally when you execute these kinds of scripts, you get a more detailed output. That is, almost for every operation a log stating the operation being done is printed in the output.

The following is an excerpt from an admanagedsrvctl.sh execution:

```
admanagedsrvctl.sh: check the logfile /somepath/fs1/inst/apps/VIS_demor12/logs/appl/admin/
log/adoacorectl.txt for more information.
```

So, these logs are sufficiently detailed and can be used to diagnose script execution problems, as in this example:

```
07/20/15-13:40:15 :: admanagedsrvctl.sh version 120.14.12020000.9
Calling txkChkEBSDependecies.pl to perform dependency checks for SERVER_NAME
Program : /somepath/fs1/EBSapps/appl/fnd/12.0.0/patch/115/bin/txkChkEBSDependecies.pl
started @ Mon Jul 20 13:40:20 2015
*** Log File = /somepath/fs1/inst/apps/VIS_demor12/logs/appl/rgf/TXK/txkChkEBSDependecies_
Mon_Jul_20_13_40_20_2015/txkChkEBSDependecies_Mon_Jul_20_13_40_20_2015.log
Perl script txkChkEBSDependecies.pl got executed successfully
Validated the past arguments for the option ebs-nmstart-managedservice
Checking if the Node Manager is already up..
Connecting to Node Manager ...
Successfully Connected to Node Manager.
```

```
The Node Manager is already up.
The Server oacore_server1 is not up. Proceeding to start the server.
Connecting to Node Manager
Successfully Connected to Node Manager.
Connecting to t3://somehost.somedomain:7001 with userid weblogic ...
Successfully connected to Admin Server 'AdminServer' that belongs to domain 'EBS_domain_VIS'.
Warning: An insecure protocol was used to connect to the
server. To ensure on-the-wire security, the SSL port or
Admin port should be used instead.
Starting server oacore_server1 ...
Successfully started server oacore_server1 ...
Started up the Managed Server oacore_server1
07/20/15-13:41:53: admanagedsrvctl.sh: exiting with status 0
```

As shown in the example log file, you can see almost every operation that the applications DBA FMW control scripts have done. You can see the connection to the Node Manager (Successfully Connected to Node Manager) and AdminServer (Successfully connected to Admin Server 'AdminServer'), you can see the other script executions like txkChkEBSDependecies.pl (Perl script txkChkEBSDependecies.pl got executed successfully) and their exit statuses, and you can see the log line stating the relevant operation is done (Started up the Managed Server oacore_server1).

Any problem that may be encountered while these scripts are executing can be identified by analyzing these log files.

Lastly in this section, we want to talk about the provisioning script named adProvisionEBS.pl. adProvisionEBS.pl is an applications DBA script located in the $AD_TOP/bin directory in EBS 12.2. This script is like a centralized operation center that can get the status of a Managed Server, start or stop a Managed Server, start or stop a Node manager, and start or stop an Admin server. All the applications DBA scripts use this provisioning script on the back end to control the FMW components.

The provisioning script is a wrapper script to call the Provisioning API (oracle.apps.ad.tools. configuration.EBSProvisioner) to provision E-Business Suite.

In this manner, the provisioning script and provisioning API are two important applications DBA tools, and that's why we wanted to cover them in this book, even though they are used by the applications DBA scripts internally.

In this section, we have explained what needs to be controlled in the scope of FMW in EBS 12.2. In addition, we have declared and shown the applications DBA scripts by showing the script executions one by one to make your understanding clearer.

As shown in this section, EBS supplies the applications DBA scripts for controlling the FMW system components and logs for these control operations, but this is not the only control mechanism for FMW components in EBS 12.2. Because FMW is a complete middleware product, it has its own sophisticated utilities named FMW Control and WebLogic Administration Console for controlling the system components belonging to it, and these utilities are useful for you as an apps DBAs.

We usually do operations such as starting and stopping the FMW system components using the applications DBA scripts from the OS terminal, but there are times when we use the sophisticated FMW utilities to manage the FMW environment inside EBS 12.2. Besides, the capabilities of these FMW utilities are so wide that using them allows you to have full control over FMW in an EBS 12.2 environment.

Let's take a look at these utilities.

Using the FMW Control and the WebLogic Console

The FMW Control and the WebLogic console are two web-based console applications that enable the FMW components to be monitored and administered with graphical user interfaces. These two applications together with WebLogic Scripting Tool (WLST) and Fusion Middleware Control MBean Browser are considered Oracle Fusion Middleware administration tools.

In this section, we will explain the FMW console and the WebLogic console, as we have reserved a separate section for WLST and do not see a requirement to go into detail about MBean Browser.

In general, both the FMW and WebLogic console applications supply rich graphical administration and monitoring with web page interfaces equipped with tree-based component panels, charts, and diagrams in order to create a user-friendly environment for easily managing the components in the complex FMW architecture. The interfaces supply several functionalities that make almost all FMW administration possible through a browser without a need for a terminal login.

Although these two applications seem similar and have several capabilities, they actually differ from each other by the kinds of functionalities they provide. Thus, you need to use them together to manage FMW efficiently.

Before showing some examples of the FMW Control and WebLogic console applications, we'll start by explaining the capabilities of these applications and the management activities that can be done using them, as this will be like a comparison report to help you to understand the potentials of these two administration applications.

Here are the tasks that can be accomplished using the FMW Control:

- Start and stop WebLogic Server

- Deploy SOA composite applications

- Monitor SOA composite applications

- Modify Oracle BPEL Process Manager MBean properties

- Debug applications such as Oracle BPEL Process Manager applications

- Deploy ADF applications

- Deploy Java EE applications

- Configure and manage auditing

- Configure SSL for Java and system components

- View and manage most of the log files

- Change ports of some of the system components

- Manage Oracle HTTP Server

- Manage Oracle Web Cache

- Start and stop components

- Start and stop applications

As you see, there are several things you can do using the FMW Control. Although some of these things such as configuring SSL for Java are a little internal and some of them such as the Monitor SOA composite application or the Modify BFEL process Manager MBean properties are not related to standard EBS configuration, there are still a lot of critical tasks that can done using the FMW Control, such as managing Oracle HTTP Server or starting and stopping applications.

Although Oracle recommends using the AD scripts for managing the FMW components on EBS 12.2, Oracle documents such as "Oracle E-Business Suite Setup Guide Release 12.2, Part No. E22953-14" state that the WebLogic Administration Console can be used to control the WebLogic Managed Servers in EBS 12.2. Also, even though working with the EBS Managed Servers using WebLogic Administration Console is not recommended by Oracle, there are some cases where you need to use the WebLogic console to stop/start the EBS 12.2 Managed Servers, such as when you have a lost WebLogic admin password or you do not have an EBS application server connection.

Oracle recommends AD scripts for managing EBS FMW components because these scripts do the validation checks and reflect the recent changes done to the context file in the EBS WebLogic configuration files. For instance, when you look at the start flow initiated by admanagedsrvctl.sh, you can see that admanagedsrvctl.sh executes txrun.pl, which in turn executes txkChkEBSDependecies.pl located in the $FND_TOP/patch/115/bin directory. By using txkChkEBSDependecies.pl, admanagedsrvctl.sh does the validation checking, although these checks (check whether the latest FORMSAPP.EAR is deployed, check whether latest cabo files are deployed, check whether the latest Jersey and Jackson libraries are deployed, and check whether all servlets are present) only produce warnings and do not break the execution of the admanagedsrvctl.sh script. After the checks, admanagedsrvctl.sh executes adProvisionEBS.pl, which in turn executes oracle.apps.ad.tools.configuration.EBSProvisioner with the ebs-nmstart-managedsrv method call, which reads the context file for building the Java and WebLogic-related command-line arguments and starts the Managed Server via the Node Manager. In conclusion, when the EBS 12.2 environment is stable (that is when there are no updates done in the context files or any EBS FMW-related code files since the last start of the WebLogic Managed Servers), WebLogic Administration Console can be used for managing (stopping, starting, and so on) EBS 12.2 Managed Servers.

Let's continue by taking a look at what can be done using the WebLogic console.

- Create additional Managed Servers

- Clone Managed Servers

- Cluster Managed Servers

- Start and stop WebLogic Server

- Add users and groups to the default embedded LDAP

- Create data sources

- Create connection pools

- Create JMS queues

- Configure advanced queueing

- Deploy Java EE applications

- Configure SSL for Oracle WebLogic Server

- Change passwords

- View and manage some of the log files (access.log, EmbeddedLDAP.log, and EmbeddedLDAPAccess.log)

- Change ports for Oracle WebLogic Server and Java components

As you see, there are several WebLogic-related tasks that can be done using the WebLogic console. Also, some of the tasks such as creating JMB queues are actually not related to EBS 12.2, as it is a packaged application, but still there are several unavoidable tasks such as managing the Managed Servers and changing the password of WebLogic users that are done using the WebLogic console. Also, activities such as restarting a Managed Server, monitoring the usages of data sources, or increasing their limits are the things you will mostly do as an apps DBA.

Note that there are also some tasks that can be done using both the FMW Control and the WebLogic console such as starting and stopping the Managed Servers.

So far, you have been introduced to the capabilities of the FMW Control and WebLogic console applications, so now it's time to go into more depth. Let's start with the Fusion Middleware Control.

The FMW Control is an Oracle Enterprise Manager, which is designed for controlling Fusion Middleware. That's why it is also called the Oracle Enterprise Manager Fusion Middleware Control. Basically, the Enterprise Manager Fusion Middleware Control is a web-based administration center, and it can be thought of as the FMW version of the Oracle Enterprise Manager Database Control tool, which core DBAs are quite familiar with.

The Enterprise Manager Fusion Middleware Control runs as an application on the WebLogic Admin Server. It works on the Admin Server's port and can be displayed using the following URL:

```
http://hostname.domain:port_of_the_admin_server/em
```

Figure 7-8 shows the first page, the Fusion Middleware Control login page, in which the WebLogic admin user and password should be supplied in order to be able to log in and start using the FMW Control.

Figure 7-8. Fusion Middleware Control login page

After the login page, a web page displaying the status of the deployments in the farm appears. The term *farm* is used for describing a collection of components managed by the Fusion Middleware Control. On this page, you can quickly take a look at the conditions of the deployed applications, WebLogic servers, and Oracle HTTP Server to see whether any of them has failed or is not running.

Figure 7-9 shows an example of this web page, displaying the farm within the general and detailed statuses of all of its deployments.

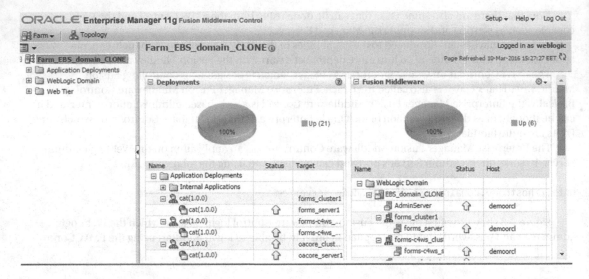

Figure 7-9. *Fusion Middleware Control, first screen displaying the status of deployments*

The panel on the left displays the components in the farm and provides a tree-based list where you can drill down to get into the details according to the component type. A right-click on any component brings a submenu onto the screen where the available actions for that component are listed, as the available actions vary from one component to another. For example, while the buttons to be used for starting and stopping a Managed Server appear in the action list for a Managed Server item, the button to be used for displaying the log files appears in the actions menu of the Oracle HTTP Server, as shown in Figure 7-10.

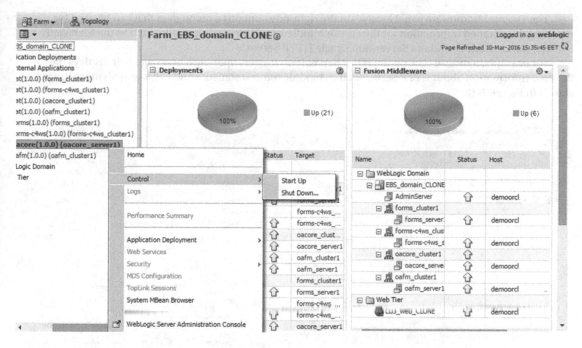

Figure 7-10. *Fusion Middleware Control displaying the action list for a component*

Figure 7-10 shows how a submenu listing the actions available for a Managed Server item appears when you right-click that Managed Server item.

The deployments panel located in the middle of the screen can be used for reaching the detailed information for the Fusion Middleware System components, and it is also interactive. A mouse click on a linked item brings another page, where the details about that item are displayed.

For example, clicking an item like the oacore server opens a page that displays quick gadgets with the response and load of the server, as well as the information such as active sessions, request-processing times, beans in use, and web entry points. Those pages look like the example shown in Figure 7-11, where the details of the oacore Managed Server are displayed.

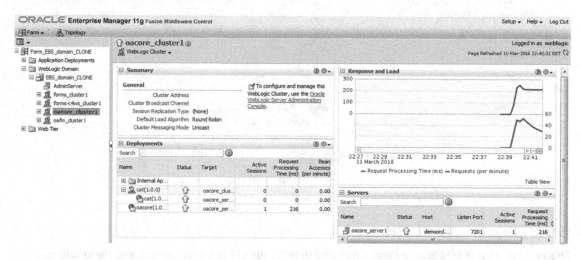

Figure 7-11. *Fusion Middleware Control page displaying details about the oacore Managed Server*

The Fusion Middleware panel located on the right side contains a menu item that can be used for reaching the detailed information for the Fusion Middleware System components such as the Managed Servers, the clusters, the Admin Server, and Oracle HTTP Server.

For example, a mouse click on the HTTP Server item triggers opening a new page that displays the detailed information about HTTP Server such as module request statistics and CPUs and Memory usages, as shown in Figure 7-12.

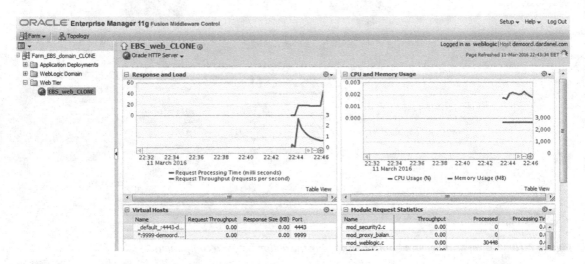

Figure 7-12. *Fusion Middleware Control page displaying the detailed information about HTTP Server*

The FMW Control also provides a Topology button in the upper-left corner of the GUI, which can be used to display a simple topology showing the web tier, FMW servers, and database in use.

Figure 7-13 shows an example topology displayed by clicking the Topology button located in the left corner of the FMW Control web pages.

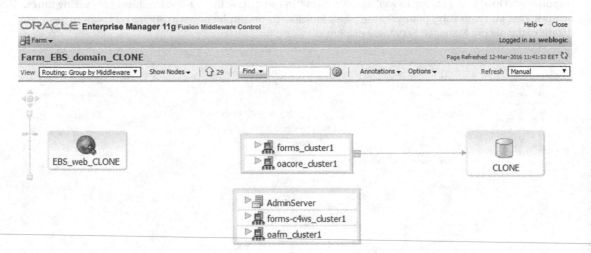

Figure 7-13. *Fusion Middleware Control topology showing the web tier, FMW servers, and the database*

It is important to mention the Farm Resource Center, which can be found almost in every page of the FMW Control. The Farm Resource Center is like a help center providing links to the Oracle Enterprise Manager Online Help, in which a lot of documents about the terms and items used in the FMW Control can be found.

As shown in Figure 7-14, using the links in the Farm Resource Center, the information about a subject can be displayed in the Oracle Enterprise Manager Online Help web pages.

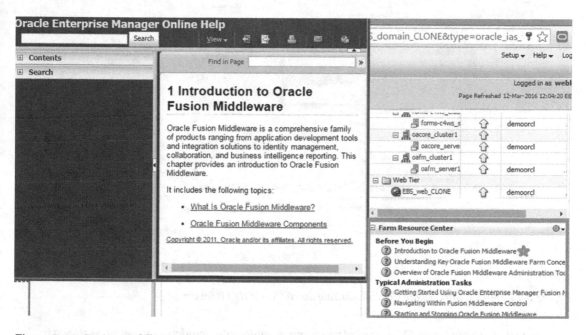

Figure 7-14. *Fusion Middleware Control Online Help*

So, the Farm Resource Center might come in handy while administering FMW for the first time, as it provides helpful information.

There are a lot of features in the FMW Control, and a lot of tasks can be accomplished using it. Thanks to Oracle, it has the look and feel that lets administrators easily get used to it. Before continuing with WebLogic console, we will give an example of the FMW Control.

In this example, we will stop Oracle HTTP Server and start it again. We have chosen to give this task as an example because it is specific to the FMW Control; in other words, this task cannot be done using other utilities like the WebLogic console.

To stop Oracle HTTP Server using the FMW Control, log in to the Enterprise Manager FMW Control as explained earlier, expand Web Tier in the tree located on the left side of the page, and right-click the EBS_web_{SID} item.

After doing this, choose the Control menu item from the submenu, and click Shut Down, as shown in Figure 7-15.

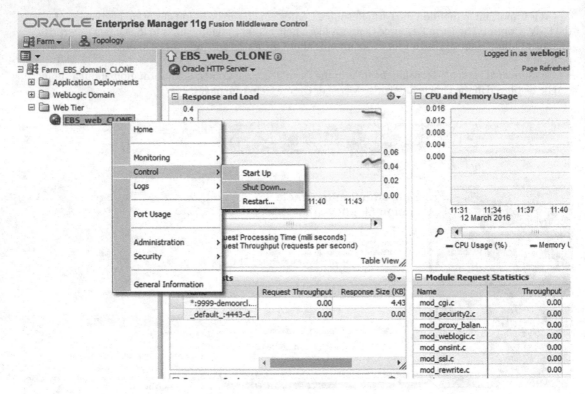

Figure 7-15. *Fusion Middleware Control shutting down Oracle HTTP Server*

After clicking Shut Down, FMW Control wants you to approve the shutdown operation, as shown in Figure 7-16.

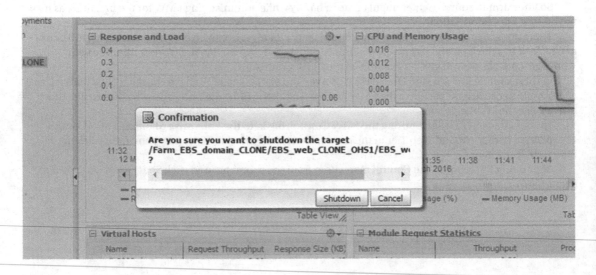

Figure 7-16. *Fusion Middleware Control Confirmation for shutting down the Oracle HTTP Server*

Click the Shutdown button in the confirmation dialog box, and the FMW Control starts the shutdown process, as shown in Figure 7-17.

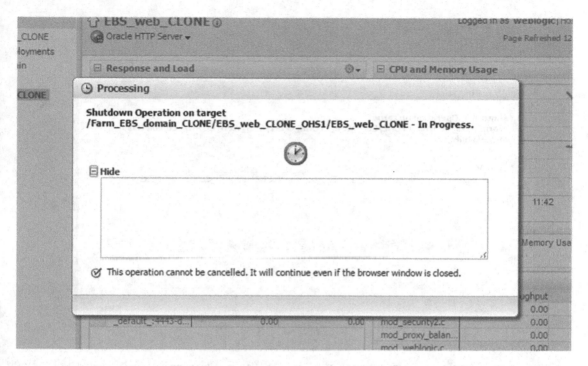

Figure 7-17. *Fusion Middleware Control shut down operation for Oracle HTTP Server in progress*

Once HTTP Server is shut down, the FMW Control displays a confirmation dialog box informing you that the shutdown operation for Oracle HTTP Server has completed successfully, as shown in Figure 7-18.

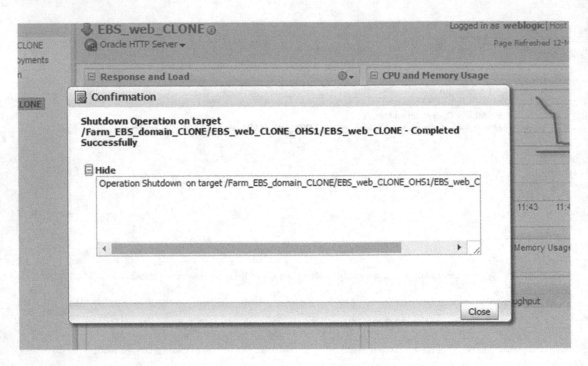

Figure 7-18. *Fusion Middleware Control shut down operation for Oracle HTTP Server completed*

The startup operation for Oracle HTTP Server is done using the same method. That is, after you expand the tree and right-click the EBS_web_{SID} item, you choose the Control from the submenu, but this time click the Start Up button afterward, as shown in Figure 7-19.

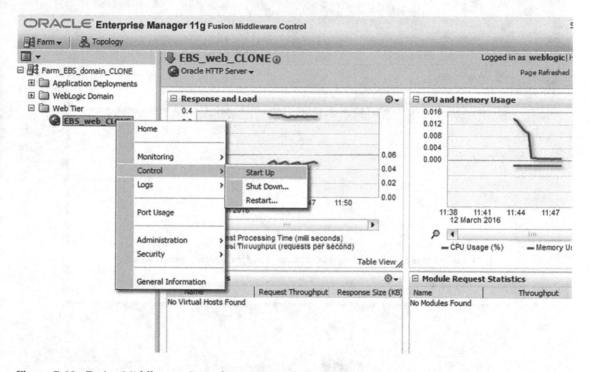

Figure 7-19. *Fusion Middleware Control starting Oracle HTTP Server*

After clicking the Startup, FMW starts Oracle HTTP Server and informs you about the continuing operation, as shown in Figure 7-20.

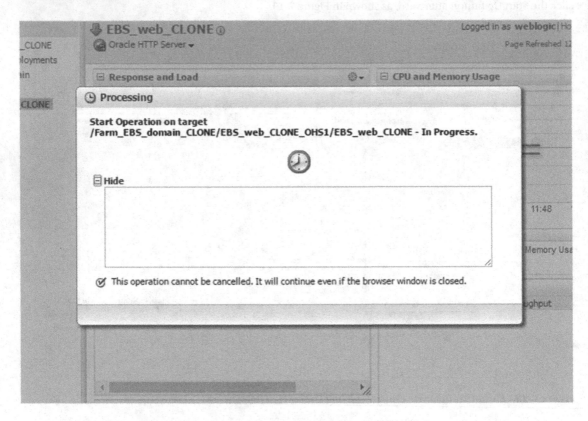

Figure 7-20. *Fusion Middleware Control starting Oracle HTTP Server, continued*

Lastly, the FMW Control displays a confirmation dialog box informing you that the startup operation for Oracle HTTP Server completed successfully, as shown in Figure 7-21.

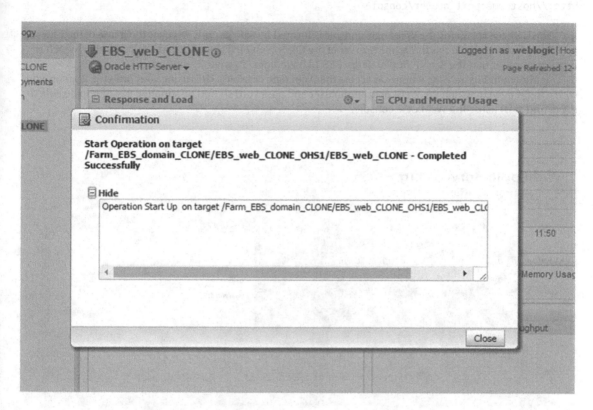

Figure 7-21. *Fusion Middleware Control starting Oracle HTTP Server, continued*

So, using the FMW Control is crucial because it saves you from using the OS terminals, navigating the directory structure using the command line, and executing the appropriate commands for every single operation. It is also easy to use, and operations that can be done using it become pretty straightforward from an administrator's point of view.

It is definitely the tool for managing FMW components generally, so it can be used for most of your FMW administration work. However, as an apps DBA, you are not dealing with FMW components mostly, and when it comes to the FMW, you are usually dealing with WebLogic.

WebLogic is the application server inside the FMW stack, and it has its own sophisticated administration tool called the WebLogic console. There are things you can do with it and things you cannot, but it is the first place to look when there is a requirement for administrating WebLogic Server instances in EBS 12.2.

The WebLogic console is an application that runs on the Admin Server of the Weblogic Domain that is part of the EBS 12.2. The WebLogic Console provides a sophisticated graphical interface, which can be accessed using a web browser, used for managing the Weblogic Domain in EBS 12.2.

Using the WebLogic console, apps DBAs can do a lot of important WebLogic-specific tasks such as configuring clusters, managing Managed Servers, deploying applications, configuring Managed Server parameters, and viewing server and domain log files.

The WebLogic console is accessible using the following URL:

```
http://hostname:port_number/console
```

The URL for accessing the WebLogic console is formed by a hostname, which is the name of the EBS application server that hosts the Admin Server of the EBS's Weblogic Domain, and a port number, which is the port number that the Admin Server of the EBS 12.2 Weblogic Domain listens on.

As shown in Figure 7-22, when you access the WebLogic console's URL using your browser, it greets you with a login page in which the WebLogic admin user and password should be supplied in order to be able to log in and start using the WebLogic console.

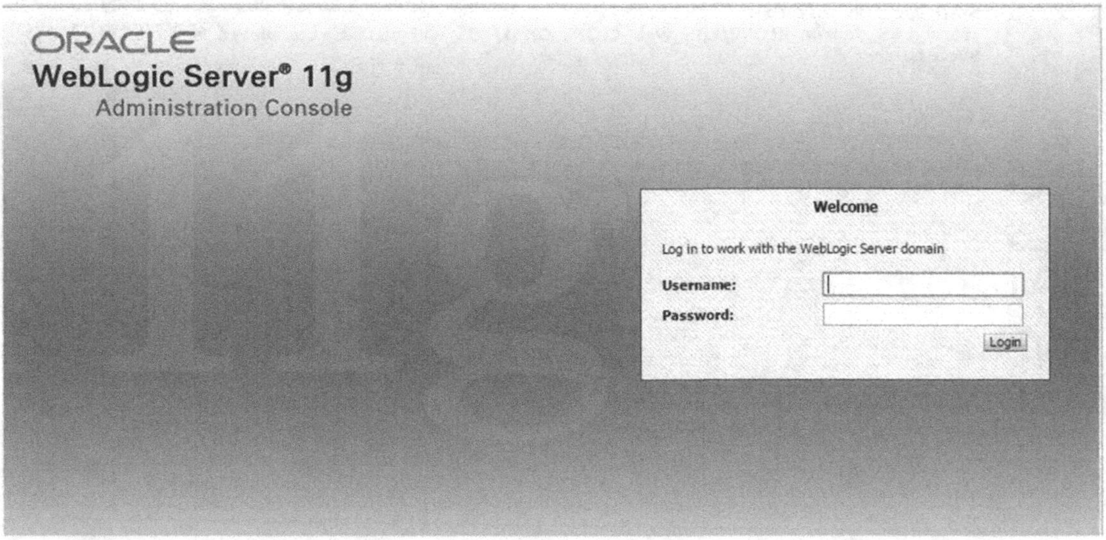

Figure 7-22. *WebLogic admin console login page*

After a successful login, the home page of the WebLogic console is displayed and several quicks links are provided for accessing the necessary WebLogic console pages to accomplish almost any task in a WebLogic environment.

On the left side of the home page, you see the Change Center tab, which has Lock & Edit and Release Configuration buttons, which in sequence can be used for getting a lock before making a change in the domain configuration and releasing a lock after making a change in the domain configuration. This is because these kinds of things are critical and should not be done simultaneously by multiple WebLogic administrators.

Just below Lock & Edit, there is a tab called Domain Structure, which is based on a tree structure. By expanding the branches of the Domain Structure tree, you can access the configuration pages for deployments, diagnostics, interoperability components such as WTC Servers (WebLogic Tuxedo Connector), and the system components that form the WebLogic environment such as servers, clusters, and machines.

Figure 7-23 shows an example WebLogic admin console home page, which is displayed after a successful login. As shown in Figure 7-23, the home page is equipped with several links to reach the necessary WebLogic admin console web pages for configuring and administrating all the WebLogic components.

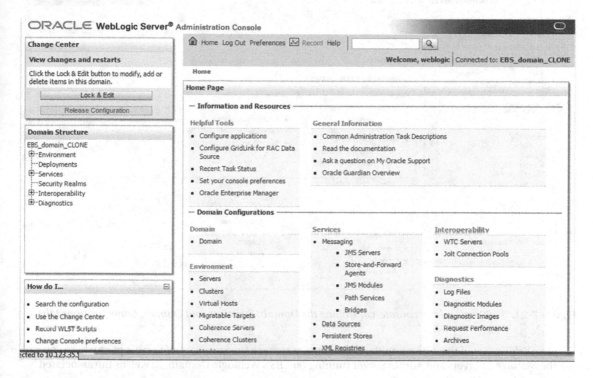

Figure 7-23. *WebLogic admin console home page*

There are several different navigation paths for accomplishing tasks in the WebLogic console, and you should be able to easily figure out how to reach the necessary pages for doing your work. Nevertheless, we will show some WebLogic console screenshots, which will give you an idea of the navigations in the WebLogic console, while we explain the WLDF watches, which retain the criteria to be used by WebLogic in identifying situations that need to be trapped while monitoring the server and application states and in tuning the Managed Server parameters in the next sections.

We'll present a WebLogic console example first. In this example, you will control the Managed Servers that host the EBS applications in EBS 12.2 using the WebLogic console.

To be able to control the WebLogic servers using the WebLogic console, the associated Node Manager must be started. This is not a thing to consider most of the time, as the Node Manager is started automatically when you start the application services using the adstrtal.sh script, which you usually use to start up the application services because it enables all the application services to be started in one go.

There are two ways to control the Managed Server in the WebLogic console. One way is to click the Servers leaf by expanding the Environment branch of the Domain Structure tree, and the other is to use the server's link located on the home page, just under the Domain Configuration title.

Figure 7-24 shows these two Domain Structure and Domain Configurations panels in which there are links that can be used for accessing the web pages for controlling the Managed Servers in the WebLogic console.

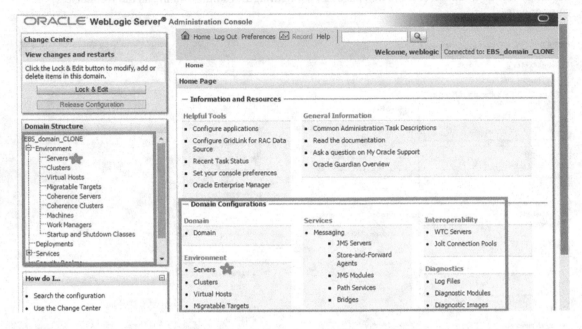

Figure 7-24. *WebLogic admin console, controlling the Domain Structure and Domain Configurations tabs*

By clicking one of these items on the home page, you reach the Summary of Servers page where you can see the Managed Servers and Admin Server running on EBS's Weblogic Domain, as well as the associated clusters and machines.

Figure 7-25 displays this Summary of Servers page, where all the WebLogic servers in the Weblogic Domain can be configured and controlled.

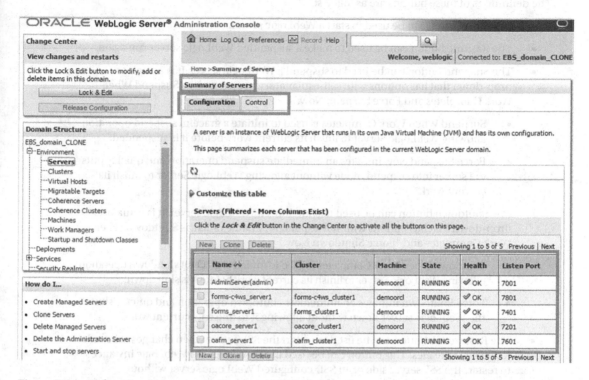

Figure 7-25. *WebLogic admin console, Summary of Servers page*

As shown in Figure 7-25, the WebLogic console also remembers and highlights the navigation path for the current page. So, while the default tab of Configuration shows the configuration summary and statuses of the WebLogic servers, you can also use the Control tab of the Summary of Servers page to control the WebLogic server resources.

When you click the Control button, the WebLogic console refreshes the Summary of Servers page and displays grayed-out control buttons such as Start, Resume, Suspend, Shut Down, and Restart SSL.

The definitions of these buttons are as follows:

- The Start button can be used to start a WebLogic server.

- The Resume button can be used to make a suspended WebLogic server run again.

- The Suspend button can be used to suspend a WebLogic server. It is actually a drop-down that has options with self-explanatory names such as Suspend When Work Completes and Force Suspend Now.

  - Suspend When Work Completes is used to initiate a graceful suspend operation allowing WebLogic Server to finish its current work before it is suspended.

  - Force Suspend Now initiates an immediate suspend operation and quickly puts the server into suspend mode without allowing WebLogic Server to finish its current work.

- The Shutdown button can be used to shut down a WebLogic server. It is actually a drop-down that has options with self-explanatory names such as Shutdown When Work Completes and "Force Shutdown Now.

  - Shutdown When Work Completes is used to initiate a graceful shutdown operation allowing WebLogic Server to finish its current work before it is shut down.

  - Force Shutdown initiates an immediate shutdown operation and quickly shuts the WebLogic server down without allowing it to finish its current work.

- The Restart SSL button can be used to restart the SSL server when changes are made to the keystore files. This button can be used in SSL-configured WebLogic instances to restart the SSL server side of an SSL-configured WebLogic server without restarting the WebLogic server itself.

Figure 7-26 shows the Summary of Servers page where the control buttons (Start, Stop, Suspend, Shutdown, Restart SSL) are grayed out and also draws the attention to the Control button located at the top of the panel to be used to activate the grayed-out control buttons.

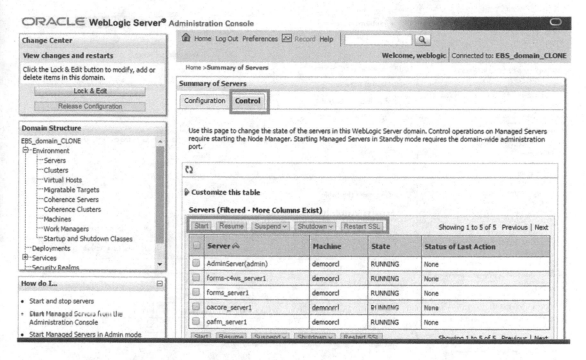

Figure 7-26. WebLogic admin console, controlling WebLogic servers

As mentioned, the control buttons appear as grayed out when the Control panel is loaded for the first time. These buttons get activated when any of the check boxes located on the left side of each manager are selected. You can select multiple check boxes to control multiple WebLogic servers in one go.

So, in this example, we will restart the oacore server, and that's why we select the check box associated with oacore_server1 and proceed as shown in Figure 7-27.

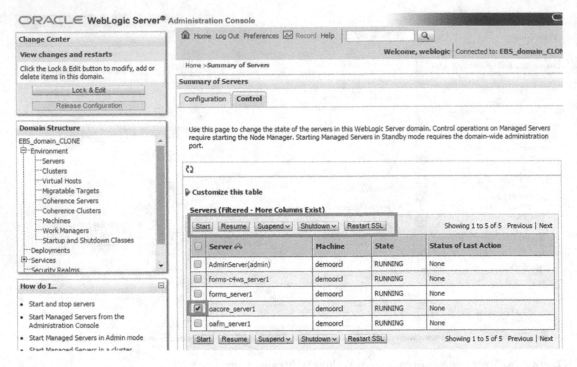

Figure 7-27. WebLogic admin console, controlling the oacore server

Click the Shutdown button and choose the Force Shutdown Now option from the drop-down list.

Note that you have shut down oacore_server1 using the option Force Shutdown Now, as this is a test server. Usually we recommend using the When Work Complete option for shutdown operations in EBS 12.2, unless a hang situation prevents WebLogic Server from being shut down gracefully. Figure 7-28 shows the drop-down menu, which lists the available shutdown options for the oacore Managed Server.

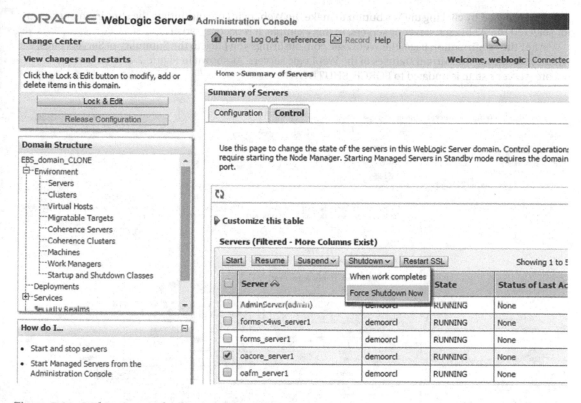

Figure 7-28. *WebLogic console, shutting down oacore server*

When you click the Force Shutdown Now drop-down item, the WebLogic console displays a web page with a confirmation about this critical event, as shown in Figure 7-29.

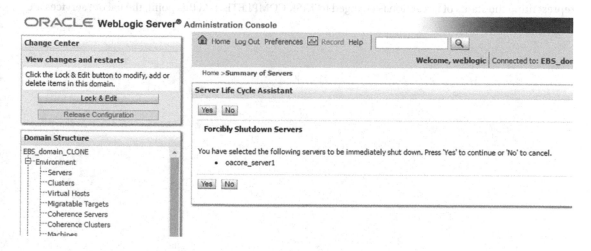

Figure 7-29. *WebLogic Administration Console, confirmation page for a forced shutdown*

You proceed by clicking the Yes button to make the WebLogic console initiate the shutdown operation for selected the WebLogic server or servers. In this example, it is oacore_server1.

After the confirmation page, the WebLogic console brings you back to the Summary of Servers page, where you can see the current statuses of the WebLogic servers. As shown in Figure 7-30, you first see oacore_server's state is updated to FORCE_SHUTDOWN.

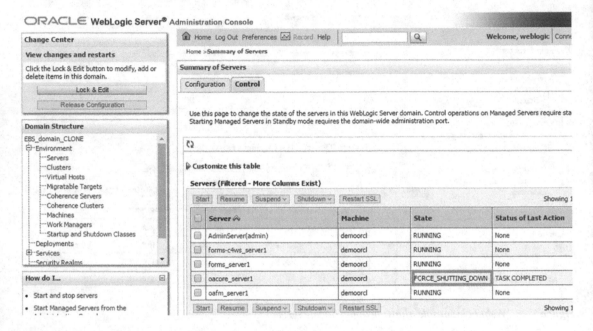

Figure 7-30. *WebLogic admin console, shutting down oacore server, continued*

After a while, you see the state of oacore_server1 is changed to SHUTDOWN and the column representing the status of last action is changed to TASK COMPLETED. At this point, the oacore services are not working anymore.

To start oacore_server1 and make oacore services be available again, you just select the check box associated with oacore_server1 and click the Start button (see Figure 7-31).

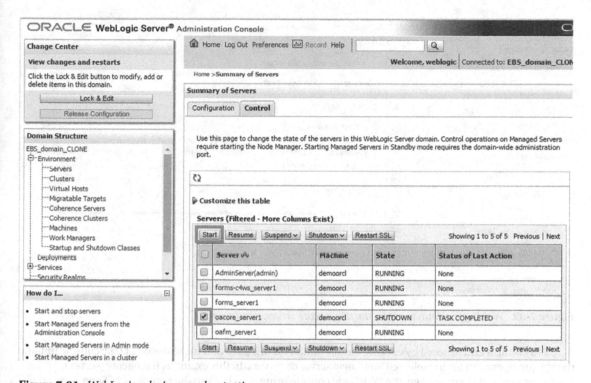

Figure 7-31. WebLogic admin console, starting oacore server

When you click the Start button, as shown in Figure 7-31, the WebLogic console displays a web page like the one shown in Figure 7-32 with the confirmation about this critical event.

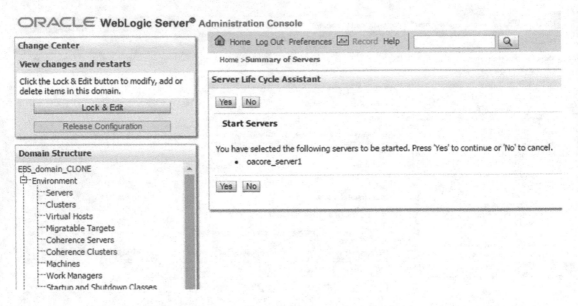

Figure 7-32. *WebLogic admin console, starting oacore server, continued*

You confirm and proceed by clicking the Yes button on this page and make the WebLogic console initiate the startup operation for the selected WebLogic server or servers. In this example, it is oacore_server1.

After the confirmation page, the WebLogic console brings you back to the Summary of Servers page, where you can see the current statuses of the WebLogic servers.

In Figure 7-33, you first see oacore_server's state is updated to STARTING. Also, a message appears on the Messages tab saying "A request has been sent to the Node Manager to start selected servers."

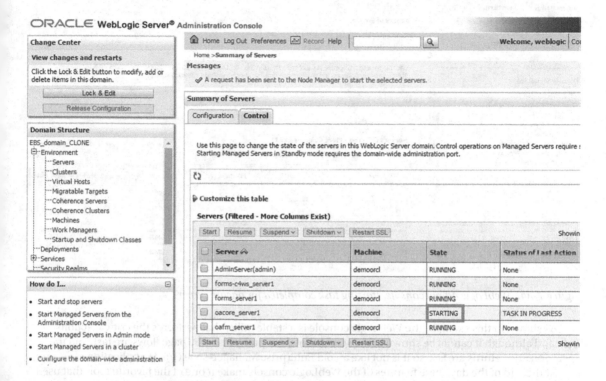

Figure 7-33. *WebLogic admin console, starting oacore server, continued*

After a while, you see the state of oacore_server1 is changed to RUNNING, and the column representing the status of last action is changed to TASK COMPLETED, as shown in the "Status of Last Action" column displayed in Figure 7-34. At this point, the oacore services have started working again, as shown in the State column displayed in Figure 7-34.

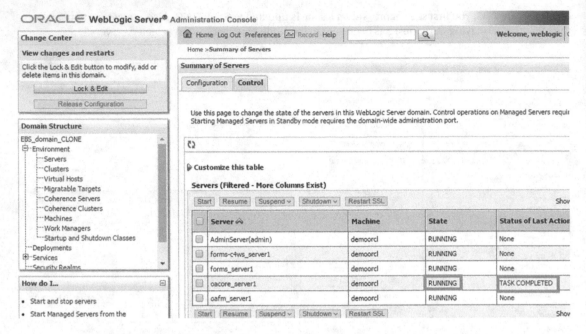

Figure 7-34. WebLogic admin console, starting task completed for oacore server

As shown in this example, the WebLogic console is a stable utility that performs the critical actions well, and although it cannot be shown in the screenshots, it is pretty fast. The page flows are fast, and the operation and returns are fast, so it is not like an old Enterprise Manager–style Oracle application.

At the end of the day, these features of the WebLogic console make it one of the favorite tools that used by apps DBAs to manage the EBS application tier components. Actually, the WebLogic admin console is not only for managing the WebLogic servers but also for configuring and maintaining almost all kinds of EBS WebLogic components. Most of the time, configuration changes for the WebLogic components are done using adProvisionEBS.pl in conjunction with the WebLogic admin console. Also, some of the changes, which are done using the WebLogic console, are reflected in the applications context file using the script called adRegisterWLSListeners.pl, which is running continuously in the background.

So, as shown, there are multiple tools used for making configuration changes, and the tools to be used depend on the configuration that you want change. Thus, apps DBAs can manage the Managed Servers using the WebLogic console, which is an alternative for the AD scripts (for example, admanagedsrvctl.sh), but to be on the safe side, in case there is a need to change a configuration in the WebLogic components, then they should also follow the documentation (Oracle Support). More specifically, as EBS 12.2 WebLogic servers are configured both with the WebLogic console and adProvisionEBS.pl, there is no single configuration tool. There are also some operations such as removing a Managed Server that should be done only by using the adProvisionEBS.pl script. That's why the documentation should be followed in cases like changing the Admin Server's port or changing the Managed Server start arguments.

In this manner, we suggest you follow Oracle Support document "Managing Configuration of Oracle HTTP Server and Web Application Services in Oracle E-Business Suite Release 12.2" (Doc ID 1905593.1) for making configuration changes on EBS 12.2's WebLogic components.

You will use the WebLogic console mostly to see the state of oacore_server when an issue about OAF screens is reported. You'll use it when there is need to increase maximum capacities of the connection pools. You'll use it to enable debug on the Managed Servers and use it to tune the Java parameters of WebLogic Server. You'll use it to view the log file on your browsers. In short, you'll use it to do pretty much everything for managing FMW inside EBS 12.2.

Of course, we can't explain everything about the WebLogic console; for example, we can't give several examples of using it, as this kind of tutorial-like explanation is beyond of the scope of this book. However, we have explained how to use the FMW Control and the WebLogic console sufficiently to give you the idea to work with them. Before explaining how to tune the Managed Server parameters and taking a look at the WLDF and Notification components, we will explain one more utility for managing the FMW components, the WebLogic Scripting Tool (WLST).

WLST and Its Typical Usages in EBS 12.2

WLST is a Java-based command-line utility to be used for monitoring and administering WebLogic Server instances and domains. It is management tool that is a little different from the WebLogic console and FMW console tools that we have talked about so far.

WLST is like a shell, so the tasks are done using WLST-based commands. It does not require any browser or graphical interface to work. Also, there is no need for the WebLogic Admin Server to be running to use WLST.

Just like the scripts that ease your daily life, WLST eases your WebLogic management activities. Once you get used to it, it may be your preferred administration tool for managing the WebLogic environment in EBS 12.2.

The tasks that can be accomplished by using WLST as a WebLogic tool are as follows:

- Creating and configuring Weblogic Domains

- Getting the runtime and configuration information for the domain

- Editing the domain configuration

- Editing custom, user-created and also non-WebLogic Server Mbeans

- Automating domain configuration tasks and application deployment

- Controlling and managing the WebLogic servers

- Starting, stopping, and suspending server instances through the Node Manager

So, by using the abilities listed, you can do several important tasks using WLST in the EBS 12.2 environments. WLST can save the day in certain circumstances such as removing a domain lock that is preventing applications DBA scripts from starting the WebLogic servers.

Actually, we will give this scenario as an example for using WLST, but before that, we'll explain a little more about WLST and its characteristics.

WLST has two types of usage: online and offline. In online mode, you can connect to admin or Managed Servers and access the Java objects called Managed Beans (Mbeans), which provide the management interfaces.

Thus, using WLST online provides several abilities such as connecting to a WebLogic Server instance, starting a server in the current domain using Node Manager, canceling an edit session, releasing the edit lock, and discarding all unsaved changes.

Offline mode, on the other hand, lets WLST work while not connected to a running WebLogic server. Working with WLST in offline mode means you have fewer capabilities when compared to WLST in online mode. In general, WLST offline only lets you access the persisted configuration information. In other words, it provides access to the configuration objects that appear only in the configuration files, but there are still some important tasks that can be accomplished in offline mode such as starting Node Manager.

Also, WLST has three types of modes, called direct/interactive/command-line mode, script mode, and embedded mode.

In interactive mode, WLST works like a standard CLI. It's like the famous utility sqlplus, which is an Oracle utility used for executing queries and a utility that apps DBAs are quite familiar with. WLST is used to execute the WebLogic-related commands supplied by the terminal. In this mode, WLST returns the response to the terminal immediately and interactively.

Script mode is useful when it is required to use a script for executing a bunch of WLST commands to accomplish a task noninteractively. To create a script for executing WLST commands, you can put the WLST commands in a text file and save that file with .py extension. Note that py is the extension used for Python, as the WLST scripts are based on Python. The resultant file can be considered a WLST script, and it can then be executed by WLST in Script mode.

Lastly, WLST commands can also be used as embedded. In embedded mode, you can embed the WLST interpreter in a custom Java code snippet and use it to run WLST commands and scripts from the custom code.

We have explained the WLST as much as is sufficient for an apps DBA, so we'll now present an example so you can see it in action. The following example will be a typical usage of WLST in an EBS 12.2 environment. As our focus is EBS 12.2, we will explain the utility from an apps DBA's perspective.

Now suppose you are in an EBS 12.2 environment and you cannot start the Managed Servers using the applications DBA scripts because of a domain lock that has been left held by some other admin. Also suppose you don't have a browser to log into the WebLogic console and release the lock using the graphical interface.

This example will show how to fix this problem and show how to use WLST in a general manner. To use the WLST, you first have to set the FMW environment. Setting the domain environment by using setDomainEnv.sh located in the $FMW_HOME/user_projects/domains/EBS_domain_<SID>/bin directory is enough for this.

After setting the environment, execute the java weblogic.WLST command to start the WLST tool. After executing the java weblogic.WLST command, the WLST tool starts working with offline mode. After a quick initialization, WLST starts waiting for the commands.

```
[applmgr@somehost bin]$ . setDomainEnv.sh
[applmgr@somehost EBS_domain_ORATEST]$ java weblogic.WLST
```

Here's the output:

```
Initializing WebLogic Scripting Tool (WLST) ..
Welcome to WebLogic Server Administration Scripting Shell
Type help () for help on available commands
wls:/offline>
```

So, you have WLST running now. Let's concentrate on the example and use some commands to check the statuses of the Managed Servers.

To do this, you connect to the Admin Server using the connect() function of WLST. Note that you supply three arguments for using the connect() function: the WebLogic admin username, the WebLogic admin password, and the Admin Server URL with the following format: t3://admin_server_hostname:admin_server_port.

After connecting the Admin Server, WLST starts working in online mode. It is important to mention that WLST works via logic based on the directory structures. That is, like you use the cd and ls commands in the shells of Linux systems, you can use functions like cd() and ls() in WLST to change the WLST directories in order to reach the information for the components you need. For example, to list the names of the servers in a Weblogic Domain, you change the WLST directory to the /EBS_domain_<SID>/serverConfig/Servers directory and use ls() to list the contents of this directory, as the subdirectories that are listed by ls are actually the names of the WebLogic servers in the domain.

So, after connecting to the Admin Server, WLST sets the current working directory to be /EBS_domain_<SID>/serverConfig by default.

At this point, you use the cd() function with the "Servers" input and then use the ls() function to list the servers, as the directories representing the names of the servers are in the /EBS_domain_<SID>/ serverConfig/Servers directory.

This approach can be described as follows:

```
wls:/offline> connect ('weblogic','welcome1','t3://somehost:7001')
wls:/EBS_domain_ORATEST/serverConfig> cd ('Servers')
wls:/EBS_domain_ORATEST/serverConfig/Servers> ls()
```

Here is the output:

```
dr--   AdminServer
dr--   forms-c4ws_server1
dr--   forms_server1
dr--   oacore_server1
dr--   oafm_server1
```

From the previous output, you can see you have five servers in this domain. This is expected, as it is a standard EBS 12.2 environment.

Let's check the status of oacore_server1.

Note that you use the print state() function to accomplish that.

```
wls:/EBS_domain_ORATEST/serverConfig/Servers> print state('oacore_server1')
```

Here's the output:

```
Current state of 'oacore_server1': SHUTDOWN
```

So, the oacore server is not running.

At this point, you have checked the status of the Managed Server named oacore_server1 and seen that it is SHUTDOWN. This is expected and consistent with the scenario, as we suppose there is a domain lock left being held, and the applications DBA Managed Server start scripts cannot start the Managed Servers when there is a domain lock in the environment. The scripts work like this by design.

```
wls:/EBS_domain_ORATEST/serverConfig> edit();
```

Here's the output:

```
Location changed to edit tree. This is a writable tree with
DomainMBean as the root.
To make changes you will need to start an edit session via startEdit ().
```

For more help, use help (edit).

```
You already have an edit session in progress and hence WLST will
continue with your edit session.
```

```
wls:/EBS_domain_ORATEST/edit> stopEdit();
```

Here's the output:

```
Sure you would like to stop your edit session? (y/n)

y
Edit session has been stopped successfully.
```

The lock is released, and now the applications DBA scripts can start the Managed Servers without any problems.

By the way, this domain lock problem may be encountered again. So, to fix this problem, the solution explained can be "scriptized," and the resultant script can be used as a wrapper for executing the EBS startup scripts.

We give the following script as an example because referring to such a script in this chapter will indeed suit our goal, and it is a real-life example that is directly related to EBS 12.2.

So, for this purpose, you can use the Python script named Example.py. What you do for preparing the script Example.py is create an empty file and basically fill it with the contents as follows.

Here's the Example.py script:

```
connect('weblogic','welcome1','t3://somehost:7001')
edit()
stopEdit(defaultAnswer='y')
exit()
```

So, the previous script Example.py is a Python script that does the same things that we have done to stop an editing session by using WLST in interactive mode. It basically written in a manner to connect to the Admin Server, stop the editing session that releases the domain lock, and exit from the WLST tool.

To execute this Python script in a single move, you can use a bash script named Example.sh. In accordance with this purpose, Example.sh is written to invoke WLST, execute the Example.py script that does actual job, and lastly start the EBS application services using the applications DBA script named adstrtal.sh.

Here's the Example.sh script:

```
# EBS 12.2 APPS START automated
# supply Apps Schema Password and Weblogic admin Password in sequence as command line
arguments
# reviewed and tested 1/15/2015
# 07/24/2015 modified to release the domain lock before starting the application services
if [ `whoami` == "root" ]
then
echo you cannot run this script with root!
echo exiting
else
. /u01/apps/EBSapps.env run
. $EBS_DOMAIN_HOME/bin/setDomainEnv.sh
java weblogic.WLST Example.py
. /u01/apps/EBSapps.env run
{ echo apps; echo $1; echo $2; } | sh $ADMIN_SCRIPTS_HOME/adstrtal.sh -nopromptmsg
fi
```

Note that in the Example.sh script we have used the command "{ echo apps; echo $1; echo $2; } | sh $ADMIN_SCRIPTS_HOME/adstrtal.sh –nopromptmsg" to start the application services. This is a special move to make the adstrtal.sh script not prompt for the WebLogic or APPS password but instead read its command-line arguments for retrieving those values.

When you execute Example.sh by supplying the APPS password and the WebLogic password as its first and second command-line arguments, it first sets the Weblogic Domain environment by using the setDomain.env script and then executes WLST with the Example.py script in script mode. This action releases the domain lock if there is any. After releasing the domain lock, Example.sh continues to run, sources the EBSapps.env file, and finally starts the application services.

Note that we have given this example to create a use case for WLST in EBS 12.2. The issue to be fixed by the script may not be reproducible in your environment because patches are released daily, but it is a good example for understanding the WLST usage in conjunction with EBS administration. We have faced with this problem in an EBS 12.2.3 environment and used the previous scripts in real life for handling it.

Well, we have explained WLST and its usages in EBS 12.2 by showing some examples. The example we have used for explaining WLS usage in script summarized all the things you need to know to use WLST. Now we can move on and take a look at what you can do in terms of tuning the WebLogic environment in EBS 12.2.

Best Practices for Tuning Fusion Middleware in EBS 12.2

So far, we have explained the Fusion Middleware (FMW) environment in general and gone through the administration activities and tool related to it. In the remaining part of this chapter, we will be focusing on activities such as tuning and diagnosing FMW and explaining the known tips for these activities in EBS 12.2 environments.

Performance tuning for FMW in EBS 12.2 is based on WebLogic Server, as it is the main component and it does all the core activities of FMW in EBS 12.2. At the same time, performance and tuning in WebLogic are big topics covering a huge number of the subjects, from tuning the pool sizes to tuning the chunk sizes.

The following are the tunable components in WebLogic:

- Pool sizes

- Connection sacklog buffering

- Chunk sizes

- HTTP sessions

- The messaging applications

Besides the tunable components, there are some optimized features that are recommended to be used for getting better performance from WebLogic.

- Prepared statement cache

- Logging last resource optimization

- Optimistic or read-only concurrency

- Local interfaces

- Eager-relationship-caching

As you may guess, tuning the components and using the features listed here can be considered as internals of WebLogic Server. So, as the main focus is EBS 12.2 and also since it is a packaged application, we will only briefly explain these tuning activities and recommended features However, we will focus more on the known tips for maximizing the performance of FMW in EBS 12.2.

Pool sizes can be tuned for JDBC connections, stateless session Enterprise Java Beans (EJBs), and Message Driven Beans (MDBs). Setting the pool sizes to the optimal values may increase the performance of FMW, as it will avoid the delays created by the pooling activities. In this manner, as for the JDBC data sources, you can increase the Maximum Capacity of Connection Pools setting to handle the probable peaks in the concurrent connections, and you can also configure the connection pool to initialize all its connections at server startup to avoid connection creation delays.

Tuning connection backlog buffering is basically telling WebLogic how many TCP connections can be buffered in a wait queue. This is useful for environments that get a continuously increasing number of connections as the wait queue is populated for the connections that the TCP stack has received but the application has not accepted yet.

Tuning the chunk sizes may be useful for applications that operate on a large volume of data per request. Chunk sizes may be increased both for the client side and for the server side as chunks are the memory portions in the Network layer, which are by default 4Kb in size.

By default WebLogic can maintain a maximum of 2,048 chunks. So, both the chunk size and the maximum number of chunks can be increased to make the WebLogic servers handle the large amount of data more efficiently.

In addition, the probable contention that can be a result of high activity in getting and using these chunks can be eliminated by increasing the partition count. That is, you can specify the number of pool partitions to be used for the chunks. Thus, the operations on these chunks can be spread to multiple partitions, and the potential for contention in using the chunks can be minimized.

By tuning the HTTP sessions, you can decrease the load for the applications by making them do as little work as possible when handling session persistence and sessions. This kind of tuning involves actions such as configuring session persistence, minimizing the sessions by developing the application accordingly, and aggregating the session data following best practices.

Tuning the messaging applications involves tuning the WebLogic persistent store, tuning WebLogic JMS, tuning WebLogic JMS Store-and-Forward, and tuning WebLogic Message Bridge by using best practices.

Prepared statement cache is a feature in WebLogic; it is a tuning that can be done in the context of data sources. The prepared statement cache is a cache for storing compiled SQL statements in memory, thus increasing the performance. By configuring the prepared statement cache, you can make WebLogic store the compiled statements in the cache and decrease the communication between the application server and database, thus getting rid of the processing overhead caused by this communication. The caching is actually related to the database cursors. The cached statements are stored in the database cursors. That is, the database maintains a cursor for each open statement.

The prepared statement cache is configured for the connection pools of the data sources. The configuration is done in two steps.

The first step is choosing a cache management algorithm, which can be either LRU (basically the Least Recently Used statement is removed when the statement cache size is met and there is a need to store a new statement in the cache) or Mixed (the first statements that are cached stay in the cache; when the cache size is met, no new statement can be cached unless the cache is manually cleared).

The second step is setting the size of the statement cache to a value, which is the desired number of prepared and callable statements stored in the cache. The statement cache size is defined for statements to cache per connection per data source instance.

Logging last resource (LLR) is an optimization that can be done for the JDBC data source to reduce the overhead of two-phase transactions, which access multiple relational databases. Logging last resource is a performance enhancement, as it relies on WebLogic Transaction Manager to do all the work for preparing the resources in the transaction and also to determine the commit decision for a global transaction. LLR uses a local database table to do its own transactional work.

LLR is effective when there is one database connection in a two-phase commit transaction, which can be thought of as a transaction that consists of a database operation (using JDBC) and another nondatabase operation, such as a message queueing operation.

LLR improves performance as it eliminates some of the XA overhead for the database processing and avoids the use of JDBC XA drivers.

Lastly, LLR can be configured while creating the JDBC data sources. So, all you need to do for enabling it is to select the Logging Last Resource option in the transaction options page while creating a JDBC data source. Also, LLR can be enabled for an already created data source using the Transaction tab present in the Settings page of that data source.

Optimistic concurrency and read-only concurrency are the optimizations that are done to minimize the locks that are created as a result of accessing the database objects concurrently. These two concurrency optimizations are done for the EJBs and they are done to configure the method followed the EJB container for dealing with the concurrent access. Optimistic concurrency is based on the assumption that the persistent states of the EJBs are changed rarely, and the read-only concurrency is based on the EJBs, which are nontransactional.

In optimistic concurrency, there are no locks held in the EJB container or in the database during a transaction. That is, the EJB container verifies that the data is not changed while the transaction is updating it. If any data that is updated but not committed by the transaction is changed by other sessions, then the EJB container rolls back the transaction.

The read-only concurrency is used for read-only EJBs. It improves the performance by increasing the parallelism, as it activates a new instance for handling the requests of each transaction.

Both of these concurrency methods take advantage of the entity bean cache provided by the EJB container.

Local interfaces, or the call-by-reference method, are development-related optimizations, and they should be done by the developers while implementing EJBS for minimizing the performance overhead that can be created when an EJB calls another EJBS or when a servlet/JSP calls an EJB. Local interfaces enable direct method invocation, which means bypassing the RMI semantics and the call-by-reference method, which eliminates the costs of copying and improves performance.

Lastly, eager-relationship-caching is a mechanism for caching the related beans and preventing multiple queries by issuing a join query and retrieving all the data needed for the related beans in one go. Eager-relationship-caching is enabled by specifying a caching name in the weblogic-query element defined in the weblogic-cmp-jar.xml file.

When eager-relationship-caching is enabled, the multiple queries that are triggered by the EJB code to load some beans are packaged as a single query according to the relationship between the beans, and a single query is issued to get the data to load the beans; thus, an increase in performance is expected.

In this section, we went through the general performance tuning recommendations for WebLogic Server in general. Some of the recommendations were internal and some of them were development related, and they were mostly appropriate for a custom application. However, since EBS 12.2 is a packaged application developed by Oracle, you actually implement administration-related WebLogic tuning activities for maximizing FMW in EBS 12.2. So, let's take a look at the best practices for maximizing FMW performance in EBS 12.2 and also examine how to make certain configuration changes for WebLogic servers in EBS 12.2.

Best Practices for FMW Performance and Managing the Configuration of WebLogic Server in EBS 12.2

The actions for implementing the best practices for FMW inside EBS 12.2 are based on increasing the server utilization by adding more JVMs and increasing the JVM's memory by tuning the JVM-related parameters such as Java heap sizes.

The Managed Servers that are deployed during the EBS 12.2 installation are configured with JVM heaps sized at 512MB. This heap size is the default, and it is normally sufficient for a test or development system, where there are fewer than 50 users. However, when it comes to production systems, JVM heaps sized at 512MB are usually not sufficient for the Managed Servers.

Especially the oacore servers need bigger heap sizes in production systems, as they are the core Managed Servers that play a part in almost every client-server connection. The recommended value for setting the heap sizes for the oacores JVM heap size is 2GB.

The oacore servers must be the first priority when increasing the heap sizes, but the heap sizes for the other Managed Servers such as forms and oafm may also be increased if there is available physical memory on the application server where they reside.

The heap sizes should be increased to the recommended values by considering the physical memory size of the application server, as these heaps are created on the physical memory of the machine that the JVMs (in other words, the Managed Servers) are running. It is important to respect the physical memory sizes, as any shortness in the machine's memory will trigger paging in the OS level and the general performance of the EBS application services will decrease in an undeniable manner.

While configuring the heap sizes, it is recommended that you set both the Xmx (Maximum heap size) values and the Xms (Minimum heap size) values of oacore servers to 2GB.

By using 2GB heap sizes, one oacore server can support almost 200 EBS users in general. Also, by configuring the minimum heap sizes to be the same as the maximum heap sizes, you eliminate the work needed for growing and shrinking the heaps. The configuration for the heap sizes can be done using the WebLogic console.

To configure the heap sizes, you connect to the WebLogic console and access the Managed Server's configuration page using the navigation Home ➤ Summary of Servers ➤ oacore_server1. Once the configuration page for the desired Managed Server is displayed, you click the Server Start tab, lock the domain configuration using the Lock & Edit button, and change the Xms and Xms values to be 2048m (2GB) in the text box Arguments.

It may have drawn your attention that you don't use AutoConfig for operations such as changing the heap size of a Managed Server. This is because now you have different tools in addition to the AutoConfig utility for managing the configurations of Oracle HTTP Server and web application services in EBS 12.2. While some of the configurations are still done using AutoConfig, some of them are done using the WebLogic Administration Console, Fusion Middleware Control, and the adProvisionEBS.pl script.

In this manner, let's take a look at the managing configuration of the EBS main FMW components, the Oracle HTTP Server, and WebLogic Server; in general, Oracle HTTP Server configurations are managed via the Fusion Middleware Control. So, you can use the Fusion Middleware Control, but as there are still some AutoConfig managed profile options regarding Oracle HTTP Servers present in the database, you can use adSyncContext.pl to reflect the configuration changes to these profile options as well. Classpaths and JVM arguments of the WebLogic Managed Servers, on the other hand, can be managed using the WebLogic console or the WLST utility or even through the command line using the adProvisionEBS.pl script.

Classpaths and JVM arguments of the Admin Server can be managed using the AutoConfig utility via the context variables named s_adminserver_classpath and s_nm_jvm_startup_properties. Changing the port numbers of the Managed Servers is done using the txkSetAppsConf.pl script located in $FND_TOP/ patch/115/bin. Adding or deleting a Managed Server is done using the adProvisionEBS.pl script in conjunction with txksetAppsConf.pl.

So, as you can conclude, there is no definable logic when choosing the utility for making the configuration changes in EBS 12.2. For some cases, you have different options, and for other cases, you have to use the right utility. That's why, as we recommended earlier in this chapter, you should follow the Oracle documentation (such as "Managing Configuration of Oracle HTTP Server and Web Application Services in Oracle E-Business Suite Release 12.2" [Doc ID 1905593.1]) for choosing the right utility to change the configuration of the FMW components in EBS 12.2.

Figure 7-35 shows such a modification in oacore server's JVM configuration, which is similar to what we have explained.

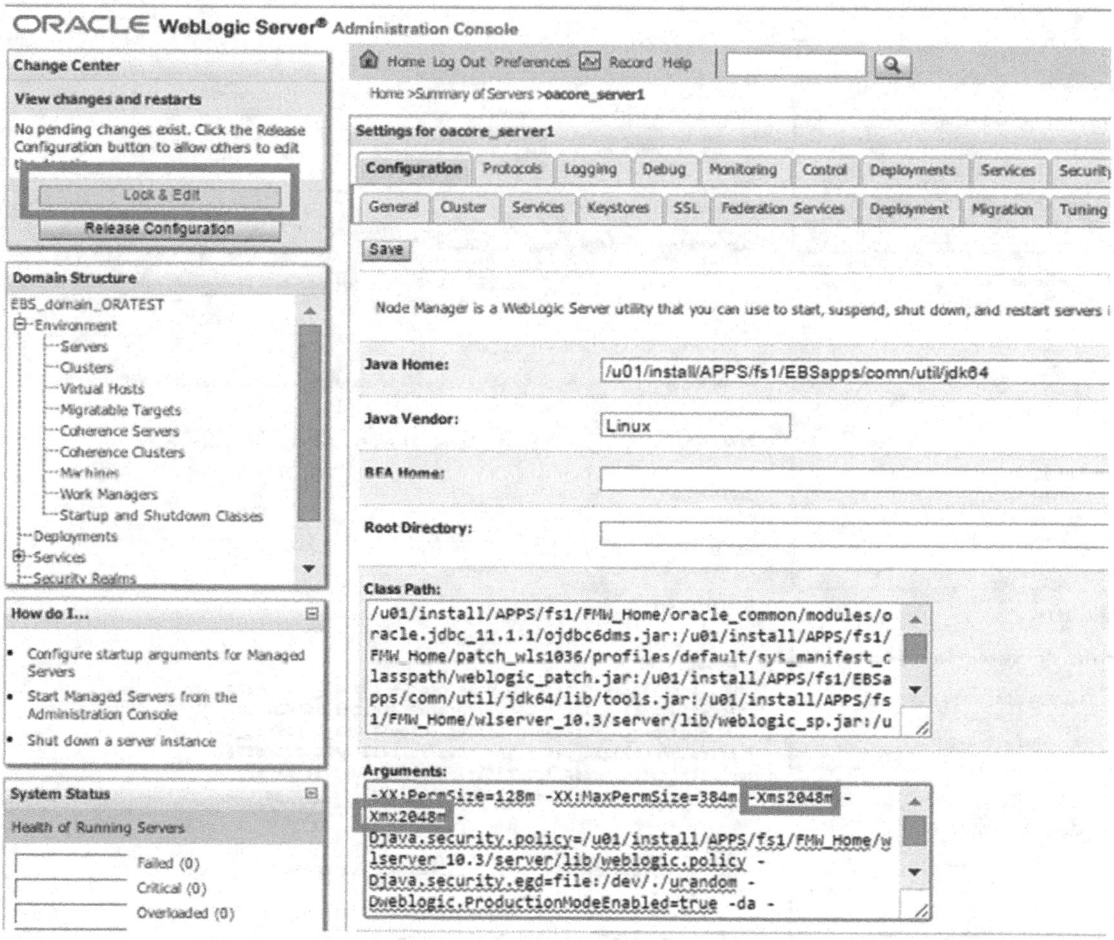

Figure 7-35. *WebLogic admin console, changing the Xms and Xmx values of a Managed Server*

After updating the Xmx and Xms values, click the Save button to see the message "Settings updated successfully" on the Messages tab. You can proceed with activating the changes using the Activate Changes button, as shown in Figure 7-36.

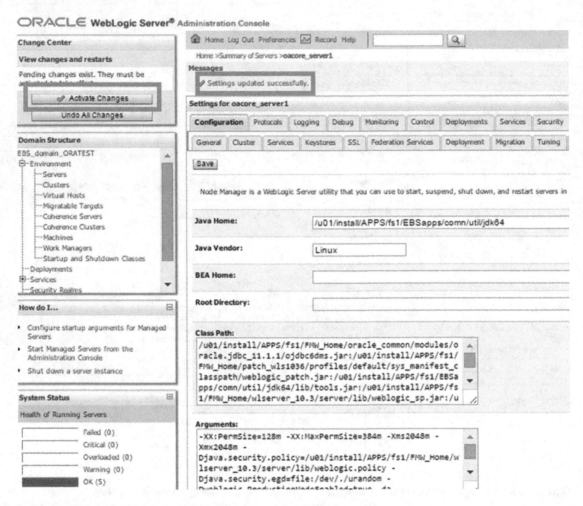

Figure 7-36. *WebLogic admin console, activating the changes*

Once the changes get activated, your domain lock gets automatically released and you restart the relevant Managed Server to make it start with the desired Xmx and Xms values.

After the restart, you use OS tools like the ps program in Linux to check the relevant Managed Server process and see whether your change is activated.

```
[root@somehost ~]# ps -ef|grep oacore
applmgr 26422  9762 99 13:33 ?        00:00:54 /u01/install/APPS/fs1/EBSapps/comn/util/
jdk64/bin/java -Dweblogic.Name=oacore_server1 -Djava.security.policy=null -
....
.......
..........
```

```
Dweblogic.security.SSL.hostnameVerifier=weblogic.security.utils.
SSLWLSWildcardHostnameVerifier -Dweblogic.ReverseDNSAllowed=false -XX: PermSize=128m
-XX:MaxPermSize=384m -Xms2048m -Xmx2048m -Djava.security.policy=/u01/install/APPS/fs1/FMW_
Home/wlserver_10.3/server/lib/
...
.....
.......
```

In addition to the heap sizes, the permanent size limits for the JVM are important for a WebLogic Managed Server.

Permanent space is used by stored classes, methods, and so on. It is controlled by the XX:PermSize parameter representing the initial value and the XX:MaxPermSize parameter representing the max value. Insufficient permanent size limits can make the WebLogic Managed Servers spin in the CPU. You can monitor this situation using the top command in Linux.

That is, just after starting your Managed Server, you can issue a top command and look for the RES column, which displays the physical memory that the Managed Server uses at that time.

The top command output also provides a column named CPU, which shows the percentage of the CPU resource that the Managed Server uses.

In a memory leak situation, you can see an increase in the RES column.

You can see that this memory usage increases until it reaches a limit that is actually the limit from your Managed Server's Java process configuration.

Well, these limits are defined with XXX:PermSize and XX:MaxPermSize. In these kinds of situations, it is advisable to increase the values of these XX:PermSize and XX:MaxPermSize parameters accordingly. The recommended values for these parameters, however, can be changed according to the environment.

We faced a problem in oacore because of the low setting of these variables. In that case, our WebLogic Managed Server was consuming all the CPU cycles in the system, and a hang situation raised because of it. So, we set both XX:PermSize and XX:MaxPermSize to 1024. By default XX:PermSize was set to 128m (XX:PermSize=128m) and XX:MaxPermsize was set to 348m (XX:MaxPermSize=384m). The XX:PermSize and XXMaxPermSize parameters can be configured using the WebLogic console via the same method covering earlier for configuring the heap sizes.

Figure 7-37 shows this type of a modification done for oacore server's PermSize and XXMaxPermSize values, using the WebLogic console.

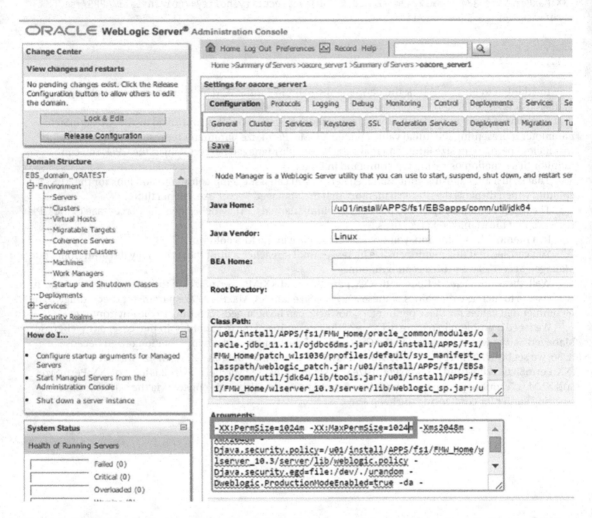

Figure 7-37. *WebLogic cdmin console , changing the Permsize and MaxPermSize values of a Managed Server*

There are some cases where one Managed Server is not sufficient to handle the EBS user load. For handling the high number of requests caused by the high user activity in crowded EBS environments, such as EBS environments operating with 1,000 concurrent users, additional Managed Servers should be created.

In these types of cases, we recommended using one Managed Server with a 2GB heap size for handling the load caused by having 200 users. We also recommend no more than one Managed Server per two CPUs.

In this manner, if you have a server with 16 CPUs and 24GB RAM and 1,000 users working mostly in the OAF pages, you can use five oacore servers to deal with the OAF user load.

By using five OAF servers, you expect to utilize 10 CPUS at most, and by setting the XX:MaxPermSize values for each of these Managed Servers to 1GB, as we recommended earlier (it actually depends according to the environment, but we recommend 1GB based on a specific real-life case), the total memory that you have to dedicate to the oacore server becomes 15GB of RAM, as the Xmx and Xms values will be 2048m for each of these Managed Servers. By making a configuration like this, the system will have room for other EBS resources.

So, the remaining system resources can be distributed among the other three Managed Server types (forms, oafm and form-c4ws), the Admin Server, other EBS system components such as concurrent managers, and the application server's operating system processes.

You use the provisioning script named adProvisionEBS.pl to create additional Managed Servers. Just after sourcing the run edition environment, you execute the provisioning script with Perl by supplying ebs-create-managed-server, the context file, the Managed Server name, the service type, the Managed Server's port, and the log file as command-line arguments.

The Managed Server port should be chosen in a way that it does not conflict with the listener ports of other Managed Servers running in both the run environment and the patch environment. That is, if you have your oacore_server1 listening on 7201, it means it will listen on 7202 after you make the cutover while applying a patch. So, in such an environment, if you want to add a new oacore server named oacore_server2, you must not configure it to listen on these ports. However, you can configure the new oracore server to listen on port 7203 for this environment, as this port is not used by the run edition or patch edition at all.

The provisioning script wants you to supply the APPS password and WebLogic admin password when we run it. So, after supplying these passwords, the script runs quietly by logging all the activity that it does to the log file that you have declared by using the log file command-line argument.

```
[applmgr@somehost ~]$ perl $AD_TOP/patch/115/bin/adProvisionEBS.pl ebs-create-
managedserver -contextfile=$CONTEXT_FILE -managedsrvname=oacore_server2 -servicetype=oacore
-managedsrvport=7203 -logfile=/tmp/add_oacoreserver2.log
Enter the APPS Schema password:
Enter the WebLogic AdminServer password:
The logfile for this session is located at /tmp/add_oacoreserver2.log
```

It is better to check the log of the adProvisionEBS.pl script to check whether there are any errors encountered. In case, any errors are reported in this log file, and the script should be executed again, of course after taking the corrective actions.

After the execution of the adProvisionEBS.pl, our new Managed Server becomes ready to be used, as the adProvision.pl script creates the Managed Server and adds a new entry to the context file for starting and stopping the new Managed Server using the applications DBA scripts.

However, the provisioning script leaves the newly added Managed Server in SHUTDOWN state.

So, you start the newly added Managed Server using the standard application DBA administration script, admanagedsrvctl.sh.

```
[applmgr@somehost scripts]$ sh admanagedsrvctl.sh start oacore_server2
You are running admanagedsrvctl.sh version 120.14.12020000.9
Enter the WebLogic Admin password:
Calling txkChkEBSDependecies.pl to perform dependency checks for oacore_server2
*** ALL THE FOLLOWING FILES ARE REQUIRED FOR RESOLVING RUNTIME ERRORS
*** Log File = /u01/install/APPS/fs1/inst/apps/ORATEST_somehost/logs/appl/rgf/TXK/
txkChkEBSDependecies_Mon_Jul_27_14_57_02_2015/txkChkEBSDependecies_Mon_Jul_27_14_57_02_2015.
log
Perl script txkChkEBSDependecies.pl got executed successfully

Starting oacore_server2...

admanagedsrvctl.sh: exiting with status 0

admanagedsrvctl.sh: check the logfile /u01/install/APPS/fs1/inst/apps/ORATEST_somehost/logs/
appl/admin/log/adoacorectl.txt for more information.
```

At this point, the newly added Managed Server starts running.

Next, you execute the txkSetAppsConf.pl script to modify the Oracle HTTP Server–related configurations by adding the information for newly added Managed Server into the Oracle HTTP Server's configuration files named mod_wl_ohs.conf and apps.conf.

The txkSetAppsConf.pl script is executed by supplying these command-line arguments:

- *Contextfile*: The path of the EBS context file. The $CONTEXT_FILE environment variable can be used here, if the environment is set properly.

- *configoption (addMS)*: Used to tell the script about the operation requested. By supplying addMS, you state that you want a Managed Server to be added.

- *oacore*: The newly added oacore server's hostname and port in the following format: hostname:port.

```
[applmgr@somehost FMW_Home]$ perl $FND_TOP/patch/115/bin/txkSetAppsConf.pl
-contextfile=$CONTEXT_FILE -configoption=addMS -oacore=somehost:7203
```

Note that the txkSetAppsConf.pl script should be executed on all the application nodes that are serving for the same cluster where the Managed Server was added.

Lastly, you restart the Oracle HTTP Server using the standard Oracle application script named adapacctl.sh.

```
[applmgr@somehost scripts]$ sh adapcctl.sh stop
You are running adapcctl.sh version 120.0.12020000.6
Stopping OPMN managed Oracle HTTP Server (OHS) instance
adapcctl.sh: exiting with status 0
adapcctl.sh: check the logfile /u01/install/APPS/fs1/inst/apps/ORATEST_somehost/logs/appl/
admin/log/adapcctl.txt for more information
[applmgr@somehost scripts]$ sh adapcctl.sh start
You are running adapcctl.sh version 120.0.12020000.6
Starting OPMN managed Oracle HTTP Server (OHS) instance
adapcctl.sh: exiting with status 0
adapcctl.sh: check the logfile /u01/install/APPS/fs1/inst/apps/ORATEST_somehost/logs/appl/
admin/log/adapcctl.txt for more information.
```

After completing these actions, the newly added Managed Server (in this example, it is oacore_server2) gets set to RUNNING and gets fully activated as being part of the same Weblogic Server Clusters as the other Managed Servers serving the same service type.

Figure 7-38 shows that the newly added Managed Server is added to the cluster named oacore_cluster1, and the state of this newly added WebLogic Managed Server named oacore_server2 is RUNNING.

Click the **Lock & Edit** button in the Change Center to activate all the buttons on this page.

| New | Clone | Delete | | | | | Showing 1 to 6 of 6 |

Name ∧	Cluster	Machine	State	Health	Listen Port
AdminServer(admin)		somehost	RUNNING	✔ OK	7001
forms-c4ws_server1	forms-c4ws_cluster1	somehost	RUNNING	✔ OK	7801
forms_server1	forms_cluster1	somehost	RUNNING	✔ OK	7401
oacore_server1	oacore_cluster1	somehost	RUNNING	✔ OK	7201
oacore_server2	oacore_cluster1	somehost	RUNNING	✔ OK	7203
oafm_server1	oafm_cluster1	somehost	RUNNING	✔ OK	7601

Figure 7-38. WebLogic admin console, Summary of Server pages displaying the newly added Managed Server

The action plan to follow for removing a Managed Server is similar to creating and adding a Managed Server, as explained earlier. Removing a Managed Server can also be done using the adProvisionEBS.pl and txkSetAppsConf.pl scripts.

In the case of removing a Managed Server, you first stop the Managed Server that you want to remove and execute the adProvisionEBS.pl script with the argument ebs-delete-Managed Server. After executing adProvisionEBS.pl, you run the txkSetAppsConf.pl script with the argument configoption=remove and finally restart HTTP Server.

By the way, changing a Managed Server's port is also done using the txkSetAppsConf.pl script.

But before running the script with the appropriate arguments, log in to the admin console, click the servers, click the Managed Server whose port needs to be changed, and change the port number specified in the text box Listen Port.

After changing the port, click Save and activate the changes in the Change Center panel located in the leftmost corner of the page.

We'll give an example of changing the port of the Managed Server named forms-c4ws from the default port (7802) to 7808.

First, log in to the WebLogic console and open the configuration page of forms-c4ws by clicking Servers ➤ forms-c4ws_server1 ➤ Configuration. Then, click the Lock & Edit button, and change the Listen Port value to be 7808, as shown in Figure 7-39.

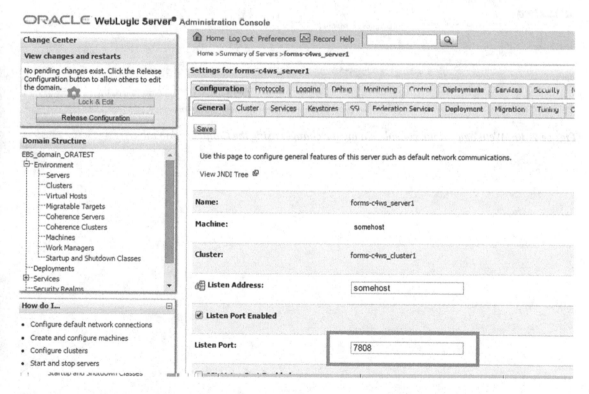

Figure 7-39. *WebLogic admin console, changing the listen port value of a Managed Server using the Configuration tab*

Save the configuration using the Save button at the bottom of the page (see Figure 7-40).

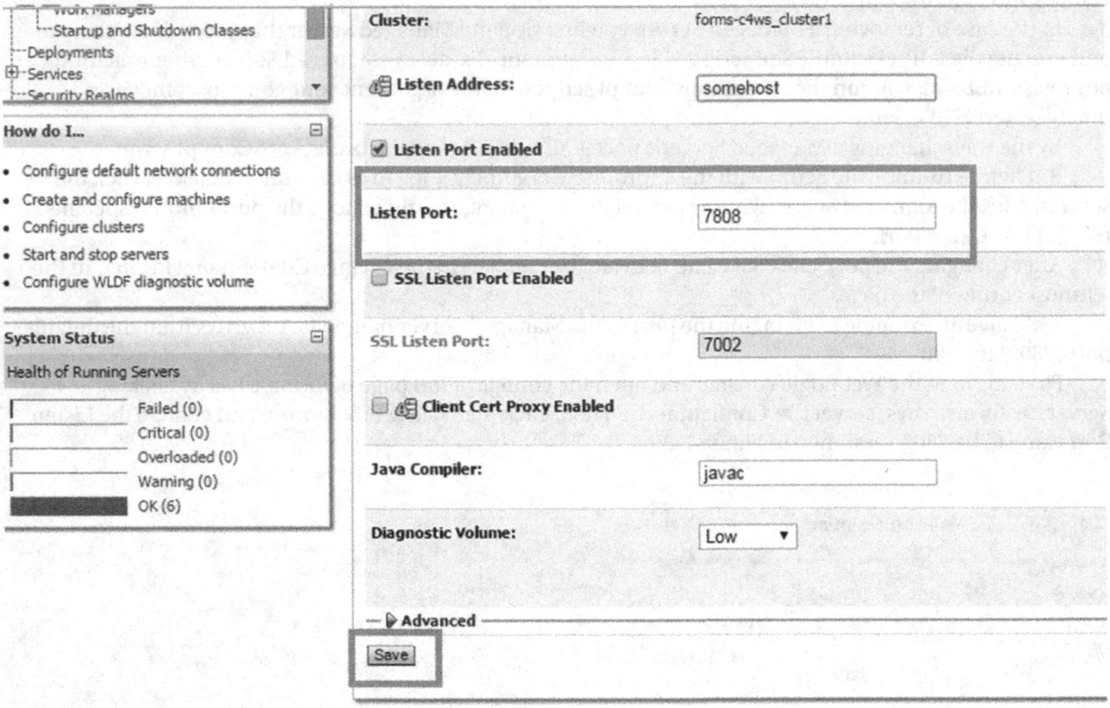

Figure 7-40. *WebLogic admin console, saving the changes using the Configuration tab*

Lastly, click the Activate Changes button, as shown in Figure 7-41.

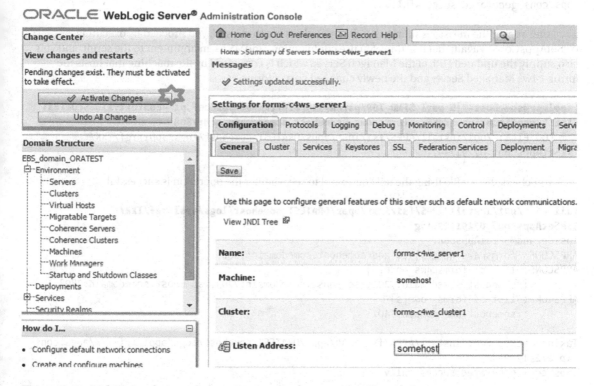

Figure 7-41. WebLogic admin console, activating the changes using Change Center

At this point, your work is done with the WebLogic console, so you can start executing the necessary scripts to make this change permanent.

First, you execute the txtkSetAppsConf.pl script with the parameter configoption=removeMs; you also supply the formc4ws Managed Server's current URL as an argument to this script in order to make the script remove the Managed Server from the configuration.

```
[applmgr@somehost ~]$  perl $FND_TOP/patch/115/bin/txkSetAppsConf.pl -contextfile=$CONTEXT_
FILE -configoption=removeMS -formsc4ws=somehost:7802

*** LOG FILE: /u01/install/APPS/fs1/inst/apps/ORATEST_somehost/logs/appl/rgf/TXK/
txkSetAppsConf_07291712.log ***
```

You use the tail command to check the log file and see that everything is OK with the script execution.

```
[applmgr@ scripts]$ tail -f /u01/install/APPS/fs1/inst/apps/ORATEST_somehost/logs/appl/rgf/
TXK/txkSetAppsConf_07291712.log
Inside removeMSFromAppsConf
APPSCONF: list of oacore_nodes
      : somehost.somedomain.com:7201,somehost.somedomain.com:7203
APPSCONF: list of forms_nodes
      : somehost.somedomain.com:7401
```

```
Taking backup /u01/install/APPS/fs1/inst/apps/ORATEST_somehost/logs/appl/rgf/TXK/apps.conf_
bkp_07291712
apps.conf generated successfully
```

After seeing the messages stating that the operations are successful, you proceed by executing txkSetAppsConf.pl again, but this time you use configoption=addMS as an argument to the script, and you also supply the updated URL of the Managed Server, which is composed by the machine that hosts the forms-c4ws Managed Server and the newly changed port of forms-c4ws.

**[applmgr@somehost ~]$ perl $FND_TOP/patch/115/bin/txkSetAppsConf.pl -contextfile=$CONTEXT_
FILE \-configoption=addMS - formsc4ws =somehost.somedomain.com:7808**
```
*** LOG FILE: /u01/install/APPS/fs1/inst/apps/ORATEST_somehost/logs/appl/rgf/TXK/
txkSetAppsConf_07291739.log ***
```

You check the log file using the tail command to see whether the operation is successful.

**tail -f /u01/install/APPS/fs1/inst/apps/ORATEST_somehost/logs/appl/rgf/TXK/
txkSetAppsConf_07291739.log**
```
Inside addMSFromAppsConf
APPSCONF: formsc4ws_node(s) to add somehost.somedomain:7808
APPSCONF: list of formsc4ws_node[s]
        : somehost.somedomain:7201, somehost.somedomain:7203, somehost.somedomain:7808
APPSCONF: list of forms_node[s]
        : somehost.somedomain:7401

Taking backup /u01/install/APPS/fs1/inst/apps/ORATEST_somehost/logs/appl/rgf/TXK/apps.conf_
bkp_07291739
apps.conf generated successfully
```

Lastly, you restart the Managed Server and the Apache server, and by using the WebLogic console and netstat and ps commands, you can see that the Managed Server named forms-c4ws starts working using the newly changed port, 7808, as shown in Figure 7-42.

Click the *Lock & Edit* button in the Change Center to activate all the buttons on this page.

New Clone Delete   Showing 1 to 6 of 6

Name ⌃	Cluster	Machine	State	Health	Listen Port
AdminServer(admin)		somehost	RUNNING	✔ OK	7001
forms-c4ws_server1	forms-c4ws_cluster1	somehost	RUNNING	✔ OK	7808
forms_server1	forms_cluster1	somehost	RUNNING	✔ OK	7401
oacore_server1	oacore_cluster1	somehost	RUNNING	✔ OK	7201
oacore_server2	oacore_cluster1	somehost	RUNNING	✔ OK	7203
oafm_server1	oafm_cluster1	somehost	RUNNING	✔ OK	7601

Figure 7-42. *WebLogic admin console, Summary of Server page displaying the newly changed port of a Managed Server (forms-c4ws_server1)*

Figure 7-42 shows an example screenshot of the Summary of Servers screen and draws your attention to the forms-c4ws server, as the listen port of this Managed Server is changed to the newly configured port after doing the port change operation explained in the previous paragraph.

To check this change from the back end, you can use the netstat utility to see whether the newly changed port is open and being listened by a process. Then by using the process ID gathered by the output of the netstat utility, you can find the command line of the process using the ps command to ensure that forms_c4ws_server1 is the process that is listening to that port number (the newly changed port).

```
[root@somehost ~]# netstat -anp |grep 10.123.35.63:7808|grep java |grep LISTEN
tcp        0      0 ::ffff:10.133.10.1:7808    :::*     LISTEN    7975/java
```

```
[root@somehost ~]# ps -ef|grep 7975
applmgr   7975  9762  0 Jul29 ?       00:03:54 /u01/install/APPS/fs1/EBSapps/comn/util/
jdk64/bin/java -Dweblogic.Name=forms-c4ws_server1
```

In addition to the Managed Server configurations, we want to mention that it is advisable to increase the Admin Server JVM's permanent and heap sizes (Xmx and Xms). Since the Admin Server is running the admin console, it is important to make it run stably.

Modifying these values for the Admin Server is not done using the admin console.

To modify these values, you modify the values represented by the tag s_nm_jvm_startup_properties in the context file and then stop the Admin Server, run AutoConfig in the application nodes, and start the Admin Server again.

The example shown in Figure 7-43 is a modified context file; the values for the JVM heap size values specified by the XML tag s_nm_jvm_startup_properties are set to the recommended values.

```
        <nm_jvm_startup_properties oa_var="s_nm_jvm_startup_properties" osd="LI
NUX_X86-64">-XX:PermSize=512m -XX:MaxPermSize=512m -Xms2048m -Xmx2048m -Djava.se
curity.policy=/u01/install/fs1/FMW_Home/wlserver_10.3/server/lib/weblogic.policy
 -Djava.security.egd=file:/dev/./urandom -Dweblogic.ProductionModeEnabled=true -
da -Dplatform.home=/u01/install/fs1/FMW_Home/wlserver_10.3 -Dwls.home=/u01/insta
ll/fs1/FMW_Home/wlserver_10.3/server -Dweblogic.home=/u01/install/fs1/FMW_Home/w
lserver_10.3/server -Dcommon.components.home=/u01/install/fs1/FMW_Home/oracle_co
mmon -Djrf.version=11.1.1 -Dorg.apache.commons.logging.Log=org.apache.commons.lo
gging.impl.Jdk14Logger -Ddomain.home=/u01/install/fs1/FMW_Home/user_projects/dom
```

Figure 7-43. *Contents of EBS 12.2 applications context file*

After modifying the context file, you shut down the Admin Server using the adadminsrvctl.sh script.

```
[applmgr@somehost scripts]$ sh adadminsrvctl.sh stop
You are running adadminsrvctl.sh version 120.10.12020000.9
Enter the WebLogic Admin password:
Enter the APPS Schema password:
Stopping WLS Admin Server...
Refer /u01/install/APPS/fs1/inst/apps/ORATEST_somehost/logs/appl/admin/log/adadminsrvctl.txt
for details
adadminsrvctl.sh: exiting with status 0
```

Next, run AutoConfig using adautocfg.sh, as we will explain in Chapter 8, to manage the EBS system configuration changes.

Basically, you use AutoConfig for propagating the changes you have made in the context file.

Note that you run AutoConfig while the application services and database are running. The only thing that is stopped is the Admin Server, as your focus is on making changes in its configuration. Thus, there is no downtime required for this operation.

[applmgr@somehost scripts]$ sh adautocfg.sh

Enter the APPS user password.

```
The log file for this session is located at: /u01/install/APPS/fs1/inst/apps/ORATEST_
somehost/admin/log/07281038/adconfig.log

AutoConfig is configuring the Applications environment...

AutoConfig will consider the custom templates if present.
        Using CONFIG_HOME location   : /u01/install/APPS/fs1/inst/apps/ORATEST_somehost
        Classpath                    : /u01/install/APPS/fs1/FMW_Home/Oracle_EBS-app1/shared-
libs/ebs-appsborg/WEB-INF/lib/ebsAppsborgManifest.jar:/u01/install/APPS/fs1/EBSapps/comn/
java/classes

        Using Context file           : /u01/install/APPS/fs1/inst/apps/ORATEST_somehost/appl/
                                       admin/ORATEST_somehost.xml

Context Value Management will now update the Context file

        Updating Context file...COMPLETED

        Attempting upload of Context file and templates to database...COMPLETED

Configuring templates from all of the product tops...
        Configuring AD_TOP........COMPLETED
        Configuring FND_TOP.......COMPLETED
        ...
        ......
        .........

AutoConfig completed successfully.
```

After completing AutoConfig successfully, you start the Admin Server.

[applmgr@somehost scripts]$ sh adadminsrvctl.sh start
```
You are running adadminsrvctl.sh version 120.10.12020000.9
Enter the WebLogic Admin password:
Enter the APPS Schema password:
Starting WLS Admin Server...
Refer /u01/install/APPS/fs1/inst/apps/ORATEST_somehost/logs/appl/admin/log/adadminsrvctl.txt
for details

adadminsrvctl.sh: exiting with status 0
```

Lastly, you check the Admin Server's operating system process using the OS tool (in our case using the Linux ps command) and see that it is started with the updated heap and permanent sizes, as shown in Figure 7-44.

```
[root@ somehost ~]$ps -ef |grep "java \-Dweblogic.Name=AdminServer"

applmgr    2281    2254   0 Feb29 ?        00:44:22 /u01/install/fs1/EBSapps/comn/util/jdk64/jre/bin/ja
va -Dweblogic.Name=AdminServer -Djava.security.policy=null -Djava.library.path=/u01/install/fs1/FMW_H
ome/patch_wls1036/profiles/default/native:/u01/install/fs1/EBSapps/10.1.2/jdk/jre/lib/i386:/u01/insta
ll/fs1/EBSapps/10.1.2/jdk/jre/lib/i386/server:/u01/install/fs1/EBSapps/10.1.2/jdk/jre/lib/i386/native
_threads:/u01/install/fs1/EBSapps/appl/cz/12.0.0/bin:/u01/install/fs1/EBSapps/10.1.2/lib32:/u01/insta
ll/fs1/EBSapps/10.1.2/lib:/usr/X11R6/lib:/usr/openwin/lib:/u01/install/fs1/EBSapps/10.1.2/jdk/jre/lib
/i386:/u01/install/fs1/EBSapps/10.1.2/jdk/jre/lib/i386/server:/u01/install/fs1/EBSapps/10.1.2/jdk/jre
/lib/i386/native_threads:/u01/install/fs1/EBSapps/appl/sht/12.0.0/lib:/u01/install/fs1/FMW_Home/wlser
ver_10.3/server/native/linux/x86_64:/u01/install/fs1/FMW_Home/wlserver_10.3/server/native/linux/x86_6
4/oci920_8:/usr/java/packages/lib/amd64:/usr/lib64:/lib64:/lib:/usr/lib -Djava.class.path=/u01/instal
l/fs1/FMW_Home/patch_wls1036/profiles/default/sys_manifest_classpath/weblogic_patch.jar:/u01/install/
fs1/FMW_Home/wlserver_10.3/server/lib/weblogic_sp.jar:/u01/install/fs1/FMW_Home/wlserver_10.3/server/
lib/weblogic.jar:/u01/install/fs1/FMW_Home/modules/features/weblogic.server.modules_10.3.6.0.jar:/u01
/install/fs1/FMW_Home/wlserver_10.3/server/lib/webservices.jar:/u01/install/fs1/FMW_Home/modules/org.
apache.ant_1.7.1/lib/ant-all.jar:/u01/install/fs1/FMW_Home/modules/net.sf.antcontrib_1.1.0.0_1-0b2/li
b/ant-contrib.jar:/u01/install/fs1/FMW_Home/oracle_common/modules/oracle.jdbc_11.1.1/ojdbc6dms.jar:/u
01/install/fs1/FMW_Home/oracle_common/webcenter/modules/oracle.portlet.server_11.1.1/oracle-portlet-a
pi.jar:/u01/install/fs1/FMW_Home/oracle_common/modules/oracle.jrf_11.1.1/jrf.jar:/u01/install/fs1/FMW
_Home/wlserver_10.3/common/derby/lib/derbyclient.jar -Dweblogic.system.BootIdentityFile=/u01/install/
fs1/FMW_Home/user_projects/domains/EBS_domain_CLONE/servers/AdminServer/security/boot_properties -Dwe
blogic.nodemanager.ServiceEnabled=true -XX:PermSize=512m -XX:MaxPermSize=512m -Xms2048m -Xmx2048m -Dj
ava.security.policy=/u01/install/fs1/FMW_Home/wlserver_10.3/server/lib/weblogic.policy -Djava.securit
```

Figure 7-44. *ps command output showing that the newly changed Permsize, MaxPermsize, Xms, and Xmx values are in use by the Admin Server*

Note that the format of the ps output in Figure 7-44 is customized for this book's page layout.

As you can see, you use the WebLogic console and sometimes AutoConfig to manage the WebLogic-related configurations in EBS 12.2. Actually, the WebLogic server is not the only system component of FMW in EBS 12.2; you also have important components such as Oracle HTTP Server to manage. So, before continuing with the next chapter, we will talk about the configuration changes in Oracle HTTP Server, too.

Managing the Configuration of Oracle HTTP Server

Oracle HTTP Server is also managed by AutoConfig partially. That is, the first instantiation of configuration files such as httpd.conf and mod_wl_ohs.conf is done by AutoConfig, but after the instantiation, the configuration of Oracle HTTP Server is managed mostly by FMW utilities. As you may guess, the utility for managing the Oracle HTTP Server configuration is the Fusion Middleware Control tool, which we have explained.

Also, when modifying the HTTP Server configurations such as port numbers, you use the Fusion Middleware Console in conjunction with AutoConfig.

■ **Note** We are explaining how to manage the configuration stored in the HTTP Server–related configuration files via the FMW Control. Alternatively, you can use your favorite text editor and the HTTP-related files located in the $IAS_ORACLE_HOME/instances/instance_id/config/OHS/component_id directory (for example, if the s_systemname is TEST, then the HTTP Server configuration files are located in $IAS_ORACLE_HOME/instances/EBS_web_TEST_OHS1/config/OHS/EBS_web_TEST) from the file system.

As a good example, let's take a look at the process for changing the default HTTP port of Oracle HTTP Server. Log in to the FMW console and drill down from the tree in the left panel until you reach Oracle HTTP Server.

Next, click the Oracle HTTP Server and choose the Advanced Configuration option located in the drop-down menu, as shown in Figure 7-45. Figure 7-45 shows the screen navigation for the Advanced Configuration page, on which the configuration changes for the HTTP Server–related files take place.

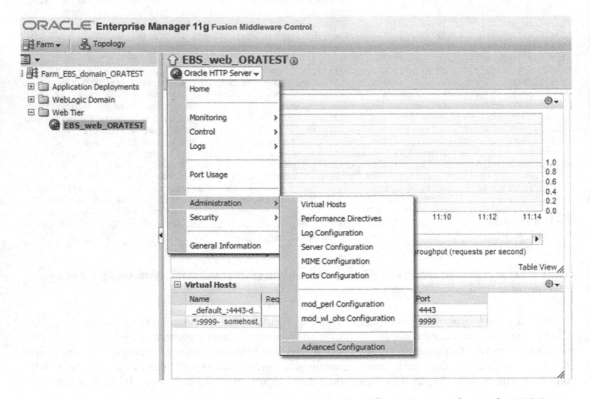

Figure 7-45. *Fusion Middleware Control, displaying the Advanced Configurations page for Oracle HTTP Server*

On the next page, choose the httpd.conf file as you want to edit the HTTP listen port in this case. Note that there are other configuration files in the list as well. So, the process for changing the configuration in those files is actually similar to this approach (see Figure 7-46).

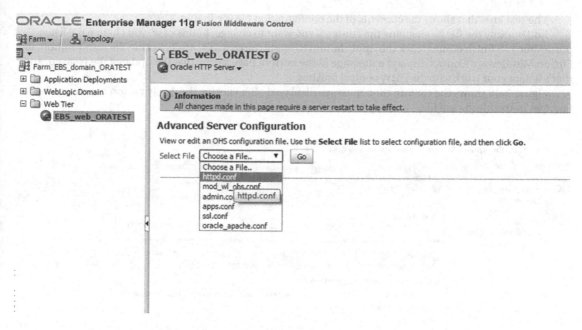

Figure 7-46. *Fusion Middleware Control, editing httpd.conf file*

Figure 7-46 shows how to start editing the httpd.conf file, which is the main configuration file of Oracle HTTP Server, using the Fusion Middleware Control in EBS 12.2.

Once you choose the configuration file that you want edit, the Fusion Middleware Control directs you to a new page displaying the contents of the configuration file.

So, as shown in Figure 7-47, you see the Fusion Middleware Control showing the contents of httpd.conf in this case.

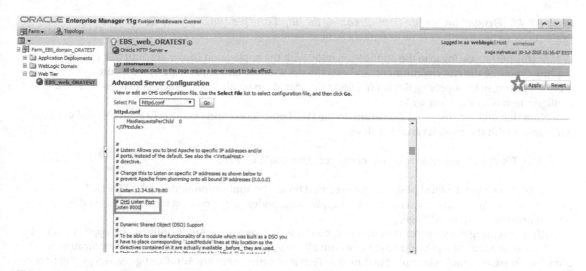

Figure 7-47. *Fusion Middleware Control, editing httpd.conf file, continued*

The text area that shows the contents of the configuration file is editable.

Edit/modify the file by changing the contents you want to change. In this case, you change the listen port. After you finish editing, click the Apply button to apply the changes. After clicking the Apply button, the Fusion Middleware Control displays a message in the current page saying that the updated file is saved, and that's where your work with the FMW control finishes.

Figure 7-48 shows the confirmation message displayed after clicking the Apply button to activate the changes in the httpd.conf file.

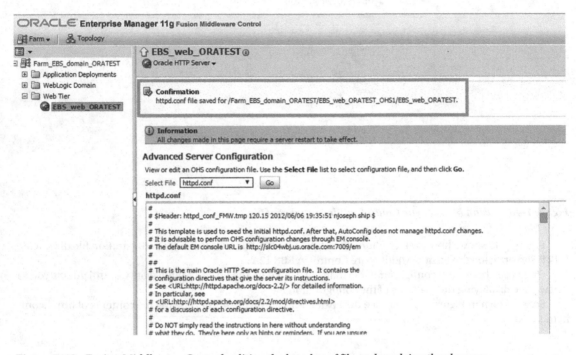

Figure 7-48. Fusion Middleware Control, editing the httpd.conf file and applying the changes

At this point, you log in to the application node with the application owner account (for example, applmgr), source the run environment, and execute the adSyncContext.pl script. You execute adSyncContext.pl by supplying the application's context file to synchronize Oracle HTTP Server's new configuration with the context file.

Note that adSyncContext.pl synchronizes the WebLogic Server and Oracle HTTP Server configuration parameters with the context variable values.

```
perl $AD_TOP/bin/adSyncContext.pl contextfile=<CONTEXT_FILE>
```

Note that adSyncContext.pl should be executed on all the application nodes if the EBS 12.2 environment in question consists of multiple application nodes, as the context files of all the nodes should be synchronized with the change.

After executing the synchronization script, continue with executing AutoConfig on the application node.

Note that AutoConfig should be executed on all the application nodes if the EBS 12.2 environment in question consists of multiple application nodes. That is because there are AutoConfig-related profile options and some related files are required to be changed.

Lastly, restart the Oracle HTTP server and see that it starts working with the new listen port.

You have now seen the tuning tips for maximizing the performance in FMW inside EBS 12.2. In addition to the tips and methods provided in this chapter, we recommend following the Oracle Support documents for the latest TXK and AD patches and applying the newly released TXK and AD patches in order to keep up with the bug fixes and performance enhancements.

Let's take a look at the FMWDFW, the Fusion Middleware Diagnostic Framework, and see what you can do with it.

EBS 12.2 FMW Diagnostics

FMW in EBS 12.2 incorporates a framework called Diagnostics Framework (DFW), which can be used to detect, diagnose, and resolve any problems that may be encountered in the Fusion Middleware components. DFW in EBS 12.2 can be used to identify the causes of any errors encountered when reaching an application's web pages, as well as the causes for performance degradation in an EBS application, which may seem causeless at first glance.

The logic behind DFW is to capture the diagnostic information and store it as an incident in the Automatic Diagnostic Repository (ADR), which can then be queried or processed by using the ADR Command Interpreter (ADRCI). The apps DBA can review and resolve the incidents or send them to Oracle Support and make a service request.

In addition to the errors or abnormal conditions such as performance degradations, you can also watch specific conditions using the Diagnostic Framework. Although conditions such as deadlocks, stuck threads, out-of-memory exceptions, and uncaught exceptions are watched by default in EBS 12.2, by declaring the necessary notification rules, you can configure EBS 12.2 to create incidents for more specific conditions too.

So, after this introduction, let's start with ADCRI. As mentioned in the previous paragraph, there are default incidents that are watched. These incidents are stored in the ADR, which is located in the application file system. These ADR locations in EBS 12.2 vary according to the WebLogic Server they are related to.

There are five WebLogic servers (admin, oacore, forms, oafm, and forms-c4ws) in a standard EBS configuration, so there are five ADR locations for storing the incidents related to these WebLogic servers. All the ADR locations are located in the EBS_DOMAIN_HOME/servers directory, but the full path of the adr location varies according to the server names.

The general pattern for the adr directory path is as follows:

```
$EBS_DOMAIN_HOME/servers/{SERVER_NAME}/adr
```

So in this context the ADR locations for Weblogic Admin Server and Managed Servers are:

```
ADR location for oacore is $EBS_DOMAIN_HOME/servers/oacore_server1/adr,
ADR location for oafm is $EBS_DOMAIN_HOME/servers/oafm_server1/adr,
ADR location for forms is $EBS_DOMAIN_HOME/servers/forms_server1/adr,
ADR location for forms-c4ws is $EBS_DOMAIN_HOME/servers/forms-c4ws1/adr and
ADR location for admin server is $EBS_DOMAIN_HOME/servers/AdminServer/adr.
```

The incidents are located in the subdirectories of these adr folders; again, the full path varies according to the server names.

The locations of the incidents are as follows:

ADR location for Admin Server:
```
$EBS_DOMAIN_HOME/servers/AdminServer/adr/diag/ofm/EBS_domain_<sid>/AdminServer/incident
```
ADR location for oacore Server:
```
$EBS_DOMAIN_HOME/servers/oacore_server1/adr/diag/ofm/EBS_domain_<sid>/oacore_server1/incident
```

ADR location for oafm Server:
$EBS_DOMAIN_HOME/servers/oafm_server1/adr/diag/ofm/EBS_domain_<sid>/oafm_server1/incident
ADR location for forms Server:
$EBS_DOMAIN_HOME/servers/forms_server1/adr/diag/ofm/EBS_domain_<sid>/forms_server1/incident
ADR location for forms-c4ws Server:
$EBS_DOMAIN_HOME/servers/forms-c4ws_server1/adr/diag/ofm/EBS_domain_<sid>/forms-c4ws_
server1/incident

So, the incidents are created as subfolders of the incidents directories. The first incident is stored in the subdirectory named incdir_1, the second is stored in incdir_2, and so on.

You don't need to memorize the directory structure of ADR, as we have a tool named adrci. adrci lets you have an analytical tool without spending any effort on analyzing the diagnostic data (such as data stored in log and trace files) located in many different locations.

Using adrci, you can see the problems and the incidents that are created because of these problems, and you can create packages consisting of the diagnostic information related to these incidents and send these packages to Oracle Support to get a more effective support service.

To be able to use adrci, you first need to set the run environment and then set the ORACLE_HOME and LD_LIBRARY_PATH environment variables.

ORACLE_HOME must be set to the $FMW_HOME/wlserver_10.3/server/adr directory, and LD_LIBRARY_PATH should be set to include $ORACLE_HOME in the first place.

```
[[applmgr@somehost]$. /u01/install/APPS/EBSapps.env run
[[applmgr@somehost]$ cd $FMW_HOME/wlserver_10.3/server/adr
[[applmgr@somehost]$ export ORACLE_HOME=`pwd`
[[applmgr@somehost]$ export LD_LIBRARY_PATH=`pwd`:$LD_LIBRARY_PATH
```

After setting the environment for adrci, we execute the utility from the "$FMW_HOME/wlserver_10.3/server/adr" directory as follows;

```
[[applmgr@somehost adr]$
ADRCI: Release 11.2.0.2.0 - Production on Tue Jul 28 15:26:26 2015
Copyright (c) 1982, 2009, Oracle and/or its affiliates. All rights reserved.
No ADR base is set
adrci>
```

After executing adrci, the tool gets initialized and gives you a message of "No ADR base is set."

To use adrci and operate on the diagnostic files, you set the base to be the ADR location of the Managed Server you want to diagnose.

Here's an example:

```
BASE should be set to "<full path of $EBS_DOMAIN_HOME>/servers/oacore_server1/adr" for
diagnosing the oacore.
```

```
adrci> SET BASE /u01/install/APPS/fs1/FMW_Home/user_projects/domains/EBS_domain_ORATEST/
servers/oacore_server1/adr
```

You also set the HOMEPATH to be the directory where the subdirectories such as incidents, trace, alert, and so on, reside (in other words, where diagnostic data resides).

Here's an example (HOMEPATH should be set to diag/ofm/EBS_domain_<s_dbSid>/oacore_server1 for diagnosing oacore):

adrci> set HOMEPATH diag/ofm/EBS_domain_ORATEST/oacore_server1

After setting BASE and HOMEPATH, you can use the adrci commands to show the problems and incidents.

adrci> show problem
```
ADR Home = /u01/install/APPS/fs1/FMW_Home/user_projects/domains/EBS_domain_ORATEST/servers/
oacore_server1/adr/diag/ofm/EBS_domain_ORATEST/oacore_server1:
*********************************************************************
PROBLEM_ID          PROBLEM_KEY                  LAST_INCIDENT        LASTINC_TIME
------------------- ---------------------------- ------------------  -------------
1                   BEA-337 [WebLogicServer]     4                    2015-07-14
18:14:19.807000 +03:00
1 rows fetched
```

We see a problem in the previous code. Although it seems a single problem was encountered in this instance, there may be many incidents created because of this problem.

adrci> show incident
```
ADR Home = /u01/install/APPS/fs1/FMW_Home/user_projects/domains/EBS_domain_ORATEST/servers/
oacore_server1/adr/diag/ofm/EBS_domain_ORATEST/oacore_server1:
*********************************************************************
INCIDENT_ID         PROBLEM_KEY                  CREATE_TIME
------------------- ---------------------------- -----------------------------------
1                   BEA-337 [WebLogicServer]     2015-07-12 16:29:17.585000 +03:00
2                   BEA-337 [WebLogicServer]     2015-07-14 10:29:18.582000 +03:00
3                   BEA-337 [WebLogicServer]     2015-07-14 16:58:19.778000 +03:00
4                   BEA-337 [WebLogicServer]     2015-07-14 18:14:19.807000 +03:00
4 rows fetched
```

As shown in the previous code, four incidents are there, and the PROBLEM_KEY column for all of these incidents shows BEA-337, which is the PROBLEM_KEY shown when you list the problem using the show problem command.

Next, you use the ips create package and ips generate package commands to create the package and put its contents in a zip file in the /tmp directory for sending it to Oracle Support.

Creating a package using the ips create commands logically puts the related diagnostic files together and relates them to the newly created logical package.

adrci> ips create package incident 1

Created package 1 based on incident id 1, correlation level typical

```
adrci> ips show files package 1
    FILE_ID              1
    FILE_LOCATION        <ADR_HOME>/incident/incdir_1
    FILE_NAME            dms_metrics2_i1.txt
    LAST_SEQUENCE        0
    EXCLUDE              Included

    FILE_ID              2
    FILE_LOCATION        <ADR_HOME>/incident/incdir_1
    FILE_NAME            jvm_threads1_i1.txt
    LAST_SEQUENCE        0
    EXCLUDE              Included

    FILE_ID              3
    FILE_LOCATION        <ADR_HOME>/incident/incdir_1
    FILE_NAME            odl_logs4_i1.txt
    LAST_SEQUENCE        0
    EXCLUDE              Included

    FILE_ID              4
    FILE_LOCATION        <ADR_HOME>/incident/incdir_1
    FILE_NAME            odl_quicktrace3_i1.txt
    LAST_SEQUENCE        0
    EXCLUDE              Included

    FILE_ID              5
    FILE_LOCATION        <ADR_HOME>/incident/incdir_1
    FILE_NAME            readme.txt
    LAST_SEQUENCE        0
    EXCLUDE              Included

    FILE_ID              6
    FILE_LOCATION        <ADR_HOME>/incident/incdir_1
    FILE_NAME            diagnostic_image_oacore_server1_2015_07_12_16_29_21.zip
    LAST_SEQUENCE        0
    EXCLUDE              Included

    FILE_ID              7
    FILE_LOCATION        <ADR_HOME>/alert
    FILE_NAME            log.xml
    LAST_SEQUENCE        0
    EXCLUDE              Included

    FILE_ID              8
    FILE_LOCATION        <ADR_HOME>/incpkg/pkg_1/seq_1/export
    FILE_NAME            IPS_CONFIGURATION.dmp
    LAST_SEQUENCE        0
    EXCLUDE              Included
```

```
FILE_ID              9
FILE_LOCATION        <ADR_HOME>/incpkg/pkg_1/seq_1/export
FILE_NAME            IPS_PACKAGE.dmp
LAST_SEQUENCE        0
EXCLUDE              Included
adrci> ips generate package 1 in /tmp
Generated package 1 in file  /tmp/BEA337_20150714439483.zip mode complete
```

The same thing and maybe more can be done using WLST. WLST is the WebLogic scripting tool, as we explained earlier.

Let's see the capabilities of WLST in diagnostics. To analyze the diagnostics, you use the WLST located in the COMMON HOME. So, you change the directory to the common/bin directory located in COMMON HOME and execute WLST from there.

```
[applmgr@somehost bin]$ cd /u01/install/APPS/fs1/FMW_Home/oracle_common/common/bin
[applmgr@somehost bin]$ ./wlst.sh
Initializing WebLogic Scripting Tool (WLST) ...
Welcome to WebLogic Server Administration Scripting Shell
Type help() for help on available commands
```

As we explained earlier, WLST starts working in offline mode when it is initialized.

So, using the connect method in WLST, you first connect to the WebLogic server that you want to diagnose.

```
wls:/offline> connect('weblogic','welcome1','t3://somehost:7201');
Connecting to t3://somehost:7201 with userid weblogic ...
Successfully connected to Managed Server 'oacore_server1' that belongs to domain 'EBS_
domain_ORATEST'.
```

After connecting the WebLogic manager server (in this case, it is oacore), you can start using diagnostics-related WLST methods.

We list the problems using listProblems() as follows;

```
wls:/EBS_domain_ORATEST/serverConfig> listProblems();
Problem Id      Problem Key
        1       BEA-337 [WebLogicServer]
```

We list the incidents using listIncidents() as follows;

```
wls:/EBS_domain_ORATEST/serverConfig> listIncidents();
Incident Id     Problem Key                   Incident Time
        4       BEA-337 [WebLogicServer]      Tue Jul 14 18:14:19 EEST 2015
        3       BEA-337 [WebLogicServer]      Tue Jul 14 16:58:19 EEST 2015
        2       BEA-337 [WebLogicServer]      Tue Jul 14 10:29:18 EEST 2015
        1       BEA-337 [WebLogicServer]      Sun Jul 12 16:29:17 EEST 2015
```

So, you have an opportunity to take a detailed look by using the showIncident method of WLST and supplying the incident ID that you have gathered via the listIncident method as an argument to the showIncident method, as follows:

```
wls:/EBS_domain_ORATEST/serverConfig> showIncident(id='1');
Incident Id: 1
Problem Id: 1
Problem Key: BEA-337 [WebLogicServer]
Incident Time:Sun Jul 12 16:29:17 EEST 2015
Error Message Id: BEA-337
Execution Context:0056epmC5KhD^ap_kP8DyZ0002Tz000dk2
Flood Controlled: false
Dump Files :
   readme.txt
   jvm_threads1_i1.txt
   dms_metrics2_i1.txt
   odl_quicktrace3_i1.txt
   odl_logs4_i1.txt
   diagnostic_image_oacore_server1_2015_07_12_16_29_21.zip  &#x00E0; this file is in "$EBS_
DOMAIN_HOME/servers/oacore_server1/adr/diag/ofm/EBS_domain_ORATEST/oacore_server1/incident/
incdir_1/diagnostic_image_oacore_server1_2015_07_12_16_29_21.zip"
```

Using the listIncident method, you can see all the diagnostic files for an incident.

By using the listIncident method, you see the diagnostics file that contributes the incident. So, you see the JVM-related diagnostics files, Dynamic Monitoring Service (DMS) diagnostic files, and the log files created by Oracle Diagnostic Logging (ODL), which is the logging service used by most of the FMW applications.

You can also see a diagnostic image file in zip format. These diagnostic image files are stored in the incident folder, and they consist of the image files to provide the necessary information about the environment that the incident you are interested in is created for.

If you unzip a diagnostic file to satisfy your curiosity, you will see a bunch of image files, as follows:

```
[applmgr@somehost incdir_2]$ unzip diagnostic_image_oacore_server1_2015_07_14_10_29_22.zip
Archive:   diagnostic_image_oacore_server1_2015_07_14_10_29_22.zip
  inflating: PathService.img
  inflating: APPLICATION.img
  inflating: PERSISTENT_STORE.img
  inflating: JTA.img
  inflating: CONNECTOR.img
  inflating: Deployment.img
  inflating: Cluster.img
  inflating: JMS.img
  inflating: ManagementRuntimeImageSource.img
  inflating: Logging.img
  inflating: HarvesterImageSource.img
  inflating: JNDI_IMAGE_SOURCE.img
  inflating: configuration.img
  inflating: SAF.img
  inflating: JVM.img
  inflating: InstrumentationImageSource.img
  inflating: WORK_MANAGER.img
```

```
inflating: JDBC.img
inflating: WatchSource.img
inflating: image.summary
```

As the names of the files imply, they are there for giving information about the components. This information can then be used by an expert to recognize the environment before analyzing it. The image file supplies environmental information such as JVM configuration, JDBC information, the cluster that the Managed Server belongs to, and so on.

Using WLST, you can also export the contents of a diagnostic file to an output file.

As shown next, you use the getIncidentFile method to create a file named jvm_threads1_forincident1.txt in the tmp folder using the diagnostic file stored in jvm_threads1_i1.txt in the ADR location.

Note that jvm_threads1diagnostics files can be used to view what the JVM thread was doing when the incident was created.

wls:/EBS_domain_ORATEST/serverConfig> getIncidentFile(id='1', name=' jvm_threads1_i1.txt', outputFile='/tmp/jvm_threads1_forincident1.txt')

Figure 7-49 shows the contents of the file /tmp/ jvm_threads1_forincident1.txt, which was created to record the JVM threads dump, later to be used to realize what the JVM threads were doing while the incident named incident1 was happening.

```
Live threads: 103
Started threads: 39637
Peak live threads: 103
Daemon threads: 99

Full Thread Dump

"oracle.dfw.impl.incident.DiagnosticsDataExtractorImpl - Incident Dump Executor (create
    at java.lang.ClassLoader.defineClass1(Native Method)
    at java.lang.ClassLoader.defineClass(ClassLoader.java:792)
    at java.security.SecureClassLoader.defineClass(SecureClassLoader.java:142)
    at java.net.URLClassLoader.defineClass(URLClassLoader.java:449)
    at java.net.URLClassLoader.access$100(URLClassLoader.java:71)
    at java.net.URLClassLoader$1.run(URLClassLoader.java:361)
    at java.net.URLClassLoader$1.run(URLClassLoader.java:355)
    at java.security.AccessController.doPrivileged(Native Method)
    at java.net.URLClassLoader.findClass(URLClassLoader.java:354)
    at java.lang.ClassLoader.loadClass(ClassLoader.java:424)
    at sun.misc.Launcher$AppClassLoader.loadClass(Launcher.java:308)
    at java.lang.ClassLoader.loadClass(ClassLoader.java:357)
    at oracle.as.management.logging.tools.QuickTraceDump.executeDump(QuickTraceDump.jav
    at oracle.dfw.impl.dump.DumpManagerImpl.executeDump(DumpManagerImpl.java:567)
    at oracle.dfw.impl.incident.DiagnosticsDataExtractorImpl$SingleDumpExecutor$2.run(D
    at oracle.dfw.impl.incident.DiagnosticsDataExtractorImpl$SingleDumpExecutor$2.run(D
    at java.security.AccessController.doPrivileged(Native Method)
    at oracle.security.jps.util.JpsSubject.doAsPrivileged(JpsSubject.java:315)
    at oracle.security.jps.internal.jaas.AccActionExecutor.execute(AccActionExecutor.ja
    at oracle.security.jps.internal.jaas.CascadeActionExecutor$SubjectPrivilegedExcepti
    at weblogic.security.acl.internal.AuthenticatedSubject.doAs(AuthenticatedSubject.ja
```

Figure 7-49. Incident file (jvm_threads1_forincident1.txt) displaying the JVM threads

Additionally, dumps can be executed on the fly. That is, you can create dump files any time you want and use them to analyze the current situation.

In WLST, you have the opportunity to execute the following dump types:

```
wls:/EBS_domain_ORATEST/serverConfig> listDumps();
odl.activeLogConfig
jvm.classhistogram
dms.ecidctx
wls.image
odl.logs
dms.metrics
odl.quicktrace
http.requests
jvm.threads
```

The describeDump method can be used to display information about the available dump types.

You can see descriptions for the odl.logs and jvm.threads dumps as follows:

```
wls:/EBS_domain_ORATEST/serverConfig> describeDump(name="odl.logs")
Name: odl.logs
Description: Dump contents of diagnostic logs
Mandatory Arguments:
Optional Arguments:
    Name        Type      Description
    match_all   BOOLEAN   Whether to match both ECID and time range or any one of them.
    timestamp   LONG      Log message timestamp in milliseconds
    ecid        STRING    Log message execution context ID (ecid)
    timerange   LONG      Time range in minutes
```

```
wls:/EBS_domain_ORATEST/serverConfig> describeDump(name='jvm.threads');
Name: jvm.threads
Description: Dumps summary statistics about the threads running in a JVM as well as
performing a full thread dump.
Mandatory Arguments:
Optional Arguments:
```

So, to execute a dump, you use the executeDump method. By supplying the dump type and an output file as arguments to the executeDump method, you can create a file containing the dump for the component you are interested in.

The following is an example of creating a JVM threads dump file named dumpout.txt in the /tmp folder:

```
wls:/EBS_domain_ORATEST/serverConfig> executeDump(name="jvm.threads", outputFile="/tmp/
dumpout.txt")
```

Figure 7-50 shows the contents of an exported JVM dump file named /tmp/dumpout.txt.

```
Live threads: 110
Started threads: 38309
Peak live threads: 115
Daemon threads: 106

Full Thread Dump

"Worker-1" id=38313 WAITING on lock=oracle.ias.cache.TaskQ@58a23694
    at java.lang.Object.wait(Native Method)
    at oracle.ias.cache.TaskQ.waitForWork(TaskQ.java:255)
    at oracle.ias.cache.TaskQ.getTask(TaskQ.java:138)
    at oracle.ias.cache.WorkerThread.run(ThreadPool.java:303)

"Worker-0" id=38312 WAITING on lock=oracle.ias.cache.TaskQ@58a23694
    at java.lang.Object.wait(Native Method)
    at oracle.ias.cache.TaskQ.waitForWork(TaskQ.java:255)
    at oracle.ias.cache.TaskQ.getTask(TaskQ.java:138)
    at oracle.ias.cache.WorkerThread.run(ThreadPool.java:303)

"Worker-4" id=38311 WAITING on lock=oracle.ias.cache.TaskQ@58a23694
    at java.lang.Object.wait(Native Method)
    at oracle.ias.cache.TaskQ.waitForWork(TaskQ.java:255)
    at oracle.ias.cache.TaskQ.getTask(TaskQ.java:138)
    at oracle.ias.cache.WorkerThread.run(ThreadPool.java:303)

"Worker-2" id=38308 WAITING on lock=oracle.ias.cache.TaskQ@58a23694
    at java.lang.Object.wait(Native Method)
```

Figure 7-50. JVM threads dump file (dumpout.txt) file contents

So far, you have seen the incidents and problems that are created by WebLogic. You also took a look at the management of these incidents and problems. You have used tools like adrci and WLST to operate on the diagnostic data captured by the WebLogic, created packages by using the data in adrci, and analyzed the problems a little bit by using WLST. Shortly, we explained the diagnostics in WebLogic by giving an introduction with a couple of examples.

Before starting a new chapter, we want explain one more thing. It is actually a little bit internal, but it is worthwhile to have some information about it.

As shown in the previous examples, there are incidents in the ADR, probably created because of the problem encountered in the applications that run on WebLogic servers. These situations or problems that are the cause of these incidents or problems are captured by the diagnostics mechanism in WebLogic by default. So, you don't need to define anything to catch the major problems such as a Deadlock, a StuckThread, or a UnexpectedException.

But, if you need to catch a nondefault problem or situation, you have the opportunity to define the diagnostic mechanism that is used to catch those problems or situations and create incidents for them. The things that can be done here are not limited to the incident creation; you also have the opportunity to do other tasks such as sending e-mails when a problem occurs.

To capture the situation or error that you want to create incidents for, you use WebLogic watches, and to create an incident, you use WebLogic notifications. Actually, the incidents you saw earlier are also created by WebLogic using the same components: the watches and the notifications. That is, when you install EBS 12.2, there are watches and notifications by default that come configured in the WebLogic Server. The default watches and notifications are created in the seeded WebLogic diagnostic module named Module-FMWDFW. If you want to create an incident for a nondefault situation or error, you just need to add a watch and a notification to this WebLogic diagnostic module.

For an example, you'll see how to add a watch to catch the server state changes and relate it to a notification to see what happens. To get the server state changes, use the log files of WebLogic Server. As you know, when a server state changes, WebLogic reflects it in the appropriate server's log file with the message ID "BEA-000365." For instance, if a server state changes to suspending, you'll see it written in the log file of the server.

So, after making a server state suspended, you will see something like the following in the log files:

```
<BEA-000365> <Server state changed to FORCE_SUSPENDING>
Likewise, after starting a server, we will see following lines in the log file;
<BEA-000365> <Server state changed to STARTING>
<BEA-000365> <Server state changed to RUNNING>
```

By keeping that in mind, you will create a watch to monitor these server log files, catch the MSG ID: BEA-000365, and trigger the creation of an ADR incident when the message BEA-000365 is seen. By configuring a watch for this purpose, you will have an incident created in your ADR repository when a server is stopped or started or suspended (in short, when a server state changes).

As for the demonstration, you start working by logging in to the WebLogic console and choosing Diagnostic Modules from the panel located on the left, as shown in Figure 7-51.

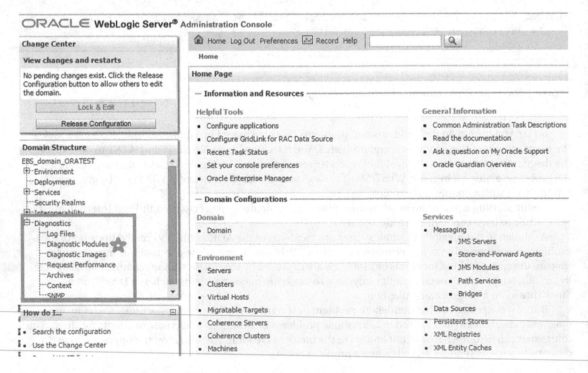

Figure 7-51. *WebLogic admin console, choosing Diagnostic Modules*

When you click Diagnostic Modules, you reach a summary page that lists the diagnostics modules present in WebLogic Server. At this point, you can create your own diagnostic module or use an existing one, which is Module-FMWDFW.

It is unnecessary to create a module for this example; you will proceed with Module-FMWDFW, as depicted in Figure 7-52.

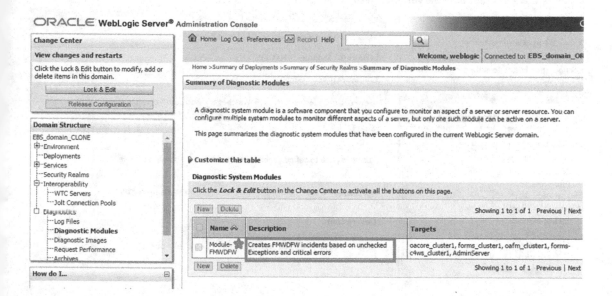

Figure 7-52. *WebLogic admin console, Summary of Diagnostic Modules page*

Figure 7-52 shows the Summary of Diagnostic Modules page and draws attention to Module-FMWDFW.

When you click Module-FMWDFW, you reach its configuration page, where you can reach the pages where you can create watches and notifications.

Next, click the Watches and Notifications tab to reach the Watches and Notification panel, as shown in Figure 7-53. Note that you don't need to associate the module with targets because Module-FMWDFW is by default associated with the all the clusters and servers in the Weblogic Domain.

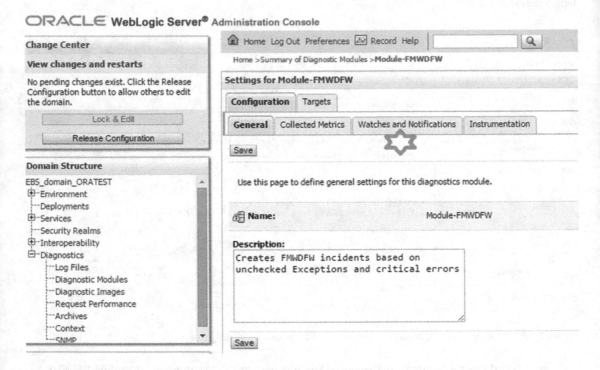

Figure 7-53. *WebLogic admin console, settings for Module-FMWDFW*

Figure 7-53 shows the settings for Module-FMWDFW and draws the attention to the Watches and Notifications tab.

After clicking the Watches and Notifications tab, you reach the page that gives information about the watches and notifications present in the system, as well as how the watch and log watch severities are configured. Choose the Notice level for both of these severities, as the message that you are trying to capture is produced in the Notice diagnostic level.

```
####<Jul 31, 2015 11:10:03 AM EEST> <Notice> <WebLogicServer> <somehost.somedomain.
com> <AdminServer> <main> <<WLS Kernel>> <> <71c2f10b37efa3eb:99451bc:14ee32
8a848:-8000-0000000000000005> <1438330203567> <BEA-000365> <Server state changed to RUNNING>
```

The default watches are also displayed in the Watches table at the bottom of the page. Here you see watches named Deadlock, StuckThread, and UnexpectedException, as briefly explained earlier.

Click the New button to add the new watch.

Figure 7-54 shows a general severity level and log watch severity level, as well as the Watches table where the watches currently defined in the system are displayed along with their type, current status (Enabled or Disabled), and alarm type.

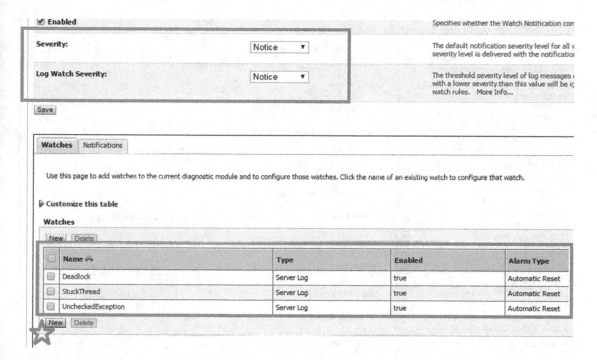

Figure 7-54. *WebLogic admin console, setting default watches and the severity levels for Module-FMWDFW*

In the opening page, you give your watch a name. In this example, it is ServerControlbylog, and also you set the watch type to Server log, as you want to catch the messages written in the server log files. The check box Enable Watch is selected by default, so you just leave it as is and click the Next button.

Figure 7-55 shows the Create Watch page where you input the name and the type of the watch that you want to create. You can use the Enable Watch check box to directly enable or disable the watch that you want to create.

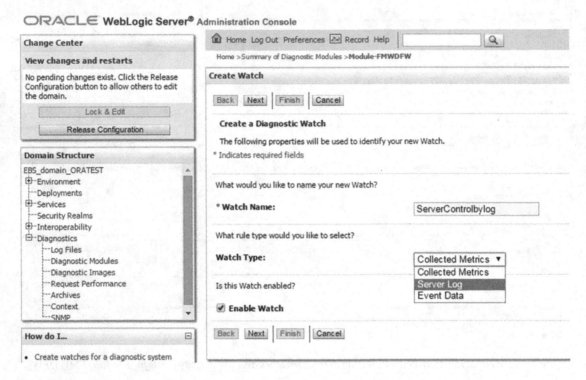

Figure 7-55. *WebLogic admin console, creating a server log type watch*

While creating your watch, you need to add an expression to it, as WebLogic will use the expression to catch the situation or the problem that you want to be caught. So, click the Add Expression button and proceed, as shown in Figure 7-56.

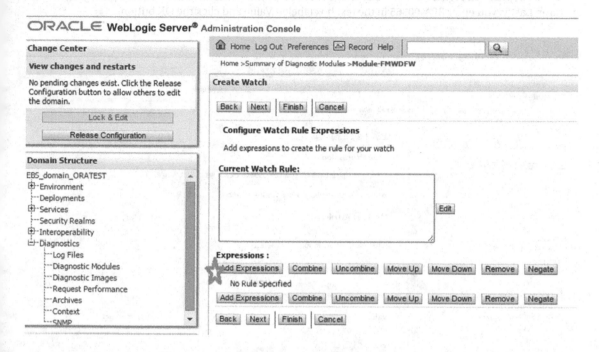

Figure 7-56. *WebLogic admin console, adding an expression for the new watch*

Figure 7-56 shows the Create Watch panel and draws attention to the Add Expression button.

The Add Expression button brings you an opportunity to choose the attribute, the operation, and the value and dynamically create an expression using them.

So, as depicted in Figure 7-57, you can choose MSGID as your attribute and an equal sign as your operator. Lastly, you enter BEA-00365 in the text box labeled Value and click the OK button.

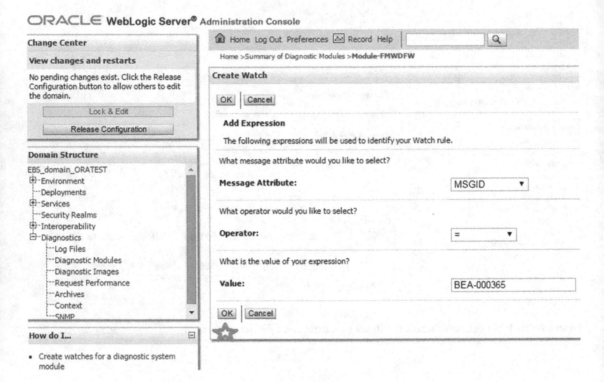

Figure 7-57. *WebLogic admin console, choosing the attributes, operator, and value for the expression*

Figure 7-57 shows the example expression that is created via the Add Expression button.

By clicking the OK button, you find yourself on the previous page where you clicked the Add Expression button, but this time, as you see in the example shown in Figure 7-58, the text area Current Watch Rule is filled with the condition you have created. At this point, the watch creation is finished. So, click the Finish button, as depicted in Figure 7-58, and continue with choosing a notification for your newly created watch.

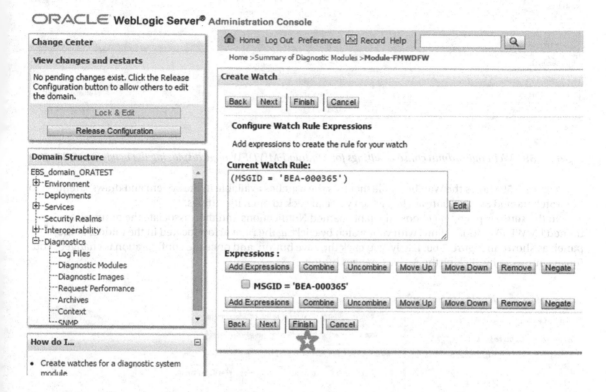

Figure 7-58. *WebLogic admin console, finishing the creation of the new watch*

Figure 7-58 shows the completion of creating a new watch.

After clicking the Finish button, the WebLogic console brings you back to the settings for Module-FMWDFW page.

To associate your newly created watch with a notification, you click the watch named ServerControlbylog and reach the setting for this watch. As you can see, it is now in the table named Watches at the bottom of this page, as shown in Figure 7-59.

Watches

New   Delete

☐	Name ⌃	Type	Enabled	Alarm Type
☐	Deadlock	Server Log	true	Automatic Reset
☐	ServerControlbylog	Server Log	true	N/A
☐	StuckThread	Server Log	true	Automatic Reset
☐	UncheckedException	Server Log	true	Automatic Reset

New   Delete

Figure 7-59. *WebLogic admin console, settings for Module-FMWDFW page displaying the newly created watch*

Figure 7-59 shows the Watches table that lists the watches available in the system and draws attention to the watch named ServerControlbylog, which you can click to open its settings.

In the settings page, you choose the table named Notifications and then associate the notification named FMWDFW-notifications with your watch by clicking the right arrow located in the middle of the panel, as shown in Figure 7-60. Lastly, you click the Save button, and once the configuration is changed, you finish your work by clicking the Active Changes button.

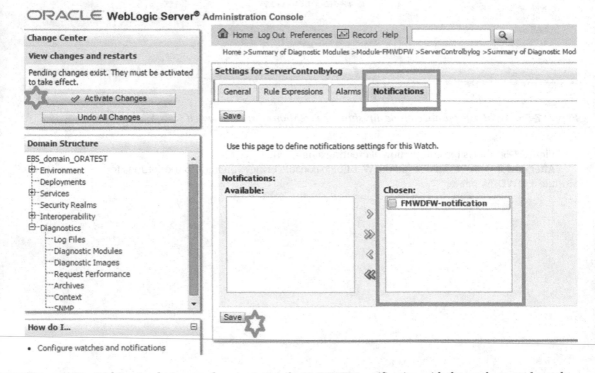

Figure 7-60. *WebLogic admin console, associating the FMWDFW notification with the newly created watch*

At this point, your watch is created, and a default notification, which will create an incident when the watch is triggered, is associated with it.

So, to see your watch in action, restart your Admin Server and during the restart operation check the Admin Server log and see that your watch is triggered.

Just after the line specifying that the watch is triggered, you see another log file that specifies an incident is created.

```
<Jul 31, 2015 9:31:02 AM EEST> <Notice> <Diagnostics> <BEA-320068> <Watch 'ServerControlbylog'
with severity 'Notice' on server 'AdminServer' has triggered at Jul 31, 2015 9:31:02 AM EEST.
Notification details:
WatchRuleType: Log
WatchRule: (MSGID = 'BEA-000365')
WatchData: DATE = Jul 31, 2015 9:31:01 AM EEST SERVER = AdminServer MESSAGE = Server state
changed to ADMIN SUBSYSTEM = WeblogicServer USERID = weblogic SEVERITY = Notice THREAD =
[ACTIVE] ExecuteThread: '1' for queue: 'weblogic.kernel.Default (self-tuning)' MSGID = BEA-
000365 MACHINE = somehost.somedomain.com TXID =  CONTEXTID = 31b4c0652d38b2a8:-44517192:14ee
2c4a3ff:-8000-0000000000000022 TIMESTAMP = 1438324261625
WatchAlarmType: None
WatchAlarmResetPeriod: 60000
>
<Jul 31, 2015 9:31:02 AM EEST> <Alert> <Diagnostics> <BEA-320016> <Creating diagnostic
image in /u01/install/APPS/fs1/FMW_Home/user_projects/domains/EBS_domain_ORATEST/servers/
AdminServer/adr/diag/ofm/EBS_domain_ORATEST/AdminServer/incident/incdir_1 with a lockout
minute period of 1.>
```

At this point, when you change your directory to the incident directory that is specified by the log messages, you see that an incident consisting of the standard diagnostic files is there.

```
[applmgr@somehost ~]$ cd /u01/install/APPS/fs1/FMW_Home/user_projects/domains/EBS_domain_
ORATEST/servers/AdminServer/adr/diag/ofm/EBS_domain_ORATEST/AdminServer/incident/incdir_1
[applmgr@somehost incdir_1]$ ls -al
-rw-r--r-- 1 applmgr oinstall 255826 Jul 31 09:31 diagnostic_image_
AdminServer_2015_07_31_09_31_02.zip
-rw-r--r-- 1 applmgr oinstall      0 Jul 31 09:31 dms_metrics2_i1.txt
-rw-r--r-- 1 applmgr oinstall  58549 Jul 31 09:31 jvm_threads1_i1.txt
-rw-r--r-- 1 applmgr oinstall  43888 Jul 31 09:31 odl_logs4_i1.txt
-rw-r--r-- 1 applmgr oinstall     30 Jul 31 09:31 odl_quicktrace3_i1.txt
-rw-r--r-- 1 applmgr oinstall   1423 Jul 31 09:31 readme.txt
```

As shown by this example, by using the diagnostic capabilities of FMW, you can configure the diagnostic mechanism according to your needs and capture what you need in case of a situation that you want to control.

Summary

It seems we have reached the end of this topic, as we have explained almost all the topics that an apps DBA should know for managing FMW in EBS 12.2. We introduced FMW, went through the concepts and the tools used for management, and covered the topics related to diagnostic and tuning activities.

We also explained which components of FMW are positioned and integrated into the EBS 12.2 technology stack. We went through the directory structure of FMW and the management activities for WebLogic servers so you have a better understanding of FMW in EBS 12.2. Moreover, by explaining the administration tools and subjects like tuning and diagnosing the FMW WebLogic components, we tried to make you more familiar with FMW in the EBS 12.2 environment.

We gave as many examples as possible, so after this point, it is in your hands to increase this knowledge by practicing the topics in this chapter. In the next chapter, we will continue explaining the AutoConfig utility, including the FMW configuration changes that are done via AutoConfig.

CHAPTER 8

■ ■ ■

AutoConfig to Manage EBS System Configuration Changes

Maintaining systems is one of the most important tasks that an apps DBA or technical owner of a system can do. For maintaining Oracle EBS, there are many tools available, and each tool has its own purpose. In this chapter, you will learn about one of the important Oracle EBS management tools, called AutoConfig (or adconfig).

Introduction to the AutoConfig Utility

Oracle E-Business Suite is tightly coupled with different technology stack components, and it provides multiple tools for managing an Oracle E-Business Suite environment. AutoConfig is one of the core utilities that is used for easier Oracle EBS configuration management. AutoConfig provides centralized management of configuration changes, and it standardizes configuration management tasks in Oracle E-Business Suite. In earlier releases (pre-11.5.4), this tool was not included in the standard installation, you have to install this tool as an add-on after installation. But in later releases like EBS 11.5.10.2 and higher, the AutoConfig tool is included in the standard installation. AutoConfig simplifies the overall Oracle E-Business Suite configuration management.

Before we jump into the technical details about AutoConfig, we'll show you a business case of how AutoConfig simplifies configuration management in Oracle EBS. For example, say that during an installation of Oracle E-Business Suite you have chosen the default ports and your environment is working without any issues. But at some point later there is an audit, which recommends that you change the default ports for the application and database. As you saw in Chapter 2, by default the database will use port 1521 and the application uses port 8000. This port information will be used and stored in many configuration files.

Consider, for example, that this port information is stored in some 50 files, and to change the configuration you have to edit those 50 files manually. If you miss any files or modify a file incorrectly, then it will affect the application availability. AutoConfig simplifies such complex configurations. You only need to update a single file (the context file) in the database tier/application tier and execute this utility. AutoConfig will automatically update all the required configuration files and maintain the change versioning, which can be used for tracking and rolling back the changes.

There are multiple options available in AutoConfig, and we will cover them in detail in the coming sections. In earlier releases (pre-12.2), AutoConfig was used for managing all the configuration changes in technology stack components. As discussed in earlier chapters, FMW is the major change introduced from EBS 12.2, and in FMW configurations, the AutoConfig role is minimized; however, for other technology stack components, all the configuration changes are managed by AutoConfig.

© Syed Zaheer and Erman Arslan 2016
S. Zaheer and E. Arslan, *Practical Oracle E-Business Suite*, DOI 10.1007/978-1-4842-1422-0_8

Understanding Configuration Management Tools and Utilities

The AutoConfig tool is a set of java classes that can be executed using Perl/shell scripts. adautoconfig.sh (the applications DBA automatic configuration) exists in both dbTier and appsTier in its respective locations. AutoConfig uses a context file for modifying the configuration changes in the database and application.

AutoConfig consists of multiple components for managing the configuration changes in Oracle E-Business Suite, as shown in Figure 8-1.

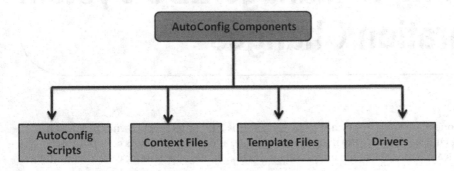

Figure 8-1. *EBS 12.2: AutoConfig components*

AutoConfig works in conjunction with its components, and each component has its own role. Now we'll discuss how to use each of these components while doing AutoConfig configuration management.

AutoConfig call certain scripts from AD_TOP whenever necessary. For example, AutoConfig will script the adgentns.pl script, and this script will connect to the database and generate tnsnames.ora files. The AutoConfig utility will call adconfig.pl from the $AD_TOP location.

AutoConfig Scripts

The scripts used for running the AutoConfig process are called AutoConfig scripts. As mentioned, AutoConfig scripts exist on all database and application nodes based on the deployment topology. You should use the AutoConfig script from the database Home while you are performing configuration changes on dbTier/ dbTechStack, and for application configuration changes you should use it from the application tier.

Starting with EBS 12.2, you have dual file system, and the AutoConfig scripts exist in both file systems. You should execute AutoConfig scripts considering the run and patch file systems, if modification is performed on RUN file system then autoconfig should be executed on RUN file system and vice versa.

Several scripts are available in Oracle EBS to support AutoConfig operations, and they are generally called AutoConfig tools. Table 8-1 describes the available AutoConfig tools that can be used while performing AutoConfig operations.

Table 8-1. EBS 12.2: AutoConfig Tools

Name	Location	Description
adautocfg.sh	Application tier: $INST_TOP/admin/scripts Database tier: $DB_HOME/appsutil/scripts/context_name	This is used for running the AutoConfig process, and it updates the changes on the system.
adchkcfg.sh	Application tier: $AD_TOP/bin Database tier: $DB_HOME/appsutil/bin	This is used for reviewing the configuration changes that AutoConfig will perform.
adtmplreport.sh	Application tier: $AD_TOP/bin Database tier: $DB_HOME/appsutil/bin	This is used to locate and gather AutoConfig template files.
admkappsutil.sh	Application tier: $AD_TOP/bin	This is used for updating the AutoConfig managed scripts on dbTier.
GenCtxInfRep.pl	Application tier: $FND_TOP/patch/115/bin Database tier: $DB_HOME/appsutil/bin	This provides the detailed information about the context file and its templates.

■ **Note** On UNIX platforms, the script extension is .sh, but if EBS is running on Windows, the script extension is .cmd.

Later in this chapter you will see how to use each of these AutoConfig tools.

Context File

The Oracle application and database configuration is stored in an XML repository file called the *context file*. There will be a separate context file for the database tier and the application tier. Suppose you have a four-node deployment topology for Oracle EBS 12.2 with split configuration, two as the database server and two as the application server. In this case, the context file will be installed and configured on all four nodes. Any configuration changes in Oracle EBS are supported via the context file. This file is an important file because it stores every bit of information related to the application and database tiers.

The context file naming is defined with a combination database SID and hostname. For example, if the database name is PROD and the hostname is erpnode1, then the context file will be generated as PROD_erpnode1.xml. Table 8-2 displays the location of the context file on the database tier and the application tier.

Table 8-2. EBS 12.2: Context File Locations

Database tier	$DB_HOME/appsutil/<context_name>.xml
Application tier	$INST_TOP/appl/admin/<context_name>.xml

■ **Note** Context files exist on each application and database node in a multinode environment.

Template Files

Oracle EBS application products contain the template files in their product top directories, and these template files are used for configuring and creating the site-level configuration in all the required files. AutoConfig will read the context variables from the template file, decide on the actual required values, and substitute these values in the required configuration files. Template files are located in the application tier and the database tier. Table 8-3 shows the location of the template files.

Table 8-3. *EBS 12.2: Template File Locations*

Database tier	$<PRODUCT_TOP>/admin/template
Application tier	$DB_HOME/appsutil/template

■ **Note**   Each configuration file has one template file associated with it. Whenever you modify a template, then each configuration file will have two template files: the original one and the customized one. During the execution of AutoConfig, the customized files are prioritized.

There are two types of AutoConfig template files. One will be used for APPL_TOP-specific configuration, and the other will be used during the Rapidwiz Install Wizard process, which creates a script for starting and stopping the application/database services. These scripts are required for starting and stopping the appropriate set of services with the configured parameters.

We will discuss AutoConfig template files more in the section "Using AutoConfig for Managing Customizations."

Driver Files

Similar to the application template files, each application product top contains the driver files. These driver files are associated with the template files and the target configuration files. Each driver file contains the command executables, and each product top in Oracle E-Business Suite contains its driver files. Table 8-4 show the location of the driver files.

Table 8-4. *EBS 12.2: Location of Driver Files*

Database tier	$<PRODUCT_TOP>/admin/driver
Application tier	$DB_HOME/appsutil/template

Working with AutoConfig

So far we have introduced AutoConfig and its components. Now you will see how AutoConfig process actually works during the configuration changes, as shown in Figure 8-2.

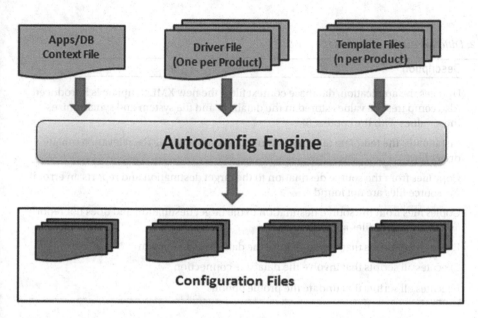

Figure 8-2. *EBS 12.2: how AutoConfig works*

To understand how the AutoConfig process works, you need to understand the terminology behind an AutoConfig instantiation. In the instantiation process, AutoConfig will create a configuration file with modified content as per the specific environment. You can use AutoConfig to instantiate and create files/scripts, and you can use these scripts for installation or configuration changes.

Template and Driver File Usage During AutoConfig Operation

AutoConfig uses template files to identify the basic settings required for configuration. As mentioned earlier, each template file will be associated with the respective driver file, and the driver file includes the names and location required to be changed for the context variables. The template and driver files are responsible for starting the instantiation process, and they also define the phases in which it should execute the instantiation process. These files are also responsible for executing set commands for all the required application products.

Later in this chapter we will explain how the template files work in detail.

Phases of AutoConfig Execution

AutoConfig executes the driver files in different phases. The driver file will perform a series of steps for installing or performing the configuration changes. Table 8-5 lists the different phases of AutoConfig driver file execution.

Table 8-5. *EBS 12.2: Different AutoConfig Phases*

Phase	Description
CVM	Updates the application/database context file if the new XML template is introduced Also compares the values stored in the database and file system and synchronizes these values with the context files
INSTE8	Instantiates the template files to the configuration files using the relevant template driver files
BINCPY	Copy files from the source destination to the target destination and reports an error if the source files are not found
BINCPY_IGERR	Copies files from the source destination to the target destination and does not report an error if source files are not found
INSTE8_SETUP	Executes all scripts that do not require the database connection
INSTE8_APPLY	Executes all scripts that involve the database connection
INSTE8_PRF	Executes all scripts that update the profile options

You have seen the different phases of AutoConfig and the set of operations performed in each phase. But AutoConfig executes the scripts in different phases, as shown in Figure 8-3.

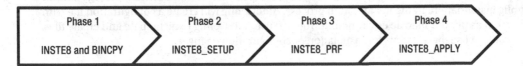

Phase 1	Phase 2	Phase 3	Phase 4
INSTE8 and BINCPY	INSTE8_SETUP	INSTE8_PRF	INSTE8_APPLY

Figure 8-3. *EBS 12.2: AutoConfig compilation order*

Phase 1: This generates all files that are part of the instantiation phase and copies the files from the source to the target destination directories.

Phase 2: This executes all setup scripts instantiated in phase 1 that do not require a database connection.

Phase 3: The executes all profile scripts instantiated in phase 1.

Phase 4: This executes all apply scripts instantiated in phase 1 that need a database connection.

The AutoConfig process requires execution of multiple scripts for installing or updating the new configuration changes to Oracle E-Business Suite systems. It works in conjunction with the context file, template files, driver files, and configuration files.

Working with the Context File

As discussed earlier, the context file is an XML repository file that will store the full configuration information of an EBS environment. The application and database tiers will have their own context files. To perform any configuration changes in the context files, you should use Context Editor from OAM because it is the recommended way of modifying the context file. You can even modify the context file using the command-line option, but this is not recommended.

Log in to the application using the SYSADMIN responsibility and navigate to the AutoConfig link (in other words, Oracle Application Dashboard (OAM) ➤ Site Map ➤ Administration), as shown in Figure 8-4.

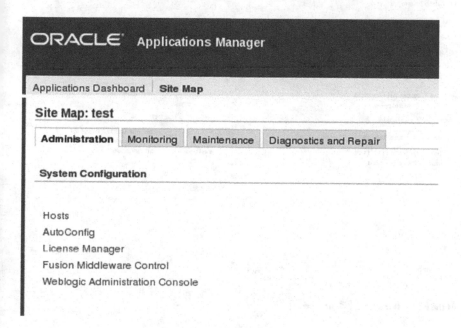

Figure 8-4. EBS 12.2: OAM AutoConfig administration

On the OAM Dashboard administration page you can see the AutoConfig option. Once you click AutoConfig, you'll see a list of the available context files. Figure 8-5 displays this list of available context files.

Context Files

Last Updated:25-Aug-2015 00:00:00

Filter | Name ▾ | | Go

Select two context files of the same tier and ... | Compare | |

Select All | Select None

Select	Details	Name	Host	Tier▲	Synchronized	Last Synchronized Date	Last Update Date	Node Status	View	Show History	Edit Parameters
☐	◢	test_erpnode3	erpnode3	Applications	✓	12-Feb-2015 11:04:24	12-Feb-2015 11:04:24	Online	6ᴏ	▥	✎
			Version	120.401.12020000.45			Path	/u01/appl_test/fs1/inst /apps/test_erpnode3/appl/admin /test_erpnode3.xml			
			Creation Date	28-Oct-2014 03:56:36			Last Updated By	APPSMGR			
			Status	Write succeeded			Comments				
☐	◢	test_erpnode3	erpnode3	Database	✓	20-Nov-2014 10:07:57	20-Nov-2014 10:07:57	Online	6ᴏ	▥	✎
			Version	120.52.12020000.2			Path	/u01/ora_test/11.2.0/appsutil /test_erpnode3.xml			
			Creation Date	27-Oct-2014 23:11:22			Last Updated By	ANONYMOUS			
			Status	Write succeeded			Comments				

Context Files

Last Updated:10-Jun-2016 00:00:00

Filter | Name ▾ | | Go

Select two context files of the same tier and ... | Compare | |

Select All | Select None

Select	Details					
☐	◢	Version	120.52.12020000.2	Path	/u01/ora_test/11.2.0/appsutil/test_erpnode3.xml	
		Creation Date	27-Oct-2014 23:11:22	Last Updated By	ANONYMOUS	
		Status	Write succeeded	Comments		
☐	◢	Version	120.52.12020000.3	Path	/u01/ora_test/12.1.0/appsutil/test_erpnode3.xml	
		Creation Date	20-Nov-2014 10:10:10	Last Updated By	ANONYMOUS	
		Status	Write succeeded	Comments		

Figure 8-5. *EBS 12.2: list of AutoConfig context files*

You can perform multiple actions on the context files from the Oracle Applications Manager Dashboard:

- Download the context file
- Show the history
- Edit the configuration parameters

AutoConfig allows you to edit the configuration changes, as shown in Figure 8-6.

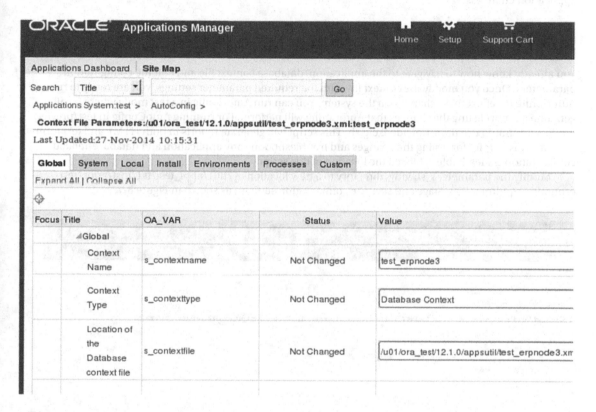

Figure 8-6. *EBS 12.2: AutoConfig, editing context file parameters*

CVM is one the components of AutoConfig that falls under the category of AutoConfig scripts shown in Figure 8-1. Whenever a value has been modified in the context file, then CVM will come in action. CVM will identify the values that need to be updated in the database and file system and will propagate the changes while executing the AutoConfig engine.

CVM will use adcvm.sh as the main script for propagating the changes to the application and database. This script will be available for the database as well as application, and it will use the template files adcvmat.xml and adcvmdb.xml for propagating the changes on the system.

Here are the application tier CVM files:

```
adcvm.sh - $AD_TOP/bin
adcvmat.xml - $AD_TOP/admin/template
```

Here are the database tier CVM files:

```
adcvm.sh - $RDBMS_HOME/appsutil/bin
adcvmdb.xml - $RDBMS_HOME/appsutil/template
```

Later in this chapter you will see how you can work with the context file for effective and centralized configuration management in Oracle E-Business Suite and how CVM works for updating the database and application changes.

Running AutoConfig in Preview Mode

You already know how to navigate to the application/database context file and edit the configuration parameters. Once you modify the context file with the required parameter settings, you are ready to run AutoConfig to reflect these changes on the system. You can run AutoConfig in a test mode where it will generate a report listing the changes that AutoConfig will perform. For running AutoConfig in test/preview mode, you should use the script adchkcfg.sh. This script will generate reports in both HTML and text format. This utility is helpful for testing the changes and troubleshooting any application and database-related configuration Issues. Table 8-1 listed the location of this script.

Modify the parameter s_staging_directory to a new location of /u01/appl_test/fs1/inst/apps/test_erpnode3/appltmp/EBS_Stage and save the configuration settings, as shown in Figure 8-7.

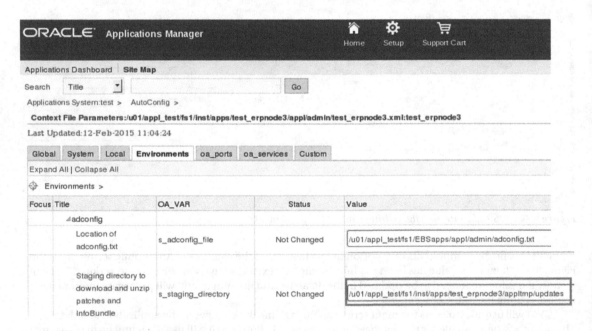

Figure 8-7. *EBS 12.2: AutoConfig, Context Editor*

After changing the value as shown in Figure 8-8, you must save the configuration. Once the new parameter is updated, it will acknowledge that the changes have been saved to the context file, and you should run AutoConfig for these parameters to be effective, as shown in Figure 8-9.

s_staging_directory	Not Changed	/u01/appl_test/fs1/inst/apps/test_erpnode3/appltmp/EBS_Stage	Temporary directory that the OAM Patch Wizard feature uses for analyzing, downloading and merging patches and InfoBundle before uploading the information to database.

onments   oa_ports   oa_services   Custom

Add to Support Cart   Save

Figure 8-8. *EBS 12.2: AutoConfig, Context Editor change parameter*

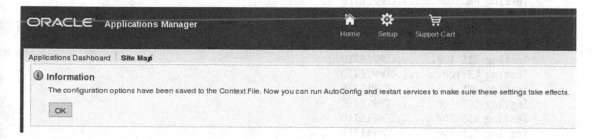

Figure 8-9. *EBS 12.2: AutoConfig, Context Editor acknowledgment*

The scripts displayed in Listing 8-1 are used for running AutoConfig in the test mode.

Listing 8-1. AutoConfig Execution in TEST Mode

```
[applebs@erpnode3 bin]$ pwd
/u01/appl_test/fs1/EBSapps/appl/ad/12.0.0/bin
[applebs@erpnode3 bin]$ ls -l adchkcfg.*
-rwxr-xr-x 1 applebs dbaerp 13143 Nov 24  2012 adchkcfg.cmd
-rwxr-xr-x 1 applebs dbaerp  4690 Nov 24  2012 adchkcfg.sh

[applebs@erpnode3 bin]$ sh adchkcfg.sh
Enter the full path to the Applications Context file:
/u01/appl_test/fs1/inst/apps/test_erpnode3/appl/admin/test_erpnode3.xml
Enter the APPS password:

The log file for this session is located at: /u01/appl_test/fs1/inst/apps/test_erpnode3/
admin/log/08251552/adconfig.log

AutoConfig is running in test mode and building diffs...
```

AutoConfig will consider the custom templates if present.
```
        Using CONFIG_HOME location     : /u01/appl_test/fs1/inst/apps/test_erpnode3
        Classpath                      : /u01/appl_test/fs1/FMW_Home/Oracle_EBS-app1/shared-
libs/ebs-appsborg/WEB-INF/lib/ebsAppsborgManifest.jar:/u01/appl_test/fs1/EBSapps/comn/java/
classes

        Using Context file             : /u01/appl_test/fs1/inst/apps/test_erpnode3/admin/
out/08251552/test_erpnode3.xml
```

Context Value Management will now update the test Context file

```
        Updating test Context file...COMPLETED
```

[**Test mode**]
No uploading of Context File and its templates to database.

```
Testing templates from all of the product tops...
        Testing AD_TOP........COMPLETED
        Testing FND_TOP.......COMPLETED
        Testing ICX_TOP.......COMPLETED
        Testing MSC_TOP.......COMPLETED
        Testing IEO_TOP.......COMPLETED
        Testing BIS_TOP.......COMPLETED
        Testing CZ_TOP........COMPLETED
        Testing AMS_TOP.......COMPLETED
        Testing CCT_TOP.......COMPLETED
        Testing WSH_TOP.......COMPLETED
        Testing CLN_TOP.......COMPLETED
        Testing OKE_TOP.......COMPLETED
        Testing OKL_TOP.......COMPLETED
        Testing OKS_TOP.......COMPLETED
        Testing CSF_TOP.......COMPLETED
        Testing IBY_TOP.......COMPLETED
        Testing JTF_TOP.......COMPLETED
        Testing MWA_TOP.......COMPLETED
        Testing CN_TOP........COMPLETED
        Testing CSI_TOP.......COMPLETED
        Testing WIP_TOP.......COMPLETED
        Testing CSE_TOP.......COMPLETED
        Testing EAM_TOP.......COMPLETED
        Testing GMF_TOP.......COMPLETED
        Testing PON_TOP.......COMPLETED
        Testing FTE_TOP.......COMPLETED
        Testing ONT_TOP.......COMPLETED
        Testing AR_TOP........COMPLETED
        Testing AHL_TOP.......COMPLETED
        Testing IES_TOP.......COMPLETED
        Testing OZF_TOP.......COMPLETED
        Testing CSD_TOP.......COMPLETED
        Testing IGC_TOP.......COMPLETED
```

```
Differences text report is located at: /u01/appl_test/fs1/inst/apps/test_erpnode3/admin/
out/08251552/cfgcheck.txt

        Generating Profile Option differences report...COMPLETED
Differences text report for the Database is located at: /u01/appl_test/fs1/inst/apps/test_
erpnode3/admin/out/08251552/ProfileReport.txt
        Generating File System differences report......COMPLETED
Differences html report is located at: /u01/appl_test/fs1/inst/apps/test_erpnode3/admin/
out/08251552/cfgcheck.html

Differences Zip report is located at: /u01/appl_test/fs1/inst/apps/test_erpnode3/admin/
out/08251552/ADXcfgcheck.zip
AutoConfig completed successfully.
[applebs@erpnode3 bin]$
```

The output report will be located under the directory $INST_TOP/admin/out /<Date>, and this report displays two different portions, in other words, the file system and the database.

File System

The file system will display all the files that will be changed at the file system level. The following are the different types of files that AutoConfig will display with respect to the changes:

> *AutoConfig context file changes:* This will display the context file changes.

> *Service group status:* This will display the services running on application tier nodes.

> *Changed configuration files:* This will list all the configuration files that will update during AutoConfig execution.

> *New configuration files:* This will list the new configuration files that are going to be created during the next AutoConfig execution.

> *Template customization:* This will display the differences between original AutoConfig templates and the customized template.

Database

This section covers the changes that will be performed on the database. The following are the different values that will be updated within the database:

> *Profile values changes*: This will display the list of profile values that it will update during the next AutoConfig execution.

> *Profile values*: This will list all the application and database profile values that will be managed by AutoConfig.

> *Database updates*: This will list the database update action that will be performed during the next AutoConfig execution.

As mentioned, after execution of AutoConfig in test mode, AutoConfig will generate the output file, as shown in Figure 8-10. This output file contains all the previously mentioned details.

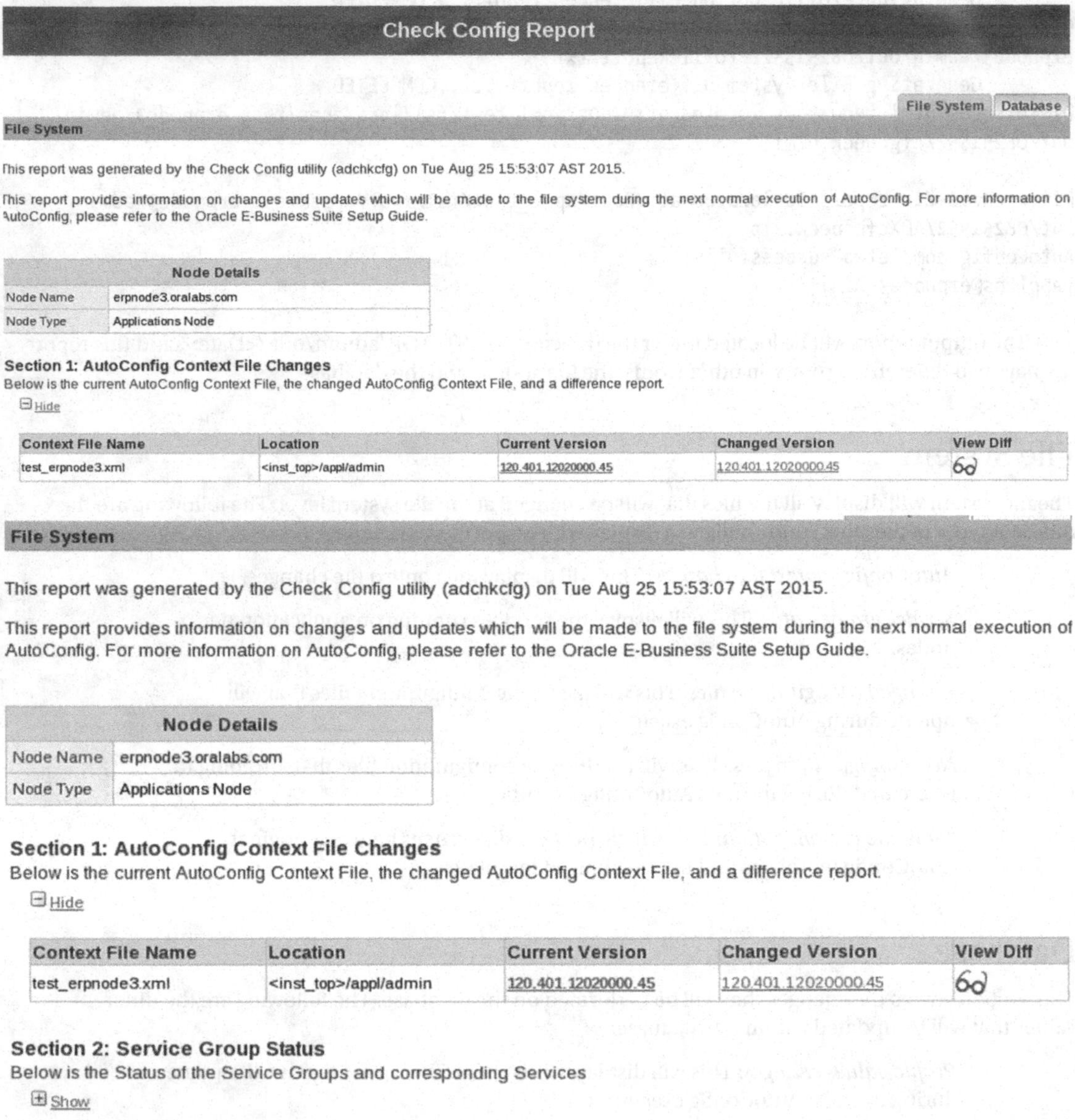

Check Config Report

	File System	Database

File System

This report was generated by the Check Config utility (adchkcfg) on Tue Aug 25 15:53:07 AST 2015.

This report provides information on changes and updates which will be made to the file system during the next normal execution of AutoConfig. For more information on AutoConfig, please refer to the Oracle E-Business Suite Setup Guide.

Node Details	
Node Name	erpnode3.oralabs.com
Node Type	Applications Node

Section 1: AutoConfig Context File Changes
Below is the current AutoConfig Context File, the changed AutoConfig Context File, and a difference report.
⊟ Hide

Context File Name	Location	Current Version	Changed Version	View Diff
test_erpnode3.xml	<inst_top>/appl/admin	120.401.12020000.45	120.401.12020000.45	6ð

File System

This report was generated by the Check Config utility (adchkcfg) on Tue Aug 25 15:53:07 AST 2015.

This report provides information on changes and updates which will be made to the file system during the next normal execution of AutoConfig. For more information on AutoConfig, please refer to the Oracle E-Business Suite Setup Guide.

Node Details	
Node Name	erpnode3.oralabs.com
Node Type	Applications Node

Section 1: AutoConfig Context File Changes
Below is the current AutoConfig Context File, the changed AutoConfig Context File, and a difference report.
⊟ Hide

Context File Name	Location	Current Version	Changed Version	View Diff
test_erpnode3.xml	<inst_top>/appl/admin	120.401.12020000.45	120.401.12020000.45	6ð

Section 2: Service Group Status
Below is the Status of the Service Groups and corresponding Services
⊞ Show

Figure 8-10. *EBS 12.2: AutoConfig, test mode output file*

You can see the differences between the old and the new context file by clicking the view differences option, as shown in Figure 8-11. The entries listed in red are the new lines that don't exist in the old context file, and the entries listed in green are the ones with a different value in the old and new context files.

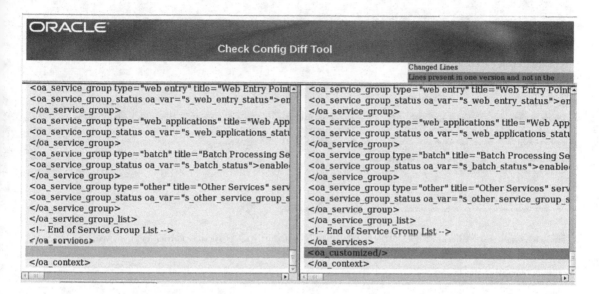

Figure 8-11. *EBS 12.2: AutoConfig, check configuration diff tool*

In the Changed Configuration Files section, you will see all the files that are going to be changed, as shown in Figure 8-12. You can also view the specific differences between the old and new files by clicking the view differences icon.

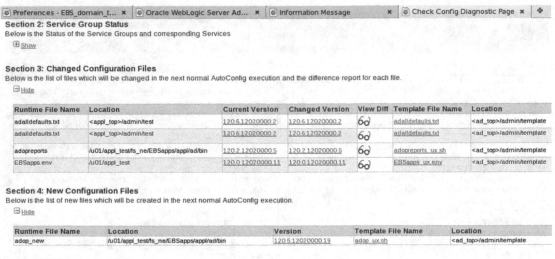

Section 3: Changed Configuration Files

Below is the list of files which will be changed in the next normal AutoConfig execution and the difference report for each file.

⊟ Hide

Runtime File Name	Location	Current Version	Changed Version	View Diff	Template File Name	Location
adalldefaults.txt	<appl_top>/admin/test	120.6.12020000.2	120.6.12020000.2	6o	adalldefaults.txt	<ad_top>/admin/template
adalldefaults.txt	<appl_top>/admin/test	120.6.12020000.2	120.6.12020000.2	6o	adalldefaults.txt	<ad_top>/admin/template
adopreports	/u01/appl_test/fs_ne/EBSapps/appl/ad/bin	120.2.12020000.5	120.2.12020000.5	6o	adopreports_ux.sh	<ad_top>/admin/template
EBSapps.env	/u01/appl_test	120.0.12020000.11	120.0.12020000.11	6o	EBSapps_ux.env	<ad_top>/admin/template

Section 4: New Configuration Files

Below is the list of new files which will be created in the next normal AutoConfig execution.

⊟ Hide

Runtime File Name	Location	Version	Template File Name	Location
adop_new	/u01/appl_test/fs_ne/EBSapps/appl/ad/bin	120.5.12020000.19	adop_ux.sh	<ad_top>/admin/template

Section 5: Template Customizations

Below is the list of custom templates.

⊞ Show

Figure 8-12. *EBS 12.2: AutoConfig, changed configuration files*

The following listing shows the customized location of the s_staging_directory in the application context file:

```
[applebs@erpnode3 admin]$ pwd
/u01/appl_test/fs1/inst/apps/test_erpnode3/appl/admin
[applebs@erpnode3 admin]$ grep s_staging_directory test_erpnode3.xml
<STAGING_DIRECTORY oa_var="s_staging_directory" customized="yes">/u01/appl_test/fs1/inst/
apps/test_erpnode3/appltmp/EBS_Stage</STAGING_DIRECTORY>
[applebs@erpnode3 admin]$
```

If you execute the adchkcfg.sh script without modifying any of the parameters in the context file, then in the output file it will not show any differences unless someone modified the scripts manually (using other command-line editors), as listed in Figure 8-13 and Figure 8-14. In addition, the view differences icon will not be displayed.

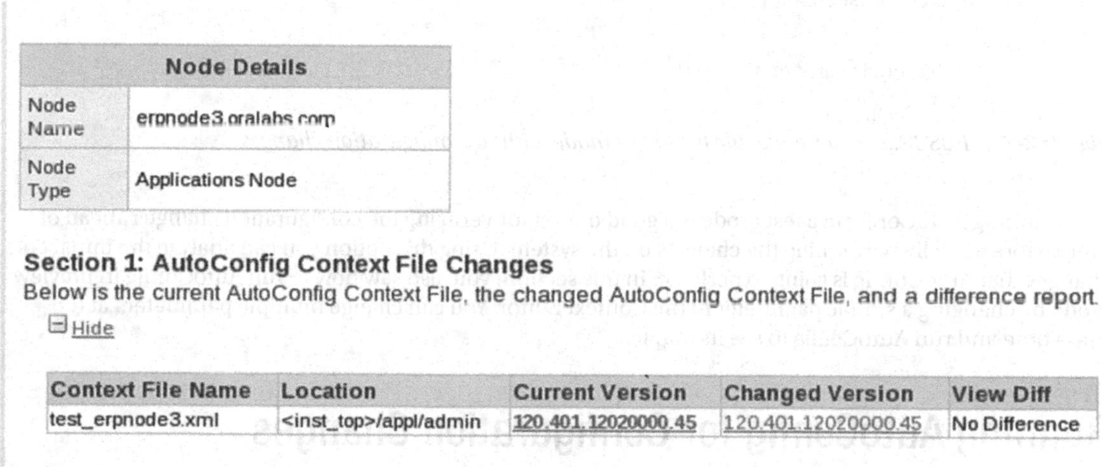

Node Details	
Node Name	erpnode3.oralabs.com
Node Type	Applications Node

Section 1: AutoConfig Context File Changes

Below is the current AutoConfig Context File, the changed AutoConfig Context File, and a difference report.

⊟ Hide

Context File Name	Location	Current Version	Changed Version	View Diff
test_erpnode3.xml	<inst_top>/appl/admin	120.401.12020000.45	120.401.12020000.45	No Difference

Figure 8-13. EBS 12.2: AutoConfig, test mode without configuration changes

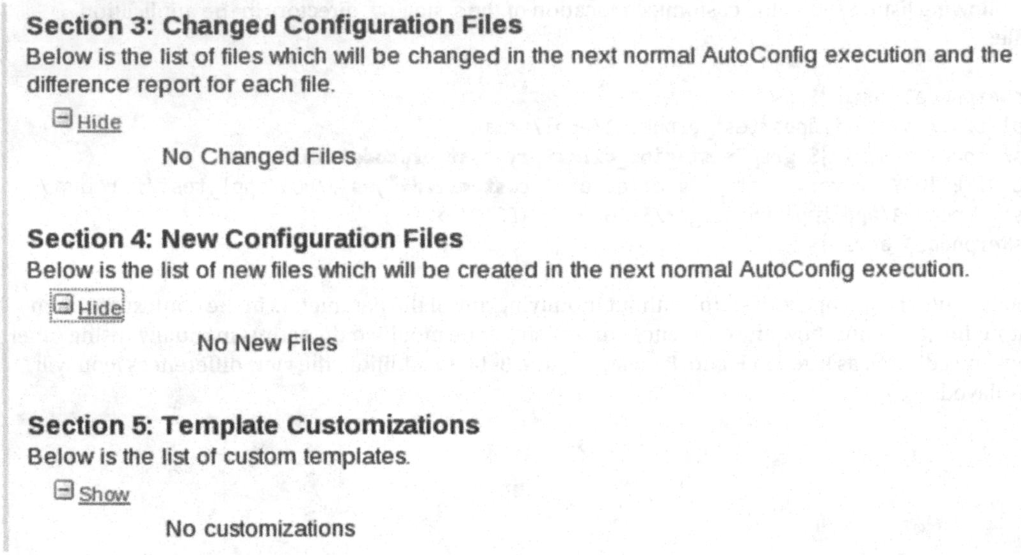

Section 3: Changed Configuration Files

Below is the list of files which will be changed in the next normal AutoConfig execution and the difference report for each file.

⊟ Hide

    No Changed Files

Section 4: New Configuration Files

Below is the list of new files which will be created in the next normal AutoConfig execution.

⊟ Hide

    No New Files

Section 5: Template Customizations

Below is the list of custom templates.

⊟ Show

    No customizations

Figure 8-14. *EBS 12.2: AutoConfig, file list in test mode without configuration changes*

Running AutoConfig in a test mode is a good option for verifying the configuration changes ahead of time before actually performing the changes on the system. Using this option you can analyze the impact of changes that AutoConfig is going to perform. In this section, you also saw how to run AutoConfig in preview mode by changing a simple parameter in the Context Editor. You can change multiple parameters at the same time and run AutoConfig to see its impact.

Running AutoConfig for Configuration Changes

We already discussed in detail how AutoConfig works. Now you will see how to execute AutoConfig and how it can be used for managing the configuration changes in Oracle E-Business Suite.

There are certain prerequisites that should be followed before executing the AutoConfig scripts:

- The database and database listener should be up and running.

- It is always recommended to shut down the application services while running AutoConfig.

- AutoConfig should be executed on the run and patch file systems individually for managing the changes. At the time of execution of the AutoConfig script, you will be prompted to choose the file system type (run or patch).

Figure 8-15 illustrates the process of using autoconfig utility in the dual file system.

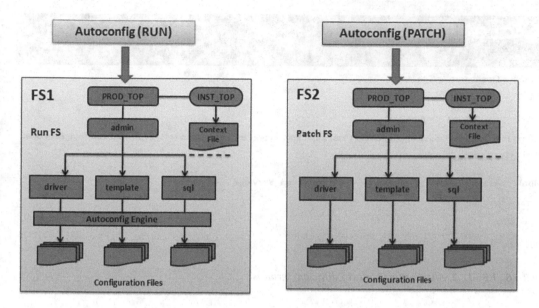

Figure 8-15. *EBS 12.2: AutoConfig, execution in dual file system*

In this demonstration, we will change the context parameters related to the concurrent manager and execute AutoConfig. You should use the Context Editor from OAM using following navigation:

Oracle Application Dashboard (OAM) ➤ Site Map ➤ Adminstration ➤ AutoConfig

Here, select the appropriate application context file, navigate to the section oa_services, and modify the parameters s_sleep_time and s_cp_diag, as shown in Figures 8-16 and 8-17.

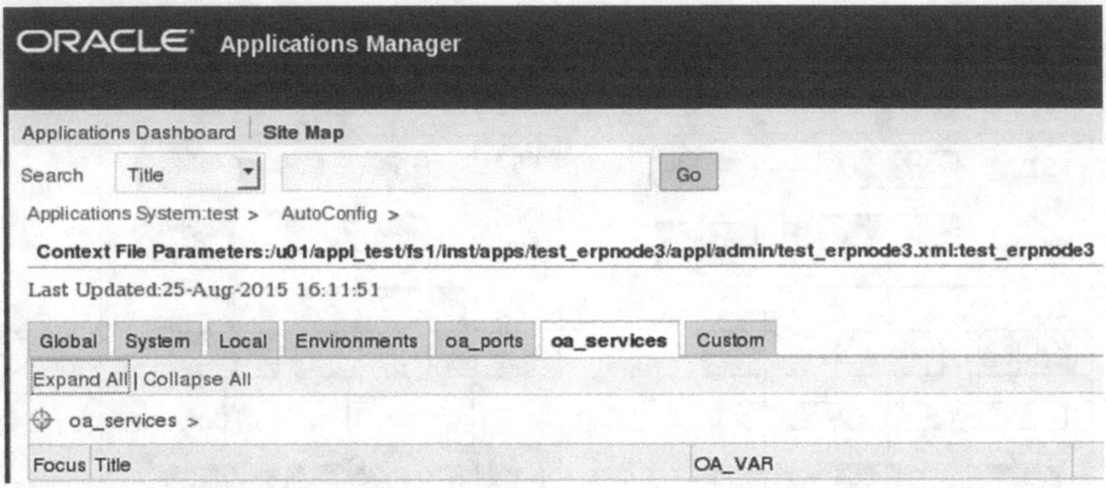

Figure 8-16. *EBS 12.2: AutoConfig Context Editor, oa_services*

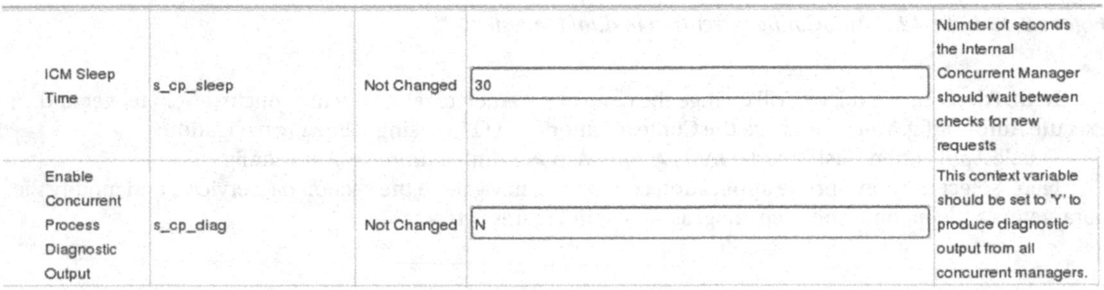

ICM Sleep Time	s_cp_sleep	Not Changed	30	Number of seconds the Internal Concurrent Manager should wait between checks for new requests
Enable Concurrent Process Diagnostic Output	s_cp_diag	Not Changed	N	This context variable should be set to 'Y' to produce diagnostic output from all concurrent managers.

Figure 8-17. *EBS 12.2: AutoConfig Context Editor, update parameters*

Once you update the parameters, you should save the settings. While saving the new settings, you will be prompted to provide the comments related to the change, as shown in Figure 8-18 and Figure 8-19. You can write any comment you like. These comments will be helpful in identifying the type of change from the context file's console. To make these changes effective on the system, you should execute AutoConfig from the run file system.

After modifying the required changes, it's now time to execute AutoConfig. You should source the environment file from the run file system and execute AutoConfig also from the run file system.

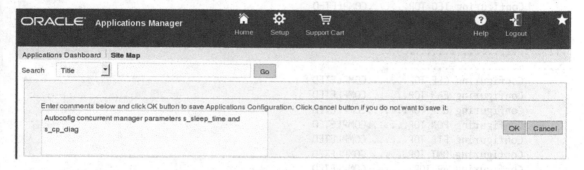

Figure 8-18. EBS 12.2: AutoConfig Context Editor, comment input

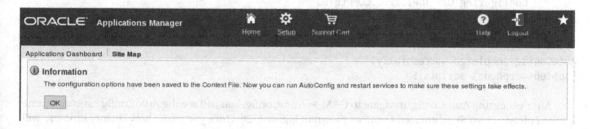

Figure 8-19. EBS 12.2: AutoConfig Context Editor, saved acknowledgment

Navigate to the $ADMIN_SCRIPTS_HOME directory and run the script adautocfg.sh, as shown in Listing 8-2.

Listing 8-2. Execution of AutoConfig

```
[applebs@erpnode3 scripts]$ adautocfg.sh
Enter the APPS user password:
The log file for this session is located at: /u01/appl_test/fs1/inst/apps/test_erpnode3/
admin/log/08262301/adconfig.log
AutoConfig is configuring the Applications environment...
AutoConfig will consider the custom templates if present.
        Using CONFIG_HOME location    : /u01/appl_test/fs1/inst/apps/test_erpnode3
        Classpath                     : /u01/appl_test/fs1/FMW_Home/Oracle_EBS-app1/shared-libs/
ebs-appsborg/WEB-INF/lib/ebsAppsborgManifest.jar:/u01/appl_test/fs1/EBSapps/comn/java/classes
        Using Context file            : /u01/appl_test/fs1/inst/apps/test_erpnode3/appl/admin/
test_erpnode3.xml
Context Value Management will now update the Context file
        Updating Context file...COMPLETED
        Attempting upload of Context file and templates to database...COMPLETED
Configuring templates from all of the product tops...
        Configuring AD_TOP........COMPLETED
```

```
        Configuring FND_TOP.......COMPLETED
        Configuring ICX_TOP.......COMPLETED
        Configuring MSC_TOP.......COMPLETED
        Configuring IEO_TOP.......COMPLETED
        Configuring BIS_TOP.......COMPLETED
        Configuring CZ_TOP........COMPLETED
..........................  ..
..........................  ..
        Configuring CSE_TOP.......COMPLETED
        Configuring EAM_TOP.......COMPLETED
        Configuring GMF_TOP.......COMPLETED
        Configuring PON_TOP.......COMPLETED
        Configuring FTE_TOP.......COMPLETED
        Configuring ONT_TOP.......COMPLETED
        Configuring AR_TOP........COMPLETED
        Configuring AHL_TOP.......COMPLETED
        Configuring IES_TOP.......COMPLETED
        Configuring OZF_TOP.......COMPLETED
        Configuring CSD_TOP.......COMPLETED
        Configuring IGC_TOP.......COMPLETED

AutoConfig completed successfully.
[applebs@erpnode3 scripts]$
```

After executing AutoConfig, navigate to OAM ➤ AutoConfig. You will see the AutoConfig execution time for the column "Last Synchronized Data," as shown in Figure 8-20. Once you click Show History link, you will see all the previous versions of the context file.

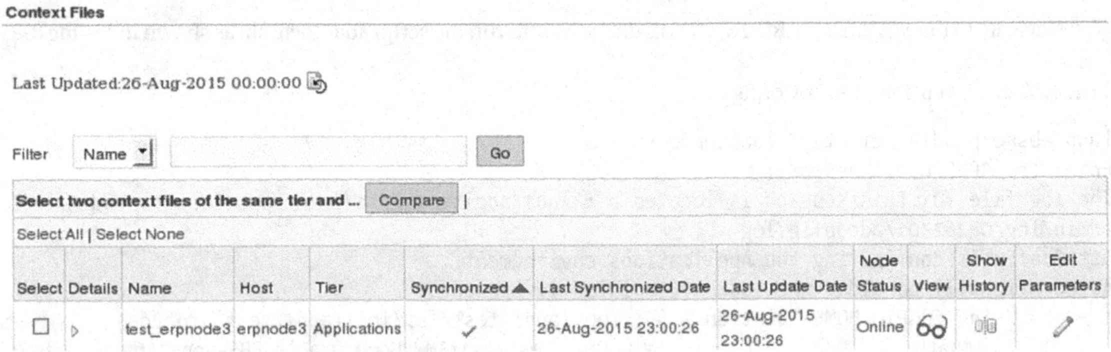

Context Files

Last Updated:26-Aug-2015 00:00:00

Filter Name ▾ [   ] Go

Select two context files of the same tier and ... Compare |

Select All | Select None

Select	Details	Name	Host	Tier	Synchronized ▲	Last Synchronized Date	Last Update Date	Node Status	View	Show History	Edit Parameters
☐	▷	test_erpnode3	erpnode3	Applications	✓	26-Aug-2015 23:00:26	26-Aug-2015 23:00:26	Online	6ð	⬓⫼	✎

Figure 8-20. *EBS 12.2: AutoConfig context file, after AutoConfig execution*

Now you can click Show Differences with the current configuration and you will see a list of the newly configured parameters, as shown in Figure 8-21.

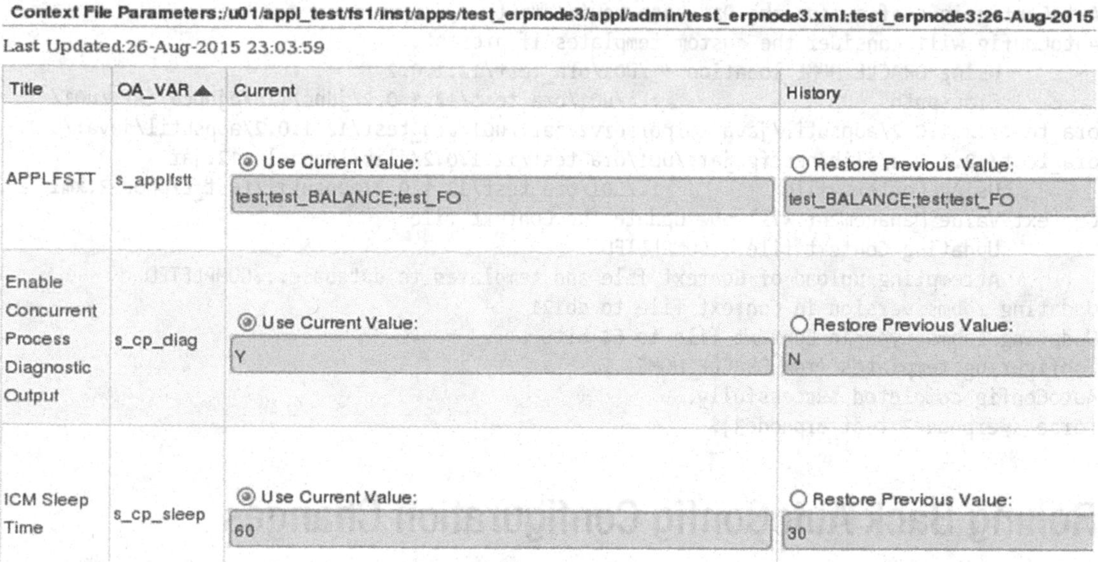

Context File Parameters:/u01/appl_test/fs1/inst/apps/test_erpnode3/appl/admin/test_erpnode3.xml:test_erpnode3:26-Aug-2015

Last Updated:26-Aug-2015 23:03:59

Title	OA_VAR ▲	Current	History
APPLFSTT	s_applfstt	⊙ Use Current Value: test;test_BALANCE;test_FO	○ Restore Previous Value: test_BALANCE;test;test_FO
Enable Concurrent Process Diagnostic Output	s_cp_diag	⊙ Use Current Value: Y	○ Restore Previous Value: N
ICM Sleep Time	s_cp_sleep	⊙ Use Current Value: 60	○ Restore Previous Value: 30

Figure 8-21. *EBS 12.2: AutoConfig context file, history*

This is how you can change as many configuration parameters in the context file as you need, and AutoConfig is responsible for reflecting these changes in all the required configuration files. If AutoConfig encounters any errors, then you should check AutoConfig and its relevant log files to identify the problem. You should check in which phase it failed. Table 8-6 lists the log file locations.

In this section, you saw how easy it is to do configuration changes using AutoConfig. If you face any issues after performing the changes, you can simply roll back those changes, as covered in the next section.

Table 8-6. *EBS 12.2: AutoConfig Log File Location*

AutoConfig Log File Location	
Location	$INST_TOP/admin/log/<date>/adconfig.log
Example	/u01/appl_test/fs1/inst/apps/test_erpnode3/admin/log/08262301/adconfig.log

Executing AutoConfig on the Database Tier

You can use Context Editor from OAM for modifying/updating the context values for the database tier as well as maintain history for all the changes in OAM. The procedure for running AutoConfig on the database tier is the same as the application tier, but while performing the configuration changes on the database tier, you must use the AutoConfig script from the RDBMS Oracle Home directory. Table 8-1 listed the database tier AutoConfig utility location.

```
[oraebs@erpnode3 test_erpnode3]$ adautocfg.sh
Enter the APPS user password:
The log file for this session is located at: /u01/ora_test/12.1.0.2/appsutil/log/test_
erpnode3/08311410/adconfig.log
```

```
AutoConfig is configuring the Database environment...
AutoConfig will consider the custom templates if present.
        Using ORACLE_HOME location : /u01/ora_test/12.1.0.2
        Classpath                  : :/u01/ora_test/12.1.0.2/jdbc/lib/ojdbc6.jar:/u01/
ora_test/12.1.0.2/appsutil/java/xmlparserv2.jar:/u01/ora_test/12.1.0.2/appsutil/java:/u01/
ora_test/12.1.0.2/jlib/netcfg.jar:/u01/ora_test/12.1.0.2/jlib/ldapjclnt12.jar
        Using Context file         : /u01/ora_test/12.1.0.2/appsutil/test_erpnode3.xml
Context Value Management will now update the Context file
        Updating Context file...COMPLETED
        Attempting upload of Context file and templates to database...COMPLETED
Updating rdbms version in Context file to db121
Updating rdbms type in Context file to 64 bits
Configuring templates from ORACLE_HOME ...
AutoConfig completed successfully.
[oraebs@erpnode3 test_erpnode3]$
```

Rolling Back AutoConfig Configuration Changes

It's a well-known rule that if you are performing any configuration changes, then you must take a backup of the existing configuration. This backup can be used if you encounter any unexpected issues and want to roll back to a previous configuration. One of the good feature of AutoConfig is that you can roll back an AutoConfig session to the previous configuration. This operation can be performed using the Context Editor from OAM or you can use the restore.sh script to roll back the configuration changes.

To restore the settings, you have to shut down the application services, execute restore.sh, and start up the application services.

```
[applebs@erpnode3 08262301]$ sh restore.sh
SQL*Plus: Release 10.1.0.5.0 - Production on Thu Aug 27 12:45:52 2015
Copyright (c) 1982, 2005, Oracle. All rights reserved.

Enter apps password

Connected.
[ CONC_GSM_ENABLED ]
Application Id : 0
Profile Value  : Y
Level Name: SITE
INFO          : Updated/created profile option value.
.
[ ICX_DEFAULT_EUL ]
Application Id : 178
Profile Value  : EUL
Level Name: SITE
INFO          : Updated/created profile option value.
```

You can use the Context Editor as well to roll back the changes (see Figure 8-22). Consider that you have changes to some set of parameters and you want to roll back only selected parameters. You can use the Context Editor and can change only the desired parameters. If you use the restore.sh script, then it will roll back all the changes performed during the last AutoConfig execution. OAM will not allow you to restore the manually made customization in the configuration files, but OAM is not a real recovery to backup. It will perform the configuration changes again using the old settings.

The previous configured value for s_cp_diag was set to yes, and the current value is set no, as listed in the figure. You can simply choose Restore Previous Value and save the configuration. After saving the configuration, you should run AutoConfig again for these parameters to take effect.

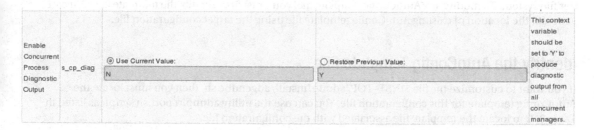

Figure 8-22. *EBS 12.2: AutoConfig context file, rollback*

Using AutoConfig for Managing Customizations

Managing customizations in EBS environment is always a big challenge for developers and DBAs. This is usually based on the requirement that the changes be performed on the configuration files directly. This will work fine until the next AutoConfig execution. After execution of AutoConfig, all these changes will be lost, and if these configuration changes are documented, then you should add them manually to all the required configuration files. This is not the correct practice of customizing the EBS configuration.

Oracle E-Business Suite is initially configured with standard configuration settings based on the user inputs from Rapidwiz. As discussed earlier, the complete Oracle E-Business Suite is configured based on the existing templates. So, for any customization requirements, you should create custom templates. If you create custom templates, the AutoConfig engine will be aware of all customizations, and it will preserve all the changes even after executing AutoConfig because it will use the customized templates.

■ **Note**   Editing the standard templates is not supported. You should create your own custom template from the standard template for customization.

The AutoConfig process supports different types of customizations. The following are the list of supported AutoConfig types:

- Modifying the existing value of the context file

- Adding a new context variable to the context file

- Customizing the existing AutoConfig template

- Creating owned custom templates

You can use the OAM Context Editor to modify and add the context variables/values to an existing context file. After performing the configuration changes, you must run AutoConfig in order to reflect these changes on the system. The process for modifying or adding the new context variables/values on the application and database tier is the same, but you should execute the AutoConfig scripts with their respective locations.

Customizing Existing AutoConfig Template

In this section, you will learn how to customize the existing AutoConfig template from the application tier file system. To modify any AutoConfig template file, you must first identify the template file. You can generate the location of existing AutoConfig template file using the target configuration file.

Identify the AutoConfig Template File

If you want to customize the file $INST_TOP/admin/install/adgendbc.sh, then you must locate the AutoConfig template for this configuration file. You can use the utility adtmplreport.sh script, as listed in Table 8-1, to locate the template file associated with the configuration file.

$AD_TOP/bin/adtmplreport.sh contextfile=<CONTEXT_FILE> target=<configurationfile>

```
[applebs@erpnode3 install]$ /u01/appl_test/fs1/EBSapps/appl/ad/12.0.0/bin/adtmplreport.sh
contextfile=$CONTEXT_FILE target=/u01/appl_test/fs1/inst/apps/test_erpnode3/admin/install/
adgendbc.sh
####################################################################
          Generating Report .....
####################################################################
For details check log file: /u01/appl_test/fs1/inst/apps/test_erpnode3/admin/log/08301040.log
```

This will generate a report in the log file, which will provide the location of the AutoConfig template file.

```
[applebs@erpnode3 install]$ cat /u01/appl_test/fs1/inst/apps/test_erpnode3/admin/log/08301040.log
==================================================================
Starting Utility to Report on Templates and their  Targets  at Sun Aug 30 10:40:48 AST 2015
Using ATTemplateReport.java version 120.0

[ INFO_REPORT ]

[AD_TOP]
TEMPLATE FILE   : /u01/appl_test/fs1/EBSapps/appl/ad/12.0.0/admin/template/adgendbc_ux.sh
TARGET FILE     : /u01/appl_test/fs1/inst/apps/test_erpnode3/admin/install/adgendbc.sh

[applebs@erpnode3 install]$
```

Create Directory and Copy Template to Custom Directory

You should create the custom directory inside the target product top and copy the required template to the custom directory.

```
[applebs@erpnode3 ~]$ mkdir -p /u01/appl_test/fs1/EBSapps/appl/ad/12.0.0/admin/template/custom
[applebs@erpnode3 ~]$ cp -i /u01/appl_test/fs1/EBSapps/appl/ad/12.0.0/admin/template/
adgendbc_ux.sh /u01/appl_test/fs1/EBSapps/appl/ad/12.0.0/admin/template/custom
[applebs@erpnode3 ~]$ ls -l /u01/appl_test/fs1/EBSapps/appl/ad/12.0.0/admin/template/custom/
adgendbc_ux.sh
```

```
-rwxr-xr-x 1 applebs dbaerp 10323 Aug 31 18:00 /u01/appl_test/fs1/EBSapps/appl/ad/12.0.0/
admin/template/custom/adgendbc_ux.sh
[applebs@erpnode3 ~]$
```

Modify the Template

You can now modify the newly copied custom template with the required changes. Note that it is not supported to edit the standard Oracle-delivered template files. You should always edit the copied custom templates.

Verify the Customization

Execute the adchkcfg.sh script to check the customized template files.

```
[applebs@erpnode3 ~]$ adchkcfg.sh contextfile=$CONTEXT_FILE
Enter the APPS password:
.........................................
..........................................
Differences text report is located at: /u01/appl_test/fs1/inst/apps/test_erpnode3/admin/
out/09011908/cfgchcck.txt

        Generating Profile Option differences report...COMPLETED
Differences text report for the Database is located at: /u01/appl_test/fs1/inst/apps/test_
erpnode3/admin/out/09011908/ProfileReport.txt
        Generating File System differences report......COMPLETED
Differences html report is located at: /u01/appl_test/fs1/inst/apps/test_erpnode3/admin/
out/09011908/cfgcheck.html

Differences Zip report is located at: /u01/appl_test/fs1/inst/apps/test_erpnode3/admin/
out/09011908/ADXcfgcheck.zip

AutoConfig completed successfully.
[applebs@erpnode3 ~]$
```

After execution of AutoConfig in test mode, you can review the generated HTML report to check the differences, as shown in Figures 8-23 and 8-24.

Section 5: Template Customizations

Below is the list of custom templates.

⊟ Show

AutoConfig Template	Version	Custom Template	Version	View Diff
<ad_top>/admin/template/adgendbc_ux.sh	120.10	<ad_top>/admin/template/custom/adgendbc_ux.sh	120.10	🔍

Figure 8-23. *EBS 12.2: AutoConfig, template customization check config*

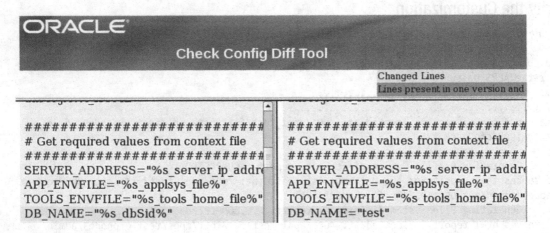

Figure 8-24. *EBS 12.2: AutoConfig, template customization differences*

Execute AutoConfig

After verifying the configuration check report, if the configuration is listed as expected, you can move forward and execute AutoConfig to reflect these changes on the system.

```
[applebs@erpnode3 ~]$ adautocfg.sh
Enter the APPS user password:

The log file for this session is located at: /u01/appl_test/fs1/inst/apps/test_erpnode3/
admin/log/09011916/adconfig.log
```

Advanced AutoConfig Features and Utilities

Oracle EBS is a highly scalable environment and may be deployed on multiple database and application nodes. In such cases you may need some advanced options for managing the systems easily and effectively. So far in this chapter we have discussed how you can use AutoConfig for managing the system, but in this section you will see advanced options available with AutoConfig.

AutoConfig Command-Line Options

The AutoConfig process provides multiple command-line options that can be executed along with the script adconfig.pl or adconfig.sh. The syntax for using these options is similar, and you will see a demonstration of some of these options later in this chapter. Table 8-7 lists the command-line options available with AutoConfig.

Table 8-7. *EBS 12.2: AutoConfig Command-Line Options*

Option	Description
Help	Provides usage information.
contextfile	Provides the application context file name.
driver	Specifies the driver file to execute.
product	Provides the product short name to execute during AutoConfig.
jdk	Provides the location (specifically, the Java location).
test	Executes AutoConfig in test mode.
promptmsg	When this parameter is set to hide, it will not prompt for some specific parameters.
nocustom	AutoConfig will not preserve any customization.
noversionchecks	AutoConfig will not maintain a version mismatch between templates.
-syncctx	It will only perform context file synchronization.
-profile	It will generate the execution statistics.
-nothreading	It will not run AutoConfig in a multithreaded mode.
-parallel	It will allow AutoConfig to execute AutoConfig on all nodes in parallel. If you do not specify this option, then it should be executed on each node after completion on respective nodes.
run	It will execute AutoConfig to a specific phase (the phases are listed in Table 8-5).

The AutoConfig utility provides some of the advanced features that can be used by the AutoConfig utility. In this section, we will discuss how you can use these advanced features and their benefits.

■ **Note** The adauotcfg.sh script internally calls the adconfig.sh script from $AD_TOP/bin. The adautocfg.sh script passes specified parameters to the adconfig.sh script for further processing. After taking inputs, adconfig. sh calls the Java API (AutoConfig engine) located in $AD_TOP/java/adconfig.zip.

Using Profiling with AutoConfig

You can use the profile option with AutoConfig to generate a performance statistics report in HTML format. The report provides a summary of product tops, consumed instantiation/execution time for its templates, and the status of templates (loaded successfully or not). Listing 8-3 shows the execution of AutoConfig with the profiling option.

Listing 8-3. Execution of AutoConfig with Profiling Pption

```
[applebs@erpnode3 bin]$ adconfig.pl contextfile=$CONTEXT_FILE -profile
Enter the APPS user password:

The log file for this session is located at: /u01/appl_test/fs1/inst/apps/test_erpnode3/
admin/log/08301203/adconfig.log
AutoConfig is configuring the Applications environment...
AutoConfig will consider the custom templates if present.
        Using CONFIG_HOME location    : /u01/appl_test/fs1/inst/apps/test_erpnode3
        Classpath                     : /u01/appl_test/fs1/FMW_Home/Oracle_EBS-app1/shared-libs/
ebs-appsborg/WEB-INF/lib/ebsAppsborgManifest.jar:/u01/appl_test/fs1/EBSapps/comn/java/classes
        Using Context file            : /u01/appl_test/fs1/inst/apps/test_erpnode3/appl/admin/
test_erpnode3.xml
Context Value Management will now update the Context file

        Updating Context file...COMPLETED

        Attempting upload of Context file and templates to database...COMPLETED

Configuring templates from all of the product tops...
        Configuring AD_TOP........COMPLETED
        Configuring FND_TOP.......COMPLETED
        Configuring ICX_TOP.......COMPLETED

        Configuring AR_TOP........COMPLETED
        Configuring AHL_TOP.......COMPLETED
        Configuring IES_TOP.......COMPLETED
        Configuring OZF_TOP.......COMPLETED
        Configuring CSD_TOP.......COMPLETED
        Configuring IGC_TOP.......COMPLETED

AutoConfig performance profile report is located at: /u01/appl_test/fs1/inst/apps/test_
erpnode3/admin/log/08301203/autoconfig_profile.html

AutoConfig completed successfully.
[applebs@erpnode3 bin]$
```

Figure 8-25 shows the results of AutoConfig executed with the profile option.

AutoConfig Performance Profile Report

AutoConfig Summary

Start Time	End Time	Total Time (sec)
2015-08-30 00:03:50	2015-08-30 12:06:35	43365.00

Context Value Management

Scripts	Instantiation Start Time (HH:mm:ss)	Instantiation End Time (HH:mm:ss)	Instantiation Time (sec)	Execution Start Time (HH:mm:ss)	Execution End Time (HH:mm:ss)	Execution Time (sec)	Total Time (sec)	Time (%)	Status
cvm	-	-	-	12:04:00	12:05:21	86.34	86.34	57.74	Passed

Product Summary Report

Product Top	Instantiation Start Time (HH:mm:ss)	Instantiation End Time (HH:mm:ss)	Instantiation Time (sec)	Execution Start Time (HH:mm:ss)	Execution End Time (HH:mm:ss)	Execution Time (sec)	Total Time (sec)	Time (%)	Status
ad/fnd	12:05:24	12:05:31	6.55	12:05:31	12:05:57	26.01	32.56	21.77	Passed
msc	12:05:57	12:05:58	0.30	12:05:58	12:06:09	11.00	11.30	7.56	Passed

Figure 8-25. EBS 12.2: AutoConfig, profile statistics

You can generate a profile report for a selected product by specifying the product for which you want to generate the report. You can provide a specific product top for which you want to execute AutoConfig with the profile option, as shown in Listing 8-4.

Listing 8-4. Execution of AutoConfig with the profile Option

```
[applebs@erpnode3 12.0.0]$ adconfig.pl contextfile=$CONTEXT_FILE product=ad -profile
Enter the APPS user password:
The log file for this session is located at: /u01/appl_test/fs1/inst/apps/test_erpnode3/
admin/log/08301341/adconfig.log
AutoConfig is configuring the Applications environment...

AutoConfig will consider the custom templates if present.
        Using CONFIG_HOME location    : /u01/appl_test/fs1/inst/apps/test_erpnode3
        Classpath                     : /u01/appl_test/fs1/FMW_Home/Oracle_EBS-app1/shared-
libs/ebs-appsborg/WEB-INF/lib/ebsAppsborgManifest.jar:/u01/appl_test/fs1/EBSapps/comn/java/
classes
        Using Context file            : /u01/appl_test/fs1/inst/apps/test_erpnode3/appl/admin/
test_erpnode3.xml
Context Value Management will now update the Context file
        Updating Context file...COMPLETED
        Attempting upload of Context file and templates to database...COMPLETED
Configuring templates from ad ...
AutoConfig performance profile report is located at: /u01/appl_test/fs1/inst/apps/test_
erpnode3/admin/log/08301341/autoconfig_profile.html
AutoConfig completed successfully.
[applebs@erpnode3 12.0.0]$
```

The HTML report is generated, and you can see the time consumed by AutoConfig for all products or selected products in their respective reports, as shown in Figure 8-26.

AutoConfig Performance Profile Report

AutoConfig Summary

Start Time	End Time	Total Time (sec)
2015-08-30 13:41:01	2015-08-30 13:43:20	139.00

Context Value Management

Scripts	Instantiation Start Time (HH:mm:ss)	Instantiation End Time (HH:mm:ss)	Instantiation Time (sec)	Execution Start Time (HH:mm:ss)	Execution End Time (HH:mm:ss)	Execution Time (sec)	Total Time (sec)	Time (%)	Status
cvm	-	-	-	13:41:11	13:42:34	88.78	88.78	68.04	Passed

Product Summary Report

Product Top	Instantiation Start Time (HH:mm:ss)	Instantiation End Time (HH:mm:ss)	Instantiation Time (sec)	Execution Start Time (HH:mm:ss)	Execution End Time (HH:mm:ss)	Execution Time (sec)	Total Time (sec)	Time (%)	Status
ad/fnd	13:42:37	13:42:43	6.40	13:42:43	13:43:19	35.30	41.70	31.96	Passed
Total	13:42:37	13:42:43	6.40	13:41:11	13:43:19	124.08	130.48	100	Passed

Figure 8-26. *EBS 12.2: AutoConfig, profile statistics for single product*

Running AutoConfig in Parallel Mode in Multinode Environment

If you are working in a multinode environment and there are certain configuration changes, to reflect these changes on the system, you have to execute AutoConfig. It has been observed that most of DBAs will execute AutoConfig node after node, which will consume a lot of time and effort. AutoConfig has a built-in feature to execute in parallel mode.

adconfig Execution on dbTier with parallel Option

In this section you will see how you can execute the AutoConfig in parallel mode on the database tier. Usually this option is helpful in RAC deployments with multiple database nodes.

```
[oraebs@erpnode3 bin]$ echo $CONTEXT_FILE
/u01/ora_test/12.1.0.2/appsutil/test_erpnode3.xml
[oraebs@erpnode3 bin]$ adconfig.pl contextfile=$CONTEXT_FILE -parallel
Enter the APPS user password:

The log file for this session is located at: /u01/ora_test/12.1.0.2/appsutil/log/test_
erpnode3/08311855/adconfig.log
```

```
............................................................
............................................................
Updating rdbms version in Context file to db121
Updating rdbms type in Context file to 64 bits
Configuring templates from ORACLE_HOME ...

AutoConfig completed successfully.
[oraebs@erpnode3 bin]$
```

adconfig Execution on appsTier with parallel Option

This section will show you how you can execute AutoConfig in parallel mode on the application tier. This option is helpful when multiple application nodes are deployed.

```
[applebs@erpnode3 bin]$ adconfig.pl contextfile=$CONTEXT_FILE -parallel
Enter the APPS user password:
The log file for this session is located at: /u01/appl_test/fs1/inst/apps/test_erpnode3/
admin/log/08311855/adconfig.log
AutoConfig is configuring the Applications environment...
AutoConfig will consider the custom templates if present.
        Attempting upload of Context file and templates to database...COMPLETED
Configuring templates from all of the product tops...
        Configuring AD_TOP........COMPLETED
        ..................................................................
        ..................................................................
        ..................................................................
        Configuring IGC_TOP.......COMPLETED
AutoConfig completed successfully.
```

The log file for both dbTier and appsTier will show adconfig.sh started in parallel synchronization mode. Listing 8-5 shows the log file of the AutoConfig execution, and you can see that it's mentioning that AutoConfig started in parallel mode.

Listing 8-5. Log File Showing AutoConfig Execution in Parallel Mode

```
=============================================================================
Initializing AutoConfigSynchronizer for AutoConfig parallel run...

Trying to obtain Database connection...

-----------------------------------------------------------------
                    ADX Database Utility
-----------------------------------------------------------------
```

If the log file fails to mention the parallel option while running AutoConfig on each node in a multinode environment, then it will result in an inconsistent file system or database across multiple nodes. The AutoConfig execution will be successful on all nodes even if you do not specify the parallel option.

AutoConfig and Fusion Middleware Home

In earlier chapters, we discussed that Fusion Middleware in Oracle EBS 12.2 has replaced the 10g Application Server OC4J components in Oracle WebLogic Server. In pre-12.2 releases, AutoConfig is the only tool for managing the configuration changes to OC4J components such as oacore, oafm, forms, and HTTP Server. But starting from EBS 12.2, AutoConfig has limited scope for performing configuration changes on these components: HTTP Server, oacore, oafm, forms and forms-c4ws.

In EBS 12.2 AutoConfig is used only for managing some specific areas of Oracle HTTP Server and it partially manages some of the configurations of oacore, oafm, forms, and forms-c4ws. The complete configuration changes of these components can be managed by the WebLogic Server Administration Console.

■ **Note**   In Oracle EBS 12.2 AutoConfig is used for the initial configuration/setup of Oracle HTTP Server during installation, and later it can be managed by WebLogic and the Fusion Middleware console.

You know the complete application configuration information will be stored in context files, and you have seen how to use AutoConfig for managing configuration changes in the context files. Now you'll see how to use the WebLogic Server Administration Console for performing changes on HTTP Server configuration files. Oracle has introduced a new process for synchronizing the OHS configuration parameters with context variables in the context file; this process is called the *feedback loop*, as shown in Figure 8-27.

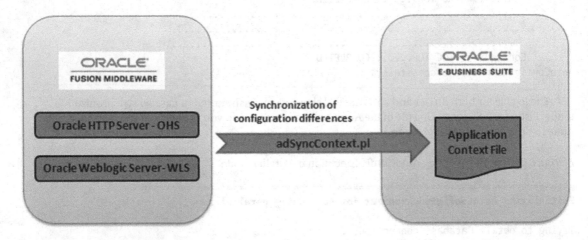

Figure 8-27.   *EBS 12.2: AutoConfig, feedback loop process*

Oracle EBS provides tools, as listed in Table 8-8, that can be used for managing this synchronization.

Table 8-8. *EBS 12.2: Tools for AutoConfig Feedback Loop*

Tool	Location	Description
adRegisterWLSListeners.pl	$AD_TOP/bin	This script will pull the changed WebLogic Server configuration parameters and update the context variables.
adSyncContext.pl	$AD_TOP/bin	This script will pull both WebLogic configuration parameters and HTTP Server configuration parameters and synchronize the respective changed values to the context variables accordingly.

■ **Note**   The script adRegisterWLSListeners.pl will only read configuration parameters related to WebLogic Server. All HTTP-related configuration will be ignored.

The admin server and Node Manager should be running while executing the adSyncContext.pl script.

The Feedback Loop

In this section, you will change the web entry port of HTTP Server in an existing environment. In earlier releases, changing the web port was managed by AutoConfig. As discussed, in EBS 12.2, the HTTP component is managed by the Fusion Middleware enterprise management console.

In the current example, you will change the web port from a value of 8008 to 8015. To perform this change, you need to follow the process of the feedback loop.

Check the web port in the existing context file. The current value is 8008.

```
[applebs@erpnode3 admin]$ grep s_login_page $CONTEXT_FILE
<login_page oa_var="s_login_page">http://erpnode3.oralabs.com:8008/OA_HTML/AppsLogin</
login_page>
[applebs@erpnode3 admin]$
```

Log in to Oracle Enterprise Manager Fusion Middleware Control and navigate to the web pages shown in Figures 8-28, 8-29, 8-30, and 8-31 by following these steps: Farm_EBS_Domian_<domain_name> ➤ Web Tier ➤ right-click ➤ Administration ➤ Port Configuration.

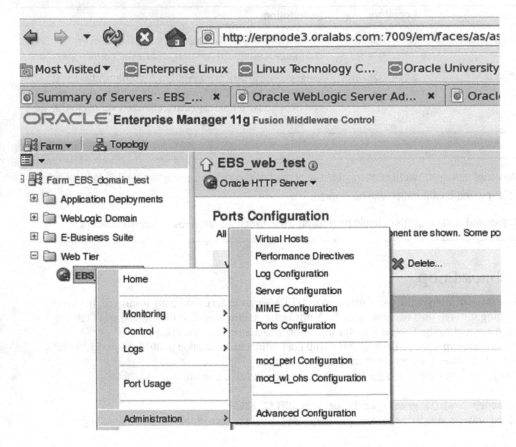

Figure 8-28. *EBS 12.2: Fusion Middleware Enterprise Manager, admin console*

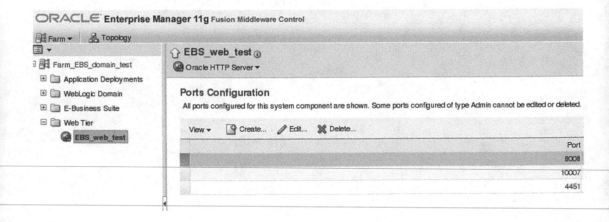

Figure 8-29. *EBS 12.2: Fusion Middleware, EM ports configuration*

476

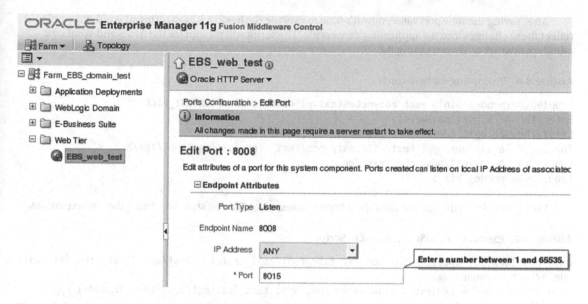

Figure 8-30. EBS 12.2: Fusion Middleware EM, editing HTTP ports

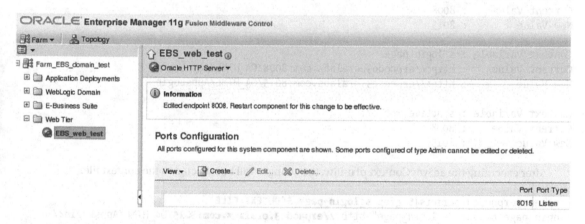

Figure 8-31. EBS 12.2: Fusion Middleware EM, saving ports

■ **Note**   The port value can be changed only when the web tier HTTP service is up and running.

The new value for the web entry port is saved in an HTTP server configuration file, but this value is not updated in the context file. Check the value of the existing port in the context file.

```
[applebs@erpnode3 admin]$ grep s_login_page $CONTEXT_FILE
<login_page oa_var="s_login_page">http://erpnode3.oralabs.com:8008/OA_HTML/AppsLogin</login_page>
[applebs@erpnode3 admin]$
```

After saving the new port value, now it's time to execute the feedback loop script adSyncContext.pl to reflect these changes into the application context file. The script will prompt for the APPS and WebLogic admin password, as shown Listing 8-6.

Listing 8-6. Prompting for Passwords

```
[applebs@erpnode3 bin]$ perl adSyncContext.pl contextfile=$CONTEXT_FILE
Enter the APPS user password:
Enter the WebLogic AdminServer password:
The log file is /u01/appl_test/fs1/inst/apps/test_erpnode3/logs/appl/rgf/Mon_
Aug_31_19_50_17_2015/adSyncContext.log
[applebs@erpnode3 bin]$
```

Listing 8-7 shows the content from the adSyncContext.pl log file that shows updating the context variable.

Listing 8-7. Execution of adSyncContext.pl Script

```
Obtained lock for updating the context file /u01/appl_test/fs1/inst/apps/test_erpnode3/appl/
admin/test_erpnode3.xml
Updating the below context variables in /u01/appl_test/fs1/inst/apps/test_erpnode3/appl/
admin/test_erpnode3.xml
Context Variable : s_webport
Current Value    : 8008
New Value        : 8015

Context Variable : s_login_page
Current Value    : http://erpnode3.oralabs.com:8008/OA_HTML/AppsLogin
New Value        : http://erpnode3.oralabs.com:8015/OA_HTML/AppsLogin

Context Variable : s_active_webport
Current Value    : 8008
New Value        : 8015
```

After executing the adSyncContext.pl utility, the changes will be reflected to the context file.

```
[applebs@erpnode3 scripts]$ grep s_login_page $CONTEXT_FILE
<login_page oa_var="s_login_page">http://erpnode3.oralabs.com:8015/OA_HTML/AppsLogin</
login_page>
[applebs@erpnode3 scripts]$
```

Once the new port value is updated in the context file, you must execute the AutoConfig.

```
[applebs@erpnode3 scripts]$ adautocfg.sh
Enter the APPS user password:

The log file for this session is located at: /u01/appl_test/fs1/inst/apps/test_erpnode3/
admin/log/08311955/adconfig.log
```

After successful completion of AutoConfig, you have to restart the HTTP service for using the newly configure port. If you do not restart the application services, then the HTTP login page will not work.

HTTP services can be restarted using the Enterprise Manager 11g Fusion Middleware Control, as shown in Figure 8-32, or it can restarted using the script adapcctl.sh from $ADMIN_SCRIPTS_HOME.

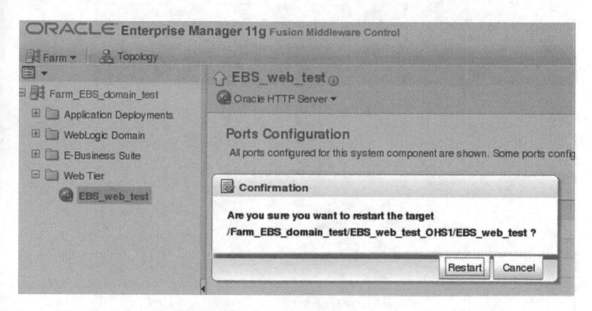

Figure 8-32. *EBS 12.2: Fusion Middleware EM, restarting HTTP Server*

After HTTP Server is restarted, you can access the application using the newly configured port value, as shown in Figure 8-33.

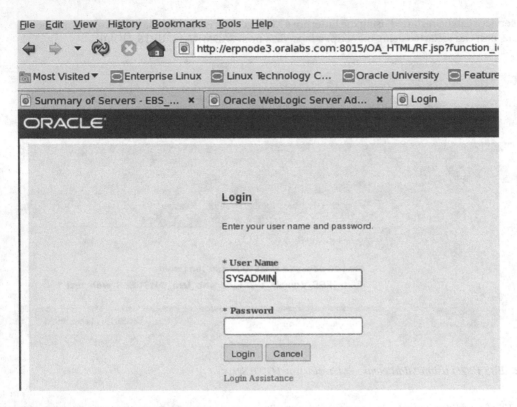

Figure 8-33. EBS 12.2: Web Server Access, using newly configured port

Adding Custom Top to EBS 12.2

Oracle EBS 12.2 is packed with 170+ product tops. But in every business organization there will be a requirement for adding the product tops based on the customization requirements Or you may need to add product tops when new products are released by Oracle. The new product tops can be added using the adsplice utility.

You need to prepare the newprods.txt, xxcustomprod.txt, and xxcustomterr.txt files in advance and then you should execute the adsplice utility for adding the custom top. These files are available after downloading patch 13725897, which is for adding the CLE product, but we will use the files from this patch as a template.

You should rename these files to the product-specific names. With this patch you will get the files cleprod.txt and cleterr.xtx. So, you should rename them to xxapressprod.txt and xxapressterr.txt.

Here's an example script of the modified newprod.txt file:

```
# Add Product,EMEA Add-On Localizations

product=xxapress
base_product_top=*APPL_TOP*
oracle_schema=xxapress
sizing_factor=100
# Table spaces may need to be edited to fit database setup
main_tspace=XXAPRESS_DATA
index_tspace=XXARESS_DATA
```

```
temp_tspace=TEMP
default_tspace=XXPRESS_DATA

#
# End control file
#
```

adsplice runs AutoConfig at the end of its processing and updates the required changes in both the database and application tiers of the run file system. The patch file system will be automatically synchronized with the next patching cycle. You should also use a unique application ID in all relevant custom files, and these files should be located under the $APPL_TOP/admin directory. adsplice also should be executed from this directory.

Adding custom product tops is simple, but you should modify all the previously listed files as appropriate according to the environment. In addition, all required tablespaces and schemas should be created well before executing adsplice.

Summary

In this chapter, you learned how to use AutoConfig to effectively manage your Oracle E-Business Suite configuration changes. You also learned how the AutoConfig process works and the set of actions it will perform in different phases of its execution. We also demonstrated how the AutoConfig process works in conjunction with Fusion Middleware Home.

CHAPTER 9

■ ■ ■

SYSADMIN Fundamentals

The Oracle application system administrator is responsible for setting up appropriate control access and managing product application files and configuration files. The activities involved for performing these functions are discussed in this chapter.

Introduction to Application Technology Layer

Oracle E-Business Suite consists of multiple application product tops. There are a certain set of products whose functionalities will be commonly used by all the other application products. These products in Oracle E-Business Suite terminology are known as the Oracle application technology layer or application technology group (ATG). Figure 9-1 shows the relationship between the application technology group and other application products.

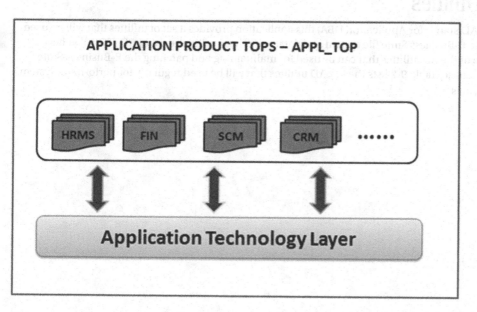

Figure 9-1. EBS 12.2: application technology layer

© Syed Zaheer and Erman Arslan 2016

S. Zaheer and E. Arslan, *Practical Oracle E-Business Suite*, DOI 10.1007/978-1-4842-1422-0_9

Table 9-1 lists the products that are part of the Oracle application technology layer.

Table 9-1. *EBS 12.2: Application Technology Layer Product Group*

Application Name	Product Top
Oracle Application DBA	AD
Oracle Application Utilities	AU
Oracle Application Object Library	FND
Oracle Common Modules	AK
Oracle Workflow	WF
Oracle Alert	ALR
Oracle Application Framework	FWK
Oracle Web Application Desktop Integrator	BNE
Oracle BI publisher	XDO

Before working with the application technology group products, we'll cover the products that are commonly used by other application products in Oracle E-Business Suite. Take AutoConfig, for example. Whenever you perform configuration changes and execute AutoConfig, changes will be applied on all application product tops wherever applicable.

Using AD Utilities

The abbreviation AD stands for Application DBA; this application provides a set of utilities that will be used for maintaining the E-Business Suite file system and database. These utilities exist in AD_TOP. You have already seen some of the AD utilities that can be used for maintaining and patching the E-Business Suite file system and database. Table 9-2 lists the key AD utilities that will be used regularly for performing system maintenance activities.

Table 9-2. *EBS 12.2: Application DBA Utilities*

Serial Number	Name	Program/Executable	Purpose
1	AD Administration	adadmin	Used to perform maintenance tasks on the database and application file systems
2	AutoPatch	adop	Used to install patches to Oracle application and database
3	AD controller	adctrl	Used to manage parallel workers invoked during adadmin, autopatch, and auto-upgrade phases
4	AD relink	adrelink	Used to relink apps executable with product libraries
5	AutoUpgrade	adaimgr	Used to upgrade database code and objects to newer version
6	AD Merge patch	admrgpch	Used to merge multiple application patches into a single patch
7	AD Splicer	adsplice	Used to register off-cycle products (not included with the base install)
8	File Character Set converter	adncnv	Used to convert a file from one character to another
9	AD configuration	$AD_TOP/sql/adutconf.sql	Used to show information about install configuration in APPS
10	AD Job Timing report	$AD_TOP/admin/sql/ adtimprpt.sql	Used to show timing information about parallel workers
11	AD file identification	adident	Used to display version and timestamp of a file
12	License manager	Oracle Applications Manager (OAM)	Used to license new products and country-specific functionalities and languages
13	Patch Wizard	Oracle Applications Manager (OAM)	Used to give information about patches applied and those that need to be applied
14	Applied Patches	Oracle Application Manager (OAM)	Used to show all applied patches on the system

adadmin is a key utility of all the AD utilities. This utility has multiple menu options and submenu options that will be used for maintaining the E-Business Suite file system and database. Table 9-3 describes the main menu and submenu items.

***Table* 9-3.** *EBS 12.2 AD Utilities: adadmin Menu Options*

adadmin		Generate Application File Menus	Generate message files
			Generates message binary files (.msb) that will be present under each product.
		Generate form files	Generates (.fmx) files from definition files (.fmb).
		Generate report files	Generates executable report files (.rdf).
		Generate product JAR files	Generates product Java archive files.
		Return to Main Menu	Returns to adadmin main menu.
	Maintain Application File Menu	Relink Applications programs	Relinks all (or product) your application binaries executables.
		Copy files to destinations	Copy files from each product area to central location.
		Convert character set	Converts character set of base language of all translatable files in APPL_TOP.
		Maintain snapshot information	Records detail information of each file under APPL_TOP. This will keep information about file versioning inside the database, and that information will be utilized later by adpatch and other ad utilities during installation and maintenance operations.
		Check for missing files	Verifies all files needed to install, upgrade, and run applications are present under APPL_TOP.
		Return to Main Menu	Return to adadmin main menu.

(continued)

Table 9-3. (*continued*)

Compile/Reload Application and Database Entities menu	**Compile APPS schema**	Complies invalid and uncompiled objects in APPS.
	Compile menu information	Compiles menu data structures.
	Compile flexfields	Compiles flexfield data structure in AOL table.
	Reload JAR files to database	Reloads all appropriate apps JAR files to database.
	Return to Main Menu	Returns to adadmin main menu.
Maintain Application Database Entities menu	**Validate APPS schema**	Run SQL script advrfapp.sql against APPS schema to verify problems you must fix.
	Re-create grants and synonyms for APPS schema	Re-creates grants and synonyms for APPLSYSPUB and re creates grants on some packages from the system to APPS.
	Maintain multi-lingual tables	Runs PL/SQLs to maintain multilingual tables.
	Check DUAL table	Useful for evaluating expressions, and most of the seeded application programs utilize the dual table for extracting outputs of functions.
	Return to Main Menu	Take you to main menu.

Using the adadmin Utility

To use the adadmin utility, you should source the correct environment file from the run file system. When you execute this utility, you will be prompted for some inputs before adadmin continues. Refer to Table 9-4 for the inputs that you need to provide while running adadmin. Figure 9-2 displays the main menu option of adadmin.

Table 9-4. EBS 12.2: adadmin Input Prompts

Explanation	Input Prompts
[applebs@erpnode3]$ adadmin	Adadmin command at shell prompt.
Is this the correct APPL_TOP [Yes] ?	Press Enter if the suggested APPL_TOP is correct. This will prompt the DBA to verify that the correct top is being selected. Usually this is helpful on TEST servers where multiple APP_TOPS exist on the same server.
Filename [adadmin.log] : adadmin_2015.log	Log file name of your choice for the logs to be generated.
Do you wish to activate this feature [No] ?	If e-mail notifications are required.
Please enter the batchsize [1000] :	This is the number of pl/sqlbatchsize.
Is this the correct database [Yes] ?	This the TNS_ADMIN/Oracle Home location.
Enter the password for your 'SYSTEM' ORACLE schema:	Enter the database password for system.
Enter the ORACLE password of Application Object Library [APPS] :	Enter the database password for apps.

```
oraebs@erpnode3:/u01/ora_test/12.1.0.2/a...  ×  applebs@erpnode3:/u01/appl_test/fs1/EBS...

Reading database for information about the modules.
Saving module information.
Reading database for information about the products.
Reading database for information about how products depend on each other.
Reading topfile.txt ...

Saving product information.

AD code level : [C.5]

*** Maintaining the Run File System (in Hotpatch mode) ***

*** Edition Enabled User ***

           AD Administration Main Menu
-----------------------------------------------------

   1.    Generate Applications Files menu

   2.    Maintain Applications Files menu

   3.    Compile/Reload Applications Database Entities menu

   4.    Maintain Applications Database Entities menu

   5.    Exit AD Administration
```

Figure 9-2. EBS 12.2: adadmin main menu options

adadmin can be run in both interactive and noninteractive modes. In interactive mode, you need to provide all the input prompts, and in noninteractive mode, you can configure the text file with all the required inputs. It will not prompt you for any inputs from the user because it will take all these inputs from the configured file.

Option 1 of adadmin is Generate Application Files. This option has suboptions, as listed in Figure 9-3. In this example, we will generate one form file from AP_TOP to show how this option works.

```
Enter your choice [5] : 1

          Generate Applications Files
-----------------------------------------------

1.     Generate message files

2.     Generate form files

3.     Generate report files

4.     Generate product JAR files

5.     Return to Main Menu
```

Figure 9-3. adadmin: generating application files

```
Enter your choice [5] : 2
Enter the number of workers [6] : 2
Do you want to generate Oracle Forms objects
using this character set [Yes] ?
Do you want to regenerate Oracle Forms PL/SQL library files [Yes] ?
Do you want to regenerate Oracle Forms menu files [Yes] ?
Do you want to regenerate Oracle Forms executable files [Yes] ?
Enter list of products ('all' for all products) [all] : AP
Generate specific forms objects for each selected product [No] ? Yes
The current set of installed languages is: US
Enter list of languages ('all' for all of the above) [all] :
You selected the following languages: US
Is this the correct set of languages [Yes] ?

Selecting library and menu files for Payables...
List of libraries and menus in Payables :

    APCACHE.pll    APPAYSHD.pll    APPREPAY.pll    APVIWPAY.pll    APXHOLDS.pll
    APXIMTCH.pll   APXINLIN.pll    APXINWKB.pll

Enter libraries and menus to generate, or enter 'all' [all] : APXINWKB.pll

List of forms in Payables :

    APPAYSHD.fmx    APPREPAY.fmx    APSTAND.fmx    APVIWPAY.fmx    APXALLOC.fmx
```

```
........................
   ......................
   APXWTRXF.fmx    APXXXDER.fmx    APXXXEER.fmx

Enter forms to generate, or enter 'all' [all] : APXINWKB.fmx
Generating Oracle Forms objects...

 Recording Adadmin action :ADADMIN_GEN_FORMS
 Tokens:GFM_USE_CHARSET=Yes,FRM_PLSQL_LIB=Yes,GEN_FRM_MENUS=Yes,GEN_FRM_EXE=Yes,GEN_FRM_
PRD=AP,GFM_SPECIFIC_OBJ=Yes,LANG_USED=all,CORRECT_LANG=Yes,SELECTED_LIB_FILES=APXINWKB.
pll,SELECTED_FILES=APXINWKB.fmx
...........................................................................
...................................................................................
.......................................................
Assigned: file APXINWKB.fmx on worker  1 for product ap  username AP.
Completed: file APXINWKB.fmx on worker  1 for product ap  username AP.

Telling workers to quit...
1 worker has quit.  Waiting for 1 more.
All workers have quit.

Dropping FND_INSTALL_PROCESSES table...
FND_INSTALL_PROCESSES table dropped.
Dropping AD_DEFERRED_JOBS table...
AD_DEFERRED_JOBS table dropped.
```

We'll show you the time stamp of the form before and after generating the new form.
Here it is before:

```
[applebs@erpnode3 US]$ ls -lrt APXINWKB.fmx
-rw-r--r-- 1 applebs dbaerp 6660376 Nov  7  2014 APXINWKB.fmx
[applebs@erpnode3 US]$
```

Here it is after:

```
[applebs@erpnode3 US]$ ls -lrt APXINWKB.fmx
-rw-r--r-- 1 applebs dbaerp 6660008 Sep  8 12:35 APXINWKB.fmx
[applebs@erpnode3 US]$
```

Usually you will use the Generate Applications Files option if the existing files are corrupted or if you are facing issues while accessing files. You can generate all the application files in a single execution or you can generate a specific set of files as per your requirements.

■ **Note** If there are any customizations on any seeded forms, then they will be lost after generating files using adadmin.

All the adadmin menu options operate in the same way, but each option has its own specific operational role. We'll cover all adadmin options next.

Generate Applications Files Menu

Oracle EBS consists of a huge number of files related to configuration and application products, and there may be certain situations where these files should be generated using seeded source files. The Generate Applications Files menu of adadmin provides multiple options that can be used for maintaining the configuration and product files.

1. Generate message files

2. Generate form files

3. Generate report files

4. Generate product JAR files

Generate message files: These files are used for printing message information to the concurrent manager log and the output files. The message file (.msb) will be in binary format, and these files will be at program run time. You can see the messages while saving a record in an application and while you are performing certain operations on forms; usually, on forms, the messages will appear in a pop-up window or be displayed at the bottom of the application screen.

This option is run when a message file (.msb) should be generated as instructed by Oracle Support or via a patch readme. This might be at the instance level, module level, or language level.

Generate form files: This compiles form executables from .fmb to .fmx. This might be at the instance level, at the product level, or in a specified form.

Generate report files: This compiles report executables as required from the instance level, from the product level, or in a selected number of forms along with pl/sql library files as selected in the options.

Generate product JAR files: This helps generate JAR files in JAVA_TOP.

Maintain Applications Files Menu

This is the second main menu option of adadmin, and it's used for maintaining existing application files. This menu has the following submenu options:

1. Relink Applications programs

2. Copy files to destinations

3. Convert character set

4. Maintain snapshot information

5. Check for missing files

Relink Applications programs: This option helps relink various application programs within applications. This can be done at the instance level or in a specific program.

Copy files to destinations: This copies files from the product location to a central location; this might be used for referencing old files.

Copy character set: This prepares and converts APPL_TOP from one character set to another.

Maintain snapshot information: Snapshots like the global or APPL_TOP snapshot contain lists of patches and versions of various other files, and they can be maintained using this option. It can be used for the following:

- Listing snapshots

- Updating current view snapshot

- Creating snapshots

491

- Updating snapshots

- Deleting snapshots

Check for missing files: This options checks for missing files in various modules.

Compile/Reload Applications Database Entities Menu

This is the third main menu option of adadmin and is used mostly for compiling objects within the EBS database. It has the following subitems:

1. Compile APPS schema

2. Compile menu information

3. Compile flexfields

4. Reload JAR files to database

Compile APPS schema: This option is used to compile invalid objects related to the APPS schema. Consider an example of applying multiple patches: by default most of the patches will compile the APPS schema as part of the patch's post-installation step. You can choose not to compile the APPS schema as part of the patch's post-installation and instead compile the APPS schema only after installing all the patches.

Compile menu information: This compiles any changes in the menu or forces all of them to compile. If there are changes to the existing menus and any new menus are added, then you must compile the menu information to ensure the proper functionalities of application.

Compile Flexfields: This feature is frequently used during a new implementation or during post patch application steps. It is used to compile the flexfields so they take effect.

A flexfield is similar to that of a normal field value, but it allows you to extend the form functionality or to capture the key information; hence, this field is known as a flexfield.

Reload JAR files: This reloads application JAR files in the database. This option should be performed if existing Java classes have been removed from the database in case a Java virtual machine is reloaded because of a corrupted database. It should also be used after upgrading a Java virtual machine in an existing application from one version to another.

Maintain Applications Database Entities Menu

This is the fourth main menu option of adadmin and is used for validating and maintaining the database objects within the EBS database. It has the following submenus:

1. Validate APPS schema

2. Re-create grants and synonyms for APPS schema

3. Maintain multi-lingual tables

4. Check DUAL table

Validate APPS schema: This option probes the APPS schema for issue that are to be fixed. They may or may not be confined to the APPS schema.

Re-create grants and synonyms for apps schema: This option creates grants and synonyms related to the APPS schema. This is an important option that is mostly used during database upgrades.

Maintain multi-lingual tables: After enabling a new language, this option has to be run to update various multilingual tables.

Check DUAL table: Certain application options require dual table access, and they must contain a single row.

Important DB Objects

All AD operations are performed using the common database objects. The following are the key database objects that are used by AD utilities.

AD_DEFERRED_JOBS, ad_timestamps, fnd_install_processes

■ **Note**   AD utilities cannot be run in parallel if the previously mentioned objects are used by running AD utilities.

Using Application DBA Reporting Utilities

Reporting the application configuration is one of the most important jobs of sysadmin/technical consultants. The adutconf.sql utility will provide the application configuration information.

adutconf.sql: Utility for Displaying Application Configuration

This utility will generate a report of a complete E-Business Suite configuration. This information is useful for troubleshooting issues and for Oracle Support, as it will list the detail configuration of the installed E-Business Suite environment.

```
[applebs@erpnode3 ~]$ sqlplus

SQL*Plus: Release 10.1.0.5.0 - Production on Tue Sep 8 13:53:12 2015

Copyright (c) 1982, 2005, Oracle. All rights reserved.

Enter user-name: apps
Enter password:

Connected to:
Oracle Database 12c Enterprise Edition Release 12.1.0.2.0 - 64bit Production
With the Partitioning, OLAP, Advanced Analytics and Real Application Testing options

SQL> @$AD_TOP/sql/adutconf.sql
```

This will generate a report in the current working directory with the name adutconf.lst. This report will be in text format and can viewed using any supported tools like the vi editor, emacs editor, and Notepad/WordPad.

Here is the sample report output:

```
--> Start of Application Information Gathering

--> Product Group Information
  ID Product Group Name            Appl Sys Name   Release      Type
---- --------------------------- --------------- ------------ ----------
Arguments
--------------------
   1 Default product group         test            12.2.4       Standard
```

```
1 row selected.
--> Multi-Org enabled?
Yes

1 row selected.
--> Existing Operating Units
no rows selected
--> Multi-Currency enabled?
No
1 row selected.
--> Registered Applications
```

adident: File Version Identification Utility

All files in Oracle E-Business Suite are maintained by their file versions for identification purposes. Oracle application patches deliver newer file versions for fixing existing problems or adding enhancement. So, you need to know the file version to help identify the problem. You can use the adident utility to find the version of any file in the E-Business Suite file system.

```
[applebs@erpnode3 bin]$ adident Header $AD_TOP/binadadmin
adadmin:
$Header adadmin_main.oc 120.12.12020000.2 2012/07/09 19:03:49 raghosh ship $
[applebs@erpnode3 bin]$
```

You can provide multiple files at the same time, as shown here:

```
[applebs@erpnode3 bin]$ adident Header $AD_TOP/bin/adadmin  $AD_TOP/bin/adctrl
adadmin:
$Header adadmin_main.oc 120.12.12020000.2 2012/07/09 19:03:49 raghosh ship $
adctrl:
$Header adctrl_main.oc 120.11.12020000.2 2012/07/09 18:55:30 raghosh ship $
[applebs@erpnode3 bin]$
```

adchkdig

This utility reports the integrity of download patches. It's a handy tool that can be executed for all downloaded patches, which will help you avoid any issue related to corrupted downloads/patches.

```
[applebs@erpnode3]$ adchkdig -file  p17766337_R12.AD.C_R12_LINUX.zip
Ad Check Digest is complete.
SHA-1 9E0F769606DF3840538D121EDF08D1432E928220
MD5   1DC21E3C8D3302C3063C5DAB320778B0
[applebs@erpnode3 EBS_patches]$
```

You can use OAM for extracting multiple reports related to installed products, applied patches, and so on. We will learn about these options later in this chapter.

Oracle Application Diagnostic

Diagnostics remains an integral and important part of any product in order to troubleshoot and analyze issues. Oracle has a diagnostics menu in the system administrator responsibility, which is separate from the diagnostics provided by the Oracle Application Manager. An organization may also opt to use the Oracle diagnostic tool (IZU_TOP), which has plenty of tests to diagnose generic issues related to setups and file versions. The results of this tool can be either downloaded for review or sent to Oracle Support for investigation. Figure 9-4 shows the tests available in the system administrator responsibility.

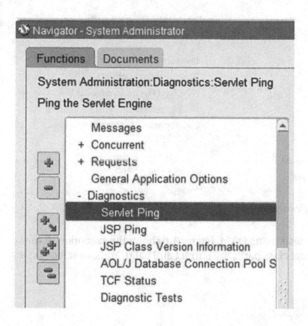

Figure 9-4. Application diagnostics: system administrator

Oracle Applications Manager has a specific tab called Diagnostic and Repair that can be used for generating diagnostic reports and troubleshooting issues related to forms, concurrent managers, and so on. Figure 9-5 displays the available diagnostic testing and troubleshooting wizard.

ORACLE Applications Manager
Home
Setup
Support Cart
Applications Dashboard
Site Map
Site Map: test
Administration
Monitoring
Maintenance
Diagnostics and Repair
Diagnostics
Execute Diagnostic Tests
View Diagnostics Reports
View Scheduled Diagnostics Tests
Diagnostics Configuration
Debug WorkBench
Troubleshooting Wizards
Concurrent Manager Recovery
Service Infrastructure
GCS and Forms Monitoring
CP Signature
Dashboard Collection Signature
TIP Only the items to which you have access are clickable.

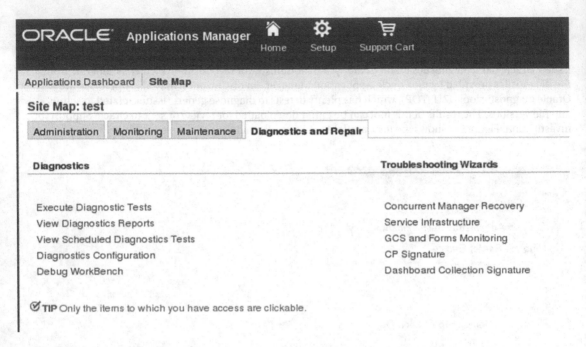

Figure 9-5. Application diagnostics: OAM Diagnostics and Repair

You'll now learn how to execute the diagnostic tests using OAM. Figure 9-6 shows the execution of the Class Path Test, which will verify that all of the existing class paths are correct and valid. You can select as many as tests as available for execution.

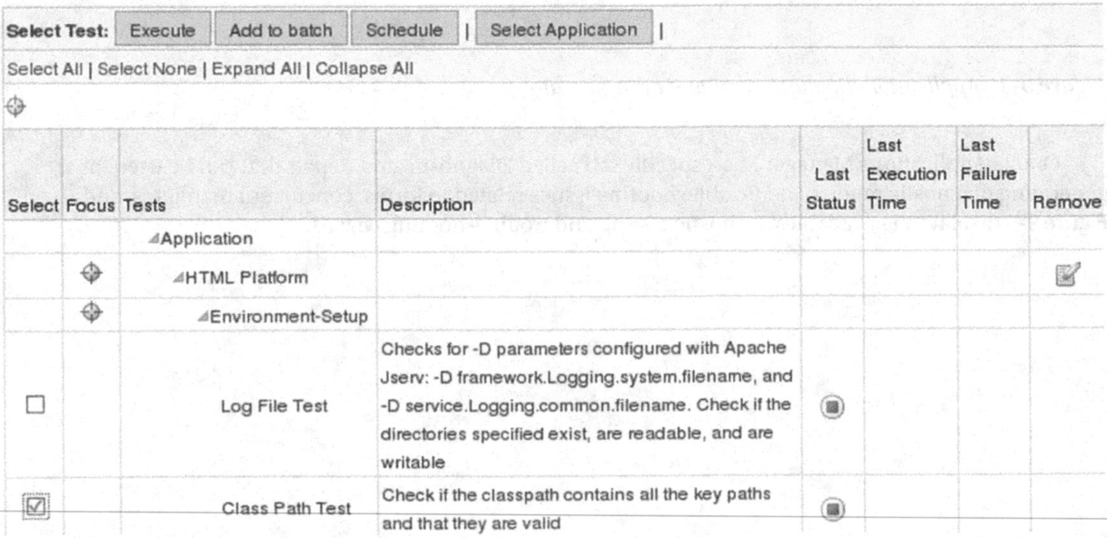

Select Test: Execute | Add to batch | Schedule | Select Application
Select All | Select None | Expand All | Collapse All
Select
Focus
Tests
Description
Last Status
Last Execution Time
Last Failure Time
Remove
Application
HTML Platform
Environment-Setup
Log File Test
Checks for -D parameters configured with Apache Jserv: -D framework.Logging.system.filename, and -D service.Logging.common.filename. Check if the directories specified exist, are readable, and are writable
Class Path Test
Check if the classpath contains all the key paths and that they are valid

Figure 9-6. OAM: diagnostic test

Click Submit to execute the test. After successful execution of the test, you can view the report or upload it for further investigation, as shown in Figures 9-7, 9-8, and 9-9.

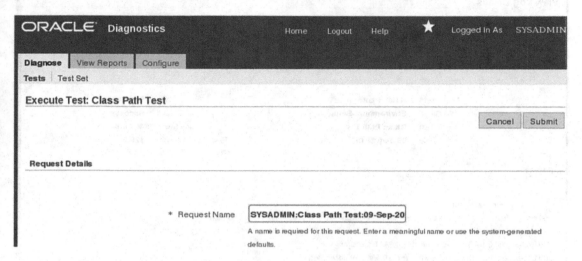

Figure 9-7. *OAM: diagnostic testing of the class paths*

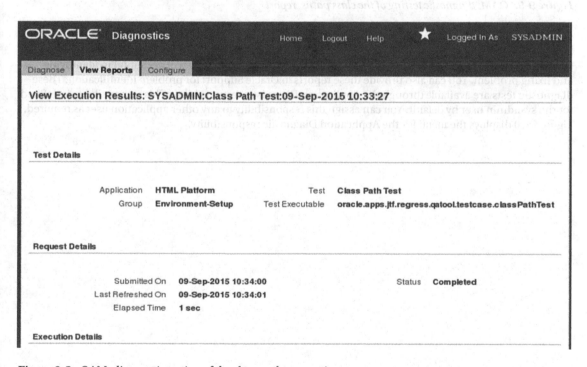

Figure 9-8. *OAM: diagnostic testing of the class paths, execution*

Figure 9-9. *OAM: diagnostic testing of the class paths, report*

Application Diagnostic Responsibility

Oracle E-Business Suite has multiple diagnostic tests, and these test reports will be helpful in identifying and fixing problem, You can also provide these reports to Oracle Support for problem identification. These diagnostic tests are available through the Application Diagnostic responsibility. This responsibility is defined for the sysadmin user by default. You can assign this responsibility to any other application user as required. Figure 9-10 displays the menu for the Application Diagnostic responsibility.

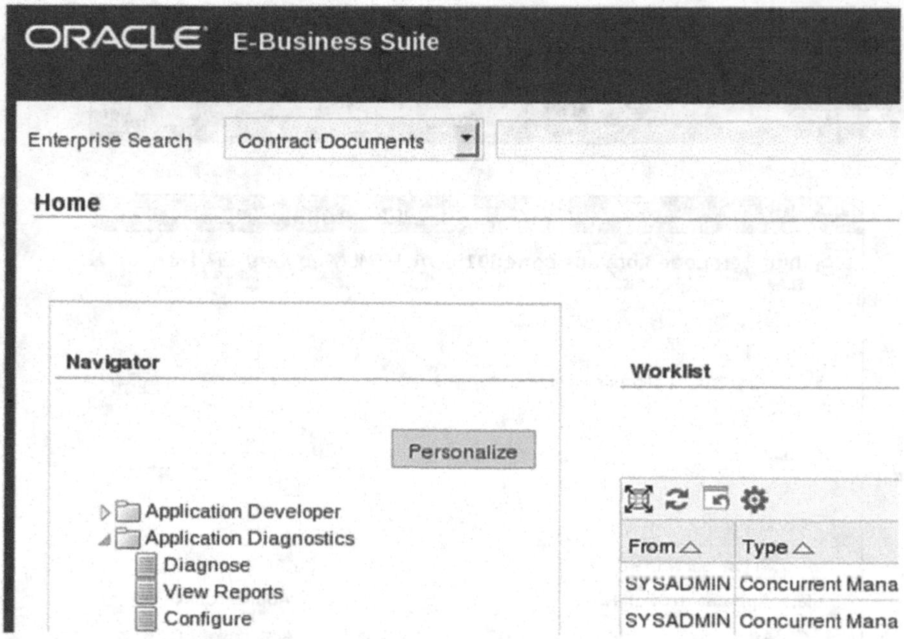

Figure 9-10. Application Diagnostic responsibility menu

Log in as the sysadmin user and then navigate to the following location:

Application Diagnostic responsibility ➤ Diagnose ➤ Select Application

Here you can select any desired application for which you want to generate the diagnostic reports. The full process of execution of reports is illustrated in Figures 9-11, 9-12, 9-13, 9-14, and 9-15.

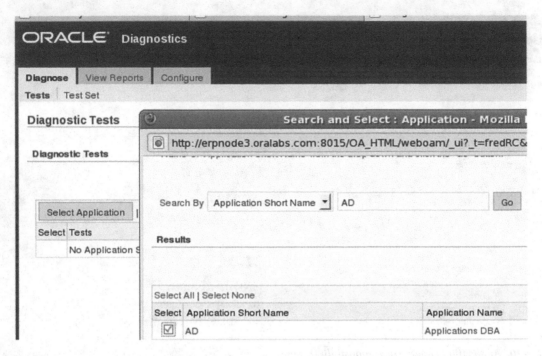

Figure 9-11. *Application Diagnostic responsibility: product selection for test*

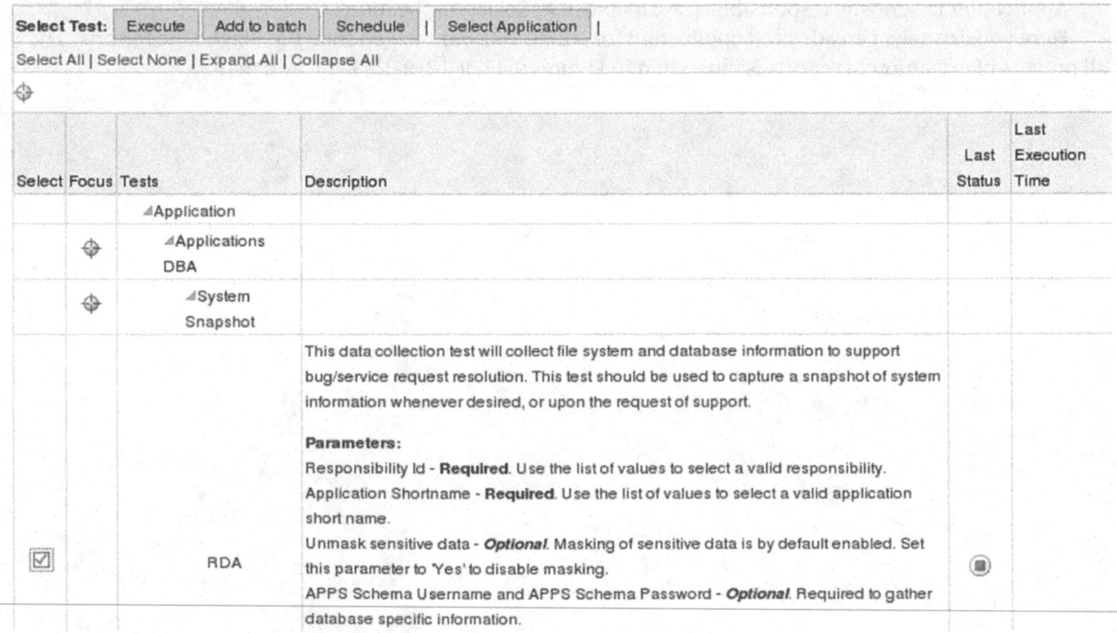

| Select Test: | Execute | Add to batch | Schedule | | Select Application | |

Select All | Select None | Expand All | Collapse All

Select	Focus	Tests	Description	Last Status	Last Execution Time
		⊿Application			
	⊕	⊿Applications DBA			
	⊕	⊿System Snapshot			
☑		RDA	This data collection test will collect file system and database information to support bug/service request resolution. This test should be used to capture a snapshot of system information whenever desired, or upon the request of support. **Parameters:** Responsibility Id - **Required**. Use the list of values to select a valid responsibility. Application Shortname - **Required**. Use the list of values to select a valid application short name. Unmask sensitive data - *Optional*. Masking of sensitive data is by default enabled. Set this parameter to 'Yes' to disable masking. APPS Schema Username and APPS Schema Password - *Optional*. Required to gather database specific information.	◉	

Figure 9-12. *Application Diagnostic responsibility: test execution*

Figure 9-13. Application Diagnostic responsibility: test execution progress

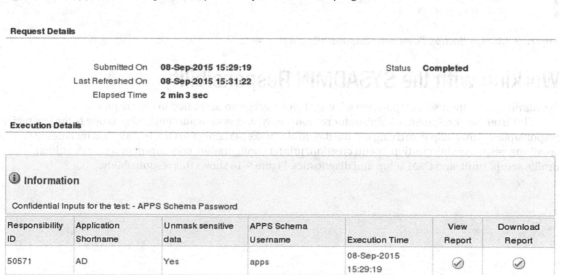

Figure 9-14. Application Diagnostic responsibility: view/download report

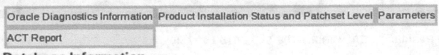

| Oracle Diagnostics Information | Product Installation Status and Patchset Level | Parameters |
| ACT Report | | |

Database Information [Top]

- Server = erpnode3.oralabs.com
- Version = Oracle Database 12c Enterprise Edition Release 12.1.0.2.0 - 64bit Production
- Name/SID = TEST
- Language = AMERICAN
- Character Set = US7ASCII

Application Information [Top]

- Release = 12.2.4
- Application = Application Object Library (0) with status of INSTALLED
- Responsibility = Application Diagnostics (50571)
- Security Group = Standard
- MultiOrg Flag = Y

Oracle Diagnostics Information [Top]

- Patch OD for R12.2 (10110972) is installed
- Patch Oracle E-Business Suite Diagnostics, R12.IZU.C (10196206) is installed
- Metalink Document Id = 420427.1

Product Installation Status and Patchset Level [Top]

Application	Short Name	Id	Installation Status	Patch Level
Application Object Library	FND	0	Installed	R12.FND.C.4
System Administration	SYSADMIN	1	Installed	Not Available

2 rows retrieved

Figure 9-15. *Application Diagnostic responsibility: test report*

Working with the SYSADMIN Responsibility

Sysadmin is the superuser compared to all other FND users given or created in Oracle EBS.

This user has the System Administrator responsibility, and system administration is one of the few main responsibilities that help in carrying out the day-to-day tasks pertaining to Oracle EBS. This includes user creations, responsibility creation, menu creation, printer configuration, concurrent program definition, profile setup, audit, and OAM setup and diagnostics. Figure 9-16 shows this responsibility.

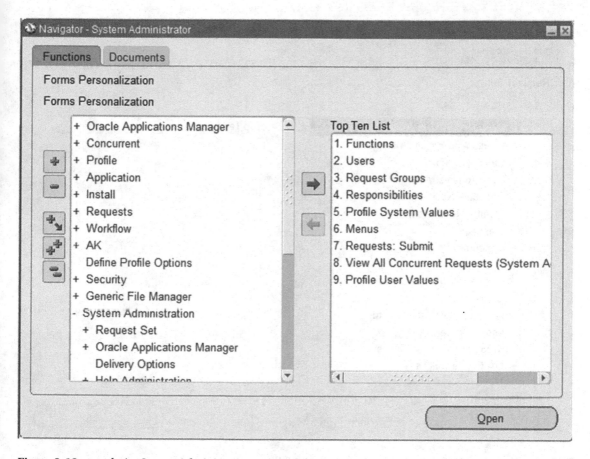

Figure 9-16. sysadmin: System Administrator responsibility

The System Administration responsibility looks the same except for a few changes; for example, Security, Application, Profile, and Concurrent are not available. This helps you carrying out the regular tasks but doesn't give you the power of an administrator. Figure 9-17 displays the main screen for the System Administration responsibility.

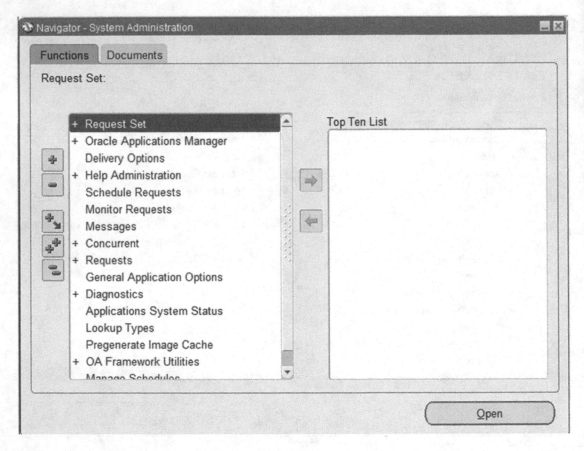

Figure 9-17. sysadmin: System Administration responsibility

As mentioned, both the System Administrator the System Administration responsibilities share a common set a menus with more or less the same privileges. The System Administrator responsibility is the super responsibility, and it has multiple menu options. You will see how to work with the regularly used System Administrator menu options later in this chapter.

Alert Manager Responsibility

The Alert Manager responsibility is capable of creating alerts that can be run either periodically or based on events.

The general usage of this responsibility is to send alerts (e-mails) to the required people so they can take a particular action. Oracle alerts can also be used to trigger a concurrent program to perform a specific request. The main screen of the Alert Manager responsibility is shown in Figure 9-18.

To get there, click the Switch Responsibility button on the front end. Then select Alert Manager to go that responsibility. Figures 9-19 and 9-20 illustrates the configuration of alert.

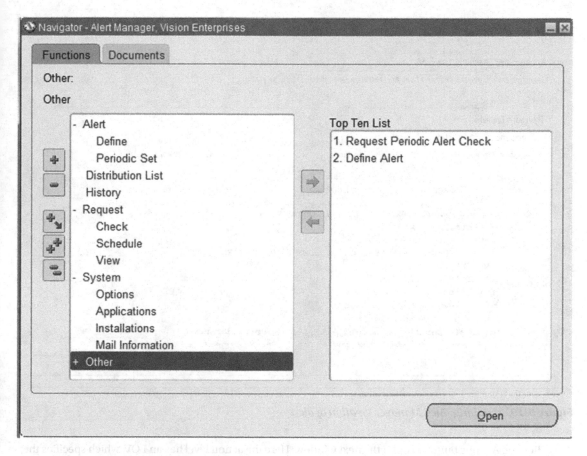

Figure 9-18. *sysadmin: Alert Manager responsibility*

To create an alert, select Alert ➤ Define.

We'll show how to use a seeded alert so you can understand how this process works. Here we have queried the seeded alert "Indexes near maximum extents."

- This is a seeded alert.

- It belongs to the application ➤ Application DBA.

- It's a periodic alert to be run daily at midnight.

- The select statement is the condition that is to be run and the results to be sent. The condition suggests all the fields that are to be printed to the alert.

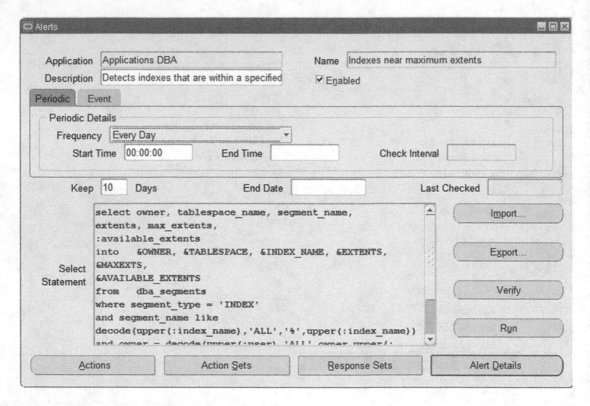

Figure 9-19. *sysadmin: Alert Manager, creation of alert*

Click the Actions button to open the next window. Here the action level has an LOV, which specifies the following:

- Detail would run the same number of alerts as the number of outputs.
- Summary would send a single alert summarized.

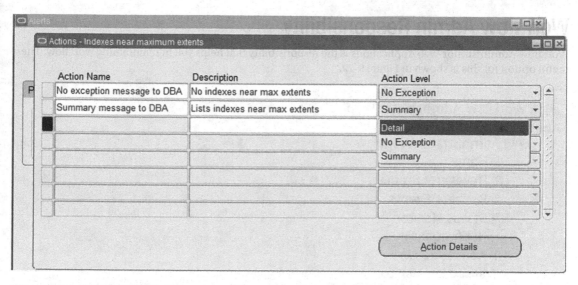

Figure 9-20. *SYSADMIN: Alert Manager, configuration of alert*

Clicking Action Details

The window shown in Figure 9-21 is used to specify the action that the alert is to take. It might be sending an e-mail or opening an alternate program to be run.

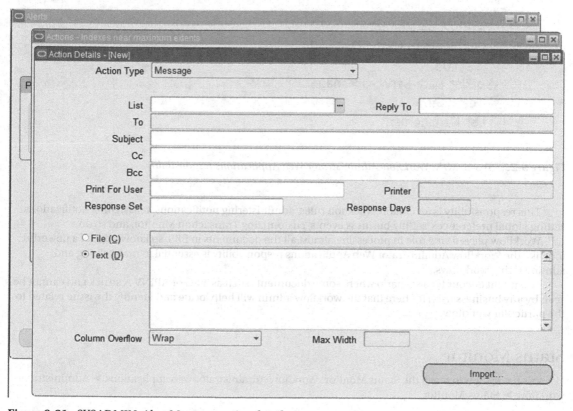

Figure 9-21. *SYSADMIN: Alert Manager, action details*

Workflow Admin Responsibility

Workflow Administrator Web Applications is the responsibility that helps you in maintaining workflow. The menu option for this is shown in Figure 9-22.

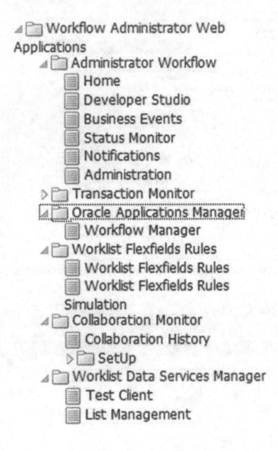

Figure 9-22. *SYSADMIN: Workflow Administrator Web Applications responsibility*

This responsibility is for creating vacation rules, administering notifications, reassigning notifications, setting global preferences, setting business events, customizing Transaction Monitor, and so on.

Workflow plays a vital role in processing almost all the documents in EBS, so knowledge of a powerful tool like the Workflow Administrator Web Applications responsibility is essential to maintaining and administering workflows.

You might encounter a scenario where some documents such as a PO or APINV is struck and cannot be seen by any business user; it's here that the workflow admin will help locate and identify the issue related to the particular workflow.

Status Monitor

Use this navigation to reach the Status Monitor: Workflow Administrator web applications ➤ Administrator workflow ➤ Status Monitor.

This navigation is used to identify the status of a particular document by its workflow name and key. The window shown in Figure 9-23 can take parameters such as internal name, workflow type, item key, user key, and status. In this example, we were in a position to query a purchase order approval document with a status error.

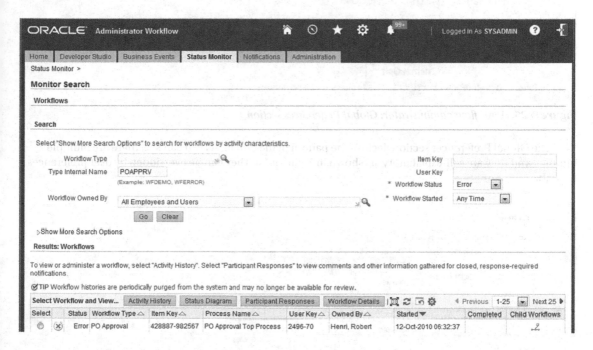

Figure 9-23. *Workflow administrator: Status Monitor*

Administration

On the Administration tab, you can set vacation rules and search notifications, as shown in Figure 9-24.

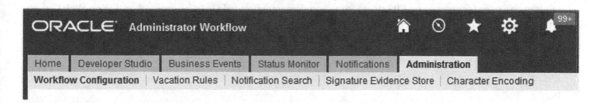

Figure 9-24. *Workflow administrator: Administration tab*

The Workflow Configuration subtab is not the same configuration as the workflow mailer configuration, but these settings are essential in determining whether the notifications are enabled or disabled globally. Figure 9-25 shows the available LOV.

Any change performed here will affect the entire system.

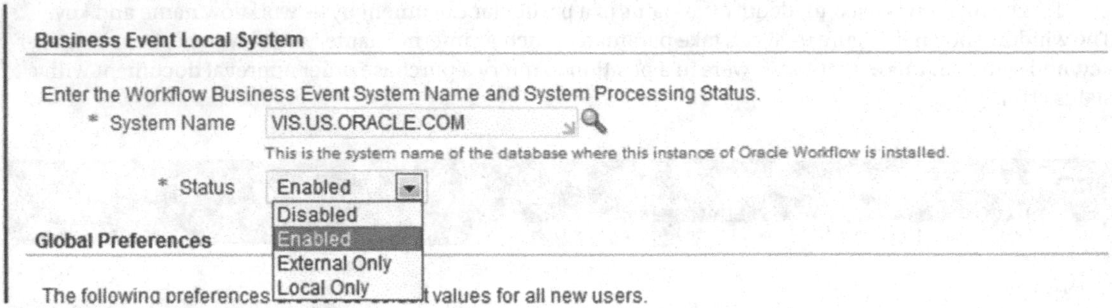

Business Event Local System

Enter the Workflow Business Event System Name and System Processing Status.

* System Name VIS.US.ORACLE.COM

This is the system name of the database where this instance of Oracle Workflow is installed.

* Status   Enabled

Disabled

Enabled

External Only

Local Only

Global Preferences

The following preferences   values for all new users.

Figure 9-25. Workflow administrator: Global Preferences section

The Global Preferences section decides the pattern of the e-mail. As you can see, there are multiple options, and they are self-explanatory, as shown in Figure 9-26. They can be overridden by user preferences, though.

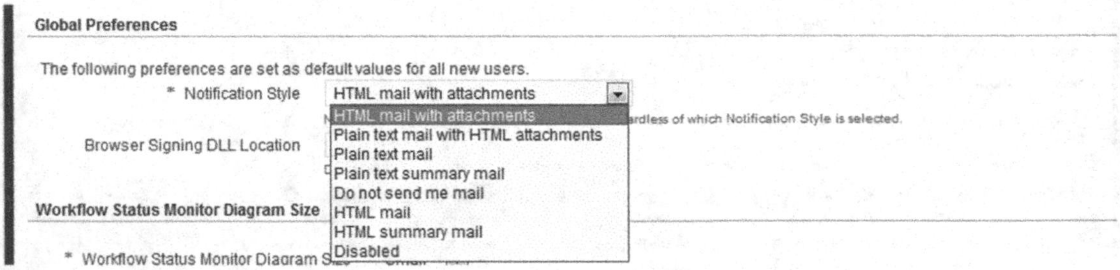

Global Preferences

The following preferences are set as default values for all new users.

* Notification Style   HTML mail with attachments

HTML mail with attachments   rdless of which Notification Style is selected.

Plain text mail with HTML attachments

Browser Signing DLL Location   Plain text mail

Plain text summary mail

Do not send me mail

Workflow Status Monitor Diagram Size   HTML mail

HTML summary mail

* Workflow Status Monitor Diagram S   Disabled

Figure 9-26. Workflow administrator: Global Preferences section, Notification Style list

Vacation Rule

The function of this option is to create a vacation rule for all those business users who either have not set a vacation rule or who don't have the required expertise to do so.

Select the user (employee or EBS user) for whom the vacation rule is to be created and then click Go, as shown in Figure 9-27.

Click Create Rule and select the types of notifications that should be forwarded.

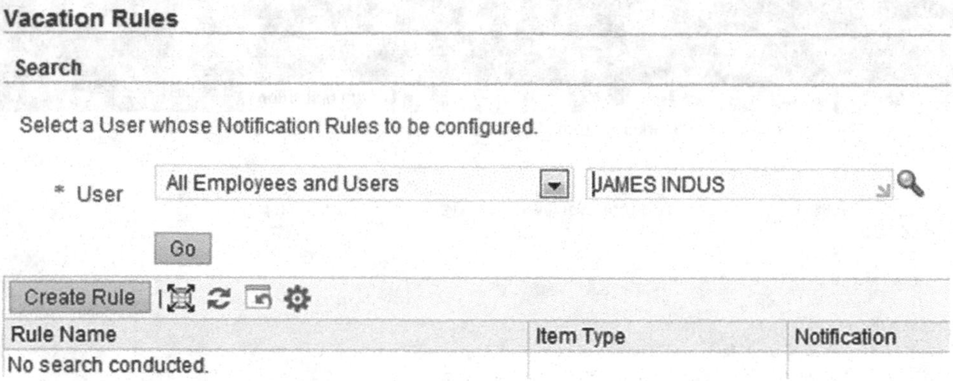

Vacation Rules

Search

Select a User whose Notification Rules to be configured.

* User [All Employees and Users ▼] [JAMES INDUS ⌄🔍]

[Go]

[Create Rule] | 🖼 ⮂ 🔚 ⚙

Rule Name	Item Type	Notification
No search conducted.		

Figure 9-27. Workflow administrator: Vacation Rules section

Select the From and To dates of the vacation and select the assignee (PDAVIS is the example used here), as shown in Figure 9-28.

This will be automatically activated and disabled at the defined times. You can also choose the type of notification that should be included.

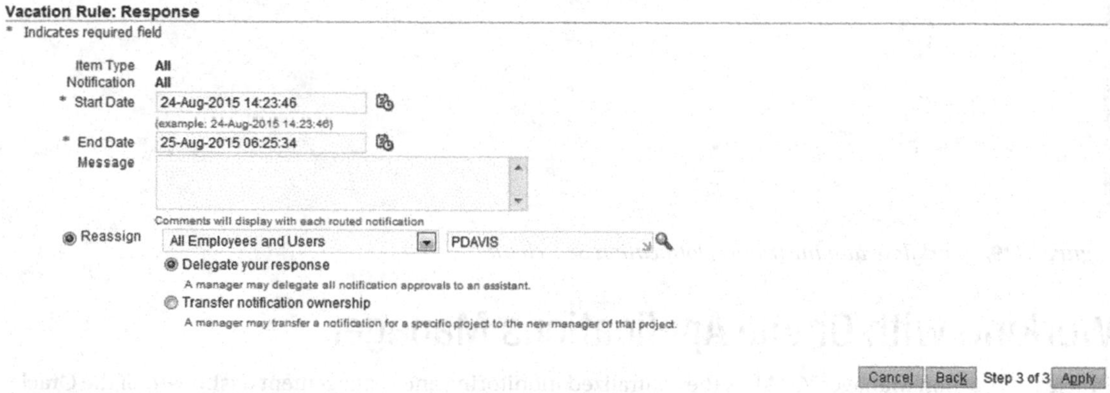

Vacation Rule: Response
* Indicates required field

Item Type **All**
Notification **All**
* Start Date [24-Aug-2015 14:23:46] 📖
(example: 24-Aug-2015 14:23:46)
* End Date [25-Aug-2015 06:25:34] 📖
Message [   ]

Comments will display with each routed notification
◉ Reassign [All Employees and Users ▼] [PDAVIS ⌄🔍]
◉ Delegate your response
A manager may delegate all notification approvals to an assistant.
○ Transfer notification ownership
A manager may transfer a notification for a specific project to the new manager of that project.

[Cancel] [Back] Step 3 of 3 [Apply]

Figure 9-28. Workflow administrator: creation of vacation rule

Notification Search

The Notification Search tab is used to find notifications based on the owner, To and From fields, status, and dates. This is quite similar to the Status Monitor except that it can be searched with the username. The benefit of doing this is that you can easily identify the pending notifications with a particular user or pending notifications on a particular day and time. This window also gives you the functionality of reassigning the notifications from one user to another. Figure 9-29 displays all the options that can be used for searching the notification.

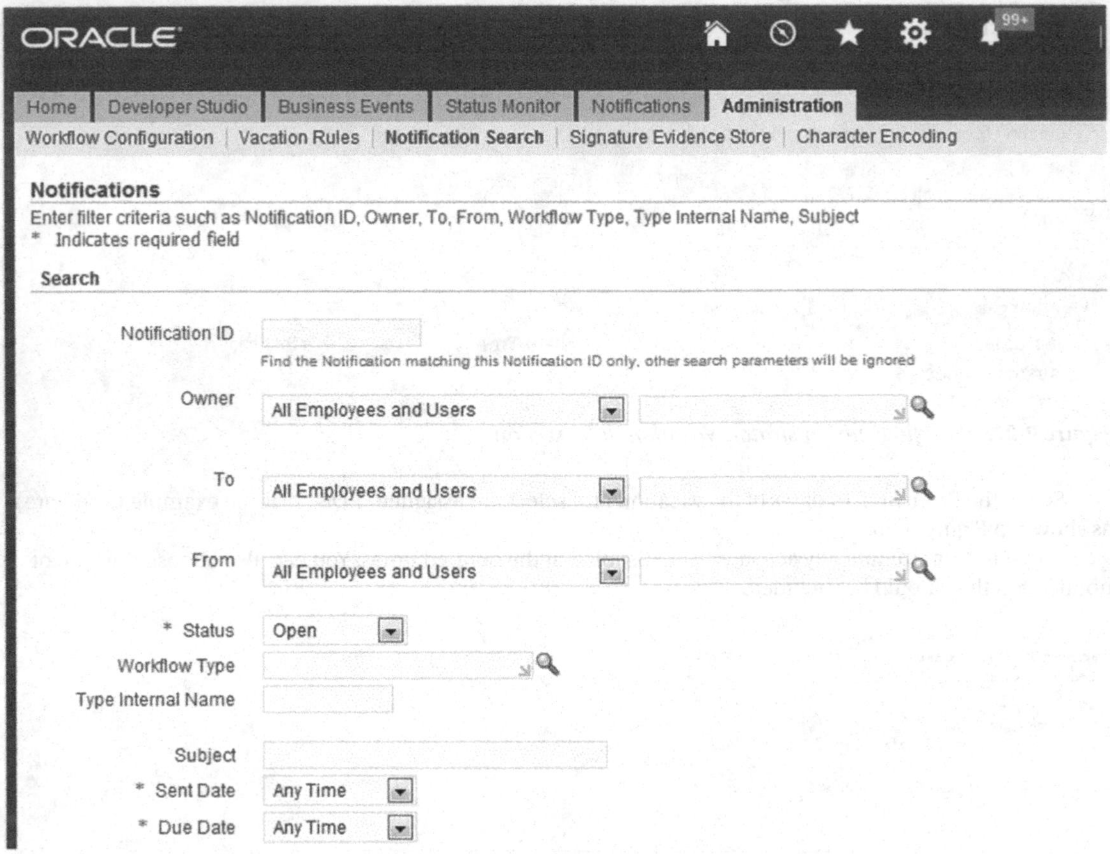

Figure 9-29. Workflow administrator: Notification Search tab

Working with Oracle Applications Manager

Oracle Application Manager (OAM) is the centralized monitoring and management dashboard of the Oracle E-Business Suite system. OAM is part of the System Administrator responsibility, and its submenu has lots of pages (OA pages).

To navigate to it, select System Administrator and then Oracle Applications Manager.

This menu, once clicked, splits into two. One side is the Application Dashboard , which informs the admin about the health of general changes that happened over a period of time. Figure 9-30 displays the available menu options under Oracle Applications Manager, and Figure 9-31 shows the two major navigations available in Oracle Applications Manager (Application Dashboard and Site Map).

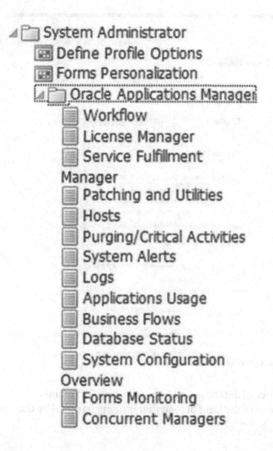

Figure 9-30. *SYSADMIN: Oracle Applications Manager menu*

Figure 9-31. *SYSADMIN: Oracle Application Dashboard and Site Map options*

The Application Dashboard has these tabs: Overview, Performance, Critical Activities, Business Flows, Security, and Software Updates.

The Overview tab gives the overall status, system alerts, and configuration changes that occurred in past 24 hours, as shown in Figure 9-32.

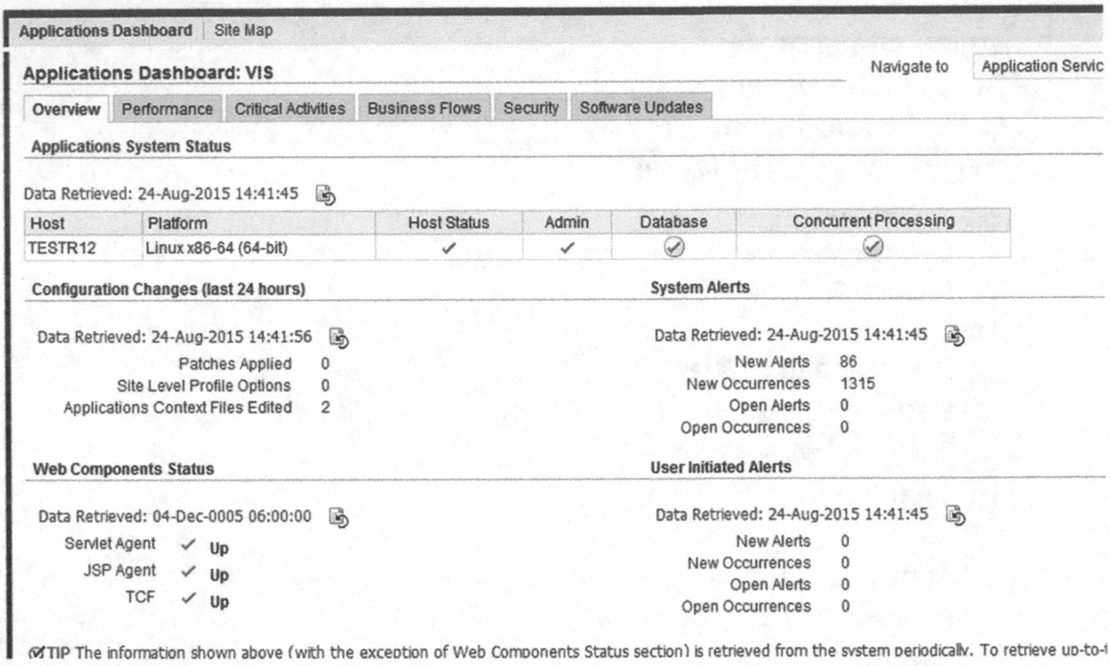

Figure 9-32. *SYSADMIN: Oracle Application Dashboard, Overview tab*

The Performance tab gives information on the number of database sessions, forms sessions, and concurrent requests running on EBS. This gives you a sense of the kind of load that is being handled by the instance, as shown in Figure 9-33.

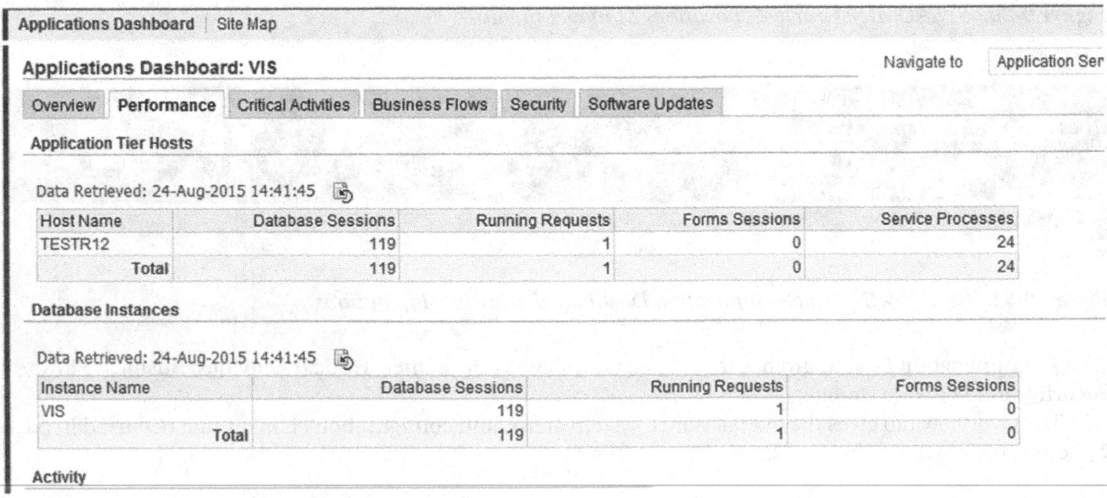

Figure 9-33. *SYSADMIN: Oracle Application Dashboard, Performance tab*

The Critical Activities tab gives you a sense of the regular required programs that are or are not being run periodically for the upkeep of the instance, as shown in Figure 9-34.

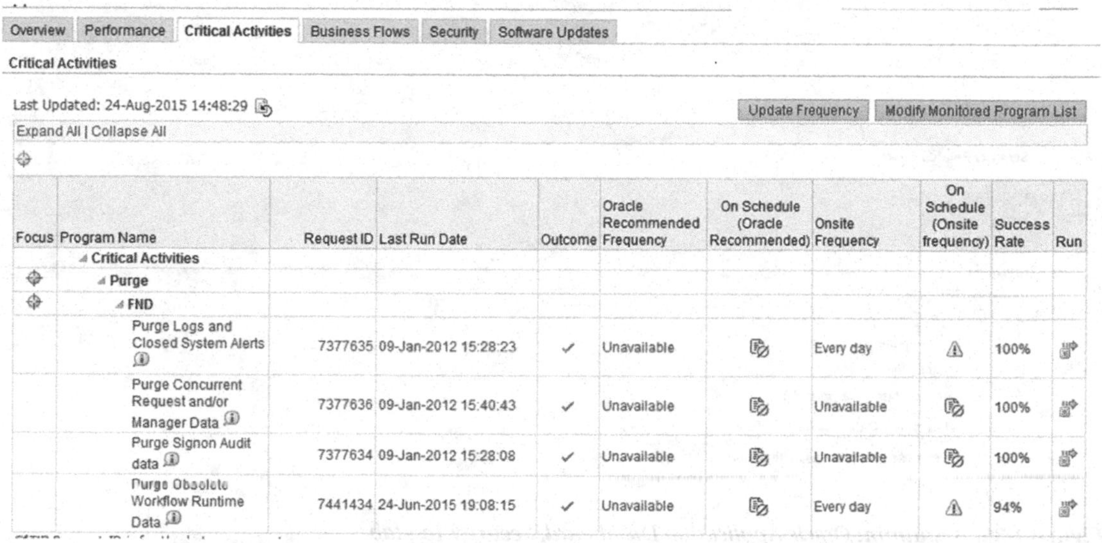

Focus	Program Name	Request ID	Last Run Date	Outcome	Oracle Recommended Frequency	On Schedule (Oracle Recommended)	Onsite Frequency	On Schedule (Onsite frequency)	Success Rate	Run
⬦	⊿ Critical Activities									
⬦	⊿ Purge									
⬦	⊿ FND									
	Purge Logs and Closed System Alerts ⓘ	7377635	09-Jan-2012 15:28:23	✓	Unavailable	🗎	Every day	⚠	100%	🗎
	Purge Concurrent Request and/or Manager Data ⓘ	7377636	09-Jan-2012 15:40:43	✓	Unavailable	🗎	Unavailable	🗎	100%	🗎
	Purge Signon Audit data ⓘ	7377634	09-Jan-2012 15:28:08	✓	Unavailable	🗎	Unavailable	🗎	100%	🗎
	Purge Obsolete Workflow Runtime Data ⓘ	7441434	24-Jun-2015 19:08:15	✓	Unavailable	🗎	Every day	⚠	94%	🗎

Figure 9-34. SYSADMIN: Oracle Application Dashboard, Critical Activities tab

The Security tab has important tests such as Best Practices: Database Security Tests and Best Practices: E-Business Suite Security Tests that can be run to obtain important security alerts to keep the system secure, as shown in Figures 9-35 and 9-36 displays OAM dashboard security tab.

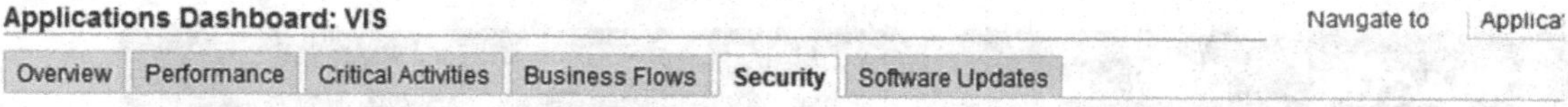

Applications Dashboard: VIS

Navigate to   Applica

Overview   Performance   Critical Activities   Business Flows   **Security**   Software Updates

Figure 9-35. SYSADMIN: Oracle Application Dashboard, Security

Security Test Failures

Last Updated: 24-Aug-2015 14:52:52
Expand All | Collapse All

Focus	Test Name	Failure Time	Diagnose	Schedule
	⊿ Failure Level			
⊕	⊿ Error			
⊕	▷ Application Object Library			

Available Security Related Tests

Last Updated: 24-Aug-2015 14:52:52
Expand All | Collapse All

Focus	Test Name	Last Status	Diagnose	Schedule
	⊿ Application			
⊕	⊿ CRM Foundation			
	SYSADMIN Role	⊗	▦	▦
⊕	⊿ Application Object Library			
	Ensure guest user has userid 6	⊗	▦	▦
	Best Practices : Database Security Tests	⊗	▦	▦
	Best Practices : E-Business Suite Security Tests	⊗	▦	▦

Figure 9-36. sysadmin: Oracle Application Dashboard, Security Test tab

We will discuss more about Oracle Application security in Chapter 12.

The Software Updates tab gives details on the patches that have been applied on the application along with cod-level histories, file histories, products installed, and maintenance activities.

The Site Map tab has four subtabs: Administration, Monitoring, Maintenance, Diagnostics and Repair (as shown in Figure 9-37).

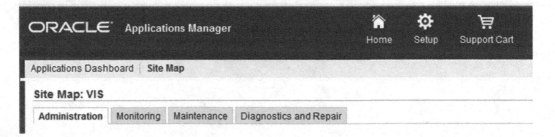

Figure 9-37. SYSADMIN: Oracle Application Dashboard, Site Map tab

Administration

This tab consists of some of the most important admin features required such as license managers, the Fusion Middleware Control, and WebLogic Administration Control. This is in addition to the workflow notification mailer, purge, background engine, and service components and work item metrics.

The License Manager tool is required to license products and languages that an organization might require to run their organization. This tool is split into two parts; one is the admin part and the other is for reporting, as shown in Figure 9-38.

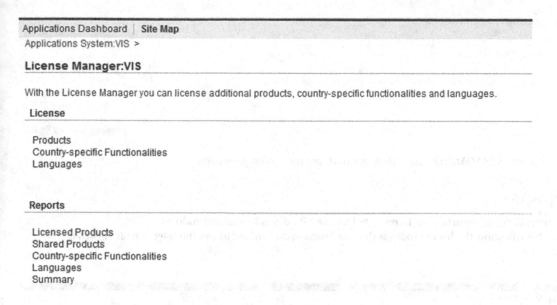

Figure 9-38. *SYSADMIN: Oracle Application Dashboard, License Manager tool*

Products in any instance can be either installed, shared, or not installed. It's only when an organization needs a product to be fully installed that this tool is used.

How to License a Product

To get to the License Manager, navigate to the Oracle Application manager's Site Map tab. Then click Administration and then License Manager.

Please refer to Figures 9-39 and 9-40 for how to add products.

To add a product, click License ➤ Products ➤ License E-Business Suite. Then click the required product and then Submit.

Figure 9-39. *SYSADMIN: License Manager, adding products*

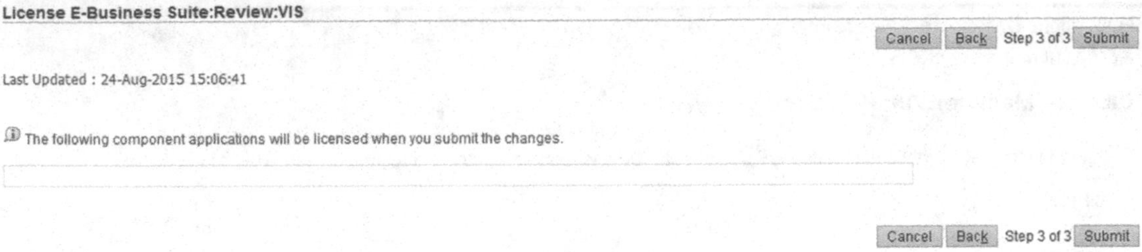

License E-Business Suite:Review:VIS

Cancel | Back | Step 3 of 3 | Submit

Last Updated : 24-Aug-2015 15:06:41

ⓘ The following component applications will be licensed when you submit the changes.

Cancel | Back | Step 3 of 3 | Submit

Figure 9-40. *SYSADMIN: License Manager, adding products confirmation*

Reports

To generate some reports, click Reports ➤ Licensed Products ➤ Shared Products.

This will show the list of products that are licensed and shared as per the selection, as shown in Figure 9-41.

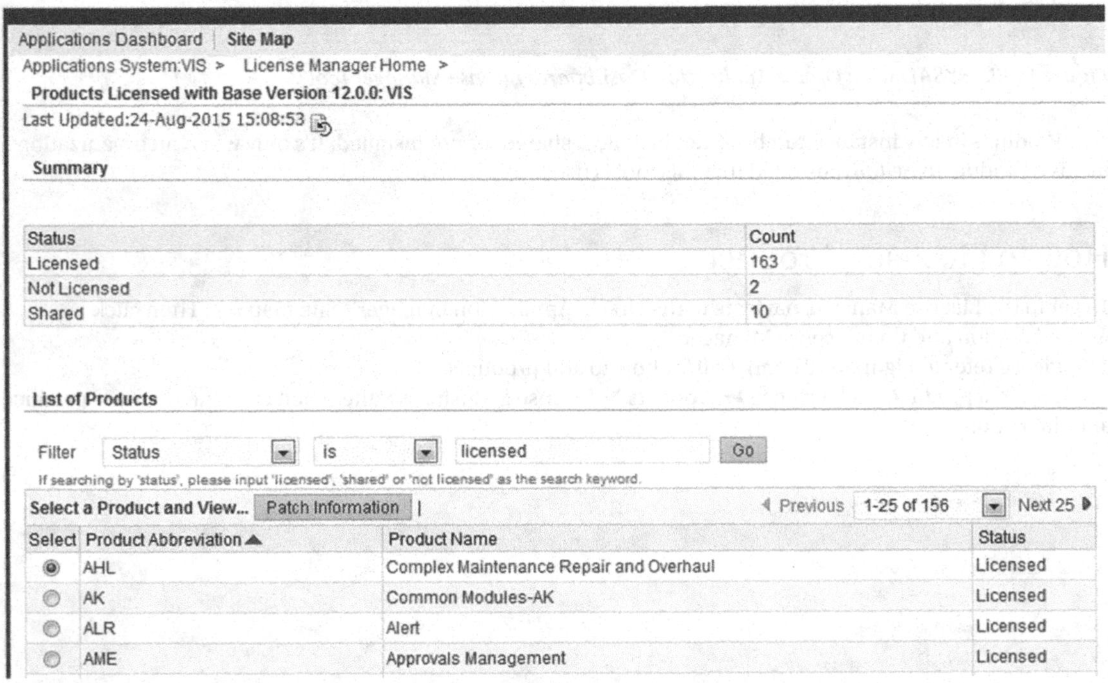

Applications Dashboard | Site Map
Applications System:VIS > License Manager Home >
Products Licensed with Base Version 12.0.0: VIS
Last Updated:24-Aug-2015 15:08:53

Summary

Status	Count
Licensed	163
Not Licensed	2
Shared	10

List of Products

Filter | Status [▼] | is [▼] | licensed | Go
If searching by 'status', please input 'licensed', 'shared' or 'not licensed' as the search keyword.

Select a Product and View... Patch Information | ◀ Previous | 1-25 of 156 [▼] Next 25 ▶

Select	Product Abbreviation ▲	Product Name	Status
◉	AHL	Complex Maintenance Repair and Overhaul	Licensed
○	AK	Common Modules-AK	Licensed
○	ALR	Alert	Licensed
○	AME	Approvals Management	Licensed

Figure 9-41. *SYSADMIN: License Manager, installed reports*

The Workflow mailer as a concept is a process that connects to an e-mail server to send and receive e-mails for various tasks such as notifying, approvals, alerts, and so on.

Workflow Mailer Configuration

To get to the Workflow mailer, navigate as follows: Application manager ➤ Site Map ➤ Administration ➤ Workflow ➤ Notification Mailer.

Figure 9-42 shows the default Workflow notification mailer.

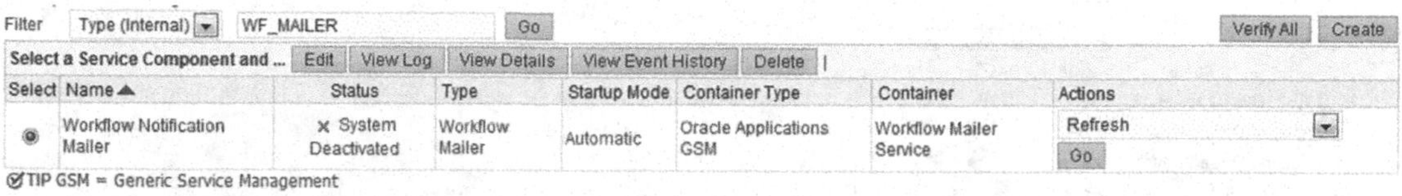

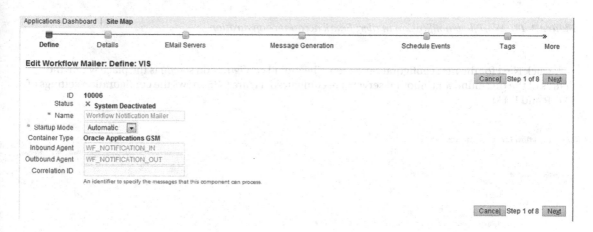

Figure 9-42. Workflow notification mailer

Click Workflow Notification Mailer, select Edit, and click Advanced.

Figure 9-43 shows how to edit the Workflow notification mailer configuration.

Figure 9-43. Workflow Notification Mailer: edit configuration

Using the drop-down list for the startup mode; you can make it either automatic, manual, or on demand.

Click Next for the next configuration screen.

In the details screen shown in Figure 9-44, the two most important parameters are for inbound and outbound thread counts.

- A 0 switch means not being configured.

- A 1 switch means being configured.

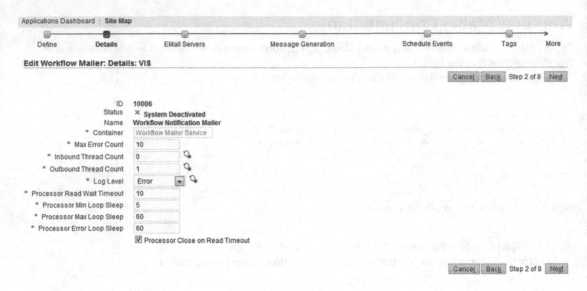

Figure 9-44. *Workflow notification mailer: Email account configuration*

Click Next for the next configuration screen. The e-mail configuration screen is the place where the details of the outbound and inbound servers are configured. Figure 9-45 shows the configuration settings of SMTP and IMAP.

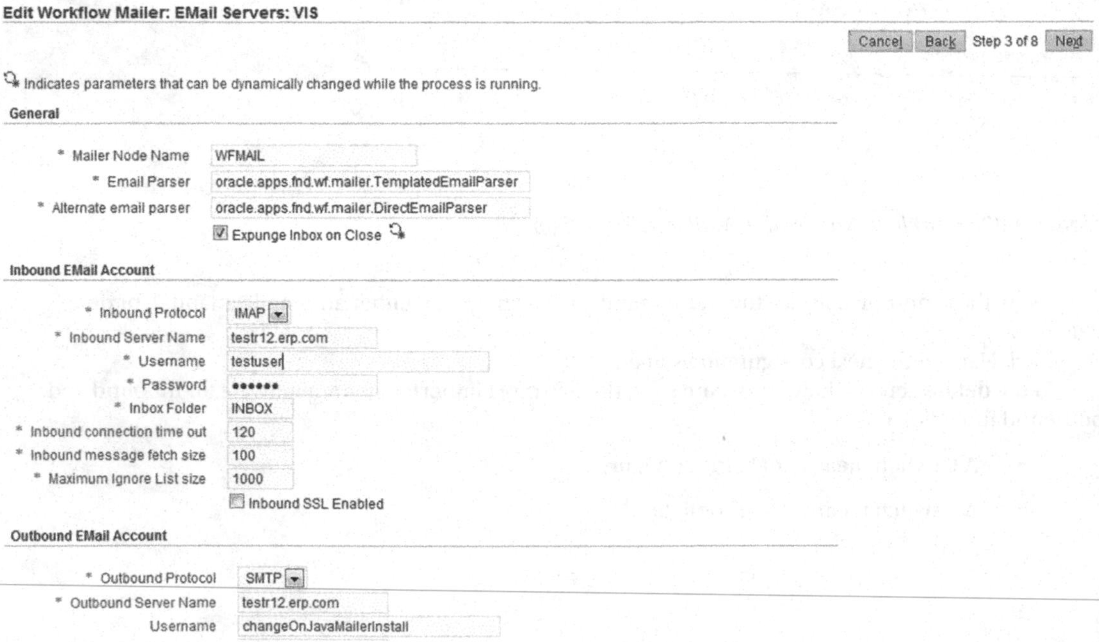

Figure 9-45. *Workflow notification mailer: SMTP and IMAP settings*

The outbound server sends e-mails to the configured e-mail addresses; it requires an SMTP server. The inbound server is the server where the e-mail would be sent back; for processing IMAP is required. A user account should be created and should have three folders, namely, INBOX, DISCARD, and PROCESS. These are case sensitive. The inbox will receive the e-mails, and the workflow will process the e-mails and move them to either PROCESS or DISCARD according to the action taken. A commonly used server for SMTP and IMAP is Microsoft Exchange Server or Lotus Notes.

Click Next and proceed until the end and then click Apply. The configuration part is done. Start the mailer with the following steps.

Here is the navigation: Application Manager ➤ Site Map ➤ Administration ➤ Workflow ➤ Notification Mailer.

Select from the actions LOV and then click Go, as shown in Figure 9-46.

Select	Name ▲	Status	Type	Startup Mode	Container Type	Container	Actions
◉	Workflow Notification Mailer	✗ System Deactivated	Workflow Mailer	Automatic	Oracle Applications GSM	Workflow Mailer Service	Start ▼
							Go

Figure 9-46. Workflow notification mailer: start/stop

Workflow Metrics is for gathering information on the number of requests being processed by the workflow.

Here is the navigation: Application Manager ➤ Site Map ➤ Administration ➤ Workflow ➤ Notification Mailer.

Workflow Metrics is the second section. Clicking the individual statuses will give a detailed breakdown of the processes used by the workflow, as shown in Figure 9-47.

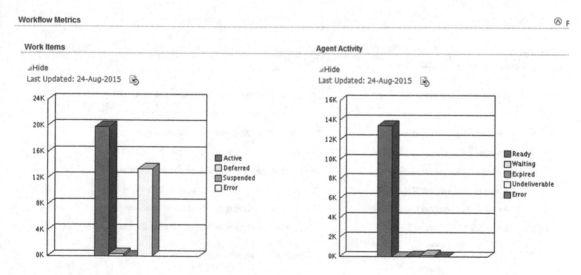

Figure 9-47. Workflow requests: Metrics

Monitoring

This tab gives you the required tools to monitor the instance, from the host status to the database, and by using these links you can proactively monitor the system. The Monitoring tab has multiple links, as shown in Figure 9-48.

Site Map: VIS

Administration	Monitoring	Maintenance	Diagnostics and Repair

Availability	Performance	Current Activity
Hosts	SQL Activity	System Alerts
Database	Forms Sessions	Database Sessions
Web Components	Forms Runtime Processes	User Monitoring
Internal Concurrent Manager	Concurrent Processing Reports	Invalid Objects
Request Processing Managers	Concurrent Processing Charts	Forms Runaway Processes
Transaction Managers	Concurrent Request Runaways	Forms Sessions
Forms	Workflow	Forms Runtime Processes
Workflow		Application Services
Business Flows		Activity Monitors
Fusion Middleware Control		Concurrent Requests
Weblogic Administration Console		Critical Activities
		Logs

Figure 9-48. *Oracle Applications Manager Dashboard: Monitoring*

There are links that open a new browser window for the Fusion Middleware Control or the WebLogic Administration Console.

The performance-monitoring links are for monitoring forms and concurrent requests.

Concurrent processing reports give you some good insight and analysis on whom and what related to the concurrent programs are being run, as shown in Figure 9-49.

Applications Dashboard	Site Map

Applications System:VIS >

Concurrent Processing Performance Charts:VIS

Last Updated : 24-Aug-2015 15:45:33

Expand All | Collapse All

Focus	Name	Description	Chart Setting
	◢Concurrent Processing Chart Group		
	◢Concurrent Requests		
	Concurrent Requests by Status	The counts of concurrent requests grouped by status	
	Running Requests per User	The counts of running requests grouped by user	
	Pending Requests per User	The counts of pending requests grouped by user	
	Running Requests per Application	The counts of running requests grouped by application	
	Pending Requests per Application	The counts of pending requests grouped by application	
	Running Requests per Responsibility	The counts of running requests grouped by responsibility	
	Pending Requests per Responsibility	The counts of pending requests grouped by responsibility	
	Completed Requests by Status	The completed requests for the last hour grouped by status	
	Top Running Requests by Buffer Gets	The top running requests by buffer gets	
	Top Running Requests by Disk Reads	The top running requests by disk reads	
	Top Running Requests by CPU	The top running requests by CPU	
	Top Running Requests by PGA	The top running requests by PGA memory	
	Top Running Requests by UGA	The top running requests by UGA memory	
	Longest Running Requests	The longest running requests	

Figure 9-49. *Oracle Applications Manager: concurrent processing performance*

User, Role, and Responsibility Management

Front-end users (business users, admins, functional consultants, technical consultants) are the ones who can access instances from URLs and forms. To access an instance, users should have access on the system with the required privileges. Using the System Administrator responsibility, you can create, deactivate, and modify users on Oracle E-Business Suite system. Figure 9-50 shows how to create a user with the mandatory and optional fields.

To get here, navigate to System Administrator, click Security, click User, and click Define.

The following fields are mandatory:

- Username
- Password

The following fields are optional :

- Description
- Person
- Customer
- Supplier
- Email
- Fax
- Responsibility

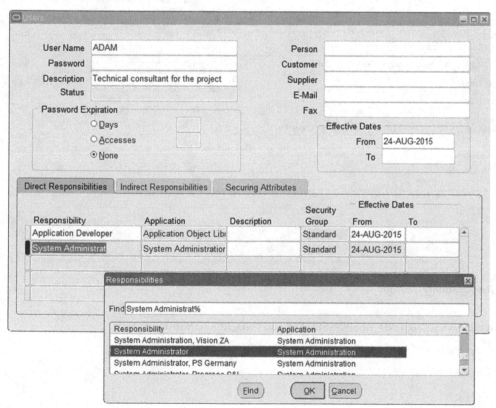

Figure 9-50. *SYSADMIN: user creation*

As shown in this example, we have created a user called Adam, and the password field has to be entered twice to verify the password. Responsibilities are assigned per the requirements of the job role, and you can give effective dates for both the responsibility and the user to restrict the use of the application. Password expiry can also be set as governed by the IT policies of a company.

An important table/view is FND_USER.

Responsibilities are a combination of menus and request groups. Menus are set of forms grouped under a name. Request sets are group of requests (programs) under a name. To create a responsibility, navigate to System Administrator, click Security, click Responsibility, and click Define.

The responsibility name and responsibility key should be unique and are mandatory fields. The application, menu, and data group are mandatory.

Responsibility usage can be controlled by setting an end date after which no user will be in a position to use the responsibility. Menu and request groups are assigned to get the required form and programs to perform the assigned task. Menu exclusions are used to exclude a particular function or menu from the granted menu.

Figure 9-51 shows how to create a responsibility.

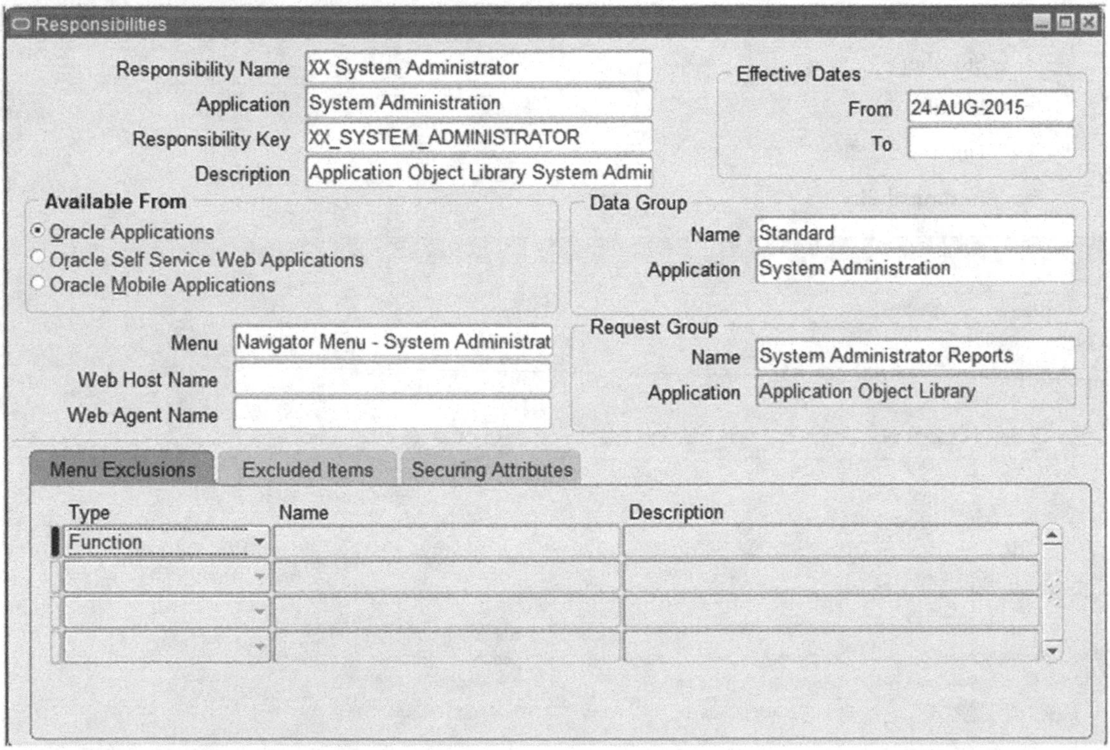

Figure 9-51. *Responsibility creation*

Important table/views are FND_RESPONSBILITY and FND_RESPONSBILITY_TL.

Managing Profiles and Profile Levels

Profiles are variables that determine the behavior of functionality at multiple levels. Profiles can be set at the following levels: user, application, responsibility, server, and organization. Navigate to System Administrator and click Profile.

Figure 9-52 shows the profile option menu from the System Administrator responsibility.

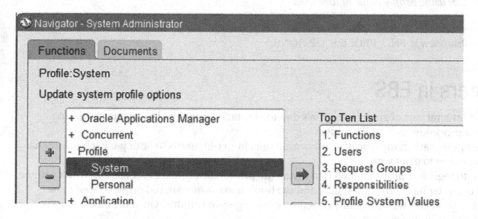

Figure 9-52. *SYSADMIN: profile menu*

In Figure 9-53, we will change the color scheme of forms for the user Adam.

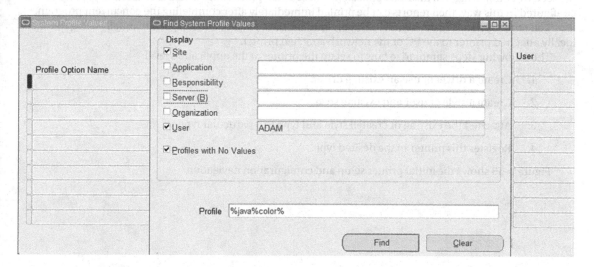

Figure 9-53. *SYSADMIN: profile value at the user level*

The profile for user Adam has been changed to red, and it remains standard for all other users. The changed profile value is shown in Figure 9-54. But for the profile value to be effective, the user needs to log off and log in with a new session.

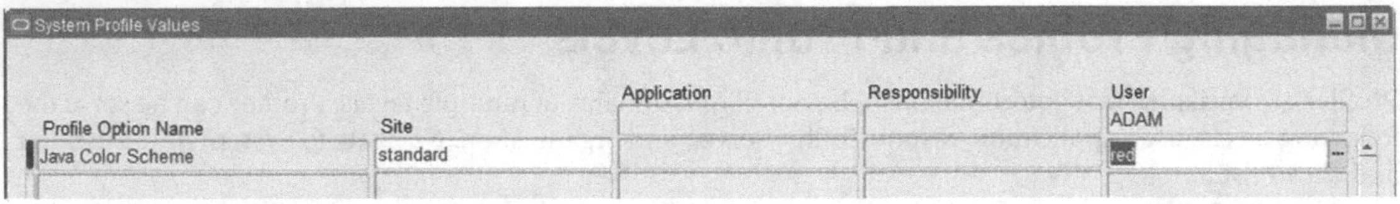

Figure 9-54. *sysadmin: using profile value at user level*

An important table/view is FND_PROFILE_OPTIONS.

Using Printers in EBS

Printing forms is an integral part of an organization's day-to-day tasks, from invoices to check printing. Therefore, EBS has a procedure to install a printer.

In today's world, there are many type of printers available, from dot matrix to laser jet. Each printer has a separate style and driver to print with.

The procedure to register a printer in EBS is to install the printer locally to a PC or use a network printer. The locally installed printer has to be shared first, and the both network and shared printers need to be communicated to the server on which the EBS concurrent managers in running. Once the basic setup is done, you can perform the following steps.

There are two supported options for printing reports for EBS applications. The printer should be registered as a network printer on the server where the batch processing service is running, and the operating system should be able to print files using OS commands like lp. Once this is set up, you can proceed by configuring it in the EBS application where batch processing service is enabled. If printers are configured in this way, then reports can be printed immediately after completing the concurrent program.

The other option is to download the report onto the user's local PC and print it manually using the locally attached printer to the PC or the network-attached printer.

The following steps summarize how to set up the printer at the application level:

1. Create a driver or use an existing driver.

2. Create a style or user and existing style.

3. Attached the existing or created style and type to a particular type.

4. Register this printer to the desired type.

Figure 9-55 shows the initial printer setup and configuration navigation.

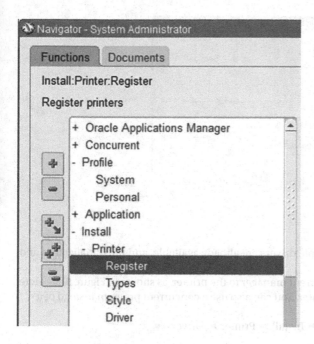

Figure 9-55. *SYSADMIN: printer configuration*

Most of the print styles are already predefined. If you need a different style, you can create one. The following fields are mandatory: Seq, User Style, Style Name, Columns, and Rows. Figures 9-56 and 9-57 show the printer style configuration screens.

This is the navigation: System Administrator ➤ Install ➤ Printer ➤ Style.

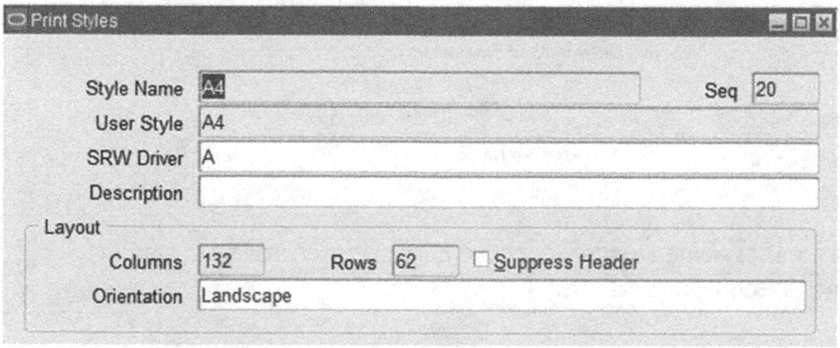

Figure 9-56. *SYSADMIN: Print Styles configuration*

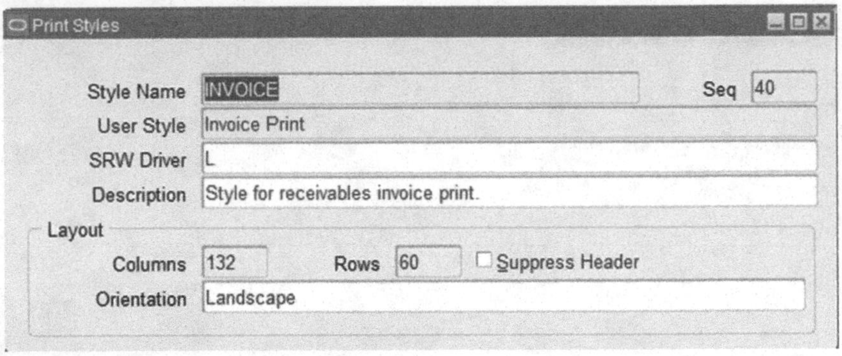

Figure 9-57. syadmin: configuring printer styles

The same is the case for printer drivers; multiple drivers are already available, and the initialization and arguments play the key roles in printing.

Arguments are commands given by the concurrent manager to the printer, as shown in Figure 9-58. Here, lp is a UNIX command that is being sent to the printer. You can also use a concurrent program instead of a command shown here.

This is the navigation: System Administrator ➤ Install ➤ Printer ➤ Driver.

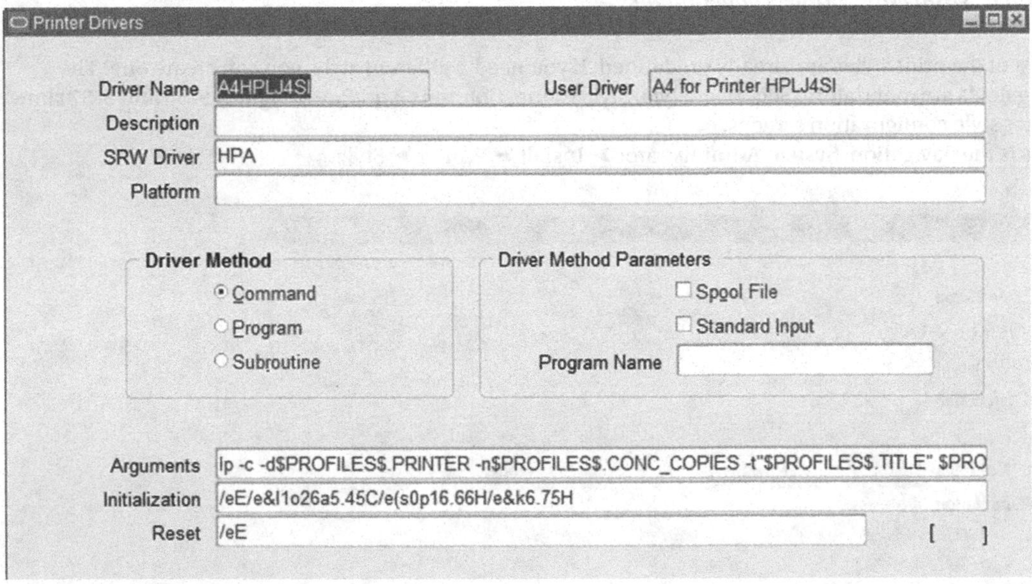

Figure 9-58. SYSADMIN: printer driver configuration

Printer Types

Once the driver and the style are ready, open the Printer Types dialog and create a printer type with all the required styles and drivers, as shown in Figure 9-59.

Here is the navigation: System Administrator ➤ Install ➤ Printer ➤ Types.

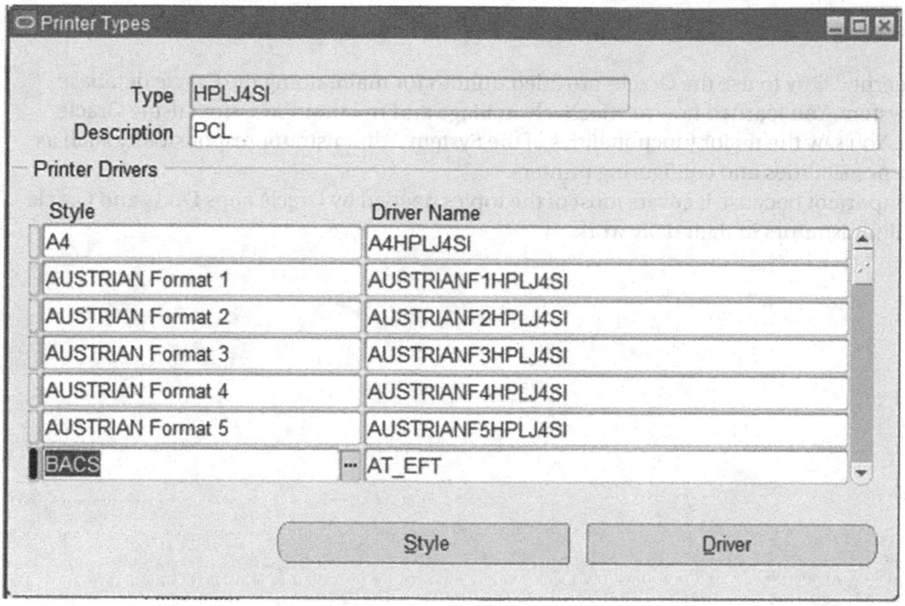

Figure 9-59. *SYSADMIN: printer types*

After performing these steps, you can directly register the printer with a name that is recognized by the OS (the printer is configured on the OS with the entered name), as shown in Figure 9-60.

Here is the navigation: System Administrator ➤ Install ➤ Printer ➤ Register.

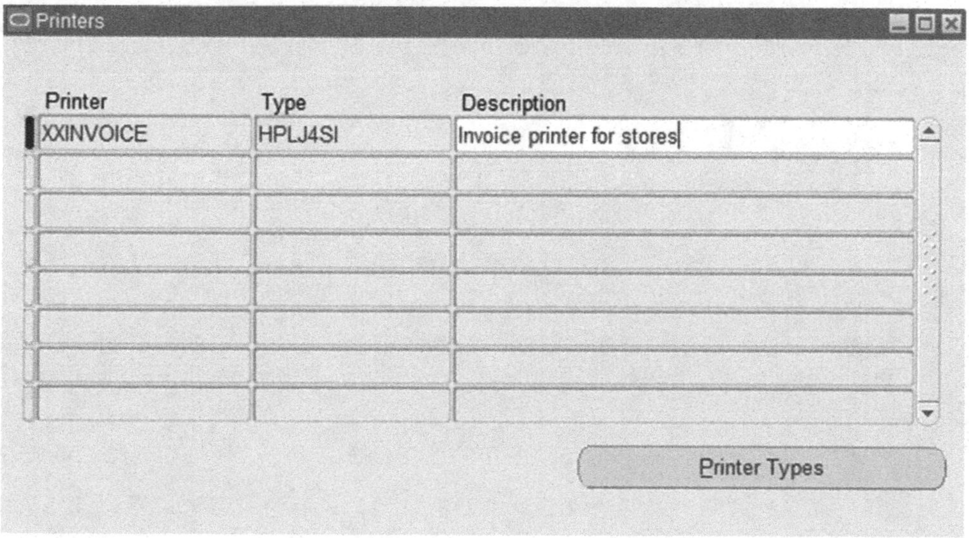

Figure 9-60. *SYSADMIN: registering a printer*

Summary

In this chapter, you learned how to use the Oracle-provided utilities for maintaining the Oracle database and application file system. You learned how to effectively manage and monitor the system using Oracle Application Manager. You saw the major functionalities of the System Administrator responsibility such as creating users and responsibilities and configuring printers.

This chapter is important because it covers most of the topics needed by Oracle apps DBAs and Oracle application system administrators in their daily work.

CHAPTER 10

■ ■ ■

Oracle EBS Concurrent Managers

Oracle concurrent processing is one of the key components of Oracle EBS systems. This chapter covers the different types of concurrent managers and how you can utilize them to meet the enterprise business requirements. It's a primary duty of an apps DBA to maintain the concurrent managers without disruption. Any failure on the concurrent processing node will impact the business. So, in this chapter, you will see how you can monitor, use, and manage concurrent processing.

Introduction to Oracle Concurrent Processing

Oracle E-Business Suite is built on multiple technology components, and each of its components has its own set of responsibilities. If there is a failure or problem in any of these components, then it will directly impact the business services. The concurrent managers are also one of the key components that are responsible for executing batch jobs in the background.

Consider a simple example of extracting a report of all active users of applications from the database. You can submit a standard seeded report named "Active users" provided within the application, and this report will generate the output with the list of active users in the applications. The concurrent manager is responsible for taking input from the users as a concurrent request, processing it on the required manager as a batch job, and generating results for the submitted job. Whenever a user submits a concurrent request, then this information is updated in the database, and the request is identified by a unique request ID. The concurrent manager will read the request information from the database to process further.

All business users can work on applications without any interruption because all concurrent processing will be performed in a background session.

Understanding Terms Concurrent Requests, Program, and Processes

Before going further, you should understand these definitions of concurrent requests, programs, and processes:

> *Concurrent request*: Whenever there is a business requirement for generating a report or performing any business transaction as a batch, then the Oracle end user will submit a request from the provided application responsibility. The execution of the program for the report is the concurrent request.

> *Concurrent program*: This is the program responsible for implementing the business functionality and generating the required results.

> *Concurrent process*: A concurrent program that is scheduled to run for performing a business transaction is known a concurrent process, and the concurrent process will get associated with the OS process.

© Syed Zaheer and Erman Arslan 2016
S. Zaheer and E. Arslan, *Practical Oracle E-Business Suite*, DOI 10.1007/978-1-4842-1422-0_10

Service Management Architecture

As discussed, Oracle EBS system services are dependent on each other. If any one service is affected, in turn it will affect other services. These services run with one or more mandatory processes that are required for the application to work.

Service management facilitates the management of the application service processes in a much simpler manner compared to earlier systems. Service management provides a fault-tolerant process management framework with centralized management of all concurrent manager processes. You can interact with the Generic Service Management (GSM) framework using Oracle Application Manager, the Administer Manager application form, or OS scripts.

This GSM service management framework is a sophisticated framework that facilitates the management of application service process on multiple nodes. This framework supports the integration of other services such as Java services and Oracle Workflow mailer.

■ **Note**   How the internal concurrent manager works is discussed in the next section.

How the Service Manager Works

As part of GSM, the service manager is responsible for starting and terminating the concurrent manager and service processes. The service processes could be any process like web listeners, forms, or any other application process that is part of GSM. If the internal concurrent manager (ICM) terminates on a node, then the service manager running on that specific node will also terminate. The internal concurrent manager and the service manager are linked to each other.

As shown in Figure 10-1, the concurrent manager and other services are distributed across three application nodes. Consider node2 is terminated because of some error; then the service manager and internal concurrent manager running on node1 will migrate the process from the failed node to any available active service manager node. ICM keeps on monitoring the processes running on all application nodes, and if for some reason the process fails on any of the nodes, the ICM will try to restart this process. ICM will migrate the processes from one node to another node only when there is a node failure.

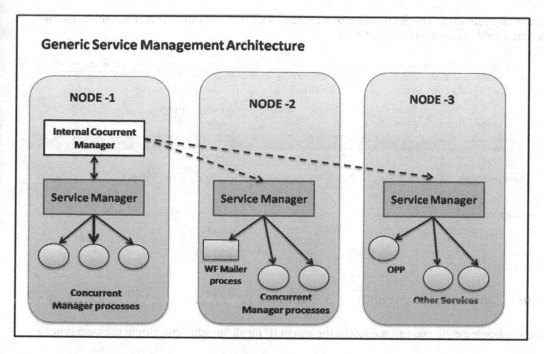

Figure 10-1. *Concurrent manager: GSM architecture*

Consider a situation where there a failure on node1; this node is one that is running the internal concurrent manager process that is required by other nodes as well for proper functioning of the application services. ICM is monitored by the internal monitor process (FNDIMON), and it keeps in constant communication with the internal concurrent manager. If there is a failure because of a network connection or node failure, then ICM will be started on any one of the surviving application nodes. You can configure the reviver process, which will monitor the connectivity. Whenever there is a disconnection, ICM terminates itself and spawns the reviver process. Once the connectivity is established, then the reviver starts the ICM and exits.

You can start multiple ICMs on all participating application nodes, but all ICM processes will get terminated, and only one will remain active—the one that was started first.

■ **Tip** The internal monitor process should be defined on each participating application node so that the failed ICM process can migrate to the surviving application node.

The overall concept of running the concurrent manager processes on more than one node is known as *parallel concurrent processing* (PCP). We'll discuss PCP later in this chapter in more detail.

Figure 10-2 shows the process ID of the service manager. PID 5590 is an operating system ID for the service manager that is running on ERPNODE3.

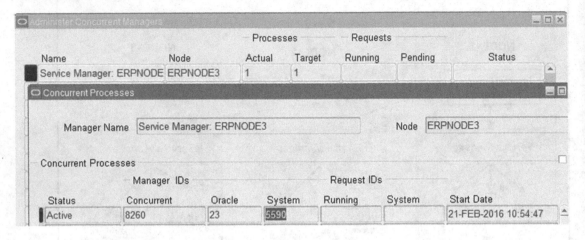

Figure 10-2. *Service manager: process ID*

In the following code, you can see 5590 is the parent ID for all the other concurrent manager processes.

```
[applebs@erpnode3 ~]$ ps -ef | grep 5590
applebs  5590     1  0 10:54 ?        00:00:00 FNDSM
applebs  5766  5590  0 10:54 ?        00:00:00 RCVOLTM
applebs  5767  5590  0 10:54 ?        00:00:00 INCTM
applebs  5768  5590  0 10:54 ?        00:00:00 POXCON
applebs  5782  5590  0 10:55 ?        00:00:00 FNDCRM
applebs  5783  5590  0 10:55 ?        00:00:00 FNDSCH
applebs  5784  5590  0 10:55 ?        00:00:00 FNDLIBR
applebs  5792  5590  0 10:55 ?        00:00:00 FNDLIBR
applebs  5818  5590  0 10:55 ?        00:00:00 INVLIBR
applebs  5826  5590  0 10:55 ?        00:00:00 PALIBR
applebs  5827  5590  0 10:55 ?        00:00:00 FNDLIBR
applebs  5832  5590  0 10:55 ?        00:00:00 FNDLIBR
applebs  5845  5590  0 10:55 ?        00:00:00 FNDLIBR
applebs  5850  5590  0 10:55 ?        00:00:00 FNDLIBR
applebs  8863  8740  0 11:36 pts/4    00:00:00 grep 5590
[applebs@erpnode3 ~]$
```

Different Types of Concurrent Managers

Different types of concurrent managers are available within Oracle E-Business Suite, and each manager has its own purpose that is required for the application to work. The following are the different types of concurrent managers:

- Internal concurrent managers

- Standard manager

- Conflict resolution manager

- Transaction manager

We'll briefly cover each of these managers and their role in an Oracle E-Business Suite system.

Internal Concurrent Managers

The internal concurrent manager is the backbone of the concurrent manager and the concurrent processing node. The ICM is the first manager started during the startup phase of the concurrent managers; it will initiate the first application process for the concurrent manager. The ICM starts the FNDLIBR application process. It is also responsible for monitoring, restarting, and terminating the other concurrent processes through communication with the service manager (FNDSM). ICM is responsible only for starting, stopping, and restarting of the service manager on all participating application nodes. In a multinode environment, the ICM will be active only on single node where PCP is configured for fault tolerance. ICM is responsible only for migrating processes from one node to another node during a node's failure.

Standard Manager

The standard manager is also one of the important concurrent managers; it is responsible for running most of the business requests. This manager will communicate only with the node service manager and client application processes. This concurrent manager will accept any requests that have no specialization rules defined. The standard manager also uses the FNDLIBR application process.

Conflict Resolution Manager

The conflict resolution manager is another type of concurrent manager, and its main responsibility is to check the concurrent program definition for incompatibility rules.

We'll cover some concurrent manager incompatibilities later in this chapter.

Transaction Manager

The transaction manager is responsible for taking the load from the concurrent request table for pooling the requests submitted by the users, and these requests are sent to the standard manager. In a RAC environment, it is required to activate the transaction managers on each cluster node.

Figure 10-3 shows the different concurrent managers actively running on ERPNODE3.

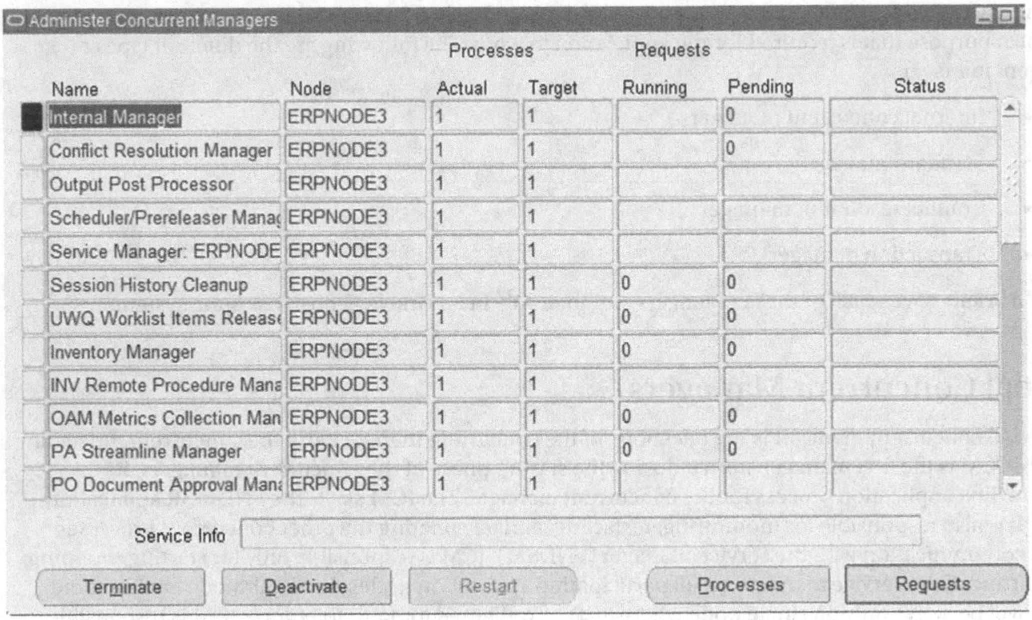

Figure 10-3. *Oracle EBS concurrent managers*

```
[applebs@erpnode3 ~]$ ps -ef | grep 5381
applebs   5381   5375  0 10:53 pts/2    00:00:00 FNDLIBR
applebs   8777   8740  0 11:31 pts/4    00:00:00 grep 5381
[applebs@erpnode3 ~]$
```

As discussed, each concurrent manager will be associated with the operating system process. Figure 10-4 shows the operating system process ID 5381 for the internal concurrent manager. At the OS level, you can see the same process ID is running the executable FNDLIBR.

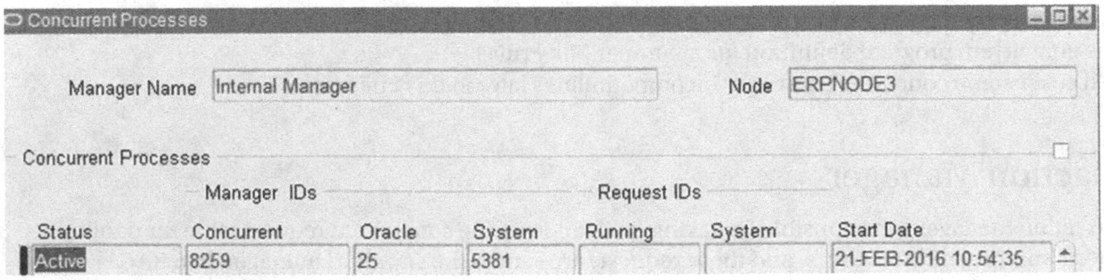

Figure 10-4. *Internal concurrent manager*

Understanding Concurrent Request Phases

So far, we have discussed some information about the concurrent managers. Now you will see the different phases of a concurrent manager that a request has to go through for processing a user request. The concurrent request will have following list of phases:

1. INACTIVE

2. PENDING

3. RUNNING

4. COMPLETED

Whenever a user submits a concurrent request the request is updated in the database table, this request will be identified with a unique request ID, and concurrent manager will read this request from the FND_CONCURRENT_REQUESTS table.

Once the request is submitted, first it will go into the PENDING state based on the sleep time value configured for that particular manager processing that specific concurrent request. It will also read the information of that particular request from database. This request will move into the RUNNING state after checking the incompatibilities and concurrent request priority. In COMPLETED, the request will be processed on the assigned concurrent manager, and the output will be generated. During the INACTIVE phase, there will be no manager available to proceed with the execution of the concurrent request.

Parent Request and Child Request

In enterprise business environments there are certain batch jobs that have to be executed in sequence. The requests are submitted in a set called a *request set*. A request set may contain multiple concurrent requests. The request set will have its unique request ID, which is known as *parent request*, and all concurrent requests running within that request set are known as *child requests*.

Table 10-1 lists the different statuses of the concurrent manager phases.

Table 10-1. Concurrent Manager: Phases and Status

Phase	PHASE_CODE	Status	STATUS_CODE	Description
PENDING	**P**	Normal	**R**	The request is waiting for the manager to be available.
		Standby	**Q**	The program is incompatible with other running programs.
		Scheduled	**F**	The request is scheduled to start at a specific time.
		Waiting	**Z**	A child request is waiting for a parent request action to process.

(continued)

Table 10-1. (*continued*)

Phase	PHASE_CODE	Status	STATUS_CODE	Description
RUNNING	**R**	Normal	**I**	The request is running normally without issues.
		Paused	**W**	All child requests will be paused until further action is requested by the parent request.
		Resuming	**B**	The request submitted by the parent request completed, and the parent request is waiting to restart.
		Terminating	**T**	The running request is terminated by selecting the Terminate action.
COMPLETED	**C**	Normal	**I**	The request completed normally.
		Error	**E**	The request completed with some errors.
		Warning	**G**	The request completed with some warnings.
		Cancelled	**D**	Requests that are in a pending/inactive state are cancelled using the cancel action.
		Terminated	**X**	The running request is terminated by selecting the Terminate action.
INACTIVE	**I**	Disabled	**U**	The program is not enabled to run.
		On Hold		The pending request is put on hold by selecting the "on Hold" action.
		No Manager	**M**	No manager is defined or available to run the request.

Table 10-1 lists two columns, PHASE_CODE and STATUS_CODE, of table FND_CONCURRENT_REQUEST. The values of these columns change based on the concurrent request lifecycle. FND_CONCURRENT_REQUESTS is the key table that keeps records about all the Oracle applications' concurrent requests.

Working with Concurrent Requests (Standard Requests, Custom Requests, and Request Arguments)

Now that you have a good understanding of how concurrent managers work, let's see how you can use a concurrent manager for generating the reports. Oracle delivers a set of seeded concurrent programs for generating reports and performing business transactions, and the requests that use these standard programs are known as *standard requests*. There may be certain business requirements that a standard manager is not capable of performing. In that situation, you may need to create the custom concurrent program, and the request that will use this custom program for performing a business transaction is known as the *custom request*.

Concurrent requests need a certain set of arguments for processing the business transaction, and these arguments are purely specific to the concurrent requests and will not be the same for all requests. The arguments that are passed on by a user to a concurrent request are known as *request arguments*.

Submitting a Standard Concurrent Request

Navigate to System Administrator ➤ Concurrent ➤ Request to get to the Request form shown in Figure 10-5.

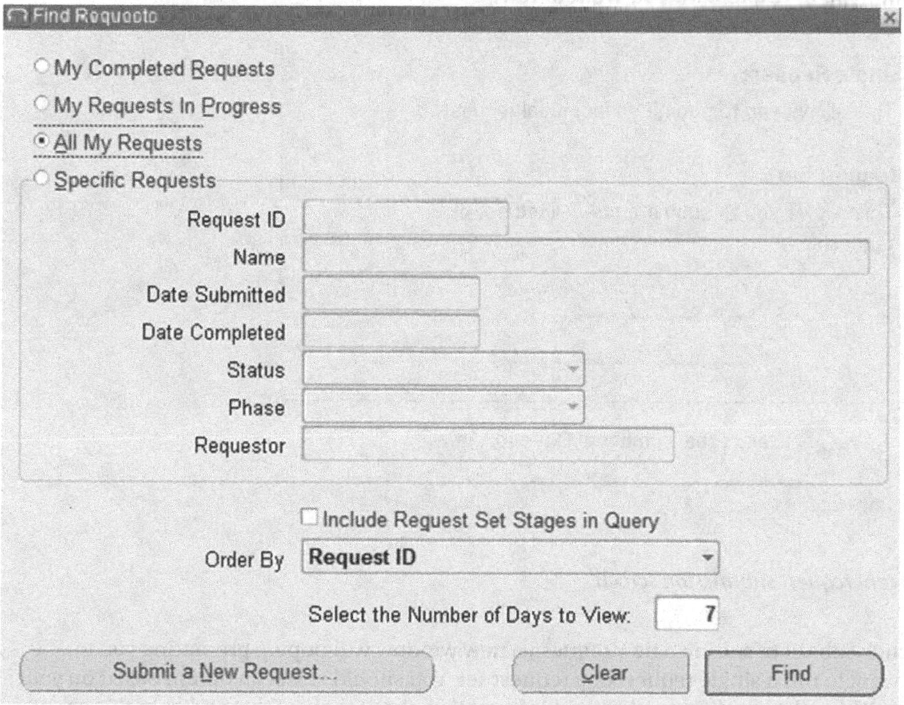

Figure 10-5. Concurrent manager: Request form

Multiple options are available on this screen, and each option is described here:

My Completed requests: Shows all requests completed by the user who is currently logged in

My Requests in Progress: Shows all requests that are still in progress

All My Requests: Shows all requests regardless of the phase for the user who is currently logged in

Specific Requests: Allows you to narrow down the search for concurrent requests with more specific information, as shown in Figure 10-6

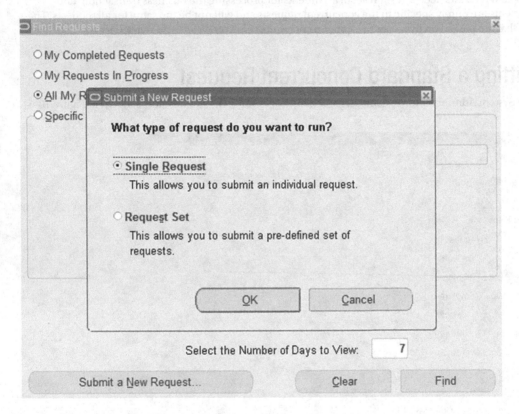

Figure 10-6. Concurrent request submission screen

Whenever you click Submit to submit a new request, a new window will pop up prompting you to choose whether you want to run a single request or a request set. You should select an option based on your business requirement. We've already discussed certain information about request sets earlier in this chapter, including the parent and child concurrent request relationship, and we'll discuss them in more depth later in this chapter.

For this example, select the option Single Request and click OK then we will get the screen for submitting concurrent request as shown in Figure 10-7.

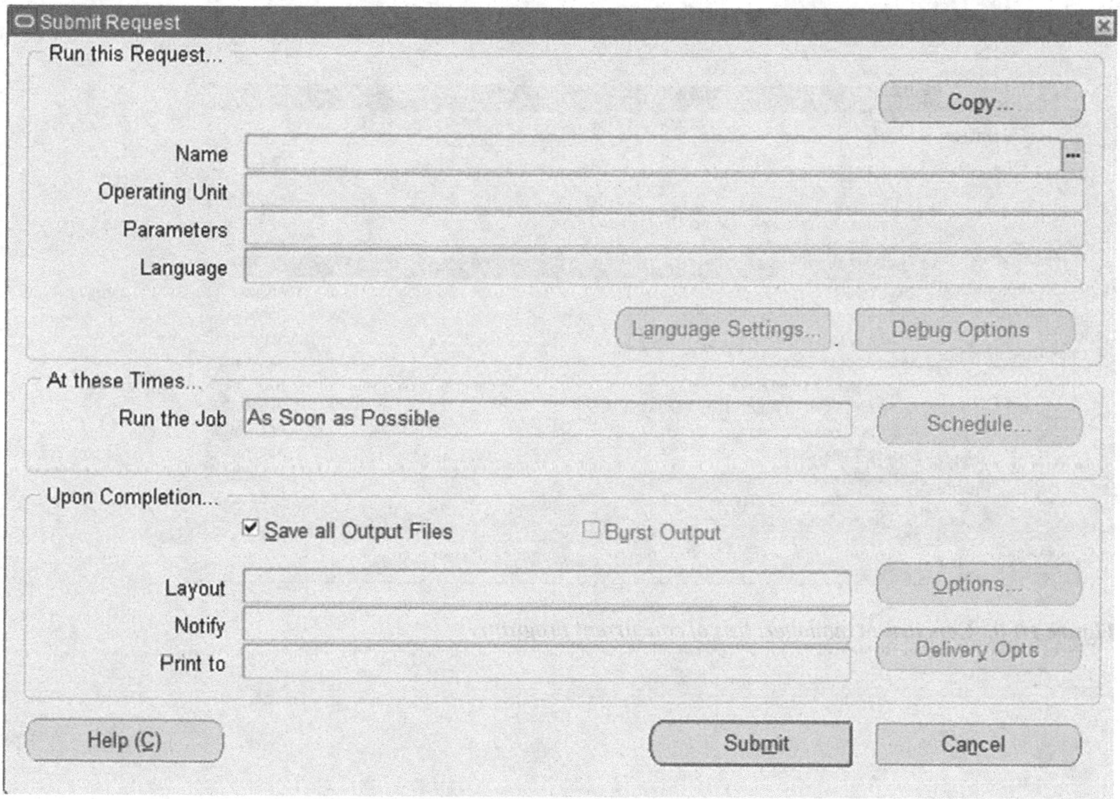

Figure 10-7. Concurrent manager: submitting a concurrent request

Again, there are multiple options available, and you should provide inputs as per your requirements.

Figure 10-8 lists the standard requests that are available within that responsibility.

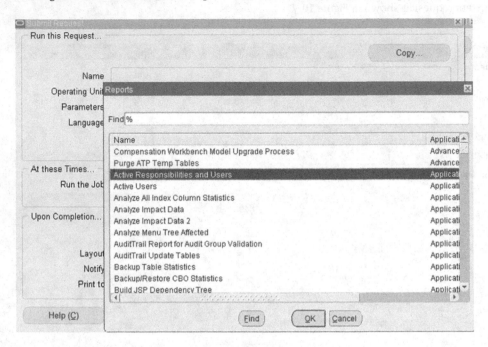

Figure 10-8. *Concurrent manager: lists of concurrent programs*

You can select any request from the available list, as shown in Figure 10-9. Here we have selected Active Responsibilities and Users, which is a standard report provided by Oracle.

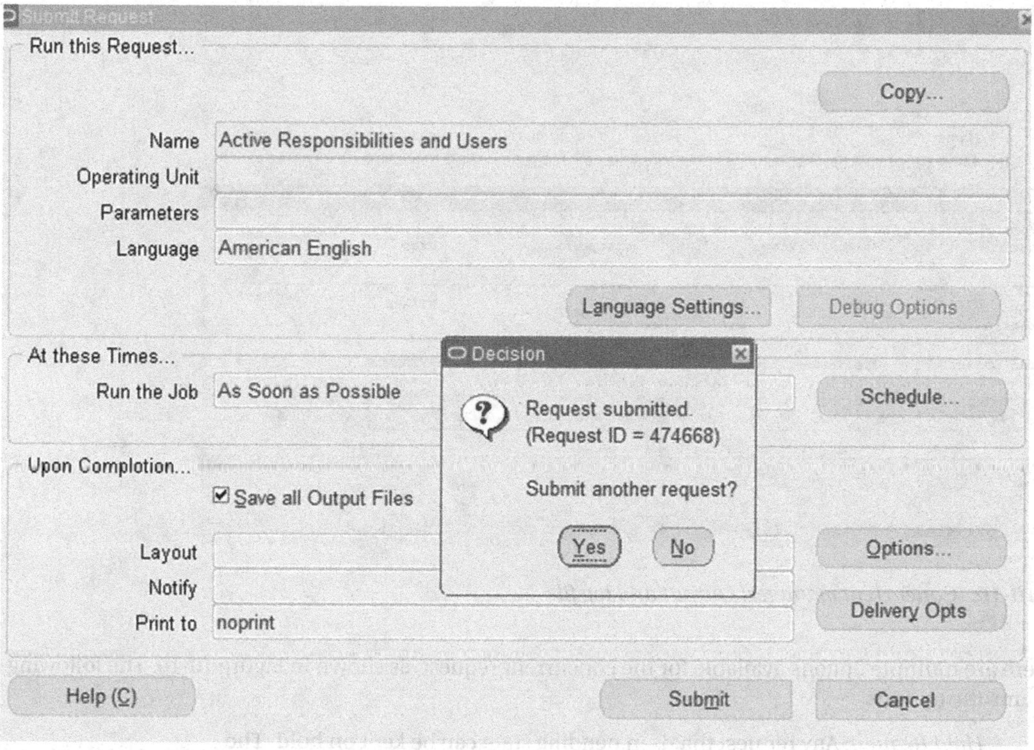

Figure 10-9. *Concurrent manager: request ID*

Once you submit a request, the system will generate a unique request ID. Figure 10-10 shows the unique request ID generated for our submitted request.

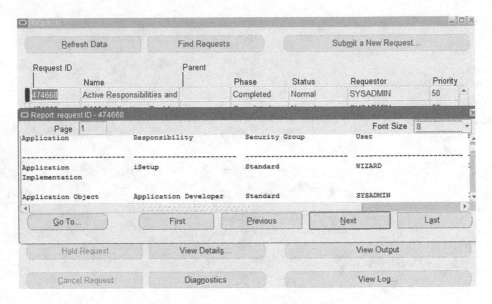

Figure 10-10. *Concurrent manager: Output and log file*

There are multiple options available for the concurrent request, as shown in Figure 10-10. The following list explains the options:

> *Hold Request*: Any request that is in pending state can be kept on hold. The system will not run these requests until the hold status has been removed.

> *View Details*: This will provide detailed information about a specific request.

> *View output*: This will provide the output file for the executed concurrent request in HTML, text, PDF, and so on.

> *Cancel request*: Any scheduled or running request can be cancelled.

> *Diagnostic*: This will show the start time and end time of the particular concurrent request.

> *View Log*: This will show the log file for that particular concurrent request, which can be helpful in troubleshooting the concurrent requests that complete with a status warning or error.

Request Arguments

Oracle concurrent requests have multiple options available to support the business needs. These options, listed in Figure 10-11, are generic for all concurrent requests. We will now discuss these options briefly.

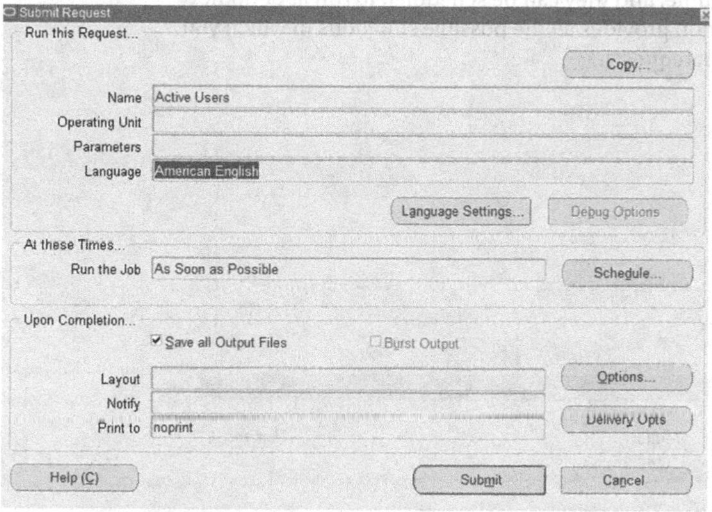

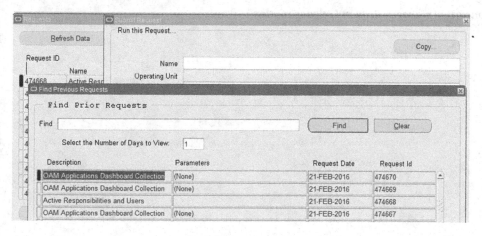

Figure 10-11. *Concurrent manager: request arguments*

> *Copy*: This will allow you to copy any previously completed concurrent request, as shown in Figure 10-12.

Figure 10-12. *Concurrent manager: request copy option*

Language Setting: This will provide an option to choose the languages in which the report must be generated. As shown in Figure 10-13, only US English is listed as there is no additional language currently installed. If there are any additional languages installed, then you can select them here.*Schedule*: This is an important feature of the concurrent manager. The concurrent requests can be scheduled to execute at some specific time, and they can be scheduled to run at periodic intervals. This schedule option provides all the possible situations in which you can schedule the concurrent requests.

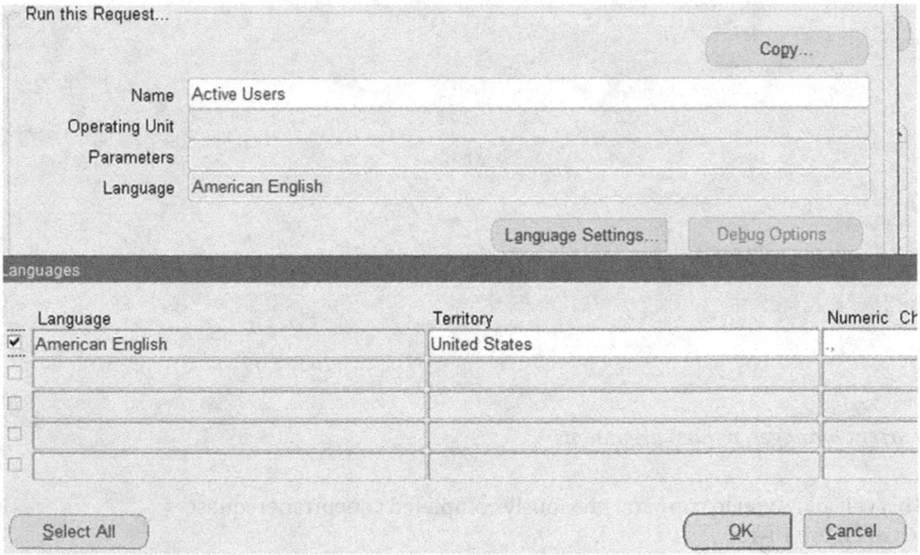

Figure 10-13. *Concurrent manager: Request Language option*

By default the value is As Soon as Possible, as shown in Figure 10-14. This means the request will run immediately if the manager is available, or it will wait for the next manager to be available.

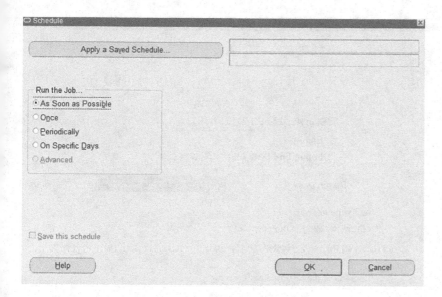

Figure 10-14. *Concurrent manager: scheduling option, As Soon as Possible*

Figure 10-15 shows the next option for the concurrent schedule: Once. This means you can schedule the execution of the concurrent request for a specific date and time. The concurrent request will run at the specified time.

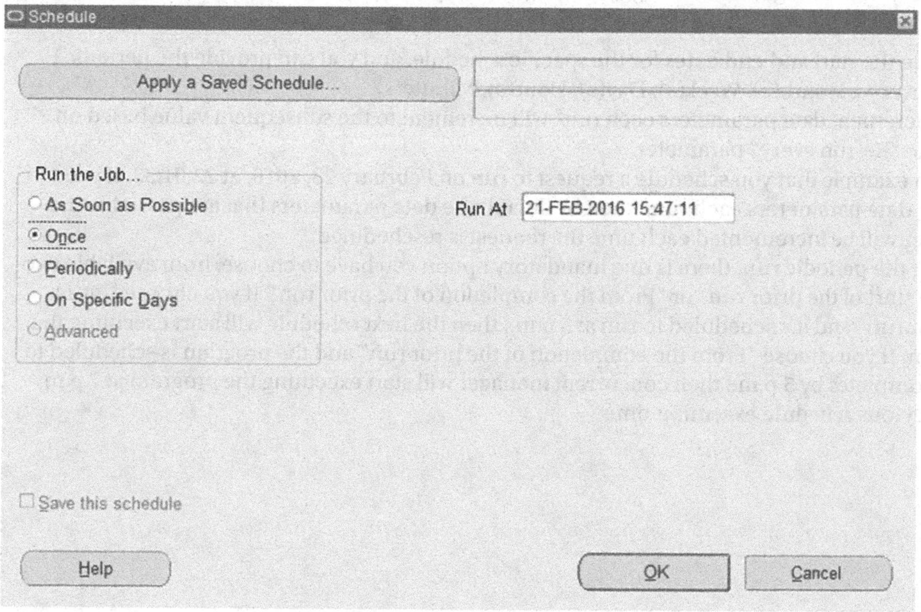

Figure 10-15. *Concurrent manager: scheduling option, Once*

The concurrent request can be scheduled to run periodically. Figure 10-16 shows that the periodic option has multiple settings for scheduling the concurrent request based on the business requirement.

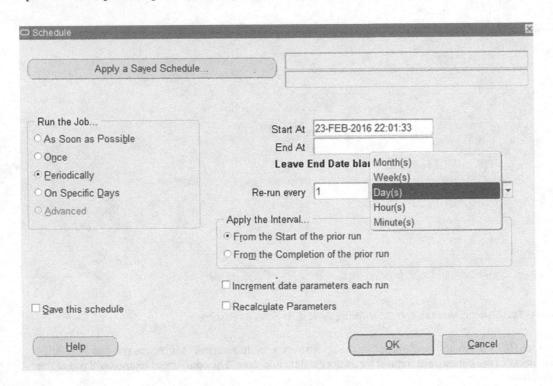

Figure 10-16. *Concurrent manager: scheduling option, Periodically*

You can provide the start and end dates for the specific schedule, and you can provide the periodic parameter Re-run every *x* Month(s), Week(s), Day(s), Hour(s), Minute(s).

The option "Increment date parameters each run" will increment to the subsequent value based on your selection of the "Re-run every" parameter.

Consider as an example that you schedule a request to run on February 23, 2016, at 22:01:33. If you choose "Increment date parameters each run," then by default the date parameters that are passed to the concurrent manager will be incremented each time the request is rescheduled.

For scheduling the periodic run, there is one mandatory option you have to choose, from available two options: "From the start of the prior run" or "From the completion of the prior run." If you choose "From the start of the prior run" and it's scheduled to run at 3 p.m., then the next schedule will start executing the program from 3 p.m. If you choose "From the completion of the prior run" and the program is scheduled to run at 3 p.m. and completes by 5 p.m., then concurrent manager will start executing the program at 7 p.m. considering the previous schedule execution time.

The On Specific Days scheduling option is simple; you can choose any specific calendar day or any day of the week for the provided period, as shown in Figure 10-17.

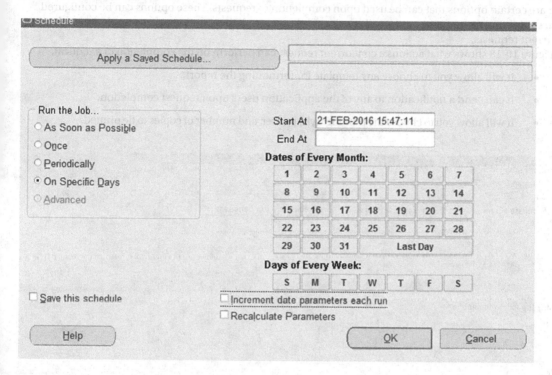

Figure 10-17. Concurrent manager: scheduling option, On Specific Days

Upon Completion

There are certain options that can be used upon completion of requests. These options can be configured before submitting the requests, and it will consider and execute all these options after completion of the concurrent requests.

Figure 10-18 shows what actions a concurrent request can perform on the completion of a request.

- It will allow you to choose any template for formatting the report.

- It can send a notification to any of the application users upon request completion.

- It will allow you to choose the printing style, printer, and number of copies to be printed.

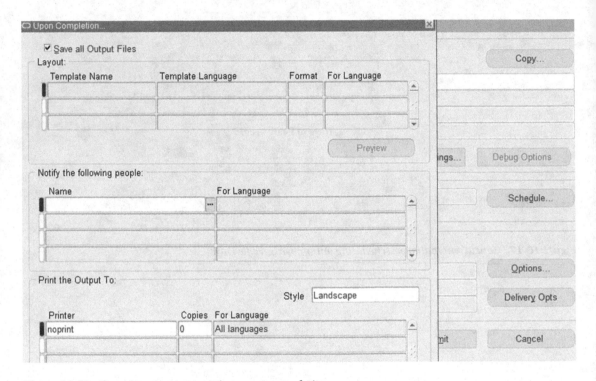

Figure 10-18. *Concurrent request: options upon completion*

Figure 10-19 shows the possible ways in which a report can be delivered. But practically we've never seen this option used. Still, it's always a good idea to be aware of capabilities of the software you are using.

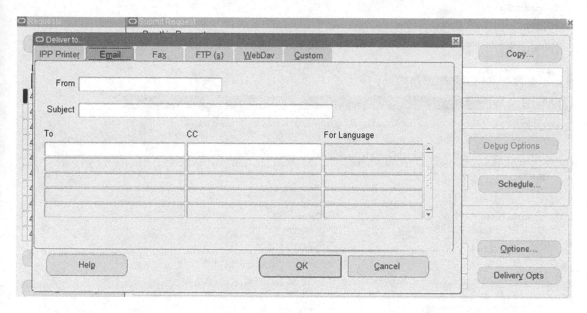

Figure 10-19. *Concurrent manager: Request, options to deliver*

Working with Concurrent Request Sets

A request set is a set of individual programs that are combined to run in a predefined sequence. This is the built-in capability of an Oracle EBS system. You saw earlier while submitting concurrent requests that it will provide two options to choose from, Single Request or Request Set. Request sets can be run in parallel or sequential mode.

These are the key benefits of request sets:

- Easy to deploy using the Request Set Wizard

- Simplify the work of a business user

- Simplify the periodic scheduling of multiple concurrent requests

- Allow you to combine requests from multiple application modules including custom modules into a single request set

- Effectively utilize concurrent resources

In this chapter, you will see how to create a request set using the Request Set Wizard. Figure 10-20 shows the Request Set Wizard.

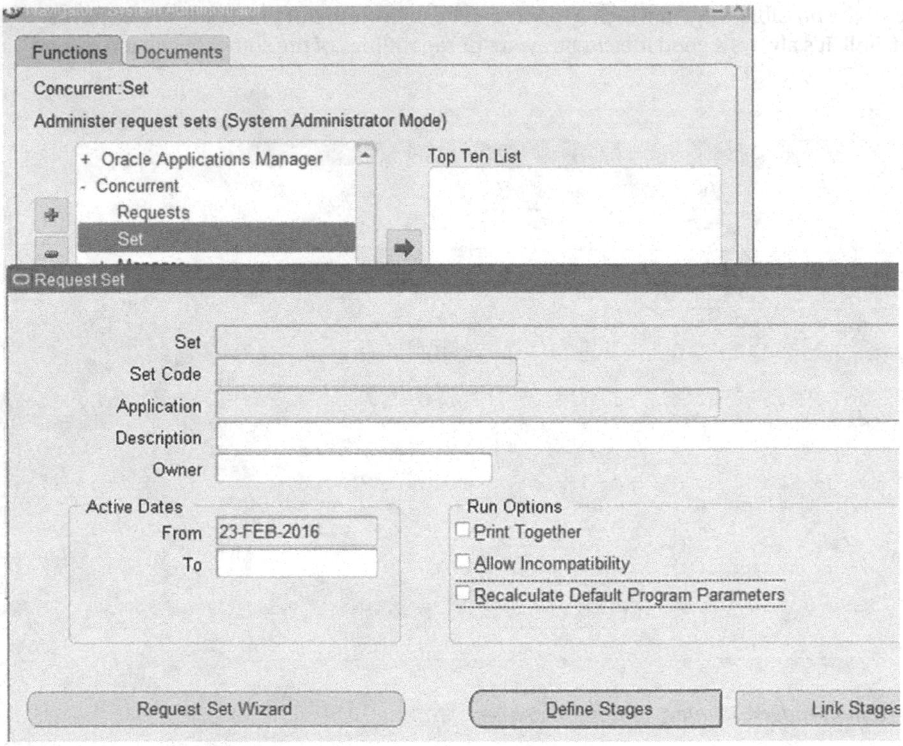

Figure 10-20. *Concurrent request set screen*

To navigate to the Request Set Wizard, select **System Administrator ➤ Concurrent ➤ Requests ➤ Set.**
Figure 10-21 provides two options to choose from: whether the requests in a request set should execute in a sequential fashion or in a parallel fashion. Individual requests will be executed based on this selection. In sequential request sets, the next request will start only after completion of the prior request. In parallel, all requests will be started in parallel.

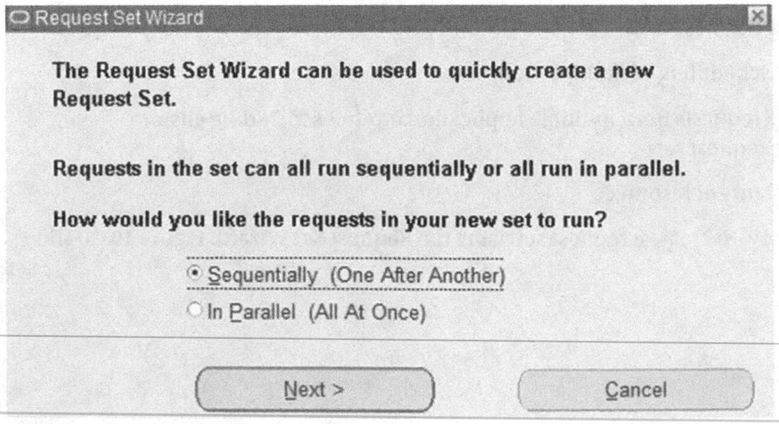

Figure 10-21. *Concurrent Request Set Wizard: sequential or parallel*

■ **Tip**   You should be very careful while defining the request sets with the parallel execution option. This should be decided based on the load capabilities of your system. Business transactions will be affected if you fail to evaluate the existing resources.

Figure 10-22 provides two available options that a request set can perform in case a concurrent request completes with the status Error. Say that there are three requests in a request set and each is request is dependent on other request successfully completing. In such cases you should select the option Abort Processing. If there are no dependencies between the requests, then you can choose Continue Processing. So, based on the nature of requests and dependencies between the concurrent requests in a request set, you should select an appropriate option.

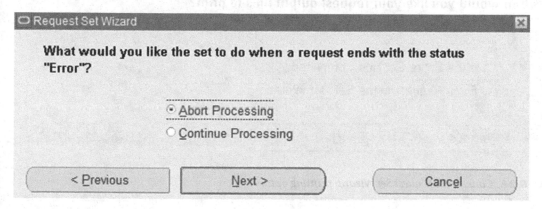

Figure 10-22.   *Concurrent Request Set Wizard: On Error, abort or continue*

Figure 10-23 requests the input for creating the request set.

Set: Any desired name can be provided, but it's always recommended that you use a relevant name.

Application: You should select the registered application.

Description: This is a brief description about the requests and request set.

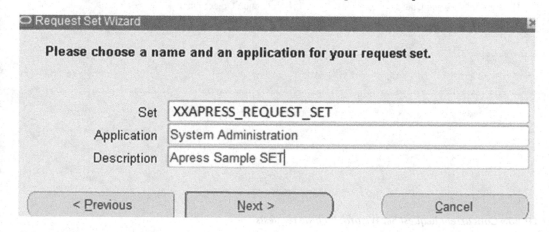

Figure 10-23.   *Concurrent Request Set Wizard: input parameters*

■ **Note**   For custom applications it's always recommended to define requests/request sets with names that start with XX_Custom_request_set.

Figure 10-24 shows how to configure the printing option for the request set. You can print requests for each individual request in a request set, or you can print all requests together after the successful completion of a request set.

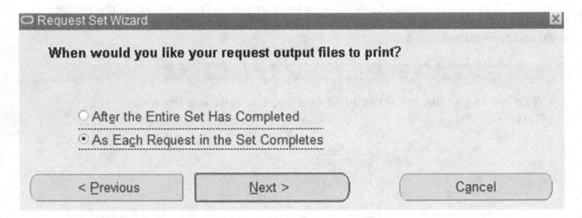

Figure 10-24. *Concurrent Request Set Wizard: printing options*

Figure 10-25 shows how to add individual requests in a request set. Here we have selected two concurrent programs: Active Responsibilities and Users and Active Users.

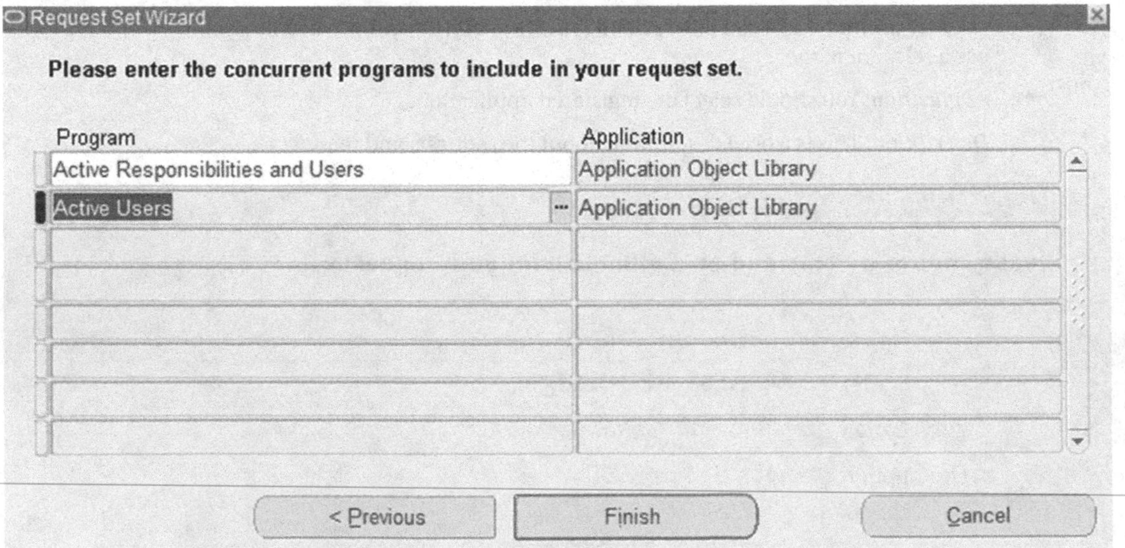

Figure 10-25. *Concurrent Request Set Wizard: include requests*

Figure 10-26 confirms the creation of the request set.

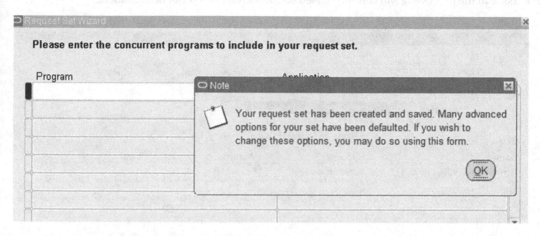

Figure 10-26. *Concurrent Request Set Wizard: request set completed*

Figure 10-27 displays the created request set and also displays other actions that can be configured for a request set such as Define Stages and Link Stages.

Set	XXAPRESS_REQUEST_SET
Set Code	FNDRSSUB933
Application	System Administration
Description	Apress Sample SET
Owner	SYSADMIN

Active Dates
From 23-FEB-2016
To

Run Options
☐ Print Together
☐ Allow Incompatibility
☐ Recalculate Default Program Parameters

Request Set Wizard   Define Stages   Link Stages

Figure 10-27. *Concurrent Request Set Wizard: Define Stages and Link Stages*

Figure 10-28 shows the sequence of execution of the individual requests. The request with sequence 10 will start first, and the processing will continue based on the incremental sequence numbers.

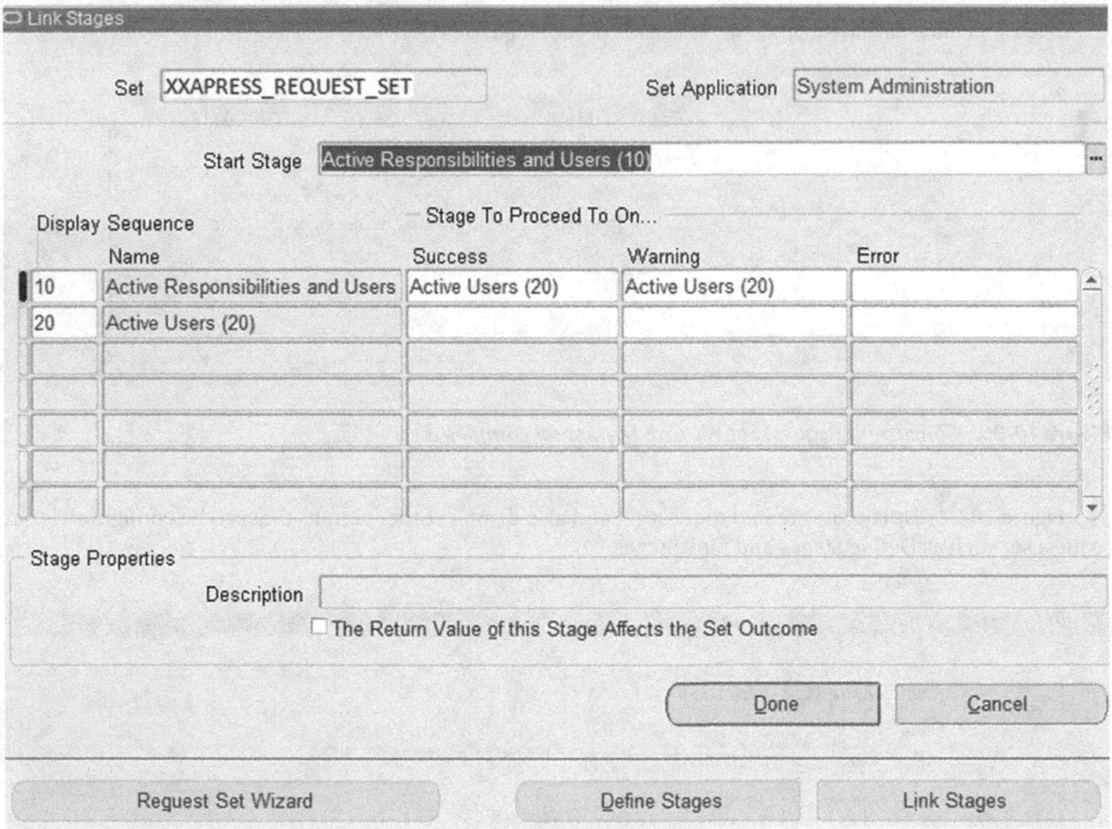

Figure 10-28. *Concurrent Request Set Wizard: request execution sequence*

Figure 10-29 shows the Link Stages option of a concurrent request set.

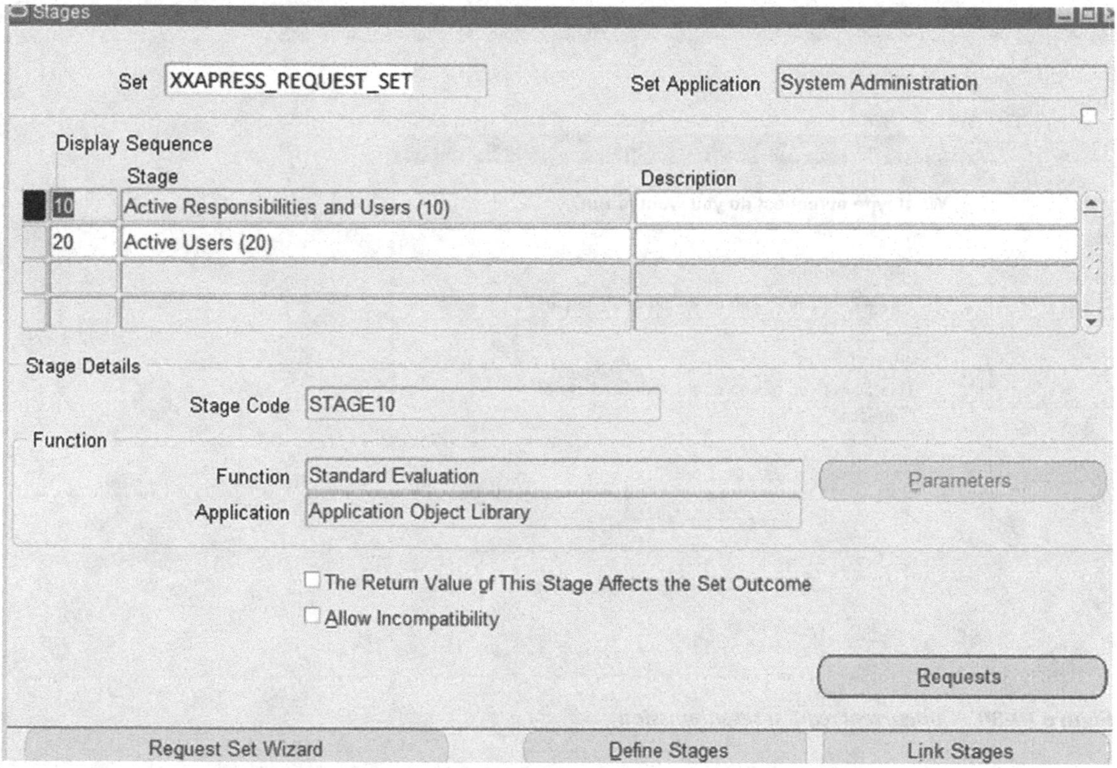

Figure 10-29. *Concurrent Request Set Wizard: Link Stages option*

Let's see the execution of a request set. The submission process of a request set is similar to a single request. Figure 10-30 shows the selection of the Request Set option.

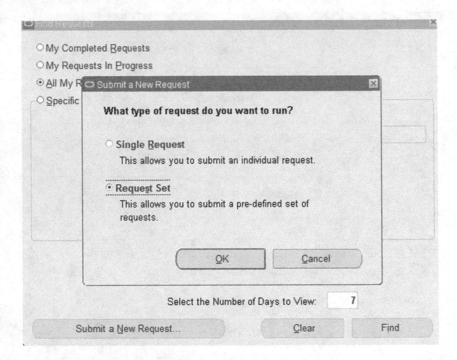

Figure 10-30. *Concurrent request set submission*

Figure 10-31 show the submission screen of newly created request set.

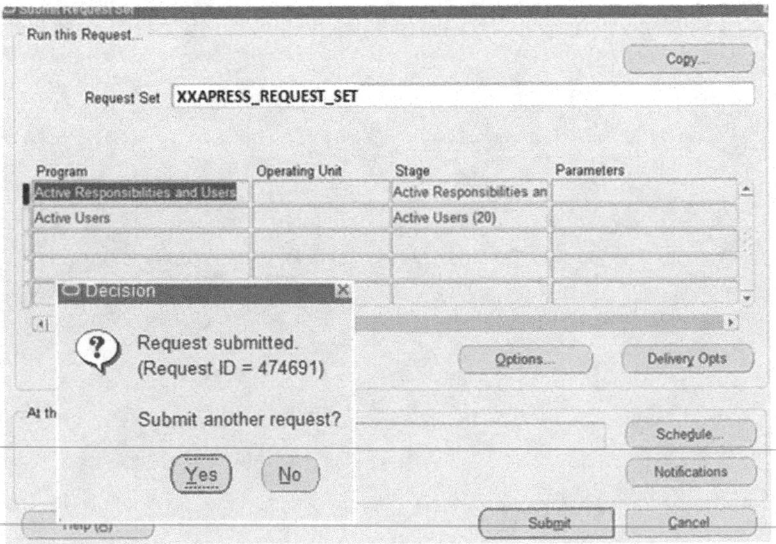

Figure 10-31. *Concurrent request set: request ID*

Once you click Submit, it will generate the new request ID for the submitted request set. This ID will be identified as the parent ID, and all requests running under that request set will be identified as child requests.

Figure 10-32 shows the successful completion of request set Apress Request SET. Here you can see that Active Responsibilities and Users completed first according to the defined sequence.

Request ID	Name	Parent	Phase	Status	Requestor	Priority
474695	Active Users	474691	Completed	Normal	SYSADMIN	50
474693	Active Responsibilities and	474691	Completed	Normal	SYSADMIN	50
474691	XXAPRESS_REQUEST_SET		Completed	Normal	SYSADMIN	50
474690	OAM Applications Dashbo:		Pending	Scheduled	SYSADMIN	50

Figure 10-32. *Concurrent request set completion*

The request set provides robust capabilities for scheduling and executing the concurrent programs. These options are designed to meet all business probabilities for scheduling concurrent requests. Request sets also provide great security. System administrators only are allowed to add requests and link these request sets to the desired responsibilities.

Managing Concurrent Manager Incompatibilities

The concurrent manager's main role is to extract or update business data. There are certain situations in which the same set of data can be accessed or updated by two different concurrent requests, which can create problems for business transactions. To overcome such situations, Oracle has a built-in feature for managing such incompatibilities with different concurrent requests.

You can define that a concurrent program is incompatible with other concurrent programs. Say that you define an incompatible rule for concurrent program A with program B. As a results, program A will not run in parallel with program B. Whenever the request is being submitted, it will check for any incompatible rules, and if it finds any incompatibilities, then that request will go in the pending phase and wait for other dependent requests to complete. It will continue to run only after the completion of the currently running dependent incompatible concurrent request. These concurrent manager dependencies are managed by the conflict resolution manager.

Concurrent program incompatibilities are managed by conflict domains. The following are the possibilities of concurrent manager incompatibilities:

- A concurrent program can defined to be incompatible with a specific concurrent program or with multiple concurrent programs.

- A concurrent program can be defined to be incompatible with itself so that it will not allow two of the same programs to run simultaneously.

- A concurrent program can be defined to be incompatible with all other programs, so that program will run alone.

- A concurrent manager incompatibility can be defined for request sets.

We'll show you a simple demonstration for defining a concurrent manager incompatibility. We will use the same request set we created earlier in this chapter.

To navigate to the right spot, select System Administrator ➤ Concurrent ➤ Set and search for the request set called Apress Request SET.

In Figure 10-33 you can see the option Allow Incompatibility. If you check that box, then the incompatibility will be defined for that concurrent request set. After saving the record, the system will generate a new request set with the name Request SET Apress Request SET. This newly created request set will allow you to choose other concurrent programs for defining incompatible rules.

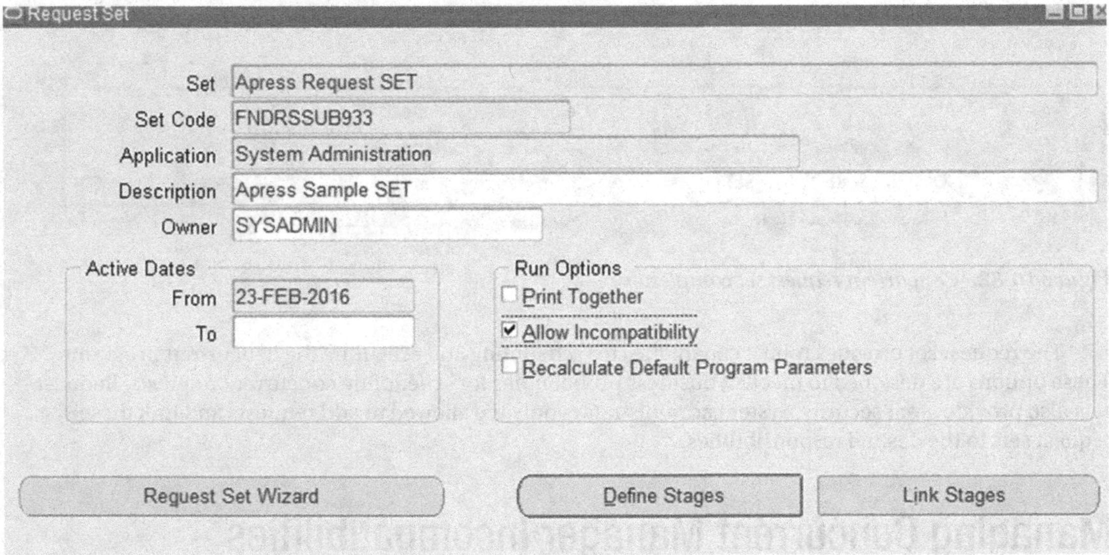

Figure 10-33. Concurrent request se: Allow Incompatibility option

To navigate here, select System Administrator ➤ Concurrent ➤ Program ➤ Define and search for Request Set Apress Request SET. Then click Incompatibilities.

Figure 10-34 displays the newly created concurrent request set on which you can define the incompatible concurrent programs.

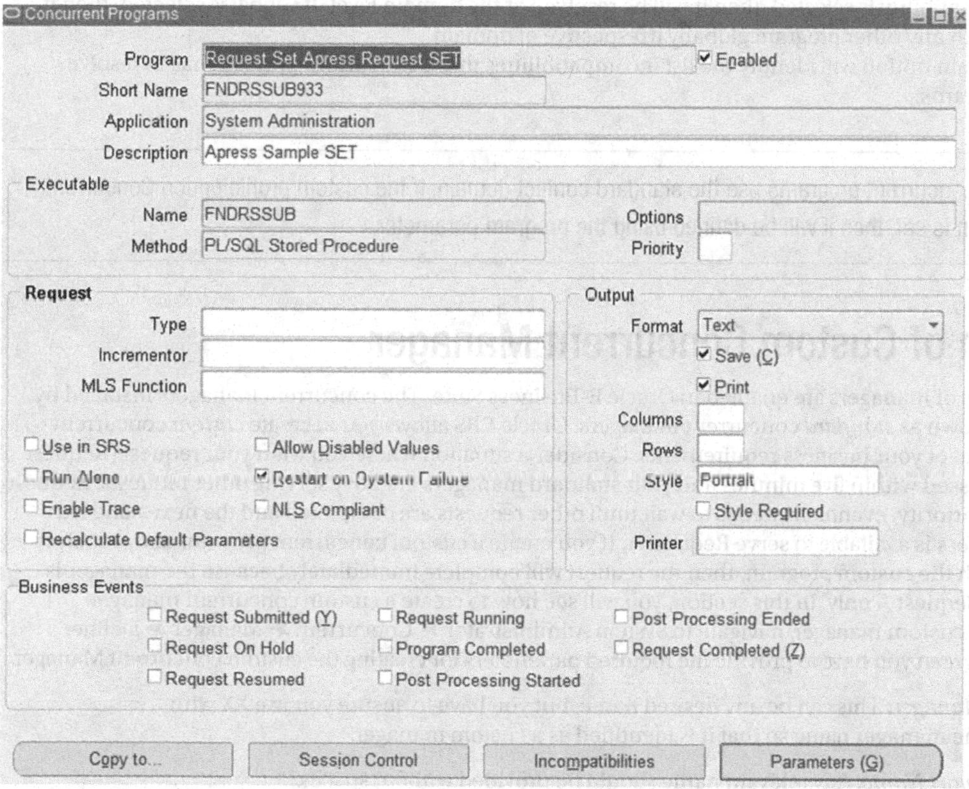

Figure 10-34. *Custom concurrent request set for incompatibilities*

You can define as many incompatible concurrent programs as possible for Request Set Apress Request SET, as shown in Figure 10-35.

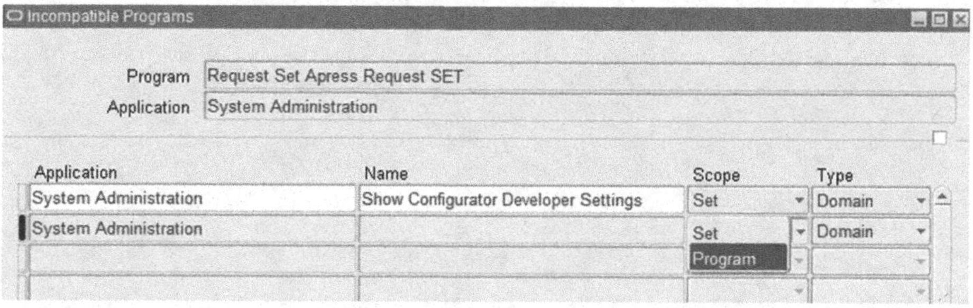

Figure 10-35. *Custom concurrent request set: adding incompatibilities*

The concurrent program can be a request set or individual program, and it can be selected from the Scope option, as shown in Figure 10-34.

Two options are available for managing the incompatibility for the concurrent program. If the Domain type of incompatibility is selected, then it will be resolved at the domain level. If Global is selected, then it cannot run with any other program globally irrespective of domain.

The Domain option will identify the list incompatibilities that a concurrent program has to resolve between programs.

■ **Note**   All concurrent programs use the standard conflict domain. If the custom profile option Concurrent: Conflict Domain is set, then it will be defined using the program parameter.

Creation of Custom Concurrent Manager

Different types of managers are enabled in Oracle E-Business Suite. The concurrent managers installed by default are known as *standard* concurrent managers. Oracle EBS allows you to create *custom* concurrent managers to meet your business requirements. Consider a situation where you want your request (Request A) to be processed within five minutes and your standard managers are busy serving other requests. Request A, which has priority, eventually needs to wait until other requests are completed and the next standard manager process is available to serve Request A. If you create a custom concurrent program and associate Request A with the custom program, then the request will complete immediately because the manager is available for Request A only. In this section, you will see how to create a custom concurrent manager.

To create custom manager, navigate to System Administrator ➤ Concurrent ➤ Manager ➤ Define.

On this screen you have to provide the required parameters for creating the custom concurrent Manager.

> *Manager*: This can be any desired name, but you have to ensure you use XX with the manager name so that it is identified as a custom manager.

> *Short Name*: Any relevant name should be provided without spaces.

> *Application Name*: You can select any application name for which the custom manager is being created.

> *Type*: This will list all the possible types of services of the GSM, and you can select any value based on the requirement.

> *Program Library*: Here you can use any other custom library as well if created.

Figure 10-36 shows all the required parameters for creating a custom concurrent manager. After inputting all these parameters, you should save the records.

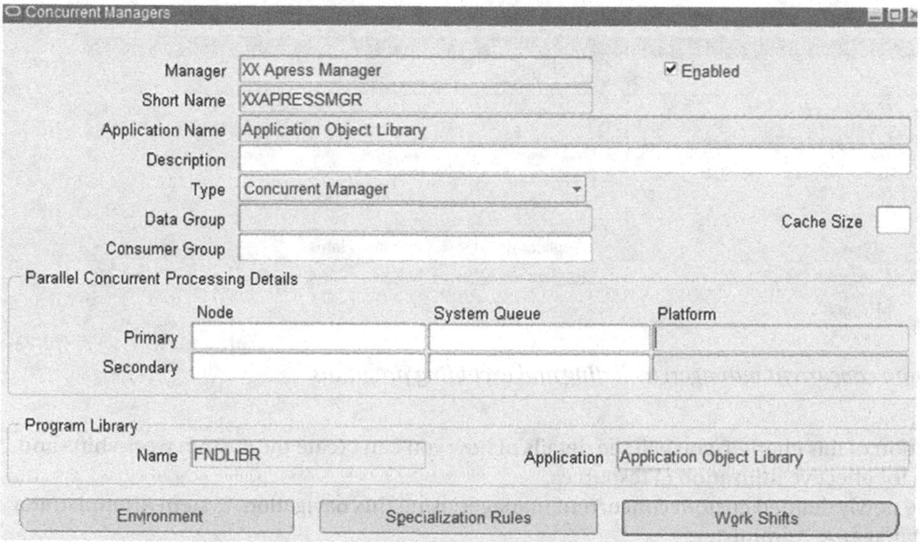

Figure 10-36. *Custom concurrent manager creation*

Once the creation of the concurrent manager completes, then you have to define specialization rules and work shifts for this custom concurrent manager. In this example, we have provided the standard work shift, which will run 24 hours every day with three processes. Figure 10-37 shows the work shift of the custom manager XX Apress Manager.

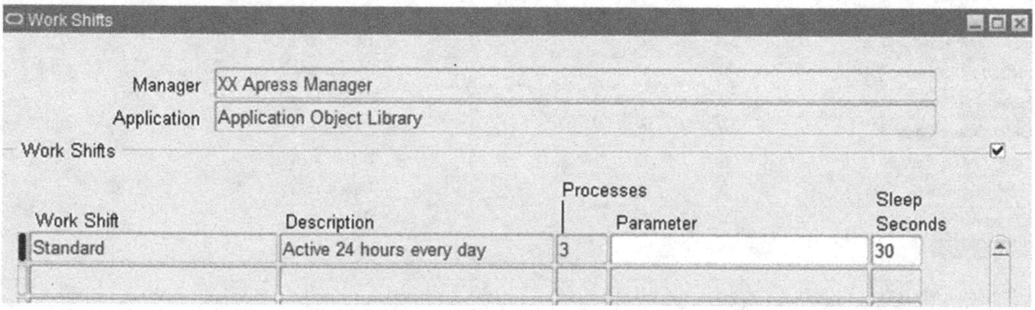

Figure 10-37. *Custom concurrent manager: work shift*

Now you will define the specialization rule for the newly created concurrent program. You will define a rule for this manager to include only the Active Users concurrent program. Figure 10-38 shows the specialization rule for XX Apress Manager.

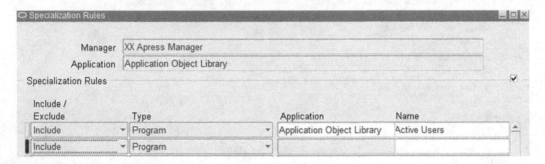

Figure 10-38. *Custom concurrent manager: including and excluding programs*

In the next section of this chapter, you will see details of how you can create the custom work shifts and specialization rules for effective utilization of resources.

You can see the newly defined custom concurrent manager using this navigation: System Administrator ➤ Concurrent ➤ Manager ➤ Administer.

Figure 10-39 displays the newly created custom manager XX Apress Manager.

		Processes		Requests		
Name	Node	Actual	Target	Running	Pending	Status
SFM Application Monitoring !		0	0			Deactivated
SFM Controller Service		0	0			Deactivated
Oracle Provisioning Manager	ERPNODE3	0	0	0	0	
SFM Event Manager Queue !		0	0			Deactivated
SFM Fulfillment Actions Que		0	0			Deactivated
SFM Fulfillment Element Rea		0	0			Deactivated
SFM Inbound Messages Que		0	0			Deactivated
SFM Order Queue Service		0	0			Deactivated
SFM Timer Queue Service		0	0			Deactivated
SFM Work Item Queue Servi		0	0			Deactivated
SFM SM Interface Test Servi		0	0			Deactivated
XX Apress Manager		0	0	0	0	Deactivated

Service Info

Terminate	Deactivate	Activate		Processes	Requests
Suspend	Resume	Verify		Refresh	

Figure 10-39. *Custom concurrent manager: administer screen*

By default the manager will be deactivated, so you need to activate it from the same Administer Concurrent Manager screen. Figure 10-40 and Figure 10-41 display the activated manager and the processes running for the new manager.

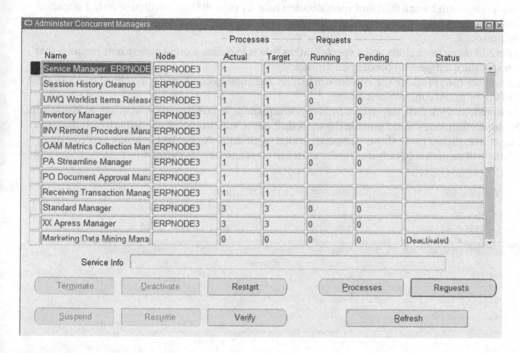

Figure 10-40. *Activated custom concurrent manager*

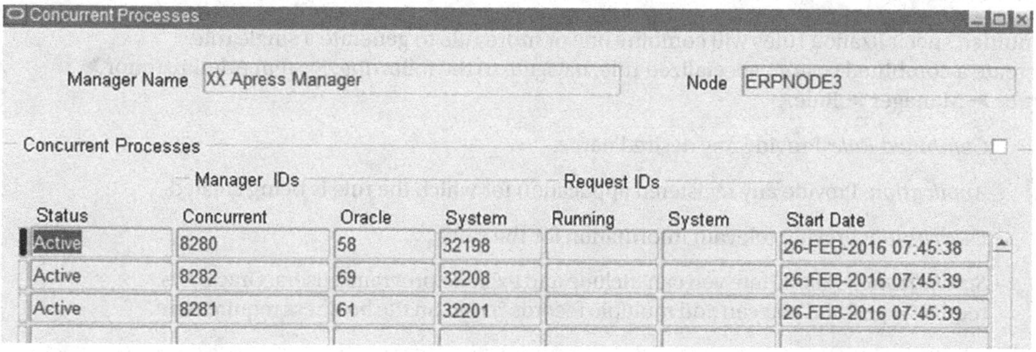

Figure 10-41. *Custom concurrent manager: processes*

Working with the Specialization Rule and Work Shifts

The terms *work shift* and *specialization rule* are self-explanatory. In concurrent processing, each concurrent manager is associated with a work shift and specialization rule. By default Oracle will have only a standard work shift that will run 24 hours every day. If you do not specify any specialization rule, then it will accept all concurrent requests.

The purpose of using work shifts and a specialization rule is to define a set of concurrent requests that should run on specific managers on predefined timings.

Here you will see how to create the custom work shifts and custom combined specialized rule and then assign these to the required concurrent manager.

To create a custom work shift, navigate to System Administrator ➤ Concurrent ➤ Manager ➤ Workshifts.

In the Name section, you should provide the work shift name and provide the time for which the work shift should be active. Figure 10-42 shows two newly added work shifts: Night Data Loading and Weekend. These work shifts will be activated only during the specified days and time as defined.

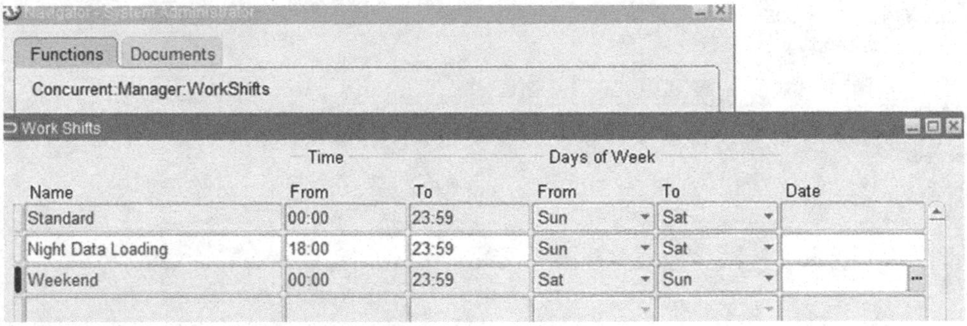

Figure 10-42. Concurrent manager: defining work shifts

Combined specialization rules will combine one or more rule to generate a single rule.

To create a combined custom specialized rule, navigate to the following: System Administrator ➤ Concurrent ➤ Manager ➤ Rule.

> *Combined Rule*: Provide any desired name.

> *Application*: Provide any registered application for which the rule is being created.

> *Description*: Provide relevant information for the rule.

> *Specialization Rules*: Here you can include and exclude programs, users, Oracle IDs, request types, and you can add multiple records based on the business requirement.

Figure 10-43 shows the specialization rule that includes two concurrent programs and excludes one user, so this rule will accept only these two listed concurrent programs and excludes user FINADMIN for running these requests.

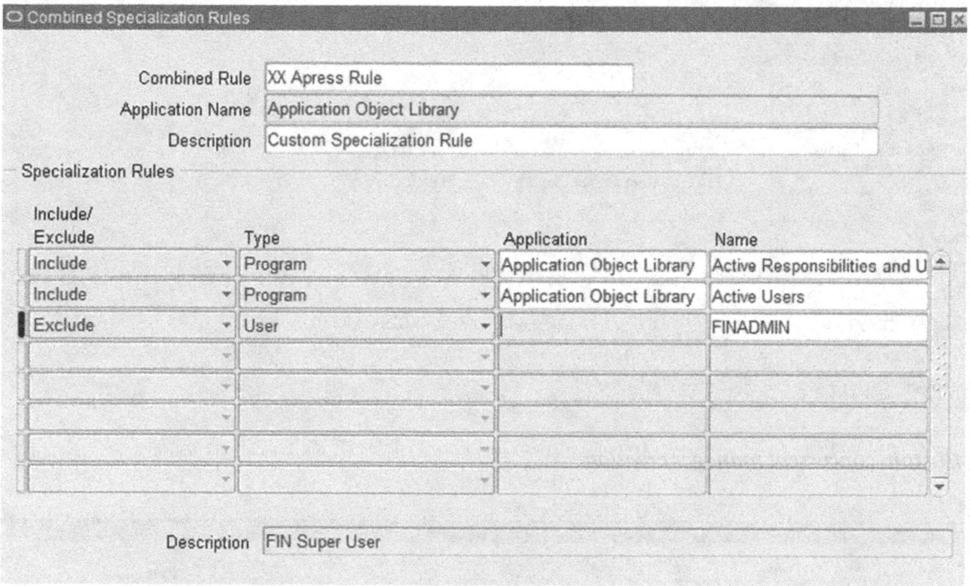

Figure 10-43. Concurrent manager: create specialization rule

Now you will add the newly created work shift and combined specialization rule to the custom manager. Figure 10-42 shows the creation of a custom manager named XX Apress Weekend Manager. The process of creating a custom manager is the same as discussed in the previous section.

Figure 10-44 and Figure10-45 show how to assign the custom specialization rule and work shift to the required concurrent manager. Modifying specialization rules requires the concurrent manager to be restarted. So, you must consider whether it's possible to reboot the managers after modifying the specialization rules.

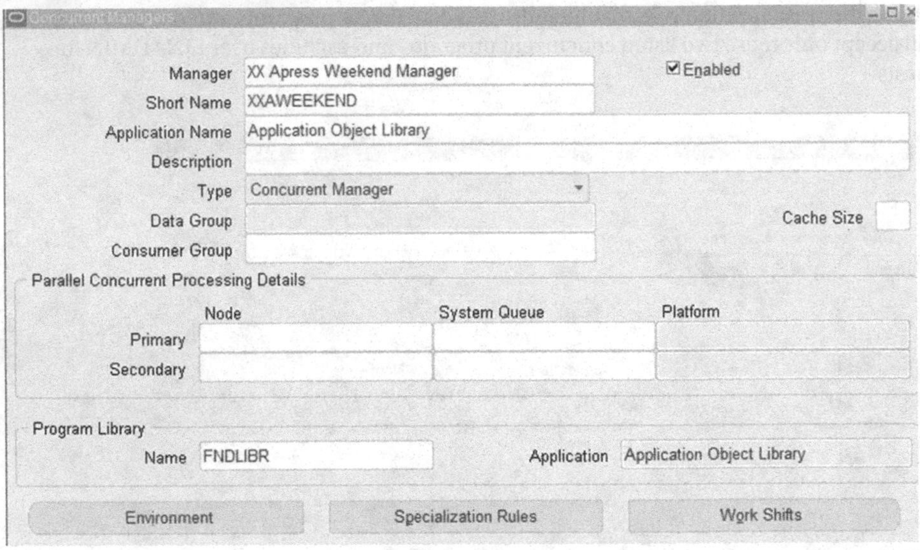

Figure 10-44. Custom concurrent manager creation

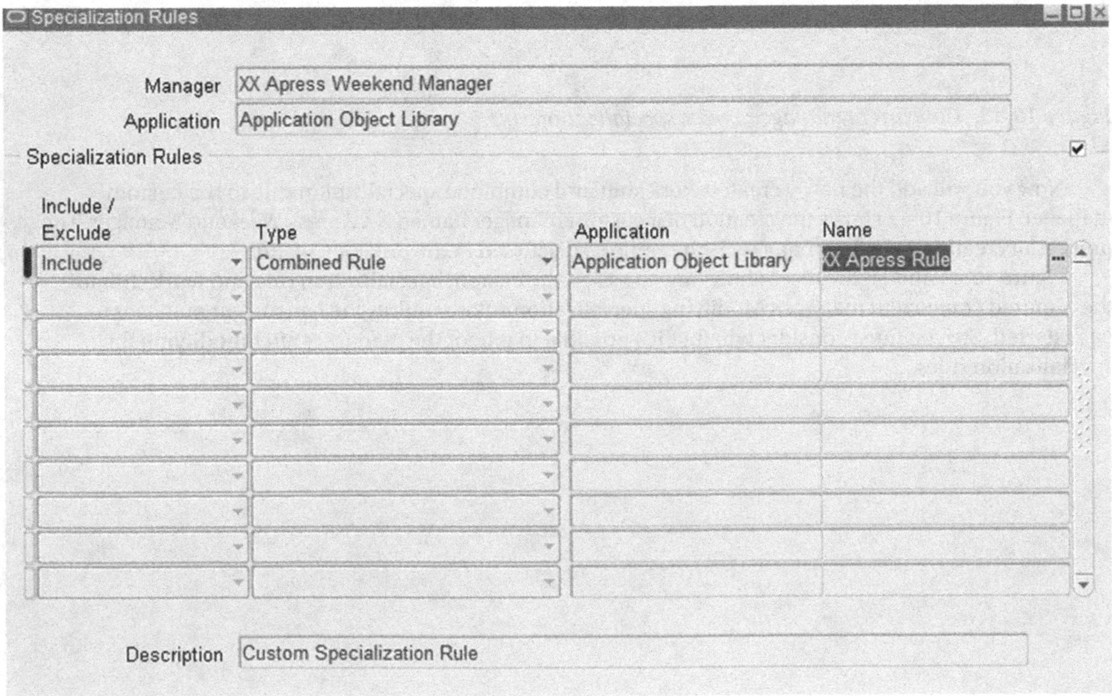

Figure 10-45. Custom concurrent manager: specialization rule

The XX Apress Weekend Manager will activate only on the weekend, as defined in the Work Shifts window, and it will run only one process with this work shift (see Figure 10-46).

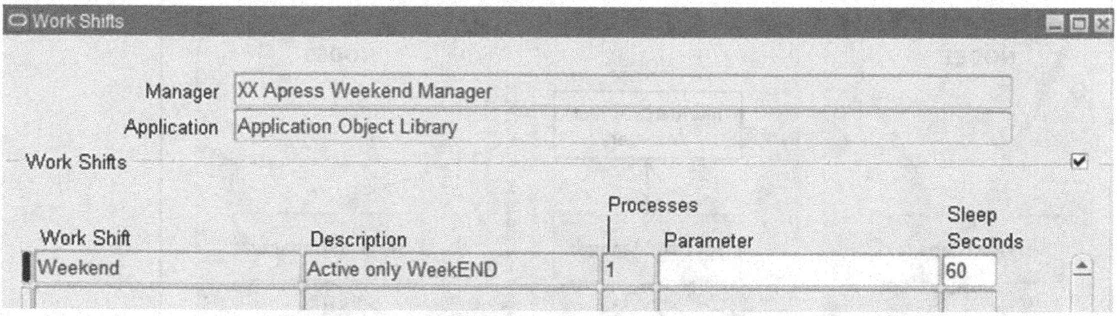

Work Shifts				_ □ ☒
Manager	XX Apress Weekend Manager			
Application	Application Object Library			

Work Shifts ☑

Work Shift	Description	Processes Parameter	Sleep Seconds
Weekend	Active only WeekEND	1	60

Figure 10-46. *Custom concurrent manager: work shift*

You have seen how to create a custom manager, a customized specialization rule, and work shifts. The examples used in the demonstration were simple, but you would apply the same logic to create complex specialization rules and work shifts. Remember to evaluate the system resources before defining the number of process for a specific work shift.

Understanding Parallel Concurrent Processing (PCP)

Parallel concurrent processing consists of distributing the concurrent manager process on more than one node. Oracle E-Business Suite is a highly scalable environment, and it supports multiple nodes for distributing the workload. PCP also provides high availability of services during the failure of nodes or applications. During failure, the PCP-enabled systems will migrate the processes from the failed application node to the surviving application node.

There is a rumor about PCP that it can be configured only on RAC-enabled systems. But this is a misconception; parallel concurrent processing can be enabled for single database instances with multiple concurrent manager nodes. Earlier in this chapter we explored the GSM architecture, and that architecture is an example of a parallel concurrent processing architecture.

Figure 10-47 shows how PCP works during a node failure. Node1, Node2, and Node3 are active concurrent processing nodes. As discussed earlier, the internal concurrent manager can be started and remain active on only one node, regardless of the number of participating nodes. Here the ICM is running on Node2. When Node1 fails, the concurrent processing services will be migrated from Node1 to Node2, or they can be migrated to any other node based on the load.

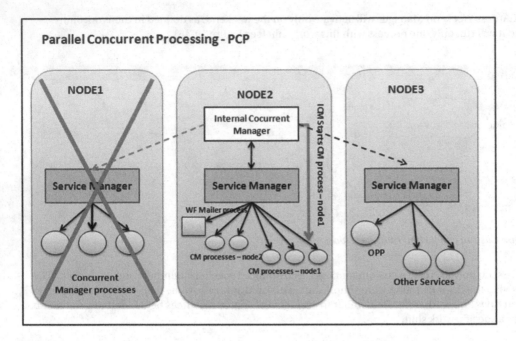

Figure 10-47. Concurrent manager: Parallel concurrent processing - PCP

All concurrent managers will connect to the database using sqlnet for all configuration (PCP and non-PCP). The concurrent manager uses the TWO_TASK (Instance name) value in adcmctl.sh and gmstart.sh on all participating concurrent manager nodes.

When there is node failure, the ICM will try to contact the service manager on the failed node (Node1). When there is communication, the ICM will start concurrent processes of the failed node on any other surviving node. If there is failure of a node where the ICM is running, then the internal monitor process (FNDIMON) spawns a new ICM process. Once the failed node is back in service, then all processes belonging to that node will move back to the primary nodes.

Role of ICM in Parallel Concurrent Processing

The role of ICM in parallel concurrent processing is as follows:

- The ICM is responsible for activating and deactivating the concurrent managers on all active PCP nodes.

- The ICM is responsible for migrating concurrent managers during instance/node failure, and it's also responsible for failback of concurrent managers on actual nodes when it's available.

- The ICM communicates with the service manager (FNDSM) for starting and stopping the concurrent manager processes.

- The ICM communicates with the FNDSM service for starting and stopping of services such as the Workflow mailer, output post processor (OPP), and other services.

- The ICM communicates with the APPS TNS listener on the respective local node and remote concurrent processing node for starting the service manager, and it will not start the service manager if it's unable to communicate with the APPS listener.

Role of Service Manager (FNDSM) in PCP

The role of the service manager is as follows:

- The service manager is the key component of PCP. It is responsible only for communicating with the ICM and PCP, and PCP cannot be configured without the service manager.

- The service manager is started only after successful communication with the APPS TNS listener.

- The service manager uses the gmstart.sh and APPSORA.env files as defined in listener.ora for setting up its environment.

Role of Internal Monitor Process (FNDIMON) in PCP

The role of the internal monitor process is as follows:

- The internal monitor process keeps monitoring the ICM process and will restart the ICM process in case of failures.

- The internal monitors are configured by default by AutoConfig on all participating concurrent manager nodes.

- The internal monitor process should be activated on all nodes where you want the ICM to start in case of failure (by default it will be inactive).

For setting up PCP with RAC in Oracle EBS 12.2, refer to MOS tech note "Configuring and Managing Oracle E-Business Suite Release 12.2.x Forms and Concurrent Processing for Oracle RAC" (Doc ID 2029173.1).

In this section, we will not cover how to set up PCP. But we will list how you can better utilize the PCP setup for distributing the workload. Say that PCP is configured on two nodes. Then by default all managers will run on one node, and the other node will remain idle and will activate managers when a node failure happens. So, in such situation, to utilize the other node, you must distribute the managers across nodes. You can enable standard managers to run on node1 and enable the inventory manager, receiving transaction managers, and so on, on node2.

You can also define a custom manager for distributing the workload across multiple nodes. You should choose the primary node for that custom manager as node2, and you can set up the specialization rule for that manager to exclude it.

Using the CLI for Submitting Concurrent Requests

So far you have seen how you can submit concurrent request using the GUI form. In this section you will see how you can submit a concurrent request from the command line. The question may arise, "Why do we need the CLI for submitting a concurrent request?" The answer is that there are certain situations in which you do not have access to a form-based application. Or you may need to troubleshoot a specific issue at the command line. So, as an apps DBA or technical consultant, you should know how to submit a concurrent request using the command line.

CONCSUB is the utility that you can use at an OS command/shell script for submitting concurrent request from command line.

Here's the syntax:

```
CONCSUB <APPS username>/<APPS password> \
<responsibility application short name> \
<responsibility name> \
<username> \
[WAIT=N|Y|<n seconds>] \
CONCURRENT \
<program application short name> \
<program name> \
[PROGRAM_NAME="<description>"] \
[REPEAT_TIME=<resubmission time>] \
[REPEAT_INTERVAL= <number>] \
[REPEAT_INTERVAL_UNIT=< resubmission unit>] \
[REPEAT_INTERVAL_TYPE=< resubmission type>] \
[REPEAT_END=<resubmission end date and time>] \
[NLS_LANGUAGE=<language of the request>] \
[NLS_TERRITORY=<territory of the request>] \
[START=<date>] \
[IMPLICIT=< type of concurrent request> \
[<parameter 1> … <parameter n>] \
```

```
[applebs@erpnode3 appl_test]$ CONCSUB apps/apps SYSADMIN "System Administrator" SYSADMIN
WAIT=N CONCURRENT FND FNDSCURS
Submitted request 474742 for CONCURRENT FND FNDSCURS
[applebs@erpnode3 appl_test]$
```

The request has been submitted with a unique request ID of 474742, and it will generate the log file and output file in $APPLCSF.

```
[applebs@erpnode3 out]$ pwd
/u01/appl_test/fs_ne/inst/test_erpnode3/logs/appl/conc/out
[applebs@erpnode3 out]$ ls -l *474742*
-rw-r--r-- 1 applebs dbaerp 6253 Feb 27 14:37 o474742.out
```

Troubleshooting Concurrent Manager Issues

As discussed earlier, the concurrent manager is a key component of Oracle E-Business Suite. If there is any problem with it, then it will affect the business transactions. Therefore, it's a primary responsibility of an Oracle apps DBA to ensure all concurrent managers and concurrent programs are working properly.

When there is problem with the concurrent managers, you should address the issue immediately. Proactive monitoring is always recommended for avoiding issues. In this section, we will give the basic troubleshooting steps you should follow for issues related to the concurrent manager.

The first step is to ensure all actual and target processes are the same for the defined concurrent managers.

Figure 10-48 is the concurrent manager's administer form. The Target column shows the defined value of the concurrent manager, and the Actual column shows the actual running processes for that concurrent manager. If there is a difference in the process count between the two columns, then you must investigate the relevant manager log files.

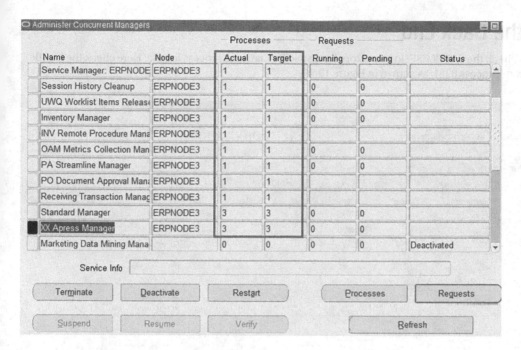

Figure 10-48. Concurrent manager administration

To view the log files, navigate to the following location: System Administrator ➤ Concurrent ➤ Manager ➤ Administer.

Select the respective manager and click Processes.

From the Back End

You should check the $APPLCSF/log directory for a specific manager process log file. Here check the log file for concurrent process 8281, as shown in Figure 10-49.

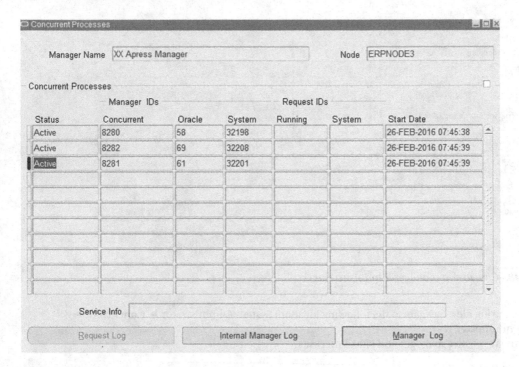

Figure 10-49. *Concurrent manager log files*

Concurrent Manager Process log File

Here's the log file:

```
[applebs@erpnode3 log]$ cd $APPLCSF/log
[applebs@erpnode3 log]$ ls -l *8281*
-rw-r--r-- 1 applebs dbaerp 362 Feb 26 07:45 w8281.mgr
[applebs@erpnode3 log]$ cat w8281.mgr

+-----------------------------------------------------------------------------+
Application Object Library: Concurrent Processing version 12.2

Copyright (c) 1998, 2013, Oracle and/or its affiliates. All rights reserved.

XXAPRESSMGR Concurrent Manager started : 26-FEB-2016 07:45:39

+-----------------------------------------------------------------------------+
[applebs@erpnode3 log]$
```

Internal Manager Log File

You should search for log file starting with the instance name in the same directory as $APPLCFS/log. There are multiple files, so look for the file with the current time stamp.

```
[applebs@erpnode3 ~]$ cd $APPLCSF/log
[applebs@erpnode3 log]$ ls -lrt test_*
-rw-r--r-- 1 applebs dbaerp  74542 Jun  3 2015 test_0212.mgr
-rw-r--r-- 1 applebs dbaerp 307058 Dec 16 15:29 test_0603.mgr
-rw-r--r-- 1 applebs dbaerp  11636 Jan  4 15:12 test_0104.mgr
-rw-r--r-- 1 applebs dbaerp   3501 Jan 18 22:58 test_0118.mgr
-rw-r--r-- 1 applebs dbaerp  61806 Feb 27 15:30 test_0221.mgr
[applebs@erpnode3 log]$
```

This is the internal manager log file, and it records all the information for other concurrent managers.

Using Concurrent Manager Recover Wizard

The Concurrent Manager Recovery Wizard is an Oracle-recommended method for fixing and troubleshooting concurrent manager issues in Oracle E-Business Suite. This wizard is available in the 12.1 release. It is available in the Oracle Application Manager, and it can be executed from the command line too. The following notes are helpful for using the Concurrent Manager Recovery Wizard.

- "Concurrent Processing - Command-Line Utility OR Recovery Wizard" (Doc ID 134007.1)

- "Concurrent Manager Recovery Wizard - Oracle Applications Manager Troubleshooting and Diagnostics" (Doc ID 2130545.1)

This is how you navigate to the Concurrent Manager Recovery Wizard: Oracle Application Manager ➤ Site Map ➤ Diagnostic and Repair ➤ Concurrent Manager Recovery.

Figure 10-50 shows the navigation path for using the Concurrent Manager Recovery Wizard.

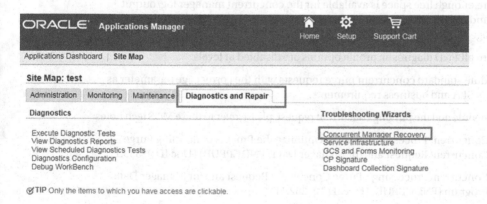

Figure 10-50. *Concurrent manager Recovery Wizard: navigation*

This is the first screen of the Concurrent Manager Recovery Wizard. To start the wizard, click Run Wizard, as shown in Figure 10-51.

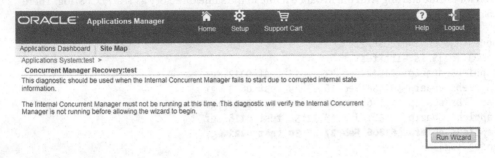

Figure 10-51. *Concurrent manager Recovery Wizard: Run Wizard button*

Problems with Printing Reports

We regularly see problems with printing reports with Oracle E-Business Suite. The reports developed in other NLS languages face issues because of incorrect printer driver, pasta configuration, and environment-related issues. So, you must ensure that all these settings are appropriate based on the NLS languages installed on the system.

The Oracle Support tech note "EBS Reports & Printing Analyzer" (Doc ID 1610143.1) will be helpful for troubleshooting report-printing issues.

Proactive Maintenance

To ensure that the concurrent managers work 24/7, you need to monitor and perform proactive maintenance on Oracle EBS systems.

1. Ensure enough free space is available for the concurrent manager log/output files and also that there is enough space available in the FND_FILE (utl_file package) directory.

2. Ensure all FND diagnostic profile options are disabled at levels.

3. Schedule standard concurrent purge requests with the correct age parameter as per the SLA and business requirements.

    To schedule and the purging concurrent request, please refer to these MOS tech notes:

    - Concurrent Processing - How to Optimize the Process of Running Purge Concurrent Request and/or Manager Data (FNDCPPUR) (Doc ID 92333.1)

    - Concurrent Processing - Purge Concurrent Request and/or Manager Data Program (FNDCPPUR) (Doc ID 104282.1)

4. Ensure there is enough free space available on the database tablespaces, especially APPS_TS_TX_DATA and APPS_TS_TX_IDX.

5. Monitor pending concurrent requests on the respective managers. If the value is increasing for pending requests, then increase the processes for the respective manager. But before increasing the concurrent manager processes, you should evaluate the existing hardware resources. For example, if you have a concurrent node with 12 CPUs, then you can define 10 processes for the concurrent manager. It's always recommended to maintain room for other operations.

These are some of the key areas that you should focus on for troubleshooting and proactively managing the concurrent managers. The following MOS tech notes are specific for release 11i and 12.1, but the information listed in these document is still valid for troubleshooting issues on 12.2.

- "Concurrent Processing - Creating Concurrent Manager Diagnostic and Debug files (troubleshooting)" (Doc ID 1312980.1)

- "Concurrent Processing - Troubleshooting Concurrent Manager Issues (Unix specific)" (Doc ID 104452.1)

Important Concurrent Manager Tables

The concurrent manager uses a database for processing concurrent transactions on the system. Table 10-2 shows the important tables used by the concurrent manager.

Table 10-2. Important Concurrent Manager Tables

Table Name	Description
FND_CONCURRENT_QUEUES	This stores information related to the concurrent manager.
FND_CONCURRENT_PROGRAMS	This stores information related to the concurrent program.
FND_CONCURRENT_REQUESTS	This stores information related to concurrent requests.
FND_CONCURRENT_PROCESSES	This stores information about the concurrent manager OS processes.
FND_CONCURRENT_QUEUE_SIZE	This stores information about the number of requests a manager can process at one time.
FND_EXECUTABLES	This stores information about the concurrent program executables.

Summary

In this chapter, you learned about the different types of concurrent managers and their purpose. You also saw how to use concurrent managers to meet business requirements, including scheduling concurrent requests with specialization rules and work shifts. We also talked about the architecture of GSM and how parallel concurrent processing (PCP) works. Finally, you learned what measures you should take for the proactive maintenance of concurrent managers and presented some generic steps for troubleshooting concurrent manager issues.

CHAPTER 11

■ ■ ■

Cloning Oracle EBS Systems

This chapter briefly introduces the importance of clone environments in business environments running production systems. It covers the detailed procedures of cloning in the Oracle EBS environment for different deployment topologies like single node to multinode, multinode to single node, and RAC to non-RAC.

Introduction to OracleApplication Cloning and Its Purpose

Cloning is the process of creating an identical copy of an existing system. Before we begin with the technical concepts, we'll explain the purpose of cloning. A clone environment is highly recommended if an existing EBS system is in production (live). There are many situations in which you should have a clone environment where you can apply and test changes. You can analyze the impact of these changes on the test environment and later move these changes to the production environments as applicable. This is the general rule followed in the software industry.

The changes could be the installation of new EBS patches for fixing bugs or adding enhancements, new customization, data fixes, and new development activities. These changes cannot be applied directly on production systems, so you must have an identical test environment to test them.

The following are some of the situations in which the cloning process is beneficial:

- Creating an existing copy of the production system

- Upgrading or migrating the operating system

- Migrating the server

- Adding nodes (scalability)

Using Rapid Clone and Its Options

Oracle E-Business Suite ships with the Rapid Clone utility, which is used to create and configure identical clone environments from existing production environments. The Rapid Clone utility simplifies the overall process of cloning an existing E-Business Suite system.

The Rapid Clone utilities are the set of scripts that must be executed on the source and target systems for creating an identical copy of the existing production environment. In Oracle E-Business Suite clone terminology, *source system* refers to the existing system from which you are creating a copy, and *target system* refers to the system on which you are creating and configuring an identical copy.

The Rapid Clone process will not modify any configuration on the source system. The adpreclone.pl script will be used on the source system, and the adcfgclone.pl script will be used on the target system.

© Syed Zaheer and Erman Arslan 2016
S. Zaheer and E. Arslan, *Practical Oracle E-Business Suite*, DOI 10.1007/978-1-4842-1422-0_11

The cloning utilities are delivered by the AD and TKX patches, and every newer version of the AD and TKX patches will have enhancements and bug fixes. Most of the systems in production are using either TKX and AD Delta6 or TKX and AD Delta7. Until Delta6, the process of cloning for the application tier was the same, but starting with Delta7, the dualfs option was introduced; it simplifies the overall application cloning process compared to Delta6.

High-Level Clone Process with AD and TKX Delta6

Follow these steps:

1. Execute adpreclone.pl dbTier and appsTier.

2. Copy the database and application files (run file system) from the source to the target.

3. Configure the database tier on the target server.

4. Configure the application tier on the run edition.

5. Copy the run edition to the patch edition.

6. Configure the application tier patch edition.

High-Level Clone Process with AD and TKX Delta7

Follow these steps:

1. Execute adpreclone.pl dbTier and appsTier.

2. Copy the database and application files (run file system) from the source to the target.

3. Configure the database tier on the target server.

4. Configure the application tier on the run edition with the dualfs option.

When using the dualfs option, you don't have to copy the patch file system from the run file system. Rapid Clone will copy the patch file system and configure both file systems. This chapter covers cloning options with Delta6 and Delta7.

■ **Note** In Delta6 code, the Leveladcfgclone.pl script must be executed twice for configuring the run and patch file systems bin with code. In Delta7 code, you need to execute it only once with the dualfs option.

---

adpreclone.pl Operations

This script will collect the information from the database, read the configuration from the existing configuration files, and create the template files based on the existing configuration. These template files will be used at a later stage for creating a new clone environment on the target server. There will be two scripts of adpreclone.pl: one on the database tier and another on the application tier. This script will prompt for the APPS password on the dbTier, but it doesn't require the APPS password while running on appsTier.

adcfgclone.pl Operations

This script should be executed once after copying the required files from the source system. This script will prompt for various inputs, and these inputs will be used for configuring the target server. This script will use the copied source system template files, and based on these templates, it will prompt for the new values during the execution of the script.

Figures 11-1 and 11-2 illustrate the sequence of steps that the adcfgclone.pl script will perform on the database and application tiers.

Figure 11-1. *Rapid Clone database tier configuration: database tier*

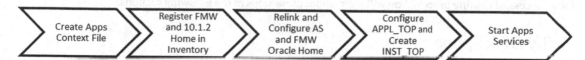

Figure 11-2. *Rapid Clone application tier configuration: application tier*

adpreclone.pl and adcfgclone.pl Options

Table 11-1 describes the options available with the adpreclone.pl script on the database and application tiers.

Table 11-1. *Rapid Clone Script Options*

adpreclone.pl/adcfgclone.pl Options: dbTier	
dbTier	Prepares/configures information for the database and database tech stack
dbTechStack	Prepares/configures information for the database tech stack component only
database	Prepares/configures information associated with the database tech stack
dbconfig	Prepares/configures the database but the database should be created and up and running
addracnode	Scales up the RAC instances
adpreclone.pl/adcfgclone.pl Options: appsTier	
appsTier	Prepares/configures appltop and atTechStack
atTechStack	Prepares/configures dev10gHome and fmwHome and wlsConfig and ohsConfig
dev10gHome	Prepares/configures ORACLE_HOMEs associated with appctx (AS and Forms)
fmwHome	Prepares/configures ORACLE_HOMEs associated with FMW_HOME
wlsConfig	Prepares/configures WebLogic Server domain configuration
ohsConfig	Prepares/configures OHS configuration
appltop	Prepares/configures appltop associated with appctx

These options can be used with the adpreclone.pl, adcfgclone.pl, or adclone.pl script based on your requirements.

Prerequisites for a New Clone Environment

In Chapter 2 you saw the prerequisite steps you should perform before kicking off the Rapidwiz Install Wizard. Failing to perform these prerequisites will eventually make the installation fail. Similarly, Rapid Clone is the utility responsible for configuring the database and application components on the new server that houses the backup of the source system. If any of these prerequisites are not available, the Rapid Clone process will not be able to configure the target system successfully.

■ **Note** The same OS prerequisites should be performed that were performed before the installation.

Prepare the Clone Systems

There are certain prerequisite steps you should perform on the source and target systems that are required for a successful cloning process. You will learn about these steps in the following sections.

Verify Disk Space

Rapid Clone requires additional disk space on the source system, and you have to calculate the disk space of the target system based on the source system utilization.

On the source system, Rapid Clone needs 6GB of free space in the $COMMON_TOP directory to create an archive of the Fusion Middleware Home, and an additional 6GB should be available in the /tmp directory. So, before running the adpreclone.pl script, you must ensure that the listed free space is available in the respective directories.

The target system space should be configured based on the sizing of the source system database and application file system. In addition to the size of the database and application tier file systems, you must ensure that at least 6GB of free space is available in the /tmp directory.

OS Prerequisites

You have to perform all the OS prerequisite steps on the target system, as discussed in Chapter 2. On target environments you have to create the operating system group and users. After this we should ensure the required capacity exists on the file system and we should change permissions and ownership of this file system to the os user with which we are going to execute the clone process.

■ **Tip** If the target system is a TEST/DEV/UAT system, then always use a group and username different from the source system. For example, in production, if the usernames are oraprod and applprod, then on the test system, the users should be oratest and appltest, respectively.

Apply Required Patches

Oracle always recommends that you apply the latest technology patches on source systems. The newest versions of technology patches include the maximum number of bug fixes and deliver the newest enhancements. Technology (AD/TKX) patches are updated regularly in Oracle Support note Doc ID 1583092.1. At the time of writing this book, the latest AD/TKX patches are R12.AD.C.Delta.7 and R12. TXK.C.Delta.7. In addition, you must install the EBS Technology Code Checker (ETCC) patch before installing the latest AD/TKX patches.

> ■ **Note** ETCC patch installation is not required if you have the current EBS version (12.2.2/12.2.3/12.2.4/12.2.5) because this patch will already be installed as part of the upgrade.

Oracle EBS Inventory Requirements

You should create and configure the directory for the new Oracle inventory on the target system. In Chapter 2 you saw how to configure the inventory for EBS installation. Similarly, you should create the new inventory on all target systems. The global inventory files must be configured as discussed in Chapter 2.

The Rapid Clone configuration script will encounter issues if the inventory files are not configured appropriately.

Validate AutoConfig on the Source System

You must ensure that AutoConfig is working fine on both the application and database tiers on the source system. You should also synchronize appsutil on dbTier if it hasn't been executed after applying the latest AD/TKX patches.

> ■ **Tip** If the source system is configured in a multinode environment, then you must ensure that AutoConfig is running fine on all active EBS nodes.

Execute and Maintain Snapshot Information from adadmin

The maintain snapshot information should be executed on each application tier node before executing the adpreclone.pl script. In Chapter 9 we discussed how to execute the maintain snapshot information from adadmin.

Executing the maintain snapshot information for the first time will consume a significant amount of time, but subsequent executions won't take as long. The snapshot information will be maintained by the adpatch and ad utilities at the time of its execution.

> ■ **Note** For detailed information of the Rapid Clone prerequisites, refer to MOS note "Cloning Oracle E-Business Suite Release 12.2 with Rapid Clone" (Doc ID 1383621.1).

Rapid Clone supports multiple configurations for cloning an Oracle E-Business Suite system. The following list illustrates the cloning options available with Rapid Clone. We will use the Delta6 code level for most of our demonstrations and will use the Delta7 code level for a single-node to multinode clone.

- Single-node to single-node clone
- Single-node to multinode clone
- Multinode to single-node clone using online backup
- Cloning in a RAC environment

Cloning from a Single Node to a Single Node

The phrase *single node to single node* clearly indicates that all EBS service components running on one server will be configured on another server for creating an identical copy that will be used for testing. In Chapter 2 you saw different types of installations supported by Rapidwiz such as single-node installations and multinode installations. In a single-node configuration, all database and application services will be configured on the same server, whereas in a multinode installation, the database and application services can be distributed based on the workload and security requirements. Usually, in most organizations the databases will be in a more protected network zone compared to the internal/external application servers. In this section, you will see how to create an identical copy of Oracle EBS 12.2 running on one server onto another server.

Starting with Oracle EBS 12.2, the cloning process is quite different for the application tier because of the introduction of the dual file system, and the dbTier cloning process is the same as earlier releases with some enhancements. On the application tier you need to execute adcfgclone.pl twice. First it should be executed on the run file system, and after successful execution on the run file system, you should execute it on the patch file system.

Steps of Rapid Clone EBS 12.2 on the Source and Target Systems

Follow these steps:

1. Execute adpreclone.pl on the dbTier source system.

2. Execute adpreclone.pl on the appsTier source system.

3. Copy dbTier from the source system to the target system.

4. Copy the apps Tier (run edition) file system to the target system.

5. Execute the adcfgclone.pl dbTier on the target system.

6. Execute the adcfgclone.pl appsTier on the target system (run edition).

7. Copy the run edition file system to the patch edition file system.

8. Execute adcfgclone.pl on the patch edition file system.

Figure 11-3 illustrates the complete process of a single to single-node clone; it includes the steps that need to be executed on the source system and the steps that need to be executed on the target system.

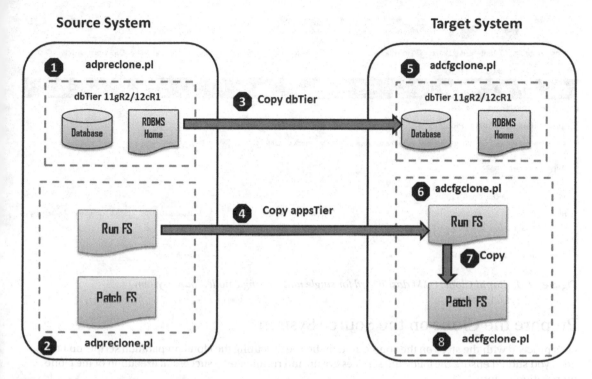

Figure 11-3. *Rapid Clone: single-node to single-node clone process*

Environment Details

Table 11-2 displays the example environment and lists the information of the source and target systems for a single-node to single-node clone process. Figure 11-4 shows the Rapid Clone OAM dashboard for a single-node to single-node process on the source system.

Table 11-2. *Rapid Clone Single-Node to Single-Node Environment Details*

	Source System	Target System
Host name	ERPNODE3	ERPTEST1
Instance name	PROD	TEST
Location of dbTier	/u01/ora_prod	/d01/ora_test
Location of appsTier	/u01/appl_prod	/d01/appl_test
OS users/group	applebs, oraebs	appltest, oratest
OS version	OEL 5.7, 64-bit	OEL 5.7, 64-bit
DB version	12.1.0.2	12.1.0.2
Apps version	12.2.4	12.2.4

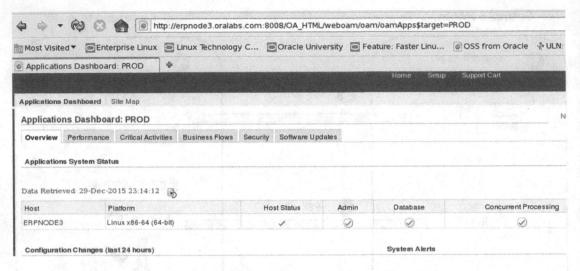

Figure 11-4. *Rapid Clone: OAM dashboard for single node to single node, source system*

Prepare the Clone on the Source System

Let's proceed with the steps on the source system. Before executing the clone preparation scripts on both tiers, you should ensure the following services are up and running for a successful execution of the clone preparation script:

- The database should be running in open mode.
- The database listener must be running.
- The WebLogic admin server should be up and running.
- There should be no active patching cycle (adop).

Execute the Clone Preparation Script on the Database Tier (dbTier)

Follow these steps:

1. Log in to the system as an Oracle database owned user.
2. Source the dbTier environment file.
3. Navigate to the clone preparation script.
4. Execute the clone preparation script.

```
[oraebs@erpnode3 PROD_erpnode3]$ perl adpreclone.pl dbTier
Copyright (c) 2011, 2014 Oracle Corporation
Redwood Shores, California, USA
Oracle E-Business Suite Rapid Clone
Version 12.2
adpreclone Version 120.31.12020000.16
Enter the APPS User Password:
```

```
Running:
perl /u01/ora_prod/12.1.0.2/appsutil/bin/adclone.pl java=/u01/ora_prod/12.1.0.2/appsutil/
jre mode=stage stage=/u01/ora_prod/12.1.0.2/appsutil/clone component=dbTier method=CUSTOM
dbctx=/u01/ora_prod/12.1.0.2/appsutil/PROD_erpnode3.xml showProgress
Beginning database tier Stage - Tue Dec 29 23:38:05 2015
----------
---------
APPS Password :
Log file located at /u01/ora_prod/12.1.0.2/appsutil/log/PROD_erpnode3/StageDBTier_12292338.
log\ 50% completed
Completed Stage...
Tue Dec 29 23:38:48 2015
[oraebs@erpnode3 PROD_erpnode3]$
```

Execute the Clone Preparation Script on the Application Tier (appsTier)

The steps are similar for executing the clone preparation script on the application tier.

1. Log in to the system with the application tier owned user.

2. Source the run edition environment file.

3. Navigate to the clone preparation script.

4. Execute the clone preparation script.

```
[applebs@erpnode3 scripts]$ adpreclone.pl appsTier

Copyright (c) 2011, 2014 Oracle Corporation
Redwood Shores, California, USA

Oracle E-Business Suite Rapid Clone

Version 12.2

adpreclone Version 120.31.12020000.16

Enter the APPS User Password:
Enter the Weblogic AdminServer password :

Checking the status of the Oracle WebLogic Administration Server....
Running perl /u01/appl_prod/fs1/EBSapps/appl/ad/12.0.0/patch/115/bin/adProvisionEBS.pl
ebs-get-serverstatus -contextfile=/u01/appl_prod/fs1/inst/apps/PROD_erpnode3/appl/admin/
PROD_erpnode3.xml -servername=AdminServer -promptmsg=hide
The Oracle WebLogic Administration Server is up.
Running:

perl /u01/appl_prod/fs1/EBSapps/appl/ad/12.0.0/bin/adclone.pl java=/u01/appl_prod/
fs1/EBSapps/comn/util/jdk64 mode=stage stage=/u01/appl_prod/fs1/EBSapps/comn/clone
component=appsTier method= appctx=/u01/appl_prod/fs1/inst/apps/PROD

_erpnode3/appl/admin/PROD_erpnode3.xml showProgress

Setting the wls environment
```

```
Beginning application tier Stage - Tue Dec 29 23:57:09 2015

Log file located at /u01/appl_prod/fs1/inst/apps/PROD_erpnode3/admin/log/clone/
StageAppsTier_12292357.log

/ 20% completed

Completed Stage...
Wed Dec 30 00:18:11 2015
[applebs@erpnode3 scripts]$
```

The preparation of clone scripts on the source system completed successfully. Now you are ready to copy the source database tier and application tier file system on the target machine.

You will use the cold backup of the application and database tiers. Once the clone preparation scripts are completed, you should shut down the database and application tier services and copy the required file systems to the target machine, as shown in Figure 11-3.

Stop Application Tier Services

Follow these steps:

1. Log in as the OS application user.

2. Source the run edition file system environment variable.

3. Navigate to the application control script's location.

4. Stop the application tier services.

```
[applebs@erpnode3 scripts]$ adstpall.sh apps/apps

You are running adstpall.sh version 120.22.12020000.7

Enter the WebLogic Server password:
The logfile for this session is located at /u01/appl_prod/fs1/inst/apps/PROD_erpnode3/logs/
appl/admin/log/adstpall.log
```

Stop Database Tier Services

Follow these steps:

1. Log in as the OS database user owner.

2. Source the database environment file.

3. Shut down the database listener.

4. Shut down the database.

```
[oraebs@erpnode3 PROD_erpnode3]$ lsnrctl stop PROD

LSNRCTL for Linux: Version 12.1.0.2.0 - Production on 30-DEC-2015 00:24:42

Copyright (c) 1991, 2014, Oracle.All rights reserved.

Connecting to (DESCRIPTION=(ADDRESS=(PROTOCOL=TCP)(HOST=erpnode3.oralabs.com)(PORT=1529)))
The command completed successfully
[oraebs@erpnode3 PROD_erpnode3]$ sqlplus / as sysdba

SQL*Plus: Release 12.1.0.2.0 Production on Wed Dec 30 00:24:48 2015

Copyright (c) 1982, 2014, Oracle.All rights reserved.

Connected to:
Oracle Database 12c Enterprise Edition Release 12.1.0.2.0 - 64bit Production
With the Partitioning, OLAP, Advanced Analytics and Real Application Testing options

SQL> shut immediate;
Database closed.
Database dismounted.
ORACLE instance shut down.
SQL>
```

After stopping the database and application services, you are ready to move the source application and database tier files on the target system. In most enterprise organizations, different backup technologies will be used for backup/restore operations. These backups are performed on tape drives and can be restored on target servers as required. The backup on tape media is cheaper compared to disk and easy to manage. If there is no centralized backup in the organization, then you will end up utilizing the operating system– and application-provided backup tools. In this section, you will use simple tar commands for backing up both the database and application file systems, and you can copy these backed-up files to the target server using sftp/ftp/scp or other OS-supported utilities. Later in the chapter you will see how to use rman database backup for cloning applications online.

Configure the Clone on the Target System

As discussed earlier, the configuration utility for cloning on a target system is the adcfgclone.pl script, and it must be executed on all the database and application tiers based on the target system topology. In the current scenario, the target system is a single node; hence, all application and database services will be configured on a single server. Table 11-1 displays the location of the source directories that are required to be copied on the target server.

For the database you should copy the RDBMS Oracle Home and all the database files (control files, redolog files, data files), and for the application tier, you must copy only the run edition file system.

You have to create users/groups and change ownership of the target system directories.

The adfcgclone.pl -clone configuration script requests some inputs during its execution in order to configure the target system. The script inputs will be different on the database tier and application tier. Table 11-3 lists the prompts required while executing adcfgclone.pl on the database tier, and Table 11-4 lists the prompts required while executing adcfgclone.plon the application tier.

Table 11-3. Rapid Clone Configuration: Database Tier Prompts

Prompt	Description
Target System Hostname (virtual or normal)	Provide the host name of the target system.
Target Instance is RAC (y/n) [n]	By default the value is no; if the target system is RAC, then you should select yes.
Target System Database SID	Provide the target system SID for the new clone environment.
Target System Base Directory	Base location of Oracle RDBMS Home.
Target System utl_file_dir Directory List	Location of configure utl_file_dir.
Number of DATA_TOPs on the Target System	Based on the location of data files, this value should be provided. If data files are stored on two different locations from source system, then you should provide two.
Target System DATA_TOP Directory	Location of the data file directories.
Target System RDBMS ORACLE_HOME Directory	Location of the RDBMS Home.
Target System Display	By default, this will select the source system display; you should select the correct display variable for target system.
Do you want the target system to have the same port values as the source system (y/n)	By default this will be yes; usually we will choose some other ports for target system.
Target System Port Pool [0-99]	The port number for database listener should be provided (and the port should be free).

Table 11-4. Rapid Clone Configuration: Application Tier Prompts

Prompt	Description
Do you want to add a node (yes/no) [no]	This option can be used while adding nodes (scalingout).
Target System File Edition type [run] :	By default this will show the run edition; you should provide the appropriate value based on the file system type (run/patch).
Target System Hostname (virtual or normal)	Host name of the target system.
Target System Database SID	Target system database SID.
Target System Database Server Node	Target system database server host name.
Target System Database Domain Name	Target system database domain name (usually the same: DB and Apps).
Target System Base Directory	Location of target system's application base directory.

(contineud)

Table 11-4. (*continued*)

Prompt	Description
Target System Instance Home Directory	Location of target system's application INST_TOP directory.
Do you want to preserve the Display	Display variable.
Target System Display	By default this will select the source system display; you should select the correct display variable for target system.
Target System Root Service [enabled] **Target System Web Administration [enabled]** **Target System Web Entry Point Services [enabled]** **Target System Web Application Services [enabled]** **Target System Batch Processing Services [enabled]** **Target System Other Services [disabled]**	By default this will be enabled, but you should choose the group of services that you want to enable on the target node.
Do you want the target system to have the same port values as the source system (y/n) [y]	By default this will be yes; usually you will choose some other ports for target system.
Target System Port Pool [0-99]	You should provide the free port that you want to configure for the application.
Choose a value which will be set as APPLPTMP value on the target node [1]	This will list all the configured directories in the database, but you should select the appropriate directory based on the target system configuration.
Enter the full path of Run File System Context file	Once you set the file system type to patch, this will prompt you for the configured context file from the run edition.

Create a Group and Users on the Target System

As listed in Table 11-1, the target system dbatest is the group in this example, and the users are oratest and appltest for the database and application tier file systems.

```
[root@erptest1 ~]# groupadd dbatest
[root@erptest1 ~]# useradd -g dbatest oratest
[root@erptest1 ~]# useradd -g dbatest appltest
[root@erptest1 ~]# passwd oratest
Changing password for user oratest.
New UNIX password:
BAD PASSWORD: it is based on a dictionary word
Retype new UNIX password:
passwd: all authentication tokens updated successfully.
[root@erptest1 ~]# passwd appltest
Changing password for user appltest.
New UNIX password:
BAD PASSWORD: it is based on a dictionary word
Retype new UNIX password:
passwd: all authentication tokens updated successfully.
[root@erptest1 ~]#
```

Change Ownership of the Target System Directories

Change the ownership of the target system directories to the users and group respective to the database and application tier users.

```
[root@erptest1 d01]# ls -ld *_test
drwxrwxr-x5 applebs dbaerp 4096 Dec 30 00:07 appl_test
drwxrwxr-x 11 oraebsdbaerp 4096 Feb 102015 ora_test
[root@erptest1 d01]# chown -R oratest:dbatest /d01/ora_test
[root@erptest1 d01]# chown -R appltest:dbatest /d01/appl_test
[root@erptest1 d01]# ls -ld *_test
drwxrwxr-x5 appltest dbatest 4096 Dec 30 00:07 appl_test
drwxrwxr-x 11 oratestdbatest 4096 Feb 102015 ora_test
[root@erptest1 d01]#
```

Configure the inventory on the target system.

The Rapid Clone process requires the central inventory, so you should create the central inventory file before executing the clone configuration scripts.

```
[root@erptest1 ~]# mkdir -p /d01/oracle/oraInventory
[root@erptest1 ~]# chmod -R 777 /d01/oracle/oraInventory
[root@erptest1 ~]#
[root@erptest1 data]# cat /etc/oraInst.loc
inventory_loc=/d01/oracle/oraInventory
[root@erptest1 data]#
```

Execute the Clone Configuration Script on the Database Tier on the Target System

Here is the script:

```
[oratest@erptest1 bin]$ perl adcfgclone.pl dbTier

Copyright (c) 2011 Oracle Corporation
Redwood Shores, California, USA

Oracle E-Business Suite Rapid Clone

Version 12.2

adcfgclone Version 120.63.12020000.37

Enter the APPS password :

Running:
```

Log file located at /d01/ora_test/12.1.0.2/appsutil/clone/bin/CloneContext_1230195552.log

Provide the values required for creation of the new Database Context file.

```
Target System Hostname (virtual or normal) [erptest1] :

Target Instance is RAC (y/n) [n] :

Target System Database SID : TEST

Target System Base Directory : /d01/ora_test

Target System utl_file_dir Directory List : /usr/tmp

Number of DATA_TOP's on the Target System [1] :

Target System DATA_TOP Directory 1 [/d01/ora_test/data] :

Target System RDBMS ORACLE_HOME Directory [/d01/ora_test/12.1.0] : /d01/ora_test/12.1.0.2

Do you want to preserve the Display [:0.0] (y/n): n

Target System Display [erptest1:0.0] :

Do you want the target system to have the same port values as the source system (y/n) [y] ? : n

Target System Port Pool [0-99] : 6

Checking the port pool 6
done: Port Pool 6 is free
Report file located at /d01/ora_test/12.1.0.2/appsutil/temp/portpool.lst
Complete port information available at /d01/ora_test/12.1.0.2/appsutil/temp/portpool.lst

Creating the new Database Context file from :
/d01/ora_test/12.1.0.2/appsutil/clone/context/db/adxdbctx.tmp

The new database context file has been created :
/d01/ora_test/12.1.0.2/appsutil/TEST_erptest1.xml

Log file located at /d01/ora_test/12.1.0.2/appsutil/clone/bin/CloneContext_1230195552.log
Check Clone Context logfile /d01/ora_test/12.1.0.2/appsutil/clone/bin/
CloneContext_1230195552.log for details.

Running Rapid Clone with command:
Running:
perl /d01/ora_test/12.1.0.2/appsutil/clone/bin/adclone.pl java=/d01/ora_test/12.1.0.2/
appsutil/clone/bin/../jre mode=apply stage=/d01/ora_test/12.1.0.2/appsutil/clone
component=dbTier method=CUSTOM dbctxtg=/d01/ora_test/12.1.0.2/appsutil/TEST_erptest1.xml
showProgress contextValidated=true

Beginning database tier Apply - Wed Dec 30 19:57:23 2015

.........................................
.........................................
|0% completed Determining Source system database type ("single" or "rac").
```

```
Source system indentified as being of type "single"!
- 15% completed

Completed Apply...
Wed Dec 30 20:14:32 2015

Starting database listener for TEST:
Running:
/d01/ora_test/12.1.0.2/appsutil/scripts/TEST_erptest1/addlnctl.sh start TEST
Logfile: /d01/ora_test/12.1.0.2/appsutil/log/TEST_erptest1/addlnctl.txt

You are running addlnctl.sh version 120.4

Starting listener process TEST ...

Listener TEST has already been started.

addlnctl.sh: exiting with status 0

addlnctl.sh: check the logfile /d01/ora_test/12.1.0.2/appsutil/log/TEST_erptest1/addlnctl.
txt for more information ...

Do you want to change the password for all EBS Schemas? (y/n) [n]) :

Do you want to change the apps password? (y/n) [n]) :

Do you want to change the sys and system passwords? (y/n) [n]) :
[oratest@erptest1 bin]$
```

The password for users and EBS schemas such as APPS, SYS, and SYSTEM can be changed while configuring the database tier on the target system. This is a new feature introduced in 12.2 Rapid Clone. But in this demonstration, none of the passwords has been changed during clone configuration; you will see this option in the next scenario (a single-node to multinode clone).

So, the configuration of the database tier completed successfully. You should connect to the database and verify all the components were configured properly. Also, you should verify the database listener is configured properly and you are able to make a connection using the service name.

Execute the Clone Configuration Script on the Application Tier on the Target System

This is for the run edition:

```
[appltest@erptest1 bin]$ perl adcfgclone.pl appsTier

Copyright (c) 2011 Oracle Corporation
Redwood Shores, California, USA

Oracle E-Business Suite Rapid Clone

Version 12.2

adcfgclone Version 120.63.12020000.37
```

```
Enter the APPS password :
Running:
/d01/appl_test/fs1/EBSapps/comn/clone/bin/../jre/bin/java -Xmx600M -classpath /d01/appl_
test/fs1/EBSapps/comn/clone/jlib/obfuscatepassword.jar:/d01/appl_test/fs1/EBSapps/comn/
clone/jlib/ojmisc.jar:/d01/appl_test/fs1/EBSapps/comn/clone/jlib/java:/d01/appl_test/fs1/
EBSapps/comn/clone/jlib/emCfg.jar oracle.apps.ad.clone.util.OPWrapper -encryptpwd /d01/
appl_test/fs1/EBSapps/comn/clone/bin/../FMW/tempinfoApps.txt

Enter the Weblogic AdminServer password :

Do you want to add a node (yes/no) [no] :

Running:

Log file located at /d01/appl_test/fs1/EBSapps/comn/clone/bin/CloneContext_1230202552.log

Target System File Edition type [run] :

Provide the values required for creation of the new APPL_TOP Context file.

Target System Hostname (virtual or normal) [erptest1] :

Target System Database SID : TEST

Target System Database Server Node [erptest1] :

Target System Database Domain Name [oralabs.com] :

Target System Base Directory : /d01/appl_test/

Target System Base Directory set to /d01/appl_test

Target System Current File System Base set to /d01/appl_test/fs1

Target System Other File System Base set to /d01/appl_test/fs2

Target System Fusion Middleware Home set to /d01/appl_test/fs1/FMW_Home

Target System Web Oracle Home set to /d01/appl_test/fs1/FMW_Home/webtier

Target System Appl TOP set to /d01/appl_test/fs1/EBSapps/appl
Target System COMMON TOP set to /d01/appl_test/fs1/EBSapps/comn

Target System Instance Home Directory [/d01/appl_test] :

Target System Instance Top set to /d01/appl_test/fs1/inst/apps/TEST_erptest1

Do you want to preserve the Display [erpnode3:0.0] (y/n): n
```

Target System Display [erptest1:0.0] :

Target System Root Service [enabled] :

Target System Web Administration [enabled] :

Target System Web Entry Point Services [enabled] :

Target System Web Application Services [enabled] :

Target System Batch Processing Services [enabled] :

Target System Other Services [disabled] :

Do you want the target system to have the same port values as the source system (y/n) [y] ? : n

Target System Port Pool [0-99] : 6

Checking the port pool 6
done: Port Pool 6 is free
Report file located at /d01/appl_test/fs1/inst/apps/TEST_erptest1/admin/out/portpool.lst
Complete port information available at /d01/appl_test/fs1/inst/apps/TEST_erptest1/admin/out/
portpool.lst

UTL_FILE_DIR on database tier consists of the following directories.

1. /usr/tmp
2. /usr/tmp
3. /d01/ora_test/12.1.0.2/appsutil/outbound/TEST_erptest1
4. /usr/tmp
Choose a value which will be set as APPLPTMP value on the target node [1] : 3

Creating the new APPL_TOP Context file from :
/d01/appl_test/fs1/EBSapps/comn/clone/context/apps/adxmlctx.tmp

The new APPL_TOP context file has been created :
/d01/appl_test/fs1/inst/apps/TEST_erptest1/appl/admin/TEST_erptest1.xml

Beginning application tier Apply - Wed Dec 30 20:27:28 2015

/d01/appl_test/fs1/EBSapps/comn/clone/bin/../jre/bin/java -Xmx600M -DCONTEXT_VALIDATED=true
-Doracle.installer.oui_loc=/oui -classpath /d01/appl_test/fs1/EBSapps/comn/clone/jlib/
xmlparserv2.jar:/d01/appl_test/fs1/EBSapps/comn/clone/jlib/ojdbc6.jar:Log file located at /
d01/appl_test/fs1/inst/apps/TEST_erptest1/admin/log/clone/ApplyAppsTier_12302027.log
|100% completed

Completed Apply...
Wed Dec 30 21:00:12 2015

Executing command: /d01/appl_test/fs1/EBSapps/10.1.2/bin/sqlplus @/d01/appl_test/fs1/
EBSapps/appl/ad/12.0.0/patch/115/sql/truncate_ad_nodes_config_status.sql

```
Do you want to startup the Application Services for TEST? (y/n) [n] :

Services not started

[appltest@erptest1 bin]$
```

As discussed earlier, you have to execute adcfgclone.pl twice on the application tier—first on the run file system and then on the patch file system. The patch file system should be configured only after the successful completion of the run file system. Now that you have seen the adcfgclone.pl script complete successfully on the run file system, you can proceed with the configuration of the patch file system.

As mentioned, we copied only the run edition file system from the source system and executed the clone configuration script on the run edition. After successful completion of the clone on the run edition, then you should copy the run file system to the patch file system.

```
[appltest@erptest1 appl_test]$ cp -pr fs1 fs2 &
[1] 5207
[appltest@erptest1 appl_test]$ jobs
[1]+Donecp -pr fs1 fs2
[appltest@erptest1 appl_test]$
```

This is for the patch edition:

```
[appltest@erptest1 bin]$ perl adcfgclone.pl appsTier

 Copyright (c) 2011 Oracle Corporation
Redwood Shores, California, USA

Oracle E-Business Suite Rapid Clone

Version 12.2

adcfgclone Version 120.63.12020000.37

Enter the APPS password :
Running:
/d01/appl_test/fs2/EBSapps/comn/clone/bin/../jre/bin/java -Xmx600M -classpath /d01/appl_
test/fs2/EBSapps/comn/clone/jlib/obfuscatepassword.jar:/d01/appl_test/fs2/EBSapps/comn/
clone/jlib/ojmisc.jar:/d01/appl_test/fs2/EBSapps/comn/clone/jlib/java:/d01/appl_test/fs2/
EBSapps/comn/clone/jlib/emCfg.jar oracle.apps.ad.clone.util.OPWrapper -encryptpwd /d01/
appl_test/fs2/EBSapps/comn/clone/bin/../FMW/tempinfoApps.txt

Enter the Weblogic AdminServer password :
Running:

Do you want to add a node (yes/no) [no] :

Running:

Log file located at /d01/appl_test/fs2/EBSapps/comn/clone/bin/CloneContext_1230233845.log

Target System File Edition type [run] : patch
```

Enter the full path of Run File System Context file : /d01/appl_test/fs1/inst/apps/TEST_
erptest1/appl/admin/TEST_erptest1.xml

Provide the values required for creation of the new APPL_TOP Context file.

Target System Fusion Middleware Home set to /d01/appl_test/fs2/FMW_Home

Target System Web Oracle Home set to /d01/appl_test/fs2/FMW_Home/webtier

Target System Appl TOP set to /d01/appl_test/fs2/EBSapps/appl

Target System COMMON TOP set to /d01/appl_test/fs2/EBSapps/comn

RC-00217: Warning: Configuration home directory (s_config_home) evaluates to /d01/appl_test/
fs2/inst/apps/TEST_erptest1. A directory with this name already exists and is not empty.

Do you want to continue (y/n) : y

Target System Instance Top set to /d01/appl_test/fs2/inst/apps/TEST_erptest1

Target System Port Pool [0-99] : 7

Checking the port pool 7
done: Port Pool 7 is free
Report file located at /d01/appl_test/fs2/inst/apps/TEST_erptest1/temp/portpool.lst
Complete port information available at /d01/appl_test/fs2/inst/apps/TEST_erptest1/temp/
portpool.lst

UTL_FILE_DIR on database tier consists of the following directories.

1. /usr/tmp
2. /usr/tmp
3. /d01/ora_test/12.1.0.2/appsutil/outbound/TEST_erptest1
4. /usr/tmp
Choose a value which will be set as APPLPTMP value on the target node [1] : 3

Backing up /d01/appl_test/fs2/inst/apps/TEST_erptest1/appl/admin/TEST_erptest1.xml to /d01/
appl_test/fs2/inst/apps/TEST_erptest1/appl/admin/TEST_erptest1.xml.bak

Creating the new APPL_TOP Context file from :
/d01/appl_test/fs2/EBSapps/comn/clone/context/apps/adxmlctx.tmp

The new APPL_TOP context file has been created :
/d01/appl_test/fs2/inst/apps/TEST_erptest1/appl/admin/TEST_erptest1.xml

Log file located at /d01/appl_test/fs2/EBSapps/comn/clone/bin/CloneContext_1230233845.log
Check Clone Context logfile /d01/appl_test/fs2/EBSapps/comn/clone/bin/
CloneContext_1230233845.log for details.

Running Rapid Clone with command:
Running:

```
perl /d01/appl_test/fs2/EBSapps/comn/clone/bin/adclone.pl java=/d01/appl_test/fs2/
EBSapps/comn/clone/bin/../jre mode=apply stage=/d01/appl_test/fs2/EBSapps/comn/clone
component=appsTier method=CUSTOM appctxtg=/d01/appl_test/fs2/inst/apps/TEST_erptest1/appl/
admin/TEST_erptest1.xml showProgress contextValidated=true

FMW Pre-requisite check log file location : /d01/appl_test/fs2/EBSapps/comn/clone/FMW/logs/
prereqcheck.log
 /d01/appl_test/fs2/EBSapps/comn/clone -log /d01/appl_test/fs2/EBSapps/comn/clone/FMW/logs/
prereqcheck.log

Beginning application tier Apply - Wed Dec 30 23:40:36 2015

/d01/appl_test/fs2/EBSapps/comn/clone/bin/../jre/bin/java -Xmx600M -DCONTEXT_VALIDATED=true
-Doracle.installer.oui_loc=/oui -classpath Log file located at /d01/appl_test/fs2/inst/apps/
TEST_erptest1/admin/log/clone/ApplyAppsTier_12302340.log
-100% completed 1

Completed Apply...
Thu Dec 31 00:11:07 2015

Looking for incomplete CLONE record in ad_adop_session_patches table

The CLONE record status is no rows selected
[appltest@erptest1 bin]$ l
```

The adcfgclone.pl script on the patch file system will prompt for the location of the context file from the run edition; it will also prompt for the target file system port pool number. You should provide a different number from the source system.

Figure 11-5 shows the OAM dashboard of the recently configured EBS cloned system.

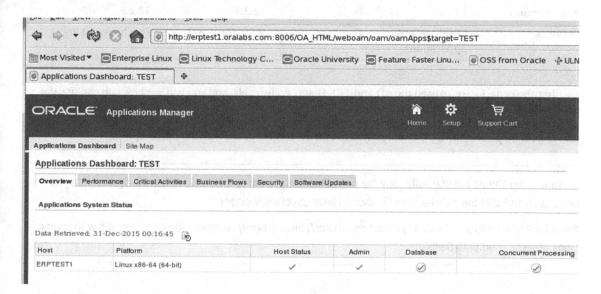

Figure 11-5. *Rapid Clone: OAM dashboard, single node to single node (target system)*

After completion of the script adfcgclone.pl on the application tier's patch edition, you know the cloning completed successfully. But you still need to perform the post-cloning steps on the configured target system. In this chapter, we are demonstrating different cloning scenarios, and after every clone execution, there must be some post-cloning tasks performed before releasing the system for development use. All these post-cloning tasks are demonstrated later in this chapter.

Cloning from a Single Node to a Multinode

In an earlier section, you saw how you can clone the E-Business Suite system from a single node to a single node. In this section, you will see how you can clone the E-Business Suite system from a single node to a multinode environment. Table 11-5 lists the example environment that will be used for demonstrating the single-node to multinode clone. Figure 11-5 displays the dashboard of the source system.

Table 11-5. *Rapid Clone: Single-Node to Multinode Clone Environment Details*

	Source System	Target System		
		DB Node	Primary App Node	Secondary App Node
Host name	ERPNODE3	ERPDB1	ERPAPP1	ERPAPP2
Instance name	TEST	EBSPROD	EBSPROD	EBSPROD
Location of dbTier	/d01/ora_test	/u01/appl_EBS		
Location of appsTier	/d01/appl_test		/u01/appl_EBS	/u01/appl_EBS
OS users/group	appltest, oratest	oracle	applmgr	applmgr
OS version	OEL 5.7: 64-bit	OEL7.2: 64-bit	OEL 7.2: 64-bit	OEL7.2: 64-bit
DB version	12.1.0.2	12.1.0.2		
Apps version	12.2.5		12.2.5	12.2.5
Services	Database and applications	Database	Root, form, web	Batch processing

In this scenario, we've used the AD and TKX Delta7 code levels, and you will see how you can use the dualfs option for configuring the target system. Some notable enhancements introduced with Delta7 are the OS prerequisite checks that take place before configuring the clone. Figure 11-4 explains the detailed steps that should be performed on the source system and the target system with the dualfs option.

■ **Note** You should not manually copy the run edition file system to the patch edition file system. You just need to ensure that the patch edition file system base directory is empty.

It's not mandatory to use the dualfs option with Delta7, but it's highly recommended. You can follow the same clone process used until Delta6.

Execute the Clone Preparation Script on the Source System

We have already discussed in detail the process of preparing the clone. You have to ensure that all listed clone preparation tasks have been performed before proceeding with the adpreclone.pl script on both the database and application tier file systems.

You've already seen the execution of the clone preparation script for both the database and applications.

After successful execution of the adpreclon.pl script on both the database and application tiers, you are now ready to copy the files from the source system to the target system. The database and application files should be copied, and the clone configuration scripts should be executed in the same sequence as listed in Figure 11-4.

Execute the Clone Configuration Scripts on the Database and Application Tiers

As per the procedure, you have to configure the database tier first. You need to ensure that all files are copied/restored on the target system successfully.

Here is adcfgclone.pl executing on dbTier:

Script Location: $ORACLE_HOME/appsutil/clone/bin

```
[oracle@erpdb1 bin]$ perl adcfgclone.pl dbTier

Copyright (c) 2011 Oracle Corporation
Redwood Shores, California, USA

Oracle E-Business Suite Rapid Clone

Version 12.2

adcfgclone Version 120.63.12020000.37

Enter the APPS password :

Running:
/
Log file located at /u01/ora_EBS/12.1.0.2/appsutil/clone/bin/CloneContext_0103001614.log

Provide the values required for creation of the new Database Context file.

Target System Hostname (virtual or normal) [erpdb1] :

Target Instance is RAC (y/n) [n] :

Target System Database SID : EBSPROD

Target System Base Directory : /u01/ora_EBS

Target System utl_file_dir Directory List : /usr/tmp
```

```
Number of DATA_TOP's on the Target System [1] :

Target System DATA_TOP Directory 1 [/u01/ora_EBS/data] :

Target System RDBMS ORACLE_HOME Directory [/u01/ora_EBS/12.1.0] : /u01/ora_EBS/12.1.0.2

Do you want to preserve the Display [erptest1:0.0] (y/n): n

Target System Display [erpdb1:0.0] :

Do you want the target system to have the same port values as the source system (y/n) [y] ? : n

Target System Port Pool [0-99] : 3

Checking the port pool 3
done: Port Pool 3 is free
Report file located at /u01/ora_EBS/12.1.0.2/appsutil/temp/portpool.lst
Complete port information available at /u01/ora_EBS/12.1.0.2/appsutil/temp/portpool.lst

Creating the new Database Context file from :
/u01/ora_EBS/12.1.0.2/appsutil/clone/context/db/adxdbctx.tmp

The new database context file has been created :
/u01/ora_EBS/12.1.0.2/appsutil/EBSPROD_erpdb1.xml

Log file located at /u01/ora_EBS/12.1.0.2/appsutil/clone/bin/CloneContext_0103001614.log
Check Clone Context logfile /u01/ora_EBS/12.1.0.2/appsutil/clone/bin/
CloneContext_0103001614.log for details.

Running Rapid Clone with command:
Running:
perl /u01/ora_EBS/12.1.0.2/appsutil/clone/bin/adclone.pl java=/u01/ora_EBS/12.1.0.2/
appsutil/clone/bin/../jre mode=apply stage=/u01/ora_EBS/12.1.0.2/appsutil/clone
component=dbTier method=CUSTOM dbctxtg=/u01/ora_EBS/12.1.0.2/appsutil/EBSPROD_erpdb1.xml
showProgress contextValidated=true

Beginning database tier Apply - Sun Jan3 00:17:04 2016

APPS Password : Log file located at /u01/ora_EBS/12.1.0.2/appsutil/log/EBSPROD_erpdb1/
ApplyDBTier_01030017.log
|0% completed Determining Source system database type ("single" or "rac").
Source system indentified as being of type "single"!
- 15% completed

Completed Apply...
Sun Jan3 00:30:14 2016
```

```
Starting database listener for EBSPROD:
Running:
/u01/ora_EBS/12.1.0.2/appsutil/scripts/EBSPROD_erpdb1/addlnctl.sh start EBSPROD
Logfile: /u01/ora_EBS/12.1.0.2/appsutil/log/EBSPROD_erpdb1/addlnctl.txt
```

You are running addlnctl.sh version 120.4

Starting listener process EBSPROD ...

Listener EBSPROD has already been started.

addlnctl.sh: exiting with status 0

addlnctl.sh: check the logfile /u01/ora_EBS/12.1.0.2/appsutil/log/EBSPROD_erpdb1/addlnctl.
txt for more information ...

Do you want to change the password for all EBS Schemas? (y/n) [n]) : y

Enter the new EBS Schema password :
Running:
/u01/ora_EBS/12.1.0.2/bin/sqlplus -s /nolog @/u01/ora_EBS/12.1.0.2/appsutil/clone/bin/
ebsUsers.sql > /u01/ora_EBS/12.1.0.2/appsutil/clone/bin/ebsUsersPasswordChange.sql 2>&1

Executing command /u01/ora_EBS/12.1.0.2/bin/sqlplus -s / as sysdba @/u01/ora_EBS/12.1.0.2/
appsutil/clone/bin/ebsUsersPasswordChange.sql > /u01/ora_EBS/12.1.0.2/appsutil/clone/bin/
ebsUsersPasswordChange.log 2>&1Running:
/u01/ora_EBS/12.1.0.2/bin/sqlplus -s / as sysdba @/u01/ora_EBS/12.1.0.2/appsutil/
clone/bin/ebsUsersPasswordChange.sql > /u01/ora_EBS/12.1.0.2/appsutil/clone/bin/
ebsUsersPasswordChange.log 2>&1

Successfully changed the EBS schema passwords

Do you want to change the apps password? (y/n) [n]) : y

Enter the new APPS password :
Running:
/u01/ora_EBS/12.1.0.2/bin/sqlplus -s apps/apps @/u01/ora_EBS/12.1.0.2/appsutil/clone/bin/
appsPasswordChange.sql > /u01/ora_EBS/12.1.0.2/appsutil/clone/bin/appsPasswordChange.log 2>&1

Apps and applsys passwords were successfully changed

Do you want to change the sys and system passwords? (y/n) [n]) : y

Enter the new sys/system password :
Running:
/u01/ora_EBS/12.1.0.2/bin/sqlplus -s /nolog @/u01/ora_EBS/12.1.0.2/appsutil/clone/
bin/systemPasswordChangeSqlFile.sql > /u01/ora_EBS/12.1.0.2/appsutil/clone/bin/
systemPasswordChange.log 2>&1

Successfully changed the sys and system passwords
[oracle@erpdb1 bin]$

In this scenario, the passwords for the APPS, SYS, and SYSTEM EBS schemas have been changed from the source system password. The database tier cloning has completed successfully. Now you should proceed with configuring the application tier.

Executing adcfglcone.pl on Primary Application Node with dualfs:

-bash-4.2$ perl adcfgclone.pl appsTier dualfs

Copyright (c) 2002, 2015 Oracle Corporation
Redwood Shores, California, USA

Oracle E-Business Suite Rapid Clone

Version 12.2

adcfgclone Version 120.63.12020000.56

Enter the APPS password :

Enter the Weblogic AdminServer password :

Do you want to add a node (yes/no) [no] :

Running: Context clone...

Log file located at /u01/appl_EBS/EBSPROD/fs1/EBSapps/comn/clone/bin/
CloneContext_0326202707.log

Provide the values required for creation of the new APPL_TOP Context file.

Target System Hostname (virtual or normal) [erpapp1] :

Target System Database SID : EBSPROD

Target System Database Server Node [erpapp1] :

Target System Database Domain Name [orasol.com] :

Target System Base Directory : /u01/appl_EBS/EBSPROD

Target System Base Directory set to /u01/appl_EBS/EBSPROD

Target System Current File System Base set to /u01/appl_EBS/EBSPROD/fs1

Target System Other File System Base set to /u01/appl_EBS/EBSPROD/fs2

Target System Fusion Middleware Home set to /u01/appl_EBS/EBSPROD/fs1/FMW_Home
Target System Other File System Fusion Middleware Home set to /u01/appl_EBS/EBSPROD/fs2/
FMW_Home

Target System Web Oracle Home set to /u01/appl_EBS/EBSPROD/fs1/FMW_Home/webtier

Target System Other File System Web Oracle Home set to /u01/appl_EBS/EBSPROD/fs2/FMW_Home/
webtier

Target System Appl TOP set to /u01/appl_EBS/EBSPROD/fs1/EBSapps/appl
Target System Other File System Appl TOP set to /u01/appl_EBS/EBSPROD/fs2/EBSapps/appl

Target System COMMON TOP set to /u01/appl_EBS/EBSPROD/fs1/EBSapps/comn
Target System Other File System COMMON TOP set to /u01/appl_EBS/EBSPROD/fs2/EBSapps/comn
Target System Instance Home Directory [/u01/appl_EBS/EBSPROD] :

Target System Current File System Instance Top set to /u01/appl_EBS/EBSPROD/fs1/inst/apps/
EBSPROD_erpapp1

Do you want to preserve the Display [erpnode2:0.0] (y/n): n

Target System Display [erpapp1:0.0] :

Target System Root Service [enabled] :

Target System Web Entry Point Services [enabled] :

Target System Web Application Services [enabled] :

Target System Batch Processing Services [enabled] : disabled

Target System Other Services [disabled] :

Do you want the target system to have the same port values as the source system (y/n) [y] ? : n

Target System Port Pool [0-99] : 3

Checking the port pool 3
done: Port Pool 3 is free
Report file located at /u01/appl_EBS/EBSPROD/fs1/inst/apps/EBSPROD_erpapp1/admin/out/
portpool.lst

UTL_FILE_DIR on database tier consists of the following directories.

1. /usr/tmp
2. /usr/tmp
3. /d01/EBSDB/ora_EBSPROD/EBSPROD/12.1.0/appsutil/outbound/EBSPROD_erpapp1
4. /usr/tmp
Choose a value which will be set as APPLPTMP value on the target node [1] : 3
The new APPL_TOP context file has been created :
/u01/appl_EBS/EBSPROD/fs1/inst/apps/EBSPROD_erpapp1/appl/admin/EBSPROD_erpapp1.xml
Check Clone Context logfile /u01/appl_EBS/EBSPROD/fs1/EBSapps/comn/clone/bin/
CloneContext_0326202707.log for details.

Creating Patch file system context file.....

Log file located at /u01/appl_EBS/EBSPROD/fs1/EBSapps/comn/clone/bin/
CloneContextPatch_0326202744.log

Target System Other File System Instance Top set to /u01/appl_EBS/EBSPROD/fs2/inst/apps/
EBSPROD_erpapp1

Target System Port Pool [0-99] : 4

Checking the port pool 3
done: Port Pool 3 is free
Report file located at /u01/appl_EBS/EBSPROD/fs2/inst/apps/EBSPROD_erpapp1/admin/out/portpool.lst
The new APPL_TOP context file has been created :
/u01/appl_EBS/EBSPROD/fs2/inst/apps/EBSPROD_erpapp1/appl/admin/EBSPROD_erpapp1.xml
Check Clone Context logfile /u01/appl_EBS/EBSPROD/fs1/EBSapps/comn/clone/bin/
CloneContextPatch_0326202744.log for details.

FMW Pre-requisite check log file location : /u01/appl_EBS/EBSPROD/fs1/EBSapps/comn/clone/
FMW/logs/prereqcheck.log
Running: FMW pre-req check...
Global inventory loc = /etc/oraInst.loc
Log: /d01/EBSDB/ora_EBSPROD/oraInventory/logs/install2016-03-26_08-27-52PM.log
contextFile:/u01/appl_EBS/EBSPROD/fs1/EBSapps/comn/clone/prereq/webtier/Scripts/prereq/oui/
agent_prereq_context.xml
The entry point is: oracle.installType.all
Check Name:CertifiedVersions
Check Description:This is a prerequisite condition to test whether the Oracle software is
certified on the current O/S or not.
/etc/inittab does not seem to contain default runlevel information.
Expected result: One of oracle-7,redhat-7,redhat-6,oracle-6,oracle-5,enterprise-
5.4,enterprise-4,enterprise-5,redhat-5.4,redhat-4,redhat-5,SuSE-10,SuSE-11
Actual Result: oracle-7
Check complete. The overall result of this check is: Passed

Check Name:Packages
Check Description:This is a prerequisite condition to test whether the packages recommended
for installing the EBSPRODuct are available on the system.
Checking for binutils-2.23.52.0.1; found binutils-2.23.52.0.1-55.el7-x86_64.   Passed
Checking for compat-libcap1-1.10; found compat-libcap1-1.10-7.el7-x86_64.   Passed
....
....
Check complete. The overall result of this check is: Passed

Check Name:Kernel
Check Description:This is a prerequisite condition to test whether the minimum required
kernel parameters are configured.
Checking for VERSION=3.8.0; found VERSION=3.8.13-98.7.1.el7uek.x86_64.   Passed
Checking for hardnofiles=4096; found hardnofiles=65536.Passed
Checking for softnofiles=4096; found softnofiles=65536.Passed
Check complete. The overall result of this check is: Passed

```
Check Name:GLIBC
Check Description:This is a prerequisite condition to check whether the recommended glibc
version is available on the system
Expected result: ATLEAST=2.17
Actual Result: 2.17-105.0.1.el7
Check complete. The overall result of this check is: Passed

Check Name:TotalMemory
Check Description:This is a prerequisite condition to test whether the system has sufficient
physical memory.
Expected result: 1024MB
Actual Result: 11760MB
Check complete. The overall result of this check is: Passed

Check Name:Check Env Variable
Check Description:Check for LD_ASSUME_KERNEL
Expected result: LD_ASSUME_KERNEL environment variable should not be set in the environment.
Actual Result: Variable Not set.
Check complete. The overall result of this check is: Passed

Summary : 0 requirements failed, 0 requirements to be verified.

Configuring: Run file system....
LogFile located at /u01/appl_EBS/EBSPROD/fs1/inst/apps/EBSPROD_erpapp1/admin/log/clone/run/
RCloneApplyAppstier_03262027.log

Configuring: Patch file system....
LogFile located at /u01/appl_EBS/EBSPROD/fs1/inst/apps/EBSPROD_erpapp1/admin/log/clone/
patch/RCloneApplyAppstier_03262101.log

Do you want to startup the Application Services for EBSPROD? (y/n) [n] : y

Starting application Services for EBSPROD:

You are running adstrtal.sh version 120.24.12020000.11
```

Similarly, you should execute adcfglcone.pl on the secondary application node on the run edition file system with dualfs. The process is similar; the only differences are that you should select the Yes option when prompted with "Do you want to add node[yes/No]:" and you should select that batch processing services are enabled.

The full process of cloning from a single-node system to a multinode system has completed successfully. Figure 11-6 shows the multinode environment created from the single-node EBS system. As discussed, for every cloning activity you may need to perform the post-cloning steps discussed later in this chapter.

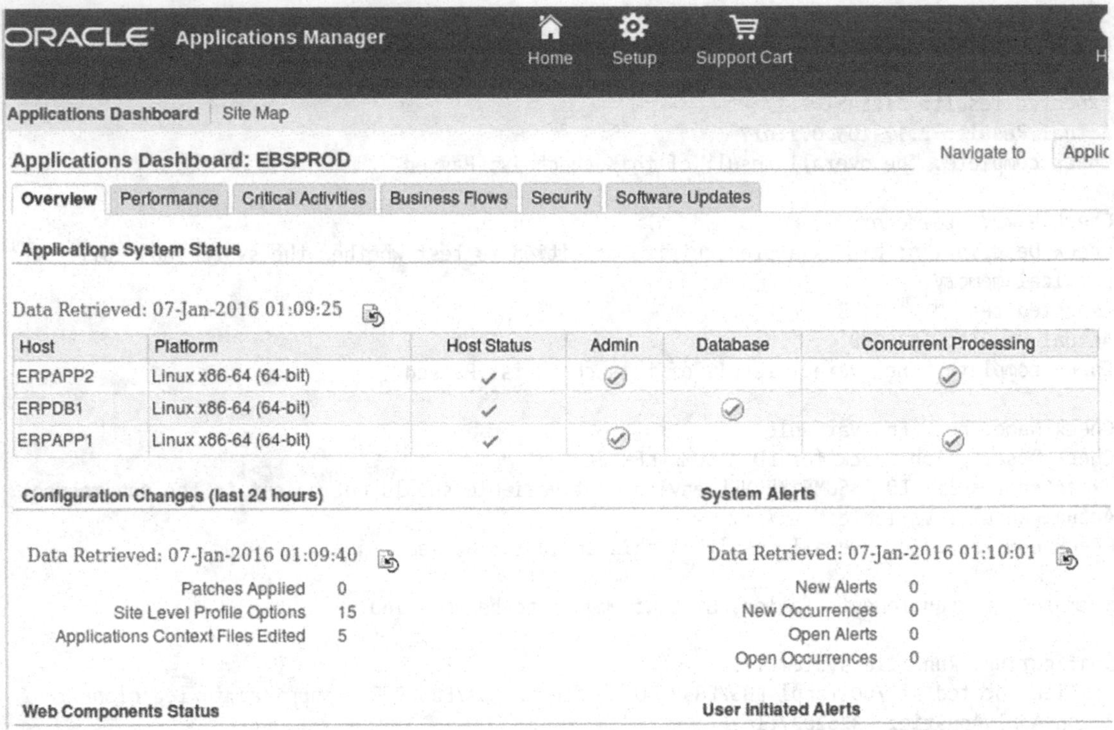

Figure 11-6. *Rapid Clone: OAM dashboard, single node to multinode (target system)*

Cloning from a Multinode to a Single-Node Clone Using Online Backup

So far we have discussed two clone scenarios: single to single and single to multinode. Both of these clone scenarios used a cold database and application backup. In this scenario, you will see how to clone a multinode E-Business Suite system using online backup to a single-node system.

Figure 11-7 illustrates the high-level steps that need to be considered for online cloning.

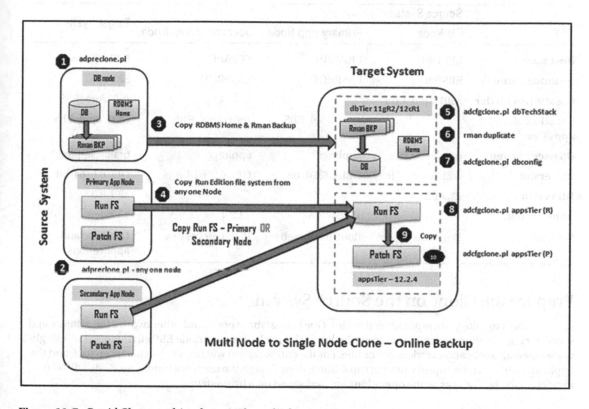

Figure 11-7. *Rapid Clone: multinode to single-node clone process*

In this demonstration, we will use same multinode system configured earlier from a single node. Table 11-6 displays the source system and target system environment details involved in the multinode to single-node clone.

Table 11-6. Rapid Clone: Multinode to Single-Node Clone Environment Details

	Source System			Target System
	DB Node	Primary App Node	Secondary App Node	
Host name	ERPDB1	ERPAPP1	ERPAPP2	ERPNODE5
Instance name	EBSPROD	EBSPROD	EBSPROD	EBSTEST
Location of dbTier	/u01/appl_EBS			/u01/ora_EBS
Location of appsTier		/u01/appl_EBS	/u01/appl_EBS	/d01/appl_EBS
OS users/group	oracle	applmgr	applmgr	oralce, applmgr
OS version	OEL 6.6: 64-bit	OEL 6.6: 64-bit	OEL 6.6: 64-bit	OEL 6.6: 64-bit
DB version	12.1.0.2			12.1.0.2
Apps version		12.2.4	12.2.4	12.2.4
Services	Database	Root, form, web	Batch processing	Database and applications

Prepare the Clone on the Source System

In the current topology, there are several nodes. One is a database node, and other two are the primary and secondary application nodes. In this scenario, the goal is to clone a multinode EBS environment to a single node when all application services are online. For the database, you will use the rman backup tool, and the application files can be copied from the run edition, even though the users are online. So, there will be no impact on the business as all the operations are performed on a live system.

■ **Note**   In a multinode environment, you should copy the application tier file system from any one of the active application nodes.

Execute the adpreclone.pl Script on dbTier

Here's the script:

```
[oracle@erpdb1 EBSPROD_erpdb1]$ adpreclone.pl dbTier
Copyright (c) 2011, 2014 Oracle Corporation
Redwood Shores, California, USA
Oracle E-Business Suite Rapid Clone
Version 12.2
adpreclone Version 120.31.12020000.16

Enter the APPS User Password:
Running:
perl /u01/ora_EBS/12.1.0.2/appsutil/bin/adclone.pl java=/u01/ora_EBS/12.1.0.2/appsutil/jre
mode=stage stage=/u01/ora_EBS/12.1.0.2/appsutil/clone component=dbTier method=CUSTOM dbctx=/
u01/ora_EBS/12.1.0.2/appsutil/EBSPROD_erpdb1.xml showProgress
Beginning database tier Stage - Sat Jan9 16:41:15 2016
```

```
/u01/ora_EBS/12.1.0.2/appsutil/jre/bin/java -Xmx600M -DCONTEXT_VALIDATED=false -Doracle.
installer.oui_loc=/u01/ora_EBS/12.1.0.2/oui -classpath /u01/ora_EBS/12.1.0.2/lib/
xmlparserv2.jar:/u01/ora_EBS/12.1.0.2/jdbc/lib/ojdbc6.jar:/u01/ora_EBS/12.1.0.2/appsutil/
java:/u01/ora_EBS/12.1.0.2/oui/jlib/OraInstaller.jar:/u01/ora_EBS/12.1.0.2/oui/jlib/ewt3.
jar:/u01/ora_EBS/12.1.0.2/oui/jlib/share.jar:/u01/ora_EBS/12.1.0.2/oui/jlib/srvm.jar:/u01/
ora_EBS/12.1.0.2/jlib/ojmisc.jar oracle.apps.ad.clone.StageDBTier -e /u01/ora_EBS/12.1.0.2/
appsutil/EBSPROD_erpdb1.xml -stage /u01/ora_EBS/12.1.0.2/appsutil/clone -tmp /tmp -method
CUSTOM-showProgress
APPS Password :
Log file located at /u01/ora_EBS/12.1.0.2/appsutil/log/EBSPROD_erpdb1/StageDBTier_01091641.log
- 50% completed
Completed Stage...
Sat Jan9 16:41:44 2016
[oracle@erpdb1 EBSPROD_erpdb1]$
```

Perform a Full Database rman Backup

rman is the tool used for Oracle database backup, restore, and recover operations. If the database sizes are really large, it will take a significant time for the backup restore operations. In such environments, storage-based snapshots are used. But in this section, we will discuss the rman backup/restore method. Using rman, you can perform database backup online while all users are connected and the business transactions are live. To perform an rman backup, the main prerequisite is to have the archive log mode enabled. By default with this installation, the archive mode of the database will be disabled.

Enable archive log mode, as shown here:

```
SQL> startup mount;
ORACLE instance started.

Total System Global Area 2147483648 bytes
Fixed Size3712904 bytes
Variable Size486541432 bytes
Database Buffers1644167168 bytes
Redo Buffers 13062144 bytes
Database mounted.

SQL> archive log list;
Database log mode No Archive Mode
Automatic archivalDisabled
Archive destination /u01/ora_EBS/data/archive
Oldest online log sequence 1
Current log sequence 2
SQL>

SQL> alter database archivelog;

Database altered.
SQL> archive log list;
Database log mode Archive Mode
Automatic archival Enabled
Archive destination/u01/ora_EBS/data/archive
Oldest online log sequence 1
```

```
Next log sequence to archive 2
Current log sequence2
SQL>

SQL> alter database open;

Database altered.

SQL>
```

Execute a Full Database Backup rman Script

In this demonstration, Disk is used as the default device type. You can use a device type of SBT if there is a tape library configured with vendor media management layer software.

```
[oracle@erpdb1 ~]$ rman target /

Recovery Manager: Release 12.1.0.2.0 - Production on Sat Jan 9 14:44:31 2016

Copyright (c) 1982, 2014, Oracle and/or its affiliates.All rights reserved.

connected to target database: EBSPROD (DBID=3543505515)

RMAN> RUN {
2> configure controlfile autobackup format for device type disks to '/u01/ora_EBS/rman_bkp/
control_%F';
3> configure controlfile autobackup on;
4>allocate channel d1 type disk;
5>allocate channel d2 type disk;
6>allocate channel d3 type disk;
7>allocate channel d4 type disk;
8>backup tag FULL_DB database plus archivelog format '/u01/ora_EBS/rman_bkp/b_%t_%s.bkp';
9>release channel d1;
10>release channel d2;
11>release channel d3;
12>release channel d4;
13>}

using target database control file instead of recovery catalog
new RMAN configuration parameters:
CONFIGURE CONTROLFILE AUTOBACKUP FORMAT FOR DEVICE TYPE 'DIKS' TO '/u01/ora_EBS/rman_bkp/
control_%F';
new RMAN configuration parameters are successfully stored

new RMAN configuration parameters:
CONFIGURE CONTROLFILE AUTOBACKUP ON;
new RMAN configuration parameters are successfully stored

allocated channel: d1
channel d1: SID=324 device type=DISK
```

```
allocated channel: d2
channel d2: SID=403 device type=DISK

allocated channel: d3
channel d3: SID=9 device type=DISK

allocated channel: d4
channel d4: SID=88 device type=DISK

Starting backup at 09-JAN-16
current log archived
channel d1: starting archived log backup set
channel d1: specifying archived log(s) in backup set
input archived log thread=1 sequence=2 RECID=1 STAMP=900686048
channel d1: starting piece 1 at 09-JAN-16
channel d2: starting archived log backup set
channel d2: specifying archived log(s) in backup set
input archived log thread=1 sequence=4 RECID=3 STAMP=900686782
channel d2: starting piece 1 at 09-JAN-16
channel d3: starting archived log backup set
channel d3: specifying archived log(s) in backup set
input archived log thread=1 sequence=3 RECID=2 STAMP=900686054
channel d3: starting piece 1 at 09-JAN-16
channel d1: finished piece 1 at 09-JAN-16
piece handle=/u01/ora_EBS/rman_bkp/b_900686783_1.bkp tag=FULL_DB comment=NONE
channel d1: backup set complete, elapsed time: 00:00:05
channel d2: finished piece 1 at 09-JAN-16
piece handle=/u01/ora_EBS/rman_bkp/b_900686785_2.bkp tag=FULL_DB comment=NONE
channel d2: backup set complete, elapsed time: 00:00:04
channel d3: finished piece 1 at 09-JAN-16
piece handle=/u01/ora_EBS/rman_bkp/b_900686787_3.bkp tag=FULL_DB comment=NONE
channel d3: backup set complete, elapsed time: 00:00:03
Finished backup at 09-JAN-16

Starting backup at 09-JAN-16
channel d1: starting full datafile backup set
channel d1: specifying datafile(s) in backup set
input datafile file number=00019 name=/u01/ora_EBS/data/system13.dbf
channel d1: starting piece 1 at 09-JAN-16
channel d2: starting full datafile backup set
channel d2: specifying datafile(s) in backup set
input datafile file number=00022 name=/u01/ora_EBS/data/system16.dbf
channel d2: starting piece 1 at 09-JAN-16
channel d3: starting full datafile backup set
channel d3: specifying datafile(s) in backup set
input datafile file number=00021 name=/u01/ora_EBS/data/system15.dbf
channel d3: starting piece 1 at 09-JAN-16
channel d4: starting full datafile backup set
channel d4: specifying datafile(s) in backup set
input datafile file number=00020 name=/u01/ora_EBS/data/system14.dbf
channel d4: starting piece 1 at 09-JAN-16
piece handle=/u01/ora_EBS/12.1.0.2/dbs/04qquou9_1_1 tag=FULL_DB comment=NONE
```

```
channel d1: backup set complete, elapsed time: 01:32:51
Finished backup at 09-JAN-16
Starting backup at 09-JAN-16
current log archived
channel d1: starting archived log backup set
channel d1: specifying archived log(s) in backup set
channel d1: backup set complete, elapsed time: 00:00:01
Finished backup at 09-JAN-16

Starting Control File Autobackup at 09-JAN-16
piece handle=/u01/ora_EBS/12.1.0.2/dbs/c-3543505515-20160109-00 comment=NONE
Finished Control File Autobackup at 09-JAN-16

released channel: d1

released channel: d2

released channel: d3

released channel: d4

RMAN>
```

The backup has been completed successfully on the source system, so you are ready to proceed with the application tier.

Execute the adpreclone.pl Script on appsTier (Run Edition)

There are no changes in the procedure of executing the script; the only difference from the previous cloning scenarios is that you need to ensure that all application services are up and running.

Execute the adpreclone.pl script on the run edition file system.

Here is the status of the application services:

```
applmgr@erpapp1 scripts]$ adopmnctl.sh status

You are running adopmnctl.sh version 120.0.12020000.2

Checking status of OPMN managed processes...

Processes in Instance: EBS_web_EBSPROD_OHS1
----------------------------------+--------------------+---------+---------
ias-component| process-type | pid | status
----------------------------------+--------------------+---------+---------
EBS_web_EBSPROD| OHS| 13366 | Alive

adopmnctl.sh: exiting with status 0

adopmnctl.sh: check the logfile /u01/appl_EBS/fs1/inst/apps/EBSPROD_erpapp1/logs/appl/admin/
log/adopmnctl.txt for more information ...
```

```
[applmgr@erpapp1 scripts]$ adpreclone.pl appsTier

Copyright (c) 2011, 2014 Oracle Corporation
Redwood Shores, California, USA

Oracle E-Business Suite Rapid Clone

Version 12.2

adpreclone Version 120.31.12020000.16

Enter the APPS User Password:
Enter the Weblogic AdminServer password :

Checking the status of the Oracle WebLogic Administration Server....

Running perl /u01/appl_EBS/fs1/EBSapps/appl/ad/12.0.0/patch/115/bin/adProvisionEBS.pl
ebs-get-serverstatus -contextfile=/u01/appl_EBS/fs1/inst/apps/EBSPROD_erpapp1/appl/admin/
EBSPROD_erpapp1.xml -servername=AdminServer -promptmsg=hide

The Oracle WebLogic Administration Server is up.

Running:
perl /u01/appl_EBS/fs1/EBSapps/appl/ad/12.0.0/bin/adclone.pl java=/u01/appl_EBS/fs1/EBSapps/
comn/util/jdk64 mode=stage stage=/u01/appl_EBS/fs1/EBSapps/comn/clone component=appsTier
method= appctx=/u01/appl_EBS/fs1/inst/apps/EBSPROD_erpapp1/appl/admin/EBSPROD_erpapp1.xml
showProgress

Setting the wls environment

Beginning application tier Stage - Sat Jan9 17:31:44 2016

Log file located at /u01/appl_EBS/fs1/inst/apps/EBSPROD_erpapp1/admin/log/clone/
StageAppsTier_09011741.log

\ 20% completed

Completed Stage...
Sat Jan9 17:41:44 2016
[applmgr@erpapp1 scripts]$
```

Configure the Target System

You need to perform all the steps listed in the previous section. In this scenario, you are using online backup, so you should have additional space on the target system to place the rman backup pieces. As shown in Figure 11-5, you should copy all the required files from the source system to the target system, including the rman backup pieces.

Execute the adcfgclone.pl Script with the dbTechStack Option

rman backup is used for configuring the database on the target system, and hence the dbTier option with the adcfgclone.pl script is not applicable. Instead, the dbTechStack option should be used to configure the tech stack components on the target database server.

The dbTechStack option is a useful option while performing clone configuration using the rman backup utility or another third-party solution like storage snapshots. It will not create control files or configure the database. It will create the context file, environment files, listener files, and database scripts and will start up the database listener.

■ **Note**   The adfcglclone.pl script has multiple configuration options and was discussed earlier in this chapter.

```
[oracle@erpnode5 bin]$ perl adcfgclone.pl dbTechStack

Copyright (c) 2011 Oracle Corporation
Redwood Shores, California, USA

Oracle E-Business Suite Rapid Clone

Version 12.2

adcfgclone Version 120.63.12020000.37

Enter the APPS password :

Running:
 /tmp/adcfgclone_11259.res

Log file located at /u01/ora_EBS/12.1.0.2/appsutil/clone/bin/CloneContext_0109230236.log

Provide the values required for creation of the new Database Context file.

Target System Hostname (virtual or normal) [erpnode5] :

Target Instance is RAC (y/n) [n] :

Target System Database SID : EBSTEST

Target System Base Directory : /u01/ora_EBS

Target System utl_file_dir Directory List : /usr/tmp

Number of DATA_TOP's on the Target System [1] :

Target System DATA_TOP Directory 1 [/u01/ora_EBS/data] :

Target System RDBMS ORACLE_HOME Directory [/u01/ora_EBS/12.1.0] : /u01/ora_EBS/12.1.0.2

Do you want to preserve the Display [erpdb1:0.0] (y/n): n
```

Target System Display [erpnode5:0.0] :

Do you want the target system to have the same port values as the source system (y/n) [y] ? : n

Target System Port Pool [0-99] : 15

Checking the port pool 15
done: Port Pool 15 is free
Report file located at /u01/ora_EBS/12.1.0.2/appsutil/temp/portpool.lst
Complete port information available at /u01/ora_EBS/12.1.0.2/appsutil/temp/portpool.lst

Creating the new Database Context file from :
/u01/ora_EBS/12.1.0.2/appsutil/clone/context/db/adxdbctx.tmp

The new database context file has been created :
/u01/ora_EBS/12.1.0.2/appsutil/EBSTEST_erpnode5.xml

Log file located at /u01/ora_EBS/12.1.0.2/appsutil/clone/bin/CloneContext_0109230236.log
Check Clone Context logfile /u01/ora_EBS/12.1.0.2/appsutil/clone/bin/
CloneContext_0109230236.log for details.

Running Rapid Clone with command:
Running:
perl /u01/ora_EBS/12.1.0.2/appsutil/clone/bin/adclone.pl java=/u01/ora_EBS/12.1.0.2/
appsutil/clone/bin/../jre mode=apply stage=/u01/ora_EBS/12.1.0.2/appsutil/clone
component=dbTechStack method=CUSTOM dbctxtg=/u01/ora_EBS/12.1.0.2/appsutil/EBSTEST_erpnode5.
xml showProgress contextValidated=true

Beginning rdbms home Apply - Sat Jan9 23:03:17 2016

APPS Password : Log file located at /u01/ora_EBS/12.1.0.2/appsutil/log/EBSTEST_erpnode5/
ApplyDBTechStack_01092303.log
|0% completed Determining Source system database type ("single" or "rac").
Source system indentified as being of type "single"!
-0% completed

Completed Apply…
Sat Jan9 23:08:35 2016

Starting database listener for EBSTEST:
Running:
/u01/ora_EBS/12.1.0.2/appsutil/scripts/EBSTEST_erpnode5/addlnctl.sh start EBSTEST
Logfile: /u01/ora_EBS/12.1.0.2/appsutil/log/EBSTEST_erpnode5/addlnctl.txt

You are running addlnctl.sh version 120.4

Starting listener process EBSTEST …

LSNRCTL for Linux: Version 12.1.0.2.0 - Production on 09-JAN-2016 23:08:35

Copyright (c) 1991, 2014, Oracle.All rights reserved.

Starting /u01/ora_EBS/12.1.0.2/bin/tnslsnr: please wait…

TNSLSNR for Linux: Version 12.1.0.2.0 - Production
System parameter file is /u01/ora_EBS/12.1.0.2/network/admin/EBSTEST_erpnode5/listener.ora
Log messages written to /u01/ora_EBS/12.1.0.2/admin/EBSTEST_erpnode5/diag/tnslsnr/erpnode5/
ebstest/alert/log.xml
Listening on: (DESCRIPTION=(ADDRESS=(PROTOCOL=tcp)(HOST=erpnode5.oralabs.com)(PORT=1536)))

Connecting to (DESCRIPTION=(ADDRESS=(PROTOCOL=TCP)(HOST=erpnode5.oralabs.com)(PORT=1536)))
STATUS of the LISTENER

Alias EBSTEST
Version TNSLSNR for Linux: Version 12.1.0.2.0 - Production
Start Date09-JAN-2016 23:08:40
Uptime0 days 0 hr. 0 min. 15 sec
Trace Level off
SecurityON: Local OS Authentication
SNMPOFF
Listener Parameter File /u01/ora_EBS/12.1.0.2/network/admin/EBSTEST_erpnode5/listener.ora
Listener Log File /u01/ora_EBS/12.1.0.2/admin/EBSTEST_erpnode5/diag/tnslsnr/erpnode5/
ebstest/alert/log.xml
Listening Endpoints Summary…
(DESCRIPTION=(ADDRESS=(PROTOCOL=tcp)(HOST=erpnode5.oralabs.com)(PORT=1536)))
Services Summary…
Service "EBSTEST" has 1 instance(s).
Instance "EBSTEST", status UNKNOWN, has 1 handler(s) for this service…
The command completed successfully

addlnctl.sh: exiting with status 0

addlnctl.sh: check the logfile /u01/ora_EBS/12.1.0.2/appsutil/log/EBSTEST_erpnode5/addlnctl.
txt for more information …

[oracle@erpnode5 bin]$

The target database tech stack configuration has completed successfully, so now you are ready to
execute the rman duplicate command.

Execute rman duplicate

The rman duplicate command clones the existing database to the new database. The rman duplicate
command can be executed by connecting to the target database, or you can use the backup pieces of the
target database to perform duplication without actually connecting to the database.

■ **Note**   In rman duplication, the target database is referred to as the *source database*, and the auxiliary
database is referred as the *clone database*.

For more information about rman duplication, please refer to "Perform Backup-Based RMAN DUPLICATE Without Connecting to Target Database for Both Disk and Tape Backups" (Doc ID 1375864.1), available at https://docs.oracle.com/database/121/BRADV/rcmdupdb.htm#BRADV010.

1. Source the new environment variable and start the database in nomount mode.

```
[oracle@erpnode5 12.1.0.2]$ sqlplus / as sysdba

SQL*Plus: Release 12.1.0.2.0 Production on Sat Jan 9 23:33:20 2016

Copyright (c) 1982, 2014, Oracle.All rights reserved.

Connected to an idle instance.

SQL> startup nomount;
ORACLE instance started.

Total System Global Area 2147483648 bytes
Fixed Size3712904 bytes
Variable Size486541432 bytes
Database Buffers 164416/168 bytes
Redo Buffers 13062144 bytes
SQL>
```

2. - Ensure all the backup pieces are copied and have valid permissions.

This step is not applicable if using tape media as the source of the backup.

```
[root@erpnode5 rman_bkp]# pwd
/d01/oracle/rman_bkp
[root@erpnode5 rman_bkp]# ls
04qquou9_1_106qquoua_1_1b_900686783_1.bkpb_900686787_3.bkpc-3543505515-20160109-00
05qquou9_1_107qquouc_1_1b_900686785_2.bkpb_900692367_8.bkpsnapcf_EBSPROD.f
[root@erpnode5 rman_bkp]#
```

3. Connect the auxiliary and execute the rman duplicate command.

If the source database and target database have different directory structures, then the db_file_name_convert and log_file_name_convert parameters should be used. In this demonstration, the same location has been used for the source and target database servers.

```
[oracle@erpnode5 data]$ rman auxiliary /

Recovery Manager: Release 12.1.0.2.0 - Production on Sun Jan 10 00:28:01 2016
Copyright (c) 1982, 2014, Oracle and/or its affiliates.All rights reserved.
connected to auxiliary database: EBSTEST (not mounted)

RMAN> spool log to '/u01/ora_EBS/data/rman_duplicate.log'
RMAN> duplicate target database to EBSTEST backup location '/d01/oracle/rman_bkp'
nofilenamecheck;
RMAN>
```

The duplication of the database from EBSPROD to EBSTEST completed successfully. You can now connect to the newly duplicate database and verify the status of the database.

```
[oracle@erpnode5 dbs]$ sqlplus / as sysdba

SQL*Plus: Release 12.1.0.2.0 Production on Sun Jan 10 01:11:39 2016

Copyright (c) 1982, 2014, Oracle.All rights reserved.

Connected to:
Oracle Database 12c Enterprise Edition Release 12.1.0.2.0 - 64bit Production
With the Partitioning, OLAP, Advanced Analytics and Real Application Testing options

SQL>
SQL> select open_mode, name from v$database;

OPEN_MODE NAME
-------------------- ---------
READ WRITE EBSTEST

SQL>
```

4. Execute the script adupdlib.sql to update libraries.

```
[oracle@erpnode5 EBSTEST_erpnode5]$ pwd
/u01/ora_EBS/12.1.0.2/appsutil/install/EBSTEST_erpnode5
[oracle@erpnode5 EBSTEST_erpnode5]$ sqlplus / as sysdba

SQL*Plus: Release 12.1.0.2.0 Production on Sun Jan 10 01:14:22 2016

Copyright (c) 1982, 2014, Oracle.All rights reserved.

Connected to:
Oracle Database 12c Enterprise Edition Release 12.1.0.2.0 - 64bit Production
With the Partitioning, OLAP, Advanced Analytics and Real Application Testing options

SQL> @adupdlib.sql so

PL/SQL procedure successfully completed.

SQL>
```

5. Execute adcfgclon.pl with the dbconfig option.

This is required for configuring the target database, and adcfgclon.pl can be executed only when the database tech stack part is completed with the database running in open mode.

This option will prompt for the context file, and you should provide the newly created context file during the dbTechStack option.

```
[oracle@erpnode5 bin]$ perl adcfgclone.pl dbconfig /u01/ora_EBS/12.1.0.2/appsutil/EBSTEST_
erpnode5.xml

 Copyright (c) 2011 Oracle Corporation
Redwood Shores, California, USA

Oracle E-Business Suite Rapid Clone

 Version 12.2

adcfgclone Version 120.63.12020000.37

Enter the APPS password :

Running Rapid Clone with command:
Running:

Beginning dbconfig Apply - Sun Jan 10 01:16:55 2016

 /u01/ora_EBS/12.1.0.2/appsutil/log/EBSTEST_erpnode5/ApplyDatabase_01100116.log
/0% completed
Log file located at /u01/ora_EBS/12.1.0.2/appsutil/log/EBSTEST_erpnode5/
ApplyDatabase_01100116.log
\ 30% completed

Completed Apply...
Sun Jan 10 01:21:32 2016

Starting database listener for EBSTEST:
Running:
/u01/ora_EBS/12.1.0.2/appsutil/scripts/EBSTEST_erpnode5/addlnctl.sh start EBSTEST
Logfile: /u01/ora_EBS/12.1.0.2/appsutil/log/EBSTEST_erpnode5/addlnctl.txt

You are running addlnctl.sh version 120.4

Starting listener process EBSTEST ...

Listener EBSTEST has already been started.

addlnctl.sh: exiting with status 0

addlnctl.sh: check the logfile /u01/ora_EBS/12.1.0.2/appsutil/log/EBSTEST_erpnode5/addlnctl.
txt for more information ...
[oracle@erpnode5 bin]$
```

This is the last step of configuring the target system clone of the database tier. Now you are ready to proceed with the configuration of the application tier.

Configure the Target System Application Tier

The process of application cloning is similar to the previous cloning scenarios. You should proceed first with configuring the run edition file system and then configure the patch edition file system.

Here is the execution of adcfgclone.pl appsTier (run edition):

```
[applmgr@erpnode5 bin]$ perl adcfgclone.pl appsTier

Copyright (c) 2011 Oracle Corporation
Redwood Shores, California, USA

Oracle E-Business Suite Rapid Clone

Version 12.2

adcfgclone Version 120.63.12020000.37

Enter the APPS password :

Enter the Weblogic AdminServer password :
Running:
Running:

Do you want to add a node (yes/no) [no] :

Running:

Log file located at /d01/appl_EBS/fs1/EBSapps/comn/clone/bin/CloneContext_0110071848.log

Target System File Edition type [run] :

Provide the values required for creation of the new APPL_TOP Context file.

Target System Hostname (virtual or normal) [erpnode5] :
Target System Database SID : EBSTEST

Target System Database Server Node [erpnode5] :

Target System Database Domain Name [oralabs.com] :

Target System Base Directory : /d01/appl_EBS

Target System Base Directory set to /d01/appl_EBS

Target System Current File System Base set to /d01/appl_EBS/fs1

Target System Other File System Base set to /d01/appl_EBS/fs2

Target System Fusion Middleware Home set to /d01/appl_EBS/fs1/FMW_Home

Target System Web Oracle Home set to /d01/appl_EBS/fs1/FMW_Home/webtier
```

Target System Appl TOP set to /d01/appl_EBS/fs1/EBSapps/appl

Target System COMMON TOP set to /d01/appl_EBS/fs1/EBSapps/comn

Target System Instance Home Directory [/d01/appl_EBS] :

Target System Instance Top set to /d01/appl_EBS/fs1/inst/apps/EBSTEST_erpnode5

Do you want to preserve the Display [erptest1:0.0] (y/n): n

Target System Display [erpnode5:0.0] :

Target System Root Service [enabled] :

Target System Web Administration [enabled] :

Target System Web Entry Point Services [enabled] :

Target System Web Application Services [enabled] :

Target System Batch Processing Services [enabled] :

Target System Other Services [disabled] :

Do you want the target system to have the same port values as the source system (y/n) [y] ? : n

Target System Port Pool [0-99] : 15
Checking the port pool 15
done: Port Pool 15 is free
Report file located at /d01/appl_EBS/fs1/inst/apps/EBSTEST_erpnode5/admin/out/portpool.lst
Complete port information available at /d01/appl_EBS/fs1/inst/apps/EBSTEST_erpnode5/admin/
out/portpool.lst

UTL_FILE_DIR on database tier consists of the following directories.

1. /usr/tmp
2. /usr/tmp
3. /u01/ora_EBS/12.1.0.2/appsutil/outbound/EBSTEST_erpnode5
4. /usr/tmp
Choose a value which will be set as APPLPTMP value on the target node [1] : 3
Log file located at /d01/appl_EBS/fs1/inst/apps/EBSTEST_erpnode5/admin/log/clone/
ApplyAppsTier_01100720.log
|100% completed

Completed Apply...
Sun Jan 10 07:44:23 2016

Executing command: /d01/appl_EBS/fs1/EBSapps/10.1.2/bin/sqlplus @/d01/appl_EBS/fs1/EBSapps/
appl/ad/12.0.0/patch/115/sql/truncate_ad_nodes_config_status.sql

```
Do you want to startup the Application Services for EBSTEST? (y/n) [n] : n
```

```
Services not started
```

```
[applmgr@erpnode5 bin]$
```

After the execution of clone configuration script on RUN Edition we must execute it on patch edition.

Cloning in RAC-Enabled Systems

Rapid Clone supports both RAC to RAC cloning and RAC to non-RAC cloning, but in this scenario, you will see how to clone a multinode RAC-enabled system to a non-RAC single-node system. Table 11-7 describes the source and target EBS node configuration.

Table 11-7. Rapid Clone: RAC to Non-RAC Clone Environment Details

	Source System		Target System
	DB Nodes	**App Nodes**	**DB, App Nodes**
Host name	ebsnode1, ebsnode2	ebsnode1	erptest1
Instance name	PROD1, PROD2	PROD	ERPTEST
Location of dbTier	/u01/oraprod/11.2.0		/u01/oraebs_R12
Datafile location	+EBSDATA		/u01/oraebs_R12/data
Location of appsTier		/applebs	/u01/applebs_R12
OS users/group	oraprod	applprod	oraerp, applerp
OS version	OEL 5.6: 64-bit	OEL 5.6: 64-bit	OEL 6.6: 64-bit
DB version	11.2.0.3: RAC		11.2.0.3: Standalone
Apps version	-	12.2.0	12.2.0
Services	Database: Cluster	Root, form, web, batch processing	Database and application services

In this scenario, we will not discuss the cloning of the application tier because there are no changes in the steps of the application tier. The appsTier can be copied to the target machine from any of the source machines where the adpreclone.pl script was executed. Figure 11-8 provides the detailed steps that should be performed to clone an RAC-based system to a non-RAC system.

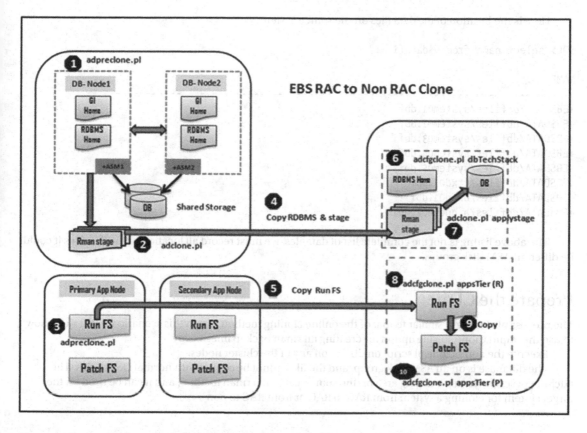

Figure 11-8. Rapid Clone: RAC to non-RAC clone process

We'll now talk about the source system instance details.

The following are the active instances running on ebsnode1 and ebsnode2:

```
SQL> select instance_name, status from gv$instance;

INSTANCE_NAMESTATUS
---------------- ------------
PROD1OPEN
PROD2OPEN

SQL>
```

Here is the location of the data files on the source system:

```
SQL> select name from v$datafile;

NAME
--------------------------------------------------------------------------
+EBSDATA/dbfiles/system01.dbf
+EBSDATA/dbfiles/system02.dbf
+EBSDATA/dbfiles/system03.dbf
+EBSDATA/dbfiles/system04.dbf
+EBSDATA/dbfiles/system05.dbf
+EBSDATA/dbfiles/ctxd01.dbf
+EBSDATA/dbfiles/owad01.dbf
+EBSDATA/dbfiles/a_queue02.dbf
```

The above listing is not the complete list of datafiles, we must record all location of the datafiles it could be different ASM disk groups.

Prepare the Clone

The process of cloning is similar to that of the online cloning method, but in this scenario we will show how to use the Rapid Clone staging option for creating an rman backup image copy.

Execute the adpreclone.pl script on dbTier on any of the cluster nodes.

The database is on an ASM disk group, and the file cannot be copied with normal OS utilities. The adclone.pl script creates a staging area on the source using the rman method, and it can be used on the target system for cloning a system from RAC to RAC or from RAC to non-RAC.

Execute the adclone.pl Script for Staging

The following output displays the options supported by the adclone.pl script:

```
$ perl adclone.pl

Copyright (c) 2011 Oracle Corporation
Redwood Shores, California, USA
Oracle E-Business Suite Rapid Clone
Version 12.2
adclone Version 120.69.12020000.47

USAGE:

perl adclone.pl java=<JDKTOP> \
mode=<MODE> \
stage=<STAGE> \
[component=<COMPONENT>] \
[method=<METHOD>] \
[appctx=<APPCTX>] \
[dbctx=<DBCTX>] \
[appctxtg=<APPCTXTG>] \
```

```
[dbctxtg=<DBCTXTG>] \
[<optional args>]

WHERE:

<JDKTOP>: Path to JDK location (1.5.0 or higher).
<MODE>: { stage | apply | clone | oamstage | oamapply |
fsclonestage | fscloneapply}
<STAGE> : Cloning Stage directory
<COMPONENT> : { all | appsTier | atTechStack | appltop| fmwHome | dev10gHome | ohsConfig
wlsConfig | cloneContext | dbTier | dbTechStack |
database | dbconfig | addracnode }
cloneContext correctly is applicable with
fsclonestage/apply mode.
<METHOD>: { CUSTOM | ZIP | RMAN | COPY | LINK }
<APPCTX>: Application Context File (for AT related components)
<DBCTX> : Database Context File (for DB related components)
<APPCTXTG>: Target Application Context File (in clone and apply mode)
<DBCTXTG> : Target Database Context File (in clone and apply mode)

[<optional args>]

  merge : To merge appltops
  pwd=<pwd> : Apps password. Default prompt interactively
  noprompt: No prompt before dbUp or dbDown. Default prompt
  noinventory : Clone without oraInventory. Only if SRC binary inventory is missing
  nthreads=<n>: Number of threads to be used for zip and unzip cloning
  temp=<temp> : Directory for temporary files. Default /tmp
  jobid=<jobid> : Jobid assigned by OAM. Applicable in "oamstage"/"oamapply" mode
  showProgress: Displays progress of the process
  orgctx=<ctx>: Applications Context File of the original or live source instance
  orgctx will be used only for preparing backup or nonlive Applications instance

"perl adclone.pl help" for more information
"perl adclone.pl examples" for usage examples
```

```
[oraprod@ebsnode1 bin]$ perl adclone.pl java=/u01/oraprod/PROD/11.2.0/jdk mode=stage stage=/
u01/oraprod/rman_bkp component=database method=RMAN dbctx=/u01/oraprod/PROD/11.2.0/appsutil/
PROD1_ebsnode1.xml pwd=apps showProgress

Beginning database Stage - Thu Jan 14 23:02:50 2016

/u01/oraprod/PROD/11.2.0/jdk/bin/java -Xmx600M -DCONTEXT_VALIDATED=false-Doracle.installer.
oui_loc=/u01/oraprod/PROD/11.2.0/oui -classpath /u01/oraprod/PROD/11.2.0/lib/xmlparserv2.
jar:/u01/oraprod/PROD/11.2.0/jdbc/lib/ojdbc6.jar:/u01/oraprod/PROD/11.2.0/appsutil/java:/
u01/oraprod/PROD/11.2.0/oui/jlib/OraInstaller.jar:/u01/oraprod/PROD/11.2.0/oui/jlib/ewt3.
jar:/u01/oraprod/PROD/11.2.0/oui/jlib/share.jar:/u01/oraprod/PROD/11.2.0/oui/jlib/srvm.jar:/
u01/oraprod/PROD/11.2.0/jlib/ojmisc.jaroracle.apps.ad.clone.StageDatabase -e /u01/oraprod/
PROD/11.2.0/appsutil/PROD1_ebsnode1.xml -stage /u01/oraprod/rman_bkp -tmp /tmp -method RMAN
-pwd apps -showProgress
```

```
Log file located at /u01/oraprod/PROD/11.2.0/appsutil/log/PROD1_ebsnode1/
StageDatabase_01142302.log
| 58% completed
Checking to determine if this environment is a Single Instance or a RAC Enabled system...
Database is ENABLED for RAC : RMAN Back Up Database beginning now...
This process usually takes quite some time, please wait for the staging process to complete.

Staging RAC Datafiles...This process will take quite a while to complete. Please be patient
and wait for the command to finish.

| 58% completed

Completed Stage...
Thu Jan 14 23:25:36 2016
[oraprod@ebsnode1 bin]$
```

After the successful creation of the stage area, you must copy the RDBMS Home, staging area, and application tier on the target system. Figure 11-8 illustrates the scenario of EBS RAC to a non-RAC clone and displays the required files that should be copied on the target system.

Configure the Clone on the Target System

First you should configure the target database tier with the dbTechStack option. Then you can apply the stage for configuring the target database. In the stage application phase, the adclone.pl script will restore the rman backup in "scaled-down" mode as you are cloning from RAC to non-RAC.

Here is the execution of adcfgclone.pl dbTechStack:

```
[oraerp@erptest1 bin]$ perl adcfgclone.pl dbtechStack

Copyright (c) 2011 Oracle Corporation
Redwood Shores, California, USA

Oracle E-Business Suite Rapid Clone

Version 12.2

adcfgclone Version 120.63.12020000.7.1202010.2
adcfgclone: unrecognized action specified: "dbtechStack"
[oraerp@erptest1 bin]$ perl adcfgclone.pl dbTechStack

Copyright (c) 2011 Oracle Corporation
Redwood Shores, California, USA

Oracle E-Business Suite Rapid Clone

Version 12.2

adcfgclone Version 120.63.12020000.7.1202010.2

Enter the APPS password :
```

Running:
/u01/oraebs_R12/11.2.0/appsutil/clone/bin/../jre/bin/java -Xmx600M -cp /u01/oraebs_
R12/11.2.0/appsutil/clone/jlib/java:/u01/oraebs_R12/11.2.0/appsutil/clone/jlib/xmlparserv2.
jar:/u01/oraebs_R12/11.2.0/appsutil/clone/jlib/ojdbc5.jar oracle.apps.ad.context.
CloneContext -e /u01/oraebs_R12/11.2.0/appsutil/clone/bin/../context/db/CTXORIG.xml
-validate -pairsfile /tmp/adpairsfile_8750.lst -stage /u01/oraebs_R12/11.2.0/appsutil/clone
-dbTechStack 2> /tmp/adcfgclone_8750.err; echo $? > /tmp/adcfgclone_8750.res

Log file located at /u01/oraebs_R12/11.2.0/appsutil/clone/bin/CloneContext_0116004502.log

Provide the values required for creation of the new Database Context file.
Target System Hostname (virtual or normal) [erptest1] :

Target Instance is RAC (y/n) [y] : n

Target System Database SID : TESTERP

Target System Base Directory : /u01/oraebs_R12

Target System utl_file_dir Directory List : /usr/tmp

Number of DATA_TOP's on the Target System [3] : 1

Target System DATA_TOP Directory 1 : /u01/oraebs_R12/data

Target System RDBMS ORACLE_HOME Directory [/u01/oraebs_R12/11.2.0] :

Target System Archive Log Directory [/u01/oraebs_R12/data/archive] :

Do you want to preserve the Display [localhost:10.0] (y/n): n

Target System Display [erptest1:0.0] :

Do you want the target system to have the same port values as the source system (y/n) [y] ? : n

Target System Port Pool [0-99] : 25

Checking the port pool 25
done: Port Pool 25 is free
Report file located at /u01/oraebs_R12/11.2.0/appsutil/temp/portpool.lst
Complete port information available at /u01/oraebs_R12/11.2.0/appsutil/temp/portpool.lst

Creating the new Database Context file from :
/u01/oraebs_R12/11.2.0/appsutil/template/adxdbctx.tmp

The new database context file has been created :
/u01/oraebs_R12/11.2.0/appsutil/TESTERP_erptest1.xml

Log file located at /u01/oraebs_R12/11.2.0/appsutil/clone/bin/CloneContext_0116004502.log
Check Clone Context logfile /u01/oraebs_R12/11.2.0/appsutil/clone/bin/
CloneContext_0116004502.log for details.

```
Running Rapid Clone with command:
Running:
perl /u01/oraebs_R12/11.2.0/appsutil/clone/bin/adclone.pl java=/u01/oraebs_R12/11.2.0/
appsutil/clone/bin/../jre mode=apply stage=/u01/oraebs_R12/11.2.0/appsutil/clone
component=dbTechStack method=CUSTOM dbctxtg=/u01/oraebs_R12/11.2.0/appsutil/TESTERP_
erptest1.xml showProgress contextValidated=true

Beginning rdbms home Apply - Sat Jan 16 00:46:02 2016

/u01/oraebs_R12/11.2.0/appsutil/clone/bin/../jre/bin/java -Xmx600M -DCONTEXT_VALIDATED=true-
Doracle.installer.oui_loc=/u01/oraebs_R12/11.2.0/oui -classpath /u01/oraebs_R12/11.2.0/
appsutil/clone/jlib/xmlparserv2.jar:/u01/oraebs_R12/11.2.0/appsutil/clone/jlib/ojdbc6.jar:/
u01/oraebs_R12/11.2.0/appsutil/clone/jlib/java:/u01/oraebs_R12/11.2.0/appsutil/clone/jlib/
oui/OraInstaller.jar:/u01/oraebs_R12/11.2.0/appsutil/clone/jlib/oui/ewt3.jar:/u01/oraebs_
R12/11.2.0/appsutil/clone/jlib/oui/share.jar:/u01/oraebs_R12/11.2.0/appsutil/clone/jlib/
oui/srvm.jar:/u01/oraebs_R12/11.2.0/appsutil/clone/jlib/ojmisc.jar oracle.apps.ad.clone.
ApplyDBTechStack -e /u01/oraebs_R12/11.2.0/appsutil/TESTERP_erptest1.xml -stage /u01/oraebs_
R12/11.2.0/appsutil/clone -showProgress
APPS Password : Log file located at /u01/oraebs_R12/11.2.0/appsutil/log/TESTERP_erptest1/
ApplyDBTechStack_01160046.log
-100% completed

Completed Apply...
Sat Jan 16 00:53:06 2016

Starting database listener for TESTERP:
Running:
/u01/oraebs_R12/11.2.0/appsutil/scripts/TESTERP_erptest1/addlnctl.sh start TESTERP
Logfile: /u01/oraebs_R12/11.2.0/appsutil/log/TESTERP_erptest1/addlnctl.txt

You are running addlnctl.sh version 120.4

Starting listener process TESTERP ...

LSNRCTL for Linux: Version 11.2.0.3.0 - Production on 16-JAN-2016 00:53:09

Copyright (c) 1991, 2011, Oracle.All rights reserved.

Starting /u01/oraebs_R12/11.2.0/bin/tnslsnr: please wait...

TNSLSNR for Linux: Version 11.2.0.3.0 - Production
System parameter file is /u01/oraebs_R12/11.2.0/network/admin/TESTERP_erptest1/listener.ora
Log messages written to /u01/oraebs_R12/11.2.0/admin/TESTERP_erptest1/diag/tnslsnr/erptest1/
testerp/alert/log.xml
Listening on: (DESCRIPTION=(ADDRESS=(PROTOCOL=tcp)(HOST=erptest1.oralabs.com)(PORT=1546)))

Connecting to (DESCRIPTION=(ADDRESS=(PROTOCOL=TCP)(HOST=erptest1.oralabs.com)(PORT=1546)))
STATUS of the LISTENER
------------------------
Alias TESTERP
```

```
Version TNSLSNR for Linux: Version 11.2.0.3.0 - Production
Start Date16-JAN-2016 00:53:10
Uptime0 days 0 hr. 0 min. 0 sec
Trace Level off
SecurityON: Local OS Authentication
SNMPOFF
Listener Parameter File /u01/oraebs_R12/11.2.0/network/admin/TESTERP_erptest1/listener.ora
Listener Log File /u01/oraebs_R12/11.2.0/admin/TESTERP_erptest1/diag/tnslsnr/erptest1/
testerp/alert/log.xml
Listening Endpoints Summary...
(DESCRIPTION=(ADDRESS=(PROTOCOL=tcp)(HOST=erptest1.oralabs.com)(PORT=1546)))
Services Summary...
Service "TESTERP" has 1 instance(s).
Instance "TESTERP", status UNKNOWN, has 1 handler(s) for this service...
The command completed successfully

addlnctl.sh: exiting with status 0

addlnctl.sh: check the logfile /u01/oraebs_R12/11.2.0/appsutil/log/TESTERP_erptest1/
addlnctl.txt for more information ...

[oraerp@erptest1 bin]$
```

After successful completion of dbTechStack, the stage can be applied on the target system.

■ **Tip** Shut down the listener started in earlier stages or else adclone.pl will fail while applying the stage. As a part of configuration, adclone.pl will try to start the listener, and if it's already started, it will fail.

Execute adclone.pl on the Target System

Here is the execution:

```
[oraerp@erptest1 bin]$ perl adclone.pl java=/u01/oraebs_R12/11.2.0/jdk component=dbTier
mode=apply stage=/u01/oraebs_R12/11.2.0/appsutil/clonemethod=RMAN dbctxtg=/u01/oraebs_
R12/11.2.0/appsutil/TESTERP_erptest1.xml rmanstage=/u01/rman_bkp/rman_backup rmantgtloc=/
u01/oraebs_R12/data srcdbname=PROD pwd=apps showProgress

Beginning database tier Apply - Sun Jan 17 21:33:56 2016

|0% completed
Log file located at /u01/oraebs_R12/11.2.0/appsutil/log/TESTERP_erptest1/
ApplyDBTier_01172133.log
/ 50% completed Determining Source system database type ("single" or "rac").
Source system indentified as being of type "rac"!

The system is identified as being a RAC Scale Down!
```

```
- 50% completed
Restoring RAC database in "Scale Down" mode onto new target system via RMAN.

In scale down mode rapidclone will remove the unwanted redo threads and undo tablespaces.

THIS PROCESS TAKES SIGNIFICANT TIME TO COMPLETE AND DEPENDS UPON THE SOURCE SYSTEM DB SIZE
```

As a last step on the database tier, you must execute AutoConfig to make sure the dbTier configuration completed successfully without any issues and that you are ready to proceed with the application tier services.

On the application tier, you must enable all application services on the same node, as illustrated during the multinode to single-node clone earlier in this chapter.

Adding Nodes and Configuring Shared APPL_TOP

In Chapter 2 we discussed that multiple application tier node deployment is not supported with the Rapidwiz Install Wizard, so you have to add nodes to the existing topology after upgrading it to 12.2.4/12.2.5 with code level Delta6/Delta7. In this section, you will see how you can add a secondary application node to the existing topology using the Shared APPL_TOP option.

The detailed steps for configuring the Shared APPL_TOP is discussed in MOS note "Sharing the Application Tier File System in Oracle E-Business Suite Release 12.2" (Doc ID 1375769.1). In this note, the NFS option for sharing a file system is discussed in detail. But in this section, you will see how to configure OCFS2 for sharing the application tier file system. The detailed steps for configuring OCFS2 for the Shared APPL_TOP can be downloaded from the source code.

Points to Be Considered for Shared APPL_TOP Deployment

Consider these points:

- The sharing of APPL_TOP in a Windows environment is not supported.

- INST_TOP also will be in shared locations unlike earlier releases.

- All application tiers sharing the file system should be running on the same operating system.

- Shared application tier file systems should be in read-write mode on all application tiers.

- If using the OCFS2 file system, then it's recommended that you use the default block size.

Figure 11-9 provides the deployment topology of the Shared APPL_TOP in a multinode environment.

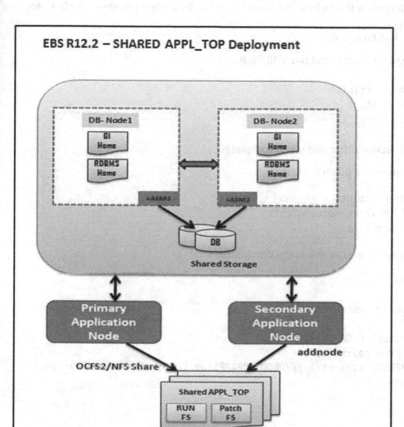

Figure 11-9. *Rapid Clone: Shared APPL_TOP deployment*

- Before starting, ensure the full patching cycle has completed without issues. You can run an empty patching cycle to verify this.

```
adop phase=finalize
adop phase=cutover
adop phase=cleanup
```

- Synchronize the application file system if this wasn't done earlier. This step can be skipped if it was performed earlier as part of the 12.2.4/12.2.5 upgrade.

```
adop phase=fs_clone
```

Once these steps have completed successfully, now you are ready to add the secondary application tier. The node addition process is different for the Delta6 and Delta7 code levels, so the procedures for both are discussed in this section.

Here are the steps for the Delta6 code level:

1. Execute adpreclone.pl on the run and patch file systems.

```
$ cd $INST_TOP/admin/scripts
$ ./adadminsrvctl.sh start
$ perl adpreclone.pl appsTier
```

You should stop application services after this script completes.

2. Execute adpreclone.pl on the patch file system.

```
$ cd $INST_TOP/admin/scripts
$ ./adadminsrvctl.sh start forcepatchfs
$ ./adpreclone.pl appsTier
```

You should stop application services after this script completes.

```
$ ./adstpall.sh apps/apps
```

3. Create the pairsfile for the run file system.

```
$ mkdir -p /u01/oraEBS/PROD/pairsfile/run
$ cd /u01/oraEBS/PROD/pairsfile/run
$ cp /u01/oraEBS/PROD/fs1/inst/apps/PROD_ERPAPP1/appl/admin/PROD_ERPAPP1_run.txt
myrunpairsfile.txt
```

Edit the following:

```
[Instance Specific]

s_temp=/u01/oraEBS/PROD/fs1/inst/apps/PROD_ERPAPP2/temp
s_contextname=PROD_ERPAPP2
s_hostname=ERPAPP2
s_domainname=oralabs.com
s_cphost=ERPAPP2
s_webhost=ERPAPP2
s_config_home=/u01/oraEBS/PROD/fs1/inst/apps/PROD_ERPAPP2
s_display=ERPAPP2:0.0
s_forms-c4ws_display=ERPAPP2:0.0
s_ohs_instance=EBS_web_PROD_OHS2

[Services]

s_web_applications_status=enabled
s_web_entry_status=enabled
s_apcstatus=enabled
s_root_status=enabled
s_batch_status=enabled
s_other_service_group_status=disabled
s_adminserverstatus=disabled
```

4. Configure the run file system on the secondary node.

```
export PATH=/u01/oraEBS/PROD/fs1/FMW_Home/webtier/perl/bin:$PATH
cd /u01/oraEBS/PROD/fs1/EBSapps/comn/clone/bin

[applmgr@ERPAPP2 bin]$ perl ./adclonectx.pl \
> addnode contextfile=/u01/oraEBS/PROD/fs1/inst/apps/PROD_ERPAPP1/appl/admin/PROD_ERPAPP1.
xml \
> pairsfile=/u01/oraEBS/PROD/pairsfile/run/myrunpairsfile.txt \
> outfile=/u01/oraEBS/PROD/fs1/inst/apps/PROD_ERPAPP2/appl/admin/PROD_ERPAPP2.xml

Copyright (c) 2011 Oracle Corporation
Redwood Shores, California, USA

Oracle E-Business Suite Rapid Clone
Version 12.2
adclonectx Version 120.30.12020000.10

...

Creating the new APPL_TOP Context file from :
/u01/oraEBS/PROD/fs1/EBSapps/appl/ad/12.0.0/admin/template/adxmlctx.tmp

The new APPL_TOP context file has been created :
/u01/oraEBS/PROD/fs1/inst/apps/PROD_ERPAPP2/appl/admin/PROD_ERPAPP2.xml

Log file located at /u01/oraEBS/PROD/fs1/EBSapps/comn/clone/bin/EBSProvision.log
contextfile=/u01/oraEBS/PROD/fs1/inst/apps/PROD_ERPAPP2/appl/admin/PROD_ERPAPP2.xml

Node ERPAPP2.oralabs.com is added successfully
```

5. Now you should have a pairsfile for the RUN file system.

The process for creating the pairsfile for the patch file system is identical, but in the patch file system pairsfile you should provide the location of the patch file system. The previously listed parameters for the run pairsfile can remain the same.

6. Configure the patch file system on the secondary application tier.

On the primary application node, start the admin server for the patch file system.

```
$ cd /u01/oraEBS/PROD/fs2/inst/apps/PROD_ERPAPP1/admin/scripts

./adadminsrvctl.sh start forcepatchfs

export PATH=/u01/oraEBS/PROD/fs2/FMW_Home/webtier/perl/bin:$PATH
cd /u01/oraEBS/PROD/fs2/EBSapps/comn/clone/bin
[applmgr@ERPAPP2 bin]$ perl ./adclonectx.pl \
> addnode contextfile=/u01/oraEBS/PROD/fs2/inst/apps/PROD_ERPAPP1/appl/admin/PROD_ERPAPP1.xml \
> pairsfile=/u01/oraEBS/PROD/pairsfile/patch/mypatchpairsfile.txt \
> outfile=/u01/oraEBS/PROD/fs2/inst/apps/PROD_ERPAPP2/appl/admin/PROD_ERPAPP2.xml
```

```
Copyright (c) 2011 Oracle Corporation
Redwood Shores, California, USA

Oracle E-Business Suite Rapid Clone

Version 12.2

adclonectx Version 120.30.12020000.10

....
....

Node ERPAPP2.oralabs.com is added successfully
```

Now we'll discuss the Delta7 code-level changes.

As discussed earlier, the dualfs Rapid Clone option was introduced in the version Delta7 code level, so there are slight changes even while adding secondary application nodes.

1. The Perl utility should point to the FMW Home.

```
$ which perl
/u01/appl_PROD/fs1/FMW_Home/webtier/perl/bin/perl
```

2. The WebLogic admin server should be running on both file systems (run and patch).

3. The creation of the pairsfile is the same as was illustrated with the Delta6 code level.

4. Configure the run edition and patch edition at one time with the dualfs option.

```
[applmgr@ERPAPP2 bin]$ perl ./adclonectx.pl \
> addnode contextfile=/u01/oraEBS/PROD/fs2/inst/apps/PROD_ERPAPP1/appl/admin/PROD_ERPAPP1.xml \
> pairsfile=/u01/oraEBS/PROD/pairsfile/patch/mypatchpairsfile.txt \
>  dualfs=yes
```

Here are some additional post-node steps:

1. Configure the load balancer in front of the application tiers.

The load balancer virtual host is globalebs.oralabs.com, and the load balancer port is 80.
The following entries should be added to both the application tier context files.

```
s_webentryhost APP
s_webentrydomain: oralabs.com
s_active_webport: 80
s_login_page:http://globalebs.oralabs.com/OA_HTML/AppsLogin
s_external_url: http://globalebs.oralabs.com
```

After completing these changes, do the following:

2. Execute AutoConfig on both the primary and secondary application nodes.

3. Restart application services on both the primary and secondary application nodes.

4. Test the connectivity of the application from the load balancer entry point URL.

Post-cloning Steps

So far we have discussed multiple supported scenarios of cloning an Oracle E-Business Suite environment, but we have not covered the post-cloning steps in each scenario. This section covers all the steps that should be performed on the target (newly cloned) environment.

Change Passwords for All Superusers

It is highly recommended that you change the password for all the superuser accounts during cloning or immediately after finishing the clone activity. In Oracle EBS, the following are considered superuser accounts: SYS, SYSTEM, APPS, SYSADMIN, WEBLOGIC, and ADMIN. Since EBS 12.2, all the user passwords of these accounts can be changed during the execution of Rapid Clone (adcfgclone.pl) on dbTier. In fact, you already saw how to use this option for changing the passwords during the execution of Rapidwiz during the multinode cloning example.

Please refer to Chapter 12, for changing the passwords for these superuser accounts.

Configure the Workflow Mailer

The Workflow (WF) notification mailer is configured to use an SMTP e-mail account for business event notifications, and in some configurations, a POP3/IMAP account will also be configured if inbound processing is enabled. In most of these cases, the WF notification mailer is not required in test environments; therefore, you should remove the production WF mailer configuration to avoid any issues related to the WF mailer in the production environment.

If there is a requirement to have a WF notification mailer in the test environment, then you should ensure different SMTP and IMAP accounts are being configured in the target system WF configuration.

Size the Target System

If the target system is a nonproduction system, then the resources on the target system should be scaled down. On test and development systems, the same amount of resources are not required as production. Hence, based on the sizing requirement discussed in Chapter 2, you should reduce the number of concurrent managers and SGA size accordingly. If the clone is prepared for load/performance testing, it's recommended that you use the same size of compute nodes.

Change System Profiles

There are certain profile options that must be changed on a cloned system if it's a nonproduction system. It's recommended that you change the following profile options after finishing the clone:

```
Java Color scheme=>Choose any other color from PROD system (Example: Olive Green)
Site Name=>Change it to any desired name (Example: TEST - clone 18jan2016)
```

These profile options are used to differentiate between test and production systems.

Update Printer Settings

Mostly Oracle EBS concurrent requests use the network printer for printing reports. If the test system is in a different VLAN or there is a requirement to use a different type of printer on the cloned system, then you must delete the existing printer and configure a new printer, as discussed in Chapter 9.

Cancel Scheduled Concurrent Requests

On a production system there may be multiple scheduled concurrent requests that may not be required to run on the test system. In those cases, we recommend you cancel the scheduled concurrent requests on the test system to avoid unnecessary consumption of system resources.

Troubleshooting Cloning Issues

Troubleshooting the issue specific to cloning requires analysis of multiple log files. To avoid any issues on the source and target systems during clone preparation and configuration, you should ensure that all prerequisites are in place, and it's highly recommended that you have applied the latest AD and TKX patches.

Log Files on the Source System

Here we give the locations of the log files on the source system.

- adpreclone.pldbTier:

```
Location==>$ORACLE_HOME/appsutil/<context_name>/SatgeDBTier_MMDDHHMM.log
Example : /d01/ora_test/12.1.0.2/appsutil/log/TEST_erptest1/StageDBTier_01012218.log
```

- adpreclone.plappsTier:

```
Location ==> $INST_TOP/admin/log/StageAppsTier_MMDDHHMM.log
```

```
Example : /d01/appl_test/fs1/inst/apps/TEST_erptest1/admin/log/clone/StageAppsTier_01012224.log
```

Log Files on the Target System

Here we give the locations of the log files on the target system.

- adcfgclone.pldbTier:

```
Location==>$ORACLE_HOME/appsutil/<context_name>/ApplyDBTier_<TIME>.log
Example : /u01/ora_EBS/12.1.0.2/appsutil/log/EBSPROD_erpdb1/ApplyDBTier_01030017.log
```

- Clone context file logs:

```
Location==>$ORACLE_HOME/appsutil/clone/bin/ CloneContext_<TIME>.log
```

Example : /u01/ora_EBS/12.1.0.2/appsutil/clone/bin/CloneContext_0103001614.log

- adcfgclone.plappsTier:

Location ==> $INST_TOP/admin/log/clone/ApplyAppsTier_<TIME>.log

Example: /u01/appl_EBS/fs1/inst/apps/EBSPROD_erpapp1/admin/log/clone/ApplyAppsTier_01052252.log

- Clone context file logs:

Location ==>$COMMON_TOP/clone/bin/CloneContext_<TIME>.log

Example : /u01/appl_EBS/fs1/EBSapps/comn/clone/bin/CloneContext_0105225137.log

- FMW prerequisite check logs:

Location ==> $COMMON_TOP/clone/FMW/logs/prereqcheck.log

Example : /u01/appl_EBS/fs1/EBSapps/comn/clone/FMW/logs/prereqcheck.log

The following are the MOS tech notes related to 12.2 cloning and illustrating the generic issues you may encounter during cloning:

- "12.2.X Rapid Clone fails with error 'Exiting cloning as FMW Home already exists'" (Doc ID 1900583.1)

- "12.2 Adpreclone Fails with ERROR: The context variable s_apps_jdbc_connect_ descriptor is" (Doc ID 1997026.1)

- "12.2 Cloning Fails As Adpreclone Does Not Generate FMW_home.jar Correctly" (Doc ID 2076461.1)

- "EBS 12.2 adcfgclone.pl on AP Tier failed with ERROR: Script failed, exit code 255 when creating new wls domain" (Doc ID 1986208.1)

- "Cloning E-business Suite 12.2 - Hangs Stopping Derby Server at command perl adcfgclone.pl appsTier" (Doc ID 1990435.1)

- "R12.2 adpreclone Fails On Applications Tier, txkSetOHSConfig.pl preClone Instance failing with "Script failed, exit code 9" (Doc ID 1586101.1)

- "Adcfgclone AppsTier Failing During Clone Into When Source And Target Are On Same Host" (Doc ID 2002613.1)

Summary

In this chapter, we walked you through the basic concepts of cloning and the execution procedure of the Rapid Clone utility on the source and target systems. We covered different cloning scenarios, from a simple single-node to single-node clone to a complex multinode E-Business Suite environment. The new clone configuration option called dualfs was also demonstrated in this chapter.

## CHAPTER 12

An Introduction to Oracle EBS Security

Security is one of the most critical aspects of any business application. With increased sophistication in which the business applications are attacked and the continuous demands of business in the wake of competition, it is becoming more challenging to provide mechanisms to protect from all kinds of vulnerabilities.

Oracle is at the forefront of innovation and technology and provides security options at each level. Oracle EBS is a three-tier architecture, and the security should be considered at all layers as well as its underlying components.

Starting from the installation and configuration up to the access and control process, Oracle provides all kinds of options to run the business application securely.

Figure 12-1 shows the typical security model that can be used for securing environments at all layers.

The client connects to the application from supported web browsers using the HTTP/HTTPS protocol. All incoming client requests will be processed through the network firewall, which will allow only authorized clients based on the rules configured in it. After that, the network firewall user access is processed through the middle tiers to the database using sqlnet authentication. In Figure 12-1 there are multiple security options available to secure the database layer. Let's see how you can configure the secure socket in an Oracle EBS 12.2 environment.

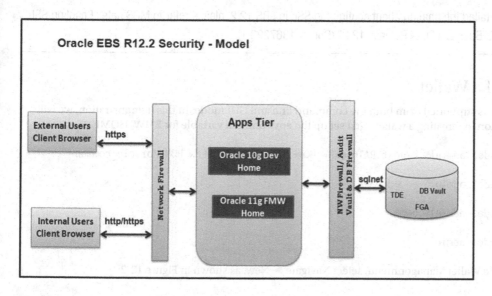

Figure 12-1. *Oracle EBS high-level security model*

© Syed Zaheer and Erman Arslan 2016
S. Zaheer and E. Arslan, *Practical Oracle E-Business Suite*, DOI 10.1007/978-1-4842-1422-0_12

Oracle E-Business Suite security is a very big topic in itself, so in this chapter we will cover some of the key security-related topics.

We suggest you refer to "Oracle E-Business Suite Security Guide, Release 12.2, Part Number E22952-13" to know more about security-specific functionalities. You can find it here:

```
http://docs.oracle.com/cd/E26401_01/doc.122/e22952/T156458T156461.htm#T156495
```

Configuring SSL/TSL with Oracle EBS 12.2

Secure Sockets Layer (SSL) is a protocol that is used to establish a secure and encrypted link between a web server and a browser. In a nutshell, it manages the server authentication, client authentication, and encrypted communication between the web server and the browser.

With EBS 12.2, Oracle Fusion Middleware supports SSL version 3 and TLS version 1. But it's not recommended that you use SSL 3 because of "POODLE exlpoit." Transport Layer Security (TLS) is much secure so far. For web tier components, EBS still uses Oracle Wallet to store and manage certificates. EBS 12.2 supports wildcard characters.

SSL is a protocol that will be used as the medium of encrypted communication between the clients and the servers. By default Oracle EBS is configured to use the HTTP protocol for the web server and SSL for forms services. The data being transferred with these protocols is clear-text packets, and anyone can use a packet sniffer on a client machine to read all the transmitted data between the client machine and the server. Hackers can even get the sysadmin username and password and steal data or damage the whole system.

To overcome this issue, it's highly recommended to configure SSL for both internal and external networks. In recent studies, most of the data theft cases were reported on internal networks; many customers still have not been convinced to use SSL for internal networks, which itself is a high risk.

EBS 12.2 SSL certificates management will be done by FMW_HOME, accessible using the Oracle Wallet Manager (OWM), which is a graphical user interface, or the new ORAPKI, which is a command-line utility.

As part of implementing SSL, it is important to review the current JRE deployment and also look into enhanced JAR file signing. By default 12 uses the forms listener servlet. Hence, it will share the same wallet as Oracle HTTP Server; a separate certificate is no longer needed for forms.

■ **Note** For detailed information about configuring SSL in EBS 12.2, please refer to MOS note "Enabling SSL or TLS in Oracle E-Business Suite Release 12.2" (Doc ID 1367293.1).

Creation of a Wallet

Creating a wallet is supported from both the command line and GUI mode. In this demonstration, we will use the GUI option for creating a wallet. First set up the environment variable for FMW_HOME.

```
[applebs@erpnode2 admin]$ export PATH=$FMW_HOME/webtier/bin:$FMW_HOME/oracle_common/
bin:$PATH
[applebs@erpnode2 admin]$

[applebs@erpnode2 admin]$ owm&
[1] 23233
[applebs@erpnode2 admin]$
```

In the Oracle Wallet Manager menu, select Navigate ➤ New, as shown in Figure 12-2.

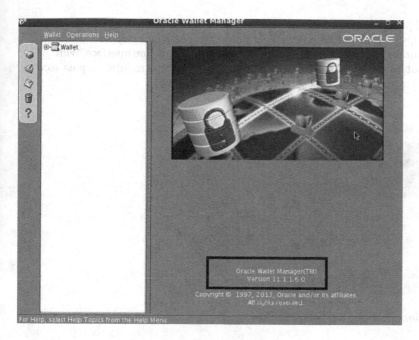

Figure 12-2. *Oracle Wallet Manager: creating a wallet*

1. Click No when Oracle Wallet Manager prompts for the default wallet directory creation.

2. Create a new password for the wallet, as shown in Figure 12-3.

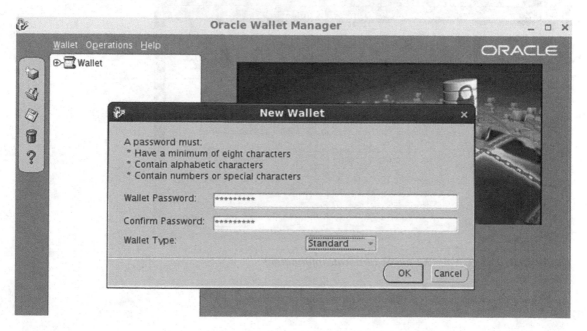

Figure 12-3. *Oracle Wallet Manager: configuring password*

The new wallet screen will prompt you to enter a password for your wallet. Configure a password that you can remember or keep a copy in a safe place because it's required for opening the wallet with Oracle Wallet Manager. Or you can perform operations on the wallet using the command-line interface. With autologin enabled, processes submitted by the OS user who created the wallet don't require the password to be entered. Click Yes when prompted, as shown in Figure 12-4.

Figure 12-4. Oracle Wallet Manager: empty wallet creation

After creating the wallet, the OWM prompts for the creation of a certificate request. Click Yes and fill the form accordingly, as shown in Figure 12-5. (You should use the information provided by your customer/company for OU, state, country, key size, and so on.)

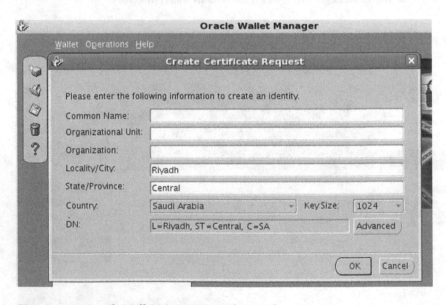

Figure 12-5. Oracle Wallet Manager: certificate information

Figure 12-6 displays the certificate request creation message.

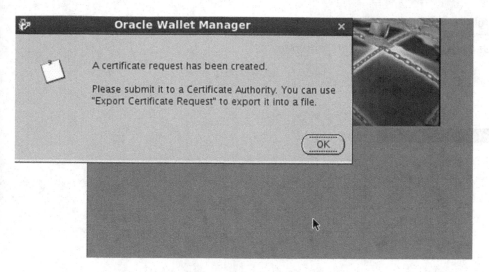

Figure 12-6. *Oracle Wallet Manager: certificate request*

3. After creating the certificate, you need to export it, as shown in Figure 12-7.

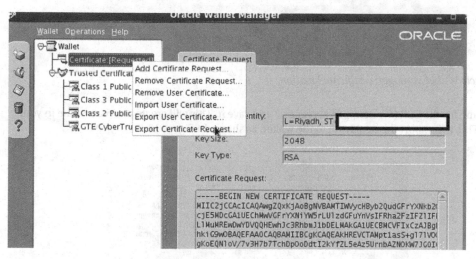

Figure 12-7. *Oracle Wallet Manager: certificate export*

4. At the time of exporting, you should write down the name of the directory as this directory location will be the default directory of the wallet, as shown in Figure 12-8.

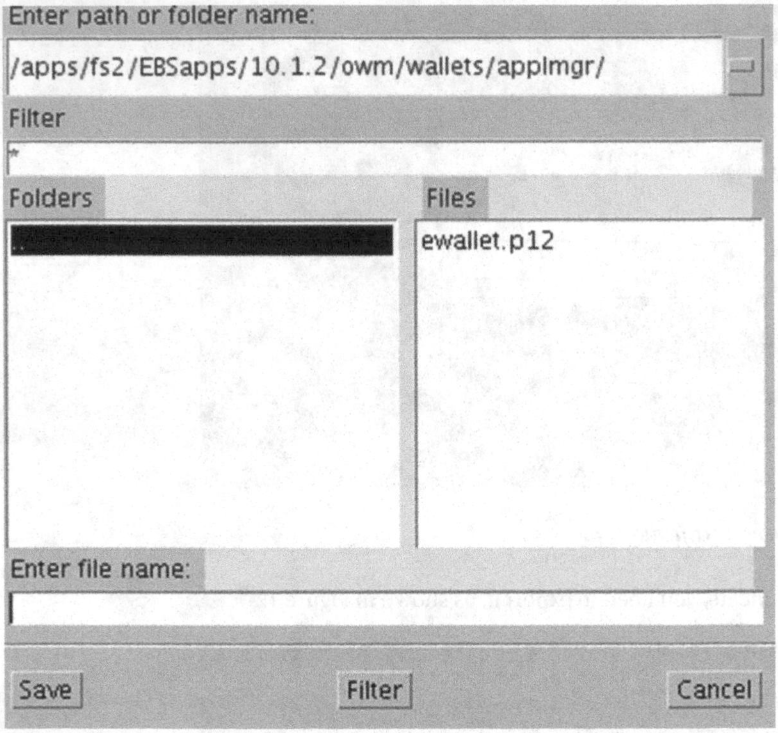

Enter path or folder name:
/apps/fs2/EBSapps/10.1.2/owm/wallets/applmgr/
Filter
*
Folders
Files
ewallet.p12
Enter file name:
Save
Filter
Cancel

***Figure 12-8.** Oracle Wallet Manager: certificate location*

Declare a name for the CSR (for example, server.csr) and save it. This will create a server.csr file in your wallet directory. This will export the certificate to the wallet, as shown in Figure 12-9.

Certificate request exported successfully to: /apps/fs2/EBSapps/10.1.2/owm/wallets/applmgr/server.csr

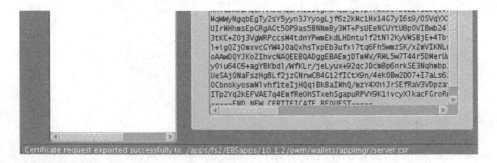

***Figure 12-9.** Oracle Wallet Manager: certificate exported*

At this stage, you should send this to your customer because they need to submit this to a certificate authority to request a server certificate. Then the certificate authority will issue a new server certificate based on the provided configuration.

If the customer/company has already acquired certification in .P12 file format, then you need to convert it to JKS format and then from JKS to Wallet.

```
keytool -v -importkeystore -srckeystore yourcert.p12 -srcstoretype PKCS12 -destkeystore
yournewkeystore.jks -deststoretype JKS
```

5. You must use the same password for the new JKS file, and the private key is mypassword. This will allow Oracle Wallet to use the server certificate and private key.

```
keytool -import -alias Root -keystore yournewkeystore.jks -trustcacerts -file root.cer
keytool -import -alias Intermediate -keystore yournewkeystore.jks -trustcacerts -file
intermediate.cer mw_home\oracle_common\bin\orapki wallet create -wallet ./ -pwd "mypassword"
mw_home\oracle_common\bin\orapki wallet jks_to_pkcs12 -wallet ./ -pwd "mypassword" -keystore
./yournewkeystore.jks -jkspwd "mypassword"
```

Verify the private key password and the wallet password match mypassword.

Open the newly created ewallet.p12 with Oracle Wallet Manager and in the Wallet menu, select autologin and then save. This creates cwallet.sso with ewallet.p12.

6. Once there is a valid wallet (ewallet.p12 and an autologin file called cwallet.sso), you can proceed with the SSL configuration.

7. While configuring autologin using Wallet Manager, you should save your wallet into the directory {s_web_ssl_directory}/Apache.

8. Curly braces are for the AutoConfig variables. This information is available in the application context file.

9. There are certain situations where the certificate authority will provide a main server certificate and an intermediate certificate's as well. This will make up the chain of certification. You should always import all certificates into Wallet Manager prior to importing the server certificate. After this, you are now ready to import the root and intermediate certificates into the b64InternetCertificate.txt file.

So, in this case, you should add the certificates to the related files.

```
cat ca.crt >> <10.1.2 ORACLE_HOME>/sysman/config/b64InternetCertificate.txt
cat intca.crt >> <10.1.2 ORACLE_HOME>/sysman/config/b64InternetCertificate.txt
```

Then you should copy the cwallet.sso file from the {s_web_ssl_directory}/Apache directory (where it was saved) to the following directories:

```
{s_ohs_instance_loc}/config/OHS/{s_ohs_component}/keystores/default
{s_ohs_instance_loc}/config/OPMN/opmn/wallet
$EBS_DOMAIN_HOME/opmn/{s_ohs_instance}/{s_ohs_component}/wallet
$EBS_DOMAIN_HOME/opmn/{s_ohs_instance}/wallet
$FMW_HOME/webtier/instances/{s_ohs_instance}/config/OHS/{s_ohs_component}/proxy-wallet
```

10. Then, you should update the cacert file (Oracle WebLogic Server, Oracle Web Services, and so on, use this file).

```
cd {s_fmw_jdktop}/jre/lib/security
chmod u+w cacerts
keytool -import -alias OHSRootCA -file ca.crt -trustcacerts -v -keystore cacerts
keytool -import -alias OHSIntCA -file intca.crt -trustcacerts -v -keystore cacerts
keytool -import -alias OHSServer -file server.crt -trustcacerts -v -keystore cacerts
```

On a UNIX system, the TCP/IP port numbers below 1024 are special. On these ports only processes with root privileges are allowed to listen. So, opening a privileged port requires extra steps, but we don't use privileged port normally. We choose to have an unknown port that is higher than port 1024.

Your cacerts and wallet files are configured now, so you are ready to continue with application configuration to use these files to supply SSL communication. These are self-signed certificates, and they should be available on client machines as trusted.

Configuration of the Web Tier (FMW)

As you know, Oracle application access works with FMW web tier components, so you must first configure the web tier components for enabling SSL. The following steps are required for configuring SSL on the web tier.

1. Log in to the Oracle Fusion Middleware Control Console. Select Web Tier Target under EBS Domain.

2. Select Administration ➤ Advanced Configuration.

3. Select the ssl.conf file to edit.

4. Update the Listen <port> and the VirtualHost _default_:<port> directives to the SSL port (for example, Listen 4443 changes to your choice -- ssl port).

5. Click Apply.

6. Execute the following command by the application owner OS user with the application environment.

    ```
    perl $AD_TOP/bin/adSyncContext.pl contextfile=$CONTEXT_FILE
    ```

7. adSyncContext.pl will propagate the changes you just made from the Oracle Fusion Middleware Control Console to the context file variables.

■ **Note** The detailed usage of this script is discussed in Chapter 8.

You should edit the context variables listed in Table 12-1 as necessary; you can edit these values using the OAM editor or at the command line using the vi editor.

Table 12-1. *Oracle EBS SSL Context Variables*

Context Variable	Non-SSL Value	SSL Value
s_url_protocol	http	https
s_local_url_protocol	http	https
s_webentryurlprotocol	http	https
s_active_webport	Same as s_webport	Same as s_webssl_port
s_webssl_port		Default is 4443
s_https_listen_parameter		Same as s_webssl_port
s_login_page	URL constructed with HTTP protocol and s_webport	URL constructed with https protocol and s_webssl_port
s_external_url	URL constructed with HTTP protocol and s_webport	URL constructed with HTTPS protocol and s_webssl_port

As a last configuration step, you must shut down all application services and execute AutoConfig to reflect the new changes. After successful execution of AutoConfig, you should start the application services and ensure SSL is working properly.

Conclusion

1. After setting up SSL , you should be able to reach the login page using https://hostname:ssl_port.

2. Even if you use http://hostname:non_ssl_port to reach the login page, then it should be redirected to the SSL-enabled URL https://hostname:ssl_port.

3. The non-SSL TCP port is still open. You can close it, but you can change httpd.conf and comment out the line starting with Listen. Then restart Apache. However, closing this port will not allow any pages to be accessed with HTTP (for example, help pages). So, you will not be able to use EBS help pages if you close that non-SSL TCP port.

4. With this configuration, your forms will be working in SSL, too. This is because EBS uses servlet architecture in the forms communication layer, and you don't need to do anything about the forms. Forms will be communicating in HTTPS.

5. We can use wildcard for certificates, A certificate with a server name *.oralabs. com work perfectly fine and i have seen many customers using certificates with wild cards.

Using a DMZ and Reverse Proxy with Oracle EBS 12.2

A demilitarized zone (DMZ) consists of the portions of a corporate network that are between the corporate intranet and the Internet.

The main purpose of a DMZ is to provide enhanced security. In case of a security breach, only the servers in the DMZ are exposed while the intranet is protected.

A DMZ configuration requires the deployment of a firewall at various levels. This is to ensure that only authorized traffic is allowed to cross the firewall. If any intrusion attempts are made, the firewall will minimize the possible communication channels that hackers can utilize using the Internet. This way, risk is reduced to a large extent, and damage is contained within the DMZ, thus protecting the internal network.

Network firewalls control access between the Internet and a corporation's internal network or intranet. Firewalls define which Internet communications will be permitted into the corporate network and which will be blocked. A well-designed firewall can foil many common Internet-based security attacks.

In a DMZ, only the required applications are deployed on the external application, and if there is a security breach, only the area that is deployed on the external tier is affected, whereas the internal web application tier remains protected.

■ **Note** For detailed DMZ configuration information, please refer to MOS tech note "Oracle E-Business Suite Release 12.2 Configuration in a DMZ" (Doc ID 1375670.1).

Oracle supports four configuration options for the DMZ:

1. DMZ configuration with external and internal application tiers

2. DMZ configuration with a reverse proxy and external application tier

3. DMZ configuration with multiple internal/external application tiers within and intranet and DMZ

4. DMZ configuration with internal and external application tiers using a shared application tier file system

DMZ Configuration with External and Internal Application Tiers (Option 1)

Configuring an external application tier as a DMZ in Oracle EBS is the simplest deployment option. In this configuration, internal users will access applications using the intranet (HTTP), and external users will access applications using the Internet (HTTPS). This will restrict external users to limited access on Oracle EBS because they are authorized to access only limited responsibilities that are assigned to external users using the external application tier. Figure 12-10 illustrates this deployment option.

Here are the advantages:

1. It's a simple configuration for external application tier and external users.

2. Internal users will access applications using the internal application tier

3. It offers restrictions for users accessing applications using the external application tier and allows those users to use those products that are deployed on external tier.

Here are the disadvantages:

4. The EBS environment will be exposed to the external world.

5. The application tier file system cannot be shared between external and internal application nodes, but it can be shared between multiple internal-to-internal application nodes and external-to-external application nodes.

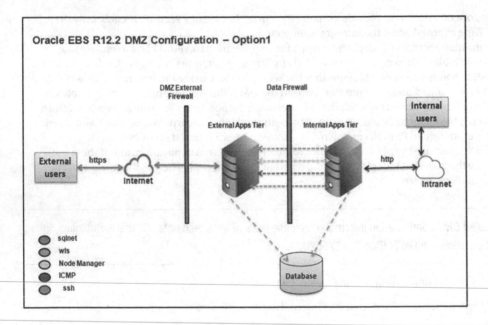

Figure 12-10. Oracle EBS DMZ configuration: option 1

DMZ Configuration with Reverse Proxy and External Application Tier (Option 2)

This configuration option is similar to the previous configuration option, but this option will not allow external application users to see the details of the external application tiers. The external application URL will be masked at the reverse proxy server level, and all external user requests are processed through the reverse proxy server. The connections are terminated at the reverse proxy layer if required, and the firewall is configured at the reverse proxy layer, so the connections are restricted at the reverse proxy layer only. If the attacker/hacker gets into the DMZ server and gets control of the reverse proxy server, then the hacker won't be able to access the data stored in the database because the reverse proxy is the only channel for routing the requests to the application server running on the other node. This is one the major improvement compared to configuration option 1.

Figure 12-11 shows a DMZ deployment with a reverse proxy in place.

Here are the advantages:

1. It restricts access to a limited set of responsibilities for the users connecting using the Internet.

2. It will allow access to only the products that are deployed on the Internet.

3. It hides the information on the application tier nodes from external users by using the reverse proxy server.

4. The firewall can be implemented at the reverse proxy layer for restricting access.

5. It terminates the connection at the reverse proxy layer if required.

Here are the disadvantages:

6. An additional server is required for the reverse proxy.

7. The application tier file system cannot be shared between external and internal application nodes, but it can be shared between multiple internal-to-internal application nodes and external-to-external application nodes.

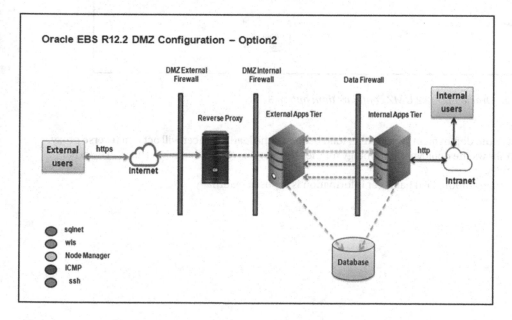

Figure 12-11. *Oracle EBS 12.2 DMZ configuration: option 2*

DMZ Configuration with Multiple Internal/External Application Tiers Within the Intranet and DMZ (Option 3 and Option 4)

This configuration is helpful if there are multiple application tier nodes configured for deployed Oracle EBS topology. Internet users are allowed to access only limited applications and responsibilities that are deployed on the external application tier. This configuration supports sharing of application tiers between internal and external application tiers. The load balancer should be configured between the external and internal application tiers for load balancing the incoming user requests between both users.

Configuration options 3 and 4 are similar and almost identical in the deployment topology; the only difference is in sharing the application tier file system. In option 3, application tiers cannot share the file system, whereas in option 4 the application tier file system can be shared across external and internal application servers. In option 4, external and internal application tiers are in an intranet zone, as shown in Figure 12-12.

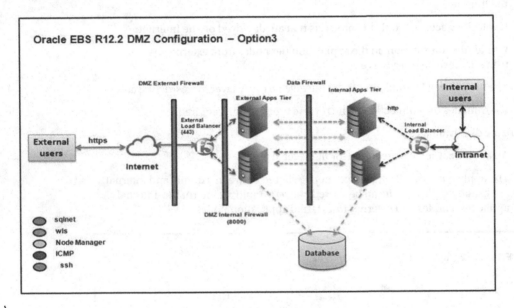

Figure 12-12. *Oracle EBS 12.2 DMZ configuration: option 3*

In most of the deployment cases with a load balancer, the load balancer will act as a reverse proxy. Figure 12-13 shows the deployment topology for the DMZ server with multiple internal and external application tiers.

In this configuration, load balancer information is exposed externally.

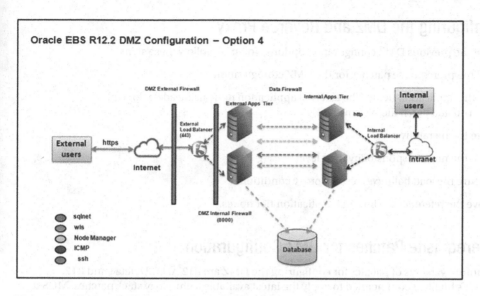

Figure 12-13. *Oracle EBS 12.2 DMZ configuration: option 4*

Here are the advantages (option 3):

1. Like options 1 and 2, it will restrict the responsibility and application level for users accessing using the Internet.

2. The application file system can be shared across all internal-to-internal nodes and external-to-external nodes.

3. Load is balanced across multiple nodes.

Here are the disadvantages (option 3):

4. The load balancer is exposed to all Internet users.

5. The application tier file system cannot be shared between internal and external application tier nodes.

Here are the advantages (option 4):

6. Like options 1 and 2, it will restrict the responsibility and application level for users accessing using the Internet.

7. The application tier file system can be shared across all nodes (internal and external).

8. Ports are not required to be open at the firewall.

9. Load is balanced across all application nodes.

Here are the disadvantages (option 4):

10. The load balancer is exposed to the external world.

Steps for Configuring the DMZ and Reverse Proxy

To configure any of the previous DMZ configuration options, you must follow these steps:

1. Install the prerequisite patches for the DMZ configuration.

2. Clone the application tier for the external application node using adcfgclone.pl for the run and patch file systems.

3. Update the hierarchy type.

4. Update the node/responsibility trust level.

5. Configure the load balancer/reverse proxy conditional.

6. Remove the references of internal application tier nodes.

Install the Prerequisite Patches for DMZ Configuration

The minimum required versions of patches for configuring the DMZ are R12.AD.C.Deleta4 and R12. TKX.C.Delta.4, but it's highly recommended to apply the latest available technology stack patches. MOS tech note 1617461.1 provides the latest available technology stack patches.

Clone the Application Tier for External Application Node Using adcfgclone.pl for the Run and Patch File Systems

The cloning procedure for configuring the DMZ's external application tier is the same as the normal cloning process. You should disable the batch processing service while configuring the external application tier node. The detailed process of cloning was discussed in Chapter 11.

```
$ perl adcfgclone.pl appsTier


                    Copyright (c) 2011 Oracle Corporation
                      Redwood Shores, California, USA
                     Oracle E-Business Suite Rapid Clone
                              Version 12.2
                       adcfgclone Version 120.63.12020000.37
Enter the APPS password :
Do you want to add a node (yes/no) [no] : yes

Target System File Edition type [run] :

Target System Root Service [enabled] :

Target System Web Administration [enabled] :

Target System Web Entry Point Services [enabled] :
```

```
Target System Web Application Services [enabled] :

Target System Batch Processing Services [enabled] :  disabled

Target System Other Services [disabled] :
```

The previous code shows the services that should be enabled while performing a clone configuration. You should choose Yes when prompted with "Do you want to add a node?"

Update the Hierarchy Type

You should update the profile options listed in Table 12-2. These profile options are used for constructing URLs.

Table 12-2. *Oracle DMZ Profile Options*

Serial Number	User Profile Name	Internal Name
1	Applications Web Agent	APPS_WEB_AGENT
2	Applications Servlet Agent	APPS_SERVLET_AGENT
3	Applications JSP Agent	APPS_JSP_AGENT
4	Applications Framework Agent	APPS_FRAMEWORK_AGENT
5	ICX:Forms Launcher	ICX_FORMS_LAUNCHER
6	ICX: Oracle Discoverer Launcher	ICX_DISCOVERER_LAUNCHER
7	ICX: Oracle Discoverer Viewer Launcher	ICX_DISCOVERER_VIEWER_LAUNCHER
8	Applications Help Web Agent	HELP_WEB_AGENT
9	Applications Portal	APPS_PORTAL
10	BOM:Configurator URL of UI Manager	CZ_UIMGR_URL
11	QP: Pricing Engine URL	QP_PRICING_ENGINE_URL
12	TCF:HOST	TCF:HOST

Figure 12-14 shows how you can modify the profile option hierarchy type.

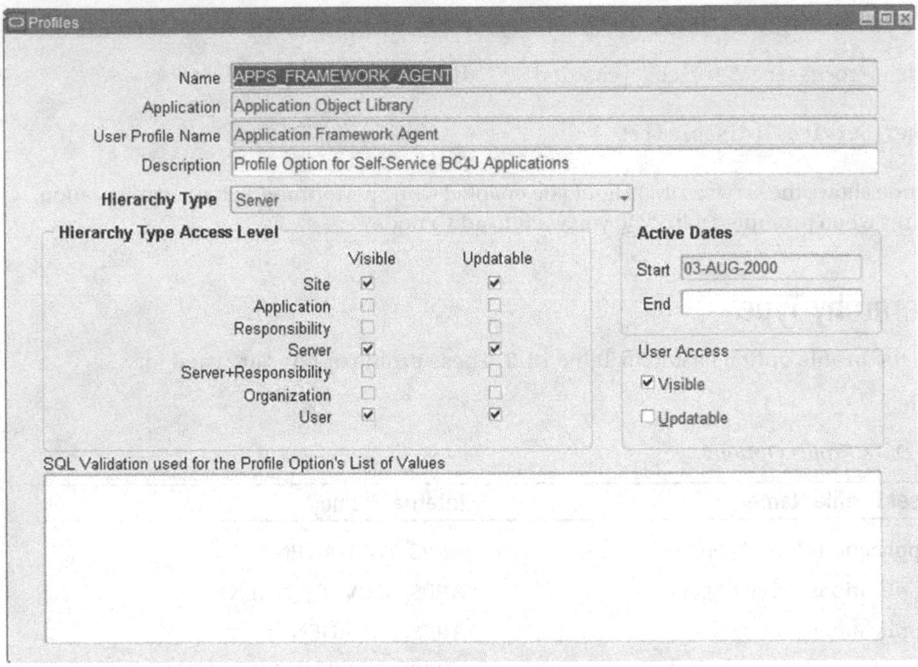

Figure 12-14. Oracle EBS: DMZ profile option

To modify the profile option hierarchy, you must execute the script txkChangeProfH.sql, as shown here. Source the run edition environment file.

```
$ . ./u01/appl_prod/APPS/EBSapps.env run

$ sqlplus apps/apps @$FND_TOP/patch/115/sql/txkChangeProfH.sql SERVRESP
```

You should run AutoConfig on all the application tier nodes after successful execution of the txkChangeProfH.sql script.

Update the Node/Responsibility Trust Level

Oracle EBS has capability to control access for users to a certain predefined set of responsibilities with respect to the server, and this restriction can be implemented using the NODE_TRUST_LEVEL profile option.

NODE_TRUST_LEVEL Profile Option Supported Values

The following are the supported values:

1. *Administrative*: These types of servers have access to a complete set of responsibilities and all business functions. These servers are considered the most secured servers.

2. *Normal*: These types of servers have access to a limited set of responsibilities.

3. *External*: These servers are considered the least secure, and they will provide access to a much more limited set of responsibilities.

Updating the Node Trust Level

To modify the Node Trust Level profile option value, you should perform the following steps:

1. Log in to Oracle E-Business Suite as the sysadmin user using the internal URL and navigate as follows:

2. Using the SYSADMIN Responsibility, select System Profile, then select the server for the external web tier, and search for NODE_TRUST_LEVEL. Finally, set the value to External at the server level.

Figure 12-15 shows the changed profile option External.

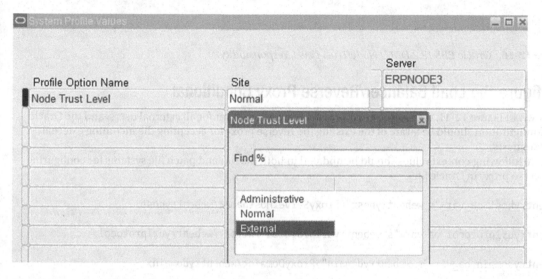

Figure 12-15. *Oracle EBS 12.2 DMZ: Node Trust Level, Server*

Updating the Responsibility Trust Level

To change the value of the Responsibility Trust Level profile option at the responsibility level for a particular responsibility, you should use following navigation:

Using the SYSADMIN responsibility, select System Profile, then select Responsibility, and then search for RES%TRUST. Finally, set the value to External at the responsibility level, but the site level should remain the same.

These steps should be performed for all responsibilities that need to be modified. Figure 12-16 shows how to set up a responsibility as external.

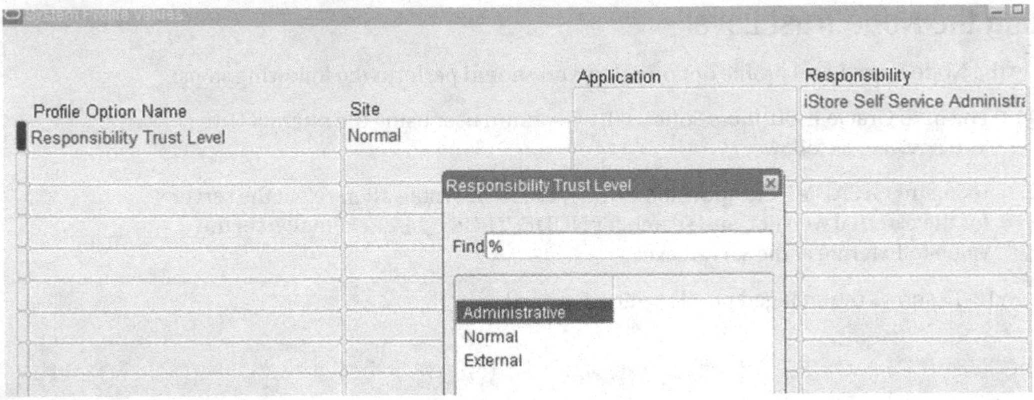

Figure 12-16. *Oracle EBS 12.2 DMZ: Node Trust Level, responsibility*

Configure the Load Balancer/Reverse Proxy Conditional

As shown in Figure 12-11, the reverse proxy is at the front access layer for all external users, and the Oracle EBS configuration should be aware of the existing the reverse proxy for accepting the incoming external client requests.

The following context values should be updated in both the run and patch file systems for configuring the reverse proxy in Oracle EBS.

```
<webentryhost oa_var="s_webentryhost">ProxyServerHostname</webentryhost>

<webentryurlprotocol oa_var="s_webentryurlprotocol">https</webentryurlprotocol>

<webentrydomain oa_var="s_webentrydomain">ProxyDomain</webentrydomain>

<activewebport oa_var="s_active_webport">443</activewebport>

<login_page oa_var="s_login_page">https://ProxyHostname.proxyDomainName:443/OA_HTML/
AppsLogin</login_page>
<externURL oa_var="s_external_url">http://ProxyHostname.proxyDomainName:443</externURL>
```

Remove References of Internal Application Tier Nodes

After adding a node to the existing Oracle EBS topology, the file mod_wl_ohs.conf will have entries for all application nodes. So, you must remove these entries from this file to ensure external nodes will not refer to internal nodes.

```
$diff mod_wl_ohs.conf mod_wl_ohs.conf.orig

33c33
<   WebLogicCluster erpnode3.oralabs.com:7209
---
>   WebLogicCluster erpnode3.oralabs.com:7209,erpnode2.oralabs.com:7208,erpnode1.oralabs.
com:7207
39c39
```

```
<   WebLogicCluster erpnode3.oralabs.com:7409
---
>   WebLogicCluster erpnode3.oralabs.com:7409,erpnode2.oralabs.com:7408,erpnode1.oralabs.
com:7407
```

Here, erpnode3 is the external node, and erpnode2 and erpnode1 are the internal nodes.

SSH Connectivity Requirements for Online Patching

The 12.2 online patching tool adop requires SSH connectivity between the primary application tier node (often called the *master node*) configured in the intranet and the other application tier nodes configured in both the intranet and the DMZ. This connectivity is required for the remote invocation of the patching procedures on all the nodes.

Sync Up the Context File and Update Configuration on All Nodes

Follow these instructions on all application tier nodes to sync up the context file and the configuration files.

1. Log in to all the application tier nodes and execute the following scripts to sync up the context file and the configuration files for the run file system and the patch file system.

2. Source the EBSapps.env file.

   ```
   $ . ./u01/R12/APPS/EBSapps.env run
   $ perl $AD_TOP/bin/adSyncContext.pl contextfile=$CONTEXT_FILE
   ```

   The following command syntax works with AD/TXK Code Level Delta4 .
   ```
   $ perl $FND_TOP/patch/115/bin/txkSetAppsConf.pl -ctxfile=$CONTEXT_FILE
   -outfile=$APPLRGF/TXK/conf.log
   ```

3. Log in to all the application tier nodes and execute the above listed scripts to sync up the context file and configuration files for the patch file system.

Perform Sanity Checks

Perform these sanity checks:

1. Start/stop the services starting with the primary application tier.

2. Launch the application and open some forms.

3. Run an empty patching cycle.

Conclusion

1. Decide which supported configuration fits your requirement.

2. EBS 12.2 requires user equivalence to be enabled between nodes.

3. It's required that you remove internal node information from the mod_wl_ohs.conf file.

Using TDE with Oracle EBS 12.2 Database

The database is the place where all the business data is stored. This data is available to users with granted privileges. But these privileges are managed logically within the database itself, and the database administrator/security administrator should ensure sensitive data is safe in case of replacement or theft of media storage (HDD) where data is stored. Oracle has a Transparent Data Encryption (TDE) database option that can be used for encrypting your databases.

Oracle TDE uses key-based access control. Encrypted data cannot be in a readable format if it's accessed without using an encryption key. The authorized users are only allowed to open the key, and then decryption occurs. The encryption can be enabled at the tablespace and table levels. Figures 12-17 and 12-18 show the column-level and tablespace-level encryption.

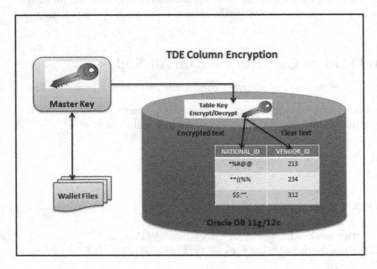

Figure 12-17. Oracle EBS column-level encryption

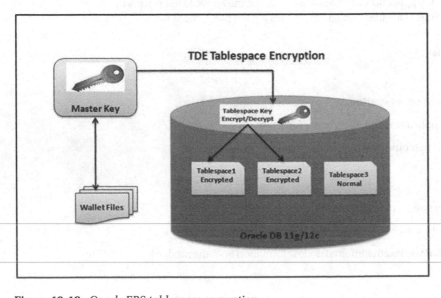

Figure 12-18. Oracle EBS tablespace encryption

Oracle transparent encryption provides encryption at two different levels.

1. TDE at the column level

2. TDE at the tablespace level

Key Points for Transparent Data Encryption

These are some key points:

1. Application and database changes are not required for implementing TDE.

2. You always need to ensure that the database wallet is open after maintenance activities.

3. Privileged and authenticated database users don't see any change.

4. There are limitations for column-level encryption.

5. To enable tablespace encryption, tablespaces must be exported and imported. The command "alter table move and create table as select * from" may also work, but it needs extra effort and is not documented.

6. Tablespace encryption will have a limited impact on performance during encrypting and decrypting.

7. The disk I/O impact is not significant.

8. Columnar encryption may have a significant impact (15 to 20 percent) based on how the data is accessed.

9. TDE needs an additional advanced security license to be used within an EBS database.

10. Data will be encrypted while it is at rest and will be decrypted automatically when it is accessed in TDE.

Let's see how you can use both supported encrypted methods within an Oracle EBS Database.

Transparent Data Encryption Column Level (CE)

TDE is supported at the column level, but there are certain limitations for using the encryption at the column level. All columns within an Oracle EBS database cannot be encrypted because all data types are not supported to be encrypted. The following are the list of data types that are supported for encryption:

1. BINARY_DOUBLE

2. BINARY_FLOAT

3. CHAR

4. DATE

5. INTERVAL DAY TO SECOND

6. INTERVAL YEAR TO MONTH

7. LOBs (internal LOBs and SECUREFILE LOBs only)

8. NCHAR

9. NUMBER

10. NVARCHAR2

11. RAW

12. TIMESTAMP (includes TIMESTAMP WITH TIME ZONE and TIMESTAMP WITH LOCAL TIME ZONE)

13. VARCHAR2

There is another limitation for column length; Table 12-3 shows the length of columns supported for encryption.

Table 12-3. Column-Level Encryption, Length Size, 11g R2

Data Type	Maximum Size
CHAR	1,932 bytes
VARCHAR2	3,932 bytes
NVARCHAR2	1,966 bytes
NCHAR	966 bytes

Configuration of TDE Wallet

There is no additional software required for configuring Oracle Wallet with an EBS database. The configuration steps are simple; all you need to do is set a valid wallet location and create/configure a wallet.

This demonstration is performed on Oracle Database 12.1.0.2.

The wallet location is /u01/ora_test/12.1.0.2/network/admin/test_erpnode3/TDE_wallet.

■ **Note**   In Oracle 12c complete wallet file configuration is performed using the ADMINISTER KEY MANAGEMENT SQL command, whereas before 12c, it was managed by the orakpki utility.

For more information on the ADMINISTER KEY MANAGEMENT command, refer to this article: http://docs.oracle.com/database/121/SQLRF/statements_1003.htm#SQLRF55976

1. Add the wallet location in sqlnet_ifile.ora.

```
[oraebs@erpnode3 test_erpnode3]$ cat sqlnet_ifile.ora
SQLNET.ALLOWED_LOGON_VERSION_SERVER = 10
###TDE WALLET Configuration
ENCRYPTION_WALLET_LOCATION=
  (SOURCE=
  (METHOD=FILE)
    (METHOD_DATA=  (DIRECTORY=/u01/ora_test/12.1.0.2/network/admin/test_erpnode3/TDE_wallet)))
[oraebs@erpnode3 test_erpnode3]$
```

2. Create an administrator password for the key store.

```
SQL> ADMINISTER KEY MANAGEMENT CREATE KEYSTORE '/u01/ora_test/12.1.0.2/network/admin/test_
erpnode3/TDE_wallet' IDENTIFIED BY "Hardpa$$word";

keystore altered.
```

3. Check the status of the wallet.

```
SQL> col WRL_PARAMETER format a40
SQL> col WRL_TYPE format a10
SQL> col STATUS format a10

SQL> select WRL_PARAMETER, WRL_TYPE, STATUS from V$ENCRYPTION_WALLET;

WRL_PARAMETER                             WRL_TYPE   STATUS
----------------------------------------- ---------- ----------
/u01/ora_test/12.1.0.2/network/admin/tes  FILE       CLOSED
t_erpnode3/TDE_wallet/
```

The status of the wallet is closed.

4. Check the wallet file.

```
SQL> !ls -lrt /u01/ora_test/12.1.0.2/network/admin/test_erpnode3/TDE_wallet
total 4
-rw-r--r-- 1 oraebs dbaerp 2408 Apr 16 20:33 ewallet.p12
```

The wallet file ewallet.p12 will be created at the specified wallet location in the spfile.

5. The wallet should be opened for the encrypt/decrypt action.

```
SQL> ADMINISTER KEY MANAGEMENT SET KEYSTORE OPEN IDENTIFIED BY "Hardpa$$word";
keystore altered.
```

6. Check again the status of the wallet.

```
SQL> select WRL_PARAMETER, WRL_TYPE, STATUS from V$ENCRYPTION_WALLET;

WRL_PARAMETER                             WRL_TYPE   STATUS
----------------------------------------- ---------- ----------
/u01/ora_test/12.1.0.2/network/admin/tes  FILE       OPEN_NO_MA
t_erpnode3/TDE_wallet/                               STER_KEY
```

7. Enable the autologin of the wallet.

If you enable autologin, then the wallet will open and close during database shutdown/startup automatically. But to configure the wallet to open automatically, you must ensure that is permitted with the organization security policies.

```
SQL> ADMINISTER KEY MANAGEMENT CREATE LOCAL AUTO_LOGIN KEYSTORE FROM KEYSTORE '/u01/ora_
test/12.1.0.2/network/admin/test_erpnode3/TDE_wallet' IDENTIFIED BY "Hardpa$$word";

keystore altered.
```

8. Check the autologin wallet file.

This will create the file cwallet.sso, which will be used to automatically open the wallet.

```
SQL> !ls -lrt /u01/ora_test/12.1.0.2/network/admin/test_erpnode3/TDE_wallet
total 8
-rw-r--r-- 1 oraebs dbaerp 2408 Apr 16 20:33 ewallet.p12
-rw-r--r-- 1 oraebs dbaerp 2461 Apr 17 10:58 cwallet.sso
```

9. Set the master key.

This is a required step to create the encrypted column and tablespaces.

```
SQL> administer key management set key identified by "Hardpa$$word" with backup;

keystore altered.
```

10. Execute the script aftdeval.sql to check for encryption readiness.

This script will perform initial assessment of whether encryption on the specified columns is possible. This script is provided by the default Oracle EBS installation, and it will be located under $FND_TOP/sql. It will generate the exact command you need to execute for encrypting the required column.

```
[applebs@erpnode3 sql]$ ls -lrt aftdeval.sql
-rwxr-xr-x 1 applebs dbaerp 7232 Nov 24  2012 aftdeval.sql
[applebs@erpnode3 sql]$ sqlplus apps/apps
SQL*Plus: Release 10.1.0.5.0 - Production on Sat Apr 16 20:22:43 2016
Copyright (c) 1982, 2005, Oracle.  All rights reserved.

Connected to:
Oracle Database 12c Enterprise Edition Release 12.1.0.2.0 - 64bit Production
With the Partitioning, OLAP, Advanced Analytics and Real Application Testing options

SQL> @aftdeval.sql HR PER_ALL_PEOPLE_F NATIONAL_IDENTIFIER E
ALTER TABLE HR.PER_ALL_PEOPLE_F modify (NATIONAL_IDENTIFIER encrypt no salt);
SQL>

SQL> @aftdeval.sql HR PER_ALL_PEOPLE_F VENDOR_ID E
ALTER TABLE HR.PER_ALL_PEOPLE_F modify (VENDOR_ID encrypt);
SQL>
```

11. Set the encryption for target columns.

Once the commands are generated using the previous script, you can enable the encryption on target columns.

```
SQL> ALTER TABLE HR.PER_ALL_PEOPLE_F modify (NATIONAL_IDENTIFIER encrypt no salt);
Table altered.
SQL>
```

```
SQL> ALTER TABLE HR.PER_ALL_PEOPLE_F modify (VENDOR_ID encrypt);
Table altered.
SQL>
```

12.   Check the encrypted columns in the database.

After the columns are encrypted, you can use check all encrypted columns in the database.

```
SQL> select table_name, column_name from dba_encrypted_columns;

TABLE_NAME                COLUMN_NAME
-------------------       --------------------
PER_ALL_PEOPLE_F          VENDOR_ID
PER_ALL_PEOPLE_F          NATIONAL_IDENTIFIER
```

Encryption of tablespaces using TDE needs additional efforts. You have to use the export/import process for migrating data to the new encrypted tablespaces. The process for creating and configuring the wallet will be the same.

The following are detailed reference notes for implementing TDE at table space level:

13.   "DB 11gR2 - Using TDE Table space Encryption with Oracle E-Business Suite Release 12.2" (Doc ID 1585296.1)

14.   "DB 12cR1 - Using TDE Table space Encryption with Oracle E-Business Suite Release 12 (Database 12c)" (Doc ID 1584458.1)

Recommendations While Using TDE in the EBS Database

These are some recommendations:

1.   Patches may fail on encrypted columns if a patch is trying to create an index on an encrypted column while increasing the column size beyond the supported value. You may need to decrypt the column before applying such patches.

2.   It's recommended that you use a shared location for the wallet in the case of a RAC database. It can be kept on ASM or ACFS volumes.

3.   During database upgrades, if using DBUA, ensure the wallet files are accessible from the new Oracle Home and autologin is enabled as the database will be restarted by DBUA.

4.   Ensure regular backup of wallet files.

5.   In Data Guard environments, update wallet files on the disaster recovery site upon changing any passwords at the primary site.

Users and Password Management in Oracle EBS 12.2

Oracle E-Business Suite 12.2 is delivered with 300+ database accounts, and almost all of these users have default passwords. These passwords should be changed periodically to ensure that only authorized users are allowed to access the application.

There are certain superuser accounts like APPS, APPLSYS, and SYSADMIN that can be used for updating and managing all the Oracle EBS schemas and configuration files. But it's been observed in many organizations that this password is shared across multiple users, so it's difficult to track who actually performed the damage on the system.

Another major problem is the read-only APPS schema is provided to almost all developers, and the read-only APPS schema can access sensitive data from the application. So, you must ensure that either data is being masked on TEST environments or developers don't have access to the sensitive data.

Let's see now how you can change the password for the APPS, APPLSYS, and APPS_NE schemas using the utilities FNDCPASS and AFPASSWD.

These are considerations for changing the APPS password:

1. To change the APPS user password, you must shut down all application services.

2. Back up the FND_USER and FND_ORACLE_USERID tables before changing the APPS password.

3. Verify the file $FND_TOP/patch/115/sql/AFSCJAVS.pls version is 120.12.12020000.8 or above. If the file version is lower, than you must apply patch 19127427 as listed in MOS note 1674462.1.

4. To use a password hashing scheme using AFPASSWD, the EBS version should be 12.2.3 or higher.

5. Stop all application services using the adstpall.sh" script.

Use the FNDCPASS Utility for Changing Passwords

Here's the syntax:

```
FNDCPASS <logon> 0 Y <SYSTEM username>/<SYSTEM password> SYSTEM APPLSYS <new_password>

[applebs@erpnode21]$ FNDCPASS apps/apps 0 Y system/manager SYSTEM APPLSYS hardpass
Log filename : L474774.log

Report filename : O474774.out

[applebs@erpnode3 sql]$ sqlplus apps/hardpass
SQL*Plus: Release 10.1.0.5.0 - Production on Sun May 8 16:12:39 2016
Copyright (c) 1982, 2005, Oracle.  All rights reserved.

Connected to:
Oracle Database 12c Enterprise Edition Release 12.1.0.2.0 - 64bit Production
With the Partitioning, OLAP, Advanced Analytics and Real Application Testing options

SQL>
```

Use AFPASSWD for Changing the APPS Password

AFPASSWD is another utility for changing the password. The AFPASSWD utility is simple and will help in segregating the duties of different administrators. It will prompt for a system password, unlike FNDCPASS where you have to provide the system password in the FNDCPASS command line.

Here's the syntax:

```
AFPASSWD [-c <APPSUSER>[@<TWO_TASK>]] -s <APPLSYS>
[applebs@erpnode2 sql]$ AFPASSWD -c apps@test -s applsys
Enter the ORACLE password of Application Object Library 'APPSUSER':
```

```
Connected successfully to APPS.
Enter the password for your 'SYSTEM' ORACLE schema:
Connected successfully to SYSTEM.
Log file: AFPWD_test_724575.log
Enter new password for user:
Verify new password for user:
AFPASSWD completed successfully.
[applebs@erpnode3 sql]$ sqlplus apps/hardpassapps
SQL*Plus: Release 10.1.0.5.0 - Production on Sun May 8 16:23:18 2016
Copyright (c) 1982, 2005, Oracle.  All rights reserved.
Connected to:
Oracle Database 12c Enterprise Edition Release 12.1.0.2.0 - 64bit Production
With the Partitioning, OLAP, Advanced Analytics and Real Application Testing options
SQL>
```

Execute AutoConfig on all application tier nodes.

```
[applebs@erpnode2 scripts]$ adautocfg.sh
Enter the APPS user password:
```

Provide the newly configured APPS password.

The APPS schema is now connected with the newly configured password, but the password changing process is not completed. You should perform the following steps to configure the new password in the data sources of WebLogic managed servers.

Start up only the WebLogic admin server.

```
[applebs@erpnode3 scripts]$ adadminsrvctl.sh start

You are running adadminsrvctl.sh version 120.10.12020000.9

Enter the WebLogic Admin password:
Enter the APPS Schema password:
Starting WLS Admin Server...
```

Steps for Changing the APPS Password in the WLS Data Source

Here are the steps:

1. Log in to the WLS Administration Console.

2. Click Lock & Edit in the Change Center, as shown in Figure 12-19.

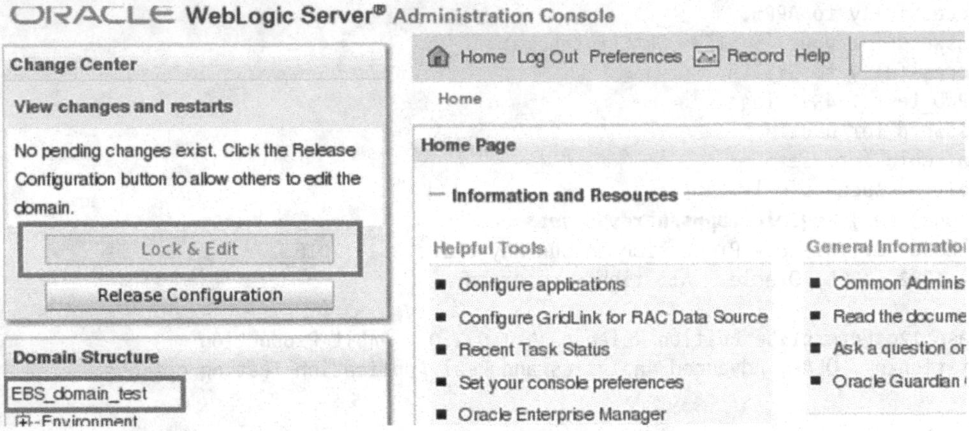

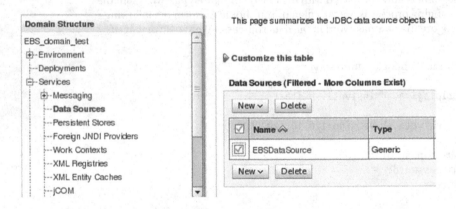

Figure 12-19. *Oracle EBS: WLS admin console, Change Center*

3. In the Domain Structure tree, expand Services and then select Data Sources.

4. On the Summary of JDBC Data Sources page, select EBSDataSource, as shown in Figure 12-20.

Figure 12-20. *Oracle EBS: JDBC DataSources, EBSDatasource*

5. On the Settings for EBSDataSource page, select the Connection Pool tab, as shown in Figure 12-21.

6. Enter the new password in the Password field, as shown in Figure 12-21.

7. Enter the new password in the Confirm Password field, as shown in Figure 12-21.

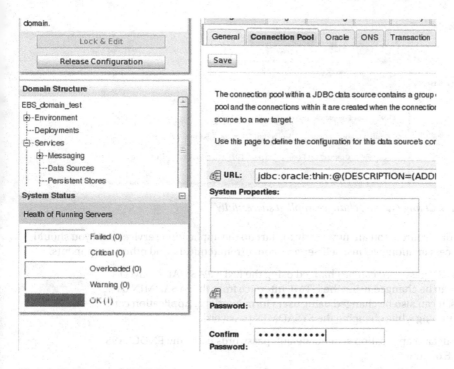

Figure 12-21. *Oracle EBS: Data source, Connection Pool and password*

8. Click Save.

9. Click Activate Changes in Change Center, as shown in Figure 12-22.

Figure 12-22. *Oracle EBS: Change Center, activating changes*

Figure 12-23 confirms the changes.

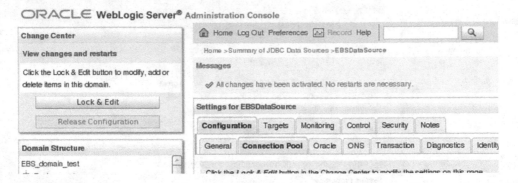

Figure 12-23. *Oracle EBS: Change Center, changes applied successfully*

After changing the data source, you are now ready to start up the application services, and you should verify the application access including forms, Self Service, concurrent requests, and other components.

1. The SYSADMIN password can be changed using the FNDCPASS/AFPASSWD utility, or it can be changed using the HTML interface from the SYSADMIN user preferences. It can also be changed using users form interface. Application can be up and running while changing the SYSADMIN password.

2. Change the default application schema default passwords using the FNDCPASS ALLORACLE option.

Here's the syntax:

```
FNDCPASS <logon> O Y <system/password> ALLORACLE <new_password>
```

3. The database default accounts either should be locked, or the default password should be changed.

4. Use the password function for custom database accounts. The password verification function will set up the rules for the user account password. You can create the password function with PASSWORD_GRACE_TIME, PASSWORD_LIFE_TIME, PASSWORD_REUSE_TIME, PASSWORD_REUSE_MAX, FAILED_LOGIN_ATTEMPTS, and PASSWORD_LOCK_TIME. These values can be customized and set based on the complexity requirement.

Securing the Database and Application Files

Oracle EBS 12.2 is divided into two major file system layers: the application tier and the database tier. These file system layers consist of multiple files. To secure the overall EBS environment, you must ensure that proper privileges have been granted to the required files. This section covers only the key files on both tiers.

1. Verify the database tier belongs to the proper OS owner and group.

2. Verify the application tier belongs to the proper OS owner and group.

3. Ensure the $ORACLE_HOME/bin permissions are set to 0751 or less and set permission to 0750 or less to the $ORACLE_HOME directory

4. Make sure listener.ora the sqlnet.ora file permissions are set to 0600.

5. Set the tnsnames.ora file to 0644.

6. Set 600 to $FND_SECURE (the location of the DBC file).

7. Ensure the concurrent log/out files have 0600 ($APPLSF/log and out).

Securing Oracle Database

Here are the steps:

1. Apply all the recommended security patches for the database and application.

2. Enable auditing in the database as and when required.

3. Configure the secure listener.

4. Revoke unwanted privileges from database accounts.

5. Lock and expire unwanted database accounts that are not related to EBS schemas, but for EBS schemas there should be a proper analysis to find the schemas that are current not being used, and rigorous testing should be done before locking the accounts on production.

6. Enable segregation of duties. Don't share apps/applsys credentials with everyone. Create a specific user for each technical consultant and grant privileges to only the required set of objects. For example, for a financial technical consultant, grant access on the AP, AR, and GL modules. He should not have access on the PAY and PER schemas.

Oracle EBS Security Profile Options

By default Oracle provides multiple security profile options, and these profile options will be helpful in managing the overall E-Business Suite security. Table 12-4 shows the default profile options related to passwords.

Table 12-4. *EBS user security profile options*

Profile Option	Value
SIGNON_PASSWORD_LENGTH	8
SIGNON_PASSWORD_HARD_TO_GUESS	YES
SIGNON_PASSWORD_NO_REUSE	180
SIGNON_PASSWORD_CASE	Sensitive
SIGNON_PASSWORD_FAILURE_LIMIT	5
ICX_SESSION_TIMEOUT	30
SIGNON_PASSWORD_CUSTOM	implement

All these profile options can be set to the desired value other than what's listed, and you can even configure and implement a custom validation function and register it with EBS.

Oracle EBS Proxy Users

There is already a feature known as a vacation rule that helps create a vacation rule and allows notifications to be assigned or transferred but never gives an opportunity for user access to be shared.

It enables a user to set up proxy access to another user for various reasons such as leave, work delegation, and so on. Using this feature proxy, the other user would get the same or selected access as the original user, and they may or may not have access to partial/full work list access. In the following demonstration, two FND_USERS are being used: SMITH and JOHN. SMITH is delegating part of his access to JOHN.

Log in to 12.2 E-business Suite as SMITH and click the Settings button. Select Manage Proxies, as shown in Figure 12-24.

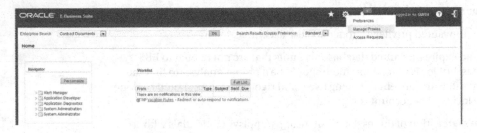

Figure 12-24. *Oracle EBS: proxy user*

Click Add Proxy, as shown in Figure 12-25.

Figure 12-25. *Oracle EBS : adding proxy*

Select the desired user to whom access is being granted; in our case, it's John, as shown in Figure 12-26. Specify the from and to date.

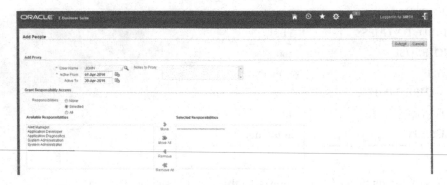

Figure 12-26. *Oracle EBS: proxy user, delegation*

Please note that dates are effective from midnight.

Select the appropriate radio buttons for the desired level of access. In the example, the following responsibilities are assigned, as shown in Figure 12-27:

Figure 12-27. *Oracle EBS: proxy user, delegation*

1. System Administrator

2. Application Developer

3. Alert Manger

The Grant Worklist Access section, as shown in Figure 12-28, allows the user to grant access to all, none, or selected item types available with the user. The user can make a choice between the three options.

Figure 12-28. *Oracle EBS: proxy user, delegation*

Once a selection has been made, click the Submit button and the access will be active on the specified date ranges, as shown in Figure 12-29.

Figure 12-29. *Oracle EBS: proxy user, confirmation*

Figure 12-29 shows that proxy user access has been completed. You should confirm that John's access has been established. As shown in Figure 12-30, a new proxy logo is now visible.

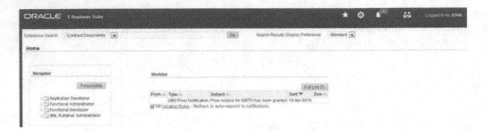

Figure 12-30. *Oracle EBS: proxy user icon*

Clicking the Switch User logo, as shown in Figure 12-31, will take you to the Switch User page where clicking the Switch logo will switch the user access.

Figure 12-31. *Oracle EBS: proxy user switch*

As shown in Figure 12-32, the pointer suggests that the access has been switched to the proxy for Smith, and the assigned responsibilities can be seen.

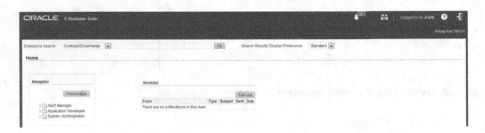

Figure 12-32. *Oracle EBS: proxy user, switch*

Please note that any action taken by John with proxy access will be updated (the Who column) in Smith's name.

Here is a sample query to get more details for proxy setup from sqlplus:

```
select * fromapps.fnd_menusfndm,apps.fnd_grantsfndg
wherefndg.menu_id=fndm.menu_id
andprogram_name='PROXY';
```

Summary

In this chapter, you learned how to configure SSL, a DMZ, and a reverse proxy in an Oracle EBS 12.2 environment. On the database layer you saw how to configure Transparent Data Encryption. Some of the new features and options introduced in EBS 12.2 were also covered in this chapter.

CHAPTER 13

■ ■ ■

Oracle E-Business Suite 12.2 Performance Recommendations

Performance tuning has been always an important task in Oracle systems. Oracle databases, Oracle applications, and even Oracle engineered systems work better in terms of performance when they are tuned properly.

Even though the latest technology delivered in Oracle databases, Oracle applications, Oracle engineered systems, and Oracle servers tunes the performance on the fly, performance tuning is still needed because all the Oracle products are tightly integrated in customer environments where there are various system resources and workload types. Besides, almost every Oracle application and Oracle system has its own performance tuning needs, and although they use almost similar Oracle technologies, the technology stacks differ according to the application type, application release, database release, and even system type and system release.

With this in mind, you can consider performance tuning to be an important task in EBS 12.2 projects, as EBS is an environment with a mixed workload (OLTP, reporting, and batches) created by the different applications. Further, the amount of data loaded by the OLTP sessions and batch jobs increases with time and affects the general system performance. That is, the reporting, the batches, and indirectly the general performance of the Oracle products, including OLTP, decrease if you don't tune your application technologies, database structures, and EBS servers. In addition to the diversity in workload and increasing data volume, there are several sophisticated Oracle technologies used in the software stack and even the most specific Oracle Database features are widely used in EBS 12.2; therefore, you need to tune the system as a whole to meet the needs of different customer environments and usage profiles.

In this chapter, we will walk you through the key performance tuning subjects in EBS 12.2 and give you recommendations about using them. While explaining performance tuning as a whole, we will cover the proactive measurements that can be done in EBS 12.2 to be aware of potential performance bottlenecks and, at the same time, give recommendations for tuning the different layers of an EBS 12.2 system.

Introduction to Oracle EBS Performance Tuning

EBS 12.2 is a complex application system consisting of a client tier, application tier, and database tier (as explained in Chapter 1), and we will cover all the areas within the scope of this tree-tier architecture. We will explain how to enhance EBS 12.2 performance mainly in five layers. That is, we will explain performance tuning for the client tier, the middle tier (application tier), the database structure, the SQL access paths, and the network in order to give you an effective approach for performance tuning.

We will also cover other tuning areas besides these five layers, such as concurrent processing, third-party reporting applications, workflow, and application debug profiles.

© Syed Zaheer and Erman Arslan 2016
S. Zaheer and E. Arslan, *Practical Oracle E-Business Suite*, DOI 10.1007/978-1-4842-1422-0_13

Specifically, we will take a look at the client operating system, client browser, and Java configurations for the client tier performance tuning.

We will go through the JVM configurations, JVM tuning, Apache/OHS tuning, and forms server tuning when we will explain middle tier performance tuning. We will also cover the AWR reports, gathering statistics, and recommended EBS parameters as well as how to choose the appropriate database block size for an EBS database. For server-side performance, we will explain the appropriate sizing of memory, the importance of disk I/O and CPU, the OS limits, the effects of paging and swapping, and some kernel parameters such as huge pages.

Inside the database, we will be concentrating on SQL tuning, SQL using literals, tables with high water marks, SQL queries with high costs, heavy custom codes and views, creating indexes (especially for reports), and analyzing AWR reports.

We will also explain the bandwidth, packet shapers, and quality-of-service implementations in routers when we explain network performance tuning in EBS 12.2.

Furthermore, we will explain actions such as decreasing the row count of the fnd_concurrent_queues table, purging concurrent manager data and logs, configuring the queue lengths, configuring the queue scan periods, and arranging dedicated custom managers, which can increase the concurrent processing performance of the EBS 12.2 environment. We will also talk about what you can do to minimize the negative performance effects that some EBS environments may face because of the heavy usage of reporting tools, especially caused by the use of Oracle Discoverer reports.

Workflow and debug profiles are other performance tuning areas that we will cover.

Let's start with the first performance tuning area, the client side.

EBS 12.2 Client-Side Performance Tuning

EBS 12.2, EBS 12, and EBS 11i are all three-tiered applications. They have a client tier, a middle tier (the application tier), and a database tier. Although the application and database tiers are the most important parts of the service that EBS provides, we will start at the client tier first, as the tools running on the client machine, basically the browsers and Java, provide the interaction between the users and the EBS applications.

The client tier is important because any performance bottleneck that our clients face could cause a performance problem or cause the clients to think that EBS 12.2 in general is a slow system. That's why you need to tune the client and be sure that it is configured as recommended by Oracle.

You can think of the clients of EBS 12.2 as thin clients because the tool used in the clients is just a browser. However, the browser also uses Java for presenting the EBS pages. Actually, when you log in and then select a function under a responsibility for opening an OAF page, the Java processing is done by the server, which is the application tier, but when you open a form, then the client Java, which is a plug-in attached to your browser, will start to work. That's why client-tier Java is important for the EBS performance. Any direct or indirect bottleneck caused by the browser or client-side Java may slow down your users and make them think that EBS is slow.

Although there are detailed approaches and configurations that can be made for increasing client-side performance, we will focus on the things that can be implemented in a corporate environment consisting of thousands of PCs. In other words, rather than giving detailed and specific tuning advice such as increasing the keyboard speed in order to increase the speed of the data load that is done by the end users or creating desktop shortcuts to let the users log in to EBS faster, we will concentrate on more general things that can affect the EBS client performance dramatically.

Basically, the client machine (Windows, Mac, or anything that is a supported EBS client) should have the necessary resources. It should have the necessary CPU and RAM to load the EBS HTML pages and to process the EBS forms pages by using the Java plug-in.

Even if there are enough resources in the client, being able to use those resources efficiently is also important on the client side. That is, there should be no sophisticated applications that may cause the client machine to be compelled to take CPU cycles and RAM from the EBS client tools and give those resources to itself. Remember, modern operating systems are time switching, so the browser that is running on the client machine and connected to EBS should have the necessary resources ready when needed because any context switch may cause the browser to wait.

The recommendations for the client-side hardware resources are classified according to the client operating systems. Thus, the operating systems must be supported by Oracle. Currently EBS 12.2 clients can use Windows or Mac OS. Currently, Windows 10, Windows 8.1, Windows 7 (32-bit or 64-bit), and Windows Vista Service Pack 1 or higher are the supported Windows operating systems for EBS 12.2 client PCs. Mac OS X 10.7.5 and higher, 10.8.2 and higher, 10.9.1, and 10.10.2 are supported for the clients that have Mac machines.

Considering the memory requirements for the operating system, the network characteristics of the environment, and the standard software (such as Word and Excel) that can be running on a client machine, we recommend at least a one-core 1.4GHz processor with 1GB memory installed in it.

■ **Note**   We recommend this hardware configuration for both Windows PCs and Macs.

Supported browsers differ according to the operating systems used at the client tier. Currently, Oracle supports Microsoft Internet Explorer 7 or higher, Firefox ESR 38.x, Chrome, and Safari 8.0.3 or higher.

■ **Note**   Chrome is not supported for Oracle Forms–based EBS applications.

Supported Java plug-ins also differ according to the operating system as well as whether the JRE is 32-bit or 64-bit.

```
At the moment; supported JRE releases for 32-bit are;
JRE 1.8.0_25 or higher 1.8.0_XX
JRE 1.7.0_10 or higher 1.7.0_XX
JRE 1.6.0_03 or higher 1.6.0_XX (not Windows 8.1 or 10)

Supported JRE releases for 32-bit for 64 bit are;
JRE 1.8.0_51 or higher 1.8.0_XX
JRE 1.7.0_85 or higher 1.7.0_XX
JRE 1.8.0_25 or higher 1.8.0_XX
JRE 1.7.0_10 or higher 1.7.0_XX
JRE 1.6.0_32 or higher 1.6.0_ (not Windows 8.1 or 10).
```

Instead of listing the supported OSs, browsers, and Java plug-ins and giving you the related OS-browser-Java matrixes, we will point you to the necessary Oracle documents where you can find the support information easily. The Oracle Support document "Recommended Browsers for Oracle E-Business Suite Release 12" (Doc ID 389422.1) includes all the supported browsers, operating systems, operating system architecture (32-bit or 64-bit), and Java plug-in matrixes. It is also gives solutions for known issues and detailed information about the browser settings (for all supported browsers) that can be configured to properly use EBS 12.2 on the client side. Additionally, increasing the heap sizes for the Java Runtime Environment (JRE) used in the EBS 12.2 client is useful for having a more stable and fast Java applet and thus a more stable client forms environment. Just like you do for the server side with Java, you can use the Xmx and Xms arguments to increase the allowed heap sizes for the client-side Java.

In Windows, you use the Java tab in the Control Panel and click the View button to open the Java Runtime Environment Settings window, where you enter the desired Xmx (1024M) and Xms (512M) values, as depicted in Figure 13-1. Note that configuring Xmx to 1024M can be tough for a 1GB client machine, so this recommendation is for client machines used specifically for connecting to an EBS environment, especially using forms-based EBS applications, and that have at least 1.5GB memory installed. Client machines that have 1GB memory installed can have the Java runtime parameters Xmx and Xms set to 512M or can be left at their default values.

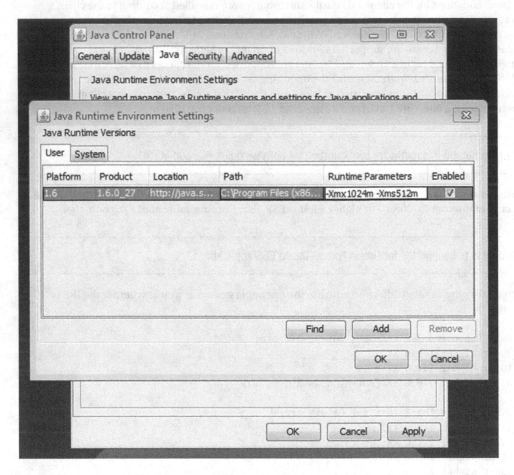

Figure 13-1. *Client-side Java runtime parameters*

In the latest version of EBS 11i (11.5.0.2), EBS 12.0, EBS 12.1 and EBS 12.2, the JRE plug-ins are installed in on the server side and deployed to EBS clients automatically by the EBS application server through the client browser when a client opens an Oracle form-based EBS application for the first time. To update the JRE for EBS clients, the server-side JRE should be updated, and the detailed instructions for deploying the JRE plug-ins can be found in Oracle Support document "Deploying JRE (Native Plug-in) for Windows Clients in Oracle E-Business Suite Release 12" (Doc ID 393931.1).

In addition to the EBS-specific client performance configurations, there are other things that can be done in the EBS client to enhance the client performance. A faster operating system, a faster Java Runtime Environment, and fewer network communication can speed up the EBS clients and indirectly increase the speed of EBS users.

Before going to the next section, we will summarize the things that should be done on the EBS client side for achieving an optimal EBS client performance.

- Arrange the client hardware to be at least 1GB RAM and a 1x1.4GHz CPU.

- Use supported operating systems on the client side.

- Use supported JRE plug-ins on the client side.

- Use supported browsers on the client side.

- Don't run any heavy programs while using EBS applications in the client applications.

- Don't install unrelated browsers plug-ins or toolbars in the EBS client machines.

- Ensure that the client-server network between the client machines and EBS servers is not too slow and can handle the environment-specific EBS workload of the clients.

- Turn off client-side automatic Java updates if possible. If this is not possible because of security requirements, implement the Dynamic Classid configuration, which is documented in Oracle Support note "Deploying JRE (Native Plug-in) for Windows Clients in Oracle E-Business Suite Release 12" (Doc ID 393931.1). Note that Dynamic Classid is applicable only when the client uses Internet Explorer.

- Always review and test the effects of operating system updates and security enhancements before applying them.

- Enable JAR file caching and configure sufficient cache sizes according to the workload.

- Enhance operating system performance if you can using operating system–specific performance software.

- Don't use high-quality wallpapers and screensavers on EBS client machines that have limited system resources.

- Check for driver updates (video cards especially).

- Check the disk fragmentations and run defragmentation software regularly.

EBS 12.2 Middle Tier Performance Tuning

The middle tier in EBS 12.2 is where the application server (or servers) on which the Oracle HTTP Server, WebLogic managed servers, and Forms and Report services are running.

The approach for getting optimal performance from the EBS 12.2 middle tier relies on having the sufficient number of application servers that can handle the user and application load, configuring the web server to work smoothly, having the sufficient number of JVMs in WebLogic instances (managed servers), configuring optimal Java memory for dealing with the application Java load, having a low latency network, using the forms in servlet mode, ensuring the application tier components to be at the latest patch level, and disabling the heavy logging and diagnostic functions.

So, the decisions for these configurations are generally made based on the expected load (before the project) or the current and future loads of your EBS environments. The decision to be made for a tuning action such as increasing the number of application servers or increasing the number of JVMs (in other words, application services) is made by answering questions such as "How many concurrent users are there in the system?" and "How many EBS modules are used in the EBS environment?" and "What are the characteristics of these EBS modules?"

Once you answer these questions, you can use rules of thumb defined in Oracle Support to decide on the application node count, the JVM heap sizes, and the WebLogic managed servers.

The recommended values for JVM (managed servers) heap sizes are roughly 512MB for 50 EBS users and 2048MB for 200 EBS users. So, when you have more than 200 users, you should add more WebLogic managed servers for the service group (for example, oacore) that is affected by the load. Likewise, if your server can't handle the load, you should add more application servers to make your EBS system meet the needs of heavy application processing.

In this manner, a load balancer can be positioned in front of the application nodes to distribute the load to several application servers without affecting any client configuration. Moreover, the work that needs to be done in the application servers for decryption and encryption in SSL-enabled EBS environments can be offloaded to the load balancers as long as it is supported by them.

Figure 13-2 shows an example EBS 12.2 system configuration consisting of a load balancer, three application nodes, and one database node. The purpose of this figure is to show you a fully load balanced application server configuration that is made possible by placing and configuring a load balancer in front of the application nodes.

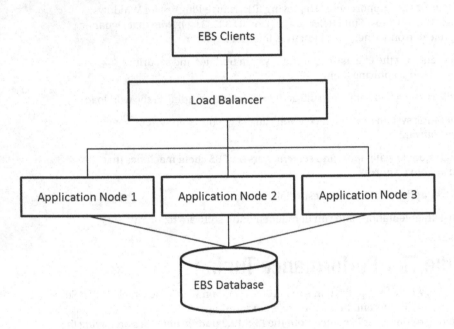

Figure 13-2. EBS 12.2 load balancer configuration

All the load balancer–related information including offloading the SSL work to the load balancers is present in My Oracle Support document "Using Load-Balancers with Oracle E-Business Suite Release 12.2" (Doc ID 1375686.1). So, if you are interested in such a configuration, please check Doc 1375686.1 for further information.

To sum up, the things that should be considered for increasing the performance of the EBS 12.2 middle tier are increasing the heap sizes according to the expected user counts, adding managed servers according to the load and expected user numbers, and adding application nodes with a load balancer in front of them according to the server load and failover needs. New managed servers can be added and the heap sizes for the WebLogic managed servers can be increased accordingly as described in Chapter 7.

Figure 13-3 shows an EBS 12.2 environment where we have added an additional oacore server named oacore_server2 to handle the load caused by oacore-related activity (OAF pages) on an EBS 12.2 application server. Figure 13-3 lists WebLogic managed servers after we added an additional oacore server, like we did while explaining WebLogic inside EBS 12.2 in Chapter 7.

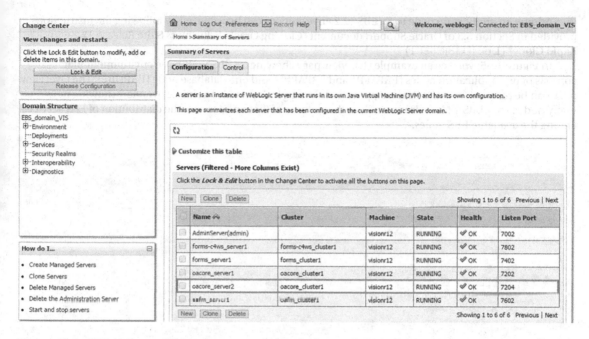

Figure 13-3. *EBS 12.2: an additional oacore server for dealing with the OAF load*

Figure 13-4 shows how we increased the JVM heap size of an oacore server for dealing with the heavy oacore-related activity. (Note that the approach for increasing the heap sizes of WebLogic servers was already explained in Chapter 7.)

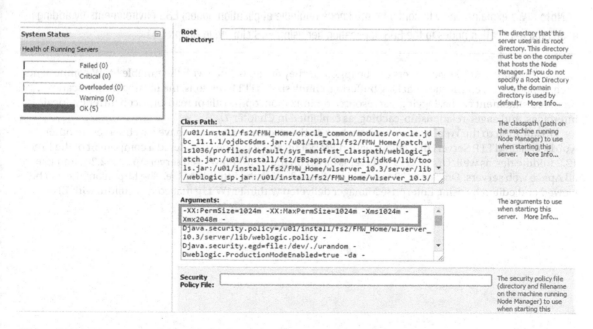

Figure 13-4. *EBS 12.2: modifying the heap sizes of a WebLogic managed server*

Adding an application node to an EBS 12.2 environment can be achieved by following the instructions provided in Section 5.3 of Oracle Support document "Cloning Oracle E-Business Suite Release 12.2 with Rapid Clone" (Doc ID 1383621.1).

In Figure 13-5, you see an example Overview page showing an EBS multinode environment that consists of two application nodes (ERPAPP1 and ERPAPP2) and one database node (ERPDB1). The Overview page can be reached from the Oracle Applications Manager; it provides a simple overview showing how many nodes your EBS 12.2 environment has, the statuses of these nodes, and the distribution of EBS services among the available EBS nodes.

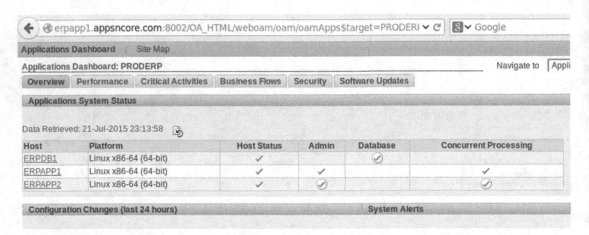

Figure 13-5. *EBS 12.2: Overview page showing multinode EBS 12.2 environment*

■ **Note** We explained how to configure multinode (multiple application nodes) EBS environments by adding additional application nodes to the EBS application tier using EBS cloning in Chapter 11.

Additionally, WebLogic servers can be tuned, as they are associated with the tunable FMW components such as pool sizes, connection backlog buffering, chunk sizes, HTTP sessions, the messaging applications, prepared statement cache, logging last resource optimization, optimistic or read-only concurrency, local interfaces, and eager-relationship-caching, as explained in Chapter 7.

In addition to the WebLogic servers you have in the middle tier, you also have a web server (in other words, Oracle HTTP Server) that comes within FMW 11g, and it can be considered a component of the EBS 12.2 middle tier, as well. Oracle HTTP Server is based on the well-known web server Apache 2.2.*x*, and like all Apace web servers, Oracle HTTP Server is configured using the httpd.conf file. The httpd.conf file can be viewed and edited by using Enterprise Manager delivered within FMW 11g that comes built-in with EBS.

As we explained in Chapter 7, we will not go into the details of viewing httpd.conf using Enterprise Manager and instead will concentrate on the performance metrics of Oracle HTTP Server and the parameters defined in httpd.conf that can affect EBS 12.2's performance. Figure 13-6 shows an example httpd.conf file opened with the Enterprise Manager Fusion Middleware Control.

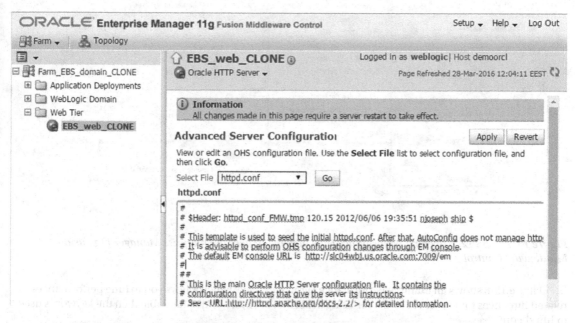

Figure 13-6. EBS 12.2: Example httpd.conf file opened with Enterprise Manager 11g Fusion Middleware Control

While the httpd.conf file can be opened and edited in place manually with the standard httpd.conf syntax, the Enterprise Manager 11g FMW Control in EBS 12.2 provides an interface called Performance Directives that can be used to change the performance-related parameters in httpd.conf, without having to edit the httpd.conf file itself.

As shown in Figure 13-7, you can right-click the icon that represents your web server (in this example, it is EBS_web_CLONE) in the tree panel located on the left of the FMW Control main page and then choose Administration and Performance Directives for opening the interface.

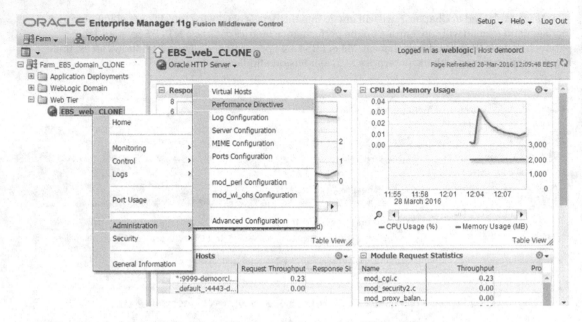

Figure 13-7. *EBS 12.2: opening Performance Directives menu item in Enterprise Manager 11g Fusion Middleware Control*

Figure 13-8 shows an example Performance Directives page, which allows you to tune performance-related directives for Oracle HTTP Server using fields that are more understandable than the keywords used in httpd.conf.

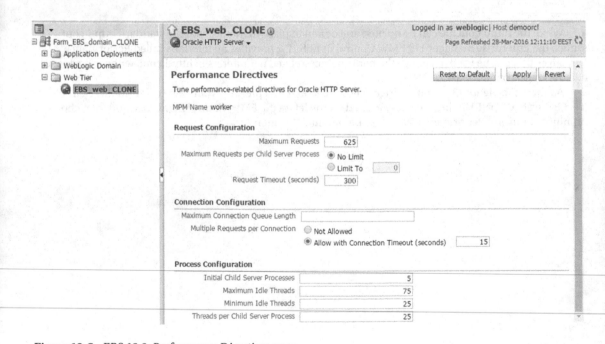

Figure 13-8. *EBS 12.2: Performance Directives page*

Using the Performance Directives page, you can control the HTTP request configuration, connection configuration, and process configuration of Oracle HTTP Server.

In the Request Configuration area of the Performance Directives page, you can see Maximum Requests, Maximum Request per Child Server Process, and Request Timeout fields.

Maximum Requests is used for setting the limit of the number of HTTP requests that can be processed by Oracle HTTP Server in one go. Maximum Request per Child Server Process can be used to limit the number of requests that an Apache child process can process during its process lifetime. Maximum Request per Child Server Process by default is set to no limit, and it should be changed only when directed by Oracle or when there is a large number of HTTP connections and the server starts to encounter memory leakages.

Request Timeout can be used to specify a limit in seconds for making Oracle HTTP Server wait for a get request; it is used for specifying the number of seconds that a single HTTP request can take. The request time is by default set to 300 but can be increased or decreased according to the situation. (Consider a scenario where some of the clients are using a low-speed network to access EBS 12.2.)

In the Connection Configuration area of the Performance Directives page, you have Maximum Connection Queue Length and Multiple Requests per Connection tunables. Maximum Connection Queue Length can be used to specify a limit on the opening of new connections, as may be necessary in some of the EBS 12.2 environments where Oracle HTTP Server becomes saturated because of the high number of HTTP connection attempts coming continuously. Multiple Requests per Connection can be used to tell Oracle HTTP Server to let single connections be free for making multiple HTTP requests. Multiple Request per Connection should be used in conjunction with Request Timeout to tell Oracle HTTP Server to wait for a single connection and keep it alive until you reach the number of seconds defined in the Request Timeout field, as there may be multiple requests that can be made by a single connection.

In the Process Configuration area of the Performance Directives page, you have the Initial Child Server Processes, Maximum Idle Threads, Minimum Idle Threads, and Threads per Child Server Process fields. Initial Child Server Processes can be used to specify the number of child server processes that are created when Oracle HTTP Server is started. The Maximum Idle Threads and Minimum Idle Threads fields can be used to specify the number of the HTTP child server processes that can be running at a time but not serving for any HTTML requests. The Threads per Child Server Process field is used to specify the number of threads that a child server process should have.

Well, we have gone through the tunables that are present on the Performance Directives page one by one. These tunables are normally sufficient for configuring Oracle HTTP Server according to the performance needs of your EBS 12.2 environments, as these tunables can be used for tuning Oracle HTTP Server in EBS 12.2. Moreover, Oracle has chosen them among several Oracle HTTP Server parameters (actually Apache parameters) and included them on the FMW Performance Directives page to make your work simpler. However, although it seems unnecessary to tune all the Oracle HTTP Server parameters in EBS 12.2, there are still some fine details in Oracle HTTP Server performance tuning, as the base of it relies on the Apache server that has several configurable parameters. So, even if it is normally not required and should not be done without obtaining the approval of Oracle, if you have such a need to tune Oracle HTTP Server at a deeper level, you can visit the Apache HTTP Server website at https://httpd.apache.org/docs/2.2.

Another key in EBS performance tuning is having a low-latency network between your client, application servers, and database server. In the Oracle EBS world, this is a network that operates at a speed that does not block the processing between the EBS 12.2 clients, database server, and application servers. However, in most cases when you identify a network latency problem, your duty is to transmit the network issue to the network team. That is, for analyzing the EBS network, you should use the Network Test form that comes with EBS 12.2, interpret the results, and transmit the issue (if there are any) to the network team.

Figure 13-9 shows the EBS navigation (System Administrator ➤ Application ➤ Network Test) for reaching the Network Test form. Note that the Network Test form is by default available under the System Administrator responsibility, but it can also be added to the user's menu so that nonadmin users can do their EBS network tests for measuring the time taken for Oracle Forms round-trips.

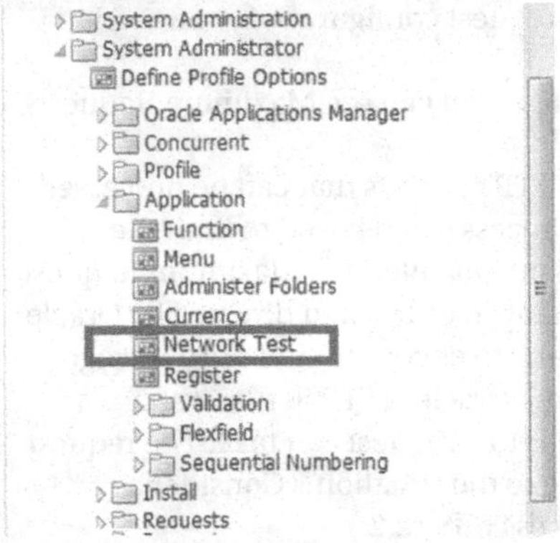

Figure 13-9. Navigation for reaching the Network Test form

Once you click the network test function shown in Figure 13-9, the Network Test form appears. In this form, you can configure the number of times that you want to send a sequence of packets (iterations) and the number of times that you want to repeat this iteration (trials). Accepting the default (Trials: 5, Iterations: 100) is enough for most cases, as the result produced for the average of 500 sequence of packets (iterations) looks promising.

To run the network test, click the Run Test button at the top right of the Network Test form, as shown in Figure 13-10.

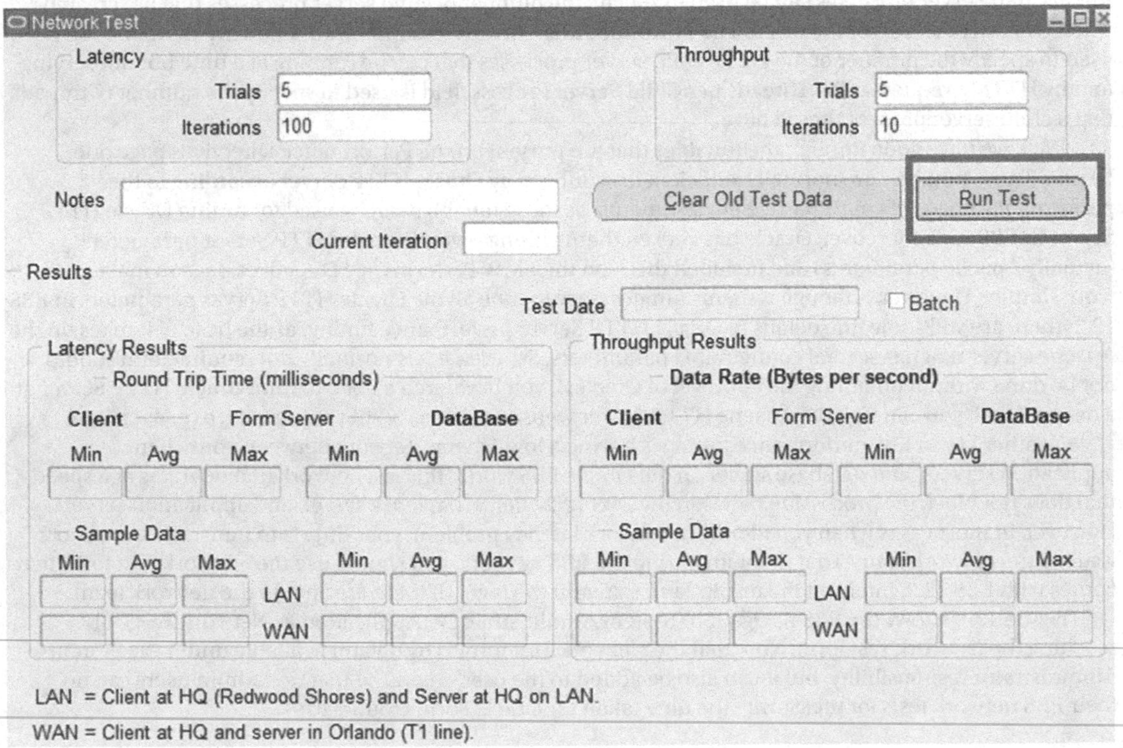

Figure 13-10. Network Test form: running a test

After clicking the Run Test button, you can wait for a while. This wait time may change according to the number of iterations and trials that you have chosen. The Network Test form measures the latency by examining the round-trip of the packets sent from the client to the application server to the database server and then back to the client.

The results of bandwidth (in other words, the results of throughput shown in the Network Test form) are also based on the client, application server, and database server communication. However, bandwidth is different from the latency. Throughput results display the data transfer rate in terms of bytes per second to show you how many bytes are transferred between the client, application server, and database server.

Figure 13-11 shows an example test result done on one of our own servers located in our lab.

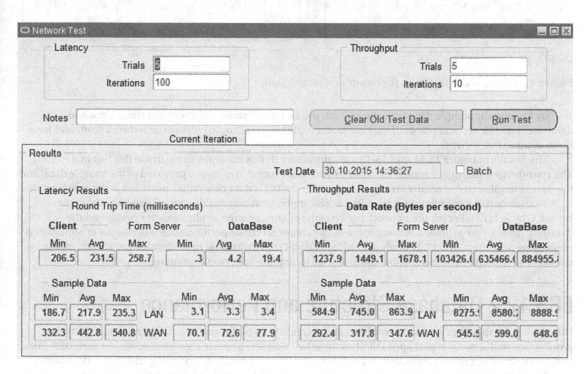

Figure 13-11. Network Test form, test results

In Figure 13-11, you can see both the latency and throughput results. Although these results seem complicated, once you know how to interpret them, it is not so hard to analyze them. Interpreting these results is not your main work, though, and probably that's why Oracle has provided some sample data to use as reference for your results. The data can be considered the minimum acceptable network values recommended by Oracle.

So, by comparing the results with the sample data results, you can understand whether the network speed between the client, form server, and database is acceptable or not. Figure 13-12 shows the sample data and example latency and throughput results more closely.

Latency Results Round Trip Time (milliseconds)						Throughput Results Data Rate (Bytes per second)					
Client			**Form Server**		**DataBase**	**Client**			**Form Server**		**DataBase**
Min	Avg	Max	Min	Avg	Max	Min	Avg	Max	Min	Avg	Max
206.5	231.5	258.7	.3	4.2	19.4	1237.9	1449.1	1678.1	103426.(	635466.(	884955.:

Sample Data						Sample Data					
Min	Avg	Max	Min	Avg	Max	Min	Avg	Max	Min	Avg	Max
186.7	217.9	235.3 LAN	3.1	3.3	3.4	584.9	745.0	863.9 LAN	8275.!	8580.:	8888.!
332.3	442.8	540.8 WAN	70.1	72.6	77.9	292.4	317.8	347.6 WAN	545.!	599.0	648.6

Figure 13-12. Network Test form, the results and sample data

By looking the sample data and your results, you can understand whether your client form and database network are acceptable. If they are not acceptable, you should consult the network team and have them analyze the network.

The results in Figure 13-11 and 13-12 are satisfactory in this example, as we made this test in a WAN. The round-trip times in our results are less than the WAN round-trip values provided in the sample data, and the data rate value in our results are much more than the WAN data rate values provided in the sample data.

To summarize, performance tuning in the EBS application tier/middle tier is based on WebLogic Server, Oracle HTTP Server, the network between the clients, and the application tier nodes and the database nodes. Any problems among these major areas can create performance bottlenecks in application processing and affect EBS 12.2 clients accordingly. If you think you need more details, you can check the documents referenced in this section and continue tuning the system components.

EBS 12.2 Database Structure and Performance

Diagnosing database performance problems and increasing its performance in EBS 12.2 are subjects that require two skill sets. An expert apps DBA has these two skill sets because they have advanced core DBA skills and EBS-related database admin skills for achieving an EBS 12.2 database operating with full performance.

The skill sets required for performance tuning require a bit more knowledge because having a high-performance EBS 12.2 database requires advanced techniques such as making EBS-specific database performance enhancements, making database configurations with an eye on performance, and taking standard database performance tuning actions without forgetting that the Oracle database you are dealing with is actually an EBS database.

EBS database performance tuning is based on two major concerns. The first one is having an Oracle database configured for performance. From the mount points where you place your database files and redolog files to the tablespace configurations, from choosing a block size for a tablespace to increasing parallelism, from memory-related Oracle database parameters to gathering statistics, and from the maintenance of big fragmented tables to the rebuilding of indexes and achieving better index clustering factors, tuning an EBS 12.2 database environment for performance requires expert Oracle core DBA abilities. In this manner, any expert core DBA can build an EBS database environment designed for performance or at least deliver acceptable database performance.

The second concern is that because EBS 12.2 is a complex application with a complex database structure consisting of a bunch of Oracle applications, it requires EBS-specific database tuning. The EBS 12.2 database is also very sensitive to some of the standard Oracle Database parameters, as a few of these parameters should not be used with EBS 12.2 databases at all. For example, you can't just partition a table or create an index on standard tables whenever you want. Moreover, duties like gathering stats and maintenance activities such as purging application tables should be done using EBS-specific programs (mostly concurrent programs) or EBS PL/SQL APIs.

These two concerns may seem separate, but to achieve performance in an EBS 12.2 database environment, you must consider both of them together while doing performance tuning work. That is, any action you plan to take or any configuration that you plan to make should conform to the rules of standard database performance tuning (concern 1) and EBS-specific database performance tuning (concern 2). You should not violate the rules of EBS-specific database performance tuning. That is, you must not take any actions that are contrary to EBS-specific database performance tuning even if those actions are correct when you look things from the viewpoint of standard database performance tuning. In other words, you should stand on the side of EBS-specific database performance tuning while planning to take any action or making any configuration that reveals a conflict between standard database performance tuning and EBS-specific database performance tuning. Also, it is better to keep in mind that although all of the Oracle Database Enterprise Edition's performance-related database features such as partitioning are by default enabled in EBS 12.2 databases and although some of the standard EBS tables are delivered with these options (partitioned tables) during the installation of EBS 12.2, you need to purchase the partitioning licenses if you need to use any of these options. For example, you need to buy a partitioning license to partition an additional EBS table.

EBS-specific database tuning should be considered with the highest priority when deciding on a performance tuning actions. This is because the performance tuning actions or configurations that may result in an increase in EBS database performance are tested and verified by Oracle. So even if Oracle (via the Oracle documents), for instance, states that a database initialization parameter is generally applicable for increasing the performance of standard Oracle databases, that parameter should be investigated and cross-checked using the EBS-specific Oracle documents. If you can't find any records about the parameter in the EBS-specific Oracle documents even after such an investigation, then you should not use that parameter in EBS 12.2 databases, as it can cause an undesired functional impact or a decrease in application performance.

Figure 13-13 depicts the tuning areas mentioned in the previous paragraph. Once you tune all these areas shown in Figure 13-13, you may consider your EBS 12.2 database to be configured for achieving acceptable database performance.

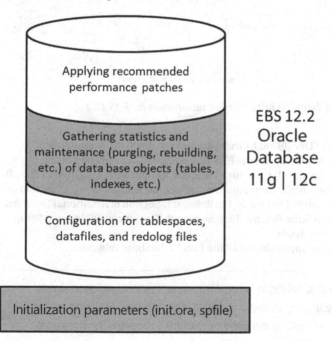

Figure 13-13. EBS 12.2: Database performance tuning areas

As Figure 13-13 implies, you take actions in four performance tuning areas. The sequence of these actions may vary, but we will start with setting database initialization parameters and then continue with the configuration for tablespaces, data files, and redolog files. Next, we will analyze the process for gathering stats and maintaining database objects for increasing the database performance in EBS 12.2. Lastly, we will mention the importance of applying recommended patches for EBS 12.2 databases.

So, let's start with database parameters, which can be considered the starting point for database performance tuning in EBS 12.2.

Initialization Parameters

The recommended database initialization parameters for EBS 12.2 are almost the same as EBS 12.0 and EBS 12.1. To set the EBS database initialization parameters, you basically follow Oracle Support document "Database Initialization Parameters for Oracle E-Business Suite Release 12" (Doc ID 396009.1). There are database release–specific database initialization parameters in Doc 396009.1. Also, there are recommendations about creating temporary tablespaces and setting the initialization parameter values according to your sizing needs.

Figure 13-14 shows Doc 396009.1, just to give you an idea about how well it is organized.

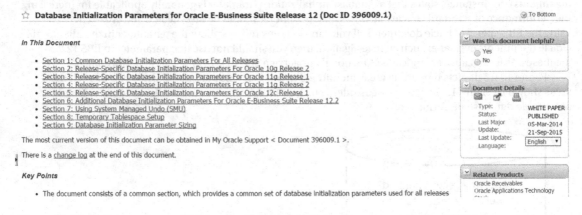

Figure 13-14. Reference document for setting database initialization parameters for EBS 12.2

As shown in Figure 13-4, in the first part of Doc 396009.1 there are links to reach the sections directly. Click the links related to EBS 12.2 to jump there quickly. As the EBS 12.2 database can only be release 11g R2 or release 12c, you can review these sections: Section 1: Common Database Initialization Parameters For All Releases, Section 4: Release-Specific Database Initialization Parameters For Oracle 11g Release 2, Section 5: Release-Specific Database Initialization Parameters For Oracle 12c Release 1, Section 6: Additional Database Initialization Parameters For Oracle E-Business Suite Release 12.2, Section 8: Temporary Tablespace Setup, and Section 9: Database Initialization Parameter Sizing.

Section 1 lists common parameters that are applicable to all the EBS 12 database releases.

■ **Note** Although the verification of EBS-specific database initialization parameters can be done simply by using bde_chk_cbo.sql documented in Oracle Support document "bde_chk_cbo.sql - EBS initialization parameters - Healthcheck" (Doc ID 174605.1), we will go through Doc 393009.1 to review the mandatory initialization parameters.

Several mandatory parameters are listed in this section; most of them are not performance-related parameters but may affect performance indirectly. Even if you accept the defaults for most of these performance parameters, it is better to know the effects of changing them generally, as it may be necessary one day.

The following list explains these parameters briefly. If you want to use them, you can get more information from the Oracle database reference documents at http://docs.oracle.com.

- *compatible*: This parameter is used to control the formats of Oracle data blocks and redo streams. It is basically controlling what is written to disk. In EBS 12.2, it is mandatory to set this parameter to 11.2.0 for 11g R2 EBS databases and to 12.1.0 for 12c EBS databases. This parameter may affect the performance of the EBS database as it is used to activate the enhancements that come with EBS's database release.

- *audit_trail*: This parameter is for enabling database audit. It may affect performance if it is turned on and if lots of operations are audited. It may bring extra I/O overhead to the EBS 12.2 database. So, if auditing is not required, you don't set it; by default it is disabled.

- *db_block_size*: This parameter is the database block size of the EBS database. It must be set to 8192.

- *timed_statistics*: This enables statistics collection for the use of SQL traces and AWR. It has a minimal performance effect but can be disabled if needed. We recommend setting it to TRUE.

- *processes*: This is the maximum process count. It should be set according to the sizing requirements. You can check Table 13-1 to have an idea about the minimum recommended values for test and development instances. We recommend this parameter be set to at least 500 for a freshly installed EBS 12.2 production database and to be increased after recognizing the load and characteristics of the EBS 12.2 environment derived from the database performance analysis such as analyzing AWR, as well.

- *sessions*: This is the maximum session count. It should be set according to the sizing requirements. You can check Table 13-1 to get an idea about the minimum recommended values for the test and development instances. We recommend this parameter be set to at least 500 for a freshly installed EBS 12.2 production database and to be increased after recognizing the load and characteristics of the EBS 12.2 environment derived from the database performance analysis such as analyzing AWR, as well.

- *dml_locks*: This is the maximum number of DML locks. Setting it to zero may increase performance, but it is not recommended for EBS at all. This parameter actually does not affect performance, but if it is set too low, it may lead to ORA-00055. Accepting the recommended value (10000) is reasonable for this parameter.

- *cursor_sharing*: This specifies which SQL statements can share the same cursors. In EBS 12.2, it is mandatory to set this parameter to EXACT. Setting it to other values (FORCE, SIMILAR) may decrease general EBS performance.

- *open_cursors*: This is the maximum number of cursors that a session opens at once. Caching cursors is done by Oracle Database, and the purpose of it is to decrease the time needed for parsing SQL statements. Oracle by default caches cursors, so open_cursors should be increased only for making sessions not get ORA-1000 errors as a result of reaching the open cursor limit defined by the open_cursors parameter. We recommend setting it to 1200 in EBS 12.2.

- *session_cached_cursors*: This is the maximum number of cached cursors (not open cursors) that a session can have. This parameter affects performance as it may decrease parse calls. We recommend setting it to 1000 in EBS 12.2. It may be increased even more if you see high soft parsing in your EBS database.

- *sga_target*: This is the total size of the Oracle's shared memory, where all the shared caches of Oracle Database named Buffer Cache, Shared Pool, Large Pool, Java Pool, and Streams Pool reside. It is one of the most important performance parameters of Oracle Database and must be set according to the load of the EBS 12.2 environment. You can check Table 13-1 to get an idea about the minimum Oracle Support–recommended sga_target values. We recommend this parameter be set to at least 8G for a freshly installed EBS 12.2 production database and to be increased after recognizing the load and characteristics of the EBS 12.2 environment derived from the database performance analysis such as analyzing AWR. This is a general recommendation, though, and it can be considered as a starting point when there is a small amount of RAM (for example, 16GB) available in the EBS database server. That is, it is no use to set this type of system resource–dependent parameter in a dedicated EBS database server environment to a low value like 8GB. In other words, when there is plenty of RAM dedicated (for example, 64BG) for the EBS database, then you can even start with a 32GB SGA or with a 48GB SGA. So, the recommended values on these parameters often depend on many factors, and our recommendations on them are just minimums. Also, with Oracle Database 11g, an alternative and more sophisticated memory_target parameter was introduced. memory_target can also be used instead of the sga_target, but as memory_target is not compatible with huge pages, we recommend using the sga_target parameter for 11g R2 EBS databases and even for 12c EBS databases.

- *db_block_checking*: This parameter makes Oracle Database processes check the memory for detecting memory errors that may corrupt the database blocks when they are in memory. It can affect performance significantly, and that's why it is set to OFF by default. On the other hand, db_block_checking can be set to LOW, MEDIUM, or FULL considering a performance overhead of 1 percent to 10 percent.

- *log_checkpoint_timeout*: This parameter is used tell Oracle Database to flush the dirty buffers to disk when the number of seconds that is defined by the log_checkpoint_timeout parameter has passed since the last redolog files were written by the last incremental checkpoint. This parameter is set to 1200 (20mins) by default. Also, you can change it according to the load characteristics of your environments. Setting it to 0 disables this timeout and makes Oracle have the checkpoints only at log switches. Having excessive checkpoints may trigger a performance issue; likewise, having long time intervals between checkpoints may create a performance issue. So, the default value is acceptable for the beginning, but we don't see any problems in tuning it as long as the new value of it is derived from the results of database performance analysis.

- *log_checkpoint_interval*: log_checkpoint_interval is specified in terms of operating system blocks (in Red Hat and Oracle Linux, 1 block equals 512 bytes), and it is used to tell Oracle Database to checkpoint if there a gap (as much as the value of log_checkpoint_interval) between the last incremental checkpoint and the last block written to the redolog. This parameter is set to 100000 by default. The default value is acceptable for the beginning, but we don't see any problems in tuning it as long as the new value of it is derived from the results of database performance analysis.

- *log_buffer*: In Oracle Database, the redo entries are first placed in redolog buffer, which is located in memory, and the LGWR process reads this buffer and writes the redo entries to the redolog files. Log_buffer controls the size of the redolog buffer, and this parameter is specified in bytes. The default value of this parameter is set to 10485760, and we can admit that it is large enough for the beginning. Also, it may be set to higher values or lower values according to the database performance analysis. While setting this parameter, you should consider the transaction count of your EBS system and the length of the statements that contribute these transactions also. Generally, setting this parameter to large values should decrease redolog file I/O, but setting this parameter to large values may also create a performance problem, as while flushing a big set of redo from the log buffer to redologs, the LGWR will need to do a lot of I/Os. Also, as LGWR has to write all the data into the redolog files and as LGWR will wait until all I/O is completed, having a big log buffer may can make LGWR write a big-sized data (redo) at once and thus may introduce I/O waits according to the performance capacity of the underlying storage.

- *shared_pool_size*: Basically, the shared pool is the memory region located in SGA of Oracle Database, and it is used by Oracle Database to cache the shared SQL and PL/SQL objects. This parameter can be set in bytes, megabytes, or gigabytes (for example, shared_pool_size-1000M). If this parameter is set to a low value, the database performance may decrease as a low setting may introduce shared pool contentions. You can check Table 13-1 to get an idea about the minimum Oracle Support–recommended shared_pool_size vales. We recommend this parameter be set to at least 2G for a freshly installed EBS 12.2 production database and to be increased after recognizing the load and characteristics of the EBS 12.2 environment derived from the database performance analysis such as analyzing AWR. If using automatic memory management (AMM) or automatic shared memory management (ASMM), there is no need to set this parameter as it is adjusted automatically. Note that AMM is enabled by setting the memory_target and memory_max_target parameters for specifying the total of SGA and PGA sizes. ASMM is enabled by setting the sga_target and sga_max_size parameters for specifying the SGA size.

- *shared_pool_reserved_size*: This parameter is specified in bytes and is used for reserving shared pool space for Oracle processes that require large and continuous shared pool space for storing shared SQL or PL/SQL objects. Although it is not mandatory at all, it is advisable to set this parameter to at least 5 percent of the shared_pool_size value to not to suffer from shared_pool waits in the case of a shortage in shared pool.

- *_shared_pool_reserved_min_alloc*: This parameter starts with an underscore; in other words, it is a hidden parameter, but it is by default set in the EBS database parameter file (pfile or spfile). The default value that comes with the initialization parameter file of the EBS database is 4100. We don't recommend changing the value of this parameter without getting Oracle's approval as it is a hidden parameter.

- *aq_tm_processes*: This parameter is used to specify the number of advanced queue processes used by some of the EBS modules, such as workflow. AQ processes handle delayed queue messages, and setting this parameter to 1 is acceptable for the beginning, but if you see any unnecessary waits in advanced queues, you should increase it accordingly.

- *job_queue_processes*: This parameter specifies how many job queue processes you want to have in your Oracle Database. Job queue processes are like background processes as they have their own dedicated OS process (ora_j* processes). The job of these processes is to execute code. Job queue processes are basically used by DBMS_JOB jobs and Oracle Scheduler (DBMS_SCHEDULER) jobs to accomplish scheduled database works, such as executing a package in regular intervals or refreshing a materialized view once a day. In addition, they can be used for executing work in the background. For instance, you can execute a package in the background using the DBMS_JOB package, which actually triggers job_queue_processes to do the work. Advanced queues use job_queue_processes to accomplish their works in the background. The recommended value of this parameter is 2 but should be increased considering the job queue–based load of your EBS database.

- *parallel_max_servers*: This parameter is used to specify the maximum count of parallel servers. As Oracle Database has parallelization capabilities and as parallelization is used in some of processes in EBS 12.2, it is a mandatory parameter, and setting this parameter to a low value may impact performance. Similarly, setting it to a very high value may impact performance, as having lots of parallel processes may result in CPU starvation in the database server. Setting this parameter too high also may create an excessive paging situation or extra waits for very short queries caused by the work transparently done for coordinating the parallel processes. The recommended value for setting this parameter is two times the available CPU cores in the database server. If you trust your machine (in other words, if your CPU cores are faster than ordinary CPUs), then you can set this parameter to even higher values. However, setting it too high may trigger a memory shortage. This parameter directly affects performance and should be set carefully.

- *parallel_min_servers*: This parameter is used to specify the minimum number of parallel servers; in other words, it is a way to tell Oracle "During the start of the database, create parallel process as many as the value of this parameter. " Setting it too low may impact performance, as new parallel processes should be started in case of a peak in the number of queries that are designed to do parallel execution. The default value of this parameter in the EBS parameter file is 0 but should be increased if parallel execution is widely used in the EBS environment. That is, if there are many Discoverer reports, many concurrent programs that do their database works in parallel, and many jobs like gathering statistics, then it is advisable to increase this parameter (while of course considering memory resources).

- *pga_aggregate_target*: This parameter is used to specify the size of process global memory in bytes or megabytes or gigabytes. Basically, Process Global Memory is the process memory where each process is and where each process puts their own (not shared) data in it. By setting pga_aggregate_target, you tell Oracle to try to keep the total process memory almost equal to the value you set for this parameter. However, as its name implies, it is not a limit; it is just a target. Even if it is just a target and not a limit, it is still important to set pga_aggregate_target to an appropriate value as there are many memory-related internal parameters derived from it. You can check Table 13-1 to get an idea about the minimum Oracle Support-recommended pga_aggregate_target values. We recommend this parameter be set to at least 4G for a freshly installed EBS 12.2 production database and to be increased after recognizing the load and characteristics of the EBS 12.2 environment derived from the database performance analysis such as analyzing AWR.

- *workarea_size_policy*: This is a mandatory parameter, and it must be set to AUTO for EBS 12.2 databases. Setting this parameter to the value AUTO enables automatic sizing of PGA work areas used by the operators. Setting this parameter to the value MANUAL may lead to a decrease in EBS database performance.

- *olap_page_pool_size*: This specifies the size of the OLAP page pool in bytes. It can be set to 4194304, as suggested in the document "Database Initialization Parameters for Oracle E-Business Suite Release 12" (Doc ID 396009.1). Setting it to a lower value may decrease OLAP performance.

The following parameters are hidden parameters, and it is mandatory to set them as documented here. The need for setting these parameters is derived by Oracle, probably as a result of several performance tests the people at Oracle did in EBS environments.

- _sort_elimination_cost_ratio=5

- _like_with_bind_as_equality =TRUE

- _fast_full_scan_enabled=FALSE

- _b_tree_bitmap_plans =FALSE

- optimizer_secure_view_merging=FALSE

- _sqlexec_progression_cost=2147483647

Table 13-1 shows the performance-related main database initialization parameters and their corresponding values, recommended by Oracle.

Table 13-1. *EBS 12.2: performance-related main database initialization parameters and sizing of memory for EBS 12.2 database*

Parameter	For Test and Development Environments	Production Environments 11 to 100 Users	Production Environments 101 to 500 Users	Production Environments 501 to 1,000 Users	Production Environments 1,001 to 2,000 Users
Processes	200	200	800	1200	2500
Sessions	400	400	1600	2400	5000
sga_target	1G	1G	2G	3G	14G
shared_pool_size	N/A	N/A	N/A	1800M	3000M
shared_pool_reserved_size	N/A	N/A	N/A	180M	300M
shared_pool_size	400M	600M	800M	1000M	2000M
shared_pool_reserved_size	40M	60M	80M	100M	100M
pga_aggregate_target	1G	2G	4G	10G	20G
Total Memory Required	~2GB	~3GB	~6GB	~13GB	~34GB

The information shown in Table 13-1 can be considered as the sizing information, as well.

The sizing of memory is important, as there may be situations where you see swapping activities in the database tier because of insufficient memory. Swapping is a need that makes the relevant kernel daemons (kswapd in Linux) search the entire memory to choose the memory pages for swapping out and also means that kernel daemons will make I/O a high priority; therefore, it may decrease the EBS database performance dramatically. That's why it is important to install the necessary amount of RAM and make the optimal configuration for SGA and PGA parameters to prevent the database server from being obliged to make swapping. It is also important to note that huge pages are not swapped out. So, the number of huge pages must be carefully adjusted, as having a high number of huge pages may introduce a memory shortage for processes that are not using these huge pages. This memory shortage in turn may result in excessive swap-out and swap-in operations for those memory pages (for example, memory used by OS processes and PGA memory). You can refer to the following Oracle Support document for the recommended values of huge pages: "Oracle Linux: Shell Script to Calculate Values Recommended Linux HugePages/HugeTLB Configuration" (Doc ID 401749.1).

■ **Note** Swap-in and swap-out operations can be monitored using OS tools such as SAR and vmstat. Swapping can also be a problem if it is encountered in the EBS application servers. For application servers, you need to install the necessary amount of RAM and set the heap sizes for both major concurrent programs and WebLogic servers to optimal values.

So far, you have seen the command initialization parameters that can be set regardless of the database versions of the EBS 12 environment. However, as our scope is EBS 12.2 and as the database version used in EBS 12.2 can be Oracle Database 11g R2 or Oracle Database 12c, it is good to take a look at the version-specific parameters as well.

Let's start with the 11g R2–specific and performance-related database initialization parameters. 11g R2 (exactly 11.2.0.4) has been the default Oracle Database version that comes with the installation of EBS 12.2 for a long time. (With the latest startCD, startCD 51, EBS 12.2 can be installed with the 12.1.0.2 database as well.)

In addition to the initialization parameters that can be specified in all the Oracle Database releases that are supported by EBS 12, you have some additional parameters that should be added to your initialization files if the database of your EBS 12.2 environment is Oracle Database 11g R2. Although the performance impact that may arise by setting these 11g R2–specific initialization parameters is small, it's worth mentioning them as these are mandatory parameters. That is, even if these parameters are not closely related to database performance, any subject that may be related with any type of performance degradation in the database tier of EBS 12.2 cannot be considered negligible.

In this scope, the compatible parameter as mentioned earlier is one of those parameters, and it is mandatory to set it to 11.2.0 for 11g R2 EBS databases and to 12.1.0 for 12c EBS databases. The hidden parameter _optimizer_autostats_jobmust also must be set to FALSE to turn off the automatic statistic collection job, as EBS is a packaged application and has logic and methods on statistics collection. (We will explain statistics collection in EBS 12.2 environments later in this chapter.) The parallel_force_local parameter, which was introduced in Oracle Database 11g, must also be set to TRUE. It forces the parallel requests for a given SQL statement to not span multiple nodes and thus may seem to be a factor that decreases parallelization. Oracle requires setting this parameter to the value TRUE probably based on the EBS 12–specific findings. The Undo_management parameter must also be set to AUTO to enable automatic undo management, which lets you minimize the undo segment performance problems by leaving the undo segment management to the Oracle database.

Lastly, the parameter memory_target introduced in 11g R2 can be used instead of the sga_target, pga_target, and sga_max_size parameters to specify a target value at one time for the total of shared (SGA) and process (PGA) memory. memory_target enables the interchange of memory buffers between process global memory and shared global memory, but as it is not compatible with huge pages, it is not recommended for large mission-critical production systems. We recommend using huge pages with the sga_max_size, sga_target, and pga_aggregate_target parameters; in addition, you should know there is a parameter called memory_target introduced in 11g R2 that eases the initialization parameter file configuration for memory-related initialization parameters and enables interchange of memory buffer between the SGA and PGA (it may be used if you haven't a big memory and thus need a solution like this). Again, we recommend using this parameter only in test/dev and small (especially in terms of memory) prod environments.

As new parameters are introduced with 11g R2 Oracle Database, some of the old parameters that were used in earlier releases such as 10g Oracle Database or 9i Oracle Database are obsoleted (in other words, deprecated in 11g R2), as these kinds of parameters are not important. Still, it is important to know what these parameters are, as you may be upgrading your EBS database to 11g R2 and need to remove those parameters as a requirement of such an upgrade. The list of parameters that should be removed when using Oracle Database 11g R2 in the EBS 12.2 database tier can be found in Section 4.2 of Doc ID 398009.1. Like in 11g R2, you have some important release-specific initialization parameters in 12c. Also, there is a parameter removal list for 12c.

Let's take a look at the Oracle Database 12c-specific EBS database parameters.

■ **Note** When EBS is installed with the latest startCD, which is startCD 51, the EBS database is delivered as 12.1.0.2 (12c Release 1). Also, as for EBS 12.2 environments, which currently have 11g R2 databases, database upgrades can be done to upgrade the 11g R2 EBS database to 12c.

Again, we start with the compatible parameter, as it is there for all Oracle Database releases. For an EBS 12c database, this parameter must be set to 12.1.0 regardless of the detailed database version string. (For example, even if your EBS database version is 12.1.0.1, you set this parameter to 12.1.0.)

Also, you must set the undo_management parameter to AUTO and the parameter parallel_force_local to TRUE for the same reason as stated earlier, for 11g R2.

In addition to the 12c parameters that are applicable to 11g R2, there are two new performance-related parameters, called Pga_aggregate_limit and temp_undo_enabled, introduced with 12c. pga_aggregate_limit is the initialization parameter that can be used for limiting the total PGA usage of the database environment, and it must be disabled by setting it to the value of 0 in order to obtain a stable EBS 12.2 environment. Setting this parameter to any value other than 0 is not recommended. Setting it to a low value may create process termination problems, as processes will fail with errors once the PGA limit is reached, and actually setting it to any other values than 0 may lead to unwanted session terminations in the EBS 12.2 database tier.

The parameter temp_undo_enabled, however, is your friend. It may increase the overall performance of your EBS 12.2 database, as it enables temporary segments (the Temp tablespace) to be used for storing temporary undo logs, caused by using objects like global temporary tables. This parameter reduces I/O as it reduces the undo and redo that are generated for that temporary transaction, and that's why it increases the overall performance of the database, as well as reduces the disk space needed for undo tablespaces, for redologs, and indirectly for the database backups.

Like with the 11g R2 EBS databases, you have a parameter remove list for 12c EBS databases. The list of parameters that should be removed in case of using Oracle Database 12c in the database tier of EBS 12.2 can be found in section 5.2 of Doc ID 398009.1.

So far, you have seen the database release–specific initialization parameters that can affect EBS 12.2 performance. Before continuing, we want to mention the database initialization parameters that are specific to EBS 12.2. These parameters can be used in any EBS 12.2 Oracle Database release because these parameters are applicable for any Oracle Database releases equal to 11.2.0.3 or higher than 11.2.0.3, because 11.2.0.3 is the base database release that comes with EBS 12.2 database installations, and because the Oracle database versions below 11.2.0.3 are not certified with EBS 12.2 at all. In other words, the Oracle database version of an EBS 12.2 database must be at least 11.2.0.3.

Actually, there are two EBS 12.2–specific database initialization parameters that are related to online patching rather than database performance. Still, as we are explaining the initialization parameters, we should talk about them. In this context, the initialization parameter recyclebin must be turned off by setting its value to "off" to support online patching (actually, to let adop execute its cleanup phase without establishing a SYS database connection). Also, the service_names parameters must include the value ebs_patch too (for example, service_names=<DB_SID>,ebs_patch). This is also required for online patching, as patching-related connections should be established using patch edition–specific database service names.

Tablespaces, Data Files, and Redolog Files

Like with any Oracle Database, there are four types of tablespaces in EBS 12.2 database environments. There are System and Sysaux tablespaces that are used by Oracle Database, EBS tablespaces that are used by EBS 12.2 applications, Temporary tablespaces that are used for placing temporary data and objects, Undo tablespaces for placing undo data, and some other tablespaces like ODM and OLAP for storing miscellaneous data that is not used or used indirectly by Oracle applications.

As the types of tablespaces in EBS 12.2 databases vary, the files that belong to these tablespaces also differ from each other. In this context, the files that belong to the System and EBS tablespaces are called *data files*, the files that belong to the temporary tablespaces are called *temporary files*, and the files belong to the Undo tablespaces are *undo files*.

As EBS databases rely on these tablespace and the files belonging to them, it is important to make performance-related configurations both in the tablespace level and in the file level to get good performance from the EBS databases. In addition, the configurations of redolog files that can be considered out of this scope are also important, as all the DML activity passes through them. Therefore, we will cover the things that should be done when configuring the tablespaces, data files, undo files, temp files, and redolog files in order to get optimal performance from EBS 12.2 databases.

Let's start with the tablespaces. When you install EBS 12.2, your EBS 12.2 database is created properly with all its tablespaces. Even so, you need to know the properties of tablespaces and the properties of the files residing in them. Moreover, it may be required to create new tablespaces by configuring their properties and configurations (if supported by Oracle and applicable for EBS 12.2) in a way that may benefit the general performance of EBS 12.2.

Well, EBS delivers built-in tablespaces, and these tablespace are optimized for performance as delivered by the EBS installer. Seven general tablespace properties may affect performance: Block Size, Extent Management, Next Extent, Logging, Force_logging, Pct Increase, and Segment Space Management. These type of properties which are also well known by Oracle Core DBAs have the same importance and they work in the same manner in EBS 12.2 databases.

Table 13-2 lists the values of these properties for a freshly installed EBS 12.2 system.

Table 13-2. Properties of EBS 12.2 Database Tablespaces

TABLESPACE_NAME	BLOCK_SIZE	EXTENT_MANAGEMENT	NEXT_EXTENT	LOGGING	FORCE_LOGGING	PCT_INCREASE	SEGMENT_SPACE_MANAGEMENT
SYSTEM	8192	DICTIONARY	106496	LOGGING	NO	100	MANUAL
CTXD	8192	LOCAL	40960	LOGGING	NO	50	MANUAL
OWAPUB	8192	LOCAL	40960	LOGGING	NO	50	MANUAL
TEMP1	8192	LOCAL	131072	NOLOGGING	NO	0	MANUAL
ODM	8192	LOCAL		LOGGING	NO		MANUAL
PORTAL	8192	LOCAL	40960	LOGGING	NO	50	MANUAL
APPS_UNDOTS1	8192	LOCAL		LOGGING	NO		MANUAL
APPS_TS_TX_DATA	8192	LOCAL	131072	LOGGING	NO	0	AUTO
APPS_TS_TX_IDX	8192	LOCAL	131072	LOGGING	NO	0	AUTO
APPS_TS_SEED	8192	LOCAL	131072	LOGGING	NO	0	AUTO
APPS_TS_INTERFACE	8192	LOCAL	131072	LOGGING	NO	0	AUTO
APPS_TS_SUMMARY	8192	LOCAL	131072	LOGGING	NO	0	AUTO
APPS_TS_NOLOGGING	8192	LOCAL	131072	LOGGING	NO	0	AUTO
APPS_TS_ARCHIVE	8192	LOCAL	131072	LOGGING	NO	0	AUTO
APPS_TS_QUEUES	8192	LOCAL	131072	LOGGING	NO	0	AUTO
APPS_TS_MEDIA	8192	LOCAL	131072	LOGGING	NO	0	AUTO
OLAP	8192	LOCAL		LOGGING	NO		MANUAL
SYSAUX	8192	LOCAL		LOGGING	NO		AUTO
APPS_TS_TOOLS	8192	LOCAL	131072	LOGGING	NO	0	AUTO
TEMP2	8192	LOCAL	1048576	NOLOGGING	NO	0	MANUAL

As you may notice, all the EBS tablespaces (APPS_TS_TX_DATA, APPS_TS_TOOLS, APPS_TS_INDEX, and so on) and the Sysaux tablespace, regardless of the type of data stored in them, have similar properties. The System tablespace, on the other hand, differs from EBS tablespaces as it has dictionary-based extent management and manual segment space management. The Temporary tablespace also differs, as it is a nologging tablespace.

You can find detailed information for these parameters by reading the release-specific Oracle Database online documentation at http://docs.oracle.com. We will give you general information about these parameters so you can understand the reasons why these tablespace configurations may benefit the database performance in EBS 12.2.

Let's start with the System tablespace. The System tablespace is the main tablespace of Oracle Database. It can be considered the internal tablespace in which the database objects used by Oracle Database internally reside. The block size of the System tablespace is 8KB, which is a must for Oracle EBS 12.2, so you can't change it. However, it is important to mention that the block size of a tablespace must be configured according to the characteristics of SQL statements and data. That is, if the SQL statements such as those coming from ETL or business intelligence applications are designed to read a big set of data, then it may be better to increase the block size of the relevant tablespaces accordingly.

The ability to have a tablespace block size that is different from the database block size was invented for transportable tablespaces, but it has been improved since then, and now it is supported and can be used generally in Oracle database environments.

Note that we are mentioning custom tablespaces, as the block sizes of the standard EBS 12.2 tablespaces should be equal to the db_block_size, which is 8KB. Also, this kind of setup should be tested before taking it to production because having a tablespace block size that is different from the database block size may provide different results based on the database activity that takes place. That is, if the tablespace is completely used by the ETL or DSS-style application schemas, then having a big tablespace block size will help the performance by helping to cache more information in memory by performing less I/O. On the other hand, if the objects in the tablespace are used by OLTP-style applications too, then this may increase block contention on the index blocks. So, this is a recommendation that is not suitable for all EBS environments, which is why it is implemented rarely and should be tested wisely.

By default the System tablespace has dictionary-based extent management, which is actually deprecated in Oracle Database 11g. Therefore, as locally managed tablespaces perform better than the dictionary managed tablespace, we recommend converting EBS's System tablespace to a locally managed tablespace.

This operation should be done by considering the following. Locally managed tablespaces don't use data dictionary tables for segment space managements, thus eliminating recursive SQLs and contention. Also, changes that are done for the segment metadata in a locally managed tablespace don't generate rollback.

However, if you are planning to migrate the System tablespace to a locally managed tablespace, then there should be no dictionary managed tablespaces in the database, because once the System tablespace is migrated, there can't be any dictionary managed tablespace opened in read-write mode. Also, after migrating the System tablespace to a locally managed tablespace, you cannot create new dictionary managed tablespaces or convert any dictionary tablespaces to locally managed tablespaces.

The procedure for this task is explained in the release-specific Oracle Database documentation at http://docs.oracle. The incremental extent size (in bytes) of the System tablespace is 104KB, which seems acceptable, but increasing it may help in the EBS environment where lots of System tablespace extents are used (for example, if database audit is in use and Oracle gets lots of extents from the System tablespace).

The System tablespace is in LOGGING mode, which makes Oracle protect this tablespace from recovery errors in case of some media failures. Although nologging mode would increase performance for the transactions that have been designed to makes changes to data stored on the System tablespace, it eliminates the media recovery option, and that's why logging mode is acceptable and actually necessary for the System tablespace.

FORCE LOGGING is not enabled for the System tablespace, as it is by design not necessary unless there is a disaster recovery (standby) database that needs to be synced with the EBS 12.2 database. Enabling FORCE LOGGING may decrease overall database performance, so it is better to leave this parameter as is, unless there is a need to have a standby EBS database environment.

The PCT_INCREASE value of the System tablespace is set to 100, which is actually acceptable, as PCT_INCREASE makes Oracle dynamically configure the NEXT extent sizes for the tablespaces. So, if a tablespace needs extents often, then it is better to increase the extent size for that tablespace (taking extends for a tablespace during a DML execution often may result in a decrease in transaction performance). By setting PCTINCREASE to 100 (meaning 100 percent), the next extents size of the System tablespace dynamically gets doubled each time an extent operation takes place. (For example, if the initial extent size is 1KB, it is set to 2KB after the first extent, it is set to 4KB after the second extent, and so on.) Note that PCT_INCREASE is applicable only for dictionary managed tablespaces. Also, it is important to consider that, in some cases, having 100 percent PCT_INCREASE may result in fragmentation, but since we are mentioning the System tablespace here, the value 100 for the PCT_ INCREASE is acceptable, as we recommend converting EBS's System tablespace to a locally managed tablespace anyway.

Lastly, the segment space management for the System tablespace is set to MANUAL; using AUTO segment space management, which could increase SQL performance, is not applicable for System tablespaces.

The tablespace properties of EBS product tablespaces and the Sysaux tablespaces, which can be considered the auxiliary tablespace of the System tablespace, are also set by the EBS installer (Rapidwiz). The EBS installer delivers these tablespaces during the installation of EBS 12.2. Some of the properties of these tablespace are different from the System tablespace, as these tablespace are not subject to restrictions such as being unable to have auto segment space management.

There is nothing to change on the configuration of these tablespaces, but still it is better to take a look at their configurations.

Like the System tablespace, the block size of the Sysaux and EBS product tablespaces is 8KB. As mentioned earlier, the 8KB block size is a must for Oracle EBS 12.2, so you can't change it even for the Sysaux and EBS product tablespaces.

By default the Sysaux and EBS product tablespaces have locally managed extents, as a result of being locally managed tablespaces. With the locally managed extents, the tablespaces perform better than the dictionary managed ones. In addition, when you have locally managed tablespaces, the need for specifying storage clause properties such as PCTINCREASE, MINEXTENTS, and MAXEXTENTS (You can't use those properties with locally managed tablespaces) is eliminated.

As EBS product tablespaces are locally managed tablespaces configured with UNIFORM extent sizes of 128KB, this is already a recommended configuration for EBS 12.2, and while these tablespaces get the benefits of being locally managed, the incremental extent size (in bytes) of these tablespaces is fixed.

The Sysaux tablespace is also a locally managed tablespace, but it is a little different than the EBS product tablespaces as it is configured to have AUTOALLOCATE extent sizes, so that's why you can't see any values set for it in the next_extent column of Table 13-2. This is an optimal setting for a tablespace like Sysaux, as the size of the data stored in Sysaux may vary according to the different database environments; leaving extent size management to Oracle brings optimal performance in most cases.

EBS product tablespaces and the Sysaux tablespace are in LOGGING mode, which makes Oracle protect Sysaux from recovery errors in case of media failures. Although nologging mode would increase performance for the transactions that have been designed to make changes to data stored on these tablespaces, it eliminates the media recovery option, and that's why logging mode is acceptable for these tablespaces.

FORCE LOGGING is not enabled for the Sysaux and EBS product tablespaces, as it is by design not necessary unless there is a disaster recovery environment (standby database) that needs to be synced with the EBS 12.2 database. Also, force logging can be enabled temporarily for ensuring all the redo data that recover the instances are recorded into the redolog files and in turn the archivelog files.

So, enabling FORCE LOGGING is good for being on the safe side against recovery problems, but as it may decrease the overall database performance, in general, we recommend leaving it as is (no force logging), unless there is a need to have a standby EBS database environment or there are any other critical operations like cloning from hot backup or doing nologging (in other words, unrecoverable operations done on the critical tables).

Of course, if the computing power, especially if the I/O file system has the required capacity that does not make you feel the impact of having additional I/O required for force logging, then there is no need to discuss enabling force logging in EBS databases.

Also, we recommend the same configuration used in EBS product tablespaces for any custom tablespace that should be created for storing the database objects of a custom schema. The only thing that we recommend is to use bigger block sizes for custom tablespaces if the applications or application modules designed to use them are reporting applications or if they are warehouse-style applications, which query lots of data but do not change the data transactionally.

The temp tablespaces are recommended to be locally managed. Their extent types should be uniform (not autoallocated), and the size of the extents should be128KB, as recommended by Oracle. This may seem a little small, but as temporary tablespaces are widely used by EBS 12.2 applications via global temporary tables and heavy SQL statements that may do excessive sorting, heaving a big extent size for temporary tablespaces may result space allocation failures. Naturally, a temporary tablespace by design should be in nologging mode (also no forcelogging) and like the System tablespace, the segment space management for temp tablespaces is set to MANUAL, as using AUTO segment space management, which could increase SQL performance, is not applicable for TEMP tablespaces.

The properties of the default Undo tablespace that is delivered with a single-node EBS 12.2 installation is APPS_UNDOTS1. APPS_UNDOTS1 is a locally managed logging undo tablespace with a block size of 8KB, which is completely acceptable for an EBS undo tablespace, and there is no performance-related configuration recommendation that can be made for the Undo tablespace at the time of writing this book. This Undo tablespace can be used as a reference for creating new Undo tablespaces in EBS 12.2 databases (consider the need for creating a new Undo tablespace for a newly added RAC node).

Lastly, the tablespaces named CTXD (the Oracle text tablespace), OWAPUB (public web applications tablespace; Oracle Application Server–related), PORTAL (portal tablespace), ODM (Data Mining Tablespace), and OLAP (OLAP tablespace) are not directly related to EBS applications data, and their default configurations are acceptable.

Now let's take a look at what we recommend for the data file, redolog, temp file, and undo data file levels. As for the data files, undo data files, temp files, and redolog files of EBS 12.2 databases, we recommend a fast I/O response. Regardless of the type of the tablespaces the data files belong to (System, Sysaux, EBS product tablespaces, and so on), the I/O response should be sufficient (based on requirements). Analyzing the Automatic Workload Repository (AWR) reports may be useful for determining whether the disks are fast enough for handling the I/O load of the EBS 12.2 databases, as the values provided for the Avg Rd(ms) metric in the File I/O Stats and Tablespace I/O Stats sections of AWR reports will give you an average time representing the average time you wait for a disk read.

Avg Rd(ms) indicates the average time to read data from disk into a buffer. So, under 20ms is acceptable for Avg Rd(ms) times. However, there is no certain value for Avg Rd(ms). Even 8ms may be slow for an EBS 12.2 database if it is an I/O-bound one. While both read and write speed requirements may change according to the load and load type of the EBS environment, we suggest you read Chapter 8 of *Oracle Database Performance Tuning Guide 11g Release 2 (11.2)* and Oracle Support document "How to Tell if the I/O of the Database is Slow" (Doc ID 1275596.1).

Having a sufficient I/O response also relies on distributing the I/O load of the EBS database in I/O-bound EBS environments, in which there may be a contention in the I/O subsystem. In this context, the data files should be placed on different disks according to their I/O load. That is, the data files of the tablespaces, which are in extensive use, should be placed on different mount points and, if possible, different disks, different local file systems, and different SAN LUNs created in different SAN volumes controlled by a different storage controller. The reason behind this approach is to distribute the extensive I/O-related tasks that may be requested by the EBS 12.2 applications into different I/O-related structures regardless of the I/O subsystem layer. Distributing the I/O load is useful for preventing the possible I/O accumulations in any of the components in the I/O path. In other words, we recommend the I/O load to be distributed in every level (from mount points to disks) of the I/O subsystem.

We make the same recommendation for temp files and undo files, as these files may be used as much as the data files in some unpredictable conditions.

In addition, we strongly recommend Oracle Automatic Storage Management (ASM) for storing Oracle database files (redolog files, data files, undo files, and temp files), as ASM uses block devices and it does not use a file system. Thus, when you use ASM, Oracle goes through a very thin layer of code on the operating system when doing I/O, which results in less code being executed on the OS layer and increases I/O performance accordingly. Another advantage of ASM is that ASM uses allocation units (multiples megabytes) for the read-write operations. Thus, when using ASM, Oracle Database writes blocks in multiples of megabytes and thus does larger I/Os but a fewer number.

Also, ASM uses direct I/O. There is no file system cache for ASM, and there is direct access to the disks. This is a good thing because when using ASM, the file system caches are not populated by Oracle Database (Oracle Database has its own buffer cache). As the file system cache of the operating system is not used as a cache by Oracle Database, having a file system cache for the database file results in double buffering. By using ASM, you prevent double buffering. The last advantage of ASM is that it has an optimized code path, which results in better performance compared to any other file systems in the scope of database I/O.

But even if ASM is in use, the distribution of I/O load in the IO subsystem levels, which are beneath the ASM, is still important. Therefore, we recommend building ASM disk groups on SAN disks that are fast enough for the I/O requirements and located on the different physical disks/LUNs/volumes on the storage side.

In the absence of ASM, asynchronous I/O and direct I/O should also be used to increase the I/O speed where it is possible. Asynchronous I/O when enabled lets the I/O done to the data files, control files, and log files be asynchronous so that processing can continue while the I/O requests of the processes are processed. While asynchronous I/O enables asynchronous I/O operations to take place, direct I/O lets Oracle bypass the file system cache and file system locking mechanisms to prevent double buffering. Modern operating systems such as Oracle Linux 6 support asynchronous I/O and direct I/O well, and they can be enabled by setting DISK_ASYNC_IO, which is the master switch of enabling or disabling the asynchronous I/O, to TRUE (the default) and by setting FILESYSTEMIO_OPTIONS to setall. However, these parameters may trigger corruptions because of an undiscovered kernel or Oracle bugs; that's why you need to use them at your own risk.

Note that you can refer to release-specific Oracle Database online documentation at http://docs.oracle.com to get details about the DISK_ASYNCH_IO and FILESYSTEMIO_OPTIONS initialization parameters.

We recommend placing redolog files into spinning disks or SSD disks that are fast enough to deliver the write requirements of LGWR. Also note that using SSD disks is a recommendation only if they are optimized for the LGWR I/O type. LGWR writes in small bursts of activity as opposed to large chunks of I/O, so the I/O subsystem that serves the redolog files must be optimized for this accordingly, like the SSD disks in Oracle engineered systems (Exadata, supercluster, and ODA), which are optimized for LGWR I/O. Therefore, if the SSD disks are not optimized for redolog write requests, we recommend a mirrored disk configuration rather than an SSD disk configuration for placing redolog files. Naturally, we do not recommend redolog files be located on RAID-5, RAID-6, or RAID DP (Double Parity) disk configurations, as the redolog files should not be placed on RAID configurations, which needs the parities to be calculated while the I/Os are taking place.

Redolog writes are important as they may create foreground waits in the database. Also, as for databases running on ASM with external redundancies and as for the non-ASM databases, we recommend placing Oracle database files into RAID mirror disks (if the capacity cost can be tolerated) or LGWR-optimized SSD disks.

Lastly, to reach the highest level in EBS database performance especially in both data file and redolog I/O, we recommend having an infrastructure that is sufficient for the workload and that has the best return on investment and total cost of ownership like the Oracle Exadata database machine.

Continuing with the next topic, the positive performance effects that can be caused by gathering statistics and performance maintenance activities in EBS 12.2 databases are not negligible. Gathering stats must be a regular maintenance activity in EBS 12.2 systems. By "gathering stats," we mean gathering statistics for EBS database objects. Well, the logic of gathering stats in an Oracle EBS 12.2 database is the same as any other Oracle database, but the method for gathering statistics is a little different.

In an EBS 12.2 database, rather than using the traditional DBMS_STATS package, you use the Gather Statistics concurrent program or the FND_STATS package delivered with EBS to collect the statistics of database objects.

Let's start with FND_STATS. FND_STATS is the package delivered with EBS used for gathering statistics in EBS databases. FND_STATS actually interacts with DBMS_STATS, but it has EBS-specific knowledge about the type of the statistics and methods for gathering statistics specifically for EBS database objects.

FND_STATS database package has a set of procedures, which are capable of gathering statistics of all the schemas, as well as for individual schemas. By using the information present in the FND_HISTOGRAM_COLUMNS table, FND_STATS knows the statistics of the columns that need to be gathered with histograms. It has the ability to collect the statistics for only the tables that have stale or missing statistics. Moreover, it has the ability to resume from the point of the failure, in case it is stopped because of a failure and rerun. Note that this capability is applicable when FND stats are triggered by the Gather Schema Statistics concurrent program.

In addition, FND_STATS records the timing information in the FND_STATS_HIST table, which later can be used for analyzing the durations of the statistics collections.

Lastly, it is important to mention that there are several other options in FND_STATS such as the ability to back up the existing statistics before collecting them, sampling options, and so on, but let's see what we recommend for gathering objects statistics to get optimal performance in EBS 12.2.

First, gathering statistics is a heavy process that introduces extra I/O and CPU consumption for the EBS database server. That's why we recommend collecting statistics in reasonable periods when the data change reaches a certain percentage. While this percentage can be determined by the management team and EBS admins, it should be something like 10 percent for big tables, such as tables with 1 million records. So, it is better to not to run a heavy process like gathering statistics when there are no big changes in the data, which may a introduce a contradiction with the current statistics and which may make the optimizer make wrong decisions.

To find the objects that have changed significantly (let's say 10 percent), you can rely on table monitoring, as described in Oracle Support note "How to List the Objects with Stale Statistics Using dbms_stats.gather_schema_stats options=>'LIST STALE'" (Doc ID 457666.1). Also, you can use the GATHER AUTO option of FND_STATS, which will be covered later in this chapter, to automatically collect the objects that have stale statistics.

Deciding on the cursor invalidations is another subject on the matter. When you gather statistics of a database object, all the SQL statements or any database object that uses the object that you gather statistics for is normally invalidated. This is the default result of gathering statistics in EBS 12.2, and this will result in a spike in hard parses. However, the Gather Statistics concurrent program has a parameter named Invalidate Dependent Cursor, and if you set this parameter to No, you can make Oracle not invalidate the objects (SQL statements, PL/SQL blocks, and so on) even if the statistics of their dependent objects are refreshed. If you set Invalidate Dependent Cursors to No, you can prevent spikes in hard parses during peak times. When you choose not to invalidate the dependent cursors, you actually postpone the required hard parses, as in this way they will happen on a cursor reload or after a manual shared pool flush. Another alternative is to use an advanced configuration like Rolling Cursor Invalidation. Rolling Cursor Invalidation is based on a hidden parameter called _optimizer_invalidation_period and is used to spread out the hard parses caused by cursor invalidations over a time period. You can check the Oracle Support document "Rolling Cursor Invalidations with DBMS_STATS.AUTO_INVALIDATE" (Doc ID 557661.1) for the details.

We recommend setting this parameter to No (considering statistics gathering is not done on peak hours) if the statistics of your EBS environment are refreshed frequently, and we recommend using this parameter as is (by default it is set to Yes) if there is a performance problem caused by the stale statistics of some database objects or if the statistics collection is done not so frequently (one a week or once in 15 days). An alternative approach for a non-24/7 EBS environment may be invalidating cursors at the beginning of the weekend.

Locking statistics for some of the database objects such as very large tables rarely change. As gathering statistics for these types of large tables may affect the duration of the Gathering Statistics program and, more importantly, the performance of the EBS system, locking the statistics for these large tables can be considered a best practice in gathering statistics of EBS 12.2 database objects. However, locking the statistics of a table may cause FND_STATS to encounter an "ORA-20005-object statistics are locked" error, so this creates a mandatory requirement to skip these kinds of objects in the statistics collections.

Note that the statistic collection for some of the seed tables in EBS 12.2 is already identified by Oracle. The global temporary tables are also by default excluded from Gathering Statistics, as gathering statistics for global temporary tables or EBS-type temporary tables such as interim tables and transactions tables is not recommended by Oracle.

You can query the FND_EXCLUDE_TABLE_STATS table, which is a table that the Gather Statistics concurrent program/FND_STATS checks to see whether there are any database objects that may be excluded from gathering statistics. You can use FND_STATS. The LOAD_XCLUD_TAB procedure adds a table, which you want to exclude from the Gathering Statistics program, to the FND_EXCLUDE_TABLE_STATS table. Alternatively, you can use DBMS_STATS.LOCK_TABLE_STATS to lock the table statistics and exclude them from FND_STATS-based gathering statistics operations to ensure that the statistics cannot be gathered for these objects either using FND_STATS or using DBMS_STATS. Although you have to use only the FND_STATS package for gathering statistics in EBS 12.2, there may be cases where DBMS_STATS is used for gathering statistics. (Consider test environments where a developer created a table in a development schema that has no appl_id to be used while executing the load_xclud_tab procedure.)

You can check the documentation for DBMS_STATS to get usage information and for FND_STATS. LOAD_XCLUD_TAB. Here is the specification:

```
PROCEDURE LOAD_XCLUD_TAB(action IN VARCHAR2,
            appl_id IN NUMBER,
            tabname IN VARCHAR2)
```

Listing 13-1 shows an example of the usage, which should help you use the LOAD_XCLUD_TABLE procedure.

Listing 13-1. Excluding AR_ARCHIVE_PURGE_INTERIM

```
EXEC FND_STATS.LOAD_XCLUD_TAB(action=>'INSERT', appl_id=>222,tabname=>'AR_ARCHIVE_PURGE_INTERIM');
```

The same situation is acceptable for the tables that are used as staging or placing temporary data. As these tables may be used for temporary work or staging, they may be truncated by the applications using them. In other words, at a certain time they contain no data. If they contain no data while you are running the Gather Statistics program, unreal statistics may be collected for these tables, which could result in database-wide performance degradation.

So, we recommend locking for the tables that don't change at all or are not changed frequently. Moreover, we recommend both deleting the statistics and locking for the tables that are used temporarily. By the way, by deleting the statistics, you actually make their statistics equal to null. This is because if an object has null statistics, then Oracle uses dynamic sampling during the executions to understand the characteristic of the table.

We also have to mention that using dynamic sampling for these types of interim tables can be considered a performance best practice because collecting statistics during the execution of a SQL statement with the wrong statistics may have a big negative performance impact. However, if the query performances with the dynamic sampling are not acceptable, you may use SQL hints or gather stats for those objects when there is a representative load on them. You can gather stats manually for those objects, lock those stats, and exclude them from the FND_STATS statistics collection to prevent the statistics of these objects from being gathered again in the future.

In addition, you can use the FND_STATS.LOAD_EXTNSTATS_COLS procedure to define the column groups to tell Oracle to populate the statistics for those columns automatically whenever the statistics of the table that you specify are gathered using the Gather Statistics concurrent program or FND_STATS package. This kind of statistic collection is called an *extended statistics collection,* and it helps Oracle's Cost Based Optimizer make better decisions by considering their precise cardinalities when the columns that you create the extended statistics on are used together in the where clauses of the queries.

You can specify four columns when using the LOAD_EXTNSTATS_COLS procedure, as shown in the following procedure specification:

```
PROCEDURE LOAD_EXTNSTATS_COLS(action     IN VARCHAR2,
                  appl_id   IN NUMBER,
                  owner     IN VARCHAR2,
                  tabname   IN VARCHAR2,
                  colname1  IN VARCHAR2,
                  colname2  IN VARCHAR2,
                  colname3  IN VARCHAR2 DEFAULT NULL,
                  colname4  IN VARCHAR2 DEFAULT NULL,
                  partname  IN VARCHAR2 DEFAULT NULL,
                  hsize     IN NUMBER DEFAULT 254,
                  commit_flag IN VARCHAR2 DEFAULT 'Y')
```

Listing 13-2 shows an example that can be used for executing LOAD_EXTNSTATS_COLS.

Listing 13-2. Defining Columns Groups That the Extended Statistics Will Be Automatically Collected For, When the Statistics of the Table Are Gathered

```
FND_STATS.LOAD_EXTNSTATS_COLS
(action =>'INSERT', appl_id=>&custom_application_id, tabname => &table_name, owner=>&owner,
colname1 =>&column_name1, colname2 =>&column_name2);
```

We also recommend gathering dictionary stats in EBS 12.2 databases, especially after large application patches, large database patches, database upgrades, and application upgrades. Listing 13-3 shows the format of a procedure call that can be used for collecting dictionary object stats.

Listing 13-3. Collecting Dictionary Stats

```
sqlplus apps/apps
SQL> EXEC DBMS_STATS.GATHER_DICTIONARY_STATS( estimate_percent => DBMS_STATS.AUTO_SAMPLE_
SIZE, options => 'GATHER AUTO' );
```

Collecting fixed object stats is also important for getting optimal performance in EBS 12.2 environments, especially after large database patches, database upgrades, workload changes, SGA/PGA-type database parameter changes, and migrations.

■ **Note** It is recommended that you gather fixed objects stats while there is workload on the system, as gathering those stats while there is no activity may result in unrepresentative objects statistics being collected.

Listing 13-4 shows the procedure call that can be used for collecting dictionary object stats.

Listing 13-4. Collecting Fixed Object Stats

```
sqlplus apps/apps
SQL>EXEC DBMS_STATS.GATHER_FIXED_OBJECTS_STATS;
```

Incremental statistics gathering is another feature that you can use for getting optimal performance for statistics gathering and thus indirectly for EBS 12.2. Incremental statistics gathering is a new feature introduced in Oracle Database 11g and is used for gathering statistics of partitioned tables by scanning only the partitions that have changed since the last time the statistics were gathered for the tables. Therefore, collecting incremental objects stats for large and partitioned tables is another recommendation, as collecting the stats for such partitioned tables incrementally dramatically decreases the time spent for collecting statistics in EBS 12.2.

Listing 13-5 shows the procedure call that can be used for marking a table part of the incremental statistics collection. Once the dbms_stats.set_table_prefs procedure is called for a table, as shown in Listing 13-5, any subsequent statistics collection done using DBMS_STATS or FND_STATS will be incremental for that table.

Listing 13-5. Collecting Incremental Stats

```
sqlplus apps/apps
SQL >exec dbms_stats.set_table_prefs('OWNER','TABLENAME','INCREMENTAL','TRUE');
```

So far, you have seen different options that can increase the quality of gathering statistics in EBS 12.2. Let's see how to gather statistics in EBS 12.2.

As mentioned earlier, there are two ways to collect stats in EBS 12.2. The first is to use the Gather Statistics concurrent program, and the second is to use the FND_STATS procedure directly for gathering statistics in EBS 12.2.

The Gather Statistics concurrent program can be executed with the SYSADMIN user. So to submit this concurrent program as a concurrent request, you log in in to the EBS 12.2 using the sysadmin user. Follow this navigation:

System Administrator Responsibility ➤ Concurrent ➤ Requests

Once you click the Request link, you reach the Submit Request form, as shown in Figure 13-15. Then, you use the keyword Gather%Stat% to list all the available gather statistics programs defined in EBS 12.2. As shown in Figure 13-15, there are four gather statistics programs: Gather All Column Statistics, Gather Column Statistics, Gather Schema Statistics, and Gather Table Statistics.

Although we recommend scheduling the Gather Schema Statistics concurrent program for gathering database objects stats in EBS 12.2 and will continue explaining the details of it, we'll take a brief look at all of these concurrent programs.

■ **Note** You can find detailed information about these programs in *Oracle E-Business Suite Maintenance Guide: Managing Query Optimization Statistics.*

- Gather All Column Statistics is used for gathering the column statistics of all the columns to determine a detailed view for the column data. Note: This concurrent program is obsolete, so we don't recommend using it.

- Gather Column Statistics is used for gathering the column statistics of a given column to determine a detailed view of the column data such as determining a histogram for a column.

- Gather Table Statistics is used for gathering the table statistics as well as the index statistics for the indexes defined on that table.

- Gather Schema Statistics is used for gathering the object statistics of the objects including tables, partition, and indexes that belong to an EBS database schema (for example, INV) or all the EBS database schemas (for example, ALL).

Figure 13-15 shows the Submit Request form that displays these gather statistics programs.

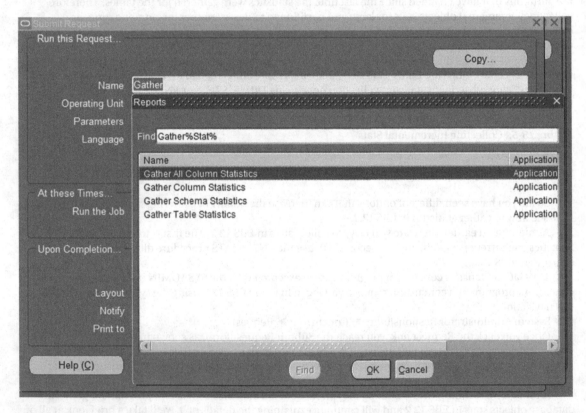

Figure 13-15. *A search that is done in the Submit Request form for displaying the available gather statistics programs*

As our focus is gathering schema stats, which we recommend scheduling for collecting EBS database object statistics, we will explain the parameters that can be used with the Gather Schema Statistics program

Figure 13-16 shows the Parameters menu that is opened when you choose the Gather Schema Statistics concurrent program after you search the available programs using the keyword Gather%Stat% in the Submit Request form.

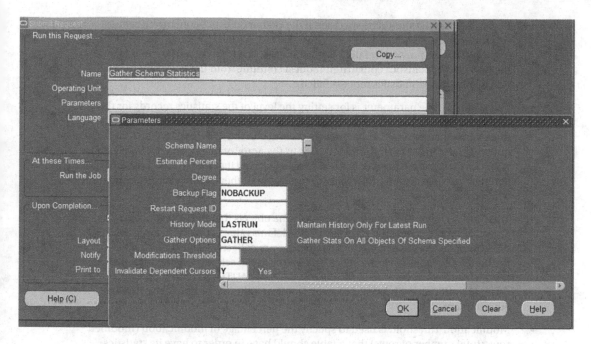

Figure 13-16. *Available parameters for Gather Schema Statistics concurrent program*

- Using the Schema Name parameter in the Parameters menu, you can define the schema to collect the statistics for.

- You can directly enter the schema name in the Schema Name text box, or you can choose the schema using the list of values displayed by clicking the LOV button located in the right corner of the Schema Name text box. Note that you can gather statistics for a single schema or for all the schemas. To gather statistics for all the application schemas in an EBS 12.2 database, you choose the keyword ALL by clicking the button labeled "…" in the right corner of the Schema Name text box.

- Using the Estimate Percent parameter, you can adjust the sampling percentage. The permitted values are between 0 to 100, and these values are used for specifying the percentage of the sampling (such as 50 or 90 percent). Note that we recommend leaving this parameter as blank or set to 0, because Oracle 11g R2 and above have an auto sampling option, which performs quite well and is triggered by setting Estimate Percent to 0 or leaving it blank.

- Using the Degree parameter, you can adjust the degree of parallelism used when gathering statistics. Its default value (when you leave it blank) is derived by the cpu_count database parameter or parallel_max_servers parameter, whichever is lower. So, as it must be set according to the environment, we can't make a recommendation on this. However, if you gather the statistics in maintenance hours when there are no other heavy activities in your EBS system, then we recommend leaving it blank.

- The Backup Flag parameter can be used for backing up the statistics, and we recommend leaving it as NOBACKUP. However, there may be situation where it may be necessary to set it to BACKUP, especially if you expect a significant change in object statistics after running the gather schema statistics concurrent program, which may affect the CBO dramatically.

- Restart Request ID should be specified if the Gather Statistics concurrent request submitted previously failed. In such cases, Restart Request ID should be set to the request ID of the previously failed Gather Statistics concurrent request to make the new Gather Statistics concurrent request continue from the point where the previously Gather Statistics request failed.

- The History Mode parameter is for setting the level of the statistics records for the Gather Schema Statistics program itself. If you set this parameter to another value than None, then the statistic records are recorded to the FND_STATS_HIST table for querying later to get the information such as the amount of time that it took to gather statistics for database objects. We recommend leaving it at the default (Last Run). Setting it to None disables the ability to restart the Gather Schema Statistics program when it fails.

- The Gather Options parameter is to specify the objects that the Gather Schema Statistics should collect the statistics for. Its default value is GATHER, and it makes the Gather Schema Statistics concurrent program collect the statistics for all the tables and indexes for the specified schema (or all schemas, if Shema Name is set to ALL). We recommend setting it to GATHER AUTO in conjunction with setting Modification Threshold to an appropriate value according to the EBS 12.2 environment.

- Modification Threshold is used to specify the percentage of modification (modified rows/total number of rows) that a table should have in order to have its statistics collected by the Gather Schema Statistics concurrent program. This parameter should be specified with the GATHER AUTO option. Note that the indexes of the tables, which have more modifications in percentage than the modification percentage defined with the Modification Threshold, are also collected.

- The Invalidate Dependent Cursor parameter has a default value of Y (Yes), and as mentioned earlier, if you set this parameter to N (No), you can make Oracle not invalidate the objects (SQL statements, PL/SQL blocks, and so on) even if the statistics of their dependent objects are refreshed. As we recommend earlier, set this parameter to N if the statistics of your EBS is environment are refreshed frequently. We recommend using this parameter as is (by default it is set to Y) if there is a performance problem caused by the stale statistics of some database objects or if the statistics collection is done not so frequently (once a week or once in 15 days).

So far, you have seen the Gather Schema Statistics concurrent program with all of its available parameters. Let's now take a look at the second option for gathering EBS database objects statistics, which is the FND_STATS package. Using FND_STATS instead of the Gather Schema Statistics concurrent program for gathering the statistics of EBS database objects may be a preferred method in cases where there is a need to execute the statistics gathering outside EBS or in cases when there is a need to programmatically start the statistics collection, such as when collecting stats for an EBS database schema when connecting to the EBS forms screens. Let's concentrate a little bit more on the FND_STATS package by going through the list of different example procedure calls shown in Listing 13-6.

Suppose you want to gather statistics for all schemas (ALL) or for only a single schema (INV) using the FND_STATS package. You connect to the EBS database using the apps user and execute the FND_STATS.gather_schema_stats procedure. Note that we are using the sqlplus tool in this example to execute the fnd_stats.gather_schema_stats procedure. Other tools can be used as well. Also note that you can even supply the parameters we explained earlier to the fnd_stats.gather_schema_stats procedure, as shown in Listing 13-6.

Listing 13-6. Executing FND_STATS.GATHER_SCHEMA_STATS for Collecting Statistics for EBS 12.2
Database Objects from the Back End

```
To gather statistics for ALL schemas;
sqlplus apps/apps
SQL> exec fnd_stats.gather_schema_statistics('ALL')

To gather statistics for only INV schemas;
SQL> exec fnd_stats.gather_schema_statistics('INV');

To gather statistics for INV schema by specifying options like Degree and estimate_percent;

SQL>fnd_stats.GATHER_SCHEMA_STATS(schemaname=>'INV', DEGREE => 4 , estimate_PERCENT=>70);
```

After explaining the statistics collection, we'll make some recommendations about scheduling statistics gathering in EBS 12.2 and then continue with the purging activities.

First, we recommend using the Gather Schema Statistics concurrent program for periodically gathering database object statistics in EBS 12.2. We recommend scheduling this concurrent program to run on a regular basis. For most environments, we recommend scheduling this concurrent program to run to collect the statistics for all the schemas once a week, and we recommend scheduling this concurrent program to run to collect the statistics of the schemas that are highly used by the applications once every three to four days. For example, you may schedule Gather Schema Statistics for INV and HR to be run every three days at night, and you may schedule Gather Schema Statistics for all schemas to be run every weekend, on Sunday night.

Purging is another activity that needs to be done on a regular basis as there are some seed application tables that may grow and affect the performance of the queries. Purging activities are done by executing some seeded concurrent programs. To purge the records of the tables that store auxiliary data such as concurrent manager log information, workflow runtime data, and the ones that are used by EBS applications internally, we recommend scheduling those concurrent programs according to the business needs.

We strongly recommend you follow the Oracle Support document "Purging Strategy for E-Business Suite" (Doc ID 732713.1), before starting these purging activities. Here is a list of the concurrent programs:

- Purge Obsolete Workflow Runtime Data (FNDWFPR)

- Purge Debug Log and System Alerts (FNDLGPRG)

- Page Access Tracking Purge Data (PATPURGE)

- Purge Obsolete Generic File Manager Data (FNDGFMPR)

- Summarize and Purge Concurrent Request Statistics (FNDCPCRS)

- Purge Inactive Sessions (ICXDLTMP)

- Purge Obsolete ECX Data (FNDECXPR)

- Purge Rule Executions (FNDDWPURG)

Maintenance of database objects from the back end is also important for getting optimal EBS 12.2 database performance. As tables and indexes are subject to fragmentation and misalignments, we will recommend some practices for them.

If there are tables that you enter increasing values such as (1, 2, 4, 5, 6, ...), then any deletes on these tables may be filled later by upcoming inserts. But this is not true for indexes. That is, as all the inserts will be based on increased values, indexes on the table will be fragmented because these new increasing values won't be stored in the index blocks from which you have deleted them.

Even if the values stored in indexes are not entered in an increasing way, there is still time needed for index blocks from which you deleted the values to be refilled. In both of these cases, performance may be affected, as there will be unnecessary empty or partially block index reads, especially when using index range scans. In fact, in such scenarios, the tables that the indexes rely on should be rebuilt using "move" operations, and indexes then need to be rebuilt as a result of these "move" operations. By using a table move operation, you can make Oracle reclaim the unused space and lower the high water mark in the offending table. By rebuilding the indexes, you can reclaim the unused space in the indexes, thus increasing the performance of index scans.

bde_rebuild.sql written by Oracle Support and available in Oracle Support document "bde_rebuild. sql - Validates and rebuilds indexes occupying more space than needed" (Doc ID 182699.1) identifies these indexes and dynamically creates a SQL file to be executed for rebuilding these kinds of indexes. We suggest using this document and bde_rebuild.sql for identifying and rebuilding these kinds of indexes. However, as stated in Doc 182699.1, bde_rebuild.sql blocks the database operations against the tables; thus, it should be executed in maintenance windows.

As for the tables that are highly fragmented because of sparse deletes or because of a purge operation, we recommend defragmentation. Defragmentation should be done carefully, as the method may change according to the application modules referencing those tables. That is, as for the concurrent tables such as FND_CONCURRENT_REQUESTS, FND_CONCURRENT_PROCESSES, FND_CRM_HISTORY, FND_ENV_CONTEXT, FND_TEMP_FILES, and FND_CONFLICTS_DOMAIN, Oracle suggests shutting down the concurrent manager and doing a table move operation such as alter table <owner>.<table_name> move; followed by index rebuilds and statistics gathering. For tables that contain LOB columns such as FND_LOBS, the procedure is the same. However, as for the tables in the INV module and tables that contain LONG or LONG RAW columns, Oracle suggests disabling triggers for the tables that are fragmented, stopping all the related transactions, doing export/import operations for those tables, and reenabling the triggers on those tables.

There is no documentation for these kinds of table defragmentation operations, but as export/import or Data Pump is an applicable method for EBS logical migration, we suggest this method for all application schemas as well. Of course, you require downtime during this operation to not to break the application-specific consistency.

The export/import method can also be used with the queue tables, but to export a queue table, you must also export the underlying queue tables and related dictionary tables. As for importing a queue table, you should import the underlying queue tables and related dictionary tables.

Although you can do a lot of things in the database level, if there is a problem in the code (application tier code or database tier PL/SQL code), then the EBS performance may not be optimal. That's why applying recommended performance patches for EBS 12.2 is a crucial activity that should be regularly done. You should regularly check Oracle Support to see whether there is any new performance-related patches released by Oracle, and when you find a new performance patch, you should plan to apply it if the module (or modules) that the patch is written for is used in your EBS 12.2 system.

Therefore, you should check the Oracle Support document "Oracle E-Business Suite Recommended Performance Patches" (Doc ID 244040.1) and apply any patches that are suitable for your EBS 12.2 environment. Doc 244040.1 lists the performance patches that are currently available for all the EBS environments including EBS 11.5.10, 12.1, and 12.2. The patches in this document are classified according to the EBS technologies such as Oracle Database 11g, 12c, Client Tools, Application Technology Products, Financial Products, Manufacturing and Supply Chain Products, Human Resources, and Sales and Marketing products. Document 244040.1 was created a long time ago (in 2008) but is updated by Oracle Support regularly to include new technologies and performance patches for these technologies. At this time, there may not be lots of EBS 12.2–specific patches in Document 244040.1, but we believe there will be more 12.2 patches as time goes on.

In addition to the Recommended Performance Patches document, we recommend applying the latest EBS version, which is 12.2.5 at the moment, and we recommend the tech stack upgrade, which consists of upgrading the database to one of the latest supported database releases (12c preferred), upgrading Forms and Reports Home to the latest versions, and applying the latest forms bundle patches to minimize the risks of encountering performance-related problems because of performance bugs that may be present in the EBS product codes and technology stack. (Remember, if EBS 12.2 is installed using the latest startCD, startCD 51, the EBS database will already be 12c.)

Note that applying the recommended patches does not guarantee getting optimal performance in every part of the EBS 12.2 environment. Still, there will be cases where you need to investigate the costly SQL statements and the modules that are executing them and make Oracle Support searches using the portion of SQL statements or module names that you have investigated as poor in performance to see whether there are any reported issues about them or any patches applicable for them.

EBS 12.2 SQL Access Paths

SQL access paths are another important performance area for optimizing EBS 12.2 performance. Below the application tier, actually inside the database tier (database server and Oracle database), you have SQL statements running and doing much of the work. Even if your database server and Oracle Database are configured perfectly for handling the expected load and even if your application tier components are optimized for dealing with the application tier load, the SQL layer not being optimized may make you unhappy with the performance of your EBS 12.2 environment. So, an optimization in this area may also affect the entire EBS 12.2 environment, and that's why EBS 12.2 performance tuning cannot be considered without tuning SQL access paths, in other words, tuning the SQL statements.

We really mean tuning the SQL statements by using the SQL access paths, but we use the phrase "access path" to describe the action, as the performance of the SQL statements is closely related with the paths that are followed by Oracle to access the data. Thus, in order to help the CBO decide on an optimal execution plan, the SQL access paths can be optimized by modifying the SQL statements. Having an optimal execution plan in turn minimizes the effort given by Oracle database processes to retrieve the records and thus increases the query performance and decreases the general load on the EBS database. In addition to the modifications that can be done in SQL statements theirselves, you can optimize the performance of SQL statements in the database layer that indirectly influences the CBO, which decides how to reach and retrieve data stored in the database.

CBO follows a cost-based approach when creating an optimal SQL access path, and basically, it creates the SQL access paths by looking at the statistics of the related objects, deciding on the join methods that are best for the SQL statements, and checking whether there are any table partitions, index partitions, or indexes that are preferred over the Full Table Scan operations to reach the data stored in the tables that are accessed by the SQL statements.

We have already explained the importance of statistics gathering in the EBS 12.2 database, so let's take a look at the modifications that can be done in SQL statements and the database objects that can be created to support these SQL statements to run optimally.

At this point, it is also important to realize that we are using the phrase "modifying SQL statements," but you cannot modify the standard SQL statements used by Oracle EBS 12.2, as that is not supported.

So, when modifying SQL statements, you first decide on the SQL statements that need to be tuned, and then if these SQL statements are executed by standard code, you just check Oracle Support to see whether there are any reported issues and patches present. If the code is good and if the slowness is caused by the big volume of data, you may consider creating indexes or partitioning the underlying tables even if the underlying tables are standard tables. That is, operations such as modifying the standard SQL statements and modifying PL/SQL procedures are not supported, but operations like creating indexes on standard tables or partitioning the standard tables are supported by Oracle.

Well, if the SQL statements that are not running well are coming from custom code, you can transfer these SQL statements to your development team by making a comment on them, such as "these sqlSQL statements do a full table scan" or "the cost of these SQL statements are very high" and so on. So, if development can't do anything about the SQL statements that you report, you may consider creating indexes or partitioning the relevant tables to make the SQL statements run faster.

Let's take a look at what you can do to find the SQL statements that need to be tuned and then continue with the opportunities that you can use for tuning them. You find the SQL statements that have performance problems (or, let's say that are under-performing or consuming lots of system resources and causing a general slowness in the EBS database) by using your own SQL statements to check the data dictionary views to list the top SQL statements, or you can use tools such as Enterprise Manager, AWR, ADDM, and ASH (also statspack if you don't have the diagnostic pack licenses) to check the top SQL statements and top sessions along with the wait events they are waiting on.

Building your own SQL statements for identifying under-performing SQL operations or the top-resource consuming SQL operations is an advanced approach as it requires you to know the data dictionary views of Oracle Database. Nevertheless, although the exploring the data dictionary views is not in the scope of this book, we thought that data dictionary views were worth mentioning because by doing a simple query against the v$sql view, you can list the top queries ordered by their CPU times.

Listing 13-7 shows a SQL query to identify the top ten SQL statements according to their CPU usage.

Listing 13-7. Query for Listing Top Ten CPU-Bound SQL Statements

```
SELECT * FROM (SELECT cpu_time, sql_text from v$sql order by cpu_time desc) WHERE ROWNUM < 10
```

So, you have several alternatives for determining the SQL statements that are on an EBS 12.2 database, and the choice is yours, as different apps DBAs can have different methods for SQL performance analysis. Some of them may use their own SQL statements, some of them may use third-party tools, and some of them may use Oracle-supplied reports such as ADDM and AWR.

Also, there are technology-specific approaches if you already know the component that has SQL performance problems. That is, for forms-specific problems, apps DBAs can use SQL Trace for the Oracle Forms sessions by enabling the forms SQL Trace using the following toolbar navigation: Help ➤ Diagnostic ➤ Trace ➤ Trace with Binds and Waits). For concurrent-specific performance problems, apps DBAs can use the Enable Trace check box present in the Concurrent Program definition form (navigation: Concurrent ➤ Program). For OAF-based performance problems, apps DBAs can enable the FND debug profiles using the Oracle Support note "How to Run Statement Level/Java trace or a SQL Trace in Self Service Application" [ID 190685.1].

The methods and approaches for determining a specific SQL performance problem may change according to layer (forms, OAF, general database, and so on), but still they are clearly documented.

Some SQL performance problems may be instance wide. That is, there may be more than one SQL performance problem that is decreasing the whole system's speed. Also, there may be some SQL statements performing not well, and you may have not even know that they exist.

For these types of diagnosis, we recommend a combination of all these alternatives that you have for determining the SQL statements that need to be tuned. You should use your own queries to find SQL performance in real time, and you should use the performance diagnostic functionalities of the tools like Toad, Enterprise Manager, and so on, if they are available in your environment. You also should analyze AWR reports and ADDM reports to get a detailed view of the problematic SQL statements and the types of problems they have.

At the moment, we are dealing with realizing SQL statement performance problems in general, so we will give an example by going through an AWR report. The AWR reports show database-wide situations, and they are well-known reports that can be interpreted by any senior apps DBA or core DBA as well as the Oracle support engineers.

AWR reports have a SQL-specific section named SQL Statistics, in which there are links defined to the SQL statement sections of the AWR reports such as "SQL ordered by Elapsed Time," "Sql ordered by CPU Time," "Sql ordered Gets," and "Sql ordered by Reads." Using these links you can directly jump to the relevant sections of the AWR reports and start analyzing unoptimized SQL statements.

"Sql ordered by Elapsed Time" is an ordered list that can be used to determine the SQL statements that are taking a long time to complete. When analyzing this table, you need to consider the execution counts and elapsed times together to decide on the problematic SQL statement.

Figure 13-18 shows an "Sql ordered by CPU Time" table, in which you can see that you have a slow-running operation executed by a custom module, as that custom module calls a PL/SQL routine with begin/end, completes its execution (Executions=1) in 147.33 (Elapsed Time) seconds, and spends most of its runtime in the CPU (%CPU=92.10).

The database operations in PL/SQL routines are actually done by the SQL statements. That is, PL/SQL routines use SQL queries for querying the database, and they use DML statements to update the database, so to investigate a poorly performing PL/SQL routine, you need to investigate the related SQL statements that are triggered from that PL/SQL routine. So, in the case shown in Figure 13-17, just below this problematic PL/SQL call, you see another SQL statement that is executed 8,736 times by the same module. The total time for its execution takes 134.37 seconds, and 99 percent of these seconds are spent on CPU.

CPU Time (s)	Executions	CPU per Exec (s)	%Total	Elapsed Time (s)	%CPU	%IO	SQL Id	SQL Module	SQL Text
135.69	1	135.69	6.80	147.33	92.10	7.47	fg4d6vgm2pq3v	e:GME:cp:custom/CUSTOM_LOT_ATTRIBU	BEGIN CUSTOM_LOT_ATTRIBUTE_MOVE...
133.62	8,736	0.02	6.69	134.37	99.44	0.00	4n9xargksst7f	e:GME:cp:custom/CUSTOM_LOT_ATTRIBU	SELECT MLNO.C_ATTRIBUTE1_SS_NO...

Figure 13-17. A portion of the "Sql ordered by CPU Time" table gathered from an AWR report

With this in mind, the SQL statement that starts with SELECT MLNO.C_ATTRIBUTE1_SS_NO must be the problem because it is executed several times by the custom PL/SQL call, and it is the reason that makes custom module consume lots of CPU resources (CPU Time).

So, you should concentrate on the SQL statement starting with SELECT MLNO.C_ATTRIBUTE1_SS_NO for SQL tuning by trying to find answers to questions like "Why is it executed so many times?" and "Is there anything that can be done to decrease the execution count?" and "Is there anything you can do for tuning the SQL itself?"

"Sql ordered by Gets" is an ordered list that can be used to determine the SQL statements that make lots of block accesses. Block accesses can be done from memory (if the requested blocks are already in memory) or from the disk (if the requested blocks are not in memory). Having excessive buffer gets is not a good thing for performance, as to able to get a buffer Oracle spends CPU cycles and sometimes makes I/O operations. In this manner, tuning to reduce buffer gets is one of the basic approaches for performance tuning. That is, if you tune your SQL statements to reduce their buffer gets, the disk I/O operation and CPU usage will also automatically reduce.

When analyzing this table, you need to consider the execution counts and buffer gets together to decide on the problematic SQL statement. Figure 13-18 shows an "Sql ordered by Gets" table, in which you see the same SQL statement that you saw in Figure 13-17 working aggressively and consuming resources. That SQL statement executed by the custom module completes its execution (Executions=1) by making 88,627,785 buffer gets.

SQL ordered by Gets

- Resources reported for PL/SQL code includes the resources used by all SQL statements called by the code.
- %Total - Buffer Gets as a percentage of Total Buffer Gets
- %CPU - CPU Time as a percentage of Elapsed Time
- %IO - User I/O Time as a percentage of Elapsed Time
- Total Buffer Gets: 187,284,454
- Captured SQL account for 83.9% of Total

Buffer Gets	Executions	Gets per Exec	%Total	Elapsed Time (s)	%CPU	%IO	SQL Id	SQL Module	SQL Text
88,627,785	1	88,627,785.00	47.32	192.75	77.1	23	fg4d6vgm2pq3v	e:GME:cp: custom LOT_ATTRIBUTES_MOVE	BEGIN custom LOT_ATTRIBUTE_MOVE...
88,120,636	9,854	8,942.63	47.05	145.98	100	0	4n9xargksst7f	e:GME:cp: custom LOT_ATTRIBUTES_MOVE	SELECT MLNO.C_ATTRIBUTE1 SS_NO...

Figure 13-18. A portion of the "Sql ordered by Gets" table gathered from an AWR report

With this in mind, we can say that this SQL statement executed by the custom module must be a problem because it does lots of buffer gets to retrieve data for processing and returns the required portion of data to the client.

In this context, you should investigate this SQL statement to answer the questions like, "Why is this SQL statement doing lots of buffer gets?" and "Is it processing unnecessary data to find the required data that the client is requesting?" and "What can be done to make it process less data?"

"Sql ordered by Elapsed Times" is an ordered list that can be used to determine the SQL statements that make lots of physical reads. Physical reads are heavy operations because Oracle must make I/O and execute its complex code to place the data coming from these reads consistently into memory.

When analyzing this table, you need to consider the execution counts and physical reads together to decide on the poorly performing SQL statements.

Figure 13-19 shows a "Sql ordered by Reads" table, in which you see a SQL statement that is processing lots of data, executed by a Discoverer report. Even if we can't say directly that it is a problem, it is obviously processing lots of data and needs to be investigated as that Discoverer report executes a SQL statement beginning with select o121863.ORGANIZATION_CO and completes its execution (Executions=1) by making 1,259 physical reads. It is an I/O-bound SQL statement as 70 percent of its execution time is spent on I/O.

SQL ordered by Reads

- %Total - Physical Reads as a percentage of Total Disk Reads
- %CPU - CPU Time as a percentage of Elapsed Time
- %IO - User I/O Time as a percentage of Elapsed Time
- Total Disk Reads: 314,826
- Captured SQL account for 44.1% of Total

Physical Reads	Executions	Reads per Exec	%Total	Elapsed Time (s)	%CPU	%IO	SQL Id	SQL Module	SQL Text
1259	1	1,259.00	52.51	5.66	30.49	70.05	fr98u6ynhv26h	Disco10, custom	Select o1213434.ORGANIZATION_CO...

Figure 13-19. *A portion of the "Sql ordered by Reads" table gathered from an AWR report*

With this in mind, we can say that this SQL statement executed by the Discoverer report can be considered inconvenient as it does lots of I/O to retrieve the records. Reports typically process lots of data, but when they are executed in peak hours, they may affect the general database performance. So, if they need to be run in peak hours, they need to be tuned. There are several things in the database configuration to support these heavy reporting activities. For instance, when you increase the parallelism for these reports, you might decrease the completion time of these reports, but you may cause your database to do more physical I/O, as parallel scans don't use buffers in the buffer cache. However, if the report is doing row-by-row operations, then tuning the database tier and even increasing the hardware resources may not affect its performance. So, the things that can be done in the database tier vary, but the things that can be done in SQL statements is certain. Therefore, there is no need to change the database configuration of an EBS system before ensuring the SQL statements (especially SQL statements executed by reporting programs) are properly tuned.

Note that although you may consider 1,259 an acceptable count for physical reads, you should think of the future, as the data that is stored in the tables that this Discoverer report uses may increase over time, so what will happen to the performance then? As the bottom line, you should analyze this SQL statement to be proactive.

"Sql ordered by Execution" is an ordered list that can be used to determine the SQL statements that are executed excessively. Executing SQL statements again and again in a loop is not a good thing for performance, because it may create a consistency problem as well as may consume system resources. Any change in the execution plan of the executed query may affect performance and can make the whole Oracle Database hang.

Figure 13-20 shows a "Sql ordered by Executions" table, in which you see a SQL statement that is executed excessively by e:FND:cp:STANDARD, which is actually the database session of the concurrent manager named Standard Manager.

Executions	Rows Processed	Rows per Exec	Elapsed Time(s)	%CPU	%IO	SQL Id	SQL Module	SQL Text
45,688	45,669	1.00	9.48	34.2	0	2mwvn9xwq1tz3	e:FND:cp:STANDARD	select (RUNNING_PROCESSES-MAX_...
45,449	35,710	0.79	18.08	57.3	0	fynt75qr1p0pg	e:FND:cp:STANDARD	SELECT R.Conc_Login_Id, R.Req...

SQL Id	SQL Text
2mwvn9xwq1tz3	select (RUNNING_PROCESSES-MAX_PROCESSES) , MAX_PROCESSES , NVL(SLEEP_SECONDS, 0) , DIAGNOSTIC_LEVEL into :b0, :b1, :b2, :b3:b4 from FND_CONCURRENT_QUEUES where ((APPLICATION_ID=:b5 and CONCURRENT_QUEUE_ID=:b6) and (TARGET_NODE=:b7 or (TARGET_NODE is null and :b7 is null)))
fynt75qr1p0pg	SELECT R.Conc_Login_Id, R.Request_Id, R.Phase_Code, R.Status_Code, P.Application_ID, P.Concurrent_Program_ID, P.Concurrent_Program_Name, R.Enable_Trace, R.Restart, DECODE(R.Increment_Dates, 'Y', 'Y', 'N'), R.NLS_Compliant, R.OUTPUT_FILE_TYPE, E.Executable_Name, E.Execution_File_Name, A2.Basepath, DECODE(R.Stale, 'Y', 'C', P.Execution_Method_Code), P.Print_Flag, P.Execution_Options, DECODE(P.Srs_Flag, 'Y', 'Y', 'Q', 'Y', 'N'), P.Argument_Method_Code, R.Print_Style, R.Argument_Input_Method_Code, R.Queue_Method_Code, R.Responsibility_ID, R.Responsibility_Application_ID, R.Requested_By, R.Number_Of_Copies, R.Save_Output_Flag, R.Printer, R.Print_Group, R.Priority, U.User_Name, O.Oracle_Username, O.Encrypted_Oracle_Password, R.Cd_Id, A.Basepath, A.Application_Short_Name, TO_CHAR(R.Requested_Start_Date, 'YYYY/MM/DD HH24:MI:SS'), R.Nls_Language, R.Nls_Territory, DECODE(R.Parent_Request_ID, NULL, 0, R.Parent_Request_ID), R.Priority_Request_ID, R.Single_Thread_Flag, R.Has_Sub_Request, R.Is_Sub_Request, R.Req_Information, R.Description, R.Resubmit_Time, TO_CHAR(R.Resubmit_Interval), R.Resubmit_Interval_Type_Code, R.Resubmit_Interval_Unit_Code, TO_CHAR(R.Resubmit_End_Date, 'YYYY/MM/DD HH24:MI:SS'), Decode(E.Execution_File_Name, NULL, 'N', Decode...

Figure 13-20. *A portion of the "Sql ordered by Executions" table gathered from an AWR report*

For this specific case, you may decrease the Standard Manager processes in your EBS 12.2 because having lots of Standard Managers (roughly, more than 40) in an EBS environment may create consistency problems as the concurrent manager by design executes the same standard queries repeatedly to see things like if they have any requests to execute.

We recommend decreasing the concurrent process counts in the environment. The process count of the concurrent managers can be increased again when it is necessary (such as at the end of the month for operations such as processing period close operations).

At the same, you can check Oracle Support to find a patch for this situation. Sometimes standard queries may be not optimized.

Well, we have tried to give you an approach for determining the SQL statements that may have performance problems. Although there are many ways for determining these kinds of SQL statements, we have walked you through the top SQL tables present in an AWR report, as it is a common and effective way for dealing with both database performance and underperforming SQL statements. Note that you can check the Oracle Support document "Performance Diagnosis with Automatic Workload Repository (AWR)" (Doc ID 1674086.1) for more details about interpreting AWR reports.

After identifying the unoptimized SQL statements and making comments about them, you can go one step further and analyze their execution plans to make a technical recommendation to the development team. There are several ways to do this, but you can use the autotrace ability of the sqlplus utility to take a look at the execution plan of the unoptimized SQL statements. In addition to the execution plans, sqlplus's autotrace can report additional statistics and predicate information for you to review the characteristics of the SQL statements in more detail.

Figure 13-21 shows how to use the sqlplus autotrace option for viewing the execution plan of a statement that may have performance problems.

```
SQL> set autotrace traceonly;
SQL> SELECT BH.BATCH_NO, BH.BATCH_ID, TH.*, BSR.RESOURCES FROM  XXHAZ.HAZ_MES_RES_TXN_HEADER TH, GME_BATCH_STEP_RESOURCES BSR,
D AND BH.BATCH_ID>10179 AND DECODE(BSR.RESOURCES , 'ET HAZ  HAZ  ', 11, 10) > NVL( TH.PROCESS_FLAG, 0)  AND START_DATE > TRUN

no rows selected


Execution Plan
----------------------------------------------------
Plan hash value: 3416302522

-------------------------------------------------------------------------------------------
| Id  | Operation                     | Name                     | Rows  | Bytes | Cost (%CPU)| Time     |
-------------------------------------------------------------------------------------------
|   0 | SELECT STATEMENT              |                          |   1 |  322 |    6  (17)| 00:00:01 |
|   1 |  SORT ORDER BY                |                          |   1 |  322 |    6  (17)| 00:00:01 |
|   2 |   NESTED LOOPS                |                          |     |      |           |          |
|   3 |    NESTED LOOPS               |                          |   1 |  322 |    5   (0)| 00:00:01 |
|   4 |     NESTED LOOPS              |                          |   1 |  291 |    5   (0)| 00:00:01 |
|*  5 |      TABLE ACCESS FULL        | XXHAZ_MES_RES_TXN_HEADER |   1 |  268 |    3   (0)| 00:00:01 |
|*  6 |      TABLE ACCESS FULL        | GME_BATCH_STEP_RESOURCES |   1 |   23 |    2   (0)| 00:00:01 |
|*  7 |     INDEX UNIQUE SCAN         | GME_BATCH_HEADER_PK      |   1 |      |    0   (0)| 00:00:01 |
|   8 |    TABLE ACCESS BY INDEX ROWID| GME_BATCH_HEADER         |   1 |   31 |    0   (0)| 00:00:01 |
-------------------------------------------------------------------------------------------
```

Figure 13-21. *Checking the execution plan of a SQL statement using sqlplus*

■ **Note** The output of the autotrace presented in Figure 13-21 is truncated, as we want you to concentrate on the execution plan rather than additional statistics.

As shown in Figure 13-21, we have two full table accesses, and one of them is done on a custom table. Although the Cost column displays very low costs, this query may be a problem when the tables that Oracle scans fully are loaded with lots of records.

An alternative approach may be using EXPLAIN PLAN to show the explain plan of a SQL statement. Figure 13-22 shows the usage of EXPLAIN PLAN for showing the explain plan of the same query used in Figure 13-21.

```
SQL> EXPLAIN PLAN FOR
SELECT BH.BATCH_NO, BH.BATCH_ID, TH.*, BSR.RESOURCES  FROM XXHAZ.XXHAZ_MES_RES_TXN_HEADER TH, GME_BATCH_STE
GME_BATCH_HEADER BH WHERE BSR.BATCH_ID = BH.BATCH_ID AND BH.BATCH_ID>10179
AND DECODE(BSR.RESOURCES , 'ET HAZ ISCISI', 11, 10) > NVL( TH.PROCESS_FLAG, 0)
AND START_DATE > TRUNC(SYSDATE-30);

Explained.

SET LINESIZE 130
SET PAGESIZE 0
SELECT * FROM    TABLE(DBMS_XPLAN.DISPLAY);

-------------------------------------------------------------------------------------------
| Id  | Operation                     | Name                     | Rows  | Bytes | Cost (%CPU)| Time     |
-------------------------------------------------------------------------------------------
|   0 | SELECT STATEMENT              |                          |   1 |  322 |    5   (0)| 00:00:01 |
|   1 |  NESTED LOOPS                 |                          |     |      |           |          |
|   2 |   NESTED LOOPS                |                          |   1 |  322 |    5   (0)| 00:00:01 |
|   3 |    NESTED LOOPS               |                          |   1 |  291 |    5   (0)| 00:00:01 |
|*  4 |     TABLE ACCESS FULL         | XXHAZ_MES_RES_TXN_HEADER |   1 |  268 |    3   (0)| 00:00:01 |
|*  5 |     TABLE ACCESS FULL         | GME_BATCH_STEP_RESOURCES |   1 |   23 |    2   (0)| 00:00:01 |
|*  6 |    INDEX UNIQUE SCAN          | GME_BATCH_HEADER_PK      |   1 |      |    0   (0)| 00:00:01 |
|   7 |   TABLE ACCESS BY INDEX ROWID | GME_BATCH_HEADER         |   1 |   31 |    0   (0)| 00:00:01 |
-------------------------------------------------------------------------------------------
```

Figure 13-22. *Using EXPLAIN PLAN for showing the explain plan of a query*

However, it is important to mention that autotrace and EXPLAIN PLAN may produce incorrect results in some cases. It is also documented in Oracle Support note "EXPLAIN PLAN and SQL*PLUS AUTOTRACE may not generate actual plans" (Doc ID 1268111.1). So, a better and guaranteed method is to use SQL TRACE (10046 trace) for generating the explain plans. Alternatively, if the sql_id of the query is known, then V$SQL_PLAN or DBMS_XPLAN.DISPLAY_CURSOR can be used to get the correct plans also.

To use DBMS_XPLAN.DISPLAY_CURSOR, you need to find the sql_id and child_number values of the SQL statement whose explain plan you want to see using the v$sql data dictionary view. After getting the sql_id and the child_number, you use the syntax table(DBMS_XPLAN.DISPLAY_CURSOR(sql_id,child_number)) to list the execution plan.

Figure 13-23 shows how to use DBMS_XPLAN.DISPLAY_CURSOR to display the explain plan of a SQL statement.

```
SQL> SELECT sql_id, child_number
FROM v$sql
WHERE sql_text LIKE '%BH.BATCH_ID>10179%ORDER BY%';

OUTPUT:
SQL ID                    CHILD NUMBER
7nvdd10043v5w                  0

SQL> SELECT * FROM table(DBMS_XPLAN.DISPLAY_CURSOR('7nvdd10043v5w',0));

SQL_ID  7nvdd10043v5w, child number 0
-------------------------------------
SELECT BH.BATCH_NO, BH.BATCH_ID, TH.*, BSR.RESOURCES  FROM
XXHAZ.XXHAZ_MES_RES_TXN_HEADER TH, GME_BATCH_STEP_RESOURCES BSR,
GME_BATCH_HEADER BH WHERE BSR.BATCH_ID = BH.BATCH_ID AND
BH.BATCH_ID>10179 AND DECODE(BSR.RESOURCES , 'ET HAZ ISCISI', 11, 10) >
NVL( TH.PROCESS_FLAG, 0) AND START_DATE > TRUNC(SYSDATE-30) ORDER BY
BATCH_ID,RES_TRX_HEADER_ID

PLAN_TABLE_OUTPUT
```

| Id | Operation | Name | Rows | Bytes |
	Cost (%CPU)| Time			
0	SELECT STATEMENT			
	6 (100)|			
1	SORT ORDER BY		1	322
	6 (17)| 00:00:01			
2	NESTED LOOPS			
3	NESTED LOOPS		1	322
	5 (0)| 00:00:01			
4	NESTED LOOPS		1	291
	5 (0)| 00:00:01			
* 5	TABLE ACCESS FULL	XXHAZ_MES_RES_TXN_HEADER	1	268
	3 (0)| 00:00:01			
* 6	TABLE ACCESS FULL	GME_BATCH_STEP_RESOURCES	1	23
	2 (0)| 00:00:01			
* 7	INDEX UNIQUE SCAN	GME_BATCH_HEADER_PK	1	
	0 (0)|			
8	TABLE ACCESS BY INDEX ROWID	GME_BATCH_HEADER	1	31
	0 (0)|			

Figure 13-23. Using DBMS_XPLAN.DISPLAY_CURSOR to show the explain plan of a SQL statement

A SQL statement like this may be reported to the development team with a comment like "This SQL statement is making full table scans and loops through the records retrieved from those full table scans. This may be a problem in the future, so please review your query and request us to create an index or configure partitioning on these tables if your query cannot be modified."

So, it is important to analyze SQL statements in this way and make comments about them, and there is always a need to look at the queries from a DBA's perspective. In the absence of your comments and findings, these SQL statements are mostly not tuned; indexes may not be created at all, and usually configurations like partitioning are not even brought on the agenda. In the absence of these analyses, you will become responsible for the performance problems at the end of the day.

Well, we have given you a general understanding of the things that can be done to analyze SQL-level performance problems and given you an approach for being proactive on the database side and making poorly written SQL statements be tuned by the development teams. Of course, this subject is a complicated one, and it is up to you to increase your knowledge and practice analyzing SQL statements and implementing SQL tuning.

EBS 12.2 Network Performance Tuning

We have given you an approach for measuring the network round-trips using the Network Test form while explaining EBS 12.2 middle tier performance tuning. Also, we have stated that the network tuning should be done by the network administrators. In this section, we will give you two recommendations about tuning the network in EBS 12.2, but you should still get the network administrators involves in this topic as network tuning is not one of the major duties of apps DBAs.

EBS 12.2 systems are part of LAN and can be reached from the WAN. All the devices connect to these networks, which is why the networks are important in our perspective. A client machine that is downloading from a location or uploading a file to a remote location or to a local location may consume the network bandwidth and capacity, which in turn can make the network traffic between the EBS clients and the EBS 12.2 application tier or even the network traffic between the EBS 12.2 application tier and EBS 12.2 database tier slow down. To prevent that, we recommend isolating the networks of the EBS users and EBS 12.2 environment from the other networks in the enterprise. However, this is not applicable most of the times as it introduces a significant implementation and operation cost.

Increasing the network capacity and bandwidth is also an effective way for dealing with these kinds of network performance problems, but it is also costly. So, what we recommend for these situations is to use some additional technologies, called *packet shapers* and *quality of service*.

Packet shapers, also known as traffic shapers, can be thought as a resource manager that lets the network be used according to the importance of the systems. By using this technology, the network can be configured in such a way that the mission-critical systems like EBS 12.2 can fully consume the bandwidth even if there are some other systems requiring network resources at the same time. So, packet shapers can be used define network allocation rules according to the priorities of the systems. This approach may be a game-changer in environments where EBS 12.2 is running along with several systems in the same physical network on which there are several subnets present and several protocols are spoken.

Quality of service (QOS) is basically used for doing the same thing in different ways. QOS is a detailed topic, and the difference between the two technologies (although from an apps DBA perspective, there is no big difference) can be stated by the vendors of these technologies. Basically, QOS too allows a priority-based network allocation like the packet shapers do, and deciding on whether to use QOS or a package shaper is something that should be done by the network administrators.

EBS 12.2 Tuning the Concurrent Processing

Prior to 12, you placed the concurrent managers in the database tier, but after 12, including EBS 12.2, concurrent processing is by default placed in the application nodes, as recommended. So, in the application tier, you have the additional service type named *concurrent processing*. It is part of the application tier, but it is considered separately from Oracle HTTP Server and middleware services, as its purpose is a lot different from the middleware and the web tier. Concurrent processing is based on the concurrent managers and on the concurrent programs that are executed by these concurrent managers. These concurrent programs can be executed for batch processing, or they can be triggered for just executing small bash scripts, Java, or C programs.

We explained concurrent processing in Chapter 10, so let's jump into the performance tuning methods for concurrent processing with some best practices for having an optimized concurrent processing environment in EBS 12.2.

Most of the tuning actions are done in the Concurrent Manager Define form, which can be reached with the following navigation: System Administrator ➤ Concurrent ➤ Manager ➤ Define.

Using the Concurrent Manager Define form, you can define a new concurrent manager or change the configuration of the existing concurrent manager.

Figure 13-24 shows an example of the Concurrent Manager Define screen in which we have chosen/queried the standard manager to display or change its configuration.

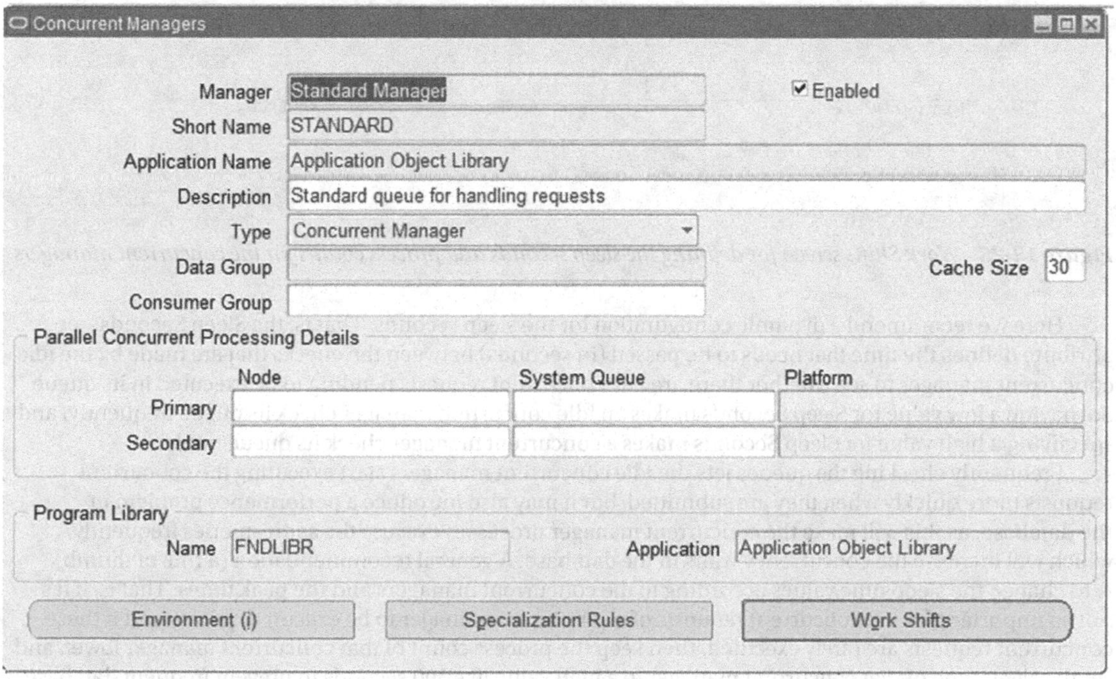

Figure 13-24. *Concurrent Manager Define form displaying Standard Manager's general definition*

As shown in the figure, there are some buttons, a check box, and some text boxes that can be used to define the work shifts (Workshifts button), add some specialization rules to specify the names of the concurrent requests that should or should not be executed by a concurrent manager (Specializations button), specify the concurrent manager node that should be used by a concurrent manager in case there is a parallel concurrent environment implemented (Primary, Secondary text boxes), enable/disable a concurrent manager (Enabled check box), associate a concurrent manager with a consumer group (Consumer Group text box), add an environment variable to the environment of a concurrent manager (Environments button), and specify the cache size for a concurrent manager (Cache Size text box).

We'll start our recommendations with the work shifts. Figure 13-25 shows the Workshifts screen that is displayed by clicking the Workshifts button in the Concurrent Manager Define form.

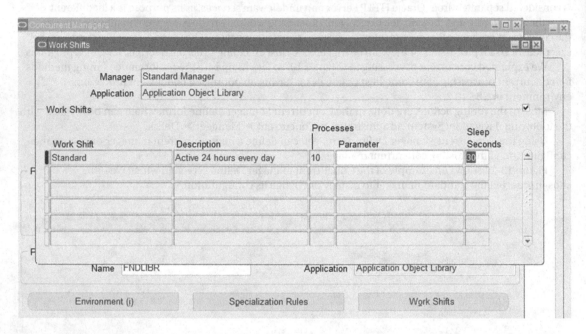

Figure 13-25. *Work Shifts screen for defining the sleep seconds and process counts for the concurrent managers*

Here we recommend a dynamic configuration for the sleep seconds. That is, the Sleep Seconds attribute defines the time that needs to be passed (in seconds) between the checks that are made by the idle concurrent manager to see whether there are any concurrent requests pending to be executed in its queue. So, having a low value for Sleep Seconds makes an idle concurrent manager check its queue frequently, and specifying a high value for Sleep Seconds makes a concurrent manager check its queue rarely.

Frequently checking the queues lets the idle concurrent managers start executing the concurrent requests more quickly when they are submitted, but it may also introduce a performance problem in the database, as this will make the concurrent manager processes execute the same queries frequently, which will increase the concurrency waits in the database. A general recommendation (a rule of thumb) is to change the sleep time values according to the concurrent managers and the peak times. That is, if it's not so important for the concurrent requests of a concurrent manager to be executed quickly and if these concurrent requests are rarely executed, then keep the process count of that concurrent manager lower, and set the sleep time of that concurrent manager to a high value like 300 seconds to prevent frequent database queries executed by this concurrent manager to check its queue.

However, if the concurrent requests defined to be executed by a concurrent manager are important enough to be executed as soon as possible and if there are lots of concurrent requests that need to be processed by that concurrent manager, then keep the process count of that concurrent manager high (like 20) and set the sleep time for that concurrent manager to be a lower value such as 30 seconds.

To summarize, a general recommendation, which we don't find accurate actually, is to change the sleep time values of the concurrent managers according to the peak times. In this context, you can lower the Sleep Seconds values for the concurrent managers when there is a peak in the concurrent program executions, and you can return the Sleep Seconds values for the concurrent managers to their original higher values when the concurrent execution load returns to normal.

Although this recommendation makes sense at first glance, it actually underestimates two facts. First, the concurrent manager sleep time is per process, and second, a concurrent manager sleeps only when it is idle.

To elaborate, the sleep time that you define for the concurrent managers is per process, so if you have 10 standard manager processes and if the sleep time for the standard manager is 30, then this means a single Standard Manager process will query the queue tables approximately 2 times in a minute. So, as you have 10 standard manager processes, then you can say that the Standard Manager processes query the fnd_concurrent_requests table 20 times in a minute, which means, with these settings, the Standard Manager processes query the fnd_concurrent_requests table every 3 seconds. In conclusion, although a sleep time of 30 seconds seems high, it does increase the frequency of the concurrent manager queries when set for a concurrent manager with a high number of processes (in this case, it is 10).

Further, the sleep time is honored only by the idle concurrent request processes. That is, the concurrent manger processes check to see whether there are any pending processes to be executed, just after they complete the processing of their current concurrent request. So, this means if a concurrent manager is nonidle all the time, then it does not sleep at all. So, setting the sleep time to a very low value for the peak times may be logical only for processing the concurrent requests that are submitted at the first points of the peak times. This is because the concurrent requests that are submitted and that are waiting to be executed in the peak times will already be executed immediately after the peak time begins. In other words, the nonidle concurrent manager processes do not sleep at all and directly check the fnd_concurrent_requests table to see whether there are any waiting concurrent requests after completing their current work. So, what value do we recommend for setting the sleep time of a concurrent manager? The answer is "it depends." It depends on three factors: the number of concurrent processes (N), the average utilization percentage of the concurrent manager (U), and the average time in seconds for a concurrent request to be allowed to wait in a pending status (T).

Once these factors are determined, the correct sleep time is derived using the following formula:

$$S=N*(1-U)*T.$$

In this scenario, where you have a concurrent manager defined with 10 concurrent manager processes, which are idle 50 percent of the time and are required to start the execution of a group of concurrent requests immediately, when they are submitted (let's say in 15 seconds), then the sleep time should be calculated as follows:

$$S=10*(1-1/2)*15=75 \text{ seconds}$$

Note that if this formula produces a sleep time (S) that is lower than T (the seconds for a concurrent request to be allowed waiting in pending status), then it means there is not enough concurrent manager processes for this concurrent manager. If that's the case, the sleep time should be recalculated after some new concurrent manager processes are added to this concurrent manager.

This method is even applicable for determining an accurate sleep time for the Conflict Resolution Manager as its sleep time is recommended to be 5 or 10 seconds regardless of the load of the environment. This manager manages the conflicts between the concurrent requests, which can be considered as a low-level and mandatory operation that needs to be done periodically.

Suppose there is a single process conflict resolution manager that is busy 50 percent of the time and must resolve the conflicts in a few seconds (i.e max 5 seconds). The formula will produce an output close to the desired value.

$$S=1*(1-1/2)*5=2.5 \text{ seconds.}$$

■ **Note**   We have referenced articles that were written by Maris Elsins on his blog (`https://me-dba.com/2013/04/performance-settings-of-concurrent-managers` and `https://me-dba.com/2016/04/internals-of-querying-the-concurrent-requests-queue-revisited-for-r122`) for the facts about the sleep time and for the formula used for determining the accurate sleep times for the concurrent managers.

The process attribute is also an important tunable that may affect performance, as it is used for specifying the process counts of the concurrent managers. Having a low value may make concurrent requests wait in the queue for a long time and sometimes may also create a hang in concurrent request execution when there are a bunch of concurrent requests that need to be executed in parallel. However, having a high value such as 70 may create a database performance problem, as it will increase the concurrent manager's queue check queries.

Table 13-3 shows a portion of an AWR report displaying the result of having a high number (120) of Standard Manager processes. As shown in Figure 13-23, the queue check queries are executed by the standard manager 27,387 times, and the total elapsed time is 184,186.61 seconds. Just imagine the performance effect of this. It will increase the CPU usage. In the case of RAC, it will increase the interconnect traffic, and if the managers are connected to different RAC nodes, it will cause concurrency waits and more.

Table 13-3. *AWR report showing the very frequently executed concurrent manager queue check queries*

Elapsed Time (s)	Executions	Elapsed Time per Exec (s)	%Total	%CPU	%IO	SQL Id	SQL Module	SQL Text
184,186.61	27,387	6.73	41.98	0.01	0.00	cpczq3f4z2hga	e:FND:cp:STANDARD	SELECT R.Conc_ Login_Id, R.Requ...

We recommend having 40 processes maximum for a concurrent manager, and we recommend this maximum value only for the peak times, like we recommended for specifying the value for sleep time.

Another recommendation is to have a dedicated custom concurrent manager for executing the custom concurrent requests. Based on our experiences, custom concurrent requests are executed often in EBS environments, and having a high number of custom concurrent requests that are waiting on the queue of the Standard Manager may prevent standard concurrent requests from being executed. So, defining a custom concurrent manager for processing these custom requests gives you an opportunity to isolate the standard and custom works, thus eliminating the delays in standard concurrent request executions caused by the high number of custom concurrent requests submitted concurrently by custom events. Having a dedicated concurrent manager also lets you isolate concurrent manager–level configurations, like sleep times and work shifts.

Custom concurrent managers can be defined using the Concurrent Manager Define form, as shown in Figure 13-26.

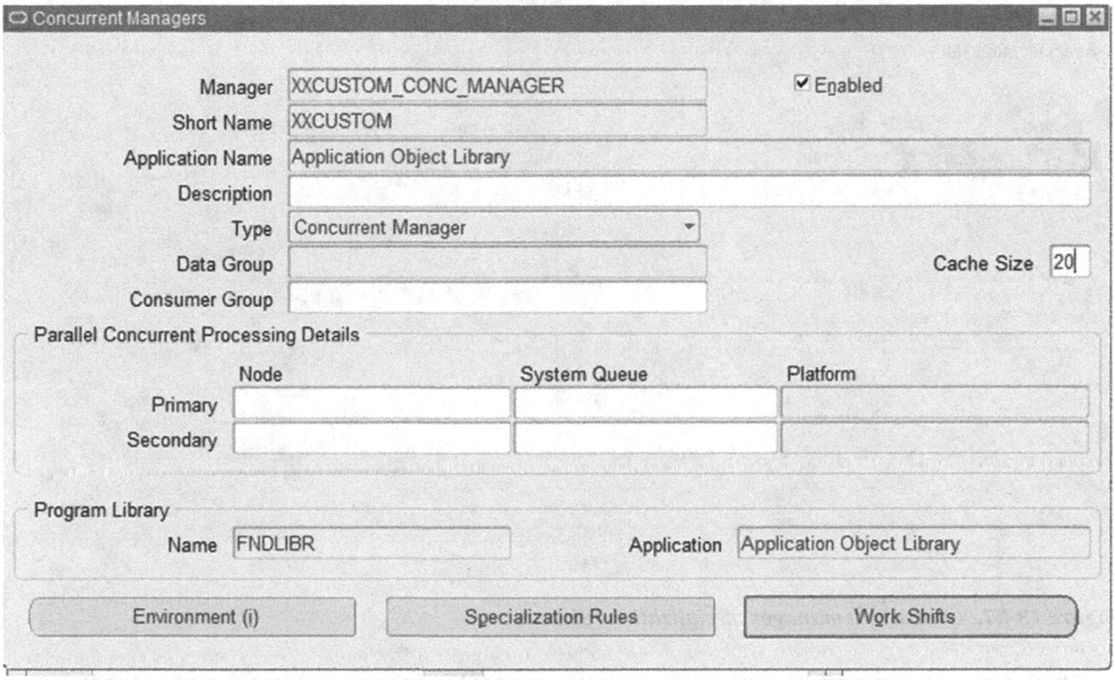

Figure 13-26. Defining custom concurrent managers

Figure 13-27 shows the Specialization Rules screen that can be reached by clicking the Specialization Rules button in the Concurrent Define form. Specialization rules can be used to tell a concurrent manager to execute a specific concurrent program (include) or to tell a concurrent manager to not execute a specific concurrent program.

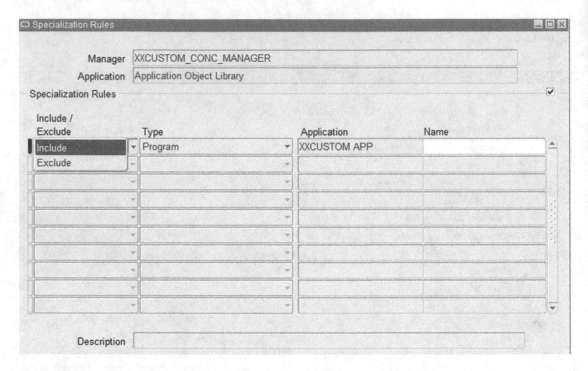

Figure 13-27. *Concurrent manager specialization rules*

In this manner, if you want a custom concurrent request to be executed only by a custom manager, you need to include that program using specialization rules of that custom manager, and also you need to exclude that same program using the specialization rules of the Standard Manager, as the Standard Manager is the concurrent manager, which by default is configured to execute all the concurrent requests.

Note that when a specialization rule of a concurrent manager is changed, the related concurrent manager is restarted automatically without a warning. So, this behavior can cause problems in production systems, as every time a specialization rule is changed, the affected manager is restarted and downtime is introduced. One alternative solution for this is to use concurrent request types. So, if you want your concurrent program named XXCUSTOM to be executed only by the concurrent manager named XXCUSTOM_MGR, you can create a request type named XXCUSTOM_TYPE and include this request type to the XXCUSTOM_MGR and exclude it from the Standard Manager.

This action will make standard and XXCUSTOM_MGR managers be restarted. However, this will be only a one-time restart. That is, at a later time, when you need to make a concurrent program be executed by XXCUSTOM_MGR only, you just need to add that custom program to the request type named XXCUSTOM_TYPE, as this will make that custom program be included in the XXCUSTOM_MGR manager and excluded from the Standard Manager automatically. The benefit of doing this is that this action will actually change the specialization rules of both the standard and XXCUSTOM_MGR managers, but it won't restart the standard and XXCUSTOM_MGR managers, because you will modify the concurrent request type, not the specialization rule.

Defining the optimal cache size for a concurrent manager is also important for concurrent processing performance in EBS 12.2. It is specified by the Cache Size check box shown in Figure 13-24 and Figure 13-26.

The cache size defines the cache length of a concurrent manager, and according to the Oracle documents, it is a way to tell a concurrent manager "Remember the cache size count of concurrent requests and execute them when you are available without going to the database and query to see whether there are pending requests available."

However, although some of the Oracle Support documents recommend setting the cache size to be at least twice the number of the concurrent manager's processes defined for a concurrent manager, we think it is unnecessary to have such a configuration unless there is a peak in the concurrent requests and as long as you properly define your concurrent process counts.

For instance, having a standard manager with ten processes as shown in the Administer Concurrent Managers screen, depicted in Figure 13-28, brings an opportunity to execute ten concurrent requests in parallel. So as long as the count of concurrent requests that are submitted all of a sudden does not exceed ten, there is no need to have a big cache for this Standard Manager.

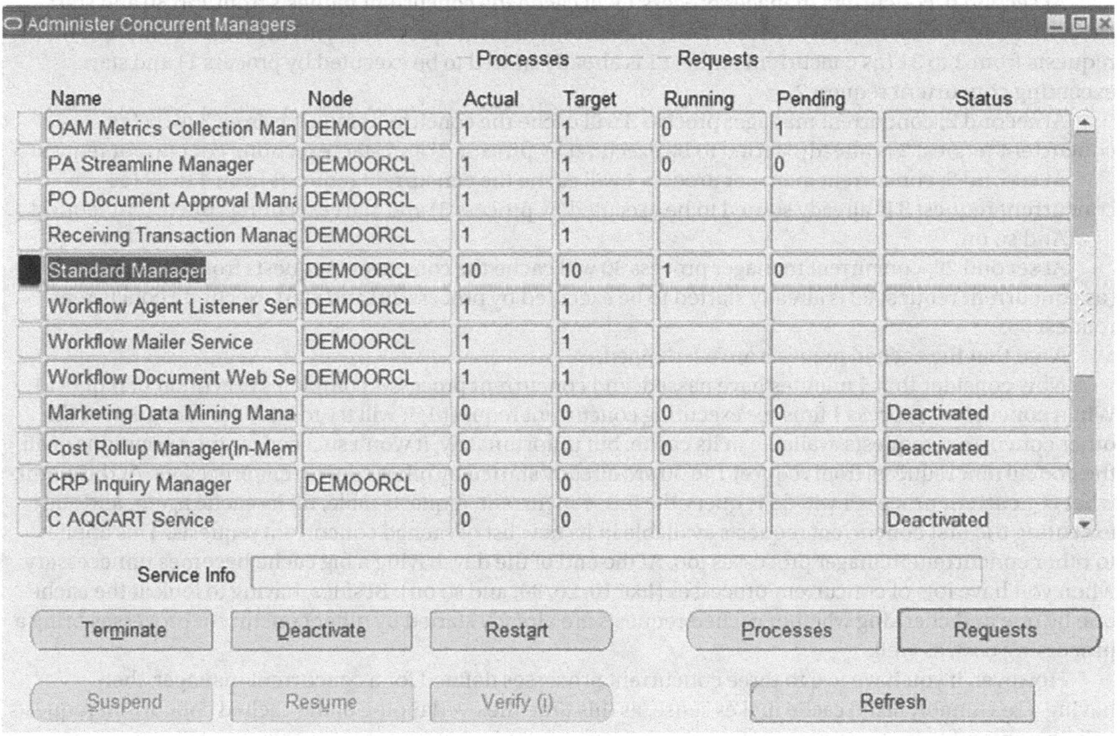

Name	Node	Processes		Requests		Status
		Actual	Target	Running	Pending	
OAM Metrics Collection Man	DEMOORCL	1	1	0	1	
PA Streamline Manager	DEMOORCL	1	1	0	0	
PO Document Approval Mana	DEMOORCL	1	1			
Receiving Transaction Manag	DEMOORCL	1	1			
Standard Manager	DEMOORCL	10	10	1	0	
Workflow Agent Listener Ser	DEMOORCL	1	1			
Workflow Mailer Service	DEMOORCL	1	1			
Workflow Document Web Se	DEMOORCL	1	1			
Marketing Data Mining Mana		0	0	0	0	Deactivated
Cost Rollup Manager(In-Mem		0	0	0	0	Deactivated
CRP Inquiry Manager	DEMOORCL	0	0			
C AQCART Service		0	0			Deactivated

Service Info

Terminate   Deactivate   Restart   Processes   Requests

Suspend   Resume   Verify (i)   Refresh

Figure 13-28. Concurrent Manager administer screen

That is, having a big cache such as 60 will make concurrent managers read the corresponding 10 rows stored in the FND_CONCURRENT_QUEUES table for caching, which is unnecessary in this case, as all of these ten concurrent requests will already be picked up and executed by the Standard Manager processes immediately and concurrently.

Actually, we don't recommend having a big cache size for any concurrent managers that have several (10, 20, or above) concurrent manager processes in general. The main reason for this is that there is no coordination between concurrent manager processes, which will be explained in the following paragraphs.

Of course, there will be cases where excessive counts of concurrent requests may be submitted by the application; for these scenarios, a general recommendation is to have a big cache size (such as twice the number of concurrent process) for the concurrent managers. That way, caching will increase the performance, and the system resources spent on these caching activities will not be for nothing. As it was in the sleep time case, this recommendation seems accurate at first glance. However, it ignores two important facts regarding how concurrent managers deal with their caches.

First, the concurrent manager cache size is actually defined per process, and second, there is no coordination between the concurrent processes to decide which requests are already cached and which are not.

Let's consider the following scenario for get a better understanding of this and see what we recommend for setting the concurrent manager cache sizes. Suppose you have 30 concurrent processes defined for a concurrent manager, and suppose you set the cache size for this concurrent manager to 30. Now suppose 1,000 concurrent requests, which generally complete in 5 minutes, are submitted to be processed by this concurrent manager. Note that we think the caching activities are done sequentially in order to give you a clear understanding about the idea.

At second 0, concurrent manager process 1 will cache the concurrent requests from 1 to 30 and start executing concurrent request 1. At second 1, concurrent manager process 2 will cache the concurrent requests from 2 to 31 (as concurrent request 1 is already started to be executed by process 1) and start executing concurrent request 2.

At second 2, concurrent manager process 3 will cache the concurrent requests from 3 to 32 (as concurrent request 2 is already started to be executed by process 2) and start executing concurrent request 3.

At second 3, concurrent manager process 4 will cache the concurrent requests from 4 to 33 (as concurrent request 3 is already started to be executed by process 3) and start executing concurrent request 4.

And so on.

At second 29, concurrent manager process 30 will cache the concurrent requests from 30 to 59 (as concurrent request 29 is already started to be executed by process 29) and start executing concurrent request 30.

Note that the cached requests are overlapped.

Now consider that 5 minutes have passed, and concurrent process 1 completes execution of request 1. When concurrent process 1 finishes executing concurrent request 1, it will try to start the execution of the other concurrent requests available in its cache, but unfortunately, it won't succeed, as the executions of all the concurrent requests from request 1 to 30 are already started by other concurrent processes. At this point, what concurrent process 1 will do is query the fnd_concurrent_requests table, fill its cache again, and start executing the first concurrent requests available in its new list of cached concurrent requests. This applies to other concurrent manager processes too. At the end of the day, having a big cache becomes unnecessary when you have lots of concurrent processes (like 10, 20, 30, and so on). Besides, having to look at the cache one by one and checking whether cached requests are already started by other concurrent processes bring a processing cost, as well.

However, if you have two to three concurrent processes defined for a concurrent manager, then having a reasonably sized cache makes sense, as this time the overlapping of the cached concurrent requests will be minimal.

To summarize, we recommend a value of 1 for setting the cache sizes of the concurrent managers that consist of several concurrent processes. Having a big cache size (like 30, 60, and so on) is only meaningful when the relevant concurrent manager has a few concurrent processes (1, 2, or 3).

■ **Note** We have referenced articles written by Maris Elsins in his blog ("https://me-dba.com/2013/04/ performance-settings-of-concurrent-managers and https://me-dba.com/2016/04/internals-of- querying-the-concurrent-requests-queue-revisited-for-r122) for the facts about the concurrent manager caches and the accurate settings for the cache sizes that we recommend for the concurrent managers, as Maris has traced the concurrent processes and seen the way they work with other.

You can see the current situations of the concurrent managers in the Administer Concurrent Manager screen. If there is an awkward situation detected there (such as an accumulation in the concurrent requests), a decision can be made for doing some modifications or taking some tuning actions for the concurrent processing. Note that these tuning actions and/or modifications should be based on the recommendations we mentioned earlier, such as increasing concurrent process counts, creating an additional concurrent manager for dealing with the custom concurrent requests, increasing the cache size of the concurrent managers, and so on.

In Figure 13-28, you see an example for the Administer Concurrent Manager screen, which can be reached by the following navigation: System ➤ Administrator ➤ Concurrent ➤ Manager ➤ Administer. In addition to the node names and statuses of the concurrent manager, Figure 13-28 displays the process values (actual and target), as well as the running and pending concurrent requests for each manager. As shown in Figure 13-28, we have ten processes configured to run for the Standard Manager, and there are no running jobs at the time of this screenshot was taken. However, other concurrent managers such as Inventory Manager and PA Streamline Manager are configured to run with single processes, as shown in Figure 13-28. The EBS environment in this example does not have a type of load that may trigger a heavy execution of the types of concurrent requests that are supposed to be executed by these kinds of managers.

■ **Note**   The values in the Target column are set to the number of processes that you configure using the Workshifts screen as mentioned earlier. The values in the Target column are the target values representing the maximum concurrent process counts that you want your concurrent managers to have in a work shift.

The Actual column lists the number of processes that are running for the concurrent managers. Usually the values shown in the Actual and Target columns should be equal unless there are some problem in the process level or unless there are some service/process deactivations or migrations happening. Process deactivations and migrations can be done automatically if the primary node for a concurrent manager is not available. Process deactivations and changing the target node for the concurrent manager in a PCP environment can be done manually by changing the primary and secondary nodes of a concurrent manager and restarting the concurrent managers.

Also note that if the value represented in the Actual column for a concurrent manager is zero, then there are no processes running for that concurrent manager. If the value represented in the Target column is not zero for that concurrent manager, then there is a problem with the concurrent manager processes that needs to be investigated.

Continuing with the more specific recommendations, we recommend you set the profile named Concurrent: Force Local Output File Mode to YES in PCP environments that employ multiple concurrent manager nodes. In EBS 12.2, this profile is set to NO by default. Setting it to YES makes the concurrent request named Purge Concurrent Request and/or Manager Data (FNDCPPUR), which is a concurrent request used to purge the expired/old concurrent request related files, run faster. The Purge Concurrent Request and/or Manager Data concurrent program is a crucial one, as it is normally scheduled in EBS 12.2 environments, and it is used to purge the old concurrent processing–related records from concurrent processing–related database tables and the old concurrent processing–related files from the application file system. This increases the EBS 12.2 performance as well as decreases the footprint of both the EBS database and application tiers.

For Oracle Reports performance, we recommend manually truncating the reports.log file that is located in $APPLCSF/$APPLLOG. This should be a regular activity for apps DBAs, as this file has a maximum size limit, which is 2GB. So if this file reaches its maximum size, Oracle report-based EBS 12.2 programs may start failing.

We recommend the Purge Concurrent Request and/or Manager Data (FNDCPPUR) program to be configured to run at night, at least once a week, to delete all the concurrent requests and manager data-related database records and files older than seven days. (The Age parameter should be used for specifying this day count, for example, Age=7.) This is an important recommendation because having lots of records in FND_CONCURRENT tables of the related queries or having lots of files in the file system directories ($APPLCSF/$APPLLOG and $APPLCSF/$APPLOUT in this case) may decrease the application performance (EBS 12.2 in this case). This is because applications may have a file system dependent operation, and it is a fact that having lots of files in a directory decreases the file system performance and may prevent the applications from being able to manage the files in that directory in a reasonable length of time.

We want to touch on the importance of the defragmentation that should be on the FND tables once again. In this context, we recommend defragmenting the FND_CONCURRENT_REQUESTS, FND_CONCURRENT_PROCESSES, FND_CRM_HISTORY, FND_ENV_CONTEXT, FND_TEMP_FILES, and FND_CONFLICTS_DOMAIN tables for both reclaiming the space and increasing the EBS 12.2 concurrent processing performance.

Another recommendation that can be made on concurrent processing performance actually relies on the parallel configuration of concurrent managers. That is, we recommend using PCP, which is an approach for having multiple concurrent processing nodes and executing the concurrent request in parallel. In addition to PCP, we recommend powering the database side of concurrent requests by using RAC and scattering the database work of the concurrent requests into multiple nodes. These two approaches will increase the performance of the concurrent processing and also supply high availability for the concurrent processing.

■ **Note**   You can get more details about PCP by reading the setup guide (*Oracle E-Business Suite Setup Guide Release 12.2*) and learn more about configuring PCP in a RAC environment by reading Appendix I of "Configure Parallel Concurrent Processing Using Oracle 11g Release 2 Real Application Clusters and Automatic storage management with Oracle E-Business Suite Release 12.2" (Doc ID 1453213.1).

It's also worth mentioning that the load balancing for the database connections of concurrent managers can be implemented even without PCP. By updating the s_cp_twotask parameter to <s_systemname>_BALANCE and running AutoConfig on the concurrent manager node, the connections of concurrent managers can be configured to a load-balanced TNS that will direct the concurrent manager connections to all the available RAC nodes in a load-balanced manner. This is basically load balancing the database sessions that are coming from concurrent managers into the RAC nodes without implementing PCP.

Well, load balancing the concurrent manager connections without implementing PCP can be a choice for EBS 12.2 environments that consist of a multinode RAC database and a single concurrent processing node. This method is a little dangerous, though, as when you use it, there is no load balancing based on EBS modules or EBS concurrent managers. The load balancing in this method is in the database level, so it is random from the EBS application perspective. Thus, a situation such as a data block that may be needed by a concurrent program running on a database node can be modified in the memory of another database node. This will result in an increase of the RAC interconnect usage, and that's why it decreases the EBS performance. Well, load balancing the database connections of the concurrent manager may increase or decrease the EBS 12.2 performance, so it should depend on the environment, and care must be taken when implementing this configuration.

Lastly, we recommend using the Concurrent Processing Analyzer (CP Analyzer) from time to time to check the concurrent processing tier. The CP Analyzer is a health check tool that can be used in EBS 12.2 to produce rich HTML files to get a detailed view of your concurrent processing environments. In addition to its health check design, it does lots of checks to produce outputs for you to use in diagnosing performance problems for your concurrent processing environment such as Total Purge Eligible Records in FND_CONCURRENT_REQUESTS, Long Running Reports During Business Hours, FND_CONCURRENT_REQUESTS Totals, Concurrent Manager Processes by Workshift, Request Managers with Incorrect Cache Size, Total Target Processes for Request Managers (Excluding Off-Hours), and so on.

■ **Note** You can get more details about the CP Analyzer by reading Oracle Support document "Concurrent Processing - CP Analyzer for E-Business Suite" (Doc ID 1411723.1).

Performance Recommendations for Reporting, Workflow, and Application Debug Profiles

In this last section, we will make some general performance recommendations that you should consider while reporting in EBS 12.2, as well as when using the standard workflow and application debug profiles.

Reporting in EBS 12.2 can be done in four main ways: using the reports (Oracle Reports) that come built in with EBS, using the custom reports created by development teams and deployed in EBS 12.2, using the custom report applications in EBS (for example, creating a custom concurrent program to produce report outputs), and using third-party web-based or client-server reporting applications such as Oracle Discoverer Desktop or Oracle Web Discoverer.

Although the approaches for taking reports from EBS 12.2 may vary, different reporting activities have lots in common. Even though they mostly have complex and costly queries, they all need significant CPU and I/O resources, and they all are just reports, which are not major concerns in EBS 12.2. That's why they should not be considered as critical activities in EBS 12.2. Nevertheless, there are still some business needs in several EBS environments that make these kinds of reporting activities critical and mandatory.

We have two types of recommendations. First, if the business is highly dependent on the reports and if these reports have to be taken during peak hours, then we recommend SQL tuning for the report queries. The queries of the reports should be reviewed, and SQL tuning should be made if necessary before deploying these reports into production. In addition to SQL tuning, creating indexes, using materialized views, using partitions, and so on, can help on this kind of query performance. Parallelism can be increased for the tables that are used by these reports, which require scanning large volumes of data, as well.

Also, if it is applicable, we recommend preventing ad hoc report queries that may be created by the reporting applications on the fly based on the user choices. As for the situation where SQL queries of these kinds of reports cannot be tuned or taking ad hoc reports cannot be prevented, we recommend using the Resource Manager of Oracle Database to give the EBS applications the needed space to do the most important work, which is processing the module-specific transactions without any performance-related interruption.

■ **Note** You can get more details about Database Resource Manager by reading the Oracle Support note "Overview of Oracle Resource Manager and DBMS_RESOURCE_MANAGER" (Doc ID 1484302.1).

If the EBS 12.2 database is on Exadata, we recommend using the IO Resource Manager (IORM) to limit the reporting-related I/O operations.

■ **Note** You can get more details about IORM by reading the *Oracle Exadata Storage Server Software* user guide, specifically, the "Managing I/O Resources" section.

Another solution for EBS 12.2 environments that are highly queried by the costly business reports may be using an active Data Guard and enabling read-only access to the standby database for directing the reporting applications and report users to the standby. This method has some restrictions. For example, some reporting applications like Discoverer, which is a widely used reporting tool in EBS world, require the database to be in read-write mode. So, this method is not applicable for the reporting environments that need the database to be in read-write mode, but still we recommend using this configuration if it is applicable for your environment.

■ **Note**   You can get more details about this configuration by reading "Using Active Data Guard Reporting with Oracle E-Business Suite Release 12.2 and an Oracle 11g or 12c Database" (Doc ID 1944539.1).

An alternative to this solution may be creating a writable standby database environment using Oracle's snapshot technology. Having an additional, read-write EBS database may give you the opportunity to direct the reporting applications/report users to this additional database and thus isolate the reporting load from the production environment. On the other hand, because of the technical impossibilities (Data Guard services cannot be run while the standby database is in read-write mode), the reporting applications will not see the up-to-date data if you implement this method. So, if it is still applicable, we strongly recommend this approach for isolating the reporting load from the production environment.

■ **Note**   You can get more details about snapshot databases by taking a look at the document "Data Guard Concepts and Administration," specifically, Chapter 9, which is at `http://docs.oracle.com`.

The last recommendation for EBS 12.2 in which there are lots of reporting activities going on is to force the users to schedule the reports. Having a scheduling option, EBS reporting users, which are generally considered end users, can schedule their heavy reports to run at night or on weekends without affecting the EBS system performance. This recommendation can be powered by letting these scheduled reports be run only in quiet times (after work hours, on weekends, at nights). Giving the schedule workbooks privilege to only the power users, who are familiar with EBS, can be a good practice for preventing lots of Discoverer reports from being scheduled at peak times.

■ **Note**   Preventing the execution of scheduled Discoverer reports can be done at the database level by setting the job_queue_processes init.ora parameter to 0 and restarting the EBS databases. However, this setting prevents all the jobs from being executed by Oracle Database. So, if you have a requirement to execute any DBMS_JOBs jobs or Oracle Scheduler (DBMS_SCHEDULER) jobs, then it is not applicable.

As for the workflow performance, we recommend being on the latest code level and querying My Oracle Support for performance patches that can increase the performance of the specific workflow activities, such as AP Invoice Approval Workflow, PO Approval Workflow, and so on. We recommend partitioning the Workflow Runtime Tables as well so as not to use debug modes if applicable, as some of the workflows are triggered by the EBS applications. If these applications are configured to run in debug mode, then workflow performance may be affected by these debugging actions. For partitioning workflow tables, see "Step 2, Partitioning Workflow Table in Workflow Administrator Guide" in *Oracle Workflow Administrator's Guide, Release 12.2, Part Number E22008-11*.

As for our recommendation about debugging, Account Generator is a good example, as it can be configured to run in debug mode using the EBS profile named ACCOUNT GENERATOR: RUN IN DEBUG MODE. There are also other profile options that can increase specific workflows to make the process faster. The PO:Workflow processing mode is one of those profiles. Setting this profile option to online makes the purchasing workflow process the documents immediately; thus, it decreases the time elapsed for approving a purchasing order (PO) document. The last workflow performance recommendation is to purge the unneeded workflow runtime data/ historical data, as growth of the underlying workflow tables may decrease the workflow performance as well as the whole EBS 12.2 system. Especially, the records stored in the tables named WF_ITEM_ATTRIBUTE_VALUES, WF_ITEM_ACTIVITY_STATUSES, and WF_NOTIFICATION_ATTRIBUTES can grow excessively.

The master workflow runtime table is called WF_ITEMS, and all the data workflow runtime tables are the additional workflow runtime tables that are associated with the WF_ITEMS table. So, purging the WF_ITEMS using the APIs deletes all the relevant records from the associated tables, as well.

To able to purge the workflow runtime data, we recommend using bde_wf_data.sql, which can be gathered by the Oracle Support document "Query Workflow Runtime Data That Is Eligible For Purging" (Doc ID 165316.1). The bde_wf_data.sql script produces output where you can see the list of closed and purgable workflow items as a summary. After analyzing the output of bde_wf_data.sql, a decision for purging can be made, and by using the concurrent program named Purge Obsolete Workflow Runtime Data (short name FNDWFPR) or workflow purge APIS (WF_Purge), purging can be done.

We recommend using the Purge Obsolete Workflow Runtime Data concurrent program for purging the workflow runtime data, and we recommend scheduling this program to run automatically every night to purge *all* item types according to the decided retention policy (specified to the FNDWFPR program using the Age parameter).

■ **Note** You can get more details about purging workflow runtime data by taking a look at the Oracle Support documents "FAQ on Purging Oracle Workflow Data" (Doc ID 277124.1) and "Quick Reference: How To Purge Obsolete Workflow Runtime Data For Applications" (Doc ID 264191.1). Also, if you want to use the workflow APIs for purging, we suggest you read the Oracle Support document "Speeding Up And Purging Workflow" (Doc ID 132254.1).

The last performance-related recommendation is about the use of debug profiles in EBS 12.2. In EBS 12.2, there are several debug profiles that can be used to enable debugging on EBS module- or technology-specific debugging or logging. For example, FND: Debug Log can be used for enabling debugging and logging operations on the Oracle Applications Framework. Similarly, GL: Debug Mode can be used to enable debugging on the GL module. So, there are several module- and application-specific debug profiles, and any application user (superusers) can set these options to enable the debugging for any level (site, responsibility, user, and so on) in an EBS 12.2 environment that is weak in security. As enabling the debug options may decrease EBS performance, we recommend regularly checking the debug profiles to see whether there are any enabled debug profiles left, and we recommend not using the debug profiles unless it is necessary.

Listing 13-8 can be used to determine the profile options related to debugging, tracing, and logging in EBS 12.2.

Listing 13-8. Script to Check Profile Options Related to Debugging, Tracing, and Logging in EBS 12.2

```
SELECT  po.user_profile_option_name,
       po.profile_option_name "NAME" ,
       DECODE (TO_CHAR (pov.level_id), '10001', 'SITE' , '10002', 'APP', '10003', 'RESP',
'10004', 'USER', '???') "LEV",
       DECODE (TO_CHAR (pov.level_id) , '10001', '', '10002', app.application_short_name ,
'10003', rsp.responsibility_key, '10004', usr.user_name, '???') "CONTEXT",
       pov.profile_option_value "VALUE"
    FROM fnd_profile_options_vl po,
        fnd_profile_option_values pov,
        fnd_user usr,
        fnd_application app,
        fnd_responsibility rsp
  WHERE (upper(po.profile_option_name) like '%DEBUG%' or upper(po.profile_option_name) like
'%TRACE%' or upper(po.profile_option_name) like '%LOG%')
    AND pov.application_id = po.application_id
    AND pov.profile_option_id =  po.profile_option_id
    AND usr.user_id(+) = pov.level_value
    AND rsp.application_id(+) = pov.level_value_application_id
    AND rsp.responsibility_id(+) = pov.level_value
    AND app.application_id(+)  = pov.level_value
ORDER BY "NAME", pov.level_id, "VALUE"
```

Summary

In this chapter, you saw recommendations for getting the optimal performance from an EBS 12.2 system on all layers, from the clients to the web tier to the database tier to the inside of Oracle applications. We covered the parameters/tunables that can affect the EBS performance and explained how those parameters/tunables can affect the underlying EBS technologies. We also mentioned reference documents from Oracle Support and http://docs.oracle.com so you can learn more if you decide to implement these recommendations.

In the next chapter, we'll cover Oracle EBS 12.2 on engineered systems such as Exadata.

■ ■ ■

Oracle E-Business Suite 12.2 on Engineered Systems

Although the name of this chapter contains *Engineered Systems*, this chapter is mostly concentrates on a single engineered system named Exadata, which is the most widely used Oracle engineered system of all time. Because engineered systems such as Exalytics and SuperCluster are not that suitable for EBS 12.2, most customers prefer to place their EBS databases in Exadata to utilize an engineered system for EBS environments.

Oracle Database Appliance (ODA), which is an entry-level Oracle engineered system, is also known as Baby Exadata; it is widely used for midsize EBS environments. That's why we will take a look at the EBS implementation process on ODA systems as well.

Exalogic is an Oracle engineered system developed for enterprise applications, and although it is not as widespread for EBS implementations, we will take a quick look at EBS on Exalogic at the end of this chapter, as it is considered a best practice for placing EBS application tiers.

So, in this chapter, we will introduce you to Oracle's database machine called Exadata and explain how to run Oracle E-Business Suite 12.2 in an Exadata environment.

Then, we will give you instructions for installing EBS 12.2 in an environment that houses Exadata X5, which is the latest, most widely implemented Exadata version at the time of writing this book. Next, we will explain the migration process that needs to be implemented to migrate an EBS 12.2 system from a traditional environment to an Exadata environment. Then, we will explain how to manage EBS 12.2 on Exadata and detail the benefits of running an EBS 12.2 database on an Exadata database machine.

Finally, we will introduce Oracle Database Appliance and Oracle Exalogic, which can be considered suitable engineered systems for EBS 12.2 implementations. In this context, we will show how to implement EBS 12.2 on these engineered systems.

Introduction to Oracle Engineered Systems

The journey for engineered systems began in 2008 with the release of Exadata V1, which was a database machine consisting of HP hardware and Oracle software components. Exadata V1 was designed to accelerate datawarehouses rather than OLTP systems, and maybe that's why it was not widely used in EBS environments. In 2009, Oracle announced Exadata V2, which was also a database machine consisting of HP hardware and Oracle software components. This time, Oracle promised that this machine was designed for both OLTP and datawarehouse environments, as Exadata V2 was utilizing a smart flash cache residing on Sun F20 flash cards. This seemed to be the only improvement done in Exadata for supporting fast OLTP processing, and maybe that's why we didn't see this machine in many EBS environments either.

The situation was completely different for the next releases of Exadata. After acquiring Sun Microsystems, Oracle announced its new database machine and released Exadata X2 in 2010.

© Syed Zaheer and Erman Arslan 2016
S. Zaheer and E. Arslan, *Practical Oracle E-Business Suite*, DOI 10.1007/978-1-4842-1422-0_14

The naming convention for this new Exadata machine, X/X2-2, was for specifying the Exadata machine type. The servers in Exadata X2 had Intel CPUs, so the X was associated with Intel/x86. The 2 was used to represent the version of the Exadata machine. The remaining number—after the dash (-), as in Exadata X2-2 or Exadata X2-8—was there to describe the CPUs per database/compute nodes.

■ **Note** This naming method is still applicable in the recent Exadata database machines.

The idea behind the X/X2-2 machine was to supply both the hardware and software by Oracle. The hardware stack was as a box, which consisted of industry-standard Intel-based Sun servers. Of course, there were some other hardware components delivered with the Exadata box such as switches supplied by Cisco, but the most crucial part of the hardware components was supplied by Sun.

The software stack consisted of Oracle Linux, Oracle Database, and Oracle Grid. The software stack was powered with the intelligent Storage Server software that made Exadata the one and only database machine that was optimized specifically for Oracle Database. By using the intelligent storage software and Infiniband technology powered by RDMA, Exadata could decrease the I/O requested by Oracle Database and decrease the elapsed times for executing the database queries dramatically without increasing the server loads (10 to 20 times faster query execution).

Similarly, DML operations were accelerated by the advantage of having the tightly integrated software stack and the flash cards. The version of Oracle RDBMS delivered with Exadata was 11g R2. 11g R2 was an Exadata-aware Oracle Database, which had the capabilities to offload database-processing work to Exadata storage servers and speak the intelligent DB protocol (iDB) with the storage servers.

Moreover, all the hardware resources used in Exadata were fault tolerant, which eliminated the risk of a single point of failure. From software (Scan Listeners, Virtual IP address, Oracle Database, RAC, ASM) to hardware (multiple compute nodes, multiple storage cells, multiple hardware cards, cabling, and so on), the Exadata X2 was promising full path redundancies. The machine had quarter, half, and full rack options, and the capacity could be expanded both horizontally (connecting multiple Exadata boxes together) and vertically (quarter to half or half to full). Regardless of being quarter, half, or full rack, Exadata X2 was a consolidation machine because it was supplying powerful hardware and optimized hardware-software pairs powered with the Exadata-specific compression methods.

Exadata X2 was designed both for OLTP and for datawarehouse environments, and as this was promised by Oracle, EBS on Exadata implementations have begun with the Exadata X2, and customers have started to see the benefits of running their EBS systems on this new Exadata X2 database machine. Maximum Availability Architecture (MAA) documents have been released for EBS on Exadata implementations, and we have started to do Fresh implementations and/or EBS Exadata migrations little by little.

■ **Note** The document named "E-Business Suite on Exadata Oracle Maximum Availability Architecture White Paper October 2012" addresses an EBS 12.1.2 implementation on an Exadata X2. This document is available at www.oracle.com/au/products/database/maa-ebs-exadata-197298.pdf.

Exadata X3 was released in 2012 and had some more improvements for OLTP. This machine had a writeback cache to improve database write performance using the flash cards. In addition, Exadata X3 was designed to improve read performance by storing the active data in the flash cards and by keeping the rarely used data in hard disks. With the release of Exadata X3, both EBS implementations and Exadata sales of Oracle increased.

In December 2013, Exadata X4 was released. Exadata X4 had faster Intel processors and more DRAM, as well as more flash cache and disk capacity.

In addition, the Infiniband network was started to be delivered with the active-active fault tolerance. (It was active-passive in the earlier Exadata releases.) So, EBS on Exadata implementations and EBS Exadata migration projects continued with Exadata X4. EBS 12.2, which has brought an opportunity for installing

Oracle Database delivered with Rapidwiz directly to ASM, was released at the same time (September 2013) with Exadata X4. With the release of EBS 12.2, the EBS Fresh Exadata installation has become easier, as the Rapidwiz version delivered with EBS 12.2 can directly place the EBS database into the ASM disk groups.

The latest release of Exadata is Exadata X5, which has brought capacity-on-demand options for limiting the Exadata configurations, as well as the ability for using Oracle virtual machines on the compute/database nodes. One of the biggest performance improvements has been the Extreme Flash Storage servers consisting of Intel solid-state-based PCIe flash cards, which replaced the old-style Exadata storage servers that had high-performance disk configurations. Exadata X5 was released at the start of 2015, and it seems EBS 12.2 Fresh implementations and EBS 12.2 Exadata migrations will continue to increase.

■ **Note**   Just before we finished writing this book, a new update came from Oracle saying that Exadata X6 was just released. It is quite a new Exadata environment; as far as we know, there are no EBS implementations done on it so far. However, the procedures to be followed for EBS on Exadata 6 implementations and EBS on Exadata X6 migrations will not differ from the procedures to be followed for EBS on Exadata X5 implementations or migrations. So, during this book, we will stick to Exadata X5.

Oracle Database Appliance is also an engineered system, which can be considered as an entry point for Oracle engineered systems. It is a 4U consolidation machine, consisting of integrated Sun hardware and Oracle software. ODA brings a ready-to-use Oracle RAC environment but doesn't have the intelligent storage server that you get in Exadata. It is not as fast as Exadata, and it does not use the high technology that Exadata uses, but still it is a consolidation machine, which supplies a ready-to-run and fault-tolerant Oracle Database environment for midsize databases. The oldest version of this machine was ODA V1, and it has been continued to be improved by ODA X3-2, ODA X4-2, and the latest ODA version, which is ODA X5-2. Although the technology delivered with ODA has been stabilized with the new releases, we have had the ability to use a ready-to-use Oracle VM Server–based virtualized environment since the first release of ODA V1. Having such an option has made ODA a consolidation environment for consolidating both the application and database servers.

Fresh EBS 12.2 on ODA implementations, as well as EBS 12.2-ODA migrations, are done in midsize companies. EBS customers who choose to purchase ODA machines usually prefer a virtualized ODA environment rather than using the machine as bare metal. In addition, these kinds of EBS on ODA migrations and implementations involve placing EBS application servers and EBS Test and Development Environments in the ODA environment.

Exalogic, also called Exalogic Elastic Cloud, is another Oracle engineered system, and it is like Exadata designed for enterprise applications. Exalogic is a complete hardware and software platform to get high performance from the supported applications such as CICS applications, COBOL, Java SE, and EE applications. Exalogic has four releases: X2-2(oldest version), X3-2, X4-2, and X5-2 (latest version). Unlike Exadata and its little brother ODA, Exalogic uses Sun ZFS storage appliances for the storage layer, and similar to ODA, Exalogic offers the ability to use virtual servers on top of an Oracle VM server optimized for Exalogic.

Exalogic is fully supported with EBS 12.2, so although it is rare, operations like EBS application tier on Exalogic implementations and EBS application tier on Exalogic migrations may be waiting for us in the near future.

So, the Oracle engineered system family is an extended family whose members are Oracle Exadata (Oracle Exadata Database Machine), Oracle Database Appliance (ODA), Oracle Exalogic (Exalogic Elastic Cloud), Oracle Big Data Appliance, Oracle Supercluster, Oracle Private Cloud Appliance, Oracle Exalytics In-Memory Machine, Zero Data Loss Recovery Appliance, Oracle FS1 Flash Storage System, and Oracle ZFS Storage Appliance.

Although most of these members have lots in common (designed for maximum performance, designed for consolidation, designed for fault tolerance, and optimized for Oracle), we will concentrate on Exadata, ODA, and Exalogic in this chapter, as these three engineered systems are the most convenient environments for running EBS 12.2.

Among these three engineered systems, we will give Exadata more space, as it is the most commonly used engineered system among EBS customers.

In this chapter, we will explain how to make Fresh EBS 12.2 Exadata installations, how to migrate EBS 12.2 databases to Exadata systems, and how to manage EBS 12.2 environments built on top of Exadata systems by giving you detailed instructions. We will give you insight rather than explaining every single command and show some screenshots (like we did in Chapter 2), as the installation tool (Rapidwiz) is the same as the one you use in regular installations and as migrations are done using documented Oracle technologies.

In addition, we will explain the benefits of running EBS 12.2 databases on Exadata systems. Lastly, we will briefly explain how to implement EBS 12.2 on ODA and Exalogic, just to show you any differences from Exadata.

Exadata Fresh Installation

The installation of EBS 12.2 on Exadata is still not documented by Oracle. There are Maximum Availability Architecture (MAA) white papers at www.oracle.com, but these documents are mostly for earlier releases (11i and 12.1).

However, installing EBS 12.2 on Exadata (X2, X3, X4, or X5) is not so different from the earlier releases. The only difference (which is also an advantage) in EBS 12.2 is the new capability of the EBS Rapidwiz Install Wizard, as it can install the fresh EBS database directly as a Real Application Clusters (RAC) database residing on the ASM file systems.

■ **Note** RAC is the clustered version of Oracle Database, and it supplies both high availability and load balancing because it's a clustering infrastructure that lets Oracle Database run in active-active clusters. You can get more information about RAC using the Oracle documents available on http://docs.oracle.com (document navigation: Oracle Database Online Documentation 11g Release 2 (11.2) / Grid Computing).

So, because ASM is used as the cluster file system with Exadata, this is an advantage. Unlike the earlier releases of EBS (in earlier releases you had to install the EBS database first in a local file system and then convert it to the ASM using the rman or rconfig utility), you can directly install the EBS 12.2 database into the ASM file system that comes built-in with Exadata engineered systems. In other words, EBS 12.2's Rapidwiz now installs the EBS database to the cluster file system (ASM in Exadata) directly and configures it automatically.

The installer of EBS 12.2 also delivers an Oracle RAC installation option. Now you can specify the RAC nodes during the installation, making Oracle RAC installation much simpler.

If you take a closer look at the installation process, in the case of an EBS 12.2-RAC installation, you create your stage, which consists of the EBS installation files in a local file system in the Exadata node or in an NFS share (ACFS or Cloud FS can also be used) connected to the Exadata node from which you initiate the EBS installation and then execute Rapidwiz, which installs the database software on all the selected RAC nodes, restores the database using rman in the storage (in ASM for Exadata), and configures the restored Oracle Database for EBS 12.2. Rapidwiz lastly converts the database to Oracle RAC using rconfig and runs AutoConfig on all nodes.

■ **Note** To install EBS 12.2 on a RAC environment, you must have the Oracle Grid Infrastructure installed and the cluster services started before invoking the EBS 12.2 installer. (In Exadata, you have a built-in grid infrastructure, so this important prerequisite is already taken care of if you are planning to install the EBS 12.2 database tier on Exadata.)

Installing EBS 12.2 on Exadata actually means having a split configuration consisting of at least one application tier node residing on a different machine than Exadata and having a RAC EBS database installed on the Exadata database nodes. (A single database node install is also applicable but not preferred.)

For EBS multinode database installations, you execute Rapidwiz on the first Exadata database node to build your EBS 12.2 RAC database on the Exadata database machine, and then you execute Rapidwiz in the application tier node/nodes to build the application tier connected to the EBS 12.2 database installed on the Exadata database machine.

Also, regardless of whether the installation is done on an Exadata or a standard RAC system, all the installation screens except the Database Node configuration screen are the same as the example installation screens provided in Chapter 2. The only different selection is done on the Database Node Configuration screen of Rapidwiz, as shown in Figure 14-1.

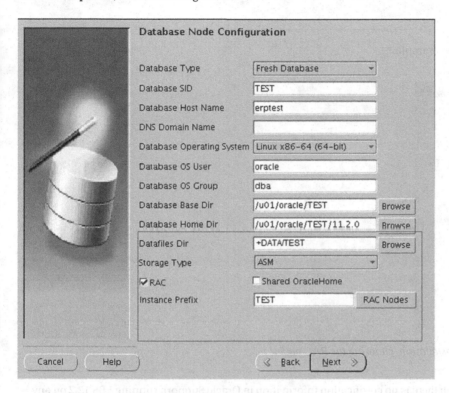

Figure 14-1. *EBS 12.2 installation, Database Node Configuration screen*

■ **Note** In Figure 14-1, you see the RAC-related options (in the red rectangle) presented in the Database Node Configuration screen of EBS 12.2's Rapidwiz.

As shown in Figure 14-1, you specify the data file directory (Datafile Dir text box) as the ASM disk group directory (+DATA in this case) with the instance prefix (TEST in this case) storage type. (We choose ASM for the Exadata installation.)

Note that you specify the instance prefix in the Datafile Dir text box just to implement the workaround for the known bug 17255876. That is, if you don't specify the instance prefix in the Datafile Dir text box, the installation may hang while performing the RAC install validations.

Select the check box named RAC to specify that you want a RAC installation; then click the RAC Nodes button and choose all the RAC nodes you want the EBS database to be part of.

Leave the check box named Shared Oracle Home unchecked, as it lets Oracle Home be shared between database nodes but not used in most of the Exadata environments. Still, if you want to use a shared Oracle Home, you can use NFS mounts for this, as Rapidwiz does not support ACFS (a cluster file system on top of ASM) but does support NFS mount for shared Oracle Home installations.

Figure 14-2 shows the dialog box that opens when clicking the RAC Nodes button.

■ **Note**   The node count depends on the underlying Exadata configuration, with Exadata being a quarter rack, half rack, or full rack.

Figure 14-2 shows an example.

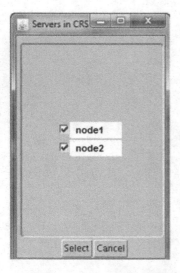

Figure 14-2. EBS 12.2 installation, choosing the RAC nodes

In addition, although there is no certification information in Oracle Support, running EBS 12.2 on any version of Exadata is considered certified, as the database versions and operating system versions that are certified by Exadata are also certified by EBS 12.2.

That is; at the time of writing this book, Oracle Database 11.2.0.3 with CPU Jul 2015, 11.2.0.4 with CPU Jul 2015, 12.1.0.1 with CPU Jul 2015 later, and 12.1.0.2 with CPU Jul 2015 were certified with Exadata. So, running an EBS 12.2 database on Exadata was certified also, as Exadata-certified database releases (Oracle Database with versions 11.2.0.3, 11.2.0.4, 12.1.0.1 and 12.1.0.2, which is delivered with the current latest EBS 12.2 installation package, startCD 51) were certified with EBS 12.2 as well.)

Similarly, as for the operating system certifications, Exadata X5 database nodes come with Oracle Linux 6 Update 6 with the Unbreakable Enterprise Kernel 2, and Exadata X4 database nodes come with Oracle Linux 5 Update 9 with the Unbreakable Enterprise Kernel 2 or Solaris 11 Update 1 (selectable at install time), and EBS 12.2 certifies all of these operating systems too.

In addition, operating systems that are used in earlier versions of Exadata (X2 and X3) are certified by EBS 12.2. As for the EBS installation, if there is a need to install additional RPM packages that are not installed in your Exadata database nodes, it is permitted to install those RPM packages into the Exadata database nodes.

So, as long as you take care of the prerequisites such as applying CPU July 2015 to your EBS database Homes, running EBS 12.2 on any Exadata system is considered certified and supported by Oracle.

As mentioned in the beginning of the chapter, there is no EBS 12.2 on Exadata documentation or white paper available on Oracle Support or http://docs.oracle.com.

So, to install the EBS 12.2 on an Exadata system, you actually determine your own way. But even if it is Exadata, it is an Oracle RAC from an apps DBA's point of view. Keeping this in mind, you can decide the documents to follow for installing EBS 12.2 on Exadata.

So, to install EBS 12.2 on an Exadata, you must follow this action plan:

1. Prepare your database nodes, and download your EBS 12.2 installation files. Unzip them and create a stage as explained in Chapter 2. The stage can be a local file system in the Exadata node, from which the EBS installation will be initiated. The stage can be placed on an NFS share, Cloud FS, or ACFS mount point.

2. Then you need to follow "Oracle E-Business Suite Installation Guide: Using Rapid Install Release 12.2 (12.2.0), Part No. E22950-18" available on http://docs. oracle.com/cd/E26401_01/doc.122/e22950.pdf and "Using Oracle 11g Release 2 Real Application Clusters and Automatic storage management with Oracle E-Business Suite Release 12.2" (Doc ID 1453213.1) to install EBS 12.2 on RAC.

3. After the initial installation, you need follow Doc ID 1617458.1 ("Oracle E-Business Suite Release 12.2.4 Readme") to upgrade your EBS 12.2.0 system to EBS 12.2.4 , as using EBS 12.2.0 that comes with the standard installation has issues, and that's why it is not supported by Oracle. 12.2.5 is the most recent release, so for upgrading to the latest EBS release, you can refer to "Oracle E-Business Suite 12.2.5 Readme" (Doc ID 1983050.1).

4. After upgrading the EBS's version, you should patch (to CPU July 2015) or upgrade (11.2.0.4 or 12c upgrade) the EBS database Homes because the EBS 12.2 installer by default installs an Oracle Database 11.2.0.3. (If installing with the latest CD, the EBS database delivered with the EBS installer will already be on the 12c release.)

5. Lastly, you should determine and apply the EBS 12.2 patches required for Exadata database machines by following these documents: "Database Patches Required by Oracle E-Business Suite on Exadata Database Machines" (Doc ID 1963786.1) and "Database Patches Required by Oracle E-Business Suite on Oracle Engineered Systems: Exadata Database Machines and SuperClusters" (Doc ID 1392527.1).

This action plan is a simplified one, so you may extend it to use multiple EBS application nodes to have parallel concurrent processing, parallel middleware, and web server processing in the EBS 12.2 application tier.

In addition, you can engage some Exadata-specific configurations such as implementing IORM, using instance caging, increasing database-level parallelization, dropping the nonseeded table indexes, using full table scans (Exadata accelerates the full table scans dramatically), and archiving (Exadata-specific archiving) to get the full advantages of having an Oracle RAC-based EBS database built on top of the processing power and technology of Exadata.

Exadata Migration

Migrating EBS 11i and 12 (12.1) to Exadata has always been important work for apps DBAs. We have done several Exadata migrations so far. When you consider the new EBS 12.2 implementations and EBS 12.2 upgrades with the increasing Exadata sales, it seems these migrations will be continuing with the new release EBS 12.2.

An EBS on Exadata migration means migrating the EBS database to the Exadata compute nodes and making the EBS application tier connect to the EBS database environment that resides on Exadata. Although it has never been necessary, some of the companies using EBS have chosen to migrate the application tier to a new machine or machines (outside of Exadata) as a subtask for these migrations.

Although you will see the EBS to Exadata migration options later in this chapter, let's go through the migration process in general by taking a look at Figure 14-3. The figure gives a schematic explanation of an example EBS 12.2 to Exadata (Quarter Rac) Data Pump migration operation, and you can see how the application tier is migrated to its new server platform, as part of this Exadata migration.

As shown in Figure 14-3, in this kind of EBS to Exadata migration, the database tier migration operations are highly dependent on the use of Oracle's Data Pump (expdp and impdp utilities). However, you see the standard cloning techniques (Rapid Clone) can be used for migrating the EBS application tier (optional) as part of this kind of EBS to Exadata migration operation.

As shown in Figure 14-3, to accomplish this kind of operation, you first patch the application tier and execute a preclone on it for the preparation phase (operation 1). You then copy the apps tier to the new application server (operation 2). After copying the application tier, you make the configurations for expdp (datapump export) and export the EBS database in place (operation 3). After exporting the datafiles, you copy the export files (datapump dump files) to a filesystem on Exadata (ext3, ext4 created on local disks of Exadata or alternatively a DBFS mount point.) (operation 4). Note that, alternatively, you can directly mount the directory, that the datapump dump files reside on source, using NFS or direct NFS to Exadata, but this is not preferred method as it may have a negative impact on the import performance. A better alternative may be export an NFS filesystem from Exadata and export the dump files there. This time, import performance will not be affected, but still the export performance should be investigated (as the export will be based on a NFS). Then you make the configurations and build the environment ready (such as creating a new and empty EBS database in Exadata) for executing impdp in Exadata and import the EBS 12.2 database using the transferred export file (operation 5). After importing the EBS database to Exadata, you continue with the EBS database tier post-cloning and post-Exadata configuration such as enabling RAC (operation 6).

Lastly, you execute post-clone in the new application server (operation 7) and do Exadata and RAC-specific EBS post-configurations such as enabling the scan listener use (operation 8).

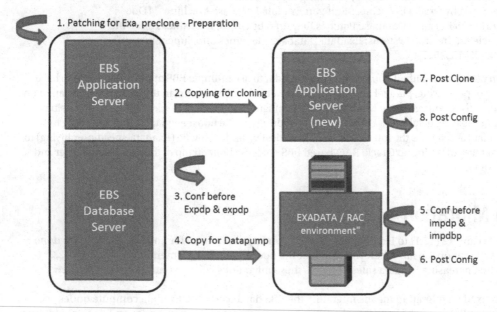

Figure 14-3. *An example diagram showing the steps to be followed for accomplishing an EBS 12.2 to Exadata migration using Data Pump*

Whether or not migrating the apps tier to the new machines, migrating the EBS database to the Exadata environment is a crucial task, as you need to combine different skills to successfully migrate your EBS environments to Exadata.

First, you need to decide on the migration method to use, as you have different options that can be used in EBS to Exadata migration, and choosing between them depends on the downtime that the chosen method requires as well as the patchsets and architecture used in your source environments.

Currently, the options you have for Exadata migration are classified into two main migration options: physical and logical.

Under physical migration, you have four migration options: Data Guard physical standby, transportable tablespace, transportable database, and Oracle EBS cloning.

However, the option for the logical migrations is Oracle Data Pump (expdp/impdp). There are also other migration methods available for generic database migrations such as Data Guard Logical Standby, Oracle GoldenGate, Oracle Streams, Create Table as Select (CTAS), and Insert as Select (IAS), but these migration methods are not supported by Oracle for migrating an EBS database, at the moment.

As you may notice, you have several migration options for migrating an EBS 12.2 database to Exadata, and these options have different characteristics, as they are built on different technologies. As you may imagine, each of these options requires its own skills. Also, the downtime that needs to be taken for the EBS to Exadata migration operation slightly differs according to the method you choose. These migration options have a different set of system requirements as well, so you can't just choose an option and plan to do your Exadata migration without satisfying its requirements.

Deciding on the best migration option for your EBS environment is important, as an optimal migration method shouldn't be too complex and should not require much downtime (if possible). To decide on your migration method among these migration options, you have to know about the options and their requirements. Let's take a look at these migration options and see what they are, what kind of downtime they can introduce, and what kind of requirements you need to satisfy before using them.

Using the physical standby method for migrating the EBS 12.2 database relies on creating a physical standby of the EBS 12.2 database on the Exadata machine, syncing it until the migration moment comes and completing the EBS 12.2 Exadata migration by doing a failover operation, which makes the physical EBS standby database on Exadata become the EBS Production database. The physical standby method requires the source platform to be on Linux, Solaris X86, or Windows, and the source database must be an Oracle RDBMS 11.2 running in archivelog mode. (Note that this version may change according to the software version in Exadata. For example, if the RDBMS version in Exadata is 12c, then the source database version must be 12c. As a requirement of Data Guard, force logging must be enabled at the source database level as well.

So, as the failover requires very little downtime, this migration method is likely to be chosen if the requirements for using it are satisfied.

Transportable database is another physical migration method; it is pretty straightforward, as it relies on converting the EBS database and restoring the EBS database on Exadata compute nodes. To implement this method, you use rman to convert the database and also rconfig on the Exadata side to write the converted database to the ASM file system.

To able to use the transportable database method for EBS 12.2 to Exadata migrations, your source EBS 12.2 database version must be at least 10.2.0.5, and the source database environment must be on little-endian platform/platforms (if the source is a multinode RAC), as Exadata database nodes are little-endian.

Endian-ness defines the order of storing the bytes of multibyte data in memory addresses. Big-endian machines store the most significant byte in the lowest memory address, and little-endian machines store the least significant byte in the lowest memory address.

Table 14-1 shows the EBS 12.2 platforms classified by their endian-ness.

Basically, if your source EBS database environment is running on one of the platforms given in the column "Little Endian Platforms," then you can use the transportable database option for your EBS to Exadata migrations.

Table 14-1. *Endian-ness of the Certified EBS Platforms*

Big-Endian Platforms	Little-Endian Platforms
IBM: Linux on POWER Systems	Oracle Solaris on x86-64
IBM: Linux on System z	Linux X86/X86-64
IBM AIX on POWER Systems	Linux Itanium
HP-UX (Itanium and PA-RISC)	HP Tru64 and OpenVMS Alpha
Oracle Solaris on SPARC	MS Windows Server x86/x64/Itanium

Using the transportable tablespace method is another option for EBS to Exadata migrations. In the transportable tablespace method, you basically complete the following steps:

1. Export the metadata of the objects that reside in the EBS-related tablespaces from the source database.

2. Transfer the data files of all the EBS-related tablespaces to the Exadata nodes.

3. Convert the data files to the Exadata endian platform.

4. Import the tablespaces exported in the first place.

5. Compile invalid objects.

Using the transportable tablespaces can be an EBS 12.2 to Exadata migration option in both little- and big-endian EBS 12.2 source database platforms. However, applying this method for these kinds of migrations may require significant downtime to complete. This is because you copy the data files containing all the actual data to the Exadata in this method, and you also do the operation that exports the EBS 12.2–related metadata from the source and imports it to Exadata. That's why this method introduces a significant amount of downtime.

Note that we suggest using transportable tablespaces (TTS) with cross-platform incremental backups technique for minimizing this downtime. Implementing TTS with cross-platform incremental backups is documented in Oracle Support note "11G - Reduce Transportable Tablespace Downtime using Cross Platform Incremental Backup" (Doc ID 1389592.1) and "12C - Reduce Transportable Tablespace Downtime using Cross Platform Incremental Backup" (Doc ID 2005729.1).

EBS standard cloning (Rapid Clone) is another option for migrating an EBS 12.2 database to Exadata. The Rapid Clone utility in EBS 12.2 can be used for migrating an EBS 12.2 database (single node or multinode) to Exadata including converting the cloned database to RAC in the target/Exadata system. Using standard cloning, however, requires the source operating system to be Linux x86-64 and the source database to be in the same version as the Oracle RDBMS software used in Exadata.

Note that the database software used in Exadata systems changes according to the Exadata environment, as you can use both Oracle Database 11g R2 and Oracle Database 12c in Exadata. This method is pretty straightforward because it relies on standard cloning. However, the downtime required in this method will be equal to the time needed for cloning an EBS 12.2 database.

Using Oracle Data Pump is a widespread method for migrating EBS 12.2 databases to Exadata, as this method relies on the well-known expdp and impdp utilities, which apps DBAs and core DBAs are quite familiar with. Moreover, migrating an EBS 12.2 database to Exadata using Data Pump can be implemented in any EBS 12.2 environment platform. The source platform is not important as the Data Pump utilities (expdp and impdp) are logical data transfer utilities. However, having a source database version exactly the same as the Oracle RDBMS version in Exadata is an advantage in this method, because EBS is highly dependent on the Oracle database and exporting a low-version EBS database and importing it to a higher-version RDBMS environment may require lots of patching in the source EBS environment, thus increasing the downtime needed for migration.

However, if you upgrade your source EBS 12.2 database in place beforehand, then you can use Data Pump without patching your EBS environment with the EBS patches. For instance, while migrating an EBS 12.2 database to an Exadata 12c environment, you need to follow EBS 12.2-RDBMS 12c interoperability documents and apply AD.C.Delta.7, AD.TXK.C.Delta7, and other interoperability patches to the source platform. So, if you upgrade your EBS 12.2 database to 12c beforehand, then you will have these patches already applied in your EBS 12.2 environment. Thus, you will have less downtime during the migration. (Again, if EBS is installed using the latest startCD, startCD 51, the EBS database will already be the 12c database release.)

Similarly, if you apply the necessary EBS apps tier and database interop patches to your source environment without performing the source database upgrade, to make your source EBS 12.2 environment interoperable with the RDBMS version used in Exadata, you can export your source EBS 12.2 database, which is a lower version than the version of Oracle RDBMS used in Exadata, and directly import it to Exadata without applying database upgrade–specific EBS patches during the migration.

As for the downtime, the downtime needed for migrating the EBS 12.2 database to Exadata Data Pump is significantly high, so this method will be your choice if the EBS 12.2 environment whose database needs to be migrated to Exadata can tolerate this kind of downtime. Nevertheless, this method is mostly used in EBS to Exadata migration projects because the EBS systems are mostly used for back-office applications. Business owners let us have big downtimes (such as a full weekend) if there is a need for a migration or upgrade operation.

There are four other undocumented EBS 12.2 to Exadata logical migration methods, which we do not recommend you implement, as these migration methods are complicated if there is an EBS database that needs to be migrated.

Two of these migration methods are using Oracle Logical Standby and using GoldenGate. These methods are two well-known logical data replication methods, but, as for the using Logical Standby, we can say that is not supported with EBS. As for the GoldenGate, maybe because GoldenGate does not support a few EBS tables, Oracle recommends using GoldenGate in only these two main cases:

- For building an alternative EBS database environment to be used for operational reporting

- For replicating databases external to the EBS database with the data stored in EBS tables

So, replicating EBS database as a whole like you do in physical standby is not one of these cases, as you may notice. That's why migrating EBS using a GoldenGate-based approach is not certified or recommended.

IAS (Insert as Select) and CTAS (Create Table As Select) are the other two migration methods. These two methods require data links such as Oracle Database Links to be present between the source and target platforms, and the execution of every statement used in these methods is done manually by apps DBAs. So, that could be why Oracle does not support these kinds of EBS migrations methods.

Even if they were supported, implementing these methods on such a complex data structure like the EBS data model would require lots of effort, not only for the migration process itself but also for controlling the migrated data and correcting possible errors. That is, as these migration methods require lots of manual operations that need to be taken care, they may introduce additional problems caused by human error.

These methods should work in theory, but we don't recommend using them for EBS to Exadata migrations. These EBS to Exadata migrations are not certified by Oracle anyway.

Currently, the supported EBS to Exadata migration methods are using Data Guard Physical Standby, transportable database, transportable tablespaces, Oracle E-Business Suite Rapid Clone, and Oracle Data Pump.

You have now seen the migration methods and the advantages and disadvantages of using them. As mentioned, the right migration methods differ according to the source environment mostly because the requirements of all these migration methods (excluding some logical migration methods like Data Guard) are highly dependent on the source platform.

However, the downtime that each migration method requires and the complexity level of each migration operation also differ.

Note that implementing complex migration methods may be not a good idea if there are other simple operations that can do the same job and satisfy the business needs such as fitting into the downtime boundaries. For example, you might implement the Data Guard Physical Standby migration method rather than the simpler Data Pump, Rapid Clone, or Transportable Database method, although there is plenty of downtime. In addition, there are white papers that explain the full EBS to Exadata migration steps by giving the commands and configuration files to be used in these kinds of migrations.

However, to an experienced apps DBA, implementing Data Guard Physical Standby for an EBS to Exadata migration may be a much simpler approach compared to performing a migration based on Data Pump. With this in mind, we believe that it is better to use the migration method that provides the downtime requirement and that the apps DBA is most comfortable with.

However, if you plan to implement a complex migration method such as Data Guard Physical Standby or any other undocumented migration method such as CTAS or IAS, you need to review all the restrictions and known issues of using these methods. Also, you need to make a full test to check every piece of data is present in your target EBS database by implementing appropriate test scenarios (especially for the undocumented methods). Although it may be possible to use the unsupported methods in EBS to Exadata migrations, we don't recommend you use them because they are implemented rarely; thus, EBS-specific restrictions and known issues about them are not documented, and any unexpected problem may result in a complete migration failure.

The bottom line is that in EBS 12.2 Exadata migrations, you need to choose the right migration method by considering your source environment, your downtime tolerance, and the complexity of the operation.

After choosing your migration method, you need to prepare an EBS 12.2 Test system (by cloning the Production environment to Test) and migrate it to Exadata by implementing the chosen migration method.

At this point, it is important to note the errors encountered during this Test system migration by recording the solutions implemented as well.

Once you complete the EBS 12.2 Test Environment Exadata migration, you need to make sure the migrated EBS 12.2 Test Environment is controlled and checked by the EBS test teams (the members of these test teams are generally functional superusers and end users), fix any errors or malfunctioning application components reported by them, and also do the required performance tuning based on the findings and performance report delivered by the EBS test teams.

Only after getting the approval of the test teams should you plan the migration of the EBS 12.2 Production Environment.

At this point, if you are using EBS 12.2 and planning to migrate it to an Exadata machine, we suggest you follow the Oracle Support document "Migrating an Oracle E-Business Suite Database to Oracle Exadata Database Machine" (Doc ID 1133355.1). In this document, you will find the links to the documentation and white papers for all the EBS to Exadata migration methods.

Although the links provided in the document are generally for describing the approaches for the EBS 12 (12.0, EBS 12.1) and EBS 11i EXADATA migrations, they are applicable for EBS 12.2 as well. (The documents and white papers written for EBS 12.1 are applicable for EBS 12.2 as well.)

■ **Note** At the moment there are no EBS 12.2–specific Exadata migration documents or white papers published by Oracle.

However, as these documents are not written specifically for EBS 12.2, there are some extra steps such as determining and applying the EBS 12.2 patches required for Exadata database machines. You can follow these documents: "Database Patches Required by Oracle E-Business Suite on Exadata Database Machines" (Doc ID 1963786.1), "Database Patches Required by Oracle E-Business Suite on Oracle Engineered Systems: Exadata Database Machines and SuperClusters" (Doc ID 1392527.1).

Configuring and Managing EBS 12.2 on Exadata

In this section, we'll list Exadata-specific EBS 12.2 management and administration activities that you should do to configure and manage EBS 12.2 in Exadata environments. The activities we will cover at this point are actually EBS on Exadata configurations that are done at the EBS database level for making EBS 12.2 use all the Exadata-specific database options to take advantage of being on an Exadata environment and provide a return of investment (purchasing Exadata and license fees are big investments) by increasing the efficiency of EBS 12.2 in terms of both the system wide performance and the consolidation abilities.

Before taking a look of this list of activities and configuration, we'll give a quick overview about the management of EBS 12.2 on Exadata environments.

System management of EBS 12.2 can be done manually by using operating system prompt (AD) scripts, database control tools such as SQL*Plus, web interfaces such as the WebLogic admin console and FMW control, and Enterprise Manager Cloud Control using the E-Business Suite plug-in for Enterprise Manager, also known as the Oracle Applications Management Pack (AMP) for E-Business Suite.

■ **Note** You can get details about AMP by reading the Oracle Support document "Getting Started with Oracle Application Management Pack (AMP) for Oracle E-Business Suite, Release 12.1.0.4.0" (Doc ID 1954099.1).

Exadata can also be managed using the operating system prompt by using Oracle-supplied utilities such as crsctl, srvctl, and sqlplus, as well as some other Exadata-specific command-line tools such as dcli and cellcli. Also, like you can manage EBS using Enterprise Manager, you can control your Exadata system using Enterprise Manager.

Figure 14-4 shows an example Enterprise Manager Cloud Control page, which can be used to monitor the Exadata database machine.

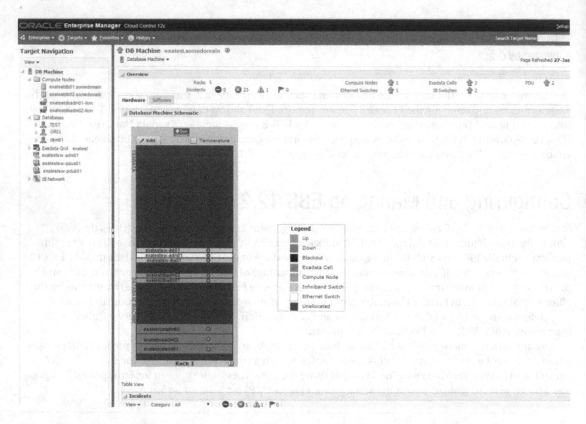

Figure 14-4. *An example Enterprise Manager Cloud Control page showing the status of Exadata components*

■ **Note** You can get details about managing Exadata using Enterprise Manager Cloud Control by reading the white paper named "Managing Oracle Exadata with Oracle Enterprise Manager 12c, An Oracle White Paper June 2012" available at www.oracle.com/us/products/middleware/exalogic/benefits-ebs-exalogic-exadata-wp-1715621.pdf.

In general, management of EBS 12.2 and Exadata are two different things and should be done by two different administrator teams. That is, Exadata admins or core DBAs should manage Exadata and all the RDBMS and Grid components on it. Apps DBAS, on the other hand, should manage the EBS 12.2 database as well as the apps data model inside the EBS 12.2 database. However, it is important to note that this is not the reality, as many companies don't separate these things. Therefore, knowing the Exadata administration is a plus for apps DBAs today.

After this management overview, let's take a look at the Exadata and EBS database-level configurations and administration activities for making EBS 12.2 get all the benefits of being on an Exadata system.

- *Determine and apply the new EBS on Exadata-specific database patches*: There are EBS 12.2 on Exadata-specific database patches, as mentioned earlier. As the supported versions and lists of these patches may change according to the new bugs and enhancements, apps DBAs should regularly check the related documents (Doc ID 1392527.1 and Doc ID 1963786.1) and, if appropriate, consider applying the new patches (if there are any).

- *Implement IORM*: I/O resource managers should be configured and used for managing the storage I/O resources according to the categories, databases, and consumer groups. IORM is a crucial component for using Exadata as a consolidation machine as it let you prioritize I/O. In this context, the general idea for using IORM is to give reports and batches a low priority and let the database processing of EBS 12.2 applications be as fast as possible.

  You can get more details by reading about this topic via Oracle Support note "Configuring Exadata I/O Resource Manager for Common Scenarios" (Doc ID 1363188.1).

- *Implement the Database Resource Manager and Auto Dop*: These options can be used to prevent a general performance decrease, which may be caused by the heavy workload in peak hours. Creating Database Resource Manager consumer groups and limiting the level of parallelism used for executing their database queries lets you have a balanced load distribution for the hardware resources of your EBS 12.2 database even in heavy workloads.

  You can get more details by reading the Oracle Support notes "Master Note: Overview of Oracle Resource Manager and DBMS_RESOURCE_MANAGER" (Doc ID 1484302.1) and "Automatic Degree of Parallelism in 11.2.0.2" (Doc ID 1269321.1).

- *Compress big application tables using Exadata-specific compression techniques*: Exadata has the Hybrid Columnar Compression (HCC) feature, which brings advanced compression methods named Query Low, Query High, Archive Low, and Archive High. These HCC compression methods let you compress the data stored in EBS 12.2 tables in a column-based manner. Compression saves you space and most of the time increases performance because having to read fewer blocks means fewer I/O operations. Based on your tests, compressing big EBS tables such as GL_JE_LINES, MT_MATERIAL_TRANSACTIONS, MTL_SYSTEM_ITEMS_B, and GL_IMPORT_PREFERENCES with the compression method named Query High has been appropriate and increases the EBS performance in general.

  So, apps DBAs should determine the tables (including the custom tables) that can benefit from this type of compression and compress the chosen tables during Exadata POCs or Exadata Test migrations to see if EBS 12.2 really gets benefit from these compressions before taking it to Production (It is better to ensure that the theory also works in real life). Take a look at the Exadata documentation, which can be downloaded from Oracle Support using the PDF documents stored in the compute nodes in the folder named /opt/oracle/cell/doc/doc.

  Also, you may find the Exadata documentation information by reading the Oracle Support note "How do I find the Exadata documentation, such as Owner and User Guide?" (Doc ID 1342281.1). This document gives the necessary information such as the names of the Exadata documents, as well as the contents of these documents.

- *Distribute EBS's database to multiple Exadata database nodes*: As mentioned earlier, there is a collection of technological components used in EBS such as forms, reports, concurrent managers, and FMW. Each of these components establishes its database connection separately. That is, each of these components reads the database connection details stored in the related configuration files and connects to the EBS database according to the connection information available for them.

  This design gives you the opportunity to configure the application component's connection details and their preferred database nodes separately. That is, while you can make concurrent managers connect to only one node, at the same time you can make forms have a scan listener–based load-balanced connection string to establish its database connections in a load-balanced manner.

These types of connection configurations are done using AutoConfig through the AutoConfig variables s_apps_jdbc_connect_descriptor, s_tools_twotask, s_weboh_twotask, and s_cp_twotask.

In this context, the connection string and tns entry pointed at by the AutoConfig variables s_apps_jdbc_connect_descriptor and s_apps_jdbc_connect_alias are used by Java applications such as the Self Service application. The Tns entry pointed at by the s_tools_twotask AutoConfig variable is used by the application components residing in 10.1.2 Oracle Home (Reports and Forms). The Tns entry pointed at by the s_weboh_twotask AutoConfig variable is used by the Oracle HTTP Server, and lastly, the tns entry pointed at by s_cp_twotask is used by the concurrent managers.

The details for configuring these variables can be found in Section 3.8.2 of Oracle Support document "Using Oracle Real Application Clusters 11g Release 2 with Oracle E-Business Suite Release 12" (Doc ID 823587.1). In this document, you will learn how to set up load-balanced connections, but you can use that information to configure the connections based on your requirements as well.

Note that s_apps_jdbc_connect_descriptor is not documented in document 823587.1, so here is the format for configuring this AutoConfig variable for a scan listener–based load-balanced configuration. (You can also use this format to configure this AutoConfig variable to point to only a single database node.)

```
<jdbc_url oa_var="s_apps_jdbc_connect_descriptor">jdbc:oracle:thin:@
(DESCRIPTION=(ADDRESS_LIST=(LOAD_BALANCE=YES)(FAILOVER=YES)
(ADDRESS=(PROTOCOL=tcp) (HOST=<NEW SCAN NAME>(PORT=<NEW SCAN PORT>)))
(CONNECT_DATA=(SERVICE_NAME=<Service Name>)))</jdbc_url>
```

- *Tuning parallelism on the database level*: Exadata has lots of CPU cores and I/O paths. So, utilizing this hardware by tuning the parallelism at the table level and configuring the parallelization-related database parameters such as parallel_max_servers to support the desired level of parallelism are good practices, which may increase performance in EBS 12.2 on Exadata environments.

In addition to the utilization on Exadata hardware, parallelism is needed for getting benefits from Exadata-specific enhancements such as Smart Scan, which is used for offloading the I/O processing to the Exadata storage nodes called Exadata cells. That is, when Smart Scan occurs, Exadata storage nodes do the database I/O processing and return smaller amounts of data to the database servers.

So, when the queries are executed in parallel, Oracle will make the direct path read operations for gathering data from the database. As the direct path read operations are eligible for Smart Scan, by having parallel queries, you can increase the chance for Smart Scans.

That's why you can say that parallel queries are eligible for Smart Scan operations. By increasing the parallelism, you can accelerate the reporting and batch processing most of the time.

We have seen these in real life. By migrating the EBS database to Exadata and by increasing the degree of parallelism on the tables that are used by the reporting tools, you can accelerate the Discoverer reports that can take hours to complete and have them completed in minutes instead.

However, increasing parallelization for all the tables may result in a performance decrease, especially for SQL statements that are short-winded and highly executed, such as SQL statements coming from forms screens and OAF pages. (The login page is an example of this.)

So, it is required that you analyze the tables and try to predict the performance effects of increasing parallelism. The effects of parallelism should also be tested wisely, and if there is uncertainty about the benefit of tuning the parallelism, we recommend giving the control to the database by configuring Auto Dop and implementing the Database Resource Manager, as explained earlier. In addition, some EBS standard tables have been configured to be serial. This means the application developers in Oracle want the operations against these kinds of tables to be done serially. This also means the queries against these tables are not suitable for parallel operations, according to the application developers at Oracle who know the EBS code.

So, the logic to decide on setting the table-level degree of parallelism should be based on the suitability of the EBS tables for parallelism. In this context, you should leave the standard tables configured to be serial the way they are and consider increasing the parallelism on the EBS standard tables, which are by default configured to have a degree of parallelism, as these tables are suitable for parallel operations.

An example configuration is setting an higher parallel degree for the custom tables used in reporting, leaving standard tables configured to be serial as the way they are, and setting a higher parallel degree for the standard tables, which are already configured to be queried parallel.

Please take a look at Oracle Support document "Using Parallel Execution" (Doc ID 203238.1) for further details about parallel processing in Oracle Database.

- *Drop indexes on custom tables if appropriate*: In addition to these parallelization settings, you should make appropriate indexes invisible to make Oracle execute the related queries with full table scan operations.

Note that you should decide on these indexes by comparing the performance of the related SQL statements. Comparing the elapsed times of the related queries by running them in both cases (when the index/or indexes on the tables are invisible and when the index/or indexes are visible) is a good practice for deciding whether to make an index invisible. If the related queries perform better without the indexes, you may consider dropping those indexes to gain free space.

- *Use instance caging when appropriate*: Exadata is a consolidation machine. In this context, you as the apps DBA would usually place the EBS 12.2 Test and Development Databases along with the EBS Production Database in the same Exadata database machine. Moreover, in most environments, you will see that there are non-EBS databases running on the same Exadata machine. So, even if the underlying hardware belongs to Exadata, it is also limited, and that's why the hardware resources in Exadata database nodes should be managed properly for preventing bottlenecks, which may be caused by the lack of hardware resources (especially CPU resources). At this point, instance caging comes into play. Instance caging can be used to limit the CPU usage in the database level. Instance caging should be configured for EBS 12.2 on Exadata environments for preventing the nonproduction and non-EBS databases from residing on the same Exadata database machine to allocate the resources excessively, leaving no space in CPU queues for the EBS Production Environment.

Note that although it is a little costly, it is a common practice to have at least two Exadata machines in the environment. It is also recommended by Oracle, as Exadata patching should be first tested on a Test Exadata machine. So, if there are two Exadata machines in the environment, you usually place the EBS Test, Clone and Dev environments on the second Exadata machine and leave the first Exadata machine for the Production Databases. Even if it is the case, the EBS Production Database. usually runs with other Production Databases in the same Exadata machine so that instance caging still comes into play.

Please take a look at the Oracle Support document "Configuring and Monitoring Instance Caging" (Doc ID 1362445.1) for further details about instance caging.

So, we have given you the list of activities and configuration for making better use of Exadata in EBS environments. Actually, when you migrate EBS (regardless of the EBS release, as long as the EBS release is supported by Exadata) to Exadata or when you install the EBS database on an Exadata system, it generally performs better than any commodity hardware without doing any Exadata-specific database-level configuration at all. However, by knowing that most of these configurations and activities are also used in EBS on Exadata POCs, we recommend implementing (or at least considering) the list of configurations and activities we have provided in this section, as they can be considered best practices for running EBS databases on Exadata.

Benefits of Running EBS on Exadata Systems

Having the EBS 12.2 database tier on Exadata brings lots of advantages in terms of being on a fully redundant machine that also enables an environment consolidation, as well as being on a platform that knows the characteristics of Oracle Database, how it is performing I/O, and what can bring it in visible benefits in terms of performance.

Actually, all the EBS installations on Exadata, all the migrations, and all the configuration we gave earlier in this chapter are done for only one general reason, which is having EBS benefit from being on the Exadata database machine.

So, the question is, Is it worth it to buy Exadata and place the latest EBS 12.2 database on it?

Well, we will give you the benefits and the results of running the EBS database tier on an Exadata machine. Specifically, we will give you a consolidated list that consists of all the benefits and results that we have gathered so far in our POCs and real-life implementations and then leave the answer to you.

Note that the results and benefits that we will give here were gathered in an EBS environment running on an Exadata X4-2 quarter rack.

Also, it is important to mention that some of the features that have helped us produce these results are features of Oracle Database, but these features conform with Exadata and produce good results in Exadata. That's why we think the results for using the database features with Exadata should be considered as benefits of Exadata.

- By using Auto Degree of Parallelism (Auto Dop) and Database Resource Manager, the performance of the system can be stabilized even in the peak times where the load is high.

- Fully I/O-bound administration operations such as tablespace creation are very fast in Exadata. By using the fast data file creation feature of Exadata, a tablespace sized 30GB can be created in 1 minute, with a throughput of 2.45 gigabytes per second.

- Using the Exadata feature Smart Scan, which is used internally by Exadata to offload SQL processing to the Intelligent Storage Server (Exadata Cells), millions of rows can be queried using a select clause such as select count(*) from testable in 30 seconds.

- Using Exadata Storage Indexes, which are used internally by Exadata to track the physical location of the data in storage level, very big EBS tables, which have no indexes on them, can be queried in seconds by eliminating most of the required (required in non-Exadata environments) read I/O operations to the tables. Although at most eight columns of a table can have storage indexes, Exadata storage creates the storage indexes automatically based on the predicates used in where clauses. So, there is a big chance of getting the storage indexes created for the highly accessed columns. By using the storage indexes transparently, Exadata can query a big table (21GB) that has no database indexes on it using a select clause such as select count(*) from testable, where id=1, in 2 seconds.

- Using the Exadata-specific compression method HCC and compression type named Query High, standard tables such as GL_JE_LINES and MTL_MATERIAL_TRANSACTIONS, as well as custom tables such as a table for storing the details of the invoices, can be compressed with quite good compression ratios. While compression decreases the size of the tables and saves space, it increases the query performance, because as the size of the tables is decreasing, the number of I/O operations that need to be done to retrieve the records from those table are decreasing too.

- By using the parallelism in Exadata, batch database operations such as building a big table using lots of records derived from other tables can run faster. We have seen an operation like creating a cost table accelerated by 11 times using a parallel degree of 8 in Exadata. Using parallelism in Exadata is different from using it in a traditional system, as parallelism in Exadata triggers Smart Scan to be used, thus increasing database operation performance significantly. This is also valid for Oracle Reports and Discoverer reports. We have seen lots of Discoverer reports accelerated by 10 times in Exadata without even touching any SQL statements used in those reports. Using parallelism in Exadata brings profit to the materialized views creation and refreshes, as well as the statistics-gathering jobs. We have seen a Gather Stats concurrent request, which was submitted for gathering statistics of all database schemas during a POC that was done on Exadata X4, accelerated by five times.

- Backup restore jobs are also very fast on Exadata. During our test, we have seen that taking a full rman backup of a 1TB EBS database took only 9 minutes. Also, taking a full compressed backup of this 1TB EBS database took 1 hour and saved 79 percent of the space that this backup would occupy without compression. Note that even if there is an Exadata-specific compression (such as HCC) in use, the backups taken for the databases, while residing on Exadata, can still be restored to a non-Exadata system. However, the tables that are compressed using HCC should be decompressed after restoring and opening these databases in a non-Exadata system (data stored on a ZFS storage appliance is an exception to these non-Exadata systems, as it can read the data stored in tables compressed using Exadata HCC). Without decompressing, the data that is stored in the HCC-compressed tables cannot be read by the databases running on non-Exadata systems.

- Using I/O Resource Manager (IORM) and instance caging in Exadata, EBS Test, Development, and Production Databases can be consolidated into a single machine, Exadata. IORM supplies a quality-of-service mechanism for disk I/O operations for ensuring the Production Database I/Os are always processed with the highest priority.

- The instance caging supplies the quality of service for the CPU resources, protecting the EBS Production Database from CPU starvation, which may be caused by excessive CPU-bound operations done in other databases running on the same Exadata machine.

- In addition to these benefits, there are also lots of other benefits such as cost savings, an ability the expand the power of the machine both vertically and horizontally, having Infiniband for the cluster interconnects, and so on. So if you are interested in those benefits, we recommend reading Exadata-specific documents and contacting an Oracle sales representative for getting a presentation of the latest Exadata machine.

So, those are the benefits of running EBS (11i 12 or 12.2) on Exadata. This machine and the intelligent software on it have the potential to bring benefits to EBS systems. We have seen in it on our POCs and real-life implementations that we have done on our customers as well.

Oracle Database Appliance Implementations

Oracle Database Appliance, sometimes called Baby Exadata, is an engineered system for midsize companies. It is a 4U machine consisting of Intel-based Sun servers for both computing and storage services. With the release of ODA X3, ODA has started to be used commonly by midsize companies, and EBS environments are starting to be migrated to ODA machines. Since ODA V1, there is a virtualization option that can be selected for creating virtual machines on top of the ODA nodes, but with the release of ODA X3, we have seen that a virtualized environment option based on Oracle VM servers has been started to be implemented commonly. With the latest release, ODA X5, the same virtualization option that was introduced in ODA V1 has been continued with its increased stability and enhancements.

Since the first version of ODA, SSD disks are used for faster redo log I/O operations. In addition to this faster redo log I/O path, the latest-release X3-2, X4-2, and X5-2 ODA machines have brought new features. For example, additional SSD storage was added to these machines, and this SSD storage is used for having an Oracle fast flash cache, giving the opportunity to store the data file on SSDs and enabling the ACFS cache. These machines can be deployed as a built-in two-node RAC called a base-metal environment or a built-in Oracle VM server–based two-node cluster virtualized environment. (Actually, starting with the ODA V1 2.5.0.0.0 release and ODA X3-2 2.5.5.0.0, you have these deployment options.)

As there is a hypervisor placed in between the hardware and the virtual machines in virtualized environments, the bare-metal ODA environment is expected to give better performance than the virtualized ODA environment. However, Oracle is ambitious in the high performance of virtualized ODA by offering a specialized virtualized domain called ODA_BASE, in which there are two virtual machines deployed to supply a two-node virtual Oracle RAC environment and configured for accessing the ODA hardware directly.

So, having bare-metal and virtual installation options brought two alternatives for EBS customers to deploy their EBS 12.2 environments to the ODA machines. In the bare-metal installation option, EBS 12.2 database tiers can be installed on a bare-metal ODA environment using almost the same steps as installing EBS 12.2 to any Oracle RAC system. The EBS 12.2 installation tool, Rapidwiz, supports direct RAC installation; thus, installing the EBS 12.2 database tier in bare-metal ODA environments is like installing EBS 12.2 on any RAC system.

In the virtualized environment option, both EBS application servers and database servers can be placed in the virtual machines created on virtualized ODA environments. In this context, having an ODA virtualized environment brings an opportunity to use the ODA machine as a consolidation environment for hosting both the databases and application tiers, as long as the ODA machine resources are sufficient for meeting the load.

Like with the virtualized ODA environments, using the ODA base servers for placing the EBS 12.2 database tier is highly recommended, because the ODA base virtual servers perform better than any virtual servers that can be created on virtualized ODA systems.

■ **Note** We have observed I/O performance problems in an EBS 12.2.4 environment (the same problems will also be there for EBS 12.2.5) where we have utilized non-ODA Base ODA X4 virtual machines for the database tier. So, we recommend using ODA base virtual machines for hosting the EBS 12.2 database tier.

We will give an overview of both of these EBS 12.2 on ODA installation methods by showing the installation processes as well as by presenting you with diagrams for giving you a better understanding of the supported and recommended EBS 12.2 on ODA configurations.

We will be focusing on the latest ODA machine (ODA X5) while giving you the installation steps. Actually, the idea behind these installation methods that we will provide applies for ODA X4, too, since the general approach for implementing EBS 12.2 on ODA X4 or implementing EBS 12.2 on ODA X5 is similar. The only difference is that in ODA X5 there is a requirement for using ACFS for storing the database files. Actually, using ACFS is a requirement of the software version that is used in ODA X5. (12.1.2.*), so storing the database files on ACFS is required in any ODA hardware that hosts one of these ODA software versions.

You can find details about this subject in the Oracle Support note "Oracle Database Appliance - 12.1.2 and 2.X Supported ODA Versions & Known Issues" (Doc ID 888888.1).

Installing EBS 12.2 on ODA Bare Metal

By "bare metal," we mean using the ODA machine without virtualization software. In bare metal, you use the ODA machine nodes by deploying Oracle Linux operating systems on them. In a bare-metal deployment, the ODA machine delivers a built-in two-node Oracle RAC environment running on top of the ODA compute nodes.

If you choose to use ODA nodes physically, also called using ODA as bare metal, you place the EBS 12.2 database tier on the ODA physical nodes as a two-node RAC database or as a single-instance database according to your choice.

In this installation type, the EBS 12.2 database tier is placed on the ODA physical nodes, and the EBS 12.2 application tier is placed on another machine or machines (if you want your EBS 12.2 to have multiple application nodes).

In Figure 14-5 you see an EBS 12.2 on ODA bare-metal implementation scheme, where the EBS 12.2 database tier is configured as a two-node RAC database running on the ODA compute nodes (ODA database servers), and the EBS 12.2 application tier is built on top of a multinode environment consisting of multiple application servers residing outside the ODA environment.

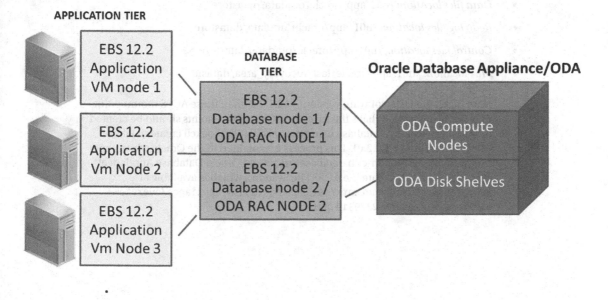

Figure 14-5. An example diagram showing the EBS 12.2 on ODA bare-metal implementation

As mentioned earlier, installing EBS 12.2 to an ODA bare-metal environment actually means installing the EBS 12.2 database tier to ODA compute nodes and installing the EBS 12.2 application tier on application servers that are external to ODA.

In this context, installing EBS 12.2 on ODA compute nodes is not actually any different than a standard EBS 12.2 RAC installation.

The action plan for this type installation is as follows:

1. Stage the EBS 12.2 database tier setup files to the ODA machine.

2. Install the required RPM files and configure the database nodes for the EBS 12.2 database installation.

3. Install the EBS 12.2 database tier using the Rapidwiz Install Wizard by invoking Rapidwiz on the first database node. Install the EBS 12.2 database tier on two ODA nodes using the RAC option. Installing EBS 12.2 on ODA RAC nodes can be done by following Section 5 of the Oracle Support document "Using Oracle 11g Release 2 Real Application Clusters and Automatic storage management with Oracle E-Business Suite Release 12.2" (Doc ID 1453213.1). If the ODA machine version is X5 or if the ODA software version is 12.1.*, then it is important to use the ACFS location for storing Oracle Database files. More specifically, if the machine that you plan to install EBS 12.2 on is an ODA X5-2 or if the machine is an earlier-version ODA 12.1.x (ODA X4, X3, or V1) and if it's upgraded to 12.1.x or reimaged with the 12.1.x ODA software version, the database should be created on top of the ACFS file system. This is because X5-2 contains 4TB disks, which exceeds the 11.2 ASM disk size limit of 2TB, and it seems the new ODA software is designed for using ACFS. This fact introduces an important requirement to install the EBS 12.2 database tier using the ACFS option. In this context, the proper locations for data files, redo log files, control files, and the flash recovery area (FRA) are as follows:

- *Data files location*: /u02/app/oracle/oradata/datastore

- *Redo log files location*: /u01/app/oracle/oradata/datastore

- *Control files location*: /u01/app/oracle/oradata/datastore

- *FRA location*: /u01/app/oracle/fast_recovery_area/datastore

  Note that if the ODA software version is 12.1.2.0, then these ACFS mount points may not be present. If that's the case, the ACFS mount points should be created by creating a dummy database using the oakcli utility (oakcli create database -db orcl -version 12.1.0.2.0). This process is explained in the Oracle white paper "Steps to migration non-cdb databases to acfs on Oracle Database Appliance 12.1.2.2.1" (Step 1: Create the ACFS File System), which is available at www.oracle.com/technetwork/database/database-appliance/overview/asm-acfs-migration-2379319.pdf.

4. Also, it is important to upgrade the database version delivered with the EBS 12.2 installation according to the ODA database support requirements. As for the latest ODA machine, ODA X5, the minimum supported version is 11.2.0.3.15 at the moment. Thus, if the EBS 12.2 database version delivered with Rapidwiz is below that version, it is required to be upgraded (remember, the latest EBS 12.2 startCD delivers a 12.1.0.2 database). Note that 11.2.0.3.15 is the minimum version of Oracle Database that supports ACFS, and that's why it is the minimum required version for ODA X5. So, if you install EBS 12.2.5, which deploys Oracle Database 11.2.0.4, then you don't need to upgrade your database. Similarly, if a newer-version startCD such as startCD 51 is used for the EBS 12.2 installation, then the EBS database will already be deployed as 12c. However, in general, we recommend the EBS 12.2 database be upgraded to the latest supported database version (12c) just after EBS 12.2 installation so that it meets the latest possible (supported with EBS 12.2) Oracle Database patch level.

So, if the EBS installation was done using a fairly old startCD, you must upgrade the database delivered with the EBS Rapidwiz Install Wizard. We recommend upgrading the EBS 12.2 database to at least 11.2.0.4 rather than upgrading it to the minimum required version, which is 11.2.0.3.15. You can find the general steps for upgrading the EBS 12.2 database tier to 11.2.0.4 here:

- Create a new 11.2.0.4 RDBMS home using oakcli (example command: oakcli create dbhome -version 11.2.0.4).

- Apply the required patches for supplying the interoperability of EBS 12.2 and Oracle RDBMS 11.2.0.4.

- Install Oracle Database examples into the newly created 11.2.0.4 Oracle Home.

- Upgrade the database from 11.2.0.3 to 11.2.0.4 using this newly created 11.2.0.4 Oracle Home.

  Note that as an alternative to 11.2.0.4, the EBS 12.2 database can be upgraded from 11.2.0.3 to 12.1.0.2.

5. After the database tier deployment is complete, proceed with the installation of the EBS 12.2 application tier using the Rapidwiz Install Wizard by invoking Rapidwiz on the application side.

The application tier installation is done on the application servers that reside outside of the ODA machine/ODA database nodes; thus, this installation can be considered as an EBS 12.2 split configuration installation or a multinode installation.

Note that for installing the application tier, you just take the necessary steps for installing the application tier as explained in Chapter 2. As for having a multinode apps tier, you install the apps tier to one of the nodes and then clone that apps tier to other application nodes using EBS's cloning techniques, as described in Chapter 11.

Installing EBS 12.2 on Virtualized ODA

The method for installing EBS 12.2 to a virtualized ODA environment is a bit different than installing EBS 12.2 on an ODA bare-metal environment. In a virtualized ODA environment, there is an Oracle VM server–based architecture, which brings a requirement to deploy both the EBS application and database tiers on virtual servers.

In virtualized ODA environments, the recommended configuration is to build an EBS environment in which the EBS application tier resides on the virtual machines presented by the Oracle VM servers running on ODA nodes and the database tier resides on the specialized virtual machines called ODA BASE virtual server/servers, which have direct access to the disk devices of the ODA machine.

In Figure 14-6, you see an EBS 12.2 on virtualized ODA implementation scheme; the EBS 12.2 database tier is configured as a two-node RAC database running on special virtual machines called ODA Base virtual machines, and a multinode EBS 12.2 application tier is built on top of the application tier virtual machines, which are presented by Oracle VM servers running on the ODA compute nodes.

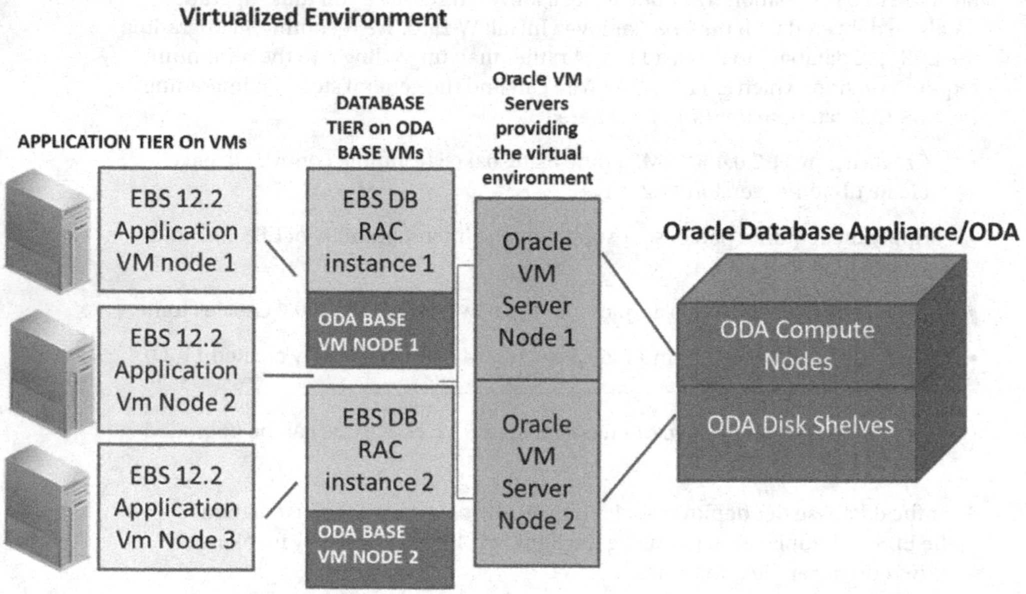

Figure 14-6. *An example diagram showing the EBS 12.2 on virtualized ODA implementation*

To get the configuration as shown in Figure 14-6, you basically install the database tier of EBS 12.2 using the EBS 12.2 Database VM template. That is, you build a one-node database tier by creating a virtual machine using the VM template, and then to have the EBS database running on specialized ODA Base nodes, you migrate the database tier to the first ODA BASE node.

After the database migration is complete, you continue with the installation of the application tier, which is done using the EBS 12.2 Application VM template. You build a one-node application tier using the EBS 12.2 Application VM template and then continue with enabling the high availability of the application and database tiers of this newly deployed EBS 12.2.

As for enabling the high availability of servers and services, you convert your newly deployed EBS 12.2 database to a two-node RAC running on both of the ODA Base nodes for having a load-balanced and highly available database tier, as shown in Figure 14-6, and you deploy additional application servers using the same method implemented for deploying the first application server node and implement the load-balanced configurations such as configuring a load balancer and configuring parallel concurrent processing (PCP) for a multinode, highly available, and load-balanced EBS 12.2 application tier, like the one shown in Figure 14-6.

Although the whole procedure for implementing an EBS 12.2 on ODA virtualized environment is documented in the Oracle white paper "Solution-in-a-box: Best practices for deploying Oracle E-Business Suite Release 12.2.4 on Oracle Database Appliance 12.1.2.2" available at www.oracle.com/technetwork/ database/database-appliance/oda-ebs-virtualized-wp-2183063.pdf, we will give you the steps here.

■ **Note** The methods and approaches given in the document "Solution-in-a-box: Best practices for deploying Oracle E-Business Suite Release 12.2.4 on Oracle Database Appliance 12.1.2" also apply to deploying EBS 12.2.5 on an Oracle database appliance. However, the references to release-specific documentation and template versions may change according to the EBS release.

Actually, the VM templates for EBS 12.2.5 are not available yet (as of June 2016). So, for deploying EBS 12.2.5 on ODA virtualized environments using EBS OVM templates, EBS 12.2.4 templates can still be used. But the EBS 12.2.4 environment deployed using these templates must be upgraded to 12.2.5 by completing the EBS upgrade tasks to have an EBS 12.2.5 instance on ODA virtualized platforms.

> **Step 1:** Perform the virtual deployment of the ODA X5 machine. (Most of the time this step is done by Oracle field engineers or the ODA presales team.)

■ **Note** You can also perform these kinds of deployments by following the release-specific ODA documents. The imaging of ODA or reimaging of ODA from a different deployment done previously can be done by following the ODA release-specific guides also. For example, for ODA X5-2, the document used in deployments is "Oracle Database Appliance Getting Started Guide Release 12.1.2.2.0 for Linux x86-64, E22692-41."

> **Step 2:** Create shared repositories for storing the application and database tier virtual machines, as well as the VM templates used for deploying the EBS application and database tiers.
>
> **Step 3:** Create a new Oracle Home according to the EBS template requirements (for example, the EBS 12.2.4 template requires 11.2.0.4.3 Oracle Home) in one of the ODA BASE servers using oakcli.
>
> **Step 4:** Install the database examples to the newly created Oracle Home and apply the RDBMS patches required by EBS 12.2 to this Oracle Home.
>
> **Step 5:** Create Oracle 9i NLS files on the newly created Oracle Home.
>
> **Step 6:** Download EBS 12.2 Database VM template files from http://edeliver. oracle.com/linux.
>
> **Step 7:** Unzip and import database VM templates (they are delivered as .ova files) to the repository created in step 2.

Step 8: Create the database virtual machine by executing the oakcli clone command on ODA BASE node1 (specify the VM template that is imported in step 7).

Step 9: Reconfigure the newly created virtual machine network by adding a network device (net1) using the oakcli modify vm <vm_name> -addnetwork command.

Step 10: Start the database virtual machine and do the EBS database configuration by connecting to the virtual console of the virtual machine and answering the questions that are asked by the scripts delivered with the EBS Database VM template. (These scripts are automatically executed at the last step of the boot cycle.)

Step 11: Migrate this newly created database virtual machine to ODA Base using Rapid Clone techniques and rman.

- Take a preclone on the source.

- Shut down the source database and mount it using the sqlplus utility and startup mount command.

- Copy the appsutil (unzip on target as well) from the source database to the ODA BASE Oracle Home created in step 3.

- Prepare the target system by executing the postclone with the tech stack option (adcfgclone dbTechStack) (on ODA Base node 1).

- Add the required tns aliases to the target Oracle Home for making the rman utility, which will be invoked from this Oracle Home to be able to connect both to the source and target databases.

- Execute the rman duplicate command by connecting the source as a target and connecting the ODA Base as the auxiliary to duplicate the database from source to target (ODA BASE).

- Run the library update script (adupdblib.sql) and configure the duplicate target database using the postclone utility (adcfgclone.pl dbconfig) (on ODA base node 1).

- Register the database to CRS using srvctl and update the necessary init.ora parameters accordingly (on ODA Base node 1).

- Restart the database using srvctl on ODA Base node 1 (on ODA Base node 1).

■ **Note** At this point, the EBS 12.2.4 database that is deployed using the EBS VM templates is migrated to ODA BASE node 1.

Continuing with the application tier, follow these steps:

Step 12: Download the EBS 12.2 Application VM template files from http://edeliver.oracle.com/linux.

Step 13: Unzip and import the Application VM templates (they are delivered as .ova files) to the repository created in step 2.

Step 14: Create the application virtual machine using the oakcli clone command by specifying the VM template that is imported in step 14. (Execute this command on ODA BASE node 1 and create the virtual machine on node 1 by specifying -node 1 as an argument to the oakcli command.)

Step 15: Reconfigure the newly created virtual machine network by adding a network device (net1) using the oakcli modify vm <vm_name> -addnetwork command.

Step 16: Start the application virtual machine and do the EBS application tier configuration by connecting to the virtual console of the virtual machine and answering the questions that are asked by the scripts delivered with the EBS Application VM template. (These scripts are automatically executed at the last step of the boot cycle.)

Continuing with enabling multiple application tier node and database tier RAC configurations, follow these steps:

Step 17: Deploy the additional application tier virtual machine by following the actions given in earlier steps (from step 12 to step 16).

Step 18: Convert the EBS database running on ODA BASE node 1 to a two-node RAC database running on ODA BASE node 1 and ODA BASE node 2 by following Section 4 of Oracle Support document "Using Oracle 11g Release 2 Real Application Clusters and Automatic storage management with Oracle E-Business Suite Release 12.2" (Doc ID 1453213.1).

Step 19: Configure PCP on concurrent processing and configure load balancing on the application tier by following Oracle Support note "380489.1: Using Load Balancers with Oracle E-Business Suite Release 12 provides detailed information on configuring load balancing."

Step 20: Delete the virtual machine created in step 8, as it was only required for the initial database VM template deployment.

In this chapter, we have gone through the methods for implementing EBS 12.2 on both ODA bare-metal and virtualized configurations. We gave you the general steps in addition to the logic behind the EBS 12.2 on ODA implementations.

Both of the implementations methods explained in this chapter were for EBS 12.2 Fresh installations. Although we have focused on the Fresh installation, migrating EBS 12.2 to ODA is not different from migrating EBS 12.2 to any other platform.

If you are interested in migrating EBS 12.2 to an ODA machine, we recommend you follow the Oracle Support note "R11i / 12: Oracle E-Business Suite Upgrades and Platform Migration" (Doc ID 1377213.1) and remind you to consider the minimum database versions that the ODA machine supports and the requirement to ACFS (if the target platform is an ODA X5).

Exalogic Implementations

Exalogic delivers high-performance, high-level fault tolerance, high parallelization, and lots of computing power for the components running on the application tier. In this context, the EBS application tier components, which enable you do online processing, batch processing, and reporting on the database, can benefit from Exalogic as well.

So, when you place EBS 12.2's application tier, which consists of Oracle Fusion Middleware, Oracle Forms, Oracle Reports, concurrent processing (batch servers), Oracle HTTP Server, and other integrated components such as applications like an HR organizational chart developed with ADF and Business Intelligence (BI) Publisher, on Exalogic, you create a load-balanced, highly available, and well-utilized EBS 12.2 application environment.

Moreover, if you empower the database tier of EBS 12.2 by using Exadata, then you determine the configuration that is called the Exastack (Exalogic+Exadata) and maximize the business gains by providing the best performance that can be delivered with an EBS 12.2 system.

That's why we recommend using Exadata with Exalogic to provide the best performance for EBS 12.2 systems, although the database tier can be deployed to Exadata or any other commodity platform regardless of the application tier being on Exalogic. It's worth mentioning that we recommend Exastack for busy EBS environments used by thousands of EBS users as well as ones employing lots of batch and parallel processing.

In this section, you will take a look at the EBS 12.2 implementations on Exalogic.

We will take a look at the recommended configuration for placing the application tier on an Exalogic environment by giving you the general steps for implementing the EBS 12.2 application tier on Exalogic, as well as the configuration that needs to be done for determining high performance and utilizing the high availability abilities of the EBS 12.2 application tier components with the Exalogic machine.

Exalogic has multiple physical servers in addition to the virtual servers that can be created on top of the Oracle VM architecture delivered with it.

Having a multiple server configured with high fault tolerance and performance makes it logical to have a multitier EBS 12.2 application tier on Exalogic.

The recommended configuration for an EBS 12.2 application on Exalogic environment is to use four application nodes in the form of two physical and two logical application servers. Of course, placing a load balancer in front is crucial for distributing the load to these multiple EBS application servers as well as for directing the traffic to the remaining application servers in case of a failure on an application server.

This configuration is not so different from what you saw in Chapter 13 while learning about middle tier performance tuning, with multiple application servers and using load balancers to distribute EBS web traffic as well as to provide parallel batch processing and so on.

Figure 14-7 depicts a recommended EBS 12.2 application tier on Exalogic configuration.

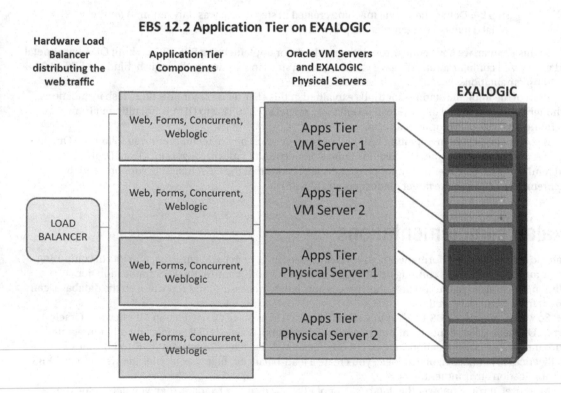

Figure 14-7. An example diagram showing the EBS 12.2 application tier implemented on virtualized and physical Exalogic nodes

In Figure 14-7, you see a multinode application tier residing on Exalogic. While two of the application servers of this application tier are running on the virtual servers delivered within the Oracle VM Server delivered with Exalogic, the other two are running on Exalogic physical servers (Currently, Oracle Linux and Oracle Solaris are the supported operating systems for Exalogic physical servers). This configuration is called a *hybrid* configuration where one-half of the compute nodes are running on the Oracle VM server and the other nodes are running on the Oracle Linux sitting on top of the Exalogic physical servers.

A hybrid configuration can be implemented in any Exalogic machine regardless of the machine size being eight, quarter, half, or full rack.

Using Oracle VM servers in addition to the physical server in your EBS 12.2 application tier brings you a higher fault tolerance, as you can configure these virtual servers to be able to run on all the available Exalogic physical servers in the case of a server failure.

On top of each EBS 12.2 application server, you see an application tier component such as Oracle HTTP Server, forms, reports, and concurrent processing (PCP enabled). Having all the application tier components running on each application server means you get better performance and fault tolerance. In front of these application servers, you see a load balancer that utilizes all of these application servers by distributing the client-server traffic.

Of course, we recommend having a high-performance and fault-tolerant database tier for the back end, such as a powerful application environment that must be supported with the proper database environment to achieve the best performance and to prevent database tier bottlenecks. In this manner, Oracle Maximum Availability Architecture (MAA) documents recommend having Exadata for supporting Exalogic, a multinode PCP-enabled application tier, and a powerful Oracle RAC on the database side.

Lastly, the documentation for implementing Exalogic or migrating to Exalogic is the same as any other hardware. So, if you are planning to implement EBS 12.2 on Exalogic, we recommend follow the basic installation manual at `http://docs.oracle.com/cd/E26401_01/doc.122/e22950.pdf` along with the Linux-specific EBS 12.2 installation guide available via Oracle Support note "Oracle E-Business Suite Installation and Upgrade Notes Release 12 (12.2) for Linux x86-64" (Doc ID 1330701.1).

Summary

In this chapter, we identified the Oracle engineered systems called Exadata, Oracle Database Appliance, and Oracle Exalogic, which are suitable platforms for implementing EBS 12.2. We gave you a detailed look at the EBS 12.2 implementation processes on these engineered systems.

We also gave a little more space to Exadata by covering EBS to Exadata migrations, the management of EBS on Exadata, and the benefits of running EBS on Exadata, as it is the engineered system that you will usually see in EBS projects.

Although this chapter was an overview, we tried to deliver the details of implementing EBS 12.2 on engineered systems, in addition to the base knowledge that is required for a starting point. The information given in this chapter can be improved on by reading the documentation on Oracle Support and the MAA documents, which we think Oracle will write specifically for EBS 12.2 in the future.

Index

■ A

Account generator, run in debug mode, 732
Accounting System, 1
Activated custom concurrent manager, 565
adadmin operational role
    main menu options, 188
    menu options, 486
    utility, 487
adadminsrvctl.sh, 367
AD and TXK release update, 120, 208
adchkdig, 494
ADMIN_SCRIPTS_HOME, 178
admrgpch (parameters and descriptions), 285
adopmnctl.sh {start|stop|status}, 366
adop patching cycles, 250
adopreports utilities, 346
adopscanlog, 347–349
adop
    outputs and logs, 346
    status command, 346
    tool, 246
adProvisionEBS.pl, 370
adrci utility, 196
ADR Command Interpreter (ADRCI), 421
adSyncContext.pl Script, 478
AD-TXK Delta 5 level, 279
Advanced Inbound Telephony, 2
Advanced Outbound Telephony, 2
Advanced procurement family, 5
AFPASSWD, 666
Application DBA online patching tool (adop)
    abort phase, 273, 275
    application nodes, 292
    APPL_TOP, 305
    APPL_TOP_NE/ad/bin, 245
    AutoConfig, 297
    cleanup phase, 272–273, 280
    CLE schema, 316
    cloning operation, 295
    command-line parameters and options, 252,
        254, 256, 258, 260

cutover phase, 270
downtime mode, 282
EBS
    application, 266
    configuration, 298
    EBS 12.2, 245
    EBS 12.2.0, 280
    patches, 246
failure node, 293
finalize phase, 269
hotpatch mode, 275–276
job timing reports, 329
localization documents and
    patches, 316, 321, 323
merging Oracle application patches, 282
MLS, 302
multi-node configuration, 289
NLS patching, 298
OAF page, 302
OAM, 303
Oracle
    HTTP Server services, 297
    marketing information and processes, 2
    Oracle Support, 344
    order management, 266
parameters, 252
patching cycle and process, 247, 262, 324
payroll, 266
phases, 248
prepare phase, 263, 265, 293
prerequisite patches, 316
run edition environment, 278–279
Subledger security, 267
synchronization patch, 307–308
system tools and commands, 324
transaction sources, 267
warehouse management, 266
Application Diagnostic responsibility
    menu options, 499
    test, 500
    test report, 502

Application technology group (ATG), 483
Application Tier (appsTier), 587
Applied patches
    pages, 325
    reporting tool, 325
APPL_TOP option
    appl directory structure, 27
    directory, 18
    snapshot, 304
    terminology, 75
APPS password
    AFPASSWD, 667
    schema, 492
appsutil directory, 166
Automatic Storage Management
        (ASM), 60
Asset lifecycle management, 3, 6
Autoconfig utilities, 583
    compilation order, 446
    components, 442
    configuration changes, 458, 464
    context file, 443, 447
    custom directory, 466
    customizations (EBS environment), 465
    customized template files, 467
    CVM, 449
    database, 453
    database tier, 463
    dbTier and appsTier, 473
    driver files, 444
    dual file system, 442
    EBS R12.2, 480
    execution, 461
    features and utilities, 468
    fusion middleware home, 474
    HTTP, 474
    OAM Dashboard administration, 448
    options, 441
    Oracle E-Business Suite, 441
    parallel mode, 473
    parameters, 450, 463
    patch file system, 481
    phases, 446
    pre-requisites, 458
    profile option and statistics, 469, 471
    RAC deployments, 472
    scripts, 442
    template file, 466–467
    template files, 444
Auto Degree of Parallelism
        (Auto Dop), 752
Automatic Storage Management
        (ASM), 703
Automatic Workload Repository
        (AWR), 702, 717

■ B

Baby Exadata, 735
BSU utility, 221–222
Bug Fixes, 332
Bundle patch, 201
Business Components for Java (BC4J) objects, 353
Business intelligence and analytics, 7
Business Process Management (BPM), 351
Business Suite 12.2 (EBS 12.2)
    application system, 675
    Avg Rd(ms), 702
    backup flag parameter, 709
    client-side performance tuning, 676–679
    Collecting Dictionary Stats, 706
    concurrent processing
        Actual column lists, 729
        Administer Concurrent Managers
            screen, 727–728
        AWR report, 724
        Concurrent Manager define form, 721–722
        Concurrent Processing Analyzer
            (CP Analyzer), 730
        Conflict Resolution Manager, 723
        custom concurrent managers,
            definition, 725
        dynamic configuration, 722
        FND_CONCURRENT_QUEUES table, 727
        FND_CONCURRENT tables, 729–730
        frequently checking, 722
        Oracle HTTP Server and middleware
            services, 721
        Oracle reports performance, 729
        Oracle Support documents, 727
        PCP, 730
        performance tuning methods, 721
        process attribute, 724
        Purge Concurrent Request and/or Manager
            Data (FNDCPPUR) program, 729
        sleep seconds values, 723
        specialization rules, 725
        Work Shifts screen, 722
        XXCUSTOM_MGR managers, 726
    database, 676
        level, 712
        structure and performance, 688–689
        tablespaces, 699
    data files, 698
    DBMS_STATS package, 704–705
    degree parameter, 709
    dynamic sampling, 705
    estimate percent parameter, 709
    export/import method, 712
    Fixed Object Stats, 707
    FND_EXCLUDE_TABLE_STATS, 705

FND_STATS, 704
FND_STATS.GATHER_SCHEMA_STATS, 711
FND_STATS.LOAD_EXTNSTATS_COLS
    procedure, 706
FND_STATS package, 710
FORCE LOGGING, 701–702
gathering statistics, 705, 707
    options parameter, 710
    schema statistics, 707, 711
    schema statistics concurrent program, 709
history mode parameter, 710
incremental stats, 707
initialization parameters
    environments, 695
    Oracle Database 12c, 697
    Oracle database reference
        documents, 691, 693–695
    Oracle Support document, 690
    parallel_force_local parameter, 696
    performance-related, 695
    reference document, 690
    SGA and PGA parameters, 696
    sizing of memory, 696
    swap-out and swap-In operations, 696
invalidate dependent cursor parameter, 710
I/O file system and load, 702–703
layers, 675
LGWR, 703
LOAD_EXTNSTATS_COLS procedure, 706
LOAD_XCLUD_TABLE procedure., 705
locking statistics, 705
LOGGING mode, 700
middle tier performance tuning
    application server, 679
    connection configuration, 685
    enterprise manager fusion middleware
        control, 683
    JVM, 679
    load balancer configuration, 680
    load balancer-related information, 680
    maximum requests, 685
    multinode environment, 682
    navigation of network test form, 686
    network test form, 686–687
    oacore server, 681
    optimal performance, 679
    Oracle HTTP Server, 685
    Oracle Support, 679
    performance directives menu item, 683–684
    process configuration, 685
    request configuration, 685
    WebLogic managed server, 681
    WebLogic managed servers, 680
    WebLogic servers, 682

modification threshold, 710
network performance tuning, 720
OLTP, 675
Oracle Database, 698
Oracle Support document, 711
PCT_INCREASE, 701
performance
    recommendations, 731, 733–734
product tablespaces, 702
recommended performance patches
    document, 712
restart request ID, 710
schema name parameter, 709
segment space management, 701
SQL access paths
    AWR reports, 714
    CBO, 713
    CPU-Bound SQL statements, 714
    database tier, 713
    DBMS_XPLAN.DISPLAY_CURSOR, 719
    discoveror report, 716
    explain plan, 718
    Oracle Support engineers, 714, 717
    PL/SQL routines, 715
    SELECT MLNO.C_ATTRIBUTE1_
        SS_NO, 715
    Sql ordered by CPU Time, 715
    Sql ordered by Elapsed Times, 716
    Sql ordered by Execution, 716
    Sql ordered by Executions, 717
    Sql ordered by Gets, 715
    Sql ordered by Reads, 716
    sqlplus autotrace option, 718
    Standard Manager processes, 717
    technology-specific approaches, 714
    types of diagnosis, 714
submit request, 708
Sysaux and EBS product
    tablespaces, 701
System tablespace, 700
table defragmentation operations, 712
tablespaces, 698
temporary files, 698
temp tablespaces, 702
Undo tablespace, 702
workflow and debug profiles, 676

■ C

checkDBpatch.sh, 113
checkMTpatch.sh, 110
Classpaths and JVM, 404
Cleanup phase, 235
CLED and CLEX tablespaces, 318

Cloning Oracle EBS Systems
  AD and TKX Delta6, 580
  AD and TKX Delta7, 580
  adcfgclone.pl operations, 581
  adpreclone.pl operations, 580–581
  application, 579
  AutoConfig, 583
  inventory requirements, 583
  maintain snapshot information, 583
  multinode to single-node
    adcfgclone.pl script, 616–618
    adpreclone.pl script, 610–611, 614–615
    configuration, 615
    database rman backup, 611–614
    environment details, 610
    execute rmanduplicate, 618–621
    online cloning, 609
    source system, 610
    target system application tier, 622–623
  OS prerequisites, 582
  patches, 582
  post-cloning steps, 637–638
  preparation, 582
  rapid clone, 579
  single node to mltinode
    AD and TKX Delta7 code levels, 600
    clone configuration scripts, 601–607
    clone preparation script, 601
    E-Business Suite system, 600
    rapid clone, 600
  single node to single node
    Application Tier (appsTier), 587
    database tier (dbTier), 586–587
    environment details, 585–586
    Oracle EBS 12.2, 584–585
    Rapidwiz, 584
    source system, 586
    stop application tier services, 588
    stop database tier services, 588–589
    target system, 589–600
  troubleshooting cloning issues, 638–639
  verify disk space, 582
Cloning procedure, 654
Clustered JDBCs, 357
Command-line interface (CLI), 571
COMMON_TOP/comn directory, 29
Compile Flexfields, 492
Component Licensing option, 61
Compress big application tables, 749
Concurrent manager
  administration, 573
  concurrent process, 531
  program, 531, 562
  recovery wizard, 575
  request ID, 543

  request set submission, 558
  request set wizard, 557
  request submission screen, 540
  schedule, 547
configoption (addMS), 410
Conflict Resolution Manager (CRM), 10, 535, 723
Context Editor change parameter, 451
Contextfile, 410
CONTEXT_FILE, 183
CONTEXT_NAME, 183
Create Table as Select (CTAS), 743, 745
Critical Activities tab, 515
Current view snapshot, 491
Cursor invalidations, 704
Custom concurrent manager, 564
  creation, 563, 568
  processes, 565
  work shift, 563
Customer support identification (CSI), 204
Custom patches, 236
Custom Tablespace, 264
Cutover phase, 270–271

■ D

Database and application files, 670
Database node configuration screen, 60
Database tech stack installation, 88
Database Tier (dbTier), 586–587
DataInstall utility, 311
DBA FMW control scripts, 370
dbTier and appsTier, 473
Demilitarized Zonezone (DMZ)
  advantages, 650
  application file system, 653
  cloning procedure, 654
  configuration, 649
  configuration option, 651
  disadvantages, 650
  EBS 12.2, 649
  external application tier, 650
  load balancer/reverse proxy, 657
  multiple application tier nodes, 652
  network firewalls control access, 649
  node/responsibility trust level, 656
  node trust level profile option, 657
  pre-requisite patches, 654
  profile options, 655–656
  responsibility trust level
        profile option, 657
  reverse proxy, 654
  SSH connectivity requirements, 659
Diagnostic modules page, 431
Diagnostic patch, 201
Diagnostics Framework (DFW), 359, 421

Domain Structure and Domain Configurations
    panels, 384, 386
Driver files, 444
Dual application file systems, 92
Dual file system and noneditioned file
    system, 228–229
Dump method, 428

■ E

Eager-relationship-caching, 403
EBS 12.2
    adop and adopreports, 160
    adrci utility, 196
    applications log files, 189–190
    application tier, 167, 183
    appsutil directory, 166
    architecture, 155
    ASM, 166, 173
    base directory, 177
    bash files, 166
    CONTEXT_FILE environment
        variable, 187
    database log files, 191
    database tiers, 156
    directories, 158
    directory structure, 161
    EBR, 156
    FMW_Home, 159
    fusion middleware
        directories, 361
    listener and database, 185
    online patching, 155
    OS terminals, 182
    patch environment, 167
    patch stores, 161
    PATH, 182
    RAC installations, 155
    SHELL, 173
    sqlplus, 169
    TEST, 186
    tnslsnr and rdbms, 193
    TWO_TASK, 167
EBS 12.2
    applications log files, 189
    database log files, 191
    database tier, 756
    dual filesystem, 24
    environment files, 26
    Exadata installations, 738
    fusion middleware subcomponents and
        technologies, 353
    installation, 740
    Rapidwiz, 36

EBS
    dual file system architecture, 158
    EBSapps, 26, 159
    file system architecture, 157
    integrated applications, 107
    multinode database installations, 739
    topology, 658
    Upgrade Activities, 154
E-Business Suite system, 600
Edition-Based Redefinition, 229
Editioned data storage, 233
Email Center, 3
Endian-ness, 744
Engineered systems
    advantages, 752
    CTAS and IAS, 746
    EBS 12.2, 747
    physical standby, 743
    software stack, 736
Enterprise Java Beans (EJBs), 401
Enterprise Manager Fusion middleware control, 373
Enterprise resource planning (ERP), 1
ETCC Summary 10g Developer Home, 115, 117
Exadata version, 735
Exadata X2, 736
Exadata X3, 736
Exadata X5, 737
Exalogic Implementations, 761
Execute adop, 251
expdb and impdp utilities, 744
External load balancer method, 357

■ F

Failed installations, 81
Farm resource center, 377
Feedback loop, 475
File system, 453
Finalize phase, 269
Financial Management Family, 3
Fix violations, 151
Flash recovery area (FRA), 756
FMWDFW, 438
FMW_Home, 159
FMW patch, 206
FNDCPASS Utility, 666
FND_NODES table, 231
FNDSM, 571
Fully I/O-bound administration operations, 752
Fusion Middleware (FMW), 17, 34, 118–119
    ADCRI, 421
    advantages, 351, 359
    application server processing, 352
    components, 351–352

Fusion Middleware (FMW) (*cont.*)
control buttons, 388–389
control online help, 373, 377, 419
deployments panel, 375
DFW, 421
directory structure, 155, 360
EBS 12.2, 401
EM, 477
enterprise, 476
features, 377
FMW_Home, 29
HTTP Server, 365
infrastructure and technology, 351
JDBC data sources, 356
log directories, 190
OPMN and OHS, 359
panel, 376
performance, 403
services and application processing, 356
subcomponents and technologies, 353
system components, 364
technologies, 352
URL, 384
WebLogic Console, 354, 371–372
WLST, 397

■ G

Generate message files, 491
Generating application files, 489
Generic database migrations, 743
Generic Service Management (GSM), 532
Global Core Human Capital Management, 4
Grid Infrastructure Flex Cluster, 75

■ H

Hotpatch mode, 275
Hotpatch parameter, 276
HR analytics, 4
HRMS legislations, 311
HTTP/HTTPS protocol, 641
Human capital management family, 4
Human resources, 4
Hybrid configuration, 763

■ I

ICM role, 570
Implement IORM, 749
Incident file, 427
Insert as Select (IAS), 743–745
Installation and configuration, EBS
Build Stage Menu options, 51
computing requirements, 38

DNS resolver parameters, 45
failed installations, 81
features, 35
guidelines, 38
hardware prerequisites, 37
kernel version, 39
multi node installation, 37
operating system packages, 40
operating systems, 37–38
ownership/permissions creations, 47
Package Installation, 42
RAC/ASM option, 35
repositories file, 42
single-node, 54
software products, 37
software requirements, 39
space requirements, 38
stage area, 47
startCD version, 54
Swap space, 44
unlink and relink library, 46
inst directory ($INST_TOP), 25
intelligent DB protocol (iDB), 736
Interaction center, 3
Internal concurrent, 535
Internal Concurrent Manager (ICM), 10, 535
Internal monitor process, 571
IORM, 741
iSupplier Portal, 5

■ J

JAR fies, 9
Java files, 211
Java Policy Store (JPS) configuration, 362
Java Runtime Environment (JRE), 677
Java Server Pages (JSP), 352
Job Timing Report, 329–330
JRE client, 80
JRIMETA.dat, 211
JVM threads dump file, 429

■ K

Kernel Versions, 40

■ L

Linux systems, 398
Logging last resource (LLR), 402

■ M

Manual method, 202
Maximum Availability Architecture (MAA), 738, 763

Merging Oracle application patches, 282
Message Driven Beans (MDBs), 401
Middle Tier Patches installation, 117
Missing database patches, 116
Multi Language Support (MLS), 302
Multi-lingual tables, 492
Multin node installation
    APPL_TOP terminology, 75
    ASM, 75
    RAC Database option, 74
Multiple database nodes (RAC), 73
My Oracle Support (MOS), 206

■ **N**

National Language settings (NLS), 64, 304
    language, 298
    patches, 282
Nocopyportion, 315
Node configuration screen, 65

■ **O**

oacore_server, 355, 403
oafm_server, 355
$OAH_TOP environment variable, 362
OAM, 496–497, 502
ODA, 760
    compute nodes, 755
    version, 737
Online patching, 151, 227, 246, 659
    architecture, 226, 236
    cycle, 158, 224, 315
    mechanism, 238
    phases, 234
    utility, 226
Oracle Application Manager
    (OAM), 299, 447, 459, 512
    applications, 78
    configuration manager, 57
    contract lifecycle management for
        public sector, 6
    channel revenue management, 2
    data pump, 744
    database appliance, 754
    dashboard, 447, 449
    security, 516
    upgrade, 129
Oracle Applications Tablespace Model (OATM), 13
Oracle Database Appliance (ODA), 735, 737
Oracle Diagnostic Logging (ODL), 426
Oracle_EBS-app1, 360
Oracle EBS concurrent managers
    active users, 531
    CLI, 571

completion, 550
concurrent requests, 531, 539, 555
developer home patch, 117
domain option, 562
EBS 12.2 proxy user, 584–585
    confirmation, 673
    database upgrade, 128
    delegation, 673
    file system structure, 19
    icon, 674
    patching utilities, 110
    switch, 674
ICM, 533
incompatibilities, 559
language setting, 546
PCP, 569
phases and status, 537
printing reports, 576
proactive maintenance, 576
request arguments, 545
request set, 551
schedule, 546
service management architecture, 532
service manager, 532
specialization rule, 567
users and password management, 665
Oracle EBS R12.2 upgrade
    demonstration, 110
    integrated applications, 107
    operating system and server upgrade, 105
    Oracle database, 106
    Purge/Archive data, 107
    RDBMS patches, 115
    space and computing capacity, 106
    virtualization, 105
Oracle EBS security
    access and control process, 641
    HTTP/HTTPS protocol, 641
    model, 641
    profile options, 671
    rapid clone, 579
    SSL context variables, 648
    SSL/TSL, 642
    wallet, 642
    Web Tier, 648
Oracle E-business suite (EBS), 50, 105, 465
    and tier, 11
    APPS, APPLSYS, and PRODUCT, 13
    architecture, 7
    concurrent processing, 10–11
    GUEST and APPLSYSPUB accounts, 12
    Java technologies, 18
    JSP compiler, 17
    installation, 54
    Release 12.2.4 Readme, 280

Oracle E-business suite (EBS) (*cont.*)
    software system, 2
    software versions, 1
    security guide, 642
    stack components, 15
    tablespaces, 13
    technology stack changes, 32
    tree-tier architecture, 8
    upgrades
        environment details, 127
        Online patching, 151
        Paths, 104
        software industry, 103
        support policies, 104
        support timeline, 105
Oracle enterprise manager, 19
Oracle fusion middleware technology, 102
Oracle_Home directory, 19, 172, 223
Oracle Home patch, 238
Oracle HTTP Server (OHS), 220, 373, 381, 417–418
Oracle Internet directory, 19
Oracle marketing, 2
Oracle order management, 2
Oracle Patch Application Assistant, 212–213,
        217–218
    initial screen, 212
Oracle procurement and spend analytics, 5
Oracle RDBMS software, 166
Oracle service, 2
Oracle software delivery, 48
Oracle supplier hub, 6
Oracle VM servers, 763
Oracle Wallet Manager (OWM), 642–644
    certificate export, 645–646
    certificate information, 644
    certificate location, 646
    certificate request, 645
    empty wallet creation, 644
Oracle WebCenter Portal, 19
Oracle Workflow Mailer Configuration, 79
Outbound server, 521

■ P, Q

Parallel concurrent processing (PCP), 533, 569, 577
Parameter skipsyncerror, 264
Patch Application Assistant method, 210
Patches and Technology Bug Fixes, 109
Patching concepts
    actions, 236
    cycle, 244, 262
    CSI, 204
    dual file system, 200
    EBS environment, 200
    FMW patch, 206

    EBS 12.2, 199
    manual method, 202
    metadata, 246
    mini packs, 201
    Oracle E-Business Suite, 199
    prerequisites, 202
    RPC, 201
    single patch, 208
    utilities (EBS 12.2), 220
patch_metadata.xml file, 211
Periodic prepaid expenses distribution, 323
PL/SQL log and out directory, 80
Post-installation
    instructions, 225
    steps, 80
    validation, 72
Post-upgrade tasks, 124
Prepared statement cache, 402
Prepare phase, 235–236
Printing forms, 526
Print Styles configuration, 527
Product value chain management, 6
Project portfolio management family
    analytics, 5
    billing, 5
    contracts, 5
    collaboration, 5
    costing, 5
    management, 5
    portfolio analysis, 5
    resource management, 5
Purge/archive EBS transaction data, 107

■ R

RAC-enabled systems
    adclone.pl Script, 626–628
    configuration, 628–630
    data files, 626
    ebsnode1 and ebsnode2, 625
    execute adclone.pl, 631
    instances, 186
    online cloning method, 626
    Rapid Clone, 624–625
Rapidwiz installation process
    application node configuration, 137
    application tier, 82
    build stage main menu, 51
    database tier, 82
    language and character set configuration, 136
    ports configuration, 133
    post-install validations, 149
    pre-install, 68
    prerequisite check, 139
    Rapidwiz Install Wizard, 35, 76, 79

replacing tools and tech stack, 94, 96–97
upgrade configuration option, 144–145
upgrade file system, 130
validation, 141, 147
WebLogic password configuration, 135
Relational Database Management System
(RDBMS), 84
patches, 115
Real Application Clusters (RAC)
database, 738
installations, 173
Recommended Patch Collection (RPC), 201
Relink Applications programs, 491
Remote Method Invocation (RMI), 357
Replacing the Oracle EBS Database Technology
Stack (RDBMS Oracle Home), 83
Rolling cursor invalidation, 704

■ **S**

Secure Sockets Layer (SSL), 642
Security patch update (SPU), 201
Service management family
cash and treasury management, 3
features, 2
financial control, 3
lease and finance management, 4
travel and expense management, 4
Shared APPL_TOP
Delta6 code level, 634–635
Delta7 code-level, 636
deployment, 632
patch file system, 635
post-node, 636
Rapidwiz Install Wizard, 632
shared_libs directory, 363
single-node installation, 54
SMTP and IMAP settings, 520
Soft and Hard Shell limits, 45
Sophisticated patching tool, 288
SQL and EXEC commands, 330
SQL statements modification, 713
SSH, 289
Standard concurrent managers, 562
Standard manager, 535
Status Monitor, 508
Suite Licensing, 61
Superuser password configuration, 66
Supply Chain Management Family, 6
asset lifecycle management, 6
business intelligence and analytics, 7
product value chain management, 6
value chain execution and planning, 6–7
Swap space, 44
Synchronization patch, 309

SYSADMIN
adadmin utility, 487
adident, 494
administration, 509, 516
AD utilities, 484, 486
alert manager, 504–505
application diagnostic responsibility, 498
compile/reload applications database, 492
configuration information, 493
database sessions, 514
diagnostic and repair, 495
generate message files, 491
license product, 517
notification search tab, 511
printer types, 528
printing forms, 526
profiles are variables, 525
role and responsibility management, 523
status monitor, 508
system administrator responsibility, 495
vacation rule, 510
SYSADMIN
password, 670
user, 299
Sys and system account passwords, 79
System administration responsibility, 495, 503–504
System configuration validations, 69

■ **T**

Talent management, 4
TCP/IP network protocol, 10
Template file locations, 444
Timing report tool, 335–336
tnslsnr and rdbms, 193
Transaction collection process, 267
Transaction manager, 535
Transparent data encryption (TDE)
column level, 661
configuration, 662
EBS database, 665
database option (levels), 661
Transportable tablespaces (TTS), 744
database, 743
method, 744
Travel and expense management, 4
Tuning parallelism, 750
txtkSetAppsConf.pl script, 413

■ **U**

UI Generator (UIX), 353
Unified driver file, 211
Updating snapshots, 492
upgrade file system, 136, 140

Upgrade Patch, 121
Upgrade file system configuration, 150
Using I/O Resource Manager (IORM), 753

V

Validate APPS schema, 492
Validate system configuration screen, 69
Value chain planning, 7
View log files page, 339
Virtualization (ODA environment), 758
Virtual private database (VPD), 233

W

WebLogic admin console, starting oacore server, 395
WebLogic patches, 121–221

WebLogic Server (WLS), 36, 112, 353
Wget utility, 42
wlserver_10.3, 360
WLST, 397–398, 425
Workflow admin responsibility, 508
Workflow mailer configuration, 519
Workflow metrics, 521
Workflow notification
        mailer, 519
Workforce management, 4

■ X, Y, Z

XML Development Kit (XDK), 16
Xmx and Xms values, 406
XXMaxPermSize values, 408
XXXPermSize and XXMaxPermSize, 407

Get the eBook for only $5!

Why limit yourself?

Now you can take the weightless companion with you wherever you go and access your content on your PC, phone, tablet, or reader.

Since you've purchased this print book, we're happy to offer you the eBook in all 3 formats for just $5.

Convenient and fully searchable, the PDF version enables you to easily find and copy code—or perform examples by quickly toggling between instructions and applications. The MOBI format is ideal for your Kindle, while the ePUB can be utilized on a variety of mobile devices.

To learn more, go to www.apress.com/companion or contact support@apress.com.

Printed in the United States
By Bookmasters